CALIFORNIA PIONEER REGISTER AND INDEX
1542 - 1848

Including
Inhabitants of California, 1769 - 1800
and
List of Pioneers

Extracted from
THE HISTORY OF CALIFORNIA
By HUBERT HOWE BANCROFT

CLEARFIELD COMPANY
REPRINTS & REMAINDERS

Extracted from
History of California. 7 volumes.
Originally published 1884-90.

Library of Congress Card Number 64-17723

REGIONAL PUBLISHING CO.
Baltimore, Md.

Reprinted for Clearfield Company Inc. by
Genealogical Publishing Co. Inc.
Baltimore, MD 1990

TABLE OF CONTENTS

PUBLISHER'S PREFACE

This volume is a compilation extracted and reassembled from the monumental seven-volume *HISTORY OF CALIFORNIA* by the able and eminent historian, Hubert Howe Bancroft. It includes all genealogical information contained in these volumes and as such should be of great interest to genealogists and to descendants of California pioneers who are interested in tracing their ancestry. The List of *Inhabitants of California, 1769-1800,* and the *List of Pioneers* were taken from volume one, the *Pioneer Register and Index* reassembled from volumes 2 to 5.

As this is an offset reprint, made by taking photographic plates of the original, the ending of one part could not be directly connected with the beginning of another. This accounts for the gaps on pages 135, 195 and 294. Nevertheless, rearrangement of most of the content was possible and so we are able to present all of the genealogical data from the set in a comprehensive and readily accessible form.

The Publishers

INHABITANTS OF CALIFORNIA,

1769-1800

This list contains the names of over 1700 male inhabitants of the province down to the year 1800. The names were selected with great care and labor from mission registers, company rosters, pueblo *padrones* and from thousands of miscellaneous documents in the archives. A few of the registers have been lost and some names, especially of children, are therefore missing.

Attempts at chronology are limited to the separation of names into four categories, putting each person in the category in which his name first appears in the records. Number 1 includes the earliest pioneers who came in 1769-73; number 2 those of 1774-80; number 3 those of 1780-90; and number 4 those of 1790-1800.

Abella, Ramon, padre.[4]
Acebedo, Francisco Ant., soldier.[2]
Acebedo, José Antonio, soldier.[2]
Acebedo, Julian, soldier.[2]
Acedo, José, settler.[4]
Aceves, Antonio, child.[2]
Aceves, José María, child.[2]
Aceves, Antonio Quiterio, soldier.[2]
Aceves, Pablo, soldier.[4]
Acosta, Antonio, soldier.[3]
Acosta, José, Cat. vol.[4]
Aguiar, Francisco.[1]
Aguila, José, settler.[4]
Aguila, Juan José, child.[4]
Aguilar, Francisco Javier.[1]
Aguilar, Luis Antonio.[1]
Alanis, Antonio, child.[3]
Alanis, Eugenio Nicolás, child.[3]
Alanis, Isidro.[4]
Alanis, Máximo, soldier.[3]
Alari, José, Cat. vol.[4]
Alberni, Pedro, lieutenant-colonel.[4]
Alcántara, Pedro, mason.[4]
Alegre, Antonio, soldier.[2]
Alegría, Norberto, soldier.[3]

Alipás, Juan N., soldier.[4]
Altamirano, José Antonio, soldier.[3]
Altamirano, Lúcas Domingo, child.[2]
Altamirano, José Marcos, child.[2]
Altamirano, Justo Roberto, soldier.[2]
Altamirano, Lúcas, soldier.[4]
Altamirano, Juan, soldier.[4]
Alvarado, Juan B.[1]
Alvarado, Bernardino.[1]
Alvarado, Ignacio, soldier.[2]
Alvarado, Francisco Javier, soldier.[3]
Alvarado, Juan B., child.[3]
Alvarado, Fran. Ma. D. C., child.[4]
Alvarado, José Vicente, child.[4]
Alvarado, Juan José, soldier.[4]
Alvarado, Juan N. D., child.[4]
Alvarez, Juan, soldier.[2]
Alvarez, Joaquin, soldier.[2]
Álvarez, Luis, soldier.[2]
Álvarez, Pedro, soldier.[2]
Álvarez, Felipe, convict.[4]
Álvarez, Doroteo.[4]
Álvarez, José, artilleryman.[4]
Álvarez, Juan, artilleryman.[4]
Álvarez, José, child.[4]

Alvires, Claudio, servant.[2]
Alvires, Juan, soldier.[3]
Alvires, Estévan.[4]
Alviso, Francisco, settler.[2]
Alviso, Domingo, soldier.[2]
Alviso, Anastasio Gerónimo, child.[4]
Alviso, Francisco Javier, soldier.[4]
Alviso, Francisco Solano, child.[4]
Alviso, Gerónimo Antonio, child.[4]
Alviso, Ignacio, soldier.[4]
Alviso, Javier, settler.[4]
Alviso, José Antonio, child.[4]
Alviso, José Gabriel L., child.[4]
Alvitre, Sebastian, soldier.[1]
Alvitre, Juan José Ma., child.[4]
Amador, Pedro, soldier.[1]
Amador, José Sinforoso, child.[3]
Amador, José Fructuoso.[3]
Amador, Juan Pablo.[3]
Amador, José María, child.[4]
Amador, Marcos Antonio, child.[4]
Amarrillas, Juan Angel, soldier.[2]
Amézquita, José Gabriel, child.[2]
Amézquita, Juan Antonio, soldier.[2]
Amézquita, Manuel Dom., settler.[2]
Amézquita, Florentino, settler.[4]
Amézquita, Gregorio, settler.[4]
Amézquita, Francisco Ma., settler.[4]
Amézquita, José, soldier.[4]
Amézquita, José Miguel, settler.[4]
Amézquita, José Reyes, settler.[4]
Amézquita, Serafin, settler.[4]
Amurrio, Gregorio, padre.[1]
Antonio, Manuel, servant.[2]
Antonio, José Crispin, child.[4]
Antonio, Macedonio, soldier.[4]
Antuña, Manuel, soldier.[2]
Arana, José, soldier.[3]
Aranguren, José, soldier.[3]
Arce, José G.[1]
Arce, Sebastian.[1]
Arce, Joaquin, child.[2]
Arcés, José, settler.[4]
Archuleta, José Ignacio, servant.[2]
Archuleta, José Norberto, child.[2]
Archuleta, Miguel Gerónimo, child.[2]
Archuleta, Gregorio, soldier.[4]
Arellanes, Teodoro.[4]
Arellano, Man. J. R., soldier.[2]
Arenaza, Pascual M., padre.[3]
Argüelles, Francisco, artilleryman.[4]
Argüello, Francisco Rafael, child.[4]
Argüello, José Dario, alférez.[3]
Argüello, José Gervacio, child.[3]
Argüello, Luis Antonio, child.[3]
Argüello, José Ignacio M., child.[4]
Armenta, Cristóbal, settler.[2]
Armenta, Joaquin, soldier.[2]
Arriola, Alejandro, soldier.[3]
Arias, Francisco, settler.[4]

Armenta, José Ma., soldier.[4]
Arriola, José Francisco, mechanic.[4]
Arriola, José Rafael B., child.[4]
Arriola, Rafael, convict.[4]
Arriz, Ignacio.[1]
Arroita, Francisco José, padre.[3]
Arroyo, José Manuel, smith.[2]
Arroyo, Juan Isidro, child.[3]
Arroyo, Vicente, soldier.[3]
Arroyo, Félix, child.[3]
Arroyo, José, sailor.[4]
Aruz, Domingo, soldier.[2]
Aruz, Martin, settler.[4]
Arvallo, Feliciano, settler.[2]
Ávalos, Nicolás.[1]
Ávalos, Joaquin, tanner.[4]
Ávila, Francisco.[4]
Ávila, Adanto, child.[4]
Ávila, Anastasio.[4]
Ávila, Antonio Ignacio.[4]
Ávila, Cornelio, settler.[4]
Ávila, Ignacio.[4]
Ávila, José, convict.[4]
Ávila, José Antonio, settler.[4]
Ávila, José María.[4]
Ávila, Miguel.[4]
Ávila, Santa Ana, soldier.[4]
Avis, Fructuoso, soldier.[4]
Ayala, José, soldier.[3]
Ayala, José C. D., child.[4]
Ayala, José Salvador, child.[4]
Ayala, Juan José G., child.[4]
Ayala, Juan P. M., child.[4]
Bacilio, Antonio, Cat. vol.[4]
Badiola, Manuel Antonio.[1]
Balderrama, convict.[4]
Ballesteros, Juan, soldier.[3]
Ballesteros, Juan Antonio, child.[3]
Ballesteros, Javier Antonio, child.[4]
Banderas, José F. de la Cruz.[4]
Barajas, José, sailor.[4]
Barbosa, José, settler.[4]
Bárcena, José, convict.[4]
Bárcenas, Marcos, settler.[4]
Barcenilla, Isidoro, padre.[4]
Barona, José, Padre.[4]
Barraza, Macedonio, soldier.[3]
Barrera, Juan Antonio, soldier.[3]
Barrientos, José, Cat. vol.[4]
Basadre y Vega, Vicente, settler.[3]
Belen, Miguel, servant.[2]
Bello, Mateo, Cat. vol.[4]
Beltran, Francisco Javier, soldier.[2]
Beltran, Joaquin, soldier.[2]
Beltran, Nicolás, soldier.[2]
Benavides, José Ma., settler.[4]
Beranzuela, Pedro, soldier.[4]
Bermudez, José, soldier.[4]
Bermudez, José S., child.[4]
Bermudez, Manuel Antonio, child.[4]

Bernal, Francisco, servant.[1]
Bernal, José Dionisio, soldier.[2]
Bernal, Juan Francisco, soldier.[2]
Bernal, Manuel Ramon, soldier.[2]
Bernal, Apolinario, child.[3]
Bernal, Juan, child.[3]
Bernal, Ramon, settler.[3]
Bernal, Bruno, child.[4]
Bernal, Joaquin, soldier.[4]
Bernal, José Agustin, child.[4]
Bernal, José Cipriano, child.[4]
Bernal, José C. Cipriano, child.[4]
Bernardo, José, settler.[4]
Berreyesa, Nicolás A., settler.[2]
Berreyesa, Juan José, child.[4]
Berreyesa, José Nazario, settler.[4]
Berreyesa, José de los Reyes, settler.[4]
Blanco, Juan, smith.[4]
Blanco, Miguel.[4]
Bojorges, José Ramon, soldier.[2]
Bojorges, Hermenegildo, child.[2]
Bojorges, Pedro Antonio, soldier.[2]
Bojorges, Francisco H., soldier.[4]
Bonnel, Ramon, Cat. vol.[1]
Borica, Diego de, governor.[4]
Boronda, Manuel, soldier.[3]
Boronda, Canuto José, child.[4]
Bosch, Buenaventura, settler.[3]
Botello, Joaquin, tailor.[4]
Bravo, José Marcelino, soldier.[1]
Briones, Ignacio Vicente, soldier.[2]
Briones, José Antonio, soldier.[1]
Briones, Ignacio Vicente, child.[3]
Briones, José Joaquin, child.[2]
Briones, Felipe Santiago, child.[3]
Briones, Nicolás María, child.[2]
Briones, Marcos, soldier.[3]
Briones, Manuel, soldier.[4]
Brito, Mariano, artilleryman.[4]
Brito, Miguel, artilleryman.[4]
Bruno, Francisco, soldier.[2]
Buelna, Eusebio José J., child.[2]
Buelna, José Antonio, soldier.[2]
Buelna, Ramon, soldier.[2]
Buelna, Eusebio J. J., child.[4]
Buelna, José Raim, child.[3]
Buelna, José María, child.[4]
Bulferig, Gerónimo, Cat. vol.[1]
Bumbau, Francisco, Cat. vol.[1]
Bustamante, José, soldier.[3]
Bustamante, Manuel, soldier.[3]
Butron, Manuel, soldier.[2]
Butron, Sebastian, settler.[4]
Caballero, José, Cat. vol.[4]
Calixto, José, soldier.[4]
Calvo, Francisco, soldier.[3]
Calzada, José Antonio, padre.[3]
Calzada, José, convict.[4]
Calzada, José Dionisio, settler.[4]
Camacho, José Antonio, soldier.[1]

Camacho, Tomás M., servant.[1]
Camacho, Juan Miguel, soldier.[1]
Camacho, Anastasio, soldier.[2]
Camacho, Antonio, soldier.[2]
Camarena, Nicolás, settler.[4]
Cambon, Pedro Benito, padre.[1]
Camero, Manuel, settler.[3]
Campa, Pedro, sailor.[2]
Campa y Coz, Miguel, padre.[1]
Campo, José, Cat. vol.[4]
Campos, Francisco, soldier.[3]
Cañedo, Albino, soldier.[2]
Cañedo, José Manuel, settler.[2]
Cañedo, Juan Ignacio, soldier.[4]
Cañizares, José, piloto.[1]
Cano, José, artilleryman.[4]
Cantua, Ignacio, soldier.[2]
Capinto, José Ma., tailor.[4]
Capinto, Mariano, tailor.[4]
Carabanas, Joaquin, soldier.[2]
Carabanas, Nicolás, soldier.[2]
Caravantes, José Salvador, soldier.[3]
Caravantes, Ventura, settler.[4]
Carcamo, José, Cat. vol.[4]
Cárdenas, Melchor, servant.[2]
Cárdenas, Cristóbal, servant.[1]
Cárdenas y Rivera, Tadeo.[1]
Cariaga, Salvador, soldier.[2]
Carlon, Hilario Ignacio, soldier.[3]
Carnicer, Baltasar, padre.[4]
Carranza, Domingo, padre.[4]
Carrillo, Guillermo, soldier.[1]
Carrillo, Mariano, sergeant.[1]
Carrillo, José Raimundo, soldier.[1]
Carrillo, Anastasio José, child.[3]
Carrillo, Cárlos Antonio, child.[3]
Carrillo, Domingo Ant. Igna., child.[4]
Carrillo, José Antonio E., child.[4]
Carrillo, Luis, sailor.[4]
Casasallas, Simon, Cat. vol.[4]
Casillas, Juan Manuel.[1]
Castañeda, José.[3]
Castañeda, José Ruiz, soldier.[3]
Castelo, Agustin, soldier.[1]
Castillo, José, phlebotomist.[4]
Castillo, José, soldier.[4]
Castro, Antonio, soldier.[2]
Castro, Ignacio, soldier.[2]
Castro, Joaquin, soldier.[2]
Castro, José, servant.[2]
Castro, Isidro.[2]
Castro, José Macario, soldier.[3]
Castro, José Simon J. N., child.[3]
Castro, Mariano, soldier.[3]
Castro, Mariano de la Cruz, child.[3]
Castro, Agapito, settler.[4]
Castro, Francisco, settler.[4]
Castro, José Joaquin, settler.[4]
Castro, José S. T., child.[4]
Castro, Simeon, settler.[4]

Cavaller, José, padre.[1]
Cayuelas, Francisco, Cat. vol.[1]
Cayuelas, Francisco, soldier.[3]
Cayuelas, Pedro, soldier.[3]
Cervantes, Juan Pablo.[1]
Cervantes, Guadalupe, soldier.[4]
Cervantes, Pablo Victoriano, soldier.[6]
Chabolla, Márcos, soldier.[3]
Chabolla, Pedro R., child.[3]
Chabolla, José, child.[4]
Chabolla, José Luis, child.[4]
Chabolla, Salvador.[4]
Chamorro, smith.[2]
Chaves, José Mateo, settler.[4]
Chaves, José, convict.[4]
Chavira, José Antonio, settler.[4]
Chavira, Jose, convict.[4]
Cibrian, Pablo, soldier.[4]
Cibrian, Leocadio, soldier.[3]
Cibrian, Pablo Antonio, smith.[4]
Ciprés, Marcelino, padre.[4]
Cisneros, José, servant.[3]
Clua, Domingo, Cat. vol.[2]
Contreras, Luis, muleteer.[2]
Contreras, José, soldier.[4]
Cordero, Joaquin Ignacio.[1]
Cordero, Francisco.[1]
Cordero, Mariano Antonio, soldier.[1]
Cordero, José E., child.[2]
Cordero, Fermin, settler.[4]
Cordero, Manuel, soldier.[2]
Cordero, José Dom., child.[4]
Cordero, Miguel E., child.[4]
Cordero, Pedro, settler.[4]
Córdoba, Alberto, engineer.[4]
Cornejo, Casimiro, settler.[4]
Cornejo, Casimiro, convict.[4]
Corona, Francisco, soldier.[4]
Coronel, Juan Antonio, muleteer.[2]
Cortés, Juan Lope, padre.[4]
Cortés, José Antonio, soldier.[3]
Cortés, Nicolás, soldier.[4]
Cortés, Nicolás Felipe, soldier.[4]
Costansó, Miguel, engineer.[1]
Cota, Antonio, soldier.[1]
Cota, Pablo Antonio, soldier.[1]
Cota, Manuel Antonio, child.[2]
Cota, Roque, soldier.[2]
Cota, Guillermo, sergeant.[3]
Cota, Juan Ignacio, soldier.[3]
Cota, Mariano, soldier.[3]
Cota, Nabor Antonio, child.[3]
Cota, Bartolomé José, child.[4]
Cota, Francisco Atanasio, child.[4]
Cota, José Manuel Ma., child.[4]
Cota, José Valentin, child.[4]
Cota, Juan Francisco, child.[4]
Cota, Manuel, soldier.[4]
Cota, Pedro Antonio, child.[4]
Crespí, Juan, padre.[1]

Cruzado, Antonio, padre.[1]
Cruz, Faustino José, soldier.[8]
Cruz y Sotomayor, Juan, soldier.[3]
Cuevas, Luis, settler.[4]
Dandricu, Andrés, soldier.[4]
Dantí, Antonio, padre.[3]
Dávila, José, surgeon.[2]
Dávila, Manuel, carpenter.[3]
Dávila, J., soldier.[3]
Dávila, José Antonio, smith.[4]
Delgado, Alonzo, Cat. vol.[4]
Diaz, Joaquin, soldier.[2]
Dominguez, Juan José, soldier.[1]
Dominguez, José Dolores, soldier.[2]
Dominguez, José Antonio, child.[3]
Dominguez, José Ma. D., child.[3]
Dominguez, Cristóbal, soldier.[4]
Dominguez, José Antonio, child.[4]
Dominguez, José Asuncion, child.[4]
Dominguez, José Francisco, child.[4]
Dominguez, Remesio, settler.[4]
Duarte, Alejo Antonio, soldier.[1]
Duarte, José Ma., soldier.[1]
Duarte, Pascual.[1]
Duarte, Francisco Javier, child.[4]
Duarte, Juan José, servant.[4]
Duarte, Leandro, soldier.[4]
Ducil, Sebastian, Cat. vol.[4]
Dumetz, Francisco, padre.[1]
Encarnacion, José, soldier.[3]
Enriquez, Antonio, servant.[3]
Enriquez, Antonio Domingo, weaver.[4]
Enriquez, Sebastian, child.[4]
Escamilla, Antonio Santos, child.[4]
Escamilla, José, soldier.[4]
Escamilla, Tomás, convict.[4]
Escribano, Sebastian, Cat. vol.[4]
Esparza, José Lorenzo, mechanic.[1]
Espí, José de la C., padre.[4]
Espinosa, Antonio, soldier.[2]
Espinosa, Joaquin, soldier.[2]
Espinosa, Juan, servant.[2]
Espinosa, Gabriel, soldier.[3]
Espinosa, José Miguel, soldier.[3]
Espinosa, Salvador, soldier.[3]
Espinosa, Tomás, soldier.[3]
Espinosa, Cayetano, soldier.[4]
Espinosa, José Gabriel S.[4]
Espinosa, José Ma. E., child.[4]
Espinosa, José Pio, Cat. vol.[4]
Espinosa, Juan Antonio J., child.[4]
Estévan, Pedro de S. José, padre.[4]
Estévan, Antonio, sailor.[1]
Estrada, José Bonifacio, soldier.[2]
Estudillo, José María, soldier.[4]
Fages, Pedro, lieutenant.[1]
Faura, José, padre.[4]
Feliciano, Alejo, settler.[2]
Feliciano, Hilario, child.[3]
Félix, Claudio Victor.[1]

Félix, Anast. Ma., soldier.[2]
Félix, Doroteo, soldier.[2]
Félix, José Vicente, soldier.[2]
Félix, José Francisco, soldier.[3]
Felix, Juan José Ignacio, child.[3]
Félix, Antonio Rafael, child.[4]
Félix, Victorino, soldier.[3]
Félix, Fernando de la T., child.[4]
Félix, José, child.[4]
Félix, José Luciano, child.[4]
Félix, José Vicente Valentin, child.[4]
Félix, Juan.[4]
Félix, Juan Jose de G., child.[4]
Félix, Leonardo Ma., child.[4]
Félix, Pedro Antonio, child.[4]
Fernandez, Gaspar Antonio, child.[3]
Fernandez, José Rosalino, soldier.[3]
Fernandez, Pedro Ignacio, child.[4]
Fernandez, Rafael Ma. de la C., child.[4]
Fernandez, Victor, Cat. vol.[4]
Fernandez, Gregorio, padre.[4]
Fernandez, José Ma., padre.[4]
Fernandez, Manuel, padre.[4]
Feyjoo, José, soldier.[3]
Ferrer, Pablo, Cat. vol.[1]
Figuer, Juan, padre.[1]
Figueroa, Manuel, soldier.[2]
Figueroa, Salvador Ignacio, child.[4]
Flores, Hermenegildo, soldier.[2]
Flores, Victoriano, servant.[2]
Flores, José Miguel, soldier.[2]
Flores, José María, soldier.[3]
Flores, José Teodosio, child.[3]
Flores, Bernardo, settler.[4]
Flores, Diego.[4]
Flores, Francisco, soldier.[4]
Flores, Isidro, soldier.[4]
Flores, José Ma. de la T., child.[4]
Flores, Leandro José, child.[4]
Flores, Pedro, soldier.[4]
Font, José, lieutenant.[4]
Fontes, Luis Ma., soldier.[3]
Fontes, Pedro, servant.[2]
Fragoso, Luis Ma., soldier.[3]
Fragoso, Rafael, Cat. vol.[4]
Franco, Juan, servant.[3]
Franco, José, convict.[4]
Franco, Pablo, convict.[4]
Fuster, Vicente, padre.[1]
Galindo, Nicolás, settler.[2]
Galindo, Francisco A., child.[2]
Galindo, José Rafael, child.[2]
Galindo, Alejandro Fidel, child.[3]
Galindo, José Leandro, child.[3]
Galindo, Juan Crisóstomo, child.[3]
Galindo, Claudio, Cat. vol.[4]
Galindo, José Cárlos H., child.[4]
Galindo, Venancio, soldier.[4]
Gallego, Cárlos, soldier.[2]
Galvez, Diego, Cat. vol.[4]

Gámez, Teodoro, soldier.[4]
Garaicoechea, José, corporal.[4]
García, Diego, padre.[3]
García, Felipe, smith.[2]
García, Francisco Bruno, soldier.[2]
García, Francisco Ma., child.[2]
García, Francisco P., soldier.[2]
García, José Reyes, child.[2]
García, Juan José, child.[2]
García, José Antonio, soldier.[2]
García, Pedro, settler.[3]
García, Pedro Gonzalez, smith.[4]
García, Cárlos Ma.[4]
García, José Antonio Inoc., child.[4]
García, José Hilario Ramon, child.[4]
García, José de las Llagas, child.[4]
Garcia, José Ma. Cancio, child.[4]
García, José Ma. Desiderio, child.[4]
García, Julian.[4]
García, Luz, soldier.[4]
García, Nicolás, Cat. vol.[4]
García, Pedro Antonio, child.[4]
García, Pedro Gonz., smith.[4]
Garibay, Jose Joaquin, child.[4]
Garibay, Vicente, soldier.[4]
Garracino, Pedro, soldier.[2]
Gerardo. (See Gonzalez G.)
German, Cris. Ant., child.[3]
German, Isidro, soldier.[3]
German, Faustin J., child.[4]
German, Manuel Ignacio, child.[4]
German, Juan, soldier.[4]
German, Juan, child.[4]
Gíol, José, servant.[2]
Gili, Bartolomé, padre.
Giribet, Miguel, padre.[3]
Gloria, Jacinto, soldier.[2]
Gloria, José Ma., soldier.[2]
Gomez, Francisco, padre.[1]
Gomez, Nicolás, settler.[2]
Gomez, Francisco, soldier.[4]
Gomez, José Antonio, Cat. vol.[4]
Gomez, Rafael, settler.[4]
Gomez, Rafael, convict.[4]
Gomez, Francisco, carpenter.[4]
Góngora, José Ma., soldier.[1]
Góngora, José Antonio, child.[2]
Gonopra, José Ma., soldier.[4]
Gonzalez, Antonio Alejo., soldier.[1]
Gonzalez, Inocencio, sailor.[1]
Gonzalez, Cirilo, servant.[2]
Gonzalez, José Antonio, soldier.[2]
Gonzalez, José Romualdo, child.[2]
Gonzalez, José Manuel, settler.[2]
Gonzalez, Mateo Jacobo, child.[2]
Gonzalez, Ramon.[2]
Gonzalez, Nicolás, soldier.[3]
Gonzalez, Alejandro, soldier.[3]
Gonzalez, Bernardo, soldier.[2]
Gonzalez, Diego, lieutenant.[2]

Gonzalez, Felipe, soldier.[3]
Gonzalez, José Eusebio, child.[3]
Gonzalez, José Feliciano, soldier.[3]
Gonzalez, Mateo Jacobo, child.[3]
Gonzalez, Tomás, soldier.[3]
Gonzalez, Alejo., Cat. vol.[4]
Gonzalez, Francisco, soldier.[4]
Gonzalez, Francisco, padre.[4]
Gonzalez, José, Cat. vol.[4]
Gonzalez, José Rafael M., child.[4]
Gonzalez, Man. Ciriaco, child.[4]
Gonzalez, Juan, soldier.[4]
Gonzalez, Pedro, mechanic.[4]
Gonzalez, Rafael, child.[4]
Gonzalez Gerardo, Rafael.[1]
Gonzalez, José Leandro, child.[4]
Goycoechea, Felipe, lieutenant.[4]
Grajera, Antonio, lieutenant.[4]
Grijalva, Juan Pablo, sergeant.[2]
Guerrero, Juan José.[1]
Guerrero, Joaquin, soldier.[2]
Guerrero, José, servant.[2]
Guerrero, José Antonio, soldier.[2]
Guerrero, Julian, soldier.[2]
Guerrero, Mateo, artilleryman.[4]
Guevara, José, soldier.[3]
Guevara, José Canuto, child.[4]
Guevara, José Sebastian, child.[4]
Guevara, Sebastian, Cat. vol.[4]
Guevara, José Francisco, child.[4]
Gutierrez, Ignacio Ma., soldier.[2]
Gutierrez, Felipe, soldier.[3]
Gutierrez, Manuel, servant.[3]
Gutierrez, Francisco, Cat. vol.[4]
Guzman, Isidro, soldier.[3]
Guzman, Juan Ma., child.[4]
Guzman, Toribio, soldier.[3]
Guztinzar, Manuel, servant.[4]
Haro, Felipe, Cat. vol.[4]
Hechedo, José Francisco.[4]
Henriquez, Antonio Dom., weaver.[4]
Heredia, Bernardino, soldier.[2]
Heredia, José Bernardo, soldier.[2]
Hernandez, José Rafael.[1]
Hernandez, Vicente Antonio.[2]
Hernandez, Justo, soldier.[3]
Hernandez, Juan José Antonio, child.[3]
Hernandez, Felipe, settler.[4]
Hernandez, Felipe, convict.[4]
Hernandez, José Antonio, settler.[4]
Hernandez, José, convict.[4]
Hernandez, J. José de la Luz, soldier.[4]
Hernandez, Antonio, saddler.[4]
Hernandez, Juan María, saddler.[4]
Hernandez, Juan, convict.[4]
Herrera, José, soldier.[4]
Higuera, Joaquin, soldier.[2]
Higuera, José Atanasio, soldier.[2]
Higuera, José Loreto, child.[2]
Higuera, José Manuel, soldier.[2]

Higuera, Juan José, soldier.[2]
Higuera, José Ignacio, soldier.[2]
Higuera, Bernardo de la Luz, child.[3]
Higuera, Juan José, child.[3]
Higuera, Salvador, soldier.[3]
Higuera, Tiburcio, child.[3]
Higuera, Tiburcio Javier, child.[4]
Higuera, Gregorio Ignacio Ma., child.[4]
Higuera, Hilario.[4]
Higuera, José 1°, soldier.[4]
Higuera, José 2°, soldier.[4]
Higuera, José Cárlos Salv., child.[4]
Higuera, José Gerónimo, child.[4]
Higuera, José Ma., child.[4]
Higuera, José Policarpo, child.[4]
Higuera, José Antonio.[4]
Higuera, José Joaquin.[4]
Higuera, Manuel, soldier.[4]
Higuera, Nicolás Antonio.[4]
Higuera, Salvador, soldier.[4]
Horchaga, José Hilario, child.[3]
Horchaga, José Manuel, child.[3]
Horchaga, Manuel, soldier.[3]
Hores, José, settler.[3]
Horra, Antonio de la C., padre.[4]
Hortel, Juan, Cat. vol.[4]
Ibarra, Francisco, servant.[2]
Ibarra, Andrés Dolores, child.[3]
Ibarra, Gil María, child.[3]
Ibarra, José Desiderio, child.[3]
Ibarra, Juan Antonio, soldier.[3]
Ibarra, Ramon, soldier.[3]
Ibarra, Albino, soldier.[4]
Ibarra, Antonio, child.[4]
Ibarra, Calixto José Antonio, child.[4]
Igadera, José, convict.[4]
Igareda, José Gordiano, settler.[4]
Iñiquez, Juan, Cat. vol.[4]
Islas, Miguel, soldier.[1]
Isvan, José Albino, soldier.[4]
Iturrate, Domingo S., padre.[4]
Izquierdo, José, soldier.[2]
Jaime, Antonio, padre.[4]
Jaume, Luis, padre.[1]
Jimenez, Francisco, Cat. vol.[4]
Jimenez, Hilario, soldier.[4]
Jimenez, Pascual Antonio, child.[4]
Juarez, Francisco, soldier.[3]
Juarez, José Joaquin, child.[4]
Juncosa, Dom, padre.[1]
Labra, Juan Antonio, soldier.[1]
Ladron de Guevara, José I., soldier.[4]
Landaeta, Martin, padre.[4]
Lasuen, Fermin Francisco, padre.[1]
Lara, José, settler.[3]
Lara, José Sostenes, child.[4]
Lara, Julian, soldier.[4]
Lara, José Antonio Seferino, child.[4]
Larios, José Ma., soldier.[3]
Lasso de la Vega, Ramon, alférez.[3]

Leal, Isidro José, servant.[2]
Leiva, Anastasio, soldier.[2]
Leiva, Agustin, soldier.[3]
Leiva, José Andrés, child.[3]
Leiva, José Antonio Ma., soldier.[1]
Leiva, Juan, soldier.[3]
Leiva, Miguel, soldier.[3]
Leiva, José Antonio.[4]
Leiva, José Rafael, child.[4]
Leiva, Manuel Ramon, child.[4]
Leiva, Rufino, soldier.[4]
Leon, José Ma., soldier.[2]
Leon, José Manuel, soldier.[2]
Lima, José, soldier.[3]
Linares, Ignacio, soldier.[2]
Linares, José de los S., child.[3]
Linares, Mariano de Dolores, child.[3]
Linares, Francisco, settler.[4]
Linares, Ramon, soldier.[4]
Linares, Salvador, soldier.[4]
Lineza, Miguel, Cat. vol.[1]
Lisalde, Diego.[4]
Lisalde, Félix, soldier.[4]
Lisalde, Juan Crisos. Antonio, child.[4]
Lizalda, Pedro Antonio, soldier.[2]
Llamas, Antonio, Cat. vol.[4]
Lledo, Rafael, carpenter.[4]
Llepis, José Mariano, servant.[2]
Lobo, José, soldier.[2]
Lobo, José Basilio, child.[3]
Lobo, Cecilio.[4]
Lobo, Pedro.[4]
Lopez, Baldomero, padre.[4]
Lopez, Jacinto, padre.[4]
Lopez, Juan Francisco, soldier.[1]
Lopez, Francisco, soldier.[2]
Lopez, Ignacio Ma. de Jesus.[2]
Lopez, Gaspar, soldier.[2]
Lopez, Joaquin, soldier.[2]
Lopez, José Ma., soldier.[2]
Lopez, Luis, soldier.[2]
Lopez, Pedro, servant.[2]
Lopez, Sebastian A., soldier.[2]
Lopez, José Antonio Gil, child.[3]
Lopez, José Ma. Ramon, child.[3]
Lopez, Juan José, child.[3]
Lopez, Melchor, soldier.[3]
Lopez, Juan, convict.[4]
Lopez, Cayetano, carpenter.[4]
Lopez, Claudio, soldier.[4]
Lopez, Cornelio Ma., child.[4]
Lopez, Ignacio, soldier.[4]
Lopez, Estévan Ignacio, child.[4]
Lopez, Juan José Trinidad, settler.[4]
Lozano, Pedro, Cat. vol.[4]
Lugo, Luis Gonzaga, soldier.[1]
Lugo, Francisco, soldier.[2]
Lugo, Ignacio, soldier.[2]
Lugo, José Ignacio, child.[2]
Lugo, Seferino, soldier.[2]

Lugo, José Antonio, soldier.[3]
Lugo, Salvador, soldier.[3]
Lugo, Ant. Ma., soldier.[4]
Lugo, José, Cat. vol.[4]
Lugo, José Antonio, child.[4]
Lugo, Juan Ma., child.[4]
Lugo, Juan, servant.[4]
Lugo, Miguel, soldier.[4]
Lugo, Pablo José, child.[4]
Lugo, Ramon Lorenzo, child.[4]
Lujan, José, alférez.[4]
Machado, José Antonio, child.[3]
Machado, José Manuel, soldier.[3]
Machado, José Agustin Ant., child.[4]
Machado, José Hilario.[4]
Machado, José Ignacio Ant., child.[4]
Machuca, José, settler.[4]
Malaret, Domingo, Cat. vol.[1]
Maldonado, Juan, Cat. vol.[4]
Mallen, Manuel, Cat. vol.[4]
Manrique, Sebastian, soldier.[1]
Manriquez, Luis, soldier.[2]
Manzana, Miguel A., Cat. vol.
Marin, Antonio, Cat. vol.[4]
Mariné y Salvatierra, J., artilleryman.[4]
Mariner, Juan, padre.[3]
Mario, Tomás, soldier.[2]
Marquez, Francisco Rafael, soldier.[2]
Marquez, José, soldier.[4]
Marron, Rafael, soldier.[3]
Martiarena, José Manuel, padre.[4]
Martin, Juan, padre.[4]
Martinez, Luis Antonio, padre.[4]
Martinez, Pedro Adriano, padre.[4]
Martinez, Luis María, soldier.[2]
Martinez, Toribio, soldier.[2]
Martinez, Dionisio, servant.[3]
Martinez, José Ma., soldier.[3]
Martinez, Juan Ignacio, soldier.[3]
Martinez, Norberto, child.[3]
Martinez, Antonio, soldier.[4]
Martinez, Bartolomé Mateo.[4]
Martinez, Gregorio, artilleryman.[4]
Martinez, José, Cat. vol.[4]
Martinez, José Leocadio, settler.[4]
Martinez, José Ma., settler.[4]
Martinez, Manuel, Cat. vol.[4]
Martinez, Máximo.[4]
Martinez, Máximo Ramon, child.[4]
Martinez, Reyes.[4]
Medina, José, artilleryman.[4]
Mejía, Pedro.[2]
Mejía, Francisco Javier, soldier.[3]
Mejía, Juan, soldier.[3]
Melecio, José, soldier.[3]
Mendoza, Manuel, soldier.[2]
Mendoza, José de los Reyes, child.[4]
Mendoza, Manuel, Cat. vol.[4]
Mendoza, Mariano, tilemaker.[4]
Mendoza, Mariano, José, weaver.[4]

Mendoza, Miguel, Cat. vol.[4]
Mequías, Juan Alberto, soldier.[3]
Mercado, Mariano, artilleryman.[4]
Merelo, Lorenzo, padre.[4]
Merino, Agustin, padre.[4]
Mesa, Nicolás Ma., child.[2]
Mesa, Valerio, soldier.[2]
Mesa, Dolores, soldier.[3]
Mesa, Ignacio, soldier.[3]
Mesa, Juan Antonio, soldier.[3]
Mesa, Luis Ma., child.[3]
Mesa, José Antonio, soldier.[4]
Mesa, José Julian Antonio, child.[4]
Mesa, Juan José, servant.[4]
Miguel, José, padre.[3]
Miranda, Juan Ma., soldier.[1]
Miranda, Alejo, soldier.[3]
Miranda, Antonio, soldier.[3]
Miranda, José Antonio, child.[3]
Miranda, Apolinario, child.[4]
Miranda, José Hilario, soldier.[4]
Miranda, José Mariano, Cat. vol.[4]
Miranda, José Santiago, child.[4]
Miranda, Juan Crisóstomo, child.[4]
Miranda, Vicente Manuel, child.[4]
Mojica, José Ma., settler.[4]
Mojica, Vicente, settler.[4]
Molas, José, Cat. vol.[1]
Molina, Joaquin, settler.[2]
Molina, Pedro, soldier.[2]
Monreal, José Antonio Nicolás, child.[4]
Monroy, José, soldier.[4]
Montaloan, Laureano, soldier.[3]
Montaña, Antonio, Cat. vol.[1]
Montaño, Antonio, soldier.[3]
Montero, Cesareo Antonio, child.[3]
Montero, Manuel, soldier.[4]
Monteverde, Francisco, artilleryman.[4]
Montial, Juan Andrés, soldier.[3]
Moraga, José Joaquin, alférez.[2]
Moraga, Gabriel, soldier.[3]
Moraga, Vicente José, child.[3]
Moreno, F. S., soldier.[4]
Moreno, Felipe Santiago, smith.[4]
Moreno, Felipe, settler.[3]
Moreno, José, settler.[3]
Moreno, Juan Francisco, child.[4]
Moreno, Manuel, soldier.[4]
Morillo, José Julian, soldier.[1]
Moumarus, Luis, Cat. vol.[1]
Muñoz, Manuel, mechanic.[3]
Mugártegui, Pablo, padre.[1]
Murguía, José Ant., padre.[1]
Murillo, Loreto, soldier.[2]
Murillo, Francisco, carpenter.[3]
Murillo, Juan, smith.[3]
Muruato, José, Cat. vol.[4]
Navarro, José Antonio, settler.[3]
Navarro, José Clemente, child.[3]
Navarro, José María, child.[3]

Nieto, José Manuel, soldier.[1]
Nieto, Juan José Ma., child.[3]
Nieto, Manuel Perez, soldier.[3]
Nieto, José Antonio Ma., soldier.[4]
Noriega, José Ramon, soldier.[1]
Noriega, José Raimundo, soldier.[2]
Noboa, Diego, padre.[3]
Nocedal, José, padre.[2]
Obaye, José Antonio, soldier.[2]
Oceguera, Faustino, Cat. vol.[4]
Ochoa, Francisco Javier.[1]
Ochoa, Felipe, soldier.[2]
Ojeda, Gabriel.[1]
Olivares, José Miguel, soldier.[2]
Olivares, José Francisco B., child.[3]
Olivares, Pedro Alcántara, child.[3]
Olivas, Juan Matias, soldier.[3]
Olivas, Cosme.[4]
Olivas, José Herculano, child.[4]
Olivas, José Lázaro Ma., child.[4]
Olivas, José Nicolás, child.[4]
Olivas, Pablo, settler.[4]
Olivera, José Ignacio, soldier.[1]
Olivera, Juan María, soldier.[1]
Olivera, Ignacio, servant.[1]
Olivera, Antonio Lúcas Ma., child.[2]
Olivera, Diego Ant. de la Luz, child.[3]
Olivera, José Desiderio, child.[3]
Olivera, José, soldier.[3]
Olivera, José Leonardo M., child.[3]
Olivera, José Ma. Matias, child.[3]
Olivera, Maximo José, child.[3]
Olivera, Tomás Antonio, child.[3]
Olivera, Higinio, soldier.[4]
Olivera, José Ant. Secundino, child.[4]
Olivera, Rosalina Ma., child.[4]
Oliveros, Lúcas.[4]
Olvera, Diego, servant.[2]
Olvera, Francisco, servant.[2]
Ontiveros, José Antonio, soldier.[1]
Ontiveros, Francisco, soldier.[3]
Ontiveros, Juan de Dios, settler.[4]
Ontiveros, Juan Ma.[4]
Ontiveros, Pacífico Juan, child.[4]
Ontiveros, Patricio, soldier.[4]
Orámas, Cristóbal, padre.[3]
Oribe, Tomás C., soldier.[3]
Orozco, José Manuel, servant.[1]
Ortega, José Francisco, sergeant.[1]
Ortega, Ignacio, soldier.[2]
Ortega, José Francisco Ma., child.[2]
Ortega, José Ma., soldier.[2]
Ortega, Juan, soldier.[2]
Ortega, Juan Cap. Ant. M. H., child.[2]
Ortega, José Ma. Martin, child.[3]
Ortega, Juan Cap., child.[3]
Ortega, Miguel, servant.[3]
Ortega, Francisco.[4]
Ortega, José Miguel, child.[4]
Ortega, José Quintin de los S., child.[4]

Ortega, José Vicente, soldier.[4]
Ortega, Antonio, convict.[4]
Ortega, Matias.[4]
Ortega, Miguel, Cat. vol.[4]
Ortel, Juan, Cat. vol.[4]
Osequera, Faustino, soldier.[4]
Osio, José Ma., Cat. vol.[4]
Osorio, José, artilleryman.[4]
Osorno, Pedro, convict.[4]
Osuna, Juan Ismerio.[1]
Osuna, Juan Luis, soldier.[2]
Osuna, Miguel, tailor.[3]
Osuna, José Joaquin, soldier.[3]
Osuna, José Ma.[4]
Osuna, Juan Nepomuceno, child.[4]
Otondo, Felipe, settler.[2]
Pacheco, Juan Salvio, soldier.[2]
Pacheco, Bartolomé Ignacio, settler.[2]
Pacheco, Rafael, convict.[4]
Pacheco, Miguel, soldier.[2]
Pacheco, Bartolo, soldier.[4]
Pacheco, Francisco, Cat. vol.[4]
Pacheco, Ignacio, child.[2]
Padilla, Juan, soldier.[3]
Padilla, Jacinto, Cat. vol.[4]
Pajarrales, settler.[4]
Palafox, José, Cat. vol.[4]
Palomares, José Cristóbal, soldier.[4]
Palomares, José Ramirez, soldier.[3]
Palou, Francisco, padre.[1]
Panella, José, padre.[4]
Parron, Fernando, padre.[1]
Paterna, Antonio, padre.[1]
Parrilla, Leon, lieutenant.[4]
Patron, Antonio José, soldier.[2]
Parra, José, soldier.[3]
Parra, José, child.[3]
Parra, José Antonio, settler.[3]
Parra, José Miguel Sabino, child.[3]
Patiño, José Victoriano, soldier.[3]
Payeras, Mariano, padre.[4]
Pedraza, José Antonio, settler.[3]
Pedro, José Antonio Ma. de S. T., child.[2]
Pedro, José Francisco de S. T., child.[2]
Pedro y Gil, Rafael, storekeeper.[2]
Peña, Francisco Ma., soldier.[1]
Peña, José Antonio, soldier.[1]
Peña, Gerardo, soldier.[2]
Peña, Luis, soldier.[2]
Peña, Eustaquio, child.[4]
Peña, José, artilleryman.[4]
Peña, Teodoro, Cat. vol.[4]
Peña y Saravia, Tomás, padre.[1]
Pengues, Miguel Sobrevía, Cat. vol.[1]
Peralta, Gabriel, soldier.[2]
Peralta, Juan José, soldier.[2]
Peralta, Luis Ma., soldier.[2]
Peralta, Pedro Regalado, soldier.[3]
Peralta, Hermenegildo Ignacio, child.[4]
Peralta, Juan.[4]

Peralta, Pantaleon, child.[4]
Perez, Juan, captain of vessel.[1]
Perez, Crispin, soldier.[2]
Perez, José Ignacio, soldier.[2]
Perez, Antonio Irimeo, child.[4]
Perez, Antonio Ma., child.[4]
Perez, Estévan.[4]
Perez, José Ma., soldier.[4]
Perez, José Ma., convict.
Perez, Juan Bautista, Cat. vol.[4]
Perez, Luis, soldier.[4]
Perez, Manuel, Cat. vol.[4]
Perez Fernandez, José, alférez.[4]
Perez de la Fuente, Pedro, settler.[3]
Pericas, Miguel, Cat. vol.[1]
Peyri, Antonio, padre.[4]
Pico, Santiago de la Cruz, soldier.[2]
Pico, Francisco Javier, soldier.[3]
Pico, José Dolores, soldier.[3]
Pico, José Ma., soldier.[3]
Pico, Juan Patricio, child.[3]
Pico, Joaquin, soldier.[4]
Pico, José Antonio Bernardo, child.[4]
Pico, José Vicente, child.[4]
Pico, Mariano.[4]
Pico, Miguel, soldier.[4]
Pico, Patricio, servant.[4]
Pieras, Miguel, padre.[1]
Piña, Juan Máximo, soldier.[3]
Piña, Mariano, servant.[3]
Piña, Pedro Rafael, child.[3]
Pinto, Juan María, soldier.[2]
Pinto, Pablo, soldier.[2]
Pinto, Marcelo, soldier.[3]
Planes, Gerónimo, Cat. vol.[1]
Plenelo, Valentin, Cat. vol.[1]
Pliego, José, settler.[4]
Palanco, José, soldier.[3]
Pollorena, Pedro.[2]
Pollorena, Juan, child.[4]
Pollorena, Rafael Eugenio, child.[4]
Portella, Francisco, Cat. vol.[1]
Portolá, Gaspar de, governor.[1]
Preciado, Venancio, servant.[3]
Prestamero, Juan, padre.[1]
Puga, Joaquin, servant.[2]
Puyol, Francisco, padre.[4]
Prat, Pedro, surgeon.[1]
Puig, Juan, sergt. Cat. vol.[1]
Quesada, Manuel, soldier.[4]
Quesada, Manuel, Cat. vol.[4]
Quijada, Ignacio Ma., child.[3]
Quijada, Vicente, soldier.[3]
Quijada, José Nazario de la T., child.[4]
Quijada, José Lorenzo, child.[4]
Quijada, Simon, child.[4]
Quintero, Luis, settler.[3]
Quintero, Clemente.[4]
Quintero, Teodosio.[4]
Quinto, Simon Tadeo.[4]

Ramirez, Francisco, soldier.[2]
Ramirez, Bernardo, soldier.[3]
Ramirez, José Antonio, carpenter.[4]
Ramirez, José Guadalupe.[4]
Ramos, José, smith.[3]
Ramos, José, convict.[4]
Ramos, Pablo Antonio, child.[3]
Rasa, Lorenzo, sailor.[2]
Rey, Cristóbal, Cat. vol.[4]
Rey, José, Cat. vol.[4]
Rey, Juan del, soldier.[4]
Reyes, Juan Francisco.[1]
Reyes, Martin, soldier.[1]
Reyes, Francisco, settler.[3]
Reyes, José Jacinto, child.[3]
Reyes, José, convict.[4]
Reyes, José, saddler.[4]
Reyes, Máximo Julian, child.[4]
Rio, Francisco del.[2]
Rioboo, Juan Antonio García, padre.[3]
Rios, Feliciano, soldier.[2]
Rios, Julian, soldier.[2]
Rios, Cayetano, child.[3]
Rios, Silverio Antonio Juan, child.[4]
Rivera, Tadeo, soldier.[2]
Rivera, Joaquin, stone-cutter.[4]
Rivera, Salvador, stone-cutter.[4]
Rivera y Moncada, Fernando, captain.[1]
Roberto, Justo, soldier.[3]
Roberto, Matias, child.[3]
Robles, Juan José, soldier.[1]
Robles, Manuel Ma., soldier.[2]
Robles, José Antonio, settler.[4]
Roca, Cárlos Pedro José, child.[4]
Roca, José, sergeant artilleryman.[4]
Rocha, Juan Estévan, soldier.[1]
Rocha, Cornelio, settler.[4]
Rocha, Cornelio, convict.[4]
Rocha, José, Cat. vol.[4]
Rocha, Juan José Lor., child.[4]
Rochin, Ignacio, soldier.[3]
Rodriguez, Manuel, carpenter.[1]
Rodriguez, José, servant.[2]
Rodriguez, Pablo, settler.[2]
Rodriguez, Vicente, soldier.[2]
Rodriguez, Alejo Máximo, child.[3]
Rodriguez, Inocencio José, child.[3]
Rodriguez, Joaquin, soldier.[3]
Rodriguez, José Antonio, soldier.[3]
Rodriguez, José Fran. Ant. L., child.[3]
Rodriguez, José Ignacio, soldier.[3]
Rodriguez, José de Jesus I., child.[3]
Rodriguez, José Leon, child.[3]
Rodriguez, José Ma., child.[3]
Rodriguez, Sebastian, child.[3]
Rodriguez, Alejandro, child.[4]
Rodriguez, Felipe Antonio, child.[4]
Rodriguez, José del Cármen S., child.[4]
Rodriguez, José Brigido, child.[4]
Rodriguez, Juan, child.[4]

Rodriguez, Juan Francisco, child.[4]
Rodriguez, Juan de Dios, child.[4]
Rodriguez, Manuel, cadet.[4]
Rodriguez, Matias, servant.[4]
Roman, José Joaquin, settler.[4]
Romero, Antonio, servant.[2]
Romero, Felipe, smith.[2]
Romero, Anselmo José Ignacio, child.[2]
Romero, José Domingo, child.[3]
Romero, José Estévan, soldier.[3]
Romero, José Ma. Basilio F., child.[3]
Romero, Juan María, child.[3]
Romero, Pedro, soldier.[3]
Romero, José Ant. Estévan, child.[4]
Romero, José Gregorio, child.[4]
Romero, José Man. Secundino, child.[4]
Romero, Juan Ma., soldier.[3]
Romero, Luis, soldier.[4]
Romero, Rafael, Cat. vol.[4]
Rosales, Bernardo, muleteer.[1]
Rosales, Cornelio, child.[2]
Rosales, José Cornelio, soldier.[4]
Rosalío, Eugenio, soldier.[2]
Rosas, Juan Estévan.[2]
Rosas, Alejo, settler.[3]
Rosas, Baltasar Juan José, child.[3]
Rosas, Basilio, settler.[3]
Rosas, Cárlos, child.[3]
Rosas, José Alejandro, settler.[3]
Rosas, José Máximo, settler.[3]
Rosas, José Máximo, child.[3]
Rosas, Gil Antonio, child.[4]
Rosas, José Darío, settler.[4]
Rosas, José, convict.[4]
Rosas, José Antonio, child.[4]
Rosas, José Antonio, soldier.[4]
Rosas, José Antonio Doroteo, child.[4]
Rosas, Leon María, child.[4]
Rosas, Luis María, child.[4]
Rubio, Ascensio Álvarez.[1]
Rubio, Bernardo.[1]
Rubio, José Cárlos.[1]
Rubio, Juan Antonio, soldier.[1]
Rubio, Cárlos, soldier.[1]
Rubio, Fran. Ramon de la L., child.[3]
Rubio, Mateo, soldier.[3]
Rubio, José Antonio, child.[4]
Rubio, Luis Ma., child.[4]
Rubio, Rafael Felipe, child.[4]
Rubiol, Francisco, Cat. vol.[4]
Rubí, Mariano, padre.[3]
Rueda, Pedro.
Ruelas, Fernando, soldier.[1]
Ruelas, Francisco, soldier.[3]
Ruelas, Venancio, Cat. vol.[4]
Ruiz, Antonio Vicente.[1]
Ruiz, Alejandro, soldier.[1]
Ruiz, Juan Ma., soldier.[1]
Ruiz, Diego Ma., soldier.[2]
Ruiz, Francisco Ma., soldier.[2]

Ruiz, Efigenio, soldier.[3]
Ruiz, Fructuoso Ma., soldier.[3]
Ruiz, Juan Pedro Jacinto, child.[3]
Ruiz, Nervo Pedro.[3]
Ruiz, Pedro José.[3]
Ruiz, Estévan, bricklayer.[4]
Ruiz, Ignacio, soldier.[4]
Ruiz, José Hilario, child.[4]
Ruiz, José Joaquin, child.[4]
Ruiz, Manuel, mechanic.[4]
Ruiz, Santiago, mason.[4]
Ruiz, Toribio, mason.[4]
Saez, Nazario, settler.[2]
Saez, Justo, soldier.[3]
Saez, Juan, settler.[4]
Saez, Miguel.[4]
Saenz, Ignacio, convict.[4]
Sajo, José, soldier.[3]
Sal, Hermenegildo, soldier.[2]
Sal, Ignacio Francisco, child.[4]
Sal, Domingo, child.[4]
Sal, Meliton, child.[4]
Salazar, Alonso Isidro, padre.[4]
Salazar, Doroteo de la Luz, child.[3]
Salazar, Doroteo, soldier.[3]
Salazar, José Loreto, soldier.[3]
Salazar, Juan José, child.[3]
Salazar, Miguel, soldier.[4]
Salas, Francisco, Cat. vol.[4]
Salazar, José Marcos, settler.[4]
Salazar, José, convict.[4]
Salazar, Miguel, soldier.[4]
Samaniego, José Ma. Gil, soldier.[3]
Samaniego, Pablo Ant. Nemesio, child.[3]
Samaniego, Tiburcio Antonio, child.[3]
Samaniego, José del Cármen, child.[4]
Sanchez, Francisco Miguel, padre.[1]
Sanchez, Joaquin, servant.[2]
Sanchez, José Antonio, soldier.[2]
Sanchez, Juan, sailor.[2]
Sanchez, Francisco, soldier.[3]
Sanchez, José Tadeo, soldier.[3]
Sanchez, José Segundo, soldier.[4]
Sanchez, José Antonio, child.[4]
Sanchez, Juan, soldier.[4]
Sanchez, Juan Ma., child.[4]
Sanchez, Vicente.[4]
Sanchez, Vicente Anastasio, child.[4]
Sangrador, Miguel, tanner.[4]
Sandoval, Antonio, servant.[2]
Sandoval, Gregorio Antonio, soldier.[3]
Santa Ana, José Francisco, child.[4]
Santa Catarina y Noriega, M., padre.[2]
Santa María, Vicente, padre.[2]
Santiago, Juan José M., padre.[3]
Sarmiento, Francisco, Cat. vol.[4]
Sarco, José Joaquin, artilleryman.[4]
Segundo, Angel, settler.[2]
Segura, Gregorio, smith.[3]
Señan, José Francisco de P., padre.[3]

Sepúlveda, Rafael, soldier.[2]
Sepúlveda, Juan José, soldier.[2]
Sepúlveda, Francisco Javier, soldier.[3]
Sepúlveda, Enrique.[4]
Sepúlveda, Francisco Javier, child.[4]
Sepúlveda, José Dolores, child.[4]
Sepúlveda, José Enrique A., child.[4]
Sepúlveda, José de los Dolores, child.[4]
Sepúlveda, Patricio.[4]
Sepúlveda, Sebastian, soldier.[4]
Serra, Junípero, padre.[1]
Serrano, Francisco, soldier.[3]
Serrano, Leandro José, child.[3]
Serrano, José María, Cat. vol.[4]
Servin, José Isidro, Cat. vol.[4]
Sierra, Benito, padre.[2]
Silva, José, settler.[2]
Silva, Hilario Leon José, child.[2]
Silva, José Manuel, servant.[2]
Silva, José Miguel, soldier.[2]
Silva, Juan de Dios J. S., child.[3]
Silva, Rafael, child.[3]
Silva, Hilario Leon José, child.[4]
Silva, José de los Santos, child.[4]
Silva, José Ma., child.[4]
Silva, José Manuel Victor, child.[4]
Silva, Teodoro.[4]
Sinova, José, soldier.[2]
Sinova, José Francisco, servant.[2]
Sitjar, Buenaventura, padre.[1]
Sola, Faustino, padre.[3]
Soberanes, José Ma., soldier.[1]
Soberanes, Agustin, servant.[2]
Soberanes, José Ma., soldier.[2]
Soler, Juan, store-keeper.[2]
Soler, Nicolás, captain.[3]
Soler, Pablo, surgeon.[4]
Solis, Alejandro, soldier.[2]
Solórzano, Francisco, soldier.[4]
Solórzano, Juan, soldier.[4]
Solórzano, Juan Mateo, child.[4]
Solórzano, Pio Antonio, child.[4]
Somera, José Antonio F., padre.[1]
Sorno, José Nolasco, settler.[4]
Sorde, José, Cat. vol.[1]
Sotelo, Francisco Antonio, soldier.[2]
Sotelo, José Antonio, soldier.[2]
Sotelo, José Gabriel, child.[3]
Sotelo, José Ma., child.[3]
Sotelo, José Antonio, child.[4]
Sotelo, José Ma. Tiburcio, child.[4]
Sotelo, Ramon, soldier.[4]
Soto, Mateo Ignacio.[1]
Soto, Alejandro, soldier.[2]
Soto, Damaso, child.[2]
Soto, Francisco José Dolores, child.[2]
Soto, Francisco Ma., child.[2]
Soto, Ignacio, soldier.[2]
Soto, Isidro, child.[2]
Soto, Francisco Rexis, soldier.[3]

Soto, Guillermo, soldier.[3]
Soto, Ignacio Javier.[3]
Soto, José Joaquin, child.[3]
Soto, Mariano, servant.[3]
Soto, Antonio, settler.[4]
Soto, José Ma. Ant., child.[4]
Soto, Juan.[4]
Soto, Miguel, soldier.[4]
Soto, Rafael.[4]
Soto, Tomás.[4]
Sotomayor, Alejandro, soldier.[1]
Sotomayor, José Crisógono.
Sotomayor, José Doroteo.
Suarez, Simon, lieutenant.[4]
Talamantes, soldier.[4]
Tapia, Felipe Santiago, soldier.[2]
Tapia, Bartolomé, servant.[3]
Tapia, Cristóbal.[3]
Tapia, José Bartolo, settler.[3]
Tapia, José Francisco, soldier.[3]
Tapia, Francisco, soldier.[4]
Tapia, José Antonio, child.[4]
Tapia, Mariano, potter.[4]
Tapinto, Mariano, tailor.[4]
Tapis, Estévan, padre.[3]
Tejo, Ignacio Antonio, Cat. vol.[4]
Ticó, José Joaquin, sergeant Cat. vol.[4]
Ticó, Fern. José Ma. Ign. M., child.[4]
Tobar, Albino, settler.[4]
Toca, José Manuel, teacher.[4]
Toral, José Perez, cadet.[4]
Torres, Victoriano, settler.[2]
Torres, Narciso, Cat. vol.[4]
Torres, Nicolás.[4]
Torrens, Hilario, padre.[3]
Trasviñas, Antonio, soldier.[1]
Trujillo, José, Cat. vol.[4]
Ulloa, José Santos, smith.[3]
Uribes, Miguel, settler.[4]
Ursetino, José, carpenter.[2]
Uría, José Antonio, padre.[4]
Usson, Ramon, padre.[1]
Valderrama, José Cornelio, settler.[4]
Valdés, Juan Bautista, soldier.[2]
Valdés, Antonio Albino, child.[3]
Valdés, Antonio Ma. de Sta M., child.[3]
Valdés, Eugenio, soldier.[3]
Valdés, José Basilio, child.[3]
Valdés, José Lorenzo, servant.[3]
Valdés, José Melesio, soldier.[3]
Valdés, Juan Melesio, soldier.[3]
Valdés, Luciano José, child.[3]
Valdés, Máximo Tomás, child.[3]
Valdés, Antonio.[4]
Valdés, Crecencio.[4]
Valdés, Francisco, Cat. vol.[4]
Valdés, Gregorio.[4]
Valdés, José Rafael, child.[4]
Valencia, José Manuel, soldier.[2]
Valencia, Francisco, soldier.[3]

Valencia, Ignacio.[3]
Valencia, Juan Ignacio, soldier.[3]
Valencia, Juan Vicente Cris., child.[3]
Valencia, Manuel, settler.[3]
Valencia, Miguel Antonio, child.[3]
Valencia, José Antonio, child.[4]
Valencia, José Manuel, child.[4]
Valenzuela, Agustin, soldier.[2]
Valenzuela, José Julian, child.[2]
Valenzuela, Rafael, soldier.[2]
Valenzuela, Angel, soldier.[3]
Valenzuela, Antonio Ma., child.[3]
Valenzuela, Gaspar José, child.[3]
Valenzuela, José.[3]
Valenzuela, José Antonio Ma., child.[3]
Valenzuela, José Manuel, soldier.[3]
Valenzuela, Antonio de Gr., child.[4]
Valenzuela, Joaquin, child.[4]
Valenzuela, José Antonio Ma., child.[4]
Valenzuela, José Candelario, child.[4]
Valenzuela, José Ignacio.[4]
Valenzuela, José Rafael, child.[4]
Valenzuela, Juan, soldier.[4]
Valenzuela, Juan Angel, child.[4]
Valenzuela, Juan Ma., child.[4]
Valenzuela, Máximo.[4]
Valenzuela, Pedro, soldier.[4]
Valenzuela, Simeon Máximo, child.[4]
Valenzuela, Vicente, soldier.[4]
Valenzuela, Vicente Antonio, child.[4]
Valenzuela, José Ma., child.[3]
Valenzuela, José Matías, child.[3]
Valenzuela, José Miguel, child.[3]
Valenzuela, José Pedro, soldier.[3]
Valenzuela, José Ramon, soldier.[3]
Valenzuela, Segundo, soldier.[3]
Valero, Ignacio, soldier.[4]
Vallejo, Ign. Vicente Ferrer, soldier.[2]
Vallejo, Juan José, soldier.[2]
Vallejo, José de Jesus, child.[4]
Vanegas, Cosme.[4]
Varelas, Casimiro, settler.[2]
Varelas, Juan, child.[2]
Varelas, José Cayetano, child.[3]
Varelas, José Manuel, child.[4]
Varelas, Juan, soldier.[4]
Vargas, Manuel, sergeant.[3]
Vazquez, Gil Anastasio, soldier.[2]
Vazquez, José Francisco, child.[2]
Vazquez, Juan Atanasio, soldier.[2]
Vazquez, Juan Silverio, child.[2]
Vazquez, José Tiburcio, settler.[2]
Vazquez, Antonio, soldier.[4]
Vazquez, José, convict.[4]
Vazquez, Faustino.[4]
Vazquez, Felipe.[4]
Vazquez, Félix.[4]
Vazquez, Hermenegildo.[4]
Vazquez, José Antonio Pablo, child.[4]
Vazquez, José Timoteo, settler.[4]

Vazquez, Julio Ma., child.[4]
Vega, José Manuel, Cat. vol.[4]
Vegas, Matías, soldier.[2]
Véjar, Pablo, carpenter.[4]
Véjar, Salv., carpenter.[4]
Velarde, José Jacobo, soldier.[2]
Velarde, José Ma., soldier.[3]
Velarde, Agustin.[4]
Velarde, José Luciano.[4]
Vegerano, José Ma., muleteer.[1]
Velasco, Fernando, soldier.[3]
Velasco, José Ignacio Mateo, child.[3]
Velazquez, José.[1]
Velazquez, José Ma., convict.[4]
Velez, José Miguel, settler.[2]
Velis, José, Cat. vol.[4]
Verdugo, Joaquin.[1]
Verdugo, José Ma., soldier.[1]
Verdugo, Francisco Ma. de la Cruz.[1]
Verdugo, Mariano de la Luz, soldier.[1]
Verdugo, Florencio, soldier.[2]
Verdugo, Ignacio Leonardo Ma.[2]
Verdugo, Juan Diego, soldier.[2]
Verdugo, Juan Ma., soldier.[3]
Verdugo, Leonardo, soldier.[3]
Verdugo, Manuel José, child.[3]
Verdugo, Anselmo José, child.[4]
Verdugo, Joaquin.[4]
Verdugo, José Francisco, child.[4]
Verdugo, Juan Andrés Dolores, child.[4]
Verdugo, Julio Antonio José, child.[4]
Verdugo, Meliton José.[4]
Verduzco, Anastasio Javier.[1]
Viader, José, padre.[4]
Victoriano, soldier.[1]
Vila, Vicente, captain of vessel.[1]
Villa, José, settler.[3]
Villa, Vicente Ferrer, child.[3]
Villa, Eleuterio.[4]

Villa, José Antonio Doroteo, child.[4]
Villa, José Francisco Antonio, child.[4]
Villa, Pascual, soldier.[4]
Villa, Rafael.[4]
Villalba, Onofre, Cat. vol.[4]
Villagomez, Francisco, soldier.[2]
Villalobos, José, soldier.[2]
Villalobos, José Ma., child.[4]
Villaseñor, José, artilleryman.[4]
Villavicencio, Rafael, soldier.[1]
Villavicencio, José Antonio, child.[2]
Villavicencio, Antonio, settler.[3]
Villavicencio, Félix, settler.[3]
Villavicencio, Pascual, settler.[4]
Villavicencio, José, soldier.[4]
Villarino, Félix Antonio, settler.[4]
Villela, Juan Manuel, soldier.[2]
Villela, Marcos, soldier.[4]
Viñals, José, padre.[4]
Virjan, Manuel, muleteer.[2]
Vizcaino, Juan, padre.[1]
Vizcarra, José, soldier.[4]
Yorba, Antonio, Cat. vol.[1]
Yorba, Francisco Javier, soldier.[4]
Yorba, José Antonio.[4]
Yorba, José Domingo, child.[4]
Yorba, Tomás.[4]
Zambrano, Nicolás, soldier.[1]
Zayas, José Salvador, soldier.[3]
Zúñiga, Pedro B., child.[2]
Zúñiga, Pio Quinto, soldier.[2]
Zúñiga, José, lieutenant.[3]
Zúñiga, José Antonio, child.[3]
Zúñiga, José Valentin Q., child.[3]
Zúñiga, Serapio Ma., child.[3]
Zúñiga, Guillermo A., child.[4]
Zúñiga, José Manuel, child.[4]
Zúñiga, Ventura.[4]

NOTE: Some of the persons mentioned in connection with the earliest expedition, especially those to whom no special occupation is assigned, never came to Alto, California at all, or only came as vaqueros or escorts to return immediately. Another source of error is the uniformity of Spanish given names and the fact that men were known at different times by different names or combination of names to avoid confusion; hence there is no doubt that the list contains a certain amount of repetitions.

Allen, Geo., 1822.
Anderson, Mary, 1829–30.
Anderson, Stephen, 1828.
Baldwin, James M., 1814–15.
Bee, Henry J., 1830.
Bob, a negro, 1816.
Bolbeda, Louis, 1826.
Bolcof, José, 1815.
Bones, John, 1821.
Bonifacio, J. B., 1822.
Borris, Wm or Jas, 1823.
Bouchet, Louis, 1828.
Bowman, Joaquin, 1826.
Breck, James, 1829.
Buckle, Sam., 1822–3.
Buckle, Wm, 1822–3.
Burke, James W., 1824.
Burns, John, 1830.
Burton, John, 1825.
Call, Daniel, 1816.
Chapman, Joseph, 1818.
Charles, Michael, 1826.
Coleman, Geo., 1827.
Cook, James, 1830.
Cooper, John B. R., 1823.
Dana, Wm G., 1826.
Davis, John, 1828.
Devoll, Phil. L., 1830.
Dillon, Joseph, 1824.
Doak, Thos, 1816.
Dodero, Nicolás, 1827.
Domingo, Juan, 1830.
Duckworth, Walter, 1829.
Elwell, Robt J., 1827.
Fellom, Matthew, 1821–4.
Ferguson, Daniel, 1824.
Ferguson, Jesse, 1828.
Fisher, a negro, 1818.
Fitch, Hen. D., 1826.
Flemming, James, 1829.
Fling, Guy F., 1826.
Foxen, Benj., 1826.
Fuller, John C., 1823.
Galbraith, Isaac, 1826.
Gale, Wm A., 1810.
Garner, Wm R., 1824.
Gilroy, John, 1814.
Glande, Giov., 1827.
Goddard, Nic., 1824.
Graham, John, 1791.
Grålbatch, Wm, 1825.
Grant, James, 1825.
Grover, Sam., 1816.
Gyzelaar, Hen., 1816.
Harris, James, 1830.
Hartnell, Wm E. P., 1822.
Higgins, John, 1830.
Hill, Daniel A., 1823.
Hinckley, Wm S., 1829.
Jackson, Joseph, 1827.

Johnson, Corn. A., 1826.
Jones, John C., 1830.
Jones, Thos J., 1821.
Kinlock, Geo., 1829.
Laughlin, Rich., 1828.
Lawrence, Jos. V., 1821.
Leandry, John B., 1827.
Lester, Thos, 1817.
Lewis, Allen, 1830.
Littlejohn, David, 1824.
Littleton, John, 1826.
Livermore, Robert, 1822–4.
Lodge, Michael, 1822.
Logan, Wm, 1826.
McAllister, Mich., 1822.
McCarty, James, 1824.
McFerion, James, 1824.
McIntosh, Ed, 1823.
McKinley, James, 1824.
Macondray, Fred. W., 1822.
Malcolm, Julian, 1814.
Martin, John, 1822.
Mason, Anthony A., 1816.
Mayo, Geo., 1816.
Moreno, Santiago, 1824.
Mulligan, John, 1814–15.
Murphy, Tim., 1828.
Mutrel, Jean B., 1827.
Nye, Gorham H., 1830.
Olivera, Manuel D., 1829.
Pacheco, Jordan, 1829.
Park, Thos B., 1826.
Pascual, Mateo J., 1818.
Pasos, Manuel D., 1822–4.
Pattie, Sylvester, 1828.
Peirce, Henry A., 1828.
Pereira, Joaquin, 1826.
Pombert, Louis, 1826.
Pope, Wm, 1828.
Prentice, Sam., 1830.
Pryor, Nath. M., 1828.
Rainsford, John, 1829.
Read, John, 1826–8.
Rice, Geo. J., 1826.
Richardson, Wm A., 1822.
Roach, John, 1830.
Robbins, Thos M., 1823.
Robinson, Alfred, 1829.
Rocha, Ant. J., 1815.
Rose, John, 1818.
Roy, Pierre, 1782.
Satte, J. J., 1827.
Sawyer, Jos., 1828.
Scott, James, 1826.
Shaw, Thos, 1824.
Slover, Isaac, 1828.
Smith, Charles, 1828.
Smith, Thos L., 1829.
Smith, Wm, 1806.
Smith, Wm, 1827.

Snook, Jos. F., 1830.
Spence, David, 1824.
Stearns, Abel, 1829.
Steel, Jos., 1826.
Stewart, Thos, 1824.
Taylor, Wm, 1828.
Temple, John, 1827.
Thomas, Ignacio, 1818.
Thompson, A. B., 1825.
Thompson, James, 1828.
Trevethen, Wm, 1826.
Turner, John S., 1826.
Vincent, Geo. W., 1826.

Warren, Wm, 1828.
Watson, Dav. or Jas, 1823–4.
Watson, Ed, 1828.
Welsh, Wm, 1821.
White, Michael, 1829.
Williams, Geo., 1829.
Willis, Wm, 1828.
Wilson, James, 1824.
Wilson, John, 1826.
Wilson, John, 1826.
Wilson, John H., 1826.
Wilson, Julian, 1828.
Wilson, Wm, 1822.

PREFACE

PIONEER REGISTER AND INDEX.

1542-1848.

ALL history, as a record of the acts of men, is biography. In these pages it is proposed by means of an alphabetic index to make available as biographical matter the first five volumes of this work, covering the annals of California from its discovery to 1848. Through this index the reader may have access directly to all that is told in the work about any man of the thousands whose acts make up the country's early history. The names will not in most cases be repeated in the general index at the end of vol. vii.; but to that index the reader is referred for additional matter relating to such of these persons as were prominent after 1848, and also for information about men who, though mentioned in the history, did not come to California.

But I propose to carry this record far beyond the limits of a mere index. To the thousands of names mentioned in the history will be added other thousands which it has not been necessary to mention there. Thus will be presented a complete register of pioneers, or early Californians. Something more is done, however, than merely to register names and dates. In many cases —indeed, in all when it is desirable and possible—information is given respecting the nationality, occupation, achievements, death, and family connections of each subject, as well as about the date and manner of his coming to California and his connection in public capacities with the country's annals. In this way the index and register is expanded into a kind of biographic dictionary.

Of foreign pioneers—that is, not of Spanish and Indian blood—including both residents and visitors, my register contains all the names I have been able to obtain, except those found in the shipping articles and crew-lists of trading vessels and muster-rolls of naval craft. Some of the former and many of the latter are accessible, but they would multiply my lists to no good purpose. Yet when a sailor returned to California in later years I have regarded him as a pioneer under the date of his earliest visit. Of Spaniards, Mexicans, and native Californians, I have not attempted to present complete lists; yet the aim has been to register all who acquired any sort of prominence in territorial or local affairs, all the well-known traders and rancheros, all the friars, all the military and civil officials, all the leading families in each section. The reader is also referred to the list published at the end of vol. i., many of the same names being repeated here with additional information.

Obviously the most rigid condensation has been necessary, and the biographic notes must be very brief; yet the natural impression at first glance that they are too short will in most cases be removed on closer examination. Seven eighths of the names—even if we could obtain additional information and had space for its presentment—would in their connection with Californian history call for nothing beyond what is here given. Of the rest, a large proportion is that of public men whose acts are sufficiently recorded and discussed elsewhere, requiring only the index reference., I would call particular attention to this phase of the matter and to a cognate one. Ask a pioneer for his reminiscences or a sketch of his life, and he will fill his narrative chiefly with the journey of his immigrant party across the plains, the organization of his regiment and its voyage round Cape Horn, his service in the California battalion, his experience in the Bear Flag revolt, or at the fight of San Pascual, or with other well-known historic happenings in which he took part, and which he remembers with pride. But these events are fully treated elsewhere, and the pages devoted to an immigrant party are added by the index to the biography of each member of the party; the chapter on the New York volunteers, or the Mormon colony, to the life of each volunteer and colonist; that on the Graham affair to the record of each exile. Thus a large amount of matter not biographical on its face is legitimately added to the Pioneer Register. It is also to be noted that the lives of many early friars and officers have been given in connection with their departure or death, requiring only a reference here. True, there remains after all a class of pioneers, a hundred or two in number, permanent residents, representative citizens, founders of families, but not directly connected with public affairs, to each of whom a few pages instead of a few lines might be devoted with interest, often with profit; yet these are the men who are given in this register the greatest average space, and it is doubtful if that space could be increased consistently with the scope of such a work.

There will be noted an entire absence of the indiscriminate eulogy so often deemed an essential feature of pioneer sketches. I have neither space nor disposition to indulge in praise or blame, either for the purpose of pleasing or displeasing pioneers or their descendants, or of adding the interest of mild scandal to my sketches. Of private individuals, as a rule, no attempt is made to depict the character, to picture them as 'nature's noblemen,' or to point out the fact that they were not members of temperance societies. It is taken for granted that they were more or less good, bad, and indifferent citizens according to circumstances; but their weaknesses and virtues, within certain limits, do not concern me or my readers. Doubtless I have recorded many items about individuals that they and their friends would prefer to have suppressed, and suppressed many items that to enemies would be most agreeable reading; but in each case I have acted on my own judgment and with strict impartiality. Where a man's distinguishing traits are so clearly marked that they may be fairly presented in few words, especially in the case of men locally famous, I have not hesitated to write the few words, whether complimentary or otherwise. Public men are freely criticised, but mainly in other parts of the work where their acts are recorded, only a summary or moderate reflection of general conclusions being introduced here. In the comparative extent and general tone of the notices, no distinction is made by reason of race between Spaniards, Mexicans, Californians, and foreigners; between soldiers and civilians, friars and laymen, sailors and immigrants, traders and rancheros, rich and poor, the living and the dead; but, other things being equal, more space is given to early pioneers than to those of later years. If a line or two of extra space is occasionally devoted to a man who has furnished documentary and other evidence on early times, and the record of another man who has shown no interest is briefer, the difference does not necessarily indicate partiality, since in many instances certain kinds of information about a man can be obtained only from himself or some member of his family.

From the nature of the case, my authorities, except in special instances, cannot be cited. Such citations would involve endless repetition, and would fill much space that can be utilized to better advantage. The reader is referred to the general list of authorities in vol. i.; but it is proper to specify here some classes that have been particularly prolific in items for this register. First in importance are the archives, public, private, and missionary; especially in their records of naturalization and passports, custom-house records, military rosters, local census lists, voting and official lists, mission registers of births and marriages and deaths, and the correspondence of officials, friars, and citizens; particularly important among the private archives being the commercial correspondence and account-books of such men as Larkin, Cooper, Hartnell, Spear, and many others. Next should be mentioned the several hundred volumes of personal reminiscences furnished for my use by early Californians, native and foreign, each containing a few—some very many—personal items in addition to those relating to the narrator and his family. Third may be noted the work of such specialists as Clark on the N. Y. volunteers, Tyler on the Mormon battalion, McGlashan on the Donner party, Kooser on the artillery company, Lancey on the conquest in general, etc.; with valuable muster-rolls kindly furnished me by the military department at Washington. Fourth, and amply worthy of separate mention, we have the biographic gleanings of Ben Hayes on the pioneers of southern California; while in the same connection may be mentioned the patient researches of Alex. S. Taylor. Fifth, the archives of the Society of Pioneers contain, besides lists of members, partials rolls of the Cal. battalion; while the government lists of those who held 'Cal. claims,' Wheeler's list of San Francisco lot-owners, the voluminous testimony in famous land cases, and especially the valuable New Helvetia diary of '45-8, furnished me by Wm F. Swasey, should not be forgotten. Sixth are to be noted the newspapers of '47-85, with their thousands of obituary and biographic items, so faulty in individual cases, so extremely valuable in the aggregate; and, similar in many respects, the county and local histories of recent years, from which I have drawn much material. Finally, I must allude to special correspondence with many pioneers from time to time as particular information has been needed; hundreds having replied, and a few—such as John Bidwell, Wm H. Davis, Wm Glover, S. H. Willey, John A. Swan, and others—meriting fuller acknowledgment than my space permits.

That this register will be appreciated in any degree commensurate with the labor it has cost is not to be expected. Within my knowledge nothing of the kind has ever been attempted in any new country. The value that in any of the older communities would now be attached to such a record, had it been made at the beginning, is my basis for estimating the prospective usefulness of this.

The references are to the *History of California*, vol. i.-v.; that is, 'iii. 475,' in connection with a man's name, indicates that on page 475, vol. iii. of the *Hist. Cal.*, some information about the man, or at least a mention, will be found; when the reference is enclosed in parentheses, as, (v. 340,) the reader is directed to some event or party with which the man was connected, without a mention of his name. With a view to condensation, abbreviations are freely used, but none, I think, which require explanation. The register will be continued alphabetically at the end of vol. iii., iv., and v.

Abbott (Austin R.), 1847, Co. K, N.Y. Vol. (v. 499), living at Sacramento '82.   Abeck (François), 1847, a Swiss in Sutter's empoy at N. Helv. in '47-8. One of the earliest gold-miners.

Abell (Alex. G.), 1847, native of N.Y., who went to Honolulu in '45; arrived at S. F. in Nov. on the *Currency Lass*. Member of the firm J. B. Mc-Clurg & Co. at Los Angeles till Feb. '48. From '49 well known as a business man at S. F., member of the state senate in '63, and prominent in the masonic order in later years. Living at S.F. in '85. A son, John, came with him in '47; another son, E. A., died in '84.

Abella (Juan), 1842, Mex. captain, of Ind. race, who came with Michel-torena and departed with him in '45. Acting comandante of the batallon fijo (iv. 287, 351, et seq.), after the departure of Tellez, and com. of the post at Monterey in '45. He left his business affairs in charge of Larkin, at whose house he had lived, and wrote to L. from S. Blas. He signed his name 'Abeya.' See vol. iv. p. 289, 357, 405, 460, 487, 514-15, 652.

Abella (Ramon), 1798, Span. friar, who served chiefly at S. F., S. Cárlos, and S. Luis Ob., dying in 1842; for many years the only survivor of those who came before 1800. Biog., iv. 647; mention in i. list of auth., p. 432, 577, 712, 732; ii. 130-2, 159-60, 198, 288, 321-3, 329-30, 373, 375, 383, 394, 616, 655; iii. 92, 96, 191, 319, 356, 396, 446, 588, 622, 679, 681, 683; iv. 46, 372, 657.

Abernethy (John J.), 1847, asst surgeon, U. S. *Lexington*.   Aborn (John), 1846, in Sta Clara val., apparently an overland immig., serving perhaps in Co. F, Cal. Bat. (v. 358-60).   Ábrego (Emigdio), 1842, Mex. lieut of the batallon fijo, '42-5. See iv. 289.

Ábrego (José), 1834, Mex. hatter and trader, who came with the H. & P. colony (iii. 259 et seq.), and opened a store at Mont. Young, intelligent, with some capital, and of good repute, he soon became a prominent citizen, holding office continuously from '36, as comisario de policía, administrator of S. Antonio mission, customs officer, member of the assembly, substitute member of the tribunal superior, and treasurer. As sub-comisario and treasurer he was in charge of the territorial finances in 1839-46, possessing the confidence of all classes. In '41-2 he was involved in controversies with Gen. Vallejo in the matter of distributing funds, as also in '45-6 with Pico's administration; but these quarrels resulted from his position rather than his character, no one questioning his integrity or ability. He revisited Mex. in '43-4. In '44 he was the grantee of the Pt Pinos rancho, and later claimant for S. Francisquito. After the U. S. occupation he deemed it his duty as a Mex. to decline office for a time, but later held some local positions. He continued his career as hatter, soap-manufacturer, and merchant, with more or less success and undiminished popularity, till his death in '78, at the age of 65. In '36 he married Josefa Estrada, half-sister of Gov. Alvarado, who survived him with six of their children. The two daughters were married to Judge Webb of Salinas and J. Bolado of S. F. One of the sons married a daughter of Jacob P. Leese. For mention of Ábrego, see vol. i. list of auth.; iii. 263, 592, 597, 601-2, 672, 675, 678, 687-8; iv. 97, 99, 198, 210, 282, 327-8, 341, 357, 377, 401-3, 432, 520, 522, 532, 540, 557-8, 563; v. 35, 38, 41, 289, 455, 570, 636.

Acacio, Indian of S. José involved in troubles with Sutter's Ind. in 1840. iv. 137-8.   Accolti (M.), 1848, Jesuit prominent in educational affairs at Sta Clara college, and St Ignatius, S. F., dying in '78; perhaps from Or. in '48.   Acebedo (Francisco), soldier who came before 1780, sergeant of the S. Diego Co. from 1798, and a settler at Los Ang. in 1808-19. i. 647; ii. 101, 350, 354.   A. (José). i. 569.   A. (Julian), i. 303. See also list i. 732.   Acedo (Ignacio), resid. of Brancif. 1801-10; com. de policía, Mont., '33; Mex. convict, '34; cavalry sold. at Mont., and employé at S. F. Solano, '36. Doubtless several distinct persons. ii. 167; iii. 673, 720.   A. (Tiburcio), had a Cal. claim in '46 (v. 462–8) for $3,670.   Aceves (Antonio), settler at S. José and grantee of Salinas rancho 1790–5. i. 478, 683; ii. 664.   A. (José), hero of the 1st marriage at Sta Cruz in 1794–5. i. 495. See also list i. 732.   Ackerman (J. Howard), 1847, clerk for Wm A. Leidesdorff at S. F., '47–8, and owner of a town lot. v. 685.   Ackley (Henry), 1847, Co. E, N. Y. Vol. (v. 499).   Acres (Hiram), 1845, Amer. immig. from Or. in the McMahon-Clyman co. (iv. 472–4, 587). At N. Helv., Sonoma, and Napa in '46–8, perhaps later.   B. Akers, probably the same or a son, served in the Cal. Bat. (v. 358–60).   Acuña, 1818, one of Bouchard's men. ii. 220–49, 232.   Adair (Wesley), 1847, Co. C, Morm. Bat. (v. 469–98). In '82 an Ariz. farmer.

Adams, 1847, mr of the *Loo Choo.* v. 511, 576.   Adams, master of the *Forrester,* on the coast perhaps in '15. ii. 274.   Adams, Amer., aged 30, at Branciforte, padron of '45.   A. (Charles), 1840, Scotch sailor, who left the *Columbia* and became a lumberman in '41.

Adams (David L.), 1846, Amer. immig. from Indiana, age 10 (v. 528). His father died on the way, and he lived on the Yuba a while with his mother —who married Abner Bryan—and sisters. At S. José '47 and from '49; Placerville mines '48–9. After a course of study at the Univ. of the Pac. in '59–61, he settled on a farm near Sta Cruz in '62, marrying Julia Bennett of the '43 immig. in '63. In '81, and I suppose later, he lived in the town of Sta Cruz with a family of 6 children, being in the lumber trade. *Sta Cruz Co. Hist.,* 27–8. In March '85 he writes me from S. Bernardino.

Adams (Elisha), 1846, said by Hall to have come to the Sta Clara val. A. (Henry), mr of the *Paradise* in '27. iii. 148.   Another Henry A. is vaguely accredited to '44. iv. 453; and another, or the same, is named by Tinkham as a boy on Howard's vessel in '46, later pres. of the Stockton Pion. Soc.

Adams (James Harmon), 1847, Co. A, N. Y. Vol., trans. to Co. G (v. 499). Born in N. Y. '19; opened a shoe-shop at L. Ang. '47, while still in the service; policeman at S. F. '49–54; at Vallejo '55–60; and at S. F. '61–85. His wife of '39, Matilda Smith, one of the original members of the 1st Presb. church of S. F., died in '79. A son, James Hardie A., born on the voy. to Cal., died in '49; a daughter died at L. Ang. in '48. Another son, John Quincy A., 3 years old on arrival, was educated in the 1st public schools at S. F.; presented with a gold nugget on the plaza by a miner as the 1st schoolboy he had seen in Cal.; played juvenile parts in the Jenny Lind theatre; served on the U. S. *Warren* '55–6; office-boy for Com. Farragut at Mare Isl. '57–8; law student at Benicia '66–7; lawyer at S. F. from '73. He has been orator at pioneer celebrations, sec. of surviving N. Y. Vol., and has afforded me some aid in the collection of historical material.

Adams (John), 1846, lieut Co. C, 1st U. S. Dragoons (v. 536).   A. (John), 1846, midshipman on the U. S. *Dale.* Another John Adams had a Cal. claim (v. 462–8) of $200 in '46; voted at S. Diego in '48; and settled near Napa—perhaps 2 or 3 different men.   A. (Jos. H.), lieut on the *Savannah* and *Levant* in '44–5.   A. (Orson B.), sergt in Co. C, Morm. Bat. '47–8. v. 477.

Adams (Walter W.), 1840, Boston sailor arrested at Mont. but not exiled. iv. 17, 120. Shipped on the *California* in '42, and later on the *Laura.* In '44 disabled at Sta B. and Mont., being aided by the U. S. consulate, and getting a carta; but in Aug. he shipped on the *Chas W. Morgan.*   A. (Washington), 1847, Co. B, N. Y. Vol. (v. 499).   A. (Wm), named by Hall as having come to Sta Clara val. in '46.

Addison (Isaac), 1846, a Mormon of the *Brooklyn* colony, v. 546, with his wife and daughter. He was excommunicated from the church, and returned east before Jan. '47.   S. K. Addison bought a town lot at S. F. in '48.

Adler (Lewis), 1846, German cooper who came from Honolulu on the *Euphemia.* Clerk for Leidesdorff and Dickson & Hay, at S. F. in '46–7, also owning a town lot. A trader from '48 at Son., where he still lived in '85, at the age of 65.

Adrian (Geo.), 1836, named in a S. José padron as a foreign resident.   Afanadon, or Afanador, chaplain who came in '22 with the Canónigo Fernandez.

ii. 458.   Agate, scientist attaché of the U. S. ex. exped. in '41. iv. 243.
Agazini (Flaminio), '25, mr of the transport *Morelos*. iii. 148.   Agnew (Hugh)
1847, Co. H, N. Y. Vol. (v. 499).   Agredo, doubtful name of a school-boy at
Mont. '15-20. ii. 429.   Agricia (José), grantee of the Laureles rancho in '44.
iv. 655.   Aguado (Ignacio), Mex. lieut of the batallon fijo in '42-5. iv. 289.
Aguiar (Francisco), soldier of 1769 et seq.; sergt at S. Diego in 1777. i. 314, 732.
     Águila (José), Mex. settler at S. F. in 1791-1800. i. 716; munic. elector at
S. F. in 1827. ii. 592.   From '28 José Águila, or José M. Aguilar (between
which names there is evident confusion), was a somewhat prominent citizen
of Mont. In '31-34 he was síndico; in '32-3 regidor and com. de policía. iii.
672-3; in '33 vocal of the diputacion. iii. 246; in '36 admin. at Soledad. iii.
690-1; in '38-9 clerk to admin. of S. Antonio. iii. 687-8; and in '44 grantee
of the Cañada de Nogales rancho. iv. 634. In a Mont. padron of '36 José
Águila is described as a painter, 50 years of age, native of Celaya, married to
María Fran. García, aged 37.   Águila (Felipe), land near
Mont. in' 35. iii. 678.   A. (Joaquin), claimant for land at Sta Inés in '47.
A. (Lugardo), resid. of S. Gabriel in '46.   A. (Ramon), soldier of S. F. in '37-
43. iv. 667. See list i. 732.
     Aguilar (Blas), son of Rosario A., born at S. Diego about 1808. In '31
majordomo of S. D. mission, and in '34 at Temécula. Lived in '38-43 at the
Palomares rancho, Los Ang. Co. In '41 got land at S. Juan Cap., where in
'46 he was living at the age of 38 with his wife Antonia Gutierrez, aged 29.
Padron; where he was alcalde in '48, and where he still lived in '76. See
mention in ii. 443, 550; iii. 620; iv. 626; v. 624.   An Aguilar is ment. as one
of Bouchard's men in '18. ii. 232.   A. (Antonio), soldier at S. F. '19-23;
resid. of Los Ang. in '38, murdered in '42. iii. 564-5; iv. 632.   A. (Casildo),
trader at Los Ang., age 26, in '39; juez de aguas in '46. iv. 625; claimant for
La Ciénega.   A. (Cristóbal), resid. of Los Ang., age 24, from '38, when he
was alcalde suplente; in '44-5, regidor. iii. 636; iv. 633.
     Aguilar (Francisco Javier), soldier of the Loreto co., who served in the
exped. of 1769 et seq. to S. Diego and Mont., but never came to live in Cal.
A sergt from 1795; in command at C. S. Lúcas of a militia co. 1795-1800.
A. (Gabino), at San Juan Cap. in '46, age 30, with his wife María Ant. Sesena
and 6 children. *Padron.*   A. (Ignacio), said to have fired the gun at Mervine's defeat '46. v. 319.   A. (José M.), settler at Los Ang. fr. '14; regidor
'21, '25-6; in trouble with Gov. Victoria in '31. In the padron of '39 he is
noted as a bricklayer, age 54. ii. 349, 359, 559-60; iii. 196. (See also Águila,
José.)   A. (Macedonio), resid. of Los Ang. in '39, age 30; juez de campo in '43-
5. iv. 632-4.   A. (Martin), Span. com. of one of Vizcaino's explor. vessels in
1602-3. i. 98, 104, 242.   A. (Ramon), killed by the Ind. in '46. v. 617.
     Aguilar (Rosario), corporal of the escolta at S. Diego and S. Luis Rey
missions from shortly after 1800. Lived at S. Diego fr. about '30, being
majordomo of the mission in '38, and getting a grant of the Paguai rancho—
which he is said to have refused—in '39. In '41 he was juez de paz at S. D.,
but obtained land at S. Juan Cap., where he was juez in '43-4, and where he
died about '45. ii. 546; iii. 612, 619, 620-3, 626-7. His daughter married José
Ant. Serrano.   A. (Santiago), Mex. sergt, age 22, at Mont. in '36. In charge
of the printing-office, and took part in the revolt against Alvarado, '37. iii.
470, 523-5.   A. (Simon), executed at Mont. '31. iii. 190-1, 669, 673, 679.
     Aguirre (José Antonio), 1834, Span. Basque, born about 1793; a wealthy
trader at Guaymas, when in '33-4 he engaged in the Cal. trade, owning several vessels, and visiting Cal. frequently. From about '38 he made Sta B. his
home, marrying María del Rosario, a daughter of José Ant. Estudillo, in '42.
His second wife was a sister of the first. Grantee of the Tejon rancho in '43,
and his wife of S. Jacinto Viejo y Nuevo in '46. On account of his great
size he was sometimes nicknamed Aguirron; of fine presence, affable in manner, and well liked by all. An excellent type of the old-time Spanish merchant, keeping aloof for the most part from smuggling and politics, though
often employed by the government. Still a resident of Sta B. after 1854.
Ment. in iii. 620, 637, 659, 660, 727; iv. 12, 61, 100, 104, 332, 621, 635; v. 587,

619.   Aguirre (Juan B.), 1775, Span. mate and master of different transport ships on the coast in 1775–90. i. 246, 287, 328, 444.   A. (Severo), 1842, Mex. sergt in the batallon fijo '43–5. iv. 289.

Ahumada, 1813, Dominican of B. Cal., preaching at S. Diego. ii. 345.

Ainsworth (John), 1828, Engl. sailor ordered to be shipped to Sand. Isl. by 1st vessel. Perhaps 'Rainsford,' q.v.

Ajuria (Gregorio), 1845, Span. supercargo of the *Hannah*, fr. Mazatlan, with a letter of introd. from Parrot to Larkin. He finally settled at Los Ang., married the daughter of John Temple, and became rich. He went to Mex. about '56 to engage in heavy and unprofitable financial operations. On the fall of Comonfort went to Paris, where he died in '64, aged 47, leaving a widow and several children.   Akers (B.), 1846, in Cal. Bat. Probably same as 'Acres,' q.v.

Alanis (Mariano), 1800, Mex. settler at Los Ang. 1800–39. ii. 349. *Padron*. A. (Máximo), 1819, resid. of Los Ang.; arrested for smuggling in '21, and for political misdeeds in '31. Owner of the S. José de Buenos Aires rancho in '40–3. ii. 354, 441; iii. 196, 634; iv. 635.   A. (Nicolás), a settler at L. Ang. in 1807. ii. 350; and Márcos A. in '46.

Alarcon (Gaspar), 1602, Span. com. of one of Vizcaino's ships. i. 98.   A. (Hernando), 1540, com. of an explor. vessel at the head of the gulf; may have seen Cal. territory. i. 68.   Alarico, 1840, Ind. chief arrested by Sutter. iv. 137.   Alariza (Juan P.), Cal. claim for $11,565 in '46 (v. 462–8).

Álava (José Manuel), 1793–4, Span. brigadier of the navy, or commodore, who visited Cal. in connection with the Nootka affair. He fell at the battle of Trafalgar in 1803. i. 509, 523–5, 533.   Alballo (Feliciano), 1777, one of the 1st settlers at S. F. i. 297.   Alberger (John), 1847, Co. A, N. Y. Vol. (v. 499).

Alberni (Pedro), 1796, Span. lieut-col, and capt. of Catalan vol., who came in connection with the project of founding Branciforte. By his rank he was com. of the S. F. post in 1796–1800, and com. de armas of Cal. at Mont. in 1801–2, dying in 1802. See biog., ii. 5–6; mention in i. 535, 539–41, 543, 565–7, 615, 630, 639, 679, 693, 705, 729; ii. 2, 140.

Albert (J. C.), 1833, mr of whaler *Isabel*. iii. 382.   Albet (Ibre), 1825–6, mr of whaler *Triton*. iii. 149.   Albin (Charles), 1845, Amer. at Mont.; prob. same as Chas Albien, who got a lot at S. F. in '47. iv. 587, 685.   Albright (James), 1845, Amer. sailor fr. the *Tasso* at S. F., aided by U. S. consul. Alcántara (Pedro), 1792–5, mason-instructor. i. 615, 684.

Alden (Fernando), 1832, at Mont. in '47. Amer. who testified at S. F. '53, in *U. S. vs Castillero*, that he came in '32, and had lived 25 years in Cal. and Mex.   A. (James), 1841, lieut in U. S. ex. exped. iv. 241. Later a commodore.   Alderman (Isaac W.), 1848, Amer. miner from Or.; killed by C. E. Pickett at Sacramento. See *Hist. Or.*, i. 459.

Aldrich (James), 1847, Co. I, N. Y. Vol. (v. 499); d. in Va '64.   A. (Prudence), 1846, widow in the Mormon col, v. 546, with son and daughter, her husband, Silas Aldrich, having died on the voyage. She was owner of a S. F. lot in '47; but returned to Utah, where she still lived with her daughter in '84. Her son Jasper died in Utah.

Alegre (Antonio), 1790–5, settler at S. José. i. 478, 683.   Aleponzoni (Flavio), 1791, alférez in Malaspina's exped. i. 490.   Alered (Jesus), 1846, resid. of S. Bernardino.   Alexander, 1834, Engl. sailor in a Mont. list.

Alexander (Cyrus), 1832, Amer. tanner born in Penn. 1805, but moving with his parents to Ill. in 1810. In '31, or perhaps earlier, after an unprofitable experience in lead-mining at Galena, he started for the far west as a trapper for the Sublette Co., and came to Cal. by way of Sta Fé. The date has been variously given from '27 to '35; but original archive evidence of '37–45 leaves no doubt that he came in '32 or '33. For 7 or 8 years he remained in the south, engaged in hunting, fishing, trading, soap-making, and stock-raising. He received Mex. naturalization papers on March 18, 1837, though he applied for new papers in '45. About '40 he came north and took charge on shares of Henry D. Fitch's Sotoyome rancho, now Healdsburg, obtaining for himself 2 leagues of the rancho in '47. In Dec. '44 he was married by Sutter to Rufina Lucero, a sister of Wm Gordon's wife, from N. Mex. There was trouble about this marriage, which had to be repeated by a priest at Sta Clara. During the flush times Alexander, though unlucky as a miner, became rich by the sale of rancho products and increase in the value of his land. His name in many ways is prominently and honorably connected with the history of Healdsburg. Unlike any other Cal. ex-trapper known to history or tradition, he was converted, joined the presbyterian church, and finally became a methodist, giving liberally to church and educational enterprises; but he was also charitable in other respects, acquiring an enviable reputation locally as an honest, unassuming citizen. He died in '72, after 7 years of partial paralysis, leaving a widow and 4 of his 12 children. Mention in iii. 388, 408; iv. 117, 674. His portrait is given in the *Sonoma Co. Hist.*, 91. A MS. in my collection—*Life and Times of Cyrus Alexander*, by his nephew Charles Alexander—contains many details.

Alexander (David W.), 1841, Irish trader from N. Mex. At first a ranchero in the S. Bernardino region, and later in trade at L. Ang. with Temple. He strongly favored the Amer. in the troubles of '46; was one of the prisoners taken at Chino (v. 311-14); and after the war was made collector of customs at S. Pedro in '47-8. Successful claimant for the ranchos of Tujunga and Providencia. In '50 regidor of Los Ang., and county sheriff in '55-6 and '76-7. His wife was a daughter of Manuel Requena. Still living, '85, in the vicinity of Los Ang. Mentioned in iv. 278-9; v. 314, 441, 572, 575, 626, 634-5. Alexander (G.), 1848, pass. from Honolulu. A. (Horace M.), 1847, Co. B, Morm. Bat. (v. 469-98). Alexy (John), 1825, mr whaler *Factor*. iii. 147. Alfaro (Joaquin), 1834, accused of murder at Mont. iii. 673. Alfe (Alfon), 1827, mr whaler *Orion*. iii. 148.

Alford (Landy), 1846, overland immig. who worked as a carpenter at Mont., and at Benicia in '47-8, afterwards settling in Suisun valley. His daughter was the wife of Nathan Barbour. v. 672.

Alipás (Dámaso), 1831, engaged in the S. Diego revolt. iii. 201. A. (Gervasio), in same revolt; also executed by the vigilantes at Los Ang., in '36. iii. 417-19. A. (José), resid. at S. Juan Cap., age 37, in '41-6; com. of a mil. force at S. Luis Rey in '46. iv. 620-1, 626. A. (Martin), 1846, resid. at Los Ang. A. (Santos), 1846, killed at the Pauma massacre. iv. 617. Allamando (Victorino), 1841, resid. at S. José, age 35.

Allen, 1832, trapper with Nidever in '30, and thought by N. to have come to Cal. a little later. iii. 408. Allen, 1847, in Sutter's employ. Allen (Albern), 1847, Co. A, Morm. Bat. (v. 469-98). A. (Andy), 1846, said by Hall to have come to Sta Clara val. with his brothers Thos and Wm, and his sisters Melissa and Rebecca. Perhaps brothers, etc., of J. M. Allen, q.v.

Allen (Daniel), 1848, a Mormon killed by Ind. in exploring for a new road over the Sierra on the return to Utah. v. 496. Tyler calls him Daniel, but there is no such name on the rolls. Bigler calls him Ezrah H. Perhaps it was Elijah or George Allen, who were privates in Co. B. Another George A. was in Co. E.

Allen (David), 1847, Amer. immig. in Brown's co. of '46, but left sick on the way, going to Or. and visiting Cal. in '47. His wife died on the overland journey (v. 526-30). See Jas M. Allen.

Allen (George), 1822, Irishman, said to have been a quaker, also called Scotch and English in some records, who landed at Mont. at age of 26. He was baptized as Josef Jorge Tomás at S. Cárlos in '24, and in '26 married Petra Boronda, a native of S. José, age 14. Naturalized in '29. He kept a little shop or inn at Mont., in comp. with Wm Gralbatch, but sold out to McIntosh in '30 for $90. In one way or another his name appears in the records of almost every year, as he was a favorite witness to divers contracts, had petty transactions with everybody, and served on occasion as surgeon and dentist. He was several times a member and oftener an employé of the ayuntamiento. In a padron of '36, when he was munic. treasurer, he is noted as a trader, 40 years old, with wife and 4 children. In '42 he was justice-of the peace, and seems to have got a lot at S. F., though he never lived there. In '44-5 teacher by the governor's appointment, and in '45-6 clerk in the U. S. consulate, being an excellent penman, and evidently a man of some education. He sometimes signed Geo. W. Allen. He died at Mont. in '47, and his widow was still living in '83; his sons were Miguel, b. in '27—in '83 living in Inyo Co.—José George, b. in '33. and Alonzo, who in '83 kept a saloon in Mont.; one daughter married Dr Martin of S. José, and the other lived in '83 with her mother. ii. 478, 496, 525, 609, 674; iii. 409, 176; iv. 117, 653, 669; v. 681.

Allen (Geo. Trail), 1848, appointed Nov. '48 Hawaiian consul in Cal. v. 615. Perhaps did not arrive till '49.   A. (Henry), 1847, owner of a S. F. lot. A. (James), capt. 1st U. S. dragoons, who organized and commanded the Morm. Bat. in '46, but died before reaching Cal. v. 473-8.

Allen (James M.), 1846, Amer. immig. from Mo. (v. 526-30), son of David Allen, q.v. With his brothers and sisters he went to Sta Clara, where he lived— also serving in Weber's company, and getting a lot at S. F.—in '46-8. He was a gold-miner in '48, also visiting Oregon. From '49, trader in live-stock, founder of the town of Frémont in '49, and sheriff of Yolo Co. in '50. From '53 in Contra Costa; from '61 at S. F., though interested in Nevada mines; and in '65-8 adj.-gen. of Cal. militia, subsequently engaging in real estate business at Livermore, where he still lived at the age of 56 in '84. His wife was Sidesia Mendenhall, his children Eugene and Delora (Mrs Biddle).   A. (Jesse H.), 1846, Co. E, Cal. Bat. (v. 358-60), under Capt. Grisby '46-7.

Allen (John), 1847, Co. E, Morm. Bat. v. 489-90. A hard case, who was drummed out of the battalion and ex-com. from the church at Los Ang. Owner of a S. F. lot in '47. v. 685. Later a 'terror' in the Placer Co. mines, being killed in a quarrel at Grass Valley in '51.   A. (Otis), 1841, named as a Maine man, resid. in Sonoma Co. '50-'77.   A. (Rufus C.), 1847, Co. A, Morm. Bat. (v. 469); a Utah farmer in '81.   A. (Theodore Henry), 1847, Pion. Soc. record. A. (Thomas), 1841, succeeded Ridley in charge of Sutter's launch.

Allgeier (Nicolaus), 1840, German trapper, some time in H. B. Co.'s employ, who came by land fr. Or. and worked for Sutter at N. Helv. His name was generally, and perhaps correctly, written Altgeier. He often quarrelled with the capt., who once accused Le Grand Nicolas of having tried to kill him; but A. was not discharged as threatened. In '42 he got from Sutter a tract of land on the Sac. just below Bear River, where he managed a ferry at the crossing between N. Helv. and Hock, building a hut of poles, and later an adobe house; and here the little town of Nicolaus bears his name. In '44 he was naturalized, and is often named in the *N. Helv. Diary* of '46-8. He still lived on his rancho in '49, and is remembered in '52-5 by Bidwell; still living in '60. He left children. Mention in iv. 117, 120, 139, 229; v. 108.

Allig, see Elick.   Allison (Francis), 1845, one of Frémont's men, though there is some doubt about the date. v. 583, 587. Wounded in '50 in a fight with Ind. in El Dorado Co. In '84 a gardener at Oakland.   Allmand (Albert), 1846-7, act. lieut U. S. N.; lieut Co. D, Stockton's Bat. v. 386.

Allred (Reddick R.), 1847, sergt Co. A, Morm. Bat. Also Q. M. sergt, and capt. of 50 on the return. v. 477, 493. In '81 a bishop and col of militia in Utah. J. R. Allred is also named by Tyler in connection with the march to Utah in '48.   Allshouse (Joseph), 1841, marine on the *Vincennes*, killed accidentally in crossing S. F. bar. iv. 279.

Allsopp (James P. C.), 1848, native of La, his father being of an old well-known Engl.-Amer. family and his mother of the Span. family of Alfaro de Villahermosa. Educated in England. A volunteer in the Mex. war, being wounded at Cerro Gordo. In '48 came overland with an immig. party from N. Orleans. v. 556; and kept a boarding-house in '48-51 at S. F., subsequently making several voyages as master of a vessel, in which he went east in '54. In '57 he made a 2d overland trip from V. Cruz to Tepic, and came to S. F., making several later voyages, and adding a shipwreck to his catalogue of adventures. In '60 a miner in Tuolumne, writing besides for the newspapers, as he did occasionally at all stages of his career. In '61 married Angelina, daughter of R. R. Hunter of N. J. In '61-'79, with a few intervals of mining and trade, he was a teacher in many public and private institutions of Cal. and Or. In '80-4 he did good service as a gleaner of historic data in my library; and in

'85 is teaching in a Berkeley institution. His *Leaves from my Log Book* is an interesting addition to my store of pioneer reminiscences; and few of the thousands named in this list have had so varied an experience. Allyn, 1848, mr of the *Isaac Walton*. v. 578.

Almenares (Fruto), resid. of S. Bern. and Los Ang. '46–8. A. (Ign.), Los Ang. 1813. ii. 359. A. (José M.), Los Ang. '46. A. (Pedro), soldier at S. F. and Sonoma, '39–42.

Alpen (James), 1828–9, Engl. sailor at Mont. Perhaps 'Halpin.'

Altamirano (Abelino), at Los Ang. '46. A. (Domingo), S. F. soldier '37–43. iii. 638, 667. A. (Francisco), S. José '41, married to Encarnacion Bernal. A. (Gonzalo), soldier at S. F. '23–9; sent to Mex. '30. iii. 85. A. (José C.), Los Ang. '46. A. (Juan C.), regidor at S. José 1809. ii. 134. A. (Justo), settler S. F. 1791–1800; inval. '19–23. i. 716. A. (Lúcas), soldier at S. Juan 1800. i. 588. A. (Luis), alférez at Los Ang. '45–8. iv. 505. A. (Marcos), soldier S. F. '19–24. A. (Rafael), at N. Helv. '47. A. (Salvador), soldier of S. F. comp. '32–42. A. (Victoriano), soldier at S. F. '23–9; sent to Mex. '30. ii. 85. See also list in i. 732.

Altimira (José), 1820, Span. friar at S. F. and Solano, of which latter he was the founder. He left Cal. in '28. A padre who had a will of his own. See biog. in ii. 579; list of auth. in vol. i.; mention in ii. 375, 394, 496–505, 595, 597, 655; iii. 24, 93–4.

Alurel (J. B.), 1836, French saddler at Mont. Perhaps 'Mutrel,' q.v.

Alva (Manuel), 1833, Mex. surgeon of the Cal. forces who came to Mont. with Gov. Figueroa, and before '36 married Nicolasa Gajiola. In '37, with other Mex., he took part in the revolt against Alvarado, for which he was arrested and confined at S. Miguel; but escaping, joined the Carrillo faction in the south, only to be rearrested in '38 by Castro at S. Buen. and released on promise of non-interference in politics. At first he was noted as a free-thinker, but with illness became devout. In '40, being disabled at the age of 53, he got a passport for Mex., and his successor was appointed. No definite record of his departure or death. iii. 236, 240, 296, 463, 523–4, 555.

Alva (Valentin). Resid. of S. Bernardino in '46.

Alvarado (Francisco Javier), soldier of S. Diego from 1780, and of Sta B. comp. from 1789. In 1795–6 corporal, and comisionado at Los Ang.; in 1805 sergt; and in 1809–10 again comisionado, dying before 1818. He married María Ignacia, daughter of Pedro Amador, about 1788. i. 601; ii. 110–11, 349, 356–7. A. (Francisco Javier), probably a son of the preceding, born in 1807, and a resid. of Los Ang., where he was suplente member of the dip. in '33, alcalde in '35, and again suplente in '37. In a padron of '39 he figures as a trader, age 32, and still lived at Los Ang. in '48. iii. 246, 282, 506, 565, 629. A. (Francisco María), perhaps a brother of the preceding, though there may be confusion between two or more of the same name. Grantee of Peñasquitos rancho in '23, '34, '36, on which he lived; regidor of S. Diego '37; grantee of Soledad rancho in '38; aux. alcalde and regidor at Los Ang. (?) '38–9; treasurer at S. Diego '40–1; and juez in '45. ii. 547, 612, 618, 663; iv. 53–4, 495, 612, 616, 619, 620–1, 636. See also list i. 732. A. (Fran. M.), at Los Ang. '39, age 25.

Alvarado (Ignacio María), witness in the Herrera trial '27; regidor at Los Ang. '32–3; juez de campo '35; síndico '37; prisoner in '38; resid. of Los Ang., age 27, in '39; juez de paz '41; still at Los Ang. '48. Very likely more than one of the name. iii. 62, 517, 554–5, 635–6; iv. 632. A. (Ignacio Rafael), 1774, soldier and later sergt of S. D. and Sta B. comp.; may have been the father of the preceding and following. Biog. i. 647, 452. A. (Isidro M.), aux. alcalde in Angeles dist. '38; age 26 in '39; grantee of Monserrate rancho '46. iii. 636; v. 619. He seems to have been the man who died at S. Luis Rey '62, and at whose grave the mourners were attacked by the sheriff and one killed. A. (Joaquin), regidor at Mont. '31–2. Born at S. D. in 1800; married to Juana de Dios Higuera; 5 children in '36, Juan José, Felipe, José A., María Ana, and Francisco. iii. 114, 672–3; iv. 653. A. (Joaquina), grantee of the Cañada Larga rancho '41. iv. 642.

Alvarado (José Francisco), 1805, sergt Mont. co. Son of Juan B., and father of Juan B. (the governor). Died in 1809. Biog. ii. 141.   A. (José M.), grantee of Vallecitos rancho '40; juez at S. D. '41–2; kiiled at Pauma '46. iii. 612; iv. 619; v. 617.   A. (Josefa), owner of house at Los Ang. '31. iii. 539; also '48; as was Juana Alv.   A. (Juan), regidor of Los Ang. '31. iii. 196.   A. (Juan A.), memb. of dip. '37. iii. 506.   A. (Juan Bautista), father of José Fran. as above, a soldier who came in the 1st exped. of 1769, but did not remain. iii. 141.

Alvarado (Juan Bautista), son of Sergt José F. Alvarado and María Josefa Vallejo, born at Mont. Feb. 14, 1809. To a man like this, who for years was a central figure in California history, and to whom many pages are devoted in other parts of this work, but scanty justice can be done in this register. I attempt no more here than to present a brief chronologic outline of salient points, to index the pages devoted to the subject in other volumes, and to add some general remarks on the man, his character, and his career. Alvarado's official life began in '27, from which date to '34 he was secretary of the diputacion, being named in '31 as comisionado for S. Luis Ob., and meanwhile employed as clerk by different Monterey merchants. From '34 to '36 he was a vista, or appraiser, in the Mont. custom-house. In '34 he was elected member of the dip. for the term of '35–6, and in '36 was president of that body. For a biog. sketch down to '36, see iii. 450–3; mention for the same period, in ii. 429; iii. 36–43, 49–50, 69, 82, 186, 216, 245, 249–50, 291, 295–6, 307, 374, 378, 422, 426, 429, 441, 443, 679, 682. Leading a revolution against Gov. Gutierrez, Alvarado was revolutionary gov. of Cal. from Dec. 7, '36, to July 9, '37; from that date, by submitting to Mex., he became regular gov. ad int. as pres. of the dip. till Nov. 24, '39, when he became constitutional gov. by Mex. appointment of Aug. On his revolution, struggle with the south, campaigns, political schemings, controversy with Carrillo, and his rule in general in '36–8—no satisfactory résumé being practicable here—see iii. 545–578, or chap. xvi.–ix.; also mention in ii. 78; iii. 614, 652, 670–1; iv. 47 et seq., 86, 87, et seq., 101, 149–50. On Alvarado's rule in '39–42, including his marriage, see iii. 579–94, 639; controversy with Vallejo, iii. 595–607; iv. 190–205, 281–4; acts in the Graham affair, iv. 1–41; policy in mission and Ind. affairs, iv. 47–73, 194–8, 330–41; commerce and finance, iv. 91–100, 206–25, 341–2; treatment of foreigners, Sutter, Russians, etc., iv. 107–89, 228–52; Com. Jones' affair, iv. 307–19; succession of Micheltorena, iv. 291–7. Alvarado's governorship ended on Dec. 31, '42; but from '43 he held a commission of colonel in the Mex. army with pay; and from '47 that of colonel of the defensores de la patria. He was a leading spirit in the revolution of '44–5 that made Pico gov., and by the latter was made admin. of the Mont. custom-house. He was elected to congress in '45, but did not go to Mex., being also the grantee of several ranchos, including the famous Mariposas. Though serving as colonel under Castro, he took but slight part in the affairs of '46, being arrested and paroled in Sept., and residing as a citizen in '47–8 at his rancho near Monterey, though the Mex. govt had appointed him ayud. inspector of the Cal. presidial companies. For mention of A. in this part of his career, '43–8, see iv. 357, 366–7, 403–4, 407–9, 453, 485, 488–508, 518–20, 524, 536–7, 539–40, 544, 556–82, 601–2, 621, 672–3; v. 5, 28, 31–2, 41, 69, 137, 231, 261, 267, 282, 289, 363, 433, 455, 561, 565–6; iii. 712. In the flush times and period of land litigation Alvarado saved no land or money; but subsequently moved to the San Pablo estate inherited by his wife—Martina, daughter of Francisco Castro, whom he married in '39— where, though the property was always in litigation, he was enabled to live comfortably until his death on July 13, 1882. His wife had died in '75, but he left several children, including two sons and a married daughter. He had also several natural daughters before his marriage. In physique Don Juan Bautista was of medium stature, stout build, fair complexion, and light hair; of genial temperament, courteous manners, and rare powers of winning friends. Respecting his character I must refer the reader to the discussion elsewhere of his various acts. Much will be found in him to praise, much to condemn. Most that is bad in his conduct may be traced to his environment, to his position as a

politician forced by circumstances to support himself by intrigue, and to his
unfortunate indulgence in intoxicating drink. From '39 he was reckless, dissipated, and in some degree disposed to permit rascalities on the part of associates
and subordinates; though, indeed, all he could have done to prevent such conduct was to resign and leave the responsibility to another. Nor can it be said
that he passed through the ordeal of later land litigation without discredit.
In his favor it may be said that he had more brains, energy, and executive
ability than any three of his contemporaries combined; that in most of his many
controversies he was right as well as successful; that he was patriotic, and at
the first full of good intentions for his country; that the politicians who forced
him to expend his energies and the country's substance in sectional quarrels
are largely responsible for his failure; that none of his countrymen could have
done so well in his place; that he was honorable in his private dealings, true
to his political friends, and never used his position to enrich himself. He has
been accused, and for the most part unjustly, through church influence, of having plundered the missions; but for their inevitable ruin he was responsible
only in being gov. while it was accomplished. Still more grossly exaggerated,
and even false, have been the accusations of such men as Farnham and Hastings,
founded on Alvarado's policy toward foreigners. In my list of authorities will
be found many of Alvarado's writings. His original letters of '36-42 merit
only praise as the best authority extant on the history of that period. His
Historia de California, dictated for my use in '76, is valuable in many parts
and worthless in many others.

Alvarado (Juan B.), son of Fran. J. Alvarado, born in 1790, regidor of Los
Ang. in '30-1; at S. D. as regidor and com. de policía in '35-6; at Los Ang. in
'37; memb. of the dip. in '39. ii. 561; iii. 509, 584, 634, 615-16. Grantee of
Rincon del Diablo in '43. He died in '47, leaving a family.   A. (Juan José),
soldier and corp. at S.Diego fr. 1793, and settler at Los Ang. in '15. ii. 350.
Another of the same name was a son of Joaquin A., born at Mont. in '26.
A. (Juan N.), settler at Los Ang. '12; regidor in '32, '35-6, age 46 in '39.   A.
(Juana), land-owner at Los Ang. '48.   A. (María Joaq.), wife of Gab. Moraga.
ii. 571.   A. (Mariano), at Los Ang. '46.   A. (Miguel), soldier of Sta B. and
S. F. '26-37; in '44 at Sonoma, age 44, and grantee of Yulupa rancho. iv.
674.   A. (N.), soldier at Mont. '45. iv. 487.   A. (Tomasa), house and lot at
S. Diego, 1830. ii. 546; iii. 612.

Álvarez, murdered at Sta B. 1794. i. 669.   A. (Felipe), settler at Mont.
1791. i. 606.   A. (José), artilleryman teacher at S. F. 1797-1800. i. 644.
A. (José F.), sec. of ayunt. S. Diego '38; clerk in Mont. custom-house '43-4.
iii. 616; iv. 377, 431.   A. (Juan), Ind. on the *S. Antonio*, 1769. i. 131; guard
at S. D. 1775. i. 250; settler at Los Ang. 1790. i. 460.   A. (Miguel), at Sta
B. '37, wife Paula Lara. At Los Ang. in '46.   A. (Pedro), at Los Ang. 1799.
ii. 340.   A. (Pedro M.), maj. at S. D., murdered '14. ii. 346.   A. (Tiburcio), plotting with Ind. '39. iii. 587.

Alvires (Claudio), settler at S. José fr. 1780; land in 1783; regidor in 1785,
1805. i. 477-8, 350; ii. 134.   A. (Francisco), settler at S. F. 1791-1800. i.
716; Id., resid. S. Gab. '46.   A. (Juan), soldier who came before 1790. i.
733.   A. (Juan), perhaps son of the preceding; alcalde of S. José 1812-13. ii.
604-5; alc. of Mont. '26. ii. 611-12; grantee of Laguna Seca rancho '34; alc.
of S. José '37. iii. 430, 712, 729-30; mention in '44-6. iv. 466, 470; v. 6, 61.

Alviso (Agustin), son of Ignacio, b. at S. F. 1809; soon going to Sta Clara;
married María Ant. Pacheco in '30; maj. of S. José mission '40-1; grantee of
Potrero de los Cerritos rancho '44. iv. 672, and later owner of Sta Rita in
Livermore Val. He was a prosperous ranchero, locally well known. Arrested
by Sutter in '44 in the Micheltorena affair. His wife died in '70; his children
were Margarita b. in '31, mar. in '59 to Andrónico Soto, at S. Luis Ob. in '85
with 5 children; José b. in '34, Salvio b. in '37, Valentin b. in '41; Jesus M.
b. in '44, mar. Ignacio Pacheco in '65, at Pleasanton in '85; José B. b. in '50,
Alam. Co. '85; Guadalupe b. in '52, Alam. Co. '85. Don Agustin died in '80.

Alviso (Anastasio), son of Francisco Jav., said not to have married.   Id.,
son of Ignacio, resid. of S. José in '41, age 40; wife María Ant. Altamirano;

child., Blas b. in '28, Isabel '32, Antonia '37, Ignacio '39. Blas Alviso is known from his connection with the affair of Arce's horses in '46, and his consequent claim on the govt. v. 106, 460.

Alviso (Domingo), son of Ignacio, b. at S. F. about 1817; in '41 a resid. of S. José; wife Maria S. Pacheco: child., Rafael and Inés. In '45 he was elected 2d alcalde. iv. 685. See also list i. 733. There was also a corporal Alviso at Sta B. in '24. ii. 531.

Alviso (Fran. Javier), bro. of Ignacio, who came as a S. F. settler with Anza in '75-6. i. 297, 716; said to have mar. María Ant. Beltran, by whom he had Nicolás, Francisco, and Anastasio; but in '17 at S. Cárlos was married Francisco—son of Francisco and María de los Reyes Duarte—to Gertrudis Villavicencio. Francisco (the son ?) was a sold. in S. F. comp. to '22; it was his daughter, perhaps, that married José M. Amador. ii. 585. Fran. ment. at Los Ang. in '31. iii. 208. In the S. José padron of '41 is Francisco (1st), Calif., age 51; wife María B. Linares; child., María S. b. in '29, María L. '32, Felipe '55, Maria H. '36, María R. '37. Also Francisco (2d), age 25; wife Maria I. Miranda; child, María B. Francisco was grantee of Cañada de los Vaqueros rancho in '44. iv. 671. Another Francisco, grantee of Agua Puerca in '43. iv. 655; alcalde of Branciforte '44, iv. 664; was in '45 living at Brancif., age 51, native of S. José; wife Bernabela García; child., Josefa b. in '29, Maria T. '32, Guillermo '35, Sabás '39, Manuelita '42.

Alviso (Gabriel), son of Ignacio, b. in 1802; soldier at S. F. '19-30, also at S. F. in '37; in '41 at S. José; wife Francisca Higuera, child., Juan Ign. b. '24, María '27, Nicolás '29, María A. '31, José R. and José S. '34, Margarita '35, Tomás '39, José E. '40. Also at S. J. in '47. v. 665.

Alviso (Ignacio), native of Sonora, b. in 1772; son of Domingo A. and Angela Trejo, Spaniards; came with his mother, brother, and sister as member of Anza's S. F. colonists in '75-6. i. 257. In '90 enlisted in S. F. comp., serving as a private till 1805, and as corp. to 1819, when he became an inválido, or pensioner, with the rank of sergt and half pay by order of the king. He remained for some years at S. F., being an elector in '27, and militiaman in '37. ii. 592. Then he went to Sta Clara; was grantee of Rincon de los Esteros rancho in '38. iii. 712; and was admin. of Sta Clara mission in '40-3; juez in '47. v. 662. He died in '48, leaving a large estate. He may be regarded as the original Alviso of Cal., and a town in Sta Clara Co. bears his name. His wife was Margarita Bernal, mar. in '94 at S. F.; his children, Agustin, José Ant., Gabriel, Anastasio, José M., Domingo, Concepcion, and Dolores. Another Ignacio A. was a native of Cal., age 65, at S. José in '41; wife Luisa Peralta.

Alviso (José Ant.), son of Ignacio. Soldier in S. F. co. down to '24; regidor at S. José '28. ii. 605; elector and militiaman S. F. '37. iii. 705; juez at S. Francisquito and S. José '39, '43. iii. 705; iv. 685. Ment. down to '55, when he was claimant for Arr. de Purisíma rancho. v. 371, 637, 677. He died before '85, leaving a large estate.   A. (José Ant.), probably another man and son of Nicolás, at Salinas in '77 gave me his interesting *Campaña de Natividad*, MS.   A. (José María), son of Ignacio, b. about 1798; sold. at S. F. '19-27; grantee of Milpitas in '35. iii. 712; alcalde at S. José '36. iii. 729-30; in '41 resid. of S. José, with wife Juana Galindo; child., Josefa b. '22, Cármen '30, Agustina '32, Florencina '34, Antonio '36, Gabriel '38.   A. (José M.), sold. at S. F. '27-32 and later; militia officer at S. José '37. iii. 732; grantee of Cañada Verde '38, and later claimant for Quito (perhaps dif. men). iii. 677; iv. 672; in '41 at S. José, age 29; wife Manuela Cantua; child., Francisco and Ignacia; with Arce in com. of troops '46. v. 106-9, 662.   A. (Juan), resid. of S. José '41, age 52, wife Lugarda Briones, child Juan.   A. (Loreto), sister of Ignacio, who came in 1776, and married Luis Peralta.   A. (Manuel), soldier at S. F. from '27; died in '64.

Alviso (Nicolás), son of Fran. J., at Mont. '26. ii. 612; grantee of Alisal, Sauzal, and Natividad. ii. 616, 664, 677; suplente of dip. '27-8. iii. 36, 41; maj. and alc. at Soledad. iii. 354, 674, 690-1; took part in arrest of Graham '40. iv. 21-2. His wife was Bárbara Butron.   Another Nic. Alviso lived at Branciforte in '45, age 28; wife Juana Lorenzana; child Rosa.   A. (Severo), soldier of S. F. comp. '23-32.

Alviso (Valentin), son of Agustin, b. at S. José in '41; educated in Mass.; married '68 Josefa Livermore, by whom he had 4 child., Cristina, Antonia, Rosa, and Ernesto. His home has been at Livermore, where he has been farmer and real estate agent, serving also as supervisor and assemblyman. In '85 he is an employé of the U. S. mint at S. F. Deeply interested in the history of his country, he has furnished me the valuable *Documentos para la Hist. Cal.*, forming the Alviso family archives; and has rendered aid in other matters, besides contributing the *Livermore Papers.*

Alvitre (Sebastian), settler and incorrigible scamp at S. José 1783 and Los Ang. fr. 1790. i. 350, 460-1, 477, 484, 640. In '40-6 a dozen Alvitres lived in the L. Ang. region, one being mentioned in iv. 637.

Amador (José María), son of Pedro, b. in 1794 at S. F. Died at Gilroy in '83. See biog. sketch ii. 585-6; also mention ii. 232, 319, 335, 339, 372, 425, 446, 599; iii. 713, 725; iv. 75, 681; i. list of auth.   A. (Marcos), sold. at S. F. '19-23; resid. of Branciforte '28-30. ii. 627.   A. (Pedro), Mex. sergt of the 1st exped. in 1769, who died in 1824. See biog. sketch in ii. 384-5; also mention in i. 141, 472, 477, 495, 510-11, 548, 551, 555-6, 566, 574, 680, 693, 710; ii. 126.   A. (Rafael), famous courier of '34. ii. 271.   A. (Valentin), militiaman at S. F. '37; in '41 at S. José, age 23, wife Ciriaca Pacheco; in '43 juez de campo. iv. 685.

Amao (Domingo), sec. of S. D. ayunt. in '36-7. iii. 508, 615-16.   Amarillas (Juan A.), sold. killed by Ind. 1781. i. 362.   Amaya (Antonio), native of Cal., age 40, at the Trinidad rancho '36; wife María Ant. Larios; children, Benito, Esperanza, Casimiro, Ezequiel, Refugio, Darío.   Amejar (Antonio), at S. Mateo '35.

Ambris (Doroteo), 1841, Ind. novice who came with the bishop. iv. 195. Sub-deacon at Sta Inés college in '44. iv. 426. He soon became a priest; officiating as curate at Mont. occasionally from '46 to '51, v. 638-40, but living at S. Antonio until his death, which occurred about 1880. He was an ignorant man, and reputed more or less vicious. However, he gave me some old papers, which covers a multitude of sins, in my eyes.   Ambrosio, Moquelumne chief shot in '38. iv. 75.

Ames, 1846, Amer. immig. from Mo., who enlisted in the Cal. Bat. under Capt. Burroughs, and like his leader was killed at Natividad in Nov. v. 371. He was buried at Gomez' rancho, and his effects were sold at N. Helv. in Sept. '47 by Peter Wimmer.   A. (Edward T.), 1847. Co. D, N. Y. Vol. (v. 499).   Ames (Josiah P.), 1847, Engl., Co. B, N. Y. Vol. (v. 499); settling at Sac., and about '55 at Half Moon Bay; farmer, supervisor, assemblyman of '77-8, and warden of state prison in '82. *Clark.*   Ames (Thaddeus M.), 1847, Co. C, N. Y. Vol. (v. 499-518); later a doctor in Mendocino Co., memb. of the assembly in '62-3, and died at Green Valley, Sonoma Co., in '76. A native of N. Y.

Amesti (José), 1822, Span. Basque, who came on the *Panther*, at the age of 30, swore allegiance to Mex., and became a prominent citizen and merchant of the Monterey district. ii. 475; iii. 51-2. In '24 he married Prudenciana, daughter of Ignacio Vallejo, by whom he had three daughters, Cármen b. in '25, Epitacia in '26, Celedonia in '29. Grantee of Corralitos rancho in '27 and '44. ii. 616, 664; iv. 655. In '32 joined the comp. extranjera. iii. 221; took slight part in the politics of '36. iii. 469; was juez in '41, and alcalde in '44 at Mont. iv. 653, 656. In '46 being plundered by the Amer., he had a Cal. claim (v. 462-8) of $7,000. v. 358-9. Though sometimes involved in quarrels by reason of a fiery temper, Amesti was a man of good character, being not only wealthy but respected. Larkin, in his *Notes* of '45, described him as a man disgusted with the Mex. govt and favoring a change. He died about '56, and his widow after '77.   A. (Felipe), alcalde at S. Juan B. in '35. iii. 692.   Amestoy (Marcos), 1804, Span. friar, who served at Sta B., and left Cal. in 1814. See ii. 364; also ii. 121, 159-60, 394.

Amézquita.   Several of the name among the early sold. and settlers of S. F. and S. José fr. 1775. See list i. 733; also mention of José, i. 679; Juan Antonio, i. 478, 617; Manuel, i. 297, 312, 350.   Juan Amézquita in '36 was a native Calif., age 40, living at Buenavista rancho near Mont. with his wife Gregoria Arceo and 6 child., Bárbara b. in '25, Tiburcio '27, Concepcion '29, Guadalupe '30, Casildo '33, Anita '34. Manuel was regidor at S. José in 1806. ii. 134. Ramon, juez de campo at Pájaro in '35. iii. 674; in '36 lived at S. Miguel rancho, age 36, with his wife Ana M. Villa and 6 child., Juan b. in '25, Vicente '28, María C. '30, Pablo '31, Refugio '32, Casimira '34. Salvador in '36 lived at the Salinas rancho, age 48, wife García Martinez; child., Salomé b. in '25, Rosa '27, Salvador '29, Ramon '32, José '35.

Amist (L.), 1834, mr of an Engl. brig. iii. 384.

Amorós (Juan), 1804, Span. friar of Cataluña, who served at S. Cárlos and S. Rafael, where he died in '32. Prominent in early annals of the northern frontier. Biog., iii. 715-16; mention in ii. 88, 147, 159-60, 218, 284, 330, 383, 394, 418, 483, 500, 587, 596, 655, 666; iii. 96, 256, 319, 351; iv. 159-60.

Amos, 1816, carpenter of the *Lydia* at Sta B. ii. 275. Amurrio (Gregorio), 1773, Span. friar; founder of S. Juan Cap.; left Cal. in 1779. See biog. in i. 458; mention in i. 194-5, 224, 248-9, 266-7, 300, 303-4. Anangua, 1813, capt. of the *Tagle*. ii. 268. Anastasio, 1831, executed at Mont. for robbery. iii. 669, 673. Anaya, 1834, lieut on the *Morelos*. iii. 269.

Anderson, 1845, doubtful name of Grigsby-Ide co. of immig. iv. 578-9. Anderson, 1848, of firm Edmondson & A. at S. F. v. 682. A. (Cameron), 1848, lot in S. F. A. (Chas), 1826-8, mr of the *Solitude*. iii. 148. A. (Chas), 1831, acting as doctor at S. Gab., prob. from a vessel. iii. 209. A. (Chas), 1846, Co. G, Cal. Bat. (v. 358), trans. to Co. B, artill. Enlisted at S. José.

Anderson (Chas C.), 1847, lieut Co. C, N. Y. Vol.; com. garrison at N. Helv. v. 504, 514, 675. He died at S. F. in Sept. '47, and his body was the 1st buried in the North Beach cemetery. A. (Frank P.), 1847, Co. D, N. Y. Vol.; printer on the *Californian*. After an adventurous career fr. '55 with Walker in Nicaragua, and as colonel in the confederate army, he returned to S. F., where he became a special policeman, dying in Oct. '81. A. (Geo.), 1844, Amer. sailor and cook on the *Hibernia*, aided by the consul, and discharged in '46. iv. 453. A. (Jacob), 1842, Amer. steward on the *California*. A. (J.), 1848, came fr. Honolulu. A. (J. D.), 1846, master's mate on the *Savannah*. A. (James), 1832, trapper of Young's co., murdered near Los Ang. iii. 388. A. (Lewis), 1843, Amer. immig. of Chiles-Walker co., iv. 392, who in '44 applied for a pass to return home via Los Ang. Anderson (Mary), 1829-30, Scotch wife of Geo. Kinlock, and the 1st foreign woman to settle in Cal. A. (Robert), 1846, Fauntleroy's dragoons (v. 232-47).

Anderson (Stephen), 1828, Scotch trader and sometimes physician, partner of Jas Goldie of Lima, who spent much of his time in Cal. from '28 to '32 as supercargo of the *Funchal*, *Thos Nowlan*, and *Ayacucho*. He was often accompanied by his family, and was known to everybody. I have much of his commercial corresp. He went to Europe from Lima in '33, and perhaps did not return to the Pacific coast, as he was at Edinburgh in '36. See mention in iii. 71, 73, 81, 99-100, 147, 178, 381. Anderson (Walter), 1848, Amer. immig. said to have come with his wife to Lake Co. in '48 (?), being the 3d settler. In '51 went to Mendocino Co., to a place named for him Anderson Valley, where he became rich, but died in poverty. *Lake Co. Hist.*, 63.

Anderson (Wm), 1837, Engl. sailor who left a whaler, or perhaps the *Kent*, at Mont. Known as 'Mountain Bill,' or 'Red Bill.' A fluent narrator in cockney dialect of his own exploits, not afraid of aguardiente. He was one of Graham's 'riflemen,' and in '40 one of the exiles to S. Blas. iv. 18, 23, 33, 37, 118, 393; but came back with a pass and claim for damages which yielded him a little money. In '42 he got a carta, and soon married a native. In '38-48 his name constantly appears in Larkin's books and other records. In '46-7—besides having a 'Cal. claim,' as who did not?—he made soap for Larkin, and had a flouring-mill on the Salinas plain, sold to Panaud in Sept. '47. A little later he was nearly killed by one Callaghan, but recovered, served as alcalde (though this may have been another Wm) at Sta Cruz in '48-9, v. 641-2, and in '84 was, I think, still in the land of the living, perhaps the latest survivor of the famous exiles. A. (Wm), 1846, an old man with a fam. desiring land on the Sac. *Lark. Doc.*, v. 74; perhaps the old bear-hunter ment. in *Colusa Co. Hist.*, 38.   A. (Wm), 1846, Co. C, 1st U. S. dragoons. (v. 336.) A. (Wm), 1846, painter on the *Dale*, who was a shipbuilder at S. F. in '49-54, according to *Lancey*.   A. (Wm), 1848, sailor-carpenter at Mont., aided by the consul, perhaps same as preceding.

Andrade (José M.), 1836, admin. at S. Antonio. iii. 687-8; arrested at Sta B. in '39. iii. 654-5; grantee of land at S. F. in '46.   A., or Andrado (Juan), 1846. Mex. said to have lost a leg at S. Pascual (v. 340-55); murdered in '63.   Andreef, 1806, pilot with Rezánof. ii. 70.   Andrés, Ind. alcalde at Sta B. '24. ii. 528-30; robber at S. Cárlos '31. iii. 191; grantee of Guajome '45.   Andrew (Hiram), 1846, Co. C, 1st U. S. dragoons (v. 336). Andrews, 1848, mr of a *Lima* ship at S. F.   Andrews, 1848, left Honolulu for S. F. on the *Sagadahoc*.   A. (Allen), 1847, Co. G, N. Y. Vol. (v. 499-518); died at Los Ang. Dec. '47.

Andrews (Augustus A.), 1840, Amer. carpenter of Mass., who at the age of 22 came on the *California* fr. Honolulu to Mont., obtaining naturalization and settling at S. F., where he married Rosalía de Haro, got a lot, and built a house. His name often appears in records of '44-6. I think he died in '47 or a little later. His widow married Chas Brown, and still lives at S. F. in '85. Mention in iv. 102, 120, 669; v. 683.   A. (Thomas), 1848, mr of the *Charles*. v. 576-7.   Anduian? (Alex.), 1845, French resid. at Branciforte.

Angel, 1848, at Sutter's in Feb.; in July one of Weber's prospectors, for whom Angel's creek and camp were named. *Carson*.   Angel (Anson), 1847, resid. of Sta Clara '47-8. *Sta Clara Co. Hist.*, 544.   Angel (Woodson), 1847, builder of a mill for Magnent at S. José; still living in that region '66. *Alta*. Angelino (Blas), resid. of S. F. dist. from '35 or earlier; síndico in '37; at Sonoma '44-6, being perhaps concerned in troubles with the Bears. iii. 705; v. 162.   Angelo (Chas A.), 1848, named in the *Annals of S. F.* as living in '54. Angle (Miles B.), 1847, on the Pion. Soc. records as a deceased member, from N. Y.   Angulo (Pedro), 1825, com. of the Span. *Aguila*. iii. 27, 146.

Anselin (Alfred), 1843, French surgeon of the batallon fijo '43-5. iv. 399; at S. F. in '44. iv. 483; had a 'Cal. claim' (v. 642-8) in '46.   He remained in Cal., and died at S. Benito rancho in '53. *S. F. Herald*.   Anson (Geo.), 1794, com. of Vancouver's storeship. i. 511.   Anthony (Alex. H.), 1847, a mason at Mont.   A. (Bascom F.), son of Elihu; b. at S. José in Oct. '47; a miner in Calaveras '84.

Anthony (Elihu), 1847, native of N. Y.; overland immig. and methodist preacher of Ind., accompanied by his wife, Sarah A. Van Anda, and infant daughter. After a short stay at S. José he settled at Sta Cruz, where he still resides in '85. Engaged in trade and prominent in religious affairs—having preached at the S. F. school-house in Sept. '48—he also takes pride in having built the 1st wharf and foundery at Sta Cruz. His children are Mrs Huntingdon of Sta Cruz, b. in '46, Bascom '47, Almon '49, Gilbert '51, Frank '55. Mention in v. 641.   A. (James), 1847, employed by Larkin at Mont. and S. F. A. (James G.), 1846, Co. G, Cal. Bat. (v. 358-60), enlisting at S. José.   A. (Louis), 1847, at N. Helv. fr. Sonoma.   A. (L. C.), 1847, sheriff at S. José. v. 662.   Antolino, 1846, neoph. of S. José mission. v. 23.

Antonio, 1838, grantee of Saca rancho. iii. 655.   Antonio, 1846, N. Mex. of the Donner party, who perished. v. 531, 534, 537.   A. (Juan), 1847, Cahuilla chief. v. 617.   A. (Manuel), 1776, at Sta Clara. i. 306.   A. (Manuel), grantee of Potrero Grande '45. iv. 635.   A., mate of *Elizabeth* in '48.

Anza (Juan Bautista), 1774, Mex. lieut-col, son of a famous officer of Sonora, who in '74 led the 1st exploring exped. from Son. to Cal. by land. i. 221-4. In '75-6 he brought a large comp. of colonists over the same route, intended for the foundation of S. F., keeping a diary of the trip which is still extant, i. 257-78, and making an exploration of the S. F. peninsula. i. 279-86. For other mention, see i. 124, 215, 218, 244, 248, 354-5, 288, 290, 294, 355, 551; ii. 43-4. Anza was an officer of marked ability and good character, making an excellent record in Cal., in Sonora, and in New Mexico, where he served as governor in 1778-87

Ánzar (José Ant.), 1832, Mex. friar of the Guadalupe college, who seems to have come at least a year before the other Zacatecanos under circumstances of which I find no record. He was in charge of a Sonora mission in 1824, and was possibly a member of the Querétaro col. transferred after his arrival. His missionary service was at S. Luis Rey in '32, and at S. Juan B. from '33, though in '44–6 he also had charge of Sta Cruz and S. Cárlos. He was also president of the Zacatecanos from '43. His name appears as curate on the S. Juan books till 1855, when I suppose he left Cal. Though involved in occasional troubles, P. Ánzar seems to have been a priest of fair character and abilities. See mention in iii. 250, 317, 622, 691; iv. 372, 453, 460, 553, 565, 638, 640, 657, 661–2.

Ánzar (Juan María), brother of the padre; grantee of Aromitas, etc., in '35, and of Sta Ana, etc., in '39. iii. 676, 679, 713; juez, acting at times as prefect, in '39–41 at S. Juan. iii. 661, 675, 693; suplente of the junta in '42–3. iii. 296; iv. 361. He was described in Larkin's *Notes* of '45 as a man of wealth and character, favoring the U. S. cause. I find no trace of him after '52, when he was claimant for certain ranchos; but in '53 María Ant. de Ánzar appears as cl. for others—apparently his widow, and daughter of A. M. Castro; though A. is said by Larkin to have been married in Mex.

Apalátegui (Antonio), 1834, Span. clerk, age 33, who came from Mex. with the H. & P. colony (iii. 259, etc.); leader in the Los Ang. revolt against Gov. Figueroa in '35, for which he was exiled to Mex. iii. 284–90. Apis (Pablo), S. Luis Rey neoph. and chief; grantee of Temécula in '45. iii. 617, 621, 624. Apolinario (Mariano), Dom. friar of B. Cal. at S. Diego 1791–1800. i. 655. Aquino (Tomás), Span. friar who acted as chaplain in Vizcaino's exped. 1602–3. i. 98, 102.

Araiza (Francisco), 1840, Mex. shop-keeper at Mont., who in '42–5 made some money under the patronage of Col Tellez; militia officer and juez in '44–5. iv. 652–6. His wife was a daughter of Capt. Segura; but soon after '46 he left his fam. and went to Mex. Aralde (Eno), doubtful name in a Los Ang. list of '46. Aralon (Wm), 1829, mr of a schr. at S. Pedro. iii. 135.

Aram (Joseph), 1846, native of N. Y., and overl. immig. from Ill. (v. 256–30), with his family. He organized and commanded a comp. of volunteers to garrison Sta Clara and protect the families of immigrants serving in the batallion '46–7, and took part in the 'battle' of Sta Clara. v. 378–81. A firm of Aram & Belcher at Mont. is ment. in '47. A miner in '48; a member of the constitutional convention in '49, and later of the 1st legislature. Then he became a farmer near S. José, where he still lived in '85. His wife died in '73.

Arana (Antonio), 1823, mr of the *Sta Apolonia*, who down to '41 had not accounted for a consignment of mission products. ii. 492, 619. Arana (Gregorio), Span. at Mont. in '36. A. (José) at Mont. '35. iii. 674; grantee of Rincon de S. Pedro, Sta Cruz, '42. iv. 656; in trouble '45. iv. 653. Aranda (María P.), 1798. i. 606.

Araujo (Buenaventura), 1834, Mex. naval capt. who came with the H. & P. colony (iii. 259, et seq.) to take com. of the Cal. fleet—of the future. Involved in the troubles of '35, he was sent to Mex. by Figueroa. iii. 266–7, 271, 281, 288–9, 378. In '38 com. of a battery at S. Juan de Ulúa; and in '47 distinguished himself during the bombardment of V. Cruz by Scott.

Araujo (Francisco), 1833, Mex. cadet with Figueroa, and ayud. de plaza at Mont. iii. 672. In '36 he was com. of the vigilante force at Los Ang., incurring the displeasure of Gov. Chico, and perhaps sent out of the country. iii. 418, 432. Arce (Bernardo), Span. who died at S. José in '57, said to have favored the Amer. in '46–7. *S: F. Bulletin.* Arce (Eugenio), settler at S. Juan Cap. '41. iv. 626.

Arce (Francisco C.), 1833, Mex. of L. Cal., who came at the age of 11 and was educated at Mont. by P. Real and at Romero's school. From '39 to '45 employed as clerk, often acting as sec. in the offices of gov. and prefect. iii. 675; iv. 294, 354. In '44 grantee of Sta Isabel rancho, and also employed to collect debts due the missions. iv. 423, 656. He declined to take part against Micheltorena. iv. 460; and after that officer's departure in '45 became sec. ad.

int. of Gen. Castro, being also alférez of auxiliaries. iv. 520; v. 41. He is best known for his part in the affair of the captured horses at the outbreak of the Bear revolt in '46, though not in command as is generally stated. He had a 'Cal claim' of $5,000; and also claimed to have a grant of S. José mission land. v. 106–9, 127. He went to Mex. with Castro, v. 277, and served throughout the war with the U. S. as lieut (nominally of the S. Diego comp.) and finally brevet capt. At one time, as a member of the S. Patricio legion of Irish deserters, being taken prisoner, he narrowly escaped death on account of his Irish physique. In '48 he served in L. Cal., and in '49 came to Mont. without leave, serving again as sec. of the prefecture. In '52 he was back in L. Cal. asking for antedated leave of absence, Mex. naturalization, and land, also marrying in '53. Subsequently he came north again; and in '77 was living on the Alisal rancho near Salinas. He gave me a collection of *Doc. Hist. Cal.;* and also dictated for my use his *Memorias Históricas,* which, notwithstanding Don Francisco's tendency to magnify his own exploits and those of his friends, have value as well as interest. He died early in '78, leaving a family in straitened circumstances.   Arce (Joaquin), sergt in the S. Diego comp. 1803–17. ii. 12–14, 101, 341, 345.   A sergt Arce is also mentioned in 1783. i. 453. See list in i. 733.   Arce (José Ign.), juez on the L. Cal. frontier in '46.

Arceo, settler of Branciforte in 1798. i. 571.   Arceo (Felipe), native of Brancif.; at Mont. '28–36, when he was 28 years old; wife Cármen Arroyo; child., Lauriano, Juan Francisco, María F., Rafaela. iii. 67, 673.   A. (José María), Mex. settler at Brancif. in 1797. i. 569; in '36 juez de campo, iii. 675, and living at Pilarcitos rancho, age 58; wife Cecilia Serrano; adopted son Juan José.   A. (Juan Ant.), at Pilarcitos '36, age 32, native of Cal.; wife Juana Vasquez; child, Guillermo.   A. (Leonardo), sent to Mex. in '30. iii. 85.

Archambeau (Auguste), 1845, Canadian, one of Frémont's mountain men. iv. 583. He served in Co. A, Cal. Bat. (v. 358–68) '46–7, but did not remain much longer in Cal. His death was in '81.

Archuleta (Florentino), alcalde at S. José in '29. ii. 605; iv. 74–5. Still a resid. in '41, age 41; native of Cal.; wife Antonia Higuera. I have doc. signed by him in '46.   A. (Ignacio), employé at S. F. mission, who in 1777 married Gertrudis Pacheco, and went to S. José, where he was alcalde in 1783, 1803, 1806. No record of him after 1807. i. 297, 312, 350, 478, 480; ii. 134–5.   A. (José), nat. of Cal., age 52, at S. José in '41; wife Juana Montero; child., Josefa b. '24, Miguel A. '27, José Ant. '30, María D. '32, Maria L. '35, Concepcion '39.   A. (José Noberto), son of Ign., b. at S. José in 1778; probably same as preceding, though age does not agree.   A. (Miguel Gerónimo), son of Ign., b. at S. F. in 1779. Became a soldier at S. F., promoted to corp.; transferred to Mont. to become a school-master about 1811. Many Calif. of later prominence attended his school in '11–20. ii. 381, 427–9. His wife was María Ant. García.   Arci (José), 1811, mr of the *Mexicana.* ii. 267.

Ardisson (Estévan), 1840–1, French trader who settled at Sta B. He was perhaps the Ed. Ardison who in July '40 had a claim against the govt. Ment. by Mofras in '41–2. His name frequently occurs in '42–7; he had a 'Cal. claim' in '46; and in '48 was alcalde. iv. 279, 587, 611, 631. Still living at El Rincon in '50.   Arellanes, maj. at Purísima '24. ii. 429.   A. (Francisco), Sta B. ranchero '37–45, with wife Petra Ruiz and 2 child.   A. (José), ditto; wife Josefa Sanchez and 5 child.   A. (José Ant.), at Sta B. '37; wife Manuela Ortega.   A. (Luis), grantee of Punta de la Laguna, S. Luis Ob. in '44. iv. 655; still in Sta B. district in '50.   A. (Teodoro), grantee of Rincon in '35, and Guadalupe in '40. iii. 655, 677. His wife was Josefa Rodriguez and they had 3 child. before '37. Still at Sta B. in '50. Don Teodoro was a very large, fine-looking man, of genial temper and gentlemanly manners, locally a kind of ranchero prince.

Arellano (Ignacio R.), a priest visiting and officiating at S. Juan Cap. in '44. v. 523.   A. (Juan R. or Manuel), settler and alcalde at Los Ang. 1790–S. i. 461, 598, 661.   A. (Luis), Mex. sold. of the Hidalgo piquete '36 at Mont.

Arenas (Cayetano), Mex. who came to Cal. as a boy. In '46 employed as clerk in the secretaria; grantee of S. Mateo rancho. v. 661. In '54–5 a resid.

of Los Ang. and witness in the Limantour case. A. (José M.), sent as a prisoner to Mex. in '30. iii. 85. A. (José), Mex. at Brancif. in '45, age 52; wife Feliciana; child., Felipe b. in '23, María '29, Florencio '31, José Ant. '33, Omebon (?) '36, Juan '38, Cármen '41, Zenona '44. A. (Luis), 1834, Mex. trader who perhaps came with the colony (iii. 259 et seq.), settled at Los Ang., where he was alcalde in '38, and was prominent in the opposition to Alvarado. iii. 491, 504, 555, 577, 636. In '37 one of the grantees of S. José rancho, and in '40-1 grantee of Azuza. iii. 633. In '44 regidor. iv. 633. In '44-5 grantee of Pauba, Los Huecos, Cahuenga, and Sta Clara orchard. iv. 621; v. 561, 665, 627. Also capt. of the defensores. v. 140. Still trading on the coast in '47; but I have no later record of him.

Arenaza (Pascual M.), 1786, Span. friar at S. Cárlos, who left Cal. in 1797 and died in '99. See i. 685; also i. 388-423, 469, 575-7, 579. Argüelles (Luis), Mex. shoemaker at Mont. in '36.

Argüello (Concepcion), daughter of José D., b. at S. F. in 1790; d. at Benicia in 1857. Famous for her romance with Rezánof in 1806, for account of which, with sketch of her life, see ii. 72-4, 77-8. Her full name was María de la Concepcion Marcela. See also mention in ii. 287; iii. 568, 660; iv. 219.

Argüello (Gervasio), son of José D., b. at Sta B. 1786. In 1804 he entered the military service as soldado distinguido of the S. F. comp., in which he was cadet 1807-17, serving also as habilitado in 1808-16. ii. 117, 125, 303, 370. Sent in '16 to Ross, writing a report of his visit. ii. 309, 631; i. list of auth. In '14 he married Encarnacion Bernal; and in '16 was sent to Mex. as habilitado general, never returning to Cal., and holding this office till '32, besides being a suplente in congress in '27-8. Meanwhile, fr. '17 he was on the payroll of the S. Diego comp. as alférez till '31, when he was promoted to lieut of the Mont. comp., and in '34 commissioned capt., but immediately retired as lieut on full pay, with permission to reside in Jalisco. ii. 213-14. 217, 261, 421-2, 514-15, 543, 671; iii. 33-4, 45, 378, 671. In Cal. Don Gervasio was reputed to be a youth of good conduct and fair abilities, though disposed to 'put on airs.' In Mex. he accomplished nothing, either as habilitado gen. or congressman, having no special fitness for the positions; yet a man of ten times his ability would very likely have failed equally in getting money for Cal. from the Mex. govt. I have private letters written by him from Guadalajara in '49 and '52, filled with pious complaints of poverty, which would be intolerable but for aid received from Cal.

Argüello (José Darío), 1781, founder of the Argüello family; Mex. alférez, later lieut and capt.; comandante at S. F., Mont., and Sta B.; acting gov. of Cal. in '14-15; gov. of L. Cal. in '15-22. Died at Guadalajara '28; his wife was Ignacia Moraga, who died at Guad. in '29. For many years Don José was the most prominent, influential, and respected man in Cal. See biog. sketch in this vol., 358-61, includ. 4 of the children who did not remain in Cal.; also mention of Don José in i. 340-2, 347, 372, 396, 445, 463, 468, 470-2, 478, 484, 498, 501-2, 511-13, 525, 531-2, 588-94, 678-80, 692-4, 708, 717, 721, and list of auth.; ii. 30, 44, 68-74, 86, 99, 117, 125, 127, 133, 135, 187, 190, 207-8, 210-11, 246, 305-7, 450, 565, 571; iii. 11. Argüello (José Ign. Máx.), oldest son of José D.; b. at S. Gabriel in 1782; educ. in Mex. as a priest; visited Cal. in 1809. ii. 359-60, 122. A. (José Ramon), son of Santiago, at San Juan Cap. in '40-1. iii. 626-7. Sec. to prefect at Los Ang. in '42. iv. 632. Suplente juez at S. Diego in '45. iv. 620. Sub-prefect in '46. v. 618. A. (José Ramon), son of Luis Ant., b. at S. F. in '28; living at Sta Clara and Mont. till '44; on the coast of Mex. '44-6; lived with his mother from '46 at Las Pulgas and Sta Clara, where he died in '76. A. (Julian), a Sonoran with Zamorano at Mont. in '36, age 16.

Argüello (Luis Antonio), son of José D., b. at S. F. in 1784; cadet at S. F. 1799; alf. 1800; lieut and com. 1806; capt. from '18. Gov. ad int. of Cal. from Nov. 22d, '22, to Nov. '25. Died at S. F. '30. First wife, Rafaela Sal, 1807-14; 2d wife, Soledad Ortega, '19, who died at Sta Clara in '74. His children were Francisco, by 1st wife, who died soon after '30; by 2d wife, Concepcion, b. in '24; Josefa, '26; José Ramon, as above; and Luis, who, I think, still lives at Sta Clara in '85. Don Luis, as military officer and gov., left an excellent record in respect of honesty and ability and popularity. Unlike his father, he had enemies, and was involved in controversies; but these were due largely to his position and the times. He often disregarded the letter of the Span. and Mex. laws, but it was always for what he believed the welfare of his country, and never for his own interests. His private record was that of a dissipated spendthrift, yet never accused of dishonorable conduct. See biog. sketch in iii. 9–13; list of auth. in i.; mention in ii. 35, 46, 48, 68 et seq., 125–6, 129–30, 137, 203–4, 210, 230–2, 243–4, 268–9, 272, 279, 284–5, 288, 300–1, 305, 307, 309, 312, 328, 330–1, 370, 372, 390, 425–6, 443–9, 451, 455, 461, 464, 466–8, 479–80, 482 et seq., 493, 510–38, 549, 551, 559, 565, 583, 591–2, 594, 596–7, 605, 607, 614, 643, 645, 647, 659, 664; iii. 2, 7, 9–10, 18–19, 24–7, 40, 75, 89, 119, 148, 712.   Argüello (Luis), lieut in the Cal. Bat. '46–7. v. 360, 386. I cannot say who he was.   A. (Romano), sec. in prefect's office in '45. *Larkin.*

Argüello (Santiago), son of José D.; b. at Mont. in 1791. He entered the military service as cadet in the S. F. comp. 1805, but was trans. in 1806 to Sta B. ii. 46, 117, 275, 361, 425. In '17–27 he was alf. of the S. F. comp., though serving from '18 as habilitado at S. Diego, where he was involved in several controversies, also visiting the north and making a trip to Ross and Sonoma. ii. 240–2, 258, 341, 370, 424, 442, 457, 470, 507, 510, 537, 542–3, 583; iii. 12, 291. In '27–31 he was lieut of the S. D. comp., being comandante from '28, in which year he was elected suplente member of congress; in '30 suplente of the diputacion. ii. 541–3; iii. 45–6, 50, 64, 135, 196. In '31–5 he was capt. of the co., taking part somewhat unwillingly in the revolt against Victoria, serving as diputado and comisionado for S. Diego mission in '33–4, and being finally retired with full pay—in theory. iii. 201, 204, 216–19, 327, 331–2, 372, 608, 612, 620; iv. 408. In '36 he was alcalde of S. Diego, using his influence against the Alvarado govt, but acting as comisionado and admin. of S. Juan Cap. in '38–40, and as vocal of the junta in '40. iii. 422, 482, 520, 590, 604, 606, 615, 626–7. In '40–3 he held the position of prefect at Los Ang., and in '41 his name was given to the pueblo of S. Juan; in '45 holding the offices of suplente of the tribunal, vocal of the junta, and sub-prefect of S. Diego. iii. 640; iv. 193, 195, 295, 319, 532, 540, 620–2, 626–7, 632–3. In '46 he was friendly to the Amer., held an honorary com. as capt. in the Cal. Bat. (?), was appointed member of the legis. council in '47, and was made collector of the port of S. Diego (?). v. 37, 282, 329, 360, 433, 446, 467, 572, 618–19. Meanwhile in '29 he had obtained the Tia Juana rancho, in '41 the Trabuco, and in '46 the S. Diego mission estate. iii. 612; iv. 635; v. 561, 619–20, 627. Argüello when very young married Pilar, daughter of Francisco Ortega of Sta B., by whom he had 22 children, among them the following, who lived and had issue: Francisco, Ignacio, José Antonio, José Ramon, Santiago E.; Refugio, who married Juan Bandini; Teresa, who married José M. Bandini; Luisa, wife of A. V. Zamorano; and Concepcion, wife of Agustin Olvera. Don Santiago was tall, stout, and of fine presence, with fair complexion and black hair; reserved in manner, yet of kindly disposition. His record, public and private, was an honorable if not a brilliant one. He was often in trouble with his brother officers and with men of other classes, and especially in the earlier years was by no means a popular man. This was chiefly due to a peculiar reserve or haughtiness of manner, attributed to family pride and regarded as an assumption of superiority. He died at Tia Juana, on the frontier, in '62, and his widow soon after '78. The rancho is still owned by the family.

Argüello (Santiago E.), son of Santiago, b. about 1813. Receptor at S. Diego '33–4. iii. 277, 609. Grantee of Melyo (Máligo?) '33. iii. 612. Took part with the south against Alvarado in '36–7, being then in charge of the ranchos Otay and S. Antonio Abad. iii. 482–3, 517, 612. Majordomo and land-owner at S. Juan Cap. '41. iv. 626–7. Suplente in assemb., and juez at S. Diego '45–6. iv. 540; v. 161. In '46 he aided the Amer., served as captain in Stockton's battalion, and had a 'Cal. claim' for $11,548 for damages to his property. v. 378, 386. I think he may have been the capt. in Cal. Bat. and collector of the port, instead of his father, as above. He died at Máligo in '57. His wife was Guadalupe Estudillo, who survived him with 2 sons and 2 (or 4) daughters; one of the latter married A. H. Wilcox and another Wm B. Coutts.

Arias (Francisco), S. F. settler of 1791–1800. i. 716. A. (Francisco), grantee of ranchos in Mont. district '39, '44. iii. 676; iv. 655; suplente prefect in '41, being juez at S. Juan '41–3, and regidor at Mont. in '46. iv. 652–3, 661; v. 636. A. (Rafael R.), 1791, contador in Malaspina's exped. i. 490.

Armas (Baltasar), 1602, piloto in Vizcaino's exped. i. 98. F., P., and J. Armas, named as at Honolulu from Cal. in '48.

Armenta (Cristóbal), sirviente at Sta Clara 1776. i. 306. A. (Joaq.), sold. at S. Diego 1775–6; later at Los Ang. i. 250, 303, 461. A. (José M.), grantee of Punta de Pinos rancho '33, '44. iii. 678. A. ('Tio'), retired soldier who kept a shop and sometimes a school at Mont. in '11–20. ii. 381–3, 420.

Armijo (Antonio), native of N. Mex., at S. José in '41, age 37; wife María D. Duarte; child., Antonio, Jesus, Félix, Matías. Probably same as the Francisco Armijo who was a S. F. militiaman in '37; and perhaps same as Antonio M. Armijo who settled in the Suisun region in '43, was in trouble '47 for outrages on Ind. v. 569, 610; and died in '50. A. (Francisco), at S. Mateo in '35; alcalde in the contra costa '37. iii. 705; at S. F. '47. *Spear, Pap.* A. (José F.), grantee of Tolenas rancho '40. iv. 674. A. (Jesus M.), at Sonoma '44, age 18. A. (Juan F.), at Sonoma '44, age 42. A. (Salvador), at Los Ang. '39–46. I have not been able to obtain much definite information about any branch of the Armijo family.

Armon (Chas), 1836, at Mont., named in Larkin's books.

Armstrong (James), 1842, com. of the *United States;* and of the *Savannah* in later visits of '44–6. iv. 307–8, 301, 313, 459, 509. A. (John), 1840, Amer. ranchero in the Mont. district; exiled to S. Blas with the Graham party. iv. 18, 120. In '46 he wrote a letter against Larkin, which appeared in a St Louis paper, causing L. to get statements in his own defence from several prominent men. A. (John), in '46 at Monterey, and in '47 employed on Larkin's Sac. rancho. Possibly same as preceding. Arnand, 1848, mr of the *Con de Valparaiso* from Honolulu for S. F.

Arnaz (José), 1841, Span. supercargo of the *Clara* in Virmond's employ. iv. 102; and later in Aguirre's *Jóven Guipuzcoana.* In '44 he opened a store at Los Ang., suffering much from depredations of the cholos. iv. 364; and in '45 leased the mission estate of S. Buen., which in '46 he purchased, as he claimed, but was not permitted to retain possession. iv. 553, 558, 561, 645; v. 400, 632, 643, 665. He still retained considerable property, however; and I found him in '74 living at his Sta Ana rancho near S. Buen., a genial gentleman of 54 years, who then and later gave me 100 pages of his interesting *Recuerdos* on the life and customs of the traders and rancheros in early times. Probably living in '85. In '47 he married Mercedes Ávila, who died in '67, leaving several children. His 2d wife was a daughter of Juan Camarrillo. Arnold (Robert), 1828, Scotch turner, age 20, at Mont. '28–9.

Arrieta (Sebastian), 1820, Span. intendente, com. of the royal order of Isabel the catholic, who came from Peru with the king's license to live in Cal.with a pension of $3,000; but died at S. Juan B. in '21, age 54.

Arrillaga (José Joaquin), 1793, Span. capt. and lieut-gov. of the Cals at Loreto '83–92; gov. ad int. '93–4 at Mont.; lieut-col and lieut-gov. at L. '94–9; gov. ad int. 1800–4; gov. of Alta Cal. from 1804—coming to Mont. in 1806—to 1814, when he died at Soledad at the age of 64. Arrillaga was an efficient and honest officer, of most excellent private character, and a model governor so far as the performance of routine duties was concerned. See biog. in ii. 204–7; i. list of auth.; also mention in i. 471, 482, 484, 488, 501–29, 531–6, 574, 602, 611, 631, 637–8, 658, 661, 663, 671, 729; ii. 2–204 passim, 269, 301–5, 386–7, 416–17, 566. Arriola (José F.), blacksmith instructor in 1792–5. i. 615. A. (María), wife of J. V. Lawrence. ii. 496. A. (Rafael), settler at Los Ang. from 1797. i. 606; ii. 350.

Arroita (Francisco José), 1786, Span. friar at Purísima, who left Cal. in '96. See biog. notice, i. 675; ment. i. 388, 423, 425, 459, 575–7. Arroyo, 1795. i.

253.   A. (Ign.), exile of 1842. iv. 653.   A. (Joaquin), grantee of Tucho '46.
v. 637.   A. (José), 1792-5. i. 615.   A. (José Man.). i. 250-3.   A. (José
Isidro); at Mont. '36, age 53, nat. of S.F.; wife Isabel; child. Ignacio, Catarina, Joaquina, Concepcion, María P.   A. (Victor), 1820-39. ii. 382; iii. 587

Arroyo de la Cuesta (Felipe), 1808, Span. friar, serving chiefly at San Juan
B.; d. at Sta Inés in '40. Noted for learning as well as piety; author of several
works on Ind. lang. See biog. in iii. 662; list of auth. i.; ment. in ii. 140, 154,
159-60, 284, 316, 338, 394, 492, 526, 655; iv. 63. See also 'Cuesta.'   Arteaga
(Ignacio), 1777-80, Span. com. of explor. and transport ships. i. 296, 323, 329.

Arther (James P.), 1829, German mate of the *Brooklyn* in '29-30. iii. 138-
9, 146, 179. Master of Bryant & Sturgis' Boston ship *California* on 4 or 5 voyages to Cal. in '34-46. iii. 381; iv. 101, 564. Mr of *Thos Perkins* in '47. v.
511, 580. Often called James D. Arthur, but I have many of his autograph
letters. A skilful mariner, though close-fisted and not very popular on the
coast. Said by Thomes to be still living in Mass. '84.

Aruz (Domingo), settler at Los Ang. 1790-1810; not allowed to devote all
his prop. to masses for his soul. i. 460; ii. 167.   A. (José), elector and memb.
of the dip. at Mont. '22-4. ii. 454, 462, 513, 536, 616.   Arzaga (Manuel), sec.
of ayunt. at Los Ang. '34-5; sec. of vigilantes '36. iii. 418, 631, 635, 638.

Ascension (Antonio), 1602, friar with Vizcaino. i. 98. I have his autograph.
Ashley (Geo. H.), 1848, native of Mass.; memb. of S. Joaquin Co. pioneers
'84 (?).   Ashmead (Geo.), 1846, Co. C, 1st U. S. dragoons; killed at S. Pascual.
v. 346.   Ashton (A. B.), 1846, clerk on the *Dale*.   A. (Geo. H.), 1847, Co.
D, N.Y. Vol.; killed by Ind. in S. Joaq. Val. in '47.   Asken (Wm), 1840,
Engl. pilot of the *Ninfa;* at Mont. '41.   Aspiroz (Salvador), 1814, teacher
with Gov. Sola. ii. 426. Quarrel with Guerra '17. ii. 382.   Asuncion (Fr. Andrés), 1602, with Vizcaino. i. 98.   Atanasio, Ind. executed at Mont. '31. iii.
190.   Atensio (Gregorio), at Los Ang. '46. v. 308; also Ign. Atensio.

Atherton (Faxon Dean), 1836, native of Mass., who as a boy went to Valparaiso; memb. of a firm engaged in the hide and tallow trade. Visited Cal. in
'36-7, and later kept up a corresp. with Larkin and others. I have many of his
letters on personal, political, and business affairs, sometimes signed Feliz D.
Atherton. Went to Honolulu and Boston in '38-9, but returned in '41. iv. 91,
103, 117-18, 141. Said to have sent descriptions of the coast to Wash., and
to have had a corresp. with Webster about Cal. Visited Cal. again in '49-50
to make investments, and became a resident in '59. Besides being the owner
of a large estate in San Mateo Co., he was prominent in building railroads,
banking, and various financial enterprises. Died at Fair Oaks in '77, leaving
a widow—native of Chile, still living in '85—and 7 children. Three of his
daughters married respectively Wm Macondray, Maj. Rathbone, U. S. A.,
and Edmunds of Valparaiso.

Atherton (Geo. D.), 1847, Co. D, N. Y. Vol. (v. 499-518).   A. (Robert),
1847, brother of Faxon D., who came with a letter of introd. to Vallejo, 'para
probar su fortuna en Cal.;' and was employed as a clerk by Larkin.   A. (Wm),
1845, mr of Parrott's *Star of the West.* iv. 568.   A. (Wm), 1846, Mormon of
the *Brooklyn* colony, with wife. v. 546. Lot at S. F. '47; also at N. Helv.; in
the mines '48. In later times a pressman on the Oakland *Transcript*.

Atillan (Pierre), 1841, French sailor married to a native at Mont. Coxswain of the custom-house boat, and tax collector. Attacked and mutilated
by the cholos in '44; got a pension from the Mex. govt till '47, when Gov.
Mason was not able to continue it; and Pierre was supported till his death by
charity. iv. 279, 339, 364, 414, 615, 653.

Atkins, 1846, mr of the *Jeanette*.   Atkinson, 1848, a physician at Sac.
according to Burnett.   Atkinson (Chas A.), 1847, Co. D, N. Y. Vol. (v. 499-
518). Called a 'judge' at S. José '77; d. at Mariposa in '82.   A. (James or
John), 1843, Amer., who after an adventurous career in Texas and Mex. came
to Cal. accord. to newspaper sketches at a date varying '40 to '46, but apparently with the Chiles-Walker party of '43. iv. 392, 399. Known as Old Wheat
for his reputed reliability; at Mont. in '45; served with Stockton in '46-7; long
a resident of Los Ang.; in '71 pensioned as a veteran of 1812; died in the (S.

Joaq.?) county hospital in '74 at the age of about 80.   Atnay, 1816, kanaka
sailor arrested at Sta B. ii. 275.   Atterville (James), 1840, doubtful name
in Farnham's list. iv. 17.   Aubens (N.), 1848, pass. from Honolulu.
    Aulick (J. H.), 1841, com. of the U. S. *Yorktown*, at Mont. and S. F.
iv. 38, 570. Later a commodore.   Auntroy (John), 1840, arrested at Los
Ang. in the Graham affair. iv. 14.   Aurelio, 1797, neoph. who killed his
wife. i. 659.   Aurweller (John), 1847, Co. C, N. Y. Vol. (v. 499); at S. F.
'82; called also Auwaerter.
    Austin, 1822, mr of the *Panther*. ii. 474.   Austin, 1847, mid. on U. S.
Independence.   A. (David), 1846, Fauntleroy's dragoons (v. 232-47).   A.
(Henry), 1838, Canadian carpenter, naturalized in '41, when he was at S. José.
iv. 119.   A. (Horace G.), 1846, on roll of Pion. Soc.; error in iv. 587.   A.
(Joseph C.), 1848, on roll of Pion. Soc.   A. (Julius C.), 1846, Mormon on the
Brooklyn, with wife and 3 children. v. 546. Ment. as a lawyer at S. Bernardino
in '81; also as in Utah, '84.   A. (J. Wemys), 1848, of Findley, Johnson & Co.
at S. F. Still at S. F. '54.   A. (Wm), 1826, mr of the *Mercury*. iii. 148.
    Ávalos (Joaquin), tanner-instructor 1792-5. i. 615.   Averett (Elisha),
1847, in com. of a party of Morm. Bat. on the return. v. 493.   Avery, 1842,
lieut with Com. Jones. iv. 308.   A. (Elihu), 1844, boy on a whaler at S. F.;
mr of *Legal Tender*, '82, accord. to a newsp. sketch.   Avieta (José Ant.),
1834, with a party from N. Mex. iii. 396.
    Ávila (Anastasio), son of Cornelio; settler at Los Ang. 1799. iii. 349; re-
gidor in 1810, '19, alcalde in '20-1. ii. 110, 337, 350-1, 354, 559; grantee of Ta-
janta in '43. iv. 635.   A. (Antonio), 1825, Mex. convict sent to Cal. for
robberies and murder in Puebla. In the Solis revolt of '29, and in the Zamorano régime of '32 he aided the govt, in the hope of getting a release; but
had to remain and serve out his time till about '38. iii. 16, 76, 83-4, 230, 669.
Another Ant. A. in '37-9 apparently. iii. 504, 639.
    Ávila (Antonio Ignacio), 1783, son of Cornelio; native of Sonora, who
settled at Los Ang.; in 1804 married Rosa Ruiz at Sta B.; in '20-1 regidor;
grantee of Sauzal Redondo in '22 and '37; juez de campo most of the time in
'35-48; and always prominent in the pursuit of Ind. horse-thieves. ii. 349-51,
353, 559, 566, 664; iii. 396, 565, 626, 632-7. He died in '58, aged 74.   A.
(Cornelio), 1783, settler Los Ang. from Sonora, with his wife Isabel Urquides and 8 children. i. 663   A. (Bruno), son of Cornelio; settler at Los Ang.
'15; later claimant of Aguage del Centinela. ii. 349-50; iv. 634.   A. (Enrique), prob. son of Anastasio; 2d alcalde at Los Ang. '47; claimant for Ta-
janta rancho. iv. 635; v. 626.   A. (Francisco), a 'hard case' at S. F. and
S. José 1783-1800. i. 350, 484, 640, 716.   A. (Francisco), drowned in the
Tulares 1796. i. 661.   A. (Francisco), son of Cornelio; in Los Ang. region
1804; alcalde in '10; applicant for dif. ranchos, and grantee of Ciénegas in '23,
'34. He had probably been a sold. at Sta B. ii. 110, 116, 172, 349-50, 354,
565, 664; iii. 633.   A. (Francisco), resid. of S. José '41, age 44; wife, María
Ant. Alviso; child., Francisco, Encarnacion, Gerónima, and Viviana.   A.
(Fran.), resid. of Brancif. '45, age 40.   A. (Guadalupe). i. 175.   A. (Ja-
nuatio), prob. son of Francisco; regidor of Los Ang. '34-9; claimant for Ciénegas. iii. 633-6.   A. (José), at Los Ang. '39-46.   A. (José), settler at S. F.
1791-1800. i. 606, 716.   A. (Joaquin), 1842, sub-lieut of the batallon. iv. 289.
A. (José Joaquin), surgeon of the Cal. forces 1774-83. His wife died at S. F.
in '79. *Prov. St. Pap.*, v. 57-8.
    Ávila (José María), son of Cornelio. Alcalde of Los Ang. in '25. In the
battle of '31 he killed Capt. Pacheco, and was himself killed. See biog. iii.
206-9; ment. ii. 559; iii. 196, 200.   A. (José de Sta Ana), son of Cornelio; maj. at Sta B. 1801-6. ii. 120; mar. María Josefa Osuna.   A. (José
de los Santos), sec. of ayunt. at Brancif. '34. iii. 696.   A. (J. S.), colegial at
Sta Inés '44. iv. 426.
    Ávila (Juan), son of Ant. Ign; eye-witness of the fight near Los Ang. in
'31. iii. 208; grantee of Miguel rancho '42. iv. 635; juez de campo at Los Ang.
'44; juez at S. Juan Cap. '46. iv. 633; v. 623; in '47 carried a flag of truce for
Stockton to the people of Los Ang. v. 396. He married Soledad Yorba; one

daughter married M. A. Forster, and another Paul Pryor. Don Juan was a man of excellent repute, who avoided political complications, but had good powers of observation and memory. At S. Juan Cap. in '77 he gave me his recollections—*Notas Californianas*—of early times, including valuable testimony on several matters.

Ávila (Miguel), son of José Sta Ana; b. at Sta B. in 1796; educ. at S. F.; served as copyist at Mont. In '16 he enlisted in the Mont. comp.; and in '24 was corporal of the escolta at S. Luis Ob., having a quarrel with the padre. ii. 516-17, 619; síndico at Mont. and alf. of militia '35-6. iii. 447, 474, 673-4. In '26 he had married María Inocenta, daughter of Dolores Pico; and in '36 lived at Mont. with 5 child., Rafaela, Jesus Domingo, Francisco de Paula, José Ant. R., Josefa de los Ang. Ment. in '37, '41. iii, 501; iv. 653; grantee of S. Miguelito in '42, '46, and Laguna in '45. iv. 637, 642, 656. Also ment. in '45-8. iv. 491; v. 321, 639. Alcalde of S. Luis Ob. in '49. He had a fondness for preserving documents, but most of his collection was burned with his house. Died in '74, leaving his S. Miguelito rancho to his widow and children. Doña María Inocenta gave me not only her own recollections on old-time *Cosas de Cal.*, ii. 242, 427, but also the remnant of Don Miguel's *Doc. Hist. Cal.*, containing several important papers.   A. (Pedro), juez de campo at Los Ang. '44. iv. 633.

Avis (Wm P.), 1842, Boston man from Honolulu, with letters from Peirce & Brewer, to go into business as a commission merchant.

Ayala (Cármen), at Sta B. '45. iv. 642.   A. (Crisógono), ranchero at Sta B. '37-50; grantee of Sta Ana; maj. of S. Buen. in '42-4. iii. 656; iv. 644-5. His wife was Bárbara Vanegas, and they had 5 children.   A. (Gervasio), juez de policía at Sta B. '48. v. 631. His wife was Rafaela Moraga, 1 child before '37.   A. (Joaquin), owner of land near Sta Inés. v. 632. A. (José), inválido at Sta B. '32; wife Juana Félix; child., María, Rafael, Juan, Prudencio, Antonio.   A. (José M.), soldier at Sta B. '32; wife Emedia Valencia.   A. (Juan B.), 1775, lieut and com. of *S. Cárlos;* explorer of S. F. bay. i. 241, 245-7.   A. (Juan Man.), 1778, com. of *Santiago.* i. 328.   A. (Juan Nepomuceno), 1834, Mex. clerk, age 20, who came with the H. & P. colony. iii. 263; took part in the revolt against Alvarado in '37. iii. 523-5.

Ayala (Juan Pablo), sergt of Sta B. comp. '35. iii. 650; lieut '38-9. iii. 583, 651. Admin. S. Luis Ob. '39-40. iii. 683; acting com. Sta B. '45; iv. 641; capt. of defensores and 2d juez '46. v. 140, 631; proposed revolt in '48. v. 586.   A. (Pablo), admin. S. F. Solano '37-8. iii. 720-1.   A. (Wm), 1832-3, mr of the *Roxana*. iii. 384.   Ayals (Manuel M.), 1837, Span. physician in Alameda Co. '76, said to have come in '37 (?). *Alam. Hist. Atlas.*

Ayer (Franklin H.), 1848, Amer. carpenter who arr. on the *Sabine* in May from Boston at S. F., and went to the Mormon Isl. mines. Ment. by Gov. Mason as having furnished gold specimens for Wash. In '52 an advertisement for him from his bro. in China and parents in Somerville, Mass., appears in the *Alta*. In '72 he wrote me a letter on his *Personal Adventures*, from Grayson, Stanislaus Co. A letter to that address in '82 brought no reply.   Ayot (Alexis), 1844, perhaps came to Cal. with Frémont. iv. 437.

Ayres (Geo. Wash.), 1812-13, mr of the *Mercury*, captured at Sta B. ii. 268-70, 295, 304, 362. In '20 he was interested with Abel Stearns in obtaining lands in the Sac. Val. for a settlement, but prob. did not revisit Cal. *Dept. Rec.*, MS., viii. 38.   A. (R. B.), 1847, lieut Co. F, 3d U. S. artillery (v. 518).   Azcona, lieut on the *Morelos* '34. iii. 269.

Babcock (Benj. E.), 1848, on the roll of Pion. Soc., died before '81.   B. (J.), 1848, sup. of the *Mary.*   Bacey (James), 1831, one of Young's trappers; perhaps did not come to Cal. iii. 388.   Bachelor (Fred.), 1841, Amer. cooper of the Workman-Rowland party from N. Mex.; went east in '42, iv. 278, but ret. to Cal. in later years, living at Noon's rancho, where he died in '76.

Bachelot (Alexis), 1832, French missionary prefect of the Sand. Isl. in exile; served at S. Gabriel in '32-7; ret. to the Isl. in '37; died '38 on a voy. to the South Sea Isl. iii. 317-18, 364, 384, 408, 643; iv. 102.   Bacon (J.), 1846,

Co. B, Cal. Bat., artillery (v. 358). Badeau (Francois), 1844, one of Frémont's Canadians. iv. 437.

Baden (James Collins), 1847, Co. F, 3d artill. (v. 518); clerk and copyist for the comp., commandant, and dept. to '51, not deserting like most of his comrades; later a teacher; d. at Watsonville '68, aged 50. He was a son of a colonel in U. S. service, and b. at Baltimore. Ment. by Gen. Sherman, *Mem.*, as his clerk; obituary in *Sta Cruz Sentinel*, Sept. '68. Bader (Christopher), 1847, Co. B, N.Y. Vol. (v. 499); a miner at Coloma and elsewhere '48–52; settled later in Butte Co., and lived for many years at Cherokee, where he was in '82, but died before '85, leaving a widow and 9 children, most of them grown. One of the sons, H. F. Bader, writes me from Cherokee April '85. Badger (Wm G. B.), 1848, pass. on the *Sabine* from Boston; at the Mormon Isl. mines. Badillo (Francisco), 1825, Mex. convict who continued his lawless career in Cal.; wife Rafaela García, 4 child.; lynched in '60 with one of his sons. iii. 16, 549, 652. Baewdsxig (?), mr of the *Nikolai* in '40. iv. 105. Bagley (Alden S.), 1848, part owner of the Coloma mill in Dec.

Bailey (Addison), 1847, Co. C, Morm. Bat. (v. 469), reënlist. at L. Ang. B. (James), 1847, Co. A, Morm. Bat.; made bricks at S.F. B. (Jefferson), 1847, Co. C, Morm. Bat., perhaps same as the Jeff. B. who had a farm in Sta Clara Co. '50–74. B. (Theodorus), 1847, lieut, com. of the U. S. *Lexington*; rear-admiral in the war of '61–5. v. 578. Portrait in the *Century*, April '85. B. (Wm J.), 1834, Engl. sailor at Mont., age 25; drove cattle to Or. '37; perhaps the Wm Bailey exiled in '40. iv. 18, 85, 412. Baillie (Thomas), 1844, com. of the Engl. *Modeste*. iv. 567. Bailon (Pascual), 1782, corporal killed on the Colorado. i. 364. Bails (Jonas), 1836, Amer. tailor at Los Ang. from N. Mex., age 29.

Baker, 1845–6, mr of the *Montezuma*. B., 1848, of the firm S. H. Williams & Co. at S. F. B. (Andy), 1846, Co. G, Cal. Bat. (v. 358); at Stockton with Weber '47–8; also employed as a builder in '47, at Mont. in '47; called also Antonio B.; ment. at N. Helv. '48; very likely the 'Antonio' employed by Larkin at S. F. B. (Isaac Munroe), 1846, nat. of Md, b. in '20; marine on the U. S. *Dale* '46–9; one of Marston's men in the Sanchez campaign (v. 379). Being disch. in N.Y. he came to S. F. in '50–65; in the east '65–8; owner of a place at La Honda, Sta Cruz mts, from '64, but in the grocery business at S. F., '75–85. Married Mary A. Smith '75, has 3 children '85. In an interview he gave many items about S. F. in '46–7. B. (John), 1846, Co. C, 1st U.S. dragoons (v. 336). B. (John F.), 1848. Passport from Honolulu. B. (Wm), 1845; Amer. sailor at Mont. Balderrama (José), 1798. i. 606, 733. Should be written Valderrama. Baldomero, grantee of Corral de Padilla '36. iii. 677.

Baldridge (Wm), 1843, Tenn. mill-wright, b. in '11, resid. of Mo. from '20; overl. immig. in the Walker-Chiles party. iv. 392, 399. After working at his trade in different places, in '45 he settled on a Napa rancho as a partner of Chiles; in '46 a member of the Bear organization, v. iii. 179, 189, and later served as lieut of Co. C, Cal. Bat. v. 361, 434. Then he resumed his trade for a time, and I have a contract signed by him in '47 to build a saw-mill for Salv. Vallejo. From '52 Baldridge lived on his rancho at Oakville, always commanding the respect of his neighbors. His *Days of '46*, written in '77, is an interesting part of my collection; and in the testimony given by him at various times for newspapers and books there is to be noted exceptional accuracy. Never married. Still living in '81, and I think in '85. A good sketch of his life, and portrait, in *Napa Co. Hist.*, 387, 20.

Baldwin (Alfred), 1846, native of N.Y.; overl. immig. to Or. in '45 and in '46 to Cal. v. 546. Served at S. José under Watmough, and went south with the Cal. Bat. (v. 358). Resid. of Sta Cruz '47–85. His wife was Fannie Willard, whom he married in '66. B. (Charles H.), 1846, passed mid. on the U.S. *Congress*, left by Stockton in com. of a guard at Mont. '46–7, until the coming of the artill. comp. v. 290, 519; lieut in war of '61–5, and com. of a gunboat in the Pacific; later an admiral in com. of North Pac. station at Mare Isl.; in Cal. '83, as was also a son. B. (James M.), 1814, Engl. sailor left at Mont. by the *Isaac Todd*. ii. 272. B. (James H.), 1847; Co. B, N.Y. Vol. (v. 499).

B. (John), 1841, at Los Ang. from the *Juan José*, but required to depart.   B. (Josiah L.), 1847, Co. I, N.Y. Vol. (v. 499); d. at S. José '50.   B. (Timothy), 1847, Co. E, N.Y. Vol.

Bale (Edward Turner), 1837, Engl. surgeon, who landed from a vessel at Mont., age 29. ii. 117–18. For 5 or 6 years he practised medicine at Mont., being in '40–3 surg. of the Cal. forces by Gen. Vallejo's appointment, and having married María Ignacia Soberanes. Bale was a man of good education, but always more or less in trouble on account of his debts and personal quarrels. In '40 he opened a liquor-shop in a room hired of Larkin for a drug-store, and was arrested in the resulting complications with the authorities. I have many original documents written by and about him; but have no intention of cataloguing his troubles. In '41 he was naturalized and got a grant of the Carne Humana rancho in Napa valley, where he went in '43, though his family lived for a time at S. F. with John Fuller. iv. 669, 671; v. 678–9. In '44, having been whipped by Salv. Vallejo, he attempted to shoot the latter, was put in jail, and narrowly saved his life. iv. 444–5, 678; the rumored intention of the Kelseys and other foreigners to rescue the doctor also caused much excitement. In '46 he built a saw-mill, and in '47–8 did a large business in lumber, the increased value of his land making him a rich man; but he died '49 or '50, leaving a widow—still living in '85—2 sons and 4 daughters. His son Edward was commissioned in '64 capt. of Co. D, 1st Bat. Nat. Cal. cavalry; and in '71 was in business at Napa.   Bale (Wm), 1831, Engl. carpenter at Los Ang. in '36, age 29. iii. 405. Possibly Wm 'Bailey,' q.v.

Ball (Franklin), 1847, Co. E, N.Y.Vol. (v. 499); blacksmith at Sta Cruz in Nov.   Ballard (John), 1847, Co. C, N.Y. Vol.   Ballenback (Wm), 1846, marine on the *Dale*, acting as baker at S. F. in '47; in the mines later.

Ballesteros (Cárlos), killed at Chino rancho '46. v. 313.   B. (Felipe) and B. (Francisco), at L. Ang. '46.   B. (Juan), regidor at L. Ang. '23, '32, '38; grantee of Rosa del Castillo rancho '31. ii. 559; iii. 633–6. He was prob. Juan Ant., son of J. de Dios.   B. (Juan de Dios), corp. of the Sta B. comp. 1787; com. of escolta at S. Ant., S. Luis Ob., and S. Juan B. 1791–7. Also named at L. Ang. 1796, 1819. His wife was Teresa Sepúlveda, and his sons Juan Antonio, b. '87, and Fran. Javier Ant., b. '97. Before '86 he had been a sergt, but was reduced to the ranks for desertion. i. 557, 718; ii. 349, 354.

Ballhaus (Fred.), 1846, German immig. (v. 526), with Hoppe and Harlan; in Cal. Bat. (v. 358), at the Natividad fight, and in Co. B artill. in the south; worked at S. F. and N. Helv. '47–8; in the mines much of the time '48–60; married Katrina Franck '53; to Frazer River '58; from '61 at S. F., brewer, vegetable gardener, and man of property; still living in '85, age 69, with wife and 3 children. He has kept a diary, and tells no end of interesting details of his Cal. experiences.   Baltasar, 1824, Ind. executed at Purísima.   Balteco (John), 1846, Fauntleroy's dragoons (v. 232).   Balygin, 1808, mr of the *Nikolai*. ii. 80.

Bancroft (Jerry), 1811, sailor at Drake's Bay. ii. 95.   B. (John), 1836, mr of the *Convoy*. iv. 103, 118. In '37–8, mr of the *Loriot* and *Llama;* killed by Ind. at the Sta B. islands. iv. 90, 105; iii. 652–3. His wife, fatally wounded at the same time, was a half-breed Hawaiian, Miss Holmes, a sister of Nathan Spear's wife.

Bandini (José), 1819, Span. b. in Andalucía 1771; came to Amer. '93; a mariner whose home was at Lima, where he married twice and had 7 children living in '28, only one of them ever known in Cal. In '19 as mr of the Span. *Reina de Los Angeles* he brought to Cal. fr. S. Blas a cargo of war supplies, making another trip in '21, and doing a little in contraband trade. ii. 253, 261, 439–40. On returning to S. Blas he raised the Mex. flag on the *Reina*, which, as he claimed, was the 1st vessel to fly independent colors in all the republic. For this and other services Don José was made by Iturbide capt. of militia, and in '22 was retired with that rank, the fuero militar, and right to wear the uniform. A few years later, being a widower, and suffering from gout, he came with his son to S. Diego, where he built a house and spent the rest of his life, taking the oath of allegiance required by the law of '27. iii. 51, 176.

In '27 he wrote a long *Carta Histórica y Descriptiva de Cal* to Eustace Barron. iv. 151. Erroneously attributed to his son in the 1st ed. of vol. i., list of auth. He died at the Sta Ana rancho in '41.

Bandini (Juan), 1824, son of José, b. at Lima in 1800, and educ. there. The exact date of arrival is not known; but in Dec. '28 his father stated that he had 4 child. by his Cal. wife. It is possible that he came with his father in '19 or '21. His public life began in '27–8 as member of the diputacion; '28–32 subcomisario of revenues at S. D.; suplente congressman '31–2. Mention in this part of his career. ii. 543, 546–7, 549, 563–4; iii. 36–42, 50, 61–5, 86, 126, 136, 217, 367, 375–6. In '31 he took a leading part in fomenting the revolution against Gov. Victoria, and in opposing Zamorano's counter-revolt of '32. iii. 188–9, 197, 200–1, 203–4, 206, 210, 225. In '33 he went to Mexico as member of congress, but came back in '34 as vice-president of Híjar and Padrés' grand colonization and commercial co., supercargo of the co.'s vessel, the *Natalia*, and inspector of customs for Cal. The disastrous failure of the colony scheme, and the refusal of Cal. to recognize his authority as inspector, were regarded by Don Juan as the most serious misfortunes of his whole life and of his adopted country's history, his failure being rendered the more humiliating by the detection of certain smuggling operations in which he had engaged. iii. 242, 246, 260–7, 297, 365, 370–3, 383, 613, 670. In '36–8 Bandini was in several respects the leading spirit of the southern opposition to Alvarado's gov't; at each triumph of the arribeños he was lucky enough to escape arrest, and lost no time in fomenting new revolts. His position was a most unwise one, productive of great harm to Cal.; his motive was chiefly personal feeling against Angel Ramirez, whom he regarded as influential in the new administration, for he had been a personal friend of the northern leaders and a supporter of their general views; and his record as a politician throughout the sectional troubles was neither dignified, patriotic, nor in any way creditable. Under Carrillo he was nominally still in charge of the S.D. custom-house. iii. 415, 419–20, 423–4, 480, 482–3, 488–90, 515–21, 539, 548, 556, 558, 564–6, 578, 609, 614; iv. 98. He was the owner of the Tecate rancho on the frontier, which was sacked by the Ind. in '37–8, B. and his family being reduced to poverty and serious want; but Gov. Alvarado made him admin. of S. Gabriel mission '38–40, granting him also in '38 Jurupa, in '39 Rincon and Cajon de Muscupiabe, and land at S. Juan Cap. '41. iii. 612, 633, 644–5; iv. 68, 92, 297, 626. He was appointed fiscal of the tribunal superior '40–2, was comisionado at the new pueblo of S. Juan de Argüello in '41, and síndico at L. Ang. '44, taking but slight part in the troubles with Gov. Micheltorena. iii. 605; iv. 196, 296, 365, 411, 624, 626–7, 633. In '45–6 Don Juan was Gov. Pico's sec., and a zealous supporter of his admin., particularly in mission affairs and opposition to Castro, being also a member of the assembly and originator of the projected consejo general. iv. 511, 519, 530–2, 540, 549; v. 35, 37, 39–40, 44–5, 48, 51, 66, 264, 278, 559. Later, however, he espoused the U.S. cause, furnished supplies for Stockton's battalion, was offered the collectorship, and named as member of the legislative council in '47, and alcalde of S.Diego in '48. v. 282, 328–30, 356, 433, 618–19. In '49 he declined a judgeship; is said to have impaired his fortune by erecting a costly building in '50 at S.D., where he kept a store; and subsequently appears to have gone across the frontier, where the estate of Guadalupe had been granted him in '46, resuming his Mex. citizenship and serving as juez in '52. He still dabbled to some extent in revolutionary politics, and as a supporter of Melendres had to quit the country with all his livestock in '55. He died at Los Angeles in '59. It is evident from the preceding résumé of what is for the most part more fully told elsewhere that Juan Bandini must be regarded as one of the most prominent men of his time in Cal. He was a man of fair abilities and education, of generous impulses, of jovial temperament, a most interesting man socially, famous for his gentlemanly manners, of good courage in the midst of personal misfortunes, and always well liked and respected; indeed, his record as a citizen was an excellent one. He also performed honestly and efficiently the duties of his various official positions. In his grander attempts as a would-be statesman, Don Juan was less fortunate. His ideas were good enough, never absurd if never brilliant; but when once an idea became fixed in his brain, he never could understand the failure of Californian affairs to revolve around that idea as a centre; and in his struggles against fate and the stupidity of his compatriots he became absurdly diplomatic and tricky as a politician. He was an eloquent speaker and fluent writer, though always disposed to use a good many long words when a few short ones would better serve the purpose. I have hundreds of his original communications, official and private, in various private archives, besides the valuable collection of *Doc. Hist. Cal.* left by Bandini and given me by his widow. By the kindness of the same lady I also obtained an original MS. *Historia de California* left by Don Juan at his death, which though brief is important, especially when supplemented and explained by the author's private correspondence. Bandini's 1st wife was Dolores, daughter of Capt. José M. Estudillo, whose children were Arcadia—Mrs Abel Stearns and later Mrs Robt S. Baker; Isidora, who married Col Cave J. Coutts; Josefa, the wife of Pedro C. Carrillo; José María, whose wife was Teresa Argüello; and Juanito. His 2d wife was Refugio, daughter of Santiago Argüello, whose children were Juan de la Cruz, Alfredo, Arturo, and two daughters, who married Chas R. Johnson and Dr James B. Winston. Bandini's daughters were famous for their beauty; all or most of his children still live in southern Cal. in '85, some wealthy, all in comfortable circumstances and of respectable family connections.

Bane (C.), 1835, mr of the *Primavera.* iii. 383.   Banks (Archibald), 1833, Scotch carpenter at Mont. '33-6; d. at S. F. '38. 409.   B. (J. H.), 1848, passp. fr. Honolulu.   Bannard (Geo.), 1847, Co. K, N. Y. Vol. (v. 499). Bantam (Geo.), 1846, Amer. sailor on the *Cyane;* in Stockton's bat., wounded at the S. Gabriel Jan. '47. v. 395.   Baptiste (Jean), 1846, French fr. N. Mex., survivor of the Donner party perhaps. v. 531-41; at N. Helv. '47-8, and one of the earliest miners. There are several of this name not to be identified. See also ' Bautista.'   Barajas, sirviente at Sta Cruz, 1795. i. 496.

Barber (A. H.), 1848, of N. Y.; vet. of the Mex. war; settled at Sutterville; lived at Chico from '51 to his death in '66, age 51.   B. and sons at Mont. '47-8. *Consul. Arch.*; perhaps the following.   B. (John and John, Jr), 1847, at Mont. and in the redwoods '47-8.   B. (John), 1848, nat. of Conn., farmer in Napa Val. to '53. *Napa Co. Reporter.*   B. (Matthew), 1847, farmer near Martinez in '60, when he testified in S. F. that he was public admin. in '47-9.   Barbosa (José), settler at Brancif. 1797. i. 569.   B. (Mariano), 1818, sailor who taught Cal. boys to make hats. Barbot (M.), 1848, at S. José '81.

Barbour (John), 1847, lot-owner at S. F. Perhaps ' Barber,' q.v.   B. (Nathan), 1846, nat. of N.Y., migrating to Ky, La, Mo., and finally overland to Cal. (v. 526), with his wife Nancy, daughter of Landy Alford. He served in Co. B, Cal. Bat. (v. 358); had a ' Cal. claim ' of $250; and in '47 settled at Benicia, where he built several houses, being in the lumber business with Alford. v. 467, 672. His daughter Amelia was the 1st child born at Benicia, and he had 6 others. In '50 the family moved to a farm in Suisun Valley, where the wife died in '68 and the husband in '82, age 69.   B. (Roswell), 1846, brother of Nathan, whom he seems to have accompanied in all his Cal. experiences until his death in '71.

Barcelo (Juain), 1826, mr of the *Mero*, doubtful record. iii. 148.   Bárcena (José), 1798. i. 606.   Barcenar (Guadalupe), drummer at S. F. '23-31.

Barcenilla (Isidoro), 1797, Span. friar; founder of the S. José mission, who left Cal. in 1804. See biog. ii. 114; mention i. 555-6, 577; ii. 131, 137, 159-60.   Bargeman (Augustus), 1847, Co. D, N.Y.Vol. (v. 499).

Barger (Wm W.), 1847, Co. D, Morm. Bat. (v. 469). At Sutter's mill when gold was discovered; said to have been the first man to whom the discoverer showed the metal. Went to Utah later. Often called James B.

Baric (Charles), 1834, French from Mex. in the H. & P. colony. iii. 263, 412. For 10 years or more a trader at Los Ang., being 27 years old at arrival, and marrying in Cal. In '37 aided Bandini to capture the town. iii. 518; in '40 had charge of Aguirre's business; interested in the S. Francisquito mines '42; iv. 297, 631; in '44 owner or mr of the *Primavera.* iv. 468.

Barker, 1838, mr of the *Rasselas*. iv. 105.   Barker (perhaps Vaca), 1846-7, mr of the *Jóven Guipuzcoana*. v. 578.   Barker, 1848, on the *Sagadahoc* fr. Honolulu.   B. (John S.), 1847, mr of the *Edward*. v. 577.   B. (Peter), 1834, Engl. carpenter working for Kinlock at Mont.   B. (Robert S.), 1852, Amer. who joined the comp. extranjera at Mont., iii. 221, 408, and whose name appears on Larkin's books to '36, getting a lot in '35.

Barmore, 1848, mr of the *Sagadahoc*. v. 580.   Barnard, 1846, mr of the *Abigail*. v. 576.   B. ('Major'), 1846, doubtful mention. v. 111.   Barnes (John), 1847, Co. F, 3d U.S. artill. (v. 518), who deserted; also named as a laborer at Mont., and ment. by Sherman. *Mem.* i. 31.   Barnes, 1822, mr of *Orion*, ii. 474.

Barnett (Elias), 1841, Amer. immig. of the Bartleson party. iv. 270, 275, 279. Lived with Yount till '43, then settled in Pope Valley, marrying the widow of Wm Pope. *Napa Co. Hist.*, 55-6. Had a house in the Sac. Valley '46, acc. to Bryant and Lancey; also seems to have signed a doc. at L. Ang. in June '46. *Dept. St. Pap.*, vii. 65. Served in Co. E, Cal. Bat. (v. 358); and had a 'Cal. claim' (v. 462) of $135. Returning to his Napa rancho, he spent the rest of his life there, dying shortly before '50.   B. (E. P.), 1848, from Or. in May on the *Mary Ann*, and after good luck in the mines went back for his family.   Barney (Walter), 1847, Co. C, Morm. Bat. (v. 469).

Barnum, 1843, in the Hastings party from Or. iv. 390. Prob. went back soon.   B. (Edgar M.), 1847, Co. I, N.Y.Vol. (v. 499); died at Mont. '47. B. (Geo.), 1845, mr of a vessel at Mont. and S. F.

Barona (José), 1798, Span. friar at S. Diego and S. Juan Cap., where he died in 1831. See biog. iii. 625; mention i. 577, 654-5; ii. 107, 110, 159, 345, 348, 394, 553, 555, 655; iii. 96, 310, 351.   Barque (Oscar de Grande), 1845-53, doubtful record. iv. 587.

Barragan (Bárbaro), Mex. soldier age 28, murdered at Mont. '36. iii. 675. B. (Manuel), settler at the Colorado pueblo, killed by Ind. 1780-1. i. 359-62. Barrena (José), juez de campo S. Dieguito '41. iv. 628.   B. (Tadeo), ditto. Barreneche (Juan Ant.), 1779-80, Franciscan missionary at the Querétaro college, killed at the Colorado River missions. i. 357-63.   Barreras (José M.), killed at Los Ang. '45. iv. 492.   B. (Juan), resid. of Los Ang. '46.

Barrett, 1845, immig. fr. Or. in McMahon-Clyman party, who prob. went back in '46. iv. 572, 587, 526. Perhaps James B.   B. (Francis H.), 1847, Co. C, N.Y.Vol., at S. F. '48.   B. (James), 1846, claimant for supplies to Frémont, and owner of S. F. lot '47. v. 676.   B. (Wm J.), 1847, accidentally killed at Sac. '80; said to have come with Stevenson's reg. *Sac. Bee.*   Barreto (Fabian), 1827, grantee of Pescadero '36; a Mex. resid. of Mont., age 26, wife Cármen García, child. Manuel Fructuoso and María Juliana.   The widow had a 'Cal. claim' of $2,582 in '46-7. v. 462.

Barron (A.), 1845, contractor at Mont.; in '58 pass. fr. Honolulu.   B. (Charles), 1846, Co. H, Cal. Bat. (v. 358).   Barroso (Leonardo Diez), 1830, Mex. lieut sent to Cal. and promoted to capt. iii. 54; employed in an investigation at Los Ang. '31. iii. 196; in com. at Paso de Bartolo and Los Ang. '32. iii. 227; departed for Mex. '33. iii. 365.

Barrowman (John), 1847, Co. B, Morm. Bat. (v. 469); tried by court-martial for sleeping on guard at S. Diego; a Utah farmer in '81.   Barrus (Ruel), 1847, lieut Co. B, Morm. Bat., also of the reënlisted co.; in com. at S. Luis Rey; sentenced by court-martial to 5 years (red. by gov. to 1 year) of hard labor for passing counterfeit coin. v. 477, 495, 610, 625. A Utah farmer in '81.

Barry (Benj.), 1847, Co. E, N.Y. Vol. (v. 499).   B. (F. E.), 1841, acting mr of the U. S. *St Louis*.   B. (Richard), 1828-9, mr of the *Vulture*. iii. 141-2, 149.   B. (W. D.), 1845 (?), immig. from Mo. at Sutter's fort. iv. 578, 587; at Sta Clara '50-76.

Bartel (Wm), 1845, Amer. immig. fr. Or. in McMahon-Clyman party. iv. 572, 587; served '46-7 in the Cal. Bat.; still in Cal. '49.   Bartels (Lewis), 1847, Co. D, N.Y.Vol. (v. 499).   Batthelow (J. M.), 1848, doubtful record. Barthote, 1846, at L. Ang., doubtful record.   Barthrop (Edward), 1847, Co. A, N.Y.Vol.; resid. of S. F. '74-85; asst sup. of the Industrial school; nat. of London; miner in Tuolumne to '61; soldier in 2d Cal. cavalry during the war of '61-5; 4 children in '85.

Bartleson (John), 1841, capt. of the 1st regular immig. party that crossed the Sierra to Cal. He returned to Mo., where he died. iv. 267–76, 342, 684. Bartlett (A.), 1848, arr. at Honolulu on the *Julian* fr. S. F.   B. (Chas H.), 1847, Co. E, N.Y.Vol.(v. 499), died at S. F. '81; a Boston man.   B. (J.), 1848, passp. fr. Honolulu.   B. (John A.), 1847, Co. E, N.Y.Vol.; nat. of Mass., b. in '28; at Sonoma and S.F. after his disch.; went to Nic. with Walker; in Boston '58–61; a vol. in the war of '61–5; at Cambridgeport, Mass., in '85.

Bartlett (Washington Allen), 1845, lieut on the U. S. *Portsmouth* '45–8; alcalde of S. F. in '46–7; captured by the Californians while out on a raid for cattle. He performed the routine duties of his position in a satisfactory manner, having the advantage of a knowledge of Spanish. See mention iv. 587; v. 126, 128–9, 137, 295, 379–80, 383, 539, 644–5, 648, 654, 659, 686. Later he commanded a vessel in coast survey service in the Pacific; was sent to Europe on a mission connected with lighthouses; and while serving on the African coast in '55 had his name stricken from the rolls of the navy by the retiring board. In *Carroll's Star of the West*, 278–344, is an elaborate defence and eulogy with favorable testimony from many naval officers, also a portrait. His daughter was the heroine of the famous 'diamond wedding' of the Cuban Oviedo. Bartlett died I think between '70 and '80.

Barton (James R. or H.), 1845, at L. Ang., serving in the Micheltorena campaign. iv. 495. Lieut in the Cal. Bat. '46–7, serving under Stockton. v. 265, 360, 435. Later a resid. of L. Ang.; killed in '57 by the ' Manilas ' while acting as sheriff in their pursuit.   B. (Wm), 1839, Amer. sailor on the *California;* one of the exiles of '40 to S. Blas, but returned with a claim for damages; at Sta Cruz '43. iv. 18, 21, 33, 119, 356.   Bartow, 1842, chaplain with Com. Jones. iv. 310.   Bartram (Wm), 1843, Scotchman who worked at the N. Almaden mine in '46; a witness in later litigation; testifying that he was at S. F. in '43, and at Sonoma in '36–7. I met him near S. Luis Ob. in '74. iv. 399.   Bartusee (Zama), 1847, Co. F, 3d artill. (v. 518).

Basadre y Vega (Vicente), 1786, Span. commissioner for estab. a fur-trade between Cal. and China. i. 438–42.   Basilio, 1824, mr of the *Rurik*. ii. 519. Basilio, 1847, in Sutter's employ.   Bassett (Nathaniel S.), 1831, mr of the *Marcus*. iii. 383.

Bassham (Wm R.), 1845, Kentuckian immig. of the Grigsby-Ide party, age 23. iv. 578, 587. He was a clerk at L. Ang. for Dalton in '46; and for Leidesdorff and later Howard & Mellus at S. F. in '47–9, being also the owner of several town lots; a member of the Cal. senate in '49–50; later a resid. of S. José and in business with Belden. In '55–6 he was a witness in the Santillan case, but I find no later record of him.   Bastian (James), 1848, Englishman fr. Honolulu who died at S. F. in Oct.   Basualdo (Francisco), 1828, Mex. artilleryman, later sergt at Sta B. and S. Diego; killed by the Ind. at Pauma '46. iii. 78, 615, 617.   Batan (Désiré), 1845, mr of the *Espadon*. iv. 565. Batchelor (Geo.), 1847, drum-major N.Y.Vol. v. 503; died before '82. Bateman (E. B.), 1847, Amer. immig. fr. Mo.; member of the 1st legislature '49–50; a physician at Stockton '75, and perhaps later.   B. (Lorenzo), 1846, Fauntleroy's dragoons at Mont. (v. 232–47).   Baten (Wm), doubtful name in a Brancif. list of '45; Amer., age 37.   Bates, 1840, purser of the *St Louis*.   Bates (Dr), 1846, had an acct with Larkin; in '47–8 often ment. at N. Helv., sometimes as a physician, oftener on the sick-list, and finally prospecting for gold and quicksilver. Possibly same as E. B. ' Bateman,' q.v. B. (Asher B), 1848, New Yorker who came round the Horn; d. at S. F. '73, age 63.   B. (Frank), 1848; alcalde at Sac.; vice-pres. of a public meeting in Jan. '49; ment. by Colton as owner of Vernon. Perhaps same as the ' doctor.' B. (Manuel), 1826; mr of the *Sta Apolonia*. iii. 148.   Bathgate (Geo.), 1848, Co. F, N.Y.Vol. (v. 499); d. before '82.

Baugh (Theodore E.), 1845, of firm Sweeny & B., who built an observatory on Telegraph Hill in '45 (?), and in '52 opened the 1st telegraph. A Pennsylvanian, who died at S.F. in '81, age 58. *S. José Pion.;* iv. 587.   Baum (John), 1848, overl. immig. fr. Ohio to Or. '47; and to the Cal. mines '48; returning to Or. in '50.   Bausford (John), 1829, Irish sawyer at S. F. '40, age 36; came by sea in '29; alias 'Solis.' *Dwinelle.* Bautista (Juan), 1846, Mexican survivor of the Donner party, said to be still living in '80. v. 531, 535, 541. Perhaps he was of French blood, and named ' Baptiste,' q.v. Bauzá (Felipe), 1791, scientist of Malaspina's exped. i. 490.

Bawden (J.), 1848, commission merchant at S. F.; advert. in *Star.* Baxter (J. G.), 1845 (?), Mass. farmer in Sta Clara '74–6. iv. 587. Baxter (Wm Owen), 1847, Co. E, N.Y.Vol.(v. 499); of Engl. birth; 30 years in the mines; living at Sta Mónica '85, age 58, with wife and 4 children. Bay, 1848, named in the *Californian* as a member of the Sonoma council. Bayley, 1848, (?), at Coloma. *El Dorado Co. Hist.,* 177. Bazard, 1847–8, at Sta Clara.

Beale (Edward F.), 1846, passed mid. and acting master of the U.S. *Congress,* serving in Stockton's battalion. With Gillespie's party sent in Dec. to meet Kearny, and sent back to S. D. with despatches after the fight of S. Pascual. v. 340, 350, 402. In Feb. '47 he was sent east with despatches. v. 430, 436; and at the end of the year was a witness in the Frémont court-martial. v. 456. Returned to Cal. in time to start east again in July '48 with despatches respecting the gold discovery. Soon left the navy, and in '52–4 was supt of Ind. affairs in Cal., and subsequently surveyor-general of the state. Becoming the owner of large Californian estates, in later years Gen. Beale became a resident of Washington, where he still lives in '85. He was at one time U.S. minister to Austria. B. (Thos W.), 1846, Co. C, 1st U.S. dragoons. (v. 534.) B. (Wm), 1845, overl. immig. of the Swasey-Todd party. iv. 576. At N. Helv.'46.

Bean (Archi), 1816, sail-maker on the *Lydia* at Sta B. ii. 275. B. (Robert or Wm), trapper with Dye and Nidever in '30; not clear that he came to Cal. Beard (E. L.), 1846–7 (?), settler in S. José valley. Beardsley (Amos F.), 1848, New Yorker who came by sea; died at S.F. '69, age 49. B. (F.), 1848, came from Honolulu on the *SS* in Jan., and ret. on the *Julian* in Nov.; possibly same as preceding.

Beasley (Jesse), 1843, perhaps an immig. of the Chiles-Walker party. iv. 393; member of the Sonoma town council '47. v. 668. In comp. with Cooper '48; had a Sonoma rancho '49; living '71 at Stony Creek, Colusa Co. Beattie (Belden), 1847, Co. H, N.Y. Vol. (v. 499); d. at S.F. '49. Beaulieu (Olivier), 1844, Canad. of Frémont's 1st exped., left in Cal. iv. 437, 439, 453. He lived at Sonoma '45–7, being occasionally ment. at N. Helv.; apparently claimant in '53 for the Cabeza de Sta Rosa rancho; still living near S. José in '81 acc. to *S. J. Pion.,* March 19, '81. Becerra, soldier at Mont. '28. ii. 615. B. (Pilar), 1824, Mex. convict liberated in '35.

Becher (Fred. G.), 1835, German assoc. in business with Virmond of Mex., supercargo of the *Catalina* and *Leonor,* who spent most of his time in Cal. fr. '35 to '37. A young man of many accomplishments, linguistic, commercial, diplomatic, and equestrian. Very popular, but in trouble with Alvarado's govt on account of his Mex. interests and sympathies. His name appears in mission accounts of '39–40. Vischer tells us that B. became head of a firm at Mazatlan, and died there at the age of 37. Ment. in iii. 288, 381, 383, 413, 429, 459, 512; iv. 102. Becker (John), 1847, Co. A, N.Y. Vol. (v. 499); at N. Helv. fr. S. Joaquin '48. Beckstead (Gordon S.), 1847, Co. A, Morm. Bat. (v. 469); reënlisted; living in Utah '81. B. (Orin M.), 1847, Co. A, Morm. Bat.; reënlisted. Beckwith (Seth Lee), 1848, nat. of Conn., who came from Honolulu on the *Kamehameha* and went to the Amador and Calaveras mines; from '50, as before '48, a traveller in many parts of the world, but regarding S.F. as his home, where he still lives in '85, at the age of 64, with a son and daughter.

Beckwourth (James P.), 1844, mulatto of Va, who became in the great west a famous hunter, guide, Indian-fighter, chief of the Crows, and horse-thief. No résumé can do justice to his adventures, nor can the slightest faith be put in his statements. See *Bonner's Life of Beckwourth.* He came to Cal. from N. Mex. '44. iv. 453, 495; and was one of the mountaineers serving against Micheltorena, at the ' battle of Cahuenga' in '45 (v. 494, 503), of which he gives an absurdly false account. Before the troubles of '46 he left Cal. with a large drove of stolen horses to continue his career in N. Mex.

and on the plains. Returning after '48 to take part in no end of stirring events in the flush times, he discovered the pass that bears his name, opening in '52 a hotel and trading-post in Beckwourth Valley. Therein he dictated to Bonner the events of his life as published in '58. But Jim was accused of divers unlawful acts, and besides was unable to content himself long in one place; so he returned to his old life of trapper and trader on the plains, and died in the North Platte country in '67, age about 70.   Bedibey (Frank), 1841, of the Workman-Rowland party from N. Mex.; did not remain in Cal. iv. 278.

Bedwell (Franklin), 1840 (?), Tennesseean who went to Mo. with his parents in '19; for many years a trapper in the Rocky Mts and great basin, from the Yellowstone to Sta Fé, with the usual adventures of his class. iv. 117, 120. Acc. to the *Sonoma Co. History*, with portraits, he came to Cal. in '40-1; continued his trapper life for several years, occasionally visiting the settlements, and working a while in the Sta Clara redwoods; but about '43 settled on a Russ. River rancho bought of Cyrus Alexander (?); joined the Bears in '46, being apparently with Ford at Olompali; went south with Frémont, being with Gillespie's garrison at L. Ang., and later one of Stockton's army; returned to his rancho after the peace; went to the mines in '48-9; and finally settled permanently in his Russ. River home. All this may be accurate, though it seems strange that of so early a man, taking part in so many events, I find no original or contemporary mention before '48. In '48 or '49 he seems to have met in Cal. his mother and brother, from whom he had been separated many years. In '58 he married Selina McMinn of Tenn., but had no children. Bedwell was still living in '83, and probably in '85, hale and hearty, though over 70 years of age.

Bee (Henry Jubilee), 1830, Engl. sailor and blacksmith who left the *Dryad* at Mont. iii. 180; joined the comp. extranjera in '31. iii. 221; and perhaps went to S. José as early as '33, though his home for some years seems to have been near Mont., and his occupation that of guiding strangers about the country; baptized as Enrique Ascension, and married in '38 to Clara Moreno. His name appears on Larkin's books and various other records nearly every year. In '36-7 Bee was one of Graham's 'riflemen.' iii. 461, 525; and in Alvarado's service performed more than one feat of valor, if we credit his own version. In '40 he was arrested but not exiled. iv. 9, 17, 23; moving soon to Sta Cruz; and living in '43 at Yerba Buena, where he got a lot, iv. 669, and another later. In '46 he carried despatches from Sloat to Frémont, v. 247, as appears from his receipt of July 12th, for $160, including the value of two horses killed in the service, in *Mont. Consul. Arch.*, though there has been some newspaper controversy on the subject. He subsequently served under Watmough at S. José; was constable at the pueblo in '47; went to the mines in '48; served as clerk in a store till '50; raised potatoes for a few years; and worked as carpenter till '60. He lost his wife in '53, his son in '60, and at the same time a leg in an encounter with the desperado Felipe Hernandez. In '77 he dictated his *Recollections* for my use; and has furnished many reminiscences for the *Pioneer* and other papers. Harry is inclined to draw somewhat heavily on his imagination for historical details; but there is generally a substratum of fact underlying his yarns. Living in '83, and I think in '85.

Beebe (J. W.), 1847, named as the 1st Amer. magistrate at S. Buenaventura. *Signal*. Perhaps same as the following.   B. (Wm L.), 1847, nat. of N. Y.; one of the 1st supervisors at S. Luis Ob.; later county judge; still living in '83. *S. Luis Ob. Co. Hist.*   Beechay, 1840, doubtful name in Farnham's list of arrested foreigners.   Beechey (Fred. Wm), 1826, com. of the Brit. exploring vessel *Blossom*, and author of a *Narrative* of the exploration. iii. 120 -5, 110, 146; i. 432; ii. 588, 590, 592, 599-600, 603, 610, 614-16.   B. (Richard B.), 1826, mid. on the *Blossom*. iii. 121.   Beener (John S.), 1847, advertises loss of a pocket-book between S. Joaq. and S.F. in *Star*; still at S.F. in '54.   Beere (Wm), 1848, cabinet-maker at S.F. v. 682.   Beers (Wm), 1847, Co. E, Morm. Bat. (v. 469).   Beeson (Henry), 1846, claimant for supplies to Frémont (v. 462). Perhaps this was ' Bee,' q.v.

Beggs (Peter), 1847, negro servant of Capt. A. J. Smith, accused of robbery at Los Ang.   Behn (John), 1841 (?), native of Baden, accredited by Wilson to the Workman party fr. N. Mex.; but not in Rowland's list, and not remembered by Given. iv. 278-9. Appears in the records fr. '44 as otter-hunter and trader at Los Ang. He quit business in '53, and died '68, leaving several children.   Béjar, see 'Véjar.'

Belcher, 1848, mr of the *Mary* at S.F. fr. Columbia Riv.   B. (Edward), 1826, lieut on the *Blossom* in Beechey's exped. iii. 121; in '37-9, com. of the *Sulphur*, and author of a *Narrative* of the expedition. iii. 614, 670, 699; iv. 93, 106, 142-6.   B. (Lewis F.), 1847, at Mont. in company with Aram; in the gold mines '48; about '50 a large dealer in cattle. An eccentric character, native of N.Y., who acquired a large property. Murdered at Mont. in '56.

Belden (Josiah), 1841, nat. of Conn., b. in '15, who after a varied commercial experience in N.Y., La, and Miss., came to Cal. in the 1st immig. party under Capt. Bartleson. iv. 267, 270, 275, 279. Going to Mont., he took charge for Larkin of a branch store and lumber business at Sta Cruz in '42-4, taking part in the raising of the U.S. flag at the time of the Com. Jones affair. iv. 312, 340, 651, 662-4. I have many of his original letters of these and later years. In '44 he obtained naturalization papers, and a grant of the Barranca Colorada rancho in the Sac. Valley. iv. 670. The firm of B. & Chard appears at Mont. in '44-5; B. took some part in preserving order during Gov. Micheltorena's absence; and in Dec. '45 went up to his rancho, returning in March '46. *N. Helv. Diary*, 22, 37. For some months in '46 B. took charge of a store for Capt. Paty at S.F., v. 682, and later in '46-7 worked as clerk and collector for Wm H. Davis, obtaining lots at S.F. and Benicia. v. 672, 676; also interested in a quicksilver mine. *Larkin's Doc.*, v. 361. In '48 he opened at S. José a branch store of Mellus & Howard, but soon followed his customers to the mines for a few weeks, leaving the store in charge of Branham. In '49 he closed up the business, and married Miss Sarah M. Jones, a pioneer of '46. In '50 he was the 1st mayor of S. José, being later member of the council, and in '76 a delegate to the republican national convention. Fortunate purchases and judicious management of S.F. real estate made Belden a capitalist. He continued to reside at S. José with his wife, two sons, and three daughters until about '81, when he changed his residence to New York, where he still lives in '85. A good sketch of his life, with portrait, is found in the *Contemp. Biog.*, i. 246; and in '78 he dictated for my use his *Historical Statement*, a MS. of 70 pp., just such a narrative as might be expected from a clear-headed man of business.

Bell (Alex.), 1842, nat. of Pa, who since '23 had lived in Mex. provinces, becoming a citizen. He came from Sonora on the *Esmeralda*, iv. 341, settling at Los Ang., where he married Nieves Guirado in '44, and engaged in trade for many years. He was prominent in '45 among the foreigners who opposed Micheltorena and Sutter. iv. 495; in '46-7, being síndico at L. Ang., v. 625, served as capt. in the Cal. Bat., v. 360, apparently quitting the town with Gillespie and returning with Stockton; and he had 'Cal. claims' of about $3,500 (v. 462). In '49 Bell built a warehouse at S. Pedro; and in later years was prominent among the vigilantes. He seems to have retired from trade about '54, but continued to reside at Los Ang. till his death in '71, age 70.   B. (Geo. W.), 1845, doubtful name of an overl. immig.; perhaps went to Or. iv. 578.   B. (John H.), 1831, mr of the *Whalehound*, said to have discov. oysters in S.F. bay. iii. 699.   B. (Richard H.), 1847, Co. F, 3d U.S. artill. v. 519.   B. (Wm), 1843, named at Los Ang., perhaps by error.

Bellomy (Geo.W.), 1843,Virginian fr. Or. in the Hastings party, wounded by Ind. on the way. iv. 390-1, 399. In '44 he got a carta de seguridad, and next year had a shop at S. José, where he complained of being robbed, and signed the call to foreigners in March. iv. 599. He does not seem to have served in the Cal. Bat. '46, but had a claim of $42, which was paid; in '47 was imprisoned for disobedience to decrees of Judge Burton's court; in '48 owner of the Sta Clara House, still in legal troubles. His wife from '45 was María de Jesus Bernal, later wife of J. T. Perez. Bellomy—or Bellamy— died in '62.   Bellow (J. Mitch.), 1846, said to have come in the navy; nat. of La, who was long a policeman at S. José, and died in '79. *S. J. Pion.*

Belt (Geo. Gordon), 1847, Q. M. sergt N.Y.Vol. v. 503; alcalde at Stockton '49; became a rich trader, and was murdered at Stockton by Wm Dennis in '69.   Beltran (Nicolás), corporal 1776–81, killed on the Colorado. i. 304, 3G3.   Belty (Wm), 1841, German immig. from Mo. in the Bartleson party. iv. 270, 275, 279. Some say he went back and died in the east; but a man of the same name served in Co. A, Cal. Bat. (v. 358); is named on Larkin's books at Mont. in '47–8; and acc. to Dally, who helped to bury him, was killed by a fall from his horse in the mines in '48.

Ben, 1846, negro servant with Gillespie. v. 24.   Benavides (Elias), 1847, at N. Helv.   B. (José), soldier at S. F. '44; grantee of a lot '46. v. 6G0. B. (José M.), settler at S. F. 1791–1800, prob. father of the preceding. i. 716. B. (María), 1847, had bonnets for sale at S. F. *Star.*   B. (Miguel), soldier at S. F. '27–31; in '41 living at S. José, age 29; wife Josefa García; child., Patricio, José Ant., Concepcion, Antonia, Nanita, Trinidad.   Benedict (C. L.), 1847, owner of a house at Benicia. v. 672.   Bengachea (José Ign.), settler at the Colorado Riv. pueblos 1780–1. i. 359, 362.   Benitez (José M.), 1803–7, surgeon of the forces at Mont. ii. 140.   Benito, neoph. rebel at Sta B. '24–6. ii. 532, 537.

Benitz (Wm), 1841–2, German in Sutter's employ. Arrived Oct. '42 acc. to rolls of the Soc. Cal. Pion.; but in applying for naturalization in '44 he claimed to have come in '41. iv. 341. After being for a time in charge of Hock farm, in '43 he took charge of the Ross estate for Sutter, succeeding Bidwell. iv. 186, 679. In '44 grantee of the Briesgau rancho in Shasta co. iv. 670; in '45 he rented the Ross rancho from Sutter, and later bought a part of it; bondsman for some of the Grigsby-Ide immig. iv. 679, 544, 581. Benitz is said to have been the man who was swindled to the extent of $6,000 by the Sutter-Muldrow claim. He lived at Ross till '67; then moved to Oakland; and in '74 went to the Argentine Republic, where he had a brother. He died there in '76, at the age of 62, leaving a family.   Benjamin (Fordyce J.), 1846, Co. H, N.Y.Vol. (v. 499); alcalde at N. Helv. '48; at Sonoma '74.

Bennett (A. B.), 1846, Co. F, Cal. Bat., enlisting at S. Juan Oct. (v. 358). B. (Charles), 1847, at Sutter's Fort fr. Or.; at the Coloma mill in '48 when gold was found; said to have been killed by Ind. in Or. about '55.   B. (Dennis), 1843, prob. son of Vardamon, fr. Or. in the Hastings party. iv. 390, 399. Named in a S. F. padron of '44 as an Amer. carpenter, age 19. B. (Jackson), 1843, brother of Dennis, age 17 in '44, said to have been slightly wounded at the 'battle' of Sta Clara in '47. iv. 390, 400; v. 381.   B. (Narciso), grantee of land at Sta Clara in '45; perhaps another son of Vardamon, who came in '43. iv. 587, 673.   B. (Thomas), 1816, sailor on the *Lydia.* ii. 275.   B. (Titus), 1847, Co. G, N.Y.Vol. (v. 499).

Bennett (Vardamon), 1843, nat. of Ga, who went to Ark. '30, crossed the plains to Or. '42, and came to Cal. in the Hastings party with a large family. iv. 390, 399. After a brief stay in the Sac. Valley B. went to S. F., where he appears in the padron of '44 as an Amer. carpenter, age 40; where he appears in other records of '45–7, including a petition for naturalization in '46; and where he kept a grog-shop, bowling alley, etc. v. 685; being also owner of a Benicia lot. v. 672. He died at S. F. in '49. His wife, Mary, was a good woman, but one of masculine attributes, who had a 'mind of her own,' and body also, in many respects head of the family. In '45 she asked for a separation, complaining to the authorities of her husband's failure to provide for herself and 8 children. In '46 she and some of the children were living at S. José, having a 'Cal. claim' (v. 462). She married Harry Love, and died near Watsonville in '68, age 66.   B. (Wm), 1845, doubtful name of an overl. immig. iv. 578.   B. (Wm), 1844, immig. fr. Or. in the Kelsey party. iv. 444, 453. Seems to have settled near S. José, where acc. to Hittell he was a wealthy man in '60; perhaps same as Wm H. on the rolls of the Soc. Cal. Pion., as having arr. March '44.

Bennett (Winston), 1843, son of Vardamon, whom he accomp. to Cal. in the Hastings party. iv. 390, 400. He is named in the S.F. padron of '44 as 25 years of age; but he did not remain long at S.F. or in any other place; roaming from the Sac. Valley to Marin Co., Yerba Buena, Sta Clara, and Sta Cruz, and taking some slight part in the troubles with Micheltorena in '45. iv. 486 -7. In '46 he enlisted in Co. G, Cal. Bat. (v. 358), took part in the fight at Natividad, and went to L. Ang. with Frémont. In '48–9 he had an adventurous career in many places as miner and trader; lived at Sta Clara and Sta Cruz in '50–3, being constable and deputy sheriff part of the time; on a rancho at Pescadero '53–65; at Sta Clara with his mother '65–72; and again on his rancho fr. '72, having married María J. Perez in '71. His *Pioneer of '43*, a narrative of his overland trip and experiences in Cal., was printed in the *S. José Pioneer* of '77, containing many interesting details. He seems to have been a very unlucky man in respect of accidents, the breaking of a leg or arm being by no means a rare occurrence; and it appears that this luck with his old propensity to roam is still retained; for as I write, in '85, the papers announce the accidental breaking of his leg at Silver City, N. Mex.

Benschoten (John W.), 1848, New Yorker who served in the Mex. war, coming to Cal. prob. with Graham's dragoons (v. 522); worked in the mines, and finally settled in S. Joaquin, where he married Jessie McKay in '66. Benson (Christian), 1847, perhaps one of the N.Y. Vol. under another name. B. (Geo.), 1847, Co. F, 3d U. S. artill. (v. 518). B. (John), 1840, Amer. sailor of the *Morse* at S.F., to be shipped on the *Don Quixote.* Bent (Silas), 1848, mr of the *Preble.* Bentley (John), 1847, Co. E, Morm. Bat. (v. 544). Benton, 1848, firm of Ross, B. & Co. at S. F.

Bercier (Francis), 1847, Engl. at N. Helv. Berdle (John), 1836, arms in his possess. seized at L. Ang. Berenback (Antoine), 1847, Co. F, 3d artill. (v. 518). Berier, 1847, at N. Helv.; prob. same as 'Bercier.' Beristain, 1847-8, mr of the *Concepcion.* v. 577. B. (Máximo), 1829, at S. Diego. iii. 141. Beritzhoff (Alex.), 1847, named in a newspaper as mate of the *Jóven Guipuzcoana.* iv. 587; went from N.Y. to Valparaiso on ship *Zenobia.* From Val. to Mont. on brig *Thos H. Benton* in '47. Owner of Stockton *Independent* '65–75. Later U.S. storekeeper int. rev. at S.F.

Bermudez (Antonio, Atansio, Dolores), at L. Ang. '46. B. (Domingo), 1832, at Sta B. B. (Francisco), 1832, soldier at Sta B., wife Concepcion Pico, 2 child. B. (José), at L. Ang. '15–28. ii. 349, 354, 560; two or three of the name at S. Bernardino and S. Gabriel '46. B. (José), at rancho nacional, Mont., '36, age 28, wife Ana M. Martinez, child. José and Martiana. Bernabé, 1824, rebel neoph. at Sta B. ii. 532, 537. Bernaci (Juan), 1791, lieut in Malaspina's exped. i. 490.

Bernal, 1826, majordomo of S. José. ii. 599. I am unable to trace definitely the dif. branches of the Bernal family in Cal., but name many individuals. See list of those in Cal. before 1800 in i. 734. B. (Agustin), soldier at S. F. '19–27; in '37 lieut of militia at S. José. iii. 732; in '41 at S. José, age 39; wife María Juana Higuera; child. José b. '25, Guadalupe '29, Presentacion '32, Abelino '34, Nicolás '37, Juana '39; in '46 juez de campo. v. 662; '53 claimant of Sta Teresa rancho. iii. 713; prob. son of Joaquin. B. (Agustin, Jr), son of the preceding, b. '48; mar. Francisca Soto in Alameda Co. '78. B. (Ana Maria), mar. 1784 to Gabriel Moraga. ii. 571. B. (Antonio), soldier at S. F. '41–3. iv. 667; still at S. José '50. B. (Apolinario), born in Cal. 1780-90; regidor at S. José 1802; killed by Ind. '13. ii. 134, 339. B. (Basilio), grantee of Sta Clara embarcadero '45–8; also claimant in '53. iv. 373; v. 665. B. (Bruno), in '41 at S. José, age 39 (prob. older); wife Antonia Ortega; children, Antonio b. in '25, Dolores '27, Francisco '31, Pedro '33, José and Gertrudis '35, Guadalupe '36, Rufina '37, Luis '39; Cal. claim of $10,000 in '46; claimant for Alisal, Mont. Co. iii. 676. B. (Jesus), juez de campo at S. José '41. iv. 684. B. (Joaquin), soldier of S. F. at Sta Cruz 1795. i. 496; invál. '19–32; grantee of Sta Teresa rancho '34, being then 94 years old. iii. 713. B. (José), soldier at S. F. '19–30. B. (José 2d), soldier at S. F. '19–24. B. (José), born at S. José in '23; married Alta Gracia Higuera in '55; 10 children; living in Alameda Co. in '80. B. (José Ant.), soldier at S. F. '29–'42. B. (José Ant.), farmer at S. José '41, age 25; wife Guadalupe Butron; children, Juan and Trinidad. B. (José Cornelio), regidor of S. José '28. ii. 605; grantee of land at Mission Dolores '34; elector and militiaman at S. F. '37. iii. 705; grantee of Rincon de Salinas, etc., and Rincon de Ballena '39. iii. 678, 712; in '42 at S. F., age 46, wife Cármen Cibrian, son José de Jesus b. '29; still living '53–4. His widow lived at the mission until after '67. i. 293.   B. (José Dionisio), soldier of the Soledad escolta 1791–1800. i. 499.   B. (José Jesus), grantee in '39 of the Cañada de Pala rancho. iii. 711; in '41 farmer at S. José, age 31; wife María Ant. Higuera; children, José Gabriel b. '34, Jesus M. '35, José Jesus '37, Dionisio '37.   B. (Juan), cattle-owners in S. F. district 1793. i. 707.   B. (Juan), soldier at S. F. '20–30; elector and militiaman at S. F. '37. iii. 705; grantee of Laguna de Palos Col. in the contra costa '35–41. iii. 712; iv. 671; in '41 at S. José, age 38; wife Encarnacion Soto (who as a widow was owner of S. F. lots fr. '44. iv. 639; v. 685); children, Guadalupe b.'31, Nicolás '35, Apolinario '37, Juan '40.   B. (Juan), farmer at S. José '41, age 31; wife Rafaela Félix; child., Francisco b. '35, Juan '38, Guadalupe '39, Refugio '40; juez de campo '44. iv. 685.   B. (Juan), son of Joaquin, at S. José in '77, age 67, who gave me his *Memoria* of several old-time occurrences; perhaps same as preceding.   B. (Juan), described by Larkin in '45 as a man of some wealth and local influence at Sta Cruz.   B. (María D. Castro de), at S. José '41, age 52; children, Juan b. '20, Gregorio and Francisco '27, Ramon '30.

Bernier (Baptiste), 1844, one of Frémont's men. iv. 437.

Berreyesa (Antonio), son of Nicolás, who in '77 at S. José gave me his *Relacion* of the murder of his uncle by Frémont's men in '46 (v. 171), and of the troubles of his father's family with the squatters and land lawyers.   B. (Félix), soldier at S. F. and musician '34–42.   B. (Francisco), soldier at S. F. '37; sergt '39; grantee in '46 of Cañada de Capay and Rincon de Musulacon. v. 669, 675; claimant for Rincon de Esteros '53. iii. 712.   B. (José Ign.), at S. José '41, age 34; children, Jesus María, José Jesus, Adelaida, María Los Angeles, and Gabriela; grantee of Chiniles rancho '46. v. 669.   B. (José Jesus), soldier at S. F. '32–3; sentenced for stealing horses at Mont. '35. iii. 674; at Sonoma, age 28, in '44; grantee of Las Putas '43, and Yacuy '46. iv. 672; v. 669.   B. (José de los Reyes), nat. of Cal., son of Nicolás, b. about 1787; sold. at S. F. '19–29, sergt from '30; also employed as a teacher at S. F. in '23. ii. 591, 584; iii. 111, 701; in '31–5 sec. of ayunt. at S. José. iii. 729–30; in '41 at S. José; wife María S. Bernal; children, Domingo b. '22, Francisco '26, Fernando '28, Encarnacion '30, Demesio '33, Madelina '34, but there were several others older; in '42 grantee of S. Vicente rancho. iv. 673. In June '46 while on his way to visit his son at Sonoma the old man was murdered at S. Rafael by Frémont's men. v. 171–4.   B. (José de los Santos), son of José Reyes; sergt S. F. comp. at Sonoma '40–2. iii. 702; iv. 678; grantee of Malacomes rancho '43. iv. 671–3; in '46 alcalde at Sonoma. v. 124, 154, 159, 668; in '55 a witness in the Santillan case.   B. (María de la Luz), mar. to Joaq. Soto 1803, the 1st marriage at S. José. ii. 138.   B. (Martin), sold. at Sonoma '42.   B. (Nasario), corporal at S. F. '19–24.   B. (Nicolás), settler at S. F. 1777–1800. i. 297, 716; wife Gertrudis Peralta, children Gabriela, María de la Luz, José de los Reyes, Nasario, Nicolás, Juan José, acc. to S. José padron of 1793.   B. (Nicolás), son of preceding; sold. at S. F. '19–30; grantee of Milpitas '34. iii. 712; regidor at S. José '36–7, iii. 730; at S. José '41. age 51, wife Gracia Padilla, children, José b. '18, Nicolás '22, Francisco '26, José '28, Antonio '31, Mariano '34, Agustin '36. The murder of his brother Reyes and the plundering of his cattle by the battalion in '46, the later lynching of his brother Demesio, the continued struggle with squatters and land lawyers, in which all his property was stripped from him, drove the old man to madness; and several of his sons also became insane. He died in '63.   B. (Rudesindo), ment. in '42. iv. 240. B. (Santiago), at S. José '41, age 37; wife María Rosario Valencia, child María Josefa.   B. (Sixto), soldier in S. F. comp. '38–42; grantee of Las Putas '43. iv. 672.

Berry, 1848, from Or., one of the 1st miners at Grass Valley. *Nev. Co. Hist.*, 52, 64.   B. (Daniel K.), 1846, overl. immig. from Mo. with his family.

v. 529; served in Co. C, Cal. Bat. (v. 358); fr. '48 one of the 1st settlers of Suisun Valley, where he still lived in '60.   B. (James Richard), 1836, Irishman who had lived long in Span. provinces, a great traveller and a man of many accomplishments; grantee of Punta de Reyes in '36. iii. 712; iv. 118; owner of lots at S.F. '41–4. iv. 669; v. 679; at Sonoma in '44, aged 52. I find no later record of him.   Bertodano (Cosme), 1794–6, Span. com. of the *Valdés, Activa, Aranzazu.* i. 523–4, 540.   Bertran (Luis), Mex. at Mont. '36, age 40, wife Tomasa Carrillo.   Bertrand (Emile), 1847, Co. C, N.Y. Vol. (v. 499).

Beston (Thos), 1847, at N. Helv., with family; apparently an immig. v. 556.   Bestor (Norman S.), 1846, assistant to Lieut Emory with Kearny's force. v. 337; at Mont. Feb. '48; had a store at Coloma '48–9. *Sherman.* Beuseman (Chris. M.), 1817, Prussian in the Russ. service, noble of the 4th class; mr of the *Chirikof*, and *Baikal*, '11–12, '25–8. ii. 298, 312, 648; iii. 146. Beverley (McKenzie), 1847, owner of S.F. lot; murderer of Dörnte; later a desperado at large. v. 586, 646, 663, 676, 684.

Bianchi (Nicholas), 1834–5, mr of the *Rosa.* iii. 384.   Bicholl (John), 1843, Amer. in charge of Sutter's cattle at Hock; naturalized '44. iv. 400; name written 'Bignol' and also 'Rignoll.'   Bickmore (Gilbert), 1847, Co. A, Morm. Bat. (v. 469).   Biddle (James), 1847–8, com. of the Pac. squadron U. S. N. on the *Columbus.* v. 437–8, 450, 577.   Bideler (Thos), 1836, Amer., doubtful name at Los. Ang.   Bidilton (John), 1828–9, Engl. catholic at Mont.

Bidwell (John), 1841, nat. of N. Y., born in 1819, who went with his parents to Penn. and Ohio; a school-teacher in Ohio and Iowa; an immig. from Mo. to Cal. in the Bartleson party. For an account of this party, including much about Bidwell personally, and about his diary sent east and published as *A Journey to California*, now of great rarity, see iv. 266–76, 279, 346–7. I have the original bond signed by Thos G. Bowen in B.'s favor on Nov. 18, '41. He entered Sutter's employ, and in '42–3 was in charge of the Ross estate at Bodega. iv. 186, 233, 665, 679; in '43–4 at Hock farm. I have much of his original corresp. of these and later years. In '44, visiting Mont. with a recommend. from Sutter to the gov., he obtained naturalization papers and a grant of the Ulpinos rancho. iv. 674.   In return Bidwell was active in support of Micheltorena, going south with Sutter's army, being taken prisoner at the 'battle' of Cahuenga, and even having something to say 40 years later in defence of that most unwise movement of the foreigners. iv. 366, 479–83, 485–6, 508.   Returning to N. Helvetia, he continued in Sutter's service as agent and clerk, being the writer of portions of the *N. Helv. Diary*, and his movements from day to day being recorded in other portions; also grantee of the Colus rancho in '45. iv. 516, 671.   His travels in the valley and foothills were extensive, and he had many narrow escapes from making the grand discovery of gold. Early in '46 he made arrangements to open a school at Mont., *Larkin's Doc.*, iv. 54; but circumstances occurred to prevent this. He did not at first take any active part in the settlers' revolt, being a Mex. citizen and apparently not warmly in sympathy with this most senseless filibusterism; but he was at one time in charge of the prisoners at the fort, and in July was sec. at the formal organization at Sonoma. v. 100, 125, 128, 179.   He went south with Frémont; was put in com. of S. Luis Rey in Aug., and made a perilous trip by sea from S. Diego to S. Pedro for supplies during the Flores revolt; ranking as capt. in the Cal. Bat., and serving as quartermaster with rank of major under Stockton in '46–7. v. 286, 317–18, 324–5, 361, 385, 420, 620–2.   Returning to the Sacramento, Bidwell continued his labors as Sutter's agent and surveyor in different parts of the valley until the discovery of gold, when he became the pioneer miner on Feather River, where Bidwell's Bar was named for him. Of his mining experience, as of his official career in later years, I shall have occasion to say something in vol. vi.–vii. of this work. Becoming owner of the Arroyo Chico ranchos granted to Dickey and Farwell, he made here his permanent home, site of the town of Chico from '60, becoming a man of great wealth, and one of the most prominent agriculturists of the state. He was chosen as a member of the constit. convention of '49, though not serving; a senator in the 1st legislature of '49–50; a delegate to the national democratic convention of '60 at Charleston; appointed brigadier-gen. of militia in '63 by Gov. Stanford; delegate to the national union convention in '64; and a member of congress '64-7, being in '75 a defeated, non-partisan, anti-monopoly candidate for gov. of Cal. But it is to the agricultural and industrial development of his county and state that he has given his chief attention, and it is his success in this direction that has evidently given him most satisfaction. His record is in all respects that of an honorable as well as successful man, one of the chief testimonials in his favor being the flimsy nature of the inevitable charges made against him as a candidate for office. His position as the leading representative of his class, that of immigrant farmers, will be questioned, as his success will be begrudged, by none. His *California in '41-8*, a MS. of 233 pages, was dictated for my use in '77, and is regarded as one of the most valuable volumes in my collection of pioneer reminiscences. He has also in later correspondence furnished many useful items for this register. In '68 he married Miss Annie Kennedy of Washington, D.C.; has no children; still residing at Chico in '85.

Biggerton (Susan), 1845, illegally married at Sac., so wrote Leidesdorff. iv. 587.   'Big Jim,' 1830, Irish trapper of Young's party, killed by Higgins. iii. 174.   Biggs (Matthew H.), 1848, mining man from Valparaiso with letters from Atherton; named also by Brooks at Mormon diggings.

Bigler (Henry W.), 1847, Virginian of Co. B, Morm. Bat. v. 478, 493, 495. His father was formerly a Methodist preacher, moving to Mo. in '38. After the mustering-out of the bat., B. entered Sutter's employ, and was one of the men working at the Coloma mill when gold was found. His *Diary of a Mormon*, copied by himself in '72, is not only an excellent narrative of the march of the battalion—one of Tyler's chief authorities—but is one of the best authorities extant on details of the gold discovery. Soon after the mining excitement began Bigler returned to Utah, where he still lived at St George in '81.   Bigley (John), 1847, owner of a S. F. lot; witness in a lawsuit of '65.

Bihler (Wm), 1848, German butcher from Baltimore round the Horn; following his trade at S. F. '48-50; on a Sonoma rancho '51-9; on a Lakeville rancho '59-80, being a large land-owner, giving particular attention to the breeding of blood stock. *Sonoma Co. Hist.*

Bill, several men known only by this name, most of whom cannot be identified, and none of the others requiring notice. Billings (Orson), 1847, Co. B, Morm. Bat. (v. 469).   'Billy the Cooper,' 1845, Engl. sailor from a whaler at Mont.; killed at the Natividad fight in Nov. '46. iv. 587; v. 371. Acc. to Swan, his full name was never known in Cal.

Bines (Robert), 1846, Fauntleroy's dragoons. (v. 232-47.)   Bingham (Erastus), 1847, Co. B, Morm. Bat. (v. 469).   B. (George), 1842, somewhat doubtfully recorded as a boy on one of Com. Jones' vessels at Mont.; returning to Cal. in '49; policeman, miner, saloon-keeper, and soldier to '79, when he lived at Vallejo. *Solano Co. Hist.*, 332-3; iv. 341.   B. (Thos), 1847, Co. B, Morm. Bat.   Binley (John), 1847, Mormon of Kearny's return escort. v. 453, 492.

Bird (David T.), 1844, overl. immig. of the Kelsey party from Or. iv. 444-5, 453. Also called David S. and David F. In '45 one of Sutter's men in the Micheltorena campaign. iv. 486; perhaps the Burt arrested by Castro at S. José in July '46. v. 136; later lieut of Co. E, Cal. Bat., enlisting at Sonoma in Oct. v. 361. He settled in Yolo Co., and was still at Woodland in '79.   B. (Wm), 1847, Co. B, Morm. Bat. (v. 469); in '81 at Paris, Id.   Birnie (James), 1857, Scotch officer of the H. B. Co. at Vancouver, who came on the *Llama* to buy cattle. iv. 85-6, 90. In '47 his name appears in a S. F. list of uncalled-for letters.   B. (Robert), 1832, Amer. who got a passport in Aug.

Birnie (Robert), 1841, son of James, born in Or. '24; came on the *Cowlitz* as clerk for Rae. iv. 217, 279; left the vessel and H. B. Co. at Honolulu in '42, but returned and worked as clerk at Sta B. and S. F., and supercargo of the *Juan José* till '45; his part in the capture of Sutter's gun '44. iv. 483; in Or. '45-7, returning to Cal. '48; clerk for Forbes at N. Almaden '49-50. After engaging in mining, farming, and various other occupations, Birnie became a real estate agent at Oakland, where he still lived in '72 with his wife and three daughters. He gave me a narrative of his *Personal Adventures.* Bishop (Stephen A.), 1846, Co. C, 1st U. S. dragoons. (v. 336). Bissie, 1848, named as a Frenchman hanged at Hangtown in Jan. '49 for robbery on the Stanislaus in '48. Black, 1827, named as one of the Jed. Smith party. iii. 160. B. (David), 1847, with the Morm. Bat. (v. 469); a step-son of Capt. Brown. B. (James), 1847, Co. I, N. Y. Vol. (v. 499); owner of lots at S.F., or this may have been the following.

Black (James), 1832, Scotch sailor left sick at Mont. in Jan., age about 25. v. 408. Other accounts represent him as having deserted at S.F. In applying for naturalization in Sept. '43 he claimed 10 years' residence. For a year or two he hunted otter with McIntosh, being named in Larkin's books from '34. A witness at Sonoma in '36; met by Edwards near S. Rafael in '37. iv. 86. About '40 he perhaps settled on the Jonive rancho, which after his naturalization and marriage in '43 was formally granted him in '45. iv. 117, 671; named in a Sonoma list of '44 as 34 years old; 2d alcalde of S. Rafael in '45. iv. 677. B. seems to have taken no part in the political troubles of '45–6. About '48 he exchanged his Jonive estate for that of Nicasio, where he spent the rest of his life. He was a judge in '50, and assessor in '52–3; evidently a man of industrious habits and good character for one of his class, though a hard drinker in the later years. Died in '70, leaving a large estate about which there was much litigation resulting from an attempt to break his will. His first wife was Agustina Sais, who died in '64, leaving a daughter, Mrs Burdell, who was living in '80. In '65 he married the widow Pacheco, who survived him. Black (Joseph), 1845, hatter at N. Helv. '45–7; often named in the *Diary.* iv. 587; lot owner at S. F.; on the 1st jury at S. José '48; perhaps his name was 'Block;' or there may have been another Block. B. (Wm), 1814, com. of the *Raccoon.* ii. 272, 304, 373.

Blackburn (Wm), 1845, Virginian cabinet-maker born in 1814; overl. immig. in the Swasey-Todd party. iv. 576, 587. He went to work at Sta Cruz as a lumberman, being a witness at the trial of Williams for killing Naile in April '46. v. 671; but after serving a while in Fauntleroy's dragoons, he joined the Cal. Bat. and was made 2d lieut of Co. A, artillery. v. 361, 435. Returning to Sta Cruz, but also obtaining a lot at S. F., B. opened a store; and served '47–9 as alcalde by the governor's appointment. v. 641–2; being also county judge in '50 after a brief experience in the mines. The decisions of his court are famous for their originality; but if technically somewhat irregular, they were always in accord with common sense and justice. He is said to have built a schooner at Sta Cruz in '48. v. 581; and was chosen a member of the convention of '49, though not serving; claimant of the Arastradero rancho. iv. 655. Blackburn was an intelligent, shrewd fellow; honest and straightforward in his dealings; always jovial and popular whether drunk or sober; in a small way a leader among his companions. After '51 he gave up politics and gave his attention to agriculture, first to raising potatoes, for which he got a premium at the N. Y. fair, and later to fruit culture, his orchard being for many years one of the chief attractions of Sta Cruz. He died in '67, leaving a widow. Several of his brothers came to Cal. after '48.

Blair (Chas D.), 1847, Co. E, N. Y. Vol. (v. 499). B. (Nicholas), 1847, ditto; d. at Los Ang. '55. B. (Wm), 1836, doubtful name in Taylor's list, from N. Mex. Blaisdle, 1837, doubtful name at Pt Reyes.

Blake (B.), 1828, agent of a Manila firm at Mont. B. (Geo. C.), 1846, com. of H. B. M. S. *Juno.* v. 579. B. (Homer C.), 1847, officer on the U. S. *Preble*; commodore '79; died '80. B. (Wm), 1832, doubtful record of a carpenter in Solano Co. '69–77. iii. 408.

Blanca (J.), 1841, mr of the *Ayacucho.* iv. 563. Blanchard, 1848, at S. F. from Honolulu in Nov. on the *Currency Lass.* B. (Ira), 1848, in the mines; furnished gold specimens to Gov. Mason; corporal of S. F. guards. B. (Wm), 1811, mr of the *Catherine.* ii. 96, 267. Blanco, at S. D. and Los Ang. '36–46. B. (Juan), 1798. i. 606. B. (Miguel), at S. Gabriel '46. B. (Thos), grantee of land, Mont. '44. iv. 656. Blanks, see 'Banks.'

Blasdell (Lewis), 1848, passp. from Honolulu. B. (Wm), 1842, German

at Mont. on the *California* from Honolulu; permitted to land; a blacksmith age 39.   Blast (Thomas), 1845, doubtful name of a trader.
    Blea (Rafael), 1846, at Los Ang. and S. Bernardino.   Blecksmith, (Leopold), 1847, Co. B, N. Y. Vol. (v. 499).   Blevins (Alex.), 1843, doubtful newspaper mention.
    'Blind Tom,' 1833, Engl. sailor at S. José. *Sta Clara Co. Hist.*   Blindenberg (L. B.), 1832-3, mr of the *Friend.* iii. 382.   Blinn (John), 1836, mr of the *Loriot* '36-7. iv. 105; mr of the *Clementina* '39 and pass. on the *Alciope.* iv. 100, 102; mr of the *Maryland* '41, in which year he died. iv. 207, 567.
    Blirkin (Wm), 1840, doubtful name in Farnham's list of arrested foreigners.   Bliss (Robert S.), 1847, Co. B, Morm. Bat. (v. 469).   Block, see 'Black.'
    Bloomfield (Wm), 1840, one of the exiled foreigners. iv. 18.   Blossom (J. W.), 1848, at S. F. from Honolulu on the *Sagadahoc.*   'Blue Jacket,' 1846, nickname of one of the guard at Sutter's Fort. v. 125.
    Blume (Fred. Gustavus), 1842, German surgeon of the whaleship *Alex. Barclay* at Sauzalito Dec. '42-March '43. iv. 341. Late in '46 he came back to Cal. on the *Currency Lass* from Honolulu with a stock of goods sold at S. F.; and again in April '47 on the *Gen. Kearny*, this time to stay, opening a store at Sonoma with M. J. Haan. In '48 he moved to a rancho in the Bodega region, near Freestone and Bloomfield—the latter named for him—where in '49 he married the widow María Ant. Cáceres de Dawson. Both were living in '80 without children. Dr B. held several local offices, and is postmaster at Freestone in '85. His portrait is found in *Sonoma Co. Hist.*, 280.   Blury (Arthur de), 1846, Fauntleroy's dragoons (v. 232-47).
    Boardman (John), 1843, overl. immig. of the Chiles-Walker party. iv. 392, 400; witness to a doc. at Sonoma '47.   'Bob,' or Juan Cristóbal, 1816, the pioneer negro, left by Capt. Smith of the *Albatross.* ii. 248, 277, 393.   'Bob,' Irish servant of Colton at Mont. '48, who made his fortune in the mines.   'Bob,' a tattooed Marquesan in the mines, ment. by Buffum.   Bobo, (Zarah), 1846, Co. C, 1st U.S. dragoons. (v. 336).   Bocalon (Agustin), 1808, com. of the *Concepcion.* ii. 87.   Bochon (Procopi), 1847, Co. D, N.Y. Vol. (v. 499).   Bode (Nicholas F.), 1847, Co. F, 3d U. S. artill. (v. 518).
    Bodega y Cuadra (Juan Francisco), 1775, Span. lieut in com. of the exploring vessel *Sonora*, discovering and naming Bodega bay. i. 241-3, 518; ii. 81; in 1779 com. of the *Favorita.* i. 329; in 1792-3, com. of the S. Blas naval establishment, and commissioner to settle the Nootka troubles with England, visiting Cal., and dying in '93. i. 506, 509-12, 519-20, 522-4, 539, 682. See also *Hist. N. W. Coast*, i.   Bodie (Waterman S.), vaguely alluded to as having come in '48.   Bogart (Henry), 1847, Co. E, N.Y.Vol. (v. 499).
    Boggs (Albert G.), 1846, son of Lilburn W., and overl. immig. with his father and brothers (v. 526); later a prominent citizen of Napa, and county treasurer; still living in '81.   B. (Guadalupe Vallejo), son of Wm M., born at Petaluma Jan. 4, '47, often named incorrectly as the 1st child of Amer. parents born in Cal.   B. (Lilburn W.), 1846, Kentuckian, b. in 1798; overl. immig. with wife and 8 children. v. 528. He lived many years in Mo., where he was a very prominent man, as pioneer, trader, and public officer, being elected gov. of the state in '36. He took a prominent part in the expulsion of the Mormons, to whose vengeance is attributed a later attempt to murder him which was very nearly successful. Spending the winter at Petaluma and settling at Sonoma he engaged in trade with Scott, and was appointed alcalde to succeed Nash from '47. v. 433, 609-10, 668-9, 681; holding the office till '49, and being elected a member of the constitutional convention, though not serving. In '52 he moved to Napa, where he died in '61. His first wife was a daughter of Silas Bent, and the second, who accompanied him to Cal., a granddaughter of Daniel Boone, dying in Napa in '80 at the age of '97. A good sketch of Ex-gov. Boggs' life is found in the *Napa Co. Hist.*, 373; and a portrait in *Menefee's Sketchbook*, 264. Many of his descendants still live in Cal., but respecting most of them I have no definite information.
    Boggs (Wm M.), 1846, son of Lilburn W., b. in Mo. '26; member of the same immigrant party, of which he was captain during part of the journey—

his bridal tour, he having married Sonora Hicklin just before the start. He took some slight part in the final campaign of the war against Sanchez in '46–7. v. 383; and after an adventurous career in the mines settled at Napa, where in '72 he wrote for me his *Reminiscences* of early life in Mo., his father's life, the trip to Cal., and his experiences in '46–8. His *Trip across the Plains*, in the newspapers, covers nearly the same ground. He has occupied several official positions, and has raised a family of five sons—Guadalupe V., Lilburn W., Jr., Angus, Jefferson, and Wm, and a daughter, to whose education special care has been devoted, several of them being teachers.   Bohorques, see 'Bojorges.'

Boinger (Fred.), 1847, Co. G, N.Y. Vol. (v. 499).   'Bois (Juan), 1828, mr of the *Wilmantic*. iii. 149.   Boissé (Gabriel), 1798, Boston sailor at S. Diego. i. 645, 654.   Bojorges—more properly written Bohorques—(Angel), at S.F. '37–9; at Sonoma '44, age 33.   B. (Bartolo), soldier at S.F. '19; inválido '22–41; regidor at S. José '24–5; elector at S.F. '35. ii. 605; iii. 704; grantee of Laguna de S. Antonio '45, and claimant '54. iv. 673.   B. (Gerardo), at S.F. '37.   B. (Hermenegildo), soldier of the S. José escolta 1797–1800. i. 556.   B. (Ignacio), soldier of the S.F. comp. '35–42; at Sonoma '44, age 26. B. (José Ramon), corporal of the Sta Clara escolta 1776–7; invál. at S. José, 1790–1821. i. 296–7, 306, 478; his wife was Francisca Romero; died '22.   B. (Juan), soldier of S.F. comp. '23–31; at Sonoma '44, age 35. iv. 363.   In '77 at Sta Clara he gave me his *Recuerdos* of Ind. campaigns.   B. (Pedro), settler at S. F. 1791–1800; regidor at S. José 1810. i. 716; ii. 134.   B. (Pedro), at S. F. '37; at Sonoma '44, age 24.

Bolan (A. J.), 1845, at Sutter's '45–6, acc. to the *N. Helv. Diary;* iv. 578. Bolaños (Francisco), 1595, one of Cermeñon's men at Pt Reyes; also with Vizcaino in 1602. i. 96, 98.   Bolbeda (Louis), 1826, French trapper of Jed. Smith's party, who rem. in Cal. iii. 160, 176.

Bolcof (José Antonio), 1815, the earliest Russian settler; native of Kamchatka, who left his vessel at Mont., age about 20. ii. 274, 393. In '17 he was baptized at Soledad, or at least had his Greek church baptism 'ratified;' in '22 married to Cándida Castro, and perhaps made a trip to Mex. ii. 479; in '24 arrested for smuggling, and from that time often named in local records of Branciforte and Sta Cruz. ii. 519, 522, 627; iv. 117, 544; in '29 named as a shoemaker of good conduct; in '31 obtained lands; naturalized in '33; alcalde at Brancif. '34, also '39–42, '45–6. iii. 695–7; iv. 662–4; v. 57, 641–2; being also in charge of the ex-mission from '39; grantee of the Refugio rancho '41. iv. 655. In the Brancif. padron of '45 B. is named with his wife and 11 children as follows: Amadeo b. '25, Francisco '27, Juan '29, Encarnacion '32, Guadalupe '36, Josefa '39, Cármen '37, José Ramon '40; José Dolores '41, María Ant. '42, and María de los Angeles '44. He took no part in the political troubles of '45–7, but in '48 engaged in mining with his sons, being very successful; but not content to let well enough alone, and imbibing somewhat too freely the new spirit of progress, the old man fell a victim to sharpers, gradually lost his lands and money, and died in poverty in '66. I have no record of his sons after '45.

Boles, see 'Bowles.'   Bollon (José María), 1834, Portuguese at Mont. Bolton (James R.), 1847, trader at Mazatlan, having some commercial relations with Cal., which country he visited for the first time in June '47 on the *Lady Shaw Stewart*. In later years he became known as the principal claimant for the Mission Dolores estate in the famous Santillan case; in '85 a capitalist residing at S. F.

Bon (John), 1829, mr of the *Wilmington*. iii. 149.   'Bonaparte,' 1836, Frenchman with Yount in Napa Val.   Bond (Thos), 1833, named as one of Walker's party. iii. 391.   B. (Wm), 1847, Co. D, N. Y. Vol. (v. 499.) Bonechu (Louis), 1824, French vineyardist at L. Ang. '40, age 57, claiming to have been 16 years in Cal.   Bones (John), 1821, Irish carpenter at S. Miguel '29–30, 31 years old, and 9 years in Cal. ii. 444; possibly 'Burns.'

Bonifacio (Juan B.), 1822, Italian or Austrian who landed from the *John Begg* with the governor's permission and was employed by Hartnell as stevedore. ii. 478; an illiterate, honest fellow about 24 years old, who married Cármen Pinto in '27; naturalized in '29; 2d in com. of the comp. extranjera '32. iii. 221, 223, 225; died about '34, leaving a widow and 3 children.

Bonilla (José Mariano), 1834, Mex. lawyer and teacher, who came with the H. & P. colony; implicated in the Apalátegui revolt, but not sent away. iii. 263, 286. A man of the same name was member of the Cal. junta in Mex. '25-7. iii. 3. A young man of 27 on his arrival, well educated at the Colegio Nacional; teacher at Sta B. '35. iii. 657; clerk and sec. in dif. public offices '36-40. iii. 463, 605, 685; admin. of S. Luis Ob., and auxiliary juez '42. iv. 331, 657-8; grantee of Huerhuero, or Huerfano, rancho in '42-4. iv. 655-6; partisan of Micheltorena in '45; sec. and appointed fiscal of the tribunal superior. iv. 532; juez and alcalde at S. Luis '46-8, being at one time arrested by Frémont. v. 638-9, 375; sub-prefect '49; later county judge, district attorney, and supervisor. Bonilla was a man who always commanded respect, though not always in sympathy with the Californians, and one whose advice, by reason of his superior education, was always in demand. In '37 he married Dolores, daughter of Inocente García, who in '78 gave me the Bonilla collection of *Doc. Hist. Cal.* He died in '78.   B. (Patricio), at Los Ang. '46.

Bonnet, 1844, mr of the *Lion* '44-5. iv. 567; iii. 382-3; also in '46; possibly in '35.   Bonney (Jarvis), 1845, Amer. immig. of Grigsby-Ide party, with his family. iv. 578, 580; v. 526. He buried two children at N. Helv. March '46, and in April went to Or., where he was in June.   B. (Truman), 1845, prob. a brother of Jarvis, whom he accomp. to Cal. and to Or. with his family. v. 578. He also lost a son at N. Helv.; and his daughter was married in Feb. '46 to A. Sanders. Next year a man named Bonny, very likely one of this family, was met on his way alone from Or. to the states. *Bryant*, 137.   Bonnycastle (John C.), 1847, lieut and adj. N. Y. Vol. v. 503; later lieut of 4th U. S. infantry '48-61; at Louisville, Ky, '82.   Bons (Wm), 1840, arrested at Branciforte, having no carta.   Bonsall—or Bonsell—(Jacob), 1848, owner of a ferry on the S. Joaquin with Doak.

Booker (Henry), 1844, Amer. named in Larkin's accounts '44-5 at Mont.; living on the Sac. '46. *Tustin.* Joining the Bears, he was the messenger who carried Ide's proclamation to Mont. Later in the year he went south with Frémont; was probably one of Gillespie's garrison at L. Ang.; with Mervine's force defeated at S. Pedro; one of Stockton's men at S. Diego; one of the party sent to reënforce Kearny; and finally killed at S. Pascual. iv. 453; v. 110, 159, 346. Perhaps no other man in Cal. had so varied an experience in this most eventful year.

Booth (J.), 1847, at S. F. on the *Currency Lass* from Honolulu.   B. (Wm), 1847, said to have settled at Sta Clara with his family. *Sta Clara Co. Hist.* Borbosa, settler at Mont. 1800. i. 679.   Borden, 1847, mr of the *Bowditch.* v. 576. Borel, 1847, at N. Helvetia.   Borenback (Antoine), 1847, Co. F, 3d artill. (v. 518), acc. to Lancey; not on the rolls.   Borgas (José M.), grantee of Pájaro in '43 (Vargas ?).

Borica (Diego), 1794, Span. colonel, gov. of Cal. from Oct. '94 to Jan. 16, 1800; dying at Durango in July 1800. See i. 530-3 and 726-30, with intervening pages, passim, for the events of Borica's rule; also list of auth. in vol. i. He was one of the ablest and best rulers the country ever had, always striving for progress in different directions, avoiding controversy, and personally interesting himself in the welfare of all classes; a jovial bon-vivant, knight of Santiago, and man of wealth. His wife, who accompanied him to Cal., was Doña Magdalena de Urquides.   Bork (Louis), 1845, Engl. who got a pass for Sonora at Los Ang.   B. (Manuel), 1845, ditto.

Boronda (José Canuto), son of Corp. Manuel B. and his wife Gertrudis Higuera, b. at S. F. 1792; soldier of Mont. comp. from 1812 in the escolta of S. Antonio, S. Miguel, and S. Juan. ii. 232; in the S. F. comp. '26-7; in '28 alcalde of Branciforte. ii. 627; wife Francisca Castro, children María, Concepcion, Antonia, Juan José, and Francisco; grantee of land in Mont. district '43. iv. 656; juez at S. Juan B. '44. iv. 661. In '78 he was living with his daughter Concepcion—grantee of the Potrero. iv. 655—near S. Luis Obispo, and dictated for me his *Notas* of old-time adventures. ii. 339, 446.   B. (José Eusebio), perhaps a brother of Canuto, in '36 majordomo of the Verjeles rancho. iii. 679; age 26, wife Josefa Buelna, children José de los Santos and

María del Cármen; in '40 grantee of Rinconada del Zanjon. iii. 678, and juez aux. '41. iv. 653; still living at Salinas in '77, but his *Apuntes Históricos* was very brief and unimportant. B. (José Manuel), prob. son of Manuel, at Salinas rancho '35–6, being juez de campo. iii. 674, 678; age 33, wife Juana Cota, children Juan de Mata b. '21, Carlota '22, Josefa '25, Isabel '28, Ascension '30, Franciso '31, Juan '33, José Manuel '36, grantee of Los Laureles in '39. iii. 667; and perhaps of Tucho in '35. iii. 679; still living in '50. B. (Juan de Mata), juez at S. Cárlos '46; named as the man who killed Capt. Burroughs at Nativi- dad. v. 370, 637; son of José Manuel. B. (Manuel), corporal and carpenter, teacher at S. F. and Mont. 1790–1818. i. 643; ii. 78, 383, 427. B. ('Tia'), woman who kept a little shop at Mont. 1811–36, perhaps a sister of Manuel. ii. 420, 614; iii. 454–5.

Borrego, 1822, Mex. priest who came as a companion of Canónigo Fernan- dez; not of the best reputation; perhaps a nickname. ii. 458. Borris (James Wm), 1823, New Yorker whose father was Engl. and mother Dutch; baptized in '24 and employed by Capt. de la Guerra as a physician for the troops at Sta B. ii. 495, 526. Very likely his name was Burroughs. Boscana (Gerónimo), 1806, Span. friar who served in the south until his death at S. Gabriel in '31; a man of learning, whose treatise on the Ind.— *Chinigchinick*—was published later, but whose conduct was not in all respects exemplary. Biog. iii. 641–2; ment. i. list of auth.; ii. 123, 159–60, 345–8, 555–6, 366, 394, 488, 517, 567, 655; iii. 96, 102, 310, 351; iv. 344–5. Bosco (John), 1847, with the Morm. Bat. (v. 469), in the fam. of Capt. Hunt. Bose (Geo. A.), 1848, German farmer in Sta Clara Val. '76. Bosque (Thomas), 1847, Co. G, N.Y.Vol. (v. 499); d. at L. Ang. '47. Bostwick (James C.), 1847, Co. D, N. Y. Vol. Botaires (Pascual), 1846, Cal. claim of $36 (v. 462). Botello (Joaquin), tailor instructor at Mont. 1792–1801. i. 615; ii. 174.

Botello (Narciso), 1833, Mex., native of Álamos, Sonora, who came with John Forster by land, and again with James Johnson in '34, age 24. Erro- neously named as sec. at Los Ang. in '26. ii. 560. At first B. tended Rice's billiard-saloon, and soon opened a grocery at L. Ang. Síndico of the ayunt. '35; sec. of the ayunt. from '36, taking a prominent part in many public mat- ters, especially in the southern opposition to Alvarado in '36–8. iii. 419, 518– 19, 550, 555, 558, 565–6, 635–6; sec. of prefecture '39–43, of the tribunal su- perior '42, and grantee of land at S. Juan Cap. '41. iii. 605, 640; iv. 626, 632 –3; vocal of the assembly '43–6, taking a leading part in all deliberations of that body, also one of the lessees of S. Buen. mission '45. iv. 361, 410–11, 425, 495, 521, 540, 553, 558, 645; active against the Amer. invasion June–Aug. '46, and also as assemblyman and sec. of Gov. Flores in '46–7, but did not go with F. to Mex. as he wished to do. v. 37–8, 50, 264, 321–2, 408, 625; grantee of La Ciénega '46. In '48–50 B. made several not very successful attempts at gold-mining, also engaging in trade at L. Ang. and S. Juan B.; in later years justice of the peace and notary public. He was a man of good abilities and fair education; always a partisan of his country, Mexico, against Cal. and the U. S., as also of the south against the north. In '78, living at the Sta María rancho near S. Diego in great poverty at the age of 63, Botello dictated for me his *Anales del Sur*, a very valuable narrative of the political and other com- plications of his Cal. experience. He had no family.

Botero (Pablo), 1801, prospective settler at Branciforte. ii. 171. Botiller (Anastasio), at Los Ang. '46. B. (Francisco and Vicente), ditto. B. (Joa- quin), teacher at Los Ang. '30. ii. 564. B. (José Ant.), at Los Ang. '19, and S. Antonio rancho '29. ii. 354, 616; in '36 at Mont., age 50, wife María de la Luz Morales, child. José de Jesus b. '14, Peregrino '24—employed by Larkin as a courier '46—José Joaq. '26. B. (José del Cármen), 1842. iv. 653. B. (Narciso), courier '46. v. 72. Botta (Paolo Emilio), 1827, Ital. scientist on the *Héros* '27–8; author of *Osservazioni*. i. list of auth.; ii. 551; iii. 128–30. Bottene, 1846, mr of the *Cabinet* at S.F.

Botts (Charles T.), 1848, Virginian, who came on the *Matilda* with an ap- pointment as U.S. naval storekeeper at Mont. I have the letter of introd. to Larkin which he brought from Com. Sloat, as well as many naval accounts

signed by B. He went to the mines with Colton; was a member of the constitutional convention in '49; member of a leading law firm in S.F. from '50; from
'58 a Sacramento journalist, publishing the *Standard*; state printer in '61; also
district judge of Sac. district. After the war he spent some years in the south,
but returned to the practice of his profession in Cal., residing chiefly at Oakland, where he died in '84 at the age of 75. His wife, who outlived their children, died a few years before her husband; but B. left two granddaughters,
daughters of Dr Aylette of Stockton. Judge Botts was a brother of John M.
Botts, the famous Virginian politician, and was himself a politician of the better
sort, a successful lawyer of marked ability, and a citizen of wide influence.

Bouchaltz (Theodore), 1847, Co. A, N.Y. Vol. (v. 499); d. at Mariposa '83.
Touchard (Hypolite), 1818, French com. of the Buenos Aires insurgents on
the Cal. coast. See ii. 220–49, 252, 348, 383, 389. Nothing is known of his
earlier or later career.   Bouchet (Louis), 1828, French cooper with Mex.
passp. at Mont. 28–9. ii. 558; iii. 178; owner of a vineyard with W. L. Hill
at Los Ang.; naturalized in '31, and soon married; one of the vigilantes '36
(iii. 430); met by Mofras in '41, who calls him Wm, also called Bauchet and
Banchot in some records. He signed a proclamation against Castro in '46; and
acc. to *Los Ang. Co. Hist.*, 33, died Oct. '47; but I find his name in an original list of '48.   Boudinet (W. E.), 1847, owner of a S.F. lot.   Bouet (Jean),
1848, French trader at Los Ang. age 30. Doubtful record.   Boulanger (Francis), 1847, Co. B, N.Y. Vol. (v. 499).   Bousol, 1846, came to S. José Valley.
Hall.   Bouzet (E. de), 1846, com. of the French corvette *Brillante*. v. 576.

Bowden (John H.), 1848, from Honolulu; kept a bakery and owned a lot at
S.F.   Bowen (Asa M.), 1846, Co. C, 1st U.S. dragoons (v. 336), who took part
in the battle of S. Pascual, on which he furnished me in '76 a *Statement*. Still
at S.F. '84–5, and in serious trouble with the officers of justice.   Bowen (Thos
G.), 1834, Amer. trapper from N. Mex.; settled at S. José from '36. iii. 117;
iv. 412. He kept a distillery, and his name, variously written, appears in Larkin's books and other records from year to year; one of Graham's riflemen '36
(iii. 457); grantee of Cañada de S. Felipe in '39, having been naturalized and
married. iii. 677, 711; arrested but not exiled '40. iv. 17; in '41, being a S.
José trader age '33, with one child, he became security for some of the Bartleson immig. iv. 275, 684, 686; failed in business '44; signed the call to foreigners '45. iv. 599. I find no record of him after '46.   B. (Thos), 1846, prob. a
son of the preceding, named by Frémont as a wild young fellow of S. José,
whose mother owned land at the mission.   B. (Wm), 1844–5, sailor from the
Sterling at Mont. iv. 587.   B. (Wm J.), 1847, came from Honolulu on the
Currency Lass; later miner, and lumberman at Bodega; part owner of the *Sabine*, making several voyages, married at Sidney. In '82 he had for many years
been a resident of Berkeley. Very likely same as preceding.

Bowers (James H.), 1847, Co. D, N.Y.Vol. (v. 499); later hotel-keeper at
Stockton; died at S. F. '70.   Bowing (Henry), 1847, Morm. Bat. (v. 469);
reënlisted at Los Ang.   Bowles or Boles (Joseph), 1838, Amer. on Larkin's
books at Mont.; somewhat prominent in the Graham affair of '40, and exiled
to S. Blas, but came back in '41 after a visit to N.Y. to urge his claim for
damages. iv. 18, 31, 33, 119. On the *Alert* at Sta B. '42; perhaps at N. Helv.
'47.   B. (Samuel), 1848, overl. immig. with Allsopp, whose partner he was
in a S. F. boarding-house till '50; when he went to the mines.   Bowman
(Joaquin, Joseph, or Gilbert), 1826, Kentuckian trapper of Jed. Smith's party.
ii. 558; iii. 155, 160, 176; settled at S. Gabriel as a miller, and still lived
there in '44 at the age of 63.

Boy (John), 1847, owner of lots at S. F.   Boyce (Geo. W.), 1847, Co. D,
Morm. Bat. (v. 469); at Salt Lake City '82.   Boyd (Wm), 1847, Co. D, Morm.
Bat.   B. (Geo.), 1848, perhaps at S. F.   B. (R.), 1848, passp. from Honolulu.
Boyer, 1848, mr of the *Persévérance*. v. 579.   Boyers (Wm), 1847, Co. E, N.
Y.Vol. (v. 499); at S. F. '82.   Boyle (Dr), 1845, doubtful name of an immig.
iv. 578.   B. (Henry G.), 1847, Co. C, Morm. Bat. v. 481, 496; in Utah '82,
chaplain of the legislature.   B. (James), 1846, Amer. carpenter at Mont. '46–8.

Brackenberry (Benj. B.), 1847, Co. B, Morm. Bat. (v. 469).   Brackenridge

(J. D.), 1841, botanist of U. S. ex. exped. iv. 241-2, 245. Brackett (John Ely), 1847, lieut 2d U. S. artillery; capt. Co. C, N.Y.Vol. v. 504; com. of the Sonoma garrison '47-8. v. 609-10, 667, 669; later a lawyer, being a member of the legislature of '49-50, and major-gen. of Cal. militia. He died at Rock Island, Ill., Jan. '55. His son or brother—for I have lost the reference—Col Albert G. Brackett, com. of the mil. district of Nevada '66, furnished me in '76 a *Sketch of the 1st Reg. N.Y. Vol.*, and several other MSS. containing useful information. See i. list of auth. Bradford (Wm), 1846, lieut on the U.S. *Warren.*

Bradley (Thomas Westly), 1843, Tennesseean immig. from Mo. in the Chiles party. iv. 392, 400; employed a while by Sutter, but in '44-9 lived in Napa Valley, joining the Bears. v. 111; but not apparently going south with the battalion, and marrying Rebecca Allen of Mo. in Dec. '46. From '49 he lived in Contra Costa county, and in '85 was still on his farm near Lafayette with a large family. Of his six sons, James Warren was b. in '47 and John Willard in '48; there were 4 daughters, 3 of them married before '85. Portrait in *Contra Costa Co. Hist.*, 296. Bradley, 1841 (?), a man who accompanied Brooks —*Four Months*, etc.—in his gold-hunting tour of '48, being named on nearly every page; claimed to have been in Cal. eight years, to have been an officer of volunteers in the war, and to be a friend of Capt. Folsom. iv. 279.

Bradshaw (John), 1827, one of the best known Boston traders on the coast; master of the *Franklin* in '27-8, of the *Pocahontas* '30-2, and of the *Lagoda* '34-5. Often in trouble with the authorities on account of his smuggling exploits, as elsewhere narrated. ii. 551; iii. 132-4, 147-8, 165-7, 176-7, 210, 382-3. Capt. B. never returned to Cal. after '35, but I have his letter to Capt. Cooper in '36; and a letter of Jan. '84 from his daughter, Mrs H. E. Roundy, informs me that he died at his home in Beverley, Mass., May '80, at the age of 94. B. (Julian), 1845, overl. immig. in the Grigsby-Ide party; bonds given by Yount; prob. went to Or. in '46. iv. 526, 578. B. (Samuel), 1848, in the mines with Brooks; formerly carpenter on a whaler. B. (Wm D.), 1846, lieut Co. D, Cal. Bat. v. 361; had a Cal. claim of $132 (v. 462). Brady, 1848, with Newell & Gilbert. B. (James), 1846, at N. Helv. in Jan.; perhaps same as preceding. B. (James), 1847, Co. K, N. Y.Vol. (v. 499). B. (John R.), 1847, Co. B, N.Y.Vol.; died at Stockton after '50.

Braham (A.), 1845, at N. Helv.; prob. 'Bruheim,' q.v. Bralee (Thomas), 1846, Engl. sailor disch. from the *Savannah;* a resid. of Mont. and Carmelo Val., except 2 years at the mines, to '77 and later, being a dairyman, with two sons and a daughter. Braley (Albert), 1845, mate on the *Morea.*

Branch (Francis Ziba), 1831, trapper of the Wolfskill party from N. Mex. iii. 387, 405; a nat. of N. Y. After a few years of hunting he opened a store and boarding-house at Sta B., though often engaging in a hunt, to keep up memories of old times. He married Manuela Carlon in '35. iv. 117; and the padron of '36 shows that he had then one son. Selling his store in '37, he applied for naturalization—obtained in '39—and got a grant of the Sta Manuela rancho near S. Luis Obispo. iii. 679; iv. 655; where he spent the rest of his life, a rich man of good repute. He died in '74 at the age of 72, leaving many children and grandchildren. His portrait is given in *S. Luis Ob. Co. Hist.*, 216. Branda (Juan), at Sonoma '44.

Brander (Wm), 1833, Scotch carpenter, 29 years old, at Mont., his name appearing often on Larkin's books and other records in '33-45. iii. 409; arrested but not exiled in '40. iv. 17; got a carta, and in '41-2 was a lumberman near Sta Cruz. In Oct. '45 he was found dead on Amesti's rancho, believed to have been killed by Ind. iv. 543.

Branham (Benj. F.), 1846, son of Isaac and overl. immig. at the age of one year; sheriff of Sta Clara Co. '85. B. (Isaac), 1846, Kentuckian immig. (v. 526), with his wife Amanda A. Bailey and son Benj. F., settling at S. José, where he was a member of the town council '46-7. v. 664; and where he still lived in '81. Portrait in *Sta Clara Co. Hist.*, 304. He had a son Charles b. '54, and a daughter Mary b. '60; besides 4 children born before he came to Cal. Branisan (Floria), 1846, pass. on the *Guipuzcoana* from Callao. Banks (Robert), 1848, visited S. F. from Honolulu on the *Julian.* Brannan (Peter),

1846, Irish bricklayer who served in the Cal. Bat. at the Natividad fight; later worked at his trade; in the mines '48; soon after drowned at S. F. *Swan.* Perhaps his name was Brennan.

Brannan (Samuel), 1846, Mormon elder and chief of the colony sent from N.Y. on the *Brooklyn.* See full account of the colony, v. 544 et seq.; mention v. 471, 644-5. B. was born at Saco, Me, in '19; learned the printer's trade in Ohio from '33; travelled as a printer through many parts of the country; and from '42 published the *N.Y. Messenger* and later the *Prophet,* as organs of the Mormon church. Of his conversion and early experience as a latter-day saint not much is known, the subject being avoided both by himself and his old associates; but he was clearly a leading spirit in the church, and was just the man to take charge of the Californian scheme. There is no good reason to doubt his devotion to the cause, but it was his firm intention to build up his own fortunes with those of his sect; he was greatly displeased with President Young's change of plans respecting Cal.; and having failed during a visit to Salt Lake to modify the president's views, it required but few years to divest himself entirely his of old-time religious fervor and become an apostate. Meanwhile, at S. F. he was a leading spirit from the first, preaching eloquently on Sundays, publishing the *Star,* buying town lots, taking part in political controversies, working zealously for the advancement of the town's educational and other interests, always aggressive but liberal in his views, showing no signs of sectarianism. For mention in this part of his career '46-7, see v. 494, 649-51, 666-8, 681-2. In '47 he established the firm of C. C. Smith & Co. at Sac., later Brannan & Co., in which Mellus & Howard and Wm Stout were partners. The immense profits of his store after the discovery of gold in '48-9, with his mining operations at Mormon Island, and the increase of S.F. real estate, made him a little later the richest man in Cal. Of his career after '48 something will be found in vol. vi. of this work; also in my *Popular Tribunals,* B. having been prominent in connection with the vigilance committees. I do not attempt even to outline his most remarkable career as capitalist and speculator. In many parts of the state and even beyond its limits he acquired immense interests, showing in their management the ability and energy so characteristic of the man. He probably did more for S.F. and for other places than was effected by the combined efforts of scores of better men; and indeed, in many respects he was not a bad man, being as a rule straightforward as well as shrewd in his dealings, as famous for his acts of charity and open-handed liberality as for his enterprise, giving also frequent proofs of personal bravery. In '59 he purchased the Calistoga estate, in connection with the improvement of which his name is perhaps most widely known. Here he established a distillery on a grand scale, and here in '68 he received eight bullets and nearly lost his life in a quarrel for possession of a mill. Meanwhile he had given himself up to strong drink; for 20 years or more he was rarely sober after noon; and he became as well known for his dissolute habits and drunken freaks as he had been for his wealth and ability. Domestic troubles led to divorce from the wife married in '44, who with their child had come with him in '46 and borne him other children in Cal.; division of the estate was followed by unlucky speculations, and Brannan's vast wealth melted gradually away. In the days of his prosperity he had liberally supported the cause of Mexico against the French invasion and its tool Maximilian, and just before 1880 he obtained in return a grant of lands in Sonora, embarking with somewhat of his old energy in a grand scheme of colonization, which has thus far proved a total failure. For the last year or two down to '85 Brannan has lived at Guaymas or on the frontier, remarried to a Mexican woman, a sorry wreck physically and financially, yet clear-headed as ever and full of courage for the future. Thousands of pioneers in Cal. remember this erratic genius with the kindliest of feelings, and hope that he may yet add a brilliant closing chapter to the record of one of the most remarkable characters in Californian annals.

Brant (Henry), 1845, one of Frémont's men. iv. 583.   Brasher (S. M.), 1841, mid. on the *St Louis.*   Brass (Benj.), 1847, Co. A, Morm. Bat. (v. 469); reënlisted at Los Ang.   Brasseau (Chas), 1847, at N. Helv.   Braun (Jean

Louis), 1831, Frenchman, 26 years old, from N. Mex. perhaps with Wolfskill or Jackson. iii. 387. Braun (Philip), 1847, Co. H, N. Y. Vol. (v. 499). Braune (Chas J. W.), 1845, perhaps cne of Frémont's men. iv. 583, 587; accidentally burned to death in El Dorado Co. '79.

Bravo (David), soldier at Mont. '36, age 43. B. (Juan de Dios), 1832, in the comp. extranjera at Mont. iii. 221; regidor at Los Ang. '35. iii. 635 B. (Juan N.), 1842–5, sub-lieut of the batallon fijo. iv. 289. B. (Manuel), 1842, ditto. iv. 289. B. (Marcelino), invál. at Brancif. 1799. i. 571.

Bray (Edmund), 1844, Irish immig. in the Stevens party, age 37. iv. 445, 453. He was employed by Sutter from '45, serving in the Micheltorena campaign. iv. 486; went to the mines in '48. He was disabled by a fall in '56, and in '72 had been for 6 years in the Sac. county hospital, where he wrote for me his *Memoir*, an excellent narrative of the journey overland. B. (Edward), 1847, mr of the *Henry*. v. 578; owner of a S. F. lot. Brazier (Richard), 1847, sergt Co. E, Morm. Bat. v. 477; prob. did not come to Cal. Breager, with a party of trappers between '32 and '40. iii. 392.

Breck (James Wm), 1829–30, Boston man who perhaps visited Cal. on a whaler, and possibly remained at that time, ii. 573, iii. 179, though some say he came back from Honolulu in '37 to become a permanent resid. of Sta B., where he married and had many children; still living in '76 at the age of 76. Also named as owner of a rancho near S. Luis Ob., and as an otter-hunter in '41–5. Information about him is very unsatisfactory. Breckenridge (Thomas E.), 1845, one of Frémont's men, serving in the Cal. Bat., and as one of the Sta B. garrison '46. v. 306, 453, 583; had a Cal. claim (v. 462) of $20, and was at Washington May '48 to testify at the court-martial.

Breen (Patrick), 1846, Irishman who came to Amer. in '28, and from Iowa overland in the Donner party (v. 530–44, where all the members of this family are named), with his wife Margaret and 7 children, the whole family surviving the perils of that terrible journey. Breen's original *Diary of the Donner Party* is one of the most highly prized treasures of my Library. The Breens lived at Murphy's on the Cosumnes till Sept. '47, then at S. José till Feb. '48, when they settled at S. Juan B. Here Patrick died in '68 and his widow in '74. Portraits and biog. sketches of the family in *McGlashan's Donner Party*. The Breens have always been regarded as honest, hard-working people. B. (Edward J.), 1846, son of Patrick. His sufferings on the overland trip were aggrayated by a broken leg; living at S. Juan in '85 with 2d wife and 5 children. B. (Isabella), 1846, infant daughter of Patrick; married Thos McMahon '69; at Hollister '85. B. (James F.), 1846, son of Patrick, b. in Iowa '41; educated at Sta Clara college; lawyer at S. Juan B. He has been district attorney, assemblyman, county judge, and from '79 superior judge of S. Benito. Married in '70, and living in '85 with wife and two children. B. (John), 1846, oldest son of Patrick, 14 years old, and strongest of the family except the mother, yet barely escaping death. In the mines at Mormon Isl. '48, and in the winter built a house where Placerville stood later. Returning to S. Juan and buying the old residence of Gen. Castro, he married a daughter of Ed. Smith in '52, and in '85 still lived there with wife and 9 children. In his *Pioneer Memoirs*, Breen has contributed an interesting narrative of 80 p. to my collection. B. (Patrick, Jr), 1846, son of Patrick, 9 years old on arrival; a farmer at S. Juan, married in '65, and living in '85 with wife and 4 children. B. (Peter), 1846, son of Patrick, a child in '46; died unmarried in '70. B. (Simon P.), 1846, son of Patrick; living '85 at S. Juan with wife and 2 children. B. (Wm M.), 1848, son of Patrick, b. at S. Juan; died '74, leaving a widow and child.

Brenard (Sam.), 1848, named as one of the murderers of the Reed family. v. 640. Brenerd (T.), 1848. at Mont. Brennan, see 'Brannan.' Bressak, 1845, at Mont. Brestone (Robert), 1838, named in *Larkin's Accts*. Bretely (Jose), 1841, at Sta B.

Brewer (Charles), 1832, mr of the *Victoria*. iii. 384. A Boston man of the well-known firm of Peirce & B. at Honolulu. Revisited Cal. in '79 with his daughter; living at Jamaica Plains, Mass., at the age of 80 in '84, when he also printed for his family a small vol. of *Reminiscences*, of which he presented a copy for my collection. B. (C, 2d, G. W., and H. B.), 1848, passp. from Honolulu. Brewerton (Geo. D.), 1847, lieut Co. C, N.Y. Vol., trans. to Co. K. v. 504; went east in '48 with Carson's party to N. Mex. (see *Brewerton's Ride*, in i. list of auth.); later lieut 1st U.S. infantry; colonel in '78; living in N.Y. '79. Brewster, 1829, said to have been master of the whaler *Alvins* (?). B. (F. M.), 1848, on the *Julian.*

Brian (Henry), 1847, Co. F, 3d U.S. artill. (v. 518). Briant (John S.), 1847, Co. A, Morm. Bat. (v. 469); reënlisted at Los Ang. Bridger (James), 1835 (?), noted trapper of the plains and mountains. It is not clear that he visited Cal. before '49, but he is likely to have done so. iii. 413. Bridges (J. C.), 1843, Kentuckian immig. from Or. in the Hastings party; employed by Sutter and perhaps by Smith at Bodega, but died in the winter of '43–4. iv. 390, 396, 400. Brien (D. L.), 1847, asst surg. U.S. *Columbus.*

Briggs (1846), in Sutter's employ. B., 1832, mr of the *Phœbe*, reported as dead the same year. B. (C. P.), 1844, sailor at S.F. from the *Morea*. iv. 453; later in Leidesdorff's employ; and perhaps one of the Bears in '46 (v. 101); but all seems to rest on his own statement in '72. He was perhaps the P. A. Briggs who joined Co. G, Cal. Bat. (v. 358), at S. José in Nov; and the C. P. A. Briggs married at S.F. '47 to Catherine Coombs. (See i. list of auth.) B. (Calvin T.), 1837 (?), overl. immig., nat. of Vt, died '68, aged 60. *Soc. Pion.*, records; also reported to have come in '32 on a whaler, to have been a trapper on the coast, and later resid. of S. Joaquin. *S. F. Examiner*, iii. 408. B. (Castor, or Caspar), 1847, Co. E, N.Y.Vol. (v. 499); at S. F. '74–82. B. (Charles), 1847, settler at Benicia; B. & Russell, lumber dealers. v. 672. B. (Francis), 1845, perhaps one of Frémont's men; in Cal. Bat. (v. 358); one of Talbot's garrison at Sta B. iv. 583; v. 316. B. (Geo.), 1847, mr of the *Isabella*. v. 511. Briggs, 1848, of sloop *Stockton* running from S. F. to Sonoma. v. 646. Brigham (E. R.), 1847, Co. B, N.Y.Vol. (v. 499). Brincken (Wilhelm), 1840, cne of the Graham exiles who did not return. iv. 18. Bringas (Luis M.), ment. in connection with J. M. Herrera's trial '27. iii. 61–2. Brinsmade (A. A.), 1848, at S. F. August–Sept., treasurer S. F. guards.

Briones (Antonio), corporal at S. Juan Cap., killed by Ind. i. 315. B. (Antonio), soldier and Ind. fighter 1810; smuggler '20–1. ii. 91, 411, 440–1, 564. B. (Canuto), S. F. militia '37. B. (Desiderio), ditto; at S. F. '41; wounded by Ind. '39; juez de campo S. José '43. iv. 76, 685. B. (Felipe), regidor at S. José '20. ii. 378; on S. Mateo rancho, elector S. F. '35. iii. 704; killed by Ind. '40. iv. 76. B. (Gregorio), soldier of S. F. comp. '16–27. ii. 371; militiaman S. F. '37; alcalde contra costa '35. iii. 704; regidor S. F. '36. iii. 705; alcalde S. Mateo '38. iii. 705; owner of lots at S. F. '41–5. iv. 669; v. 683; at Sonoma '44, age 47; juez at S. Rafael, and grantee of Baulines '46. iv. 677; v. 669–70. B. (Juana), mentioned as a widow at S. F., and also as the wife of Apolinario Miranda, noted for her kindness to sick and deserting sailors; had an adobe house in the North Beach region in '36; owner of lot '41–5. iii. 709; iv. 669; later claimant for Purísima rancho, Sta Clara Co. iii. 712; still living at Mayfield '78 at a very advanced age. B. (Manuel), soldier at S. Juan B. before 1800. i. 558. B. (Manuela Valencia de), widow at S. José '41, age 47; children, Ramon b. '13, Desiderio '16, Isidora '20, Casimiro '24, Felipa '18, María Ant. '27, Angela '30, Encarnacion '32, Marcelino '34, Vicente '36, Cármen '38. B. (Marcos), soldier at Soledad, invál. at Brancif. 1791–1800. i. 499, 571; comisionado at Brancif. 1812. ii. 390; still living at S. José '41, a native of Sinaloa, age 87. B. (Pablo), in Marin Co. and Sonoma from '37, prob. son of Gregorio. B. (Ramon), soldier at S.F. '37, '44.

Bristler (John), 1846, bugler in Co. C, 1st U.S. dragoons (v. 336). Bristow (Elijah), 1845, an old Kentuckian at N. Helv. iv. 578; an overl. immig. and called by some a Mormon. J. H. Brown says that B. came with himself and in the Grigsby-Ide party. Wintering at the fort, where he was badly hurt by being thrown from a horse, he went to Or. in '46. v. 526; where he died in '72. *Hist. Or.*, i. 568–9. Britton, 1845, at N. Helv. Dec., perhaps an error. B. (W. F.), 1848, passp. from Honolulu. Brizzee (Henry W.), 1847, Co. D, Morm. Bat. (v. 469); reënl. at L. Ang.; in Arizona '82.

Broadhurst (Stephen), 1848, overl. immig. from Mo. with his wife; in Merced Co. '73.   Brock (Elisha E.), 1848, Virginian, overl. immig., accomp. by his family; a miner on the Yuba; farmer at Sta Clara, and from '62 near Gilroy, where he died in '69. His widow, Eliza S. Day, survived him: there were 9 children, 3 of them born in Cal.   B. (Hiram), 1846, Cal. Bat. '46-7 (v. 358); in S. Joaq. Valley '48.   Brockee (Joseph), 1847, Co. E, N.Y.Vol. (v. 499); drowned in Stanislaus Riv. '47.   Broder (Andrew H.), 1847, Soc. Cal. Pion. rolls.   Brohan (John), 1847, Co. A, N.Y.Vol.; died at Stockton '50.

Brolaski (Henry Lyons), 1841, overl. immig. of the Bartleson party. iv. 267, 270, 275, 342; at Mont. Feb. '42, but soon sailed for Callao, from which place he writes in '44 to Larkin and T. H. Green. He succeeded his brother in business at Callao for three years from '44; at St Louis Sept. '48, anxious to come to Cal. and establish a saw-mill; but said to have been living in Mo. as late as '70. He sometimes signed Brolaskey.   Brooks (S. S.), 1848 (?), storekeeper at Colima. El Dorado Co. Hist.   Brooker (Alex. V.), 1846, at S. José; in '47 digging a cellar for Larkin at S.F.   Brookey, overl. immig. with Bryant. v. 528; ment. by Sherman as a worthless fellow at S.F. '47; prob. same as preceding.   Brookman (Israel), 1846, doubtful mention as a Bear Flag man living in '62.   Brooks (Chas W.), 1847, Co. K, N.Y.Vol. (v. 499).   B. (Edward J.), 1847, Co. I, N.Y.Vol.   B. (Geo.), 1848, passp. from Honolulu.   B. (H. L.), 1848, ditto.   B. (J. Tyrwhitt), 1848, Engl. physician, who came by sea from Or., and made a tour in the mines; author of Four Months among the Gold-Finders.   B. (Wm S.), 1847, on the U.S. Preble; later in govt employ at S.F. and Mare Isl., where he was in '79; twice married with 8 children. Solano Co. Hist., 334.

Brotchie (Wm), 1837, Engl. master of the Cadboro, Llama, Nereid, and Cowlitz, on the coast '37-42, in service of H. B. Co. from Vancouver. iv. 101, 105, 564.   Brothers (P.), to Honolulu from S. F. on the Francisca.   Broughton (Wm Robert), 1792, com. of the H. B. M. S. Chatham; and of the Providence 1796. i. 510-13, 538-9, 685; author of Voy. of Discov. to the North Pac. Ocean, Lond. 1804.   B. (Sam. Q.), 1846-7, Co. B, Cal. Bat. (v. 358).   Brower (Geo.), 1845, at Mont. from N. Y.   Browett (Daniel), 1847, sergt Co. E, Morm. Bat. (v. 477); in Sutter's employ '47-8 as carpenter and boat-builder; killed by Ind. on his way to Utah July '48. v. 496.

Brown, 1793, mr of an Engl. vessel. i. 514, 705.   B., 1803, mr of the Alexander. ii. 12, 15-17, 94, 103, 108, 130, 144.   B., 1831, deserter from the Fanny.   B., 1845, cook for Sutter from Oct.   B., '46-8, often named at N. Helv.; may be the preceding or one or more of the following.   B., 1848, came with Peter J. Davis; family.   B., 1848, mining at Coloma.   B., 1847, from Honolulu to S. F. on the Guipuzcoana.   Brown (Albert), 1844, Amer. 28 years old at S.F.   B. (Alex.), 1847, Co. C, Morm. Bat. (v. 469); in '82 at Lynne, Utah.   B. (Benj.), 1832, named in a board bill at Mont.

Brown (Charles), 1833, nat. of N. Y., b. in '14, who deserted from the whaler Helvetius at S. F. iii. 409, 382; ii. 590-1. In later years Brown always claimed to have come in '29; but the archive evidence is conclusive against the statement, both himself and his comrade deserters testifying in early years and in different doc. that they came in '33, to say nothing of the fact that the Helvetius does not appear in the lists of '29. He lived for a time at Pinole with Felipe Briones; served P. Quijas at S. Rafael; went to Sonoma with the H. & P. colony; got a land grant in '34 in Napa Valley, which he sold to Capt. Stokes. iii. 712; was severely wounded in an Ind. exped. to the north. iii. 360; and worked at shingle-making for Geo. Yount—all this by his own account before the end of '35, but most of these events are prob. antedated. The 1st original evidence of his presence is a permission to cut timber given by Vallejo in May '37; in '38 he was baptized by P. Quijas as Cárlos de Jesus, and about the same time married a daughter of Antonio García of S. José; arrested in '40 but not exiled, being at that time at work in the redwoods of Sta Clara Co. iv. 9, 17, 23; naturalized in '41, claiming 9 years' residence; in '44 named in a S. F. list, owning a lot at the mission. iv. 676, 673; in '45 took part in the Micheltorena campaign by exchanging himself as a prisoner for Manuel Castro. iv. 487. To about '49 he lived on a rancho near Searsville, and later at the Mission Dolores, where in '78 he gave me his narrative of *Early Events*, and where he died in '83 at the age of 69. His second wife was Rosalía de Haro, widow of A. A. Andrews, who survived him with several grown children, and who I think still lives in '85.   Brown (Chas), 1845. iv. 587; real name 'Dittmann,' q.v.   B. (Chas), 1847, Co. E, N.Y.Vol. (v. 499).   B. (Chas), 1848, at Sta Cruz '81. *S. J. Pioneer.*

Brown (Ebenezer), 1847, sergt Co. A, Morm. Bat. (v. 469); at Mont. '48. B. (Edmund Lee), 1847, sergt Co. E, Morm. Bat. v. 495; reënl. at Los Ang.; a Virginian who remained in Cal.; alcalde at S. Diego and in charge of the mission '47-8. v. 618-20; claimant for Laguna de Santos Calle rancho. iv. 671; died at Davisville '72 age 68.

Brown (Elam), 1846, nat. of N.Y., b. in 1797, moving to Mass., Ohio, Ill., Mo., and finally overland to Cal. with his children in a party of which he was captain. v. 528. He went to Sta Clara; served in Aram's comp. (v. 378); was named for the proposed legis. council in '47. v. 433; bought the Acalanes rancho. iii. 711; and was juez of the contra costa in '48. v. 662. In '49 he was a member of the constitutional convention, and also of the first two legislatures. From '48 to '85, being now 88 years old, Brown has lived on his Contra Costa farm, a rich man and respected citizen. His second wife, married in '47, was Mrs Margaret Allen, who died in '84 at the age of 89. His daughter Margeline became the wife of Napoleon B. Smith, and was still living in Contra Costa Co. '85. His sons were Thomas A., Warren J., and Lawrence M. The *Contra Costa Co. Hist.*, 515, contains Brown's reminiscences of his overland trip and Californian experience, in which as is common with '46 immig., an exaggerated importance is attached to the Sanchez campaign of Sta Clara. See also list of auth. vol. i.   Brown (E.), 1848, passp. from Honolulu.

Brown (Francis), 1847, Co. B, Morm. Bat. (v. 469).   B. (Geo.), 1844, Amer. sailor on the *Admittance*, discharged sick in '45.   B. (James), 1847, capt. Co. C, Morm. Bat.; left behind in N. Mex., but came to Cal. by the Truckee route before the end of '47. v. 477, 482, 494; delivered an oration at a battalion reunion at Salt Lake City '55.   B. (James), 1847, returned with Stockton or Frémont; a witness at Washington Jan '48. v. 454; possibly same as preceding.   B. (James), 1847, Co. D, Morm. Bat. (v. 469).   B. (James S.), 1847, Co. D, Morm. Bat.; in Sutter's employ; at the Coloma mill when gold was discov.; at Salt Lake City '82.   B. (James), 1837, named in Larkin's books; cook on the *California* in '40.   B. (Jeffery), 1836, on Larkin's books '36-40; arrested at Los Ang. in '40. iv. 14, 118.

Brown (John), 1828 (?), Swede known as Juan Flaco or 'lean John,' and famous for his ride from Los Ang. to Mont. with despatches in '46. iii. 178; v. 303-4. He claimed to have come on a Mex. vessel in '28 after an adventurous career in the Engl. navy and the service of Bolívar in S. Amer.; also to have been one of Graham's men in '36-7 (iii. 457), and one of Sutter's men in the campaign of '44-5 (iv. 476); he died at Stockton in '59. I find no original evidence of his presence before '46; but there was a John Brown on Larkin's books '37-9; a Jean Louis Braun at Los Ang. '36; and a John 'Moreno,' Dutch sawyer at S.F. '42.   B. (John), 1804, negro deserter from O'Cain's ship at S.D.; sent to S. Blas. ii. 26.   B. (John), 1825-7, mr of the *Jóven Tartar* (?). iii. 149.   B. (John), 1846, Co.C, 1st U.S. dragoons (v. 336).   B. (John), 1847, Co. A, Morm. Bat. (v. 469); Utah farmer '81.   B. (John G.), 1841, in U.S. ex. exped. iv. 241.

Brown (John Henry), 1843-5, Engl. sailor who came to Amer. about '30, wandered westward, and about '40 went to live with the Cherokee Ind. In '43, with a party of Cherokee fur-traders under Dan Coodey the half-breed, he crossed the country by the Humboldt and Truckee route, spending the winter at what was later Johnson's rancho—not visiting Sutter's fort, though some of the Ind. did so—returning in the spring of '44 eastward, and meeting the Stevens party (iv. 445) on the way. After many adventures in the great basin and Texas, Brown came back to Cal. in '45 with the Grigsby-Ide party (iv. 578). All this rests solely on his own statement; but there is little doubt that he came overland in '45, in a party that was with the Grigsby-Ide part of the way, and about which there is much confusion that I am unable to clear up (iv. 578, 587). He may have been the B. employed by Sutter as cook in Oct. '45; but the 1st definite record is that of his departure from N. Helv. for S.F. Jan. 14, '46. At S.F. he was a well-known character as bar-tender and hotel-keeper '46-50. At 1st with Ridley; kept the Portsmouth House from Oct. '46; the City Hotel, cor. Kearny and Clay streets, sometimes known as Brown's Hotel, at different times in '47-50; nominal owner of a dozen city lots or more in '48. v. 672, 680. In Dec. '46 he married Hetty C., daughter of E. Ward Pell, and in April '47 advertised her as having left him; but he soon married again and had children by his 2d wife. In '50-81 he lived at Sta Cruz, and then returned to S.F., where in '85 he keeps a grocery, being 75 years old. John Henry is one of those who claim 'to know more than any other live man' about early times in S.F., and one of these days he is going to publish what he knows, thus gaining no end of fame and money. He gave me, however, some useful items. B. (J. H.), 1847-8, made a trip to Honolulu on the *Mary Ann*, returning in Dec. '48; perhaps same as the preceding.

Brown (Lawrence M.), 1846, son of Elam; died in Contra Costa Co. '77, leaving a widow and 2 children still living in '85. B. (Martin), 1845, immig. from Or. in the McMahon-Clyman party; probably returned to Or. '46. v. 572, 526. B. (Philip), 1847, lot-owner at S.F. v. 676. B. (R.), 1848, passg. from Honolulu. B. (Richard), 1845-7, a Delaware Ind. of Frémont's comp. B. (Robert), 1847, Co. F, 3d U.S. artill. (v. 518). B. (Robt), 1828, 'Roberto el Baleado,' a horse-thief operating in Cal.; the reference may be to Peg-leg Smith or to Juan Flaco. B. (Sam.), 1946, overl. immig. of German descent who in '47 built houses for Larkin at Benicia. v. 671; in Napa Valley '48; went to Or. about '50, becoming a farmer at French Prairie, and a candidate for the state senate in '66. B. (Talbot), 1844, Amer. at Mont., who got a passport for one year. B. (Thomas), 1839, named in Larkin's books '39-40; said to have come in '34. *Sta Clara Co. Hist. Atlas.*

Brown (Thomas A.), 1847, son of Elam, b. in Ill. '23, overl. immig. to Or. '43, who visited Cal. '47. In '48 he came to Cal. to stay, settling at Martinez in '49. In Or. a surveyor; in Cal. at 1st miner and trader; holding several town and county offices, and becoming a lawyer; married in '51 to Caroline Camron. County judge '56-64, and '74-80; assemblyman '65-8; candidate for U. S. senate; judge of the superior court of Contra Costa from '80; still living '85, with wife and 3 sons. Portrait in *Contra Costa Co. Hist.*, 56. B. (Warren J.), 1847, son of Elam, b. in Ill. '26; started with his father in '46, but was left sick at Ft Bridger and went to Or., coming to Cal. in Sept. '47. Lumberman and miner '47-8; storekeeper '49-50 at Martinez, where he lived till '71, having married Laura A. Hastings in '54. He held the offices of county surveyor, assemblyman, and sheriff. From '75 he lived on a farm at Lafayette, where he was still in '85; no children. B. (Wm), 1844, sail-maker on the *Vandalia*, implicated in a robbery. B. (Wm), 1847, witness at Wash. in Frémont court-martial Jan. '48; perhaps went east with F. or Stockton. v. 454. B. (W. B.), 1847, in list of letters S. F. B. (Wm H.), 1847, N.Y.Vol., under another name; at Oakland '74. B. (W. H.), 1841, acting lieut on U.S. *St Louis*. B. (Wm W.), 1847, Co. A, Morm. Bat. (v. 469); reënlisted.

Brownell (Russell G.), 1847, musician Co. C, Morm. Bat. (v. 469). Browning (John W.), 1847, Co. K, N.Y.Vol. (v. 499). Brownlea (J. J.), 1841, assist surg. on U. S. *St Louis*.

Bruce (David), 1845-7, sail-maker on the U.S. *Portsmouth*. Brucon (John), 1840, Amer. deserter from the *Morse*, age 19, at S. F. Bruen (John H.), 1847, perhaps of N.Y.Vol. under another name; died at S. Isidro '78. Bruheim (Adolf), 1842, German, age 21, who came on the *California* from Honolulu as servant to a passenger, being permitted to remain. iv. 341; went to N. Helv.; employed by Cordua on Feather River '45-6; and named as one of the 1st Donner relief party. v. 539; no record of him after '47, but I think he lived at S. F. in later years under another name. Bruner (Christian), 1846, overl. immig. with his wife and brother; employed by Sutter '47, also owning a lot at S. F.; in '57 at S. F. he was sentenced to state prison for 11 years for murder committed when in liquor. *S. F. Herald.*   B. (Jacob), 1846, brother of the preceding; settled at Sonoma.   Brunson (Clinton D.), 1847, Co. A, Morm. Bat. (v. 469); in Utah '81.   Brusle (Jackson), 1847, Co. E, N.Y.Vol. (v. 499); d. Contra Costa Co. '54.   B. (Wash.), 1847, Co. E, N.Y.Vol.

Bryan (Abner), 1845, at N. Helv. '45-6; iv. 578, 587; testified before the land com. after '50. I am informed by D. L. Adams, whose mother B. married, that he is still living '85 in Sta B. Co.   B. (J. W.), 1847, farmer in Sta Clara Co. '47-76; a native of Mo.   B. (Wm), 1848, at Monterey; perhaps ' Bryant.'   Bryant (A.), 1847, acting mr of the U. S. *Dale.*

Bryant (Edwin), 1846, nat. of Mass., and a journalist of Ky, who came overland at the head of a party. v. 527-36. He took a prominent part in enlisting men for the Cal. Bat., in which he served as lieut of Co. H. v. 359, 361; alcalde of S. F. Feb.–May '47, also lot-owner. v. 648, 676; returned east with Gen. Kearny, and testified at the Frémont court-martial. v. 452, 456, 543. He came back across the plains in '49, and was for 4 or 5 years a prominent citizen, property owner, and politician; also visited Cal. several times after he went east to live; died at Louisville, Ky, in '69 at the age of 64. His *What I Saw in Cal.*, published just after his 1st visit, is a standard authority on events of '46-7.   B. (Nathaniel C.), 1846, mid., acting master of the U. S. *Dale.*   B. (Stephen), 1842, Amer. cook on the schr *California.* B. (Wm), 1846, overl. immig. accompanied by his wife Lucy Ann. v. 528; at Benicia '47-8, where he built houses for Larkin. v. 672; in the mines from end of '48, and died of cholera in '50. According to testimony in later litigation, he was the owner of Mare Island, living on it in '47-8. His widow married a man named Grissom, and in '77 was living in Sonoma Co.   Bryen (Geo.),· 1846, Co. C, 1st U. S. dragoons. v. 336.

Buchalas, 1846, doubtful name of an immig. v. 529.   Buchanan, 1845, Amer. immig. from Or. in the McMahon-Clyman party. iv. 572, 587; perhaps at N. Helv. '47-8.   B. (John), 1847, Co. D, Morm. Bat.; at Manti, Utah, '82.   B. (John C.), 1846, Kentuckian immig. with Bryant's party. v. 528; of the firm McDonald & B. at S.F., auctioneers, Jan.–May '48; owner of many city lots; alcalde's clerk '47. v. 648, 651, 676, 682-3. Perhaps a resid of S. F. in later years.   B. (McKean), 1846, nat. of Penn., purser of the U. S. *Dale* '46-7; died in Mass. '71; father of the actor of the same name. Buck (Nicholas), 1847, sail-maker on the U. S. *Independence.*   Buckbee (Flavius), 1847, Co. D, N.Y.Vol. (v. 499).

Buckelew (Benj. R.), 1846, New Yorker and overl. immig. with Hoppe and Harlan. (v. 526); kept a jewelry and watch-maker's shop at Clark's Point S. F. '47-8, being also publisher of the *Californian,* owner of many lots, and member of the town council. v. 648-9, 658, 672, 684. He was interested in several newspapers and was engaged in trade after '49. Claimant of the Pt Quintin rancho. iii. 712; and owner of part of the Nicasio rancho. Died in Marin Co. '59 at the age of 37, leaving a family.   Buckland (Alondus D. L.), 1846, of the Mormon colony with family. v. 546; one of the founders of New Hope on the Stanislaus, which he was the last to leave, settling at Stockton in '47-8, and later builder of the Buckland House in S. F.   B. (Hannah D.), 1846, mother of Alondus. v. 546; owner of S. F. lot; in Utah '84.   Buckle (Robert), 1847, Co. E, N.Y.Vol. (v. 499); owner of a lot at S. F.

Buckle (Samuel), 1821-3, Engl. sailor and laborer at Mont. '29, claiming 6 years' residence, age 28; in '33 a contractor to furnish lumber; in '40-1 described as an Engl. sawyer, age 45, and residence 19 years; naturalized in '41, when he lived at Branciforte, having been baptized as José Samuel, often called Manuel, and his name being written also Boc, Bocle, Bockel, Bokle, Bugle, and Buchel. ii. 445, 495; iii. 180. In '45 named in the Brancif. padron as a bachelor aged 50. No more is heard of him by the name of Buckle; but he seems to have been the Samuel Thompson who appears often in Larkin's books and corresp. as a lumberman at Sta Cruz from '33 to '48. The newspapers tell us how Samuel sailed for many years in search of his brother Wm, but gave up the search and settled at Mont., soon meeting his brother accidentally at Sta Cruz; but about dates and details of this strange meeting there is much confusion. Nor have I any clew to the motive of the two for using two names, Buckle and Thompson. Samuel died at the house of Chas Martin in the Sta Cruz Mts in '72.

Buckle (Wm), 1823, baptized as José Guillermo, brother of Samuel, at Mont. '29, age 25, and married; also claiming 16 years' residence in '39, when he was naturalized, having moved with his brother to Branciforte and obtained the grant of La Cabonera in '38. ii. 495; iii. 677; in '43 he signed a doc. against Graham, iv. 356, and obtained a license to build a vessel of 35 tons. In '45 he is named in the Brancif. padron as 42 years of age; wife Antonia Castro, children Guillermo b. '33, José Ant. '35, María Teresa 31, María Sebola (?) '36, Francisco '38, Guillerma '39, Josefa '40, and María Jesus '44—all b. at Branciforte. It was at his house that Henry Naile was killed in '46. v. 641. There is no later record of Buckle, but Wm Thompson appears in Larkin's accounts and other records from '33 to '47; was one of the foreigners arrested in '40; and was 2d juez at Sta Cruz in '46. He died about '59. ii. 479; iii. 409; iv. 17; v. 641. Buckler, 1845, a settler in the Sac. Val. Buckley (Newman), 1847, Co. E, Morm. Bat. (v. 469); a book agent in Springville, Utah, '82. Buckner (Thos M.), 1848, Kentuckian miner from Or.; at Spanish Dry Diggings, El Dorado Co., '82. Budington, 1843-4, mr of the *Wm C. Nye*. iv. 570; in Conn. '82. Budd (Chas K.), 1847, Co. D, N.Y.Vol. (v. 469); in Sonoma '68. Buel (Frederic), 1841, said to have visited Mont. by sea before '46. *Oakland Home Jour.*, Nov. 1, '73; said also to have served after graduation at Yale on the whaler *Braganza*. *Wood's Recoll.*, 39; and this vessel was on the coast in '41. v. 279. B. was a presbyterian clergyman, agent for the Amer. Bible Soc. on the Pac. coast for 20 years; d. at Oakland '73.

Buelna (Antonio), Mex. soldier before 1780; in the Soledad escolta, settler at S. F., holder of a rancho near Mont. before 1801. i. 499, 683, 716, 734; ii. 171; teacher at Mont. and S. José 1818-21, '29. ii. 378-9, 427, 603, 613. B. (Antonio), perhaps son of the preceding, also a soldier at one time, possibly confounded with his father or another Antonio in some records; member of the diputacion from '28. iii. 36, 41-3, 50, 63; alcalde of Mont. '31. iii. 187, 194, 212, 672; dip. again in '35-9; com. of S. José troops in Alvarado's revolt, sent to the south as comisionado '37. iii. 291, 454-5, 457, 460, 469, 481, 491, 506, 585, 692; grantee of S. Gregorio and S. Francisquito in '39. iii. 678, 713; in com. of exped. against Ind. and foreigners '39-40. iv. 22, 256. In '41 at S. José, age 50, wife Concepcion Valencia, children Juan b. '16, Concepcion '38; juez de paz at Sta Clara '41-2. iv. 683-6; but died in '42. Though somewhat prominent as shown above, B. was a very ignorant and commonplace man. B. (E.), prob. son of Ant., and claimant of S. Gregorio in '52. iii. 678. B. (Félix), resid. of S. José from '37; 2d alcalde '39, '44, '45. iii. 731; iv. 685; in '41, age 27, wife Bernarda Sepúlveda, child. Juliana and María; '46 2d juez. v. 664; sub-prefect '49; moved to Mont. '54. He furnished a *Narracion* for my use in '76. B. (Joaquin), brother of Antonio, writer of various verses; comisionado at Brancif. 1818. ii. 244-5, 390; teacher at S. José '21. ii. 603; alcalde or juez auxiliar at Brancif. '26, '32, '38-9. ii. 627, 696-7; grantee of Sayante rancho '33. iii. 679; sec. ayunt. '36. iii. 697; juez aux. at Pilarcitos, Refugio, etc. '40-2, '46. iii. 676; iv. 653; v. 637. B. (José F.), elector at S. José '43. iv. 361, 685. B. (José Ramon), grantee of Potrero y Rincon de S. Pedro '38. iii. 678; alcalde at Brancif. '45. v. 664; age 30, wife Rafaela Perez, child. Guadalupe, Matilde, and Juan. B. (Juan), at S. F. and Mont. from '26. ii. 612; in '41 at S. José, age 49, wife Ascension Bernal, child. Trinidad, Antonia M., Francisco, and Alta Gracia. B. (María Antonia), teacher at Mont. '18-24. B. (Ramon), soldier before 1780; settler at Los Ang. from '93-1819; regidor in 1802. ii. 110, 349-50, 354. Buenaventura (José), 1829, Irishman, family name not known; at Los Ang. with certif. of good character, age 47.

Buffin, 1845, possibly in the Grigsby-Ide party, but prob. went to Or. iv. 578-9. Buffum (Edward Gould), 1847, lieut Co. B, N.Y.Vol. v. 504; having been previously connected with the *N. Y. Herald*. After his discharge went to the mines in '48, and in '49-50 was a reporter on the *Alta*, serving also as sec. of various public meetings. Then he went east and published his *Six Months in the Gold Mines*, Phila, 1850. Returning to Cal. '53, he rejoined the *Alta* corps, acting at times as editor, notably during the time of the vigilance com. of '56; member of the legislature '55; went in '57 to Paris, where he wrote letters for the *Alta* and *N.Y. Herald*, and where he committed suicide in '67, at the age of about 45. He was a man of good character and abilities. Buhne (H. H.), 1847, Danish mate of the *Clementine*, who came back in '49, and from '50 was a pioneer of Humboldt Co., where he still lived in '82 with wife and 5 children, a prominent man of business. Portrait in *Humb. Co. Hist.*, 164. Bujan (Antonio), 1844, a militiaman at S. F., called Buyano, aged 25, and Mex., but he was a foreigner who came earlier, perhaps in '42, witness in the Santillan case; in later times he kept a wayside inn and saloon in Visitacion Valley, S.F., where he still is perhaps in '85.

Bull (James H.), 1844, at S. F.   Bull, 1848, mr of the *Olga*.   Bullard, 1846, owner of a Los Ang. rancho (?).   Bullen (Newell), 1846, of the Morm. col. with wife and 3 children. v. 546; owner of a S. F. lot '47. v. 680; died in Utah, where his family resided '84.   Bullock (Ezekial), 1847, Co. E, N.Y. Vol. (v. 499); at S. F. '74-82.   B. (James D.), 1848, mid. on the U. S. *Warren*.   Bultice (Vincent), 1847, Co. G, N.Y.Vol. (v. 499); died before '82.

Bund (John), 1847, Co. I, N.Y.Vol. (v. 499); at Hawkeye, Calaveras Co. '71-4.   Bunker (Benj.), 1841, gunner on the U. S. *St Louis*, and in '47 on the *Independence*.   B. (Alex.), 1822, mr of the *Ontario*. ii. 474.   B. (Edward), 1847, Co. E, Morm. Bat. (v. 469); a bishop in Utah '82.

Burch (Chas H.), 1846, claimant for supplies to Frémont (v. 462) to the extent of $39; at N. Helv. '47-8; went to Or. and ret. in '48.   Burger (Chas), German of the Donner party who died in the mts. v. 531, 534. Burgeman (Emil), 1847, Co. G, N.Y.Vol. (v. 499).   Burgess, 1846, immig. with Bryant; perhaps did not come to Cal.   B. (Edward), 1847, Co. B, N. Y.Vol., transf. to Co. G (v. 499); owner of a S. F. lot. v. 676; went to Honolulu on the *Julia* '47, ret. in '48; at Honolulu '71.   B. (Thos H.), 1845, Kentuckian immig. in the Grigsby-Ide party. iv. 578, 587; joined the Bears, with Ford at Olompali in '46. v. 167; Cal. claim of $35 (v. 462); went south with Frémont; with Gillespie at Los Ang., and at S. Pascual. v. 347, 350; at N. Helv. '47-8.   Burhell (Richard), 1846, Co. B, Cal. Bat. (v. 358), enlisting at S. José.   Burke (Jas), 1847, Co. A, N.Y.Vol.; died on the Stanislaus '51.

Burke (James W.), 1824, Irish trader from S. Amer. on the *Jóven Tartar*, who settled at Sta B. in '28, ii. 526, 573, being then 30 years old. His name —often Santiago and Walter—appears often in commercial and other records from '30; married Josefa Boronda, and in '36 had 6 children, being then regidor and an applicant for lands. iii. 426, 654. Still living at Sta B. '76, but seems to have died a year or two later.   Burkins (James), 1847, Co. F, 3d U. S. artill. (v. 518).   Burling (Joseph), 1795, Irish sailor at Sta B. desiring to remain, but sent to Spain '96. i. 538-40.

Burnett (Horace), 1848, nephew of Peter H., with whom he came from Or. and engaged in mining.   B. (Peter H.), 1848, nat. of Tenn., b. in 1807; a trader and lawyer in Tenn. and Mo.; overl. immig. to Or. in '43; farmer, member of legislature, and judge of supreme court in Or.; came to Cal. by land after the discov. of gold, and worked in the mines for a month or more in '48. In Dec. he came to N. Helv., and became agent for young Sutter in settling the captain's complicated business and the sale of town lots, thus paying off old debts and laying the foundation of a handsome fortune. His family came from Or. in May '49, and his management of Sutter's business ceased in July. He took a prominent part in public meetings to secure a state govt; went to S. F.; was made judge of the supreme court; sold half his Sacramento property for $50,000; moved to S. José; and was finally elected governor of Cal.—all before the end of '49. He was one of the luckiest men of the time. Resigning his office in Jan. '51, he devoted himself mainly to the management of his private business, practising law to a limited extent, residing at S. José except in '52-3 at Sac. and several long visits to the east. He was judge of the supreme court in '57-8; in '60 published *The Path Which*

Led a Protestant Lawyer to the Catholic Church; and from '63 was president of the Pacific Bank at S. F. His *Recollections*, in MS., were copied for my Library in '78 and published in '80. Still living in '85, possessing great wealth and a good reputation. Burnett has never been credited with any brilliant abilities, nor charged with any great weakness; lacking force and decision in official positions; an honest, industrious, kind-hearted, diplomatic, lucky man; of many but harmless whims in private life. His wife died in '58; but he has several sons and a married daughter.

Burnie, 1829, mr of the *Ann.* iii. 146.   Burns (Daniel M.), 1840 (?), sec. of state in '80; native of Tenn., age 49 in '79; said in newspaper sketches to have come to Cal. at the age of 10. iv. 120; his name is in a list of letters at S. F. in '48.   B. (James), 1840, in Farnham's list of arrested foreigners. B. (John), 1830, Amer. at S. Miguel. iii. 180; joined the comp. extranjera in '32. iii. 221; was perhaps the John Byrnes on Larkin's books '34.   B. (P. T.), 1847, in Sutter's employ at N. Helv.   B. (Wm), 1839, Engl. who came with Sutter. iv. 119, 138; in '40 he asked for a pass to quit N. Helv. and settle at Sta Cruz; in Farnham's list of arrested foreigners. iv. 17.   Burques (Pedro), soldier at the Colorado Riv. pueblos 1780–1, killed by Ind. i. 359, 362.

Burr (Chas C.), 1846, of the Morm. colony with wife and child, one child having died at sea. v. 546; owner of S. F. lot '47. v. 678; in Utah '84.   B. (Nathan), 1846, of the Morm. col. with wife, father of Chas. C.; died in Utah before '84. v. 546.   Burrell (Chas), 1846, sailor on the U. S. *Dale*, long a resident of S. F. in later years.   B. (Cuthbert), 1846, at Gilroy '78.

Burroughs (Chas) 1846, apparently an immig. of this year; prominent in raising men for the Cal. Bat., in which he seems to have ranked as captain— or perhaps was to have been made captain. Chief in com. at the fight of Natividad, where he was killed in Nov. v. 360, 363–71. Beyond the part that he took in this affair, and his general reputation as a brave and popular man, though a gambler, nothing seems to be known of him. His name is often written Burus and Burrows, and it is not sure that his name was Charles or that he came in '46.   B.—or Borris—(Wm), Amer. doctor at Sta B. 1823–4. ii. 495, 576.   Burrows, 1841, from Or. with wife and child in Emmon's party of the U.S. ex. exped. iv. 278.

Burt, 1846, doubtful name of a man captured with Weber by Castro. v. 136; probably 'Bird,' q. v.   B. (Wm), 1847, Co.C, Morm. Bat. (v. 469).   Burton (E. F.), 1848, memb. of N.Y. territorial pioneers '78. *Upham's Notes.*

Burton (Henry S.), 1847, lieut-col N.Y. Vol., and for a time in com. at Sta B. v. 503, 511, 513, 630–1; in com. of the exped. to La Paz '47–8. v. 583. He was a graduate of West Point and lieut of Co. F, 3d artill., of which he took com. as capt. on the mustering-out of the regt. v. 515, 520. He remained several years in Cal., and was collector of customs at Mont. '48–9. He was promoted to major in '61, and in '65 to brevet brigadier-gen., dying in R.I. '69. His wife, who survived him with two children, was Doña Amparo Ruiz of Lower Cal., whose father and grandfather were prominent in the early annals of the peninsula, and who has gained some literary as well as social distinction.   Burton (B.), 1847, lieut who raised and commanded a volunteer cavalry comp. at Mont. in April. v. 449, 521, 636. I am unable to say who he was.   B. (James), J. B. & Co. ment. at Mont. in connection with naval stores.   B. (James C.), 1847, Co. E, N.Y. Vol. (v. 499).

Burton (John), 1825 (?), Amer., who at S. José in '29 claimed to have come as master of the *Juan Battey*, lost at S. Diego, and to have been 3 years and 5 months in Cal.; a native of Provincetown, who left home in '22; then 40 years old. iii. 29, 147. In '30 a farmer, also engaged in trade. ii. 602; generally said to have arrived in '30; married in '31 Juana Galindo; often named in various records from this time; regidor of S. José '37. iii. 730; arrested in '40 as a formality, but not exiled. In '41, age 48, children José Miguel, Juan, and Silveria; witness of Naile's murder. iv. 686; signer of the call to foreigners in '45. iv. 599; alcalde in '46–7. v. 662. I have no later record of him; perhaps died in '48.   B. (John B.), 1840, Amer. mechanic who came on the *Cervantes* to

Mont. B. (Joseph), 1848, Boston man age 30, who came from Honolulu in Aug. and died at S.F. in Oct.

Burton (Lewis T.), 1831, Tennesseean from N. Mex. with the Wolfskill party. v. 386, 405; settling at Sta B., and engaging in otter-hunting, trade, and finally farming. iv. 117. In '36 he described himself as a catholic bachelor, 24 years old, in business with Branch; in '39 he married María Antonia, daughter of Cárlos Carrillo; naturalized in '42. Larkin gave him a high character in his *Notes* of '45; and he had a Cal. claim of $400 in '46 (v. 462), 304. He became a wealthy merchant and ranchero; claimant for the Jesus María and Chamizal ranchos. v. 655, 677; and died at Sta B. in '79. A second wife was the daughter of José Ant. Carrillo.

Bush (Richard), 1847, Co. B, Morm. Bat. (v. 469).   Bushane (Leandro), 1847, Helv., formerly a corporal at the fort, and apparently an Ind.; Otith B. also died.   Bustamante y Guerra (José), 1791, com. of the *Atrevida* in Malaspina's exped. i. 490.   Buten (Wm), 1845, doubtful name of an Amer. in a Branciforte padron, age 37.   Butler, 1846, bugler in Cal. Bat. v. 374.   Butler (Amos), 1847, at S. F. from Astoria on the *Henry;* in list of letters '48.   B. (Nathaniel), 1847, at Mont. July.

Butron (Felipe), named in '40 in connection with the Graham affair. iv. 6; leader in a proposed attack on Mont. '45. iv. 515, being then a capt. of aux. cavalry; in '46 a lieut in the Cal. Bat. v. 360; in '47 lieut in an exped. against Ind. v. 662.   B. (Juan de Dios), soldier in Mont. comp. '36, age 31.   B. (Manuel), soldier of Mont. comp. 1775, married to a neophyte, and the 1st grantee of land. i. 311, 608, 610, 683; a settler at S. José 1786. i. 477.   B. (Manuel), prob. son of preceding, grantee of Alisal '28, and of Natividad '30, '37. ii. 616, 664, 677; in '36 living at Natividad, age 58, wife María Ignacia Higuera, children Josefa b. 1806, Nicolás '21, Ramona '21, Manuel '24.   B. (Ramon), son of Manuel, claimant for Natividad. iii. 677.   B. (Sebastian), settler before 1800; in '41 at S. José, age 61.

Butterfield (Jacob K.), 1847, Co. A, Morm. Bat. (v. 469); at Taylorville, Utah, '81.   Butters (Thomas), 1841, Engl. sailor disch. from the *Leonor;* Bidwell mentions a Thos Battus at Bodega about the same time.   Button (Montgomery), 1847, Co. D, Morm. Bat.

Buzzell (Joseph Willard), 1841 (?), deserter from the whaler *Orizaba* at Halfmoon Bay, spending some time with Graham at Sta Cruz, later a trapper at N. Helv., till he went to Or. in '43, where he married—apparently one of the Kelsey family. This is his own statement in newspaper sketches. iv. 279. In '44 he came from Or. in the Kelsey party. v. 444; served Sutter in the Micheltorena campaign; signed the call to foreigners at S. José '45. iv. 599; and worked for Leidesdorff at S. F. His name often appears in the *N. Helv. Diary,* and occasionally in records of Mont. and S. José. A daughter Ellen is said to have been born at N. Helv. '45. In '46-7 B. served in the Cal. Bat. (v. 358), under Frémont, Gillespie, Mervine, and Stockton in the south. Returning he went to Stockton with Weber, acquiring land on which the town stood later, and building a cabin. *Tinkham, Carson,* etc. A son was born '47. *S. J. Pion.* His name appears at Sutter's fort '47-8; daughter Lizzie Agnes born at Stockton, Sept. '48. Still living in '60; acc. to *Yolo Co. Hist.* drowned at Halfmoon Bay a few years before '79.

Bybee (Henry G.), 1847, Co. C, Morm. Bat. (v. 469).   B. (John), 1847, ditto.   Byers, 1847, at Honolulu from Mont. on the *María Helena.*   B. (Josiah Stoddart), 1846, applicant for land at S. José; a mid. on the U. S. *Congress. Sta Clara Co. Hist.*, 331.   Byrens (Allen T.), 1846, mid. on the U. S. *Dale*, at S. José, Dec.   Byrnes (Ed.), 1834, Irish. in Mont. list.   B. (Wm), 1848, at Honolulu from S. F.; declined to serve as alcalde at S. José. v. 662.

Caamaño (Jacinto), 1792, Span. com. of the *Aranzazu*, engaged in northern coast explor. i. 509–11; *Hist. N. W.C.*, i. 267 et seq.; com. of the *Princesa* in 1797 and of the *Concepcion* 1798. i. 540, 543–4.   Caatrell (John), 1846, doubtful name in a Los Ang. list.   Caballer, see 'Cavaller.'

Caballero (Andrés A.), 1781, lieut of the escort to Cal. and return to

Sonora. i. 342.   C. (Felix), 1833, Dominican friar of L. Cal.; a famous missionary of the frontier, who crossed the line to Cal. '23, '29, '33, and doubtless on other occasions. ii. 486, 507; iii. 96, 557.   C. (Francisco), Sta B. ranchero '45.   C. (María Antonia), grantee of Sisquoc in '33. iii. 656.   Cabello (Martin S.), 1834, Mex. revenue officer with the H. & P. colony; receptor in charge of S. Diego custom-house '34–8; prob. left Cal. about '38. iii. 267, 377, 499–501, 609, 613; iv. 98; Cabiner, 1846, mr of the *Isaac Howland*.

Cabot (Juan), 1805, Span. friar who served for 30 years in Cal., chiefly at S. Miguel, retiring to his college in 1835. Biog. in iii. 683–4; ment. i. list auth.; ii. 123, 149, 159–60, 325, 327, 331, 375, 384–6, 393, 536, 620, 622, 655; iii. 92, 96, 169, 309.   C. (Miguel), 1836, nephew of the two friars, who came to Cal. to receive the stipend due Fr. Pedro after his death.   C. (Pedro), 1804, Span. friar, brother of Juan, who served 32 years in Cal., chiefly at S. Antonio, dying at S. Fernando '36. Biog. iii. 645–6; ment. ii. 152, 159–60, 385, 394, 621–3, 655; iii. 92, 96, 418, 686.   Cabott (F.), 1848, passp. from Honolulu.   Cabrera (Agapito), at Sta Inés college '44. iv. 426.   C. (Pedro), Peruvian, juez de policía at Los Ang. '47. v. 626.

Cabrillo (Juan Rodriguez), 1542, Portuguese discoverer of Cal., who died at the Sta B. islands in Jan. 1543. See full account of the voy. of exploration. i. 69–81; also *Hist. N. Mex. States*, i. 133.

Cace (Henry P.), 1845, nat. of R. I. at Mont; perhaps 'Case.'   Cáceres (Francisco), Span. ex-sergt of dragoons, who was regidor at Mont. in '28–29. ii. 612; iii. 51, 53; and in '31 the only Span. in S. F. district. iii. 399, 699. He is named as a resid. and house-owner of S.F. from '38, being síndico in '39. iii. 705; v. 684. He died at Freestone in '48 at the age of 76. His wife was Anastasia Boronda who died in '49. The children were Antonia, Francisco, Cármen, Guadalupe Antonio, Julian, Rafaela, Ciro, Helena, and Teresa; all dead before '85 except Ciro and Francisco. The latter is named in a Sonoma list of '44 as 18 years old. The daughter Antonia married James Dawson '40, and Dr Fred. Blume in '49, dying in '80 without children. She was the grantee and claimant of Pogolomi rancho. iv. 672.   Cacho (Rafael), grantee of S. Gerónimo rancho '44. iv. 673.

Cade (Jonathan), 1846, of the Mormon col. with wife. v. 546; perhaps his name was Kincaid; sergt-at-arms in S. F. council '49; but died in Utah. Cadel—or Kadel—(Peter), 1846, said to have arrived in July; at N. Helv. from S. Rafael and Sonoma '47–8; lot-owner S.F. '47; died at Oakland '75, age 61.   C. (Tobias), 1847, lot at S. F.; at N. Helv. '48.   Cadena (Antonio), 1836, Mex. corporal in Hidalgo bat. at Mont. age 30; tried for murder. iii. 675.   Cady (Chas L.), 1845 (?), said to have been in Lake Co. as a hunter, being also there in '75. *Lakeport Bee;* iv. 587; in '46–7 member of the 2d Donner relief. v. 539; estab. a mail service July '47 bet. S. F. and Sac. via Sauzalito and Sonoma. *Californian,* July 24th; kept a store at Coloma with Shannon '48–9. *El Dorado Co. Hist.*, 177.   Cahill (Martin), 1847, Co. A, N.Y. Vol. (v. 499); at Stockton '71–82.

Calder (Lawson M.), 1847, Co. E, N.Y.Vol. (v. 499).   Caldwell (Arthur S. C.), 1846, overl. immig. in Young's party with family. v. 529; wife Margaret, son, and three daughters; in Cal. Bat., enlisting at Mont. Nov. (v. 358); bought a house at S. José '48. *Pico, Doc.*, i. 140; named as a wealthy citizen in '60.   C. (Colohill), 1846, Cal. Bat., enlisting at S. Juan; Cal. claim of $6 (v. 462); prob. son of preceding, or possibly the same.   C. (Matthew), 1847, Co. E, Morm. Bat. (v. 469); Utah farmer '82.   Calheart (Seth), 1827, mr of the *Massachusetts*. iii. 148.   Calkin (Milo), 1846, house lately occupied by him rented to another Jan. '47.   Calkins (Ed R.), 1847, Co. A, Morm. Bat. (v. 469); reënl. at Los Ang.   C. (Sylvanus), 1847, Co. A, Morm. Bat.

Call (Daniel), 1816, Amer. carpenter, age 17, who landed from the *Atala* at Sta B., where in '36 he had a wife and two children. ii. 248, 282, 393. Callaghan, 1846, three brothers in the Los Ang. region. iv. 495; their names as signed to a doc. of June '46 seem to be 'Ein,' 'Epli,' and 'Geral,' but it appears that 2 of them were Evan and Isaac. They served under Gillespie, and were among the chino prisoners. v. 314; in '47 one was in charge of S. Buen.

mission, being juez de paz in '48. v. 634: and another had some petty position at S. Pedro. Acc. to B. D. Wilson, Evan C. came to Cal. in '44.   C. (James), 1847, drowned at S. F.'51; said to have been one of the N.Y.Vol., but not on the rolls.   C. (John), 1847, lot-owner at S. F.; still there '50.   Callahan (Carolus B.), 1846, Co. C, 1st U. S. dragoons (v. 336).   C. (Thos W.), 1847, Co. B, Morm. Bat. (v. 460); reënl. at Los Ang.   Callegan, 1769, com. of the *S. José*, lost on the voy. to Cal. i. 124.   Callender (Mills L.), 1847, Co. K, N.Y.Vol.; lots at S. F. '47-8. v. 679; sec. of town council '48; still there '52-4; d. Brooklyn, N. Y., '71 (?).   Callis (Eulalia), 1783, wife of Gov. Pedro Fages. i. 389-93, 487.

Calvin (Vincent), 1844, overl. immig. of Stevens party. iv. 445; at N. Helv. and S. José '45-8.   Calzada (José Ant.), 1787, Span. friar who served 27 years in Cal., being founder of Sta Inés, where he died 1814. Biog. ii. 368; ment. i. 388, 459, 575, 577, 664-5; ii. 28-9, 123, 159, 394.   Calzado (Dionisio), at Branciforte 1803. ii. 156.   Calzado (José), 1798. i. 606.

Cam (Isidro), 1830, New Yorker, age 26, whose only known exploit was to fight with Leandry about a dog, for which he served a month in the chain-gang at Mont.   Camacho, com. of transport vessel 1783-90. i. 444.   C., killed at Jamul '37. iii. 614.   C. (Anastasio), soldier at S. Diego 1775. i. 255. C. (Tomás M.), soldier killed on the Colorado by Ind. 1781. i. 363.   Camareno (Nicolás), settler at S. F. 1791-1800. i. 716.   Camarrillo (Juan), 1834, Mex. who came prob. with the H. & P. col. (iii. 259); trader at Sta B., where he was síndico and juez at different times '40-6. iii. 655; iv. 490, 631, 642; moved to S. Buen. '59, where he became owner of the Calleguas rancho. He died '80, at the age of 68; his wife was Martina Hernandez, married in '40; and he left 7 children, one of his daughters being the wife of José Arnaz. Portrait in *Sta B. Co. Hist.*, 392.

Cambon (Pedro Benito), 1779, Span. friar who served chiefly at S. F., but was founder of S. Gabriel and S. Buen., retiring to his college '91. Biog. i. 712; ment. i. 173, 176, 179-81, 187-9, 193-4, 265-6, 246, 255, 271, 287, 289-90. 292, 297, 329-30, 352, 373, 376, 378, 382, 388, 399, 469, 473, 575-6.   Cambuston (Henri), 1841, Frenchman from Mex., who became a teacher at Mont. iv. 279; married Gabriela Soberanes; fined for smuggling '44. iv. 566; quarrel at Mont. with Prefect Castro '46. v. 34; at the military junta. v. 61; grantee of land in Butte Co. v. 675. A man of some ability, but often in trouble on acct of intemperate habits; witness in the Limantour case; sent to the Stockton insane asylum about '56, where he died 4 or 5 years later.   Camero (Manuel), 1781, mulatto settler at Los Ang.; regidor in '89. i. 348-9, 461. Cameron, 1848, at Sutter's Fort.   C. (James),.1845, doubtful record of an overl. immig. iv. 578.   C. (John), 1847, Co. C, N.Y.Vol. (v. 499).   C. (John), real name of John 'Gilroy,' q.v.

Camp, 1837, of the Willamette cattle comp. iv. 85.   C. (J. G.), 1847, Co. B, Morm. Bat. (v. 469).   Campa y Cos (Miguel), 1775, Span friar of L. Cal. 1769-73, who was chaplain of Heceta's exped. at Mont. and on the north coast '75. i. 122-3, 194, 235, 240-2, 247.

Campbell, 1806, otter-hunter. ii. 40-1.   C. (Anthony), 1840, Engl. sailor disch. from the *Fly* at S. F., and killed by Ind. near Sta Clara on his way to Mont. April '41. iv. 120, 280, 684, 686.   C. (Benj.), 1846, Kentuckian settler at Sta Clara, building a saw-mill on Campbell's Creek in '47-8; still living in '76.   C. (Colin), 1840, Scotch sailor at Mont. iv. 120; presbyterian sawyer at Aptos '41-2.   C. (James), 1846, sailor of the *Congress* in Stockton's bat., wounded at the Mesa Jan. '47. v. 395.   C. (James T.), 1847, Co. E, N.Y.Vol. (v. 499); d. S. F. '53.   C. (John G.), 1844, one of Frémont's men; also in '45; Cal. Bat. Co. A. iv. 437, 583.   C. (Jonathan), 1847, Co. E, Morm. Bat. (v. 469).   C. (Patrick), 1846, sailor on the *Cyane*, in Stockton's bat., wounded at S. Gabriel Jan. '47. v. 395.   C. (Joseph T.), 1846, Co. C, 1st U. S. dragoons, killed at S. Pascual. v. 346.   C. (Peter), 1847, Co. H, N.Y.Vol. C. (Richard), 1827, said to have come from N. Orleans to S. Diego. iii. 162. C. (Reuben P.), 1848, lieut of Graham's dragoons. v. 522.   C. (Samuel), 1833 (?), accredited to this year by the newspapers, and said to have been a

rich merchant of S. F.; d. Red Bluff '70. iii. 409.   C. (Samuel), 1847, Co. E,
Morm. Bat. (v. 469).   C. (Thomas), 1846, Kentuckian overl. immig. from
Mo. with his wife and her parents and brothers named West. v. 528. Known
as Major C. on the trip; one of Burroughs' men at Natividad (v. 363); and
went south with the Cal. Bat.; surveyor at S. José, and member of the council
'47. v. 664; in the mines '48-9; later resid. of S. José to '77 and later.   C.
(Wm), 1842, said to have been killed. iv. 686.   C. (Wm), 1846, apparently
overl. immig. and perhaps a brother of Thomas; came to S. José with his
family; surveyor '47. v. 664. In Tulare '83, age 90, veteran of 1812 and battle
of N. Orleans; 2 sons.   C. (Wm), 1847, Co. K, N.Y.Vol. (v. 499); deserted,
and was hanged in Dec. '48 at S. José for robbery and attempted murder. v.
663-4.   C. (Wm), 1848, overl. with Lawton and Johnson; editor of *Sierra
Democrat* and clerk of legislature '56; county judge of Sierra to '63; district
attorney at Virginia City, dying '76. *Nevada Transcript*, Jan. 28, '76.   Campo,
see 'Fernandez' del C. and 'Perez' del C.

Cané (Vicente), 1825, Span. sailor landing from the *Asia* at Mont. iii. 51,
92-3; permitted to remain and marry in '28; grantee of S. Bernardo rancho
'40; admin. and juez at S. Luis Ob. '40-1. v. 657, 683.   Canedo (Dolores),
at Los Ang. '46.   C. (Gerónimo), settler at Los Ang. 1812. ii. 350.   C.
(José), soldier and corp. '23-4. ii. 555-6.   C. (José), soldier at Sta B. '32,
wife Luisa Valenzuela.   C. (José), at S. Juan Cap., age 58, wife María,
children Antonia b. '26, Felipe '28, Juliana '31, Juan '37, Leonardo '43.   C.
(José María), at S. Juan Cap. '41-6. iv. 626; age 36, wife Feliciana.   C.
(Juan), at Los Ang. '46.   C. (Juan N.), at S. Juan Cap. '41. iv. 626.   C.
(Manuel), soldier killed on the Colorado. i. 363.   C. (Rafael), at Los Ang.
'46.   C. (Silvestre), ditto.   Cañete (Joaquin), sent to escort Gov. Fages'
wife to Cal. 1783. i. 390.

Canfield (Cyrus C.), 1847, lieut Co. D, Morm. Bat. v. 477; also lieut of the
reënl. men. v. 495; collector of the port of S. D. '48. v. 619; acquitted on trial
for passing counterfeit money. v. 610-11.   C. (Geo. W.), 1847, Co. E, N.Y.
Vol. (v. 499); at Phil. '82.   C. (O. F.), 1847, in Sonoma Co. '50-77. *Sonoma
Co. Hist.*, 102.   Canian (Wm), 1832, doubtful name of a mr of the *California*.
Cañizares (José), 1769, pilotin who kept a diary of Rivera's exped. to Cal.;
com. of *S. Antonio* '74, of *S. Cárlos* '76, being an explorer of S.F. bay and
planner of the presidio; again at Mont. '84; com. of *Aranzazu* '89. i. 132, 136,
208, 225, 246, 287, 289, 329, 410-11, 438, 441, 444.   Cann (Dan. M.), 1847,
Co. F, 3d artill. (v. 518). *Lancey*, not on roll.   Cannell (John), 1847, lot at
S.F.   Cannifax (Abstrum R.), 1847, contractor at mission S. José to make
shingles for Larkin.   Cannon (Manena), 1846, one of the Mormons, who prob.
did not come to Cal. v. 547.   Cano (Gil.), com. de policía at Mont. '36. iii.
675; Mex., age 23, wife Josefa Soto, children Rafael, María, Luisa, Nicolás.

Cantan (Gustavus A.), 1847, lot at S.F.   Cantua (Dolores), soldier of S.F.
comp. '19-27; ment. in '18. ii. 232.   C. (Guadalupe), in '36 at the Guadalupe
rancho, Mont. district, age 51, wife Cármen Castro, children Josefa b. '18,
Gracia '29, Ramon '31, Ramona '33; majordomo and juez de campo '35-6; in
'41 grantee of S. Luisito near S. Luis Ob. iii. 674-7; iv. 656.   C. (Ignacio),
settler at S.F. 1791-1800. i. 716.   C. (Juan Ign.), son of Vicente, wounded
at the Natividad fight '46. v. 367.   C. (Julian), at S. Isidro rancho '36, age
40, wife Isabel Ortega, child. Manuel b. '16, Manuela '20, Faustina '22.   C.
(Manuel), soldier of S.F. comp. '32-9; at Sonoma '44, age 25; in Sutter's service '45; militia alférez killed at Olompali '46. v. 166.   C. (Manuel), son of
Julian, at S. José '50.   C. (Manuel), at Los Ang. '46; connected with the
Flores revolt, a good judge of aguardiente, nicknamed 'governor' for a time.
v. 308, 331.   C. (Pablo), soldier of S.F. comp. at Sonoma '42.   C. (Vicente),
majordomo at Patrocinio (Alisal), '36, age 45, wife Juana Soto, child. Juan
Ign. b. '28, Juan María '31, María Ant. '33, Cármen '36; juez de campo and
auxiliar '35, '39, '41. iii. 674-5; iv. 653; grantee of rancho nacional '39. iii.
677; admin. Soledad '39-40. iii. 691; Cal. claim (v. 462) of $3,661 in '46; still
in Mont. dist. '50.   Cantwell (Thos), 1847, in S. Diego district.   Caples
(James), 1847, roll of the Soc. Cal. Pion.

Carabajal (Rafael), at Los Ang. '48.   Carabanas (Nicolás), corp. of the S. Juan Cap. escolta 1776. i. 303.   Carabantes (Agustin), settler at Los Ang. 1807. ii. 350.   C. (Salvador), at Sta B. 1797.   Carbajal, surg. of the *Princesa*, 1786. i. 397.   C. (Josefa), wife of Surgeon Dávila, d. S.F. 1780. i. 468. Carbit (Thos), 1847, said to have come with the N.Y. Vol., but not on the roll; d. Oregon City, Cal. '61, age 35. *S. F. Herald.*

Card (Geo. H.), 1840, nat. of R. I., mate of a trader—probably the *Alert*— on the coast '40-2; returned in '48; wrote newspaper articles on his Cal. experiences; d. at Stockton after '68, age 74. iv. 120, 136.   Cárdenas (José), 1825, officer of the *Asia;* mr of the *Rover* '26. iii. 25-6, 120.   C. (Melchor), sirviente at S.F. 1777. i. 297.   Cardwell (Henry), 1848, sheriff at Los Ang. v. 626; perhaps same as following.   C. (Herman C.), 1844, nat. of Vt (or Va), who came to Cal. on a whaler, settling at Los Ang. perhaps in '46; in Cal. Bat. (v. 358), having a Cal. claim (v. 462) under name of H. H. C.; in the mines '48-9; memb. of 1st legisl. '49-50; seriously injured in '50 by a fall from his horse; d. at Los Ang. '59. I find little about him except in newspaper sketches.   Cariaga (Saturnino), grantee of Real de las Águilas '44. iv. 655. Carl (John), 1847, at S. Buen.   Carlon, soldier killed in 1790. i. 465.   C. (José), inválido at Sta B. '32.   C. (Seferino), soldier of Sta B. comp.; grantee of Arroyo Grande rancho '41. iv. 655; one of this family was the wife of F. Z. Branch.   Cárlos, neophyte leader of rebels at S. Diego 1775-6. i. 253, 266.   Carlton, 1848 (?), later a judge in Tuolumne Co.; d. '55.   Carlton (W. H.), 1848, clerk for A. J. Grayson, S.F.   Cármen (José del), Ind. chief killed '44. iv. 409.

Carmichael (Lawrence), 1833, Scotch trapper from N. Mex., who went to Or. '34 with Young and Kelley. iii. 388, 400; returned to drive a band of cattle to the Willamette '37. iv. 85; and again came back on the *Nereid* via Honolulu '38. iv. 105; and settled at S. José. He was one of the exiles of '40, but returned in '41 with a pass and a claim for $7,000 damages for interrupted business. iv. 18, 32-3, 116. His name often appears in the records from '41; in '45 one of the party capturing Prefect Castro. iv. 487; in July '46 had trouble with Henry Naile about a house; in Aug. sec. of the juez at Sta Cruz. v. 641; and later in '46 shot by a party of Mex. for the alleged reason that he was bearer of despatches for the Amer., but very little is known of this affair, of which I find no contemporary record.

Carnes (Henry S.), 1847, lieut Co. F, N.Y. Vol. v. 504; collector of the port of Sta B. '48. v. 575; later a member of the legisl., district judge, and postmaster at Sta B., where he lived in '79; at S. Buen. '82.   C. (Thos), 1847, Co. B, N.Y. Vol. (v. 499); drowned at Stockton '51.   Carnicer (Baltasar), 1797, Span, friar who served chiefly at S. Cárlos and retired in 1808. Biog. ii. 147; ment. i. 500, 561, 577, 686; ii. 7, 149, 159-60.

Carpenter (Benj.), 1845, Amer. immig. from Or. in the McMahon-Clyman party; prob. went back to Or. '46. iv. 572, 576.   C. (Chas R.), 1847, Co. F, N.Y. Vol. (v. 499); died in Cuba '60.   C. (Isaac), 1847, Co. C, Morm. Bat. (v. 469).   C. (John), 1845, named as a captive exchanged for Manuel Castro. iv. 487, doubtful.   C. (Lemuel or Samuel), 1832, Amer. from N. Mex. iii. 388, 408; accredited to '31 and '33 in two lists of '36; prob. came in winter of '32-3; 22 years old in '36, 28 in '40; had a soap-factory on the S. Gabriel River and a vineyard in co. with Chard; one of the vigilantes '36, and not arrested '40; served '45 against Micheltorena. iv. 495; in '48 had an orchard near S. Buen. Claimant for Sta Gertrudis '53. iii. 634; where on account of financial troubles he committed suicide in '59.   C. (Roman), 1840, named on Larkin's books; perhaps the 'Roman carpenter' or 'Roman the carpenter.'   C. (Wm), 1841, doubtful record at Los Ang.   C. (Wm M.), 1848, physician at N. Helv., room-mate of P. H. Burnett.   Carpentier, memb. of legisl. '55, accredited to '48 in the *Chart.*

Carr (Overton), 1841, lieut U. S. ex. exped. iv. 241, 567.   C. (Griffith), 1846, Co. F, Cal. Bat. (v. 358), enlisting at Sonoma.   C. (Stephen), 1847, Co. A, N.Y. Vol. (v. 499); d. Stanislaus Co. '49.   Carranza (Domingo), 1798, Span, friar, who served at Sta Cruz and S. Luis Rey, retiring in 1810. Biog. ii. 108;

ment. i. 408, 577; ii. 154–5, 159–60, 197.   Carrasco (José M.), Sonoran at Mont. '36, age 39, single; at Mont. and other places to '47.   C. (Juan), 1791, com. schr *Horcasitas*. i. 493.   C. (Juan), nat. of Buenos Aires, insane, found dead at Arroyo Mocho '38. iii. 732.   Carreaga (Saturnino), 1845, juez at S. Juan B. iv. 662; see 'Cariaga,' prob. the same man.

Carrigan (Thos), 1847, Co. H, N.Y.Vol. (v. 499).   Carriger (Daniel S.), 1846, Cal. Bat. (v. 358), enlisting at Sonoma.   C. (Nicholas), 1846, Tennesseean immig. from Mo. with family. v. 528; his father died and a daughter was born on the journey. He served in the Sonoma garrison and as mail-carrier from Sonora to S. Rafael during the war; a miner in '48–9; farmer at Sonoma from '50, where he still lived in '80, aged 64, with 9 living children. I obtained from him a brief *Autobiography;* portrait in *Sonoma Co. Hist.*, 312; a son, Dav. W., was born in '47.   Carrillo, sirviente at Sta Cruz 1795. i. 496.

Carrillo (Anastasio), son of José Raim., b. at Sta B. 1788; sergt distinguido of the Sta B. comp., named in connection with many Ind. exped., etc. 1818–30. ii. 235, 334, 361, 528–9, 561, 572; iii. 78, 103; comisionado in charge of Los Ang. '18–25. ii. 350, 559; member of the dip. '27–8; habilitado '27, '29–34. ii. 572; iii. 36–42, 63; '31–6 alférez of the comp. iii. 650–1, 281; in '32 his family consisted of his wife Concepcion García and child. Micaela, Manuela, Soledad, Francisco, and Luis; his other sons being Guillermo and Raimundo; commisionado to secularize Sta B. '34. iii. 346, 657; in '36 retired from the army on full pay; in '37 com. to treat with Alvarado, majordomo at S. Fernando, grantee of Pt Concepcion. iii. 519, 647, 655; '38 comisario sub. at Sta B. 549, 651; memb. of dip. '39–40. iii. 590; grantee of Cieneguita '45. iv. 642; sub-prefect '45–6. iv. 631, 641. Thus it will be seen that Don Anastasio was a prominent man of Sta B., where he still lived after '50.

Carrillo (Cárlos Antonio de Jesus), son of José Raimundo, b. at Sta B. 1783; soldier in the Mont. comp. from 1797, and soldado distinguido from '99; named as clerk in a murder trial 1806. ii. 191; sergt of the Sta B. comp. from '11 to about '25, taking an active part in defensive operations against Bouchard in '18 and the rebel Ind. in '24. ii. 236–7, 275–6, 361, 363, 492, 534, 537, 572. Quitting the military service, Don Cárlos was partido elector in '27, and memb. of the dip. '28. iii. 33, 41, 140, 572; being in '30 elected member of congress for '31–2, and working earnestly in Mex., if we may judge by his own corresp., for the interests of his country. iii. 50, 214, 232–5, 260, 311–13, 319, 398. He worked particularly in favor of the missions, drawing his inspiration from Capt. de la Guerra; and also in the interest of Californian as against Mex. officers. One of his speeches, the *Exposicion sobre el Fondo Piadoso*, was the first production of a native Californian printed in book form. Back in Cal., he was grantee of the Sespe rancho '33, was memb. of the dip. '34–5, and was made comisionado for the secularization of S. Buen. in '36. iii. 246, 249–50, 258, 342, 353, 421, 488, 549, 656, 660–1; iv. 46. He was a warm supporter of Alvarado's revolutionary govt in '36, and not as has been often said a leader of the southern opposition. iii. 490–2. In '37, however, his brother obtained for him in Mex. an appointment as gov.; and Don Cárlos, making Los Ang. his capital, strove ineffectually in '37–8 to assume the governorship, which Alvarado very properly refused to surrender. This interesting but somewhat ridiculous episode of Cal. history, with its attendant military campaigns, is fully recorded in iii. 534–81, 594, 612, 614, 631, 699; iv. 47, 81, 89. In '43–5 he was member of the junta, and in '45 grantee of Sta Rosa Island. iv. 157, 361, 495–6, 521, 547, 643; Cal. claim of $14,000 '46–7. v. 467; memb. of the Sta B. ayunt. '49. Carrillo died in '52 at the age of 69. In person Don Cárlos Antonio, like most of his brothers and cousins, was large and of magnificent presence; distinguished for his courteous and gentlemanly manners. In all Cal. there was no more kind-hearted, generous, popular, and inoffensive citizen than he. For public life he was much too timid and irresolute; as congressman he was but the mouth-piece of his brother-in-law Capt. de la Guerra; as politician and aspirant for the governorship he was the softest of wax in the hands of his astute brother José Antonio; as military leader in the burlesque child's-play warfare of '38 he cut but a sorry figure; yet everybody understood his character and he had no enemies. His wife was Josefa Castro, who died in '53; his sons José, Pedro C., and José Jesus; his daughters Josefa wife of Wm G. Dana, Encarnacion wife of Thos Robbins, Francisca wife of A. B. Thompson, Manuela wife of John C. Jones, and Antonia wife of Lewis Burton.   Carrillo (Dolores), at Sonoma, age 20, in '44.

Carrillo (Domingo Antonio Ignacio), son of José Raimundo, b. at S. Diego 1791; soldado distinguido in S. Diego comp. from 1807; cadet from 1809; prosecutor in a case of '11. ii. 341, 345. In '18 he had left the service, and Capt. de la Guerra wished to send him to Mex. for a few years; but failing in this had him restored as sold. disting. of the Sta B. comp., and in '21 he was transf. as cadet to S. Diego. Ment. in '24–9 at S. D., sometimes as revenue col. and habilitado, promoted to alférez in '27. ii. 536, 543, 547, 572; iii. 41, 134, 141. In '30 he was transf. to Sta B., where he was elector, acting com., and a supporter of Victoria. ii. 572; iii. 50, 99, 223; in '34 prom. to lieut, admin. of Purísima, and grantee of Las Vírgenes. iii. 346, 349, 634-5, 650–1, 665–6. In '36 com. at Sta B., and though having trouble with Gov. Chico, opposed Alvarado unlike other Barbareños, and was removed from the com.; but in '38 he opposed Carrillo. iii. 422, 436, 485, 503, 565. I find no record of Don Domingo after '37, and cannot give the date of his death. His wife, married in 1810, was Concepcion, sister of Pio Pico; his sons Joaquin, José Antonio, Francisco, Alejandro, and Felipe; daughters María wife of José M. Covarrubias, Angela wife of Ignacio del Valle, and Antonia. His widow in '78 gave me a small col. of *Doc. Hist. Cal.*, remnant of the family archives, including no less a paper than the original treaty of Cahuenga.   C. (Francisco), son of Anastasio, who died young.   C. (Francisco), son of Domingo; married Dorotea Lugo.   C. (Guillermo), 1769, corporal of the S. D. comp., and later sergt; died in 1782. i. 301–2, 314, 452. I do not know that he left any descendants.   C. (Guillermo), son of Anastasio; married Manuela Ortega; still living in '79.

Carrillo (Joaquin), nat. of Lower Cal., for 22 years a soldier, part of the time at S. Diego, where, having retired from the service, he lived with his family in '27. He was probably a cousin of José Raimundo, but I find no information about his parentage. It is related that he played well on the violin, and was once put in the stocks by Com. Ruiz because he was too long tuning his instrument for a favorite air. The romantic marriage of his daughter to Capt. Fitch in '27 is recorded in iii. 140–4; marriage of another daughter to M. G. Vallejo '32. iii. 472. In '35 he tried to get a grant of the S. D. mission estate; and the same year his wife called upon the gov. to prevent his sale of the garden given to their children by Com. Ruiz, their godfather. iii. 617. I suppose he died before '40. His widow was María Ignacia Lopez, who in '41 was grantee of the Cabeza de Sta Rosa rancho in Sonoma Co. iii. 673; and for whom was built about this time the 1st house in the Sta Rosa region. Among the sons were Joaquin, Julio, and José Ramon; daughters, Josefa wife of Hen. D. Fitch, Francisca Benicia wife of M. G. Vallejo, María de la Luz wife of Salvador Vallejo, Ramona wife of Romualdo Pacheco and later of John Wilson, Juana, and Felicidad who was claimant of part of the Sta Rosa estate and wife of Victor Castro.   C. (Joaquin), son of Joaquin, at Sonoma '44, age 24; grantee of Llano de Sta Rosa the same year, for which he was later claimant. iv. 673; first settler in Analy township. In '46 2d alcalde of Sonoma, imprisoned by the Bears. v. 129, 157, 162.

Carrillo (Joaquin), son of Domingo, who seems to have been a cadet in the Sta B. comp. '28. ii. 576; in '35 or a little later he married his cousin Manuela, daughter of Anastasio; maj. and later admin. of Purísima. iii. 353–4, 612, 666; grantee of Lompoc '37. iii. 655; juez at Sta B. '40–2, being proposed for sub-prefect. iii. 655; iv. 641–2; in '45 lessee of Sta Inés, suplente in assembly, grantee of Mision Vieja de Purísima. and S. Cárlos de Jonata. iv. 540, 553, 558, 643, 647; in '46 juez and assemblyman, and purchaser of Sta Inés. v. 38, 321, 561, 635. He was appointed prefect in '49, was subsequently county judge, and was district judge for a dozen years from '52, being a man of broad views and good sense, and though not speaking English and knowing but little of legal technicalities, he had good advisers and left a good reputation. He died in '68.   C. (José), son of Cárlos Antonio, ment. in '29 as prospective mr of a Cal. schr. iii. 140; also ment. in '31. iii. 555; grantee of Las Pozas '34. iii. 655; took some part in the political troubles of '37-9. iii. 556, 580; capt. of auxiliary cavalry and acting com. at Sta B. '45-6. iv. 538-9, 641; v. 35. Still living in '50 and later. His wife was Catarina Ortega, by whom he had 4 children before '37; his 2d wife, and widow, was Dolores Dominguez, who in '78 gave me what were left of Don José's *Doc. Hist. Cal.*, including several valuable papers.

Carrillo (José Antonio Ezequiel), son of José Raimundo, b. 1796 at S.F.; said to have been a teacher at S. Diego in 1813 and later. ii. 344; house-lot at Los Ang. '21. ii. 562; member of dip. '22-4; governor's sec. '26; alcalde of Los Ang. '27-8; elector in '29-30, but defeated for congress. ii. 462, 513, 536, 560-1, 563-4; iii. 7, 13, 50, 63, 95. In '31, having a quarrel with Alcalde Sanchez, and being arrested and exiled, he became a leading instigator of the movement against Gov. Victoria. iii. 196-7, 203-4, 206-8, 630, 652; in '32 favored Pico against Echeandía. iii. 218; in '33-4 suplente congressman, member of the dip., and alcalde of Los Ang. iii. 242, 246-50, 258, 275, 327, 342, 366, 373, 635, 637, 644. In '35-6 C. was in Mex. as member of congress; otherwise as 1st vocal of the dip. he would have been gov. ad. int. instead of Castro in '35; and might in '36-7 have given a more formidable aspect to the southern opposition to Alvarado. iii. 258, 291-2, 299. He came back at the end of '37, and from that time to the beginning of '39 engaged in fruitless efforts to rule Cal. by making his brother Don Cárlos gov., being more than once a prisoner, and on one occasion spending some months in captivity at Sonoma, where by his diplomatic skill he wellnigh won over Gen. Vallejo to his cause. iii. 534-45, 547-9, 551, 555, 558-9, 564, 566, 570-1, 573, 578, 580; memb. of the dip., ministro of the tribunal superior, believed to be engaged in various plots '40-3. iii. 602, 604-7, 632; iv. 193, 282, 284, 296, 319; in '43-4, grantee with his brother of Sta Rosa Isl., capt. of Los Ang. defensores, and not very active openly in opposition to Micheltorena. iv. 351, 407, 462, 475, 643; but finally induced in '45 to join the revolutionists. iv. 491-3, 509, 522. Under the new administration in '45, after declining the appointment of 1st justice of the tribunal, C. become lieut-col of militia, comandante de escuadron, and com. principal of the southern line. In this capacity as representative of Gen. Castro in the south he became a northern partisan in the sectional quarrels, and was banished to the frontier by Gov. Pico. iv. 520, 523, 531-2, 538-41. Returning in '46 he joined Castro at Sta Clara, as mayor-gen. of the Cal. forces, and retreated to the south in July. v. 39, 41, 53, 105, 134-5. In Flores' revolt C. was 2d in com., defeating Mervine, and frightening Stockton away from S. Pedro; then engaging in a plot against Flores, but resuming his allegiance for the final struggle against the invaders, and finally signing the treaty of Cahuenga as Mex. commissioner in Jan. '47. v. 309, 318-20, 324, 331-3, 391, 404-5. In '49 he was a member of the constitutional convention, and this would seem to have been the end of his public life. He died at Sta B. in '62. His 1st wife was Estefana Pico, and his second Jacinto Pico, both sisters of Don Pio. A daughter married Lewis T. Burton, but I know nothing of any other children. Thus Don José Antonio's name was constantly before the Cal. public for over 25 years. He was a man of remarkable natural abilities for the most part unimproved and wasted. Slight modifications in the conditions and his character might have made him the foremost of Californians—either the best or worst. None excelled him in intrigue, and he was never without a plot on hand. A gambler, of loose habits, and utterly careless in his associations, he yet never lost the privilege of associating with the best or the power of winning their friendship. There was nothing he would not do to oblige a friend or get the better of a foe; and there were few of any note who were not at one time or another both his foes and friends. No Californian could drink so much brandy as he with so little effect. A man of fine appearance and iron constitution; of generous impulses, without much principle; one of the few original and prominent characters in early Californian annals.   C. (José Antonio), son of Domingo, at school in Lima '29; grantee of Lompoc '37 and Purísima—mision vieja—'45; also in charge of S. Miguel. iii. 655; iv. 643, 660; his wife was Felicidad Gutierrez.

Carrillo (José Raimundo), 1769, nat. of Loreto, who came as a soldier and rose to be capt., dying in 1809. He may be regarded as the founder of the Carrillo family, which must be considered in several respects the leading one in Cal., by reason of the number and prominence of its members and of their connection by marriage with so many of the best families, both native and pioneer. The captain's wife was Tomasa Ignacia Lugo; his sons and some of his grandsons are named in these pages; his only daughter, María Antonia, married Capt. José de la Guerra y Noriega. See biog. ii. 99–101; ment. i. 463, 466, 551-2, 665, 679-82, 692-3, 701; ii. 28, 30, 116-19, 140, 143-4, 174. He signed his name Raymundo, dropping the José.   C. (José Ramon), son of Joaquin (of S. Diego), who in '44 was at Sonoma, age 21, having come north with his mother a few years before. In '46 he was an officer in Padilla's band of Californians who captured and killed Cowie and Fowler during the Bear revolt. v. 160-4. It was claimed by himself and friends, then and later, that the murder was committed against his protest or without his knowledge, and I have no reason to suppose that he was in any way responsible for that unfortunate occurrence. He joined Castro's force as lieut., and with him went south, taking part with his countrymen in the last campaigns of the war '46-7. v. 308, 312, 325, 329, 331, 351, 388, 617; and remained in the south. He was a rough and reckless fellow, often in bad company, but not regarded as a bad man by those who knew him best. He was tried by the courts and by the vigilantes for murder, and acquitted; but soon, in May '64, he was shot from behind the trees at Cucamonga. Whether this murder was committed by a vigilante not pleased with the verdict, by some avenger of the Sonoma victims, or by a private foe, was never known.   C. (José Ramon), at Sta B. '44; grantee of Matzultaquea rancho '45. iv. 496, 635. Perhaps same as preceding; if not, I have no idea who he was.   C. (Juan), soldier of the S.F. comp. at Sonoma '41.

Carrillo (Julio), son of Joaquin, brother of Ramon, who came north with his mother about '40, and in '44 is ment. in a Sonoma list as 19 years of age. In '46, going to visit his brother-in-law, Gen. Vallejo, a prisoner at Sutter's Fort, Don Julio was himself thrown into prison for several months. v. 124, 128, 298-9; had a Cal. claim of $17,500, most of which was disallowed. v. 467. From '49 he was a resident of Sta Rosa, where he was the owner of a large tract of his mother's rancho. iv. 673; but like most of his countrymen lost his land. Still living at Sta Rosa, '85, in poverty, but a man of good repute.   C. (Luis), son of Anastasio; married Refugio Ortega; 2d alcalde of Sta B. '47. v. 631; died in early times.   C. (María del Espíritu Santo), grantee of Loma del Esp. Sto rancho, Mont. dist. '39. iii. 677. I am unable to say who she was.

Carrillo (Mariano), 1769, brother of Guillermo, uncle of José Raim., had a brother Raimundo who never came to Cal.; their parents were Juan Carrillo and Efigenia Millar. Came as a corp. and d. as alférez in 1782; had no family. Biog. i. 385-6; ment. 252-3, 304, 315-16, 335-40, 426-7.   C. (Pedro C.), son of Cárlos Antonio, educated at Honolulu and Boston; arrested at Sta B. by Castro '38. iii. 555, 569; grantee of Álamos y Agua Caliente, and Camulos '43, and S. Diego Isl. '46. iv. 634, 642; v. 619; elector at Los. Ang. '45. iv. 540; receptor at S.D. '46. v. 618-19. In the troubles of '46-7 Don Pedro favored the Americans from the first, and was made collector at S. Pedro, S. Diego, and finally at Sta B. v. 267, 287, 402, 446, 572, 626, 631; alcalde of Sta B. '48. v. 586-7, 631, 611. He was town surveyor of Sta B.; and later justice of the peace at Los. Ang., where he still resides in '85. In '77 he allowed me to copy his col. of Doc. Hist. Cal., including his father's original commission as gov. His wife was Josefa Bandini, and there are several sons and daughters.

Carrillo (Raimundo), son of Anastasio; clerk at Sta B. mission '35, and admin. '36-8. iii. 657-8; sub-prefect '39-40. iii. 654-5; iv. 15, 641; secretary of juez, '41. iv. 632, 641; in '41 grantee of S. Miguel rancho. iv. 643; in '43 juez at Sta B. and grantee of Nojoqui. iv. 642-3; capt. of defensores '49. iv. 407; suplente of sup. court, and elector of Sta B. '45. iv. 532, 540; in '46 com. at Sta B. v. 330, 400, 630. He was alcalde of Sta B. in '49, and still lived there in '50 and later. His wife was Dolores Ortega, and there were several children.   Carrillo (Ramona), daughter of Joaquin; grantee of rancho at S. Luis Ob. '41. iv. 655; later Mrs Wilson; still living in '85.   C. (Tomás M.), 1848, named by Brooks as a robber shot by Bradley.   C. (Vicente), soldier of S.F. comp. at Sonoma '41-2.   C. (W.), 1841, nat. of L. Cal.; in Sonoma Co. '51-77.   Carrion (Manuel), 1837, Frenchman at Sta Cruz desiring to marry. iv. 118.   C., several of the name at Los Ang. '46.

Carson (Christopher), 1830 (?), Kentuckian trapper, guide, and Ind.-fighter, born in 1809, who claimed to have come to Cal. with Ewing Young, and very likely did so. iii. 175, 180. At any rate, he came in '44 as guide and hunter with Frémont; and again with the same officer in '45. iv. 437, 583. His acts in '46, in connection with F.'s operations at Gavilan in the Sac. Valley, on the Or. frontier, in the S. Rafael campaign of the Bear revolt, are mentioned in v. 3, 6, 24-5, 94, 121, 127, 171-2, 175. Going south, he was sent east with despatches in Aug., but met Kearny in N. Mex. and returned with him, taking part in the S. Pascual fight, and subsequently serving in the Los Ang. campaign. v. 216, 236-7, 350, 417. In March '47 he was again sent to Washington with despatches, accompanying Lieut Beale. At Wash. he was appointed lieut—though the appointment was not confirmed—and sent back to Cal., arriving in Dec., returning in '48, and then settling in N. Mex. Again in '53 he came to Cal. with a flock of sheep. In N. Mex. he was farmer, hunter, and guide; an Ind. agent from '54; colonel and brevet brigadier-gen. of volunteers at the end of the war of '61-5. He died at Ft Lyon, Colorado, in '68, at the age of 59. His first wife was an Indian woman, by whom he had a daughter; the 2d wife was Josefa Jaramillo, who bore him 3 children. *Peters' Life and Adven. of Kit Carson* was published in '59; *Abbott's Christopher Carson* in '76. Kit Carson was a small, wiry man, of undoubted bravery and skill in all that pertained to his profession, comparatively quiet in manner, and somewhat less garrulous and boastful than many of the frontiersmen; yet the difference between him and others of his class in character and skill was by no means so marked as has been represented in eulogistic biog. sketches. No one, however, begrudges Kit the fame his biographers have given him. It is their custom, ignoring faults, to concentrate in one trapper all the virtues of his class for dramatic effect. Carson's statements on his Cal. experience were not noticeable for their accuracy; his connection with the Haro-Berreyesa murder—though he doubtless obeyed orders—is not creditable; and I suppose his influence to have had much to do with Frémont's stupid folly of the Gavilan, and Kearny's disaster at S. Pascual.

Carson (James H.), 1847, nat. of Va; sergt in Co. F, 3d artill. v. 519-20; in the mines '48; an active prospector, who gave his name to several 'diggings,' and whose little book—*Early Recoll. of the Mines*—was pub. at Stockton in '52. He died in '53, his wife and child arriving a little later, but returning to the east.   C. (John), owner of S.F. lot '46; went to U.S.   C. (Jose Manuel,) 1840, at S. Gabriel with a Sonora pass to visit Cal.   C. (Lindsay), 1847, settler in Russ. Riv. Valley; still there after '56. *Son. Co. Hist.*, 358. Carson (Moses), 1832, brother of Kit, from N. Mex. with Ewing Young. iii. 388, 408. He remained for some time in the Los Ang. region, and in '36 obtained a certif. of 10 years' resid. in Mex. Territory and 4 in Cal., being then 31 years old. In '45 he went north to take charge of Capt. Fitch's Russ. Riv. rancho; joined the Bears in '46, and was the messenger who announced the capture of Sonoma at N. Helv.; also in Cal. Bat. (v. 358), and had a Cal. claim of $653, not allowed (v. 462). After his discharge he returned to Healdsburg, but soon after '50 recrossed the continent and soon died.   C. (Richard), 1847, sup. of the *Confederacion*. v. 577.   Carstens (H.), 1848, German said to have come this year; in S. Mateo Co. '59-78.

Carter, 1825, mr of the *Jura*. iii. 147.   C., 1845, a physician at N. Helv.

'45-6. iv. 580; perhaps Geo.		C., 1848, mr of the *Kamehameha III.*; of C.
& Davis at S.F.; perhaps Joseph O.		C. (David), 1848, at Mont. from Bos-
ton with letters from J. C. Jones.		C. (Geo.), 1845, immig. apparently of
the Grigsby-Ide party. iv. 578, 587; perhaps the G. S. Carter who served in
the Cal. Bat. (v. 358).		C. (Geo.), 1846, Co. C, 1st U.S. dragoons (v. 336).
C. (Geo.), 1847, Co. B, N.Y.Vol. (v. 499).		C. (Henry), 1831, mr of the *Wm
Little*. iii. 384.		C. (J. B.), 1846, lieut on the *Savannah*.		C. (John), 1844,
Amer. sailor from the *Tasso;* landed sick at S.D. iv. 453; sent to Mont. on
the *Admittance;* aided by the consul, and shipped in '46.		C. (John), 1847,
Co. K, N.Y.Vol. (v. 499).		C. (Joseph O.), 1831, Amer. mr of the *Volunteer*
and *Harriet Blanchard* '31-3, and of the *Rasselas* '36-8. iii. 382, 384, 405;
iv. 105, 141. His wife and child often accomp. him on his voy. bet. Cal. and
the islands. Went to Boston on the *Alciope* in '40. iv. 100; d. at Honolulu
about '51. His son Henry A. Carter was Hawaiian min. at Wash. '84. Also
called J. D. and John O.; possibly more than one man.		C. (Philo J.), 1847,
Co. B, Morm. Bat. (v. 469); reënl. at Los Ang.		C. (R.), 1847, Co. B, Morm.
Bat.		C. (R.R.), 1846, mid. on the U.S. *Savannah*.
		Cartney (Barthol.), 1847, lot-owner at S.F.		Cartwright, 1841, mr of the
Sapphire. iv. 568.		C. (H. B.), 1848, at Benicia. *Yuba Co. Hist.*, 86.		Carver
(M.M.), 1848, Kentuckian from Or., and member of the const. convention
'49.		Cary (Lewis), 1848 (?), in Colusa '80; said to have come by the isthmus
in '48. *Col. Co. Hist.*, 81.		Cásares, see 'Cáceres.'		Casarin, see 'Jimeno C.'
		Case (A. L.), 1841, lieut U.S. ex. exped. iv. 241.		C. (B. A.), 1847, nat.
of Conn.; settler at Sta Cruz; died in Mendocino '71. His wife, Mary Amney
of Vt, taught at Sta Cruz '48, and still lived there in '80.		Casement (Wm),
1847, Co. F, 3d U.S. artill. (v. 518).		Casey (Michael), 1847, Co. I, N.Y.
Vol. (v. 499).		C. (Neil), Co. B, N.Y.Vol.		Cash (A.), 1837, mr of the *Har-
vest*. iv. 104.		C. (James H.), 1844, Amer. sailor from a whaler at Mont. iv.
453; enlisted Nov. '46 in Co. G, Cal. Bat., and was wounded at Natividad.
v. 371; mentioned also in '48.		C. (John C.), 1847, lieut of marines on the
Columbus.		Casper (Wm W.), 1847, Co. A, Morm. Bat. (v. 469); Utah
farmer and col of militia '81.		Cassel (John), 1847, perhaps of N.Y.Vol., not
on roll.		Cassidy (Hugh), 1847, Co. F, 3d artill. (v. 518).		Cassin (John
W.), 1846, sergt Co. C, 1st U.S. dragoons (v. 336); went east '49, but returned
from Washington Ter. '52, settling in Tuolumne; a farmer in Tehama '62-77,
the time of his death.		Castañares (Gregorio), regidor at Mont. '44. iv. 653.
C. (José), juez de campo at Mont. '35. iii. 674.
		Castañares (José María), 1833, Mex. from Puebla; clerk for the admin.
of customs Rafael Gonzalez, whose daughter, Ana María, was his wife; 29
years old in '36, when his amours with Ildefonsa Herrera were the basis of a
causa célebre at Mont. iii. 436-9. He was a handsome fellow, but arrogant in
manner. He went to Mex. a little later, but in '40 came back on the *Catalina*.
iv. 31; in '42 fiscal and ministro suplente of the tribunal. iii. 605; iv. 299,
296; in '43 grantee of the Arroyo de los Calzoncillos rancho. iv. 671; in '44
lieut-col of the defensores and a supporter of Micheltorena. iv. 405, 407, 509,
654; in '45 sent to Mex. by Gen. Castro on a mission of which little is known,
and never returned. iv. 530, 601; v. 32. In '47 he appears as a colonel in the
Mex. army.		C. (Manuel), 1840, brother of José María, who came from
Mex. to take charge of the Mont. custom-house, but became, instead, sec. of
the prefecture '40-2. iii. 675; iv. 31, 626, 652; in '42 sent to Mex. by Alvarado as a commissioner, returning with appointment as admin. of customs;
also fiscal of the tribunal. iv. 283-5, 296, 312, 339, 341, 352, 563; in '43 still
admin. of customs, elector for Mont., grantee of Mariposas, and finally
elected member of congress. iv. 355, 357, 361, 377, 386, 672. His labors in
congress '44-5, as shown by his *Coleccion de Documentos* published in '45, are
recorded in iv. 412-18, 431, 449-50, 457, 524-5; v. 32. He never returned to
Cal., but in later years gave testimony in the Limantour case, which was
pronounced false by Judge Hoffman. He was a man of some ability, and more
popular than his brother. I think his family came and went with him.
		Castañeda (Juan), 1837, Mex. capt., nat. of Texas, and com. of the L. Cal.

frontier, who came to Cal. with José Ant. Carrillo, and took a prominent part in the mil. operations to support Cárlos Carrillo in '38, until captured. iii. 546, 549-50, 553-5, 569, 661. In '39 he was made sec. of the com. gen., and sent on a mission to Mex. by Vallejo. iii. 599; iv. 285; returned in '42 with Micheltorena, or at least about the same time; in '43-6 not much is heard of him, but he was the grantee, as was claimed, of several pieces of land, having a lot at S.F. iv. 352, 669, 671; v. 41, 561, 665, 680. After '50 a witness in land cases. A man of good manners, fair education, and little force.

Castillero (Andrés), 1836, Mex. capt. of the L. Cal. frontier comp., who came to Mont. apparently with Gov. Chico; at the downfall of Gutierrez he was not exiled, but chose to go away, perhaps to Mex. iii. 460-3; in '37 he came back as a comisionado of the Mex. govt and induced Alvarado to submit to centralism, being at once sent back to Mex. to work for Alvarado's interests. iii. 521, 526-31, 572, 624. Successful again, he returned to Cal. in '38. iii. 574-6; iv. 101; in '39 was grantee of Sta Cruz Isl., and went to Mex. as congressman and habilitado-gen. of the Cal. companies. iii. 582, 590, 656; iv. 66, 100, 102, 143. In '45 he came back once more as a comisionado of the govt to prepare for the reception of Mex. troops and defence against Amer. invaders. iv. 528, 535, 537, 602-3, 606, 614; v. 17. It was at this time that Castillero found and denounced the famous New Almaden quicksilver mine, for which he figured as claimant in the litigation of later years. v. 665. He was sent to Mex. again on govt business early in '46 and did not return till after the war. v. 32-3, 577. I have no record of him after the litigation of '49-61, during which he resided chiefly in Mex.

Castillo (Ambrosio, Enrique, Gabriel, José M., Loreto, and Manuel), at Los Ang. '46. C. (Felipe), Sonoran cigar-maker and trader, age 25, who took part in the Apalátegui revolt at Los Ang. '35. iii. 282-5; went to Son. but returned in '45. iv. 572; grantee of Valle de S. Felipe, and sent overland with despatches to Son. '46. v. 332, 619. C. (José), juez aux. Mont. '44. iv. 653. C. (José María), soldier at S. José mission 1797-1800. i. 556. C. (José María), regidor at Mont. '31-2. iii. 672-3. C. (Francisco), sec. to sub-prefect at Sta B. and to prefect at Los Ang. '39-40. iii. 640, 654-5. C. (Pedro del), Mex. infantry sergt from S. Blas about '25; elector at S.F. '27. ii. 592; regidor Mont. '33. iii. 673; receptor of customs at S.F. '33-6; iii. 377, 700. C. (Nícanor de Jesus Garnica del), 1842, came from N. Mex. in a colony, and after a short stay at S. Luis Ob. came to Mont., living later at S. José, and finally near Salinas, where in '77 he gave me some *Recuerdos* of events in '44-6.

Castillo Bueno (Juan), 1602, sergt in Vizcaino's exped. i. 98. Castillo Negrete (Francisco Javier), 1834, came from Mex. with the H. & P. col.; síndico and sec. of ayunt. at Mont. '35; sec. of Gov. Chico; grantee of Quien Sabe and Sta Ana ranchos '36; either exiled with Gutierrez or sent by Chico as an agent to Mex. a little earlier in '36. See iñ. 466; also 263, 426, 674, 678. C. N. (Luis), 1834, Span. lawyer, brother of Fran. J., who also came with the colony as district judge of Cal.; a bitter opponent of Alvarado's govt, who went away voluntarily with Gutierrez in '36; a poet as well as lawyer; later gov. of L. Cal.; died in '43. Biog. iii. 463-6; ment. iii. 263, 267, 277, 372, 415, 480, 484, 486-7, 534, 586. Castle (John), 1845, deserter from the *Hopewell*, at S. Diego. Casto (James), 1847, Co. D., Morm. Bat. (v. 469). Caston (Geo. R.), 1847, Co. D., N.Y. Vol. (v. 499).

Castro. Except in the case of a few of the most prominent of the name, no attempt is made here to follow the complicated connections of this family or group of families, doubtless the most numerous in Cal. Castro, in a S.F. padron '44, age 25. C. (Agustin), son of Mariano, at Las Ánimas '36, age 24. C. (Albino), son of Francisco M., age 16, in '41; d. without issue before '52. C. (Angel), sub-maj. of S. Juan B. '35. iii. 692; at S.F. del Rosario rancho '36. iii. 678; nat. of Cal., age 45, wife Isabel Butron, child. Ramon b. '16, Guadalupe '20, José '23, Josefa '30, Concepcion '32, Juana M. '31, José Joaq. '33, Josefa '34; ment. '40. iv. 6; in '42 grantee of Los Paicines, and com. of a militia comp. at S. José and Brancif. iv. 655, 663, 686; juez at S. Juan B. '44, '46; family insulted by Frémont's men. iv. 561; v. 9, 640; tax-payer in Mont.

Co. '50. C. (Antonio María), soldier of 1780, retired in 1809; grantee of Vega del Pájaro rancho '20. ii. 383, 664; iii. 679; supleate of dip. '22, and vocal '25. ii. 462; iii. 18. C. (Antonio), son of Francisco M. iv. 71, 544, 679. C. (Antonio), perhaps son of Ant. María, or in some items there may be confusion bet. him and his father and others; regidor of Mont. '30–1. ii. 612; iii. 212, 672; comis. of S. Antonio mis. '31. iii. 307, 687; alc. at Pájaro '35. iii. 674; supl. juez at S. Juan B. '39, '46. iii. 693; v. 640. C. (Antonio), possibly the same, or the son of Fran. M., at S. José '41, age 41, wife Bárbara Soto, child. Francisca b. '24, Concepcion '28, José de Jesus '29, María S. '30, Gabriela '12, José '36, José Ant. '39. C. (Antonio María), son of Joaquin, at S. José '41, age 16. C. (Blas), son of José Ant., at S. Antonio rancho '36, age 20. C. (Cándida), wife of José Bolcof. ii. 479; grantee in '39, with her sisters, of Refugio rancho.

Castro (Cárlos), bro. of Francisco, Ignacio, and Mariano; maj. at Sta Cruz '12. ii. 388; supl. of the dip. '22–4. ii. 462, 543–4; síndico at S. José '28, also supl. vocal '28–9. ii. 605; iii. 42–3; in '34 grantee of Las Llagas rancho, Sta Clara Co. iii. 674, 677, 712; where he lived in '36, age 60, nat. of Cal., wife María del Rosario García; supl. vocal of junta '39. iii. 590. Don Cárlos is described as an eccentric old fellow, who tempered his hospitality by an affectation of abusing his guests. By a padron of '41 he was a Sonoran, age '62, while his wife was a year younger than in '36! C. (Cárlos), ment. at S. Luis Rey '39. iii. 625. C. ('Chanate'), see 'C. (Manuel).' C. (Crisanto), son of Mariano, at S. José '41, age 11. C. (Cruz), at S. Bern. '46, age 28. C. (Evaristo), son of José, at Las Ánimas '38, age 22. C. (Felipe), prob. son of Mariano, soldier at Mont. '36, age 26. C. (Francisco), piloto and master of transport vessels 1776–8. i. 287, 266, 328.

Castro (Francisco María), nat. of Sinaloa, b. 1775; prob. bro. of Cárlos, Ign., and Mariano; for 13 years artill. soldier and corp.; settler at S.F. before 1800, in which year he was alcalde. i. 716, 718. In '22 elector, member of dip., alc. at S. José (?). ii. 454, 462, 584, 604; in '23 explor. exped. north of bay, and grant of the S. Pablo rancho, renewed in '34, where Don Francisco spent the rest of his life. ii. 497–9, 594–5, 664; iii. 713; vocal and elector '25, '27. ii. 592; iii. 17–18. Duhant-Cilly, *Viaggio* ii. 88–9, says that Don Francisco was of French descent; I find no other evidence of this fact, or of any direct relationship to the other Castros. He died in '31, leaving a widow, Gabriela Berreyesa, who died in '51; 7 sons—Alvino, Antonio, Gabriel Vicente, Jesus María, Joaquin Isidro, Juan José, and Victor; 4 daughters—María de Jesus who d. before '52 without issue, María Gregoria who married José Ramon Estrada and died without issue before '52, Francisca who married Joaq. Moraga and died before '52 leaving 5 children, and Martina the wife of Gov. Alvarado. iii. 593, 679. The San Pablo estate was left half to the widow and half to the 11 children, and by deaths and the mother's will Doña Martina C. de Alvarado became owner of 15-22. But the lawyers got in their work in the distribution, and the whole family has been kept in a state of landed poverty by litigation, which in '85 is not entirely at an end. C. (Francisco), son of Guillermo, at Mont. '36–41, age 4–7. C. (Fran.), son of Juan José, at S. José '41, age 8. C. (Fran.), son of Rafael, at Brancif. '45, age 20. C. (Fran.), son of Simeon, at Mont. '36, age 4. C. (Fran.), Cal. claim of $3,045 in '46.

Castro (Gabriel Vicente), son of Francisco M., resid. at S. Pablo; elector at S.F. '35. iii. 704; sergt in militia comp. '37; juez de campo '43. iv. 685; ment. in '44. iv. 463; lawsuit '47. v. 663. C. (Guadalupe), bro. of Rafael and Juan José at Brancif. '45, age 30, single; juez de paz '43. iv. 663. C. (Guad.), son of Angel, age 16 in '36. C. (Guad.), son of Joaquin, at Brancif. '28; claimant of S. Andrés rancho '52. iii. 678. C. (Guad.), son of Juan José, at Brancif. '45, age 19. C. (Guillermo), prob. son of Cárlos, at Las Llagas '36. iii. 677; lieut of S. José militia '37. iii. 732; grantee of S. Lorenzo rancho '38–41. iii. 711, 713; iv. 673; in '38 surveyor at S. José. iii. 730; in '41 at his rancho, age 31, wife Luisa Peralta, child. Juan b. '31, Francisco '34, José Ramon Simon '34, Concepcion '35, Encarnacion '46, Loreto '37, Luisa '38; in '41–4 juez of the contra costa. iv. 684–5; in '45 suplente min. of the sup. tribunal. iv. 532.

Castro (Ignacio), bro. of Cárlos, Fran., and Mariano; soldier of S.F. 1780; settler at S. José 1786; alcalde 1799, 1804, '9, '10. i. 477–8, 716; ii. 134; perhaps the same man who was drowned near Mission S. José in '17. ii. 382. C. (Ign.), son of Joaquin, at Brancif. '28.   C. (Ign.), son of Mariano, at S. José '41, age 20.   C. (Isidoro), his daughter married Surg. Dávila. i. 469. C. (Jesus María), son of Francisco M.; resid. of S. Pablo; age 18 in '41; in S. F. militia '37.   C. (Jesus M.), son of Juan José, at Brancif. '28, age 13. C. (Joaquin), soldier of S.F. comp. 1777; wife Martina Botiller; settler at S. José 1790, etc. i. 478, 617; perhaps the same who owned the Buenavista rancho near Mont. '95, and obtained La Brea 1801–2. i. 683; ii. 171, 664. C. (Joaquin), inválido soldier and settler at Brancif. from 1799. i. 571; married María Ant. Amador; maj. of Sta Cruz '18. ii. 244–5; fined '27. ii. 627; in '28 at Brancif., a widower, child. Guadalupe, Ignacio, Joaquin, Vicenta, Daría; Rafael, and Juan José were apparently his sons; there had also been a daughter Plácida de Jesus, b. 1803; ment. in '30. ii. 627; alcalde '31. iii. 696–7; grantee of S. Andrés rancho '33. iii. 678.   C. (Joaquin), son of preceding; at Brancif. '45, age 25, wife Eusebia Valencia, child. José and Marcelina.   C. (Joaquin), prob. son of Joaq. of '95; at La Brea '36, age 41; at S. José '41, age 47; wife María Inés Sepúlveda, child. Mariano b. '21, Antonio M. '23, Lugarda '28.   C. (Joaquin Isidro), son of Francisco M.; regidor at S.F. '35. iii. 704; lieut of the civic comp. '37. iii. 701; grantee of El Sobrante '41. iv. 673–4; ment. '41–3. iv. 199, 684, 686; Cal. claim of $8,516 (v. 462) in '46; claimant for S. Pablo, and executor of his father's estate. iii. 713.

Castro (José), son of José Tiburcio, b. about 1810; at school in Mont. '15–20. ii. 429; his 1st public service seems to have been as sec. of the Mont. ayunt. in '28. ii. 612; though in these years it is difficult to distinguish in the records between him and his father, both called generally José. Arrested by the rebels of '29. iii. 69, 89; sec. in '30, also arrested again for expressing contempt for the Mex. iii. 49–50; ii. 612. Besides being engaged to some extent in otter-hunting '31–4, Castro was still sec. of the ayunt. '31, also named as comisionado to secularize S. Miguel, and a member of the dip. which Victoria refused to convene. iii. 186 et seq., 307, 374, 394, 684–5; 7th vocal of the dip. '33. iii. 246, 249–50, 291; 3d vocal in '35, but acting as 1st in the absence of the 1st and 2d, and thus acting gov. Sept. '35 to Jan. '36. iii. 298–300, 414–16, 426; also comisionado at S. Juan B. in '35. iii. 692. He took part in the troubles with Gov. Chico. iii. 424, 440; and in Oct.–Nov. '36 was Alvarado's chief supporter as mil. com. in the overthrow of Gutierrez. iii. 453–75. From Nov. 5th, the downfall of G., he was com. gen. of Cal. to Nov. 29th, and gov.—as presid. of the dip.—to Dec. 7th; then, as lieut-col of civic militia—under Vallejo, who remained at the north as com. gen.—he went south to take charge of Alvarado's cause in the complicated campaigns of '37–8. iii. 493, 501, 503, 505, 509–10, 520–1, 522–3, 526, 546, 551–6, 558–62, 577–8, 580, 582; claiming also a grant of Yerba Buena Isl. in '38. iii. 713. In '39 he was commissioned by the Mex. govt as capt. of the Mont. comp. iii. 584, 671; was vocal of the junta, one of the terna for gov., and grantee of S. Justo rancho; and prefect of the Mont. district '39–40. iii. 584–6, 588, 590, 603–4, 675, 678; iv. 75. In '40 Castro arrested the foreigners and went with them to S. Blas, being tried by court-martial and acquitted in Mex., and returning to Cal. in '41. iv. 6, 11–35, 37, 193, 202–4; mention in '41–3 as capt., promoted to lieut-col in '42, member of the junta, etc. iv. 282, 292, 295, 313, 339, 357, 360–2, 364, 652; in '44 lieut-col of the defensores, and sent to establish a frontier garrison in the S. Joaq. Val. iv. 407–9; a leader in the revolt against Micheltorena '44–5, and after M.'s overthrow became com. gen. of Cal. iv. 458, 460, 463, 483, 485, 488–510; his official acts in '45, controversy with Gov. Pico, precautions against foreign invasion, tour in the north, treatment of immigrants, etc. iv. 518–45, 556, 558–60, 589–90, 601, 603, 606–7, 652; continuation of the controversy in '46, troubles with Frémont and the Bears, negotiations with Larkin, operations at Sta Clara, and retreat to the south in July. v. 5–53, 60–1, 72, 78–100, 105–9, 132–3, 185, 230–3, 245, 637, 661, 675; final operations in the south, negotiations with Stockton, and flight to Mex. Aug. '46. **v.** 261-78, 407-9. Don José came back to Cal. from Sinaloa in '48, **v.** 585-6, 640, 678, and lived as a private citizen at Mont. and S. Juan till '53, when he went again to Mex., being made sub-jefe politico and mil. com. of the L. Cal. frontier from about '56. In '60, while holding this office, he was killed in a drunken brawl—or, as some say, assassinated—by one Manuel Marquez. His widow, Modesta Castro, was still living in Cal. as late as '77. Thus, José Castro was the most prominent of his name as a public man. No Californian has been so thoroughly abused as he in what has passed for history. It should be stated at the outset that nine tenths of all that has been said against him by American writers has no foundation in truth. Of his conduct in the sectional quarrels of '45-6, there is not much to be said in his favor, except that it was somewhat less discreditable than that of his opponent, Pico; but with his acts in the contest with the settlers and the U.S. little fault can be justly found. He did not maltreat the exiles of '40, as charged by Farnham and others. He did not break his pledge to Frémont in the spring of '46, nor did he do any of the absurd things attributed to him in connection with the Gavilan affair; but his conduct was far more honorable, dignified, and consistent than that of Frémont. He did not threaten to drive the immigrants back into the snows of the Sierra, but treated them with uniform kindness; nor did he incite the Ind. to burn Sutter's grain-fields. In the southern negotiations of August he bore a much more honorable part than did Com. Stockton. He was not a very able man, but with ten times his ability and resources no resistance could have been offered to the U.S.; he was not a very brave man, but he showed no cowardice in the operations of '46. Indeed, his record as a public man in Upper Cal. was, on the whole, not a bad one. He had much energy, was popular with most classes, was true to his friends, and as a public officer fairly honest. About his private character there is great difference of opinion among competent witnesses, native and foreign, who knew him well. He must have had some good qualities, yet it is clear that he had some very bad ones. He was addicted to many vices, and when drunk, especially in the later years, was rough to the verge of brutality; yet a kind-hearted man when sober. Of commonplace abilities and education, in most respects inferior to such men as Vallejo, Bandini, Alvarado, and Carrillo, he was yet by no means the cowardly, incompetent braggart that he has been generally painted. Castro (José), sirviente at S.F. mis. 1777. i. 297.   C. (José), soldier of S.F. comp. '19-22; in '36 at Las Ánimas, age 39, wife Inés Robles, child. Evaristo b. '14, Juana '21, Estefana '23, Salvador '26; prob. a son of Mariano.   C. (José Antonio), nat. of Sinaloa; at S. Antonio rancho '36, age 50, wife Merced Ortega, child. Blas b. '16, Mariano '18, Rudesindo '20, Estefana '21, Bautista '23, Emiliana '24, Blanca '25, Manuel '28, Francisco '29, Perseverancia '30, Tomás '31, Juan '32, Ventura '34. iii. 678; grantee of Lomas Muertas and Estanislao '42-3. iv. 655, 672; in S. José dist. '50.   C. (José Ant.), son of Mariano, at S. José '41, age 14.   C. (José Ant.), son of Rafael, at Brancif. '45, age 18.   C. (José Ant.), son of Simeon, at Mont. '36, age 6.   C. (José Ignacio), at Brancif. '45, age '28, wife Ricarda Rodriguez, child. José Ramon b. '37, José Simon '39, María '44.   C. (José J,), at S. José '39. iii. 731.   C. (José Jesus), son of Antonio, at S. José '41, age 12.   C. (José Joaquin), son of Angel, age 3, '36.   C. (José Manuel), son of Juan José, at Brancif. '45, age 21.   C. (José María), son of Rafael, at Brancif., age 22, in '45; witness in the Santillan case.   C. (José Ramon Simon), son of Guillermo, at S. José '41, age 7.   C. (José Saturnino), soldier at S.F. '19-22.

Castro (José Tiburcio), son of Macario, nat. of Sinaloa, who came to Cal. prob. before 1800; perhaps the man ment. 1801, '16. ii, 152, 371. He was a soldier, and finally a corporal. In '19 alcalde of S. José, having a rancho in that vicinity. ii. 378; suplente or vocal of the dip. '22, '24, '27. ii. 462, 510-11, 612; iii. 36; alcalde of Mont. '27. ii. 612; in '28-9, memb. of dip. and partido elector. ii. 613; iii. '41-4; alc. '29. ii. 612; iii. 69, 73; vocal '31, taking part against Victoria. iii. 187, 189; comisionado for Soledad '31. iii. 307, 690; grantee of Sauzal rancho '34, '45. iii. 679; maj. and admin. at S. Juan B. '35-6. iii. 354, 692; memb. of the junta dip. '39. iii. 590; prefect of **the**

1st dist. in '40, succeeding his son. iii. 652, 656, 675–6. His wife seems to
have been an Álvarez; but I have no record of any children except José and
the wife of Santiago Moreno, nor of the date of his death. Don Tiburcio was
a man of little ability and still less education, but of excellent character.   C.
(Juan), had a son in the Mont. school '46.   C. (Juan), son of Guillermo, S.
José dist. '41, age 10.   C. (Juan Bautista), son of José Ant., at S. Antonio
rancho '36, age 13; perhaps the alférez of aux. cavalry at Mont. '45–6 of same
name. v. 41.   C. (Juan B.), son of Simeon, b. '35; in later years a prosperous ranchero at Castroville, where he still resides in '85.   C. (Juan José),
son of Francisco M.; militiaman S.F. '37; grantee of Y. B. Isl. '38; in '41 in
S. José dist (at S. Pablo), age 38, wife Petra Bernal, child. Maiseta (?) b. '28,
Magin '30, Francisco '33, José María and Narcisa '38; grantee of El Sobrante
and other lands in the contra costa '41, '44. iv. 671; living in '52; d. before
'82, the date of his widow's death.   C. (Juan José), bro. of Rafael and Guadalupe, at Brancif. '28, wife Manuela Juarez, son Manuel; regidor '33. ii. 627,
696; in '45 at Brancif., age 38, wife (2d) Rita Josefa, child. José Manuel b.
'24, Guadalupe '26, Trinidad '28, Jesus María '32, José Domingo '33, Cármen
'34, Amoina (?) '36, Angustias '42.   C. (Juan María), at Mont. '36, age 14;
Mrs M. Castro de Estrada apparently his sister.   C. (Leandro), son of
Simeon, b. '34; in later years ranchero near Castroville; still living '85.   C.
(Luis), Span. soldier who left the *Aquiles* at Sta B. iii. 27, 51–2; at S. Gabriel
'28–9, 60 years old, single, of good conduct.   C. (Luis), at Los Ang. '46, possibly the preceding.
   Castro (Macario), native of Sinaloa, soldier from 1778, who came to Cal.
in 1784; was corp. of the S. D. comp. at S. Juan Cap. '85–7; and at S. José
and Soledad '90–4, being comisionado of S. José '92–4. i. 479, 499, 716;
sergt from '94. i. 680; frequent mention '95–1800, in con. with Ind. affairs
and explor. exped. i. 548–9, 552, 558–9, 683, list auth.; invál. and comisionado at S. José 1788–1807, and a prominent citizen in many respects. ii.
16, 132, 134–5, 140–1. I find no record of him after 1807. His wife, who
came with him to Cal., was María Potenciana Ramirez; their children were
José Tiburcio, Agapito, Simeon, Mariano, Maria de Jesus, María Dolores,
and Cármen, all born before 1793.   Don Macario, as the grandfather of
José and Manuel, may be regarded as the most prominent among the Castro
founders.   C. (Magin), son of Juan José, S. José dist. '41, age 11.   C.
(Manuel de Jesus), son of Simeon, b. '21; sec. and collector at Mont. 39. iii.
675; sec. of the prefecture '42–3. iv. 652. He was prime mover in the revolt
against Micheltorena, taking an active part throughout in '44–5, being once
captured and exchanged, and finally comisionado to make a treaty. iv. 458–9,
462–8, 486–7, 500–509. Under the new admin. he was made prefect of the
Monterey district in '45, being also made lieut of the Mont. comp., and
taking a most prominent part in public affairs, as representative of the civil
authority and supporter of Gov. Pico against Gen. Castro in the north. iv.
533, 536–7, 606, 652. In '46, besides being promoted to capt. of the Sta B.
comp., getting a land grant, having a Cal. claim of $10,000, and continuing
his services as prefect, v. 636–7, he took a prominent and honorable part in
the troubles with Frémont. v. 4, 12, 17; quarrel with Cambuston. v. 34;
efforts for defence against the settlers and the U. S. v. 41, 45, 56, 131, 134–5;
sent south in July as comisionado to effect a reconciliation bet. the general
and gov. v. 136, 143–4, 261; left in com. at Los Ang. on Gen. C.'s departure
in Aug., but there is doubt whether he was one of the officers captured and
paroled by Stockton's men. v. 266, 282, 361. On the outbreak of Flores' revolt in Oct. Castro was put in com. of the northern division and commanded
in the Natividad campaign. v. 321, 361–72, 639; flight to Mex. with Flores
'47. v. 407–9. In Mex. Don Manuel continued his military services for several years, and in '49 was put in com. of the frontier comp. of L. Cal., in place
of Andrés Castillero, taking charge of the military colony of Santo Tomás
till '52, when he had to yield to Castillo Negrete. See *Hist. North Mex.
States*, ii. Since '52 Castro has resided for the most part in S.F. down to '85,
never becoming a citizen of the U. S., often interested in Mex. colonization.

schemes, and ranking as colonel in the Mex. army—perhaps brevet general in the last years. He was never married. Don Manuel was an abler man than his cousin, the general, and his public record in Cal. down to '47 was in most respects an excellent one. True to his country's cause, with no sympathy for foreign filibusters, he exerted himself, for the most part in vain, to heal foolish dissensions between Calif. chiefs and direct their force against the invaders. Of his later record not so much can be said in praise. Various ' ways that are dark ' are popularly attributed to him, and, while charges are doubtless exaggerated, it is possible that he has yielded somewhat to temptations offered by land litigation, politics, dislike of the Yankees, and chronic impecuniosity. But at least he has contributed grandly to the store of material for Cal. history. The *Castro, Doc. Hist. Cal.*, in 3 vols, is a most important collection of original papers presented by him in '75; and a few years later he contributed a still larger and richer col. of *Doc. Hist. Cal.*, with important L. Cal. material—somewhat unwillingly, it is true, some of my assistants having to adopt the policy of ' fighting the devil with fire;' and finally I obtained his *Relacion de Alta Cal.*, none the less valuable because after it had been written at my expense one of my wicked collaborators had to steal a copy for my use.   C. (Manuel), brother of the preceding, b. in '24; nicknamed ' Chanate;' capturer of despatches in '46. v. 235; perhaps the same who married the widow of Wm R. Garner, and a tax-payer at Mont. '50. C. (Manuel R.), soldier of the Mont. comp. from '36, sergt from '38; alférez from '46. iii. 671; v. 41; went to Mex. with Gen. Castro, continued in mil. service, and in '51 was at Sto Tomás on the frontier.   C. (Manuel), son of Juan José, at Brancif. '28; perhaps same as the preceding.   C. (Manuel), son of José Ant., at S. Antonio rancho '36, age 8.   C. (M.), sentenced to presidio '45. iv. 654.   C. (María Encarnacion), wife of Surg. Dávila 1782. i. 468.   C. (María de Los Angeles), wife of J. L. Majors; grantee of Refugio '39. iii. 678.

Castro (Mariano), apparently bro. of Cárlos and Francisco M., and perhaps cousin of Macario; came to Cal. before 1800, in 1801 went to Mex. and obtained a grant of La Brea, or Las Ánimas, rancho in Sta Clara Co., about which he had considerable trouble later, though the grant was conf. in '35. ii. 7, 153, 163, 171, 594, 603, 673, 676, 711; alcalde at S. José '27, '30. ii. 605–6. He died before '35. His wife was Josefa Romero, living at La Brea '36, age 55, with her sons Agustin b. '12 and Vicente '18. One of their daughters, Lugarda, married Thos Doak in '20. ii. 277. I think another daughter, María, was the wife of Cárlos Ant. Carrillo. There were 4 children in 1801.   C. (Mariano), son of Macario; probably the same who in '41 lived at S. José, age 57, wife Trinidad Peralta, child. Mercedes b. '13, Angela '17, Ignacio '21, José Ant. '27, Josefa '28, Crisanto '30, Susana '32; grantee of S. Ramon '33, and Solis '35, and of land in Mont. dist. '39 (Rufina C. being cl. of 2 of these ranchos and prob. his daughter). iii. 679, 713; juez de policía '42, '44. iii. 512; iv. 685. Perhaps the same man was one of the three of that name who voted at S. José in '50, or the Mont. tax-payer of the same year, or the claimant for Refugio rancho in '52; or some of these items may apply to one of the following.   C. (Mariano), soldier of S. F. comp. '19–22.   C. (Mariano), son of Joaquin, at La Brea '36, age 15.   C. (Mariano), son of José Ant., at S. Antonio rancho '36, age 18.   C. (Mariano I.), soldier of S. F. comp. '19–22.   C. (Martina), grantee of Shoquel '33, and Palo de Yesca '34, and claimant '52.   C. (Matias), settler at the Colorado pueblos 1780–1. i. 359.   C. (Miguel), soldier '30, ii. 660.   C. (Miguel), alférez of aux. cavalry Mont. '45; Cal. claim $174 in '46.   C. (Modesta), wife of Gen. C., grantee of Cañada de los Osos, '44. iv. 655.   C. (Pedro), son of Simeon, at Mont. '36, age 8.   C. (Primo), at Las Ánimas '36, age 60.

Castro (Rafael), son of Joaquin, juez de campo at Brancif. '32. iii. 696; grantee of Aptos '33. iii. 676; síndico '34. iii. 696; alcalde aux. and juez '36, '42–3. iii. 663, 697; in '45 officer of election.' iv. 664, then living at Brancif., age 40, wife Soledad Cota, child, José María b. '23, Francisco '25, José Ant. '27, Vicente '35, María '31, María de los Angeles '33, Rafaela '35, Angustias

'44. He died at Aptos in '78. Newspaper notices of his death give his age as 78, state that he was formerly a soldier and capt. before '30—doubtless an error—and that he had 11 children, 8 of them living in '78. Don Rafael, like his brothers, was an industrious and prosperous ranchero of good repute, not meddling much in politics. C. (Ramon), son of Angel, age 20 in '36. C. (Rudesindo), son of José Ant., at S. Ant. rancho '36, age 16. C. (Salvador), son of José, at Las Ánimas '36, age 10; '46 memb. of S. José council. v. 664; claimant of S. Gregorio '52. C. (Ramon), at S. Bern. '46, age 24.

Castro (Simeon), full name José Simeon Juan Nepomuceno, son of Macario, b. in 1784 at Sta B.; soldier of the Mont. comp. 1809; grantee of Bolsa Nueva y Moro Cojo '25 and later. ii. 615, 664, 672, 677; regidor at Mont. '33-4, '37. iii. 673, 675; in '36 at Mont., age 52, wife María Antonio Pico, child. Juana b. '17, Manuel J. '22, Manuel '24, María Antonio '26, Pedro '28, José Ant. '30, Francisco '32, Leandro '34, Juan B. '35. In '38-9 alcalde at Mont. iii. 577, 675; in '41 juez de paz, and grantee of Tucho. ii. 616; iv. 653, 656; in '42 grantee of Año Nuevo. iv. 655. He died about '42. His widow was the claimant for Bolsa Nueva and Corral de Padilla in '52. iii. 677; continued to live at Mont.; and died in '84. C. (Vicente), son of Mariano, at Las Ánimas '36, age 18. C. (Victor), son of Francisco M., ment. '36 in connection with Ind. affairs. iv. 71; militiaman '37; grantee of Mare Isl. '40-1. iii. 712; iv. 672; in '41 living at S. Pablo, age 24, wife Luisa Martinez (daughter of Don Ignacio), child José; juez de campo '43. iv. 685; ment. '44, '46. iv. 473; v. 105; Cal. claim (v. 462) of $12,912. Still a resid. of Contra Costa Co. '85. In early troubles with the Ind. as well as in later contests with the squatters, Don Victor has repeatedly shown himself to be a brave and determined man. His second wife was Felicidad Carrillo, and the third an American. Caswell (J. F.), 1848, passp. from Honolulu.

Catalá (Magin), 1794, Span. friar, who had previously been chaplain at Nootka, and who served at Sta Clara for 36 years, till his death in 1830. Certain miraculous powers were popularly attributed to Fray Magin, and on the strength of these, I suppose, the preliminary steps for his beatification were taken by the church in '84. Biog. in ii. 600-1; ment. in i. 523, 556-7, 576, 587, 638, 719-20, 723; ii. 137, 159, 394, 577, 655; iii. 96, 351. Catalan (Benito), 1796, Span. friar who served at S. Antonio till his retirement in 1800 on account of insanity. i. 577, 689. Catharte, (?) 1823, mr of the Massachusetts. ii. 492. Catlin (Geo. W.), 1847, Co. C, Morm. Bat. (v. 469). Catts (Samuel A.), 1847, Co. B, N.Y.Vol. (v. 499); nat. of Md; resid. of Stockton '74-84; Caulfield, (David), 1847, Co. G, N.Y.Vol. C. (Patrick), 1847, ditto. Cavaller (José), 1771, Span. friar, founder of S. Luis Ob., where he served till his death in 1789. Biog. i. 469; ment. i. 173, 176, 188, 196, 299, 388. Cavell (J.), 1848, passp. from Honolulu. Cavenecia (José), 1814; master of the Lima ship Tagle; of the S. Antonio in '17. ii. 222, 271, 282-3, 271. Cayuelas, 1790-1820, several of the name prob., soldier, corp., settler at S.F. and S. José, and inválido at Mont., in trade and known as 'Tio.' Francisco C. was in '28 a Span. inválido, age 80. i. 478, 610, 690, 716; ii. 383, 420; iii. 51.

Ceballos (Ignacio), alcalde at S. José '32. Cebet (Pierre Jean), 1831, Frenchman who got a carta in Oct. prob. 'Chevrette,' q. v. Cecil (B.), 1847, advertises for a lost pocket-book bet. S.F. and S.J. C. (T. M.), 1846, carpenter of the Savannah, who built Fort Stockton at Mont.; prob. same as preceding. Célis (Eulogio), 1836, Span. supercargo in Virmond's employ, who was on the Leonor in '36, and perhaps on the Catalina earlier, as he certainly was in '41-2; often named in various records '36-42 and later. iii. 146, 381, 428-9; iv. 198, 237, 564. Célis made Los Ang. his home; was one of the grantees of the S. Fernando estate in '46; had a famous claim for cattle furnished to Frémont; and to '48 and later was a wealthy man of business well known in all parts of Cal. v. 365, 396, 435, 448, 561, 580, 627, 630. He went to Spain in '53 and died in '68. His wife was Josefa, daughter of Luis Ant. Argüello, who came back to Cal. after her husband's death. Three sons, the eldest Eulogio, still live at Los Ang., I think, in '85; two sons and two daughters remained in Spain. Cermeñon (Sebastian Rodriguez), 1595, Span.

voyager at Pt Reyes, who prob. gave the name S. Francisco—later transferred to another bay—to his anchorage. i. 89, 96-7.   Cervantes (Andrés), Mex. artill. sergt at Mont. '29-36. iii. 69, 74, 671; age 48 in '36, wife Encarnacion Alcivar, of Tepic.   C. (Cruz), Mex. majordomo at Tucho rancho '36, age 40, wife Filomena Arroyo, child. Ancleta b. '31, Celedonia '33, Teodosio '35; grantee of S. Joaquin or Rosa Morada '36, for which he was claimant in later years. iii. 678-9.   C. (Pablo V.), soldier killed by Ind. on the Colorado 1781. i. 363.   Cesena (Ramon S.), 1846, resid. of Sta Clara Co. '81; a Mexican.

Chabolla, juez of S. Juan B. '46. v. 359, 640.   C. (Anastacio), soldier of S. F. comp. '23-31; nat. of Cal.; in '41 at S. José, age 31, wife Josefa Higuera, child. José Ant. b. '35, Fernando '37, José J. '39, Angel María '40; in '44 grantee of Sanjon de Moquelumnes. iv. 673; d. before '53.   Maria C., prob. his daughter, was claimant for this land, and also his son Angel.   C. (Antonio), grantee of Yerba Buena, Sta Clara Co. '33. iii. 713, 729-30; in '41 at S. José, age 37, wife Juliana Butron, child. Marta b. '31, Juan 36, Estefana '35, Antonia '38, Auisez (?) '39; juez de policía '43. iv. 685; claimant for Y. B. '53.   C. (Gervasio), at S. José '41, age '37, wife Miguela Linares, child. Juan b. '33, Francisco '38, Marcos '39.   C. (José de la Cruz), son of Marcos, b. 1796 at S.F.; at S. José '41, wife Máxima Vasquez, child. José de la Cruz b. '24, Tomasa '30, Soledad '35, Juana '37, Nemesio '41.   C. (Luis), son of Marcos; síndico of S. José '31, '35, '43. iii. 729-30; iv. 685; in '41, age 48, wife Guadalupe Romero.   C. (Marcos), Span. soldier, corp., and settler at S.F. before 1800; alcalde 1796-7. i. 716, 719; his wife was Teresa Bernal; child. in '93, Pedro, Salvador, and Luis.   C. (Pedro Regalado), son of Marcos, b. S.F. 1789; soldier of S.F. comp. '19-22; in '30 síndico of S. José. ii. 606; in '34 alcalde. iii. 329-30; in trouble '37-8. iii. 525, 573; juez de campo. '41, '44. iv. 684-5; age 47 acc. to padron of '41, wife Gertrudis Ortega, child. José Miguel and Josefa b. '30, José de Jesus '35, Alejandro '36, Salvador '37, María '38, Teresa '39; alcalde in '46. v. 662.   Still a resid. of S. José in '60.

Chace (Henry P.), 1843, nat. of R. I., at Mont. and Los Ang. '45-6, bound to Sonora; on Pion. Soc. roll as having arr. in Oct. '43. iv. 400.   Chaden (Charles), 1845, Amer. at Brancif., age 36, wife Mary, also Amer., child. S. Dionisio b. '31, Matilde '34, Josefa '36, Tomás '38, María '40, Elisa '42. I don't think this was the man's real name, but cannot identify him.   Chadwick (W.), 1822-5, mr of the *Plowboy*. ii. 479; iii. 148.   Chaffield, 1848, mr of the *Sabine*. v. 580.   Chaland (Fred.), 1847, lieut on the *Independence*.

Chamberlain (John), 1839, Irish blacksmith who came on the *California* from Acapulco, having deserted from a whaler on the Mex. coast. iv. 119; worked at his trade at Mont., was arrested in '40, and though not exiled was obliged to make shackles for the other prisoners. iv. 9, 17, 23, 28; on Larkin's books to '41; a little later went to the Sac.; naturalized in '44 and got a grant of Socayac. iv. 674; enlisted in Gantt's com. for Sutter's campaign of '45, but on account of illness did not go south. iv. 486; married in Jan. '46 to Nancy Hess—only one of some 19 similar contracts on his part as popular tradition has it—and soon went to Or. v. 526. But he returned after 18 or 20 years, and in '77 was working at his trade at Mont., where he dictated his *Memoirs* for my use, and where I think he still lives in '85.   C. (John), 1846, Co. C, 1st U. S. dragoons (v. 336).   C. (Levi), 1840, on the *Don Quixote* at Mont. iv. 103.   C. (Ventura), 1841, on the *Jóven Carolina*. Chamisso (Adelbert von), 1816, naturalist of Kotzebue's exped., and author of *Reise* and *Remarks* with inform. on Cal. ii. 279-81, 309-11, 372-3, 420. Champion, 1848, came on a vessel from Honolulu acc. to his later testimony. Champlain (Wm M.), 1844, from N. Y.; doubtful newspaper record.

Chana (Claude), 1846, French cooper, who came to N. Orleans in '39, to Mo. '41, and overland to Cal. in '46. He worked for Sutter; was one of the earliest gold-miners in '48; became owner of the Nemshas rancho on Bear River. iv. 672; long a resident of Wheatland, where he died in '82 at the age of 71. I suppose the original name was 'Chanon,' as indeed it is written in the *N. Helv. Diary.* Chance (Dr), 1846, overl. immig. who lived at Mont. and Stockton till '50 or later, then went to Texas, but returned, and was in southern Cal. '69; *S. F. Examiner.* Chancey (Alex.), 1847, Co. F, 3d U. S. artillery (v. 518). Chandler (David W.), 1841, overl. immig. of the Bartleson party. iv. 267, 270, 275, 279; interested at Benicia '47. v. 672; went to Honolulu, but came back in '48. I have no later record than his letter at S.F. Nov. '48, but he is said to have died in Cal. C. (John A.), 1847, Co. D, N. Y. Vol. (v. 499); at Boston '82. C. (Ralph), 1847, mid. on the U.S. *Independence.* C. (Wm), 1848, lot-owner at S.F.

. Chapel (Geo.), 1840, one of the exiles to San Blas who came back in '41 and settled in the Sta Cruz redwoods. iv. 18, 33, 37, 120; in '45 on the Brancif. padron as English, age 27, wife Josefa Soto, child. Manuel b. '40, José C. '44; at Mont. '47. Chapin (Geo.), 1847, of Morm. Bat. (v. 469); wounded by Ind.; perhaps same as following. C. (Samuel), 1847, Co. E, Morm. Bat. C. (Sam. M.), 1847, blacksmith at Mont. '47-8. Chapman (Charles), 1847, worked for Leidesdorff; witness in the Limantour case '54, residing at S.F., age 30. C. (Geo. W.), 1847, lieut of the U.S. *Independence* and *Columbus.*

Chapman (Joseph), 1818, Amer. carpenter and blacksmith, one of Bouchard's insurgentes—impressed into that service at the Sandwich Isl., as he claimed—taken prisoner at Mont., and soon finding a home in the south. ii. 229, 248, 292, 393. Foster, *First American in Los Angeles*, tells a most interesting but inaccurate story of his capture at Sta B. by Lugo. In '20 Joseph was employed at Sta Inés, where in '21 he built a grist-mill, and obtained from Gov. Sola the king's amnesty to Anglo-Amer. prisoners. ii. 444; then he went to S. Gabriel to build another mill. ii. 568; and was baptized at S. Buen. in '22 as José Juan, being married the same year at Sta Inés to Guadalupe Ortega, by whom he had five children. ii. 479. In '24–6 he bought a house at Los Ang. and got a piece of land, where he planted a vineyard of 4,000 vines. ii. 526; but still continued to do odd jobs at the missions, being a jack-of-all-trades, who apparently could make or repair anything that was needed. He was a great favorite of the friars, especially P. Sanchez, who declared it a marvel that one so long in the darkness of baptist faith could give such example of true catholic piety to older christians. In '29, armed with certificates from leading men of all classes, and defying the world to find any fault with his record, he asked for naturalization, which he got in '31, having meanwhile built a schooner and served on occasion as surgeon. ii. 558; iii. 140, 209, 363, 382. His age in '29 is variously given as 33 to 48; he himself seems to say he was 33 or 34 in '22, but is now 48. He soon moved to Sta B., where in '36, age 52, he lived with wife and 5 children; in '38 grantee of S. Pedro rancho. iii. 656; is ment. in '45, and by Bryant in '47 as living near S. Buen.; but seems to have died in '48 or '49. *Huse* and *Foster.* His widow was claimant for the rancho '52; and I think some of his descendants still live, '85, in Ventura Co. Among all the earliest pioneers of Cal. there was no more attractive character, no more popular and useful man, than Joseph Chapman the Yankee. C. (Juan), at Los Ang. '45; perhaps a son of Joseph. C. (Manuel), 1844, one of Frémont's men. iv. 437. C. (Thos), 1833, mr of the *Charles Eyes.* iii. 381. Chaquette (Heman), 1847, Co. G, N. Y. Vol. (v. 499). Charbonneau (Jean B.), 1847, guide to the Morm. Bat. v. 483; in '48 alcalde at S. Luis Rey. v. 621, 623.

Chard (Wm Geo.), 1832, New Yorker from N. Mex. with Alexander, Carpenter, etc. iii. 388, 408; at Los Ang., where he had a vineyard, till '36, appearing in several records and being one of the vigilantes (iii. 430); in '37 naturalized, being then at Sta B., protestant, age 27, a trader on the coast. The same year went north to the Sta Cruz region, apparently with Graham's comp., and his name often appears on Larkin's books from '37. In '40, living at Brancif., he was exiled to S. Blas, but returned in '41, and next to Graham was loudest in his demands for justice and damages, until the courts spoiled his little game by showing his Mex. citizenship. iv. 17–18, 24, 31, 33, 39–40, 116. In '43–5 C. had a store and sailor boarding-house at Mont. in partnership with Josiah Belden; in '44 he got a grant of Las Flores, Tehama Co., on which he put his cattle in '45. iv. 671; earlier in '45 he signed the call to foreigners at

S. José. iv. 599; in '45-7 he was employed by Andrés Castillero to work the New Almaden mine; but before the end of '47 he settled, apparently, on his Tehama rancho, where he still lived in '58, and where he died, I think, about '80. His wife was a Californian of the Robles family, who died in '72. The family seems to have resided at Sta Clara for some years after Chard went to Tehama. Stephen Chard, a son of Wm G. was still in '80 and later, a prosperous farmer of Tehama.

Charlefoux, 1837, Canadian from N. Mex. in com. of a party of ' Chaguanosos,' or Shawnees, who were trappers, soldiers, traders, or horse-thieves— whichever profession might be most profitable at the time—in '37-40. He aided Bandini and the sureños against Alvarado in '37. iii. 495, 518, 520; iv. 118. Charles, 1846, in Sutter's employ, and guard over the Sonoma prisoners '46-7. v. 125. Charley, 1845, Delaware Ind. of Frémont's party. '45-7. Charles (Michael), 1826, Irish blacksmith who landed sick from a whaler; at Mont. '40, age 57. iii. 176. Charles (Joseph), 1844, sailor on the *California*, witness at Mont. Charquin, rebel neoph. of S.F. 1793. i. 709.

Chase (Charles), 1846, on the 1st jury at Mont. v. 289. C. (C.), 1846, fleet surgeon on the *Savannah;* perhaps same as preceding. C. (Hiram), 1847, Co. J, N.Y.Vol. (v. 499); d. before '82. C. (Hiram B.), 1847, Co. A, Morm Bat. (v. 469); in Utah '81. C. (Sam.), 1844, Engl. with a pass. for a year at Mont. C. (Sam.), 1847, at Sutter's July; at Mont. Dec.; in '48 in charge of Larkin's rancho on the Sac., but soon quit farming for the mines. C. (S. M.), 1846, doubtful record of a Bear Flag man, at Sonoma in '62. C. (S.U.), 1845, New Yorker of quaker parentage, who came west in '38, crossed the plains to Or. '43, and came to Cal. '45 in the McMahon-Clyman party. iv. 572, 577, 587. After visiting Sta Cruz and Mont. he ret. to the Sac., and went to Or. in '46; came back to the mines '48-9; later a farmer in Solano and Napa; about '66 settled in Yolo, where he still lived in Capay Val. '79. Never married. Portrait in *Yolo Co. Hist.*, 26. Chaseagre? (J.), 1833-5, mr of the *Mariquita.* iii. 383. Chatard (Fred.), 1847, lieut on the U.S. *Independence.* Chatfield, 1848, mr of the *Sabine.* Chatozo (Pedro), named by Lancey as builder of a mill at N. Almaden '24. Chaudière (H.), 1835, mr of the *Grange.* iii. 382. Chauncey (Alex.), 1847, Co. F, 3d U. S. artill. (v. 518), acc. to Lancey, but not on the roll; at Livermore '48.

Chavarria (Nicolás), 1818, S. Amer. of Bouchard's insurgents, captured at Mont., and remained in Cal. ii. 227, 230-2, 241; soldier of S.F. comp. '28-31. Chavez (José Ant.), 1833, Mex. brought to Cal. by Gov. Figueroa, whose natural son he is supposed by many to have been; tax collector at Mont. '43. iv. 653; one of the prime movers in the movement against Micheltorena '44, also sec. of ayunt. iv. 588-9, 653; grantee of Ciénega del Gavilan '43, and Pleito '45. iv. 655; celador at Mont. '46. v. 570. He took part in various military operations of '46 as lieut, being sent by Castro to Frémont's camp at Gavilan. v. 11; and later the captor of Larkin and 2d in com. at Natividad, where he was wounded, escaping capture a few days later by being hidden in bed between two well-known ladies of Mont. v. 362, 364, 366-72. Leaving Cal. in '48, v. 585-6, he went to S. Blas, and was later prominent with Manuel Castro on the L. Cal. frontier. Chavez, 1818, painter at S. Juan B. ii. 356. C. (José), 1798, i. 606. C. (Julian), supl. alcalde Los Ang. '38. iii. 656; regidor '46-7, and grantee of Las Ánimas '46. v. 625-7. C. (Mariano), at Los Ang. '46. Chavira (José), 1798, i. 606. Chavira y Lerma (Josefa), wife of Pedro y Gil, 1781. i. 451. Chavon, 1847, mr of the *Adelaide.*

Check, 1816, on the *Lydia,* arrested at Sta B. ii. 275. Cheney (Zacheus), 1847, Co. B, Morm. Bat. (v. 469). Chever (Henry), 1846, nat. of Mass., who had lived long in Valparaiso and Manila; acc. to his brother's statement was mr of the *Hannah.* v. 578; but he seems to have come to S.F. from Honolulu on the *Elizabeth;* had a lot at S.F. '46; member of the firm J.B. McClurg & Co. at Los Ang., dissolved Feb. '48; also connected with Ward & Smith '47; and later with Hastings & Co. at Coloma. He was one of the founders of Yuba City; at S.F. '51-3 in poor health; died in Napa Val. '54, leaving no family. His brother Edward E. was in Cal. '49-54, and again '83-5. Chevrette (Pierre J.), 1832, signed roll of the comp. extranjera. iii. 221. Chichester (Chas), 1848, overl. immig. with Allsopp; went to the mines. C. (Henry T.), 1847, Co. E, N. Y. Vol. (v. 499); deserter. Chico, Ind. chief killed 1781. i. 466.

Chico (Mariano), 1836, Mex. col and memb. of congress from Guanajuato, appointed gov. of Cal. Dec. '35, arriving in April '36 on the *Leonor*, and assuming his office May 2d. He encountered a bitter prejudice against Mex. rulers, and his position was made so uncomfortable by an unmanageable diputacion and other soi-disant opponents of centralism that he was virtually forced to depart in Aug., his rule ending July 31st. He was a man of fair abilities and good education; by no means the villain, fool, or madman that the Californians generally represent him; but he was fussy, conceited, and gifted with no tact for making friends or overcoming obstacles. He also scandalized Mont. society by bringing a mistress, Doña Cruz, whom he introduced as his niece. On his rule, see iii. 420-44, also ment. iii. 300, 399, 652-3, 670; iv. 44-7, 72, 82-3, 102, 104-5, 112. In '43-4 Don Mariano was gov. of Aguascalientes, where he is said to have written many verses, making himself somewhat popular socially, though less so than his wife, Doña Ignacia Alegre. *Gonzalez, Hist. Aguas.* 128-30. In '46 he was com. gen. of Guanajuato. Chienes (Alex.), 1842, mr of the *Primavera.* iv. 568. Childers (Morris R.), 1845, Amer. carpenter from Or. in the McMahon-Clyman party. iv. 572; prob. went back in '46. iv. 526; but visited S.F. in '47 on the *Henry* from Astoria. C. (Moses), 1843, said to have crossed the plains and to have been in Amador Co. '48. *Amador Co. Hist.*, 182; perhaps a vague ref. to the preceding. Childs (Mark D.), 1846, Co. C, 1st U.S. dragoons; wounded at the Mesa Jan. '47. v. 395; name also given Mark A. Child.

Chiles (Joseph B.), 1841, Kentuckian b. 1810; in Mo. from '30; took part in the Florida war '38; and in '41 came overl. to Cal. with the Bartleson party. iv. 267, 270, 275, 279. After visiting Monterey, Sonoma, and other parts of the country, and obtaining from Vallejo the promise of a mill site, he returned east in '42 for the mill. iv. 276, 342. In '43 he came back with the party that bears his name, one portion of the party under Walker taking a southern route and being obliged to leave Chiles' mill on the way. iv. 392-5, 679. In '44 he was grantee of Catacula rancho in Napa Val. iv. 671; ment. also iv. 448, 453; in '45 signs bonds for some of the new immigrants. iv. 581. I do not find any definite record that he joined either the Bears or the Cal. Bat. in '46, though he may have done so, and certainly aided Frémont with supplies and information. v. 297-8. He went east in '47, prob. as guide and hunter in Stockton's party. v. 454; was at Washington to testify at the Frémont court-martial; and in '48 made his 3d overl. trip to Cal. at the head of a party, v. 557, which included his own family of a son and 3 daughters, his wife having died in '37. The son was, I suppose, the Kit Chiles named in *Yolo Co. Hist.*, 74, as having settled at Washington in '48; the daughters were Fanny wife of Jerome Davis, Elizabeth wife of Daniel Brown, and Mary, Mrs Tully. Colonel Joe Chiles, as he is familiarly known, married M. G. Garnett in '53; and has resided in Napa and Lake counties down to '85, I think, a famous hunter notwithstanding his years, and a good citizen. A brief narrative of his *Visit to Cal. in '41* was furnished by him in '78. Chinook (Wm), 1845, Ind. of Frémont's party, one of the Sta B. garrison. iv. 583. Chipman (Walter), 1847, sergt Co. A, N.Y.Vol., at Cedar Springs, Mich., '83. Chiron, 1837, in Petit-Thouar's exped., surveying S.F. Bay. iv. 149.

Choquet (Diego), 1776, mr of the *S. Antonio.* i. 287, 301. Choris (Louis), 1816, artist with Kotzebue; author of the *Voyage Pittorresque.* ii. 281, 372. Christian (Chas), 1847, perhaps of N. Y. Vol. (v. 499), under another name. C. (Chas W. H.), 1848, in charge of S.F. school Dec. *Californian.* C. (John), 1838, one of the exiles to S. Blas, not known to have returned. iv. 18. C. (Kail), 1840, mr of the *Catalina.* iv. 31. C. (W. A.), 1848, purser U.S.N., at S.F. on the *Lady Adams.* C. (Wm. H.), 1847, Co. K, N.Y.Vol. (v. 499); brig.-gen. in war of '61-5; at Los Ang. '71; at Utica, N.Y., '74-82; perhaps the Chas and Chas W. H. ment. above. A man of the same name was at S.

José in '50.   Christiancy (James), 1846, Fauntleroy's dragoons (v. 232–47).
Christie (H.), 1848, left Honolulu for S. F.   C. (John G.), 1847, at S.F. on
the *Currency Lass* from Hon.; at Mont. '48.   Chulte, in Sutter's employ '47;
perhaps an Ind.   Chumazero (Ignacio), at Sta Cruz 1794. i. 496.   Church
(Haden W.), 1847, Co. B, Morm. Bat. (v. 469).   C. (Wm S.), 1843, Amer.
carpenter from Sandwich Isl., who died at the house of Temple at Los Ang.
'43, his effects being sold Jan. '44. iv. 400.   C. (Wm S.), 1841, mate of the
Maryland, who took com. on the return from Mazatlan to Hon. '42.   Capt.
Peirce says he saw him at S.F. in '49; else he would appear same as preceding.   Churchman (T.), 1848, worked for Sutter on his mill from May.
Chute, 1847, convicted of manslaughter at S. José. v. 663.
    Cibrian (Blas), soldier of S.F. comp. '27–33; his wife was Paula Mesa,
living at Mont. '36, age 28, child. Francisco b. '23, María de la Cruz '27, José
Prudencio '30, José Blas '32, Refugio '34, José Estanislao '36.   C. (Cármen),
wife of Cornelio Bernal, resid. at S.F. mission from '38 and earlier to '07 and
later.   C. (Eusebio), at S. José '41, age 41; at S.F. mission '46; witness
in Santillan case.   C. (Francisco), soldier of S.F. comp. '39–43. iv. 667; at
S. José '50.   C. (Gabriel), at S.F. '55, age 36.   C. (Leocadio), soldier and
settler of 1791–1800. i. 499, 416.   C. (María Rosa Pacheco de), widow, at
S. José '41, age '44, child. Isidro b. '22, Ignacio '24, Eusebia '27, Florencio
'30, José Manuel '32, Cárlos '33, Encarnacion '40.   C. (Pablo), settler at S.
F. 1791–1800. i. 716.   Ciel, 1838, doubtful name at Sta. B.   Cimental,
(Cris.), reg. at Mont. 1805. ii. 156.   Cins, see 'Zinns.'   Ciprés (Marcelino),
1795, Span. friar who served at S. Antonio and S. Luis Ob. till his death in
1810. Biog. ii. 148; ment. i. 576, 689; ii. 23, 28, 50, 147, 151–2, 159–60, 191.
Cipriano, Ind. associate of Estanislao '29. iii. 110; perhaps the same who
died in '78 in the region of N. Almaden at the age of 100 or more.
    Clamp (Richard), 1847, Co. A, N. Y. Vol. (v. 499); at Chinese Camp,
Cal. '71–82.   Clap (Curtis), 1840, mr. of the *Alciope;* sup. of the *California* '42–3; a Boston and Sandw. Isl. trader. iv. 100, 564.   Clapin (Joseph),
1846, corp. Co. C, 1st U.S. dragoons (v. 336).   Clapp (Chas D.), 1847, Co.
D, N. Y. Vol. (v. 499); died in Australia after '50.   Clar (Juan), 1836,
Span. of Minorca; translator and keeper of the archives, well known in S.F.
'49–84; said to have visited Cal. as early as '36 as prof. of mathematics on a
man-of-war, and again with Com. Jones in '42. He died at S.F. '84.   Clare
(Wm), 1847, Co. F, 3d U. S. artill. (v. 518); an Engl. who joined the comp.
at Valparaiso; served as clerk in Col Mason's office, but like most of his
comrades deserted for the mines in '48. Said to have inherited a fortune later
and to have settled down at Liverpool.
    Clark, 1836, mr of *Ionic.* iv. 104.   C., 1845, in Sutter's army. iv. 486.
C., 1847, mr of the *Vesper.* v. 580.   C., 1847, 'Father Clark,' said to
have celebrated his 49th birthday at S. Diego, in '72, 25 years and 6 mo.
after his arrival. *S. D. World.*   C., 1847, left Hon. for S.F. on the *Eveline.*
C. (Albert), 1847; Co. E, Morm. Bat. (v. 469).   C. (Daniel), 1848, Irish
immig. to Or. of earlier years, who came to the Cal. mines '48–50, going
back to Or., where he has been a well-known citizen. *Hist. Or.*, i. 468.   C.
(Daniel P.), 1847, Co. B, N. Y. Vol. (v. 499); owner of S.F. lot. v. 680; at
S. Diego from '71, where he died '79.   C. (E. St Clair), 1847, sec. U. S. *Columbus.*   C. (Francis), 1843, doubtful immig. of the Hastings party. iv. 390.
C. (Francis C.), 1847, Co. D, N.Y. Vol. (v. 499); shot on Merced Riv. '53.
    Clark (Francis D.), 1847, Co. D, N. Y. Vol. (v. 499); nat. of N. Y.; a
miner in '48–9; in '49–55 trader, ferryman, and justice of the peace in S.
Joaquin; N.Y. city trader '55–60; major and mil. sec. in the war of '61–5;
and later a business man of N. Y. city. Clark has been sec. and one of the
most active members of the N.Y. society of Cal. Pioneers; and has particularly interested himself in keeping awake memories of pioneer times by the
publication of rolls of surviving comrades of '47 in '71 and '74; and finally
by *The First Regiment of N. Y. Volunteers,* bringing the record down to '83.
See v. 503, et seq. That work also contains the author's portrait. His *Pioneer
of '47* is a somewhat minute narrative of his experience in '47–55. I have

followed his record of the N. Y. Vol. with a few corrections and additions.
C. (Geo.), 1847, Co. E, N.Y.Vol. (v. 499). C. (Geo. S.), 1847, Co. B, Morm.
Bat. (v. 469). C. (H.), 1847. sup. of the *Eveline.* C. (John), 1847, Co. G,
N.Y. Vol. (v. 499); an Irishman, drowned at S.F. '54. C. (John Case), 1843,
said to have visited the coast on a man-of-war. iv. 400; miner from '49; at
Red Bluff a few years from '57; at S. Diego from '69 to his death in '73.
C. (John N.), 1847, Co. I, N. Y. Vol. (v. 499); bro. of Francis C.; miner and
painter, at Stockton '71–4; died in Fresno Co. '79. C. (Joseph), 1847, Co.
A, Morm. Bat. (v. 469). C. (Lorenzo), 1847, lieut Co. A, Morm. Bat. v. 477;
tanner in Utah '81. C. (M.), 1848, passp. from Honolulu. C. (Nicholas),
1846, at Sutter's Fort; one of the 2d Donner relief. v. 540; portrait in *Mc-
Glashan,* 184; living in '79. C. (Obed), 1822–3, mr of the *Gideon.* ii. 474,
492. C. (Ransom), 1844, perhaps of Frémont's party. iv. 437; at S. José '50.
C. (Riley P.), 1847, Co. A, Morm. Bat. (v. 409); reënl. at Los Ang. C.
(Smith Douglas), 1845, Engl. with a passp. for Sonora. C. (Sophia P.), 1846,
one of the Mormon col. v. 576; prob. Mrs King at Ogden '84. C. (Terence),
1848? an early settler at Sonora. C. (Wm), 1823–6, mr of the *Thos Nowlan.* ii. 492, 519; iii. 149.

Clark (Wm Squire), 1846, nat. of Md, b. in 1807, grandson of Abraham C.
signer of the declaration of independence; educated in Ohio; a business man
in the south and west; and an overland immig. of '46 (v. 526). He came directly to S.F., and served apparently under Marston in the Sta Clara campaign.
Obtaining a lot at what was named for him Clark's Point—which lot is still
owned by him 40 years later—he built a warehouse and a wharf, driving the
first piles in the bay. In '47–8 he was not only one of the most prominent
business men in town, becoming the owner of dozens of city lots, but he was a
member of the council, president of public meetings, and otherwise active in
public affairs. v. 648, 650, 652–4, 656, 678, 680, 685. I know of no foundation
for Gen. Sherman's statement that Clark was a Mormon. v. 547. In '48 he was
a successful miner, but soon returned to S.F., where his land investments made
him eventually a millionnaire. He married Alice A. Duncan in '68, and in '70
went to live at S. José, where he still is in '85, with a son, Wm S., Jr, and 4
daughters. He wrote his *Recollections* for my use in '85, and in an interview
gave me many details of old San Francisco. C. (W.W.), 1847, mr of a whaler.

Classen (John C.), 1848, Pion. Soc. roll. Claudio, 1837, leader of hostile
Ind. S. Diego. iii. 614. Clausen (Wm), 1847, musician Co. D, N.Y.Vol.
(v. 499). Clavell, 1844, officer on H.B.M.S. *Modeste.* Clawson (John R.),
1847, Co. D, Morm. Bat. (v. 469); reënl. at Los. Ang. Claviter (Edward),
1848, passp. from Honolulu; resid. of Mt Eden, Alameda Co. '49–78; at Alameda from '78 to his death in '84.

Clayton (Charles), 1848, nat. of Engl., who came to the U.S. in '42 and
crossed the plains to Or. in '47, coming to Cal. in April '48 on the *Henry.*
After a year in the mines he opened a store at Sta Clara, where he also held
local offices. From '53 he become a prominent commission merchant in S.F.,
filling also with credit the offices of supervisor, member of the legislature, surveyor of the port, and member of congress. He married Hannah Morgan in
'54; and still resides in S.F. in '85, age 60. Clements, 1845, at S. F., N.
Helv., and again at S.F. with a family; seems to have gone east with Clyman
in '46. iv. 526, 578. Name also written Clemence, Clement, and Clemons.
Wm Clemons is named in one list as a member of the Stevens party of '44, and
was perhaps the same, though he may have gone first to Or. Clements (Lam-
beth B.), 1847, of N.Y.Vol. (v. 499); comp. not known; lot at S.F. '47; at
S.F. '54; at Soquel '74. Cleveland (Richard J.), 1803, owner and 1st officer
of the *Lelia Byrd;* involved in smuggling exploits; author of a *Narrative.*
ii. 10–14, 21, 102–3. Clifford (Cornelius), 1847, Co. B, N.Y.Vol. (v. 499);
d. at S. Juan B. after 1850. C. (J.), 1848, passp. from Honolulu. C.
(O. G.), 1848, ditto. Clift (James), 1847, Co. C, Morm. Bat. (v. 469): reënl.
at Los Ang. C. (Robert), 1847, lieut Co. C, Morm. Bat. v. 477; lieut of the
reënl. comp. v. 495; alcalde of S. Diego '47–8. v. 491, 618–19. Clipper,
doubtful name–of a corporal killed at S. Pascual. Cloud (J. H.), 1847, major

and paymaster U.S.A., who came with the Morm. Bat. v. 483, 440; killed at Sutter's Fort Aug. 3d by a fall from his horse.   Clough (Wm), 1837, named in Larkin's accounts.

Clyman (James), 1845, Virginian who, after an adventurous career as surveyor and trapper in the great west, came overland to Or. in '44, and to Cal. the next year as a leader in the McMahon-Clyman party. v. 572-4, 587. He travelled over the country as far as Monterey; spent the winter hunting in the Napa and other valleys. v. 17; and in the spring of '46—after a union with Frémont's comp. had been declined. v. 23—returned to the states overland, meeting the Donner and other parties on the way. v. 526. He came back to Cal. in later years, and lived at Napa till his death in '81, at the age of 84. Colonel Clyman's *Note-book*, a MS. diary of his wanderings of '44-6, is one of the most complete and important records of its class in my library. *Clyman's Diary* is an abridgment of the same, with a few documentary additions. Clymer, 1842, with Com. Jones at Los Ang. iv. 321.

Coates (Geo.), 1846, served in the Cal. Bat. (v. 358), enlisting at S. Juan Oct.; prob. same as the following.   C. (James), 1843, Amer. shoemaker, farmer, tanner, and overl. immig. from Or. in the Hastings party. iv. 390. Naturalized '44, then living at Mont.; in '45 a lieut in Sutter's force, at one time a prisoner. iv. 486, 500; in '46 perhaps in the Cal. Bat. as above; in '47 lot-owner at S.F., tanner at N. Helv., and finally moving to a house on Amer. River. I have no later record than March '48, when Coates was seriously injured by a fall from his horse, being also robbed of $300.   Cobb, 1840, on the *Don Quixote* from Hon. iv. 103.   C. (Chas), 1848, owner of S.F. lots; same name in S.F. directory of '52.

Cochran (Thos), 1845, nat. of N.C., who crossed the plains to Or. '43, and came to Cal. in the McMahon-Clyman party. iv. 572, 574, 587. Named at N. Helv. several times in '45-8; in '49 built a hotel, the 1st building at Cacheville; an eccentric man, who in '51 suddenly departed for Australia.   Cocket (C.), 1848, passp. from Honolulu.   Cocks (Henry), 1846, English marine on the U. S. *Dale*, who after his disch. in '48 lived at Mont. and married a daughter of Francisco García, moving in '53 to the S. Bernabé rancho, or Cock's station, of which he was the claimant. iv. 655, 679. In '66 he went with the telegraph exped. to Alaska and Siberia; had an appointment on the Tule River Ind. reservation; accomp. Wheeler's explor. exped. on the Colorado; and in '75 was living near his old place in Mont. Co., where he still is, I think, in '85.   Coe (John J.), 1847, Co. F, N. Y. Vol. (v. 499).   Coeur (François), 1846, with Kearny's force. v. 337.

Coffelt (Geo.), 1846, teamster Co. C, 1st U.S. dragoons (v. 336).   Coffemeyer (Edward), 1846, sailor at N. Helv. '47-8; member of 1st and 4th Donner relief. v. 538, 541.   Coffin (Ephraim), 1841, of U.S. ex. exped.; died in Cal. iv. 279.   C. (Henry), 1844, Amer. sailor of the *Monmouth*, aided by the consul.   C. (Ivory), 1846, seaman or marine on the *Savannah;* wounded at the S. Gabriel Jan. 9, '47. v. 395.   C. (James), 1835, mr of the *Peor es Nada*. C. (J. W.), 1847, on a whaler; came back in '50; of S. F. firm C. & Hendry; d. before '85, leaving a son and daughter.   C. (L.), 1848, at S.F. on the *Lady Adams* from Callao.   C. (Wm), 1826, mr of the *Franklin*. iii. 147.   C. (Wm), 1847, Co. B, N.Y.Vol. (v. 499).   C., 1847, mr of the *Charles Drew.*   Coghlan (James), 1848, sailor on the *Elizabeth.*   Cogswell, 1845, at N. Helv. Dec. Cohn (Moritz), 1847, musician N.Y.Vol. (v. 499).   C. (Philip), 1847, Co. D, N.Y.Vol.

Colbath (Lemuel), 1846, mate of the *Euphemia* '46-8; a New Englander. Colbert (John), 1834, Engl. shipwright, age 26; naturalized '39; still at S. F. '40. iii. 412.   Cole (James B.), 1847, Co. D, Morm. Bat.; at Springville, Utah, '82.   C. (John), 1826, sailor on the *Rover*.   C. (Thomas), 1833, Engl. sailor whose name often appears in Larkin's accounts of '33-49. iii. 409. Acc. to John Price, in *S. Luis Ob. Co. Hist.*, 63, he deserted from the *Kent*, but I have no record of that vessel before '36. Cole was one of Graham's riflemen of '36-8. (iii. 457); arrested but not exiled '40. iv. 17; grantee of lands in Salinas Val. '42-4. iv. 656; in '44 flogged by the Calif. for revealing to Micheltorena

the place where certain powder and lead had been buried, so says Swan; in
'45–6 often employed to carry despatches, v. 29, 235, also signing the call to
foreigners at S. José, iv. 599, and accomp. Lieut Revere on a hunting trip.
Mentioned by Revere, Sherman, and Colton, the latter naming him as a man
who stole a horse. His name appears on the assessment rolls of '50; and acc.
to *Taylor's List*, he died at Mont. in '58.   Coleman (Geo.), 1827, at Sta B.
and S. Buen. '27–8. ii. 580; iii. 94, 176.   C. (Michael), 1845, overl. immig.
of Grigsby-Ide party; bonds given by Wm Benitz Nov. 21st; prob. went to
Or. in '46. iv. 526, 578.   C. (Thos), 1847, carpenter on the U. S. *Preble*.
Colespedriguez (Bruno), 1829, mr of the *Rosalía*. iii. 148.
    Colgan (James A.), 1847, Co. G, N.Y.Vol. (v. 499).   Colima (Tomás San-
chez), at Los Ang. '43; juez de campo '44. iv. 633; cl. for Sta Gertrudis '53.
iv. 629, 635. .   Collie (Alex.), 1826–7, surg. of H.B.M.S. *Blossom;* made a
trip from S.F. to Mont. and back by land. iii. 121.   Colligan, 1847, attempts
murder at Sta Cruz. *S. F. Star*, Nov. 20th; perhaps 'Callaghan.'   C. (Wm),
1846, sailor of the navy; at Mont. in July; went south with the Cal. Bat.; in
'75 and later a broker and politician of N.Y. City.   Collins (John), 1847,
boatswain of the *Cyane*.   C. (Napoleon), 1847, lot-owner at S.F.; perhaps
the C. who was wrecked in the bay and rescued by the *Tasso's* boat. *Alta*,
Feb. 17, '67.   C. (Peter), 1842, in the Sta Cruz redwoods. iv. 341; in '43
kept a bar at Mont.; killed at Pacheco Pass about '54.   C. (Robert H.), 1847,
Co. D, Morm. Bat. (v. 469); in '82 at Huntingdon, Utah.   Colombet (Clement), 1844, Frenchman who kept a hotel at S. José '49. iv. 453; made a fortune in the mines, lost later and regained; married a daughter of Thos Kell;
in '60 at Warm Springs, Alameda Co., age 43; living at S. José '81.   Colton
(Chas E.), 1847, servant to an officer in Morm. Bat. (v. 469).   C. (Patrick),
1847, Co. F, 3d U. S. artill. (v. 518).   C. (Philander), 1847, Co. B, Morm.
Bat.; a mason who made bricks and worked on 1st brick house at S. Diego.
    Colton (Walter), 1846, chaplain U.S.N., who came on the *Congress*, and
was alcalde at Mont. in '46–8; also judge of the admiralty; an earnest, kind-
hearted, and sensible man, whose official and private record in Cal. was a
most excellent one. In partnership with Robert Semple, he edited and published the *Californian*, the 1st Cal. newspaper, in '46–7, making a visit to the
mines in the autumn of '48, and causing the erection of a school-house at Mont.,
named for him Colton Hall. His *Deck and Port*, and *Three Years in Cal.*,
published in '50, are journals of his experience and observations, full of interest, and justly regarded as standard works on the annals of '46–8. He went
east early in '49, but I have no record of his later career. v. 254, 288–93, 433,
608, 637–8, 658.   Columbo (A.), 1847, Amer. farmer at S. Buen.   Colwell
(J.), 1845, doubtful name of an immig. iv. 578.
    Combs (Abram), 1847, one of the Mormon col. with wife and 3 child. **v.**
546; in Utah '84, his wife being dead.   Comelero (Pedro), 1836, Italian cook
from Lima at Los Ang.   Comfort (Geo. F.), 1838, mr of the *Ayacucho*. iv.
101.   Comstock (Cortey), 1847, Co. G, N.Y.Vol. (v. 499).
    Conanse (José), 1791–1800, visiting friar at S. Diego. i. 655.   Concha
(Juan), 1791, lieut in Malaspina's exped. i. 490.   Conde (Pedro), 1818, lieut,
com. of one of Bouchard's vessels. ii. 226–7.   Condels, 1845, doubtful name
of an Amer. at Brancif., age 24.   Condit (Jeptha), 1847, Co. C, Morm. Bat.
(v. 469); reënl. at Los Ang.   Conduian (Alex.), 1845, doubtful name of a
Frenchman at Brancif., age 25.   Conejo (Casimiro), 1798, i. 606.   Conley
(James H.), 1847, carpenter on the *Dale*.   Conley (Marston F.), 1847, perhaps of N.Y.Vol. under another name.   Conn (John), 1843, doubtful member of the Chiles-Walker party. iv. 393; in '52 claimant of a Napa Co. rancho.
Connell (John), 1847, Co. I, N.Y.Vol. (v. 499); died at sea bet. Or. and Cal.
'82.   Connell (John), 1847, sergt Co. G, N.Y.Vol. v. 504; lot-owner S. F.
v. 685.   Connelly (Michael), 1847, Co. B, N.Y.Vol. (v. 499); resid. of Stockton from '49 to his death in '57.   C. (Wm), 1847, Co. B, N.Y.Vol.   Conners
(John), 1844, said to have arrived in Sta Clara Co. iv. 453; called Conness by
Hall.   Conner (W.E.), 1848, passp. from Honolulu.   Connolly (James H.),
1846, carpenter on the U.S. *Dale*.   Connor (James), 1845, Delaware Ind. of

Frémont's comp. '45-7; wounded in the service. iv. 583.   Conover (Francis S.), 1847, mid. on the U.S. *Independence.*   Conrad (Henry), 1847, Co. C, N.Y. Vol. (v. 499); at N. Helv.; later mayor (?) at Sonoma. *Clark.*   C. (Edward), 1844, on the roll of the Pion. Soc.; at Riverside '81.   C. (John P.) 1847, Co. C, N.Y.Vol. (v. 499); at S.F. '74; d. before '82.   C. (Wm), 1848, keeper of the Colonnade House S.F. v. 683.

Coock (John), 1847, Co. F, 3d artill. (v. 518).   Cook (Chas), 1845, N. Yorker who died suddenly at Mont. iv. 587.   C. (Geo.), 1844, Amer. naturalized this year. iv. 453; ment. by Bryant as owner of a rancho at S. José, '46.   C. (Goodwin), 1848, in Sutter's employ.   C. (Grove C.), 1841, Kentuckian hunter, and overl. immig. in Bartleson party. iv. 270, 275, 279; wandering about for a few years; often named in Larkin's accounts from '43; naturalized in '44; at Sutter's fort '45 working on a distillery. His shooting of a Walla Walla chief in July caused much excitement. iv. 544-5; v. 300-1; and in Dec. he was married by Sutter to Rebecca Kelsey, who presently had some reason to regret it. In '46 Cook went to Yerba Buena, and settled more or less at S. José, where he took some slight part in the mil. campaign, was member of the council and junta, v. 664, and in '49 was a man of wealth, subsequently lost. He died at Sta Cruz in '52. He is described as a man whose wit and generosity went far to counterbalance some less desirable qualities. C. (Jackson), 1847, at N. Helv.; apparently Grove Cook, q.v.   C. (James), 1830, at work on Cooper's rancho. iii. 180; joined the comp. extranjera at Mont. '32. iii. 221.   C. (Jonas), 1846, doubtful name of the Mormon col. v. 547.   C. (Manuel), 1830, Amer. who got a carta in Oct.   C. (Sam.), 1830, mr. of the *Danube.* iii. 146.   C. (Wm), 1843, disabled seaman of the *John Jay;* aided by consul, and worked on ranchos, but shipped late in '44.

Cooke (Henry D.), 1847, sup. and part owner of the *Lambayacana* from Valparaiso; also of the *Com. Shubrick;* lot-owner at S.F.; of firm Ruckle & Co.; a prominent business man of S.F. '49-54; figuring later at Washington in the crédit mobilier and other financial operations; a relation of Jay Cooke. C. (Philip St George), 1847, capt 1st U.S. dragoons, who came to Cal. as lieut-col, commanding the Mormon Bat. v. 428, 477, 483-6. He was for a time commandant of the southern district, taking some part in the quarrel with Frémont. v. 437, 440, 445-6; resigned his com. and went east with Gen. Kearny, being a witness at the Frémont court-martial. v. 450, 452, 456, 489. His *Journal* of the march of the Bat. was published by the govt. v. 483; and was republished with additions by the author—then brevet major-general U. S.A.—in '78 as the *Conquest of Cal. and N. Mex.*, a good narrative of Cooke's experiences and those of his men, but of no value whatever in its assumed character as a complete record of the conquest. He also wrote *Scenes and Adventures in the Army.* It is noticeable that a part of his journal was lost in Cal., and in Jan. '48 was purchased by Sutter from an Ind. *N. Helv. Diary,* MS., 164.   Coombs (Chas), 1824, cook on the *Rover.*   C. (Catherine), 1847, married at S.F. to C.P.A.Briggs. *Star.*

Coombs (Nathan), 1843, native of Mass. who came to Or. overland in '42, and to Cal. in the Hastings' party at the age of about 18. v. 390, 400. After working a while for Stephen Smith, iv. 396, he went to Gordon's place on Cache Creek, where he won the heart of Uncle Billy's daughter Isabel, and was nearly killed by a grizzly bear, also asking for naturalization in '44. In '45 he seems to have served in Sutter's force. iv. 486, 501; then married and settled on a Napa Valley rancho purchased of Salv. Vallejo; took no active part in the troubles of '46; and in '48 laid out the town of Napa on his rancho. v. 670. He became wealthy, was active in local politics, served in the legislature of '55, was capt. of militia '63, but was best known as a patron of the turf and the owner of blood-stock. Portrait in *Napa Co. Hist.,* 42. He died at his Napa home in '77, leaving a widow, 4 sons—Wm, Nathan, Frank, and Levi—and a daughter, Eva, wife of John M. Coghlan.   Coon (Wm), 1846, member of the 1st Donner relief. v. 539.   C. (Wm), 1847, sergt Co. D, Morm. Bat. (v. 469).

Cooper, 1831, said to have come from N. Mex. in the Wolfskill party, and to have died at Sta B. iii. 387, 405. C. (Charles H.), 1840, Amer. exile to S. Blas, who returned before '42 to urge his claim for damages. iv. 18, 33, 120. C. (Daniel, or David), 1834, Amer. sailor with but one arm, possibly a relation of Capt. J.B.R.Cooper. I have the original Boston passport to Daniel and the Hawaiian passp. to Dav. of '34. He came on the *Ayacucho.* iv. 412; his name appears often in corresp.; mate of the *California* in '40; died at S. F. May '41 of apoplexy—which a large quantity of aguardiente had not cured. C. (Fernando M.), 1835, named in Larkin's accounts '36–8. iv. 118; in '38 at Los Ang. signs a certif. as a physician. Prob. the same who in '35 embalmed the body of Gov. Figueroa. iii. 296. C. (Henry), 1836, named in Larkin's accounts '36–43. iv. 118; arrested in '40. iv. 17; called by Morris an Ind. at Sta Cruz; apparently in Sutter's employ '47. C. (J.W.), 1846, Cal. Bat. (v. 358); enlisting at S. Juan in Nov.; perhaps same as following. C. (James), 1846, kept a hotel at Sonoma '48; ment. by Hittell as a rich man near Benicia in '60. C. (James F.), 1847, Co. F, N.Y.Vol. (v. 499). C. (John Burwood), 1830, known as 'sailor Jack,' said by some authorities to have come to S.F. as early as '24–5, or by others on a whaler in '33, or in '36. iii. 409; iv. 118. Juan Coopet, prob. the same, was an artilleryman at S.F. in '30-1; named as English at Mont. in '34; a N. York sailor and calker, age 43, at Mont. in '36 in the artill. barracks; built houses at S.F. '40, '44. v. 683–4; Engl. retired artill., age 56, in S.F. padron of '44; at S.F. also '45-6, receiving some votes for collector. v. 295. Thus there may have been two John Coopers at least. John B. settled cn a S. Mateo rancho, married a native, and died in '62, leaving a family. His monument at the S.F. mission cemetery is inscribed John Baptist Burwood Cooper, nat. of Engl., age 68; his wife was María Cecilia ——, d, '53, age 27; children María Jesus b. '41, Agapito, Juan B. Aniceto, Narciso Nieves, María Julia Dolores, and Juan Lorenzo d. '61, age 10.

Cooper (John Bautista Roger), 1823, nat. of the Alderney Isl., who came to Mass. as a boy with his mother, who by a 2d marriage became the mother of Thos O. Larkin. I have his 'protection paper' of 1816, certifying his U. S. citizenship, and describing him as 24 years old, 5 ft 5 in. in height, with light complex., sandy hair, and blue eyes, with a scar on the left arm and nerves of the left hand contracted. From this deformity he was known in Cal. as Don Juan el Manco. He came as master of the *Rover* from Boston, selling the vessel to Gov. Argüello, and continuing to command her on voyages to China till '26. ii. 492-3, 495, 519-20, 614; iii. 24, 119, 148. From '26 he became a resident of Mont., and there is not a year from '26 to '48 in which his name does not occur in many original records. In '27 he was baptized, his original name of John Roger being transformed into Juan Bautista Roger, married Encarnacion Vallejo, became a rival of Hartnell & Co. in trade, and signed bonds for Jed. Smith. ii. 616; iii. 128, 158-60. In '28 began his legal quarrels with Luis Argüello. ii.583; iii. 12; in '29 he bought for $2,000 from Joaq. de la Torre the rancho of Bolsa del Potrero y Moro Cojo, or Sagrada Familia. ii. 615; and in '30 was naturalized, being ment. besides in connection with the Solis revolt and the Fitch romance, as well as in commercial records. ii. 609; iii. 71, 83, 142, 145. His business corresp. shows not only that he was always complaining of some injustice, but that he often gave cause of complaint to those who traded with him. In '32 on the roll of the comp. extranjera. iii. 221; in '33 licensed to hunt otter, and granted the Molino rancho, Sonoma. iii. 394, 712; regidor at Mont. '34-5. iii. 673; in '36 living with wife, 2 children, mother-in-law, and her 3 daughters at Mont., having also cattle and a mill on the Sonoma rancho confirmed to him this year. iii. 429; iv. 116; his mill visited by Edwards '37. iv. 86. In '39 Capt. C. resumed his seafaring life as master of the govt schooner *California,* making many trips in the next 5 years to the Mex. coast and to the islands, of which I have his original *Log of the California.* iv. 102, 282, 289, 346, 361, 563-4; in '40 obtained land at S.F. and the Punta de Quintin rancho, iii. 706, 712, v. 683, but was in trouble about $5,250 which the govt had owed him since '26; perhaps the Juan Cooper to whom the Nicasio rancho was granted '44. iv. 672; sick at Acapulco at end of '44; but was back again in '45, only to depart for Peru. where, in '46, he was matriculated as 2d piloto. He visited Cal. in '47, and in '48 seems to have been in com. of the *Elizabeth*, wrecked at Sta B. In '49 he commanded the *Ereline* on a voy. to China; but soon quit the sea; was harbor-master at Mont. in '51; and was claimant for the Bolsas, Molino, and El Sur ranchos. iii. 679. He continued to live at Mont., much of the time on his rancho, till after 1860; and died at S.F. in '72, in his 80th year. There were few of the old Cal. pioneers more widely known or better liked than Capt. Cooper, though as a trader he had some peculiarities that, in the earlier years particularly, kept him in hot water with other traders much of the time. Besides hundreds of his letters scattered in dif. archives, his family papers fill several volumes of the *Vallejo, Doc. Hist. Cal.*, which should properly bear his name. In addition to his *Log* of '39-44, I have also a book of *Accounts* of '27. His widow still lives, '85, in S.F. His children were Ana María Guadalupe b. '29 wife of Herman Wohler, Juan Baut. Guillermo b. '31, Henry B., Francisco G., Amelia (Mrs Molera), George Howard, and Wm Roger who died in '73.   .

Cooper (J. M.), 1846, gunner on the U.S. *Savannah*.   C. (Luther), 1834, named often in Larkin's accounts '34-7. iii. 412.   C. (Martin), 1835, Amer. at S. Luis Ob.; also on Larkin's books '35-7. iii. 413.   C. (Samuel E.), 1846, teamster of Co. C, 1st U. S. dragoons (v. 336).   C. (Sarchel), 1846, son of Stephen, miner at Park's Bar '48; d. at Colusa '74.   C. (Sidney), 1831, doubtful record of a trapper of Young's party. iii. 388.

Cooper (Stephen), 1846, Kentuckian b. 1797, moved to Mo. 1817, guide and scout in the Sta Fé trade and various Ind. wars, Ind. agent and member of the legislature, who came overl. to Cal. as capt. of a small party, v. 528, with his wife Melinda and 6 children. From Yount's, in Napa Val., he went to S.F., where in Feb. '47 he presided over a public meeting of citizens dissatisfied with the composition of the proposed governor's council. *Star;* v. 433; in the autumn settled at Benicia. v. 672-3; alcalde in '48. v. 673; judge of 1st instance of the Sonoma district from Aug. '49, having also mined at Park's Bar for a short time. In '54 went to Colusa, where he was justice of the peace for 12 years, and where he still lived in '80; went later to Modoc Co., and in '85 lives at Winters, Yolo Co. Portrait in *Yolo Co. Hist.*, 26; biog. sketch from Cooper's own statement by 'F. S.' in *Colusa Sun* June 17, '71. Mrs. C. died in '72 at the age of 71. Of the two sons, Sarchel died about '74, and Thos B. lives in Modoc Co. '85; the daughters were Francis wife of Robert Semple and later of I. N. Van Winkle, living in Oakland '85, Susan wife of John Wolfskill, Elizabeth wife of Waller Calmes, and Martha wife of Amos Roberts. In '71 Maj. Cooper had 6 children and 16 grandchildren living.   C. (Wm C.), 1845, overl. immig. of the Grigsby-Ide party; prob. went to Or. in '46. iv. 526, 578.

Cope (Wm), 1846, seaman of the *Savannah*, wounded at the S. Gabriel, Jan. '47. v. 395; perhaps 'Coxe.'   Copeland (Alex.), 1843, Amer. immig. from Or. in the Hastings party; got a carta in Nov., calling himself a clerk, and was employed by Stephen Smith at Bodega. iv. 390, 396; early in '46 at Sutter's Fort; prob. identical with the following.   C. (Andrew), 1846, lieut Co. B, Cal. Bat. v. 361; Cal. claim of $82 (v. 462); A. M. Copeland voted at S. José '50.   Copenger (Chas), 1847, Co. G, N.Y. Vol. (v. 499).   Copey (John), 1832, doubtful ment. at S.F.

Coppinger (John), 1835, prob. deserter from a British vessel at S.F. iii. 413; said to have been a lieut in the British army or navy; generally called Engl., but Amer. acc. to his naturalization papers, while Quigley makes him a nat. of Cork and near relative of a Bishop Coppinger, and in a S.F. padron he appears as a Dublin sawyer. On Larkin's books from '36; in '36-8 lieut of Graham's foreign comp. in Alvarado's service. iii. 458-9, 491; naturalized '39 and juez at Corte Madera. iii. 705; arrested but not exiled in '40, being also the grantee of Cañada de Raimundo in S. Mateo. iii. 711; iv. 17. From '41 he seems to have lived on the rancho, being included in S.F. padrones, one of the defensores of the patria, 30 years old in '42 and 35 in '44; aided Michel-torena in '45. iv. 487; seems to have taken no part in the troubles of '46 except that Weber accused him of giving inform. that led to his, W.'s, arrest. I find no record of him later except an unintelligible one in *S. Mateo Co. Hist.*, 4, that during the war he was carried as a prisoner to Mex. where he died. His widow was María Luisa Soto, who before '52 married a man named Greer, and was a claimant of the rancho, living at Mayfield in late years.

Coray (Wm), 1847, sergt Co. B, Morm. Bat. v. 477, 496. Corcoran, or Corgan (Geo. A.), Co. D, N.Y. Vol. (v. 499); at Chicago '82. C. (Martin), 1844, nat. of Nova Scotia, who came from Honolulu as seaman on the U.S. *Levant.* iv. 453. In '46 he came back, on the *Savannah* probably, and was one of Bartlett's party captured by Sanchez (v. 379), prob. the only survivor of that party; disch. from the navy in N.Y.; ret. to Cal. '49 and went to the mines. From '51 he was engaged in many kinds of business, chiefly that of hotel-keeper, at S. F., Alviso, S. José, and Sta Clara, being R.R. agent, tax collector, and county treasurer. In '85, at the age of 61, wharfinger at S.F.

Cordero, killed at S. Buen. '38. iii. 554. C., a leader in disturbance at Los Ang. '45. iv. 523. C. (Ambrosio), soldier of S.F. comp. at Sonoma '41–2. C. (Clemente), Sta B. soldier before '37. C. (Fermin), settler at Brancif. 1797; regidor 1802. i. 569, 639; ii. 156. C. (Francisco), at Sta B. '37, wife Petra Pico, 1 child. C. (José), soldier of S.F. comp. '34–42. C. (Juan), at Sta B. '37, wife Antonia Valenzuela and 7 child. C. (Mariano), 1st marriage S.F., to Juana Pinto 1776. i. 296. C. (Miguel), at Sta B. before '37, wife Antonia Jimeno and 5 children; maj. at Sta Inés '40–3. iii. 646–8, 663–4; at Sta B. '50. C. (Pedro), at Sta B. '37, wife Dolores Quijada and 4 child.; juez de paz '39–40. iii. 654–5; grantee of Cañada de Salsipuedes '44. iv. 642.

Córdoba (Alberto de), 1796, Span. lieut of engineers sent to Cal. to inspect coast defences, and superintend the founding of Branciforte, 1796–8; author of an *Informe.* i. 497, 541–2, 545, 565–70, 652, 682, 700, 719. I have other engineering reports by him before his visit to Cal.

Cordua (Theodore), 1842, German trader and farmer from Honolulu on the *California*, after corresp. with Sutter, whom he had known before. iv. 229, 341. In '43 settled on Feather River near the site of the later Marysville, where Dr Sandels found him a fat, jolly, whist-loving man, popular with everybody. He had a straw hut at first, soon replaced by an adobe structure, the place being named New Mecklenburg, but better known as Cordua's rancho. In '44 he was naturalized and got the Honcut rancho. iv. 671; had a lighter, the *Yuba*, running on the river, often visiting the settlements, and his name often appeared in various commercial and other records of the time. Larkin described him in '45 as a man of 52 years, with property, respectability, and local influence; enlisted in Sutter's force, but wisely left it on the march south; often named in the *N. Helv. Diary* '45–8; took no part in the conflict of '46–7. In '48–9 sold his land and cattle for $30,000 and opened a store in the mines, where he is said to have lost his wealth; still in the Sac. Val. '54; but broken in health as well as property, he is said by Gilbert to have returned to the Sand. Isl., where he died.

Corey, 1846, mr of the *Isaac Howland.* v. 578. C. (P.), 1848, passp. from Honolulu. Corne (L. P.), 1840, sailor on the *California*. Cornelio (D.), 1828, mr of the *Minerva.* iii. 148. Corning (Otto), 1847, Co. G, N.Y. Vol. (v. 499). Cornwall (Pierre B.), 1848, nat. of N.Y. who came overland and made a large fortune in trade at Sacramento '48–9 as member of the firm Priest, Lee, & Co.; from '59 a resident and prominent business man of S.F., being at one time president of the Soc. of Cal. Pioneers. Still living in S.F., I think, in '85. Cornwell (Geo. N.), Co. H, N.Y.Vol. (v. 499); nat. of N.Y., who on his discharge, after a brief experience in the mines, settled at Napa, where as trader, farmer, owner in quicksilver mines, postmaster, member of the legislature, supervisor, deputy sheriff, and politician, he has always been a prominent man. He married Anna J. West of N.H. in '54, and in '72, when he furnished me a MS. *Sketch of My Life*, they had 3 children, Fannie L., Clara, and Norris, 3 having died. Claimant of rancho. iv. 674. Still living at Napa in '82, and I think in '85. Corona (José), com. de policía S. Diego '36 iii. 616. C. (José M.), at Los Ang. '46. C (Juan B.), com. policía (?) at S. Diego '36. iii. 613.

Coronel (Antonio Francisco), 1834, son of Ignacio, with whom he came to Cal. at the age of 17. His 1st public service seems to have been as sergt of artill. in support of Cárlos Carrillo in '38; in '41 applicant for a lot at S. Juan Cap. iv. 626; in '43 juez de paz at Los Ang., and interventor at the transfer of S. Fernando. iv. 633, 639; in '45 comisionado of the junta to treat with Micheltorena, and elector of Los Ang., declining the sub-prefecture. iv. 497, 540, 633; grantee of Sierra de los Verdugos '46. v. 628; also taking part as capt. in all the southern military operations against the U.S. in '46-7, starting at one time for Mex. with a flag taken from Mervine at S. Pedro, and narrowly escaping capture by Kearny's men on the way. v. 331-2. In '48 he was a successful miner; and in later years held many local positions, though giving chief attention to his vineyard and to agricultural interests; county assessor '50 et seq.; mayor in '53; member of the council '54-67; state treasurer '67-71. A man of wealth and influence, still residing at his Los Ang. vineyard and orange orchard in '85. In '77 he dictated for my use his *Cosas de California*, or recollections of early events, a MS. of 265 pp., and one of the best narratives of its class in my collection. He also gave me a valuable col. of *Doc. Hist. Cal.* from his family archives. C. (Guillermo), 1842-5, sub-lieut in the batallon fijo. iv. 289.   C. (Ignacio), 1834, Mex. teacher who with his family came in the H. & P. colony. iii. 263. In Mex. Don Ignacio had been a soldier from 1810 in the Span. army, being made corporal of cavalry in '14, a sergt of the Cholula *realistas urbanas* in '18, and prob. in '22 was retired with the rank of alférez; at least, he got all the necessary certificates, including one that he had served the cause of independence and had ceded all his back pay to the national treasury. *Coronel, Doc.*, MS. The failure of the colony was a bitter disappointment, as his appointment of teacher at Solano at $1,000 per year brought in no funds, and he was even ordered to be sent to Mex. for complicity in the supposed revolt of '35, but did not go. iii. 287, 291. In '36 he was living at Corralitos rancho, Mont. dist., age 41, wife Francisca Romero, child. Josefa b. '16, Antonio '18, Micaela '21, Soledad '26, and Manuel '32. iii. 677. The same year he was named as comisionado to secularize S. Miguel. iii. 685; iv. 46; and in '37 he went to Los Ang., taking com. at S. Gabriel, and aiding Carrillo in the campaign of Las Flores. iii. 520, 522, 558. In '38-9 he taught a school at Los Ang., having also a little store, and serving as sec. of the ayunt. iii. 631, 635-6; also sec. in '44-7. iv. 633-4; v. 625-6; grantee of La Cañada '43 and of Cajon de los Negros '46. iv. 635; v. 627, ministro suplente of the tribunal sup. '45. iv. 532; receptor at S. Pedro '46. v. 264, 625. He died at Los Ang. in '62.   C. (Juan Ant.), 1769, arriero in the 1st exped. i. 135.

Correa (José M.), 1842, sub-lieut of the batallon fijo '42-5. iv. 289, 407. Cortés (Anastasio), com. de policía at S. José; killed by José J. Castro '39; but named as sub-lieut of artill. at Mont. '45. iv. 731, 652.   C. (Felipe), inválido at Sta B. '32, wife María de Jesus Lara.   C. (Fernando), Mex. convict of '25. iii. 16.   C. (Juan Lope), 1796, Span. friar who served at S. Gabriel and Sta B., retiring in 1805. Biog. ii. 120-1; ment. i. 577, 588-90, 594, 664, 672; ii. 159-60.   Cortis (Henry), 1848, passp. from Honolulu.

Corville, 1847, at Sutter's Fort and New Mecklenburg.   Corvan (Toribio Gomez de), 1602, com. of one of Vizcaino's vessels. i. 98, 102.   Corwin (Mrs Fanny M.), 1846, of the Mormon colony. v. 546; remained in Cal.; prob. at S.F. '85.   Cory (Benj.), 1847, nat of Ohio, b. in '22, a physician who went to Or. '47 and came to Cal. on the *Henry* in Nov.; settled at S. José, but went to the mines in '48. A rumor like he had found new placers on the Moquelumne induced 500 men to quit the old diggings and follow his trail, so wrote Schallenberger in Aug. Member of 1st legislature '49-50; memb. of S. José council '50-4; married Sarah Ann Braly '53; trustee of normal school from '72; county physician '81. Still living at S. José in '82 with 8 children.

Cosío (Blas), 1820, mr of the *S. F. de Paula*. ii. 293.   C. (José María), sec. of the gov. '34; ayud. de plaza at Mont. and fiscal '36. iii. 672, 687. Costa (Bernabal), 1836, Ital. sailor at Los Ang. from Lima, age 36.   Costan, 1774, surg. on the *Santiago*. i. 228.   Costansó (Miguel), 1769, Span. alférez and engineer who accomp. the 1st exped. to Cal. as cosmographer, and whose *Diario Histórico* was pub. in Mex. 1776. He was later very prominent in his profession, and I have some of his original reports relating to proposed defences in Cal. 1794–5, as well as to the fortifications of V. Cruz and drainage of Mex.; still living in 1811, being then a mariscal de campo. i. 128, 131, 136, 140–1, 147–51, 154–5, 168, 171–2, 534–5, 662, 615, 624, and list of auth.; *Hist. Mex.* iv. 134.   Coster (Antonio), at Sonoma '44, age 16.

Cot (Antonio José), 1820, Span. trader from Lima, partner of Juan Ign. Mancisidor, visiting the coast apparently in '20; in '22 brought his family from Lima; named in various commercial records from '23. ii. 493. In '28 he was required to quit Cal. as a Span. supposed to be unfriendly to Mex., and after some delays to arrange his business affairs—perhaps departing and returning meanwhile—he sailed with wife and 3 child. in '30. iii. 51, 99. He came back, however, in '35–6; is ment. in mission accounts of '40. iii. 620, 637; and became a permanent resident at Los Ang., prominent in commercial affairs in '46–7, being the purchaser of S. Luis Rey, and having a claim for supplies furnished the U.S. v. 435, 464, 467, 561, 620–1. He died at Sta B. about '60. His wife was Mariana Estevanez of Lima.   C. (Daniel), at Sta B. before '37, wife Bruna García, 2 child.

Cota, see list, in vol. i. p. 735, of those of this name before 1800; information about this family is very fragmentary.   C., corporal at Sta Inés '24. ii. 528.   C. (Antonia María), cl. of Tepusquet, widow of Tomás Olivera. iii. 636.   C. (Benito), at Los Ang. '46.   C. (Francisco), soldier at Sta B. before '37; com. and admin. at Sta Inés '37–41. iii. 663–4; grantee of Sta Rosa rancho '39. iii. 636; juez at Sta Inés '41, '48. iv. 646–8; v. 635; still at Sta B. '50. His widow and cl. for the rancho '52 was María Jesus Olivera.   C. (Francisco Atanasio), elector at Sta B. '28. ii. 572; iii. 44.   C. (Guillermo), corp. of the escolta at S. Fern. 1806–10. ii. 92, 115, 192; comisionado of Los Ang. '10–17. iii. 110, 208, 349–50; sergt of Sta B. comp. from '11. ii. 361, 572; at S. Fern. '32. ii. 570; comis. at Los Ang. '23–5. ii. 559–61; alcalde '27–9. ii. 560–1; age 70 in '39, still at Los Ang.   C. (Joaquin), engaged in revolt at Sta B. '29. iii. 78; wife Ventura Ortega.   C. (José Manuel), settler at Los Ang. '15; regidor '32. ii. 349, 635; iii. 638; at La Ballona '39, age 37. C. (José María), at Sta B. '32, wife Antonia Dominguez, 2 child.   C. (Josefa), widow of A. M. Nieto, grantee of Sta Gertrudis rancho '34; at Los Ang. '48. C. (Juan), at Los Ang. '46.   C. (Leonardo), alférez of defensores '45. iv. 539; regidor of Los Ang. '45–6. iv. 633; v. 625; grantee of Rio de las Ánimas '46. v. 627; and operating against the U. S. in S. Diego region as capt. v. 325, 342, 351–2.   C. (Manuel), soldier of Sta B. comp. before 1800, and corp. of the Sta Inés escolta '28. iii. 459, 582; in '32 at Sta B., wife María Ant. Valenzuela, 4 child.; admin. Sta B. mission '38–9. iii. 656–8. In '39 a lieut. iii. 583; ment. in '47. v. 617; father and son of the same name; see also José Manuel. C. (Marcos), at Los Ang. '46.   C. (María Isabel), wife of Dolores Pico; d. '69.   C. (Mariano), soldier of Sta B. comp. before 1790; inval. 1819, when he was killed by Ind. at S. Buen. ii. 333.   C. (Martin), named in '36. iii. 491.   C. (Miguel), at Sta B. before '37, wife Manuela Ortega, 2 children; arrested in '41. iv. 642.   C. (Pablo Antonio), soldier of 1769–74; corp. at S. Antonio '78–9; sergt in com. at S. Buen. '82–7; alférez from '88; died at Sta B. 1800, age 56. Biog. i. 665; ment. i. 425, 463, 466, 477, 553, 639, list auth.; ii. 28. His wife was Rosa María Lugo; a son Manuel Ant. was b. 1779; a daughter María de los Angeles was the wife of Joaq. de la Torre.   C. (Pacífico), son of Valentin, at Sta B. '48 in con. with the 'cañon perdido.' v. 588. C. (Raimundo and Ramon), at Los Ang. '46.   C. (Roque), soldier before 1780; settler at Los Ang. 1790. i. 347, 461.   C. (Simon), sec. of alcalde at Soledad '26. ii. 623.   C. (Valentin), son of Manuel, juez aux. Sta B. '33. iii. 654; capt. of militia and later of Sta B. comp. '36–9, supporting Alvarado. iii. 474, 553, 583, 651; grantee of Rio Sta Clara rancho '37. iii. 655; in charge of Sta Inés '42. iv. 646; in '46 resigns mil. rank; sub-prefect of Sta B. iv. 538; v. 35, 49. His wife was Luz Gonzalez.

Coulter (John), 1834, visitor, perhaps; at any rate, author of a trashy book.

of *Adventures* describing a visit. iii. 411.   C. (Thomas), 1831, Engl. visitor and scientist, who joined the comp. extranjera in '32, and published valuable *Notes on Upper Cal.* I have his letter of '33 from Guanajuato; also a note due him sent for collection in '38. iii. 221, 406-8.   Coupe (Geo.), 1848, passp. from Honolulu.   Courteau (Philibert), 1844, perhaps with Frémont in 1st and 2d exped. '44, '45-7; at N. Helv. '48. iv. 437, 583. Named as ' Philibert' in Cal. Bat. '46-7. (v. 358).   Coustner (And. J.), 1846, Co. C, 1st dragoons (v. 336).   Coutan (Gustavus J.), 1847, Co. H, N.Y.Vol. (v. 499).

Coutts (Cave Johnson), 1848, nat. of Tenn. and graduate of West Point in '43. After serving in the Mex. war he came to Cal. from Coahuila with Graham's battalion as lieut of the 1st U.S. dragoons. v. 522. He subsequently went with his comp. to the frontier on boundary-survey service; but in '51 resigned his commission, married Isidora Bandini, and settled at S. Diego, where he served as county judge. In '54 he moved to the Guajome rancho, a wedding gift of Abel Stearns to Doña Isidora; and there he spent the rest of his life, becoming rich in lands and live-stock, always popular and respected, though as bitter in his enmities as warm in his friendships, making Guajome a centre of the famed hospitality of southern Cal. Claimant also for Soledad rancho. iii. 612. He gave me in '74 a copy of his *Diary* of the overland march and early experience in Cal., besides rendering other valuable aid. Col Coutts died in '74 or '75, when he was 54 years of age. His widow still lived on the rancho in '82, having 8 surviving children. Perhaps the name should be written 'Couts.' A good biog. sketch in *S. Bern. Co. Hist.*, 196-7.   Couzens (John H.), 1847, had a lot and slaughter-house at S.F.; kept sheep on Yerba Buena Isl.; owned a lot at Benicia. v. 672, 685; he went to Honolulu and returned in '48.

Covarrubias (José María), 1834, nat. of France, naturalized citizen of Mex., who came in the H. & P. col., intending to be a teacher. iii. 263, 412. In '36-7 com. for secularization of Sta Inés. iii. 663-4; sec. of the dip. '37 and in '39; a partizan of Carrillo in the contest of '38. iii. 549, 556, 569, 580; in '39 partido elector at Sta B., and sec. of the prefecture at Mont. iii. 590, 675; took part in arrest of foreigners '40, and accomp. the exiles to S. Blas, going to Mex., where he rec'd a cross of honor for services in that city during the disturbances of July; returned in '40. iv. 11, 13, 15, 23, 30, 102. He was grantee of Castac rancho in '43. iv. 634; in '44 sec. of the assembly and alcalde of Sta B. iv. 410, 642; in '45 succeeded Bandini as sec. of Gov. Pico, and was lessee of Sta Inés. iv. 490, 519, 523, 531, 553, 558, 647; sent as comisionado to Mex. in '46, also grantee of Sta Inés. v. 32, 210, 561, 632; at Sta Inés '48. v. 589, 635; being a justice of the sup. court. In '49 he was a member of the constit. convention, and of the 1st legislature, being 4 times reëlected, and county judge of Sta B. in '61. Covarrubias died in '70 at the age of 69, leaving a family. His wife was María, daughter of Domingo Carrillo; his eldest son, Nicolás, was for a long time sheriff of Sta B. County.

Covell (Hiram), 1834, mr of the *By Chance*. iii. 381.   Covil (John Q. A.), 1847, Co. C, Morm. Bat. (v. 469); reënl. at Los Ang.   Covillaud (Charles), 1846, nat. of France, who had lived in La and Mo. for some years; overl. immig. to Cal. (v. 526). He is named in the *N. Helv. Diary*, '47-8, being an overseer at Cordua's rancho, and later prospector on the Yuba; had a trading-post at Cordua's '48-9 in partnership with his brothers-in-law, and in '49-57 the post was at Sacramento. Meanwhile, in '48, C., with others, had bought Cordua's rancho at New Mecklenburg, and here in '50 they laid out a new town, named Marysville in honor of C.'s wife, Mary Murphy, a survivor of the Donner party. Judge Stephen J. Field, the 1st alcalde of Marysville, gives an interesting account of the founding. *Remin.*, 20 et seq. Here C. spent the rest of his life, gaining an enviable reputation for his open-handed liberality, and filling some local offices. He died in '67 at the age of 51; his widow died later in the same year.

Cowie (Thomas), 1843, Amer. immig. of the Chiles-Walker party. From Feb. '44, when Walker applied for a pass in his behalf, nothing appears about him till June '46, when he joined the Bears and was killed by the Californians near Sta Rosa. iv. 392-3; v. 110, 148, 160-4.   C. (R.). 1837, came from Honolulu. iv. 104.   Cox (Alex. J.), 1847, Co. C, N.Y.Vol. (v. 499); a newspaper man, founder of the Sonoma *Bulletin* and Napa *Reporter;* at Napa '71-80; in Mendocino Co. '82.   C. (Amos), 1847, Co. D, Morm. Bat. (v. 469); in Iowa '82.   C. (Henderson), 1847, Co. A, Morm. Bat.; at N. Helv. '47-8 in Sutter's employ; killed by Ind. on the return to Salt Lake '48. v. 496; prob. the man called Henry W. by Bigler.   C. (Henry), 1846, mariner on the U.S. *Dale;* one of Marston's men (v. 379); disch. in Cal.; at Colton, S. Bern. Co., '85.   C. (John), 1847, Co. E, Morm. Bat. (v. 469); in Sutter's employ '47-8. C. (John), 1846. sergt Co. C, 1st U.S. dragoons; killed at S. Pascual. v. 346. C. (Patrick), 1847, Co. F, 3d U.S. artill. (v. 518).   Coxe (Wm), 1847, wounded at the S. Gabriel. v. 395; perhaps 'Cope.'   Coyan (Fred.), 1847, Co. F, 3d U.S. artill. (v. 518); a laborer at Mont. '48.   C. (Fred.), 1847, Co. G, N.Y. Vol. (v. 499); at Vallejo '41-4; prob. some error.

Crabb (H. G. and H. N.), 1848, at Honolulu from Mont.   Crabb (Jeremiah), 1846, Co. C, 1st U.S. dragoons (v. 336).   Crafts (Albert B.), 1847, Co. H, N.Y.Vol. (v. 499); d. S.F. '49.   Crafton (T.), 1845, boy in the Grigsby-Ide immig. party. iv. 578-9, 587.   Craig (James), 1832, said by Dye to have crossed the mts with him and to be in S.F. '69; doubtful. iii. 388, 408. C. (John), 1846, leader of an immig. party, who in Apr.-May '47 was at N. Helv. preparing to return east with a party. v. 528. *Star.*   C. (Otto), 1847, Co. F, 3d U.S. artill. v. 518.   Crain (Walter C.), 1846, mid. on the U.S. *Warren.*   Crane, or Ne-ta-me-commin, 1845, Del. Ind. in Frémont's party; killed on the Or. frontier '46. iv. 583; v. 25.   C., 1847, had a restaurant at Mont.   C. (Geo. W.), 1846, Virginian said to have arr. in May; served in the Cal. Bat. (v. 358); miner in '48; became a lawyer; memb. of legisl. from Yolo '50. and from Mont. '57; d. at S. Juan B. '68, age 41, leaving a widow and several children. All this comes from his obituary as memb. of Soc. Cal. Pion.   C. (J. C.), 1848, on the *Charles* at Honolulu from Mont.; in Cal. '55. C. (W. O.), 1846, mid. on the U.S. *Warren.*   Craven (James A. M.), 1846, lieut on the U.S. *Dale;* nat. of N. H., and brother of Rear-adm. C.; killed at Mobile '64 in com. of the monitor *Tecumseh. Lancey.*   Crawford (Geo.), 1846, boatswain's mate on the U.S. *Cyane;* wounded at the Mesa Jan. '47. v. 395.   Crawley (Philip), 1843, worked for Steph. Smith at Bodega acc. to the county histories. iv. 396.

Crebbe, 1847, doubtful name, in Sutter's employ '47-8.   Creen (Hugh W.), 1847, purser on the U.S. *Independence.*   Creighton (James), 1848, at Benicia, prospective partner of Pfister; vice-pres. of S.F. guards '48-9; elected to legisl. from S. F. '49.   C. (Johnston Blakely), 1846, passed mid. on the *Dale* and *Lexington* '47; in '77-8 com. of Norfolk navy-yard.   Crélis (Michel), 1844, perhaps one of Frémont's men. iv. 437.

Crespí (Juan), 1769, Span. friar who came with the 1st exped. by land to Cal. after 17 years of missionary service in New Spain; wrote a diary of the 1st *Viaje* by land from S. Diego to Mont., and several other important diaries of early years. i. list of auth., also i. 141, 151, 224, 284, 386; and served 13 years in Cal., chiefly at S. Cárlos, till his death in 1782. Biog. i. 386; ment. i. 121-2, 132-6, 140-4, 148-52, 158, 165, 167-9, 171, 175-6, 183-9, 196, 227, 231, 284-5, 351, 388, 410, 473-6; ii. 44.   Crespo (Manuel), Mex. phlebotomist and teacher at Mont. from '29 or earlier. ii. 613; comisionado of S. Cárlos '31. iii. 307, 679; vocal of the dip. '33. iii. 246; in '35 comisionado to secularize S. Antonio. iii. 354, 687-8. In '36 C. was living at Mont., age 28, wife Nicolasa Velarde, child. Tomasa A. b. '19 at Tepic, Adelaida '32, Manuel '33, Carolina '36; also vocal of the dip., taking part in a small way in the stirring political events. iii. 426, 454-5, 460, 463, 469. I have no record of him after his arrest in '37 for plotting against Alvarado. iii. 525.   Cretaine (Julio), 1846, at Los Ang.; made a claim for supplies of stationery and clothing (v. 462).   Creutzfeldt (F.), 1845, probably one of Frémont's men '45-7, as he was in '48. iv. 583; v. 453.   Cristan (Joseph), 1840, permitted to settle at S. Juan Cap. iv. 626.   Cristen (C.), 1830, mr of the *Catalina;* doubtful. iii. 146.   Cristóbal, neoph. grantee of Ulistac '45.   C. (Juan), or 'Bob,' 1816, negro settler. ii. 393.

Crocker (David), 1847, Co. F, 3d U.S. artill. (v. 518).   Crockett, 1848, at S.F. from Hon. on the *Sagadahoc*.   Cromwell, 1848(?), Winters & C., hotel at Coloma.   Cronstead (Philip), 1845, deserter from the *Hopewell* at S. Diego; prob. 'Crossthwaite,' q.v.   Crooks (Stephen), 1847, apparently an overl. immig.; in Sutter's employ '48.   Crosby, 1847, mr of the *Toulon*. v. 580. C. (A. H.), 1845, Amer. carpenter and overl. immig. of the Hastings-Semple party; employed by Sutter; prob. went back in '46. iv. 586; v. 526.   C. (Edmund P.), 1847, sergt Co. C, N.Y.Vol. v. 504.   C. (Thos), 1846, Co. C, 1st U.S. dragoons (v. 336).   Cross (Alex.), 1848, S.F. merchant, of C., Hobson, & Co. v. 681.   C. (Geo.), 1846, overl. immig. who served in the Cal. Bat. (v. 358), enlisting at S. Juan in Oct.; in Sta Clara Co. '76.   C. (John), 1846, prob. a brother of Geo.; in Cal. Bat.; on 1st jury at S. José '48.   C. (John), 1838, named in Larkin's accounts.   Crossman (Gideon), 1847, Amer. at N. Helv.   Crossthwaite (Philip), 1845, landed from a vessel at S. Diego. iv. 587; ment. in '46. v. 352; 2d juez at S. D. '47. v. 618; married Josefa Lopez '48, also lessee of S. Diego mission. v. 620; went to the mines; memb. of ayunt. '49–50; county clerk '52; later deputy sheriff; still at S. D. '72.

Crouch (Henry), 1847, builder of a house at Benicia. v. 672; a Baltimore carpenter who went to the mines in '48.   W. A. Crouch is also named as having settled at Benicia '47, perhaps another man.   C. (Henry J.), 1841, mr of the *Rosalind* '41–2. iv. 196, 568.   Crowell (Joseph), 1836, Engl. sailor from a whaler at Sta B.   C. (Wm H.), 1835(?), nat. of Conn., somewhat prominent from '49 as trader and local official in Sac., S.F., Sonoma, and Mendocino; said as a ship's boy to have touched at S.F. and other points as early as '35; died at Ukiah '69. *Mendoc. Dem.*, Aug. 6, '69; iii. 413.   Crowley, 1846, overl. immig. with Boggs. v. 528.   C. (Michael), 1847, Co. K, N. Y. Vol. (v. 499).   C. (Philip), 1846, Cal. claim $50. (v. 462); perhaps 'Crawley,' q.v. Crowninshields (Jacob), 1848, lot-owner at S.F.   Cruceno (Antonio), at Sta B. '32, wife Teresa Verdugo, 5 child.   Cruell (Robert), 1846, doubtful name in Sta B. region. v. 330.   Cruz (Faustino José), settler at Los Ang. 1790. i. 461.   C. (José), killed by Ind. at Pauma '46. v. 617.   C. (José M.), grantee of Cañada de Pinacates in '35. iii. 633.   C. (Santiago), at Los Ang. '46. C. (Tomás), sirv. at S.F. 1777. i. 297.   C. (Trinidad), convict from Mex. '29–33.   Cruzado (Antonio), 1771, Span. friar who served at S. Gabriel for 33 years and died in 1804. Biog. ii. 113; ment. i. 173, 176, 181, 196, 223, 299, 388, 459, 575, 664; ii. 159–60.

Cuani (Keaniu), 1847, lot-owner at S. F. v. 679.   Cucar (Thos), 1819, Engl. ii. 293.   Cuculla (Fran.), Dom. friar of L. Cal., at S. Gabriel '31–2. iii. 311, 641.   Cue (James), 1828, Engl. sailor, age 26, at Mont. '28–9. Cuesta, additional mention omitted by error on p. 704 for 'Arroyo de la Cuesta,' q.v. ii. 166, 386, 398, 496, 623; iii. 92, 96, 664, 681, 683, 691.   Cueva (Pedro), 1804, Span. friar who served at S. José mission two years, being wounded by the Ind. in 1805, and retiring 1806. Biog. ii 137–8; ment. ii. 34, 107, 109–10, 159–60.   Cuevas, 1834, mate of the *Natalia*. iii. 268.   Culebras (Miguel), 1828, Span. trader, who had been a lieut in the war of Indep., apparently not allowed to remain after '30. iii. 51–2.   Cullingham (James), 1847, locksmith at Mont.; name variously written.   Culverwell (Stephen S.), 1842, boy on the *United States* in Jones' fleet at the taking of Mont.; living in S.F. '85. iv. 304, 341.

Cummings (James), 1847, Co. G, N. Y. Vol. (v. 499).   C. (Joseph W.), 1847, Co. F, 3d U. S. artill. v. 518.   Cummins (Thos), 1842, Amer. trader who came from Hon. on the *Fama* for his health, age 38. iv. 141, 341; again at S. F. '48.   Cumuchi, chief of horse-thieves shot at Sonoma. iv. 73. Cunningham (Alex. S.), Co. B, N. Y. Vol. (v. 499); in Fresno Co. '82.   C. (Stephen), 1847, perhaps of N. Y. Vol. under another name.   C. (Wm H.), 1826, Mass. man, mr of the *Courier* '26–8, spending much of his time on shore, befriending Jed. Smith and Pattie, taking an active part in trade at all the ports, and vainly attempting to establish himself on Sta Catalina Isl. iii. 128, 146, 154, 165, 176. In '31 at Boston, but thinking of another trip to Cal.; said by Peirce to have been still living in Mass. after '80.   Cupper (Geo.), 1847, at Hon. from Mont. on the *Xylon*.

Curiel (Bernardo), Mex. soldier at Mont. '36, age 32, single. C. (Fernando), arrested '29. iii. 69. Curier (Anastase), 1830, French trapper of Young's party. iii. 174. Curl (James D.), 1846, Co. F, Cal. Bat. (v. 358); lot at S.F. '47; at S. José '50, as was Robert C. Curman (Lewis), 1847, sergt Co. F, 3d U.S. artill. v. 519. Curphey, 1847, mr of the *Maria Helena*. v. 579. Curran (Edward), 1846, Co. C, 1st U.S. dragoons (v. 336). C. (Michael), 1846, ditto. Curren (Edward), 1847, Co. A, N. Y. Vol. (v. 499); died in Cal. '60.

Curtis (Dabney), 1846, asst draughtsman with Kearny. *Lancey.* C. (Dorr P.), 1847, Co. B, Morm. Bat. (v. 469). C. (Foster), 1847, Co. D, Morm. Bat. C. (Josiah), 1847, Co. A, Morm. Bat. C. (Jotham), 1846, overl. immig. with his wife; connected with the 1st Donner relief, and roundly abused—with how much of reason I know not—by McCutchen and Thornton; owner of a lot at S.F. '47. v. 538-9, 678. C. (Wm), 1846, Kentuckian in Cal. Bat. (v. 358). Curus, 1847, mr of the *Europa.* v. 578.

Cushing, 1843, sup. of the *Admittance*, who had much trouble with the capt. and consignee, and was sent home. *Thomes.* Cushing (Bela), 1847, Co. C, N. Y. Vol. (v. 499); a printer of Boston; d. Sonoma '48. Cushman (Benj.), 1845, mr of the *Morea.* iv. 567. C. (James and Stephen), 1837, named in Larkin's accounts. Custer (John), 1846, Fauntleroy's dragoons (v. 232); Co. G, Cal. Bat. (v. 358); settled near Napa '48. Custot (Octave), 1837, Frenchman who signed a contract to take charge of Rafael Gomez' rancho in May. iv. 118; at S. Pablo '38 trying to make beet sugar; later induced Vallejo to employ him to superintend this industry at Petaluma on a larger scale, but failed to produce any sugar except some cakes of an imported article remelted to keep the general in good courage. In '39 he joined Sutter, and for several years was a kind of superintendent at N. Helv. iv. 219. He seems to have disappeared before '45, as his name does not occur in the *N. Helv. Diary.*

Cutler (John), 1846, Co. C, 1st U.S. dragoons (v. 336). Cutrell (Wm E.), 1847, lieut Co. E, N.Y.Vol. v. 504; went to Sandw. Isl., where he married and had several children; returned to S. F., where he died '68. Cutting, 1848, doubtful record of a man who came overl. to Or. from Ind. in '47, and ret. from Cal. in '48 with large quantities of gold-dust. *Solano Co. Hist.*, 380. Cuvellier (Emil), 1847, Co. G, N.Y.Vol. (v. 499).

Cyrus (Enoch), 1846, overl. immig. with wife and 3 sons, who settled in Napa Valley. v. 529. C. and two of the sons died of small-pox in '53, and the widow, Rebecca Cook, died in '73, age 77, at the farm near Calistoga, where the family had lived since '50. C. (John), 1846, son of Enoch, b. in Ill. '31; married Lovina Graves of the Donner party in '50; still living with 5 children near Calistoga in '81.

Daggett (Ed), 1832, mr of the *Balance.* iii. 381, D. (Timothy), 1822-3, mr of the *Almira.* ii. 474, 492. Dailey (Peter), 1847, Co. F, 3d U.S. artill. (v. 518). Daily, 1833, possibly in Walker's comp. iii. 391. Dailey and Daily, see 'Daly.' Dake (Morris B.), 1842, asst surg. on the *United States.* Daleman (John), 1846, marine on the *Dale;* in Phil. '84. Dall (John), 1847, Co. F, 3d U.S. artill. *Lancey.* Dally, 1846, mr of the *Golden Gate.*

Dally (Henry J.), 1843, nat. of N.Y., who after an adventurous career as sailor in many parts of the world landed at Mont. from the whaler *Chas W. Morgan.* iv. 400. He worked at Mont. for Kinlock, Larkin, and others; made an otter-hunting trip in '45; soon went to S. Luis Ob., where he married a Rodriguez and lived—but for a brief tour in the mines '48—till '52, serving as sheriff in '49-51; then settled at Sta B., where he still lived in '78, age 63. His MS. *Narrative*, besides an account of his early wanderings, contains testimony on early affairs at S. Luis, especially in '46, v. 375, and on the acts of outlaws in the south after '49.

Dalton (Henry), 1843, Engl. trader from Lima; sup. of the *Soledad.* iv. 400, 568. In his *Notes* of '45 Larkin describes D. as 40 years old, a man of property, intelligence, and local influence; and from that time his name often appears in commercial records, his home being at Los Ang. In '45 he served against Micheltorena, bought land at S. Gabriel, was sup. of the *Star of the West*, and grantee of S. Francisquito. iv. 495, 548, 568, 635; in '46 encargado at S. Gabriel, affording important financial aid to his brother-in-law Gen. Flores. v. 332, 628; in '47 purchaser of Sta Anita, for which and for Azuza, his permanent home, he was claimant in '52. v. 628, 633, 635.   Still living in '80. His wife was the daughter of A. V. Zamorano. iii. 561; and his son, Henry, Jr, was probably born before the end of '48.   D. (John), 1844, mr of the *Julian*.   D. (Wm), 1846, Co. C, 1st U.S. dragoons (v. 336); killed at S. Pascual. **v.** 346.

Daly, 1842, doubtful record at Mont.; perhaps Nathan.   D. (Henry), 1844, mentioned at Mont.   D. (J. and S.), 1846, Co. F, Cal. Bat. (v. 358); prob. one man.   D. (Nathan), 1834, Amer. named in Larkin's books '34-40. iii. 412; exiled in '40 and not known to have returned. iv. 18, 24.   D. (Wm), 1834 (?), said to have arrived in Sta Clara Co.; arrested '43, as appears from a letter of Forbes inquiring about him as a British subject; at Sutter's Fort with his wife '47; in the mines '48; had a rancho on the Cosumnes '49.   Perhaps more than one man of the name. iii. 412.   Dana (James D.), 1841, mineralogist of U.S. ex. exped. iv. 241-3.   D. (Richard H., Jr), 1835, Boston sailor on the *Pilgrim;* author of the famous *Two Years Before the Mast;* later an eminent lawyer and writer. iii. 367, 412-13, 613, 652; iv. 140, 142.

Dana (Wm Goodwin), 1826, nat. of Boston, and mr of the *Waverly* '26-8. iii. 118, 149, 154, 176.   Among his first acts was falling in love with Josefa Carrillo, daughter of Don Cárlos, and he was greatly troubled at having to wait for baptism and naturalization before getting married. I have his original letter to Capt. Cooper in '27-8 on this subject, with a quaint intermixture of business affairs. He had no objection to changing his religion and country, but damned the institutions that forced him to lose time. However, he was baptized in '27, got provisional papers in '28, was married to Doña Josefa, age 16, the same year, and in July '30 in a business letter announced the birth and death of his 2d child, cheerfully adding, ' We will soon have enough'—as they did, 21 in all. Meanwhile he had engaged in trade, agriculture, stock-raising, and soap-making, besides building the schr *Sta Bárbara* and buying the wreck and cargo of the *Danube*. ii. 573; iii. 140, 146. Every branch of his business was always on the point of going to the dogs, if we credit the letters of this inveterate grumbler. One source of revenue was the letting-out for a percentage of results of his otter license to foreigners, who could get no such paper. Final naturalization in '35; appraiser at Purísima. iii. 665; capt. of the port. iii. 654; in '36 alcalde of Sta B. iii. 483, 654; iv. 117. In '37 he was grantee of the Nipomo rancho, S. Luis Ob., iii. 655, on which he lived from about '39, having in '38 rendered some aid to his father-in-law in his political troubles. iii. 569. Sometimes named as a physician and architect. In '45 Larkin gave him an excellent character as a man of greater influence than any other foreigner of Sta B. region. Ment. '46, having also a Cal. claim. v. 321, 639. Prefect in '49; county treasurer in '51. Of his children 8 died in infancy, one, Mrs. Pollard, in '78, and in '83 the survivors were Chas C. at S. Luis, Wm C. at Los Berros, and on the home farm, John F., Henry C., Frank, Edward G., Fred. A., Adelina E., David A., Eliseo C., and Samuel A.

Daniel, 1824, Amer., surname not given, said to have been killed by Ind. at Sta B. ii. 527, 534.   Daniels, 1836, Boston cook, age 26, with Angel Ramirez at Mont. iv. 118; arrested in '40.   Daniels, 1816, mr of the *Colonel*. ii. 278, 382.   D. (John), 1839, Scotch in El Dorado Co.; doubtful date. iv. 119.   D. (Wm), 1846, nat. of Engl.; overl. immig. with family; settled at S. José; known as judge; died '73, age 71.   Danti (Antonio), 1790, Span. friar who served at S.F., retiring in 1796. Biog. i. 712-13; ment. i. 388, 474, 492, 510, 551-2, 552, 575-6, 679, 709, list auth.   Dare (Robert H.), 1838, mr of the *Fearnaught* and of the *Ayucucho* '39-40. iv. 101, 103.   Darley (Henry L.), 1846, at Mont.   Darlington (B. S. B.), 1841, lieut on the U. S. *St Louis*.   Darrah (Decatur), 1847, Co. D, N. Y. Vol. (v. 499).   Darren (Henry E.), 1847, Co. A, N.Y.Vol.; drowned in the Sac. Riv. '49.

Daubenbiss (John), 1843, nat. of Bavaria, who came to Amer. '35 at the age of 19, and found his way westward by short stages for 7 years, coming overland to Or. in '42 and to Cal. next year in the Hastings party. iv. 390, 400. After working on mills for Smith at Bodega, iv. 396, and Vallejo at Mission S. José, he served Sutter in the Micheltorena campaign, was naturalized and got a grant of Coluses rancho in '44. iv. 671; in '45 signed the S. José call to foreigners. iv. 599; and in '46 carried despatches between Sloat and Frémont, v. 16, 245, 247, then going south with the Cal. Bat. to S. Diego and Los Ang., but returning with Maddox. Later he reënlisted in Co. F of the Bat. to take part in the final campaign. Returning to S. José early in '47, he married Sarah C. Lard and moved to his rancho at Soquel, where he built a flour-mill. In partnership with John Haines '48, also going to the mines; elected to constit. convention '49, though not serving. In '79 he had 8 children; prob. still living in '85. His *Biog. Sketch* contains many interesting adventures; portrait in *Sta Cruz Co. Hist.*, 26.

Dávalos (Miguel), 1780-2, chaplain of the *Santiago* and *Princesa*. i. 329, 378. D. (Teresa), wife of Rivera y Moncada. i. 364. Davenport (Alfred), 1846, Co. A, Cal. Bat. (v. 358). Daveson (Peter), 1841 (?), nat. of the Ionic Isl., who came in '41-3, acc. to dif. authorities. iv. 279; signed the S. José call to foreigners '45. iv. 599; ment. in '45-7 in employ of Weber and Southward; also kept an inn, and went to the mines in '48; still living in '84 at S. José. His wife was a granddaughter of Luis Peralta. David (Alex.), 1845, in Cal. iv. 587; perhaps Davis. David (Edward), 1827, mr of the *Isabella* or *Sarah and Elizabeth*. iii. 147. Davidof, 1806, lieut with Rezánof at S.F. ii. 68, 70. Davidson, 1843, mate of the *Admittance*, nat. of N.H.; killed at ·S.F. '44 by falling from the ship's foretopsail yard. *Thomes.* D. (Hunter), 1845, mid. on the *Portsmouth.* D. (John W.), 1846, lieut 1st U.S. dragoons, who came with Kearny and fought at S. Pascual and the later conflicts of '46-7. v. 336-7, 340, 343-7, 385-6, 446; later col of 2d cavalry and brevet brig.-gen., serving on the Pac. coast to '59, and dying in Minn. '81. Dávila (Agustin), sec. to juez at Brancif. '41-2. iv. 663; grantee of Corral de Cuati '45. iv. 642; killed by Foxen near Sta Inés '48. v. 611, 631. D. (Jose), 1771, surg. of the Cal. forces at Mont. '71-83. Biog. i. 668; ment. i. 224, 228, 385. Davis, 1811-12, mr of the *Isabella.* ii. 93, 267, 269, 282; possibly Wm H., Sr. D., 1845, doubtful memb. of Grigsby-Ide party. iv. 579. D., 1846, said to have been mr of a coaster; later a highwayman known as Red Davis, hanged at Stockton about '52. D., 1847, memb. of Sonoma council. D., 1848, two of the name on the *Sagadahoc* from Honolulu. D., 1848, miner at Thompson's Flat.

Davis (Benj. B.), 1847, Co. H, N.Y.Vol. (v. 499); miner in Mariposa; vol. in war of '61-5; died at Merced Aug. '78. D. (Daniel C.), 1847, capt. Co. E, Morm. Bat., and of the reënl. comp.; in com. at S. Diego. v. 477, 490, 495, 617; accomp. by his wife and son, Dan. C., Jr, the latter being wounded in a fight with wild cattle on the march to Cal. D. (David A.), 1846, at S. José in April; perhaps an immig. of '45; one of Fauntleroy's dragoons (v. 232); lieut of Co. G, Cal. Bat. v. 361; in '47-8 had a store and ferry at Benicia. v. 673. D. (David A.), 1847, Co. H, N. Y. Vol. (v. 499); a deserter who was hanged at S. José for robbery and attempted murder in Dec. '48. v. 663-4. D. (Eleazer), 1847, Co. D, Morm. Bat. (v. 469).

Davis (Geo.), 1843, Irish immig. from Or. in the Hastings party. iv. 390-2, 400. Married by Sutter to Lizzie Sumner, whose parents came in the same party; naturalized in '44; often named in the *N. Helv. Diary* '45-6; later engaged in tanning and raising stock in the Sta Cruz region; in '60 settled in S. Luis Ob. Co., where he still lived in '83. D. (Isaac), 1848, sentenced for larceny at S. F. *Californian.* D. (Jerome C.), 1845, apparently one of Frémont's men, who served in the Cal. Bat. '46-7. v. 358. It was for him, I think, that the town of Davisville was named; still living at Sac. in '78. D. (John), 1828, Norwegian carpenter, age 23, who came from the Sandw. Isl. and in '30-6 was a resid. of Los Ang. ñ. 558; iii. 178. D. (John), 1848, passp. from Honolulu; letters at S.F.

Davis (John Calvert), 1839, Engl. ship-carpenter and blacksmith, who had been a sailor, and for 5 years on Mex. vessels, probably touching in Cal. ports some years earlier; naturalized, got a lot, and built a house and shop at S. F. '39. iii. 705; iv. 119; v. 682-3. In Nov. '41 he had built, in Napa Creek, a schr called the *Susana*, for which he asked permission to use the Mex. flag, and in her made a trip to Mazatlan and back in '42-3. In records of the time he is often mentioned as a Yerba Buena blacksmith, and was 32 years old in '42; formed a partnership with Rose and Reynolds, and the firm built houses as well as boats, including a mill for Salv. Vallejo in Napa Val.; corporal of S. F. defensores '44, when he got new naturalization papers, having lost the original on his trip down the coast. He married a daughter of Geo. Yount, prob. in '44, since in April he writes to Larkin for gold earrings and material for a lady's dress—all to be kept a profound secret, though L. may guess the object. The same year he built the *Londresa;* often named in records of '44-7, being a witness at the Rae inquest in '45, iv. 593, and town treasurer in '46. v. 648. I find no later record than Nov. '47, and he is said to have died in '48, committing suicide, according to Sutter. His widow married Eugene Sullivan. He left a son—John D., living at Napa '85—and 2 daughters.   D. (Joseph), 1845. Amer. sailor and immig. from Or. in the McMahon-Clyman party. iv. 572, 587. Lived for a time at Gordon's; served '46-7 in Co. B, Cal. Bat. (v. 358); claimant for supplies to Frémont. (v. 462); called also M. J. Davis.   D. (J. H.), 1848, passp. from Honolulu.

Davis (Pedro), 1843-5, Ital. resid. of Mont. iv. 400.   D. (Peter), 1848 (?), nat. of Mass., long a resid. of Loreto, perhaps came to Cal. before end of '48; Capt. D. died at Mont. '53.   D. (Peter J.), 1848, nat. of N.C., overl. immig. with family; miner on Feather River '48-50; later farmer in S. Joaquin; d.. in Humboldt '73. His 1st wife, Phœbe Hunter, died in '49; in '73 there were 3 surviving children.   D. (Robert G.), 1839, clerk on the *Monsoon*. iv. 105, 279; nat. of Honolulu, bro. of Wm H., educated in Boston. He came back on the *Julia Ann* with goods, which were sold at S. F. '41-2. iv. 566; later in trade at Honolulu, being also Peruvian consul and a judge; died about '72. D. (Robert P.), 1848, nat. of Mo., overl. immig., miner and resid. of Coloma till his death by a fall from his wagon in '57.   D. (Samuel H.), 1843, Amer. immig. from Or. in the Hastings party. iv. 390; prob. returned to Or. in '43-4.   D. (Sterling), 1847, Co. D, Morm. Bat. (v. 469).   D. (Thos), 1846, one of Fauntleroy's dragoons (v. 232); Co. G, Cal. Bat., enlisting at S. José Nov. (v. 358); perhaps the 'Uncle Tommy' Davis who died at Sta Cruz '83. A lumberman of same name ment. at S. Buen. '47.   D. (W.), 1825, mr of the *Maria Ester*. iii. 147.

Davis (Wm Heath), 1816 (?), Boston ship-master who, according to the statement of his son, was owner and mr of the *Eagle* from Boston to the Sandw. Isl. about '14, for some years in the China trade, and visited Cal. accomp. by his wife, still on the *Eagle*, about '16, making other trips to the N. W. coast and perhaps to Cal. I have no record of any such vessel on the coast, and there is probably some error in the dates; indeed, it is not unlikely that this was Capt. Davis of the *Isabella*, 1811-13, whose presence on the coast is ment. in ii. 93, 267, 269, 282. He was related to Gen. Heath, of revolutionary fame; and was for years U.S. commercial agent at Honolulu. His wife was a daughter of Oliver Holmes, another Mass. ship-master who lived long at the Sandwich Isl., being at one time gov. of Oahu under Kamehameha 1st. Another daughter of Holmes was the wife of Nathan Spear. Capt. D. died at Honolulu in '23, leaving two sons, Robert G. and Wm H., both named in this register.   D. (Wm Heath, Jr), 1831, son of the preceding, b. at Honolulu in '22, came to Cal. as a boy on the *Louisa*. iii. 383, 405; again on the *Volunteer* in '33; and a 3d time on the *Don Quixote* in '38. iv. 103, having meanwhile attended school and worked as clerk for a Boston firm at Honolulu. From '38 D. was clerk and manager for his uncle, Nathan Spear, at S. F., much of his time being spent in trading trips around the bay. iv. 82, 116, 245, 250-1; in '39 he commanded the 'fleet' that took John A. Sutter and his company up the Sac. Riv. to N. Helv. iv. 130-1; in '40 was arrested as a matter of form, but not sent farther than the mission, though the troubles of this year prob. prevented the granting of his petition for naturalization. iv. 10, 17. In '42 he left Spear's service, and made a trip to Hon. as sup. of the *Don Quixote*, Capt. Paty, returning in '43, and in '43–5 acted as agent at S.F. for the firm of Paty, McKinley, & Co. iv. 314, 565; v. 679; in '45 at Los Ang. during the Michel-torena campaign, though not a combatant, bought a lot at S.F., and went to Honolulu on the *Don Quixote*. iv. 505, 512: v. 679. He now formed a partner-ship with Hiram Grimes, buying the *Euphemia* with a cargo of merchandise, and returning on her to Cal. in '46, from which date he was a prominent mer-chant under his own name at S.F., owning several lots and buildings, but spending much of his time on the vessel, which visited the islands and all the ports. v. 240, 578, 653, 681, 683. He took but slight part in political affairs, though acting as inspector of elections, as school trustee, and in '49 as mem-ber of the town council. v. 295, 646, 651–2, 656–7; Cal. claim of $3,000 in '46–7 (v. 462); in Nov. '47 married María de Jesus, daughter of Joaquin Estudillo. iv. 305; v. 686; in '48 of the firm Davis & Carter; in '49 memb. of the S.F. guard, and vice-president of mass-meeting. His name was given to Davis street, S.F. All the records of early times point to Davis as an honest, genial, industrious, and successful merchant, who laid well the foun-dations of a handsome fortune, which, however, in one way or another, slipped from his grasp in the later years. In '85, as for a long time preceding, he re-sides at Oakland with his family. In various private archives of my collection I have many of his original business letters, in personal interviews much use-ful information has been obtained from him, and he has besides dictated for my use over 300 pages of his *Glimpses of the Past*, which contains not only his own experiences, but hundreds of interesting items respecting early men and times, especially on commercial methods, and social manners and customs of native and foreign pioneers. His memory is excellent, and has been re-freshed by frequent reference to his original correspondence. The value of his historical testimony is somewhat impaired by a tendency to eulogize every-body, or to suppress in the narrative such happenings as might call for un-friendly comment. If he ever had enemies, there is no indication of the fact in his statements or in any other records that I have seen. Let us hope that all the early Californians were as good as he paints them.   David (John W.), 1845, one of the *Warren's* men, lost in S.F. bay '46. iv. 587; v. 384.

Dawson, 1846, from Honolulu on the *Euphemia*.   D. (J.), 1848, passp. from Honolulu.   D. (Fleurnaye), 1843, Amer immig. of the Walker-Chiles party, who applied for a passport in '44. iv. 392–3.   D. (James), 1824(?), Irish sailor on the *Rover* in '26, who possibly came on the same vessel in '23, and who, in Dec. '41, at Sonoma, asking for naturalization, claimed a residence of 17 years. I have his autograph on a contract to employ John Fuller in '39. He married María Antonia Cáceres in '40, and settled on the Estero Ameri-cano rancho near Bodega. Quarrelling with his partner about the title, Dawson sawed their house in two parts and moved his half to the Pogolomi rancho, for a grant of which he applied, but died in Oct. '43, and the rancho was granted in '44 to his widow, who was married to Fred. Blume in '49. Though D. is said on good authority to have died in '43, I find records in the archives which seem to show that he was alive in July '44. iv. 448; *Vallejo Doc.*, xii. 55.   D. (James), 1841, immig. of the Bartleson party. iv. 270; also known as V. W. 'Cheyenne,' John, and 'Long Jim' Dawson; said to have been drowned in the Columbia River.   D. (Nicholas), 1841, prob. a bro. of James, also in Bartleson party. iv. 270, 275, 279. Known also as 'Bear,' 'Berry,' and 'Birny' Dawson; kept a store at Sta Cruz in '43, but closed it and went away; said to have left Cal. and died.

Day (Abraham), 1847, Co. E, Morm. Bat. (v. 469).   D. (Benj.), 1831–2, perhaps of Young's trappers from N. Mex. iii. 388, 408; Amer. hatter at Mont. '34–6.   D. (Edward), 1847, perhaps of N.Y. Vol. (v. 499) under an-other name.   D. (Francis), 1840, naturalized citizen at Brancif.; licensed to hunt otter '43; ment. in '46. iv. 120; v. 23.   D. (John S.), 1847, lieut Co. H, N.Y. Vol. v. 504; died at Chicago '51.   D. (Manuel), 1838, named in Larkin's books.　D. (Wm), 1832, Kentuckian hatter at Mont. '34; very likely one of Young's trappers, and perhaps same as Benjamin. iii. 388, 408. In '35, keeping a liquor-shop at Los Ang., he stabbed Abel Stearns in a quarrel and was kept in prison a year. iii. 631; acc. to the *County Hist.* died in Sonora, having settled at Los Ang. in '31.

Daylor (Wm), 1835 (?), Engl. sailor said to have left his vessel this year, to have entered Sutter's service in '40-1, and to have settled on the Cosumnes with Sheldon, his brother-in-law, about '44. iii. 413; iv. 138. Yates met him in '42-3 and speaks in high praise of his character. From '45 he is often named in the *N. Helv. Diary*, having fights with Hess and Kampt in '46; Cal. claim of $50 in '46-7 (v. 462); Gen. Kearny camped on his rancho '47. v. 452; mining with Weber '48; Ind. killed on his rancho '49. *Placer Times.* He died of cholera in '50. His widow—originally Sarah Rhoads married in '47—was married in '51 to Wm R. Grimshaw, whose *Narrative*, MS., is the best authority on Daylor's life.　Days (Wolberton), 1841, New Yorker who lived long in Brazil, hospital steward on U. S. ex. exped., who came back to Cal. in '49, settling at Grass Val. iv. 279; *Nevada Co. Hist.*　Dayton (W.), 1848, passp. from Honolulu.　D. (Wm J.), 1847, Co. B, Morm. Bat. (v. 469); reënlisted; also called Willard Y.

Deal (John), 1844, Amer. sailor of the *Benj. Morgan*, landed sick, aided by the consul at Mont. '44-5.　Dean (Geo. C.), 1847, Co. F, 3d artill. (v. 518); at Mont. to '49.　D. (Geo. C.), 1847, Co. D, N.Y.Vol. (v. 499); at Visalia '74-82, *Clark;* prob. some confusion bet. him and the preceding.　D. (Gilbert E.), 1847, Co. A, N.Y.Vol.; at Fort Lee, N.J., '74-82.　D. (James), 1837, at Mont.　Deas (James), 1847, Co. E, N.Y.Vol. (v. 499).　Deck (Augustus), 1846, owner of S.F. lot. v. 685.　Decker (Zachariah B.), 1847, Co. A, Morm. Bat. (v. 469); at Sutter's Fort '48; in Utah '81.

Dedmond (Joel P.), 1838 (?), Amer. carpenter who in '44, returning apparently from Honolulu on the *Fama*, claimed a residence of 6 years, obtaining naturalization, a lot at S.F., and the S. Juan rancho in the Sac. Val. iv. 119, 669, 673, 683. He prob. served Micheltorena under Sutter; appears in the *N. Helv. Diary* '45-7; but seems to have made a trip to Honolulu in '46. In '47 he sold out his land to Sutter and was employed at S.F. by Larkin as surveyor.　Defleet (Wm H.), 1847, owner of S.F. lot.　Deford (Isaac), 1847, Co. F, 3d U.S. artill. (v. 518).　Deitch (Lewis), 1847, ditto.　Dekin (Anthony), 1847, owner of S.F. lot.　Deland (Francis), 1844, Canad. immig. of the Stevens party. iv. 445; perhaps went to Or., as nothing more is known of him, unless it was 'Delone,' q.v.　Delaney (Rich. E.), 1847, Co. F, N.Y. Vol. (v. 499); d. S.F. '76.　Delehaye (Chas), 1847, Co. C, N.Y.Vol.

Deleissèques (Olivier), 1838, Frenchman in Mont. district, chiefly at S. Juan B., '38-47; possibly as early as '36. iii. 469; iv. 119; síndico at Mont. '45. iv. 653; purchaser of S. Juan B. orchard '46. v. 561, 637, 640-1. He had a family, but I know nothing of them or him after '47. His name is variously written, Mofras calling him Leyssegues, which is perhaps the correct form. He may have come in the colony of '34.　Delenau (Philibert), 1846, doubtful name of the Cal. Bat.　Delfin, neoph. at S. Juan Cap. iii. 626.　Delgadillo (Ignacio), 1829-33, Mex. convict.　Delgado (Cristina), grantee of Rincon de Salinas rancho '33.　D. (Gerónimo), 1791, piloto in Malaspina's exped. i. 490.　D. (Ignacio), 1819, Mex. alférez of the Mazatlan comp. at Sta B.; prob. died or left Cal. soon after '27. His wife is said to have been very skilful in fine needle-work, making artificial flowers, etc., and to have taught her art to several Cal. girls; perhaps she was the Cristina named above. ii. 254, 361, 573, 675.　Delick (John), 1847, Co. D, N.Y.Vol. (v. 499).　Delone (Francis), 1846, at N. Helv. '46-8, being under arrest in June '46; also called Delong; prob. same as 'Deland' of '44, q.v.　Delong (Wm F.), 1846, master U.S.N. in Marston's force against Sanchez. v. 380.

Demarante (Manuel), 1836, Portuguese skipper of S. F. mission launch, also farmer and sawyer who, in '41, asking for naturalization, claimed a resid. of 4½ years in Cal. iv. 118.　Demard, 1848, doubtful mention of a Mormon preacher at S. F.　Demedrion (Juan B.), 1834, Greek fisherman at Mont.

'34-7; two Italians, Luis and Matias, with him.   Demetrius, 1839, mr of the *Baikal.* iv. 101.

Den (Nicholas Augustus), 1836, Irish physician who came on the *Kent*, landing in Dec. at Sta B., where he became a permanent settler, often named in records of later years. iv. 117-18. In '39 not permitted to build on his lot; in '40 applied for naturalization, which was prob. obtained in '41; soon married a daughter of Daniel Hill. In '42 collector at Sta B., and grantee of Dos Pueblos rancho. iv. 642; in '43 grantee of S. Antonio rancho. iv. 635; in '45 alcalde of Sta B., and with his father-in-law lessee of the mission. iv. 426, 542, 553, 642, 644; v. 558; in '46 grantee of S. Marcos, Cal. claim of about $2,000. v. 632-3, 365 (462). Dr Den is said to have been of good family, and became in Cal. a most popular stock-raiser of considerable wealth and excellent reputation. He died at Sta B. in '62 at the age of 50; his children were Catherine wife of John Bell, Mary wife of Thos More, d. '78, Susan, Emmanuel, Nicholas, Wm, Alfred, Alphonso, and Augustus. Portrait in *Sta B. Co. Hist.*, 46.   D. (Richard Somerset), 1843, Irish physician, bro. of Nicholas A., who settled at Los Ang. iv. 400; ment. at Los Ang. '46. v. 3'4; purchaser of Sta B. mission estate. v. 561, 632-3; Cal. claim of $1,020 (v. 462); ment. in '47. v. 365; cl. for S. Antonio rancho. iv. 635. Living at Los Ang. '80.   Deng (Fred.), 1848, left Gen. Lane's party and settled at Yreka.

Denike (Geo.), 1846, baker and saloon-keeper at S.F. '46-8. v. 646, 684; perhaps correctly written 'Denecke.'   Deniston (Garrett V.), 1847, mid. on the U.S. *Independence.*   Denkers (Chas W.), 1847, Co. A, N.Y.Vol. (v. 499); died at Sac. '71 ('81 ?).   Dennett (Daniel Q.), 1847, Co. E, Morm. Bat. (v. 469).   Dennis (Jemmy), 1831, doubtful men. of an Irishman at Reed's rancho, Marin Co.   Dennison (Nathaniel), 1816, on the *Lydia* at Sta B. ii. 275.

Denniston (James G.), 1847, sergt Co. B, N.Y.Vol. v. 504; nat. of N. J.; twice a member of the legisl. from S. Mateo; died at S.F. '69, leaving a widow and 3 children.   Denny, 1845, Ind. of Frémont's party. iv. 583, 587; perhaps killed on the Or. frontier '46.   Dent (Lewis), 1847, nat. of Mo., lawyer at Mont.; of firm D. & Martin; in '49 member of the constit. convention, and from '49 judge of the superior and circuit court; later a lawyer and politician in Miss., Mo., and Washington; a brother-in-law of Gen. Grant. Died in '74 at the age of 51.   Denton, 1831-2, one of Young's trappers, said to have remained some years in Cal. iii. 388, 408.   Denton (David), 1846, doubtful name at Los Ang.   D. (John), 1846, one of the Donner party from Ill., who died in the mts. v. 530, 534.   Deny (Wm), 1828, mr of the *Verale.* iii. 149. Depeaux (Louis), 1847, resid. at Sta Cruz '47-65 acc. to his testimony in '65. Depen (Joseph H.), 1848, visited S.F. on the *Julian* from Honolulu.

Deppe (Ferdinand), 1832, German supercargo of Virmond's vessels, often in Cal. '32-6; perhaps from '29-30. iii. 350, 408, 105, 142. Said to have made a drawing of S. Gabriel in '35. iii. 644. Also a naturalist devoting his spare time to the collection of birds, plants, and shells. Sailed with his specimens on the *Rasselas* '36; and acc. to Vischer subsequently devoted himself to horticulture in the royal gardens at Pottsdam. David Spence is said to have received a letter from Deppe at Berlin in '73.   Derby (J.), 1848, passp. from Honolulu.   Derosier (Baptiste), 1844, one of Frémont's party, who wandered from camp in Cal. and was not heard of again. iv. 437, 439.

Desforges (Auguste), 1834, Frenchman who came with the H. & P. col. from Mex. (iii. 249), though in '40, being then a bachelor, age 28, in the Mont. district, he claimed a resid. of 8 years. Janssens, *Vida*, 32 et seq., his companion in the trip from S. Diego to Sonoma, has much to say of him. In '36 he worked on the Palo Colorado rancho; named in Larkin's accounts '34-43; in '49 aux. alcalde of S. José.   Despau, 1837, one of the party from Or. for cattle. iv. 85.   Desprairies, 1846, mr of the *Valiant.* v. 580.   Deston (Geo.), 1843, mr of the *North America.* iv. 567.   Devoll (Philip H.), 1830 (?), said to have been on the coast on a whaler as early as '30; resid. of Stockton and Sta Cruz from '68. iii. 180.

Dewell (Benj.), 1845, nat. of Ohio, overl. immig. from Ind. in Grigsby-Ide party. iv. 579, 587. Spending the winter in Napa Val., he joined the

Bears in '46. v. 79, 110, 148; remained in the Sonoma garrison after the U.S. occupation, but in Oct. enlisted in the Cal. Bat. (v. 358), Co. E, and served in the southern campaign. Returning, he lived '47–54 in the Guilicos valley of Sonoma Co., and then moved to a farm near Upper Lake, where he still lived in '81 at the age of 58. His wife was Celia H. Elliott, married in '50, and in '81 they had 8 surviving children. *Lake Co. Hist.*, 230. De Witt (Alfred), 1848, cf S.F. firm of De Witt & Harrison. v. 685; remained at S.F. till '54. Dexter, 1848, from Honolulu, according to his later testimony.   Dey (Nathan B.), 1847, Co. E, N.Y.Vol. (v. 499).

Diaz, 1824, soldier at Sta B. ii. 532.   D. (Benito), Mex. receptor of customs at Sta B. '35–7. iii. 377, 491, 654; iv. 98; celador at Mont. '42–3. iv. 330, 377; receptor at S.F. '44–5, being also agente de policía, owner of lots, builder of the custom-house, and locally prominent in other ways. iv. 423, 430–1, 463, 557, 654, 666, 669, 684; again ment. as in charge of the revenues in '46, S.F. delegate to the consejo gen., and grantee, as was claimed, of Pt Lobos and the Sta Clara orchard. v. 36, 45, 561, 570, 644, 660, 665–6, 681; had a Cal. claim of $1,500 (v. 462). Witness in the Santillan and N. Almaden cases '55, '57, age 43, still living in '68.   D. (Francisco), juez de paz at S. Juan B. '43–5. iv. 661–2; at S. José '50.   D. (Gabriel), soldier killed at the Colorado pueblos 1781. i. 359–62.   D., chaplain of the S. Cárlos, at Serra's funeral. i. 411.   D. (Juan M.), 1774, Span. friar who came to Cal. with Anza, and was missionary on the Colorado, where he was killed by Ind. in 1781. i. 221, 223, 259, 362.   D. (Manuel), Mex. trader, mr of the *Trinidad* '43; perhaps had visited Cal. before. iv. 569. In '46 alcalde of Mont., grantee of Sacramento rancho, on the 1st jury, and memb. of the council after U. S. occupation. v. 15, 234, 289, 636–8, 675. He is said to have bought the schr *Sta Cruz*, and in her to have removed his family and effects to L. Cal. about '48; but there was a Manuel D. at Mont. in '51. In '45 Larkin described him as aged 35, a quiet man, of some influence and property, well disposed to the U.S.   D. (Melchor), 1540, one of Coronado's officers, who crossed the Colorado, and perhaps looked upon Cal. territory. i. 68.   D. (Nicolás), Los Ang. hatter '39–46.   Dibble (Jonas), 1847, advertises sale of the schr *William* in *Mont. Californian;* he was carpenter on the *Columbus.*   'Dick,' 1846, Cal. Bat. v. 358.   Dickens (Wm), 1836, doubtful name in a Los Ang. list; perhaps 'Dickey,' q.v.

Dickenson (Gallant Duncan), 1846, nat. of Penn., reared in Va, who came overland from Mo. with his wife—Isabella McCrary, married '28—4 sons, and 2 daughters. v. 528–9. He spent the winter at Sta Clara, being a member of Aram's garrison, going thence to Sta Cruz and Mont., where in '47 he made bricks and built the 1st brick house in Cal. v. 636. Going to the mines in '48, he gave his name to Dickenson Gulch, Tuolumne Co.; in '49 settled at Stockton as a hotel-keeper, being also alcalde and memb. of the constit. convention. His daughters are said to have been the 1st Amer. women married at Stockton, Margaret to A. G. Lawrey, and the other to N. B. Stoneroad. In '52 D. moved to the Tuolumne River, where he kept a ferry and hotel, and from '67 lived in Merced Co., dying in '70. As a methodist he took an active part in church affairs. His widow died at S. José in '77.   D. (Geo. W.), 1846, son of G. D., b. in Mo.; settled in Merced Co. '58; in '81 had a farm and hotel at Chester, or Dickenson's Ferry. His wife was Mary Ann Brooks, and they had 5 children.   D. (W. L.), 1846, bro. of Geo. W., representing Merced and Stanislaus in the legisl. of '63; resid. Horr's rancho, nat. of Tenn., age 32. Dickey (D.), 1848, memb. of 1st Mont. jury; perhaps David who was at S. José in '50.   D. (H. W.), 1848, passp. from Honolulu.

Dickey (Wm), 1832, Irishman who got a pass in July, iii. 408, though there may possibly be an error in the year. From '33 his name appears in Larkin's accts and other records; arrested in '40, but not exiled. iii. 408; iv. 17; in '42 obtained a renewal of his pass, claiming about 7 years' residence; and about the same time he moved from the Sta Cruz region to N. Helvetia. In '43 he accomp. Dr Sandels in his travels through the Sac. Val., where he had already selected a rancho, the Arroyo Chico adjoining Keyser's, for which he petitioned the same year. In '44 he was naturalized and got his rancho, iv. 670, being recom. by Sutter, under whom he prob. served in the Michcltorena campaign. iv. 486; signed the order for Weber's arrest. iv. 483; appears in the list of Cal. claimants (v. 462); and is named in the *N. Helv. Diary* '46-8. He may have been the 'Dick ' of the Cal. Bat. as above. In '48 he was a partner of Bidwell in the Feather River mines; went east in '49, living at Liberty, Penn., and dying before '66. Dickinson (F.), 1848, of U.S.N., at S.F. on the *Lady Adams*. D. (M.), 1848, alcalde in Calaveras Co. acc. to a newspaper mention. Dickson, 1847, S. F. merchant of firm D. & Hay, of the Beehive store; owner of town-lots '47-8. v. 644-5, 684; the firm still in business in '50. I suppose this may have been John Dickson, who came from Honolulu on the *Providence;* name often written 'Dixon.'

Diddleson (Augustus), 1847, Co. G, N.Y.Vol. (v. 499). Diel (J.F.), 1846, Co. F, Cal. Bat. (v. 358). D. (Valentine), 1846, ditto; lot at S.F. '48. The name was perhaps ' Diehl,' who, acc. to Ballhaus, was an overl. immig. with Hoppe and Harlan; still at S.F., a grocer, '52-4; later a farmer near Mayfield, where he died about '82. Dierkin (A.), 1848, corporal of S. F. guards. Digg (Henry), 1846, Fauntleroy's dragoons. v. 232. Dillaway (John), 1813, pilot of the *Mercury*. ii. 268. Dillon (James, 1847, Co. F, 3d U.S. artill. (v. 518). D. (Joseph), 1824, Amer. quarryman at Mont. '29, age 28, 5 years in Cal. ii. 526.

Dimmick (Kimball H.), 1847, nat. of Conn., N.Y. lawyer and militia officer, who came as capt. of Co. K, N.Y.Vol. v. 504; election inspector at S.F. '48. v. 652; alcalde of S. José '49. v. 662; also judge of the sup. tribunal and memb. of the constit. convention; a Sac. printer '50; went east '51, but returned to Los Ang., where he was district attorney, justice of the peace, and county judge. He died in '61 at the age of 50. Dimond (J.), 1847, at S. F. from Or. on the *Henry*. Dittmann (Carl), 1844, German sailor, known in Cal. as Charley Brown, who came on the *Euphemia*, engaging in otter-hunting with Nidever and others, an occupation interrupted by mining in '48-50. Sta B. was his home down to '78, when he dictated for me his *Narrative of a Sea-faring Life*, an interesting record of many adventures. iv. 453; v. 317. Dix (J.), 1848, on the *Julian* from Honolulu. Dixon (James), 1846, Fauntleroy's dragoons (v. 232). D. (J.), 1847, at Honolulu from Cal.; perhaps ' Dickson ' of D. & Hay, q.v. D. (James F.), 1847, Co. A, N.Y.Vol. (v. 499); drowned in Gold Lake '80. D. (Joseph), 1832, Amer. who joined the comp. extranjera at Mont. iii. 221, 408; on Larkin's books and other records '34-48; got a pass '44; in Sutter's employ '45-6; sometimes called an Englishman, and there may have been two of the name.

Doak (Thomas W.), 1816, the 1st Amer. settler in Cal., nat. of Boston, who came on the *Albatross*, name often written Duke and Doc. ii. 275, 277, 393. He was baptized at S. Cárlos in '16 as Felipe Santiago; in '18 employed to paint the mission church of S. Juan B., where he was married in '20, by viceregal permission of '19, to María Lugarda, daughter of Mariano Castro. ii. 248, 272, 386; in '29 his age is given as 42, and from this time his name appears in various records as a carpenter of good habits. He lived for some years at Sta Cruz, or at least two of his children were born there; in '32 joined the comp. extranjera at Mont. iii. 221; said to have been at S. José in '33; on Larkin's books from '33; in '34 had 6 children acc. to the padron; in '36 living in the Mont. dist., at or near Las Ánimas, age 50, wife Lugarda Castro age 36, child. Juan B. b. '21, Valeriano '23, Ana María '29, and Cecilio '33. I have his autograph of '27 and '47, but no later record of him or his family. Taylor says he died before '48. D. (John), 1847, overl. immig., who went 1st to Sta Cruz and then to the mines in '48, presently establishing a ferry on the S. Joaquin, and becoming one of the earliest business men of Stockton. I believe that he, or one of his sons, was somewhat prominent in S. Joaq. politics in later years. Doatey, 1847, at N. Helv.

Dobson, 1846, doubtful name in a Los Ang. list. D. (Joseph), 1847, Co. A, Morm. Bat. (v. 469). Docente (Chas), 1847, owner of S. F. lot. v. 676. Dockrill (Joseph, or James), 1847, printer from Canada, whose real name is said to have been Joseph Armstrong; foreman and perhaps part owner of the *Californian* '47–8. v. 658; worked in newspaper offices S.F. till '52, becoming dissipated and losing his property; then went to the mines; died at Dry Creek '56. Dodd (Matthew), 1847, carpenter on the U.S. *Cyane*. D. (Solomon), 1848, name in list of letters; at S. José '50. Dodero (Nicolás), 1827, Italian sailor who left the *María Ester* at S. F., was sent to Mont., and in '29 was living at S. José, age 25. iii. 176; married an Higuera; in '40 a naturalized citizen at Branciforte; in '44 grantee of Tres Ojos de Agua, Sta Cruz Co. iv. 656; in '46 had a son in the Mont. school. Dodge (Augustus), 1847, Co. C, Morm. Bat. (v. 469); Utah farmer '82. Dodge (Chas F. and Theophilus), 1848 (?), early settlers of Sonora. D. (Edwin T.), 1847 (?), policeman and sheriff of Yuba Co., who in '58 went to B. Col., and later to Wash. Ter.; said to have been a sergt in N.Y.Vol., but there is no such name on the roll. Dodson (Eli), 1847, Co. A, Morm Bat. (v. 469). D. (Jacob), 1844, servant of Frémont in 1st and 2d exped.; F.'s companion in the famous ride of '47. iv. 437; v. 443. D. (Wm), 1845, overl. immig. from Ill. iv. 578; who went to Or. with Bristow in '46. v. 526. Doekin (Anthony), 1847, owner of S. F. lot. Dofar, or Dojan (Matthew), 1847, named as one of the 2d Donner relief. v. 540. Dofit (Joseph), 1831, named as one of Young's trappers. iii. 388. Doge (J. F.), 1847, doubtful name at Mont. Doggte (Tim.), 1823, mr of the *Balance;* perhaps Daggett. ii. 492. Dohling (Geo.), 1846, at S.F. and N. Helv.; owner of lots. v. 684; Cal. claim, apparently for service in Cal. Bat. (v. 358); owner of land at S. José '48. Doiron (A.), 1848, passp. from Honolulu. Doke (James), 1841, from N. Mex. in the Workman-Rowland party. iv. 278; a nat. of Tenn.; started to return to Sta Fé with Rowland in '43, and was drowned in Green River. *Given.* Dolan (Patrick), 1846, Irishman of the Donner party, from Keokuk, Iowa; died in an attempt to obtain relief for the rest. v. 530, 534, 537. Doliver, 1816, carpenter of the *Lydia.* ii. 275. Dolman (John), 1846, seaman in the navy; later Phil. lawyer. *S.J. Pioneer.* Doll (John), 1847, Co. F, 3d U. S. artill. (v. 518). Dollman (Fred.), 1847, Co. A, N.Y.Vol. (v. 499). Dolton (Henry S.), 1847, Co. B, Morm. Bat. (v. 469); at Cacheville, Utah, '81. Dom (Antonio), weaver instructor 1792–5. i. 615. Domer (Peter), 1847, Co. I, N.Y.Vol. (v. 499); d. S. Diego '48. Domingo, neophyte leader in the fight at S. Buen. 1795. i. 675. D. (Juan), 1830, Dutch ship-carpenter on the *Danube* from Lima, age about 28. iii. 180; settled at Los Ang., where he was living in '36; married a Félix before '40; became a man of some wealth; had a Cal. claim in '46 (v. 462), 627; died in '58.

Dominguez, known as Dominguito, killed at Pauma '46. v. 617. D. (Antonio), soldier of Sta B. comp. before '37. D. (Cárlos), at Los Ang. '39, age 29. D. (Cármen), juez de campo at Sta B. '35. iii. 654; wife Isabel Romero, 6 children. D. (Cristóbal), soldier of S. Diego comp. before 1800; sergt 1817–25; grantee of S. Pedro rancho '22; nephew of Juan José; died '25. i. 662; ii. 341, 424, 563. His wife was Maria de los Reyes Ibañes; child. Maria Victoria wife of José Ant. Estudillo, Luis Gonzaga, Manuel, María Fran. Marcelina wife of Wm A. Gale, María Elena Ramona, José Nasario, and Pedro Juan Agapito. D. (Demesio), mentioned '31–47. iii. 196; v. 400; at Los Ang. '39, age 48, on the Vírgenes rancho. D. (Domingo), soldier of Sta B. comp. '32; another at S. Bern. '46, age 24. D. (Francisco), son of José Ant., cl. of S. Emigdio rancho. iv. 635. D. (Jesus), 1846, at Los Ang. D. (José), comisionado at S. José 1785, when he died. i. 478. D. (José Ant.), grantee of S. Emigdio '42. iv. 635. D. (José Dolores), soldier of S. D. at S. Juan Cap. 1776. i. 303; corporal of the S. Antonio escolta 1780; prob. the José who died in '85 as above. D. (José María), soldier at Sta B. 1800. i. 639; invál. at Sta B. '32, wife Marcelina Félix, 4 children; grantee of Las Vírgenes '37. iii. 634; died in '45 at age of about 100; his widow died '65 at age of 105, leaving over 100 descendants through 7 sons and 7 daughters. One son was José; 2 daughters were Luisa and María. D. (José María), at Los Ang. '39, age 39; also '43. iv. 642. D. (José María), at Brancif. '45, age 25, wife Concepcion Galatan, child. Manuel and Guadalupe. D. (Juan José), settler of Los Ang. 1785-90, soldier in earlier years. i. 346, 461; grantee of S. Pedro rancho 1800-22. i. 662; ii. 111, 350, 353, 634, 663.

Dominguez (Manuel), son of Cristóbal, who from about '25 lived on the S. Pedro rancho. In '27-8, of terna for contador, suplente of the dip., and elector for Los Ang. ii. 560; iii. 42, 44, 63; in '29 regidor. ii. 561; in '32 alcalde of Los Ang. iii. 216, 635; in '33-6 aux. alcalde at S. Pedro. iii. 635-6; opposition to Gov. Alvarado '36-7. iii. 491, 496; in '39 2d alcalde Los Ang. iii. 636; '42-3 juez de paz. iv. 632-3; in '43 prefect of 2d district. iv. 632-3; in '44 capt. of defensores. iv. 407. In '46 his rancho was occupied by the Amer. in Oct. v. 319; in '49 he was a member of the constit. convention; in '52 county supervisor, cl. for the S. Pedro rancho. iii. 634. Don Manuel was always a man of influence and of excellent repute. Still living on his home rancho in '80 at the age of 77, entirely blind for some years; died, I think, a few years later. His wife was María Alta Gracia Cota, and they had 10 children, of whom 6 daughters survived in '80.   D. (Mariano), Los Ang. trader, age 50, in '39.   D. (Nasario), bro. of Manuel, a wild fellow, but a successful ranchero. He sold his share of the rancho to his brother.   D. (Nemesio), soldier at Sonoma '41.   D. (Pedro), at Los Ang. '38; juez de campo at S. Pedro '40. iii. 564-5, 637; age 29 in '39.   D. (Serapio), Mex. soldier of the piquete de Hidalgo at Mont. '36, age 23.   D. (Vicente), at Los Ang. '46.   D. (Vicente Sotelo de), at Los Ang. '38. iii. 566.

Dominis (John), 1835, mr of the *Bolívar*. iii. 381; mr of the *Joseph Peabody* '39-42. iv. 104, 566; native of Trieste, who was lost on the *Noble* about '45. His widow lived at Honolulu '84, and his son John O. was brother-in-law of the king. *Peirce.*   Donald (M.), 1848, miner said to have been drowned in the Yuba.   D. (Neal), 1847, Co. C, Morm. Bat. (v. 469); reënl.; died at S. Diego Nov.   Donaldson (A. C.), 1846, Co. C, 1st U.S. dragoons (v. 336). Donegan (John), 1847, Co. C, N. Y. Vol. (v. 499).   Donnelly, 1848, kept a gambling and grog shop at Sta B., ordered to be broken up by govt.   D. (John), 1847, Co. F, 3d U.S. artill. (v. 518).

Donner (Geo.), 1846, nat. of N. C., who came from Springfield, Ill., in the famous immig. party that bears his name. For a full account of this terrible journey, see v. 530-44. He was accompanied by his wife—Tamsen, widow Dozier, maiden name Eustis, a woman of culture and education, formerly a teacher. v. 530, 541, 544; two daughters by a former wife, Elitha C., v. 534, and Leanna C., v. 534; and three daughters by Tamsen, Frances E., Georgia A., and Eliza P. v. 535. The father and mother both perished, the latter deliberately sacrificing her own life in order to cheer the dying hours of her husband; but the children were all rescued. Elitha married Perry McCoon in '47, and after his death Benj. W. Wilder; and in '80 lived at Elk Grove, Sac. Co., with 6 children. Leanna married John App in '52, and in '80 lived at Jamestown, Tuol. Co., with 3 children. Frances married Wm R. Wilder, and in '80 lived in Contra Costa Co. with 5 children. Georgia married W. A. Babcock in '63, and in '80 lived at Mountain View, Sta Clara Co., with 3 children. Eliza, the youngest, a small child in '46, married S. O. Houghton in '61, and in '80 was living at S. José with 6 children. McGlashan gives many details about the members of this family, with a portrait of Georgia.

Donner (Jacob), 1846, brother of Geo., and member of the same party, with his wife Elizabeth, 4 sons, and a daughter. v. 530-44. The father, mother, and 3 sons—Isaac, Lewis, and Samuel—perished in the mountains; but one son and the daughter survived. Geo. D., Jr, married Margaret J. Watson in '62, and died at Sebastopol, Sonoma Co., in '74, leaving a widow and 6 children living in '80. A S.F. lot was granted him in '47. His sister, Mary M. Donner, was married in '59 to S. O. Houghton, and died in '60, leaving a daughter, still living in '80.   Mrs Elizabeth D. also had two sons by a former marriage, named 'Hook,' q.v.   Donnavan (B.), 1848, passp. from Honolulu. Doody (Patrick), 1847, Co. I, N.Y. Vol. (v. 499); at Coloma '49 with his wife. Doolan (John), 1847, Co. D, N. Y. Vol. (v. 499).   Dooley (Thomas), 1846, Co. C, 1st U.S. dragoons (v. 336).   D. (Thos), 1847, Co. G, N.Y. Vol. *Clark;* prob. an error.   Door (James), 1840, arrested foreigner, doubtful. iv. 14.

Döpken (Jacob), 1845, at S. F. '45–6; Johana D., apparently his wife; at N. Helv. '47; lot at S.F. iv. 587; v. 678. Doran (John), 1847, Co. F, 3d U. S. artill. (v. 518). Dorman (Henry), 1846, overl. immig. with Ballhaus (v. 526); vineyardist in Sac. Val.; d. about '54. D. (John), 1834, Engl. tailor at Mont. Dornin (Thomas), 1842, com. of the U. S. *Dale.* iv. 314, 565. Dörnte (C.), 1845, at N. Helv. with a family. iv. 578; possibly went to Or. v. 526; but was probably the D. who settled at S. F. in '46, and was murdered by Beverley in Nov. '47. v. 646, 684. Dorr (Ebenezer), 1796, mr of the *Otter*, the 1st Amer. vessel in a Cal. port. i. 539–40, 618, 644, 685. Dorset, 1847, on the *Currency Lass* from Honolulu. Dorty (Wm), 1841, employed on Leese's launch. Dotson, 1846, doubtful name at Chino rancho. v. 314. Dotter (Wm C.), 1847, Co. C, N.Y.Vol. (v. 499); lot at S. F., where he still lived '71–82; ex-member of the legislature.

Doucett (Louis), 1847, lot-owner at S.F. Dougherty, 1846, at S.F. with family; prob. 'Dörnte,' q. v. D. (James), 1847, Co. C, N. Y. Vol. (v. 499). D. (John), 1847, Irish, at N. Helv. D. (Joseph), 1832, one of Young's trappers who perhaps remained in Cal. iii. 388. Douglas, 1845, Engl. pass to Sonora. D. (David), 1830, Scotch botanist on the *Dryad* from the Columbia Riv.; joined the comp. extranjera at Mont. '32; touched again at S. F. '33; died at the Sandw. Isl. '34. iii. 221, 382, 403–5, 699. D. (David F.), 1848, nat. of Tenn. who came as wagoner from Mex. with Graham's dragoons (v. 522); memb. of 1st legisl. '49–50; U.S. marshal; sec. of state '55–7; from '57 on a farm in S. Joaq. to his death in '72, age 51. D. (Sir James), 1841, agent of the H.B.Co., who came on the *Columbia.* iv. 80, 194, 209–17, 564, 619, 650, 665. See also *Hist. Brit. Col.,* this series. My collection contains his *Private Papers* and *Journal,* including the *Voyage to Cal.* He died at Victoria in '77. D. (James), 1847, Co. D, Morm. Bat. (v. 469); later in Sutter's employ. D. (John), 1823, sailor on the *Rover.* D. (Thos), 1847, teacher and graduate of Yale, who came from Honolulu on the *Francesca* with letters from Judd to Larkin, and in '48 took charge of the S. F. public school. v. 656–7. D. (Thos A.), 1846, Co. C, 1st U.S. dragoons (v. 336).

Dove (James G.), 1833, Engl. sailor from the whaler *Kitty* at Mont. iii. 409; named in a Los Ang. list of '36 as a single London carpenter, age 22, from Peru; a trapper for some years; in '40 exiled to S. Blas, but came back with a pass and claim for damages. iv. 18, 33, 37. He is named in a S. Gabriel list of '44; but I find no trace of him in '46–7; in the mines '48–52, and later at Stockton, Fresno, and Tuolumne, where he lived in '71. Dow (Joseph G.), 1847, Co. C, N.Y.Vol. (v. 499); memb. of leg'sl. '62; in Sonoma Co. '71–9; in Mendocino '82. Dowd (Michael), 1841, mr of the *Corsair.* iv. 564. Dowling (Geo.), 1847, owner of S.F. lots; prob. same as ' Dohling,' q.v. D. (John), 1848, in the mines with Brooks; wounded by Ind. D. (Thos H.), 1848, Irish overl. immig.; claimant for Yerba Buena Isl.; left Cal. '67; died at Wash. '72, age 62. Downes (John), 1846, passed mid. on the U. S. *Dale;* acting mr of the *Portsmouth* '47. Downey (Chas H.), 1847, Co. F, 3d U.S. artill. (v. 518). D. (Joseph), 1846, doubtful name at S. F. v. 649. Downing (Helms), 1845, overl. immig. in the Hastings party. iv. 586–7; at N. Helv. '46; served in the Cal. Bat. (v. 358); prob. went east soon after '47. Doyle (James), 1836, employee of Leese at S.F., who on being dismissed engaged in stealing horses in the interior, for which he was arrested and brought to Sonoma for trial. iii. 722; iv. 113, 118. It may have been the same or another James D. who appears as a laborer on Larkin's books from '44 and got land at S.F. and Mont. in '46–7.

Drabe (David R.), 1845, mr of the *Martha.* iv. 567. Drake (Andrew J.), 1847, lieut on the U. S. *Columbus.* D. (Francis), 1579, Engl. navigator on the coast of Cal.; full account of his visit in i. 81–94. Drayton (Joseph), 1841, artist in U.S. ex. exped. iv. 241. D. (Percival), 1847, lieut on the U. S. *Columbus.* Drear, see 'Dryer.' Drennan (James), 1847, Co. B, N. Y. Vol. (v. 499); d. Tuolumne '71. Dresher (Jacob), 1846, Co. C, 1st U. S. dragoons (v. 336). Dreyer (Henry), 1847, Co. F, 3d U. S. artill. (v. 518). Drieher (Jacob), 1847, Co. E, N. Y. Vol. (v. 499). Dring (David), 1847, mr of the *Janet*. v. 578; a business man of S. F. '48–9 and later. Driscoll, 1848, at S.F. from Tahiti. Druce (Lozuel), 1841, carpenter from the *Alert* at S. Pedro; ordered to reëmbark, Stearns being fined for keeping D. at his house; written also ' Dince ' and ' Dance.' Drummond (John W. H.), 1847, had a lot and house at Benicia. v. 672. Dryer (John), 1847, Co. B, N.Y.Vol. (v. 499); at Sta Cruz '71–82.

Duarte (Alberto), soldier in S.F. militia comp. '37. D. (Andrés), grantee of Azuza '41, and of a S. Gabriel lot '46. v. 628, 634; his name is still retained by a settlement in this region. D. (Angel, Felipe, Francisco, José, Julio, Manuel, Martin, Nasario, Rafael, Ramon, Vicente), living in the Los Ang. region '46. D. (Antonio Ign.), soldier at Sta B. '32, wife Eulalia Higuera. D. (Cayetano), settler at Los Ang. '13. ii. 350. D. (José), ranchero and militiaman in S.F. dist '35–7; at S. José '41, age 33, wife María Soto, child Antonio. D. (José), shot for murder at Los Ang. '41. iv. 630. D. (Juan José), settler at Los Ang. '14. ii. 350. D. (Juan José), soldier at Sta B. '32, wife María Serrano. D. (Juan María), soldier at Sta B. before '37. D. (Leandro), settler at Los Ang. ii. 350. D. (Manuel), soldier at the Colorado pueblos, killed by Ind. 1781. i. 359, 362. D. (Manuel), síndico at S. José '27. ii. 605; aux. alcalde at Sta Gertrudis '37. iii. 636. D. (Mariano), soldier of S.F. comp. '19; alcalde of S. José '31, in controversy with Gov. Victoria. iii. 194–5, 669, 729; in '41 at S. José, age 68, nat. of Cal., wife Teodora Peralta, child. Albino b. '21, Loreto '27, Luisa '32; in '45 a school-master on trial for grave crimes. iv. 686.

Dubosc (Pierre), 1840, Frenchman killed by an Ind. at McIntosh's rancho. Mofras blamed the authorities for neglect to arrest the murderer. iv. 120, 252. Duchène, 1845, perhaps with Frémont. iv. 583. Duckworth (Walter), 1829 (?), Engl. sailor who in '32 joined the comp. extranjera at Mont. iii. 179–80, 221, 408; often named in records of '32–43; in '36 at Mont., age 32, wife Antonia Armenta, child. Guillermo b. '30, Santiago '32, María Adelaida '35. The age of his son is the only evidence I have that he came before '32. In '41 he accompanied Douglas on a trip from Mont. to S.F.; prob. died soon after '43. He was often called Santiago, and was juez del monte at Mont. '35. iii. 674. The son Santiago had a Cal. claim of $3,950 in '46–7 (v. 462). Ducoigne (Eugène), 1846, Cal. Bat., artill. Co. B (v. 358), enlisting at S.F. Oct.; Cal. claim for services, $161. Dueñas, 1842, perhaps an alférez of the batallon fijo, said to have remained in Cal. '45. iv. 513.

Dufrá (Jacques), 1840, arrested at Los Ang. iv. 14; prob. the name was ' Dufras.' Duhaut-Cilly (Auguste), 1827–8, mr of the French trader *Héros*, and author of the *Voyage autour du Monde*, containing much valuable matter about Cal. iii. 94–5, 128–31, 133, 147; also ment. of his work and local descriptions. ii. 548, 550–1, 563–4, 574–5, 579, 589–90, 595, 598, 603, 610–11, 614, 616, 626, 631, 650. Duhy (John), 1848, came from Sandw. Isl. *Hist. Or.*, ii. 334. Duisenberg (Edward), 1848, German business man of S.F. '80, who may have arrived from Valparaiso before the end of '48. *Contemp. Biog.* i. 416. Duketel (Sidney), 1845, perhaps one of Frémont's men, as he was in '48–9. v. 453, 583. Dulanto (Andrés), 1804, Span. friar who served at S. Juan B., and died in 1808. ii. 154, 159–60. Dulany, 1842, lieut U.S.N. with Com. Jones. iv. 308. Dumetz (Francisco), 1771, Span. friar who served as missionary for 40 years, chiefly at S. Buen., S. Fern., and S. Gabriel, where he died in 1811. Biog. ii. 355; ment. i. 173, 175–6, 178–9, 187–9, 196, 237, 246, 255, 276, 282, 351, 388, 405, 466, 562, 575, 578, 674; ii. 113–15, 159, 394.

Duncan, 1815, on the *Columbia*, not permitted to remain in Cal. ii. 273. D., 1845, immig. from Or. in the McMahon-Clyman party, prob. went back in '46. iv. 572, 526. D. (Alex.), 1843, mr of the *Vancouver*. iv. 569; perhaps of the *Columbia* '47. v. 577. D. (James M.), 1846, passed mid. on the *Congress;* acting capt. of Co. F, Stockton's Bat. '46–7, and in Gillespie's party meeting Kearny. v. 340, 385. D. (Robert), 1846, Scotchman from New Zealand with his wife and 4 children; lived at S.F., where he owned a lot in '47; in the mines '48–9; settled in Sta Clara Co., where he died '57. Portrait in *Hesperian* Nov. '59. D. (Thomas), 1839, Scotch mr of the *Juan José* '39–

44; naturalized in '44; at Mont. '45. iv. 104, 119, 566.　D. (Thos). 1846 (?), Kentuckian; at Sac. '48–9; at Emigrant Gap, Nev. '82. *Reno Gazette.*　Duncomb (C.), 1848, nat. of Conn.; doctor and farmer; in legisl. '63 from Sac., age 70.　D. (John), 1846, owner of S.F. lot. v. 684.　Dundas, 1844, officer on the *Modeste.*　Dunderfeldt (John), 1816, sailor on the *Lydia* at Sta B. ii. 275.　Dunham (Albert), 1847, Co. B, Morm. Bat. (v. 469); died at S. Diego '47.　Dunitch (Ernest F.), 1847, musician of N.Y.Vol. (v. 499); near Placerville '83.　Dunlap (John), 1846, Co. C, 1st U. S. dragoons (v. 336).　D. (John G.), 1847, Co. F, 3d U. S. artill. (v. 518).　Dunleavy (James G. T.), 1846, overl. immig. and methodist preacher, who was a lot-owner at S. F., and was prominent in town affairs of '47, being municipal clerk and taking part in public meetings. v. 528–9, 645, 648–9, 653; in '47–8 preacher and acting alcalde at Sta Cruz. v. 641–2; also preached at the gold-mines '48. I find no later record of him. His 3d initial is often printed S. or W., but I have his autograph.　Dunlevy (James), 1847, Co. F, N.Y.Vol. (v. 499).

Dunn (Alex.), 1836, Amer. hatter from N. Mex. at Los Ang., age 29. D. (Alex.), 1847, Co. F, 3d U. S. artill.; in the mines from '48; in Mariposa '51–2; from '56 at Stockton, where he was drowned in '77.　D. (E. H.), 1846, 1st officer of the *Fama*, in trouble with the capt.　D. (Ed. T.), 1847, purser of the U.S. *Columbus.*　D. (James H.), 1846, Fauntleroy's dragoons (v. 232). D. (Patrick H.), 1846, nat. of Me, who landed from a whaler and went to Sonoma Co.; also accredited to N.Y.Vol.; a printer; said to have frozen his feet in one of the Donner relief parties. In southern Cal. he belonged to a gang of desperadoes, being twice tried for murder. Went to Ariz. in '57; edited a paper; served in the legisl., and as county judge; and died near Tucson in '71, or, as some say, in '66. See John 'Dunne.'　D. (Thos), 1847, Co. B, Morm. Bat. (v. 469); at Goose Creek, Id., '81.　Dunne (John), 1847, Co. G, N.Y.Vol. (v. 499); a printer from Me, who lived 3 years at Sonoma; badly wounded in a fight with desperadoes at Sta B. about '53; drowned in Kern Riv. '55. Evidently there is much confusion between this man and Pat. H. 'Dunn,' q.v.　D. (Wm Burden), 1846, Co. C, 1st U.S. dragoons (v. 336); nat. of Ireland and resid. of Los Ang. '76. I have his MS. *Notes on S. Pascual.*　Dunklemugger (John), 1846, doubtful name in '71. *Alta.*　Dupas (J.), 1845, in Sutter's employ '45–8. iv. 587; often named in the *N. Helv. Diary*; also written 'Dupeé,' and 'Dupeis,' 'Dupont,' and 'Dupos'; perhaps the man called 'Dofar,' q.v.　Dupont (Samuel F.), 1846, com. of the U. S. *Congress*, transferred to the *Cyane*. v. 251, 253, 267, 284, 577; nat. of N. J.; rear-admiral in the war of '61–5; d. in '65.

Duran (Narciso), 1806, Span. friar, who served 40 years as missionary in Cal., chiefly at S. José and Sta B.; one of the most prominent and influential of the Franciscans, especially in the later years; president and prefect; died at Sta B. in '46, the last survivor but two of the Fernandinos in Cal. Biog. v. 633–4; ment. ii. 136, 138, 159–60, 163, 218, 329–30, 335, 375, 387, 394, 493, 500, 502, 504, 518, 599–600, 644, 655, 657; iii. 18–20, 74–5, 87, 89, 96, 114, 156, 198–9, 250, 257–8, 308–10, 316, 318, 320, 328–36, 338, 346–7, 423, 434–6, 492, 510, 530, 550, 566, 577, 582, 595, 611, 652–3, 656, 733–4; iv. 45–8, 57, 60, 63–4, 159, 253, 331, 371–2, 423, 546–51, 553, 565, 643.　Durand (St Vrain), 1845, Canadian sawyer from Or. in the McMahon-Clyman party. iv. 572, 587. He went south with Frémont in '46, and was one of Talbot's men at Sta B. v. 316; later served in Co. A, Cal. Bat. (v. 358), enlisting at Mont. in Sept.　Durbin (Daniel), 1844, possibly of the Stevens' immig. party (iv. 445), but prob. went to Or.　D. (M. L.), 1848, nat. of Cal., farmer in Solano Co. '78; prob. son of the following.　D. (W. Perry), 1846, nat. of Mo., prob. overl. immig.; farmer in Solano Co. '51–78.　Durick (Patrick), 1842, Irish carpenter from Honolulu on the *Fama*, age 31; still at Mont. '46.　Durivage, 1848 (?), editorial writer on the *Alta* and other papers from '49; left N. Orleans for Cal. via Chihuahua in '48 and possibly arrived at the end of the year. Durkue (Anthony), 1847, Co. K, N.Y. Vol. (v. 499).　Dustin (C. H.), 1848, nat. of Vt; in Sta Clara '53–76.

Dutcher (Thomas P.), 1847, Co. B, Morm. Bat. (v. 469); reënlisted.　Du-tra de Vargas (Manuel), 1841, Portug. trader, age 19, who came from S. Amer. on the *Jóven Carolina*, and was naturalized in '42, having a Mex. wife. He kept a saloon at Mont. in '43, and was prob. the 'Dutre' named by Colton in '47. iv. 279.   Dutton (C.), 1846, at Sutter's Fort in Feb.

Dutton (David Dewey), 1840, nat. of Mass. who crossed the plains to Or. in '39, and in '40 was a passenger on the *Lausanne*, touching at Bodega and going to Honolulu. iv. 104, 117, 120-1. In '43 he came back from S. Amer. with Stephen Smith. iv. 396; worked a while at Bodega; went to N. Helv., being employed as cook by Sutter, and settled on Butte Cr., being naturalized in '44. iv. 229, 396. v. 102. Soon after '48 he moved to Solano Co., where he still lived at Vacaville after '80. His wife was Martha J. Pearson, married in '56; and they had 7 children in '79. Portrait in *Solano Co. Hist.*, 80.   Dutton (Daniel), 1847, owner of lot at S.F.   Duval, 1843, mr of the *Fanny*. iv. 565; mr of the *Parachute* and *Covington* '46-7, perhaps the same man. v. 577, 579.   D. (J., or Marius), 1846, asst surg. on the *Portsmouth;* visited N. Helv.; in Marston's exped. Jan. '47. v. 102, 380.   Duvall (Robert C.), 1846. mid. on the U.S. *Savannah;* acting lieut in Stockton's Bat. '46-7. v. 366. Duvanchelle (E.), 1848, passp. from Honolulu.   Dwyer (Wm), 1846 (?), Irish cabin-boy on a trader; came back after '48; famous as a saloon-keeper and bruiser; killed in S.F. '73.   Dye (Hazard), 1847, Co. K, N.Y.Vol. (v. 499).

Dye (Job Francis), 1832, Kentuckian trapper from N. Mex. in Young's party. iii. 388, 408. For a year or more Dye engaged in otter-hunting on the coast, iii. 394, and late in '33 took charge of Capt. Cooper's live-stock at the Rancho del Sur; from this date his name appears on Larkin's books; and he still made occasional otter-hunting trips. In '35 he established a distillery at Sayante near Sta Cruz, at first with Tomlinson, later with Majors, whom he bought out in '40, having applied for naturalization in '39. Met by Edwards '37. iv. 86; arrested but not exiled in '40, being accused by Morris of taking part against the foreigners. iv. 9, 17, 22. He had a store and mill as well as distillery at Sta Cruz; but claims, rather unintelligibly, that his business was ruined by Castro and other Mex. officials, and he was forced to start anew in a small way as trader at Mont. In '44 he got a grant of the Rio de Berrendos rancho, Tehama Co. iv. 672; and in '45 put stock on the place, *N. Helv. Diary*, though still residing at Mont. In '46 he was regidor, served as guide for Fauntleroy's dragoons, and was employed to carry despatches from Sloat at Mont. to S.F. v. 238, 636. In '47 he advertised his house for sale, but continued his business in partnership with Packard, and perhaps built an adobe house on his Antelope Cr. property. In '48 he made a successful tour in the mines, and in company with Larkin chartered the *Mary*, on which he brought a cargo of goods from Mazatlan, bringing a drove of mules from Sonora by land the next year; in '50 a trader at Sacramento, and later engaged in stock-raising on his Tehama rancho. In '77 he lived on his farm near Corralitos, Sta Cruz, and gave me his *Recollections of Cal.* in MS., substantially the same narrative being that printed in the Sta Cruz *Sentinel* of '69. Here he died in '83 at the age of 78, leaving 4 grown children, James and Newton Dye of Sta Cruz Co., Mrs J. S. Butler of Oakland, and Mrs C. M. Hays of Silver City, Id. *S. J. Pioneer*.   Dyer (W.H.), 1847, nat. of Mass.; in Alameda Co. '56-78. *Alam. Co. Hist. Atlas.*   Dyes (W. W.), 1841, taxidermist in U. S. ex. exped. iv. 241.   Dyke (Simon), 1847, Co. E, Morm. Bat. (v. 469); in Arizona '82.   Dykes (Geo. P.), 1847, lieut Co. D, Morm. Bat., and adj. of the battalion; his actions severely criticised by the Mormons. v. 477, 480, 482-3.

Eagar (John), 1846, nat. of N.Y., one of the Mormon colony, with his mother Mrs Lucy E., brother, and two sisters. v. 546. He was Brannan's clerk, also printer, and for a time associate editor of the *Star*, being owner of lots at S.F. in '47. v. 658, 682. I have his original application to Larkin for a clerkship, dated Feb. 21, '47. His mother had been excommunicated from the church on the voy., and wished to remove her children from Mormon influences. Lieut W. A. Bartlett, at her request, wrote a very flattering recommendation for John, adding his opinion that E.'s absence would 'kill this lying Mormon paper and its editor at once!' The plan was not successful, or at least John did not apostatize, but went to Utah, where he died. I have a brief narrative by him of the voyage of the colony. Mrs E. kept a little store at S.F. in '46, also obtaining a lot; but she went to Mont. with her daughters in '47, where one of them taught a school. v. 636. Mary Eagar married Milton Little in '48, and as a widow is perhaps still living at Mont. in '85. The other daughter, Arabella, married a man named Knapp, and was at S.F. about '81. E. (Thomas), 1846, bro. of John, also on the *Brooklyn*, age 18; owner of a S. F. lot '47; clerk at Mont. and Los Ang. '47–8; in the mines '48; at S.F. '49– 54. From '54 he was in the lumber business at East Oakland, where in '54 he married Angelina A. Tupper, and where he lived with his family in '78; a member of the legisl. '59, '60, '65; living in Nevada '85; portrait in *Halley's Cent. Year-Book*, 544.   Eagle (F.), 1840, doubtful name in Farnham's list of arrested foreigners. iv. 17.   E. (Robert Nelson), 1842, trader, age 22, who came from Hon. on the *California* for his health.   Eames, see 'Ames.'

Earl (Jacob), 1847, Co. E, Morm. Bat. (v. 469); reënl.   E. (James C.), 1847, Co. A, Morm. Bat.   E. (Jesse), 1847, musician Co. E, Morm. Bat. E. (Justice C.), 1847, Co. E, Morm. Bat.   Earle (Peter), 1847, Co. E, N.Y. Vol. (v. 499); later an actor and cultivator of hops; d. at Sac. '71.   Earley (James), 1847, owner of lots at S.F.; perhaps with Kearny in '46. v. 337, 683. Eastham, 1848, mr of the *Luia Perry*.   Eastin (James W.), 1847, Ken-tuckian overl. immig. with wife; at Sonoma '47–8, also at Mormon Isl. and S.F., where twins were born '48, one of them, a son, still living in '83; at Sta Clara from '50, and still living in '83, when his wife died.   Eastland (Addi-son G.), 1847, Co. F, 3d U.S. artill. (v. 518).·   Eastman (Isaac E.), 1848, miner near Volcano. *Amador Co. Hist.*   E. (Marcus N.), 1847, Co. B, Morm. Bat. (v. 469).   Eaton, 1847, at Hon. from S. F. on the *Georgiana*.   E. (Geo.), 1847, Co. G, N.Y. Vol. (v. 499).   E. (Henry), 1839, sailor on the *Monsoon*, who went up the Sac. with Sutter; remained on the coast till '41; at S.F. '73. His *Pioneer of '38* is a letter of '73 to Benj. Hayes narrating the visit. iv. 119. E. (Thos), 1836, doubtful name of an Amer., age 60, in a Los Ang. list.

Ebbetts (John, Jr), 1830, Amer. sup. of the *Volunteer* '30–1. iii. 180, 384; on the coast again in '32–4 on the *Henriqueta;* and again in '34–5, being men-tioned in mission accts in '39–40. iiii. 623. Peirce says that he died in N.Y. soon after '42, and his father—prob. Thos J. of '36, iv. 141—at Honolulu in '41. I have many of E.'s business letters; and some of them, besides dry details of hides, tallow, and goods, reveal in sentimental phrases the writer's attach-ment to a well-known señorita of Mont., who, greatly to the sorrow of John, Jr, preferred another Americano.   Eberhardt, see 'Everhart.'   Echeandía (José María), 1825, Mex. lieut-col of engineers, who was gov. and com. gen. of Cal. from Nov. '25 to end of Jan. '31, and again—if there was any such official—from Dec. '31 to Jan. '33, though Pio Pico is generally and inaccurately named as gov. He left Cal. in May '33, was still living in Mex. '56, but seems to have died before '71. See biog. with references. iii. 243–5; mention i. 364; ii. 543–54, 560, 572, 574, 587, 592, 637, 614, 648–52, 664, 674, 680; on appointment, arrival, and acts in '25. iii. 8–30; '26–30, rule, politics, etc. iii. 31–55; acts on finance, Solis revolt, 56 –86; mission and Ind. affairs, 87–115; maritime and commercial affairs, Fitch romance, 116–46; policy with foreigners, Smith and Pattie, 150–80; acts of '31. iii. 181–7, 195, 201–4, 203, 209, 212, 301–6; acts of '32. iii. 217–39, 314–15; acts of '33. iii. 238–9, 326, 335, 613. It was Echeandía's fortune to rule Cal. at a time when secularization of the missions was first seriously agitated, and he has been a shining mark for severe criticism, and even abuse, from partisans of the friars, for the most part undeserved. His views were sound and his in-tentions good, but he lacked firmness and energy, and made some mistakes. His character is fully discussed elsewhere.   Echevarría (Nicolás), at La Brea, Mont. district, '36, age 45, wife María del Pilar Larios, child. Juliana b. '23, María '30, Juan. '32, Antonio '35.   Echeverría (Agustin), 1782, com. of the *Favorita*. i. 378.   Ecker (John), 1847, musician N.Y. Vol. (v. 499).

Eddy (Wm H.), 1846, one of the Donner party from Belleville, Ill. His wife Eleanor, son James P., and daughter Mary all perished in the Sierra, but the father survived, being one of the most active in saving other members of the party. vt 531, 234, 540–4. Eddy married Mrs F. Alfred at Gilroy in '48, and Miss A. M. Pardoe in '56, dying at Petaluma in '59. A son James, with family, and daughter Eleanor (Mrs S.B. Anderson), lived at S. José '80; and a son Alonzo was a physician in Colorado. Eddy, 1844, mr of the *Jane.* iv. 566. Edelin (James), 1847, capt. of marines on the *Independence.* Edgington (Wm), 1846, overl. immig., who served in Co. F, Cal. Bat. (v. 358); lived from '48 near Napa, where he died in '84, leaving a widow, 9 children, and a fortune. Edmonds (Nathan), 1834, Amer. in a Mont list. Edmonson (Alfred), 1847, Co. G, N.Y.Vol. (v. 499); lot in S.F. '47; of E. & Anderson, butchers and market-men '48. v. 682. E, 1847, Co. H, N.Y.Vol.; at S.F. '82; perhaps same as preceding.

Edwards, 1847, mr of the *Euphrates.* v. 578. * E, 1847, mr of the *Pacific.* v. 579. E. (David), 1826, mr of the *Paragon.* iii. 148. E. (John), 1846, negro imprisoned at Mont. for robbery; shot in attempting to escape. E. (John S.), 1847, Co. D, N. Y. Vol. (v. 499); drowned in S. Joaq. Riv. '54. E. (Philip L.), 1837, nat. of Ky, who came overl. to Or. in '34, and in '37 visited Cal. to purchase cattle for the Willamette Valley. iii. 358, 699; iv. 85–7, 117–18. He went east the same year, studied law, married Mary Allen in '40, and practised his profession at Richmond, being a memb. of the Va legislature, and taking an active part in politics; came again to Cal. in '50 and lived at Sac. till his death in '69; prominent as a lawyer and orator, memb. of legisl., and candidate for congress; a man of exceptional ability and attainments. His MS. *Diary of a Visit to Cal. in 1837* is an interesting narrative of personal observations, presented by his daughter.

Egbert (Robert C.), 1847, Co. A, Morm. Bat. (v. 469). Egger (John W.), 1847, tried for murder of Ind. in the Sac. Val., but apparently acquitted. v. 569, 610. Eggleston (Geo.), 1848, had a market at S. F. v. 683. E. (J. W.), 1847, had a lot at Benicia. v. 672; very likely the same as Geo. Eguren (Francisco), 1842, Mex. lieut of the batallon fijo '42–5, who was still in Cal. '46. iv. 289; v. 41, 49. Ehlers (August), 1847, Co. A, N.Y.Vol. (v. 499); at Los Ang. '74–82. Ehrenberg (Herman), 1847, German engineer and explorer, who after many adventures as revolutionist in Texas crossed the plains to Or. in '44, and came to Cal. by sea, visiting also the Sandw. Isl. and Mex. coast in '47. In the mines '48–9; discoverer of the mouth of the Klamath and Gold Bluff '50, publishing a map of that region; and in '54 a filibuster in Sonora. He became a pioneer of Ariz., where a town bears his name; and was murdered by an Ind. at Dos Palmas in '66. Eixarch (Tomás), 1775, Franciscan with Anza; remained on the Colorado while A. came to Cal. i. 258, 273, 354.

Elb (Fred.), 1847, Co. C, N.Y.Vol. (v. 499); German aged about 45, who died in '48 on the *Carolina* bet. S. F. and Sac. Elbourne (John), 1846, mr of a whaler. Eld, 1841, mid. in U. S. ex. exped. iv. 245. E. (Henry N.), 1848, owner of lots at S. F. Elder (Turner), 1846, prob. overl. immig. with wife and 3 children, who built a cabin on Dry Creek, S. Joaq. Co.; moved in '47 to the Moquelumne; later at Daylor's rancho and in the mines; went to Mo. '49, and was still there in '79. His wife was a daughter of Thos Rhoads; twin children were born in '47, John living in Fresno Co. '79, Nancy (Mrs Reese) in Mo. *S. Joaq. Co. Hist.,* 19. Eldred (Nathaniel B.), 1848, came from Honolulu to S. F.; went to the Sandw. Isl. '50–1; wandered over Ariz., Utah, and Or.; near Stockton '66, and perhaps died in '69. Eldridge (Geo.), 1848, on the first jury at S. José.

Elijah, 1833, Ind. cook from Conn. on the *Helvetius;* went to Japan with Capt. Cooper in '42. *Chas Brown.* Elijah, 1845, Walla Walla Ind. shot by Grove Cook at N. Helv. v. 300–1. Eliot de Castro (John), 1814, sup. of the *Ilmen,* arrested in '15, left Cal. with Kotzebue in '16. ii. 210, 274, 279, 307–11, 373, 384. Elisa (Francisco), 1790–2, Span. com. of the *Concepcion* and *Activa* in Cal. and at Nootka. i. 493, 506, 517; see also *Hist. N. W. Coast,* index. and list of auth. Elizalde (Joaquin), at Los Ang. '46. E. (José), his doggerel of '38. iii. 577. E. (Juan), ment. in '29. iii. 68–9; soldier at

Sonoma '41.   E. (Mariano), attacked by the Bears '46. v. 162.   E. (Nicolás), at Los Ang. '39.   E. (Vicente), at Los Ang. '46.

Ellick (John), 1845, German shoemaker from Or. in McMahon-Clyman party. iv. 572, 587. In '46, applying for naturalization, he claimed 3 years' residence, and may, therefore, have visited Cal. before going to Or. He settled at S. F., where he got a lot and kept a bakery with Denike, also a grogshop. v. 684–5. Still at S. F. '48–9; name written Alleck, Allig, Ellig, and Ilig, the last being perhaps the correct form.   Elliott (Albion R.), 1845, Co. E, Cal. Bat. (v. 358), enlisting at Sonoma; prob. a son of W. B.   E. (Ems), 1845, a son of Wm B; said to have been one of a party that discov. the Geysers.   E. (J. L.), 1841, chaplain of U. S. ex. exped., detached at S. F. E. (Milton), 1846, one of the Donner party from Ill.; perished. v. 530, 534. The Milton Elliott of Or. named by McBride in *Tullidge's Mag.*, July '84, is not the Donner-party man, as he writes me from Astoria in '85.   E. (Thos), 1847, Co. F, 3d U. S. artill. (v. 518); later in the mines.

Elliott (Wm B.), 1845, nat. of N.C., overl. immig. of the Grigsby-Ide party from Mo. with wife—Elizabeth Patton, married in '21—and 7 children. v. 579, 587; summoned before Castro as a repres. of the immig. iv. 606. He became a famous hunter, and on one of his early exped. is credited with having discovered the Geysers. He built a cabin on Mark West Cr., worked for Smith at Bodega, but left his family in Napa Val. He joined the Bears in '46, and Mrs E. is said to have furnished cloth and needles for the famous flag. v. 110, 148. One or more of his sons went south with the Cal. Bat. (v. 358). The old hunter raised grain and cattle in Napa and Sonoma; kept a hotel in '49; and in '54 moved to a farm in Lake Co., near Upper Lake, where he died in '76 at the age of 78. One of his daughters married Benj. Dewell, another pioneer.

Ellis (Alfred J.), 1847, nat. of N.Y., who came from Honolulu with wife and 3 children on the *Francisca;* owner of a lot and keeper of a boarding-house at S.F. from '47. v. 684; made a trip to Hon. and back with his son in '48 on the *Euphemia;* member of S.F. guard '48-9, and of city council '49; member of the constit. convention '49. Still at S.F. in '54 and later.   E. (Robert), 1826, sailor on the *Rover.*   E. (Thos W.), 1847, Co. D, N.Y.Vol. (v. 499). Ellison (Pleasant), 1836, named in Larkin's books.   Ellsworth, 1845, from Hon. on the *Fama.*   Elmer (Elijah), 1847, sergt Co. C, Morm. Bat. v. 477; a carpenter at Mont. '48; d. in Utah '80.   Elson (Thos), 1826–7, mr of the *Blossom.* iii. 121.

Elwell (Robert J.), 1827, nat. of Mass. who went to Honolulu in '23, and came to Cal. '27 as mr of the *Tamaahmaah*, and of the *Washington* in '28. ii. 573; iii. 149, 176–7. Often said to have come in '25 or earlier, and this may be so, though in a padron of '36 he is said to have come 9 years before. He settled at Sta B., was naturalized '28, and in '29 married Vicenta Sanchez, being engaged in trade. iv. 117. Many of his commercial letters for the following years are extant. In '36, age 39, with 4 children; in '42 got a grant of land at S.F. iv. 673; in '45 grantee of Sacramento Isl.; died at Sta B. '53. He is remembered by Davis and others as a comical genius, and his wife as a handsome woman.

Embly (James), 1846, doubtful member of the Mormon col. v. 547.   Emerson (John Calvin), 1847, Co. I, N.Y.Vol. (v. 499); at Bath, N.Y., '82.   E. (Wm), 1832, one of Young's trappers, still at Los Ang. '34. iii. 388.   Emery (John), 1847, a resid. of S. F. from '52.   Emmett, 1837, mr of the *Toward Castle.* iv. 106.   Emmons (Geo. F.), 1841, lieut U.S.N., of U. S. ex. exped. iv. 232, 241–5, 278; visited Cal. again in '48 on the *Ohio*, being owner of S.F. lots; later rear-admiral; died in N. J. '84 at age of 72.   Emory (Oliver C.), 1846, came as wagon-master (with Kearny?); kept a livery-stable at Stockton and a ferry on the Stanislaus; in '50 county judge of S. Joaq.; later a farmer.

Emory (Wm H.), 1846, lieut of topographical engineers U.S.A., who came with Kearny from N.Mex. and took part in the fight at S. Pascual. v. 336–7, 343–7, 350. Having acted as adj.-gen. of Stockton's force in the campaign of '46-7, and planned the fortifications of Los Ang., he was sent east with despatches, and testified at the Frémont court-martial. v. 385, 398–9, 420, 428,

456. His *Notes of a Mil. Reconnoissance* pub. by govt in '48 is a valuable record of the march across the continent and the final campaign of the war. He ret. to Cal. in '49, and was prominent in the surveys of the Mex. boundary commission. In the war of 1861-5 he rose to the rank of maj.-general.

Engelberg (Emil August), 1847, Co. F, N. Y. Vol. (v. 499); at S. F. '82. English, 1845, doubtful name of an overl. immig.; prob. went to Or. iv. 578. E. (Earl), 1847, mid. on the U. S. *Independence.* E. (John), 1832, ment. in '32; perhaps 'English John.' Ennis (John), 1847, Co. A, N.Y.Vol. (v. 499). Ennughty (Thos), 1846, Fauntleroy's dragoons (v. 232). Enright (James), 1846, nat. of Ireland, who settled in Sta Clara Co. with his wife; prob. overl. immig.; lots at S.F. '47; still living in Sta Clara '81, cl. for a rancho. iv. 673. Enriquez (Antonio), weaver and soldier before 1800. i. 558, 676, 684. Ensign (Elias), 1846, of the Morm. col. who died at sea, as did his daughter Eliza. The widow, Jerusha, and a son arrived at S. F. v. 546. Ensloe (Hiram), 1848, had a store at Mormon Diggings. *Brooks.* Entinin (Francis), 1845, doubtful name of an Amer. in a Brancif. padron, age 29.

Erequette, 1837, doubtful name of one of Young's men driving cattle to Or. iv. 85. Erickson (L.), 1848, at Hon. from S.F. on the *Julian.* Ermatinger (Francis), 1831, in com. of the H.B. Co.'s trappers in Cal. '41-4. iv. 218, 220, 279. Ernest (Valentine), 1846, Co. C, 1st U.S. dragoons (v. 336).

Escalante (Gregorio), 1833, nat. of Manila, who deserted from the *Helvetius.* Lived at S.F. '40-4, owning a lot, being síndico in '42, and 40 years old in '44. iv. 655, 665, 684. Acc. to Chas Brown he married, raised a family, made and lost a fortune, and in '78 was in the poor-house at Mayfield. Escamilla (Blas A.), grantee of S. Vicente '46. v. 641. E. (Joaquin de los Santos), lieut of aux. cavalry at Mont. '44. iv. 652; elector '45. iv. 540, 651; 2d alcalde '45-6. iv. 653; v. 134, 636. E. (Serapio), soldier of S.F. comp. '22-3; concerned in revolt of '28, and sent to Mex. '30. ii. 615; iii. 85. E. (Tomás), Mex. convict 1797. i. 606. Escherick (Carl), 1847, musician N. Y. Vol. (v. 499); died in southern Cal. '74.

Escobar (Agustin), juez de campo at Mont. '46. v. 637; in '77 at Mont. gave me his recollections of the *Campaña de '46.* E. (Marcelino), Mex., who in '24 made a trip to China on the *Rover.* ii. 520; síndico at Mont. '30. ii. 612; alcalde '33, '36-7; iii. 673-5; in '36 at Mont., age 39, wife Tomasa García, child. Agustin b. '17, Juan '22, Josefa '23, José María '26, Nicolás Antonio '27, Jacoba '29, Amparo '31, Refugio '32, Fernanda '34; in '39 grantee of S. José y Sur Chiquito, and juez int. at S. Cárlos. iii. 678, 680; in '44 regidor, in '45 alcalde. iv. 653-6. Escudé (Jaime), 1812, Span. friar of S. Fern. college, b. at Gandesa, Cataluña, 1779; took the habit 1799; left Cádiz 1810; left Mex. for Cal. 1811. He served as missionary at Sta Cruz '12-18, and at S. Luis Rey '18-22, after which I have no record of him, and suppose him to have retired. He was reported by his superiors as a zealous worker of excellent character. *Autob. Autog. de los Padres,* MS.; *Arch. Sta B.,* iii. 124; see mention in ii. 246, 346, 387, 394, 452-3, 553, 655.

Esparza (Lorenzo), carpenter at S. D. 1779; wife María Dávila d. '81; pension granted in '95. i. 636. Espeleta, 1825, sup. of the *Merope.* iii. 148. Espí (José de la Cruz), 1792, Span. friar who served for short terms at several northern missions, retiring in 1800. Biog. i. 712; ment. i. 498, 500, 576-7, 617, 689. Espindola (Ramon), Span. artilleryman, age 60, with wife and 3 child. named in list sent to Mex. '28.

Espinosa, soldier killed by Ind. 1790. i. 465. E., mr of the *Magallanes.* i. 544. E., punished in 1821. ii. 660. E., corporal at Sta B. '24. ii. 531. E., soldier wounded by Ind. '29. iii. 113. E., guard of courier '34. iii. 271. E. (Antonio), soldier killed on the Colorado 1781. i. 363. E. (Ascension), at Sta B. '32, wife Nicolasa Pico, 6 children. E. (Cárlos), grantee of Poza de los Ositos '39. iii. 678; ment. in '46. v. 363; in Mont. Co. '50. E. (Cayetano), soldier at Soledad 1791-1800. i. 499. E. (Clemente), soldier at Mont. '36, age 20; an alférez '38-9. iii. 566, 583; at Sta Rita, near S. José, in '77 he gave me some brief *Apuntes.* E. (Estévan), ment. in the revolt of '29. iii. 69; grantee of rancho '40. iii. 679; in '36 at Salinas rancho, age 25, wife Antonia Amézquita, child Antonio b. '32.   E. (Feliciano), juez de campo at Mont. '36. iii. 675.   E. (Gabriel), ment. in '22. ii. 614; in revolt of '29. iii. 68-9; in trouble '31. iii. 673; grantee of Salinas in '36. iii. 678. In '36 he lived at Salinas, age 38, wife Mauricia Tapia, child. José María b. '19, Estefana '22, Antonio '25, Marcelino '29, Juana '28, Francisca '30, Bárbara '31, Juan '35.   E. (Gabriel), grantee of Pilarcitos '35. iii. 678; in '36 at the rancho, age 46, wife Guadalupe Boronda, child. Gabriel b. '22, Ignacia '25, Pedro '26, María '27, Francisco '30, Juan M. '33, Guillermo '35.   E. (Gregoria), wife of Sergt Verdugo before 1800. i. 663.   E. (Joaquin), soldier killed on the Colorado 1781. i. 303.   E. (Hipólito), at Los Ang. '46, age 30. E. (José), 1791, lieut in Malaspina's exped. i. 490.   E. (José), regidor of Mont. '30. ii. 612; at Mont. '50.   E. (Juan), sirviente at S. F. 1777. i. 297. E. (Juan B.), in comp. extranjera '32. iii. 672.   E. (Luis), Mex. soldier of the Hidalgo piquete at Mont. '36, age 34.   E. (Manuel), at S. Bern. '46, had Cal. claim (v. 462).   E. (Miguel), soldier of Mont. comp. 1791-1800. i. 499; sergt 1809-13. ii. 141, 339.   E. (Prudencio), at Alisal, Mont. '36, age 33, wife Antonia Buelna, child. José Manuel b. '28, Antonio '31, Ramon '32, Leonardo '33, Trinidad '36, Concepcion '27. In '46 he was juez suplente of the valley ranchos, and carried a message from Larkin to Frémont. v. 14-15, 637.   E. (Salvador), named as sirviente and soldier 1777-1800. i. 297, 499. E. (Salvador), alcalde at Mont. '31-2. iii. 223, 225, 672-3; in '35 regidor. iii. 673; in '36 at San Miguel rancho, age 40, wife Lugarda Castro, child. Cárlos b. '16, José Ant. '18, José María '20, Asuncion '24; in '37 grantee of S. Miguel, or Escarpin. ii. 616, 664, 677-8; admin. of Soledad '35. iii. 690-1; in '43 juez at Refugio. iii. 653.   E. (Trinidad), grantee of Los Gatos, or Sta Rita '20, '37. iii. 677, 672; at S. Miguel rancho '36, being juez de campo. iii. 675, 678, age 43, wife Jacinta Archuleta, son Mariano b. '17; in '45 at battle of Cahuenga and juez at Refugio. iv. 506, 653.   E. (Vicente), Cal. claim '46 of $2,285 (v. 462).

Esquerra (Cayetano), messenger Sta Cruz '18. ii. 225.   E. (Manuel), 1791, contador in Malaspina's exped. i. 490.   Est, 1817, left at Sta B. ii. 286; prob. 'Lester,' q.v.   Estabrook (Ethan), 1840, left at Mont. as U. S. consular agent to attend to the claims of the Graham exiles. He was not recog. by the govt, and sailed for Mazatlan in '41; at Mazatlan in '46. iv. 36-7, 194, 207, 214.   Estanislao, kills his wife 1792. i. 687-8.   Estanislao, renegade neophyte and hostile chief. 29-35; the name of Stanislaus County comes indirectly from him. ii. 110-14, 362.

Esténega (Tomás Eleuterio), 1820, Span. friar who served at S. Miguel, S. F., and S. Gabriel, dying at the latter mission in '47. Biog. v. 629; ment. ii. 384, 394, 440, 595-6, 620, 655; iii. 7, 12, 19, 91, 96, 121, 257, 319, 349, 359, 642-3, 713, 716; iv. 331, 371, 422, 549-50, 623, 629, 636-7.   Estévan (José), settler at the Colorado pueblos, killed by Ind. 1781. i. 359-62.   E. (José), 1821, Span. capt. and com. of Horcasitas, Sonora, who fled to Cal. on refusing oath of indep., on the Zertaje. ii. 431.   E. (Pedro de S. José), 1794, Span. friar who served at S. Diego and S. Gabriel. retiring in 1802. Biog. ii. 113; ment. i. 576, 655, 657, 664; ii. 159.   E., executed at Purísima '24. Estirten (Félix), 1829, mr of the Trident; doubtful. iii. 149.

Estrada (Francisco), at Chualar rancho '36. iii. 677; at S. José '41, age 23, wife Inés Castro; grantee of Pastoría de las Borregas and Refugio '42. iv. 672.   E. (Joaquin), in '36 at Chualar, age 19, single. iii. 677; grantee of Sta Margarita '41. iv. 656; juez de paz at S. Luis Ob. '45. iv. 658-9; arrested by Frémont '46. v. 375; county judge '53; still at S. Luis '77.   E. (José Ant.), represented Gov. Alvarado at his wedding '39. iii. 593; admin. of S. José mission '40-1. iii. 725; iv. 681, 684.   E. (José María), alférez of the Loreto comp., prob. father of José Mariano and Raimundo, died 1791; never in Cal. Estrada (José Mariano), 1806, born at Loreto 1784. enlisted 1797, came to Cal. as alférez of the Mont. comp., which position he held for 12 years, being habilitado most of the time. ii. 140, 206, 379-89. He was made brevet lieut in '18 for his services against Bouchard, and lieut '24 for services in suppressing the Ind. revolt. ii. 225-33, 243-4, 247, 531-3, 536, 608; also habilitado and sometimes acting com.; ment. in connection with various affairs. i. 170; ii. 451, 454, 461, 510; grantee of Buenavista ranchos '22–3. ii. 615, 664; iii. 677; admin. gen. of provincial finances '24. ii. 513, 521; mention '25–9, quarrel with Capt. Gonzalez, vocal in diputacion, Herrera trial, revenue affairs. ii. 612; iii. 25, 36–7, 39–40, 62–5, 159. He retired from the mil. service in '29; in '30 executor of Luis Argüello's estate. iii. 12; in '32–3 sub-comisario at Mont. iii. 376, 672; juez de campo '35. iii. 674; in '36 at Buenavista, a widower, child. Julian b. '16, and Francisco '20; ment. in the troubles at Mont. '36, also in '44. iii. 439; iv. 408. I have no record of him after '45. Don Mariano was one of the most respected and influential men in northern California. E. (José Raimundo), 1806, brother of José Mariano, who was cadet of the Mont. comp. to '18. ii. 56, 88, 379; in 1812 married the widow Josefa Vallejo de Alvarado. ii. 141; iii. 451 (where 'Ramon' should read 'Raimundo'); ment. perhaps in '24. ii. 537. In '24–30 Raimundo Estrada was cadet in the S.F. comp. ii. 584, 669; and would seem to be the same man, though he appears as a soldier at S.F. in '23; thus there may have been another of the name.

Estrada (José Ramon), son of José Mariano; in school at Mont. '15–20. ii. 429; hunting otter '32–4. iii. 374, 394; grantee of El Toro '35. iii. 679; in '36 alcalde at Mont. iii. 430, 439, 674; being at that time 25 years of age, wife María Castro; in '37 memb. of dip., in com. at Mont., and comisionado and admin. at Sta Clara. iii. 507, 511, 672, 728; iv. 47; vocal again '39. iii. 585, 590. In '41–3 Estrada was prefect of the 1st district. iv. 357, 652, 656; in '42 grantee of S. Simeon. iv. 656; and in '42–5 memb. of the junta. iv. 295, 360–1, 410, 521, 540. He seems to have died in '45. E. (Julian), son of José Mariano, grantee of Sta Rosa rancho '41. iv. 656; still in S. Luis Ob. Co. '50–60. E. (Nicanor), 1834, Mex. blacksmith and political exile with the H. & P. col., who had been a capt. in Mex., and whose rank was restored in '35; went to the L. Cal. frontier in '36 on the fall of Gutierrez. iii. 263, 467; being at this time 30 years old, wife Guadalupe Diaz, child. Gumesinda b. '31, Elena '34. In '37 he aided Bandini and others in their preparations against Alvarado, and was perhaps sent as a comisionado to Mex. iii. 516, 520, 531; but came back with Micheltorena in '42, and was capt. of the Mont. comp. in '43–4. iv. 290, 357, 652. I have no later record of him.

Estrada (Patricio), 1825, alférez of the piquete de Hidalgo who came with Echeandía, and in '36 was sent away with Gutierrez. iii. 13–15, 463, 467, 672. He was 19 years old and single in '36. E. (Pedro), owner of lot at S.F. '41–5. iv. 669; sub-lieut of militia; grantee of Asuncion in '45. iv. 655; still at S. Luis Ob. '50–1. E. (Rafael), celador of Mont. custom-house '42–4. iv. 339, 377, 431; grantee of S. Lúcas rancho '42, and alf. of aux. cavalry. 655, 652; in '46 regidor at Mont. v. 636; still in Mont. Co. '53. E. (Raimundo), cadet in S. F. comp. '24–30; prob. same as José Raimundo, q.v. E. (Santiago), son of José Mariano, grantee with his brothers of Buenavista rancho '22–3. ii. 615; iii. 677; made a trip to China on the *Rover* '24. ii. 520; síndico at Mont. '33. iii. 673; in '35–6 aux. alcalde and juez de campo. iii. 674–5; then living at Buevavista, age 27, wife Isidora Soto, child. Mariano, Francisco, María de los Angeles, and Juana. In '36–7 also named as sub-comisario and comandante at Mont. iii. 513, 524, 672; iv. 96; in '38 courier and com. of prisoners' guard. iii. 552, 567; in '39 partido elector. iii. 590; in '39–45 capt. of aux. comp. at Mont. iv. 75, 197–8, 407, 515, 652; in '46 juez of the valley ranchos. v. 637; still in Mont. Co. '50–1.

Estudillo (José Antonio), son of José María, b. at Mont. 1805.; in '27 of terna for treasurer, and grantee of S. Diego lot. ii. 546–7; iii. 63; in '28–30, revenue collector and treasurer at S.D. ii. 543; iii. 137; in '29 grantee of Otay rancho. ii. 542, 547, 663; iii. 612. In '33–5 he was a memb. of the dip. iii. 246, 249–50; in '35 had a claim to the temporary governorship. iii. 299–300, 414–15; grantee of Temécula. iii. 612; in '36–8 alcalde and juez of S. Diego. iii. 485, 616; in '36–8 took part against Alvarado's govt. iv. 491, 548–9, 557, 568, 578; elector '39, treasurer '40, and justice of the sup. tribunal '40–2. iii. 605, 614, 616; iv. 296; admin. and maj. at S. Luis Rey '40–3, also owner of land at S. Juan Cap. '41. iii. 623–4, 627; iv. 619, 623, 626; grantee of S. Jacinto '42. iv. 621, 618; claim against the govt '45. iv. 561; in '45-6 juez de paz at S. Diego, iv. 618-20, but was neutral in the troubles with the U.S. v. 329; ment. '47. v. 620. In later years he served under the U.S. rule as town treasurer and county assessor. Died in '52. Don José Antonio was a man of excellent character, of good education for his time and country, and of wide influence in the south. His wife was María Victoria Dominguez, locally well known for her charities, who died in '73 at the age of 72, leaving 30 grandchildren. The sons were José María, Salvador, José Guadalupe, José Antonio, and Francisco. Of the daughters, two, Francisca and Rosario, married José Ant. Aguirre, and another seems to have married Manuel A. Ferrer.   E. (José Guadalupe), son of José Antonio, b. '38; connected with a S. Diego bank; county treasurer from '63; state treasurer from '75; still living in Southern Cal. '85.

Estudillo (José Joaquin), son of José María, b. 1798, who entered the mil. service in '15 as soldado distinguido of the Mont. comp., but was transferred to the S.F. comp. in '16 as cadet, which place he held until he left the service in '23, having accompanied Luis Argüello on the famous exped. to the far north in '21. ii. 370, 445, 584. Ment. at S.F. '26-7. iii. 33, 63; munic. elector '27, and supl. member of dip. '27, '29. ii. 592; iii. 36-41; in '34-5 comisionado to secularize S.F. mission. iii. 346, 354, 714-15; in '35 elector, in '36 alcalde at S.F. iii. 703-5; in '38 living at S. Leandro rancho, which in '42 was granted to him. iii. 713; iv. 673, 314. In a padron of the S. José dist. of '41 he is named, with wife Juana Martinez, child. Concepcion b. '25, Ramon '27, Gertrudis '29, Antonio '30, María de Jesus '31, José Vicente '33, José Luis '36, María Guadalupe '38. Don Joaquin was juez de la contra costa in '43, also in '46-7, taking but slight part in the war. iv. 685; v. 17, 129, 662. He died in '52. I have much of his corresp. in dif. private archives; and also 2 vols of *Estudillo, Doc. Hist. Cal.*, presented by his son Jesus María in '75. He left 9 children, some of whom in '85 still own a part of the original S. Leandro estate. Of his daughters, the oldest, Concepcion, married John B. Ward, María de Jesus in '47 became the wife of Wm H. Davis, Magdalena married John Nugent, and Dolores married Chas H. Cushing. Of the sons Antonio lives in '85 at S. Leandro, Luis at Oakland, Ramon and Vicente at S. Luis Ob., and Jesus María at S.F.

Estudillo (José María), 1806, Span. lieut of the Mont. comp. 1806-27, and capt. of the S. Diego comp. from '27 to his death in '30. Biog. ii. 541-2; ment. ii. 140, 171, 192, 226, 230, 234, 271, 285, 309, 335-6, 340-1, 379, 382, 383-4, 387-8, 412, 433, 442, 451, 454-5, 461, 467, 507-8, 512-13, 517, 523, 525, 539, 608; iii. 13, 39, 51-3, 60, 291, 422. Don José María was the founder of the Estudillo family in Cal., one of the best of the old families, as judged by the average prominence and character of its members. A faithful officer, though of only medium abilities, he had some disagreeable qualities—notably that of vanity—which made him at one time or another heartily disliked by most of his brother officers, who were disposed to ridicule him and make him the butt of practical jokes. His wife was Gertrudis Horcasitas. His daughter, Magdalena, was grantee of part of Otay in '29. ii. 209, 373, 542, 547; v. 619. A daughter married Lieut Manuel Gomez. ii. 470.   E. (José María), cadet at S.F. 1803-7. ii. 135. I do not know who he was.   E. (José María), son of José Ant., b. at S. Diego '31; educ. at Sta B., Mont., and Lima '39-48; in '50 agent for Aguirre, his brother-in-law; later a ranchero in the S.D. mission valley, where, in '77, he gave me some interesting *Datos Históricos.* His wife was a daughter of Juan María Marron.

Etholin (Adolf), 1827, mr of the Russian *Baikal* '27-30. ii. 649-51; iii. 146; i. list auth.   Eusebio, Ind. in Sutter's employ '45-6; induced to testify that Castro had instigated him to burn grain-fields, etc.   Eustice (Dabney), 1846, with Kearny from N. Mex. v. 337.   Eustis, 1845, at N. Helv., perhaps an overl. immig. iv. 578.   Euth (John), 1847, Co. G, N.Y. Vol. (v. 499).

Evans (Geo. M.), 1847, brick-maker and owner of a S.F. lot. v. 685; published an article in defense of the Mormons in *S.F. Californian* July 31, '47. E. (Israel), 1847, Co. B, Morm. Bat. (v. 469); in Sutter's employ; went to

Utah '48. E. (John), 1826-7, clerk on the *Blossom;* trip from S.F. to Mont. by land. iii. 121. E. (John), 1842, Austrian sailor and carpenter, landed from a whaler with a broken leg. iv. 341; hunted otter with Dittmann '45; at S.F. '46 with a family, getting a lot in '47. The original name was Evanowitz; still at S.F. '79. E. (John), 1847, Co. F, 3d artillery. *Lancey;* not on roll. E. (Joseph), 1847, sergt Co. I, N.Y. Vol. v. 504; 15 years in Cal.; at Newark N. J. '84; a brother Geo. at S. José '78. E. (O. H.), 1847, at S. F. from Or. on the *Henry.* E. (Parley P.), 1847, nat. of Penn.; son of Wm, age 6 years; in '55 messenger in the assembly at Sac.; I have a letter from him in Utah '84. E. (Plummer B.), 1847, Co. I, N.Y. Vol. (v. 499); at Hampton, Va. '82. E. (Randolph), 1847, Co. F, N.Y. Vol. (v. 499). E. (Wm), 1846, of the Morm. col., with wife Hannah R., and 4 child. Amanda M., Jonathan B., Parley P., and Wm. v. 546; owner of S.F. lot '47. v. 682; d. S.F. '52; the family went to Utah '57, where the mother died in '84, when the children were all living. E. (Wm), 1847, Co. B, Morm. Bat. (v. 469); reënl.; a mason who in '48 was judge of election at S. Diego. v. 652.

Everett (C. T.), 1846, mr of a whaler at S. Pedro. E. (Elisha), 1847, musician Co. B, Morm. Bat. (v. 469); capt. of a party on the return. *Bigler.* E. (John C.), 1844, mr of the *Vandalia* '44-7; owner of S. F. lot. iv. 569; v. 580. E. (John H.), 1836, at Mont., prob. as clerk on the *Alert.* iv. 118, 141; and again in '41-4 as sup. of the *Tasso.* iv. 460, 569. He is said to have been much less popular with the Californians than other traders of the period. Everhart (Lazarus), 1845, tailor in the McMahon-Clyman party from Or. iv. 572, 587; had crossed the plains from Mich. in '44. He went first to Mont., but from '47 had a tailor-shop at S. F., where he was the owner of several lots, a candidate for alcalde, and in '49 member of the council. v. 650, 676, 683. Eversfield (Chas), 1846, asst surg. on the U. S. *Congress;* acting as surg. in Stockton's Bat. '47. v. 385. Everts (Henry), 1845, doubtful name of an overl. immig. iv. 578. Evrett (Solomon), 1845, Del. Ind. in Frémont's party.

Ewel (James D.), 1846, came to S. José Valley. *Hall.* Ewer, 1847, mr of the *Emily Morgan.* v. 577. Exter (Richard), 1828, licensed by Mex. govt to hunt in Cal. with Julian Wilson; no definite record of operations. iii. 172-3. Eymerlun, 1845, doubtful name of a negro deserter from the *Héroine.* Ezquer (Ignacio), 1833, Mex. clerk who came by sea at the age of 15; served as clerk for dif. admin. of missions; kept a bar '42-5, later a store and billiard-room; in '38 temp. in charge of S. Juan Cap. iii. 558; in '48 candidate for munic. treasurer. iv. 653; in '46 regidor and acting alcalde of Mont. v. 233, 636; in '49 again alcalde. He lived at Alisal '50-3, and in '54 went to S. Luis Ob., where he served several years as justice of the peace. There in '78 he gave me his *Memorias* on early events. His first wife was Josefa, daughter of Rafael Pico; the second a daughter of Gov. Alvarado.

Fabbol, 1845, one of Frémont's men '45-7. iv. 583.   Fabregat (Narciso), 1819, Span. lieut of the Mazatlan cavalry, who served chiefly at Sta B., being often mentioned in the military records down to '30; being suspended for a time in '27-8 on account of his Span. birth, though he took the oath and gave no cause of suspicion; retired from mil. service in '33. ii. 254, 336, 361, 441, 533-4, 572-3, 575, 675; iii. 51-3. In '29 he was 67 years old, had been three times married, had a daughter in Sin. to whom he allowed one third of his pay, and two small children by his last wife. He became a trader at Sta B., and in '43 was grantee of the Catera or Pozitas rancho. iii. 655; iv. 642; ment. in '44. iv. 408. I have no later record than '45, but think the old lieut was murdered by robbers soon after '48.

Fages (Pedro), 1769, Span. lieut of Catalan volunteers, who accomp. the 1st exped. as com. of the forces that came by sea; mil. com. of Cal. July '70 to May '74, being capt. from '71; came back as gov. and com. gen. of Cal. Sept. '82 to April '91, being colonel from '89; in the city of Mex. '94, the date of his death not being known. See biog. i. 481-7; his *Voyage* and other writings, i. list of auth., 141, 396, 408, 443, 486; mention '69-74, including his explor. of S.F. Bay and his quarrels with P. Serra. i. 117, 119, 128, 131, 134, 136, 140-1, 147, 151, 153, 168-9, 171-2, 175-6, 178-9, 181-92, 195-6, 207, 210, 213, 215, 217-19, 223, 225-7, 229, 231-2, 245, 283-6, 290, 386, 671; ii. 44; ment. in '81-2, including his appt as gov. and operations on the Colorado. i. 363, 366-70, 373, 376, 378, 383-5; mention in 1783-90, gen. record, includ. family troubles. i. 387-408; mission affairs during his rule. i. 409-25; foreign relations and commerce. i. 426-49; occasional ment. in con. with local matters. i. 450-80; 1791-2, end of rule, departure, biog. i. 481-7; additional references. i. 492, 534, 583, 605, 609, 619, 625, 661-2, 666-7; ii. 44. Don Pedro was a central figure in early Californian annals; his character has been to me a most attractive one; but I refer the reader to i. 486-7, for my views on the subject.   Fagins (Lucius), 1847, owner of a S.F. lot.

Fairbanks (Henry), 1847, Co. A, Morm. Bat. (v. 469); at Payson, Utah, '82. F. (W.R.), 1848, nat. of Vt, who came by sea with his cousins, named Heyman, at the age of 10; in the mines to '55; 10 years in N.Y.; at Tomales '80 with wife, Belinda Scanlan, and 4 children. *Marin Co. Hist.*, 493.   Fairchild (Ephraim), 1847, prob. overl. immig. v. 556; blacksmith and wagon-maker, who worked at N. Helv. '47-9; at Sac. in '71.   F. (Wm H.), 1846, connected with the Mormon settlement on the Stanislaus in '46-7, though prob. not a Mormon; settled at Stockton '47; county surveyor and supervisor '78-9. Fairfax (D.M.), 1847, mid. on the *Columbus*, acting master of the *Erie*.   Fairfield (Levi), 1848, miner from whom Gov. Mason obtained specimens of gold. Fala (Francis), 1847, owner of lot at S.F.   Fales (Bounty), 1846-7, doubtful name, Cal. claims (v. 462).   Falker (Joseph K.), 1844, Amer. who got a pass for 1 year.   Falkner (E.R.), 1848, clerk of Starky, Junion, & Co. at S. F.   Fallet (1847), at N. Helv.   Fallon (Daniel), 1826, mr of the *Adam*. iii. 145.   F. (D.), 1846-7, in list of Cal. claims (v. 462).   F. (Jeremiah), 1847, owner of S.F. lot; also at S. José.

Fallon (Thomas), 1844, Canadian generally said to have come with Frémont, though there is some doubt in the matter. iv. 453; also said by the county histories to have lived for a time in Butte Co. The earliest original

records of his presence are in Oct.-Nov. '45, when he was at Branciforte, age
26. In '46 he took part in enlisting men south of the bay to coöperate with the
Bear filibusters. v. 137; and in July, being known as 'captain,' raised the U.
S. flag at S. José. v. 245-6. Later in '46-7 he served in Co. F, Cal. Bat., enlisting at S. Juan in Oct. (v. 358); several times named in the *N. Helv. Diary*
'46-7; in the list of Cal. claimants (v. 462); in '48-9 a successful miner; mayor
of S. José in '51; absent in Texas '52-4; later a capitalist of S.F. and S. José,
where he still lives in '85. His 1st wife, by whom he had 5 children, was, I
think, a daughter of Michael Lodge, the Irish pioneer of '22. She obtained a
divorce, as did the 2d wife; and in '84-5 the amorous old captain had to pay
damages in a breach-of-promise suit.   F. (Wm O.), 1845, Irish trapper,
known as 'Mountaineer,' 'Big,' or 'Le Gros' Fallon, who came from N. Mex.
with a party of which little is known, and in Feb. '45 took part with the
Calif. against Micheltorena in the south. iv. 495, 587. In Aug. he was at N.
Helv. intending to start soon for the states; early in '46 he found Frémont's
men in the S. Joaq. Val. v. 6; in June joined the Bears in the capture of Sonoma, and his signature appears in the original procl. of June 14th in my
possession. v. 110, 114. He served prob. in Co. F, Cal. Bat. (v. 358), and had
a Cal. claim of $50 for a mule (v. 462); was a member of the 4th Donner re-
lief, and his diary, published in the *Star*, was the foundation of the absurd
charges against Keseburg. v. 541-3. He went east with Gen. Kearny as guide.
v. 452; and in the *S.F. Calif.* of Sept. 2, '48, we read that he had started alone
from Ft Hall for Cal., and it was feared he had been killed by Ind.
    Falls (Richard J.), 1846, nat. of N.Y.; sergt Co. C, 1st U.S. dragoons, who
served under Kearny at S. Pascual, the S. Gabriel, and the Mesa '46-7. v.
347. He remained in Cal. after his disch., living on a Napa farm till '62, when
he went east to serve in the war with distinction and wounds for 3 years, rising to the rank of colonel. Returning to Cal. he was in '69 an officer in the
custom-house; and in '83-5 a sergt of police in S. F. His daughter, Ivy I.
Falls, was appointed postmistress at Vallejo in '69.   Famin (Ign.), 1847,
doubtful name of an Englishman at N. Helv.
    Fannier (M.), 1846, doubtful name of the Cal. Bat. (v. 358).   Fanning
(H.F.), 1847, resid. of Stockton. *Tinkham.*   F. (R.C.), 1846, Co. F, Cal.
Bat. (v. 358); enlist at S. Juan, Oct.   Farías (José María), settler at Los
Ang. '15. ii. 350; still there '39-48.   F. (Santiago), 1827, Scotchman, bapt.
at S. Diego; prob. James 'McFerion,' q.v.   Farley (Anderson), 1846, Co. F,
Cal. Bat. (v. 358); prob. an overl. immig., cl. for a Napa rancho '52.   F.
(Geo.), 1847, Co. B, N.Y.Vol. (v. 499); at The Dalles, Or., '82.   F., 1846,
said by Lancey to have come with Kearny; owner of a S. F. lot '47.   F.
(John F.), 1847, Co. B, N.Y.Vol. (v. 499); died at Portland, Or., '69. *Hist.
Or.*, i. 630.   F. (John G.), 1847, father of John F., Co. B, N.Y.Vol.; d. S.F.
'49.   F. (Thos P.), 1847, Co. B, N.Y.Vol.; at Portland, Or., '82.   Farnesio
(Francisco), 1805, priest from Manila, at Mont., sent to Mex. ii. 31, 160.
    Farnham (Thos Jefferson), 1840, nat. of Me, who came overl. to Or. in '39,
and to Cal. via Honolulu on the *Don Quixote*, returning east by S. Blas and
across Mex., and writing books on Or., Mex., and Cal. as a result. See iii.
680; iv. 2, 4, 6-7, 10, 15-17, 25-8, 95, 103, 117, 120, 156-7, 192, 266. F. was
a lawyer of some ability, and a writer of somewhat fertile imagination. His
work on Cal. is criticised elsewhere in this work; here it must suffice to say
that in all those parts resting on his own observations it is worthless trash,
and in all that relates to the Californian people a tissue of falsehoods. He
came back to Cal. in '47—perhaps in '46, as he took part in a public meeting
at S.F. in June '47, v. 455—and died at S. F. in Sept. '48, age 42. He left a
widow and 3 children in N.Y. The former, Eliza W. Farnham, came to Cal.
by sea in '50, and in '56 published her *California Indoors and Out*, a pleasing
picture of life on the Pacific coast. She was a woman bent on doing the world
as much good as possible, and one of her hobbies was the bringing eastern
girls to Cal. in quest of husbands. She died in '64 at the age of 49.   Farns-
worth (J.B.), 1839, Engl. at Mont. acc. to newsp. item of '72.   F. (J.M.),
1846, doubtful memb. of the Mormon col. v. 547.   Farnum, 1848, mr of a

vessel at Sta Cruz and Mont. Farr (Philip), 1847, Co. G, N.Y.Vol. (v. 499); d. at Dutch Flat '83.

Farwell (Edward Augustus), 1842, Boston printer and sailor who came from Honolulu with Capt. Cooper on the *California*, perhaps as mate, with letters from Reynolds to Larkin, age 27. iv. 341. In '43 he was naturalized, and in '44 got a grant of the Arroyo Chico rancho, Butte Co. iv. 670; I have a letter of '45 from his brother Joseph R. in Bost. to the U.S. consul asking for information about him. He went east overl. in '45, seeking relief from weak eyes, returning in '48; was for a time in charge of Sutter's launch running on the Sac., and died at S. F. in Jan. '49. F. (James), 1840, doubtful name in Farnham's list of arrested foreigners. iv. 17. Fatoute (Ezra), 1847, Co. B, Morm. Bat. (v. 469); reënl. Faucon (Edward H.), 1835, mr of the Boston ships *Alert* and *Pilgrim* '35-7. iii. 381, 383; iv. 105, 141. Wm H. Thomes informs me that Capt. F. is still living in Mass. '85. Fauffer (Johann), 1847, musician of N.Y.Vol. (v. 499); d. Wash. '64. Faulkner (James Y.), 1847, Co. G, N.Y.Vol. (v. 499); at S. José '50 and '74; S.F. '71; in Or. '78.

Fauntleroy (Daingerfield), 1844, nat. of Va, b. 1799; capt. of state militia about 1838; purser U.S.N. from '33; on the *Savannah* '44-7. iv. 453. The service that has made him best known in Cal. was as capt. of a comp. of volunteer dragoons to which was intrusted the preservation of order in the Mont. district July-Sept. '46, F. commanding the garrison of S. Juan B. and making an exped. against hostile Ind. v. 232, 247-8, 254, 293-4. Died at Pensacola navy-yard in '53. His son W.H.F., in interviews and letters of '77, being then in S.F., gave me information about his father's life.

Faura (José), 1798, Span. friar who served 12 years as missionary at S. Luis Rey and S. Juan Cap. Biog. ii. 110; ment. i. 564, 577, 654, 657; ii. 110, 159-60. Faust (John B.), 1847, owner of S.F. lot. v. 685; in May intending to start from Sonoma with a party to explore Trinidad Bay; in March '48 digging wells at 'Benicia. v. 673; d. at the Yuba mines Aug. 18th. Faustino, 1845, leader in a disturbance at Los Ang. iv. 523. Fautrel, 1837, mr of the *Nancy*. iv. 105. Faxon (Wm. T.), 1840, Amer. trader who came by sea and took charge of Larkin's store at Mont. '41. iv. 120. He went to Hon. in '42 but returned in '44, his name frequently occurring in commercial corresp. He left the country on the *California* in '46, and in a later letter Capt. Arther gave a very unfavorable report of his conduct on the voyage.

Febiger (Geo. Carson), 1846, lieut on the *Dale*, on land service at S.F. F. (John C.), 1846, passed mid. on the *Dale;* at Wash. '78. Feil (J.), 1837, owner of S.F. lot. iii. 705; doubtful name. Feliciano (Alejo), 1777, sirviente at S.F. i. 297. Felipe, executed at Sta. B. '24. F. (A.), 1848, passp. from Hon.

Félix, see list in i. 735-6 of those who came before 1800. Félix (Anastasio), at Los Ang. '46. F. (Antonio), at Los Ang. '39, age 28. F. (Antonio), soldier at S.F. '44, age 21. F. (Diego), at Mont. '36, age 26, wife María del Rosario, child Andrés; maj. at San Antonio '39. iii. 688; executed for the murder of his wife '40. iii. 676. F. (Dolores), alférez of cavalry at Mont. '45. iv. 652. Still at Mont. '48. F. (Domingo), murdered by his wife and her paramour at Los Ang. '36, a crime that resulted in the 1st Cal. vigilance com. iii. 417-19, 631. F. (Domingo), militia sergt at S.F. '37 and later; owner of S.F. lot '43, and grantee of S. Mateo rancho '44. iv. 669, 671, 673, 676, 683; still at S.F. '55, a witness in the Santillan case. F. (Doroteo), settler at Los Ang. 1803. ii. 350. F. (Fernando), regidor at S. José '31. iii. 729; at S. Mateo '35; grantee of Novato '39. iii. 712, and of Sanel '44. iv. 673; age 46 in '44; ment. by Revere. '46. ii. 297. F. (Francisco), settler at Los Ang. 1791. ii. 350. F. (Hipólito), French, at Brancif. '45, age 27. F. (Ignacio), soldier at Sta. B. before '37. F. (Jacoba), cl. of S. Fran. rancho. iii. 633. F. (Jesus), aux. alcalde at S. José '36. iii. 636. F. (José), settler at Los Ang. '13-19; ii. 349, 354. F. (José), at S.F. and Son. '42-4, age 15-20. F. (José), juez de campo S. José. v. 662. F. (José Antonio), killed by Ind. about '24. F. (José Antonio), at Los Ang. '46. F. (Juan), soldier at Sta. B. '32. F. (Juan), at Los Ang. '39, age 57. F. (Juan), killed by

Ind. at Refugio '45. iv. 642. F. (Juan José), at Brancif. '28–45, age at latter date 45; wife Antonia Castro, child. Rafaela, Miguel b. '22, Leon '25, Angel '27, Antonio '32, Victoria '31, Josefa '39; juez de paz in '43. ii. 677; iv. 663. F. (Julian), at S. Mateo '35. F. (Leonardo), soldier at S.F. '19–27; arrested at Mont. '37. iii. 525. F. (Luciano), sentinel at S. Buen. '19. ii. 333; in revolt at Sta B. '29. iii. 78; at the Natividad fight '46; in 49 juez de policía at S. Luis Ob. F. (Luis), soldier at S.F. '44, age 17. F. (Luis), soldier at Sta B. '32–7, wife Secundina Cordero, 3 children. F. (Manuel), in Los Ang. dist. '46–56. F. (Nicolás), at Los Ang. '46. F. (Rafael), at S. Mateo '35; S.F. militia '37; in '41 in S. José dist., age 44, wife Juana Amézquita, child. Ramon b. '28, Urbano '29, Macario '31, Julia '27, Sinforosa '34, Jose d. '40. F. (Rafael), soldier of S.F. comp. '39–42; detailed in '41 to accomp. capt. Castañeda to Mex.; grantee of Pescadero, S. Joaq., '43. iv. 672; ment. in '46. F. (Santiago), at S. Juan Cap. '46, age 30, wife Juana Riola, child. Juan, Andrea, Alonza, and Ascension. F. (Tomás), soldier at Sta B. before '37. F. (Vicente), inválido corp. in charge of Los Ang. as comisionado much of the time 1785–1800. i. 347, 461, 479, 661; owner of the Félix rancho, 1802–16. ii. 111, 185, 353. F. (Vicente), soldier at Sta B. before '37, wife Filomena Valenzuela; 5 children; in '36 maj. at Buena Esperanza rancho. iii. 677; widower, age 26, child. Casiana, Gerónimo, Juan, and José; grantee of Moro y Cayucos, S. Luis Ob., '42. iv. 655; in trouble with the auth. at S. Luis '47. Perhaps 2 or 3 men of this name.

Fellom (Caius Julius), 1845(?), Danish sailor, brother of Matthew, who came to Cal. in '52 and again in '62, and at S. José in '78 claimed to have touched at Sta B. before '46 on the whaler *Waverly*. *S. J. Pion.* Jul. 6, '78. F. (Matthew, or Felipe), 1821(?), Danish hatter and sailor, who landed from a whaler all the way from '21 to '24 acc. to dif. records. ii. 444, 526–7. He settled in the Gilroy region, and married after '34, when his age was 32. Felipe was prob. his baptismal name in Cal.; on Larkin's books '41–7: in '42 making soap at Gilroy's; in '46 juez at S. Juan B. v. 640. He is said to have become rich in lands and cattle, and to have died in '68 or '73. Fellows (C.J.), 1845, doubtful arrival. iv. 587. F. (Hiram W.), 1847, Co. C, Morm. Bat. (v. 469); reënl. Fendero (Jesus), Mex. soldier of the piquete de Hidalgo at Mont. '36, age 29. Fenley (Daniel), 1847, Co. A, N.Y.Vol. (v. 499).

Ferguson, 1846, doubtful memb. of the Mormon Col. v. 547. F. (Adrian), 1835, at S. José; prob. Geo. A., q. v. F. (Daniel), 1824, Irish shoemaker from N. Mex. ii. 526; iii. 156; joined the comp. extranjera at Mont. '32. iii. 221; in '36 a resid. of Los Ang., age 30, with a Cal. wife. He was one of the vigilantes (iii. 430); but failed to secure a lot; and in '39 or earlier came north, his name appearing on Larkin's books in '39–40. He was murdered in Salinas Val. '41 by Arana, the paramour of F.'s wife, Cármen Ruiz. iv. 280, 653. F. (Geo. A.), 1831, Amer. sailor, cooper, and lumberman, who deserted from the *Fanny*, working at S. Rafael, S. F. iv. 708–9, Mont. in '33, and S. José from '34. iii. 405; arrested but not exiled in '40. iv. 17; in the contra costa '44; signed the S. José call to foreigners '45. iv. 599; lot at S.F. '47; perhaps had a store at Stockton '48; in '78–83 a resid. of Mayfield. F. (James), 1847, sergt-maj. of Morm. Bat. v. 477, 483; in '58 adj.-gen. Utah; delivered a lecture in Liverpool '55. F. (Jesse), 1828, Amer. trapper of Pattie's party, who remained in Cal., settling at Los Ang.; married a Rendon in '31; named in '36 as a trader, age 36; said to have died in L. Cal. a few years later. ii. 558; iii. 163, 178. F. (J.C.), 1846, overl. immig., named by Bryant; Co. C, Cal. Bat., enlisting at S. Juan in Oct. (v. 358); Joseph F. had a Cal. claim (v. 462); Josiah F. was a witness in the Cal. claims and in the Frémont court-martial. v. 454. These may have been all the same man; but there was also a Ferguson at Sonoma in June before the arrival of the immig. v. 110, 128. Fermor (Edward), 1847, Co. D, N.Y.Vol. (v. 499).

Fernandez (Antonio), regidor of Mont. '27–8. ii. 612. F. (Diego), 1827, Span. trader on the *Waverly;* teacher at Sta B. '30. ii. 574; wife Brígida Navarro, 2 child.; widower in '36, age 51, 3 child.; maj. at Purísima '42. iv. 648. F. (Dionisio), grantee with his bro. Máximo of land in Butte '46. v.

675. F. (Francisco), 1825, Span. from the *Aquiles;* ordered away in '28–30. iii. 51. F. (Gregorio), 1794, Span. friar, who served at S. Luis Ob. and Purísima, retiring 1805. Biog. ii. 123; ment. i. 547, 576, 675, 689; ii. 159–60.

Fernandez (José), 1817, Span. sailor who came from Peru with Rocquefeuil as a sailor on the *Bordelais*, and served in the S. F. comp. as soldier and corporal in '19–27, going with Argüello in '21 on the exped. to the north. ii. 232, 289, 446. In '28–9, like other Span., he was in some trouble with the Mex. auth. but was allowed to remain. iii. 51–2, 75; in '30 sec. of the ayunt. at S. José. iii. 730; in '39 partido elector. iii. 590, 731; in '44 síndico. iv. 685; in '46 juez de paz, capt. of defensores, serving in the south under Castro to Aug., and after U.S. occupation memb. of the council. v. 140, 295, 662, 664; in '49 2d alcalde. In later years he resided at Sta Clara, being a witness in the N. Almaden and many other cases. In '74 he dictated his recollections of early days, a most interesting narrative called *Cosas de California.* He died a year or two later, over 75 years of age. Capt. F. was a man who always merited the respect and esteem of those who knew him.

Fernandez (José María), 1796, Span. friar, who served at S. F., but was obliged to retire in '97, insane from the effects of a blow on the head. i. 712–13; also i. 577, 711. F. (José Perez), see 'Perez Fernandez.' F. (José Zenon), 1834, Mex. teacher who came in the H. & P. col., iii. 263, teaching for a short time at Sta Clara. iii. 728. In '39 he was sec. of the S. José ayunt. and suplente juez de paz. iii. 731; in '40–1 sec. of the junta and ad int. of the govt. iii. 604, 193; and grantee of Quito rancho, Sta Clara, in '41. iv. 672; in '42 juez de paz at Mont., administering justice in a way not quite satisfactory to Com. Jones, and going south with Jimeno Casarin as sec. iv. 39, 294, 653, 656; in '44 sec. of the assembly down to his death in Aug. iv. 410. F. (Manuel), 1794, Span. friar who served at Sta Clara and Sta Cruz, retiring in 1798. Biog. i. 498; ment. i. 576–7, 618, 723. F. (Mariano), artillery corporal at S.D. 1803–6. ii. 102–3. F. (Mariano), of the custom-house guard at Mont. '45, perhaps the same. F. (Máximo), grantee of rancho in Butte, and S. F. lot '46. v. 675, 684. F. (Pedro), builder of 1st frame house at S. José '41. iv. 684. F. (Sabás), Mex. corporal sent to Cal. for the Mont. comp. '37; employed at Sonoma as lieut in com. of an Ind. comp. iii. 511; iv. 72. F. (Santiago), soldier of S.F. comp. '41.

Fernandez del Campo (José), 1828, Mex. lieut in com. of Cal. artill., stationed at Mont.; arrested by insurgents '29; died in '31. ii. 608, 674; iii. 68, 70, 89, 190, 239. Fernandez de San Vicente (Agustin), 1822, Mex. priest and canónigo, sent to Cal. as commissioner by Iturbide to superintend the change of govt; skillful in politics and intrigue, a bon-vivant and gambler, whose character was not admired by the friars. He departed in '23, and a few years later was vicar at Sta Fé, N. Mex. ii. 457–70, 483, 496, 550, 591, 597, 631, 643–4, 661; iii. 11. Fernando, neoph. grantee of Rincon del Alisal '44. Fernando, at Soledad '27. ii. 623.

Ferrelo (Bartolomé), 1542, piloto mayor in com. of one of Cabrillo's vessels in the discov. of Cal.; com. of the exped. after Cabrillo's death, continuing the voyage to the north. i. 77–81. Ferrer (Antonio), 1825, on the *Asia.* iii. 26. Ferrill (Thos J.), 1846, Fauntleroy's dragoons (v. 232, 247). Fetzchoror (Christian), 1847, musician of N.Y.Vol. (v. 499). Fetzer (John), 1846, Co. C, 1st U.S. dragoons (v. 336).

Fich (Henry), 1846, owner of S.F. lot; prob. Hen. D. 'Fitch,' q.v. Fickett (S.H.), 1847, nat. of N.Y.; memb. of S. Joaq. pioneers '84. Fidalgo (Salvador), 1790, Span. naval lieut, com. of the transports and explor. vessels *S. Cárlos* and *Princesa*, on the Cal. coast and at Nootka 1790–5. i. 444, 506, 509, 513, 517, 524, 533, 535, 543, list. of auth.; also *Hist. N. W. Coast*, index. Fiel (W.H.), 1846, Co. C, 1st U.S. dragoons, trans. from Co. K.; killed at S. Pascual. v. 346. Field (B. Oscar), 1847, nat. of Penn., captured as a boy by Ind., and later interpreter and courier for the govt. Said to have come to Cal. '47; in Sac. Val. '48; at S.F. from '50. Died at S.F. '64. *Bulletin.* F. (Daniel), 1847, Co. F, N.Y.Vol. (v. 499). F. (John), 1847, ditto. F. (Samuel), 1845, overl. immig., perhaps of the Grigsby-Ide party. iv. 579.

Fife (John), 1847, Co. C, Morm. Bat. (v. 469).   F. (Peter), 1847, Co. B, ditto.   F. (Wm), 1841, Scotch otter-hunter in Sta B. region from '45, and prob. several years earlier. iv. 279; v. 317; went to the mines '48, but resumed his hunting to '58 and later; murdered by a Sonoran at Sta B. in '66.   Fifer, see 'Pfeifer.'   Fifield (Ira), 1848, furnished specimens of gold to Gov. Mason; prob. same as following.   F. (Levi), 1847, Co. C, Morm. Bat. (v. 469); in Sutter's employ '47-8.

Figuer (Juan), 1772, Span. friar who served at S. Gabriel, San Luis Ob., and S. Diego, dying in 1784. Biog. i. 455; ment. i. 107, 192-3, 196, 272, 299, 316, 388, 457-9, 654, 106-7.   Figueroa (Felipe), soldier at Sta B. '32, wife Ignacia Lopez; still at Sta B. in '50.   F. (Francisco), 1833, Mex. capt. who came with his brother, the gov., and was appointed contador at Mont. in '34. iii. 236, 240, 378. In '36 he lived at Mont., age 32, wife María de Jesus Palomares, age 18, son Guadalupe b. '36; in '37 involved in the revolt against Alvarado. iii. 513, 523-6; from '39 in charge of his brother's Alamitos rancho near Los Ang. iii. 633, 637. In '44-6 he was a member of the assembly, being president of that body under Flores' administration, and taking some part against the U.S. iv. 361, 411, 495-6. 521; v. 37-8, 49-50, 264, 321-2. Don Francisco was city treasurer of Los Ang. in '50.   F. (Guadalupe), grantee of Corral de Tierra '36.

Figueroa (José), 1833, Mex. brigadier-gen. who had been com. gen. of Son. and Sin., and who was gov. and com. gen. of Cal. from Jan. 14, '33, to his death on Sept. 29, '35. See full account of his arrival, rule, and death, including his troubles with Híjar, Padrés, and Apalátegui, in iii. 234-98, espec. on biog. and character, 234, 296-7; also ment. i. 662; ii. 508, 594; iii. 16, 365, 414, 613, 633, 652, 669-71; acts and policy in mission and Ind. affairs. iii. 318, 321-36, 339-62, 620; commercial and financial affairs. iii. 368-80; the Russians. iv. 161-3. Figueroa is known as the best of California's Mex. governors, and in many respects merits his reputation. He was an intelligent man, of good intentions and liberal views; not a model in respect of private morality, and not always to be fully trusted; well versed in the arts of making friends and of gaining popularity by overcoming imaginary obstacles; was fortunate in the circumstances under which he was called to rule the country; and made no serious mistakes.   F. (Manuel), settler at Los Ang. in '79. i. 461.   Filibert (Francisco), 1825, Span. from the *Aquiles*, in list sent to Mex. '28; perhaps not sent away. iii. 51.

Finch (John), 1838, Engl. tinker and blacksmith who came to Mont. by sea, age 28. iv. 119. From '40 he lived at S.F., getting a lot, and keeping a saloon and bowling-alley at the cor. of Washington and Kearny streets. v. 683. He was more commonly known as John 'Tinker'; died Aug. 20, '47. Finch, 1847, mr of the *Com. Stockton*.   Findla (James), 1847, overl. immig. and carpenter from Mo., who worked at S.F. and became the owner of many town lots in '47-8. v. 556. Went to the mines in '48-9; later in the real estate business at S.F., where in '78 he dictated for my use his *Statement of Early Events*, and where I think he still lives in '85.   Findlay (John), 1847, Co. E, Morm. Bat. (v. 469).   F. (Wm), 1846, lieut and later capt. of Co. A, Cal. Bat. v. 361, 434; went east with Stockton or Kearny in '47. v. 454; at Wash. as a witness Jan. '48; perhaps the Wm Finlay at S. José '54 accredited to '45. *Annals of S.F.*, 822.

Fine (J. H.), 1846, nat. of Ky; claimant for Suisun rancho. iv. 674; died at Paso de Robles in '79, age 58.   F. (Quin?), 1847, blacksmith at Benicia; member of Sonoma council; died in '48. v. 668, 672-3.   Fink (Nicholas), 1836, German shoemaker who came to Los Ang. with a Mex. passp. of '35; age 30, and single in '40, when, having a shop in town, he was robbed and murdered, the 3 assassins being executed '41. iv. 118, 280, 629-30.

Finlay (Thomas), 1847, Co. D, Morm. Bat. (v. 469).   Finlayson (Duncan), 1833, agent of the H.B. Co., touched at S.F. on the *Dryad*. iii. 382, 404. Finley (Asa W.), 1846, overl. immig. with wife and 2 children; served under Aram at Sta Clara (v. 378); a farmer at S. José for 17 years; later in Linn Val., Kern Co., where he was in '79, having 2 sons, 3 married daughters, Mrs

Henry Pascoe, L. A. Beardsley, and J. P. Wilkes in Kern Co., and 2 daughters in Or. *Bakersfield Gazette.* Finley, 1844, a half-breed assistant of Laframboise. *Yolo Co. Hist.* F. (James), 1848, owner of lots at S.F. F. (John), 1847, Co. F, 3d U.S. artill. (v. 518). F. (John M.), 1848, of firm F., Johnson, & Co., traders at S.F. v. 680. F. (Richard), 1848, miner from Or., where he still lived in '82. Finley (S.), 1846, Cal. claim of $15 for a rifle (v. 462). Fippard (Chas), 1833, Engl. carpenter from the *Catalina*, who asked for a carta in '34, and was still at Mont. '35. iii. 409.

Fish (Wm), 1834, doubtful name in a Los Ang. list. Fisher, or Norris, 1818, negro of Bouchard's force, who rem. in Cal. There is no definite record of his later career, he being perhaps confounded in such vague allusions as exist with the following. ii. 248, 393. F., or Fisar, 1825, negro from Penn., who came to Sta B. on the *Sta Rosa;* in '29 at Los Ang., a farmer 35 years old, without religion, but of good conduct. iii. 29; ment. by Coronel, for whom he had worked, in '46-7; and perhaps by Foster in '48-9. It is possible, however, that this F. and the preceding were the same. F., 1846, of Cal. Bat., said to have been attacked by Ind. near Los Ang. in '47. *Frémont's Court-martial,* 233. F., 1847, mr of the *California.* v. 576. F., 1848, at Sutter's Fort from the quicksilver mines.

Fisher (Adam), 1843, named by Baldridge as a memb. of the Chiles-Walker immig. party. F. (Daniel), 1845, signer of the S. José call to foreigners. iv. 599. F. (Daniel), 1847, asst quartermaster in Stockton's Bat. Jan. v. 385. F. (F.), 1839, captain ment. in Larkin's accts as being at Mont. Aug. F. (Herman), 1848, German resid. of Sonoma Co. '73-7. *Son. Co. Hist.* F. (Joseph R.), 1846, one of the Mormon col., who rem. in Cal. v. 546. Fisher (Mary Ann), 1846, ditto; died in the faith at Mission S. José. v. 546. F. (Thomas M.), 1846, son of Wm, age 4, who settled in Sta Clara Co., married Anna Hanks in '61, and was still living, in '81, near Gilroy, with 5 children.

Fisher (Wm), 1845, nat. of Mass. who lived many years at Cape S. Lúcas, L. Cal., marrying Liberata Ceseña, trading on the coast, possibly visiting Upper Cal. earlier, but apparently coming for the 1st time in '45, when he got a S.F. lot, and is mentioned in Larkin's corresp. iv. 587, 669, 684. It was prob. on this visit that he purchased the Alvires, or Laguna Seca, rancho near S. José, for which his heirs were claimants in later years. iii. 712. In '46 he brought his family and settled at Laguna Seca, being also engaged in trade at S. José; it was on his rancho that Frémont encamped. v. 6, 660; in Dec. '46 memb. of council, v. 664, having declined the office of alcalde. v. 662. In '49 he sold his S. José business to Belden, and died in '50. His children were Mary C. wife of D. Murphy, Thos M., Cipriano W. (died), and Uloga Frico(?), as named in *Sta Clara Co. Hist.* The widow married Geo. H. Ball of N. Y. F. (Wm), 1825, mr of the *Recovery.* iii. 148. F. (Wm), 1830, at Los Ang. ii. 555. Fishpan (?), (John), 1846, Fauntleroy's dragoons (v. 232, 247). Fisk (Daniel), 1844, deserter from the *Warren.* Fiske (F.), 1841, mid. on the U.S. *St Louis.*

Fitch (Henry Delano), 1826, nat. of New Bedford, Mass., b. 1799, who came to Cal. as mr of Virmond's Mex. brig. *María Ester.* iii. 147, 176. In '27 he announced his intention of becoming a Mex. citizen; in '29 was baptized at S. Diego as Enrique Domingo Fitch; and was married at Valparaíso in July of the same year to Josefa Carrillo, daughter of Don Joaquin of S. Diego. For an account of his romantic elopement, return, and ecclesiastical trial, see iii. 140-4; ii. 551, 562, 569, 615. In '30-1 he was mr of the *Leonor,* iii. 49, 147, 383, his home being at S. Diego after his family troubles had been settled; in '32 already applying for lands north of S.F. bay. *Sup. Govt St. Pap.,* viii. 37; sons were born '30, '32, '34; naturalized in '33. He had a store at S. Diego; síndico in '35. iii. 615; com. de policía '36. iii. 616; afforded some aid —moistened powder, etc.—to the sureños in the political quarrels of '37-8. iii. 495, 553; in '39-40 presid. of election and juez de paz. iii. 614, 616-17. In '40 Capt. Fitch went to Hon. as sup. of the *California,* and at the Isl. bought of Peirce & Brewer for 2,500 hides a half-interest in the *Morse,* which he brought to Cal., renamed her the *Ninfa,* and made a trip to Mazatlan in

'41. iv. 102, 105, 209, 249, 567. Stearns, McKinley, and Temple were his partners in this venture, and Paty a little later. In '41 he was grantee of the Sotoyomi rancho, iv. 674; v. 297, 358, later Healdsburg, which was put in charge of his agents, as he still lived at S. Diego, being much of the time at sea. Receptor at S.D. '45–6; made a survey of town lands; juez de paz '46–7, grantee of lands at S.F., being also ment. in connection with various matters. iv. 345, 557, 620; v. 267, 317, 618–20, 659–60, 679. He died at S. Diego in '49, and was the last person buried on Presidio Hill. Capt. Fitch was one of the earliest, most prominent, and most popular of the early pioneers; straightforward in his dealings, generous in disposition, frank and cheerful in manner, in physique a very tall man inclined to corpulency. Dana is the only man that has anything unfavorable to say of him, and it is hinted that D., a wild young sailor disposed to put on airs by reason of his education and high connections, was once rather summarily ejected from Don Enrique's house, when he and his companions applied for grog. I have hundreds of the captain's business and personal letters in the collections of Vallejo and Cooper, besides an immense vol. of the *Fitch, Doc. Hist. Cal.*, presented by his widow in '75. Doña Josefa—born at S. D. 1810, and baptized as María Ant. Natalia Elijia Carrillo, being called Josefa later because her godmother forgot the names, and thought that one of them was Josefa!—moved to the Healdsburg rancho soon after her husband's death, and was still living there in '80, dictating for my use in '75 a most interesting *Narracion*, besides presenting the doc. cited above, including her marriage certificate and the captain's naturalization papers. There were 11 children, as follows: Henry E. b. '30, Fred. '32, Wm '34, Joseph '36, Josefa '37, John B. '39, Isabella '40, Charles '42, Michael '44, María Ant. Natalia '45, and Anita '48. The last two died in '50–4; Josefa became the wife of John Grant and a locally famous singer; Isabella married John Balash; Wm, in '75, had a vineyard on Russian River; John B. was a newspaper man, who visited my Library in '83.

Fitch, 1847, mr of the *Armalta*. v. 576. F. (Worthington L.), 1847, Co. B, N.Y.Vol. (v. 499); d. S.F. '50. Fitzhugh (John W.), 1848, immig. whose widow lived at Snelling in '77. *S. J. Pion.* Fitzpatrick (John), 1836, Engl. on a Los Ang. list, age 40. F. (Thos), well-known trapper and guide; possibly came to Cal. before '40; guide of Bartleson party '41 and Frémont '44, but did not come to Cal. then. iii. 392; iv. 268, 437. Fitzsimmons (James), 1847, Co. G, N.Y.Vol. (v. 499).

Flaco (Juan), see John Brown. Flandrew (J.B.), 1848, passp. from Hon. Flanning (H.T.), 1845, nat. of N.Y.; on the U.S. *Portsmouth;* later member of S. Joaq. pioneers. iv. 587. Fleet (Wm H.), 1847, lot at S.F. Fleetwood (Robert), 1847, Co. F, N.Y.Vol. (v. 499). Flemming (James), 1829, Irish 'jack-at-all-trades,' age 40, working for Cooper at Mont. iii. 179; in '36 living with Larkin, age 52! often named in records of '36–8. In '41–4 he appears in the Sonoma and Bodega regions. Fletcher, 1579, chaplain of Francis Drake's vessel, and author of a narrative of the voyage. i. 85 et seq. F. (Philander), 1847, Co. D, Morm. Bat. (v. 469); reënl. Fleury (Ernest de), 1848, the Baron de Lisle, a French traveller and officer in Mex. under Maximilian; said to have visited Cal. in '48; died in N.Y. '67. *Alta.*

Fling (Guy Freeman), 1826, nat. of Me, on the *Courier* '26–8. iii. 176. In '31 he came back from the Sandwich Islands to settle permanently, at the age of 34, getting a carta from Gov. Victoria, and in '32 joining the comp. extranjera at Mont. iii. 221. From that time his name often appears on Larkin's books and other records. He worked at his trade as blacksmith at Mont., and in '36 at the Buenavista rancho, being then only 26 years old, acc. to the padron. In '40 he had a shop at Natividad, and is accredited by tradition with having refused to iron the foreign exiles, though John Chamberlain says this was not so, as Fling was absent at the time. iv. 28. I find no definite trace of him in '41–7, but he was prob. engaged in hunting, as he is said to have been with Geo. Yount in Napa Val., and to have spent much of his time among the Ind. He lived at Sonoma for some years; went to Napa about '50, and died in the county infirmary in '70, at the reputed age of 80 years.

144   FLINT—FLÜGGE.

Flint (Amos E.), 1847, Co. F, 3d U. S. artill. (v. 518).   F. (Isaac A.), 1845, overl. immig. perhaps of the Grigsby-Ide party, who prob. went back east with Clyman in '46. iv. 579; v. 526.   F. (Wm), 1846, doubtful member of the Mormon col. v. 547.   Flomboy (John), 1844, half-breed Ind. and overl. immig. of the Stevens party, acc. to Schallenberger and some of the county histories. iv. 445.   Flood (John), 1847, Co. A, N.Y.Vol. (v. 499); at S.F. '71–4.

Flores (Amando), 1836, Mex. convict; later one of Murrieta's band.   F. (Antonio), 1602, piloto of one of Vizcaino's vessels; died on the voy. i. 98, 104.   F. (Bernardo), settler at S.F. 1791–1800. i. 716.   F. (Francisco), 1791, surgeon of Malaspina's exped. i. 490.   F. (Francisco), soldier at mission S. José 1797–1800. i. 556.   F. (Gumesindo), 1834, Mex. capt. and brevet lieut-col, who came as a kind of political exile with the H. & P. col. iii. 263. In '35–6 maj. and admin. of S.F. iii. 354, 714–15; in '39–42, having been rein-stated in his mil. rank, he was com. of the post at Mont. iii. 671; iv. 33, 652; in '42–6 com. at Sta B.; in '45 leader in an outbreak of the troops. iv. 541, 641; v. 317, 630. Capt. F. continued to reside at Sta B. until shot and killed in '60. His widow and daughter were still at Sta B. in '78.   F. (Hermene-gildo), killed 1794. i. 454.   F. (Isidro), soldier at S. Juan B. before 1800. i. 558.   F. (José Bern.), sirviente at Soledad 1791–1800. i. 499.

Flores (José María), 1842, Mex. capt. in the batallon fijo, who came with Micheltorena as secretary. iv. 289; in '44 named as instructor of the Sta B. defensores (?). iv. 407; but sent to Mex. as comisionado by the gov. to obtain aid. iv. 402, 414, 534, 564, 568. Returning in '45, he remained after Michel-torena's departure, and was the commissioner sent by Castro to treat with Stockton in Aug. iv. 513; v. 41, 268–9, 280. On the revolt of the Californians in Sept., Flores was made gov. and com. gen. from Oct., in this capacity di-recting all the operations of this final campaign of the war, and finally re-treating to Sonora in Jan. '47. See v. 37–8, 309–25, 329–56, 365, 389–410, 563–5. In breaking his parole, Gen. Flores of course committed a most dishon-orable act, though much may be said in defence of the general rising against the U.S. In other respects he acted with commendable energy, skill, and pa-triotism under difficult circumstances, meriting but little of the ridicule and abuse of which he has been the object. After leaving Cal. he served in the Mex. army, being in '49–50 sub-inspector, and in '51 et seq. com. gen. of the military colonies of the west; visiting Cal. in '50 to bring his family; but I think his wife, a daughter of A. V. Zamorano, did not leave Cal. He was at Mazatlan in '55, and is said to have died there in '66, *Los Ang. Co. Hist.*, 24, though a colonel of the same name was serving in Michoacan in '67 against Maximilian.

Flores (José María), at S. José '25. ii. 605; in '41, age 48, wife Josefa Se-púlveda, child. Miguel b. '23, Sebastian '31, Cármen '27, José María '32, Juan B. '34, José '37, Paula '40, Fernando '41; juez de policía '43. iv. 685; in '46 juez de campo at S.F. v. 648.   F. (José María), soldier at Sta B. from 1788. F. (José María), grantee of Liebre rancho '46, also claimant in '53. v. 632. F. (José Miguel), maj. at S. Gabriel, 1791–6. i. 664.   F. (José S.), Mex. con-vict '29–34.   F. (Leandro), soldier in S. F. comp. '19–29; regidor at S. José '31. iii. 212, 729; in '41, age 42, wife Romana Martinez, child. José Ant. b. '33, María Ant. '16, María del Sac. '26, Refugio '34; in '43 juez del campo. iv. 685.   F. (M.), 1848, passp. from Hon.   F. (Manuel), artilleryman at Sta B. '24. ii. 532.   F. (Manuel), in Hidalgo piquete at Mont. '36.   F. (Miguel), son of José María, at S. José from '23 to '77, when he gave me his *Recuerdos Históricos*. v. 137.   F. (Teodosio), alcalde of S. José—and also of Mont?—in '20. ii. 378, 611; at S. José '41, age 52.   F. (Victoriano), sirviente at S.F. 1777. i. 297.   Florin (Joseph), 1833, Canadian gardener from Colom-bia at Los Ang. '36, '40, age 27, 31, and married. iii. 409. One record puts his arrival in '30.

Flügge (Chas W.), 1841, German of the Bartleson immig. party who went 1st to Or., but came down by land to Cal. before the end of the year. iv. 269, 276, 279. In '42–3 he was employed by Sutter, who had known him before, as clerk and adviser, F. being a man of many accomplishments and having some knowledge of law. He was sent by Sutter to conciliate Micheltorena. iv. 389; got a lot at S.F. iv. 669, 678; was naturalized at the end of '43; and in '44 was grantee of a rancho on Feather River. iv. 670-1. He opened a store at Los Ang.; used his influence for Sutter and Micheltorena. iv. 490; and at the end of '45 went to Honolulu, returning on the *Don Quixote* early in '46. He had a Cal. claim (v. 462), continuing in trade at Los Ang., and serving as a messenger from Flores to Stockton in Jan. '47. v. 387. He is mentioned with a wife (?) at N. Helv. in Sept. '47. *N. Helv. Diary,* 110; perhaps an error. At the end of '48 he left Cal., though McKinley, his partner, made efforts to prevent his departure, and is said to have gone to Germany with a considerable sum of money. Though admired for his accomplishments, he had quarrelled sooner or later with most of those who were intimate with him, showing divers eccentricities of conduct. In the winter of '51-2 he returned to Los Ang., secluding himself from old friends, acting strangely in other respects, and evidently insane. In Sept. '52 he wandered off into the country and was found dead some 12 miles from town. Flundin (Joseph), 1842, French steward of a hospital in Oakland '77, said to have visited S.F. in June '42. iv. 341; *S.J.Pion.* Flying (Andrew), 1847, Co. F, N. Y. Vol. (v. 499); at Sta B. '71-82.

Fogo (Manuel), 1825, Span. from the *Asia;* still in Cal. '30. iii. 27, 51-2. Foisy (M.G.), 1846, Or. pioneer of '44; a printer still in Or. '76, for whom it is claimed that he published (?) the *Californian* at Mont. *Hist. Or.,* i. 467. He may possibly have been a printer on that paper in '46 or '47, but prob. not. v. 293. Foley (Alfred), 1847, Co. E, N.Y.Vol. (v. 499). F. (Michael), 1846, Irish. of the Cal. Bat. (v. 358); owner of S.F. lot '47. v. 685; said to have been killed in a brawl at the mission a few years later. Folger (Edward F.), 1847, at S.F., agent, or perhaps partner, of Gelston & Co. F. (Wm D.), 1847, on roll of Soc. Cal. Pion. Follansbee (S.), 1846, doubtful newsp. ment. of a Shasta Co. pion. Follen (Julian), 1845, petitioner for land for a colony; perhaps not in Cal. iv. 571. Follett (Wm A.), 1847, Co. B, Morm. Bat. (v. 469); in Ariz. '81. F. (Wm T.), 1847, Co. E, Morm. Bat.; at St George, Utah, '82.

Folsom (Joseph Libbey), 1847, nat. of N. H., graduate of West Point in '40, and later instructor in that institution; came to Cal. as capt. U.S.A. and asst quartermaster in the N.Y.Vol.; and was chief of the Q.M. department station at S.F., being also collector of the port for a time in '47-9. v. 98, 503, 511-13, 650, 659-60, 673. Capt. F. invested all the money he could raise in town lots, which in a few years made him a rich man. During a trip to the east in '49 he was smart and lucky enough to find the heirs of Wm A. Leidesdorff and buy of them for a song their title to the immense Leidesdorff estate in S.F. He thus became one of the wealthiest men in Cal., owning large estates in the country, including the Amer. River rancho on which the town of Folsom now bears his name, as does Folsom Street in S.F. His reputation is that of a most enterprising man of business, an honorable gentleman of superior education and refinement, somewhat formal and haughty in manner. He died at Mission San José in '55 at the age of 38. F. (Wm H.), 1847, Co. H, N.Y.Vol. (v. 499); in N.Y. city '82.

Font (José), 1796, Span. lieut of Catalan volunteers, com. of the comp. after Alberni's death, also com. at S. Diego '99. Left Cal. with the Cal. Vol. 1803. i. 541, 647-8; ii. 5, 18-19, 78, 107, 153. F. (Pedro), 1775-6, Span. friar, prob. of the Querétaro Franciscans, who was chaplain of Anza's exped. to Cal., of which he left an important *Diario* and map. i. 258-60, 262-4, 267-9, 280-6, 330; ii. 44. Fontes (Pedro), sirviente at S.F. 1777. i. 297. Forbagh, 1847, at Benicia. v. 672; prob. 'Forbush,' q.v.

Forbes (Alexander), Scotch merchant of Tepic; author of the standard work on *California* pub. in '39. iv. 150-2. He had never visited Cal., though meditating a visit in '26. iii. 176. It is stated, however, that later, in '46-8, he came to Cal. in con. with the N. Almaden affairs; but I have no definite record of his presence. He has often been confounded by writers with James

146 FORBES—FORD.

A. Forbes. F. (Eli B.), 1847, Co. E, N.Y.Vol. (v. 499); carpenter at Mont.
'47-8. F. (Hector M.), 1847, Co. D, N.Y.Vol. (v. 499).

Forbes (James Alex.), 1831, nat. of Scotland, who had lived for some years
in Span. countries, prob. in Chili or Peru. The first that is definitely known
of him is that in a trip to the isl. of the S. Amer. coast he was wrecked,
picked up by the *Nelson* at or near the Galápagos, and transferred to the
whaler *Fanny*, which brought him, rating as 4th mate, by way of the Mar-
quesas to S.F. in Oct. '31, or possibly '30. iii. 405. In '32 he was acting as a
kind of clerk or majordomo for P. Viader at Sta Clara; early in '33 asked for
naturalization, which he obtained in April '34, and in July married Ana María, daughter of Juan C. Galindo, being then 27 years old, and having as witnesses Geo. Ferguson and Jas W. Weeks, who had come with him on the
Fanny. For several years his name does not appear, but he was doubtless engaged in trade and farming at S. José, where from '36 he acted as agent for
the H.B.Co., being elector in '38 and síndico in '39, trying in '40—to obtain
a loan of mission sheep in comp. with Dr Marsh, signing bonds for some
of the Bartleson immig., and, acc. to the padron of '41, having two sons, Cárlos b. '37, and Alejandro in '39. iii. 731; iv. 86, 117, 217-18, 275, 684. In '42
Forbes was appointed British vice-consul at Mont., assuming the office in Oct.
'43, and performing some acts in his official capacity in the next few years,
though not residing at Mont. iv. 384, 479, 563, 651. Grantee of the Potrero
de Sta Clara '44. iv. 673; in '45-6 at S.F. in charge of the H.B.Co. property
after Rae's death, having apparently used his influence against Sutter and
Micheltorena, being involved in a controversy with Leidesdorff, and obtaining for himself and wife some beach lots in town. v. 486, 590-1, 649, 679-80.
In '46 Larkin reported F. to the Wash. govt as a man of moderate property,
whose private interests and official position clashed, but who wished the U.
S. to have Cal. F. asserted at the time, and in later years, that he had nothing to do with schemes for an English protectorate, and it is certain that those
schemes, as well as the vice-consul's agency, have been greatly exaggerated.
v. 68, 70, 614. In the troubles of '46-7 he took but slight part. v. 298, 378,
380, 382. Gov. Mason declined to permit F., as vice-consul, to introduce
goods free of duties. Don Diego was an intelligent man of good education,
whose knowledge of Spanish gave him an advantage, though he never lost his
broad Scotch accent, and whose record in early times was an excellent one,
though many writers have exaggerated his prominence. After the U.S. occupation, he became interested in the New Almaden mines, and was involved
in the complicated litigation that lasted for years, to the serious detriment of
his financial hopes, of his reputation, and especially of his temper. In later
years he led a life of retirement, nursing his intense, and perhaps not unfounded, bitterness against all that was American, and died at Oakland in
'81, at the age of 77. His children, as named by his son in '85, were Cárlos
H., residing at Los Ang. with 10 children, Martha (deceased), James Alex.,
Jr, Michael, Frederick, James Alonzo, Luis Felipe (deceased), María Clara,
Juan Telésforo, Margaret, Francis H., and Alfred O. James Alex., Jr, was educated at Sta Clara college, has been state translator of the laws, and in '85
for some years has been employed as translator and keeper of the archives in
the U.S. surveyor-general's office. Though not in charge when my search of
the archives was made, he has afforded me aid on several points.

Forbes (John), 1833, Engl. on Larkin's books '33-5. iii. 409. F. (Robert
B.), 1825, mr of the *Nile*. iii. 148. Visiting S.F. again in '70, he delivered a
lecture which included reminiscences of '25; and in '78 he published his *Personal Reminiscences*, which describes both the visits and the lecture; still
living at Milton, Mass., in '85. F. (Wm), 1835, Engl. who worked for Larkin at Mont. '35-6. iii. 413; one of the exiles of '40. iv. 18; perhaps cl. for a
Sonoma Co. rancho '52. iv. 671. Forbush (Benj.), 1847, from Hon. on the
Euphemia; at Benicia; perhaps Forbagh. F. (Lorin), 1847, Co. C, Morm.
Bat. (v. 469).

Ford (Henry L.), 1842-4, nat. of Vt or N.H., who prob. came by sea. He
claimed to have come in '42; the 1st original record is a certificate of his U.S.

citizenship, dated at Mont. April 19, '44. iv. 341. He seems to have been one
of Capt. Gantt's men in the Micheltorena campaign of '45 (v. 484), and was
prominent among the Bears in '46, taking part in the stealing of Arce's horses
and the capture of Sonoma. v. 78, 107, 110, 147. As lieut of the Bear army
he commanded in the fight at Olompali, the only one of the revolt. v. 153,
164-9; went south with Frémont; returned with Maddox in Aug.; and later
served in the final campaign as capt. of Co. B, Cal. Bat. v. 184, 282, 289, 361,
434. In '48 he settled in Tehama Co., where in '51 he married Susan Wilson,
and in '56 was accidentally shot and killed at the age of 33. Ford's narrative
of the *Bear Flag Revolt*, a MS. furnished to me by Rev. S. H. Willey, for
whom it was written in '51, is noticed in v. 189. Not much is definitely
known of Ford, but he appears to have been a good man of strong prejudices.
F. (Henry). 1847, perhaps of N.Y.Vol. under another name.   F. (John),
1827, mr of the *Favorite*. iii. 147.   F. (Noah E.), 1847, in letter list at S.F.
'47-8.   F. (Patrick), 1847, Co. E, N.Y.Vol. (v. 499); a deserter in '48; killed
by Rogue Riv. Ind. '66.   Forero (Ramon), doubtful name in a S.F. list '35.
     Forney (Peter), 1846, Co. C, 1st U.S. dragoons (v. 336).   Forrest (B.),
1841, clerk on the U.S. *St Louis*.   F. (French), 1840-1, com. of the U.S. *St
Louis*. iv. 36-7, 106; commodore in Confed. navy '62.   F. (Richard), 1846,
lieut on the *Portsmouth* and *Levant*.   F. (Sam.), 1848, lot at S.F.   Forrester (Geo. H. H.), 1847, Co. K, N.Y.Vol. (v. 499).   Forsgreen (John),
1847, Co. D, Morm. Bat. (v. 469).
     Forster (John), 1833, nat. of England, who came to Guaymas in '31, and
in '33 on the *Facio*—belonging to his uncle James Johnson—to Cal., returning to Sonora on the vessel as master, and coming back to Los Ang. by land
the same year. iii. 365, 382, 389, 397, 509. He made other trips to Son. for
his uncle, and in '36 announced his intention to remain permanently, claiming
7 years' residence in Mex. territory and 4 in Cal.; in '37 married Isidora, sister of Pio Pico; in '40-3 at S. Pedro as shipping agent, part of the time capt.
of the port. iv. 322, 636. In '44 he settled at S. Juan Cap., purchasing the
ex-mission estate in '45, and living there for 20 years. iv. 553, 558, 621, 627;
grantee of rancho de la Nacion '45. iv. 621; juez de paz '45-7. iv. 627; v. 623-
4; in '46 for a time in charge of S. Luis Rey, having trouble with Frémont,
and aiding Gov. Pico to escape. v. 267, 278, 620; grantee of Trabuco. iv. 635;
had a Cal. claim (v. 462); aided Stockton in the campaign of '47. v. 388. In
'64 Forster bought the Sta Margarita rancho of Pio Pico, where he spent the
rest of his life, dying in '84 at the age of 70. Don Juan was a man who was
liked and respected by all who knew him, that is, by everybody in southern
Cal. and hundreds more, a genial ranchero, famous for the hospitalities of his
Sta Margarita home. He was for many years a man of immense wealth;
formed several plans for colonization on a grand scale, which were never carried out; but was harassed in the later years by litigation and other troubles;
and the estate was sold before his death. At his rancho in '74 he gave me a
narrative of early experiences; and in '78 dictated his more complete *Pioneer
Data*, giving also a few original papers. His wife died a short time before his
death. In '46, acc. to the S. Juan padron, there were 6 children: Emerico and
Dolores (perhaps error of copyist), Marcos Antonio b. '40, Francisco '42, Ana
María '43, Juan Fernando '45. Francisco, or 'Chico,' killed by a woman at
Los Angeles after '80. Mark Antony and John still live in S. Diego Co. '85.
Two of Don Juan's brothers, Hugh and Thomas, came to Cal. after '48.
Fort, see 'Ford.'   Forsyth (Thomas), 1834, Irish ship-carpenter who came on
the *Leonor;* still at Mont. '37.
     Fortuni (Buenaventura), 1806, Span. friar who served 34 years as a mis-
sionary in Cal., chiefly at S. José and Solano, dying at Sta B. in '40. Biog.
iii. 659; ment. ii. 138, 159-60, 322, 375, 394, 505, 598-9, 623, 655; iii. 96, 318,
346, 622-3, 658, 660, 719; iv. 63, 66. Fosdick (Jay), 1846, of the Donner
party from Ill.; died in the mts. v. 530, 534, 537. His wife, Sarah Graves, survived, marrying Wm Ritchie in '48, and Samuel Spiers in '56; died near
Watsonville in '71.
     Foster, 1833, one of Hall J. Kelley's companions in the trip across Mex.,

whom K. denounces as a rascal, and who, as he learned, came to Mont. on a
whaler, was ordered away, shipped on a man-of-war, and in trying to desert
was drowned in the bay as a punishment for his sins. iii. 409; perhaps Chas
or Ed. C. described as Amer. at Mont. in '34.   F., 1846, of F. & Patterson,
Cal. claim (v. 462).   F. (Benj. F.), 1847, Co. C, N.Y.Vol. (v. 499); a printer
and part proprietor of the *Californian* in '48; later foreman in the *Alta* office
and connected with the *Standard* and other S. F. papers; making two trips
to the Sandw. Isl. He went east and died at Portsmouth, N.H., in '65, at the
age of 49.
        Foster (Geo.), 1846, a Mo. immig. prob. of this year, who was killed at
Natividad in Nov. v. 367. He was known as Captain Foster. Possibly came
earlier, though those who imply this seem to confound him with another man.
F. (James), 1841, mid. on the U. S. *St Louis*.   F. (John), 1847, apparently
sold lumber at Mont.   F. (John R.), 1848, named by Lancey as a brother of
the man killed at Natividad.   F. (Joseph), 1846, Co. F, Cal. Bat. (v. 358),
enlisting at S. Juan, Oct.; possibly identical with Geo. ' F. (Joseph), 1847,
member of the 4th, and perhaps 1st, Donner relief. v. 538, 541; said to have
been a sailor.   F. (Joseph), 1846, Engl. who kept a saloon in S.F. '53-9; lost
a leg in '49; died in '59. *Herald;* perhaps same as preceding.   F. (Joseph
E.), 1844, overl. immig. of the Stevens party. iv. 445, 453; named at N.
Helv. '45-6; served in Co. B, Cal. Bat. (v. 358); prob. identical with one of
the preceding.   F. (Joseph R.), 1846, in the vicinity of Sta Cruz.   F. (O.
H.), 1846, Co. F, Cal. Bat. (v. 358).
        Foster (Stephen Clark), 1847, nat. of Me, b. in '20; graduate of Yale in
'40; teacher and medical student in Va, Ala, and La; physician in Mo.; trader
in N. Mex. and Sonora; come to Cal. as interpreter with the Morm. Bat.
v. 483. He was alcalde at Los Ang. in '48-9. v. 610, 626-7; memb. of the
constit. convention in '49, also prefect; member of the Cal. senate '50-3;
memb. of Los Ang. council '51, '58; mayor '54, '56. He married a Lugo, and
is still living at Los Ang. in '85. He has written to some extent on pioneer
topics for the newspapers. ii. 221, 292; and in '77 furnished for my use a
fragment on *Los Angeles in '47-9*. He has had much to do with the Span.
archives of the south, in familiarity with which he is excelled by few, if any.
His official record in the early time, and so far as I know in later years, has
been a good one. He was a man of remarkable natural abilities and of fine
education. His prominent position in the past as a public man makes it
necessary to add that in respect of morality and sobriety his conduct in later
times is not exemplary.   F. (Wm M.), 1846, surviving memb. of the Donner
party, from Penn. with wife and infant son George, the latter dying in the
mts. F. was also an active memb. of the 4th relief party. v. 531-5, 540-1. At
N. Helv. '47; had a furniture store at S.F. '47-8. v. 678; later kept a store
at the mines, giving his name to Foster's Bar. He died at S.F. in '74. His
wife, Sarah A. C. Murphy, was living at Marysville with her brother in '80.
F. (Wm S.), 1847, Co. A, N.Y.Vol. (v. 499).
        Fourcade (Richard), 1841, named in Larkin's books '41-8; called also Al-
bert R., and John R. Fouchade. iv. 279.   Fourgeaud (G.), 1847, brother of
Victor J., and overl. immig. at N. Helv.; owner of lot at S.F.   F. (Victor
J.), 1847, nat. of N.C., physician at St Louis, and overl. immig., with his wife,
son, and brother. v. 556. He practised medicine at S.F. in '47-8, being a
school trustee and otherwise prominent. v. 651, 656-7, 680; also owner of
town lots, and author of an article on the *Prospects of Cal.* in the *Star* of '48.
He moved later to Sac., but returned about '63, and died at S.F. in '75 at the
age of 60. His widow died in '83, age 74.   Fourri (François le), 1831, from
N. Mex. in the Wolfskill party. iii. 387.
        Fowler, 1846, Amer. of the Bear party murdered by the Californians near
Sta Rosa in June. v. 110, 160-4. I cannot identify him; possibly Wm, Jr, of
'44; called B. Fowler of '45; also George.   F. (Henry), 1844, son of Wm,
nat. of Ill. who came overl. to Or. in '43 and to Cal. in the Kelsey party
with his father and brother. iv. 444-5. In '45 he worked for Sutter, asked
for naturalization, and perhaps settled in Napa. With his father he purchased,

later, a farm near Calistoga; and in '71 was a resident of Napa City.   F. (James E.), 1841, resid. of Sonoma Co. '51-77; nat. of N.Y. *Son. Co. Hist.*   F. (Jerusha), 1846, of the Mormon col. with 4 children. v. 546; rem. in Cal.   F. (John), 1843, overl. immig. who joined the Bears. v. 111; went south with Frémont, but returned with a broken arm in Nov. '46. This is his own statement in a narrative of the *Bear Flag* given by him at Napa in '78. He may be a brother of Henry, or possibly the name may be John Henry. There was a J. W. Fowler in the Cal. Bat.   F. (John S.), 1847, nat. of N.J.; 2d alcalde at Sac. '48-9; died at Sac. '60, age 42.

Fowler (Wm), 1844, nat. of N.Y., from Ill. to Or. in '43, and to Cal. in the Kelsey party with 2 or more sons. iv. 444-5. He brought a letter of recommendation as a good catholic and carpenter from P. Dimers of the Walamet to P. Quijas. Worked for a time at Sonoma, after spending some time in Pope Valley; was at N. Helv. in '47, and finally with his son Henry bought a farm of Dr Bale near Calistoga, where at the age of 72 he married a 2d wife, and died in '65, at the age of 86.   F. (Wm, Jr), 1844, son of Wm, who came in the same party from Or., and worked as a carpenter at Sonoma, N. Helv., and S. Rafael. iv. 444-5. In Or. he married Rebecca Kelsey, who left him on arrival in Cal. Application was made to Larkin for a divorce, and despite his lack of authority to grant it, she was married by Sutter to another man. As I find no record of F. after '46, it is possible that he was the man killed with Cowie during the Bear revolt.   F. (Wm), immig. of the Bartleson party, '41, going to Or. iv. 269; perhaps the Wm named above.   F. (W.), 1843, mr of the *Diamond.* iv. 565.   Fowrklinot (Jacobo), 1844, otter-hunter at Los Ang., prob. 'Frankfort.'

Fox (J.), 1848, passp. from Honolulu.   Foxen (Benj.), 1826, Engl. sailor who came on the *Courier* and left that vessel in '28. iii. 176; ii. 573. He was baptized as Wm Domingo, though often called Julian; married Eduarda Osuna (or Olivera); was naturalized in '37, when he was 38 years old, and had 3 children, being in trade at Sta B. A few years later he became owner of the Tinaquaic rancho, iii. 656, where he spent the rest of his life, dying in '74 and leaving 10 children and a large estate. He was a rough and violent man, often in trouble with other rough men and with the authorities, being sentenced to 4 years in prison in '48 for killing Agustin Dávila. v. 611, 613; yet accredited with good qualities, such as bravery and honesty. His three daughters married respectively C. W. Goodchild, F. Wickenden, and John R. Stone. His son, Wm J.J., born in '33, was in '83 a ranchero in Sta B. Co. Portrait of Benj. and his wife in *Sta B. Co. Hist.*, 322.

Fraezher (Geo.), see 'Frazer.'   Framier (R.), 1846, Cal. Bat. (v. 358). France (Joseph), 1846, doubtful memb. of the Mormon col. v. 547.   Francis (Alex.), 1842, Florida Ind., deserter from the U. S. *Cyane* '43.   F. (Wm), 1847, lot at S.F.   Francisco, neoph. at S. Diego 1775. i. 253.   Francisco, 1818, negro of Bouchard's force captured at Mont. ii. 232.   Franco (Jose), convict settler 1797. i. 606.   F. (Juan José), a recruit who came with José de la Guerra y Noriega and J. J. de la Torre in 1801.   F. (Pablo), convict settler 1798; at Los Ang. '19. i. 606; ii. 354.   Franec (Wm), 1845, doubtful name of an Irishman at Branciforte, age 45, single.

Frank (Manuel), 1841, 1st frame house at S. José built for. iv. 684. Frankfort (Jacob), 1841, German tailor from N. Mex. in the Workman party. iv. 278-9; at Los Ang. '46; up and down the coast '47-8, making a trip to Hon. and back on the *Gen. Kearny* and *Eveline*, and obtaining a lot at S. F. Franz (Fred W.), 1845, at Mont. iv. 587; lot at S. F. '47.   Frapp, '32-40, doubtful name of a trapper chief. iii. 392.   Frare (Wm), 1844, Irish. who got a pass for 1 year; prob. same as 'Frere,' q.v.   Fraser, see 'Frazer.' Frawell (Ephraim P.), 1853, Phil. tailor who deserted from the whaler *Helvetius*, and worked at his trade at dif. points round S.F. bay. iii. 409. He was met by Wilkes at Mission S. José in '41; lived from '43 at S. José, where he died about '78; name also written 'Fravel.'   Frayer (Henry or Eugene), 1844, German who got a pass.

Frazer (Abner), 1845, Amer. carpenter from Or. in the McMahon-Clyman party, and returned to Or. in '46, where he still lived after '75. iv. 572, 526; written also ' Frazier.'   F. (Alex.), 1827, signs as a witness at Mont.   F. (Geo. W.), 1833, Amer. trapper with Walker's party. iii. 391; iv. 409. He is ment. in Mont. records of '34–5; in '40 exiled to S. Blas, but returned, obtaining cartas in '41–2, when he lived near Sta Cruz. iv. 18, 33; in '43 at Alviso's; in '45 signed the call to foreigners at S. José. iv. 599; applied for land at S. José '46; visited N. Helv. '45–8; at Stockton '47–8. Name also written ' Fraezher,' which was perhaps the correct form.   F. (M.), 1836, lumberman at S. Rafael. iv. 118.   F. (Thos), 1847, Co. D, Morm. Bat. (v. 469); in Sutter's employ '47–8; name prob. ' Frazier.'   F. (Wm), 1845, Amer. farmer from Or. in the McM.-Clyman party; prob. went back '46 with Abner F., who was perhaps his brother. iv. 572–3, 526.

Frederick (J.), 1846, Co. F, Cal. Bat. (v. 358).   Fredingburg (H.), 1848, passp. from Honolulu.   Freeborn (John), 1847, Co. K, N. Y. Vol. (v. 499); passp. from Hon. '48.   Freeman, 1837, mr of the *Indian*. iv. 104.   F. (Duric), 1844, Amer. who obtained a carta at Mont.   F. (Elijah), 1847, Morm. Bat. (v. 469); prob. not in Cal.   F. (F.), Co. G, Cal. Bat. (v. 358), enlisting at S. José, Nov.   F. (Isam), 1840, doubtful name of a naturalized foreigner at Sta B.   F. (Richard), 1846, bought a house of Capt. Fitch at S. Diego.   F. (Truman), 1844, Amer. age 25, in a S.F. padron.   F. (W), 1848, passp. from Hon.   Freer (Matthew), 1848, hanged at S. José for highway robbery and attempted murder. v. 663–4.

Frémont (John Charles), 1844, nat. of Ga, b. in '13, sometime teacher of mathematics and surveyor, lieut of top. engineers from '38, and husband of a daughter of Thos H. Benton from '41. He is in some respects the most famous of all the pioneers named in this register, and his Californian career was the foundation of his fame. Full details of that career will be found in other volumes of this work. His three exploring exped. of '42, '43–4, and '45, in the 2d and 3d of which he reached Cal., are described, with their results, in iv. 434–44, 452, 581–5, 679. Exploring and mapping regions before known only to trappers and immigrants, narrating his labors with modesty and full credit to those who preceded and accompanied him, he gained much credit at home and abroad for his skill in the field and for his reports. As the pioneer of scientific exploration in the far west, he deserves only praise. The ridicule of which he has been the object in this connection resulted mainly from the campaign of '56, in which his achievements as pathfinder were so magnified for effect in the east as to excite the jealousy of western pioneers, a feeling fomented by partisans for political purposes. Frémont's acts of Jan.–May '46 in Cal. are given in v. 1–29, 58–9, 644, 660. Being permitted by Gen. Castro to rest his men and animals in the S. Joaquin Valley for a continuation of his exploring trip to Or., he forfeited the privilege by marching his party into S. José and encamping for a week at Fisher's rancho; grossly insulted the alcalde who, in the discharge of his routine duties, served a legal notice on him; and finally marched over the Sta Cruz Mts and down the coast—for Oregon! When the authorities very properly ordered him to leave Cal., he fortified a position on Gavilan Peak and raised the U. S. flag. This was foolish bravado, as he realized after a day or two of reflection, in connection with Consul Larkin's advice and the sight of military preparations at San Juan; so he ran away in the night. The current version of Castro's broken promise and subsequent cowardly bluster is pure fiction, but it has long served its purpose—that of covering Frémont's folly. He was overtaken on the Or. frontier by despatches from Wash. which required him to remain in Cal. His part in the Bear revolt of June–July is recorded in v. 77–190. That most indefensible rising of the settlers, which interrupted negotiations for a pacific change of flag, would not have occurred but for F.'s promise of active support when needed; therefore he must be held responsible, not only for the bloodshed and bitterness of feeling that attended the conflict of '46–7, but for the much more disastrous state of affairs that, but for the sheerest good luck, must have resulted. His alleged motives were three fold: 1st, The welfare of Amer. settlers threatened with oppression and expulsion—a mere pretext, since the danger was wholly imaginary, as F. and the leaders well knew, though a few settlers were led to believe it real; 2d, the necessity of prompt action to save Cal. from England—an excuse invented later, which has had a success out of all proportion to its merits, for had England entertained the idea of a protectorate the settlers' revolt would have afforded the best possible occasion for interference; and 3d, the receipt of instructions from Wash. to seize the first opportunity to wrest Cal. from Mex. In a statement of '85—a MS. furnished by Gen. and Mrs F. to Dr Josiah Royce, and by the kindness of the latter added, with the authors' consent, to my collection—he relies mainly on this 3d plea, and alleges positively, as he and his friends have always implied, that he received such instructions, guardedly expressed by Sec. Buchanan, and more openly by Benton in a private letter. This is simply not true. I have the instructions sent from Wash. in '45, both the original, signed by Buchanan, and the copy written by Gillespie from memory on arrival, and they contain not a word to justify any but conciliatory measures. The lieut disobeyed the letter and spirit of his orders, unless deceived by Gillespie at Benton's instigation. His real motive was a desire to make himself more prominent in the approaching occupation by the U.S. than he could be if the whole matter were left to Larkin and the naval officers. Doubtless he drew his inspiration largely from his brilliant father-in-law. He saw several plausible avenues of escape from disgrace should there be no war or should matters otherwise go wrong; but it is likely that the young filibuster was far from anticipating the full measure of success that good fortune was to give his deception. Once committed to the Bear cause, he acted in most respects with commendable energy and consistency; yet it must be stated that he meanly assumed for himself credit for the Bears' warlike acts, in which he took no active part; that never in his Cal. career was he in the actual presence of an armed foe; that in his S. Rafael campaign, represented by him as a grand victory, he was completely outwitted by Joaq. de la Torre; and that the murder of the Haro brothers and Berreyesa is an ineffaceable stain on his record. This deed F. and his friends have chosen to ignore as far as possible, alluding to it as a trivial occurrence incidental to a state of war, falsely representing the Haros as spies, on whose bodies murderous instructions from Castro were found; and finally, F. has the assurance to refer to it as the act of his Delawares out on a scout, unknown to him till later. For his part in the conquest proper, from July '46 to Jan. '47, see v. 231, 246-53, 266-7, 283, 286-7, 290, 295, 302, 304-5, 357-60, 372-6, 385-410, 412, 617, 630, 634, 639. At Mont., though Com. Sloat would not adopt his views, F. found in Stockton a filibuster after his own heart, willing to incorporate the Gavilan episode and the Bear revolt in the sacred cause of the U.S. As major of the Cal. battalion, he aided in the occupation of S. Diego and Los Ang. in Aug., returning north as mil. com. of Cal. Later he reorganized the battalion, and marched south to take part in the final campaign, concluded by his treaty of Cahuenga in Jan. '47. In all this period the major and commodore merely overcame obstacles of their own creation, but the former efficiently performed somewhat difficult duties, and merits but little of the blame and derision heaped upon him for his methods of obtaining supplies, for his disastrous crossing of the Sta Inés Mountain, and for his cautious approach to Los Ang. His policy at Cahuenga deserves no more severe adjective than the slangy one of 'cheeky.' Next we have his proceedings at the capital in Jan.-May as gov. of Cal. by Stockton's appointment, and his connection with the complicated controversies of the commodore and general, as related in v. 421-68. In general terms, it may be said of these quarrels that Kearny was in the right, Stockton in the wrong, and Frémont first right, then wrong. Though technically disobeying mil. orders, F. could not, consistently with the honor that should prevail among filibusters as well as thieves, abandon the chief who had fathered his cause and given him office; but at last his disobedience was renewed in so offensive a form as to move Kearny to wrath and the fullest exercise of his authority. Crossing the continent in disgrace, he was condemned by court-martial to dismissal from the army. v. 455-62. The verdict was technically a just one, but the lieut-colonel refused to accept the presi-

dent's proffered pardon. He had just then no further use for the army; the
trial had been a splendid advertisement; and the popular verdict had doubtless been in his favor. The evidence had been skilfully made to include as
much as possible of such Cal. annals as could be made to appear flattering to
the accused and unfavorable to his rivals; but if the accusers had had the
wish and power to present all the facts in their true light, the popular hero's
career might have been nipped in the bud. Something will be said in vol. vi.
of his later career so far as it pertains to Cal.; of the rest my study has been
comparatively superficial, but before beginning work was elected, in '50, to the U. S.
shown in the early record. In a 4th explor. exped. of '48 many of his men
perished in the snow before reaching N. Mex., but the leader kept on and
reached Cal. in '49. He accepted an appointment as commissioner of the
boundary survey, but before beginning work was elected, in '50, to the U. S.
senate from Cal., doing no harm during his brief term as senator, which expired in March '51. In '52, spending a year in Europe, he was once put in a
London jail on charges growing out of his Cal. operations of '47. In '53-4 he
made a 5th and last exploring tour across the continent between 38° and 39°.
He had bought of ex-Gov. Alvarado in '46 the famous Mariposas estate, which
now bade fair to make him the richest man in America; and in '56 he was
nominated for the presidency by the republicans. He had no qualifications
for the office, but it was hoped, with much reason, that his fame as 'pathfinder' and 'conqueror of Cal.' would make him an available candidate. At
this period appeared many biographic sketches, notably those of Bigelow,
Smucker, and Upham. Defeated by Buchanan, he lived a year or two in Cal.,
visited Europe, and in '61-2 served in the war as maj.-gen. of volunteers; but
the govt not appreciating his military genius, he resigned, and devoted himself to grand schemes of speculation in connection with railroads, being temporarily the candidate of a few dissatisfied republicans for the presidency,
and in '73 sentenced to fine and imprisonment for fraud by a French court.
In '78, when reduced to extreme poverty, he was appointed gov. of Ariz.,
serving for a brief term, and subsequently resuming his speculations, which
are always on the point of making him rich. In '85 he resides with his wife
in N.Y. City, a venerable couple with several grown children. Frémont did
more than any other to prevent or retard the conquest of Cal., yet his fame
as 'conqueror' is the corner-stone of his greatness, and in all the structure
there are few blocks more solid. He is to be regarded as an adventurer of
marvellous good fortune, if it be good fortune for a man of moderate abilities
to be made conspicuous before the world, or to enjoy opportunities that cannot be utilized. He was, moreover, intelligent, well educated, brilliant within
certain limits, of gentlemanly manners, personally magnetic, full of enthusi-
asm. Abuse has done more for him than eulogy; and doubtless from his
standpoint he has been a successful man.

French (Erasmus D.), 1846, Co. C, 1st U. S. dragoons (v. 336); nat of N.
Y., educated as a physician, a miner '48-9, at S. José '50-8, then at Chico
and the Coso mines; from '69 a farmer in S. Diego, where he still lived in '83,
age 60, with his wife, C.S. Cowles. S. Bern. Co. Hist.   F. (H.), 1847, lieut on
the U.S. Columbus.   F. (Wm), 1827, Amer. trader of Honolulu at Mont. in
'27, '30; sup. of the Europe in '36-7, aiding Alvarado in his revolution. Very
likely visited Cal. on other occasions. iii. 461; iv. 103, 141.   Frere (Alex.
W.), 1842, Amer. who got a carta, in '32 acc. to one record; named in Cal.
till '44. iv. 341.   Fresche (Francis), 1847, Co. G, N.Y.Vol. (v. 499); at S.F.
'74.   Freverdon (Wm), 1848, doubtful name of a lumberman at S. José.
Frew (Alex.), 1828, trader on the coast; d. before '32.

Frias (Mariano), Mex. soldier at Mont. '33-6, age 33.   Fricher (John),
1842, Amer. blacksmith at S.F., age 36.   Frink (Chris. L.), 1848, at Mont.
F. (Daniel), 1847, Co. K, N.Y.Vol. (v. 499); miner in El Dorado '48; made a
trip to Chile and back; lumberman in Sonoma Co. '49-50; later owner of part
of Nicasio rancho, Marin Co. iv. 672; justice of the peace and assoc. judge;
memb. of legisl. '79; married in '52 to Pauline H. Reynolds; living '83 at
Mountain View, Sta Clara Co., with 6 children. Portrait in Sta Clara Co.

Hist., 256.   Frisbie (Eleazer), 1847, sergt Co. H, N.Y.Vol. v. 504; kept a store at Sonoma '48-50; settled in Solano Co., and lived at Vallejo in '82 with his wife, Carrie E. Klink, and 7 children; a brother of John B.

Frisbie (John B.), 1847, capt. Co. H, N.Y.Vol. v. 504, 667; nat of N.Y., b. in '23; a lawyer, politician, and militia officer in N. Y. After leaving the mil. service Capt. F. was a candidate for lieut-gov. in '49; married a daughter of Gen. Vallejo; and became a prominent business man of the town of Vallejo, interested in the building of railroads, president of a bank, and a man of considerable wealth; in '60 sent the 1st cargo of wheat to Europe; a member of the legislature in '67. Losing his fortune just before 1880, he moved with his family to Mexico, where he still resides in '85, being engaged in mining operations. He furnished me his *Reminiscences*, containing information on Mex. as well as on early times in Cal. Portrait in *Solano Co. Hist.*, 48.   Friund (Henry J.), 1847, Co. D, N.Y.Vol. (v. 499); died before '82.   Froelich (Rosa), 1847, in Amador Co. from '54.   Frost (Lafayette N.), 1847, Co. A, Morm. Bat. (v. 469); d. S. Diego Sept.   Fructuoso, grantee of Potrero de S. Cárlos '37. iii. 678.   Frymire (Walter), 1846, Co. F, Cal. Bat. (v. 358).   Fuentes (José M.), grantee of Potrero '43. iv. 672.   Fuller (Hazel), 1832, Amer. blacksmith, deserter from the whaler *Friends;* still at Mont. '34. iii. 408.

Fuller (John Casimiro), 1823, Engl. sailor on the *Rover;* prob. made other visits; well known from about '27; on Larkin's books at Mont. from '33. He had been baptized at S. Blas, and married—apparently at Sta B—to Concepcion Ávila; in '36 at Mont. with wife and a daughter, born in '36 at the Sandwich Isl. In '37 he got a lot at S. F. iii. 705; v. 678; but also bought of Watson the Beltran house at Mont., retransferred 2 years later; moved to S. F. in '38; had a house there in '49. iii. 609, 678; being also síndico. iii. 705; worked for Dawson at Sonoma '39; in Farnham's list of arrested foreigners '40. iv. 17; naturalized '41, being also síndico. iv. 665; from 40 to 45 years old in '42, when he had 5 children, 2 of whom were Concepcion and Santiago. His name appears often in S.F. records to '47, when he took part in efforts for the relief of the Donner party, v. 539, and advertised that he would not be responsible for his wife's debts; and he seems to have died in '49. He was a butcher and cook well known to all the early traders; an alley in the city still bears his name; and his widow and children were still at S.F. in '63.

Fuller (Thos), 1831, Engl. carpenter, landed sick at Mont., and still there in '40, age 34. iii. 405.   F. (Wm M.), 1847, Co. F, N.Y.Vol. (v. 499); lot at S.F.; claimant in '53 for a Marin Co. rancho. iv. 674.   Fulma (Mores), 1846, came to S. José. *Hall.*   Funk (John), 1847, Co. B, N. Y. Vol. (v. 499); in Shasta Co. '74; doubtful name.   Furbush, 1847, came from Hon. on the *Euphemia;* prob. 'Forbush,' q.v.   Fuster (Vicente), 1773, Span. friar who served chiefly at S. Diego and S. Juan Cap., dying in 1800. See biog. i. 657; ment. i. 194-5, 250-3, 266-7, 300, 302, 377, 388, 425, 453, 575, 577; ii. 109-10.

Gabel (Ludovico), 1843, German sailor from Boston on the *Admittance*, under the name of Robt Foster, known as 'Bob the fisherman;' d. at Mont. '72, *Swan.*   Gabriel (Ralph), 1847, at S.F. to '70. *Alta.*   Gafan (Cárlos V.), 1837, mr of the *Veloz Asturiano*. iv. 106.   Gaitan (Cayetano), at Jamacha rancho '36. iii. 611.   G. (José M.), Mex. convict '29-35.   Gajiola (José Ant.), sec. of ayunt. at Mont. '29. ii. 612; clerk at Soledad '36. iii. 690-1; sec. at S. José '42-3. iv. 684.   G. (Valentin), alférez and habilitado at Mont '45-6. iv. 652; v. 41.   Galbraith (Isaac), 1826, Amer. blacksmith and hunter who came with Jed. Smith's party and settled at San Gabriel. ii. 558; iii. 153, 155-6, 158, 160, 176; a crack shot, and a man of gigantic size and strength. I find no record of him after '29, when his age was 34.   Gale (Joseph), 1841-2, mr of the *State of Oregon*. iv. 568.   G. (Joseph), 1831, doubtful member of Young's party. iii. 388.

Gale (Wm Alden), 1810, Boston trader, who 1st visited Cal. as clerk on the *Albatross*, which did a large business in furs about the Farallones. ii. 93-4. In '22-3 he came back as sup. of the *Sachem*, the pioneer in the hide trade with Boston. ii. 474-5, 478, 492-3, 614. Again he returned in '25-7, still on the *Sachem*, taking back as wife Marcelina Estudillo, the 1st Cal. woman to visit the 'hub,' who seems never to have returned to Cal. iii. 24, 62, 118, 148. His next trip was on the *Brookline* in '29-30; and his last on the *Roxana* '32, when he remained on the coast as agent of Bryant & Sturgis's ships till '35, getting a carta in '33. iii. 137-8, 146, 381. He died in Mass. '41. He was a most popular trader, famous for the zeal with which he drove his bargains in broken Spanish. His most common nickname was Cuatro Ojos, by reason of his spectacles; but his name was also translated into Tormenta, 'a gale;' and he was sometimes called Cambalache, or 'barter.' Galente (Rafael), 1847, lot at S.F. Gali (Francisco), 1584, Span. voyager down the Cal. coast. i. 94-6. Galiano (Dionisio), 1792, Span. com. of the *Sutil* and *Mexicana* in an explor. exped. to Cal. and the N.W. Coast; killed at Trafalgar. i. 490. 506-9; see also *Hist. N. W. Coast*, i.

Galindo (Bautista), soldier at S.F. '37; at S. José '41, age 27, wife Alvisa (?) Moreno. G. (Crisóstomo), at S. José '41, age 67, wife Jacoba Bernal, child. Francisco b. '24, Antonio '26, José '29, Agustin '31, Juan '39. His daughter Ana María married J. A. Forbes; and the family home was at Milpitas; grantee and cl. of S. José mission land. v. 665. The full name was Juan C. See also José Jesus and Juan. G. (Eusebio), b. at S.F. 1802; soldier in S.F. comp. '28-9; ment. in '40. iv. 23; juez de paz at Sta Clara '45. iv. 683. Still at Sta Clara in '77, when he gave me some historical *Apuntes.* G. (Francisco), son of Crisóstomo or José Jesus; in Alameda Co. '78. G. (Francisco), Span. not required to quit Cal. in '30. iii. 52. G. (José), soldier of S.F. comp. '37-43. iv. 667. G. (José), soldier of S.F. comp. '38-9. G. (José Ant.), grantee of Laguna de la Merced and Sauzalito '35. iii. 712-15; corp. S.F. militia '37; killed José Peralta at S.F. in '38. G. (José de Jesus), died at Milpitas in '77, at the reputed age of 106; his son Francisco was then a resid. of Oakland; and his daughter Juana was the wife of José M. Alviso and later of José Uridias, still living in '77. José Jesus may have been Crisóstomo, q.v., whose age in '77 would have been 103. G. (Juan), corporal in S.F. comp. '19-29; very likely Juan Crisóstomo, q.v. G. (Leandro), regidor at S. José '22. ii. 604; militiaman and elector at S.F. '37. iii. 705; lot at S.F. mission '40. iv. 706; in '42 at S.F., age 55, wife Dominga Alaman, child. Seferino b. '30, María '33, Antonio '35, Francisco '38, Gregoria '39, Genaro '40, and Mariano '41; militia corporal '44; juez de campo and grantee of a lot '46. v. 648, 684. G. (Manuel), 1825, Span. officer on the *Constante*. iii. 26. G. (Nasario), son of Leandro; soldier, corp., and sergt of S.F. comp. '32-43. iii. 567, 667, 678; in '55 near mission S. José, age 40. G. (Nicolás), settler at S.F. 1791-1800. i. 716. G. (Rafael), soldier of S.F. comp. 1797-1800. i. 556; also '34-7, perhaps another man. Galista (José Ant.), Mex. clerk at Mont. '36, age 50, wife Andrea Jimeno, child. Darío b. '22 at Mont., Valentin '24, Domitila '27, José '29, Felipe '31, María G. '33, José Ant. '36.

Gallagher (John), 1847, Co. B, N.Y.Vol. (v. 499); an Irish farmer in Sonoma Co. '71-83, when he was at Bodega. Gallant (Victor), 1846, Co. E, Cal. Bat. (v. 358), enlist. at Sonoma, Oct. Gallardo (Anastasio), Mex. convict '29-35. G. (Félix), at Los Ang. '36. iii. 491; and '40. v. 312; 2 of the name in '46. G. (José Ant.), a settler at Brancif. 1797. i. 569. G. (Juan), soldier killed by Ind. at the Colorado 1781. i. 359-62. G. (Juan), Mex. shoemaker, and leader in the Apalátegui revolt of '35. iii. 282-6; still at Los Ang. to '46, when he was alcalde. iii. 504, 564; v. 50, 143, 625-6; claimant in '52 for land granted '38. G. (Rafael), at Los Ang. from '36; juez de paz '43. iv. 633; regidor '47. v. 626. G. (Simon), at Los Ang. '48. Gallego (Cárlos), settler on the Colorado, killed 1781. i. 359-62. G., trader forbidden to hold raffles 1798. i. 642. G. (Pablo), at Sonoma '44, age 35. Gallegos, drowned at Sta B. '30. ii. 576. Galusha (Elon A.), 1847, Co. F, N.Y.Vol. (v. 499); d. at Rochester, N.Y., before '83. Galway (James), 1847 (?), said to have come with his parents at the age of 5; page in the convention of '49; with Walker in Nic.; lieut in war of '61-5; editor of Sta Cruz *Journal;* d. in '70. *Sta Clara News*, Sept. 24, '70.

Gamble (Wm), 1841, a young naturalist sent out from Phil. by Nuttall to collect specimens; came from N. Mex. in the Workman party. iv. 278-9. Being financially crippled, he was employed by Com. Jones in '42 as clerk on the *Cyane*, and perhaps went away on that vessel; in '44 at Callao; said by Given to have ret. to Cal. about '49.   G. (Wm M.), 1845, mid. on the U. S. *Portsmouth*.   Gamon (José M.), 1844, mr of the *Trinidad*. iv. 569.   G. (Thos), 1826, at Mont.   Gándara (Pedro), apparently a clerk of Pedrorena '40-1.   Gann (Nicholas), 1847, overl. immig. with wife Ruth, to whom, in camp at Stockton, Oct., was born the 1st child in S. Joaq., named Wm; at Gilroy '79-82.   Gannon (Thos), 1847, Co. F, N. Y. Vol. (v. 499); d. Sta B. '55.   Gansevoort (Stanwix), 1845, mid. on U.S. *Portsmouth*.

Gantt (John), 1843, member of the Chiles-Walker immig. party. iv. 392-4, 400. In earlier times said to have been an officer in the U.S. army. Capt. G. commanded Sutter's force in Micheltorena's service '44-5; and after the campaign made a contract to attack Ind. horse-thieves for a share of the recovered animals. iv. 480, 485-6, 506-7, 516-17, 543.   In Sept. '46 Bryant found him ill at Dr Marsh's rancho, and it is likely that sickness prevented his taking part in the troubles of '46-7. In '47 he wrote from Sonoma asking an appointment as sub-Ind. agent, and from Yount's place in Napa, proposing to build a saw-mill on his ' mountain tract;' in '48 of firm G. & Hannah at Napa; in '49 mining on Feather River; died in Napa Val. later in '49.

Garaycoechea (José), at S. F. 1795. i. 700.   Garcés (Francisco T. H.), 1774, Span. friar of Querétaro college, and missionary in Sonora from '68; with Anza in his exped. to Cal. 1774-6; the 1st to explore the Tulare valley and the route from Mojave to S. Gabriel; later missionary at the Colorado pueblos, where he was killed by the Ind. in 1781. i. 221-3, 258-62, 273-8, 354-67, 573, and list of auth. ii. 43-4.

García (Anastasio), a desperado who killed Joaq. de la Torre and several other men in the Sta B. region '55.   G. (Anselmo), at S. José '47.   G. (Antonio), at Los Ang. '46.   G. (Bernardino), son of Francisco, age 19 in '41, when he enlisted in the S.F. comp. at Sonoma. iv. 667. He was the desperado, ' Four-fingered Jack,' who killed Cowie and Fowler in '46. v. 161-2; also ment. at Natividad. v. 370; Cal. claim of $1,375; I think he was hanged in later years.   G. (Bibiana Romero de), widow at J. José '41, age 21, child. José Ant. b. '34, Francisco '36.   G. (Bruno), settler at Los Ang. 1796. ii. 350. G. (Cárlos), ditto 1813.   G. (Cármen), Cal. claim $2,152 (v. 462).

García (Diego), 1787, Span. friar, who served chiefly at S.F. and retired in '97. Biog. i. 713; ment. i. 388, 474, 498-500, 575, 577.   G. (Dionisio), Mex. sold. at Mont. '36, age 37; owner of S. F. lots '39-46. v. 676, 682.   G. (Eugenio), soldier at Sta B. '32.   G. (Faustino), at Mont. '47.   G. (Felipe), Span. sold. of the Mont. comp. before 1780; had a garden at Mont. about 1815. ii. 209; his wife was Petra Lugo (or Rincon), and they had 20 children. G. (Felipe Santiago), regidor at Los Ang. 1789-90. i. 461; perhaps same as preceding.   G. (Felipe Santiago), son of preceding, b. at Mont. 1782; in '35, '46, juez de campo. iii. 674; v. 637; in '36 at Mont., wife Jacinta Fernandez, child. José de Jesus b. '22, Antonia '25, Manuel Estévan '27, Encarnacion '29. In '54 he gave Taylor, *Discov. and Founders*, ii. 25, his recollections; Cal. claim in '46 of $1,042 (v. 462); still living after '60.   G. (Felipe), in Los Ang. region '46, age 25.   G. (Francisco), maj. at Sta B. 1811-1820. ii. 364. G. (Francisco), Span. invalido of Sta B. comp. in '28-9, age 60. iii. 51.   G. (Francisco), soldier of S. F. '34-5.   G. (Francisco), Mex. at Mont. '36, age 34, wife Josefa Gonzalez, child. Bernabé b. '23, Pedro '25, José '26, Epitacio '28, Lugarda '30, Bonifacia '31, María Jesus '33, Micaela '34; grantee of ranchos in Mont. and Sta Clara '42, '45. iv. 655, 673; juez at S. Feliciano '45-6; iv. 625, 634, 637. Cal. claims of $14,625 and $2,170 in '46-7. (v. 462); still in Mont. Co. '50.   G. (Francisco), at Los Ang '46.   G. (Francisco), one of the Jack Powers gang hanged near S. Luis Ob. about '55; ment. in '46. v. 162; perhaps confounded with Bernardino.   G. (Gabriel), at the S. Pascual fight '46. v. 352; a soldier at Sta B. before '37.   G. (Hilarion), maj. at S. Diego '30. ii. 549; alférez at Sta B. '39-46. iii. 583; iv. 642; v. 35.

García (Inocente), son of Felipe, b. at Los Ang. 1791; soldier in Mont.

comp. from 1807, serving in the escolta of S. Miguel and Soledad; from '13 trader and soap-maker; maj. of S. Juan B. '22-3. ii. 624; ment. at Mont. '28-30. ii. 612; iii. 41; took part in Alvarado's revolt of '36, and in Ind. exped. of '37-9. iii. 457, 460. 469; iv. 75; admin. of S. Miguel '37-45. iii. 555, 587, 685; iv. 659; arrested by Frémont '46. v. 375-6. He went to the mines in '48; and for years supposed himself to be owner of a rancho near S. Luis Ob., but lost it. His wife was María del Cármen Ramirez, and there were many children. In '78 living at S. Luis in poverty, strong in body and mind, though 83 years old, and of good repute. He gave me his *Hechos Históricos*, a MS. full of interesting details of the old soldier's life and observations. ii. 232, 336-9, 366. In '85 I have not heard of his death.   G. (Jacinto), soldier at S.F. '27-40.   G. (Jesus), at Los Ang. '46.   G. (Joaq.), sent to Mex. '30. iii. 85. García (José), 1800, Span. friar who served at S. Luis Rey, and retired in 1808. Biog. ii. 108; ment. i. 577; ii. 159-60.   G. (José), settler at Los Ang. 1808. ii. 350.   G. (José), soldier at S.F. '28-33.   G. (José), sent as prisoner to Sonora '37. iii. 638.   G. (José), came in '36 from S. Amer.; flogged for forgery at Mont. '37; clerk at S. José '41-2. iv. 684-5; ment. in '46. v. 321; said to have been killed at Natividad. v. 372.   G. (José Ant.), 1st death at Sta Clara. i. 306.   G. (José Ant.), petitioner for lands for N. Mex. colony '45. iv. 572, 635, 637.   G. (José Dolores), ment. at Sta B. '48, in con. with the Cañon Perdido. v. 588.   G. (José E.), son of José Maria, worked at Sta B. for Capt. Robbins '45; served under Carrillo and Flores '46. v. 400; took part in hiding the cannon in '48; and in '78 gave me his *Episodios*.   G. (José Manuel), lots at S.F. '39.   G. (José María), nat. of Sonora, of Span. parentage; síndico at Sta B. '31-2. iii. 653, 212; maj. and admin. of Sta B. '34-6. iii. 346, 353, 657-8; alcalde in '34. iii. 654. His wife was María Ant. Ayala. G. (José Miguel), militiaman at S.F. '37; age 21, wife Rafaela Miranda, child. Guadalupe b. '39.   G. (José Norberto), murdered at S. Juan B. '44. iv. 662.   G. (Juan), soldier at S.F. 1797-1800. i. 556.   G. (Juan), soldier at Mont. '36, age 26.   G. (Juan and Juan José), at Los Ang. '46. G. (Juan B.), soldier of S. F. comp. '34-42.   G. (Julian), at Los Ang. '46; S. Luis Ob. '58.   G. (Luis), at Brancif. '30. ii. 627; at S. José '41, age 28. G. (Luz), comisionado at Brancif. '15. ii. 390; inválido '28, wife Rosalía Vazquez, child. Rufino, Antonio, José María.

García (M.), grantee of S. Miguel rancho '46. v. 637.   G. (Manuel), 1822, mr of the *S.F. de Paula*. ii. 457, 474.   G. (Manuel), at Los Ang. '46.   G. (Marcelino), 1844, one of the Bat. fijo. iv. 289, 405; in '77 at Salinas City, where he gave me his *Apunte sobre Micheltorena*.   G. (Matias and Miguel), at Los Ang. '46.   G. (Máximo), soldier of the piquete de Hidalgo at Mont. '36, age 45.   G. (Miguel), grantee of S. Miguel '46.   G. (Norberto), at Salinas '36, age 35, wife María Victoria Gomez, child. María Francita b. '20, Rita '23, José '25, Juan José '28, Guadalupe '31, Teodora '34.   G. (Pascual), soldier at Sta B. before '37.   G. (Pascual), at La Brea '36, age 49, wife Juliana Sanchez.   G. (Pedro), 1842, lieut of the batallon fijo. iv. 389.   G. (Pedro Gonzalez), armorer and instructor 1792-5. i. 615, 684.   G. (Rafael), soldier of S. F. comp. '23-33; at S. Rafael '24. ii. 598; grantee of Tamales and Baulinas '36. iii. 713; grantee of land in Mendocino '44. iv. 672; raid on the Ind. '45. iv. 541, 679. He died in '66 in Marin Co., age 75.   G. (Rafael), at Los Ang. '46; soldier at Sta B. '32.   G. (Ramon), at S. José '41, age 27. G. (Reyes), in piquete de Hidalgo at Mont. '36.   G. (Rosalio), son of Felipe; went to Chili to avoid mil. service.   G. (Salvador), Span. sailor of the *Asia;* rem. in Cal. iii. 51-2.   G. (Tomás), soldier at Sta B. before '37.   G. (Trifion), grantee of Atascadero '42. iv. 655.

García Diego (Francisco), 1833, Mex. friar of the Zacatecanos, who served at Sta Clara to '35, being prefect of the northern missions, and in '41 came back as bishop of Cal., dying in '46. Biog. v. 632-3; ment. iii. 318-24, 328-36, 338, 347-8, 351-2, 726; iv. 63-5, 195-6, 219, 332-8, 372-4, 424-7, 519, 554, 565, 619, 640.   Gard (Chas and John), 1848, at Mont.   Gardner (Geo. W.), 1844, mr of the *Nantucket*. iv. 567.   G. (Wyman), 1840, at Mont. (?). G., 1848, worked for John Williams on Butte Cr.   Gareolo (Valentin), lieut

in Cal. '45 (?). Garfias (Manuel), 1842, Mex. lieut in the batallon fijo '42–5.
iv. 289; grantee of S. Pascual '43. iv. 635; rem. in Cal., and took part in the
war against the U.S. '46–7, going to Mex. with Flores. iv. 513; v. 41, 49, 391,
391, 457. He came back to Cal., and was county treasurer of Los Ang. '50–1;
in later years U.S. consul at Mazatlan, where he still lived, perhaps, in '77.
G. (Salvador), Span. at S. José '41, age 41, wife Crecencia Cibrian, child. Salvador b. 31, Ascension '36, José Jesus, '34, Felicidad '29, Encarnacion '30,
Cármen '38, Josefa '40.   Garibay (Gertrudis), accused of murder at Mont.
'34. iii. 673.   Garner (Philip), 1847, Co. B, Morm. Bat. (v. 469).   G. (R.),
1848, landed at Sta B. (?).   G. (Wm A.), 1847, ditto, made bricks and dug
a well at S. Diego.

Garner (Wm Robert), 1824, nat. of London, b. in 1803, who deserted from
an English whaler at Sta B., the date being often given as '26. ii. 526. In '29
he was refused naturalization; in '31 married a daughter of Manuel Butron;
in '32 joined the comp. extranjera at Mont. iii. 221. He was a lumberman,
and appears on Larkin's books from '33; in '36–7 was a lieut of Graham's
comp. in Alvarado's service. iii. 458–9, 512; and in '39 was naturalized, then
living at S. Juan B. His part in the Graham affair of '40 is recorded in iv. 5–
6, 10, 12, 21, 27, he being the man who revealed the plot of Graham and his
associates. It is not quite clear whether he simply acted in good faith as a
Mex. citizen, was prompted by hostility to G., or was entrapped by Castro
into confession for self-protection. Continuing his lumber business for a few
years, in '44–8 he kept a boarding-house at Mont., being also at times clerk,
policeman, translator, auctioneer, and alcalde's sec., besides serving apparently in the campaign against Micheltorena. iv. 495; v. 637. He went to the
mines with Colton, and with his sons made several mining trips, and then
moved to S. Luis Ob., from which point, in '49, he made an exped. against
the Ind. of the interior and was killed with 6 of his men. His son José C., b.
about '32, in a letter of '75, gave me some information about his father; also
to the *S. José Pion.* of '78, when he lived at S. José, as he does still, perhaps,
in '85. In their anger at the affair of '40, Graham and his friends accused Garner not only of treachery in that matter, but of having been an Australian
convict, murderer, and desperado; but in the absence of proofs, it is well to
judge the man's character by his Cal. record, which is in every respect better
than that of his accusers. He is said to have been of a good family, and was
an intelligent man of some education.   Garnica del 'Castillo,' q.v.

Garra, Ind. chief at Pauma '46. v. 567–8.   Garraleta (Antonio), clerk at
Sta B. mission '39. iii. 657.   G. (José Ant.), lieut of the frontier comp.,
sometimes visiting S. Diego; killed in '41 by his wife. iv. 619.   Garrick
(Peter), 1834, Engl. carpenter at Mont. in Spear's service; written Garruk
and Garrenk.   Garriger (Solomon), 1846, Co. E, Cal. Bat. (v. 358), enlisting
at N. Helv. Oct.   Garter (David), 1848, doubtful name.   Garue (Wm),
1834, nat. of Sto Domingo, from Hon.; cooper at Los Ang. '36. iii. 412.

Gasquet (Louis), 1845, French consul at Mont. '45–7. iv. 385, 587, 590; v.
34, 60. 232–3, 364.   Gastelum (Francisco J.), at Los Ang. '39–45.   Gaten
(H.), 1846, Co. B, artill., Cal. Bat. (v. 358).   Gautier (Julian), 1843, d. at
Los Ang.; his widow at Sonoma, Dec.   Gavitt (John), 1847, lot at S. F.
Gay (Geo.), 1832, Engl. deserter from a whaler. iii. 408; went to Or. in '35,
and came back in '37 in the cattle exped. iv. 85; *see Hist. Or.,* i. 98.

Geddes (Paul), see Green (Talbot H.).   Gehringer (Andrew), 1847, Co.
H, N.Y. Vol. (v. 499); miner in '48–50; Sta Clara farmer '51–63; in '63–83
near Concord, Contra Costa.   Geiger (Wm), 1841, N.Y. teacher, age 24,
who came from Hon. on the *Thos Perkins.* iv. 104, 569; later in the year at
N. Helv.   Gelabert (Wm), 1846, Span. in U.S.N.; settled later at Stockton,
where he died in '82, leaving a wife and 3 children.   Gelston (Roland), 1847,
mr of the *Whiton,* and a S. F. merchant of G. & Co. in '47–9; owner of town
lot and building; in '53 claimant for lands in Sac. and S.F. v. 581, 676, 678,
683.   Gendreau (François), 1844, Canadian in Sutter's employ '45–8; com.
of an Ind. comp. in '46. iv. 453; v. 360. He, or his son Joseph, was in the 2d
Donner relief '47. v. 540. His wife was a Walla Walla Ind., and their child

was buried at S. José Mission in Dec. '44. His name is often written Gendran, Gendron, Geandreau, and even Jondro.   Genks, 1846, named at N. Helv. Genling (Joaquin), doubtful name of a juez in Mont. dist. iv. 653.   Gennon (John), 1847, named by Lancey as a member of Co. F, 3d U.S. artill.   Genoa y Aguirre (Fermin), 1817-18, sup. of the *Hermosa Mexicana*. ii. 282-3, 424. George (J.), 1848, from Hon. on the *Julian*.

Gerardo (Rafael), maj. at Sta B. 1793-4. ii. 120.   Gerke (Henry), 1847, German immig. at N. Helv. and S.F. in Oct. v. 556; lot-owner at S.F. '47-8. v. 656; later a well-known vineyardist in Tehama Co., where he still lived in '80.   German (Antonio), juez de campo at La Brea and grantee of Juristac, iii. 674, 676, 711-12, being 50 years old in '36, wife María de la Luz Peña, child. Antonio b. '18, Juan '20, José '22, Luis '24. In early times he had been a soldier at Sta B.   G. (Cayetano), at Los Ang. '46; cl. for the rancho in '53. G. (Faustino), brother of Antonio, at Mont. '26. ii. 612; juez de campo '31, '35. iii. 672, 674; grantee with Ant. of Juristac '35. iii. 712; in '36 at La Brea, age 48, wife María Ant. García, age 40. Faustino, like his brother, lost all his land under the manipulations of Amer. sharpers, and died in poverty at S. Juan in '83, at the age of 95, leaving his widow, aged 87, but no children.   G. (John), 1847, Co. F, 3d U.S. artill. (v. 518).   G. (Juan), vecino of S. Diego, killed in '26. ii. 549.   G. (José de los Santos), son of Antonio, b. at Sta B. '23; in '78 at Tres Pinos, S. Benito Co., engaged in raising cattle with his brother Luis C. German. The two gave me their recollections of Californian *Sucesos*, which, on several points, have proved valuable material for history. iv. 359, 463; v. 167.   G. (Manuel), soldier at Sta B. before '37; at Los Ang. '30-48. Gerónimo, Ind. alcalde at Soledad '26. ii. 623.   Gervasio (José), soldier of S.F. comp. '37-42.   Gessen, 1845, a German in the south. iv. 490.   Gettinger (Peter), 1847, Co. F, 3d U.S. artill. (v. 518). Geurron (J.A.), 1846, Co. G, Cal. Bat. (v. 358).   Gholston (Wm C.), 1846, Co. K, 1st dragoons; killed at S. Pascual. v. 346.

Gibbins, 1840, at Mont.   Gibbon (L.), 1841, mid. on U. S. *St Louis*. Gibbs (John), 1845, overl. immig. of the Grigsby-Ide party. iv. 579, 587; of committee repres. the immig. before Castro. iv. 606; prob. of the Bears. v. 110; settled in Napa; at N. Helv. Nov. '47.   G., 1845, Amer. at Brancif., age 40.   Gibson, 1842, purser with Com. Jones. iv. 308.   G. (Horatio Gates), 1847-8 (?), lieut in 3d U.S. artill.; at S. Diego, S.F., and other points in Cal. to '61; colonel in war of '61-5; in '77 in com. of Fort Wardsworth, N. Y.; president of eastern assoc. of pioneers. I find no original record of such an officer before '49.   G. (Joseph), 1831, Amer. trapper and tailor of 'Haquinsor' (Arkansas!), from N. Mex. with Jackson or Wolfskill. iii. 387, 405; at Los Ang. and S. Pedro '34-6; 44 years old in '36 and single.   G. (Marion), 1845, Amer. farmer from Or. in the McM.-Clyman party. iv. 572, 587; in the mines with Job Dye '48; died at a date not recorded.   G. (Samuel), 1845, Amer. immig. from Or., prob. in the McM.-Clyman party, and possibly identical with the preceding. iv. 578, 587. He took a prominent part in the proceedings of the Bears, being sergt. v. 110, 153, 163-4, 168; went south with Frémont, remaining with Gillespie at Los Ang. and S. Diego, ranking as capt. in the Cal. Bat., wounded at S. Pascual, and serving under Stockton in the final campaign. v. 326-7, 340, 343-7, 360, 386, 434. In '48 he mined on Feather River in partnership with G.P. Swift, and was drowned in the winter of '48-9. *Bidwell*.   G. (Thos), 1847, Co. C, Morm. Bat. (v. 469).

Gifford (James), 1846, applicant for timber-land near S. Diego.   Gift (Geo. W.), 1848, nat. of Tenn.; mid. on the U.S. *St Mary*; left navy in '52; banker at Sac. from '55; lieut in confed. navy from '61; newspaper man at S. Rafael and Napa till his death in '79, leaving a wife and 4 children.   Gil y Taboada (Luis), 1801, Mex. friar of S. Fern. college, who served at many missions, being founder of S. Rafael, and died at S. Luis Ob. '33. Biog. iii. 660-1, ment. ii. 29, 121, 131, 135, 137, 159, 329-30, 337, 351, 355, 364, 366, 387, 394, 425, 562, 618, 623, 625, 627, 655.   Gilbert (Albert), 1830, from N. Mex. to buy cattle; in trouble with the authorities; went to Hon. on the *Volunteer* in '32.

Gilbert (Edward), 1847, N.Y. printer, and lieut Co. H, N.Y.Vol. v. 504. He made a census of S.F. and wrote an article on the town published in the *Star*. v. 647, 656; was a candidate for alcalde, and declined the collectorship. v. 575, 652, 659; but seems to have acted as Collector Folsom's deputy. He took a prominent part from '48 in public affairs; was editor of the *Alta* from its beginning in Jan. '49. v. 659; was a member of the constit. convention; and in Nov. '49 was elected as the 1st congressman from Cal. One of his editorial articles drew out a letter which led him to challenge Gen. Jas W. Denver, by whom he was killed in a duel near Sac. in '52 at the age of 33. He was regarded as a man of unusual ability and promise.   G., 1848, at Mont.; of firm Newell, Brady, & G.   G. (James), 1845, at N.Helv. in Sutter's service '45-6.   G. (John), 1847, Co. D, Morm. Bat. (v. 469).   G. (Wm), 1846, said to have been steward on the U.S. *Savannah;* at Stockton '79.

Gilchrist (Edward), 1846, surgeon on the *Congress* and *Cyane;* justice of the peace at Mont.; acted as surg. of the Cal. Bat. v. 231, 361, 637-8.   Gildea (Wm B.), 1845, Amer. physician who came overl. in the Swasey-Todd party; died at N.Helv. Jan. '46. iv. 576, 580, 587.   Gili (Bartolomé), 1791, Span. friar, who served chiefly at S. Antonio and retired in '94. Biog. i. 689; ment. i. 496, 500, 523-4, 576, 597.   Gill (James), 1846, Co. F, Cal. Bat. (v. 358); enlisting at S. Juan Oct.; lot at S.F. '47.

Gillespie (Archibald H.), 1846, nat. of Penn. and lieut. of marines U.S.N., who was sent in Oct. '45 from Wash. to Cal. as a bearer of a duplicate of secret instructions to Larkin, with whom he was to coöperate, as was Frémont, in carrying out those instructions. He crossed Mex., destroying his official despatch after committing its contents to memory, and arrived at Mont. in April '46 on the *Cyane* via Honolulu, thence proceeding to the Oregon frontier to overtake Frémont. v. 24-9, 200, 636, 644. The original of his despatch is now in my possession, and also the copy written by him from memory at Mont. Frémont claims to have received a very different despatch, and there is a bare possibility that Gillespie deceived him. In the various events of May-July, G. took an active part, being made adjutant of the Cal. Bat. at its 1st organization. v. 79-80, 101-2, 127, 177, 184, 247, 252-3. Going south in July, he was left at Los Ang. in com. of the garrison, and by his unwise policy caused the people to revolt and drive him out in Oct. v. 286, 306-15, 319. Joining Stockton at S. Diego, he was sent with a reënforcement to meet Kearny, and was wounded in the fight at S. Pascual in Dec. v. 328-9, 340, 343-7. Ranking as major of the battalion, G. commanded a division of Stockton's army, and was again wounded at the S. Gabriel in Jan. '47. v. 360, 386, 391-5. Declining the secretaryship of state under Frémont, he was relieved from duty in Cal., and reported to Com. Biddle in May. v. 433, 437, 440, 445, 450. He went east overland with Stockton, and testified for Frémont at the court-martial; also in the Cal. claims investigation. v. 453-6. He seems to have returned overland to Cal. in '48, and to have spent much of his later life here, though for some years previous to '61 he was in Mex., perhaps as sec. of legation. He was never prominent after '49, having to a certain extent 'lost his grip' in the battle of life. He died at S.F. in '73, at the age of 60.

Gillespie (Chas V.), 1848, bro. of Arch. H., nat. of N. Y., who came on the *Eagle* from China with his family, a cargo of merchandise, and 2 Chinese servants. He advertised in the *Star* as a merchant and conveyancer; and was made notary public and judge of election. v. 648, 652, 680. He also made inquiries for a rancho, and wrote, 'One of my favorite projects is to introduce Chinese immigrants into this country.' He took a prominent part under Howard in settling the Leidesdorff estate. In '85 he still lives in S.F., where he has been well known as a lawyer and searcher of records. In '75 he contributed for my use a statement on the *Vigilance Committee* and other topics of early S.F. life; and later gave me some items about early buildings in the city. Mrs G. organized a sabbath-school in '48, and has since been prominent in church affairs. v. 657.   G. (James), 1828, mr of the *Telemachus*. iii. 149; a Mass. man who was lost with the same vessel near Mazatlan. *Forbes' Pers. Remin.*, 90.   G. (J.), 1848, mr of a vessel, or sup.   Gillingham (Henry),

1847, musician Co. I, N.Y.Vol. (v. 499); owner of S.F. lots '48.   Gilman (G. D.), 1848, from Honolulu; of firm Wetmore & G. at S.F. '48–9.

Gilroy (John), 1814, Scotch sailor, and the 1st foreigner to settle permanently in Cal., being left sick at Mont. by the *Isaac Todd*. ii. 204, 248, 272, 382, 393. His real name was John Cameron, but having run away from home as a minor, he changed it to avoid being arrested and sent back. His parents moved to England when John was very young; and indeed, he often claimed to be a native of Sunderland, Engl. In Sept. '14 he was baptized at S. Cárlos by P. Sarría as Juan Antonio María Gilroy. In '18 Capt. Guerra, at Sta B., sent to the viceroy his petition as an 'Amer. cooper' for permission to remain and marry in Cal., which was granted in '19; and in '21 he was married at S. Juan B. to María Clara de la Asuncion, daughter of Ignacio Ortega. The same year he accompanied Capt. Argüello in his famous exped. 'to the Columbia' as guide, or rather, interpreter, for Amer. intruders were to be met and talked to. ii. 444–5. The next we hear of him was in '33, when he obtained naturalization, producing certificates that he was a soap-maker and millwright of good character, with wife and 4 children, having also some livestock on the S. Isidro rancho. This rancho was granted the same year to the Ortegas; G. owned a league of it, on which he built an adobe house and spent the rest of his life. His name appears on Larkin's books from '34, when his age was given as 45. In '35 he was aux. alcalde at 'Los Ortegas.' iii. 674; by the padron of '36, age 40, wife age 28, child. Nicodemus b. '26, Miguel '28. iv. 117; age 46 in '40; not arrested in the Graham affair; often named in records of most years; said to have been sent to Frémont's Gavilan camp in '46. v. 18. In '51 for the 1st time Gilroy wrote to his family in England, and I have the original reply—presented by Valentin Alviso—of his brother Alex. Cameron, tanner, at Newton Heath, near Manchester, dated June 29, '52. Alex. is glad to learn that he has a brother living, for father, mother, and the other brothers are all dead. John Gilroy was an honest, good-natured old sailor-ranchero, well liked by everybody, much too fond of his grog and cards, careless and improvident, and as powerless in the hands of land-lawyers as were the natives themselves. He lost all his lands and cattle, but he lived to see his old rancho the site of a flourishing town, which bears his adopted name, Gilroy; and he died, as poor as when he landed in Cal. more than half a century before, in '69, at the age of about '75. I have no definite record of his sons since '48. 'Juanita' (McPherson) has given many items on G.'s early life, obtained from himself, in the *Sta Clara Argus* and other papers.   Gilt (Henry), 1840, at Brancif.; prob. 'Hill.'

Gines, executed at Purísima '24.   Gingery, 1847, in Sutter's employ '47–8; millwright and blacksmith.   Gios (José), sirv. S.F. 1777. i. 297.   Girard (A.), 1846, lieut in com. of Co. B, artill., Cal. Bat., v. 361, enlisting at S.F. Oct.   G. (Wm), 1846, came to S. José. *Hall.*   Giraudeau, 1841, French viniculturist at Los Ang.; named by Mofras.   Giribet (Miguel), 1785, Span. friar who served at S.F. and S. Luis Ob., retiring in 1800. Biog. i. 689; ment. i. 388, 422, 469, 473–4, 575, 577.   Gitt, 1847, a physician named in the *N. Helv. Diary* '47–8.

Given (Isaac L.), 1841, nat. of Ohio and civil engineer, who, on a visit to the Missouri River region in '40, heard of Cal., and failing to reach Independence in time to join the Bartleson party, went to Sta Fé, and with 4 of his comrades joined the Workman-Rowland party, or in a sense originated that party. v. 278–9. His 1st work in Cal. was to survey the Rowland rancho. In '42 he came north to apply for land for himself; explored the Sac. Val. with Capt. Merritt and others; visited Napa and Russian Riv.; and ret. to Mont. to get naturalization. Here he found letters from home which caused him to go east as clerk on the *Dale*. He came back in '49 by the Panamá route, worked as a surveyor at Sac., and was later engaged for many years in mining operations. His wife is Mary A. Thomes, sister of Rob. H. Thomes, a pioneer of '41. In '79–85 Maj. Given resides at Oakland, and his *Immigrant of '41* is a MS. narrative of much value and interest.   Given, 1847, mr of the *Mt Vernon*. v. 579.

Glande (Giovanni), 1827, Ital. trader still at Mont. '29, age 25. iii. 176.
Gleason (James H.), 1846, trader at Mont. '46–9; owner of S.F. lot. He came
from Hon. on the *Don Quixote*, and was agent for Paty & Co.; one record has
it that he died in '60.   G. (John), 1848, roll of Soc. Cal. Pion.

Glein (Cárlos F.), 1844, German blacksmith who came from Mazatlan on
the *California*, settling at S.F., obtaining naturalization and a town lot the
same year, and having a blacksmith shop at the cor. of Montgom. and Pacific
streets from '45 to '49 and later. iv. 453, 563, 669; v. 684; also owner of a
Sonoma Co. rancho in '47; made a trip to Honolulu in '48. Later for many
years a dealer in hardware in S.F., where he still lives in '85.   Gliddon
(Geo. R.), 1846, sup. of the *Barnstable*, at S.F., Sonoma, Petaluma, and N.
Helv. '46–8.   Glines (James H.), sergt-major of Morm. Bat. v. 477; did not
come to Cal.   Gloria (Jacinto), at S. Juan Cap. 1776. i. 303.   Gloss (John),
1847. Co. C, N.Y.Vol. (v. 499).

Glover (Aquilla), 1846, memb. of 1st Donner relief. v. 538; owner of S.F.
lots '47–8. v. 685.   G. (Wm), 1846, member of the Mormon colony with
wife and 3 children. v. 546. He was the owner of S.F. lots, member of the
town council and of the school committee in '47. v. 648, 656, 682; a mason and
builder; also com. for settling the affairs of Brannan & Co.; a miner in '48,
being one of those who furnished Gov. Mason specimens of gold. He went a
little later with his family to Utah, where he still lives in '85 at Farmington.
His *Mormons in Cal.* is an important source of information on its topic, and
he has also sent me valuable items about early buildings in S.F.   G. (R. O.),
1841, purser on the U.S. *St Louis*.   Glynn (James), 1847, com. of the U.S.
Preble. v. 580.

Goche (Wm), 1838, Fr. shoemaker from N. Mex., age 31, at Los Ang. '40.
iv. 119.   Goddard (Nicodemus), 1824, Amer. shoemaker on the *Sachem*. v.
526; at Sta B. '40, age 31, single and catholic.   Godey (Alexis), 1844, nat.
of Mo., of Fr. Canadian parentage, a hunter in Frémont's 2d, 3d, and 4th
exped. iv. 437, 453, 583. He is named in connection with several of F.'s operations in '46. v. 4, 15, 22, 24; went south and remained with Gillespie, was
for a time in charge at S. Luis Rey, and took part in the fight at S. Pascual, ranking as lieut in the Cal. Bat. v. 314, 347, 353, 360. He went east
with his party but came back in '49; married a sister of A. F. Coronel, and
became a farmer and sheep-raiser, like his old associate, Kit Carson. As late as
'78 he was still living in southern Cal.   Gooway (J. M.), 1847, from Or. on
the *Henry*.   Goff (Daniel), 1840, one of the exiles to S. Blas, who did not
return. iv. 18.   Golden (Edward), 1847, Co. E, N.Y.Vol. (v. 499).   Gold-
smith (Sam.), 1845, doubtful member of Frémont's party. iv. 583; said to
have died in Valparaíso in '69, leaving a fortune. *Nev. Gazette*.   Goldwaite
(Richard M.), 1847, Co. H, N.Y.Vol. (v. 499); at Albany, N.Y., in '82.   Go-
lovnin (V. M.), 1818, Russian visitor and author of *Voy. of the Kamchatka*.
ii. 251, 291, 317–18, 383, 416.

Gomez, killed at Mont. '31. iii. 673.   G. (Ambrosio), sec. of ayunt. at
Mont. v. 636–7.   G. (Felipe), at S.F. '37–44; owner of S.F. lot '40. iii. 706;
age 57 in '44.   G. (Felipe), son of Rafael, trader at Mont., and sometime
postmaster, to '85.   G. (Francisco), 1769, Span. friar with the 1st division of
the 1st exped.; one of the party discovering S.F. bay; at S. Diego and Mont.
'70; retired in '71. Mention i. 127, 136, 140, 147, 151, 167, 175–6, 178.   G.
(Francisco), at Sta Cruz 1794. i. 496.   G. (Francisco), Mex. teacher at Mont.
'45.   G. (Guillermo), policeman at Mont. '46. v. 637.

Gomez (José Joaquin), 1830, Mex. trader who came on the *Leonor;* customs officer and comisario subalterno at Mont. '31–2. iii. 224–5, 376, 672; in
'34 regidor and builder of the *Peor es Nada*. iii. 383, 673; in '35 regidor,
comisionado to secularize S. Cárlos, and grantee of Los Verjeles. iii. 354, 673,
679, 680; in '36 member of the dip., being then 48 years old, having a wife
and children in Mex. iii. 426, 454, 460, 469. From '40 his rancho of Verjeles
is often mentioned, being on the way from Mont. to S. José; here Larkin was
captured in '46, and the fight of Natividad was in the vicinity; he was also
grantee of Tucho in '43. ii. 616; iv. 134, 212, 453, 656; v. 4, 14, 364. In '46

Don Joaquin was reported to the govt at Wash. by Larkin as a man of property and character, friendly to the U.S.; in '48 Los Verjeles was advertised for sale for the benefit of creditors. He had a son and a daughter, Dolores, who came to Cal. after his arrival. The latter married and died at Mont. after '78. G. (José María), soldier in S.F. comp. '19–26; killed by Ind. '29. iii. 110.

Gomez (José Miguel), 1842, Mex. priest who served as curate at Purísima in '42–4, and at S. Luis Ob. in '44–56; claimant for S. Simeon rancho. iv. 371, 421, 426, 647–8, 656–7, 659; v. 638–9.   G. (Juan), soldier of S.F. comp. '19. G. (Juan), 1834, mr of the *Natalia*, and of the *Leonidas* '36. iii. 265–7, 383; iv. 104.   G. (Juan), son of Rafael, resid. of Mont. and S.F. in '75–85, who gave me the privilege of copying a col. of his father's *Doc. Hist. Cal.*   G. (Manuel), Mex. sergt of artill. at S. F. and Mont. from '16; lieut from '19; left Cal. in '22. Biog. ii. 470; ment. ii. 225–32, 247, 263, 371, 422, 451, 454, 461.   G. (Nicolás), one of the mission guard at S. Juan Cap. 1776. i. 303. G. (Pedro), executed at Sta Cruz '47 for killing his wife. v. 641.   G. (Rafael), convict settler at S. José 1798–1808. i. 606, 638; ii. 192.

Gomez (Rafael), 1830, Mex. lawyer who came to Cal. as asesor, or legal adviser of the govt, a relation of Joaquin. ii. 607, 677; ii. 46, 54. As a supporter of Gov. Victoria, or rather by his legal opinions in the criminal cases of '31, he excited considerable opposition among the Californians, and tried to escape after V.'s downfall; but failed and was not molested. iii. 190–2, 195, 213, 660–1; grantee of Sta Rosa in '31. iii. 713, 721; iv. 160; supports Zamorano '32. iii. 222–3; action in P. Mercado's case '33. iii. 324; supports Figueroa '34. iii. 277; but resigned his office. He was grantee of Tularcitos in '34. iii. 679; regidor at Mont. '35. iii. 673; memb. of the dip. in '36, also appointed agent in Mex., but did not go. iii. 426, 454; being at this time 36 years old; wife Josefa Estrada, child. Felipe b. '33, María Isabel '34, Juan '35. His *Diario de Cosas Notables de '36* (erroneously accredited to his son in list of auth.) I have found to be a very useful document. iii. 422. A few years after '36, at his rancho of Tularcitos, he was accidentally killed by being entangled in the reata of a horse he was trying to drive away from his grain. Don Rafael was a man of good character and a lawyer of much ability, who came to Cal. in reality as a kind of political exile.   G. (Teodoro), soldier at Soledad 1791–1800. i. 499.   G. (Vicente), 1825. Mex. guerrillero chief in the war of independence; a fiend known as El Capador, who, however, behaved well enough in Cal. during his stay of a few months. iii. 16.

Gomez (Vicente Perfecto), 1842, son of José Joaquin and nat. of Guadalajara, who came to Cal. as a clerk with Gov. Micheltorena. In '44 he was, or at least claimed later to have been, the grantee of the Panocha Grande rancho. iv. 655, 672. This grant, rejected by the courts, was the foundation of the famous McGarragan claim to the New Idria quicksilver mines; and Don Vicente is the villain of Bret Harte's *Story of a Mine.* He was also the unsuccessful claimant for Tucho. iv. 656. In '45 he was sec. of the juzgado at Mont. iv. 653; aided Manuel Castro in Nov. '46. v. 366; had a Cal. claim of $11,500, of which $500 was paid (v. 462); and in '47–8 was for a time in charge of S. Antonio mission. v. 640. As a witness in later land litigation he met with some severe criticism, much of it doubtless undeserved; and though an intelligent clerk and good penman, knowing little English, he had a hard time in the later years to pay his grog bills. In '75–6 he worked for me in the Library and various archives, doing much faithful service. Many were the stories he told of old times in Cal.; his fellow-laborers were instructed to write out his yarns; and the result is a large vol. of MS. called *Gomez, Lo Que Sabe,* full of interest, and by no means devoid of historic value. He died at Mont. in '84 at the age of about 60, a better man in several respects than he has been given credit for. He had no family.

Góngora (José Ant.), son of José M., b. 1778 at S. Antonio; ment. in '22. ii. 614; sergt of S. Diego comp. '25–8. ii. 543; in '42–3 juez at S. Diego. iv. 619–21.   G. (José María), soldier of S.D. comp. 1771; corp. of the guard at S. Antonio '73; sergt from '75; ment. in connection with Anza's exped. '76. i. 269–71, 287. In '79 Gov. Neve reported against his promotion; and in '82 he was retired as an inválido and went to Loreto. His wife was Rosalía Maximiana Verdugo, married in '76, died '79 at S. Antonio. Gönnefgen (John A.), 1840, copy of his German passport of '24 made at Los Ang. by Fink '40. Gonzalez, soldier poisoned at Sta B. 1796. i. 670. G. (Alejo Ant.), of the S.D. guard. 1775. i. 250. G. (Bernardo), settler at S. José 1791-1800. i. 716; wife Mónica, child. Petra and Antonia. G. (Cirilo), sirv. at Sta Clara 1776. i. 306. G. (Diego), 1781, Span. lieut in com. at Mont. '81-5, and S.F. '85-7; an incompetent officer, of bad conduct, sent to the frontier in '87 and dropped from the rolls in '93. i. 340-2, 466-70, 484, 678; ii. 44. G. (Dionisio), 1842, Mex. capt. of the batallon fijo with Micheltorena. Nothing is recorded of him in Cal. iv. 289. G. (Felipe), at Brancif. '45, age 24, wife María Soria, child Antonio. G. (Francisco), 1797, Span. friar who served at Sta Cruz and retired in 1805. i. 498, 577; ii. 154-5, 159-60. G. (Francisco), settler at S. José 1791-1800; regidor in 1803. i. 716; ii. 134. G. (Francisco), soldier of S.F. comp. '19-24; also '37-40, perhaps another. G. (Francisco), corp. of the guard at Sta Inés '24. ii. 582. G. (Francisco), at Brancif. '28-30, wife María Engracia, child. Felipe, Margarita, and Natividad. ii. 627. G. (Fran.), at S. Felipe rancho, Mont., '36, age 30. G. (Fran.), said to have been drowned '44-5. G. (Francisco), Cal. claim of $15,850, '46-7 (v. 462). G. (Jacinto), síndico at Sta B. '28. ii. 572. G. (José), soldier of S.F. comp. '23-32. G. (José Ant.), at Sta Clara 1776. i. 306.

Gonzalez (José María de Jesus), 1833, Mex. friar of the Guadalupe college at Zacatecas, a nat. of Guadalajara, b. in 1803, coming to Cal. with the other Zacatecanos in '33. He served at S. José mission '33-42, being president and vice-prefect of the northern missions in '38-43. iii. 318, 577, 593, 724; iv. 61, 64, 372, 680. From '43 he served at Sta B. iv. 426, 643. From '46 he was the bishop's vicar, and after the bishop's death the same year was governor of the diocese. v. 565, 634; thus being the chief ecclesiastical authority in Cal. until the coming of Bishop Alemany in '50, and later vicar; president of the Sta B. college of Franciscans '58-72; died at Sta B. in '75, the last survivor of the Cal. missionaries, a man respected and beloved by all from the beginning to the end of his career; one of the few Zacatecanos who in ability, missionary zeal, and purity of life were the equals of the Span. Fernandinos. Gonzalez Rubio was his full name. G. (J. M. J.), com. de policía Sta Inés '35. iii. 291. G. (Juan), at Brancif. '28, wife Eusebia Pinto. G. (Juan), at Brancif. '30. ii. 627; maj. and admin. of Sta Cruz '34-9. iii. 346, 694-5; juez in '42. iv. 663; in '45, age 40, wife María Ana Rodriguez, both nat. of Cal., child. Ramona b. '23. Melanía '29, Francisca '30, Petra '33, Juana '35, Tomasa '38, Refugia '40, Rosa '36, Pedro '38, Gabriela '42. G. (Juan José), soldier in S.F. comp. '23-33; grantee of Pescadero, Sta Cruz, '33. iii. 678. G. (Juan Pablo), officer in Mont. custom-house '27.

Gonzalez (Leandro), juez de campo at Sta B. '34; admin. and maj. of the mission '40-3. iii. 657-8; iv. 643; his wife was Josefa Guevara, with 4 child. before '37; still at Sta B. '50. G. (Macedonio), Mex. half-breed alférez on the L. Cal. frontier from about '36; a famous Ind. fighter, who took some part with the sureños in the troubles of '37-40, being once arrested and sent to Sonoma. iii. 549, 606-7; iv. 68-9. In later years he lived in Cal., and was in S. Diego Co. '64, age over 70. G. (Manuel), settler at S. José and S.F. from 1777; alcalde of S. José '85. v. 297, 312, 350, 478; wife Gertrudis Acebedo, child. Francisco, Romualdo, Antonia, in '93. G. (Manuel), settler at Los Ang. '14. ii. 350. G. (Manuel), at Sta B. '37. iii. 657; perhaps still there in '52. G. (Manuel), executed at Mont. for murder '42. iv. 653-4, 686. G. (Mauricio), son of Rafael, appointed guarda of Mont. customs '29, but did not come from Mex. till '40. iii. 136; iv. 31; grantee of Cholam, S. Luis Ob. iv. 655; with Micheltorena in '45. iv. 511. In '77, living at Mont. with his wife, the daughter of Manuel Crespo, he gave me his *Memorias*, and a col. of *Papeles Originales*, that had belonged to his father; still living in '85. G. (Miguel), 1825, Mex. capt. of artill., comandante de armas at Mont. '26-8, a bad fellow, if we credit the Californians, often in trouble, and finally sent away in '30. His daughter, Ildefonsa G. de Herrera, was more or less a famous character at Mont. iii. 39–41; also ii. 576, 605, 608, 610–11, 614, 624, 674; iii. 15, 44, 93, 121, 437. His full name was Gonzalez de Ávila. G. (Pablo), of terna for contador '27. iii. 63. G. (Pedro), 1791, surg. in Malaspina's exped. i. 490.

Gonzalez (Rafael), 1833, Mex. admin. of customs and sub-comisario at Mont. '33–4, having been appointed in '29, but coming to Cal. with Figueroa in '33. iii. 46, 136, 237–8, 240, 376–7, 437, 672. His *Diario* is an important record of '32–3. He had been a lieut in the war of independence, and was an ignorant man of good character. In '35 he was alcalde at Mont. iii. 673, 441; also governor's sec. iii. 463; and grantee of S. Justo, ii. 678, being then 48 years old, wife Cármen Sierra, a Mex. He was arrested in the troubles of '37. iii. 513; comandante de celadores at the custom-house '37–46. iv. 339, 97, 210, 357, 377, 431, 577; v. 570; member of the junta '39–43, being also delegate to the consejo general of '46. iii. 590, 604; iv. 294–5, 360, 460; v. 45, 61; grantee of S. Miguelito in '41, being cl. in '53. iv. 656; had a Cal. claim of $26,200. Larkin reported him as a man of property and influence. He died at Mont. in '68, at the age of 82. His *Doc. Hist. Cal.* were given me by his son Mauricio; his daughter, Ana G. de Castañares, was a woman with a will. iii. 437–8. G. (Rafael), 2d alcalde at S. Juan B. '35. iii. 692. G. (Rafael), son of Raf. Gerardo, b. at Sta B. in 1797, sold. of the Sta B. comp. '16–27. ii. 223, 235, 237–8, 337, 429, 508, 536. In '29–32 he was alcalde of Sta B., and again in '35 and '45. ii. 572; iii. 78, 212, 653–4; iv. 642; admin. and maj. of S. Buen. '38–42. iii. 660–1; iv. 644–5. His wife was Antonia Guevara, and there were 3 child. before '37. In '78 he was still living at Sta B., where he gave me an interesting narrative of his early *Experiencias.* G. (Rafael G.), Mex. soldier before 1800; wife Tomasa Quinteros. G. (Ramon T.), clerk of Célis at Los Ang. '40; at Sta Inés '44. iv. 426; perhaps at S. Luis Ob. '50.

Gonzalez (Teodoro), 1825, Mex. who lived at Mont. from his arrival; licensed to hunt otters '33. iii. 374; in '36 regidor and acting alcalde during the troubles with Gov. Chico. iii. 439, 675; grantee in '36 of Rincon de la Puente and Sur Chiquito. iii. 678; being then 30 years old, wife Guadalupe Villarnel de Rico, the mother of Francisco Rico. Alcalde in '37; at Buena-vista '40; juez de paz '42–3; aux. de policía in '46. iii. 525; iv. 24, 637, 653–4, 656. He became a man of wealth and good standing in Cal.; and in '78, though his memory was failing with age, gave me some information about the *Revoluciones de Cal.* His death occurred a few years later. His sons Mariano and Alfredo were prominently connected with the Monterey and Salinas R. R., and in '85 reside in S.F. with their mother. G. (Tiburcio), at Mont. '36, age 28, nat. of Cal., wife Cruz Espinosa, child. Ramona and José. Gonzalvo (M.), 1848, passp. from Honolulu.

Goodhue, 1843, mate of the *Admittance*, died at sea on the passage home '45. Goodsell (J.), 1846, on the *Cyane*, acting commandant's clerk. Goodspeed (Galen), 1824, sailor and mate on the *Rover* '24–6. Goodwell (James F.), 1847, Co. H, N.Y.Vol. (v. 499). G. (James T.), 1847, Co. G, N.Y.Vol. Goodwin, 1847, mr of the *Eveline* from Hon., with wife. v. 578. G. (Andrew), 1847, Co. A, Morm. Bat. (v. 469). G. (Isaac), 1846, one of the Mormon col., with 6 children, his wife dying on the voyage. v. 546; nat. of Conn., and a mason who built a house for Larkin. Sent east to report to Brigham Young on Cal. prospects; interviewed in Utah '78 by Codman. *Round Trip*, 198–201. Goodyear (Andrew), 1847, nat. of Conn. and overl. immig.; at Benicia from '49; still living in '79. G. (Miles), 1847, trapper and trader at Los Ang., with a Cal. claim of $1,800 (v. 462); a nat. of Conn. who died in '49; perhaps a brother of Andrew. Goosebfh, 1809, mr of the *Coniach.* ii. 81.

Gordon, 1844, officer on H.B.M.S. *Modeste.* G. (A. J.), 1846, nat. of Mo. and overl. immig.; prob. son of Joseph; perhaps the G. at N. Helv. from Benicia '47; in Sonoma Co. from '48; in Mendocino '77. G. (Benj.), 1848, in the mines on Amer. Riv.; at S. José '50. G. (B.H.), 1846, married a daughter of Ed. Pyle; father of John M. G. of Los Gatos in '80. G. (Gilman), 1847, Co. A, Morm. Bat. (v. 469). G. (G. van), 1846, nat. of Mich.; in S. Luis Ob. '66–83. G. (Ira van), 1846, nat. of Penn. and overl. immig., prob.

with Harlan, whose daughter Rebecca he married in '41; one of Aram's men at Sta Clara; lot at S.F. '47; after several changes of residence and employment, became a farmer from '68 in S. Luis Ob., where he still lived '83. By some authorities he has been accredited to '43. iv. 393, 400. Either identical with or a brother of the preceding or following.   G. (John van), 1846, perhaps same as G., at N. Helv. May; not of '43. iv. 393, 400.   G. (John), 1845, com. of H.B.M.S. *America*. iv. 562.   G. (Jacob), 1846, overl. immig. with Young, v. 529, with family; perhaps went to Or.; perhaps one of the van G.'s.   G. (Joseph), 1846, overl. immig. ment. by Bryant; with fam.; perhaps went to Or. or back east. v. 528-9.   G. (Julian), 1844, in Sonoma dist. '44-6; age 45 in '46.   G. (Jemima), 1847, owner of S. F. lot.   G. (Nicholas), 1845, blacksmith at Mont. '45-8. iv. 587.   G. (Robert), 1846, came from Hon. on the *Elizabeth;* in '47-8 editor of the *Californian* at S.F., and judge of election. v. 650, 658; at Sac. '48-9, active in politics.

Gordon (Wm), 1841, nat. of Ohio, who became a Mex. citizen in N. Mex., where he married María Lucero, and came to Cal. in the Rowland-Workman party. iv. 277-9. In '42 came north to Sonoma, original passp. in my col.; and in '43 was grantee of Quesesosi rancho on Cache Cr., becoming the pioneer settler of Yolo Co. Here he lived till about '66, then moved to Cobb Valley, Lake Co., where he died in '76, at the age of 75. His wife died in '44, her sister being the wife of Cyrus Alexander; and in '55 G. married Elizabeth Corum. One of his daughters, Mrs Sarah Ingraham, died in Gordon Val. '68; another, Isabel, was the wife of Nathan Coombs. 'Uncle Billy' had been a trapper in his early years, and continued to be fond of the hunt in Cal.; a rough, uneducated, honest, and hospitable man. In '43-6 his place on Cache Cr. was a general rendezvous for settlers and hunters, and is oftener mentioned than any other place except Sutter's Fort and Sonoma. It was in the vicinity of the modern town of Frémont. Portrait *Yolo Co. Hist.*, 26; ment. iv. 573, 672; v. iii. 672.   Gorgonio, neoph. who killed his wife at S. Buen. '17. ii. 424.   G. (José), grantee of Purísima, Sta Clara, in '40. iii. 712. Gorgy (D.), doubtful name of a Russian owner of land near Bodega '37. ii. 638. Gorman (Geo.), 1843, at Mont.   G. (John), 1831, Irish. from Hon. with a letter from P. Short. iii. 405; joined the comp. extranjera in '32. iii. 221; got a lot in '35; in '36 at Hartnell's rancho, age 50 and single.   Gormly (Martin F.), 1847, Co. F, N.Y.Vol. (v. 499); claimant for a Marin Co. rancho. iv. 674; mr of the *Bostonian*, and killed by explosion of the *Secretary* in '54. Goss, 1847, on the *Currency Lass* from Hon.

Gould, 1848, mr of the *Mary Frances*.   G. (John C.), 1847, Co. C, Morm. Bat. (v. 469).   G. (John R.), 1846, assisted in printing the Mont. *Californian*. v. 293.   G. (Samuel), 1847, Co. C, Morm. Bat. (v. 489). Gouldin, 1847, doubtful name, Alameda Co. '55-78.   Goulet (G.), 1845, in Sutter's employ '45-6; and Geo. Goutler had a Cal. claim of $60 for shoeing horses (v. 462).   Gourville (Jean), 1836, Fr. laborer at Los Verjeles rancho, age 27. Goycoechea (Felipe), 1783, Mex. lieut and com. of the Sta B. comp. 1784-1802, being brevet capt. from 1797; habilitado gen. of Cal. in Mex. 1802-5; gov. of L. Cal. 1806-14, where he died at Loreto. A prominent and able officer. Biog. ii. 116-17; ment. i. list of auth., 396, 461-3, 464-6, 484, 501-2, 517, 521-2, 532, 537, 542, 573, 583, 588-94, 639; ii. 28, 30, 32-3, 36, 111, 154-6, 186, 188, 665, 669.

Grable (Benj.), 1841(?), nat. of Ohio; d. S. Luis Ob. '76. iv. 279; date of arrival prob. a misprint in *Cal. Christ. Adv.*, Jul. 30, '76.   Grady (Thomas), 1846, Co. C, 1st U.S. dragoons (v. 336).   Graf (Joseph), 1848, overl. immig. with wife, who settled at Nicolaus; a teamster.   Graff (Geo. J.), 1847, Co. E, N. Y. Vol. (v. 499); at S.F. '74-82.   Grafton (Ed. C.), 1845, mid. on the U.S. *Portsmouth;* acting lieut Co. C, Stockton's bat. '46-7. v. 385.   Graham, 1848, from Or. with Martin; supposed to have been killed by Ind. the same year at Murderers bar.   G. (Chas K.), 1847, mid. on the U. S. *Columbus;* maj.-gen. in war of '61-5; surveyor of port of N. Y. '79.   G. (Geo.), 1847, Co. F, N.Y.Vol. (v. 499); passp. from Hon. '48.

Graham (Isaac), 1833-5, nat. of Ky, and for many years a trapper in the

great basin and N.Mex., whence he is generally said to have come to Cal. in
'33. iii. 388, 409. I have found no details of his arrival, which was very likely
in '34 or '35. In '36 he had a distillery and drinking-place at Natividad, and
from the loafers about his place, chiefly deserting sailors, raised a comp. of
' riflemen ' to support Alvarado in his revolution, going south in that cause in
'37. See full details in iii. 454–9, 491, 524, 685. In '38 he was condemned to
8 months in the chain-gang for killing cattle on Gomez' rancho. *Mont. Arch.;*
and in '39 he and Naile tried to organize a comp. to cross the mts eastward.
In '40, with a dozen of his associates and enough other foreigners to make up
the number of 47, G. was sent to S. Blas on a charge of plotting against the
govt; but with 18 of the exiles came back the next year. iv. 2–41, 95, 116,
348. The current versions of this affair, as fully explained elsewhere, have but
a slight foundation in truth; the exiles were for the most part foreigners of
the worst class, who had come to Cal. in defiance of the laws; and while the
definite charges of conspiracy could not be proved, the arrest was only tech-
nical, and in the case of a few, an outrage, for which Gov. Alvarado was
willing that Mex. should pay damages. Statements that Alvarado broke his
promises to G., and that the prisoners were brutally treated, have no better
foundation than the absurd ravings of Farnham and the complaints of the
victims hungry for damages. After his return, G., with Majors and others,
bought the Sayante rancho near Sta Cruz, built a saw-mill, and engaged also
to some extent in tanning. His name appears constantly on Larkin's books.
He made desperate efforts to get damages from Mex. through the U. S. govt
for his exile; it is a popular tradition that he succeeded in getting $36,000,
and possibly he did in later years get a small sum, but I find no definite evidence to that effect. iv. 40–1. In '43 he offered his support and that of his
associates—without their knowledge—to Gov. Micheltorena, who declined at
first. iv. 356; but he finally went south with Sutter's force in defense of the
gov. in '44–5; iv. 472, 478, 483, 486, 507. In '45 he induced a young American woman to live with him, her mother making an effort through Consul
Larkin and the alcalde to oblige him to marry, but apparently without success; though G. claimed that she was his wife, and she so appears in the padron of '45, when G. was 46 years old. I have much of the original corresp. connected with the scandal. At this time 20 of G.'s foreign fellow-citizens signed
a petition to the prefect for his expulsion from the community, as a dissolute,
lawless, quarrelsome corruptor of the public peace and morals. I think the
woman left him in '49, about the time that some of his children by a former
marriage came to Cal. The case of Graham vs Roussillon in '46 was the 1st
tried by a jury in Cal. v. 289. After the U.S. occupation, G. continued to live
on his Sta Cruz rancho, for which he was the claimant. iv. 656; and died at
S. F. in '63 at the age of nearly 70. Two of his daughters, very respectable
people, live in Sta Cruz Co. '85; and his brother also resided in Cal. for many
years. Respecting Graham's character, much is said in my narrative of the
events of '40. But for the unmerited praise that has been so profusely accorded
him, and his own never-ending abuse of better men, it might be in doubtful
taste to dwell on the man's true character. In N. Mex. and on the plains,
where he was well known by Nidever, B. D. Wilson, Job Dye, and others, he
had the worst of reputations, amply justified by his career in Cal. At the best,
he was a loud-mouthed, unprincipled, profligate, and reckless man, whose only
good qualities seem to have been the personal bravery and prodigal hospitality of his class, with undoubted skill as a hunter, and a degree of industry.
    Graham (John), 1791, Boston boy of Malaspina's exped. who died at Mont.,
called Groem. i. 491.   G. (John), 1841, lieut on the U.S. *St Louis.*   G. (Lawrence P.), 1848, brevet major 2d U. S. drag., in com. of a dragoon battalion
from Mex. arriving at the end of Dec.; mil. com. of the southern dist in '49.
v. 522, 618.   G. (Wm), 1841, doubtful name at S. José. *Bidwell.*   Grajera
(Antonio), Mex. lieut in com. of the S. Diego comp. 1793–9; capt. from '98;
conduct far from exemplary; left Cal. Jan. 1800, and died at sea 3 days after
sailing. Biog. i. 676; ment. i. 522, 532, 538, 543, 563, 588–94, 630, 634, 653,
656, 730.   Gralbatch (Wm), 1825, Engl. sailor and cooper who landed at

Mont. ii. 609; iii. 29. In '29 he kept a shop with Geo. Allen and applied for naturalization, age 26; a memb. of the comp. extranjera in '32. iii. 221; on Larkin's books from '33. In '36 he lived at S. Isidro rancho, being then single, but married before '40. I find no later record than Oct. '41; generally called Graybatch or Grayback, but I have his autographs. Grambis (Fred.), 1847, chief musician N. Y. Vol. v. 503; d. before '82. Grams (Philip), 1847, Co. K, N.Y.Vol. (v. 499); died at Milwaukee, Wis., '80. Granados (Fran.), 1846, aux. de policía. Mont. v. 637. Grant, 1844, off. on H.B.M.S. *Modeste*. G. (B.), 1845, doubtful name of the Grigsby-Ide immig. party. iv. 579; prob. went to Or. G. (James), 1825, Engl. waterman, age 25, protestant and single; in Mont. dist. '25-9. iii. 29. G. (Thos), 1832, got a carta. iii. 408.

Graves (Franklin W.), 1846, member of the Donner party from Ill., accompanied by wife Elizabeth, 3 sons, and 6 daughters. The father, mother, and one son—Franklin W., Jr, age 5—died in the Sierra. v. 528, 530, 534, 537. Eight of the children survived. Jonathan B., age 7, and Elizabeth, Jr, died near Sutter's Fort in '47. v. 530, 534. Wm C. was, in '80-1, a blacksmith at Calistoga, and in '84 writes me from Merrimac, Plumas Co.; he also wrote for the newspapers a narrative of *Crossing the Plains in '46*. v. 530, 534, 536, 541. Eleanor married Wm McDonald in '49, and in '81 lived at Knight's Val., Sonoma, with 8 children. v. 530, 534. Mary Ann married Ed. Pyle in '47, and J. T. Clarke in '52, and in '81 lived at White River, Tulare, with 5 children. Lovina married John Cyrus in '56, and in '81 lived near Calistoga with 5 children. Nancy married R. W. Williamson in '55, and in '81 lived at Los Gatos, also with 5 children. A married daughter, also a survivor, was Mrs 'Fosdick,' q.v. G. (Hiram), 1848, at S.F. acc. to his later testimony.

Gray (Andrew F. V.), 1846, lieut on the U.S. *Congress;* com. of the force sent by Stockton to Kearny's relief at S. Pascual; served as S.'s aide in the final campaign of '47; went east overland with despatches; and testified at the Frémont court-martial in Wash. v. 328, 350, 385, 420, 456. G. (Alonzo), 1847, Co. D, N.Y.Vol. (v. 499). G. (E.), 1847, mr of the *Antonita*. v. 576. G. (E. L.), 1846, from Hon. on the *Euphemia;* perhaps same as preceding. G. (G. R.), 1841, lieut on the U.S. *St Louis.* G. (G.L.), 1847, at Hon. from Cal. twice, 1st on the *Currency Lass,* 2d on the *Gen. Kearny.* G. (James A.), 1847, Co. D, N.Y.Vol. (v. 499); nat. of Penn.; and memb. of 1st Cal. legisl. '49-50; resid. at Salinas City '82. G. (John B.), 1847, came from Va with letters from Fauntleroy and Minor to Larkin; at N.Helv. '48, interested in mines. G. (L. C.), 1847, trader on the coast '47-8 from Honolulu on the *Gen. Kearny, Louise,* and *Undine;* owner of S.F. lot. v. 679; at Benicia '49-50, and perhaps the S. C. Gray whose lecture in Benicia is published in the *Solano Co. Hist.*, 146; still living, I think, in '85. G. (Robt), 1788, mr of the *Washington,* sighting the Cal. coast on his way north. i. 445, 499; see *Hist. N. W. Coast.* G. (Wm), 1837, lumberman and militiaman at Sonoma. G. (Wm D.), 1847, Co. K, N.Y.Vol. (v. 499).

Grayson (Andrew J.), 1846, nat. of La, and overl. immig.—being at the start in com. of a small party—with wife and child, living for a time in the Upper Sac. Val. v. 528. Active in raising men for the Cal. Bat., in which he ranked as lieut; but remained in the north, and took part in the campaign against Sanchez. v. 359, 361, 383. Mrs G. seems to have remained at Sonoma, where she is named as a witness in Jan. '47. In '47-8 G. obtained lots at Benicia and S.F., where he kept a little stationery shop in the City Hotel. v. 672, 680; also acting as Capt. Folsom's agent at Corte Madera, Marin Co., and soon founding—on paper—the town of Graysonville on the S. Joaq. Riv. In these days, though a gambler and associate of Lippincott, McDougal, and other like characters, he was regarded as a man of good abilities and character. In '50 he settled at S. José and gave his attention to the study of ornithology, in which branch, and as an artist, he became widely known to scientific men in all parts of the world. In '57 he went with his wife to Mex., and died at Mazatlan in '69 at the age of 50. His descrip. and paintings of Pac. coast birds have as yet, unfortunately, remained unpublished. His widow returned to Cal., married Dr G. B. Crane, and was still living at St Helena in '77, as she is, I think, in '85.   G. (Ned), 1846, at S. José '54.   *Annals of S.F.*, 822; perhaps the preceding or his son.

Green (Alfred A.), 1847, Co. B, N.Y.Vol. v. 513, 610; a nat. of New Bruns-wick, who after a brief experience in the mines became a somewhat promi-nent lawyer at S.F., being at one time memb. of the legislature, and well known in connection with the pueblo land question, Santillan claim, and vigi-lance committee. In '78 he gave me a narrative of the *Adventures of a '47er*, containing many interesting details of early S.F. annals; still living in S.F. '82, and I think in '85. There is some confusion in the records between him and H.A. Green, at Sonoma in '47-8.   G. (Alonzo), 1848 (?), doubtful date of a Sonora settler.   G. (Cambridge), 1832, one of Young's trappers, who killed a man named Anderson, and is said to have been imprisoned at Los Ang.; also had a brother in the same party. iii. 388.   G. (Daniel S. or C.), 1846, surgeon on the U. S. *Dale;* in confed. service '61-5.   G. (Ephraim), 1847, Co. B, Morm. Bat. (v. 469); at Sutter's and in the mines '48.   G. (Francis), 1836, Amer. age 40, in a Los Ang. list; perhaps at Sta Cruz '39.   G. (Geo. W.), 1829, on the *Brookline.* iii. 138-9; living in Mass. '72.   G. (Harry), 1848, named by Glover as a Mormon who went to Utah '49.   G. (Henry A.), 1844 (?), a lumberman and builder—possibly the G. at Sta Cruz '39—named in various records of '44-6 at Mont. and Sta Cruz. iv. 455; Cal. claim of $76 (v. 462). In '47 he was at Sonoma, being a member of the town council, v. 668, and employed in preparing material, under a contract with Larkin, for houses which were erected at Benicia in '48. v. 671-3. There was a Mrs G., perhaps his wife, at Sonoma in '47.   G. (H.F.A.), 1848, at Mont., acc. to consulate arch.   G. (Hugh W.), 1847, purser on the U. S. *Independence.* G. (Jacob), 1846, Swiss trapper at N. Helv. '46-7; Cal. claim $25 (v. 462); ment. by Ward in '48.   G. (J.L.), 1848, owner of a S.F. lot.   G. (James), 1847, doubtful member of N.Y.Vol. (v. 499); at S.F. '74.   G. (James), 1831, perhaps of Young's party. iii. 388.   G. (James M.), 1845, nat. of Conn., who came on a whaler. iv. 587; long a resid. of Hon., and mr of vessels running to Cal.; memb. of firm C. A. Williams & Co.; also ship-chandler at S.F.; died in Stockton insane asylum '68. Newspapers.   G. (John), 1847, Co. C, Morm. Bat. (v. 469).   G. (John D.), 1847, resid. at Sta Cruz, acc. to the county hist.   G. (Judson), 1846, overl. immig. with Steph. Cooper.   G. (Lewis), 1846 (?), at Los Ang. '59-76.   G. (Michael), 1846, Co. C, 1st U.S. .dragoons (v. 388).   G. (T.C.), 1847, at N. Helv.

Green (Talbot H.), 1841, nat. of Penn., and overl. immig. of the Bartleson party. iv. 268, 270, 275, 279. Early in '42 he entered Larkin's service at Mont. as clerk; and in May '43 made a contract to carry on L.'s business for one year for $400 and 5 per cent of the profits. This arrangement was contin-ued to the end of '45, and in Jan. '46 G. made a contract for 3 years to take the business, with $10,000 worth of goods, for one third of the profits. v. 55-6. I have much of his business corresp. In '44 he got a renewal of his pass-port, possibly naturalization; in '46 served on the 1st jury, v. 289, and was grantee of land near Mont. v. 637; and in '46-7 was collector of the port, having also a Cal. claim of $10,855, and obtaining a lot at S.F. v. 289, 433, 467, 570, 572. He made a trip to Mazatlan, and contributed items for the *Californian.* In '48 visited the mines. From Jan. '49 he was a member of the S.F. firm of Mellus & Howard, a prosperous and popular man of business, mem-ber of the town council, and taking an active part in political affairs. He married the widow Montgomery, of the Stevens immig. party of '44, by whom he had a son, in '85 state librarian at Sac., his mother, now Mrs Wallis, being a resident of Mayfield. In '51 Green, being then a prominent candidate for mayor, was recognized and denounced as Paul Geddes of Penn., a default-ing bank clerk, who had left a wife and children in the east. There is no agreement about the circumstances of the discovery. The charge proved true, but G. protested his innocence, and went east via Panamá for the avowed purpose of clearing his reputation, being escorted to the boat by a large com-pany of prominent citizens. There are several confused versions of his later life. I have his letter to Larkin in '53, in which he expresses shame and penitence for the deception he had practised; says he has lost $3,200 from his trunk, and is 'penniless and destitute, with spirits broken and energy gone;' begs L., 'for God's sake,' to send him his share of the proceeds of the Cal. claims and other debts; confesses that he has deceived Thompson; but intends to buy a small farm in Tenn. Some day he will send a full history of his life. In '54 he visited Cal. and was seen by Wm F. White—whose *Grey's Picture of Pion. Times*, 124-31, contains a good account of G.'s life—and in '55 he writes to Larkin from N.Y. that he had settled with Mr H. (Howard ?); that Mr B. (Brannan) had settled the Penn. affair; and that he is about to start for Tenn. He is understood to have rejoined his 1st wife and to be still living in '85. In the *S. J. Pion.* of Apr. 21, '77, it is stated that G. had been for some time asst sec. of the U.S. senate, and that he visited Cal. in '76. Lieut Maddox accused Green of dishonorable conduct in '46-7, and there are some slight indications that his Penn. defalcation was not his only transgression; but his Cal. record, as a whole, was excellent.

Green (Theodore P.), 1846, lieut on the U.S. *Congress*. G. (Wm), 1840, one of the S. Blas exiles, arrested in the south. iv. 14, 18. G. (Wm G), 1847, Co. C, N.Y.Vol. (v. 499); d. S. Rafael '71. Greenman (J. D.), 1848, passp. from Honolulu. Greenock, 1846, ment. by Revere as the frontier settler on a journey from Napa Val. to Clear Lake. I think there may be some connection between this name and 'Guenoc,' that of a Lake Co. rancho granted in '45 to Geo. 'Rock.' Guenoc is still the name in use.

Greenwood (Caleb), 1844, trapper and mountaineer, who, with his two sons, Britain and John, by a Crow wife, guided the Stevens immig. party across the plains; and performed like service for other parties in '45-6, being sent to Ft Hall to divert the Or. immig. to Cal. They served in Sutter's force '45; Bryant met the old man in Lake Co. '46, when he claimed to be 83 years old; Britain was with the 2d Donner relief of '47, and lived in Mendocino Co. '84; S. S. Greenwood, apparently one of the 3, is said to have been a nat. of Nova Scotia, to have come with Frémont, and to have been justice of the peace and assessor at Sac., where he died in '78. John served in Co. E, Cal. Bat. (v. 358), and had a trading-post in Greenwood Val. '48. It is impossible to distinguish between the 3, or to locate any one of them at any definite time. iv. 445, 453-4, 486, 539, 575, 579.

Gregory (John), 1844, Engl. in Cal. '44-6; came back in '55; in Sonoma Co. '61-80 with wife and 3 child. *Son. Co. Hist.*, 691. G. (Robert), 1846, Co. K, 1st U.S. drag., killed at S. Pascual. v. 346. G. (Thos), 1848, at S. F. from Honolulu. Gregson (James), 1845, Engl. who came to Phil. as a boy, and overl. to Cal. in the Grigsby-Ide party, with his wife, Elizabeth Marshall, and her two brothers, mother, and sister. v. 579, 587. In '45-8 he worked as a blacksmith for Sutter, serving in the Sac. garrison during the Bear revolt. v. 79; and later in Co. B, Cal. Bat. (v. 358), being perhaps at the Natividad fight, and taking part in the southern campaign of '46-7. Returning, he resumed work for Sutter, got a lot at S.F. v. 685, and was at work at the famous mill when gold was discovered. Mrs G. is mentioned in '47 as passenger on the 1st steamboat to Sac. v. 579. In '50-80 he lived in Green Val., Sonoma Co., with 9 children. His daughter, Annie, b. Sept. 3, '46, married Robert Reid of S. Luis Ob.; another, Mary Ellen, b. '48, married McChristian. Prob. still alive in '85. I have a MS. *Statement* from him. Portrait in *Son. Co. Hist.*, 509. G. (Wm), 1834, Amer., age 29, in Spear's service at Mont. Gremell, 1848, in list of letters, S.F. Grems, 1821, mr of the *Sigloe* (?), at Sta B. ii. 440. Grey (Wm), 1837, in S. F. militia. G. (Louisa C.), 1848, wife of W.L.G., d. Stockton '79, age 31; named as 1st Amer. child born in Sonoma.

Grien (Carl), 1844, blacksmith at Mont. Griffin, 1847, from Honolulu on the *Euphemia;* in '48 mr of the *Ariel.* v. 576. G. (John S.), 1846, asst surg. U. S. A. from '40, prob. nat. of Ky, who came with Kearny from N. Mex., being present in the fights of S. Pascual, S. Gabriel, and the Mesa. v. 336-7, 385. His *Journal* of '46-7 is one of the best authorities extant, and is supplemented by his original *Doc. Hist. Cal.* in my collection. He was stationed at S.D. and Los Ang. in charge of the mil. hospital; visited the mines

on leave of absence in '49, became interested with Vallejo and Frisbie in Napa
lands, and was stationed at Benicia till '52, when he was transferred to the
south; went east in '53, and in '54 resigned and settled at Los Ang., where he
has since resided and practiced medicine down to '85.   G. (M.), 1847, at S.
F. from Honolulu.   G. (Peter K.), 1844, Amer. at Mont., getting a pass for
a year.   G. (Sam. P.), 1846, mid. on the U.S. *Savannah;* serving in garrison
at S. José, v. 378, where he applied for land.

   Griffith (Calvin C.), 1845, nat. of N.C., who came with his parents in the
Grigsby-Ide party. iv. 579, 587. He served with the Bears, v. 110, and in the
Cal. Bat. (v. 358), later becoming a miner and farmer. In '81 he lived at Rutherford, Napa Co., with his wife, Lydia Lensibaugh, mar. in '55, and 7 children.
G. (F.G.), 1846, in Cal. Bat., and named in a list of Bears; perhaps a brother
of Calvin.   G. (James A.), 1845, overl. immig. of Grigsby-Ide party, with
wife, Elizabeth R., and one or more sons. Bonds given by Yount Nov. 19th.
iv. 579, 587. The family settled in Napa Val.; Cal. claim of $1,000 for repair-
ing barracks (v. 462); died in Sonoma '68.   G. (Jonathan), 1846, one of the
Morm. Col. with wife and 2 children. v. 546; lot at S.F. '47; Mrs G. and son
at Mont. '48. G. did not go to Utah.   G. (Thomas), 1846, doubtful name of
a Bear; possibly a son of James A.   G. (Joseph), doubtful name of a trapper
in S. Joaq. Val. in very early times. *Mont. Co. Hist.*, 29.

   Grigsby (Franklin F.), 1845, Co. E, Cal. Bat. '46–7 (v. 358); prob. a son
of John and immig. of '45.   G. (Granville W.), 1845, ditto.   G. (John), 1845,
nat. of Tenn., came to Cal. from Mo. in the immig. party that bears his name,
with his family. iv. 578–81, 587. He was one of the most active in fomenting the
Bear revolt of '46; was for a few hours leader at Sonoma on June 14th; com. the
guard that took the prisoners to N. Helv.; and after the U. S. occup. was in
com. of the Sonoma garrison, being capt. of Co. B, Cal. Bat. v. 110, 114–19,
164, 168, 175, 184, 242–3, 296, 298. After the reorganization of the battalion
in Nov. Capt. G. com. Co. E, in the southern campaign. v. 358–61. He had a
Cal. claim (v. 462); and in '47 is mentioned in connection with political affairs
at Sonoma. v. 433, 609. He settled in Napa, where he continued to live till
about '72, when he went to Texas, and died in Mo. '76, at the age of 70. There
is a strange lack of information about him and his family after '46. Two of
the name, perhaps his sons, have been mentioned; his daughter was the wife
of Wm Edgington; and he had a brother Jesse in Cal. I have copies of a small
col. of *Grigsby Papers* furnished by the Sonoma Pion. Soc.   Grijalva (Juan
Pablo), 1776, Mex. sergt with Anza's exped.; served at S.F. '76–86; alf. of S.
Diego comp. '86–96; retired as lieut '96–1806, the date of his death. His
daughters married Ant. Yorba and Pedro Peralta. Biog. ii. 104; ment. i. 258,
262–7, 286–7, 296–7, 359, 362, 452, 472–3, 547, 553, 647, 652–3, 663; ii. 57.
G. (Luciano), at Los Ang. in '33.

   Grimes (Eliab), 1838, nat. of Mass.; lieut on a privateer in the war of
1812; later for 20 years a well-known merchant of Honolulu, of firm E. & H.
Grimes. iv. 141. In '38 he visited Cal. on the *Rasselas*, of which he was
owner, and went to Boston. iv. 105, 117, 119. His next visit was on the schr
California in '42, at which time he selected a rancho in the Sac. Val., which,
after he had returned from a trip to Hon. on the *Fama*, was granted to him
in '44. iv. 672. From this time Capt. G. may be regarded as a permanent resid.
of S.F., though he made another trip to Hon. on the *Don Quixote* in '47. He
had a lot and house, was a well-known trader, and was a memb. of the legisl.
council in '47. v. 433, 653, 678, 680. G. & Sinclair had a Cal. claim for horses
(v. 462). For some years he made 'Kent Hall' his home while in town, and
kept there a case of extra fine liquors, which nothing would induce the old
man to open for convivial purposes but a story that could arouse his interest;
hence there was a continual rivalry in yarn-spinning among the younger merchants. As a boat was going up the Sac., after the gold excitement, the occu-
pants were asked who was left at S.F., and 'nobody but old Grimes' was the
reply; but 'old Grimes' died in Oct. '48, at the age of 69.   G. (Hiram), 1847,
nephew and partner of Eliab at Honolulu; partner of Wm. H. Davis in '45–
6; came to Cal. in Feb. '47 on the *Don Quixote;* and again on the *Euphemia*

in July with his wife and child. Often named in S.F. annals of '48-9; claimant for several ranchos. iv. 672-3; still in Cal. '54.   G. (A. J. and B.), 1847-8, doubtful mention; prob. confounded with the preceding.

Grimshaw (Wm Robinson), 1848, nat. of N.Y. city, b. in 1826 of Engl. parents; sailor on the *Isaac Walton*, and after arrival on the tender *Anita*, U.S.N.; also mr of the launch *Susanita*, on the trip up the Sac. v. 580. He worked as book-keeper for Brannan & Co. at Sac. in '48-9; and from Nov. '49 was partner of Wm Daylor in a store or Ind. trading-post on the Cosumnes. Daylor having died in '50, G. married his widow in '51, and continued to reside on the rancho, where in '72 he wrote for me his *Narrative*. This is not only an interesting sketch of his own life and adventures, but one of the best accounts extant of the events of '48-50 in the Sac. region. Still living in '80, with 7 children, Wm R., Jr, Thos W., Emma (Mrs W. D. Lawton of S.F.), George, Francis, Frederick, and Walter.   Grinnell, 1848, from Hon. on the *Starling*.   G. (Chas C.), 1847, Co. G, N. Y. Vol. (v. 499); d. before '82. Griswold (Theodore), 1847, at N.Helv.; lot at S.F.; named in '48.

Groem, 1791, see 'Graham.' i. 491.   Groh (Jacob), 1847, Co. F, 3d artill. (v. 518).   Grogan (Alex.), 1848, from Valparaíso with letter from Atherton; clerk for C. L. Ross at S.F. '48-9; still in S.F. after '80.   Grove (Wm), 1848, lieut of S.F. guards.   Grovecot, 1846, perhaps in Sta Clara.   Grover (Sam.), 1816, Mass. sailor bapt. at S. Cárlos. ii. 276-7.   Grow (Wm), 1847, sergt Co. H, N.Y.Vol. v. 504; at Yreka '78; at Deadwood, Dakota, '83.   Guadalupe (José M.), soldier at S. Miguel 1797. i. 560.   Guat (Santiago), 1836, juez de de campo at Mont. iii. 678; prob. James 'Watt.'   Guchapa, Ind. chief at S. Miguel 1804. ii. 150.

Guerra (Antonio María), son of José de la G. y N., b. '25; reg. and sec. of ayunt. '49; memb. of the Cal. senate in '53, several times mayor of Sta. B., holding other local offices; in the war of '61-5 a capt. of Cal. volunteers serving in Ariz. He is said to have been one of the ablest of the family; but in later years the loss of his palate and of his eyesight obliged him to lead a life of retirement. He never married, and died at Sta B. in '81 at the age of 56. G. (Bautista), 1831, from N. Mex. with Wolfskill. iii. 387.   G. (Francisco), son of José de la G. y N., b. '18; acc. to the padron of '32 there were two Franciscos; from '43 member of the junta, elector at Sta B. '45, taking a somewhat prominent part in political and mil. affairs in '46-7, and involved in the imaginary Sta B. revolt of '48. iv. 361, 522, 540; v. 38-9, 404, 586. He took no pains to conceal his hostility to Amer., but after the change of flag was mayor of Sta B. for several years from '51. He inherited a rancho, but died poor in '78. His 1st wife was María Asuncion Sepúlveda, by whom he had Francisco, Jr (county assessor of Sta B. in '82), and María Antonia; the 2d wife was Concepcion Sepúlveda, sister of the 1st, and her children were Juan, Osbaldo, José, Hércules, Pablo, Aníbal, Anita (Mrs F. W. Thompson), Erlinda, Rosa, and Diana. There were also two natural children legitimated. G. (Joaquin), son of G. y N., b. '22; once sheriff; no family; d. before '70.

Guerra (José Antonio), son of G. y N., b. 1805; cadet in the Sta B. comp. '18-28. ii. 572, 576; accomp. his father to Mex. '19; síndico '29 and alcalde '33. ii. 572; iii. 654; elector in '34. From '35 a memb. of the dip., taking a prominent part in support of Alvarado's govt in '36-7. iii. 291, 426, 454-5, 461, 506; in '37-40 capt. of the port of Sta B., being made capt. by Vallejo, and at times acting as mil. com. iii. 583, 601-2, 651, 654; iv. 98; vocal of the dip., and grantee of Los Álamos '39. iii. 585, 655. Prop. for sub-prefect '41. iv. 641; admin. at Purísima '41-2. iv. 647-8; where there were serious charges against him by P. Abella and others. In '43 he was capt. of the port, and in '44 receptor. iv. 431-2, 640, 642; and in '44-6 a memb. of the assembly, being in '45 leader in an outbreak at Sta B. iv. 410, 497-8, 541, 559; v. 37-8, 142, 264, 280, 321-2. In '48 took part in the affair of the lost cannon at Sta B. v. 588. In later years he was several times sheriff of S. Luis Ob., holding that office—or his son—in '69. He had the whim of signing his name José Noriega, as he had no right to do. Don José Antonio's record was, in several respects, not of the best, though there is nothing very bad to be said of him.

His wife was María Concepcion Ortega, and his children—6 of them born before '40—were José Ant. J., Ramon (sheriff of S. Luis Ob.), Alejandro, Guillermo, Dolores, Catarina, Sola (?), Cristina, and Juana.   G. (Juan J.), son of G. y N., b. about 1810, educ. in England; later at the Mont. school under Hartnell and P. Short; died in '33, unmarried; ment. i. 432. I have a long letter, in good English, written by him in '28 from Stonyhurst College, Engl. G. (Máximo), said to have been exiled in '29, and again in '39. iii. 78, 84-5, 580.   G. (Miguel), son of G. y N., b. '23, wife Trinidad Ortega, child. Gaspar, Ulpiano, Leon, María (wife of Alex. S. Taylor), Josefa, Olimpia, Joaquina, and Paulina. Died at Sta B. in '78.

Guerra (Pablo), son of G. y N., b. '19, educated in Hartnell's school at Mont., where he is ment. in the padron of '36. His baptismal name was Pablo Andrés Antonio María Saturnino; and in '40 he is called Pablo Gaspar. From '38 he was vista, and from '42 contador and acting administrator of the Mont. custom-house. iii. 598; iv. 97, 309, 339, 353, 357, 364, 377, 431, 556, 570, 590; in '44 grantee of Nicasio rancho. iv. 672; in '45 elector de partido. iv. 515, 540, 651. In '46 Don Pablo was active against the Amer., trying to reconcile the hostile factions of his people, and favoring an Engl. protectorate. v. 43-4, 61, 68-9. On the raising of the U. S. flag he went south; served as Castro's commissioner to Stockton. v. 235, 268-9; and after Castro's departure returned to Mont., where he was arrested in Nov. on the outbreak of Flores' revolt, and kept a prisoner till Feb. '47. v. 363. He was alcalde of Sta B. in '47, and was suspected of complicity in a revolutionary movement in '48. v. 631, 586. His next public service was as memb. of the constit. convention in '49; and subsequently he was state senator for several terms, acting lieut-gov., U.S. marshal, and district judge from '64 to within a short time before his death, in '74. Don Pablo was by far the most prominent of the Guerra family, except his father; a man of good ability and education; of gentlemanly manners, though somewhat haughty and overbearing; a good speaker in Spanish and English; and one whose family name gave him an influence in the south greater than he could otherwise have acquired. It has been customary to eulogize him far beyond his merits; he was a politician of not the best type, trimming his sails adroitly to catch the breeze of popularity, and changing somewhat abruptly from secessionist to union man in the race for office; yet his record in office seems always to have been an honorable one. In private life also he is reported to have been liberal and honest, though health and property were largely sacrificed to his fondness for brandy and cards. He married Josefa Moreno in '47 at S. Cárlos; his children were Francisca (Mrs Dibblee), Delfina, Ernina, Paulina, and a son whose name I do not find.

Guerra y Noriega (José de la), 1801, nat. of Spain, b. Mar. 6, 1779, son of Juan José de la G. (died 1820) and María Teresa de Noriega (died 1815), both, and especially the mother, of old and distinguished Span. families. In boyhood he wished to be a friar, a freak that caused his parents much sorrow; but soon he went to Mex. to be a clerk in the store of his uncle, Pedro Noriega. In 1793 he left the store—much to the displeasure of Don Pedro, who afterwards relented and gave him much aid—and became asst in the office of Habilitado gen. Cárcaba, by whose influence he was enrolled as cadet in the army and attached to the S. Diego comp. Respecting this and most other parts of his life I have more original corresp. than I have room to utilize. In 1800 he was promoted to alférez of the Mont. comp., and came to Cal. on the *Concepcion* in Aug. 1801. At Mont. he was habilitado, and acting com. much of the time, in 1802-6, being mentioned in con. with many minor affairs. ii. 50, 78, 132-3, 135, 140, 150, 153, 155; having in 1804, with permission of the king, married Antonia, daughter of Raimundo Carrillo, with the condition that she and her children should not be entitled to montepio unless he were killed in battle. In 1806 he was promoted to lieut of the Sta B. comp., and sent to S. Diego as habilitado in 1806-9, being knocked down in a quarrel with Lieut Ruiz, which greatly alarmed his friends as likely to interfere with his rapid promotion. ii. 85, 99-100, 117, 540. From 1808 he received large consignments of goods from his uncle Pedro in Mex., the sale of which greatly improved his financial condition. ii. 186. In 1810 he was sent to Mex. as habilitado gen. of the Cals, but being arrested by insurgents at S. Blas, was unable to reach the capital, and returned to Cal. in '11, taking his position at Sta B., and continuing his commercial operations, though going to S. Diego again as habilitado in '13-15. ii. 98, 188-9, 197-8, 341, 419-21. From '15 he was com. at Sta B., taking part in the arrest of foreign smugglers, in defensive operations against Bouchard, having a quarrel with P. Señan, and being promoted to Capt. in '18. ii. 222-5, 235-42, 275, 284-5, 317, 332, 361, 382, 405, 416, 424. In '19 he was sent again to Mex. as repres. of the Cal. companies to obtain supplies, and prob. with a hope of getting an appointment as gov., returning in '20 after accomplishing very little, though all that was possible. ii. 260-2, 265, 354, 422. He was busied, besides his official duties, in '21-2 in obtaining ranchos, quarrelling with the friars on the subject, and getting a grant of Conejo in '22. ii. 441, 566, 569-70, 580. In '22 he was a candidate for gov., and but for his Span. birth and Canónigo Fernandez' consequent opposition, would have been chosen; being also favored by the friars for congressman. ii. 451, 453-4, 465-8. There is no truth in the statement of Wilkes, *U.S. Explor. Exped.*, v. 173, on this matter, and but little in that of Petit-Thouars, *Voy.*, ii. 90; though his disappointment may have had an influence on Don José's later policy between Mexicans and natives. Mention in '23-5, including his acts in suppressing the Ind. revolt of '24. ii. 495, 510, 530, 533, 536-7, 561, 576; iii. 27. He was elected dip. to congress in '27, and against the advice of many went to Mex. in '28, but was not given his seat, returned in '29, and was for some time, as a Span., nominally suspended from his command. ii. 570-1, 574-5, 676; iii. 33-4, 51-2, 61, 127; iv. 343. In '29-30 he bought a schr, perhaps had another built, and bought the cargo of a wrecked vessel. iii. 140, 146. He did not join the movement against Victoria in '31. iii. 205, 210; controlled the policy of Cárlos Carrillo in congress. iii. 214; and in all these years acted as a kind of treasurer and confidential adviser of the friars—síndico apostólico; accused in '34 of being engaged in a conspiracy against the govt. iii. 250, 257-8. In the sectional troubles of '36-8 Capt. G. was a firm supporter of Alvarado's cause, though personally a friend of Carrillo. Alvarado wished to make him com. gen., and did grant him the S. Julian or Nacional rancho. iii. 436, 492, 510, 533, 550, 582, 650-1. In '39 he made vain attempts to collect his back pay, being still com. at Sta B. iii. 584, 651; and having to his credit, including extra allowances, 51 years, 9 months, and 1 day of mil. service on May 10th. In '40 he asked for retirement because he could not get the $12,000 due him, nor the promotion to which he was entitled, and because of his ailments and age of 62. He finally retired from the mil. service on April 1, '42. Ment. in '40-2. iii. 655; iv. 199, 632, 640-1; ment. '44-6. iv. 403, 408, 530; v. 282. Though not friendly to the U. S., he kept quiet for the most part, and did not indulge in any offensive partisanship. In later years he was claimant for several ranchos. iv. 643, 655-6; living quietly at Sta B., and being a man of great wealth, most of which his sons managed to squander even before their father's death. He died in '58, leaving over 100 direct descendants. None of the pioneers here registered exerted for so long a period so wide and good an influence as Capt. de la Guerra. He was a man of excellent character and conduct throughout his career, though no great or brilliant achievements can be placed to his credit, though he had the advantage of rich and influential friends from the first, and though his Span. birth prevented his reaching the highest rank; yet his honest and efficient performance of each duty, his well-balanced judgment, his dignified conservatism, command admiration. At Sta B. he was known as the patriarch, to whom the people were wont to apply as a matter of course to settle their controversies; and he was famous for his charities. No man in Cal. ever came so near, by peaceful, legitimate means, absolute control of his district. He did not purchase popularity at the cost of independence, for many were his controversies, even with the friars, though their life-long friend and a devout churchman. The *Guerra, Doc. Hist. Cal.*, copies of which I was permitted to make by the kindness of Mr Dibblee, executor of the estate, are the most extensive and valuable family archives in Cal. except those of Vallejo. In person, Don José was short and stout, with a flat nose and an ugly face. His intimate friends in their letters were fond of applying nicknames. Gen. Cárcaba and the leading friars used such endearing epithets as *corcobado*, *chato maldito*, *chato flojo*, etc. On account of pride in his wife's family he had a fondness for her name, and was as often called Capt. Noriega as by his proper name; in the case of his sons this became ridiculous affectation. His wife, María Antonia Carrillo, died in '43. His 5 sons have been named in this list, being for the most part prominent citizens of good enough abilities and character, yet hardly what a union of the two best families of Cal. should have produced. The daughters, noted for beauty and intelligence, were 4, all of whom eventually married foreigners. Teresa de Jesus, b. 1809, married W. E. P. Hartnell, and still lives in '85, having furnished for my use valuable documents of the family archives and a *Narrative* of personal recollections. María de las Angustias, b. 1815, married Manuel Jimeno Casarin, and later Dr J. D. Ord; and she also is living in '85, her *Ocurrencias* being one of the best personal narratives in my collection. Ana María, b. '20, married Alfred Robinson and died in '55. María Antonia, b. '27, married Cesario Lataillade, and later Gaspar Oreña, a Span. with whom she still lives at Sta B. in '85.

Guerrero y Palomares (Francisco), 1834, Mex. who came from Tepic, I think, in the H. & P. colony, at the age of 23. iii. 263; but possibly in '28, as per Soc. Cal. Pion. rolls and Lancey. He perhaps obtained a S.F. mission lot in '36; was elector '37, '39. iii. 705, 590; receptor and admin. of customs from '39 to '44. iii. 700; iv. 98, 375, 431, 483, 670; in '39–41 juez de paz and alcalde. iii. 705–6; iv. 247, 665; grantee of several town lots and the rancho de los Putos. iv. 669, 673, 676, 682. In '42 he was 31 years old, wife Josefa de Haro, age 17, and one child; in '44 grantee of Corral de Tierra rancho; in '45–6 sub-prefect at S.F., being often mentioned in local annals of the north. iv. 667; v. 17, 129, 239, 241, 295, 455, 644, 648; in '49 again sub-prefect. He continued to reside at the mission, where in '51 he was murdered, and where his widow still lived in '80. A street in S.F. bears his name. Don Francisco seems to have been a kind-hearted, genial man, of much intelligence, and good character.   G. (José M.), at Los Ang. '46.   G. (José Vicente), ditto; síndico '41; 2d alcalde '48. v. 626.   G. (Joaquin), soldier killed on the Col. 1781. i. 363.   G. (Matias), teacher at Mont. about '15. ii. 427; sec. at S. José '24. ii. 605.   G. (Pedro), ment. in '29–31. iii. 68–9, 208.   Guescote (Fran.), armero of S.F. comp. '42; perhaps 'Westcot.'   Guest (John), 1846, passed mid. on U.S. *Congress*, and act. lieut on the *Warren;* capt. in Stockton's bat. v. 350, 386; commodore in '72; d. '79, in com. of Portsmouth navy-yard.   Gueval (P.), 1848, passp. from Hon.   Guevara (Antonio), in revolt at Sta B.; sent to Mex. '29–30. iii. 78, 85.   G. (Canuto), at Sta B. before '37; wife Rafaela Lugo, 3 children.

Guibal (Eugene), 1847, Co. I, N.Y.Vol. (v. 499); in S. Joaquin '71–5; d. at Gilroy '83.   Guilcost (Wm), 1826, mr of the *María Teresa.* iii. 148. Guild (H.M.), 1847, Co. B, N.Y.Vol. (v. 499); carpenter at Mont. '48.   Guile (Wm), 1847, musician Co. K, N.Y.Vol. (v. 499).   Guillen (Antonio), guard at S. Diego 1803. ii. 13.   G. (Isidoro), son of Eulalia Perez de G., sergt of Sta B. comp., made alf. in '39. iii. 583, 650; juez de paz at S. José '41–3. iv. 684–6.   Guillon (Chas F.B.), 1847, asst surg. on the U.S. *Columbus.*   Guirado (Bernardino), trader at Los Ang. from '39; supervisor in '58–9.   G. (Rafael), 1833, Mex. trader from Sonora, owner and sup. of the *Leonidas*, who settled at Los Ang., age 32; in '35–6 regidor. iii. 283, 635–6; in '39 clerk at S. Gabriel. iii. 645; owner of S.F. lot in '47. v. 684; coroner in '52; died at Los Ang. in '72.

Gulnac (Wm), 1833, nat. of N.Y., who had lived long in L. Cal., and who came on the *Volunteer*, via Honolulu, with his family, settling at S. José. iii. 400; iv. 86, 117. He was naturalized in '34; in '38 owner of S. F. land, and employed to survey S. José town lands. iii. 705, 730; in '39 regidor, and possibly arrested in '40. iii. 731; iv. 17, 120. In the padron of '41, age 40, wife Isabel Ceseña, child. José Ramon b. '26, Juan Pánfilo '31, Cárlos María '33,

Susana '34, Isabel '36, and Luisa '38. In '44–5 he joined Sutter's army, somewhat reluctantly, and was grantee of the French Camp rancho, sold to Weber. iv. 462, 486, 671, 674; signed the S. José call to foreigners in '45. iv. 599; on the 1st jury '48; and died in '51. Two of the sons, Cárlos and Juan, served with Fauntleroy's dragoons in '46 (v. 232, 247); and another, Pedro, is named in '43. Gunn, see 'Gann.'

Gutche (Valentin), 1848, in Sutter's employ. Guthrie, 1845, apparently one of Frémont's men. iv. 583. G. (Alfred), 1847, Co. G, N.Y.Vol. (v. 499); doubtful; at S.F. '74. G. (Dexter), 1846, overl. immig. from Ill., who lived in Napa Val. till his death by suicide in '81. G. (R.), 1846, one of Fauntleroy's dragoons. v. 332, 347. G. (Wm), 1847, Co. H, N.Y.Vol. (v. 499); at Coulterville '82.

Gutierrez, carpenter at S. Juan Cap. 1797. i. 658. G. (Cirilo), at S. Juan Cap. '46, age 51, wife Ana M. Romero, child Pablo, b. '38. G. (Fran.), sergt Catalan vol. 1796. i. 540. G. (Fran.), 1825, Span. prob. from the *Asia*, iii. 27. G. (Joaquin), soldier at Mont. '36, age 20; juez aux. Mont. dist '42. iv. 653; cl. for Potrero de S. Cárlos. '52. iii. 678. G. (José M.), Mex. at Brancif. '45, age 40, wife Guadalupe. G. (José de Jesus María), 1833, Mex. friar of the Zacatecanos, who served at Solano, S.F., and S. Antonio till '45, after which I find no record of him; prob. left Cal. iv. 680–1; iii. 318, 322, 353–4, 392, 399, 553, 660, 686–8, 713, 719. G. (Juan), 1842, sub-lieut of the batallon fijo '42–5. iv. 289. G. (Manuel), Span. who came to Cal. before 1790; on the Dominguez rancho, Los Ang. dist. from 1811. ii. 350, 353, 386; ment. '19. ii. 292; alcalde of Los Ang. '22–3. ii. 559; in '28–30, 80 years old, claiming exemption from expulsion as a Span. iii. 51–2. G. (Manuel), Span. who came in '21, age 43 in '28, claimed exemption. iii. 51–2; had a vineyard at Los Ang.; alcalde at S. Pedro '36. iii. 635; at Sta Inés '42. iv. 646.

Gutierrez (Nicolás), 1833, Span. capt. in Mex. army, who came with Gov. Figueroa and was prom. the same year to lieut-col. He was comisionado for the secul. of S. Gabriel in '34–6; acting com. gen. Oct. 8, '35, to Jan. 2, '36, and from that date gefe pol. and com. gen. to May 3d; mil. com. in the south during Chico's rule; again gov. and com. gen. on Chico's departure from Sept. 6th to his own overthrow by Alvarado on Nov. 4, '36. See his rule and the revolution, iii. 445–66, with biog. 448; ment. iii. 236, 240, 258, 281, 284–5, 288, 298–300, 346, 414–20, 422, 431, 433, 442, 644–5; iv. 83, 102, 112, 141, 164. Gov. Gutierrez was an easy-going, faithful officer, of ordinary abilities and not very strict morals, the current charges against whom in justification of the revolt have but slight foundation in fact. Nothing is known of his later career. G. (Octaviano), Mex. artill. corp. at Sta B. from '24. ii. 532; lieut in '39. iii. 583, 651; in '46 juez de paz, v. 635, and again in '49; claimant for the Laguna rancho '53. iv. 642. G. (Pablo), Mex. grantee of rancho in Yuba Co. '44. iv. 671; in Sutter's employ '44–5; made plans with Bidwell to seek for gold on Bear Riv., but B. says he was captured and hanged by Castro in the Micheltorena campaign. Sutter tells a similar story; but I know nothing further of the matter. G. (Romualdo), 1804, Span. friar who served at Sta Inés, and retired on account of ill health in 1806. Biog. ii. 29; ment. ii. 122, 159–60. G. (Tomás), grantee of land at S. Juan Cap. '41. iv. 626; in '46 at S. Juan, age 63, wife María Ant. Cota, child. Luis b. '33, Ignacia '34, Francisco '37, Petra '39, Mariano '41, Ramona '45. Guy (Omnes), 1842, Fr. sawyer at Sta Cruz who was naturalized in '44. iv. 341. Guzman, settler at Brancif. 1797. i. 569. G. (Laureano), 1842, fifer in the batallon fijo '42–5. iv. 289. G. (Manuel), 1829, mex. convict, pardoned in '34.

Gwinn (Frank), 1841, blacksmith from N. Mex. in the Workman-Rowland party; went back the next year. iv. 278. Gyzelaar (Henry), 1816, mr. of the *Lydia*, arrested at Sta B. ii. 275–8, 362–3, 382. In '18 he came back as mr of the *Clarion* with a warning against Bouchard. ii. 222, 291. In '22–3 he returned again as mr of the pioneer Boston trader *Sachem*, and remained in Cal., ii. 474–5, 478, 492–3, being drowned in '25 or '26 in trying to cross Russian River. iii. 29.

Haag (Fred.), 1847, Co. D, N.Y.Vol. (v. 499).   Haan (Matthew J.), 1846, from Hon. on the *Elizabeth*; trader at Sonoma '47, in partnership with Fred. G. Blume, and later Victor Prudon; owner of S.F. lots. v. 680.   Hace, 1831, perhaps of Young's trappers. iii. 388.   Hacker (Wm), 1846, bugler Co. C, 1st U.S. dragoons (v. 336).   Hackett (Pat.), 1847, Co. D, N.Y.Vol. (v. 499).   Haenck (Tadeo), 1791, apothecary with Malaspina. i. 490.   Hageman (Chas K.), 1847, Co. D, N.Y.Vol. (v. 499).   Hagemeister, 1817, Russ. gov. of Alaska who visited Cal. on the *Kutusof* '17–18. ii. 216, 251, 283, 291, 315–18, 373, 383.   Haggerty (John K.), 1847, Co. F, 3d U.S. artill. (v. 518); a miner in '48.   Hägler (Henry), 1843, German ship-carpenter and mill-wright with Stephen Smith from Baltimore. iv. 395, 460. He worked at Bodega; in '47–8 in charge of the farm of his brother-in-law F. G. Blume; seems to have spent his life in Sonoma Co.; died at Bodega in '73. His name was perhaps Hegelar.

Haig (A.), 1822, mr of the *Snipe*. ii. 474.   Haight (Jacob), 1846, artill. of Stockton's bat., killed at the S. Gabriel, Jan. '47. v. 395.   H. (Sam. W.), 1847, sutler of N.Y.Vol. (v. 503); often named in commercial records of '47–8, being interested at Benicia; d. S.F. '56.   Hails (R. C.), 1846, nat. of Tenn. and overl. immig.; several times memb. of the legisl. from Napa and Solano down to '78, when he was 62 years old.   Haines (John), 1837, named in Larkin's books; in Sutter's employ '44; also ment. at N. Helv. '46.   Hairbird (John), 1846, doubtful memb. of the Mormon col. v. 547.

Hale (Horatio), 1841, on the *Cowlitz;* of scientific corps U. S. ex. ex. IV. 218, 241–2, 246, 250.   Haler (Lorenzo), 1845, one of Frémont's men in '48–9, and perhaps in '45. iv. 583; v. 453.   Halee, 1842, doubtful name at S. F.   Haley (John), 1828, Irish cooper at S. Pedro from an Engl. vessel; in '29–30 at S. Gab., age 34. ii. 558; written 'Geli.'   Hall (Basil), 1847, owner of S.F. lot. v. 678.   H. (Chas), 1832, Boston trader at Los Ang. '33–6; d. before '62. iii. 408.   H. (James), 1826, mate on the *Rover*.   H. (James), 1831 (?), mate of a trader, perhaps same as preceding; visited S.F. '81 from Me.   H. (James), 1844, disabled Amer. sailor aided by the consul; sailed on the *Nantucket*.   H. (James), 1843, at Mont., perhaps J. T.   H. (J.T.), 1846, mr of the *Barnstable* and *Elizabeth* '46–8, perhaps 2 men. v. 576–7.   H. (John), 1822, mr of the *Lady Blackwood*, author of notes on Cal. harbors. ii. 474; iv. 151.   H. (John or Chas), 1847, Co. E, N.Y.Vol. (v. 499); for many years a miner in Nev., where he died in '77, leaving a widow and daughter.   H. (John T.), 1847, mr of the *Malek Adhel*.   H. (R.R.), 1847, boatswain on the *Columbus*.   H. (Willard P.), 1847, memb. of congress from Mo., who came as guide (?) with the Morm. Bat. v. 483; served in Co. C, Cal. Bat. (v. 358); went east with Kearny. v. 452; and testified at Wash. in the Frémont court-martial. v. 456.

Halleck (Henry Wager), 1847, nat. of N.Y., graduate of West Point, and lieut of engineers U. S.A., who came with Co. F, 3d U.S. artill. to inspect Pacific coast fortifications. v. 518–20. Besides attending to his duties as engineer officer, being soon brevetted captain, he went down the coast to take part in the military operations at Mazatlan and in L. Cal.; prepared a report on Cal. land titles; and acted in '48–9 as gov't secretary and auditor of revenues. In '49 he was an active and influential member of the constitutional convention; and in '50–4 acted as inspector of light-houses on the Pac. coast. Then he resigned his commission, and in '54–60 was a member of the law firm of Halleck, Peachy, & Billings in S.F., taking part as counsellor in many of the great land suits, acting as a kind of director of the New Almaden mines, acquiring a vast estate, and in '60–1 serving as major-gen. of militia. In '61 he went east and was commissioned major-gen.; commanded the dept. of Mo. in '61–2; was the highest mil. authority at Wash. as senior general, and later as chief of staff in '62–5; commanded for a time at Richmond; was in '65–9 com. of the dept. of the Pacific; and from '69 of the dept of the South until his death at Louisville, Ky, in '72, at the age of 56. No analysis of Gen. Halleck's character is called for here; his reputation is national, though he was essentially a Californian; and the positions held by him are sufficient to show his abilities. He was a cold-blooded, generally unpopular man; plodding rather than brilliant in all his efforts; arousing bitter enmity as well as profound admiration. He was the author of several professional works and translations, and his treatises on military, mining, and international law are regarded as of standard value. His wife was a daughter of John C. Hamilton, and survived him with a son. H., 1847, brother of H.W., said to have been in the Q.M. dept., and to have died at Mont. '48. It may be that there is an error in the date of death, and that this was Jabez Halleck, who was collector, harbor-master, and com. of deeds in '49.

Haller (John J.), 1847, owner of S.F. lot. Halloran (Luke), 1846, memb. of the Donner party, who died before reaching Cal. v. 531. Halls (John), 1847, surveyor at S.F., Mont., and N. Helv. '47–8. v. 683. Halpin (Michael), 1846, Irish bugler of Co. C, 1st U.S. dragoons (v. 336). Halsey, 1846, mr of the *Caroline*. v. 576.

Ham (Hiram), 1847, owner of S. F. lot. H. (R.S.), 1848, early settler and alcalde at Sonora. H. (Zacarias), 1831, with Wolfskill from N. Mex.; said to have been drowned in the Col. a little later. iii. 387. Hamel (Wm), 1847, Co. F, 3d U.S. artill. (v. 518); died in '84. *Swan*. Hamell (Dr) 1847, doubtful name at N. Helv. Hames (John), 1844 (?), named at Soquel. iv. 453; in '45 signed the S. José call to foreigners. iv. 599; ment. in '46. v. 641; memb. of Sta Cruz council '48. v. 642; alcalde in '49; claimant of Arroyo del Rodeo '53. iii. 677. Hamilton, 1847, of firm H. & Foster, Mont. H., 1845, one of Frémont's men. iv. 583. H. (Geo. W.), 1846, of Cal. Bat. (v. 358); lumber dealer at Mont. '48; at S. José '50. H. (James), 1847, Co. A, N.Y. Vol. (v. 499); d. at Jackson, Amador Co., '58. H. (J.R.), 1846, act. mid. on the *Dale;* lieut confed. navy '61–5. H. (Mary), 1846, one of the Mormon col., perhaps with family. v. 546; Mary Sparks was her daughter.

Hamlen (Mortimer J.), 1847, Co. E, N.Y.Vol. (v. 409). Hamley (Geo. W.), 1846, mr of the *Stonington*. v. 578, 580; bearer of despatches from Stockton to Frémont in Jan. '47. v. 401; and in Dec. witness at Wash., D. C.; in '53 cl. for Güejito rancho. v. 621. His name is written in many ways, but I have his autograph. Hammer (Robert), 1847, Co. G, N.Y.Vol. (v. 499); d. on Amer. Riv. '49. Hammond (Francis A.), 1847, from Hon. on the *Currency Lass;* kept a shoe-shop in S.F. '48. v. 685. H. (Thos C.), 1846, lieut Co. K, 1st U.S. dragoons. v. 336, 341, 343; died of his wounds at S. Pascual. v. 343–7. Hampton (Wade), 1841, Amer. gunsmith in Workman-Rowland party from N. Mex. iv. 278; at Los Ang. '42; returned via Mazatlan in '43, and was mysteriously killed on the way. *Given.*

Hance (Wm), 1838, Amer. sailor, who deserted from the *Sarah and Caroline*, perhaps in '36. iv. 118; arrested, but not exiled, in '40. iv. 17; got a pass in '41, being then a lumberman near Monterey. In '42 he signed an appeal on the sufferings of the arrested party; in '44 got his pass renewed, living at S. F., age 35. Hancock (Chas), 1847, Co. C, Morm. Bat. (v. 469). H. (Geo. W.), 1847, Co. C, ditto. H. (Levi W.), 1847, musician Co. E, Morm. Bat., being also poet, preacher, and spiritual director of the battalion. v. 477, 485, 488, 493–4; in Utah '82. Hand, 1841, mr of the *Hamilton*. iv. 566. H. (Chas S.), 1847, at Benicia '47–8. v. 673. H. (Patrick), 1847, sergt Co. F. 3d U.S. artill. v. 519. Handerick (James), 1847, owner of S.F. lots. v. 679. Handford, 1847, mr of the *Jóven Guipuzcoana*. Handley (Wm), 1837, mr of the *Loriot*. iv. 105. Hands, 1848, arrested at S. José. v. 662.

Hanks (Ephraim), 1847, Co. B, Morm. Bat. (v. 469). H. (Ebenezer), 1847, sergt ditto. v. 477. H. (Julian), 1845, mr of the *María Teresa*. v. 587, 579; perhaps came earlier; at S. José from '46, being member of the council. v. 664; in '49 memb. of the constit. convention, a nat. of Conn. age 37. He went later to L. Cal. Hanley (James), 1835–7, mr of the *Clementine*. iii. 382, 442; iv. 102. Hann (Wm), 1847, owner of S.F. lot. Hanna, 1848, mr of the *Lady Adams*. v. 579. Hannah (Dolphus), 1845, doubtful overl. immig. iv. 578. Hanner (Joseph), 1842, Amer. from N. Mex. at Los Ang. '42–3. Hannoah (Baptiste), 1848, d. at N. Helv. Hanns (H.), 1848, at Hon. from S.F. on the *Julian*. Hansen (Christian), 1840, mr of the *Catalina*

'40-2. iv. 192, 564; lieut in Mex. navy.   Hanson (Geo. M.), 1846 (?), miner
in early times, and later publisher of newspapers; perhaps an immig. of '46,
died in Lake Co. '78.   Hanton (Matthew O.), 1847, Co. G, N.Y. Vol. (v.
499).   Harbin (James M.), 1846, overl. immig. (v. 526), who settled in Yolo
'47, and about '57 at the springs in Lake that bear his name; sometimes accredited to '44. iv. 446; cl. for land in Napa and Yolo; d. Lake Co. '77.   H.
(Joshua), 1846, Co. E, Cal. Bat. (v. 358), enlisting at Son., Oct.   H. (Matthew), 1844, son of J. M., and overl. immig. of the Stevens party. iv. 445,
453. He went south and was one of the prisoners at Chino. v. 313–14; later
a resid. of Napa and Lake, and about '75 went to Mexico to engage in stock-
raising.   Harcourt (Geo.), 1846, Fauntleroy's dragoons (v. 232, 247); Co. G,
Cal. Bat. (v. 358).

Hardcoop, 1846, Belgian of the Donner party, who died before reaching
the Sierra. v. 531-2.   Hardie (James A.), 1847, lieut 3d artill. U.S.A.,
major N.Y.Vol. v. 574; in com. of S.F. garrison '47-8. v. 513, 515, 649, 659;
owner of town lots. In the war of '61-5 a brig.-gen.; d. Wash. '76.   Hard-
ing, 1846, doubtful name at Los Ang.   H., 1847, mr of the *Thos H. Benton.*
H. (Francis), 1847, owner of S.F. lot.   H. (James), 1846, Co. G, Cal. Bat.
(v. 358).   H. (Thomas), 1845, Amer. sailor of the *Tasso* and *Vandalia*, aided
by the consul. v. 587.   Hardmont (Wm), 1847, Co. I, N.Y. Vol. (v. 499),
at S. José '50; d. before '82.   Hardy, 1848, com. of the U.S. *Ohio.* v. 579.
H. (Daniel), 1848, newspaper record.   H. (H. C.), 1848, owner of S.F. lot.

Hardy (Thomas M.), 1843, Canadian who possibly came earlier or had
been naturalized in some other Mex. province. iv. 400; grantee this year of
Rio de Jesus María on the Sac. near mouth of Cache cr.; in '44 named in several records as carpenter and translator in Sonoma district, age 43. iv. 448;
in '45-8 often named in *N. Helv. Diary* as visiting Sutter's Fort. I have an
original letter in Span. of May '46. The Bear captors of Vallejo and Prudon
spent the night at H.'s place. v. 120. He was unpopular with the settlers,
perhaps because of his sympathy for the Mex. Had a Cal. claim for
horses; in the gold mines May '48; and a little later in '48 or '49 he
was drowned in Suisun Bay, perhaps accidentally. His property was sold by
the public administrator, and as late as '70 the sons of John Hardy—claimed
to be identical with Thos M.—were trying in the courts to overthrow the
title of J. M. Harbin and other holders under the administrator's sale and
U.S. patent to the rancho.   H. (Thos), 1847, at Benicia; perhaps same as
preceding.   H. (Wm H.), 1845, landed at Sta Cruz from a whaler. v. 587;
worked for Larkin and others as a carpenter and lumberman, building a
schooner '46; of H. & Jenkins '48; still at Sta Cruz '80.   Hare (Henry),
1836, Engl. clerk with Jas Watson at Mont., age 26, and single.

Hargrave (Wm), 1844, Amer. immig. from Or. in the Kelsey party. iv.
444-5, 453; settling in Napa as a hunter. He was prominent in the Bear revolt. v. 78-9, 95, 104, .110, 119; and later served in the south as lieut of Co.
C, Cal. Bat. v. 361, 283. He is occasionally ment. in divers records of '45-8.
In '78 he still lived in Napa, where he dictated for my use an interesting narrative of *California in '46.*   Harlan (Geo.), 1846, overl. immig. from Ind.
with wife—Elizabeth Duncan—2 sons, and 2 daughters. v. 528-30. He lived
at S.F., and later in Contra Costa, dying in Sta Clara '50, and his wife in '48.
H. (Elisha), 1846, son of Geo., in same party.   H. (Joel), 1846, son of Geo.,
b. Ind. '28; in '49 married Minerva, daughter of Wm Fowler; lived at many
dif. places, and from '82 in Amador Val., where he died in '72, leaving a
widow and 7 children. Portrait in *Contra Costa Co. Hist.,* 78.   Harlem (P.
W.), 1846, Co. F, Cal. Bat. (v. 358).   Harley (Henry), 1847, Co. D, N.Y.Vol.
(v. 499); d. near Sac. after '70.

Harmand, see 'Harmon.'   Harmes (Henry), 1847, owner of S. F. lot.
H. (Wm), 1847, ditto.   Harmon (De Witt J.), 1847, Co. I, N.Y.Vol. (v.
499); at Murphy's, Calav. Co., '71-4.   H. (Ebenezer), 1847, Co. C, Morm.
Bat. (v. 469).   H. (Jacob), 1847, owner of lot at S.F. v. 685; in '48 had a
garden at the mission, and a wife, Elenora, who obtained a divorce in '49. He
died at S.F. '50, leaving a widow and 2 children, Mary Ann and Jacob. The

widow married Michael Foley in '50, and died at Sta Clara '60.   H. (Lorenzo
F.), 1847, Co. C, Morm. Bat. (v. 469); reënl.   H. (Oliver N.), 1847, Co. E,
ditto; home missionary at Hoytsville, Utah, '82.

Harnden, 1847, mr of the *Naslednik.* v. 579.   Harner (Jóseph), 1843,
Amer. tailor from N. Mex., who had a shop at Mont., where he worked at
his trade, sold grog, and smuggled in a small way. Died in '44 of small-pox,
leaving property worth about $2,000, of which the consul wrote to his mother,
Dolly H. of Va.   Harnes (Henry), 1847, Co. H, N.Y.Vol. (v. 499).   Har-
ness (Wm), 1846, at N. Helv. Jan.–March.

Haro (Francisco de), 1819, Mex. sub-lieut of the S. Blas infantry comp.
in Cal. ii. 253, 371. In '21 accomp. Argüello on his trip to the north. ii. 445;
and in '22–3 served as sec. of the govt and dip. ii. 461–3, 486, 676. In '24 2d
in com. of the exped. against revolted neophytes. ii. 531–2; and the same
year retired from mil. service. ii. 675 (error in ii. 585); elector de partido '27.
ii. 584, 592; iii. 33; land grants in '29. ii. 595; iii. 75; suplente of the dip.
'30–1. iii. 50, 187; vocal '33–4. iii. 246, 249–50. In '35 and '38 he was alcalde
at S.F., and elector in '37. iii. 703–5; in '41–4 sec. of the juzgado, and owner
of town lots. iv. 665–6, 669, 676, 683. In '42, age 50, apparently a widower
(his wife had been a daughter of José Sanchez), child. Francisco and Ramon
b. '27, Rosalía '28, Natividad '29, Prudencio '31, Carlota '33, Dolores '36, Jesus Felipe '40, Alonzo. The oldest daughter, Josefa, b. '25, was the wife of
Fran. Guerrero, and cl. for the ranchos granted to her father and brothers.
Rosalía became the wife of A. A. Andrews, and later of Chas Brown. iv. 669.
In '46 Don Francisco was at times acting sub-prefect, inspector of election,
and candidate for alcalde. v. 295, 648. He died in '48. His twin sons, Francisco and Ramon, were militiamen at S.F. in '43; were granted, or permitted
to occupy, the Potrero in '44. iv. 673; Ramon, or 'Chico,' was involved in
the Libbey assault of '45 (iv. 569); and both were murdered by Frémont's
men at S. Rafael in June '46. v. 171–4.   H. (Ignacio), at Sonoma '44, age 20.

Harper (Thos W.), 1847, Co. B, N.Y. Vol. (v. 499); d. Sta B. '56.   Har-
ran (Geo. and Joel), 1847, lots at S.F., prob. 'Harlan,' q.v.   Harriens (David),
1826, mr of the *Cyrus;* also in '30. iii. 146.   Harrington (John), 1847, Co.
D, N.Y. Vol. (v. 499).   Harris, 1847, in prison at N. Helv. for stealing horses.
H., 1847, from Hon. on the *Currency Lass.*   H. (Austin), 1848, passed mid.
on the U.S. *Independence.*   H. (Geo. Aug.), 1826, trader who had a quarrel
with Dav. Spence.   H. (Geo. C.), 1846, on the *Sarah Parker* acc. to *Swan.*
H. (Henry), 1846, of the Mormon col., joining at Hon., and somewhat prominent by reason of his suit against Brannan. *Annals of S.F.*, 750. At S.F.
'47–8; owner of town lots. v. 685. His wife was Mary ——, and their only
child, Henry Wm, died in '48.   H. (James), 1830, shipwrecked sailor of the
Danube; still at Sta B. '36. iii. 180.   H. (John), 1844, Engl. at Mont.   H.
(John D.), 1847, owner of S.F. lot. v. 685.   H. (J. H.), 1848, subscribes for
a ball at Mont.   H. (Robert), 1847, captain's clerk on the *Columbus;* perhaps
same as preceding.   H. (Robert), 1847, Co. E, Morm. Bat. (v. 469).   H.
(Silas), 1847, Co. B, ditto; a Utah farmer '81; mail-carrier '48.

Harris (Stephen), 1847, Q. M. sergt N.Y. Vol. v. 503; with wife and 2
daughters. One of the latter died at S.F. in Aug.; the other was born on the
voy., and christened Alta California at Rio Janeiro with much ceremony, v.
512, getting a S.F. lot in '48, as her father had in '47; candidate for council
in '47. v. 650; still in Cal. '54.   H. (Stephen A.), 1848, owner of S.F. lot;
left Cal. in '50 and d. '67. His lot was claimed in '54 by Stephen, whose grantees
held it from '64; and the heirs of Stephen A., in '70–9, were unable to recover the
land in the courts.   H. (Mrs S. E.), 1845, at Sonoma '77; maiden name not
given.   H. (Wm), 1844, Amer. sailor put ashore by the *Vandalia;* shipped
by the consul on the *C. W. Morgan.*   H. (Wm), 1846, Fauntleroy's dragoons
(v. 232, 247).   H. (Wm A.), 1847, asst surg. on the *Independence* '47–8.

Harrison (Ed. H.), 1847, Q.M. clerk of N.Y.Vol. and of the dept at S.F.;
a prominent man from '48, school trustee, president of public meetings, owner
of lots, and collector of the port. v. 575, 650–1, 656–7, 659, 678, 685; apparently of DeWitt & H., a well-known S.F. firm.   H. (G.), 1847, mid. on the

U.S. *Columbus.*   H. (Henry A.), 1848, had a store in S.F.; memb. of council '49; died in N. Y. '57.   H. (H.H.), 1841, mid. on the U. S. *St Louis.*
H. (Isaac), 1847, Co. E, Morm. Bat. (v. 469); at Sandy, Utah, '81.   H.
(Israel), 1847, Co. E, Morm. Bat.   H. (N.B.), 1846, mid. and act. master of
the U.S.*Portsmouth:* sent by Montgomery to Sloat with despatches. v. 228;
at Mont. '48.   H. (Thos), 1846, doubtful mention; a Mrs Russell is also said
to have come in '46 with her father and mother named Harrison.   Harron
(James), 1847, Co. D, N. Y. Vol. (v. 499); at Sentinel, Fresno, '83.   Harsh
(Dan.), 1847, in Napa Val.

Hart, 1839, mr of the *Flibberty-gibbet.* iv. 103–4.   H. (Henry L.), 1847,
Co. A, N. Y. Vol. (v. 499); d. in L. Cal. '48.   H. (James S.), 1847, Co. E,
Morm. Bat. (v. 469); reënl.   H. (Jerome), 1847, Co. G, N. Y. Vol. (v. 499);
d. in Shasta '52.   H. (John), 1829–30, mr of a vessel on the coast.   H.
(John), 1847, Co. D, ditto; at S.F. '71–4; d. before '82.   H. (Joseph), 1846,
Co. G, Cal. Bat. (v. 358); enlisted at S. José, Oct.   Hartcell (David), 1847,
Co. F, 3d U. S. artill. (v. 518).   Hartman (Henry), 1847, owner of S.F. lot,
who had a tin-shop in '48. v. 684.   Hartnell (Horatio Nelson), see 'Hartwell.'   H. (Jack), 1834, at Mont.   H. (Wm A.), 1846, celador of Mont.
custom-house. v. 570.

Hartnell (Wm Edward Petty), 1822, nat. of Lancashire, Engl., b. 1798,
who, after a resid. of several years in S. Amer., came to Cal. on the *John Begg,*
as member of the firm McCulloch, H., & Co., agents of Begg & Co. of Lima,
and of the Brothertons in Liverpool and Edinburgh. This firm made a contract to take mission produce for 3 years from '23, and for some years did a
large business. ii. 474–9, 564, 591, 603, 659; iii. 24, 28. In '24 he was baptized at S. Cárlos, the name Edward being added at that time (the 'Paty'
of ii. 475 is prob. an error); and in '25 married María Teresa de la Guerra.
iii. 27, 29.   His business was prosperous down to '26, and some loans were
made to the govt; but in '27–9 there came reverses that caused him to go to
S. Amer. in '29 to close the partnership, leaving him with a heavy burden of
debt. iii. 49, 57–8, 71, 118, 121–2, 127–8, 138, 147, 176. In '30 he was naturalized, and in '31 undertook the life of a ranchero at Alisal in partnership with
the Soberanes. In '32 he com. the comp. extranjera at Monterey in support of
Zamorano. iii. 221–5, 672; and in '33–6 acted as Cal. agent of the Russian
comp. iv. 162–4; grantee in '34 of the Alisal, or Patrocinio, rancho, ii. 616,
where with Father Short he established a kind of college, called sometimes
Seminario de S. José. iii. 317, 670, 677–8. In '35–6 he was regidor. iii. 293,
673, 675; his children then being Guillermo Ant. b. '27, Adalberto '32, José
'34, and Matilde '36, one or two having died and others perhaps not living at
the college, where there were then 13 students. He was also collector of taxes
and customs in '36–7, and employed to make a padron of the district. iii. 672;
iv. 96, 116; but about this time the school was given up as unprofitable, and
H. found it difficult to support his family. In '39–40 he served by Alvarado's
appointment as visitador general of missions, at a salary of $2,000, his faith-
ful efforts for reform being recorded, with his reports, in iii. 600-1, 620, 624–
8, 645, 657–8, 661, 664, 666, 683, 685, 688, 691, 718, 720, 725, 728; iv. 9, 55–
62, 194–5. Visited by Douglas '41. iv. 212; interpreter in '42 for Com. Jones'
investig. of the Graham affair; in '43 an officer of customs, iv. 377, tithe collector, court clerk, and teacher; in '44, 1st officer, inspector, interpreter, and
acting admin. of the custom-house, having also an interesting corresp. with
Wyllie on plans of Engl. colonization. iv. 403, 430–1, 451–2, 654; ment. in
'45. iv. 515, 559; being still in the custom-house '45–6, somewhat unfriendly
to the U.S. until he lost all hope of an Engl. protectorate. v. 7, 9, 61, 235,
570. After the change of flag he was appointed by Stockton surveyor and
appraiser of customs, being elected councillor, serving on the 1st jury, and
making a trip to Honolulu in Dec. v. 289, 293, 637. In '47–50 H. was employed by the U.S. authorities as official interpreter and translator, v. 609, in
which capacity he rendered most important services, both in connection with
legal and land matters and the constit. convention. Later he was county
assessor and held other positions, being claimant for two ranchos. iv. 643; iii.

676; dying in '54 at the age of 56. Hartnell was a man who enjoyed and merited the respect and friendship of all who knew him, being perfectly honest and straightforward in all his transactions, of most genial temperament, and too liberal for his own interests. In some directions he was a man of rare ability, being a master of the Spanish, French, and German languages besides his own. He was not a good business manager, lacking application, method, and energy, and being always in financial trouble; but in any clerical or subordinate capacity he was most reliable and efficient. In the later years he drank to excess. Besides the original records of the *Convention of '49* and the valuable *Diario del Visitador Gen. '39-40*, I have hundreds of his letters in various private archives; and indeed, his family doc. form more than one vol. of the Vallejo collection, which should bear his name. His correspondents were men of education and standing in many parts of the world. His widow still lives at Salinas in '85, at the age of 76, being still owner of the Alisal rancho. She gave me a personal *Narrativa.* There were 20 sons and 5 daughters acc. to her own statement. In '40 there had been 13, of whom 9 were living. Besides the 4 named above, I find the following in the *Sta B. Co. Hist.*: Juan, Uldarico, Pablo, Alvano (?), Nathaniel (died), George, Frank, Benjamin, Teresa, Anita, Magdalena, and Amelia. There was also an Estévan. Ramon (perhaps José) was majordomo at S. Juan in '40; Wm A. was customhouse guard in '45-6. Most of the sons seem to have inherited the father's weaknesses rather than his abilities; but several became respectable citizens.

Hartwell (Lorenzo Nelson), 1834, Amer. sailor from the *Catalina* at S. Diego. iii. 412; still there in '40, naturalized and married. Called generally Horatio and Lawrence Hartnell, but I have his authograph of '38. H. (Wm), 1834, Engl., age 36, testifies in favor of John Reed. Hartwig, 1847, a naturalist at N. Helv. in June. Harvan (Wm), 1846, doubtful name at Los Ang. Harvey (Thos), 1831, mate of the *Catalina.*

Hashagen, 1847, mr of the *Clementine.* v. 577. Haschal (A. G.), 1846, one of the Mormon col. v. 546; lot at S.F. '47; did not go to Utah; perhaps 'Haskell.' Thales Haskell is also named. Haskell (Geo.), 1847, Co. B, Morm. Bat. (v. 469). H. (J. G.), 1847, owner of S.F. lot. H. (John W.), 1847, Co. F, N.Y. Vol. (v. 499); d. Sta B. '78. Hasking (Henry), 1847, at Hon. from S.F. on the *Julia.* Haslitt (Geo.), 1845, perhaps one of Frémont's men. iv. 583, 587; in Sonoma Co. '74; a Cherokee Ind. Hassard (J. G.), 1848, passp. from Hon. Hassel (H.), 1848, ditto. Hastie, 1848, from Hon. on the *Sagadahoc.*

Hastings (Lansford W.), 1843, nat. of Ohio, b. '19, a lawyer who com. a party crossing the plains to Or. '42, and came to Cal. '43 in com. of the immig. party that bears his name. iv. 389-92, 400, 444. His views were those of a filibuster, but he found that the time had not come for a successful movement; so he went back in '44, by sea and across Mex., to publish a worthless book called an *Emigrant's Guide*, and to attract settlers and prospective revolutionists by lectures and other methods. iv. 396-9, 355-6, 2, 6, 20, 26. In '45 he returned with another party overland to Cal. iv. 585-6; but in the spring of '46. after the settlers' revolt had been postponed, went with Clyman's party to Salt Lake in search of more immig., and thus missed the Bear movement. v. 526, 529; but returned in the autumn with Harlan's party, by H.'s new cutoff, which proved so fatal to the Donners, in time to serve as capt. of Co. F, Cal. Bat. v. 529-30, 359, 361. Before going east, however, he and Bidwell had laid out the new town of Sutterville, reported at the time to be intended for a Mormon town, v. 58; and indeed, H. was an agent for the Mormons in the secular phases of their enterprise. v. 548; selecting a site at Montezuma, Solano, where some time in '47-8 he built an adobe house, still standing in '80, and established a ferry across the S. Joaquin. v. 552. In '47-8 he also practised law at S.F., being the owner of town lots. v. 579, 645, 678, 681. In March –April '48 he was trying to recruit a battalion of volunteers to put down an imaginary revolt in the south; in May was elected school trustee at S.F.; in July married Charlotte Catherine, daughter of Hopeful Toler, at Sac., and in Sept. was appointed judge of the northern district. In '49 he was a member

of the constit. convention, utilizing his geographical acquirements in the fixing
of a boundary. He lived at or near Sac. till '57; then went to Arizona; came
back on a visit in '64; and is said to have died in Brazil about '70. He was an
intelligent, active man, never without some grand scheme on hand, not overburdened with conscientious scruples, but never getting caught in anything very
disreputable.   H. (Sam. J.), 1841, mr of the *Tasso* '41–4. iv. 569.   Haswell
(Robert), 1788, Engl. mate of the *Washington* in voy. to N. W. coast, the 1st
Amer. vessel to enter Cal. waters. H. kept a diary which was furnished me
by his daughter, Mrs John J. Clark, who died at Roxbury, Mass., in '83, at the
age of 80.

Hatch (James B.), 1842, mr of the *Barnstable* '42–3, '44–5; possibly on the
coast before. iv. 341, 563, 101; iii. 381; also mr of the *Loo Choo* in '47. v. 511.
H. (J. W.), 1848 (?), killed accidentally at Napa '79.   H. (Meltliah), 1847,
Co. C, Morm. Bat. (v. 469); at Panguich, Utah, '82,   H. (Orin), 1847, ditto,
at Bountiful, Utah, '82.   H. (Prince G.), 1847, in S.F. list of letters.   H.
(Sam. B.), 1843, at Sta Cruz.   Hathaway (Humphrey), 1838, came on a vessel com. by Capt. Howland, and worked as a carpenter at Mont. On Larkin's
books '38–43; in Farnham's list of arrests in '40; left Mont.—and his debts—
on the *Rajah* in '43. iv. 17, 119.   H. (James M.), 1847, Co. A, N.Y.Vol. (v.
499); d. Downieville '51.   H. 1848, from Hon. on the *Sagadahoc*.   Hatler
(Alex.), 1847, owner of S.F. lots. v. 685.   Hatton (Wm), 1826, on the *Rover*.
Hauff (Ernest), 1847, musician N.Y.Vol. (v. 499); at S.F. '71–4; in Mendocino Co. '83.   Haughty (Michael), 1847, Co. I, ditto.   Haulstorn (Alex.),
1830, doubtful name in a business account.   Haun (John S.), 1846(?), nat. of
Mo.; in Sta Clara Co. '76; perhaps son of Wm.   H. (Wm), 1846, settler at
Sta Clara with wife, Lavinia Whisman, the latter still living in '80.   Haust
(Joseph), 1847, owner of S.F. lot.   Havey (John), 1847, Co. D, N.Y.Vol. (v.
499); at West Point, Calaveras Co., '71–82.

Hawes (Horace), 1847, nat. of N. Y., who visited Cal. from Hon. on the
Angola, en route to Tahiti, where he had been appointed U.S. consul. In '49
he came back and was prefect at S.F., where he spent the rest of his life as a
prominent lawyer and legislator. He was the author of an important treatise
on the Cal. mission cases, and of many other well-known briefs, political
pamphlets, and speeches; also of the S.F. consolidation bill of '56 and registry
law of '66; a member of the assembly for two terms, and of the state senate
in '63–4. Hawes was a self-made man, a shrewd lawyer, a man of powerful
mind, original in his views and methods, but full of conceit, suspicious by
nature, always unpopular, and eccentric to the verge of insanity in his later
years. He became a millionaire, and by his will of '71—the year of his death
at the age of 58—left the bulk of his estate for the foundation of Mount Eagle
University and a Chamber of Industry, making but a comfortable provision
for his heirs and relations. But the heirs, in a suit that is one of the *causas
célebres* of Cal., succeeded in breaking the will on the ground of the testator's
insanity, and thus defeated his plans for the public good and his own permanent fame. His 2d wife, married in '58, was Catherine Coombs, who survived
him with a son, Horace, who died in '84, and a daughter, Caroline, who married James, the son of Alfred Robinson, and is still living in '85.

Hawk (Nathan), 1847, Co. B, Morm. Bat. (v. 469); overland mail-carrier
in '48, being employed by Brannan.   H. (Wm), 1847, ditto; at Salt Lake
City '81.   Hawkhurst, 1837, perhaps one of the men employed to drive cattle to Or. iv. 85.   Hawkins, 1848, lieut with Gen. Lane, Sta Fé to Or. via
S. Diego. *Coutts*.   H. (Benj.), 1847, Co. A, Morm. Bat. (v. 469); in S. F.
letter list '48.   H. (John A. or P.), 1847, perhaps of N.Y.Vol. under another
name (v. 499); d. at S. F.   H. (Sam.), 1845, doubtful name of an overl.
immig. iv. 578.   H. (Wm), 1830 (?), trapper of Ashley's comp., said to have
hunted in the S. Joaquin Val. in very early times, and again in '33. *Mont.
Co. Hist.*, 29.   H. (Zacarias), 1845, doctor and overl. immig. prob. to Or.,
and not Cal. iv. 578.   Hawley (Jos.), 1842, mr of the whaler *Hague* '42, '44;
iv. 566.   Haws (Alpheus P.), 1847, sergt Co. D, Morm. Bat. v. 477.

Hay, 1847, Scotchman, of H. & Dickson, S.F. traders at the 'Beehive' store '47-50; owner of town lots. v. 675, 684; left Cal. after '50. H. (G.C.), 1848, treasurer of S.F.; called 'Dr'; perhaps same as preceding. Hayden (Geo. W.), 1847, Co. D, N.Y.Vol. (v. 499). Hayes, 1845, Amer. immig. from Or. in the McM.-Clyman party; prob. went back in '46; but may have been the H. wounded at Natividad. iv. 572; v. 526, 367. H., 1848, at Mont. from Hon. on the *S. Francisco.* H. (Elias), 1833, Amer. at Mont. '33-6; in '34-5 making shingles for Abel Stearns. iii. 409. H. (Jacob), 1846, one of the Mormon col. v. 546; did not go to Utah; d. before '80; called also 'Hayse.' H. (James), 1846, at Mont. as a kind of policeman; in the Cal. Bat., wounded at Natividad in Nov. v. 367; also called John. H. (Wm B.), 1847, mid. on the U.S. *Dale;* died at sea in '49. Hayt (Elisha), 1848, doubtful name at Mont.; prob. 'Hyatt.' Haywood (Philip H.), 1846, mid. on the *Independence;* lieut in Stockton's bat. '47. v. 386, 391-5.

Healy, 1845, on the *Sterling* at Mont. Hearn (Thos), 1847, Co. E, N.Y. Vol. (v. 499). Heartstene (H.T.), 1842, lieut U. S. N., sent east by Com. Jones with despatches. iv. 313. Heath (Chas), 1843, nat. of N.Y., who got a carta in Oct., living at Sta Cruz. iv. 400, 356; ment. at N. Helv. '45-7; in '47 owner of S.F. lot, and builder of a ferry-boat at Benicia. v. 671, 673, 678. H. (Rich. W.), 1846 (?), came as quartermaster U.S.A., and later had a ferry on the Stanislaus. *Tinkham.* H. (Russell), 1847, doubtful mention at S. Buen. H. (W.), 1848, passp. from Hon. Heathcoat, 1847, possibly of N. Y.Vol. under another name. Heathcote (Theodore), 1846, sergt Co. C, 1st U.S. dragoons; in '48 ordnance sergt at Los Ang.

Heceta (Bruno), 1775, Span. capt. and com. of the *Santiago* in explor. voy. to Cal. and the N. W. coast. i. 241, 247-8, 280, 330. Hecox (Adna A.), 1846, nat. of Mich., b. 1806, and overland immig. with wife, Margaret M. Hamer, and 3 children. v. 529. Remaining at Sta Clara during the winter— that is, 'taking an active part in the war with Mexicans'—he went to the Sta Cruz region, where he built a saw-mill, and worked as carpenter and builder; went to the mines for a short time in '48; alcalde at Sta Cruz '48-9. v. 642; later justice of the peace; county treasurer '61-3; from '70 in charge of the Sta Cruz light-house till his death, in '83. He was a methodist, and one of the first who preached protestant sermons in Cal. v. 641. His narr. of his early life, overl. trip, and experience in Cal., was published in the S. José *Pioneer* of '77, and was embodied by Willey in the *Sta Cruz Co. Hist.* His testimony on events connected with the 'war' in '46-7, like that of so many other immigrants, has little value. His widow survived him, with the following child.: Mrs M. E. Stampley of Carson, Nev., Mrs C. M. Brown of S. F., and Adna H. Hecox of S. Luis Ob., all pioneers of '46, and of those born in Cal. Mrs M. Longley of Sta Cruz, Mrs A. Rigg, Laura J., and Orville S. Portrait of Adna A. in *Sta Cruz Hist.*, 44. He was an active and respectable man of business. Hedges, 1844, mr of the *Monmouth.* iv. 567.

Heeney (Robert), 1846, marine on the U.S. *Dale;* one of Marston's men in the Sanchez campaign of '47; slightly wounded. v. 381. Hefferman (Chas), 1847, Co. F, N. Y.Vol. (v. 499); in the mines '48; died at S.F. before '82. Heft (Geo.), 1816, sailor on the *Lydia.* ii. 275. Hegarty (Peter), 1845, signer of the S. José call to foreigners. iv. 599; on the 1st S.José jury '48. Hegel (Fred.), 1841, named in Larkin's accts '41-2. iv. 279; said to have been in the Bodega region '48-9; perhaps some confusion or relationship bet. him and 'Hägler;' also 'Hugel,' q.v. Hehn (Henry), 1847, musician of N.Y.Vol. (v. 499). Heil (Fred.), 1832, passp. at Mont.; perhaps 'Hegel' or 'Hugel.' Heinrich (Chas), 1847, Co. B, N.Y.Vol. (v. 299); in the mines '48; later a trader at Sac., where he still lived in '82; nat. of Germany, b. '24; wife from '50, Sarah Neubauer. Heinricks (Ed.), 1846, Co. C, 1st U.S. dragoons (v. 336). Heitleman, 1847, from Mazatlan with letters from Talbot & Co.

Heleno, grantee of Cosumnes rancho '44. Helmstadler (James), 1847, Co. B, N.Y.Vol. (v. 499). Hembkey (Conrad), 1846, Co. C, 1st U.S. dragoons (v. 336). Hemen (James), 1828, Irish sailor, age 40. at Mont. '28-9. Hemenror (M. W.), 1846, doubtful name at Los Ang. Hemerle (John), 1846, Co. C, 1st U.S. dragoons (v. 336). Hempstead, 1847, mr of the *Corea.* v. 577.

Hempstead (Sidney C.), 1831, trader on the coast.   Hen (Wm), 1846, doubtful name. *Hittell*, and Soc. Cal. Pion. roll. See ' Haun.'   Henderson (And. J.), 1846, asst surg. on the U.S. *Portsmouth;* at N.Helv. and Sonoma in Bear times. v. 126, 128, 300; surg. of Stockton's bat. '47. v. 385.   H. (Christian), 1846, Fauntleroy's dragoons (v. 232, 247).   H. (James), 1842, lieut U.S.N. *Maxwell.*   H. (Levin), 1846, sailor in navy, on sentry duty at Mont.; deserts with his escaping prisoners.   H. (Moses), 1847, in S.F. letter list.   H. (T.), 1848, passp. from Hon.   H. (Wm,) 1826, mr of the *Olive Branch* '26-7. iii. 148, 154.   H. (Wm), 1870, doubtful name in Farnham's list; perhaps 'Anderson,' q.v.   H. (W. T.), 1848, nat. of Tenn., arr. S.F.June; perhaps same as T. above; in '50 slayer of Joaq. Murieta; in Fresno '80.   Hendricks (Joseph), 1844, at Sonoma, age 54.   H. (Wm), 1848, barber at S.F. v. 682. H. (Wm D.), 1847, Co. D, Morm. Bat. (v. 469); at Richmond, Utah, '82. Hendrickson (Henry), 1847, Co. D, N.Y.Vol. (v. 499); at Vallejo '74.   H. (James), 1847, Co. C, Morm Bat. (v. 469).   Hendy (James), 1846, marine on the *Congress*, wounded at the S. Gabriel, Jan. '47. v. 395.   Henge (T.), 1848, passp. from Hon.

Hennet, 1829, mr of the *John Coleman.* iii. 147.   Henriquez (Antonio), artisan at Sta Cruz, 1795. i. 496.   H. (Abraham), 1847, Co. F, 3d U.S. artill. (v. 518).   Henry (Dan.), 1847, Co. D, Morm. Bat. (v. 469); at Monte, Utah, '82.   H. (Francis), 1844, Irish sailor of the *Vandalia*, arrested at Mont. H. (James), 1844, Scotch sailor on the *Vandalia;* prob. same as preceding. iv. 453. Known as ' Scotch Harry;' at Mont. and Sta Cruz '45-6; in Fallon's comp. at S. José; then served 2 years on the *Portsmouth* and *Cyane*. In '48 kept a shop at Mont.; in the mines '49-52; traveled 10 years in dif. parts of the world; went to Frazer River, and died in the Sonoma Co. hospital '76. His narr. was pub. in the Stockton *Indep.* of July 14, '76, but no reliance can be put in details.   H. (James), 1847, Co. E, N. Y. Vol. (v. 499).   H. (Robert), 1847, owner of S.F. lot. v. 683.   Henschel (H. L), 1848, German custom-house broker in S.F. from '52 to '68, the year of his death; left a wife and two daughters.   Henshaw (Geo.), 1841, overl. immig. of the Bartleson party, who went back in '42. iv. 266, 270, 275.   H. (Hiram), 1846, doubtful name in list of Cal. claimants (v. 462).

Hensley (Samuel J.), 1843, nat. of Ky, and overl. immig. of the Chiles-Walker party. iv. 392, 394, 400. He had been a trapper and had spent some years in N. Mex. In '44 he was naturalized, got a grant of the Agua de Nieves rancho, iv. 670, and entered Sutter's service as supercargo of the launch; signing the order for Weber's arrest. iv. 483. He served as commissary in Sutter's army during the Micheltorena campaign. iv. 485-7, 517. Returning to the north, he took charge of Hock farm and attended to Sutter's general business, being often named in the *N. Helv. Diary.* In '46 he was prominent in fomenting the Bear revolt. v. 80, 104, 127-8, 170; was capt., and later major, of the Cal. Bat. in the south. v. 309, 328, 356, 360, 386, 391-5, 435; had a Cal. claim (v. 462); and a S.F. lot. v. 685. Going east with Stockton in '47, he testified at the Frémont court-martial. v. 454, 456; but returned to Cal. in '48, and after a brief experience in the mines opened a store at Sac. in partnership with Reading. From '50 he engaged in navigation of the Sac. river, and a little later was one of the founders of the Cal. Steam Nav. Co., of which he became president. His residence for many years was at S. José, and he died at Warm Springs, Alameda Co., in '66, at the age of 49. Of his career and that of his fellow-filibusters in '46 enough is said elsewhere; otherwise Maj. Hensley's record is that of an honest and successful man of business, of strong will and well-balanced mind, generous, temperate, and brave. His wife was Helen, daughter of E. O. Crosby, who survived him with a son and daughter.

Henysey (James), 1842, Scotch sawyer in a S.F. list.

Herbert (Thos), 1842, Engl. lumberman at S.F., age 33.   Herd (Henry), 1834, Amer. in Mont. dist. '34-7. iii. 412.   Heredia (Bernardo), settler at S. José from 1791; in '95 owner of Chupadero rancho; in 1803 regidor at S. José. i. 683, 716; ii. 134.   Herman (Jacob), 1845, overl. immig. iv. 578, 587; lived at S.F. mission '46-9 with a family; d. before '55.   Hermosillo (Nicolás), leader of a revolt at Los Ang. and S. Diego '46. v. 308, 329.

PIONEER REGISTER AND INDEX. 185

Hernandez (Antonio), saddler instructor 1792-6. i, 615, 684. H. (Antonio), soldier in S.F. comp. '19-35. H. (Cornelio), at S. José '49, a soapmaker. H. (Domingo), a Mex. convict whose term expired in '35. H. (Dom.), nat. of Cal. and a noted desperado and murderer from '45-6; sentenced to be hanged on one occasion, but saved by the breaking of the rope, only to be hanged by vigilantes in later years. Some of his brothers and sisters are said to have been criminals; but there is little definite information about any of them. H. (Encarnacion), soldier murdered at Mont. '34. iii. 673. H. (Felipe), convict settler of 1798; alcalde of Branciforte 1805; grantee of Laguna de Calabazas '33. i. 606; ii. 156; iii. 677. H. (José), convict settler of 1798, pardoned 1803, grantee of Rinconada de los Gatos '40. i. 606; ii. 156; iii. 712. H. (Juan), convict settler of 1798. i. 606. H. (Juan), regidor at S. José '22; stabbed by Mojica. ii. 604-5. H. (Juan Ant.), at S. José '41, age 58. H. (Juan María), Mex. at S. José '41, age 65, wife Francisca Lorenzana, child. Pedro b. '20, José Jesus '25; grantee of Ojo de Agua '35. iii. 712. H. (Juana), poisoned her husband '43. iv. 364. H. (Mariano), at S. José '41, age 29, wife Rosario Bernal, child. Fernando b. '37, María '38, and 2 others; grantee of Puerto in '44. iv. 672. H. (Santiago), soldier of S.F. comp. '39-43. iv. 667. H. (Simon), soldier in the Hidalgo piquete at Mont. '36, age 32. H. (Tomasa), Cal. claim $100 (v. 462). Hernano (Antonio), ment. of his lawsuit '47. v. 663.

Herrera (Dolores), 1840, nat. of N. Mex., at S. Luis Ob. to '83. H. (Ignacio), took church asylum '30. ii. 660. H. (José), corp. of S.F. comp. prom. to sergt 1811 for bravery in Ind. exped. ii. 91. Still sergt '20-4. H. (José María), 1825, Mex. sub-comisario at Mont., who was involved in controversies with Gov. Echeandía and was sent to Mex. for alleged complicity in the Solis revolt. ii. 551, 607, 614, 648; iii. 14, 33, 38, 59-85, 117, 125, 159. In '34 he came back in the same capacity with the H. & P. colony; was in new troubles arising from the amours of his wife, Ildefonsa Gonzalez; and was again exiled in '36 because he refused to support the Alvarado govt. iii. 261-7, 377, 436-9, 672; iv. 96. See also biog. ment. in iii. 466. He was a man of much ability and good education, to whom the Californians, without much apparent reason, give a bad character. In '36 he was 33 years old, and had 2 children at Mont., Vicente b. '33, and Eulalia b. '35. H. (José M.), regidor at Los Ang. '36-8; age 33 in '39; served under Castro '47. iii. 481, 509, 564-5, 636; v. 363. H. (Tomás) grantee of S. Juan Cap. del Camote '46. v. 637; still a ranchero in S. Luis Ob. '60, having held several local offices after '48. H. (Trineo), Mex. at S. Miguel rancho, Mont., '36, age 28, wife Antonia García, child Teresa b. 32.

Herriot (Adam), 1846, at Sta Cruz. Herron (James C.), 1845, mid. on the U.S. *Portsmouth*. H. (Walter), 1846, one of the Donner party from Ill. v. 530, 532. He came in advance over the mts with Reed; served in the Cal. Bat., Co. B; got a S.F. lot in '47, and aided O'Farrell as a surveyor at Stockton; but I find no later record of him. Hersey (Stephen), 1832, mr of the *Newcastle*. iii. 383. Herven (Jon.), 1840, doubtful name of Farnham's list. iv. 17. Hescock (Isaac), 1845, doubtful name of an Amer. in the Brancif. padron, age 65, in the family of Isabel Patterson (?). Hess, 1845, at N. Helv., prob. overl. immig. of Grigsby-Ide party. iv. 578-80. His daughter Nancy married John Chamberlain in Jan. '46, and all the fam. went to Or.

Hetherington (Wm E.), 1847, Co. D, N.Y.Vol. (v. 499). Hense (Sam. E.), 1846, sailor in the navy; in Amador Co. '52-79, the date of his death. Hewen (Jon.), 1840, in Farnham's list. Hewes, 1847, mr of the *Iris*. v. 578. Hewitt (A.), 1846, Co. F, Cal. Bat. (v. 358); perhaps at N. Helv. '48; see also 'Huet' of '45. H. (Geo.), 1839, Amer. sailor and otter-hunter in Sta B. dist. '39-41. iv. 119, 24. Hewlett (Palmer B.), 1847, lieut Co. I, N.Y.Vol. v. 504; later militia gen.; in Sonoma Co. '71-82. Heydenrich (Wm), 1847, Co. D, N.Y.Vol. (v. 499). Heyerman (A.), 1847 (?), doctor said to have left the *Clementine;* at N. Helv. May '48, on his way to the mines; also said to have lived at Petaluma from '45 (?) to '52, and to have returned in '73. Heyland (John), 1847, Co. A, N.Y. Vol. (v. 499). Heyward (James), 1847, nephew of Com. Shubrick, at Mont. with letters to Larkin; returned to Hon olulu '48.   Heywood (Chas), 1847, lieut on the U.S. *Independence.*

Hibler (Geo.), 1845, Amer. immig. from Or. in McM.-Clyman party. iv. 572, 526; prob. went back in '46.   Hickenlooper (Wm F.), 1847, Co. A, Morm. Bat. (v. 469); reënl.   Hickey, 1818, com. of an Engl. vessel at Mont. ii. 291.   Hickman (Thos), 1842(?), German butcher in Alameda '70-8. iv. 341. Hickmot (John), 1847, Co. E, Morm. Bat. (v. 469).   Hicks (Harry), 1833, Amer. in Mont. dist. '33-5; also called George. iii. 409.   H. (Henry), 1839, negro cook on the *California.*   H. (Joseph), 1833, Amer. tailor on the *Leonor;* at Sta B. '36; perhaps same as Harry. iii. 409.   H. (Joseph), 1846, one of the Mormon col. who remained in Cal.; owner of S.F. lot '47; died before '80. v. 546, 678.   H. (Joseph Henry), 1841, built a house for Prudon at Sonoma; prob. same as Harry and Joseph of '33.   H. (Wm), 1843, nat. of Tenn., overl. immig. from Mo. in Walker-Chiles party. iv. 392, 400; at Sutter's Fort '47; claimed a land grant on the Cosumnes, iv. 671, where the town of Hicksville was named for him, and where he died in '84, at the age of 67. His wife was a Mrs Wilson, who died a few years before him.   Hicky, 1847, at N. Helv.; prob. Hicks.   Hidalgo (Miguel), at Mont. and Los Ang. '35. iii. 285.

Higares (Francisco), 1833, named as a Dutch shoemaker from the U.S. at Los Ang. in '36, age 29. iii. 409.   Higgins, 1846, in Pt Reyes region. *Marin Co. Hist.*   H., 1848, from Australia with his family. *El Dorado Co. Hist.* H., 1848, with Buffum in the mines.   H., 1848, deserter arrested at S. José. v. 663.   H. (Edward), 1847, at work on Larkin's house at Benicia '48. v. 673.   H. (Edward), 1846, act. lieut U.S.N., and capt. Stockton's bat. '46-7; later capt. in merchant marine N.Y., and officer in confed. navy; in '75 agent of P.M.S.S.Co. at S. F., where he died in that year. v. 386.   H. (Isaac), 1848, in S.F. letter list.   H. (James), 1841, mid. on the U.S. *St Louis.*   H. (James), 1830, one of Young's party. iii. 174.   H. (John), 1830, Irish trapper of Young's party from N. Mex., where he had been naturalized. iii. 180, 388. At Sta B. in '36, age 39, and single, being often a companion of Nidever in hunting tours. From '37 named on Larkin's books at Mont.; in '40 a lumberman on Carmelo Creek, where he was arrested and sent to S. Blas. iv. 18, 23; never came back.   H. (Nelson), 1847, capt. Co. D, Morm. Bat. v. 477; with wife and 4 children, but did not reach Cal. v. 477, 482.   H. (N.D.), 1847, servant to officer of Morm. Bat. (v. 469).   H. (Silas G.), 1847, Co. C, N.Y.Vol. (v. 499).   H. (W.D.), 1848, passp. from Hon.

Higuera, ment. in 1793-1808. i. 617, 640; ii. 192.   H. in Mont. revolt '37. iii. 525.   H. (Antonino), in S. José district '41, age 38, wife Josefa Alviso, 5 children named, but all called Alviso in the padron. The date of this man's death, in '46, is the turning-point in litigation for the Livermore rancho now in progress '85. Some papers of my col. bearing on the case—in which Antonino's name seems to have been rather clumsily forged before the papers came into my hands—were introduced as evidence.   H. (Antonio), soldier of S.F. comp. '19-22; at S. Mateo '35.   H. (Bernarda Soto de), widow at S. José '41, age 52, child. Joaquin b. '15, José Ant. '18, Ramona '22, Juan María '25, Dominga '32, Encarnacion '36.   H. (Bernardo), in Los Ang. dist. '19-43; grantee of Rincon de los Bueyes. ii. 355, 565; iv. 635.   H. (Dolores), arrested at Los Ang. '45. iv. 541.   H. (Doroteo), at Los Ang. '46.   H. (Estévan), soldier of S. F. comp. '19-30; militiaman '37.   H. (Francisco), soldier of S.F. comp. '19-24; elector '27; drowned in '30. ii. 592, 594.   H. (Fran.), soldier of S. F. comp. '37-42.   H. (Fran.), son of Bernardo; at S. Pascual '46. v. 352; claimant of Rincon de Bueyes '52. iv. 635.   H. (Fulgencio), son of José; soldier of S.F. comp. '19-30; alf. of militia at S. José '37. iii. 732; grantee of Agua Caliente, Alam. Co., '39. iii. 711; in '41 living at his rancho, age 42, wife Clara Pacheco, child. Albino b. '24, Tomás '26, Narciso '29, Gabriel '31, José Jesus '32, Fernando '35, Leandro '37, Francisca '22, María L. '27, María de los Ang. '36.   H. (Gregorio), at Los Ang. '39, prob. son of Bernardo, age 29.

Higuera (Ignacio), settler at S. José 1790; majordomo in 1805, killed by Ind., but ment. in 1807. i. 478; ii. 34, 135.   H. (Ignacio), soldier of S. F.

comp. '30-40; at Sonoma in '44, age 33.   H. (Ignacio), soldier of S.F. comp. '35-6; sergt '39-40. iii. 702; encargado of the contra costa '39. iii. 705.   H. (Ignacio), soldier of Mont. comp. '36, age 24.   H. (Ignacio), maj. at Sta B. 1799-1801. ii. 120.   H. (Ignacio), soldier at Sta B. before '37.   H. (Jerónimo), at S. José '41, age 23, wife Rosario Félix, one child.   H. (Joaquin), settler at Los Ang. 1790; alcalde in 1800. i. 461, 661; ii. 349.   H. (Joaquin), regidor, alcalde, and juez de campo at S. José at dif. times '20-46. ii. 378, 604-5; iii. 729; iv. 662, 684; Cal. claim '46-7 (v. 462); claimant for Pala, Sta Clara Co., '52.

Higuera (José), soldier of S.F. comp. '19-41; perhaps the man who settled in Napa.   H., at S. José '41, age 66, wife Ramona García, child. Florencio b. '36, Encarnacion '18 (?), Miguel '37, Rita '40.   H. (José), grantee of Tularcitos and Llano del Abrevadero '21-2, and of Pala '35. ii. 594, 664, 712-13; Antonia H. et al. were claimants.   H. (José), perhaps the same; the distrib. of his estate took place in March '46, and I have the orig. expediente in *Pico* (*Ramon*), *Doc. Hist. Cal.*, i. 107-24, which shows the following heirs: Fulgencio, Valentin, Mariano, 5 minors whose guardian was Mariano (prob. their father by a daughter of José), Mrs Robert Livermore, wife of Lázaro H., Florentino Archuleta, and Antonio Mesa, each receiving 133 cattle, 88 vines, and 10 fruit-trees. It was in these papers that the name of Antonino was fraudulently introduced, as noted above.   H. (José), ment. in '46. v. 235. H. (José Ant.), son of Manuel; at S. José '41, age 52, wife Ambrosia Pacheco, child. Ricardo b. '22, Juan '24, Miguel '26, Leonardo '27, Isidro '29, Fernando '33, and Encarnacion '31.   H. (José María), at Salinas rancho '36, age 50, wife María de Jesus Cota, child. Juan b. '14, Tomás '18, Pilar '19, Blas '21, José '26, Encarnacion '28, Gertrudis '31, Manuel '33, and Luisa '35.

Higuera (Juan), in '31 comisionado of S. Juan B., and regidor of Mont. iii. 212, 307, 672, 692; juez aux. '42. iv. 653; at S. José '50.   H. (Juan), of Sta Cruz, killed at Los Ang. '45. iv. 492.   H. (Juan), at Los Ang. '39, age 45.   H. (Juan José), soldier at S. José mission 1797-1800. i. 556.   H. (Juan José), juez at S. Juan B. '42. iv. 661.   H. (Juan José), at Los Ang. '19, '25. ii. 354; iii. 7.   H. (Lázaro), at N. Helv. '47; his wife was an Higuera, daughter of José.   H. (Leonardo), in Los Ang. revolt '46. v. 308; Cal. claim of $12,072 (v. 462); age 37 in '39.   H. (Manuel), soldier and settler at S. José and S. Juan B. before 1800. i. 477, 558; in 1793 named in S. José padron as a soldier, wife Antonia Arredondo, child. Ignacia, Ana María, Gabriela, José Joaquin, and José Ant.   H. (Manuel), inválido of S.F. comp. '19-29, perhaps the same.   H. (Manuel), at S. José '41; age 52, wife María N. Mesa, child. Antonio M. b. '30, José Jesus '32, José Balfino '37, José María '40, Argentina '34, María Ant. '36.   H. (Manuel), at Los Ang. '46.   H. (Mariano), at Los Ang. '39-46.   H. (Mariano), at S. José '41, age 26, wife Maria Antonia Higuera, child. Emilio b. '39, José '41, Rosario '32, María Ascension '34, Inés '38.   H. (Marta Frias de), cl. of Entre Napa rancho.

Higuera (Nicolás), soldier of S.F. comp. '19-23; alcalde on the frontier and grantee of Entre Napa and Carneros ranchos '36. iii. 705, 711, 722; at N. Helv. '48.   H. (Policarpo), soldier at Sta B. before '37.   H. (Salvador), soldier and settler at Sta Cruz and S. José 1791-1800. i. 495, 556, 716.   H. (Secundino), at Los Ang. '46.   H. (Tomás), soldier of S.F. comp. '30-2.   H. (Valentin), resid. of Sta Clara region from '41, grantee of Pescadero rancho '43. iv. 672; juez de paz, suplente, '46, at S. José '46. v. 662; died '79, age 70. Híjar (Cárlos N.), 1834, nephew of José M., with whom he came in the colony in '34, and again in '45; and in '77, then a resident of S. José, gave me his recollections of *California in '34.*   H. (José María), 1834, a wealthy and influential Mex. of Jalisco who joined J. M. Padrés and others in organizing the Cal. colony that bears their name. He also got an appointment as gov.; but Gov. Figueroa refused to recognize his title, the colony was a failure, and H. was sent to Mex. in '35 on a charge of conspiracy, which was but very slightly founded in fact. iii. 259-69, 272-91, 344-5, 383, 613, 652, 670. Nothing is known of his experience in Mex.; but in '45 he was sent back to Cal. as a commissioner of the govt to prepare for resisting the U.S. He died at Los Ang. very soon after his arrival. iv. 526-31, 631. He was an honorable man of many accomplishments and frail health, with little fitness or fondness for political wrangles.   Hilgers (Gerard), 1846, at Mont.; owner of S.F. lot '47.

Hill, 1848, called major at Mont.   H., 1847, at N. Helv.; brother of Tom Hill, Delaware Ind.   H., 1848, mr of the *Rhone.* v. 580.   H. (Daniel Antonio), 1823, nat. of Mass., who came from Hon. on the *Rover*, and settled at Sta B. ii. 495, 573; iv. 117. He was baptized by P. Ripoll in '25, iii. 29, being then 26 years old; and soon married Rafaela Ortega, being naturalized in '29. Robinson, *Life in Cal.*, 89, describes him as 'a sort of factotum for the whole town, carpenter or mason by turns as his services were needed.' In '36 he had 6 children. In '45 he leased the Sta B. mission. iv. 553, 558, 644; in '46 was the grantee of La Goleta rancho, having some trouble with the Flores govt. v. 317, 330, 632, 644; regidor in '49; went east in '60 on a visit; and died at Sta B. in '65. A son, Ramon J., was assemblyman and court interpreter, dying in '84. One of his daughters married Dr Nicholas Den, and another, Susana, married T. W. More in '53.   H. (Henry de Jesus), 1840, German who got a pass. in June; perhaps Jos. Henry.   H. (Henry), 1847, owner of S.F. lot; nat. of Va, and memb. of the constit. convention in '49.   H. (John), 1846, sailor of the navy, on sentry duty at Mont.; deserts with his prisoners. H. (John), 1847, later policeman.   H. (John E.), 1847, Co. D, N.Y.Vol. (v. 499.); d. at Pendleton, Or., '82.   H. (Joseph Henry), 1834, German from Mex. in the H. & P. col. iii. 412; at Sta Cruz '42-3.   H. (Thos), 1845, Delaware Ind. in Frémont's party, who distinguished himself by bravery on several occasions. iv. 583; v. 367, 371, 400.   H. (Thos J.), 1847, Co. A, N. Y. Vol. (v. 499); at S.F. '71-82.   H. (Wm Luther), 1831, nat. of N.Y. and partner of Louis Bouchet in a Los Ang. vineyard; died this year, making his will on the *Catalina* in July. There was a property of $406 for his father, Peter Hill. iii. 405.   Hilton (Benj.), 1847, Co. D, N. Y. Vol. (v. 499); d. Mont. '47.   H. (Gilman), 1845, one of the men lost on the *Warren's* launch. iv. 587; v. 384.   Hilts, 1848, mate of the *Isaac Walton* from N.Y.   *Grimshaw.*

Hina (Jack), 1847, owner of S.F. lot.   Hinckley, 1847, mr of the *Alice.* v. 576.   H., 1848, mr of the *Starling.* v. 400.   H., 1848, from Hon. on the *Currency Lass.*   H. (Azra E.), 1837, Co. B, Morm. Bat. (v. 469); a Utah farmer '81.   H. (F. G.), 1842, in Dwinelle's list; wife Susana Suart (?); doubtless a confused ref. to Capt. Wm S.   H. (Sam. A.), 1844, Amer. who rec'd naturalization in June. iv. 453.   H. (Thomas), 1831-2, mr or sup. of the *Crusader.* iii. 382. He was a brother of Wm S., a partner of Henry A. Peirce at Honolulu, and died in Cent. America on his voy. home.   H. (Wm Crawley), 1847, nat. of Mass., from Valparaíso on the *Georgiana;* mr of the *Providence* in '47-8, to Tahiti, Hon., Mazatlan, then up the Sac. from Sta Cruz with a cargo of goods, converting the vessel temporarily into a country store; at S.F. from '49 to '72, when he gave me an autobiog. sketch. v. 580.

Hinckley (Wm Sturgis), 1830, nat. of Mass., nephew of Wm Sturgis, for several years a trader at Honolulu, and mr of the *Volunteer*, going to the U. S. iii. 85, 149, 170, 179. In '33-4 he came again as sup. of the *Don Quixote*, and in '34-5 mr of the *Avon.* iii. 381-2. After rendering aid to Alvarado in his revolution of '36, for which he was poetically and otherwise sharply criticised by Mexicans, his vessel having been wrecked, apparently, he went to Hon. on the *Quixote.* iii. 466-1, 487; iv. 82, 103, 116, 141. In '37-8 he was mr of the *Diana* or *Kamamalu*, being arrested at S.F. for smuggling, still a confidential friend of the gov., and from this time interested in business with Nathan Spear and Leese at S.F., obtaining and occupying a lot on Montgomery St. iii. 549, 699, 705, 709-10; iv. 699. In '39 he was mr and owner of the *Corsair*, being again in trouble with the revenue authorities, also grantee of town lot. iii. 705; iv. 103, 130; v. 681. In '42, dating his permanent residence from '40, he was naturalized and married; in '44 was alcalde, getting more lots. iv. 666, 676, 679, 683; in '45-6 capt. of the port, having much controversy with Leidesdorff and Forbes, escaping arrest by Frémont's men as a Mex. official by death in June '46, at the age of 39. iv. 593, 666; v. 3, 131, 136, 178, 649, 681. His

1st wife went east in '37, iv. 101, and died in Mass. '40; his 2d wife was Susana, daughter of Ignacio Martinez, who, after H.'s death, married Wm M. Smith in '48. I have no record of children. Capt. Hinckley was a handsome, jovial, intelligent man, immensely popular with the natives, somewhat reckless in the use of his tongue when under the influence of liquor. If there was anything he liked better than contraband trade it was probably practical joking. Some of his jokes, like the one of Christmas night at S. Juan in '37, are not exactly adapted to print; and for others space is lacking; but I may note how, in an interview with Gov. Alvarado on matters of state, he disposed of an over-inquisitive secretary who came in too often to snuff the candle, by filling the snuffers with powder; also how Gen. Vallejo avenged himself for some prank by mounting H. on a bear-hunting horse at Sonoma. The horse made it very lively for the mariner, who returned on foot with tales of encounters with grizzlies not wholly credited by the listeners.   Hinds (R. B.), 1837-9, surgeon in Belcher's exped.; author of *Regions of Vegetation, Botany* and *Zoölogy* of the exped. iv. 143-6.   Hinton, see 'Hoornbeck.'   Hintz (Herman), 1847, owner of S.F. lot.

Hipwood (Thos), 1847, sergt Co. F, N. Y. Vol. v. 504; killed in L. Cal. '48.   Hitchcock, 1844, guide of the Stevens immig. party. iv. 475-6. Acc. to Schallenberger he had no family, the boy generally called H., Jr, being Patterson. Mrs P. of that party with 3 children was apparently H.'s daughter. He claimed to have visited Cal. 11 years before, and had possibly been one of Walker's party in '33.   H. (Isaac), 1847, Co. F, 3d U. S. artill. (v. 518); in the mines '49; in Salinas Val. '77-80; d. at Sta Rita, from an accident, in '81, at the age of 64.   H. (John C.), 1847, Co. E, N. Y. Vol. (v. 499).   H. (R. B.), 1845, lieut on the U. S. *Savannah.*   H. (Rufus), 1848, overl. immig., who kept a boarding-house at N.Helv. in '48, with son and 2 daughters; later kept a hotel on the Amer. Riv. and at Green Springs, where H. and wife died of small-pox. One of the daughters, Mrs Lappeus, was in Or. '72; the other dead.   Hitt (Calvin), 1848, Co. H, N.Y.Vol. (v. 499); at Winona, Minn., '82.

Hoar (John A.), 1843 (?), prob. error in a list of pioneers; in S. F. '54. Hoarde (John), 1833, said to have been a member of Walker's party. iii. 391.   Hoban (Chas F.), 1847, nat. of N. Y., from Honolulu on the *Com. Shubrick;* Brannan's clerk at Mormon Isl. '49; d. S.F. '63, age 43.   Hobson (Joseph), 1848, nat. of Md, perhaps came on the *Lady Adams* from Callao; memb. of constit. conven. in '49.   H. (Wm L.), 1847, from Valparaíso with letters from Atherton; at Hon. as sup. of the *María Helena;* of S. F. guard '49.   Hodges (Hiram B.), mr of the *Monmouth.*   Hoen (Francis), 1845, overl. immig. of the Swasey-Todd party. iv. 576, 587; for a time in Sutter's employ; in '46 owner of S.F. lots and candidate for treasurer. v. 295, 684-5; kept a cigar-store; still in S.F. '54.

Hoeppner (Andrew), 1844, German long in Russian employ at Sitka, where he married a half-breed wife. The exact date and manner of his coming to Cal. are not known, but he was here in '45. iv. 453. Lived at Yerba Buena and Sonoma '45-9; a musician and man of many accomplishments, besides defeating Vioget in an eating-match, as Davis relates. In '47 he had great expectations from his warm springs of Annenthal, near Sonoma, as advertised in the *Star.* v. 667. Markof visited him in '45 and Sherman in '47. In '48 he was 2d alcalde at Sonoma. v. 668; and is named at N. Helv. on his way to the gold mines. About '49 he left his wife and went to Hon. and Chile, where he is said to have died about '55.   Hoffheins (Jacob), 1847, Co. B, Morm. Bat. (v. 469).   Hoffman (Chas), 1847, perhaps of N.Y.Vol. under another name. H. (Geo. W.), 1847, Co. A, N.Y.Vol. (v. 499).   H. (Henry), 1847, Co. F, 3d U.S. artill. (v. 528).   H. (Henry A.), 1847, ditto; corporal. v. 519.   Hoffstetter (John J.), 1847, died at N. Helv.; property sold at auction.   Hoit (John), 1846, Co. G, Cal. Bat. (v. 358).

Holbrook (Washington), 1848, sup. of the *Sabine;* came back on the *Elizabeth* from Hon.; negotiates for lot at S.F. v. 681.   Holdaway (Shadrach), 1847, Co. C, Morm. Bat. (v. 469); at Provo. Utah, '82.   Holden (Dr), 1848, with Gen. Lane from N. Mex. for Or.; in S. Diego region Dec.   H. (W. S.),

1848, passp. from Hon. Holland (F. S.), 1847, at Benicia. v. 673. H.
(J.), 1847, in S.F. letter list. Hollingsworth (John McHenry), 1847, lieut
Co. I, N.Y.Vol. v. 504; memb. of the constit. conven. '49; at Georgetown, D.
C., '74–82. H. (Z.), 1846, an overl. immig. with Russell, at Sonoma; killed
by Ind. in the mines '48; left a family in Solano, consisting of Harriet (later
Mrs Anderson), John D., Hezekiah S., Joseph B., Wm T., and Sarah E.
(later Mrs Duncan). Holloway (Adam), 1847, doubtful date; veteran of the
Mex. war; at S. José '52–79; brewer and chief of fire dept; left a family at
his death in '79; also accredited to '46. H. (M.), 1846, came to Sta Clara
Co. (?). Holly (Gray), 1834, named in Larkin's accts. Holman (James D.),
1848, left Cal. a week after the discov. of gold; d. at Portland, Or., '82. H.
1847, lieut of Morm. Bat. (?); prob. 'Holmes.'
　　Holmes, 1848, Conn. mechanic in the mines. H., 1841; surgeon of U.S.
ex. ex. (?). H. (H. P.), 1846, in Sonoma Co. '52–77; doubtful date of arrival.
H. (John Andrew Christian), 1827, Boston trader, sup. and mr of the *Franklin*, *Maria Ester*, and *Catalina* '27–32. iii. 147–8, 176–7, 381. He died in
March '32 between Acapulco and Callao. His wife Rachel came from Hon. to
Cal. the same year to meet him, but only to hear of his death; and she soon
married Thos O. Larkin, a fellow-passenger on the *Newcastle*. iii. 408. H.
(Jonathan), 1847, Co. L, Morm. Bat., and presid. of a party on the return in
'48, after working as shoemaker at N. Helv. v. 496. Holstein (W.), 1845,
mr of the *Maria*. iv. 567. Holt (John), 1846, veteran of 1812, sailor in the
navy, in Stockton's bat., at S. Gabriel '72, age 81. *Los Ang. Express.* H.
(Wm), 1847, Co. C, Morm. Bat. (v. 469). Holton (Benj. D.), 1847, Co. F,
3d U.S. artill. (v. 518). Hommitch (John), 1847, Co. K, N.Y.Vol. (v. 499).
Honey (Wm), 1847, owner of S.F. lot.
　　Hood (Frisbie), 1848, negro steward on the *Isaac Walton;* at Mokelumne
Hill '52. *Grimshaw.* H. (Wm), 1846, Scotch carpenter at S.F. '47–8, of H.
& Wilson; owner of lots and a house. v. 650, 684–5; in Sonoma Co. '50–77.
Hook (Henry), 1831, writes to Cooper from Sta Fé; connected with the *Globe*,
and had apparently been in Cal. H. (Solomon), 1846, one of the Donner
party who survived; a son of Mrs Elizabeth Donner. v. 530, 534. W. C.
Graves tells me he saw H. in Lake Co. in '63–4. H. (Wm), 1846, brother
of Sol., who died in the Sierra. v. 530, 534. Hooker, 1841, sec. of Sir Geo.
Simpson. Hooker (Wm), 1840, sent to Mont. from Branciforte; written
'Guca.' Hooper (Simon), 1846, Co. C, 1st U. S. dragoons (v. 336). H.
(Wm M.), 1833, from Boston, with a letter from Childs to Larkin. iii. 409;
went to Hon. in '45, and returned in '48; prob. the same who advertised as a
merchant at S. F. '48–9; of the firm Cross, Hobson & Co. Hoornbeck (A.
T.D.), 1848, known as Francis Hinton; died at S. Luis Rey '70. Hoover
(Westley), 1846, overl. immig. with a family, who settled at S. José, where
he served on the 1st jury in '48. v. 529. H., 1846, at N. Helv. in charge of
a launch in Feb.; Sutter mentions him as a scientific man who superintended
his farm for several years, and who was thought to be living at Sta Clara in
'76; perhaps Westley, though he could not have been an immig. of '46.
　　Hope (Alex. W.), 1848, nat. of Va, who had been surg. in U.S.A.; at Los
Ang. '48–56, where he died; memb. of 1st Cal. senate. H. (Gerard), 1834,
Irish hatter of H. & Day at Mont. '34–6, age 30. iii. 412. H. (John), 1833,
named in Larkin's accts '33–4; perhaps the same. Hoppe (Jacob D.), 1846,
nat. of Md, and overl. immig.; owner of town lots, proprietor and editor of
the *Californian*, and candidate for alcalde in '47–8. v. 652, 658, 685; projector
of the new town of Halo Chemuck. v. 674; went to the mines, was a memb. of
the constit. convention of '49, and settled at S. José, where he made a fortune in trade and lost it by speculation. Claimant of Ulistac rancho. v. 674;
killed by the explosion of the *Jenny Lind* in '53, at the age of about 40. He
was an enterprising and popular man, against whom nothing appears.
　　Hopper (Chas), 1841, nat. of N. C., a hunter who came with the Bartleson
party, but went back as guide with part of the comp. in '42. iv. 270–1, 275–6,
279, 342. In '47 he came back overl. to Cal. with his family, v. 556, and bought
a Napa farm, where he spent the rest of his life, dying in '80, at the age of 81,

and leaving 5 children. *Hopper's Narrative* in my col. was written from conversations with H. by R. T. Montgomery in '71. Portrait in *Menefee's Hist. Sketch-book*, 128.   H. (James), 184, in Sta Clara Val. '60. *Ilittell.*   H. (John), 1848, on 1st S. José jury.   H. (Thomas), 1847, nat. of Mo., and overl. immig. with his wife, Minerva Young; in Sta Cruz region '47-8; in the mines '48-9. From '49 at dif. places in Sonoma Co., being in '80 a rich landowner with 7 children. Portrait in *Sonoma Co. Hist.*, 384.   H. (Wm), 1847, Co. G, N.Y.Vol. (v. 499); d. Los Ang. '47.

Horden (Stephen), 1844, doubtful name of an Amer. in S.F. list.   Horn (Wm), 1846, settler in Sta Clara Val. with fam.; Cal. claim (v. 462).   Horndell (Joseph), 1847, Co. B, N.Y. Vol. (v. 499); at St Louis, Mo., '82.   Horner (John M.), 1846, one of the Mormon col. from N. J. with wife. v. 546; settled as a farmer at mission S. José, with a variation of mining experience in '48. In partnership with his brother, who came in '49-50; he took a prominent part in the early annals of Alameda Co. By agriculture, trade in farm produce, and land speculations, the Horners became rich and extended their operations to the peninsula of S.F., where their name is preserved in Horner's Addition. They lost their property in '54, and from that time lived on their Alameda farm till '80, when they went to the Sandwich Islands.   Horra (Antonio de la Concepcion), 1796, Span. friar who served at S. Miguel for a very brief term, and was sent away by Pres. Lasuen in '97 on a charge of insanity. In Mex. he made a long report against the Cal. friars, and the investigation of his charges formed one of the causas célebres of mission annals. i. 560-1, 567, 587-97.   Horry (Irwin), 1847, owner of S.F. lot.   H. (James), 1848, servant of Brooks' party in the mines; killed by Ind. in Bear Valley.   Horsely (Joseph), 1833, at Mont. '33-4; also called Horseman.   Horton, 1847, mr of the *Triad*. v. 580.   H. (Wm), 1840, in Farnham's list of arrested foreigners. iv. 17.   Hoseir (E.), 1848, in S.F. letter list.   Hoskins (Henry), 1847, Co. E, Morm. Bat. (v. 469.)   Hotchkiss (H.), 1848, passp. from Hon.

Houck (James), 1845, Amer. immig. from Or. in the McM.-Clyman party. iv. 572; about 10 days after arrival at Sutter's Fort he was charged with an attempt at rape, and nothing more is known of him.   Hough (H.), 1845, purser's clerk on the *Savannah*.   Houghtailing, 1847, at Hon. from S.F. Houghton (Sherman O.), 1847, sergt of Co. A, N.Y. Vol. v. 503. A nat. of N. Y., who became a prominent lawyer of Sta Clara Co., being mayor of S. José, county recorder, and member of congress '71-5. His 1st wife was Mary M. Donner, who died in '60 leaving one daughter, Mary M.; the 2d wife was Eliza P. Donner, who still lived in '85 with 7 children, Eliza P., Sherman O., Clara H., Chas D., Francis J., Stanley W., and Herbert S. (died '76). Portrait of S. O. H. in *Sta Clara Co. Hist.*, 32.   Houptman (Wm), 1840, German who got passports in '40 and '44, the former in Mex., so that he may have come later. iv. 120.   House (James), 1844, at Sonoma, age 50.   H. (Joseph), 1846, came to S. José. *Hall*.   Houston (Thos B. or T.), 1846, act. mid. on the U. S. *Dale;* died '63, as lieut, at Naples.

How (Oliver H.), 1847, Co. C, N.Y.Vol. (v. 499).   Howard (Wm), 1848, Swedish sailor on the U.S. *St Mary*, who quit the service at S.F., went to the mines, and in '50 settled in Sonoma Co., where he still lived in '80, at a R.R. station bearing his name; wife from '55 Caroline Kolmer of '46; 9 children. Portrait in *Sonoma Co. Hist.*, 296.   H. (Wm Davis Merry), 1839, nat. of Boston, sent to sea by his mother with a view to needed discipline, who came to Cal. as a cabin-boy on the *California*. iv. 117, 119; and worked for a while as clerk for Stearns at Los Ang. He went east in '40, and came back in '42 as sup. of the *California*. At Honolulu, on the way, he married Mary Warren, adopted daughter of Capt. Grimes, a native of Hon. and daughter of Wm Warren, q.v., who was returning on the vessel from Boston, where she had been educated. In '43-5 H. acted as sup. of the *Vandalia* and *California*. iv. 564, 569, 640; and in '45 opened a store at S.F. with Henry Mellus, buying the H.B.Co. establishment. In '46-9 Mellus & H. were the leading firm in town, and after the gold excitement did an immense business, having branches at Sac. in charge of Brannan, and at S. José under Belden's care, both being partners in the interior business, as was Talbot H. Green in the city. The firm was dissolved in '50, and H. retired a rich man. See mention of H. in various minor matters, he being a member of the council, and admin. of the Leidesdorff estate. v. 240, 321, 359, 539, 648–52, 678; cl. for the S. Mateo rancho. v. 660. After a visit to the east in '53 his health failed, and he died in '56, at the age of about 37. Howard was a large man, of fine personal appearance; jovial, generous, and humorous; fond of practical jokes, late suppers, and private theatricals; but always attentive to business. He had no political ambitions, but was fond of helping his friends into office. Among all the pioneer traders of S.F. there was probably no better man, nor more deservedly popular. A street in the city bears his name. His 1st wife died in '49, leaving one child, who died; and his 2d wife, Agnes Poett, married in '49, survived him, marrying his brother George, and later a man named Bowie. A son by the 2d wife was still living in '80.

Howe (Elisha W.), 1848, nat. of R. I., who came by sea and went to the mines; in S. Luis Ob. '50–83; married Gabriela Estudillo, and had 6 children. H. (Franklin), 1846, Co. C, 1st U.S. dragoons (v. 336).   H. (Henry), 1848, in Sonoma, as he stated later.   Howell, 1848, from Honolulu.   H. (Chas), 1848, mining at Rose Bar.   H. (Isaac), 1846, nat. of N.Y., and overl. immig., settling in Napa Co. with his family. In '69 he moved to S. Luis Ob., where he died in '78, at the age of 80; known as Father Howell; left a widow and 7 children, one or more of whom came with him in '46. A son is ment. at N. Helv. in '48; the widow died in '83, also aged 80; two of the sons were John and Joseph.   H. (John), 1846, Cal. Bat. (v. 358); at Sonoma and N. Helv. '47–8; perhaps son of Isaac.   H. (T.C.D.), 1847, Co. E, Morm. Bat. (v. 469); in '82 a farmer at Clifton. Id.   H. (Wm), 1847, Co. E, Morm. Bat. (v. 469).   Howes (Horan), 1847, Soc. Cal. Pion. roll.   Howland (Henry S.), 1837, mr of the *Com. Rodgers* '37–8. iv. 103.   H. (Wm), 1848, sailor on *I. Walton.*

Hoxie, 1847, mr of the *S. Boston.* v. 550.   Hoyer (Cornelius), 1842, mr of the *Fama* '42–3, and perhaps '41; at Hon. '36. iv. 141, 565; passp. from Hon. '48.   Hoyt (Aug. A.), 1846, Fauntleroy's dragoons (v. 232, 247); Co. F, Cal. Bat. (v. 358).   H. (C.), 1847, at Mont. '47–8.   H. (Daniel C.), 1847, Co. K, N.Y.Vol. (v. 499).   H. (Henry P.), 1847, Co. A, Morm. Bat. (v. 469); d. on the return journey.   H. (R.C.M.), 1846, leased land and house at Mont.; Taber & H., hotel-keepers at Mont. '47–8; at S. José '50.

Hubbard, 1845, apparently one of Frémont's men; v. 453, 583, 587; at N. Helv. Feb. '46; in F.'s exped. of '48, when he died.   H. (Charles), 1834, German and naturalized Mex.; mr of the *Peor es Nada* '34–5, and of the Soledad '43. iii. 383, 412; iv. 568.   H. (Geo. C.), 1847, lieut Co. K, N.Y.Vol. v. 504; a printer; memb. of legisl. '49; d. in Ill. before '60.   H. (John E.), 1848, nat. of Chile, who came with his parents to S.F. at the age of 6; liquor-dealer at Vallejo '79. *Solano Co. Hist.*   H. (T. W.), 1845, nat. of N.Y.; came at age of 5; messenger in assembly '55.   H. (W. H.), 1847, rented a house at Sonoma.   Hubbell (Ezekiel), 1801, mr of the *Enterprise.* ii. 2. Huber (Henry), 1841, overl. immig. of the Bartleson party. iv. 270, 275, 279; grantee of Honcut rancho '45, for which he was an unsuccessful claimant in '53. iv. 671; ment. at Sutter's Fort '46; owner of lots at S.F. '47–8. v. 676. I think he is the man who for 15 years or more, down to '85, has kept a well-known liquor-store at S.F.   Hubert (Nicholas), 1844, deserter from the *Warren.*   Huchas (Heinrich), 1847, musician N.Y.Vol. (v. 499).

Huddart (John M.), 1847, lieut Co. F, N.Y.Vol. v. 504; d. at the Sandw. Isl. before '60.   Hudgekison (David), 1847, contract to haul lumber at N. Helv. Dec.   Hudson (A. J.), 1845, at S. Luis Ob. '68–83. *S. Luis Ob. Co. Hist.*, 388.   H. (Benj.), 1847, Co. K, N.Y.Vol. (v. 499).   H. (David), 1845, nat. of Mo., b. '20, overl. immig. of the Grigsby-Ide party, iv. 578, 587, with his brother, Wm, and sister, Mrs York; settled in Napa Val., where—but for his service with the Bears, v. 110, later in the Cal. Bat. (v. 356), and a brief mining experience in the mines '48—he lived till '73. Then he moved to a farm in Coyote Val., Lake Co., where he lived in '81 with wife—Francis

Griffith, married in '47—and 6 children, Rodney J. b. '50, Lavonia, Elbert, Ella, Ada, Bertha (died), and Robert L. Prob. still alive in '85. In '72, at Calistoga, he wrote his *Autobiography* for me. Portrait in *Lake Co. Hist.*, 188. Six of his brothers and sisters came to Cal., sooner or later.   H. (Edward), 1847, owner of S.F. lot. v. 682; still in S.F. '52, a carpenter.   H. (Hiram), 1847, laborer and watchman at Mont.   H. (James T.), 1845, a trader at S. Pedro.   H. (John T.), 1805–6, mr of the *Tamana*. ii. 24.   H. (Martin), 1848, nat. of Va, brother of David, and overl. immig. with wife and 5 children; settled in Guilicos Val., Son. Co., '48–9 and lived there until his death in '71, at the age of 64.   His widow, Elizabeth McAlroy, and 7 children were living in '80. The sons who came in '48, and were still living in '80, were Michael E, John W., David A., and Matthew T.   H. (Thos), 1844, said to have come to Sta Clara Val. iv. 453; at Mont. '45; in '46–7 of Co. B, Cal. Bat. (v. 358), serving also a courier in Oct. '46; at Mont. '47–8.   H. (T. F.), 1848, settler in Sonoma Co.; at Sta Rosa '77.   H. (Wilford), 1847, Co. A, Morm. Bat. (v. 469); at Sutter's Fort in '48 when gold was discovered.   H. (Wm), 1845, brother of David, overl. immig. of the Grigsby-Ide party, apparently with a family. iv. 579, 587; at Sta Rosa from '46, in which year his daughter Mary, later Mrs McCormick, was born. His wife is credited with having furnished some material for the famous Bear flag. v. 148. He died in '66, leaving a large family.   H. (Wm L.), 1841, com. of the U.S. *Peacock* in U.S. ex. ex. iv. 241.

Hudspeth (Benj. M. or N.), 1846, lieut, and later capt., Co. A, Cal. Bat. v. 361. I find nothing more about him.   H. (James M.), 1843, nat. of Ala, who crossed the plains to Or. in '42, and came to Cal. in the Hastings party. iv. 390, 400. He worked for Stephen Smith at Bodega for a while. iv. 396; and subsequently visited various parts of Cal., working as a lumberman at Sauzalito, and hunting in the Sac. Val.; served, perhaps, as a 2d lieut of Gantt's comp. during the Micheltorena war of '44–5; and in the spring of '46 went east to the Salt Lake region with Hastings and Clyman to aid in diverting immig. and prospective filibusters from Or. to Cal. v. 526, 529.   He returned in the autumn, v. 530, and served as lieut of Co. F, Cal. Bat., in '46–7. v. 361, 435. After the war he bought land in Sonoma, and worked with O'Farrell as surveyor at Benicia—where he owned a lot, v. 672, as also at S. F., v. 679—Napa, and other places; in the mines '49–50; later a farmer in Sonoma Co.; memb. of legislature '52–5; and still living in '85, at the age of 63. His wife, from '54, was Matilda Fuller, and he had no children. Portrait in *Son. Co. Hist.*, 160.

Huefner (Wm), 1847, Co. C, N. Y. Vol. (v. 499); ment. at Sonoma, where he took part in theatrical performances, and at N. Helv.; resid. of S. F. and for a long time marshal of the pioneer society to '82; but I think died before '85.   Huerstel (Laurent), 1844 (?), in S.F. '81, said to have arrived in '44. Soc. Cal. Pion. roll. iv. 453.   Huet, 1845, Amer. farmer from Or. in McM.-Clyman party, who prob. went back in '46. iv. 572, 526; perhaps 'Hewitt.' Huff (Columbus), 1847, Co. F, 3d U.S. artill. (v. 518); in Napa '48.

Hugel (Fred.), 1837, German who had been in Cal. 5 years when applying for a pass in '42. iv. 118; at Sutter's Fort '46; in '47 bought land of Rufus in Son. Co.; perhaps 'Hegel,' q.v.   Hugenin (Dan. C.), 1846, mid. on the U. S. *Portsmouth;* lost on the *Warren's* launch. iv. 587; v. 384.   Hughes (H. M.), 1839 (?), in Sonoma Co. '74–7.   H. (John), 1847, Co. D, N. Y. Vol. (v. 499).   H. (Wm), 1845, one of Frémont's men. iv. 583; Cal. claim '46–7 (v. 462). He was a nephew of Cyrus Alexander, and also in the exped. of '48. H. (Wm), 1847, Co. F, N.Y.Vol. (v. 499).   H. (Wm O.), 1836, on Larkin's books '36–7; perhaps 'Hewes.'   Huguee, 1845, mr of the *Medicis*. iv. 567. Huie (Geo. W.), 1847, physician said to have come with Lieut Thompson of the U.S.N.; joined by his family '49 at S. F.; at Petaluma '53–68, and later at S.F., where he died in '77.

Hulett (Sylvester), 1847, lieut Co. D, Morm. Bat. v. 477; in '82 at Manti, Utah.   Hull, 1844, mr of the *Georgia*. iv. 566.   H. (Isaac), 1848, passp. from Hon.   H. (Joseph), 1848, nat. of Ohio, who came to Or. in '45, and to

Cal. on the discov. of gold; joined by his family '49; from '50 on a Sac. farm, where he still lived in '80 with wife and 4 children.   H. (Joseph B.), 1843, com. of the U.S. *Warren* '43-7; in com. at S.F. '46-7, succeeding Mont-gomery. iv. 569; v. 284, 289, 380, 434, 539, 581, 649, 659.

Humphrey, 1840, at Mont.; Larkin urged to use his influence to start him for home.   H. (Benj. F.), 1847, Co. E, N.Y.Vol. (v. 499).   H. (Geo. L.), 1847, Co. H, N.Y.Vol. (v. 499); at Coulterville '74.   H. (Isaac), 1848, nat. of Ga, at Sutter's Fort when gold was discovered; having been a miner in Ga, he hastened to the mill, made a rocker, and thus became the pioneer in a new industry. Ment. in *N. Helv. Diary* in April. Died at Victoria in '67.   H. (Wm), 1847, Co. G, N.Y.Vol. (v. 499); at Coulterville '71-4; perhaps con-founded with Geo. L.   H. (W.), 1848, passp. from Hon.   Humphries, 1840, mr of the *Columbia* '40-1. iv. 102-3, 564.   H. (Stephen), 1848, in S.F. list.

Hunnewell (James), 1830, a well-known Boston trader in business at Hon. for some years.   The only evidence I have that he ever came to Cal. is a letter of Oct. '30, in which he hopes to visit the country 'again;' but in '33 he was in Mass. and intended to stay there. He died in '69. He may have visited Cal. before '20.   Hunsacker (Abraham), 1847, Co. D, Morm. Bat. (v. 469); later sergt; in '82 a bishop at Brigham City, Utah.   H. (Daniel), 1847, overl. immig. from Mo. with his family; ment. at N. Helv. in Aug. with news of approaching immigration. v. 556. Settled at Benicia, and later in Contra Costa, where he was treasurer of the county. Of his sons who came in '47, Harrison K. was at one time deputy sheriff of Contra Costa; James C. was sheriff, and lost on the *Brother Jonathan;* and Nicholas, also sheriff, was a miner at Park's Bar in '48, and a resid. of S. Diego '74.

Hunt, 1813, agent of Astor's fur company, on the *Pedler.* ii. 271.   H. (Gilbert), 1847, Co. A, Morm. Bat. (v. 469).   H. (Jefferson), 1847, capt. Co. A, Morm. Bat., and also preacher. v. 477-80, 488, 493; had a project for raising a new battalion. v. 496. He was accomp. by his wife and 4 sons, Hiram, John, Joseph, and Martial; and three daughters, Jane, Harriet, and Mary; but it is doubtful if all the family came to Cal. In later years Capt. H. came back to Cal. and represented S. Bernardino in the legisl. of '55. H. (Martial), 1847, son of Capt. H., Co. A, Morm. Bat.; in '81 at Snowflake, Ariz.   H. (Timothy Dwight), 1841, protestant clergyman who came from Honolulu in Nov., and was employed for a time as city chaplain. In '55 he was in Cal. as the agent of the Amer. Home Miss. Soc. v. 657.

Hunter (Barry), 1846, doubtful name in a Los Ang. list.   H. (Benj. F.), 1846, lieut on the U. S. *Portsmouth;* at N.Helv. June. v. 102; acting capt. of Co. C, Stockton's bat. '46-7. v. 385.   H. (Edward), 1847, Co. B, Morm. Bat. (v. 469); in '82 a bishop in Utah.   H. (Jesse D.), 1847, nat. of Ky, and capt. Co. B, Morm. Bat. v. 477; in com. of S. Diego garrison. v. 488, 617. Ind. agent for southern Cal. at S. Luis Rey from Aug. v. 492, 568, 621-2. His wife died at S.D. in '47. v. 490. He remained in Cal., went to the mines in '48, but returned to the south to act again as Ind. agent. He died at Los Ang. in '77, at the age of 73, leaving 7 grown children with families.   H. (Wm), 1847, musician of Morm. Bat., Co. B. (v. 469).   Huntington (Dimick B.), 1847, Co. D, Morm. Bat. (v. 499); at Salt Lake City '55.   Huntley (Ezra), 1847, Co. K, N. Y. Vol. (v. 499).   Huntsman (Isaiah), 1847, Co. B, Morm. Bat. (v. 469); in Utah '81.

Huppertz (Gerard), 1834, succeeded Sill & Co. as baker at Sta B.   Hurst, 1847, at N. Helv. from S.F., Oct.   Hurtado (Joaquin), 1791, piloto in Malas-pina's exped. i. 490.   Huse (Sam. E.), 1846, gunner on the U.S. *Congress,* and in com. of a gun in Stockton's campaign of '46-7; in Amador Co. from '51; died at Yount in '79.   Hutcheon (Walter), 1847, Co. E, N.Y.Vol. (v. 499); d. Brooklyn, N.Y., '80.   Hutcheson, 1848, sentenced to corporal punishment by court-martial.   Hutchins, 1846, mr of the whaler *Columbus.*   Hutchin-son (G.N.), 1846, in the U.S.N.; drowned in '78 at Vallejo, where he was mr of the navy-yard yacht *Freda,* and had lived for 20 years.

Hutchinson (Jacob A.), 1846, overl. immig. with family, who in '49 set-tled on the Cosumnes River, and soon started on a prospecting tour, from which he never returned.   H. (Jacob A., Jr), 1847, son of the preceding; living on the Cosumnes with family in '80; perhaps date of arrival should be '46, or that of his father '47. The H. brothers are named as having bought Isbel's claim in S. Joaq. '48.   H. (Joseph), 1846, Fauntleroy's dragoons (v. 232, 247).   H. (Wm A.), 1848, advertised for a lost rifle at S.F.   Hütt- mann (Francis), 1847, mr and sup. of the *Matilda*, *Primavera*, and *Callao* in '47–8; made advances of money to Frémont, about which there was much trouble later. v. 441, 465–6, 576.   Hutton (James D.), 1847, surveyor of pueblo lands at S. José; appointed official surveyor of the southern dept, but the appointment was withdrawn on account of charges in connection with his S. José work. v. 665.   Huxley (J. Mead), 1847, Co. A, N.Y.Vol. (v. 499); at S.F. '54; officer in the war of '61–5; died before '82.

Hyatt (Elisha), 1846, one of the Mormon col. with wife and son. v. 546; excommunicated at S. F.; and in Oct. at Mont., making tubs, etc.   Hyde (Geo.), 1846, nat. of Penn., who came on the U.S. *Congress* as Com. Stockton's sec. For a time, in Aug., he was alcalde at S. José. v. 294–5, 662; then came to S.F., where he was 2d alcalde with Bartlett, and 1st alcalde from June '47 to March '48, having much trouble in his administration of the office, as fully explained in v. 648–52, 680. There seems to have been but slight foundation for the many and bitter charges against him. He was a lawyer, of good abil- ities and character. He was somewhat prominent in city politics in '49 and the few years following; and has resided in S. F. ever since to '85, being in the real estate business. In '78 he gave me a valuable statement of *Historical Facts*, including not only his own controversies, but many other points of in- terest connected with early S.F. annals.   Hyde (Wm), 1847, sergt Co. B, Morm. Bat., being also an elder and preacher, and a capt. of 50 on the return. v. 477, 488, 490–1, 493.

Ibañez (Florencio), 1801, Span. friar who served at S. Antonio and Soledad, dying in '18. Biog. ii. 385-6; ment. 152, 159, 205, 230, 394, 427. I.
(Doña Maria), mentioned at S. Diego '21 and '46. ii. 546; v. 329. I. (Sebastian), Mex. at Mont. '48.

Ibarra (Agustin), at Los Ang. '46. I. (Andrés), at Los Ang. '19. ii. 357;
took part in revol. of '31. iii. 201; juez de campo at S. Diego '36. iii. 615-16;
kept a dram-shop '41. iv. 619; grantee of Encinitos '42. iv. 620. I. (Antonio), at Los Ang. '19, taking part in revol. of '31. ii. 357; iii. 201; at Sta
Gertrudis rancho '39, age 37. I. (Calixto), at Los Ang. '46. I. (Desiderio), settler at Los. Ang. '14, and regidor in '26-8. ii. 349, 560; still there
in '48. I. (Francisco), sirviente at Sta Clara 1776. i. 306. I. (Francisco
Gonzalez de), 1820, Span. friar who served at S. Fernando and S. Luis Rey,
dying in '42. Biog. iv. 622-3; ment. ii. 357, 394, 436, 569-70, 580; iii. 20-1,
96, 205, 353, 622-4, 641, 646-7. I. (Gabriel), at Los Coyotes rancho, Los
Ang. '39, age 35. I. (Gerónimo), at Los Ang. '46, wounded at the Chino
fight. v. 314.

Ibarra (Gil), síndico of Los Ang. '31. iii. 634. He was born at S. Diego in
1784. In '36-7 he was alcalde of Los Ang., and was prominent as a partisan of
the south against Alvarado's govt in '37-8, being more than once arrested by the
norteños. iii, 485, 509, 518, 548, 555, 558, 565-6, 636; grantee of Rincon de la
Brea in '41. iv. 635; and still at Los Ang. '48. I. (Isidro), said to have
been the man who killed Ávila in the battle of '31. iii. 208; at S. Luis Ob.
from '33. iii. 682. I. (José M.), at Los Ang. '46.

Ibarra (Juan María), 1819, Mex. lieut of the escuadron de Mazatlan. ii. 254;
stationed at S. Diego '21-30, taking part in Ind. exped. and other affairs. ii.
534-6, 543, 549, 675; iii. 88, 109; in '30-1 memb. of the junta to try P. Martinez, fiscal in the trial of Atanasio, and defender of Alcalde Duarte. iii. 99,
190, 195. In '32 he was a prominent supporter of Zamorano, being sent south
in command of the northern forces. iii. 222-7; and in '33-6 was comandante
at Sta B. iii. 650-1; but was unwilling to submit to the new govt, and left
Cal. in '36. He is described as a rough, coarse man of very dark complexion,
but energetic and brave. He had a wife in Sinaloa. I. (Leonardo, Luis, and
Pedro), at Los Ang. '46. I. (Rafael), at S. Juan Cap. '46, age 48. I. (Ramon L.), juez de campo at Los Ang. '40, '42-4. iii. 637; iv. 632-3; still at Los
Ang. '46-8. I. (Severiano), at Los Ang. '39-48. Ibera (Nicolás), 1779,
chaplain of the *Santiago*. i. 328. Idahl (Christopher), 1847, Co. F, 3d U. S.
artill. (v. 518).

Ide (Wm Brown), 1845, nat. of Mass. of pilgrim ancestry, b. in 1786,
who worked as a carpenter in Vt and N. H. to '33, and in '34-44 as carpenter,
farmer, and sometimes teacher, in Ohio and Ill. In '45 he came overland in
the Grigsby-Ide party with his wife (Susan G. Haskell, married in '20), 4 sons,
and a daughter. iv. 578-81, 587. He encamped for the winter on Thomes'
rancho, and in the spring of '46 moved into a cabin on Belden's rancho, Tehama Co., owned by Ide later. In June '46 he joined the Bear party, being
apparently one of the few settlers who acted in good faith and was induced
to believe the false reports that the Americans were in danger. After the occupation of Sonora and the departure of Capt. Grigsby, Ide was chosen commandant of the Bears, and held that position until the reorganization of the

forces under Frémont in July, just before the cause was merged in that of the U. S. For his acts in this capacity, including much that throws light on the peculiar character of the man, see v. 78–100, 104, 110, 115–19, 145–69, 175, 179–84, 231; or, better still, all the chapters relating to the Bear movement. Ide soon came to regard himself as leader in a grand revolutionary movement, as the conqueror of Cal.; his men regarded him simply as temporary commandant at Sonora, chosen to that position for his zeal in the cause and some educational advantages, and they were willing to indulge him in harmless eccentricities, paying but slight attention to his grandiloquent proclamations, or to his peculiar views of himself and the republic he thought he had founded. The assumption of the command by Frémont was regarded by Ide as a grievous wrong to himself; but his views and writings on this subject—respecting which his idiosyncrasy came very near to insanity—are fully presented elsewhere. After the change he served as a private in the Cal. Bat. during the first expedition to the south, but returned to Sonoma in Sept. v. 298; and to the Sac. Valley in Nov. In April '47 he was at Sonoma, taking part in a public meeting in behalf of Alcalde Nash. v. 609; on June 7th he was appointed by Gov. Mason surveyor for the northern department; on the 17th he married a couple at Cache Cr.; in July was referee in a slander case at Sonoma; and in '48 was at Mont. In '48–9 he had some experience in the mines, but the home of his family in these and later years was on the rancho Barranca Colorada, bought of Belden, near Red Bluff, claimed by him in '52. iv. 670; and confirmed to his heirs in '55. In '51–2 he seems to have held pretty nearly all the county offices in Colusa at the same time, the highest being that of county judge, and the seat of his govt being at Monroe's rancho, where he died in Dec. '52. He retained to the end his fondness for long reports and for political theorizing, but with all his eccentricity he was always a most worthy and honest man, and had somewhat remarkable tact and executive ability in several directions. The *Biographic Sketch* published in '80 by his brother is noticed in v. 188–9. It is stated by several writers, including Belden and Baldridge, that Ide was a Mormon, but I have found no positive evidence on the subject. Mrs I. died a few years before her husband. Information about the children is meagre. The oldest son, James M., lived long in Colusa and Tehama counties, then went to Utah, where he died in '78. Wm H. worked for Sutter a while in '45, then went south to the Sta Cruz region, and is said to have been held a prisoner by Castro for a while in '46. Daniel and Lemuel, small children in '45, lived with the family in Tehama, and I think one of them still survived in '85. The daughter, Sarah E., became Mrs Healy, and lived at Sta Cruz in '80, when she contributed her recollections of the overland trip, with other material, for the *Biog. Sketch.* There were 4 other children, but of the 9 only 2 survived in '80.

Idirbe (Basilio), 1834, mr of the *Urup.* iii. 384. Igadera (José), 1798, convict settler. i. 606. Iglesias (José M.), 1825, Span. from the *Aquiles;* named in list sent to Mex. '28, and passport ordered in '30. iii. 51–2; in '32 joined the comp. extranjera at Mont. iii. 221. Ihre (Geo.), 1847, Co. B, N.Y.Vol. (v. 499). Iliasovich (Livovich), 1831–3, mr of the *Baikal,* doubtful name. iii. 381. Illyn, 1806, pilot with Rezánof from Sitka. ii. 70. Illig, see 'Ellick.' Imman, 1848, at N.Helv. Imparan (José), 1779, com. of the 1st galleon that touched at Mont. i. 330.

Imus (Chas), 1846, nat. of N.Y. who came overland from Ill., being capt. of a party, and accompanied by his nephew, Chas A. Imus. v. 529. Both are said to have served in the Cal. Bat. (v. 358); and later were stock-raisers on the S. Joaquin. Their parents came to Cal. in '50. The capt. died at Sta Cruz in '56, and the nephew was perhaps still living in '77. Inciarte (Juan), 1791, piloto in Malaspina's exped. i. 490. Indart, 1845, mr of a vessel. Inestrumo, 1826; mr of the *Argosy.* iii. 146. Ingals (Dav.), 1845, doubtful name of an overl. immig. iv. 578. Ingalls (Rufus), 1848, nat. of Me, lieut 1st U.S. dragoons, came on the *Huntress* to act as asst Q.M.; in N.Y. '81 at a pioneer reunion. Ingersoll (Chester), 1847, overl. immig. from Ill., who bought land at Napa in Dec. In '48 he is said to have sent instructions east to sell his property, purchase 500 bbls of dried apples, and distribute the balance among relatives, as he had made a fortune in Cal. He died in S.F. '49, leaving a family.   Initia (C.), doubtful name of grantee of Olompali '43. iv. 672.   Inwood (Geo.), 1846, Co. B, Cal. Bat. (v. 358).   Iñigo (Lope), grantee of Posolomi and Pozito, Sta Clara, '44. iv. 672.   Iñigues (Juan), 1796, sergt Catalan volunteers. i. 540.   Iquina, 1793, Nootka Ind. baptized at Mont. i. 498.

Ira, or Irea (Cyrus), 1846, one of the Mormon colony. v. 546; left the church, and was living in the eastern states '84.   Irante (Antonio), at Los Ang. '46.   Irish, 1846, said to have been in the Pt Reyes region.   Irvin (John), 1840, one of the exiles to S. Blas. iv. 18.   Irwin (Edward), 1847, sergt Co. A, N. Y.Vol. v. 503; in the mines '48–50; then—after a year or two in Nicaragua —a resident of Sierra Co., where he was sheriff '55–9; lived 3 years in Napa and went to Nev. in '63, serving as sheriff and U.S. marshal in Nye and White Pine counties. In '70 he returned to Cal. and settled in Lake Co., where he still lived at Middleton in '83.   I. (Wm), 1847, doubtful memb. of N.Y.Vol. (v. 499); at S.F. '74.   Irwood (Henry), 1848, at Benicia. *Yuba Co. Hist.*

Isbel (James C.), 1846, physician from Ohio, overl. immig. accomp. by his wife. v. 529; settled in S. Joaquin '47, where he is mentioned in connection with various mining operations in '48. His wife, Olive M., taught the 1st English school in Sta Clara—possibly in Cal.—in the spring of '47, while the immig. families were gathered there awaiting the close of the war. Both the doctor and his wife were living in Ventura Co. as late as '79, the former disabled and the latter still a teacher. The name is also written Isbell and Isabell.   Isidoro, Ind. said to have been killed at Olompali '46. v. 166.   Isidro, Ind. mentioned at Soledad '26. ii. 623.   Islas (Santiago), Mex. alférez commanding guard at the Colorado pueblos 1780–1; killed by Ind. i. 359–63.   Iturrate (Domingo Santiago), 1800, Span. friar, who served at S. Juan B. until his departure from Cal. in 1809. Biog. ii. 154; ment. i. 577; ii. 100, 159–60.   Iven (Alfred), 1847. Co. D, N.Y.Vol. (v. 499); died at Acapulco '49.   Ives, 1845, at N. Helv. with family; prob. error for 'Ide.'   Ivie (Thomas C.), 1847, Co. C, Morm. Bat. (v. 469); farmer at Scipo, Utah, '82.   Ivy (Richard A.), 1847, Co. A, Morm. Bat. (v. 469); farmer in Utah '81.

Jackson, 1845, at N.Helv., prob. an overl. immig. iv. 578, 587; said to have come to Napa with N. Coombs in '45, and to be living at Oakland '78.   J. (Mrs), 1846, Mormon woman on the *Brooklyn* (v. 544), wife of Col J. Tulidge.   J. (A.), 1848, steward in the City Hotel at Mont.   J. (B), 1848, from Hon. on the *Sagadahoc.*   J. (Dav. E.), 1831, of the Rocky Mt. Fur Co., formerly partner of Jed. Smith and Sublette; came from N. Mex. in com. of a trading party. iii. 387, 613; iv. 264.   J. (Geo.), 1847, sergt Co. G, N.Y.Vol. v. 504.   J. (Henry W.), 1847, musician Co. D, Morm. Bat. (v. 469); reënl.   J. (James), 1845, passport from Los Ang. to Sonora.   J. (James M.), 1846, coxswain of *Dale's* launch, disch. at S.F. '49; later mr of a vessel, and in the war of '61–5 ensign on the *Comanche;* at S.F. '84. *Lancey.*   J. (Joseph), 1827, Irish shoemaker in Mont. dist. '29, age 27. iii. 176.   J. (Joseph), 1848, passp. from Hon.   J. (Sam.), 1847, asst surg. on the U.S. *Independence.*   J. (Wm), 1848, in S.F. list of letters.

Jacob (Richard Taylor), 1846, Kentuckian who accomp. Bryant on the overland trip, and was capt. of Co. H, Cal. Bat. in the campaign of '46–7, returning east probably by way of Panamá with Lieut Emory, and being in Wash. at the time of Frémont's court-martial. v. 359, 361, 454, 528. He later married a daughter of Thos H. Benton; was col of the 9th Ky cavalry in the war of '61–5; and became lieut-gov. of Ky.   Jacobs (Sanford), 1847, Co. D, Morm. Bat. (v. 469); employed by Brannan as mail-carrier in '48.   Jacobson (Andrés), 1848, at S.F. from Valparaíso.

James, 1846, boy on the *Savannah,* said to be at Oakland in '76. *Alta.*   Jaime (Antonio), 1795, Span. friar who served chiefly at Soledad, and died at Sta B. in '29. Biog. ii. 576–8; ment. i. 500, 576, 686; ii. 152, 159, 385, 394,

491, 530, 622, 655; iii. 96–7.　Jalapa (Fran.), soldier of S.F. comp. '39–42; at Sonoma '44, age 25.　J., 1848, one of the Weber's prospectors, for whom Jamestown was named.　J. (Antonio), 1847, lumberman in S.F. dist.　J. (Noah), 1846, memb. of the Donner party from Ill., believed to be still living in '80. v. 530, 534.　J. (Zacarias), 1832, debtor of Purísima mission.　Jameson (F. A.), 1848, passp. from Hon.　Jamieson (Geo. Wm), 1847, Co. E, N.Y. Vol. (v. 499).

Jan (Barnaby), 1798, Boston sailor at S. Diego. i. 545, 654.　Janes (Alden W.), 1847, Co. D, N. Y. Vol. (v. 499); at Kenton, Ohio, '83; present at a review of survivors in N.Y. '84.　Janion (R. C.), 1847, Engl. trader who came from Hon. on the *Laura Ann;* member of the S.F. firm of Starkey, J., & Co. in '47–9, making several trips to the islands; died in England some years later.　Jansen (Cornelio), see 'Johnson.'

Janssens (Victor Eugène Auguste), 1834, Belgian who came from Mex. in the H. & P. colony at the age of 17. iii. 263, 412. After the colony was broken up he worked at the Corralitos rancho with the Coronel family in '35–6. Later, in '36, he kept a shop at Mont. with Ayala, but on the downfall of Gov. Gutierrez he wished to return to Mex., where his mother still lived, and failing in this he went south, and in '37–8 took part in many of the Abajeños' operations against Alvarado, besides serving against the Ind. on the S. Diego frontier. iii. 504, 516–20, 558. Later he had an orchard and worked as a distiller at Los Ang.; and in '40–2 he lived at S. Juan Cap., acting as majordomo and juez. iii. 627–8; iv. 624–7; naturalized in '41, and in '42 married María Antonia, daughter of Vicente Pico. Subsequently he was agent for Aguirre and partner of Lataillade at Sta B., obtaining the rancho of Lomas de la Puríficacion in '44. iv. 642; and perhaps elected alcalde for '45, but not serving. iv. 491, 672. In '46 he was justice of the peace at Sta Inés, and under the Flores govt was mil. com. of that region. v. 320, 635. He was again juez in '48–9, and lived on his rancho, confirmed to him by the courts, till about '56, going to the mines in '48 for a time, but later residing at Sta B., where at various times in '61–8 he served as county assessor, postmaster, trustee, and deputy collector and sheriff. In '78, residing at Sta B., he dictated to me his *Vida y Adventuras,* an excellent narrative of colony affairs and of later Cal. events; and also permitted me to copy his col. of *Doc. Hist. Cal.,* containing several important records. He was an intelligent man of good repute, a widower with two sons and a daughter. I think he is still living in '85.　Janston, 1846, mid. U. S. N. at Mont. with Baldwin in com. of guard. *Lancey.*　Jantzen (Fred.), 1847, Co. G, N. Y. Vol. (v. 499); liv-at S. F. '74–83.　Jaramillo (Juan José), at S. Bern. '46, age 30.　Jarvis (James J.), 1847, at S. Diego and Mont. '47–8, representing Everett of Hon. Jatiñil, Ind. chief on the S. Diego frontier, a faithful ally of the whites.

Jauffrey (Agustin), maj. at S. Juan Cap. '41.　Jaume (Luis), 1771, Span. friar, who served as missionary at S. Diego until killed by the Ind. on Nov. 5, 1775. i. 173, 176, 195, 229, 250–2, 255, 455, 654, 657; ii. 106–7.　Javier (Fran.), Ind. chief on the Colorado 1781. i. 361.　Jaw, or Jay, at N. Helv. '47–8; doubtful name of a N. Y. vol.　Jaynith (Ed.), 1847, doubtful name of a Benicia settler.

Jefferson (Geo.), 1843–4, at S. F. in trouble about debts, etc.; prob. a sailor.　Jeffray (Wm), 1848, memb. of Soc. Cal. Pioneers; in S. F. '81–3. Jegge (Jacob), 1846, Co. C, 1st U. S. dragoons (v. 336).　Jelvero (Fran.), 1825, Span. who came on the *Aquiles;* at Sta B. '36, age 36, with wife and 5 children.　Jena (N.), 1840, mr of the *Angelina.* iv. 101.　Jenkins, named by the Los Ang. vigilantes in '36 as having been killed, perhaps some years earlier. iii. 419.　J., 1848, of J. & Hardy, at Mont. (?)　J. (A. and H.), 1848, passp. from Hon.　J. (Jackson W.), 1846, overl. immig. apparently with Aram.　J. (John W.) 1846, Co. F, Cal. Bat. (v. 358); perhaps same as preceding.　J. (Wm K.), 1847, Co. D, N. Y. Vol. (v. 499).　Jenks (Chas N.), 1845, Amer., at Mont.　Jennings, 1848, in the mines, from Or., later asst Q. M. Gen.; in real estate business at Sac., but returned to Or.　J. (John), 1815, mr of the *Columbia.* ii. 273–4.　Jennison (Dan.), 1823, at Sta B. ii. 495.

Jesse (Archer C., or Archibald C.), 1846, overl. immig. who settled in Napa Val., served as lieut of Co. E, Cal. Bat. v. 361, 529; and had a Cal. claim of $13.50 (v. 462). I have no later information about him.   Jesus (Felipe de), at Soledad '26. ii. 623.   J. (José), Ind. chief of S. Joaq., aiding the whites '46-8. v. 360, 662.   J. (José Ant.), Mex. convict, set free in '33. J. (Serafin), grantee of lot at S. Gabriel '43. iv. 637.   Jeupas, 1847, mr of the *Keone Ana.* v. 579.   Jewell (Ben.), 1848, in Son. Co.; prob. 'Dewell,' q. v.   Jewett (Enoch P.), 1847, from Hon. on the *Eveline;* owner of S. F. lot. v. 685.   J. (Geo.), 1836, Amer. who landed from a whaler at Sta B., age 21.   J. (Thomas), 1836, Amer. cooper, age 28, who came with Geo., and was perhaps his brother. iv. 118; in Larkin's employ at Mont. '40.   Jim ('Kanaka,' or 'Yankee'), in charge of Hock for Sutter '46.

Jimenez, 1791-1800, chaplain on one of the S. Blas transports.   J. (Antonio M.), Mex. priest at S. Gabriel and curate of Los Ang. from '44. iv. 422, 634, 637. He died at S. Gabriel in '53.   Jimeno (Antonio), 1827, Mex. friar of the S. Fernando college, who served as missionary or curate at Sta Cruz in '27-8, at S. Buen. '40-3, and at Sta B. '29-40 and '44-56, being chosen supiente president in '30. ii. 576, 625, 655; iii. 87, 433-4, 656, 658; iv. 45, 421-2, 426, 643-5. Padre Antonio is remembered as stout and dark in person, amiable in disposition, kind to his neophytes, but strict in all religious matters. He left Cal. in '56 or a little later, and in '71 was still living in the city of Mex., blind and indigent, probably the last survivor of the Fernandinos.   J. (José Joaquin), 1827, or perhaps '28, Mex. friar of S. Fernando college, brother of Antonio, whose missionary service was at S. Luis Rey in '27-30, Sta Cruz '30-3, Sta Inés '33-50, S. Gabriel '50-3, and Sta B. '54-6. From '38 he was president of the Fernandinos, being vicar in '38-9, and prefect after Duran's death in '46. In '44 he was the founder of the Sta Inés seminary, of which he was the rector to '50. In '54 he founded the missionary college of Dolores at Sta B., of which he was president to his death in '56, at the age of 52. ii. 553, 618-19, 625, 655; iii. 309, 319, 433-4, 661, 693-4; iv. 63-4, 372, 421, 425-6, 549, 645; v. 620, 635. A good account of his life is given by P. Gonzalez in his burial record. *Savage, Doc.,* ii. 144-6. Padre Joaquin resembled Antonio in most respects, being somewhat shorter in stature and less affable or more reserved in manner, being a very zealous missionary, though sometimes in trouble with his ecclesiastical superiors.

Jimeno Casarin (Manuel), 1828, nat. of Mex., and brother of the friars Jimeno, sub. comisario and contador in the Mont. custom-house in '28-30. ii. 607; iii. 46, 65, 69, 86, 136. In '32 he was síndico of the Mont. ayunt.; in '34 alcalde, and grantee of Salsipuedes; in '35 member of the diputacion and comisionado for the secularization of S. Luis Ob. iii. 291, 354, 673, 678, 682. In '37 he was again vocal, and in '39-42 was Alvarado's sec. of state, besides being 1st vocal and often acting gov. during Alvarado's illness, and grantee of Sta Rosa, Sta B. Co. in '39. iii. 506, 585, 590, 593-9, 604; iv. 133, 137, 193, 282, 294-5. Under Micheltorena he continued to serve as sec. in '43-5, being the grantee of Sta Paula in '43, and the Jimeno rancho, Colusa Co., in '44. iv. 357, 360, 403, 409, 643, 671. In the troubles of '45-7 Don Manuel seems to have taken no active part, but in these and later years gave his whole attention to private business, being also in bad health. He does not appear as claimant for any of the ranchos granted to him. He went to Mex. early in '53, and died there in Dec. of that year. Jimeno was a man of good character and abilities; a faithful official, well fitted for his position as govt secretary; devoted to Mexico, but not bitter in his prejudices against foreigners; small and lean in physique; vivacious and witty in conversation. His wife, married about '32, was Doña Angustias de la Guerra, who later married Dr Ord, and is still living in '85. There were 11 children, only 2 or 3 of whom survive. Two of the sons—Antonio and Porfirio—were sent east with Lieut Sherman in '50 to be educated, and Porfirio was a capt. of Cal. volunteers in the war of '61-5.   Jimkins (Henry), 1848, lumberman and farmer at Sta Cruz to '61, later a soldier and miner in Nev.   Jimmerson (Chas), 1847, Co. E, Morm. Bat. (v. 469).   Joaquin (Emilio), Ind. grantee of S. Gabriel land '43. iv. 637.

John, 1836, cook from Coromandel, age 40, at Mont. John, 1836, Amer. at Salinas, age 18. John (James), 1841, overl. immig. of the Bartlesa u party; went soon to Or. iv. 234, 270, 272, 275. Johns (Juan C.), 1833, at Sonoma. Johnson, 1834, doubtful name of an Engl. sailor at Gomez' rancho. J., 1840, blacksmith arrested at Los Ang., but escaped. J., 1843, doubtful mention as an overl. immig.; perhaps of Chiles-Walker party. iv. 392. J., 1846, midshipman arrested by Capt. Montgomery. J., 1847, carpenter at Mont. J., 1847, fined at S. Diego for stabbing. v. 618. J., 1848, overl. immig. with Lawton.

Johnson (Archibald), 1832, testified in '68 that he had lived in Cal. since '32. iii. 408. J. (A. B.), 1837, trader on the coast; also called Benjamin. J. (A. M.), 1846, mid. on the U.S. *Warren*. J. (Chas), 1840, doubtful mention. J. (Chas F.), 1847, Co. K, N.Y. Vol. (v. 499); owner of S.F. lot. J. (Chas B.), 1848, memb. of Pion. Soc., at Los Ang. '54. *Annals.* J. (Chas H.), 1848, nat. of Md; S.F. trader in '48-9, of firm Findley, J., & Co.; in '61 represented S. Luis Ob. in the legislature. J. (Chas R.), 1846, auctioneer in S.F. '48, who at Los Ang. '76 testified that he was in Cal. '46. There is prob. some confusion between this man and the 2 preceding. J. (Cornelius Adré), 1826, German soldier from Mex. iii. 176; at work on Hartnell's rancho '36, age 60; in '40 worked for Leese at S.F. His name was perhaps Jansen.

Johnson (David W.), 1846, farrier Co. K, C, 1st U.S. dragoons; killed at S. Pascual. v. 346. J. (Ed.), 1845, nat. of Md, sailor on the U.S. *Erie* '45-8. iv. 587; came back to Cal. '49-50, and again in '54; lived at S. José '58-81 and later. *S. J. Pion.* J. (Francis), 1840, sup. of the *D. Quixote* and *Maryland* '40-1. iv. 103, 120, 567. He was a Mass. man who had been clerk for Peirce & Brewer at Hon., and later in business for himself. He died in Mass. abt '48. J. (Francis), 1845, at Los Ang., pleading exemption from mil. service; went to Hon. on the *Portsmouth;* perhaps the son of Don Santiago. J. (Fred.), 1847, Co. G, N.Y. Vol. (v. 499). J. (Geo. A.), 1848, nat. of N.Y., who in the legislature of '63 represented S. Diego Co., age 37. J. (Henry), 1847, Co. A, Morm. Bat. (v. 469). J. (Ira), 1847, Co. I, N.Y. Vol. (v. 469); smuggler at S. Diego and builder at Mont. '48. J. (Isaac C.), 1847, Co. E, N.Y. Vol. (v. 469); at Astoria, Or., '82.

Johnson (James), 1833, Engl. trader at Guaymas, engaged also in pearl-fishing, who came to Cal. both by land and on the *Facio*, making several trips to Sonora and back in '33-4. iii. 382, 409. He represented some kind of a Sonora company and bought the right of Manuel Gutierrez in the S. Pedro rancho, with large quantities of live-stock; but presently became financially embarrassed. He was accused of complicity in the Apalátegui revolt of '35, and is mentioned occasionally in Los Ang. annals of '36-40. iii. 285, 519; iv. 14, 117. Grantee of S. Jacinto and S. Gregorio, S. Diego Co., in '43. iv. 621, 563. Don Santiago was a large stout man of variable temperament. He died in '47. His widow, Cármen Guirado, sister of Rafael G. and Mrs Manuel Requena, still survived in '78, as does a son Francis in '85, he being mentioned at Hartnell's school in '36, and as the owner of Los Ang. lands in '48. There was another son named Santiago. The 3 daughters, Anita, Adelaide, and Margarita, married respectively Henry and Francis Mellus and James H. Lander. J. (James), 1836, Amer., age 32, who worked for Spear at Mont. J. (John), 1845, at Mont. J. (John Michael), 1821, Scotchman baptized at S. Buen. ii. 444. J. (John W.), 1846, Fauntleroy's dragoons (v. 232. 247). J. (Joseph), 1845, deserter from the *Hopewell* at S. Diego; in '47 sentenced to 2 months of public works and $50 fine for stabbing García at Sta Isabel.

Johnson (Robert E.), 1841, in U.S. ex. ex. iv. 241. J. (Sampson W.), 1846, Virginian and overl. immig., perhaps via Or., who served in Co. E, Cal. Bat. (v. 358); in the mines '48-9; at S. José '50-4, serving as constable; farmer in S. Joaq. '54-9; keeper of a stable at Pacheco and Martinez '60-80. He married Annie McClellan in '50. J. (Sam.), of Morm. col., see 'Ladd.' J. (Wm), 1832, memb. of the comp. extranjera at Mont. iii. 221.

Johnson (Wm), 1840, nat. of Boston and mate of the *Alciope*, engaged in trade at S.F. and getting a pass. in June '41; also grantee of town lot in '44. iv. 669; v. 679. From '42 he owned a lighter in company with Leese; asking in '44 for a license for his boat, he called himself an Irishman and naturalized Mex. (There are indications that in '40-1 there were 2 of the name at S.F., one of whom came as pilot on the *Trinidad*.) In '45 he bought the Gutierrez rancho on Bear River, where he lived from that time, being often named in the *N.Helv.Diary* as making trips up and down the river. His ranch was on the immig. route and is mentioned by all parties from '45. v. 23, 452, 484. In June '47 he married Mary Murphy, who in Nov. was advertised as having left him and later became Mrs Covillaud. In '52 he was the claimant for his rancho. iv. 671; and a little later (or earlier, as would appear but for the land claim) he either died or went to the Sandwich Islands.   J. (Wm), 1842, surg. U.S.N. at Mont. *Maxwell*.   J. (Wm), 1847, sergt Co. C, N.Y.Vol. v. 504; owner of S.F. lot.   J. (Wm S.), 1847, Co. D, N.Y.Vol. (v. 499); later a prominent citizen of Monterey Co., holding several county offices; claimant for El Pleito. iv. 655; cashier of the Salinas City bank '82. He is also said to have lived in '48-9 and '75 at Stockton.

Johnston (Abraham R.), 1846, capt Co. C, 1st U.S. dragoons, who came with Kearny from N. Mex., and was killed at S. Pascual. v. 336, 343-4; author of a published *Journal* of the march.   J. (Wm J.), 1847, Co. C, Morm. Bat. (v. 469); in Sutter's employ in '47-8, and at the Coloma mill when gold was discovered.   Johnstone (A.), 1847, at S.F. from Hon. on the *Currency Lass*; went back on the *Columbia*.   J. (Charles), 1834, Dane in the Mont. dist '34-7. iii. 412. *Larkin's Accts*.   Jonas, 1840, doubtful name in Farnham's list of arrested foreigners.

Jones, 1841, com. of H. B. M. S. *Curaçoa*. iv. 38, 564.   J., 1841, mr of the *Llama*. iv. 567.   J., 1846, orderly sergt Cal. Bat. *Lancey*.   J., 1846, sailor of the *Savannah;* in the mines '48.   J., 1847, mr of the *Confederacion*. v. 577.

Jones (A. F.), 1846, came to S. José with wife and 3 children. *Hall;* perhaps the J. ment. in the mines from S. José '48.   J. (Albert G.), 1844, Amer. who got naturalization papers. iv. 453.   J. (C.), 1848, passp. from Hon. J. (Cárlos), 1847, Co. F, 3d U.S. artill. (v. 518).   J. (Chas E.), 1847, in S.F. list of letters.   J. (David H.), 1847, Co. B, Morm. Bat. (v. 469).   J. (E.), 1846, purser's clerk on the *Warren;* at Mont. '48.

Jones (Elbert P.), 1846, Kentuckian lawyer and overl. immig. who practised law in S.F., was the 1st editor of the *Star* in '47, kept the Portsmouth House, was member and sec. of the town council, took an active part in political wrangles, became the owner of many city lots, and I think gave his name to Jones St. v. 645, 648-53, 657-8, 676, 678, 680, 685. He married Sarah Kittleman of the Mormon colony in '47, and lived in S.F. till after '50, dying at Charleston S.C. in '52. Jones was a man of much talent and versatility, not in all respects of model character.   J. (Eli), 1847, at Hon. from S.F. on the *Currency Lass*.   J. (H. L.), 1847, blacksmith in Sutter's employ '47-8; had a family.   J. (Harold), 1846, sailor on the U.S. *Dale*.

Jones (Mrs Isabella), 1846, one of the Mormon col. v. 546; owner of a S.F. lot '47; never went to Utah.   J. (James H.), 1842, Amer. farmer naturalized in '44 claiming 2 years' residence, being then a resident of N.Helv., where he still lived apparently in '45-7. iv. 341.   J. (John), 1837, trader at S.F.   J. (John), 1846, at S. José. *Hall*.   J. (John), 1847, Co. G, N.Y.Vol. (v. 499); d. before '53, when his widow, Sarah—who came with him in '47—married D. McC. Murray. She lived at Healdsburg, where she died in '79.

Jones (John Coffin, Jr), 1830, Boston man and long a merchant at Honolulu, where he was also U.S. consul. He had large transactions with Cal. which he visited nearly every year in '30-8, as mr or sup. of his own vessels, the *Volunteer, Louisa, Harriet Blanchard, Avon, Bolívar, Griffon*, and *Rasselas*, finally marrying Manuela, daughter of Cárlos Carrillo. iii. 85, 145, 180, 381, 383-4, 461; iv. 101, 104-5, 117, 141. After settling his affairs at the Islands and making a visit east, he came back on the *Julia Ann* from Panamá in '41 and settled at Sta B., though still making visits to Hon. I have many of his original business letters, and others on current events in the south which have much historical value. iv. 291, 333, 523, 563, 566, 640. Early in '46 he sailed with his family on the *Admittance* for Boston, where he died a few years later. His widow was claimant for Sta Rosa Isl. iv. 643; which Jones with A. B. Thompson had stocked with cattle and sheep; also for La Calera. She is still living in '85, having married, I think, a man named Kittle.   J. (John M.), 1846, nat. of Ky and prob. overl. immig.; at S.F. and S. José '48-50; memb. of constit. convention '49.

Jones (Nathaniel), 1846, nat. of Tenn.; overl. immig. with wife and son from Mo. Leaving his family at Chiles' rancho in Napa Val., he served in the Sanchez, or Sta Clara, campaign, and then settled in Contra Costa, where he still lived in '82 with wife and 5 children. Portrait in *Contra C. Co. Hist.*, 264. He served as sheriff, public administrator, and county supervisor. His daughter, Martha A., born in '47, married John Slitz. The son who came with him, at the age of 2 years, was Robinson M., a newspaper man, farmer, teacher, county surveyor, and warehouseman, living at Martinez in '82 with wife, Nettie Renwick, and 3 children.   J. (Nathaniel V.), 1847, sergt Co. D, Morm. Bat.; in Kearny's return escort. v. 453, 477, 492.   J. (Owen), 1841, at S.F.   J. (Peter), 1834-5, Frenchman at Mont.   J. (Robert), 1836, named in Mont. accounts.   J. (Sam. E.), 1846, son of Zacarias; resident of Mont. Co. '59-70.   J. (T.), 1848, passp. from Hon.   J. (Thomas), 1840, one of the S. Blas exiles, arrested at Los Ang. iv. 14, 18.   J. (Thomas), 1841, Amer. immig. of Bartleson party. iv. 270, 272, 275, 279; in '45 signed the S. José call to foreigners. iv. 599; in '46 applied for land at S. José.   J. (T. H. or M.), 1848, at N. Helv. May.

Jones (Thos Ap Catesby), 1842, commodore U.S.N., in com. of the Pac. squadron, taking possession of Mont. See iv. 39, 298-329, 569, 631. 636, 640, 652, 665; v. 579. He was again in com. of the squadron in '48-9.   J. (Thomas Jeremiah), 1821, Engl. sawyer, baptized at S. Juan B. in '23, and naturalized in '41, at which time he had a native wife. Jeremiah J., often ment. in records of '39-40, and perhaps one of the arrested foreigners, may have been the same man. ii. 444, 496; iv. 17.

Jones (Walter), 1846, at S. José. *Hall.*   J. (Wm), 1838, doubtful name of an Amer. captured by Mex. pirates and forced to work as a slave in the mines; at Mont. with wife and 2 children in '44, acc. to Geo. Reed, in *S.F. Calif.*, May 22, '47. iv. 119.   J. (Wm), 1843, immig. from Or. in the Hastings party. iv. 390; nothing more known of him unless he is the J. who left N. Helv. for Or. in '46. v. 526.   J. (Wm), 1847, Co. C, N.Y.Vol. (v. 499); at Sonoma '71-4.   J. (W.D.), 1847, in U.S.N. '47-54, spending the rest of his life at Vallejo, where he died in '76.   J. (Wm Owen), 1816, pilot of the *Lydia.* ii. 275.   J. (Zachariah), 1846, overl. immig. who settled at S. José with wife and 5 children, Margaret, Reuben, Sam. E., and Clark. He kept a hotel in '47, built a saw-mill at Los Gatos '48, and was still living in '60. One of his daughters married Josiah Belden in '49.   Jongh (Wm F.D.), 1846, in com. of a gun in Marston's Sta Clara campaign.   Jonvera (Louis), 1829, Frenchman, age 28, at S. José April.

Jordan (J.), 1841, carpenter on the U.S. *St Louis.*   J. (Jackson), 1848, owner of S.F. lot; perhaps the same.   J. (Louis), 1842, trader at Los Ang. '42-6, being regidor in '45-6. iv. 341, 633-4; v. 625.   J. (Mariano), 1846, at Los Ang.   J. (Philip), 1847, Co. F, N.Y.Vol. (v. 499).   Jourdain (Étienne), 1847, at Los Ang.; Fr. consular agent at S.F. '48. v. 614-15.   Joy (Manuel), 1846, Co. F, Cal. Bat. (v. 358); Cal. claim of $20 (v. 462).   J. (Wm), 1848, clerk for C. L. Ross at S.F.; still in S.F. '54.   Joyce (John), 1846, one of the Mormon col., with wife, Caroline, and 2 daughters, Augusta and Helen F. v. 546. He was a carpenter who got a town lot in '47. v. 686; went to the mines in '48; was still at S.F. in '50; and in '64 lived at Centreville, Alameda Co., age 42. Possibly there was another Mrs J. and fam., who went to Utah and died before '84.   J. (Thos), 1848, passp. from Hon.   Joynes (J.), 1845, sailmaker on the U.S. *Warren.*

Juan (Luiz), 1840, reward offered for the discov. of his murderers at S. Diego. Juan (Ricardo), 1845, Frenchman at Branciforte, age 28, wife Maria Cota, child Jesus. Juan Bautista, 1836, Greek fisherman at Mont. Juan de Dios, executed at Mont. '45. Juan Evangelista, neophyte taken to Mex. by P. Serra. i. 321. Juarez (Andrés), soldier of Mont. comp. '36, age 19; juez of valley ranchos '46. v. 637.

Juarez (Cayetano), nat. of Cal.; soldier of S. F. comp. '28-31, corp. '32-5; but apparently acting as sergt from '33, being majordomo at Solano in '36, and later capt. of militia, engaged in many Ind. exped. iii. 701-2, 705, 720. In '41 he was grantee of the Tulucay rancho in Napa Val., where he built an adobe house and spent the rest of his life, being alcalde at Sonoma in '45, and grantee of Yukaya (Ukiah) in the same year. iv. 674, 678. In '46 he somewhat distinguished himself by his plans to rescue the Bear prisoners. v. 120; and by a famous swim of some 9 miles to escape capture. In '75 he gave me some rambling *Notas*. He died at Napa in '83, at the age of about 75. Portrait in *Napa Co. Hist.* J. (Francisco), at Branciforte '28-30. ii. 627; síndico '36. iii. 697; his wife was Dolores Cota; children in '28, Mateo and Antonio. J. (Francisco), at S. José '41, age 35, wife Andrea Pinto, child. Narciso b. '29, Juan '31, María '32, Jesus '34, Paula '36, Juan de Dios '38, Natividad '40. J. (Joaquin), at Brancif. '30-45, age 60 in '45, wife Pascuala Lorenzana, child. Luis b. '17, Solano '33. ii. 627. J. (José), soldier of S.F. comp. '37-9. J. (José C.), at Brancif. '45, age 26, wife Fernanda Figueroa, child José. J. (José Manuel), at Brancif. '28; at S. Isidro '36; at S. José '41, age 39, wife Pascuala Figueroa, children Benjamin b. '29, Gertrudis '30, Andrea, '35, José M., Jr, '36. J. (José María), at Brancif. '30. ii. 627. J. (Marcos), soldier at Mont. '34. iii. 673; at Sonoma '44, age 45. J. (Mateo), at La Brea, Mont., '36, age 23, wife Tomasa Galindo, child Trinidad. J. (Vicente), at S. José '33-41, age 23 in '41; also a soldier in S.F. comp. '37.

Judd (Hiram), 1847, Co. E, Morm. Bat. (v. 469). Judd (Zadock K.), 1847, ditto; in Utah '82. Judson (Henry), 1847, Co. D, N.Y. Vol. (v. 499); died Mokelumne Hill '49. Julian, 1845, at N. Helv. iv. 578, 587. He was a French Canadian who settled on a rancho in the upper Sac. Val., and is said by Bidwell to have joined Gillespie and Frémont, and to have been killed by the Ind. in May '46. Julio, neophyte alcalde killed in '13 near Mission S. José. ii. 324-5. Julio César, ex-neophyte of S. Luis Rey, living in '78 with a son and 3 grandchidren at Tres Pinos, S. Benito Co., where he gave me an interesting narrative of old-time *Cosas de Indios*. Juncosa (Domingo), 1771, Span. friar, nat. of Cataluña, who came on the *S. Antonio*. He was one of the first missionaries of S. Luis Ob., though not present at the founding, and he served there until 1774, when he retired to his college. Very little appears in the records about this padre; mention in i. 173, 176, 178, 188-9, 196.

Kaan, 1848, at N. Helv. Kal (C.), 1846, doubtful name at Los Ang. Kalohe, 1848, passp. from Hon., with wife. Kamp (Harold), 1847, Co. C, N.Y. Vol. (v. 499); at Sonoma '71-82. Kampt, 1846, blacksmith at N. Helv., had a fight with Daylor. Kane (Elias K.), 1848, lieut of dragoons in Graham's battalion from Mex. v. 522; capt. and asst Q. M. at Mont. '50. K. (Peter), 1847, Co. I, N.Y. Vol. (v. 499); died before '82. K. (Wm S.), 1847, at S. Pedro. Kapawa, 1848, passp. from Hon. Kappis (Geo.), 1847, Co. C, N.Y. Vol. (v. 499). Karr (Wm), 1847, Co. F, 3d U.S. artill. (v. 518). Katt (Wm), 1798, Boston sailor at S. Diego. i. 545, 654. Kaufman (Julius), 1837, Co. G, N.Y.Vol. (v. 499). Kay (James), 1838, at Mont. Kays (John C.), 1846, at Los Ang.; at Sta B. from '48 to '85; his wife was Josefa Burke. See 'Keyes.'

Keapnell (Fred.), 1847, Co, D, N.Y. Vol. (v. 499). Kearney, 1843, com. of the U.S. *Constellation*. iv. 564. K. (James), 1847, Co. F, 3d U.S. artill. (v. 518). K. (John), 1846, Co. F, Cal. Bat., enlisting at S. Juan Oct. (v. 358). Kearny (Stephen W.), 1846, nat. of N.J.; lieut of 13th U.S. infantry from 1812; col 1st dragoons '36-46, stationed much of the time at Ft Leavenworth. In '46, being put in com. of the exped. to N. Mex., he

was made brigadier-gen. and sent across the continent to occupy Cal. His march to Cal., defeat at S. Pascual, and final mil. operations of '47 with Stockton are recorded in v. 197, 328, 334-56, 385-99, 473, 483. For his controversies with Stockton and Frémont, his rule as mil. gov. from March 1 to May 31, '47, his return east overland, and his prosecution of Frémont, see v. 411-62, 489-90, 543, 564, 645, 460-2. The affair at S. Pascual must be regarded as an inexcusable blunder on Kearny's part, but otherwise his course in Cal. was consistent and dignified in the midst of difficult circumstances, and his military record throughout his whole career was an honorable one, the violent tirades of Benton and other partisans of Stockton and Frémont being for the most part without foundation in justice. He died in '48. His name is borne by one of San Francisco's principal streets. His wife was a step-daughter of Clarke, of Lewis and Clarke exploring fame.

Keeney (Jonathan), 1848, miner from Or., where he still lived in '82. Keeny, 1845, of Grigsby-Ide party. iv. 579; prob. 'Kinney,' q. v. Keffer (J. L.), 1847, commander's clerk on the U.S. *Columbus.* Kehoe (Joseph H.), 1847, Co. D, N.Y. Vol. (v. 499); d. at Mont. '48. Keith (Wm), 1833, Amer. physician who had lived some years in Sonora. He came to Cal. prob. with Santiago Johnson and John Forster. iii. 409; and lived at Los Ang. for 3 years as surgeon and trader, going back to Hermosillo in '36. He returned to Cal. in '48, went to the mines, and died at or near Stockton soon after '49. The *Sonorense* of Oct. 6, '48, contains a very flattering notice of his services in Sonora. Kekuacaca, 1848, passp. from Hon.

Kell (John M.), 1846, mid. U.S.N., who took part in Marston's Sta Clara campaign of '46-7. v. 380. K. (Thomas), 1846, nat. of Engl. and overl. immig. from Mo. In the mines '48-9, and later a resident of S. José or vicinity, till his death in '78 at the age of 84. He left 4 or more sons and 2 daughters, the latter being the wives of C. Colombet and T. Carrol. Kellett, 1837, lieut in com. of H. B. M. S. *Starling* of Belcher's exped. '37, '39. iv. 106, 142-6; capt. of the *Herald* in '46. v. 578.

Kelley, 1846, at N. Helv. K. (Geo.), 1847, Co. E, Morm. Bat. (v. 469). K. (Hall J.), 1834, Amer. enthusiast on the subject of Pacific coast colonization, who visited Cal. en route to Or.; writer of books, pamphlets, and letters on his favorite subject. See iii. 409-11; iv. 129, 147; also *Hist. Or.* K. (Henry), 1831, Amer. sailor on the *Leonor.* iii. 405; at Sta B. '36, age 46 and single. K. (James), 1840, in Farnham's list of arrested foreigners. iv. 17. K. (John H.), 1842, sailor in Sutter's employ at Ross; at S. José '44; at N. Helv. '45. iv. 578, 587; prob. one of the Bears in '46. v. 110; in Co. E, Cal. Bat. (v. 358); in the mines '48-50; last seen by Bidwell '51. K. (Nicholas), 1847, Co. A, Morm. Bat. (v. 469). K. (Wm), 1847, Co. A, Morm. Bat. (v. 469); in Sutter's employ '47-8 as boat-builder and lumberman. K. (Wm), 1826, mr of the *Washington.* iii. 149. See also 'Kelly.'

Kelliher (Jeremiah), 1846, Co. C, 1st U.S. dragoons (v. 336). Kellogg (Benjamin F.), 1846, Co. E, Cal. Bat. (v. 358). The K. family seem to have been overl. immig. of this year, but I am unable to distinguish between the members. K. (Frank), 1846, resid. of Napa Co. to '68 and later. K. (F. E.), 1846, overl. immig. from Ill. with a family; Napa Co. official '50, '56; perhaps same as Frank. K. (Fred.), 1845, mid. on U.S. *Warren.* K. (H.), 1848, named in Mont. accounts. K. (Irwin), 1846, near St Helena '69; father-in-law of Wm Nash.

Kelly, 1816, mr of the *Atala.* ii. 282. K., 1824, mr of the *Hawaii.* ii. 519. K. (James), 1847, musician Co. I, N.Y.Vol. (v. 499). K. (John), 1847, Co. K, ditto; at N. Helv.; owner of S.F. lot. K. (Philip), 1847, Co. I, ditto; died in Calaveras '60. K. (Thomas). 1839, pilot of a Peruv. brig at S.F. K. (Wm H.), 1847, mr of the American whaler *Georgian;* died '72.

Kelsey (Andrew), 1841, overl. immig. of the Bartleson party. iv. 270, 275, 279; went to Or. in '43 with his brothers, but returned in '44 with the party bearing his name. iv. 390, 444-5. He prob. served under Capt. Gantt in the Micheltorena campaign of '44-5. iv. 486; and took part in the Bear revolt.

v. 110; perhaps joining the Cal. Bat., though I find no definite record of his name. In '47 he and his brother with others bought live-stock of Salvador Vallejo and obtained the privilege of grazing their cattle near Clear Lake. Andrew and a man named Stone went to live at the place where Kelseyville —so named for him—now stands, thus becoming the 1st settlers of Lake Co. The natives were numerous, and under oppression became hostile; K. and S. were men who scorned to use conciliatory methods with 'Injuns and such varmint;' and they were both killed, as they well deserved to be, in '49; but soon a force was sent to butcher hundreds of the Ind. in vengeance.

Kelsey (Benj.), 1841, brother of Andrew, and one of the Bartleson party, accomp. by his wife, Nancy A., the 1st woman who came to Cal. by the direct overland route. iv. 270, 272, 275, 279. What has been said of Andrew above may be applied to Benj., except what relates to the former's death. iv. 390, 444-5; v. 110, 148. The brothers called Napa Val. their home from '45, and though they worked sometimes at N.Helv. they preferred the adventurous life of hunters. They were rough men, often in trouble with the authorities. Though one of the owners, Benj. did not live at the Clear Lake establishment, but his treatment of Ind. carried practically as slaves to the mines did much to provoke the killing of his brother. The family lived in Or.·again '51-5, later in Texas, and at various points of southern Cal. in '60-78 or later. There were 2 children in '45, and the scalping of a daughter on the way to Texas is mentioned. Ellen K., said to have been born at N.Helv. Aug. 2, '45, may have been his daughter.

Kelsey (David), 1844, brother (or possibly father) of Andrew and Benj.; came to Or. in '43, and to Cal. in the Kelsey party of '44 with his wife, 3 daughters, and perhaps a son. iv. 444-5. He settled at French Camp, but died at Stockton in '45 of small-pox, from the effects of which disease Mrs K. became blind. v. 674. Of the son nothing appears. A married daughter, Mrs Rebecca Fowler, left her husband and was married by Sutter, in Dec. '45, to Grove Cook. Josephine married Dr C. Grattan, and died at Stockton in '71. America married Geo F. Wyman in '46; and a 4th daughter became the wife of Willard Buzzell. K. (Samuel), 1844, brother of Andrew and Benj., and member of the Kelsey party from Or., having started with Hastings in '43, but turned back on meeting his brothers. iv. 269, 444-5, 453. I have his autog. letter of Sept. 7, '44, at Sonoma, on troubles in which the brothers were involved in connection with the Bale affair. He was prominent in the Bear revolt and a signer of the original proclamation of June 14th, in my possession. v. 95, 104, 110, 153; also one of the Cal. claimants (v. 462). Nothing appears about his family or what became of him.   K. (Wm) 1847, boat-builder at N.Helv.

Kemble (Edward C.), 1846, printer who came with the Mormon colony, though possibly not a member of the church. v. 546. He served in Co. G, Cal. Bat. (v. 358); and from April '47 was editor of the *S. F. Star*, succeeding Jones. v. 657-9. His connection with the *Star* and its successors, the *Star and Californian* and *Alta California*, as editor or proprietor continued to '55, though he was also the founder of the Sac. *Placer Times* and its editor in April-June '49. He was sec. of the S.F. council in '48, and somewhat prominent in local matters. vi. 649, 656; being regarded as a young man of good abilities and character. After '55 he went east, and in the war of '61-5 was connected with the army as paymaster, subsequently spending some years from '67 on the Pacific coast as inspector of Ind. affairs; and being later connected with the Associated Press in N.Y., where he still lives in '85, a card from him on 'Early journalism in S.F.' appearing in the *Bulletin* of Feb. Kempsey (Bartholomew.), 1848, died in '61. *Herald.*   Kempst (Geo. W.), 1847, Co. I, N.Y.Vol. (v. 499).   Kemsey (Thomas), 1846, Co. F, Cal. Bat. (v. 358).

Ken (John M.), 1845, mid. on the U.S. *Savannah*.   Kendall (Alva), 1847, Co. K, N.Y.Vol. (v. 499).   Kendrick (John), 1789, mr of the *Columbia*, the 1st Amer. vessel to visit the N.W. coast, sighting the Cal. coast on the way north. He visited Mont. in com. of the *Aranzazu* in 1794, and in

'99 was perhaps sup. of the *Eliza*. i. 445, 523-4, 545. Kennedy (Andy), 1848, said to have come to Cal. with Col Davis. K. (Edm. P.), 1836, com. of the U.S. *Peacock*. iv. 104-5, 140-1. K. (Edw. P.), 1847, Co. D, N.Y.Vol. (v. 499). K. (James), 1831, Irishman who in '35 got a lot at Mont., and in '36 was a clerk for Watson, age 46, and single. iii. 405. Naturalized in '41, when he lived at S. José, and claimed 10 years of residence in Cal.; at Sta Cruz, '42-3. K. (Joseph), 1846, Co. C, 1st U.S. dragoons; fatally wounded at S. Pascual. v. 346, 345. K. (Wm A.), 1847, Co. G, N.Y.Vol. (v. 499). Kennersly (A. J.), 1847, Co. E, ditto. Kenney (Chas), 1847, watchman at Mont. '47-8. K. (Wm S.), 1847, inspector of hides at S. Pedro; called Guillermo S. Kene. Keno (T.), 1846, one of the Donner relief party (?); had a claim on the Cosumnes; at Stockton in '80. *Sac. Co. Hist.* Kentzburg (Adolphus), 1847, Co. C, N.Y.Vol. (v. 499). Kenway (Geo. S.), 1847, from Hon. on the *Gen. Kearny,* and went back on the *Toulon.*

Kerby (John), 1844, sailor on the schr *California.* Kern (Edward M.), 1845, artist of Frémont's exped., and author of a published *Journal.* From the outbreak of the Bear Revolt he commanded the garrison at N. Helvetia, ranking as lieut in the Cal. Bat. He started east with Stockton in '47, but was left behind ill, and sailed from S. F. in Oct. on the *Com. Shubrick;* owner of a S. F. lot; Kern river and county are named for him. iv. 583, 585; v. 3, 6, 123, 244, 298-9, 359-60, 450, 453-4, 538, 675. Kerphy, 1847, mr of the *Maria Helena.* Kerr (Thomas), 1847, owner of S. F. lot.

Keseberg (Louis), 1846, Prussian, member of the Donner party, with wife Philipine, and children Louis and Ada. Both the children perished, the parents surviving. v. 531, 534, 541, 544. K. was the last of the party to be rescued; was forced to subsist on human flesh longer than his companions, among whom he had been unpopular from the first, and by some of whom— but chiefly by Capt. Fallon and his disappointed treasure-seekers of the last relief party—he was charged with robbery and murder. On this man have been concentrated in the public mind all the horror and loathing arising from the events of that terrible winter; he has been pictured as a fiend exulting in his cannibalism. It is fair to state that the charges rest on no tangible evidence, and that K. is entitled to be regarded as an unfortunate victim. His narrative as given by McGlashan bears every mark of truth, while the statements of his accusers are clearly tainted with exaggeration and falsehood. A portrait is given by McG., p. 220. Keseberg worked for Sutter as supercargo of his launch in '47, and later for Vallejo at Sonoma; went to the mines in 48-9; kept a boarding-house and hotel at Sac.; and was later a brewer at Calistoga and Sac. He made and lost several fortunes, being the victim of successive reverses by fire and flood. His wife died in '77; and in '80 he was living at Brighton, at the age of 66, in extreme poverty, with two grown-up daughters, both idiots. Two other married daughters survived, and 7 of his children had died. He was a man of intelligence, good education, and much business ability; and his record in Cal., except as affected by suspicions growing out of the affair of '46, was a good one. In '85 I have not heard of his death.

Ketchum (Thomas E.), 1847, lieut Co. B, N.Y.Vol., leaving N.Y. with recruits after the departure of the regiment. v. 503-4, 511; capt. of Cal. volunteers in the war of '61-5; and later brigadier-gen. of militia. A resident of Stockton, '71-82. Kettle, 1848, at S. F. from Tahiti. Kettleman, see Kittleman. Keyes (John), 1843, Irish steward on the *Soledad,* who had a barber-shop at Mont., but went soon to Los Ang. and Sta B., where he married a Miss Burke, and still lived in '70; claimant for Cañada de Salsipuedes. iv. 400, 642. Apparently identical with John C. 'Kays,' q. v. K. (Robert C.), 1845, overl. immig. of the Grigsby-Ide party, who went to Or. early in '46, but came back in '47; at Mont. '48; sheriff at S. José '49. v. 526, 576, 579, 587. K. (Mrs), 1846, of the Donner party, but died before reaching the Sierra. She had a son in Or., whom she expected to meet at Ft Hall, and who was possibly Robt C. Keyser (Guy M.), 1847, Co. B, Morm. Bat. (v. 469); in Utah '81.

Keyser (Sebastian), 1840, nat. of the Austrian Tyrol, a trapper who came overland to Or. with Sutter in '38, and again joined him at N. Helv., possibly not till '41. The first definite record is a letter of introd. from Sutter to Suñol in Aug. '41. iv. 117, 120, 139. He accompanied Dr Sandels in his valley travels of '43, having then selected a rancho adjoining Dickey's; was naturalized in '44, getting a grant of the Llano Seco rancho in Butte co. iv. 671; in '45 settled on Bear River as half owner of Johnson's rancho, serving also in Capt. Gantt's company. iv. 486. In '46 he was probably a Bear Flag man; may have served in the Cal. Bat. (v. 358); had part of his left hand blown off; and married Elizabeth Rhoads, who left him soon, but returned to make him happy in '47. He was one of the 4th Donner relief party. v. 541; sold his interest in the rancho in '49; and subsequently lived on Daylor's place, running a ferry on the Cosumnes for Daylor and Grimshaw, by the sinking of which craft he was drowned in '50. He left one child and $15,000 in gold-dust. His widow became Mrs Pierce, and was living in Fresno Co. '72. I have a letter of that year, in which she gives information about Keyser. Khlébnikof (Cyril), 1820, agent of the Russ. Amer. Fur Co. at Sitka, who visited Cal. in '20, '25-6, and '30-1. ii. 263, 317-19, 383, 644, 648; iii. 146, 213; iv. 160.   Khorstof (Nicholas), 1806, mr of the *Juno*. ii. 70.

Kilbey (James), 1847, Co. A, Morm. Bat. (v. 469), reënl.   Kiddey (Wm), 1848(?), Engl. liquor dealer at Sta Clara '76.   Kiernan (John B.), 1847, Co. E, N.Y.Vol. (v. 499); d. Stockton after '60.   Kiesler (Lafayette), 1847, Co. C, N.Y.Vol. (v. 499); at Sonoma '48.   Kilborn (Wm K.), 1847, mr and owner of the *Henry* '47-8. v. 578; of the S.F. firm K., Lawton, & Co. '48-9. Kilburn (Benj.), 1846, Cal. Bat. Co. B, artill., enlisting at S. José (v. 358); owner of a S.F. lot '47. v. 676.   K. (Ralph L.), 1842(?), a settler of Napa Val. from '44, but generally accredited to '42. iv. 341. In later years he stated that he built a mill on Dr Bale's rancho in 43. I find nothing about the manner of his coming. Naturalized '45, and subsequently married by Sutter; in '47-8 had an interest at Benicia, where he built houses for Larkin. v. 673. Alcalde at Napa '49; county treasurer '50; cl. for lands in '52. He died at Rutherford in '79, age 70. His daughter married a man named Lockwood. Kild (Adam H.), 1835, named as one of the owners of Palo Colorado rancho, Mont.   Kileven (Tom), 1806, mate of the *Peacock*, in prison at S. Juan Cap. ii. 38; perhaps the following.

Kimball, 1806, mr of the *Peacock*. ii. 37-8, 109.   K. (Hazen), 1848, overland Mormon immig. met by Bigler at the Humboldt sink in Aug.; memb. of Soc. Cal. Pion., and a resident of S.F. '83.   Kimsey (Alvis and Thos L.), 1847, owners of S.F. lots.   Kinch, 1847, mr of the *Com. Stockton*. v. 577.   King (Ed A.), 1847, mr of the *Elizabeth* and purchaser of the *Primavera;* mr of the *Hope* in '48. v. 577, 580; lumber dealer and underwriters' agent at Mont. '48; harbormaster '49 at S.F., where he still lived in '54.   K. (Henry), 1839, clerk in Sutter's employ.

King (Henry), 1845, one of Frémont's party, who served as capt. and commissary of the Cal. Bat., and went east on the *Com. Shubrick* in Oct. '47. v. 94, 360, 450, 453-4, 583. Joining Frémont's 4th exped. in '48, he was frozen to death before reaching Sta Fé, and probably eaten by his companion. He seems to have been a brother of James King of William.   K. (John H.), 1846, overland immig. who played poker in Eureka down to a late date acc. to the papers.   K. (John M.), 1847, Co. B, Morm. Bat. (v. 469).   K. (Manuel), 1835, Portuguese on Larkin's books '35-8. iii. 413.   K. (Robert), 1834, Engl. lumberman, who was one of Graham's men in '36-8, and was arrested in '40, but left at Sta B. sick. iii. 412; iv. 17. Naturalized in '41 and arrested for stealing lumber at Sta Cruz in '42, but escaped from jail; perhaps the man named in *Larkin's Accts* '45.   K. (Thomas), 1848, passp. from Hon.   K. (Wm), 1846, came to S. José. *Hall.*   K. (Wm), 1847, Co. F, N.Y.Vol. (v. 499).

King of William (James), 1848, nat. of Georgetown, D. C., assuming the affix 'of William' at the age of 16, from his father's given name, to distinguish himself from others named James King. He came to Cal. by way of Panamá and Valparaíso in Nov. '48, made some money in the mines, worked as clerk for Reading & Co. at Sac., and in '49 opened a bank at S.F., his family from the east joining him in '51. In '54-5 he was obliged to close his business, and was employed by Adams & Co. until the failure of that firm. In Oct. '55 he started the S.F. *Evening Bulletin,* and began a violent, fearless, and desperate crusade against prevalent corruption in the city. Though harsh and often injudicious in his methods, bitter in his prejudices, and generally disposed to abuse all who did not agree with his ideas of reform, he was honest in stating facts and aimed to be just in his attacks; and he was indirectly the instrument of great good to the community. He was shot in May '56 by James P. Casey, a politician and newspaper man whose unsavory record he had exposed, and his murder led to the organization of the famous Vigilance Committee. In my *Popular Tribunals,* vol. ii., the reader will find much information about King; and there is a sketch of his life and a portrait in the *Contemp. Biography.* He left a widow and 6 children, some of whom still live in S.F. in '85. Kingery (Sam.), 1848, nat. of Ohio; resid. of S. Luis Ob. Co. '68-83. Kingsbury, 1846, doubtful mention of a major at Sutterville. *SutterCo.Hist.,*18. K. (Elisha), 1848, on roll of Soc. Cal. Pion. Kingsley (Francis), 1846, Fauntleroy's dragoons (v. 232, 247). Kink (Robert), 1843, doubtful name of an Englishman at Branciforte in '45, age 36, wife Estefana Juarez, child Robert. v. 43. Kinley, 1846, doubtful mention at Hock Farm.

Kinlock (Geo.), 1830, Scotch carpenter and trader at Mont. with his wife, Mary Anderson, also Scotch, and the 1st foreign woman who lived in Cal. As their son Geo. David—the 1st child of foreign parents born in Cal.—was born in '30, they may have arrived a year or two earlier. From '30 K.'s name appears constantly in all kinds of Monterey records. In '36 his age was 39. He died about '58. His son Geo. D. in '48-9 was with Rose & Reynolds at Rose Bar. There was a daughter Catalina, born in '33. iii. 179-80, 221, 609; iv. 17. Kinnane (Patrick), 1847, Co. F. 3d U.S. artill. (v. 518). Kinney (A. and S.), 1845, overl. immig., perhaps of the Grigsby-Ide party. A. had a family and perhaps went to Or. in '46; S. was a 'hard case,' employed by Sutter during the winter, and went back east in the spring. v. 526, 579. K. (James), 1847, teamster in Co. F, 3d U.S. artill. (v. 518). Kinns (Alex.), 1847, Co. C, N.Y.Vol. (v. 499); d. at Sonoma Dec. '47. Kinsey, 1845, at N. Helv.: and a Dan. D. Kinsey is named in one list as one of the Stevens party of '44. Kintring (Chas M.), 1847, Co. E, N.Y.Vol. (v. 499).

Kirby (Henry), 1839, Engl. steward of the *Corsair,* who kept a restaurant at S. F. in '40; a witness against Capt. Hinckley in '40-1. iv. 119. K. (James), 1844, attendant of a sick sailor at Mont.; perhaps same as John K., a sailor. K. (Richard C.), 1846, Engl. tanner, who left a whaler on the Or. coast in '45, and came by land to Cal. with a party the next year. v. 526. He worked at his trade for Sutter during Bear Flag times, and later had a small tannery in the North Beach region at S. F. In '47-8 he worked at Sta Cruz; as miner and trader in the mines '48-9 he made a small fortune, which he soon lost in a city speculation; and from '50 he was engaged in the manufacture of leather at Sta Cruz, where he still lived in '79, and I think in '85. Portrait in *Sta Cruz Co. Hist.,* 16. Kirchner (Henry), 1848, partner of Weber at Stockton. *Tinkham.* Kirk (Thomas), 1847, Co. B, Morm. Bat. (v. 469). Kirkwood (James and John), 1846, Co. B, Cal. Bat. (v. 338); there was also a James, Jr, at Mont. in '47. The K.'s were overl. immig. mentioned by Bryant. Kisling (John W.), 1846, Danish sailor at S. F., who got a lot in '47, went to the mines in '48, and returning lived in town to '59, later at S. Mateo, and died in '61, leaving a widow and 2 children.

Kittleman (John), 1846, one of the Mormon colony with a family; owner of S.F. lot '47; died at Sta Cruz '52. His children, each of them obtaining a S.F. lot, were George; Thomas, who married Angeline Lovett at S.F. in '47, and was a constable in the same year; Sarah, who married E. P. Jones; and Wm, who died in Utah '55, leaving a widow and 6 children living at Centreville, Utah, '85. None of John's 4 children survives in '85. v. 546, 678, 680,

685.   Kleinbroth (John), 1847, musician N.Y.Vol. (v. 499); owner of S.F. lot. v. 678.   Kleinschrooth (John), 1847, Co. G, ditto; owner of S.F. lot; in S F. '52; in Germany '82.   Klengel (Francis), 1847, Co. C, ditto.   Klier (Wm), 1847, Co. F, 3d U.S. artill. (v. 518).   Klopper (Michael), 1847, Co. K, N.Y.Vol. (v. 499).

Knapp (Albert), 1847, Co. E, Morm. Bat. (v. 469); at Mont. '48.   K. (Joel B.), 1848, came from Hon. and went to the mines.   K. (M.), 1848, from Hon. on the *Julian*.   Knight, 1846, said by Lancey to have come with Kearny; a newspaper writer in S.F. '84.   Knight (Henry), 1840, one of the S. Blas exiles. iv. 18.   K. (Henry), 1844, Swiss, at S. F.; age 40; perhaps same as preceding.   K. (John), 1847, Co. K, N.Y.Vol. (v. 499); at Ukiah '71–82.   K. (Thomas), 1841, German sailor and sawyer, who left the *Alert* and got a passport.   K. (Thomas), 1845, native of Me; trader in La, Ark., and Mo.; overl. immig. of the Grigsby-Ide party, or of the Swasey-Todd branch of that party. iv. 576, 579, 587. All his property, including a stock of goods for sale, was destroyed by the explosion of a keg of powder under his wagon in the Sierra. He settled in Napa Val., took part in the Bear revolt. v. 110; and had some experience in the mines. In '51–70 he was a farmer in Napa and Sonoma counties, being owner of the Moristal or Berreyesa rancho. v. 671–2; and later a dealer in real estate at S.F. In '72 he wrote for me his *Recollections*, containing much information about early times and men; and in '79 he dictated another and briefer statement of *Early Events in Cal.* His wife was Serena Haines, married in '54; and in '72 they had two children, Chas P. S. and Thos G. He still resides in S.F. '85, at the age of 65.

Knight (Wm), 1841, nat. of Ind., naturalized and married to a native in N. Mex., who came with the Workman-Rowland party, returning in '42 to bring his family. v. 278–9. He settled in '43 on the Sacramento, at the place named for him, Knight's Landing—obtaining in '44 a renewal of his naturalization papers that had been lost. He served Micheltorena in Gantt's comp.; was a signer of the S. José call to foreigners; got a land-grant in '46; and took an active part in the Bear revolt, perhaps serving in the Cal. Bat. iv. 486, 501, 573, 599: v. 106, 110, 114–19, 637. After the discovery of gold he established Knight's Ferry on the Stanislaus, where he died in '49. He was a great hunter, and though said to have been educated as a physician, was a man of very rough ways, violent in temper, always ready to take offence, and to settle all differences by force. His title to lands, resting on Sutter's general title and a fraudulent grant from Pico, was not confirmed; and though reputed to be rich, his heirs are said to have received very little. Three of his daughters, still living in '85, I think, married respectively Chas F. Reed, J. N. Snowball, and Nathaniel Jacobs. A good sketch of Knight is given in *Yolo Co. Hist.*, 31.

Knoss (M.), 1846, Co. B, artill. Cal. Bat., enlisting at Sac. in Oct. (v. 358).   Knott, 1847, mr of the *Sweden*, bringing recruits for the N.Y.Vol. v. 511.   Knowles (Richard), 1846, one of the Mormon colony, with his wife; owner of S.F. lot '47. v. 546, 678. He died in the faith, and his widow was living in Utah '84.   Knox (Sam. P.), 1841, com. of the *Flying Fish*, of U.S. ex. ex. iv. 241, 565.

Kob (Geo.), 1847, Co. K, N.Y.Vol. (v. 499).   Koeger (Henry E.), 1846, at S. José. *Hall.*   Kohler (Deoden), 1847, owner of S.F. lot.   K. (Theodore G.), 1845, said to have arrived this year. iv. 587; in '49 a clerk for Wells & Co., S.F.; later connected with the Cal. press; died at S.F. '75.   Kolan, 1846, doubtful name in a Los Ang. list.   Kolmer (Michael), 1846, accomp. by wife and 3 children; settled near Bodega, one daughter marrying Wm Howard and another Wm Benitz. *Sonoma Co. Hist.*, 201.   Köenig (Wm), 1847, Co. C, N.Y.Vol. (v. 499); drowned in Sac. Riv. '47.   Kontz (John G.), 1847, Co. F, ditto.   Kook (Chas), 1847, Co. F, 3d U.S. artill. (v. 518).   K. (Theodore), 1839, at S. Diego.

Kooser (Benj. Park), 1847, Co. F, 3d U.S. artill.; nat. of Pa. He was a printer and connected with the press, even before his discharge, working as pressman on the *Californian* in '47, and writing letters for the eastern

papers. To one of his letters on the gold discov. in the N.Y. *Herald* is attributed much influence in directing the 1st stream of gold-seekers to Cal. After quitting the mil. service he was connected chiefly with S. Joaquin Co. papers till '65, having married Belle Ward of S. José in '62. Then he became editor and publisher of the Sta Cruz *Sentinel* for 11 years, his valedictory address appearing May 27, '76. He took a deep interest in pioneer reminiscences, and wrote many articles on the subject, his *Pioneer Soldiers of Cal.*, an account of the artill. company, being published in the *Alta* of '64. v. 520. In '76 he went east as centennial commissioner for Cal.; and died at Sta Cruz in '78, at the age of 56.   Korn (Julius), 1847, perhaps of N.Y.Vol. under another name.   Kornish, 1847, ditto.   Kosier, 1848, mr of a launch at N. Helv.   Kostromitinof (Peter), 1829, Russ. manager of Ross. '29-36; and in '40-1 agent for the sale of Ross and settling up all Russian business in Cal.; also visiting the country several times in later years on the same mission. ii. 651; iii. 426; iv. 161-4, 174-5, 178-80.   Kotzebue (Otto von), 1816, com. of the Russ. exploring ship *Rurik*, and author of a *Voyage of Discovery;* and again com. of the *Predpriate* in '24, and author of a *New Voyage*. For notice of his visit and writings, containing much useful information about Cal., see ii. 212-13, 278-80, 299, 309-10, 373, 517, 519, 522-5, 587, 590, 592, 597, 602-3, 645-6.   Kountze (Wm), 1847-8, Mormon, at Sutter's mill. *Bigler.*
Kraft (Chas), 1847, Co. F, 3d U. S. artill. (v. 518).   Krauss (Chas), 1847, musician, N.Y.Vol. (v. 499).   Kreutzer (John), 1847, Co. F, 3d artill. (v. 518).   Krewzburg, 1847, named at N. Helv. as one of the N.Y.Vol.   Krienan, 1847, named in '48 as a deserter from the N.Y.Vol.   Krohn (John M.), 1847, Co. C, N.Y.Vol. (v. 499).   Krusof (Stephen), 1822, mr of the *Apollo.* ii. 643.
Kunhardt, 1848, from Hon. on the *Sagudahoc.*   Kuntze (John C.), 1847, at N. Helv. and S.F., where he owned a lot.   Kuppertz (Gerard), 1836, mr of the *Peor es Nada.* iv. 105; in '37 (or '34) he announces that he has succeeded Sill & Co. as a baker at Sta B.   Kuprianof (Ivan), 1840, ex-gov. of the Russ. estab. in Alaska; visited Cal. on the *Nikolai.* iv. 105, 167, 174-6.   Kurtz (Lewis), 1847, Co. G, N.Y.Vol. (v. 499).   Kuskof (Ivan A.), 1808, Russ. explorer of the coast in 1808-11; founder of Ross in '12, and manager of that establishment until succeeded by Schmidt in '21, having visited S.F. in '16. ii. 80-2, 88, 198, 203-4, 210, 212-13, 267, 280, 294-318, 373, 630, 672-3.   Kutchback (Chas), 1847, Co. D, N.Y.Vol. (v. 499).
Kyburz (Daniel), 1847, owner of S.F. lot.   K. (Sam. E.), 1846, overl. immig. from Wisconsin with his wife and her brothers. Entered Sutter's employ as a kind of superintendent, and is often mentioned in the *N. Helv. Diary* '47-8, also owning a S.F. lot in '47. He took an active part in events connected with the gold discovery; and in '48-9 kept a hotel at Sac. In '50-4 he seems to have been a trader at S. F. Mrs K. had two children born at Sutter's Fort, one of them, a son, in Feb. '48; and she was living at Clarksville, El Dorado Co., in '80.

Labastida, soldier-teacher at S. José '22. ii. 603.   Labra (Juan Ant.), soldier, sentenced to death at Mont. for robbery 1781.   Lacousse, 1848, Canadian at Bear River and Mormon Diggings. *Brooks.*   Lacy (Sam.), 1839, mr of a Peruv. brig at S.F.   Ladd (Milton), 1845, one of the men lost on the *Warren's* launch '46. iv. 384, 587.   L. (Sam.), 1846, one of the Mormon colony, who went by the name of Johnson; formerly a soldier, being a teacher of tactics on the *Brooklyn;* went to Utah, where he still lived in '84. v. 546, 550.   L. (S. G.), 1847, at Benicia.   Laez (Mazario), claimed to have been grantee of land in Sta Clara Co. 1785.
Lafleur (Louis), 1846, Canadian in Co. G, Cal. Bat., enlisting at S. José Nov.; went east with Com. Stockton '47. v. 454; but returned, and in Dec. '48 was drowned in the Yuba.   Laframboise (Michel), 1832 (?), chief of the H. B. Co. hunters in Cal., making half a dozen or more visits in '32-46, especially in '35-42. The date of the 1st visit is uncertain. iii. 392-3, 408; iv. 135, 213, 220.   Lafrenz (C. F.), 1847, from Hon. on the *Xylon.*   L. (J. H.),

1848, passp. from Hon.   Lagos (J. B.), 1848, ditto.   Lagrace (Fran.), 1840, perhaps one of the arrested foreigners. iv. 17.
Laidlaw (Geo.), 1847, Co. B, N.Y.Vol. (v. 499).   Laighton (John B.), 1835, lieut in Mex. navy stationed at Mont.; went to S. Blas to join his corps in '36. He was an American.   Laine (Thos H.), 1847, nat. of Mo., who came to Cal. at the age of 15, and became a prominent lawyer of Sta Clara; memb. of the state senate '74-7, and of the constit. convention of '78.   Laird (John W.), 1847, nat. of Pa and overl. immig. with his family. In Feb. '48 he kept a ferry on the Sac. Riv. at Montezuma. v. 674; acc. to the newspapers Mrs L. had a son born on the Amer. Riv. in May, '47, but it was prob. in '48. Laird kept a store at Angels, living also at Stockton and other places; but in '50 settled in Stanislaus Co., where he died in '78, leaving a widow—a sister of Thos Pyle—and 3 children.
Lajeunesse (Basil), 1845, Canadian trapper and member of Frémont's exploring party, who was killed by Ind. on the Or. frontier in the night attack on Frémont's camp, April '46. iv. 583, 587; v. 24.   L. (François), 1833 (?), probably brother of Basil, said to have visited Cal. either in the Walker party or in one of the H. B. Co. parties. He was one of Frémont's men in '44, but did not reach Cal. iii. 391.   Lake (John), 1846, Fauntleroy's dragoons (v. 232, 247).
Lamanon, 1786, with La Pérouse. i. 435.   Lambaren (Juan), 1842, adj. of the batallon fijo, who died '44. iv. 289.   Lambdon, 1847, at N. Helv. Lambert (John A.), 1847, Co. E, N.Y.Vol. (v. 499).   Lamoine, 1847, mr of the *François*.   Lamoreux (Louis), 1840, Canadian carpenter, age 37, at Los Ang. with a N. Mex. passport; perhaps his name was Lamoreau, still at Los Ang. '48.   Lamotte (François), 1845, negro deserter from the *Héroine* at Mont.   Lamplicie (Wm), 1824, mate of the *Rover*.   Lampman (Wm L.), 1847, Co. A, N.Y.Vol. (v. 499); in Mexico '82.   Lance (Wm), 1847, Co. E, Morm. Bat. (v. 469); reënl.
Lancey (Thomas Crosby), 1846, nat. of Me., born in '24, and a sailor from '42; a coxswain on the U.S. *Dale* in '46-9. After his discharge from the navy in '49 he took charge of a store at Mormon Isl., and later was drayman, teamster, and stage-driver in the Sac. region till '51, when he came to S. F., and has since resided here as mining agent and painter. For 4 or 5 years, in '85, he has been confined to his room, and much of the time to his bed. He kept a journal during his service in the navy, supplemented with many items obtained from later observations, reading, and association with pioneers, with a view to publication in book form as material for history. Being prevented by failing health from carrying out his purpose, he furnished a part of his historical gleanings to the S. J. *Pioneer* for publication in '79-81. The result, *Lancey's Cruise of the Dale*, preserved in my Library in scrap-book form, v. 190, is in many respects the most complete collection extant of data on the conquest of Cal. The author has shown not only indefatigable zeal, but marked ability in his researches. The matter is not always systematically arranged; the effect is marred by typographic errors, resulting chiefly from the newspaper medium of publication; the author is often in error respecting matters resting on Spanish documentary evidence; and he is, in my opinion, excessively American in his views; but with all its faults, the work merits praise, and justifies me in placing the author high in the list of those who have done faithful work on Cal. history. Lancey also wrote a sketch of the N.Y.Volunteers, published in *Clark's First Regiment*. (Died in '85.)
Landaeta (Martin), 1791, Span. friar, who served chiefly at S.F., and died at S. Fern. in 1810. Biog. ii. 115-16; mention i. 510, 514, 576-7, 706, 712, 721; ii. 130-1, 159-60.   Landers (Ebenezer), 1847, Co. C, Morm. Bat. (v. 469); at Salem, Utah, '82.   L. (Wm), 1847, Co. H, N.Y.Vol. (v. 499); sheriff in '48; died at S. F. '50.   Lane, 1848, sutler in Graham's battalion (v. 522).   L. (Emmeline A.), 1846, one of the Mormon colony. v. 546.   L. (Joseph), 1848, passed through Cal. on his way from Sta Fé to Or.; a prominent man in the north. See *Hist. Or.*   L. (Lewis), 1847, sergt Co. D, Morm. Bat. (v. 469).   L. (Samuel), 1846, one of the men lost on the *Warren's* launch. v. 364.   Lané, 1842, doubtful name of a ranch owner near S. Luis Ob.

Lang (Charles), 1828, Amer. smuggler at S. Diego '28–9; ii. 551; iii. 139, 168. L. (Chas), 1848, from Boston on the *Sabine*. L. (John P. and Willis), 1848, brothers from Mo., at Sutter's Fort and in the mines. Langdon (Maurice), 1846, came with Kearny. *Lancey.* Langenberger (A.), 1848, German miner on the Yuba and Stanislaus '48–9; later a trader at S. Gabriel and Anaheim, where he lived in '80 with 7 children by his 1st wife, a daughter of Juan P. Ontiveros, married in '50. Langle, 1786, with La Pérouse. i. 428, 431–3. Langlois (A.), 1848, passp. from Hon. Langlois (William), 1840, Canadian, exiled with the Graham party, who returned in '41; perhaps the Laingles named at Sonoma in '50. iv. 18, 33, 37, 120. Langsdorff (G. H. von), 1806, German naturalist with Rezánof at S.F., and author of a book of *Voyages and Travels*, containing a narrative of the author's visit and observations in Cal. ii. 46–7, 65–76, 115, 128, 130, 138–40, 164, 176. Lanman (Joseph), 1847, lieut U.S.N., com. of the *Warren* '47–8. v. 581. L. (Stephen), 1846, sailmaker on the U.S. *Dale*. Lansing, 1847, mr of the *Citizen*. v. 577. Lanson (J.), 1847, blacksmith at S. Diego.

La Pérouse (Jean F. G.), 1786, French navigator, the first foreign voyager to touch the coast of Cal. after Span. occupation; and author of a *Voyage* which contains much valuable information about Cal. See account of his visit and book in i. 428–40; also ment. i. 282, 475, 509, 512, 519, 527, 619; ii. 23, 131, 616. Lapierre (Louis), 1845, Canadian boat-maker of Frémont's party. iv. 583. He is said to have built a schooner for Sainsevain at Sta Cruz in later years. Laplace (Cyrille P. T.), 1839, com. of the French man-of-war *Artémise*, and author of a *Campagne de Circumnavigation*. iv. 152–5; ment. iii. 695, 700; iv. 93, 101, 165. Lappeus (James H.), 1847, Co. H, N.Y.Vol. (v. 499); owner of S.F. lot; trader at Sac. '48; married in '49 to Ann Hitchcock. He went later to N.Y. and Idaho, and in '82 lived at Portland, Or., where he had been city marshal, and for 12 years chief of police.

Lara, sentinel at Los Ang. '37. iii. 519. L. (Antonio), alguacil at Mont. '36. iii. 675. L. (Casimiro), inválido of Sta B. comp. '32. L. (Fran.), soldier of S. F. comp. '39–42. L. (Fran.), killed at S. Pascual. v. 179. L. (José), one of the 1st settlers at Los Ang. 1781; Span., with an Ind. wife. L. (Juan), soldier and corp. S.F. comp. '37–42. L. (Julian), soldier at Sta B. before '37. L. (Romualdo), 1837, Mex. of the H. & P. colony, implicated in the troubles of '35, and sent to Mex. under arrest. iii. 281, 286, 288.

Lard (Fielding), 1846, overl. immig. with his family. The marriage of his daughter (Mary to R. S. Moultrie) on the trip is mentioned by Bryant; at Sutter's Fort in '47, and owner of a S.F. lot, but settled in Sta Clara Val., where he still lived in '60; often called Wm. L. (Joseph A.), 1846, came to Sta Clara; prob. son of Fielding. Lardner, 1842, lieut U.S.N., with Jones at Mont. iv. 308. La Reintrie (Henry), 1842, commander's sec. on the *Yorktown*.

Larios (Gracia), sent to Mex. as a prisoner '30. iii. 85. L. (José María), Mex. sold. who came between 1780 and '90; from '91 a settler at S. José, and later at Las Aromas, near S. Juan B. He was a blacksmith and builder of mills, but was chiefly noted as a bear-hunter, being killed by a grizzly in 1818. i. 642, 716, 718; ii. 135, 170, 387. His first wife was Juliana Linares, and the 2d Eusebia Álvarez; his children were Antonio, Manuel, José Dolores, Justo, María del Pilar, Antonia, and Antonina. L. (Justo), son of José M., b. at S. José 1808; soap-maker and ranchero who served as miltia artilleryman in the war against Micheltorena '44–5, and for a short time under Castro in '46; grantee of Cañada de los Capitancillos in '42. iv. 671; all his horses were taken by Frémont. He made two successful visits to the mines in '49–50, but in later years lost all his land and other property, through no fault of his own, as he believes. In '78, living at Gilroy, he gave me an interesting narrative called *Convulsiones en California*. His wife was Cecilia, daughter of Joaquin Castro, married in '33; children '41, Adelino b. '34, Juan '36, Olivero '39, Soledad '38. L. (Manuel), son of José M., b. at S. José 1798. He seems to have served as a soldier in '15–29, and was later an alférez of militia, serving in Gov. Alvarado's time. In '39 he was grantee of Sta.

Ana rancho near S. Juan B., which was finally confirmed to him. iii. **679,** **713.** In '40 he was juez at S. Juan, and took part in the arrest of the foreigners. iii, 693; iv. 20. He was, like his father, a famous bear-hunter, took part in various exped., and his rancho suffered much from Ind. depredations. iv. 362; v. 662. He died in '63. His wives were successively María A. Pacheco, Guadalupe Castro, and Rosario Arnas, by whom he is said to have had 22 children. In '78 his son (or grandson), Estolano Larios, gave me some information on the *Vida y Adventures* of Don Manuel.

　　Larkin (Thomas Oliver), 1832, nat. of Mass., b. at Charlestown in 1802, in business at Wilmington, N.C., from '21 to '30, and in '31 accepting an invitation from Capt. Cooper, his half-brother, to join him at Monterey. His mother was then married to a 3d husband, Mr Childs. L.'s passport from the gov. of Mass. is dated Sept. 2, '31, and he came on the *Newcastle* via Honolulu, arriving in April '32. iii. 364, 408. In '32 he was employed by Cooper as clerk, or accountant; in Feb.–Sept. '33 he did a small commission business, and then with a capital of $500 he opened a little store at Mont. for the sale of groceries, grog, produce, and dry goods, starting a flour-mill the next year, and dealing to a considerable extent in lumber. In '33 he was also married on board the *Volunteer* at Sta B., by Consul Jones of Honolulu, to Mrs Rachel Holmes, née Hobson, his fellow-passenger on the *Newcastle*, who had come to join her husband, Capt. John C. Holmes, but on arrival had found herself a widow. iii. 365, 408, 652. She was the 1st Amer. woman to live in Cal., and her son Thomas O., born in April '34, was the 1st child born of Amer. parents in Cal. Having the proverbial Yankee shrewdness in trade, with no inconvenient veneration for the revenue laws, Larkin prospered from the first. In his ledgers he has left careful memoranda of his wealth on Jan. 1st of each year as follows: '35, $2,650; '36, $4,708; '37, $5,626 (chiefly in house and mill, for he had spent all his money on the house and had no goods); '38, $11,013; '39, $13,788; '40, $15,895; '41, $21,493; '42, $37,958; '43, $49,147; '44, $46,-505; '45, $60,175; '46, $66,644. He did not seek to become a Mex. citizen, but in '36 obtained a carta, which was renewed from year to year. He took no part openly in politics, but quietly supported Alvarado's movement in '36. iii. 461; iv. 141. I have much of his business corresp. from the first. In '39 he made a special effort to induce whalers to touch at Mont. iv. 92. In '40 he did all that he could for the comfort of the arrested foreigners, but because he did not join in the loud protests and absurd threats of Graham and his gang he was the subject of some unfavorable criticism at the time and later. iv. 8, 9, 24, 32–3. He visited Mex. in '40–1 on business. iv. 102, 207; on his return took a contract to build the Mont. custom-house; and in '42 did good service in maintaining friendly relations between Com. Jones and the Californians. iv. 307, 310, 329. The same year he established a branch store at Sta Cruz in charge of Josiah Belden; but an incendiary fire destroying $6,000 worth of lumber in '43 made this part of his business unprofitable. In '43–4 he had somewhat intimate business relations with Gov. Micheltorena, making loans to the govt, and doubtless was induced by personal interests to look with too much favor on the cholo cause, making also another visit to Mex. on govt business, and bringing back the small-pox, among other results. iv. 364, 366, 401–3, 405, 473, 478–9, 558–9, 563, 651. On his return he assumed the position of U.S. consul at Mont., his appointment having been made at Wash. in '43 and renewed in '44, and from the first was active in sending accurate information to his govt respecting Cal. affairs, as well as in the routine duties of his office. iv. 385, 408, 428, 430, 450, 454, 561, 589–98. Larkin's closeness in money matters, in contrast with the reckless prodigality affected by many, prevented his ever reaching in a certain sense the highest popularity, but he was always respected by the better classes of natives and foreigners as a man of honorable conduct, of sound judgment, and of conservative though not selfish views on general topics. He was a man of slight education, but of much tact and practical good sense. Duly devoted to the interests of his govt and of the Amer. immigrants, he had no sympathy with filibusterism, and did not ignore the rights and prejudices of the Californians. He fully believed that, either in the event of war with Mex. or by purchase, the people and local rulers might be induced voluntarily to transfer their allegiance to the U.S. At the end of '45 he was formally appointed a secret and confidential agent of the adminis- tration at Wash. to bring about this result; and from the beginning of '46, turning over his private business to Talbot H. Green, he worked earnestly, and as he believed with good prospects of success, to make friends for the U.S. and to counteract the effects of the few who favored an English protectorate. v. 4-28, 54-76, 109, 142, 219-20. Frémont's foolish bravado at Gavilan, and the still more foolish and criminal Bear revolt, were wellnigh fatal blows to his plans; but still he did not despair, and having used his influence with Com. Sloat successfully in favor of a conservative policy, v. 224-54, he went south with Stockton, hoping with the aid of his associate, Abel Stearns, to induce Castro and Pico, with the people of the south, to submit without re- sistance, artfully presenting to them the danger that the U.S. forces, in case the report of war should prove unfounded as in '42, would retire and leave Cal. at the mercy of the Bears. That Stockton took effective and dishonorable steps to prevent the success of these plans, fearing that the submission of the gov. and general would interfere with the immediate prospects of himself and his associate filibusters, is no discredit to Larkin, whose course through- out is worthy of all praise, his statesmanship being incomparably superior to that of the opera-bouffe 'conquerors' of Cal. v. 271-2, 281. Returning to Mont., L. was appointed acting U.S. naval agent, interesting himself also in the release of the Bears' captives at N. Helvetia. v. 281, 298-9, 304. In '45-6 he was a correspondent of the N.Y. *Herald* and *Sun*. In Nov., while on his way to visit a sick daughter at S.F., L. was captured by the Califor- nians under Manuel Castro, became a witness of the fight at Natividad, and was carried south to be retained as a captive till the end of the war. He was kindly treated, there being no ill-will toward him, and the intention being to utilize the possession of so prominent a man either in exchange or in making favorable terms of capitulation. v. 358, 364-5, 367-70, 402. Returning north in '47, he served as naval store-keeper, and his appointment as naval agent was confirmed in Wash. v. 614. He was also a member of the legislative council which never met. v. 433. He took, however, but slight part in public affairs. v. 443, 448, 455, 571; being notified in June '48 that his functions as counsel and confidential agent terminated in May with the treaty of peace. He had become the owner of various S.F. lots, and in partnership with Sem- ple, the founder of Benicia in '47. v. 653, 660, 671-4. In '49 he was a member of the constit. convention, and his naval agency was discontinued by orders from Wash. In '50-3 he resided with his family in N.Y., but returned to S.F. and gave his attention to the care of his property. Though unable to sustain his title to a S.F. grant and the Sta Clara orchard, he was the successful claimant for the Flügge and Jimeno ranchos in the Sac. Val. v. 665-6, 670-1; and these, with his possessions in S.F., Mont., and Benicia, made him a very rich man. His sons had also been the grantees in '44 of a rancho in Colusa. iv. 671. Larkin died at S.F. in '58. He was a man to whom nothing like just credit has hitherto been given for his public services in '45-6. Portraits are given in *Colton's Three Years in Cal.*, *Annals of S.F.*, and there are photographs in the library of the Soc. Cal. Pion. A street in S.F. bears his name. Mrs L. died in '73, at the age of 66. The children were Thos O. b. in '34; an infant son who died in '36; Fred. H. b. in '37, d. '69; Adelaide who died at S.F. in '46; Francis R. b. '40, d. '74; Alfred O. born in '48; and a daughter who married Sampson Tams. Thomas, Alfred, and Mrs Tams are still living, I think, in '85. The Larkin manuscripts furnished for my use as material for history by representatives of the family have been named in my list of au- thorities, with some comments, in i: 49-50. They constitute a most magnifi- cent and unequalled contribution to the history in which the father of the donors took so prominent and honorable a part. L. (Wm M.), 1843, on the roll of the Soc. Cal. Pion. iv. 400.   Larragoyli (Rafael), 1822, mr of the *S.F. de Paula*. ii. 474.   La Roche (Eugene), 1846, witness in the Santillan case '55, age 33.   La Rocque (Geo.), 1848, Canadian miner from Or. on the

Henry; went back in '49 to Or., where he died in '77, leaving a widow and 4 children. Laskey (Alex. B.), 1847, Co. D, N.Y.Vol. (v. 499); killed by Ind. '48.

Lassen (Peter), 1840, Danish blacksmith who came to Amer. in '19, to Or. overland in '39, and to Cal. by the *Lausanne,* landing at Bodega, and thence proceeding to Sutter's Fort, S.F., and S. José, where he worked at his trade though the winter of '40-1. iv. 117, 120-1, 136. In the spring of '41 he built a saw-mill near Sta Cruz, which he sold to Graham early in '43. Dr Sandels describes him this year as a travelling blacksmith and hunter between S.José and Sac.; he had a hut on the Cosumnes in Nov.; applied for naturalization, and selected a rancho. In '44 he got his papers and his land-grant of Bosquejo on Deer Cr., Tehama Co. iv. 670-1. His place is often mentioned in '45-6. iv. 229, 580; v. 22, 24-5, 102; he was with Gillespie and Frémont and probably one of the Bears in '46; but is said to have gone east in the Stockton party of '47, returning, prob. with Chiles, in '48; but I think there may be an error in this, and that L. went no farther east than Fort Hall, his mission being to divert immigration into the Lassen route to the upper Sac. Val. He was owner of a S.F. lot in '47. In '50 he sold half of his rancho and stock, engaging in unfortunate steamboat speculation at Sac. which soon ruined him financially. In '51 he settled in Indian Val., Plumas Co.; and in '55, as miner and farmer in Honey Lake Val., Lassen Co. In '59, while on a prospecting tour in the region north of Pyramid Lake, he was killed by Ind., or possibly white man disguised as Ind., being then 59 years old. Portrait in *Plumas, Lassen, and Sierra Co. Hist.,* 56. His memory is preserved in the name of Lassen peak and county.

Lasso de la Vega (Ramon), 1781, Mex. alférez of the S.F. comp., and sometimes habilitado; retired on half pay in '94; later a teacher at S. José; died in 1821, at the age of 64. Biog. i. 470-1; ment. 340, 342-3, 385, 584, 642, 693, 716. Lasuen (Fermin Francisco), 1773, Span. friar who served as missionary, chiefly at S. Diego till 1785, when he was chosen president of the missions, a position held until his death at S. Cárlos in 1803. In all the annals of the Fernandinos there is presented no more admirable character than that of Padre Fermin. Biog. ii. 8-10; ment. i. 122, 194-6, 248-9, 266-7, 300, 302-4, 316, 328, 388, 398-406, 417, 422-5, 432, 439, 441, 454-9, 469, 471, 474, 476, 480, 491-3, 498-9, 512-13, 522, 531, 537, 542, 544, 553-5, 557, 559-64, 568, 573-4, 576, 578-99, 600-23, 626, 655, 686, 689, 709-11, 727-8; ii. 3, 146, 159, 165, 378, 623.

Lataillade (Cesáreo), 1842, Span. of French descent, and member of a Mex. trading firm, who came as sup. of the *Trinidad.* iv. 341, 569. He became well known as a man of business, making Sta B. his home. From '46 he was vice-consul of Spain at Mont., being allowed to reside at Sta B. from '47, and being the grantee of Cuyamas rancho in '46. iv. 590; v. 218, 615, 632. His name often appears in official commun. during the mil. régime of '47-8; he was mentioned in connection with idle rumors of revolts. v. 586; and took a prominent part in arresting the murderers of the Reed family. v. 640. He accidentally shot and killed himself at Sta B. in '49. His wife was María Antonia de la Guerra, who was claimant for several ranchos, iii. 655; iv. 642, became the wife of Gaspar de Oreña, and is still living in '85. Latham, 1846, Cal. Bat. (v. 358). Lathrop (Geo. W.), 1847, Co. H, N.Y.Vol. (v. 499).

Lauber (Matthew), 1846, Co. C, 1st U.S. dragoons (v. 336). Lauff (Chas August), 1844, German sailor on the Whaler *Warren,* transferred to the *Tasso,* and making a trip to Callao with Capt. Cooper. iv. 453. In '45-6, he worked as a lumberman in Marin; in '46-7 served in the Cal. Bat., Co. B, artill. (v. 358); went to the mines in '48-9; and in '49 was pilot on the bay and S. Joaquin. From '50 he lived at different places in Marin Co., being in '80 on a rancho near Bolinas, with wife—María J. Cibrian, daughter of Gregorio Briones, married in '62—and 9 children. Portrait in *Marin Co. Hist.,* 64. Laughlin, 1827, see iii. 160. L. (James), 1848, nat. of S.C., who came from Or. to the mines; died in Stanislaus Co. '78. L. (Richard), 1828, Amer. trapper who came from N. Mex. with Pattie's party, with a passport dated

Paso del Norte, Apr. 18, '27. iii. 163, 178. He settled at Los Ang. as a carpenter. ii. 558; got a carta in '31; and later owned a vineyard, perhaps marrying a native. He is named in various records of '34-43, took part in the Micheltorena campaign of '45. iv. 495; and is said to have had a garden near S. Buen. in '46. He died at the end of that year, at the age of 44. Laure, 1830, drowned at S. Luis Ob. in attempting to land from a ship. iii. 180. Laurend (M.), 1848, passp. from Hon. Laurencel (Henry), 1848, roll of Soc. Cal. Pion. Lavallette (Eric A. F.), 1847, com. of the U.S. *Independence.* Lavin (Thos), 1844, Engl. who received a pass.

Lawlor (John), 1827-8, mr of the *Karimoko*, in trouble in the south by reason of his smuggling operations. ii. 551, 564; iii. 94-5, 134-5, 147. He was lost on a voy. from Hon. to Australia in '34, as mr of the *Alpha.* Lawrence, 1848, sailor on the *Isaac Walton.* L. (Henry), 1847, Co. G, N.Y.Vol. (v. 499). L. (J. C.), 1848, died in Utah before '77. L. (John), 1846. Fauntleroy's dragoons (v. 232, 247). L. (Joseph Vicente), 1821, nat. of N.Y. who landed from the *Blackwood* at Bodega and came to S.F. in a boat. ii. 478. In '23 he went to Los Ang., where he was baptized in '24, married María Arriola, and in '29 was still there with wife and son, age 32. ii. 496, 526, 558; iii. 179.

Lawrey (Amos G.), 1846, Amer. mason and perhaps overl. immig., who in '47 worked on the 1st brick house built at Mont. for G. D. Dickenson, whose daughter Margaret he married a little later. In the *Salinas Index*, Oct. 26, '76, 'Jack the Pioneer' (Swan) tells how the young man went to Hon. for a wedding outfit, and attempting to smuggle the goods ashore, had to purchase them anew at a round price; and indeed his arrival at Hon. on the *Charles* in Feb. '48 is recorded. L. died at S. José in '81, having been blind for many years. He left a widow and 3 grown children, one of them Mrs Hollenbach. Lawson (Henry), 1847, Co. H, N.Y.Vol. (v. 499). L. (John), 1847, Co. B, ditto; died at Mont. '49. L. (John), 1847, Co. B, Morm. Bat. (v. 469). Lawton, 1848, overl. immig. with Johnson. L., 1848, of Kilborn, L., & Co., S. F. L. (Benj. H.), 1834, mr of the *S. Feighton.* iii. 384.

Layden (Wm), 1847, Co. C, N. Y. Vol. (v. 499); died at Honolulu '54. Layton (Chas), 1847, ordnance sergt Co. F, 3d U.S. artill. v. 519. A nat. of Engl. who had served in the British army; in the mines '49-52; later lighthouse keeper at Pt Pinos; died at Mont. '55, being fatally wounded while attempting to capture the outlaw García. His widow—née Charlotte Wade, and mar. in '43—was in '78 the wife of Geo. C. Harris at S.F., where a daughter, Mrs Amos Burr, also lived. One son was a sailor and another lived in N. South Wales. *Swan.* L. (Christopher), 1847, Co. C, Morm. Bat. (v. 469); in '82 at Kaysville, Utah. Lazaref (Andrew), 1815, mr of the *Suvárof*, and of the *Ladoga* in '23. iii. 307, 492. L. (Michael), 1823, mr of the *Creiser.* ii. 492, 519. Lázaro (Nicolás), 1805, Span. friar who served for a brief term at S. Fern. and S. Diego, where he died in 1807. ii. 115; iii. 159-60.

Leach (Kendrick N.), 1847, Co. K, N.Y.Vol. (v. 499); in '83 at Fountain Green, Ill. Leahy (Dan.), 1845, Irish cooper at Sutter's Fort '45-6, and prob. an overl. immig. iv. 578, 587. In '47 owner of a lot at S.F., where he still lived in '48-54. He died in Nevada '75, leaving a family in Or. Leandry (Juan B.), 1827, Ital. who came by sea at the age of '23. iii. 176. In '32 he joined the comp. extranjera at Mont. iv. 221; in '36 kept a store at Los Ang.; was naturalized in '39. Juez de paz '40-1, holding other local offices; owner of part of S. Pedro, and grantee of Los Coyotes, where he died in '43. iii. 614, 633, 637; iv. 629, 633. Leary (Wm), 1844, deserter from the *Warren* near Mont.; perhaps at Sonoma '48.

Leavens (Wm), 1846, one of the men captured with Alcalde Bartlett by Sanchez at S.F. (v. 377). Leavenworth (Thaddeus M.), 1847, nat. of Conn., physician and episcopal clergyman, who came as chaplain of the N.Y.Vol. v. 504, 511. He took some part in matters pertaining to church and schools, and was alcalde of S.F. in '47-9. v. 648-52, 657. He was also owner of town lots, and a street in the city bears his name. His official acts have been severely criticised, but I find no data for a just estimate of his character. In '50 he went to Sonoma Co., where he was claimant for a part of Agua Caliente ran-

cho, iii. 711, and where he still lived in '82.   Leavy (Owen), 1847, corp. Co.
F, 3d U.S. artill. The name was perhaps Leary. v. 529.   Lebeau (Joseph),
1846, Cal. Bat. (v. 358).   Lecky (Wm C.), 1846, Co. C, 1st U.S. dragoons,
killed at S. Pascual. v. 346.   Lecointe, 1845, com. of the *Héroine.* iv. 566.
Lecoq (Martin), 1834, Frenchman in a Mont. list.   Leddy (Michael), 1847,
Co. H, N.Y.Vol. (v. 499); died in Mendocino Co. bef. '83.   Ledesma (José),
grantee of land at S. Gabriel. v. 628.
    Lee, 1847, a son said to have been born to Mrs Lee in Jan., at N. Helv.
L., 1847, of L. & Reily, bakers, Mont.   L., 1848, flogged and imprisoned
for attempt at murder near S. José.   L. (Barton), 1848, nat. of N.Y., who
came from Or. to the mines; member and successor of the Sac. firm of Priest,
L., & Co.; prominent also in local politics. He failed for a large amount in '50,
and went to live in the Sandwich Isl., but returned to Cal., and died at Sac.
in '56.   L. (Cornelius R.V.), 1847, Co. F, N.Y.Vol. (v. 499); presid. of the
regulators at S.F. '49; died at Sta B. in '63.   L. (Elisha), 1847, owner of
S.F. lot.   L. (James R.), 1847, Co. H, N.Y.Vol. (v. 499); at Vallejo in '82.
L. (John C.), 1847, Co. F, ditto.   L. (Lawton), 1845, one of the men lost on
the *Warren's* launch in '46. iv. 587; v. 384.   L. (Milton), 1847, trader at
Mont.   L. (Sam.), 1846, mate of the *Euphemia* '46-8.   L. (Theodore), 1846,
mid. on the *Congress;* act. lieut Co. A, Stockton's naval bat., '46-7. v. 386.
Levy (Wm), 1848, miner on the Yuba.
    Leese (Jacob Primer), 1833, native of Ohio, b. in 1809, and engaged in the
Sta Fé trade from '30, who seems to have come from N. Mex. late in '33, but
perhaps went back and came again in July '34, engaging in trade at Los Ang.
iii. 388, 409. In '36 he came to Mont. with Gov. Chico, whose good-will he
succeeded in gaining, formed a partnership with Nathan Spear and Wm S.
Hinckley, obtained a lot at S.F., and on it built the 1st solid structure in
town before July 4th, being naturalized in Sept. iii. 421, 431, 705, 709; iv.
86, 116; v. 680. The next year he erected a larger store on the beach, and
married Rosalía, sister of Gen. Vallejo, much against the general's wishes.
He had a lighter, the *Isabella,* running on the bay and rivers, and the business of the firm, in exchanging goods for rancho products, was profitable;
but he quarrelled with Spear and Hinckley about the division of the $13,000
profits, and the partnership was dissolved in '38, though L. continued the
business for several years, failing to get the appointment of receptor in '39,
and getting another town lot in '40. iii. 700, 705-6, 709-10; iv. 98; v. 679.
In '41 he was grantee of the Cañada de Guadalupe, Visitacion, y Rodeo Viejo
rancho at S.F., and of Huichica at Sonoma; and this year he sold out his
store to the H. B. Co. iv. 37, 179, 217, 671. He also transferred his residence
and place of business to Sonoma, owning one lighter in comp. with Wm Johnson, and another, the *Rosalía,* with Salv. Vallejo. In '43 he went to Or. with
a drove of cattle. iv. 377, 390; and in '44-5 he was alcalde at Sonoma, having serious quarrels with Victor Prudon. iv. 445, 448, 678-9. In '46 he was to
a certain extent a sub-agent for the carrying-out of Larkin's plans. v. 63;
and for this reason, perhaps, having accompanied the Bears to Sac. as interpreter, was thrown into prison by Frémont with the Vallejos and Prudon. v.
112, 119-21, 298-9. His *Bear Flag Revolt,* an original MS. in my col., is one
of the best narratives extant on the subject. v. 187. He had a 'Cal. claim'
of $6,189, besides a claim for the construction of a wharf at Mont. v. 467; i.
list auth. In '47 he is named as a member of the Sonoma council. v. 668; and
is said to have made considerable money in the mines '48-9. He made a voyage to China in '49 on the *Eveline,* under an arrangement with Larkin; and
subsequently resided at Mont., holding some local offices; being the claimant
for several ranchos. iii. 678-9; iv. 671; and in '55 vice-president of the Soc.
Cal. Pion. He was an uneducated and not very intelligent man, active and
enterprising in business, whose many speculations were marked by boldness
rather than ability; and his large property, with that of his wife, all disappeared. In '63 he obtained, in company with others, a concession of lands for
colonization in L. Cal., but the scheme was a failure; and about '65 he left
Cal. for the east. I have no definite record of his subsequent career, but in

Feb. '85 an apparently reliable newspaper report represents him as living at S. Antonio, Texas, in good health, but extreme poverty, an appeal being made to pioneers in his behalf. Portrait in *Annals of S. F.* and *Hesperian.* Mrs Leese lives at Mont. in '85, and has 7 grown children. She furnished for my use a *History of the Osos*, of no special value. A daughter, Rosalía, born at S.F. in '38, and the 1st child born at Yerba Buena, iii. 710, died, and her name was given to a younger daughter. The oldest son, Jacob, was born in '39, and resides in '85 at Salinas, where he has been county clerk and deputy sheriff, his wife being an Estrada, a niece of Gov. Alvarado. One of Leese's daughters married a son of José Ábrego. (L. returned to Cal. in '85.)

Lefèvre (Minard J.), 1846, Co. C, 1st U.S. dragoons (v. 336). Lefort (Geo.), 1847, Co. F, N.Y.Vol. (v. 499). Le Fourri (François), 1831, fro.n N. Mex. with Wolfskill or Jackson. Legar (Miguel), 1602, sergt in Vizcai-no's exped. i. 98. Legarda (José), 1841, mr of the *Jóven Carolina.* iv. 593. Legare (Burnett), 1847, Co. E, N.Y.Vol. (v. 499); died at sea '66. L. (Wm H.), 1847, ditto; died at Los Ang. '47. v. 625. Legendre (Louis), 1847, Fr. settler in Russ. Riv. township, where he was murdered after '52. *Son. Co. Hist.*, 358–60. Legge, 1844, officer in the *Modeste.* Leggett (Wm), 1847, Co. H, N.Y.Vol. (v. 499). Lehigh, 1847, son said to have been born to Mrs L.; perhaps 'Leahy,' q. v. Leicer, 1844, Walla Walla chief. iv. 545; see 'Elijah.' Leick (Chas), 1847, Co. D, N.Y.Vol. (v. 499).

Leidesdorff (Wm Alex.), 1841, nat. of the Danish West Indies, son of a Dane by a mulattress, who came to the U.S. as a boy, and became a master of vessels sailing from N.Y. and N. Orleans. He came to Cal. as mr of the *Julia Ann*, on which he made later trips to the Islands down to '45. iv. 279, 566. Engaging in trade at S.F., he got a lot in '43 at the cor. of Clay and Kearny streets, and in '44 or '45 built a warehouse on the beach at Cal. and Leidesdorff streets. iv. 669, 678; in '46 building the City Hotel on his 1st lot, and in '47 buying from Ridley the cottage at the cor. of Montgomery and CaL streets, where he passed the rest of his life. iv. 678, 680. In '44 he obtained naturalization papers and a grant of the Rio de los Americanos rancho. iv. 673; and from Oct. '45 served as U.S. vice-consul by Larkin's appointment. iv. 188, 557, 589–90, 665. His corresp. of these years, especially with Larkin, is a most valuable source of historical information. In '46 he had controversies with Forbes, Ridley, and Hinckley, who were not intensely American enough to suit this Danish citizen of Mex.; visiting N. Helv. and Monterey; and in this and the following years becoming owner of many city lots. v. 3–4, 28, 136, 178, 239, 295, 648–9, 678, 680. In '47, having a Cal. claim of $8,740 (v. 462), and launching the 1st steamer that ever sailed on S.F. bay, v. 577–8, 646, he was not only one of the town's most prominent business men, but a member of the council, treasurer, and member of the school committee, tak- ing an active part in local politics. v. 455, 648–52, 656. He died in May '48, at the age of 38. He was an intelligent man of fair education, speaking sev- eral languages; active, enterprising, and public-spirited; honorable for the most part in his transactions; but jealous, quick-tempered, often quarrel- some, and disagreeable. His estate, burdened by heavy debts at the time of his death, after the gold excitement became of immense value. It was ad- ministered by W. D. M. Howard, with the assistance of C. V. Gillespie, and was for years the subject of complicated litigation; but the title of Capt. Folsom, who had found the mother and other heirs of Leidesdorff at St Croix Isl., and had bought their interests, was finally adjudged to be valid.

Leigh (Isaac), 1846, one of the Mormon Col. with his wife. v. 546; never went to Utah. Leighton (James C.), 1848, at S.F. from Tahiti; lieut of S. F. guards; of firm L., Swasey, & Co. v. 681. L. (Nathaniel S.), 1840, Amer. carpenter who got a carta at S F. in Oct.; at Mont. in '42. iv. 120. L. (Peter), 1838, named in Larkin's accts. Leinhard (J. H.), 1847, in Sut- ter's employ '47–8. Leister (Thomas), 1846, Co. C, 1st U.S. dragoons (v. 336). Leiva, maj. of Jamul near S. Diego, killed by Ind. '37. iii. 614; iv. 68. L. (Antonio), at S. Juan Cap. '46, age 23. L. (Francisco), soldier at Sta B. '32; wife María C. Valencia; at Sta B. '50. L. (José), soldier of S.F.

comp. '39-42; at Los Ang. '46. L. (Juan), corporal at Sta B. before '37; at Los Ang, '46. L. (Miguel), soldier at Sta B. '33. L. (Ramon), ditto. L. (Rufino), corp. of Sta B. comp., in com. of escolta at S. Buen., where he was killed by Ind. in '19. ii. 333. L. (Santiago and Teodoro), at Los Ang. '46. Lelland (John M.), 1847, owner of S.F. lot; perhaps McLelland. Lelong (Martin), 1847, Co. G, N.Y.Vol. (v. 499).

Lem (Wm), 1828, Engl. sailor who deserted from a Fr. whaler at Todos Santos and came to S. Diego; or perhaps left drunk at S. D. by the *General Sucre.* Leman (John), 1846, Co. B, Cal. Bat. (v. 358), enlisting at S. José Nov. Lemoine (G. D.), 1846-7, mr of the *Francisca* and pass. on the *Elizabeth;* owner of S.F. lot. v. 578, 679. Lemon (Geo. F.), 1847, lieut Co. A, N.Y.Vol. v. 503; S.F. assessor '51; lieut-col N.Y.Vol. in the war of the rebellion; killed in battle '62. L. (James W.), 1847, Co. A, Morm. Bat. (v. 469); reënl.; at Weston, Utah, '81.

Le Netrel (Ed.), Fr. lieut on the *Héros.* iii. 129. Lenoir, 1845, Fr. hatter from Or. in the McM.-Clyman party; prob. returned to Or. '46. iv. 572, 526. Lenox (E. H.), 1848, Kentuckian in Sta Clara '68-76. L. (John A.), 1846, overl. immig. with his parents at the age of 2 years. The family settled at Sonoma, where John died in '74. *Sac. Union.* L. (J. W.), 1848, nat. of Ind.; in Sonoma Co. '48-77. *Son. Co. Hist.* L. (T.), 1847, in Sutter's employ '47-8; had a family; prob. came in '46. All the preceding are prob. vague ref. to the same family. Leon (Andrés), in the Mont. revolt of '29; sent as prisoner to Mex. '30. iii. 69, 71, 85. Leon y Luna, 1793, mr of the *Activo.* i. 544. Leonard (Geo. W. M.), 1847, Co. E, N.Y.Vol. (v. 499); a colonel under Walker in Nicaragua; in N.Y. city '82. L. (Louis), 1846, overl. immig. with Hoppe and Harlan; went back east and died. *Balhaus.* Leonardo (Pedro B.), sirviente at Soledad 1791-1800. i. 499.

Lepage (François), 1842, Frenchman who got a carta at S.F.; owner of a lot in '45, which he sold to James Lick in '48. iv. 341, 669. L. (Nicholas), 1842, brother of François, who also got a carta. Lequez (J. V.), 1831, doubtful name of a Scotchman permitted to marry. Lerma, soldier killed by Ind. in '21. ii. 550. Leroux, 1847, guide to Morm. Bat. v. 483. Leroy (Joseph), 1836, Frenchman, aged 29, at the Verjeles rancho near Mont.; perhaps the same man was an otter-hunter with Nidever in '39-40. iv. 119. L. (R.), 1839, Fr. surgeon at Sta B. and Mont. Lester (Thomas), 1817, Engl. sailor baptized as José Tomás Ignacio, and living at S. José '29-33. ii. 284, 286, 393, 602; perhaps the same who went to Hon. on the *Mary Ann* in '47. Letterman (Henry), 1846, Co. F, Cal. Bat. (v. 358).

Levelain (Chas), 1843-4, Fr. boy who left the *Ferdinand* (?), and lived with Capt. Richardson at Sauzalito. iv. 400; at S.F. from '49; married a daughter of Eusebio Soto in '50; at Butte City '60; at S.F. '64-7. Levitt, 1848, mr of the *Eagle.* v. 577. Levick (Isaac), 1845, at S.F.; also in '54. L. (John), 1837, deserter from an Engl. schr with a man named Morgan. They built a cabin at what became the cor of Dupont and Broadway, S.F. (?), and acquired a large fortune. He left Cal. in '57, and was lost on the *Central America. Herald,* Oct. 31, '57. iv. 118. Levin (Louis), 1835, at Los Ang. Levy (Thos), 1848, overl. immig. to Or. in '46, and came from Or. to the mines; found dead at Mosquito '74, age 49. *Sac. Union.*

Lewis, 1847, of firm of L. & Lynch, Mont. '47-8. L. 1846, deserter from an Engl. man-of-war, who on pretence of having great wealth married an orphan who left him when she learned the truth; so wrote Leidesdorff. Perhaps Wm Lewis of '40. L., 1846, overl. immig. with Stephen Cooper. L., 1848, from Honolulu. L. (Abraham), 1848, nat. of N.Y.; in Sta Clara Co. '76. L. (Allen), 1830, Amer. blacksmith, age 25, who came on the *Planet.* iii. 180; at Sta B. '36. L. (F. W.) 1847, mate of the *Elizabeth;* perhaps at Sta B. '50. L. (Geo W.), 1846, nat. of Mo., said to have come with his father's family and to have settled at Sonoma, where his mother lived in '80, and he was candidate for county assessor. L. (Henry), 1847, Co. G, N.Y.Vol. (v. 499). L. (H. E.), 1847, Co. E, ditto; at S. José '71-4; not in Clark's latest list. L. (Henry H.), 1847, lieut on the U.S. *Independence.* L. (J.), 1848, passp. from Hon. L. (James), 1845, doubtful name of the McM.-Clyman party. iv. 573. L. (James D.), 1843, sailor on the *Admittance*, disch. in '45. *Peterson's Diary*. L. (John B.), 1845, overl. immig. of the Swasey-Todd party. iv. 576, 587; one of the committee representing new-comers in the treaty with Castro in Nov. iv. 606; at Sonoma and Napa '46-8, and member of the Sonoma council '47. v. 668; at S. José '50. L. (John), 1847, Co. F, N.Y. Vol. (v. 499); d. Sta B. '48. L. (John), 1834, at Los Ang.; doubtful name. L. (Joseph), 1847, commander's clerk on the *Columbus*. L. (Joseph B.) 1847, Co. A, N.Y.Vol. (v. 499); d. in Texas '82. L. (Louis), 1835, nat. of Pa, trader at Los Ang., age 25; accused of complicity in the Apalátegui revolt (iii. 282). L. (Sam.), 1847, Co. C, Morm. Bat. (v. 469); at Panguich, Utah, '82. L. (Thomas), 1833, Amer. from S. Blas, accused of illegal otter-hunting in Sept. In '36 he was at Los Ang., a single carpenter, aged 25. In '40 one of the Graham exiles, who returned in '41 and worked at Sta Cruz as a lumberman in '42-3. He may have been the Tom Lewis who accompanied John Brown on his famous ride of '46. iii. 393, 409; iv. 18, 33; v. 304. L. (Thomas), 1844, Engl., age 30, at S.F. L. (Wm), 1840, naturalized this year and named on Larkin's books. iv. 120. At S.F. and S. José in '41; in '45 at N. Helv., where he was married in Dec. His wife may be the Mrs L. who married Perry McCoon in Feb '46 and died in June.

Libbey (Elliott), 1845, mr of the *Tasso* '45-8; also of the *Com. Shubrick* in '47. iv. 569; v. 577, 580. For assault on him and Spear at S.F., see iv. 589, 665-6. According to Thomes there was a 'woman in the case.' Capt. L. was the owner of a town lot in '46 (v. 685), and in 54 lived at S. Rafael. It is possible that he visited Cal. on some vessel from Hon. earlier than '45. Lichtenstein, see 'Lightstone.' Lick (James), 1848, nat. of Pa, a piano-maker by trade, who had lived for over 20 years in Buenos Aires, Chile, and Peru, and who came to S.F. from Callao on the *Lady Adams*, arriving Jan. 7, '48. He had already a small fortune, which he invested in S.F. lands (v. 678), and patiently waited for the increase in the value of his real estate to make him immensely wealthy. Among his enterprises of later years were a grand flouring mill at S. José, finished with mahogany in the interior, and the Lick House, in which some of the fine decorations in wood are the work of his own hands. He was an honest, industrious man, of much common sense, though noted for his many eccentricities and whims, and in his later years of irritable and thoroughly disagreeable temperament. He had no family, except an illegitimate son, who was recognized by him and spent some years with him in Cal. He took a deep interest from the first in the Society of Cal. Pioneers, to which he made liberal gifts. His great and well-merited fame rests on the final disposition of his millions, which, after provision for his relatives, were devoted to various scientific, charitable, and educational enterprises, for the benefit of the donor's adopted state. He died in '76, at the age of '80; and after the usual delays caused by financial and legal complications, the results of Lick's bequests are beginning, in '85, to assume practical shape.

Light (Allen B.), 1835, negro, who deserted from the *Pilgrim*, or some other vessel, and became an otter-hunter. iii. 413. He was known as Black Steward, his encounter with a grizzly bear in the Sta B. region being mentioned by Alfred Robinson, and other adventures by Nidever. He was one of Graham's men in '36-8; and in '39, being a naturalized resident of Sta B., was appointed by the govt agent to prevent illegal otter-hunting. iv. 91; at Los Ang. in '41, and in '46-8 at S. Diego, still a hunter. L. (James), 1846, nat. of Me, and one of the Mormon Col., with wife and child, though sometimes accredited to the N.Y.Vol. v. 546. He lived in S. Joaq., and later at Sauzalito; but from '50 was a resident of Humboldt Co., where he died at Arcata in '81. His wife, Mary J., died in '75. Lightstone (Frank), 1845, German soap-maker and chandler; original name Franz Lichtenstein, who came from Or. in the McMahon-Clyman party, and settled at S. José '46. iv. 572, 487; still living in Sta Clara Co., I think, in '85.

Lillie (Leonard G.), 1846, nat. of N.Y., prob. overl. immig. from Ill., and settler in Napa Val. He died at Calistoga in '72, age 48, leaving a widow and

6 children.   Limantour (Joseph Yves), 1841, Fr. trader in Mex., who came
to Cal. as sup. of the *Ayacucho*. iv. 279, 563.   The schr was wrecked near
Pt Reyes, and L. opened a store at S.F. to dispose of the cargo '41-2. He
came back in '43-4, '47, and '52-3. v. 449, 576.   During the visit of '43-4 he
furnished aid to Gov. Micheltorena, and received in return, as there seems to
be no reason to doubt, several grants of land.   In '52-3 he presented his claims
before the land commission. iv. 352, 386, 402, 511, 559, 634, 655, 671-4.   His chief
claim, to about half the site of San Francisco, was at first confirmed by the
commission; but in '58 was rejected by the district court, the grant being
pronounced a forgery supported by false testimony. This famous case is more
fully noticed elsewhere (see vol. vi.).   The truth would seem to be that L.
had really obtained grants of land at S.F. and elsewhere; but that in later
years, by forged papers and with the aid of Ex-gov. Micheltorena, he overreached himself by attempting to improve the location and extent of his
grants. He is still, in '85, a wealthy resident of the City of Mexico.   Lim-
cante (Blas), 1806, sailor on the *Peacock*, arrested at S. Juan Cap. ii. 38.
Limon (Cayetano), 1781-2, Mex. alférez, who came to Cal. in com. of escort
to Rivera's colony. i. 342-4, 361, 364-5.   Limon (Fran.), criminal at S. Fern.
'39. iii. 638.   L. (Fran.), apparently a lieut.; at Mont. '46; went to Mex.
with Flores '48. v. 41, 407-8.   L. (José M.), 1842; sub-lieut of the batallon
fijo; suspended in '43. iv. 289, 354, 364.
    Linares (Fran.), at Los Ang. '46.   L. (Ignacio), settler at S. José 1786.
i. 477. In 1793 inválido, wife Gertrudis Rivas, child. Salvador, Marcela,
Francisco, Mariano, Nicolasa, Santos, Antonia, and Rosa.   L. (José), lla-
vero, at Sta Inés '39. iii. 664.   L. (José de la Cruz), grantee of Nogales '40.
iii. 633; at S. Gabriel '46.   L. (Juan José), soldier of the guard at S. José
mission 1797-1800. i. 556.   L. (Margarito), Mex. soldier at Mont. '36.   L.
(María Ant.), grantee of Los Carneros '42. iv. 655.   L. (Miguel), at Los Ang.
'46.   L. (Ramon), soldier at Sta Cruz and S. José 1795-1800. i. 496, 556;
inválido of the S.F. comp. 1819-21.   L. (Rafael), at the Natividad fight (v.
363).   L. (Rosa), had a son in the Mont. school '46.   L. (Santiago), shot
for murder at Los Ang. '41. iv. 630.   L. (Vicente), grantee of rancho at S.
Luis Ob. '42. iv. 656.   L. (Victor), soldier at S. Diego '26. ii. 549; in '37
grantee of Tinaquaic. iii. 656, 557; in 39-40 maj. at S. Luis Ob., and militia
alférez. iii. 683; iv. 13; in '42 grantee of Cañada de los Osos. iv. 655; in '46
juez at S. Luis, v. 638, where he still lived in '51.   Linch, see 'Lynch.'
    Lincoln (John), 1822, mr of the *John Begg*. ii. 474.   L. (Jonas), 1847,
son of Seth, who came at the age of 10, born in Engl. He was later a member
of the Pac. Stock Exchange, S.F., and died, as did his wife, in '76, leaving 7
children.   L. (J. S.), 1847, candidate for the S.F. council. v. 650; prob.
same as the following.   L. (Seth S.), 1847, from Hon. with wife and 2 children on the *Francesca*. He was the owner of several town lots in '47-8, and
by some is said to have been a Mormon preacher. v. 547. All the family except Jonas left S.F. for Australia and were lost at sea.
    Linder (Francis), 1847, Co. G, N.Y.Vol. (v. 499).   Lindsay, 1848, mr of
the *Tasso*.   L. (J. H.), 1845, at S.F. June '46. *Terr. Pion., 1st An.*   L.
(Thomas), 1841, immig. from N. Mex. in the Workman-Rowland party,
called a 'mineralogist' in the Rowland list. iv. 278-9. In '44 he settled at
what was later Stockton, building a tule hut. He went south—as the entire
pop. of Stockton—with Sutter in the Micheltorena campaign. iv. 486; and
soon after his return, in the spring of '45, was killed by Indians, his body being burned with the hut. iv. 516, 543, 674.   Lineda (Arcadio), 1789, lieut
in Malaspina's exped. i. 490.   Linel (Joseph), 1847, owner of a S.F. lot.
Link, 1848, from S. José to the mines.   Linn (James S.), 1847, owner of S.
F. lot; also at N. Helv., Sta Clara, and in the mines '47-8; had a family.
Lino, neoph. at Sta Cruz 1817. ii. 388.   L., sacristain at Sta B. '38. iii. 656.
Linson (Fran.), a litigant in Los Ang. district '39.   Linton (James), 1847,
Co. E, N.Y.Vol. (v. 499).   Linty (J.), 1846, Cal. Bat., Co. B, artill. v. 358.
    Lipp (Carl), 1847, Co. D, N.Y.Vol. (v. 499); at Vallejo '71-82.   Lipper
(Augustus), 1847, Co. G, ditto.   Lippincott (Benj. S.), 1846, nat. of N.Y.

who came overland with Bryant, being wounded on the way by Ind. v. 528. He was active in raising recruits for the war, and served as lieut of Co. H, Cal. Bat., acting also as asst Q. M. v. 359, 361. In this connection he is often called Geo. M. Lippincott, but I find no evidence that there were two of the name. In '47–8 he lived at S.F., being a gambler by profession, owner of town lots, v. 678, and a candidate for the council. v. 650. He was a member of the constit. convention of '49, representing S. Joaq. Co. in the 1st legislature, and Calaveras in those of '55 and '61. He was a popular man as trader, politician, and 'one of the boys.' He died in N. J. '70, at the age of 55.   Lippett (Francis J.), 1847, nat. of R. I., capt. Co. F, N.Y.Vol., and in com. of the garrison at Sta B. v. 504, 514, 584, 631; owner of a town lot, v. 685, and from '48 a lawyer at S.F. to '52 or later. v. 686; member of the constit. convention of '49; col of 1st Cal. infantry in war of '61–5; at Providence, R. I., '71; Boston, '74, and Washington, D.C.,'82.   Lisa (Dan.), 1816, nat. of Mass. who came on the *Lydia*, and was baptized at Sta B. in '18 as Daniel Mártir José de Sta Rosa. The name was prob. Daniel Eleazer, the surname being unknown.   L. (José Manuel), 1816, brother of Dan., bapt. at Sta B. '16. ii. 277.   Lisárraga (José M.), 1842. iv. 642.

Little, 1837, mr of the *Griffon*. iv. 104; perhaps Wm C. iv. 141.   L. (August), 1847, owner of S.F. lot.   L. (John), 1848(?), trader and postmaster at Coloma.   L. (Milton), 1843, nat. of N. Y. and overl. immig. of the Walker-Chiles party, being wounded by Ind. on the trip. iv. 392, 394, 400. He settled at Mont. as a trader in '44, and from that time his name constantly appears in various records. ·He got a carta in '44, was a partner of Belden in '45, was 2d alcalde in '46, serving on the 1st jury, and having a Cal. claim. v. 289, 637 (462). In '48 he married Mary Eagar, also visiting the gold mines, After '49 he continued to trade at Mont., holding several county offices, being claimant for lands, iv. 656, and dying in '79 at the age of '67. He left a widow and several children.   Littlefield (Geo.), 1845, mr of the *Hopewell*. iv. 566.

Littlejohn (David), 1824, Scotch farmer and carpenter from Callao on one of Hartnell's vessels. ii. 526; baptized in '25 at S. Cárlos as Francisco Javier David; joined the comp. extranjera in '32. iii. 221; naturalized in '33, being then 40 years old, married to a native, and owner of some cattle. In '34 he was grantee of Carneros rancho, Mont. Co., later confirmed to his heirs. iii. 677; named often in Larkin's accounts and other records '34–46. Being partially insane (?), he objected to the plundering of his rancho by Frémont's men and narrowly escaped with his life. He died a little later, and his widow married José M. Castro before '50.   Littleton (John), 1826, Engl. sailor who landed sick at Mont. from the *Rover*. iii. 176; ii. 609. In '29, being 22 years old, he worked at the inn when able; lived with Larkin in '36; and is last mentioned in '37.

Livermore (Robert), 1822, nat. of London, b. 1799, apprenticed to a mason, from whom he ran away in '16 and went to sea. After serving in the U.S. navy he left that service on the S. Amer. coast, and joined the allied fleet under Lord Cochrane, taking part on the *Esmeralda* in the naval operations at Callao (which were in '20–1), and perhaps joining an exped. to the north (though he could not apparently have been in the Gulf of Cal. in '22. See *Hist. N. Mex. St.*, ii.). Leaving the naval service, he shipped on the *Colonel Young*, a trading craft, from which he deserted in Cal., probably in '22, the date of her arrival, ii. 478, but possibly later on another trip of '25. iii. 29. There is a strange confusion in records of his coming, the date being given by different writers all the way from '16 to '29. He is understood to have lived some years on the Laguna, or Alvires, rancho, spending some time in the south at S. Gabriel, and working in the Sta Clara redwoods; but this was prob. later, as Geo. Frazer, of '33, is named as his comrade. The earliest original record is in '29, when, being maj. on the rancho of Torre and Mulligan, he claimed to be 23 years old, and to have come in '19, intending to remain and marry, *St. Pap. Sac.*, xiii. 3, both of which statements must be erroneous. In another record of '29, being a resident of S. José, 'Roberto' said he had deserted from the *Conoliango* about '21, was 22 years old, and had been bap-tized at Sta Clara (as Juan Bautista Roberto). *Dept. St. Pap.*, xix. 3. I have a receipt of money from L., dated Los Pozitos, in '25. *Alviso, Doc.*, 6; but this may be a slip of the pen for '35. He is mentioned at S. José in '30 and '31, but as intending to quit the place. *Vallejo, Doc.*, xxx. 61, 313. In '42 he writes of a cattle-brand that he had used for 15 years (since '27). *Estudillo, Doc.*, ii. 54. Soon after '30 he went to the Tularcitos rancho, where he married Josefa Higuera, widow of Fuentes Molina, as early as '34, if we follow the padron of '41, which makes his daughter Casimira 6 years old, though the date is gen-erally given as later; and before '37—when Edwards visited him—he had es-tablished himself on the Pozitos rancho, in what was later called Livermore Valley, and where he spent the rest of his life. iv. 86, 117. In '39 he was ap-parently granted the rancho on Apr. 8th. *Leg. Rec.*, iii. 61; but 2 days later it was granted to Salvio Pacheco, prob. as a formality, L. not being a citizen. He at once bought the property in partnership with José Noriega, whose in-terest he purchased later. In a list of foreigners of '40—when L. was per-haps arrested, iv. 17—as per extract furnished by J. A. Forbes for my use, L. is said to be 36 years old, and to have come with Mancisidor on the *Coro-nel Yon* 20 years ago. In '40-1 he had some dealings with Sutter, iv. 134, 233, being called 39 years old in a padron; and in all these years he had much trouble with the Ind., being wounded in one of his exped. In '44 he was naturalized, being a resid. for 'over 20 years,' and having a large family. In '46 he rendered some service in carrying despatches. v. 246-7; about this time purchased the Cañada de los Vaqueros of the Alvisos; and his place was a well-known station on the route from Mont. and S. José to Sac. The two ranchos were later confirmed to him. iii. 712; iv. 671; and the former sailor became a rich man. His reputation is that of a hospitable and honest man, a good representative of his class. In '51, through the medium of a neighbor named Strickland, who had a sister living in England, L. resumed commun. with his relatives after 35 years of silence. The original corresp., *Livermore Papers*, MS., chiefly of his brother, Wm C., in London, has been furnished to me by Valentin Alviso, his son-in-law. The corresp. extended from '51 to '57, showing L.'s father to have died in '26 and his mother in '48, but several brothers, sisters, and other relatives still survived; and the English builder's views and advice respecting Cal. ranchero life must have been more amusing than instructive to Don Roberto. One suggestion was to surround his rancho with a ditch, and another to brand his cattle. Livermore died in '58. Portrait in *Halley's Centen. Year-Book*, 563. He left a widow and 8 children. His son Robert, b. in '40, still resides, '85, in Livermore Valley with wife, Teresa Ber-nal, and 6 children. Portrait in *Alam. Co. Hist.*, 16. One of the daughters, Josefa, is the wife of Valentin Alviso.

Livingstone (John W.), 1846, lieut U.S.N., com. of the *Congress* '46-8. v. 253, 577; rear-admiral living in N.Y. '77. L. (Peter F.), 1847, Co. K, N.Y. Vol. (v. 499); I have his letter of Apr. '48, at S.F., in which he expresses his desire to buy a tract of land near the presidio as discharged; alcalde at S. José '49. He died at Sonora '73. Lizalde (Ignacio), at Sta B. '37, wife María Ign. Arellanes, 3 children. L. (Juan), soldier of S.F. comp. '39-42. L. (Pedro), corporal of S. Diego comp. 1797. i. 562; settler at Los Ang. 1808. ii. 349. Llanos (Wm), 1846, doubtful name in a N.Y. age. list. Llepe (Jerome), 1834, doubtful name of an Engl. hatter at Mont., age 27. Lloyd (Horace), 1847, Co. F, 3d U.S. artill. (v. 518); perhaps the L. in Alameda Co. '55-78. Lobar (Juan), 1831, from N. Mex. in the Wolfskill party. iii. 387. Lobato (Miguel García), Mex. lieut. of engineers, who perhaps came with Echeandía in '25. He is mentioned in connection with the trial of P. Martinez in '29-30. iii. 84, 99; and was sent to Mex. in '30 as a comisionado by the junta de guerra. L. (Diego), at S. Gabriel '46. Lobo (Juan), resid. of Los Ang. '46; prominent at the fight of S. Pascual. v. 352. L. (Juan José), set-tler at Los Ang. 1790. i. 461. L. (Juan José and Santiago), at Los Ang. '46. L. (Marcial), at S. Diego '26. L. (Pedro), sergt at S. Diego '25-8. ii. 543.

Locke, 1795, mr of the *Resolution.* i. 538, 625. L. (James O.), 1829, mr of the *Brookline* '29–30. iii. 146. In '40, at Boston, he jumped from a 3d-story window and fractured his skull.   Lockwood (Isaac), 1847, Co. D, N.Y.Vol. (v. 499); at S. José '50.   L. (Wm A.), 1842, prof. of mathematics on Com. Jones' fleet. iv. 308.

Lodge (Michael), 1822, Irish carpenter, who, in '29, was living at Mont., age 30, married to Martina Castro. ii. 479. I have his autograph letter of May '28. His name appears on Larkin's books in '33–47, his business being that of lumberman, and from about '37 owner of a rancho near Sta Cruz. In '40 he was arrested but not exiled (iv. 17), though in '41 fined $20 for applying an opprobrious epithet to the Mex. govt. In '45 he is named in the Branciforte padron as 50 years old, wife 39, children Refugio, b. '32, María Ant. 35, Miguel '39, Joaquin '41, and María '42. In Nov. '47 he was still a lumberman at Soquel, but I have no later record of him, or of his family, except that one of his daughters married Thos Fallon.   Loesa, chaplain of the S. Blas transports, 1791–1800. i. 655.   Loeser (Lucien), 1847, lieut Co. F, 3d U.S. artill. v. 518; sent east with despatches '48.

Logan (Joseph B.), 1847, sergt Co. I, N. Y. Vol. v. 504; died at Springfield, Tuol. Co., '57.   L. (L. L.), 1846, from Mich.; a soldier in N. Mex. '61–4, when he was fatally wounded by the Ind. *Watsonville Pájaro Times.* L. (Wm), 1824, owner of a vineyard at Los Ang. '31. ii. 526; prob. same as Wm Lobe, named in '40 as an Amer. carpenter from N. Mex., who had been 14 years in Cal., married, and 38 years old. iii. 176.   Loker (Wm N.), 1845, Amer. trader from Mo., and overl. immig. of the Hastings party. iv. 586–7; clerk in Sutter's employ from Jan. '46; in charge of the Bear prisoners. v. 125, 80; lieut Co. A, Cal. Bat., and later adjutant; had a Cal. claim (v. 462); went east with Frémont, and testified at the court-martial. v. 453–456. In '76 he is named as a broker at St Louis.   Lomer, 1848, Mont. firm of Copman & L. '48–9.

Londerman, 1848, at N. Helv.   Long (Dr), 1847, at N. Helv.; mining at Parks Bar '48, with his brothers.   L. (A. K.), 1841, com. of the *Relief*, U.S. ex. iv. 271.   L. (A. R.), 1848, capt U.S.N., on the *Warren;* com. of marine guard at S.F.   L. (David), 1847, came on the *Fama*, perhaps earlier, and worked at S.F., '47–8, for Ward & Smith, and for Leidesdorff; at N. Helv., on Leidesdorff's launch, '48.   L. (John), 1847, Co. F, 3d U.S. artill. (v. 518). L. (John P.), 1846, Co. B, Cal. Bat. (v. 358), enlisting at Mont. Oct.; had a Cal. claim for quarters and clothing (v. 462); in the mines at Park and Long bars '48.   L. (Wm or Willis), 1846, Co. B, Cal. Bat. (v. 358); living in Vaca Valley '74.   Longdeau (Maurice), 1846, with Kearny from N. Mex. v. 337. Longley (Wm Rufus), 1846, came from Hon. on the *Euphemia*, as clerk for Davis, '46–7; clerk at Mont. for naval store-keeper, and agent for McClurg & Co.; 2d alcalde at Mont. '48; also trading in the mines. v. 637.   Look, 1843, doubtful name of a saloon-keeper at Mont. acc. to newspapers.   Loper (Andrew J.), 1846, Co. E, Cal. Bat., enlisting at Sonoma Oct. (v. 358).

Lopez, sailor sirviente at Sta Cruz. i. 496.   L.(Alejandro), at Los Ang. '46. L. (Antonio), settler at Los Ang. '13. ii. 359; in '32 invál. of the Sta B. comp., wife Gertrudis Félix, child. Josefa, Filomena, Juan José, Bernardino, and José María.   L. (Baldomero), 1791, Span. friar; founder of Sta Cruz, where he served till his retirement in '96; guardian of S. Fernando College '18–25. Biog. i. 497–9; ment. i. 494, 576; ii. 397–8, 402, 431–2; iii. 21.   L. (Bernardino), son of Antonio; regidor at Los Ang. '37–8. iii. 509, 636; encargado of S. Gabriel '47. v. 628; had a Cal. claim (v. 462); still at Los Ang. '48.   L. (Bonifacio), juez del campo at S. Diego '35. iii. 615; in charge of the mission '43. v. 620.   L. (Capistrano), at S. Juan B. '44; mentioned in connection with the Frémont-Gavilan affair of '46. v. 18; in later years a noted desperado finally hanged at Sta Cruz.   L. (Cayetano), artisan-instructor 1792–5; i. 615, 725.   L. (Claudio), settler at Los Ang. '11; maj. at S. Gabriel '21–30; alcalde at Los Ang. '26. ii. 349, 560, 568.   L. (Cornelio), resid. of Los Ang. '36–48.   L. (Estévan), 1602, corp. in Vizcaino's exped. i. 98.   L. (Estévan), at Los Ang. '28–39.   L. (Francisco), at S. Fern. '39; sec. in the juzgado at Los Ang. '41. iv. 641; named as discov. of the southern gold mines in '42. iv. 630–1; grantee of Los Álamos '46. v. 627; clerk in governor's office '45; juez de campo '48. v. 626.   L. (Francisco), corp. of Sta B. comp. '32; wife María Ant. Félix; grantee of Temescal '43. iv. 643; living on his rancho '45.   L. (Gerónimo), at Los Ang. '46.   L. (Gregorio), at Sta B. before '37; wife Antonia María Ortega, and one child; in '46 maj. of S. Julian rancho. v. 282.   L. (Ignacio), soldier of S. Diego comp.; partido elector of S. Diego '22, and elected to legislature. ii. 454, 462, 543; took part in revolution of '31. iii. 201; juez de campo '36. iii. 616.   L. (Jacinto), 1799, Span. friar who served for brief terms at S. Antonio and S. Juan B., retiring in 1801. i. 558, 577; ii. 153, 159.   L. (Joaquin), soldier killed on the Colorado 1781. i. 363.   L. (José), brother of Ignacio, at S. Diego, engaged in the revolution of '31. iii. 201; owner of land at S. Juan Cap. '41–3. iv. 371, 624, 626; killed by Ind. at Puma '46. v. 617; but another of the same name was regidor at S. Diego '49.   L. (José Ant.), Mex. convict '29–34.   L. (José de Jesus), soldier of the S.F. comp. '39–42.   L. (José M.), at Sta Cruz 1794. i. 496.   L. (José M.), soldier of Sta B. comp. before '37; at Los Ang. '39–48, being zanjero in '44. iv. 633.   L. (Juan), settler at Los Ang. 1798-9; i. 606; ii. 349.   L. (Juan), at S. Diego, engaged in revolt of '31. iii. 200–1; grantee of Cañada de S. Vicente '46. v. 619; iii. 612.   L. (Juan José), 1842, Mex. cornet in batallon fijo '42–5. iv. 289.   L. (Juan B.), killed at Mont. '25. iii. 26.   L. (J. B.), otter-hunter '30. iii. 145.   L. (Leandro), at Los Ang. '46.   L. (Manuel), ex-llavero S. Antonio '40. iii. 687.   L. (M. J.), owner of Jesus rancho, S. Diego, '36. iii. 611–12.   L. (María Ign.), wife of Joaq. Carrillo; grantee of Sta Rosa '41. iv. 673. She was a half-sister of Pio Pico's mother, Ignacio and José being her brothers. Her sisters were Josefa, wife of Véjar, Juana, wife of Juan Osuna, and María Ant., wife of José M. Aguilar.   L. (Nicolás), owner of a house at Sta B. '48. v. 632.   L. (Pedro), sirviente at S.F. 1777. i. 297.   L. (Pedro), at S. Fern. '39, age 28; grantee of Tujunga '40. iii. 634; still at S. Fern. '56.   L. (Rafael), soldier at Sta B. '32, wife María Ortega.   L. (Ramon), Dominican friar from L. Cal., at S. Diego occasionally 1791-1800. i. 655.   L. (Tiburcio), soldier of Sta B. comp. before '37; at Los Ang. '46.   L. (Theodore), 1847, Co. F, N.Y.Vol. (v. 499); in Tuol. Co. 77.   Lord (Joseph M.), 1847, owner of boats on bay and river '48–9; in S.F. after '70.

Lorenzana (Apolinaria), 1800, one of the foundlings sent from Mex. to Cal., who lived at Sta B. and S. Diego, never married, and became known as La Beata, devoting her life to charity and teaching, a favorite godmother at baptisms. i. 606; ii. 169. She was at S. Luis Rey '21–30. ii. 553; and was grantee of Jamacho and Cañada de los Coches in '40, '43, iii. 611, 621, the former being confirmed to her by the land commission, but taken from her by some legal hocus pocus that the old woman never understood. In '78 she was living at Sta B., entirely blind and supported by friends and the county. Her *Memorias de La Beata*, dictated for my use, contains many interesting items on early times. Her name of Lorenzana is that of the archbishop of Mex. given to all foundlings from that asylum.   L. (Felipe), at Sta B. before '37, wife Natividad Ruiz, 4 children; ranchero in '45.   L. (Inocente), juez de policía at Sta B. before '48. v. 631.   L. (Jacinto), at Sta B. '37, wife Cármen Rodriguez, 3 children; síndico in '40. iii. 655.   L. (José), at Branciforte '45, age 29, wife Manuela Salazar, child. Josefa b. '36, Prudencio '37, Benita '38, Juan José '40, Rosario '42; a man of same name at Sta B. '50–5.   L. (Macedonio), soldier of S.F. comp. '19–22; at Brancif. '28, wife Romualda Vasquez, child. José, Apolinario b. '19, Bernarda, Juana, Arcadio '24, and Pedro. ii. 627; in '35, '39, síndico. iii. 696–7; '38 regidor. iii. 637; '45–6 2d alcalde. iv. 641, 664; in '45, age 53, additional children, Juan b. '25, Matias '26, Fernando '30, Jesus '35, Faustino '36, José '37, Ricardo '40, Trinidad '44.   L. (Manuel), alguacil at Sta B. '39. iii. 654.   L. (Timoteo), killed in '31. iii. 673.   L. (Tomás), soldier at Sta B. before '37.   L. (Vicente), at Los Ang. '12–48, a carpenter, age 50 in '39. ii. 350.

Loring (Sam.), 1836, Amer. cooper, age 26, in a Sta B. list. iv. 118; died at Los Ang. '43.   L. ('Major'), 1846, doubtful name in a Los Ang. list.

LORING—LUGO.   227

Lornes (John), 1846, Co. F, Cal. Bat. (v. 358).   Losaya (José M.), killed a
man at Sta B. '40. iii. 655.   Loughray (Andrew), 1847, Co. K, N.Y.Vol.
(v. 499).   Louis, 1847, mr of the *Providence*.   L. (Henry), 1846, Fauntleroy's
dragoons (v. 232, 247).   L. (J. Gros and P. Gros), 1846, Cal. Bat., Co. B,
artill. (v. 358).   Lount (Seth H.), 1847, Co. I, N.Y.Vol. (v. 499); killed by
Rogue Riv. Ind. '55.   Louzade (James), 1840, one of the exiles to S. Blas.
iv. 18.
    Love (Harry), 1843(?), arrived in Oct. acc. to records of the Soc. Cal.
Pion. iv. 400. His wife was Mary Bennett, widow of Vardamon B. of '43.
She was living in Sta Clara Co. '55.   L. (John), 1846, lieut Co. C, 1st U.S.
dragoons, as per muster-roll; prob. did not come to Cal.   Loveall (Stephen),
1847, Co. F, 3d U.S. artill. (v. 518).   Lovejoy (A. L.), 1848, Or. lawyer in
the mines. *Burnett.*   Lovelain (L. F.), 1846, Cal. Bat. (v. 358).   Loveland
(Cyrus C.), 1847, Co. K, N.Y.Vol. (v. 499); in Sta Co. '83.   L. (J. B.),
1848, at Monterey.   Lovett, 1848, mr of the *Eagle*.   L. (Angeline M.), 1846,
a woman of the Mormon colony. v. 546; married to Thos Kittleman in Dec.
'47 at S.F.
    Low (James C.), 1847, Q. M. sergt N.Y.Vol. v. 503; acting order. sergt;
disch. for physical disability Sept.; owner of S.F. lots; in S.F. '54; d. at S.
Rafael before '82.   L. (Thomas), 1831, perhaps one of Young's trappers. iii.
388; at S.F. in '40.   Lowe, 1847, mr of the *Sta Cruz* schr '46-8. v. 580.
Lowe (Mrs W. H.), 1846, at S. José '81.   Lowery (Anthony W.), 1847, Co.
E, N.Y.Vol. (v. 499); at S.F. '74-8.   Loy (Horace), 1848, teamster in Sutter's employ.   Loze (M. M.), 1846, Cal. Bat. (v. 358).
    Lucas (John), 1838, Engl. lumberman in the Sta Cruz region named in
Larkin's accounts. iv. 119; one of the exiles of '40, who returned in '41. iv.
18, 33.   Luce, 1848, mr of the *Tepic*. v. 580.   L. (S. B.), 1847, mid. on the
U.S. *Columbus*.   Lucío (Juan Saenz de), 1806, Span. friar who served at
S.F., retiring in '16. ii. 374-5, 131, 159-60, 386, 394.   Luco (Juan M.),
1847, Chilian and mr of the *Natalia* '47-8. v. 579; claimant for the Ulpinos
rancho. iv. 674; somewhat prominent in land matters, and still in S.F. '85.
Ludloff (Charles), 1847, Co. B, N.Y.Vol. (v. 499).
    Lugo (Antonio María), son of Francisco, nat. of Cal., b. at S. Antonio
1775, and a soldier till 1809, when he settled near Los Angeles. ii. 350, 353.
In 1810 he was grantee of S. Antonio rancho, confirmed to him in later years.
ii. 112, 352, 565-6, 633, 664. In '16 and '18 he was alcalde at Los Ang. ii.
350; juez del campo '33-4. iii. 635, 257-8; in '37-8 memb. of the ayunt.,
taking some part as commissioner in the troubles between north and south.
iii. 509, 519, 556, 636; grantee of Chino in '41. iv. 634; ment. occasionally
in connection with Ind. affairs and other public matters, having a claim of
$5,000 against the govt '42-6. iv. 338, 497, 626, 629, 634. He was a wealthy
and widely known ranchero, uneducated but of good character. He died in
'60. His wife was María Dolores Ruiz; and his daughter Merced married
Stephen C. Foster. José del Cármen and Felipe were his sons.   L. (Bernardino), at Sta B. before '37, wife Isabel Leiva.   L. (Felipe), son, I
think, of Ant. M., born about 1808; regidor at Los Ang. '32-3, '36-7, '44-5.
iii. 635-6; iv. 633; in '39 a lieut. iii. 583; and partido elector. iii. 590; and
juez in '40. iii. 637. After the Amer. occupation he was justice of the peace
and supervisor, residing at La Mesa; still living in '78.
    Lugo (Francisco), Mex. soldier who came from Sinaloa with his family
soon after 1769, living at Los Ang. and Sta B. i. 461; ii. 100. He died at
Sta B. in 1805, and may be regarded as the founder of the Lugo family in
Cal. His wife was Juana Vianazul (one record seems to say Juana M. Rita
Martinez), and he brought four children from Sin., Salvador killed when a
boy by being thrown from a horse, José Antonio a soldier at Sta B. who left
a family, Tomasa who married Capt. Raimundo Carrillo, ii. 100, and Rosa
who married Alférez Cota and was the mother of Joaq. de la Torre's wife,
dying in 1790. i. 665. Five children were born in Cal., José Ignacio, Antonio María, and Juan, all soldiers; María Antonia who married Ignacio Vallejo, and María Ignacia who married José Ruiz.   L. (Francisco), at Pilar-

citos rancho '25-6, being juez de campo '35, iii. 674, age 37, wife Juana Briones, child. Cayetano b. '31 (at Sta B. '51), Juan de Mata '34, Francisco '36; in '39 grantee of Paraje de Sanchez, iii. 677, for which his widow was claimant in '52; juez auxiliar '44. iv. 653.

Lugo (José), sergt of the Sta B. comp., and alférez '39-46, involved in several revolts and in the affair of the cañon perdido of '48. iii. 651; iv. 476, 539, 541, 651; v. 35, 586, 588. Known as El Chato.   L. (José del Cármen), son of Antonio María, b. at Los Ang. '13; regidor at Los Ang. '38-9. iii. 636; grantee of S. Bernardino '42. iv. 635; juez de campo '44. iv. 633; prominent in the chino fight and in several Ind. exped. of '46-7. v. 312-14, 408, 566, 617, 625; alcalde of Los Ang. '49. About '51 he sold his rancho to the Mormons, and from that time has lived at Los Ang., in good circumstances till about '63, when he lost his property. In '78 he dictated his *Vida de un Ranchero* for my use. He had a wife and 4 daughters.   L. (José Ignacio), son of Francisco, soldier at San Juan B. before 1800, and later settler at Los Ang. i. 558; ii. 350; maj. at S. Fern. '17; in '32 inval. of Sta B. comp.: wife Rafaela Romero, child. Magdalena and Luis; at Los Ang. '46.   L. (José María), juez del campo at Los Ang. '36, '38. iii. 636; one of the grantees of S. Bernardino '42; a son of Ant. María; still living at S. Bern. '50.   L. (Juan), corp. at Sta B. before '37; at Los Ang. '48.   L. (Luis), at Sta B. 1790, when his wife died in giving birth to twins.   L. (María Guadalupe), wife of Sergt Verdugo, d. 1780. i. 663.   L. (Miguel), at Sta B. '37, wife Isabel Fernandez, 2 children.   L. (Nicanor), had a Cal. claim for horses $1,970 (v. 462).   L. (Rafael), soldier at Sta B. before '37. L. (Santiago), appraiser at Purísima '35. iii. 665; regidor at Sta B. '37. iii. 654; juez de paz '41. iv. 641.   L. (Seferino), soldier in 1777; one of the earliest settlers at S. José. i. 312, 477-8; wife Gertrudis Pacheco.   L. (Trinidad), soldier at Sta B. '32, wife Rosario Dominguez, 6 children.   L. (Vicente), one of the grantees of S. Bern. '42, son of Antonio M.; justice at S. Gabriel '50; supervisor Los Ang. Co. '62-3.

Luis, 1836, Ital. fisherman at Mont., age 26.   Luis, Ind. in Sutter's employ; one of the 1st Donner relief; refused to eat human flesh, and was himself killed and eaten. v. 531-2, 534, 537.   Lujan (José), 1797, Span. alférez of S. Diego comp. to 1806, when he left the country. i. 544, 647; ii. 101. L. (José María), at Los Ang. '46.   Luker (Wm), 1847, Co. I, N.Y.Vol. (v. 499); at Sonora, Cal., '83.   Lumsden (Wm), 1834, Engl. pilot on the *Margarita*, age 31, registered at S. Blas. iii. 412; in '36-7 at S. Diego. iii. 618; in '40 arrested at Sta B., but released at S. Diego. iv. 14, 17; in '44 at S.F. and in '48 at Mont.   Luna, Dominican friar from L. Cal., at S. Gabriel '29. iii. 96.   Lunia (Joseph), 1834, Frenchman in a Mont. list.   Lunt (Dan.), 1848, mate of the *Euphemia*.   Lupton (Durah), 1848, at S. José '76.   Luque (Gabriel), soldier killed by Ind. on the Colorado 1782. i. 359, 362.   Lusiano Basilio), zanjero at Los Ang. '47. v. 626.   Luskey (Joseph), 1847, Co. A, N.Y. Vol. (v. 499); died before '80.   Luther, 1848, at Sutter's Fort with family. Lutz (Wm D.), 1846, sailor on the *Cyane;* at Phil '77.

Lyman (Chester S.), 1847, clergyman who came from Hon. on the *Euphemia*, with letters to Colton and Larkin. In Sept. he was appointed surveyor for the middle department, and in '48 made surveys at S. José and N. Almaden. v. 665. He remained in Cal. till '50, returning in '54 from New Haven to testify in the N. Almaden case.   L. (J. H.), 1841, physician from Mass. who came from N. Mex. with the Workman-Rowland party. iv. 278. He returned East in '43, perhaps via Oregon as he had intended. Wilson says he came back with his family and was in S.F. '77; but Given thinks he never returned but is still in Mass., though G. could not find him in '83.

Lynch, 1838, at Mont. '38-9.   L., 1847, of the firm L. & Lewis Mont. '47-8.   L. (Ferdinand), 1847, Co. C, N.Y. Vol. (v. 499).   L. (James), 1847, Co. F, ditto; nat. of Pa, of Irish parentage; on a rancho at Pleito, S. Luis Ob., '71-4; at Jolon, Mont. Co., '82. Quigley tells some very absurd stories about him.   L. (John), 1842, Engl. sailor on the *Jóven Guipuzcoana*, arrested at S.F. for mutiny; still in S.F. '44, age 30.   L. (Joseph Peter), 1847, corp. Co.

G, N.Y. Vol. (v. 499); one of the murderers of the Reed family at S. Miguel, executed at Sta B. '48. v. 632, 640.   L. (Patrick), 1847, Co. B, N.Y. Vol. (v. 199); at S.F. '71–82.
Lyon (Albert G.), 1846, nat. of Va and overl. immig. from Mo.; in Sonoma from '48; died '79, leaving a widow and 9 children.   Lyons (Aaron), 1847, sergt Co. D, N.Y. Vol. v. 504; sheriff of Mont. Co.; died '65.   L. (Geo.), 1848, at S. Diego; possibly in '42.   L. (Peter), 1840, at Mont. '40–1; said to have aided in the arrest of the foreigners. iv. 22, 120; later in Sutter's employ, which he left in '46.   L. (R. M.), 1846, Co. F, Cal. Bat. (v. 358); at Sonoma '47.   Lytle (Andrew), 1847, lieut Co. E, Morm. Bat.; capt. of 100 on the return. v. 477, 493.

M. (J. F. B.), 1840, from Hon. on the *Don Quixote*, author of *Leaves from my Journal.* iv. 157.   McAllister (Michael James), 1822, Irish blacksmith, known at Mont. '29 as 'el herrero loco,' age 38.   Still worked at his trade and drank his aguardiente in '31–40, as shown by various records, also selling grog at his shop, without much profit perhaps, as he is said to have taken no pay from sailors.   He had been an Australian convict for 7 years before coming to Cal.; also called Patrick; died at Mont. '54.   McA. (Robert), 1840, one of the Graham exiles. iv. 18, 33; perhaps returned, as there was a lumberman of his name in S.F. district '42, age 29.   McArran (Robert M.), 1846, mid. on the U. S. *Independence.*   McArthur (Henry), 1847, Co. D, Morm. Bat. (v. 469); at Scipio, Utah, '82.   McA. (Wm P.), 1848, ment. in *Alta* '51.   McAulley (Alex.), 1847, Co. B, N.Y. Vol. (v. 499).   McBride (Haslam), 1847, Co. E, Morm. Bat. (v. 469); reënl.
McCaffery (Hugh), 1846, Co. C, 1st U. S. dragoons (v. 336).   McCallum (James), 1828, Scotch carpenter at Mont. '28–9, age 22.   McCann (Dan.), 1847, Co. F, 3d U.S. artill. (v. 518).   McCarran (Joseph), 1847, Co. D, N. Y. Vol. (v. 499).   McCartney (Bartholomew), 1847, Co. H, N.Y. Vol. (v. 499); owner of S.F. lot.   McCarty (Dav. C.), 1847, Co. C, ditto; later a real estate agent and inspector of customs at S.F., where he died in '62 at the age of 41; an Irishman.   McC. (Edward), 1847, Co. C, ditto; d. Sta B. '52.   McC. (James), 1825, signs a receipt of payment from Robt Livermore; perhaps an error in date.   McC. (Nelson), 1847, Co. B, Morm. Bat. (v. 469).   McC. (Wm), 1832, one of the comp. extranjera at Mont. iii. 221; named on Larkin's books '33–4.   McCarver (M. M.), 1848, Kentuckian from Or.; memb. of the constit. convention '49; went to Idaho later.   McCaulley (James), 1846, Fauntleroy's dragoons (v. 232, 247); also ment. in Pt Reyes region.
McChristian (Patrick), 1845, overl. immig. of the Grigsby-Ide party. iv. 579, 587; one of the Bears in '46, having given Robt A. Thompson a narrative of that affair, of which I have a copy. v. 110; in the mines '48–9; and after a short residence at Sta Cruz, a farmer at Sonoma, where he prob. still lives in '85.   McClain (John L.), 1847, owner of a S.F. lot.   McClarcklin 1845, at S. José (McLaughlin?).   McClary (James), 1846, overl. immig. in Bryant's party. v. 528; served in Co. F, Cal. Bat. (v. 358); in lists of S.F. lot-owners and Cal. claimants. v. 685 (462); interested at Benicia '47; perhaps in some cases confounded with McClurg.   McClaskey (Wm I.), 1847, Co. D, N.Y. Vol. (v. 499); d. S.F. '66.
McClellan, 1842, went to Or. with Joel Walker in '43.   McC., 1847, at Sutter's Fort June–July.   McC. (Dav. Frank), 1843, nat. of Tenn. and overl. immig. of the Walker-Chiles party (iv. 392). He went east in '46 with his uncle, Jos. Walker, but came back in '48, being a trader and butcher in the mines, with several visits to the east, until '53, when he settled on a Contra Costa farm, where he still lived in '80.   McC. (John), 1848, nat. of Pa, who died at S.F. '63, age 73.   McC. (Michael T.), 1848, brother of Dav. F., and overl. immig. of the Chiles party with family; in Sonoma Co. '80. He had 15 children; one of his daughters was the wife of John A. Paxton, a well-known banker of Marysville and Austin, Nev.   McCloud (Wm), 1847, from Hon. on the *Xylon.*
McClure (James), 1847, owner of S.F. lot; at Benicia; perhaps 'McClary,'

q.v. McC. (John), 1841, from N. Mex. in the Workman-Rowland party. iv. 278; in '43 he went with Leese to Or. iv. 390; and was still there as late as '60. McC. (Wm), 1845, doubtful name of an overl. immig.; prob. went to Or. and not Cal. iv. 578. McClurg (James B.), 1847, trader from Hon. on the *Xylon*, also sup. of the *Francesca;* member of the firm McC. & Co. (Abell and Chever) at Los Ang. to Feb. '48; owner of S.F. lots '47. v. 678; at Mont. '48; at S.F. from '48; also interested at Benicia. He died at S.F. '57, age 42. McClusky (Philip), 1847, Co. D, N.Y.Vol. (v. 499).

McComb (Benj.), 1848, overl. immig. from Mo.; perhaps his family were cl. for parts of the Entre Napa rancho. McCoon (Perry), 1844, Engl. sailor who may have come in '43. iv. 453. In Dec. '44 he was sent by Sutter to S. Rafael to obtain recruits for the Micheltorena campaign. iv. 486-501. Re-turning he worked a while at the fort, but in Dec. '45 moved to a farm of his own near by. In Feb. '46 he married Mrs Lewis, who died in June; and in '47 he married Elitha C. Donner, having a launch on the bay and river. Men-tioned as a miner at Weber Cr. and Hangtown '48-9. He became locally some-what famous for his skill as a vaquero; but in '51 was thrown from his horse and dragged to death by the riata at his home on the Cosumnes. His widow married Benj. Wilder and was still living in '80 at Elk Grove. McC. (Rob-ert), 1848, owner of S.F. lot. McCord (Alex.), 1847, sergt Co. A, Morm. Bat. v. 477. McCormick (James), 1847, left an Engl. vessel at Mont.; owner of a S.F. lot; in the mines '48; later a resid. of S. José. McCoy (Redding), 1845, nat. of N. J. and mate on the *Dromo;* disch. at Mont. iv. 587. Ship-ping on the *Fama* he was wrecked at Sta. B. in '46; became an otter-hunter, having also several startling adventures with bears; got a S.F. lot in '47; at Bodega '48, and went to the mines McCracken (John C.), 1846, at N. Helv., prob. an overl. immig.; nat. of N. C.; died at Sonoma '70, age 55. McC. (Wm R.), 1847, Co. F, N.Y.Vol. (v. 499). McCrady, 1845, one of Frémont's party. iv. 583.

McCue (Patrick), 1846, one of the Mormon col. with wife and 4 children. v. 546; owner of S.F. lot; worked as a blacksmith at Bodega and other places; going east in '52. McCulloch (Hugh), 1822, merchant of Lima and member of the Cal. branch of McC., Hartnell, & Co., who visited Cal. on the *John Begg.* ii. 474-7, 479, 492-3, 519, 613-14; iii. 24, 71. He died in Liverpool in '42. McC. (James), 1831, brother of Hugh, at Mont. '31-2; not behaving in a man-ner satisfactory to his relatives. McC. (Levi H.), 1847, Co. C, Morm. Bat. (v. 469); at Fillmore, Utah, '82. McCusker (Mrs T. C.), 1843, nat. of Ga, from Or., maiden name not given; married in '45, at Sta Cruz to '59, in Mont. Co. to '81. McCutchen (John), 1846, overl. immig.; perhaps went to Or. v. 529. McC. (Wm), 1846, nat. of Tenn. and one of the Donner party with wife and daughter. He left the party before reaching the Sierra and from Cal. went back with the 2d relief party. The daughter Harriet died, but the father and mother, Amanda M., survived, settling 1st at Sonoma, and in '48 at S. José, where McC. still lived in '80. v. 531-2, 534. Portrait in *McGlashan*, 244.

McDermott (Chas), 1848 (?), pres. of a Benicia lumber comp. in '48-9. McD. (David), 1847, mid. on the U. S. *Columbus.* McD. (D. A.), 1846, at S.F. '54. McD. (H.), 1848, from Hon. on the *Euphemia;* new passp. from Hon. Aug. McDonald, 1845, in Sutter's employ '45-6. iv. 578, 587; went to Or. Apr. '46. v. 526; but was perhaps back again in '48. McD. (Alex.), 1845, one of the men lost on the *Warren's* launch '46. v. 384, 587. McD. (Alex. C.), 1847, sergt-major N.Y.Vol. v. 503; at Sonoma to '59, and later on a rancho known as McD.'s station, between Cloverdale and Ukiah, where he died in '80 at the age of 65, leaving a widow, and of the pioneer Smith family. McD. (Benj.), 1847, settler at Benicia. v. 672; married a daughter of Lundy Alford. McD. (Chas), 1847, perhaps of N. Y. Vol. under another name. McD. (D.), 1847, from Or. on the *Henry.* McD. (Wm.), 1847, Co. G, N.Y. Vol. (v. 499). McD. (Wm), 1847, auctioneer at S.F. '47-8, of firm McD. & Buchanan. v. 680, 682; owner of town lots; died '48 at the age of 35. McD. (Wm), 1847, Engl. at Benicia '47-8. *Tustin;* perhaps same as Benj. McD. (Wm), 1846, testified at Napa '68 that he lived in Napa Val. '46-50; prob.

same as following. McDonnell (Wm), 1846, nat. of Mo. and overl. immig.;
Co. E, Cal. Bat. (v. 358); disch. in Nov. at S. Diego; lived in Napa Co. to '50,
marrying Eleanor Graves of the Donner party in '49. Later in Sonoma Co.,
acting as guide to the Geysers for many years; in '80 at Knight's Val. with
family of 9 children. McDonough (Joseph), 1847, Co. A, N.Y.Vol. (v. 499);
capt. in Meagher's brigade war of '61–5; at S.F. '82. McD. (Nicholas), 1847,
Co. A, N.Y.Vol. (v. 499); in L. Cal. '71–4; killed at La Paz. McDormaut,
1847, at Sutter's Fort.

McDougal, 1816, sup. of the *Colonel*. ii. 278. McD. (Geo.), 1845, nat. of
Ohio, and overl. immig. from Ind. in the Swasey-Todd party. v. 575–6, 587.
He lived at Sta Cruz and Gilroy; served as a kind of unattached volunteer in
the Cal. Bat. '46–7; was a 'broker'—that is, a gambler—at S.F. '47–8, becoming the owner of many town lots in partnership with Lippincott. v. 676, 679,
680; and a trader at Sac. in '48–9. His movements in later years were too numerous and complicated to be recorded here. He made several trips to the East,
where he had a family, and about '53 began a roving life, rarely making his
whereabouts known, and spending much of his time among the Ind. in Arizona
and Mexico. In '67 he was found by a naval commander in Patagonia, but
returned to Ind., and in '69 went to Washington, D. C., when he died in '72.
He was an eccentric but brave and popular man. McD. (John), 1848, brother
of Geo., and overl. immig. from Ind.; a member of the constit. convention
'49, and elected lieut-gov., becoming gov. on the resignation of Burnett. He
died at S.F. in '66 at the age of 49.

McDowell (Dugald), 1837, named in Larkin's books. McD. (James),
1845, overland immig., with his wife, Margaret Pyles, and daughter, Maggie
A., age 3 years. iv. 578, 587. He came in a party which I am unable to identify, and most of the members of which went to Or. from Ft Hall. He was
employed as a gunsmith by Sutter in '45–7, and possibly served in the Cal.
Bat., having a Cal. claim for work (v. 462). In Aug. '47 he moved with his
family across the Sac. Riv., where he bought a rancho and built a house. He
was murdered in May '49. In '50 the widow had the town site of Washington
laid out on her land; married Dr E. C. Taylor in '51; and died at Washington in '83. The daughter Maggie became Mrs M. A. Hunt, and in '84, living
at Washington, furnished me information about her family. Another daughter, Harriet, in '81 Mrs Cooke, was born—prob. at the fort, though Mrs
Hunt is sure it was at Washington—Feb. 21, '47; and a son Wm according
to the newspapers in '48. McD. (John), 1841, overl. immig. of the Bartleson party, who went back to Mo. in '42. iv. 270, 275, 342. McDuff (J.),
1848, passp. from Hon. McDuffee (And. J.), 1847, connected in some way
with the N.Y. Vol. (v. 499), but not on the roll; clerk in the naval store office at Mont. '47–8, and named in many records; trading at the dry diggings
'48; at S. José '50. Clark calls him McDuff.

McElroy (Alex.), 1848 (?), long a resid. of Mariposa Co.; d. at Merced '82, leaving a widow and a married daughter; perhaps of Graham's dragoons (v. 522).
McElroy (Hugh), 1846, Co. C, 1st U.S. dragoons (v. 336). McElvain (J.),
1846, lieut of Co. C, 1st U. S. dragoons (v. 336); not in Cal. McFerion
(James), 1824, Scotch tailor from Lima. ii. 526; at S. Diego '28. v. 545; at
Los Ang. '36, age 50 and single. McGee (Milton), 1843, overl. immig. of
the Chiles-Walker party. iv. 392, 394. McGeehan (Patrick), 1847, Co. F,
3d U. S. artill. (v. 518). McGhee (John), 1847, Co. B, N. Y. Vol. (v. 499);
d. at S.F. '61. McGill (James), 1847, Co. E, ditto. McG. (Pat.), 1847,
Co. A, ditto. McGilvery, 1841, on the *Cowlitz*, from Columbia Riv. Mc-
Gloene (James), 1847, perhaps of N.Y. Vol. under another name. McGlone
(Wm), 1837, Irish sailor on the wrecked whaler *Com. Rogers*. iv. 118; employed in Graham's distillery and known as 'Billy the Brewer.' He was
exiled in '40 but returned. iv. 18, 33; and I have his letter of '44 in which
he complains that he has been 7 days in jail without food! Worked in Larkin's soap factory '45; perhaps joined Fauntleroy's dragoons '46 (v. 232, 247);
and later Co. B, Cal. Bat., being wounded at Natividad. v. 371. He was at
N. Helv. '47, in the mines '48; at Mont. '57, and a few years later was drowned

at Sta B.   McGranaghan (Wm G.), 1847, Co. E, N.Y. Vol. (v. 499).   Mc-
Guier (A.), 1848, passp. from Hon.   McGuire (John), 1847, Co. B, N.Y.
Vol. (v. 499).   McHollingworth (J.), 1846 (?), in S. Joaq. Co. '49.   *Tinkham.*
   McIntosh (Chas), 1843, Cherokee or Delaware half-breed, in the Walker-
Chiles party. iv. 392, 400; at Mont. and N. Helv. '45, serving in the Micheltorena campaign. iv. 486, 501; served in Cal. Bat. '46-7, taking part in the
Natividad fight.   McI. (Edward), 1823 (?), Scotch sailor who landed at Mont.
from a trader. ii. 475, 495. In a record of '29 he claimed to have come in '23;
in another of Dec. '33, to have been 12 years in Cal., or since '22; while in
some accounts he is said to have visited Cal. in '13 and returned in '23. I
think it likely he came on the *Rover* with Capt. Cooper., In '28 he was baptized at S. Cárlos as Edward Manuel. I have his letter of May '28. In '29
he appears in a Mont. list as a single carpenter, age 34. In '30 he bought Geo.
Allen's interest in a Mont. inn for $90, becoming a partner of Wm Gralbatch.
ii. 609; was naturalized in '33; got an otter-hunting license in '34, making a
trip with Dye. iii. 395; still at Mont. '35. In '38, or perhaps a year or two
earlier, he settled with James Dawson on the Estero Americano rancho near
Bodega, iv. 117, being recorded in that year as agent for Vallejo and for the
H. B. Co. In '39 he obtained a grant of the rancho, and is said to have left
his partner's name out of the title, for which he was flogged by the irate Daw-
som, who proceeded to saw their house in two and move his half to another
rancho. iii. 712; iv. 129. In '40 he guided Spalding of the *Lausanne* to S.F.
iv. 172; and was in trouble on account of a Frenchman found murdered on
his place. He was at N. Helv. in '44-5, taking part in the Micheltorena campaign. iv. 483; but does not figure in the war records of '46-7. Owner of a
S.F. lot '46. v. 685; alcalde at Sonoma '46. v. 297, 663; alcalde of S. Rafael
'47. v. 668; when he leased his rancho to O'Farrell and went to live with his
old comrade James Black, both of them dying in '70, McI. at the age of 75.
McI. (Jas W.), 1837, pass. on the *Europa* to Hon. iv. 103.   McIntyre, 1845,
making shingles at Larkin's soap factory.   McI. (H.), 1848, passp. from
Hon. with family.   McI. (John), 1843, overl. immig. of the Chiles-Walker
party. iv. 392-3; nothing more known of him.   McI. (Terance), 1847, Co.
D, N.Y. Vol. (v. 499).   McI. (Wm L.), 1847, asst surg. Morm. Bat. v. 477,
480.
   McKaffray (Hugh), 1846, perhaps killed at S. Pascual. v. 346.   McKay,
1846, mid. U. S. N., bearer of despatches from Wash.; perhaps ' Mackae.'
McK. (Jean B. D.), 1825, hunter of the H. B. Co., who visited Cal. in '41 and
prob. several times before. iii. 151; iv. 212, 214.   McK. (John H.), 1847,
Co. K, N.Y. Vol. (v. 499); in '80 claimed to have aided at Benicia in '48 in
making the 1st casting in Cal.—a faucet for a still, made of copper balls.
McKay (Thos), 1848, guide to Burnett's party from Or.   McKean, 1847,
mid. on the U. S. *Independence*.   McK. (Wm W.), 1846, com. of the U. S.
Dale, '46-7; v. 577; d. '65.   McKee (James), 1848, at S.F. from Hon. June.
McK. (James), 1847, murdered by B. K. Thompson at Stockton Jan. '48.
McK. (James M.), 1847, Co. D, N.Y. Vol. (v. 499); d. Mont. Dec.   McK.
(James R.), 1846, bugler Co. C, 1st U. S. dragoons. v. 336.   McK. (Wm
H.), 1846, Scotch physician at Mont., who possibly came a year or two earlier;
often named in records of '46-8 at Mont., S. José, and Sac., where in '48 he
seems to have been engaged in trade. In '52 he was claimant for the Jacinto
rancho, Colusa. iv. 671. He married, I think, a daughter of Estévan Munrás;
and his son Robert, who in '76 gave me a valuable vol. of old mission records,
still lives in '85 at Mont. or S.F.   McKeever (James), 1844, hunter and adventurer of the plains known as Capt. Jack, killed in Idaho '77; claimed to
have landed at S.F. in 44, to have aided in the revolt and war of '46-7, and
to have a family at Sta Rosa. *S. F. Chronicle;* iv. 453.   McKenzie, 1845, at
N. Helv. '45, '47; with Arce in '46. iv. 578, 587; v. 109; perhaps same as the
following.   McK. (Bernard), 1846, carpenter and mason at Mont. '46-8; in
the mines '48, discovering the dry diggings at Placerville. *Carson* and *Swan.*
A ' Capt.' McK. died at S. F. in '54.   McK. (D'l), 1843, trader at S. Diego.
McKern (Ed.), 1847, owner of S. F. lot; prob. ' Kern,' q. v.

McKinley (James), 1824, Scotch sailor boy left at S. F. or Sta B. by a
whaler. ii. 526. This is the statement usually made in accounts of his life,
and it is also said that he was but 11 years old, all of which may be erroneous. He is constantly named in commercial records from '30, when he was
agent for Capt. Cooper at Mont., travelling much of the time, but making
Mont. his home, and joining the comp. extranjera in '32. iii. 221. In '35 he
went to Los Ang. as agent for Larkin; in '36 is named in a padron as a trader,
aged 33; and from this year to '40 and later was owner of the *Ayacucho* schr,
making trips up and down the coast. iv. 101, 117. Perhaps arrested as a matter of form in '40. iv. 17. From '42 in partnership with Fitch and Paty, but
it is hard to say what place he regarded as home; I have many letters written by him at different points. From '43 the firm had a store at S.F. v. 682;
in '44–5 McK. took a leading part at Los Ang. in the movement of southern
foreigners against Micheltorena. iv. 495, 505–8; also in '44–5 was one of the
purchasers of the mission estates of S. Juan Cap. and S. Luis Ob. iv. 553, 627,
655, 659; v. 558. In '46 he seems to have transferred his residence from Los
Ang. to Mont., where in Jan.'47 he was placed under arrest by Lieut Maddox
with a view of extorting information about Calif. operations in the south. *Alviso Doc.*, 209–10. He married Cármen, daughter of José Amesti, in '48; was
claimant in '52 for ranchos in Mont. and S. Luis Ob. counties. iv. 655; and
died at Mont. in '75, leaving several children. Don Santiago was a man of
good repute throughout his long career in Cal. I have a letter from his mother
in '43.   McK. (J.), 1841, boatswain on the U. S. *St Louis*.   McKinney
(Wm S.), 1847, mr of the *Primavera*. v. 580.   McKinstry (Geo., Jr), 1846,
overl. immig., who became the 1st sheriff of the northern district at Sutter's
Fort '46–7. v. 675; active in relief measures for the Donner party, v. 538, on
which subject his letters were published in the S.F. *Star;* passenger on the
1st steamer to Sac. '47. v. 579; also owner of a S.F. lot. v. 678. He was somewhat prominent in public affairs at Sac. in early mining times; and had a
trading post on the Cosumnes '49–50. I find no record of him from that time
till '71–4, when he was a physician at Old S. Diego, and gave me the valuable
original *McKinstry Papers*, including some of his summons to jurors, etc., as
sheriff; and also some important records on the Donner party. He was an
eccentric character while at S. Diego, spending much of his time in long tours
among the Ind. Beyond a vague rumor of his death before '80, I have no trace
of him after '74.

McLanahan (T.), 1847, mid. on the U.S. *Columbus;* doubtful.   McLane,
1846, mr of the *Paladin*. v. 579.   McL. (Geo.), 1839, at Mont. '39–40;
named in Larkin's books.   McL. (Louis), 1846, nat. of Del., b. '19, entered
the navy '35, and came to Cal. as passed mid. on the *Savannah*. He served
with Fauntleroy's dragoons. v. 232, 289; and took a prominent part in recruit-
ing and organizing the Cal. Bat., becoming capt. of the artill. comp., and
later in the campaign ranking as major. vi. 359, 361. He was one of Frémont's
commissioners who signed the treaty of Cahuenga, closing the war. v. 404–5,
434. In '50 he resigned his position in the navy and returned to Cal. to engage in a series of important industrial and financial enterprises, being manager of Wells, Fargo & Co.'s express from '55 to '68, and of the Nevada Bank
from '75 to '82. He left Cal. a little later, but is still living in '85. His wife
was Sophie Hoffman of Baltimore, and there were 8 children. Portrait in
Contemp. Biog.   McLannan, 1846, from Hon. on the *Euphemia*.   McLarcy,
1846, sergt Co. B. artill. Cal. Bat. v. 358.   McLean (Geo.), 1817, mr of the
Currency Lass. '47–8; perhaps 'McLane' of '39.   McLean, 1848, kept a
furniture shop at S.F., of firm McL. & Osburn. v. 678. ,   McL. (James
D.), 1846, Cal. Bat. (v. 358).   McL. (Wm S.), 1846, ditto.   McL., 1848, at
S.F. from Tahiti.   McLeod (Alex. R.), 1828, in com. of H. B. Co. hunters
from the N. iii. 151; iv. 263.   McL. (Francis J.), 1847, Co. F, N. Y. Vol.
(v. 499).   McL. (John C.), 1834, Scotch sailor on the *Bonanza* (?), in '34–6,
iii. 412; returned to Cal. '50; and lived at Vallejo '60–79. *Solano Co. Hist.*
McL. (John M.), 1838, on the *Cadboro*, agent of H.B.Co.   McLine (Joseph),
1848, owner of a S. F. lot.   McLoughlin (John), 1841, chief factor of the H.

B. Co., who visited Cal. on the *Cowlitz.* iv. 216-18, 250, 564; see also *Hist. B. Col.* and *Hist. Or.*   McLown (Wm), 1839, sailor under arrest at S. F. McMahon (Green), 1841, nat. of Mo., and overl. immig. of the Bartleson party. iv. 270, 275, 279. He went to Or., but returned in '45 with a party to which I have given his name. iv. 572-4. Possibly there was a James Mc-M. in the same party. v. 573. He settled on Putah Creek, Solano Co., and died at Dixon in '84 at the age of 65. By the death notice it appears that his name was Samuel G.   McM. (Jeremiah), 1848, Irishman at Mont. '47-8; seems to have died about '56.   McM. (Nelson), 1841, brother of Green, and one of the Bartleson party. iv. 270, 275. He went East or to Or., and I think did not return to Cal., though he is mentioned also as one of the Clyman party of '45. iv. 573.   McM. (Patrick), 1847, Co. F, 3d U. S. artill. (v. 518).   McManus (James), 1847, Co. E, N. Y. Vol. (v. 499); d. S. F. '52. McMichael (Grove C.), 1848, nat. of Mo.; a gambler of good repute, killed in S. F. '54.   McM. (Wm), 1831 (?), a sailor said to have visited Cal. about this time. iii. 405; settled at S. F. '51; a wharf superintendent '53-4; d. at sea '59, at the age of 55.   McMillan, 1845, in charge of Sutter's launch; also called McMullen.   McM. (Chas), 1847, Co. E, N. Y. Vol. (v. 499); d. S. F. after '60.   McMonigle (Simpson), 1846, overl. immig. with Young. v. 529; served in Co. E, Cal. Bat. (v. 358); at Los Ang. '48.

McNamara (Eugene), 1846, Irish priest who had a grand scheme for colonizing Cal. with Irishmen to the glory of God and the discomfiture of the Yankees. His project has been generally given more importance in connection with English plans than it deserved. McM. came to Cal. on the *Juno.* iv. 592; v. 37, 215-23, 577, 636.   McNeilly (John), 1846, Co. C, 1st U. S. dragoons (v. 336).   McPhail, 1848, from Or. with Brooks.   McPherson (Chas J.), 1847, musician Co. B, N. Y. Vol. (v. 499); living in N. Y. '84. McP. (Geo.), 1847, musician, ditto; d. Morrisania, N.Y.,'69.   McP. (James), 1826, on the *Rover;* on Larkin's books at Mont. '38; I have his autograph of '43.

McPherson (John C.), 1848; Scotchman of good education and considerable ability as a writer; but eccentric to the verge of insanity, and almost constantly under the influence of liquor in his later years. It is not quite clear how he came, but apparently overl. from Mo., where he had been a teacher; though it is also said that he went to Texas and served in the Mex. war. He appeared in the mines in '48, and is mentioned by Burnett and others as the author of a popular song, ' Yuba, dear Yuba,' and other poetical effusions. He spent his later years in wandering about the country and writing pioneer sketches for the newspapers, under the signature of Juanita. Many of his sketches were of real value, though generally overburdened with eulogy; and the author was always an inoffensive, kind-hearted man. In '80 he fell through the trestle-work of a railroad bridge over the Tuolumne Riv. and was killed.   McQuade (Peter), 1836, at Mont.   McQuien (D.), 1848, passp. from Hon.

McRae (Arch.), 1846, mid. U. S. N., bearer of despatches from Wash. v. 287.   McRice, 1848, murdered by Scott at Sonoma.   McSpadden (James), 1847, Co. F, N. Y. Vol. (v. 499).   McRoberts (J.), 1845; mid. on the U. S. *Warren.*   McTavish (Donald), 1826, sup. of the *Colonel.* ii. 278.   McT. (Dugald), 1846, agent of the H. B. Co., visiting Cal. to sell the property of the comp. iv. 594.   McVicker (Henry), 1837, Amer. named in Larkin's book '37-41 as being in the Mont. district; perhaps arrested in '40. iv. 118, 17. In '42 he was in com. of Sutter's trappers, but quarrelled with S.; in '44 at S. F., age 24, took part in the Michel torena campaign, capturing Manuel Castro. iv. 486-7; in '45 named at Mont. and at N. Helv., where he had a fight with Geo. Davis. The latest record that I have found is that he left the fort Jan. '46 for Sonoma.

Mace (P.), 1845, doubtful name of a man at Cahuenga. iv. 595.   Machado, ment. in '19, '23. ii. 354, 550.   M., 1875, mr of the *Republicano.* iv. 568.   M. (Agustin), at Los Ang. from '24. ii. 526: juez de campo '38, and grantee of Ballona '39. iii. 633, 636; age 42 in '39; juez de campo '48. v.

626; justice of peace in '56.   M. (Andrés), at Los Ang. '46.   M. (Antonio Ignacio), regidor at Los Ang. '33, '38–9 acting síndico and alcalde. iii. 635–6; died in '78 at the age of '81.   M. (Bárbara), at Los Ang. '48.   M. (Benito), 1834, mr of the *Jóven Dorotea.* iii. 382.   M. (Eugenio), celador at Mont. '44. iv. 431.   M. (Dolores and Francisco), at Los Ang. '46.   M. (Hilario), at Los Ang. '19–27.   M. (Ignacio), at Los Ang. '38–48; grantee of Aguaje del Centinela '44; age 33 in '39. iii. 565; iv. 634.   M. (Jesus), at S. Bern. '46; cl. for Buenavista '52. iv. 620.   M. (José), at S. Bern. '46, age 27.   M. (José Ant.), at Los Ang. '46.   M. (José María), soldier of S.F. comp. '39; at Los Ang. '46.   M. (Juan), at S. Diego '40. iii. 610; at Los Ang. '46.   M. (Juana), daughter of José Manuel, a corp. of the S. Diego comp., and widow of Thos Ridington, who at S. Diego in '78, at the age of 64—though apparently about 40—gave me an interesting narrative of *Tiempos Pasados de Cal.* She has a son and 4 married daughters.   M. (Manuel), regidor at S. Diego and in charge of Rosario rancho in '36. iii. 612, 615.   M. (María Ant.), claimant for Las Vírgenes rancho. iii. 634.   Machuca (José S.), settler at Branciforte 1797. i. 569.

Maciel (Luis G.), 1842, Mex. lieut of the batallon fijo, suspended from his rank '43. iv. 289, 354, 364; but signed the treaty of Sta Teresa in '44. iv. 470.   Mack (John W.), 1847, carpenter at Mont. '47–8; at Angel's Camp '49. M. (Wm), 1846, one of the Mormon col., who prob. did not come to Cal. v. 547.   Macomb (Wm H.), 1847, lieut U. S. N., and acting mr of the *Lexington.*

Macondray (Fred. W.), 1822, nat. of Mass. and sailor on the *Panther,* which touched at Mont. from Chile. ii. 478. Subsequently he was mr of trading craft and remained some years in China. In '49 he came back to Cal. with his family and established the firm of M. & Co., being a prominent citizen of S. F. to the date of his death in '62.   M. (John Oliver E.), 1832, brother of Fred. W., who came from Boston on the *Newcastle* with Larkin, having a consignment of goods. iii. 208. His name appears on Larkin's books '33–7; in '36 he was a clerk for Watson, being then 29 years old; taking some part with other foreigners in the revolutionary events of '36, and especially aiding in retaking Mont. from the Mex. who had revolted against Alvarado. For this service he thought he had a claim on the U.S. (!) for 3 leagues of land in Cal., writing from Dorchester in Oct. '46 to Larkin on the subject, and enclosing a letter from his brother. He was about to sail for China, proposing to come to Cal. later.   Macy (Alex.), 1826, mr of the *Peruvian.*

Madariaga (Bonifacio), Mex. clerk at Mont. from about '30; comis. de policía and regidor in '36–7. iii. 675. In '36 age 27, wife Josefa Vallejo de Estrada (mother of Gov. Alvarado), children Dolores b. '32, Francisco '33. He went to Mex. in '42.   Maddox (Wm A. T.), 1846, lieut of marines U.S.N. on the *Cyane* and *Congress.* After the occupation of Los Ang. he came to Mont. by land, capturing some Cal. officers on the way, and was made com. of the garrison and of the central district, ranking as capt. in the Cal. Bat. He made an exped. to S. Juan B., and marched to Sta Clara with his comp. to take part in the final Sanchez campaign. v. 282, 289–90, 294, 358, 360, 383, 519, 639. I have no record of him after '47.   Madison (Geo.), 1839, sailor sent away on the *California* for robbing Spear's store; perhaps also Joseph M.   Madox (James), 1841, doubtful name at Mont.   Madrazo (José M.), Mex. sergt of artill. who signed the Zamorano pronunciamiento of '32. iii. 223.

Magee (Henry), 1847, lieut Co. I, N. Y. Vol. v. 504; at S. Diego '71–9. Mager (Adam), 1847, Co. D, ditto.   Maggard (Benj.), 1847, Co. C, Morm. Bat. (v. 469).   Magnent (Ollivier), 1844, Canadian immig. of the Stevens party. iv. 445, 453. He built a flour-mill at S. José, which he advertises for sale in the *S. F. Californian* of Apr. '48. Called also Magnet, Magnand, and Marquet. Acc. to the *Fresno Co. Hist.* there were two, Oliver and Francis, but the ref. is prob. to Deland.   Mahon, see 'McMahon.'   Mahony (John), 1848, in S.F. list of letters.

Main (James), 1844, at Mont. '44–5.   M. (Russell M.), 1847, Co. F, 3d U. S. artill. (v. 518).   Mainsford (John), 1836, Irish sawyer at Mont., age 30;

perhaps 'Rainsford,' q. v.   Maison (Joseph), 1846, Co. C, 1st U. S. dragoons
(v. 336).   Maitorena (José Joaquin), 1861, came to Cal. as cadet of the Sta
B. comp.; alférez from 1806; lieut from '27; elected to congress in '28; died
in Mex. '30. He was a drunken, good-natured fellow, with some skil as an
accountant when sober. Biog. iii. 45–6; ment. ii. 47, 100, 109, 117, 228, 361,
364, 424, 530–1, 536–7, 571–2, 570, 676; iii. 61, 64, 88.   Majors (Alex.),
1845 (?); later of the pony-express firm of Russell, M., & Waddell; doubtful
date of arrival. iv. 587. At S.F. '70.

Majors (Joseph L.), 1834, nat. of Tenn.—some accounts say of Ky, Va,
or Ohio—who came from N. Mex., perhaps with Graham. iii. 388, 412. At
Los Ang. in Nov. '34 he signed, with other foreigners, a protest against being
obliged to do military duty. In '35 he seems to have settled in the Sta Cruz
region, and from that year his name appears often in Larkin's accounts and
other records. He was one of Graham's men in the troubles of '36–S; and acc.
to Job Dye's statement bought Tomlinson's interest in the Zayante distillery
about '37, selling out to Dye a few years later. In '39 he was naturalized,
calling himself Juan José Crisóstomo, prob. a name received at baptism in N.
Mex. or Cal. About the same time he married María de los Angeles Castro,
by whom he had 19 children. (See 'Marones.') He was arrested in '40 but
soon released. iv. 17, 22, 24; receiving in '41 grants of the S. Agustin and
Zayante ranchos, the latter of which he sold to Graham. iv. 655–6; yet in '42
he signed an appeal to the U. S. for indemnity for sufferings while under
arrest! In '43 he signed a protest against Graham's offer of the services of
foreigners to Micheltorena. iv. 356; and served as juez de campo at Branciforte. iv. 663; in '46 juez de paz, and a witness at the trial of Naile's murderer.
v. 641–2; perhaps juez in '47; member of the Sta Cruz council '48. v. 642; alcalde and sub-prefect '49–50, and chosen delegate to the constit. convention.
Sta Cruz Arch., 102. He was claimant for the S. Agustin rancho, and a rich
man in those years, but subsequently lost most of his property, dying in '68
at Sta Cruz, where his widow still lived in '80.   Makárof, 1814, mr of the
Suvárof '14–15. ii. 274, 306, 373.   Malaco, a Suisun chief '17. ii. 339.

Malarin (Juan), 1820, nat. of Peru, and mr of the Señoriano in Cal. '20–2.
ii. 293, 439–40, 467. In '24 he came back as mr of the Apolonia. ii. 518; and
in '25 was chosen by Gov. Argüello to take the Asia and Constante prizes to
Acapulco. iii. 26; for which service he was made a lieut in the Mex. navy.
About the same time he married Josefa Estrada, and made Monterey his home,
though still going to sea. Mentioned in '29–30, being partido-elector. ii. 613;
iii. 49–50, 76, 82; signed the Zamorano pronunc. '32, being called into service
as alférez. iii. 223, 672; in '33 mr of the Leónidas, capt. of the port, and grantee of Guadalupe rancho. iii. 383, 673, 677; ment. in '37–8. iii. 501; iv. 104;
grantee of Chualar and mr of the Cervantes '39. iii. 677; iv. 102; justice and
president of the tribunal superior '41–5. iii. 605; iv. 296, 357, 532; in '46 member of the Mont. council and of the 1st jury. v. 289, 637. He died in '49 or
'50 at the age of nearly 60, leaving a large estate. Don Juan was a quiet, un-
obtrusive man of excellent character and much influence. His children in
'36 were María Isabel b. '26, Mariano '28, Concepcion '32, Urbano '35. One
of the daughters married Cárlos Olvera, and lives, as does Urbano, at Chualar, and there was another son, Ignacio, a money-broker at S.F. in '83.   M.
(Mariano), son of Juan, educated in Peru; executor of his father's estate, and
in that capacity successful claimant for the ranchos of Zanjones, Guadalupe,
and Chualar; judge of 1st instance at Mont. '49; coroner '50–1; supervisor '56;
member of the assembly '59–60; later a wealthy resident of Sta Clara, where
he still lives in '85.

Malaspina (Alejandro), 1791, Span. com. of an exploring exped. touching
at Mont. i. 490–2, 498, 506; ii. 61.   Malcolm, 1848, from Or. by sea, a companion of Brooks in the mines.   M. (Alex. B.), 1847, Co. G, N.Y.Vol. (v.
499).   M. (Julian), 1814, sailor left at Mont. by the Isaac Todd. ii. 272, 277.
Malculia, 1848, passp. from Hon.   Maldonado, 1821, an actor or revo
lutionary agent. ii. 431.   M. (José María), perhaps the same. Mex. clerk
from Tepic; receptor of customs at Sta B. '33–5. iii. 377, 654; sec. of the

diputacion '34–6. iii. 250, 291, 426, 673; síndico and sec. of Mont. ayunt. '35 –6. iii. 674–5. In '36 at Mont. age 38, wife Antonia Velarde, child Vicente, b. in Tepic '26. I have no record of him after his arrest in connection with the revolt of Mexicans against Alvarado in '37. iii. 525. Malherbe, mr of the *Eliza.* iv. 505. Mallett (Chas G.), 1845, Amer. sailor in care of the consul, from the *Warsaw;* shipped for Boston on the *California* or *Vandalia.* Mallogh, 1846, doubtful Irish settler at S. Luis Ob. *Quigley.* Mallory, 1846, mr of the *Prescott.* v. 580. Malloy (Ed.), 1845, deserter from the *Hopewell* at S. Diego. Malo (José Ramon), grantee of Purísima and Sta Rita ranchos, Sta B. '45. iv. 653; v. 558; at Sta Inés '54. Maltok (Richard), 1842, Engl. lumberman at S.F.

Manchester (Alex.), 1845, sailor on the *María,* or *Morea.* M. (Thomas), 1846, overl. immig.; served in Co. F, Cal. Bat. (v. 358); owner of S.F. lot '48; in the mines '48; drowned in S.F. bay before '69. Mancilla (Tomás), Dominican friar in L. Cal. who visited S. Diego '29–30. ii. 552; v. 620. Mancisidor (Juan Ignacio), 1822, Span. supercargo of the *Col Young,* '22–3. ii. 474, 293; iii. 118. He came back in '25 on the *Thos Nowlan* and remained as agent of a Lima firm, being a resident of Los Ang. from '27. He was obliged to quit the country in '30 under the law expelling Span., and in spite of his petition of '28 to be allowed to remain. iii. 51–2, 100, 145. He had no family. Mangot, 1848, mr of the *Con de Talcahuano.* Manjares (Graciano), Mex. grantee of Saucito '33. iii. 679; in '36, age 35, wife Maximiana Góngora, child. Domingo b. '29, José '30, Ponciano '31, Estanislao '32, Juana '35; juez auxiliar in '42. iv. 653. Manrique (Miguel), com. of transports 1775, 1797. i. 241, 543. M. (Jose Ant.), at Los Ang. '46. M. (Juan), soldier of Sta B. comp. '32. M. (Julian), at Sta Ana rancho, Los. Ang. '39, age 35; in '44 grantee of Laguna. iv. 621. Mansaneli (María Ant.), at Mont. '36, nat. of Tepic, apparently the sister of the wife of Munrás. Manser (Jacob), 1846, Co. C, 1st U. S. dragoons (v. 336). Manso (Juan), 1844, Span. trader in Virmond's employ; in '45 appointed commissioner to form inventories of the mission estates, and lessee of S. Fernando. iv. 550, 553, 637-8, 643, 683; v. 558, 630. M. (Lúcas F.), 1834, com. of the *Morelos* which brought part of the colony. iii. 267, 269, 383. Manson (Cephus), 1846, Fauntleroy's dragoons (v. 232, 247). Manuel, N. Mex. of Sta B. garrison '46. v. 316. M. (Andrés and José), grantees of Guajome '45. iv. 621. Maqueda (Juan D.), 1791, piloto in Malaspina's exped. i. 490.

Mapes (Geo. W. and Walker B.), 1847, Co. I, N.Y.Vol. (v. 499). Maple (Dav.), 1847, carpenter on the *Independence.* M. (John), 1847, Co. H, N.Y. Vol. (v. 499). Marago (V.), grantee of Pauba. iv. 621 (Moraga?). · Maranasio (Tom), 1845, nat. of Oahu, in charge of custom-house boat at Mont. Maraviof, 1825, mr of the *Elena* '26-6. iii. 146. March (Edwin), 1847, Co. K, N.Y.Vol. (v. 499); d. '60. M. (Wm J.), 1847, employed at Fitch's Sotoyoma rancho '77-8. Marchand (J. B.), 1848, owner of S.F. lot. Marchena (Fern.), 1844, ditto. iv. 673. Marcy (Sam.), 1847, 2d mr on the U. S. *Independence.*

Marcy (Wm G.), 1847, A. A. Q. M., U. S. A., commissary of N.Y.Vol. v. 503, 511. A son of the sec. of state at Wash.; went to the mines with Colton in '48; sec. of the constit. conven. '49; member of the legislature '55; pay-master in the navy from '61; at Wash. 71–4; living at Alameda '82. María de Jesus (Madre), 1800, sent from Mex. in charge of foundlings. i. 606. Mariano, leader in Sta B. outbreak '24, ii. 532. M. (Man.), 1828, Mex. convict released in '36. Marin, Ind. chief for whom Marin Co. was named; vaguely mentioned '16-24. ii. 328, 538, 598. Mariné (Fruto), soldier of Mont. comp. '39. M. (Juan), 1795, Span. artilleryman retired after '21 with rank of lieut de premio from '27; at S. Gabriel '28, age 60. ii. 543; iii. 51; perhaps his name was 'Mariner.' Mariner (Juan), 1785, Span. friar who served at S. Diego till his death in 1800. Biog. i. 654; ment. i. 388, 422, 455, 459, 553, 576-7; ii. 106-7.

Mark (Joseph), 1847, Co. G, N.Y.Vol. (v. 499). M. (Louis), 1847, Co. E, ditto; d. before '80. Market (Augustine), 1847, Co. D, ditto. Markham

(Mrs E.), 1846, came to Sta Clara Co.; maiden name not given.   Markof
(Alex.), 1845, Russ. visitor, who published a narrative. iv. 562.   Marks (Chas),
1846, Fauntleroy's dragoons (v. 232, 247).   Marlin (Hen.), 1845, doubtful
name of an immig. iv. 578.   Marones (José), at Branciforte '45, age 33, wife
María Castro, child. José Joaq. b. '40, María '41, Danira (?) '42, Santa (?)
'43, Roberto '44. I think this may be intended for ' Majors,' q.v.   Maroni
(Fran.), at Mont. '39–41.   Marple (Dav.), see ' Maple.'   Marquet, 1845,
doubtful member of Frémont's party. iv. 583. *Martin.*   Marquez (Fran.),
grantee of Boca de Sta Mónica. iii. 633; a blacksmith, age 47.

Marquez (Manuel), 1842, Mex. lieut of the batallon fijo '42–5. iv. 289;
implicated as an accomplice in a poisoning case and transferred to Sta B. '43.
iv. 364, 641; adj. and instructor of the S. Luis Ob. defensores '44. iv. 407; at
Mont. Apr. '46. v. 41.   M. (Rafael), soldier killed by Ind. on the Colorado
1781. i. 363.   Marquinez (Marcelino), 1810, Span. friar who served chiefly
at Sta Cruz, and left Cal. in '17. Biog. ii. 387; ment. ii. 149, 159–60, 218, 326,
384, 394, 421.

Marron (Jesus), at Los Ang. '46.   M. (Juan María), had a house at S.
Diego '21. ii. 546; took part in the revolution of '31. iii. 201; regidor '35–6,
and elector in '36, being owner of the Cueros de Venado rancho attacked by
Ind. iii. 483, 611, 615; iv. 67. He was juez suplente in '39–40. iii. 616; owner
of land at S. Juan Cap. '41. iv. 626; grantee of Agua Hedionda '42. iv. 620;
and juez in '44. iv. 540. In '45 he was elector de partido and admin. of S. Luis
Rey. iv. 540, 620–1; 623–4; and in '46 alcalde. v. 325, 329, 618–19. He died
in '56. His widow, Felipa Osuna, b. at S. D. 1809, and still living there in '78,
gave me her *Recuerdos* of early times, to which is attached a col. of original
Doc. Hist. Cal. presented by her brother.   Marsh (Eton S.), 1847, owner
of S. F. lot. v. 685.   M. (Geo.), 1826, purser of H. B. M. S. *Blossom* in
Beechey's exped. iii. 121.

Marsh (John), 1836, nat. of Mass. and graduate of Harvard, who after
residing in Wisconsin and Mo. spent 6 years in New Mex. and Sonora, and
came to Cal. early in Jan. '36 from Sta Fé. iv. 117–18. Presenting his diploma
as a physician to the ayunt. of Los Ang. he got in Feb. a license to practise
medicine; but came to the north early in '37, in which year Edwards met him
in the Mont. district, v. 86, and from which time his name appears on Larkin's books. He seems to have travelled considerably in the northern districts,
but in a year or two became the owner of the rancho of Los Médanos—also
called Pulpunes, Umpines, and later New York, at the foot of Mt Diablo,
near the modern Antioch—granted to Noriega in '35. Here he built a rude
hut and spent the rest of his life, gradually accumulating wealth in live-stock.
In '40 he was arrested but not exiled, had some dealings with Sutter, and
wrote letters to Mo. for the purpose of encouraging immigration. iv. 9, 17,
23–4, 134, 265. In '41 he received the 1st immig. party, Bartleson's, at his
rancho, and afforded them much assistance, though he made the new-comers
pay well for his services and grievously offended many of them by his mean-
ness. iv. 272–5, 347. The officers of the U. S. ex. ex. also came in contact
with him this year, and Dr Pickering, *Races of Men*, 102; *Wilkes' Narr.*, v.
193–4, mentions the Dr as his former classmate and friend. His *Letter to Com.
Jones*, of '42, on the state of the country, is a doc. of some value, as the writer
was an intelligent, observant man. iv. 348. In '44 he was naturalized; and
in '44–5 joined Sutter's force against the Californians, with a view to disor-
ganize it, made a contract with the govt to furnish Ind. horse-thieves in
comp. with Capt. Gantt, and signed at S. José the call to foreigners. iv. 486,
491, 516–17, 543, 599. He took but slight part in the troubles of '46–7, v. 7,
17, 641, leading for the most part the life of a hermit, though he wrote a long
letter to Lewis Cass on the country and its prospects. He took much interest
in politics, desiring to see Cal. in possession of the U. S., but not favoring
filibusterism. In '48 his house was robbed, and he tried his fortune in the
mines. He was murdered, by a party of young Californians, on the road between his rancho and Martinez in '56, at the age of 52. One of the murderers
was sent to prison for life some 10 years later. Dr M. was a peculiar and gen-

erally disagreeable man, whose notorious parsimony kept him constantly in trouble with most that came in contact with him; yet he was apparently an honest man, of more than ordinary ability, and several of the Californians, among them Vallejo, speak of him in terms of warm praise. He left a son in the East, who is said to have joined him just before his death; he seems to have had some children by an Indian woman; and John Currey, who was his attorney and gives much information about him, states that about '51 he married a teacher from Mass., who died a few years later.

Marshall, 1846, widow, married to James Smith at N. Helv.; perhaps mother of Henry. M. (Earl), 1846, nat. of N. J. and one of the Mormon col., with his wife, Letitia Dorsey. v. 46. A milkman at S. F.; in Alameda co. from '50; died '81, leaving a widow. Portrait in *Alam. Co. Hist.*, 24. M. (Henry), 1845, Engl. immig. of the Grigsby-Ide party, with mother, brother, and sisters. iv. 579, 587. He was employed by Sutter, and during the Bear revolt was stationed at the fort, v. 79, 125, but later enlisted in the Cal. Bat. and was wounded at Natividad, v. 369, 371, recovering in time to serve with Weber in the Sta Clara campaign (v. 379). After the war he lived at Sonoma, Petaluma, and Benicia, going to the mines in '48. In '50 he settled in Green Valley, Sonoma co., where he still lived in '78. His reminiscences as given to R. A. Thompson are in my collection, and were published in the *S. J. Pion.*, Aug. 10, '78. His sister Eliza was the wife of James Gregson; another was Mary A. Marshall (James W.), 1845, nat. of N. J., a carriage-maker and carpenter by trade, who came overland to Or. in '44, and in the McMahon-Clyman party to Cal. the next year. iv. 572, 574, 587. He entered Sutter's employ and is often named in the *N. Helv. Diary* '45-8. He seems to have taken part in the Bear revolt (v. 101), and to have gone south with the Cal. Bat. (v. 358). Returning north he resumed his work at the fort, and in Aug. formed a partnership with Sutter to build a saw-mill on the Amer. river, selecting a site at Coloma and beginning work at once, with half a dozen workmen. Here in Jan. '48 he made the famous discovery of gold, for full particulars of which see vol. vi. There have been attempts to show that M.'s companions have been deprived of the credit due them in this connection; but it seems clear that M. was the first to see the metal, and his visit to the fort Jan. 28th on 'very important business' is recorded in the *Diary*. He is doubtless entitled to his fame as the discoverer of gold. Sutter has also been praised as the real discoverer, and indeed if he had not settled in the Sac. Val., or Cabrillo had not discovered Cal., or Columbus America, the 'glittering particles' might have been found by another man under different circumstances. Marshall was not able to protect his mill and land at Coloma from the raids of miners and lawyers, and for many years led the life of a miner and prospector without much luck. In '70 his *Life and Adventures*, by Geo. F. Parsons, was published at Sac.; and subsequently a small pension was paid M. for some years by act of the legislature. He is still living in '85 at the age of 73, and seems always to have borne a good character. I have an original daguerreotype taken in early years; and his portrait may also be found in the *Annals of S. F.; Plumas Co. Hist.*, etc. (He died near Coloma in Aug. '85, after the above was written.)

Marshall (John), 1845, brother of Henry and overl. immig. of the Grigsby-Ide party. iv. 579, 587; at Sonoma '47. M. (John), 1836, Amer. age 45, in a Los Ang. list. M. (Joseph), 1836, on Larkin's books '36-7. M. (Robert), 1834, mr of the *Catalina* '34-5, '43. iii. 381; iv. 564. M. (Wm), 1845, Amer. deserter from the *Hopewell* at S. D. iv. 587; in '46 in charge of Warner's rancho charged with theft in April. *S. D. Arch.*, 320; and in Dec. entertained Kearny and his dragoons. v. 339. A little later he was an instigator of the Pauma massacre, for which crime he was hanged in '51. v. 589. M. (Wm P.), 1841, Engl. physician on the *Index;* at Mont. '42. Marst (Wm), 1847, owner of a S. F. lot. Marston, (J. D.), 1847, teacher at S. F. v. 656-7, 685; married Mar. '48 to Miss S. Still. M. (Ward), 1846, capt. of marines on the U. S. *Savannah;* in com. of S. F. garrison; and of the force that marched to Sta Clara against Sanchez Jan. '47. v. 380-3, 359.

Martell (James L.), 1843, purser's clerk on the U. S. *Dale* and *Southhampton;* disch. '49 and lived at S. F. to '85, being part of the time a custom-house officer.   Martiarena (José Manuel), 1794, Span. friar and founder of S. Juan Bautista, where he served to 1804 when he left Cal. Biog. ii. 153–4; ment. i. 500, 557–8, 576, 689, 712; ii. 131, 159–60.   Martin, 1847, of M. & Dent, Mont., '47–8.   M., 1848, came with family in party of Peter J. Davis. *Sta Clara Co. Hist.*, 660.   M., 1848, leader of a party from Or. *El Dorado Co. Hist.*, 182.   M. (Augustus), 1847, a witness at Los Ang.

Martin (Dennis), 1844, overl. immig. of the Stevens party, iv. 445, with his father and brother, returning in '45 to rescue Schallenberger at Donner Lake and the party left on the Yuba. iv. 454. He worked for Sutter in '45–6, but I find no definite record of him in the troubles of '46–7, or in mining times of '48–9. He was a hunter and lumberman, settling in S. Mateo Co., where he still lived in '78 and later.   M. (Ed.), 1847, sergt Co. C, Morm. Bat. v. 477; in '82 at Salt Lake City.   M. (Edw. J.), 1848, nat. of Ireland, who came by sea from Chile in Nov. He became prominent in various enterprises, being for many years treasurer and sec. of the Hibernia Bank. He died in '80 at the age of 61, leaving 8 children.   M. (Jesse B.), 1847, Co. B, Morm. Bat. (v. 469); in Sutter's service at the discov. of gold '48.

Martin (Fernando), 1811, Span. friar who served at S. Diego till his death in '38. Biog. iii. 619; ment. ii. 345, 394, 551–2, 655; iii. 19, 91, 96, 102, 317; iv. 63.   M. (John), 1822, Engl. or Scotch sailor who left the *Orion*. ii. 478. In '24 he was admitted to the church at S. Juan B. ii. 526; in '29 had been living for several years at S. F. presidio; in '30 was at Mont. ii. 609; in '31 he got permission to cultivate a league of land at Gotoqui, or S. Patricio; at S. F. '32. He was known as the 'old Scotch carpenter' and lived for some time at Reed's rancho, being in '37 on the Corte de Madera de Novato rancho, Marin Co., which was granted him in '39. iv. 86, 117; iii. 711; owner of S. F. lots '41–5. iv. 669; v. 684; in '46 applied for land in S. José dist. I find nothing about him after his claim before the land com. in '52.   M. (John), 1848, passp. from Hon.   M. (Juan), 1794, Span. friar who served 27 years at S. Miguel, where he died in '24. Biog. ii. 620; ment. i. 561, 576, 664, 675; ii. 45, 149–50, 159, 325–6, 384, 394, 655.

Martin (Julius), 1843, nat. of N. C. and overl. immig. of the Walker-Chiles party, with wife, Elizabeth McPherson, and 3 daughters. iv. 393, 400. Early in '44 he settled, or established his family, in the Gilroy region, working at different places for a few years; prob. in Sutter's force '44–5. iv. 486. I have his letter of July '45. In '46 he served under Frémont and Fauntleroy. v. 16, 22 (232); and later commanded a comp. of S. F. volunteers in the Sanchez campaign. v. 381; owner of S. F. lots '47. v. 684; at N. Helv. '48. From '50 he lived on his farm near Gilroy, owning also land in Napa, though he finally lost most of his property. He was blind from about '61; still living in '81, and I think in '85 at the age of 81. His 3 daughters that crossed the plains were Mary wife of P. B. Tully, Arzelia Mrs Lewis, and Martha Mrs Oldham; three others born in Cal.—one of them perhaps in '44—were Susan Mrs Bartlett, Georgie Mrs Johnson, and Julia Mrs Hornback.   M. (J.B.), 1847, nat. of Va, and one of the earliest settlers of Ione Val., having crossed the plains with Childers and Hicks. Claimant for the Cosumnes rancho. iv. 671; still living at Sutter Cr.'81.   M. (Montgomery), 1846, lieut in Cal. Bat. on detached service. v. 360; clerk for Larkin '47; and still at Mont. '48. M. (Patrick), 1844, Irish immig. of the Stevens party with his sons Dennis and Patrick, Jr. iv. 445, 453; owner of S. F. lot '47. His daughter married James Murphy.

Martin (Thomas S.), 1845, nat. of Tenn. b. '18, resid. of St Louis '40–5, and one of Frémont's party in '45. v. 583, 587. He served in Co. A, Cal. Bat. (v. 358); went East with F. in '47; and came back in the exped. of '48–9. In '49–53 a horse-trader in dif. regions; then settled with a wife at Sta B., still to some extent a trader and hunter, also serving as city marshal and deputy sheriff. In '78 he gave me a *Narrative of Frémont's Exped.*, which is in some respects valuable, as the official journal has never been published, but is marred by the author's tendency to claim participation in many Cal. events which he can only have known by hearsay. Many parts are notably accurate; and others have but slight foundation in truth. iv. 505; v. 107, 168–9, 172, 189. M. (Wm H.), 1847, Co. H, N.Y.Vol. (v. 499); owner of a S.F. lot; at Oakland '71; d. Stanislaus Co. 74.   M. (Wm J.), 1843, Amer. mason who came overland in the Chiles-Walker party. iv. 393, 400; though sometimes accredited to the Stevens party of '44. iv. 446; still living '72.   Martinau (A.), 1846, Co. B, artill. Cal. Bat. (v. 358).

Martinez (Agustin), juez de campo '31,'46, in Mont. dist. iii. 672, 637, 566. M. (Andrés), at S.José '41, age 40, wife María de J. Narvaez, child. Jesus M. b. '34, Antonio '36, Luciana '21, Mariana '27, Cármen '28, Flavia '31, Concepcion '33; Cal. claim '46–7 (v. 462). Still at S. José '50.   M. (Bartolomé) soldier at Soledad 1791–1800. i. 499.   M. (Blas), at Salinas, Mont., '36, age 40, wife Josefa Amézquita, child. Eugenio b. '21, María Josefa '23, José '26, Emiliana '27, Francisca '30, Leon '32, Juan '33; grantee of Tucho '35, iii. 679, and of Laureles '39.   M. (E.), sentenced to presidio '45. iv. 654.   M. (Estévan), 1779, com. of the S. Blas transports on the coast, 1779–99. i. 328–9, 378, 430, 444, 505.   M. (Felipe), at Los Ang. '46.   M. (Francisco), Span., age 45, who left Cal. on the *Thos Nowlan*. iii. 51.

Martinez (Ignacio), 1800, nat. of the city of Mex. b. 1774, who entered the mil. service as cadet of the Sta B. comp. in 1799. i. 639; promoted to alférez of the S. Diego comp. from 1806, being also much of the time habilitado. ii. 99–101, 110, 341, 424–5, 540. In '17 he was recommended for promotion to lieut of the Sta B. comp., but by some error at Madrid or Mex. the commission was made out for the S.F. comp., and to S.F. he had to go much against his will, his name appearing on the rolls—as comandante in '22–7 and from '28—down to '32, taking part in some Ind. exped., as fiscal in some criminal cases, and being otherwise mentioned in connection with routine duties of his position, besides being a member of the junta, or diputacion in '24, '27. ii. 235, 361, 370, 440, 500, 512–13, 537–8, 583–4, 592, 640; iii. 20, 36–7, 64, 75, 88, 110, 121, 132, 156, 186, 191–2, 701. In '31 he was retired with use of uniform and full pay, being credited with 41 years of service. Meanwhile he had obtained, in '29, the Pinole rancho, Contra Costa, regranted in '42. iv. 672; and here—after having apparently lived at S. José for several years, being regidor in '34–5, and serving as comisionado for the secularization of S. Rafael in '34—he went to live in '36 or a little later. ii. 594, 664; iii. 193, 346, 716, 718, 730. In '37 he was alcalde at S.F. iii. 703, 705, 552; suplente of the junta '39. iii. 590; a creditor of Sutter. iv. 132, 134; defeated the Ind. in 40. iv. 76; and entertained Wilkes in '41. iv. 245. He was living at Pinole in '41 with his wife, Martina Arellanes, age 53, and 6 daughters, Encarnacion b. 1808, Susana '24 (who soon married Capt. Hinckley, and after his death Wm M. Smith), Francisco '24, Rafaela '27, María '29, and Dolores '31. Another daughter, María Antonia, was the wife of Capt. Richardson; others married Victor Castro and Dr Tennant. His son Vicente J., b. in '18, was still living in Contra Costa '82, with seven children by two wives, Guadulupe Moraga and Nieves Soto. I cannot give the date of Don Ignacio's death, but it was before '52, when his heirs were claimants for Pinole. He was not popular as an officer, being haughty and despotic, as it seemed to his men, and he was several times reproved and unfavorably criticised by his superior officers; but as a ranchero he is spoken of as a very courteous and hospitable man. The town of Martinez takes its name from him or his family.   M. (Ignacio), at S.F. '43, age 23; also named—perhaps another—as lieut of militia at S. José '37. iii. 732.

Martinez (José), 1875, com. of the *Asia*. iii. 24–5, 146.   M. (José), son of Ignacio, lieut of militia at S.F. '37. iii. 701; in '41 living in S. José dist., age 27, wife Cármen Peralta, children Rafael b. '39, Alejandro '41; Cal. claim '46–7 (v. 462). He was noted for his liberality and for his skilful horsemanship, but was killed in '64 from an entanglement with his riata. A second wife was an English woman named Tennant.   M. (José Ignacio), soldier killed by Ind. on the Colorado, 1781. i. 359–62.   M. (José de Jesus), at Los Ang. '46.

M. (José Manuel), ditto.   M. (José María), settler at S. José before 1800; alcalde in 1797 and 1806. i. 716, 719; ii. 134. His wife was María García, son Máximo, brother Reyes, sister Juana.   M. (Josefa), grantee of land in Mont. Co. '44–5. iv. 656.   M. (Juan), soldier killed on the Colorado, 1781. i. 359, 362.   M. (Juan), at Mont. '36, age 36, wife Francisco García, child. Cármen b. '25, José Blas '26, Francisco' 29, María '34.   M. (Juan, Juan Andrés, and Leonor), at Los. Aug. '46.   M. (Juan de Jesus María), 1831, Dominican from L. Cal., at San Gabriel, '31–2. iii. 311, 641.   M. (Leocadio), carpenter and settler at S.F. and S. José before 1800. i. 499, 634, 716, 718.

Martinez (Luis Antonio), 1798, Span. friar who served at S. Luis Ob. for 32 years. A very able man and prominent in missionary annals, but rather in the industrial and political than in ecclesiastical phases of his profession. He was banished in '30 for alleged complicity in the Solis revolt, and wrote from Madrid '32–3. Biog. ii. 618–19; ment. i. 689; ii. 148, 204, 219, 224, 235–6, 255, 276, 311, 327, 384, 394, 438, 441, 479, 493, 516–17, 576, 655; iii. 21, 51, 84–5, 92, 94, 98–100.   M. (Máximo), soldier of S.F. comp. '19–23; in '33 and '44 grantee of Corte de Madera, Sta Clara. iii. 711; iv. 671; regidor at S. José '33–4. iii. 729–30; in '41 age 51, wife Damiana Padilla, child. Nicolás b. '28, Evinisa (?) '26, José Ant. '33, Dolores '34, José María '35, Guadalupe '38, Clara '41.   M. (Miguel), at S. Bern. '46, age 50.   M. (Pedro Adriano), 1797, Span. friar who served at S. Juan B. and S. Miguel, retiring in 1804. Biog. ii. 149; ment. i. 558, 577; ii. 159–60.   M. (Rafael), at Los Ang. '46. M. (Santiago), N. Mex. at Los Ang. with families, applying for land '42–6. iv. 343, 572, 635.   M. (Sixto), at Los Ang. '46.   M. (Vicente), son of Igna-cio; militiaman S. F. '37; at S. José dist. '41, age 29, wife Guad. Moraga, child. Francisco b. '38, Merced '39; síndico of S. José '43. iv. 685; Cal. claim '46–7 (v. 462).   Marx (Ernest), 1847, musician N. Y. Vol. (v. 499).   Mas-carel (Joseph), 1844 (?), French mayor of Los Ang. '65, and resident '80. iv. 453.   Mashim (Rosistof), 1840, mr of the *Baikal.* iv. 101.   Mason, 1848, keeper of a gambling and grog shop at Sta B.   M. (Alfred), 1847, Co. F, N. Y. Vol. (v. 499); d. Sac. before '83.   M. (E.), 1846, Cal. Bat. (v. 358). Mason (Ignacio), at S. Gabriel '39, age 27, a jeweller; perhaps ' Mazon.'   M. (John), 1847, Co. B, N.Y.Vol. (v. 499).   M. (Marcos or Anthony A.), 1816, 'Anglo-Amer. Irishman from Boston,' baptized at S. Cárlos, and recommended by P. Sarría in '17 as about to go to the Philippines. ii. 276–7, 288.   M. (M.), 1842, lieut on the U. S. *Cyane.*   M. (Richard B.), 1847, colonel 1st U. S. dra-goons who arrived in Feb., and on May 31st succeeded Kearny as mil. gov. of Cal., holding that position till Feb. '49. For account of his rule, including his controversy and proposed duel with Frémont, see v. 582, 615; also 416, 436–7, 443–4, 446–7, 451, 455, 464, 515, 571–5, 646, 666, 675; also vol. vi. He per-formed most satisfactorily the duties of a difficult position, and though by his strict discipline and apparent harshness of manner he made an unfavor-able impression in some quarters and inspired bitter enmities, yet his record is that of an honest, faithful, and able officer. He went East by steamer in in May '49, and died of cholera at St Louis in that year or the next. His widow married Gen. Don Carlos Buell, and still lived in '75.   Mast (Her-man), 1847, perhaps of N.Y.Vol. under another name; at S. F. '74.

Mata, member of a court-martial at S. Diego '26. ii. 549.   M. (Juan de Dios), Mex. convict released in '35.   Matamoros (Tomás), murdered in 1805. ii. 191.   Matchin (C. F.), 1845, mr of the *Matador.* iv. 567.   Mateo, 1818, mulatto from Bouchard's fleet. ii. 230.   Mathias (Thos), 1828, in Cal.; autog. letter.   Mathers (James), 1846, nat. of N.Y.; settled in Sta Clara; at S. Luis Ob. '58 to his death in '70 at the age of 80.   Matias (Juan), at Los Ang. '46.   Mathurin (Louis), 1833, Fr. sailor at S. F. '40–1. iii. 409.   Matsell (Henry C.), 1847, lieut Co. B, N.Y.Vol. v. 504; trader at S. Diego; in Kan-sas '71–9.   Matt (James), 1848, at Sutter's Fort April.   Mattheson (Alex. J.), 1839, Engl. pilot on the schr *California*, implicated in a plot against the capt.; on Larkin's books '40.

Matthews, 1836, Amer. otter-hunter with Nidever.   M., 1847, in Sut-ter's service.   M., 1846, at S. José with a son-in-law. *Hittell.*   M. (Geo.),

1839, named in Larkin's books '39-40. M. (H.), 1843, witness at S. F. '66. M. (Henry), 1846, arr. in Sept., acc. to Sac. Cal. Pion. rolls; at Benicia '47. iii. 673; at S. F. '60. M. (James), 1834. at Mont. M. (John), 1831, Engl. sailor, who landed from a whaler at S. F. iii. 405, 708-9. On Larkin's books '33-42; naturalized before '40; but this may be one of the following. M. (John), 1836, Italian fisherman, living with the Greek Demedrion at Mont. M., 1836, Amer., age 35, at S. Isidro (Gilroy's); perhaps Matthew, a given name, who was a cook for Murphy in '30. M. (Wm), 1831, Engl. sailor who landed from a whaler at S. Luis Ob. iii. 405. In '36 at Sta B.; came north and appears in various records from '34; in '70 permitted to live at S. F. or Sonoma; arrested but not exiled. iv. 17; from '44 or earlier at Mont., keeping a boarding-house. Matthews' mill is also mentioned in '42. He may be the M. whose wife is said to have furnished some material for the Bear flag. v. 148; and in July he carried despatches from Mont. to S. F. v. 255; starting with Larkin in Nov. at the time of the latter's capture. v. 364. He is vaguely said to have died about '58.

Matute (Juan B.), 1791, com. of the *Aranzazu*, explor. and transport on the coast '91-2, '95-6. i. 493, 506, 517, 537-8. Maube (Arno), 1843, French grantee of land near S. Gabriel; at Sta Cruz '47 with claim against the govt. iv. 400, 615, 637. M. (Henry), 1847, held Larkin's note for $120; perhaps same as preceding. Mauët (John), 1847, at Sutter's Fort. Maun (Francis), 1842, at Sta Cruz. M. (James), 1845, employed at Larkin's soap factory. Maurelle (Antonio), 1775, Span. naval officer on the coast '75, '79, '84; author of a *Journal*. i. 241, 329, 444, 509; see also *Hist. N. W. Coast*, i. Maury (Wm L.), 1841, lieut U. S. N. on the U. S. ex. ex. iv. 241; on the *Warren* '46-7. v. 539. Mavilla (Antonio), 1846, at S. Gabriel '46. Mawrey (James), 1847, servant to an officer in the Morm. Bat. (v. 469).

Maxfield (Wm C.), 1847, owner of S. F. lot. Maxim (Harvey), 1847, sergt Co. F, 3d U. S. artill. i. 519. Maximo, 1799, negro slave of Alberni. i. 639. Maxwell (Chas), 1847, owner of S. F. lot. M. (H.), 1848, settler at Stockton. M. (James W.), 1847, Co. K, N.Y. Vol. (v. 499). M. (Lucien). 1845, hunter and guide of Frémont's party. iv. 583; v. 24. M. (Richard T.), 1842, nat. of Penn. and asst surg. U. S. N. on the *United States*. iv. 304, 308-9, 341, 348. He returned to Cal. in '54, and became a prominent physician of S. F. In '77 he gave me his *Monterey in '42*, or recollections of the capture of that town by Com. Jones, and also a MS. furnished by Dr Marsh to Jones at that time. He died in '83 at the age of 62, leaving an estate which has been the occasion of much litigation arising from the doctor's death-bed marriage. M. (Wm), 1847, Co. D, Morm. Bat. (v. 469); a farmer in Williams Val., N. Mex., '82. M. (Wm C.), 1847, Co. F, N. Y. Vol. (v. 499); died before '82. M. (Wm H.), 1847, Co. B, ditto; d. N. Y. city '76.

May (Henry), 1835, nephew of Larkin, bound to Cal. on the *Alert;* no record of arrival. Maya (Ign.), at S. Bern. '46. Mayan (Mrs), 1847, died at N. Helv. July. Mayberry (Ebenezer), 1847, Co. F, 3d U. S. artill. (v. 518). Mayer, 1832, about to visit Cal. from Sitka for scientific purposes; letter of introd. from Khlébnikof to Hartnell. M. (John), 1840, Engl. at Mont. and S. F. Jan., Nov. M. (Lewis W.), 1847, Co. F, 3d U. S. artill. (v. 518); in the mines '49-50; a German wine-maker, who lived in Sonoma '65-80. Mayfield (Benj. F.), 1847, Co. A, Morm. Bat. (v. 469); sergt of reënlisted comp. v. 495; a resid. of S. Luis Ob. Co. '68-83; a nat. of Tenn. Mayhew (John), 1826, on the *Eliza*. Maynard (James), 1837, on Larkin's books; perhaps same as John. M. (John), 1840, Engl. exile with the Graham party; not known to have returned, though he got a license to do so. Maynes (James), 1845, laborer at Mont. Mayo (Geo.), 1816, Mass. sailor, baptized at S. Cárlos. *Taylor;* ii. 276-7. Mazateco (Juan), at Sonoma '44, age 19; prob. a 'Mazateco' Ind. or from Mazatlan.

Mead (James D.), 1841, nat. of Ia, episcopal clergyman, and perhaps physician in the West Indies, who came from N. Mex. in the Workman party, and in '42 went to the Sandwich Isl. or China. iv. 278; said to have been a

bishop later.   M. (Orlando F.), 1847, Co. C, Morm. Bat. (v. 469); later at
Sutter's Fort; at Spanish Fork '82.   M. (Sam.), 1832, one of the comp. extranjera at Mont. iii. 221.   Meadows (James), 1837, Engl. sailor, who deserted from a whaler at Mont. iv. 117-18. His name appears in the records
from '38; one of Graham's riflemen '36-8 (iii. 457); later a lumberman; exiled
to S. Blas in '40, but returned in '41 to live as a sawyer in Mont. dist. iv. 18,
23, 33. Not much is known of him in '43-8, except that he is mentioned from
time to time as at S. José, Sacramento, or in the mines. He finally settled on
the Palo Escrito rancho near Mont., which was confirmed to him in '54, iii.
679, and where he was living in '77 with a native wife and several children.
He gave me an interesting narrative of the *Graham Affair*, he being one of the
last survivors of the exiles. In respect of accuracy, his account compares favorably with the testimony of others on the subject—which is not paying it
a very high compliment. I have not heard in '85 of his death.   Mechacken
(John C.), 1846, Co. F, Cal. Bat. (v. 358).   Mecham (Henry), 1848 (?), nat.
of N. Y. and resid. of Sonoma Co. '53-77.
   Meder (Moses A.), 1846, one of the Mormon colony with wife and child.
v. 546. A nat. of Ohio, who engaged in the lumber business at Sta Cruz, the
firm of Stout, Sirrine, & M. advertising in the *Star* of '47. He worked also
for Graham, whose receipt of $36,000 indemnity he claims to have witnessed.
Still a resid. of Sta Cruz in '80 and prob. in '85; portrait in *Sta Cruz Co.
Hist.*, 44. His 1st wife, Sarah D. Blod, died in '72, and in '73 he married
Olive A. Linnett.   Medina (Guadalupe), 1842, Mex. lieut of the batallon
fijo '42-5; teacher at Los Ang. '43-4; com of the garrison '45. iv. 289, 321,
403, 492, 629.   M. (José), ship's boy and teacher at Sta B. 1797-1800. i.
643.   Medrano (José Maria), artill. sergt at Mont. '26-32. iii. 77, 671-2.
   Meehan (Dennis), 1847, Co. E, N. Y. Vol. (v. 499); killed at Stockton '49.
M. (James), 1847, Co. G, ditto, killed at Los Ang. about '50.   M. (Thos),
1847, Co. E, ditto; killed by a steamboat explosion on the S. Joaq. '53.
Meek (John), 1829, mr of the *Tamaahmaah* '29, possibly of another craft '25,
and of the *D. Quixote* '33-6. iii. 149, 179, 382; iv. 103, 141. He is also said
by Wm H. Davis to have visited Cal. as mate of the *Eagle* before '20, possibly
M. of the *Amethyst* '11-12. ii. 267. He was a nat. of Mass. who came to the
Isl. about '12, and died at Hon. '74 at the age of 85.   M. (Joseph), 1833,
Rocky Mt. trapper who came with Walker's party, going back to Salt Lake
in '34. iii. 390. He visited Cal. again in '48 and later, and died in Or. '75, his
adventures being the basis of Mrs Victor's *River of the West.*   M. (Stephen
II. L.), 1833, nat. of Va and brother of Joseph, also a mountain man who
came and departed with Walker. iii. 390, 409. He came back to Cal. after
the discov. of gold, possibly having made intermediate trips, and in '76 wrote
me a letter from Etna, Siskiyou Co., Cal.   M. (Stephen H. L.), 1843, signed
a certificate for a sailor at Mont. Sept., and in Jan '44 he got a passport.
Apparently not the preceding. A Dr Meek at Mont. '33 is mentioned by a
newspaper writer.   M. (Thomas), 1811, perhaps on the *Amethyst* '11-12.
ii. 96, 267. Said by Brewer to have gone to Hon. on the *Chinchilla* from Boston
in '23; at Hon. '36. iv. 141; d. at Marblehead, Mass., about '41. *Peirce.*   M.
(Wm), 1848, nat. of Ohio who came from Or. to the mines and went back.
In '59 returned to Cal. and settled at S. Lorenzo, Alameda Co., where he
became a wealthy farmer, serving also as county supervisor and regent of the
university. He died '81 at the age of 65, leaving a widow and 5 children.
Portrait in *Alam. Co. Hist.*, 937.   Meel (Robert), 1846, Co. F, Cal. Bat.
(v. 358).   Meeres, 1845, possibly of the Grigsby-Ide immig. party. iv. 579.
   Mein (John), 1842, mr of the *Bertha & Jenny.* iv. 563.   Meineke (A.
and D.), 1848, passp. from Hon.   Mejía (Hipólito), 1838, killed by Ind. iii.
693.   M. (José María), 1842, Mex. capt. in the batallon fijo, who was sent
to Mex. by Micheltorena in '44 to obtain aid. iv. 289, 308, 364, 404-5, 461,
471.   M. (Juan), settler at S. José 1791-1800. i. 716.   Meldguem (John),
1814, Irish deserter from a vessel; in Mont. dist '29, age 40, and single.
Melendez, 1796, com. of the *Concepcion.* i. 538.   M., 1826, mr of the *Gen.
Lravo.* iii. 147.   M. (Sebastian), 1602, alférez in Vizcaino's exped. i. 98.

Melleck (Joseph), 1837, in charge of the *Clementina.* M. (Vicente), at Los Ang. '46. Mellish (J.), 1835, at Sta Cruz.

Mellus (Francis), 1839, nat. of Boston, who came on the *California* at the age of 15. iv. 117, 119. He became clerk for A. B. Thompson at Sta B., and on the *Bolivar;* and his *Diary* of trips up and down the coast in '39–40 is an interesting MS. of my collection. In later years he was clerk, traveling agent, and from Jan. '49 partner with his brother in the firm of M., Howard, & Co. at S. F.; and in '50–6 with D. W. Alexander in charge of a branch of the business at Los Ang., where he settled permanently; claimant for Providencia rancho. iv. 635. In '52–3 he was county treasurer, in '54 councilman, in '55 memb. of the legislature, and later in charge of Wells, Fargo, & Co.'s express. He died in '63, leaving a widow—Adelaida, daughter of Santiago Johnson—and 7 children. M. (Henry), 1835, brother of Francis, who came before the mast with Rich. H. Dana on the *Pilgrim.* iii. 413. He left the ship to be agent's clerk, and is named in a Los Ang. list of '36 as 26 years old; but in '37–8 made a trip to the states. Returning in '39 he remained on the coast as agent or supercargo of the vessels of Appleton & Co., including the *Admittance* and *Tasso,* iv. 562, 569, and his name often appears in commercial records of the time, making his home chiefly at Los Ang. In '45 he formed a partnership with W. D. M. Howard, and the firm of M. & H. soon became the most prominent in S. F., buying the H. B. Co. property in '46, v. 699, building the 1st brick store in town, and establishing branches at S. José, Los Ang., and Sac. He became owner of many town lots and a very rich man. In '47 he married Anita, daughter of James Johnson of Los Ang., and in '48 made a visit to the East, and on his return had a stroke of apoplexy, from the effects of which he never entirely recovered. In '50 he sold his interest in the firm and went East, subsequently losing most of his wealth in unfortunate business enterprises. About '53 he brought a suit, finally abandoned, against Howard on the plea that he had not been of sound mind at the time of settlement. This created some ill feeling against him in S.F., and it is said that by H.'s influence the name of Mellus St was changed to Natoma. In '59 he came back to Cal. and settled at Los Ang., where he was elected mayor in May '60, but died in Dec. of the same year at the age of 45, leaving a family. Mellus was a man of remarkable business ability, of good character, and of courteous, pleasing manners. Melros (M.), 1846, doubtful name in a Los Ang. list. Mcluren (Louis), see 'Mathurin.' Melville, 1848, at S. F. from Tahiti. M. (Hugh), 1845, sailor of the *Morea,* disch. at S.F., and sent to the Mont. hospital. Melvin (James W.), 1847, Co. B, N.Y.Vol. (v. 499); d. S. F. '74.

Ménard (François), 1846, teamster with Kearny's force from N. Mex. v. 337; killed at S. Pascual. v. 346. M. (Louis), 1844, doubtful member of Frémont's party. iv. 437. Menchaca (R.), 1842, mr of the *Trinidad.* iv. 569. Mendenhall (Wm M), 1845, nat. of Ohio, and overl. immig. of the Hastings party. iv. 586–7; at Sutter's Fort in '46. I find no further original record of him in early times, but in the county history it is said that in '46–7 he took part in the Bear revolt, went south with Frémont, was commissary at S. José in the Sanchez campaign, kept a bakery at S.F., and married Mary Allen; in the mines '48; in Or. '49; Sta Clara Co. '50–3, '68–76; Contra Costa '53–60, '65–8, and Alameda Co. '60–65, and from '76 to '85, where he is a prosperous farmer at Livermore, age 62, with 9 surviving children: James M., Lizzie Mrs C. H. Lindley, Emma Mrs Black, Eila, Archer, Wm Oswald, Ascey, and Etta. In the earlier records he is called H. and Philip Mendenhall. Portrait in *Alam. Co. Hist.,* 56.

Mendez (Antonio), Mex. com. of artill. at S.F. '31–2. iii. 702; at Mont. '36, age 38, wife Juana Soto, child. Baltasar b. '29, Sofia '31, Evaristo '33; juez aux. '44. iv. 653; had a store, which in '46 was broken open and robbed. M. (Juan Ign.), trader and carpenter from 1798; had a grand commercial scheme 1800. i. 628. M. (Pedro), at Los Ang. '46–8. Mendoza (Antonino), at S. José '41. M. (Antonio), settler killed by Ind. 1781. i. 359, 362. M. (Henriquez), weaver-instructor 1792–5. i. 615. M. (Jaime), resid. of Branciforte '30. ii. 627.   M. (Manuel), soldier at Soledad 1791–1800. i. 499.   M. (Mariano José), weaver-instructor 1792–1801. i. 615, 658; ii. 174.   Menendez (Antonio), 1825, Span. Dominican friar of the L. Cal. frontier, relieved from missionary work for irregular conduct, and employed as chaplain of the troops at S. Diego from '25. ii. 425, 544, 552, 658; iii. 8; quarrelled with Alvarado. iii. 41; in the '28 list of Span., iii. 51, but not sent away; teacher and chaplain of the dip. '29. ii. 548; iii. 43, 77, 141; transferred to Mont. '30. ii 609; iii. 144, 451; died at Sta B. '32. iii. 317, 656.   M., 1792, com. of the Aranzazu. i. 517; and of the Concepcion in '94. i. 523.   M. (José Ant.), Mex. trader '33–9. iii. 242, 623.   Meneses (José H.), artilleryman at S. Diego '20. Mensing, 1846, mr of the Patriot. v. 579.   Menzies, 1847, mr of the Gen. Kearny. v. 578; and of the Louise in '48.   Mequelixt (Michael), 1822. ii. 479; prob. 'McAllister,' q. v.

Mercado (Jesus María Vasquez del), 1833, Mex. friar of the Zacatecanos, who served at S. Rafael, S. Antonio, and Sta Clara, leaving Cal. in '44; a quarrelsome and vicious padre who did much harm, though of good abilities and education. Biog. iv. 682; ment., with record of his controversies, iii. 300, 319, 321–4, 354, 426, 477, 586–7, 686–90, 716, 726; iv. 162, 373, 423, 473.   M., sergt at S. Diego, and sometime teacher, '10–11. ii. 424.   M. (Mariano), 1842, cornet of batallon fijo. iv. 289.   Mercure (H.), 1848, in S. F. letter list. Merelo (Lorenzo), 1799, Span. friar who served for brief term in S.F. and S. Antonio, retiring in 1801. Biog. ii. 152; ment. i. 577, 712; ii. 147, 159.   Merino (Agustin), 1797, Span. friar who served at S. José until forced by illness to retire in 1800. i. 555, 577.   Merium (W.), 1846, Co. G, Cal. Bat. (v. 358). Merrick, 1847, lieut ill at Los Ang.; doubtful name.   Merrilies (Robert), 1847, Co. F, 3d U.S. artill. (v. 518); a Scotchman with no antipathy to whiskey, and fond of Burns' poetry, who deserted, like most of his comrades, for the mines in '48; was at Mont. '58–9; and later a sheep-herder in the south. 'Mirilies' on the roll.

Merrill, 1831, at Los Ang.   M. (Ferdinand), 1847, Co. D, Morm. Bat. (v. 469); farmer at Salt Lake '82.   M. (John H.), 1847, Co. K, N.Y. Vol. (v. 499); owner of S.F. lots, and superintendent of sabbath-school. v. 657. I have his letter of '48 complaining of various persecutions by Lieut Brewerton. He was later a resid. of S. José, and in '82 at Wash., D.C.   M. (Philemon C.), 1847, lieut Co. B, Morm. Bat., and acting adjutant. v. 477, 483; in '81 at St David, Ariz.   M. (Squire G.), 1847, son of John H., and drummer of Co. H, N.Y.Vol. (v. 499; age 12; attended school at S. F.; clerk for Belden at S. José; in trade at Alviso, and later at S. F. He went East in '59, served in the war of '61–5, and in '77 had been 10 years a clerk in the adj.-gen. office at Wash., D.C., where he still lived in '82.   M. (W. H.), 1847, builder and keeper of a boarding-house at S. F. '47–8. v. 681, 685; possibly same as John H.   Merriner (Nicholas), 1847, owner of S. F. lot. Mrs M. with sons in Marin Co. '46.

Merritt (Ezekiel), 1841 (?), Amer. trapper, the exact date and circumstances of whose arrival are not known. He may be the man who appears on Larkin's books in '37. iv. 117–18; is ment. as one of Walker's men in '33. iii. 391; was at N. Helv. '41. iv. 233; in the Sac. Val. '43; implicated in the attempt to release Dr Bale in '44. iv. 445; in which year, in getting naturalization papers, he claimed to have been in Cal. 2 years! He was one of Capt. Gantt's men in the Micheltorena campaign of '44–5. iv. 486; and from '45 is often mentioned in the N. Helv. Diary. He commanded the party that stole Arce's horses in '46, and was nominally in com. of the Bears at first, his name appearing on the original proclamation of June 14th. v. 107–9, 114, 121, 127, 169. Returning with the prisoners to the fort, he subsequently went south with Frémont, and remained with Gillespie at Los Ang., being sent at one time with a small garrison to S. Diego. v. 308, 317, 324–5, 617. Bidwell says that he became partner with Wm C. Moon on a Tehama rancho, and died in the winter of '47–8, though possibly it was a little later, as there are vague references to his presence in the mines. Merritt was a coarse-grained, loudmouthed, unprincipled, whiskey-drinking, quarrelsome fellow, well adapted

to the use that was made of him in promoting the filibusters' schemes.   M.
(Robert G.), 1847, Co. K, N.Y. Vol. (v. 499); in Napa Co. '75; d. at Ukiah
'83.   M. (Thos), 1837, named in Larkin's accounts.   Mervine (Wm), 1846,
commander U.S.N. in com. of the *Cyane* and *Savannah*, the officer who raised
the U. S. flag at Mont. and took com. on shore. After the outbreak of the
Flores revolt he went south to S. Pedro, and was defeated by the Californians in Oct. while attempting to march inland to Los Ang. He took no further active part in the war; was owner of a S.F. lot in '47, negotiating also
for land at Sonoma; and started for the East in March. He was capt. in the
war of '61–5. v. 27, 200–3, 224, 229–31, 253, 289–90, 296, 304, 318–20, 327,
383, 539, 580.

Mesa (Alejandro), Cal. claim of $4,220 for horses in '46–7 (v. 462).   M.
(Andrés) soldier of the S.F. comp. '23–9.   M. (Antonio), 1781, negro settler
of Los Ang., with wife and 2 children. i. 345.   M. (Antonio), soldier of S.F.
comp. '19–30; militiaman at S.F. '37; in '41 at S. José, age 46, wife Dolores
Higuera, child. Alejandro b. '34, Isidro '37, Benedicto '39.   M. (Cayetano),
soldier killed by Ind. on the Colorado. i. 359–62.   M. (Dolores), settler at
S. José 1791–1800; regidor in 1806. i. 716; ii. 134, 171.   M. (Dolores), at S.
José '41, age 48.   M. (Domingo), soldier of S.F. comp. '28–31; named in '46.
v. 162.   M. (Encarnacion), claimant for S. Antonio, Sta Clara. iii. 712.   M.
(Francisco), soldier of S.F. comp. '34–5; in '36 maj. of the rancho nacional,
age 37. iii. 677; drowned near Mont. in '45.   M. (Gerónimo), soldier of S.F.
comp. '41–3. iv. 667.   M. (Hilario), corporal of the guard at S. José 1783–98;
settler '86. i. 477–8, 495.   M. (Joaquin), soldier at Sta Cruz and settler at
S. José before 1800. i. 496, 716.   M. (José), 1791, chaplain in Malaspina's
exped. i. 490.   M. (José Ant.), grantee of Los Médanos, Contra Costa, '39.
iii. 712.   M. (José Ign.), soldier at Soledad 1791–1800. i. 499.   M. (José
de Jesus), soldier of S.F. comp. '23–33, '38–9; two of the name as militiamen
at S.F. '37; in '41 at S. José, age 39, wife Juana Miranda, child. María b.
'36, Trinidad '38.   M. (Juan B.), owner of S.F. lot '44. v. 684.   M. (Juan
Prado), soldier of S.F. comp. from '28; corporal from '32, in com. of Sta
Clara escolta. iii. 728; sergt 36, and acting alf. from '37. iii. 511, 522; in '39
full alférez, com. of the S.F. garrison, grantee of S. Antonio rancho, and engaged in Ind. fights. iii. 701–2, 712, 722; iv. 75–6. On the roll as alf. to '42,
and mentioned occasionally as in mil. com. at S.F., where he was owner of a
lot. iv. 665, 666–7, 669, 678. He seems to have died at his rancho in '45.
M. (Luis), at Pilarcitos rancho '36, age 43, wife María Ant. Martinez, child.
Juan b. '21, Serafina '24; juez del campo. iii. 674–5, 678.   M. (María Ant.),
grantee of Rinconada del Arroyo de S. Francisquito '41. iv. 672–3.   M.
(Miguel), at S. José '41, age 30, wife Hilaria Benavides, child. Francisco b.
'34, Agueda '37; juez de campo '43. iv. 685.   M. (Nicolás), regidor at S.
José 1805. ii. 134.   M. (Pedro), sold. of S.F. comp. '27–37; juez de campo
at S. José '39. iii. 731; in '41 age 24, wife Teresa Higuera, child. Joaquin b.
'39, José Ant. '41; another of the name at S. José '41, age 33.   M. (Petra
Higuera de), widow at S. José '41, age 38, child. José b. '28, Domingo '30,
Guadalupe '31, Rufina '32, Albino '33, Pamela '37, José Ant. '39.   M. (Rafael), one of the original settlers at Los Ang. 1782. i. 345–6.   M. (Rafael),
soldier of the S.F. comp. '23–31; at S. José '41, age 34.   M. (Ramon), soldier of S.F. comp. '34–42; at Sonoma '44, age 25; grantee of Soulajule, Marin
Co., '44. iv. 674; named in connection with the Bear war '46. iv. 674; v. 162.
M. (Santiago), at S. Mateo '35.   M. (Valerio), corp. of S. F. comp. 1777. i.
297, 312; at S. José '93, wife Leonor Barboa, child Nicolás.

Mesnard, 1837, connected with Petit-Thouars' exped. iv. 149.   Metcalf
(T.), 1848, from Hon. on the *Hope*.   Metzger (Jacob N.), 1848, came from
Or. in May, and after a successful visit to the mines went to Or. in Aug. to
bring his family.   Mexica (Teodora), at Sta Cruz '18, ii. 225.   Mexwell
(Wm H.), 1848, at Stockton. *Herald;* prob. ' Maxwell,' q. v.

Meyer (Chas), 1847, owner of S.F. lot.   M. (Francis), 1847, Co. F, 3d U.S.
artill. (v. 518).   M. (Geo. S.), 1847, Co. D, N.Y.Vol. (v. 499); a German in
the mines '48–9, kept a hotel at S.F.; and settled at Mt Eden, Alameda Co.,

in 53. Still living in '83, age 71, with wife Sophia Prüger, and 4 children, Geo. A., Henry H., Matilda Mrs Martin, and Amelia. Portrait in *Alam. Co. Hist.*, 520.   M. (John Daniel), 1832, from Strassburg and Mex., a blacksmith at Los Ang. naturalized in '34, age 27. iii. 408. He was one of the vigilantes in '36 (iii. 130), and was at S. Diego in '40.   Meyers (R. G.), 1848, nat. of Pa, resid. of S. Joaquin '50-78, being several times member of the legislature.   M., see also 'Myers.'   Meyerholz, 1847, at N. Helv.

Micheltorena (Manuel), 1842, Mex. brigadier-gen., governor and com. gen. of Cal. from '42—appointed Jan. 22d, took possession formally Dec. 31 to Feb. 22, '45, when he signed the treaty of surrender to the revolutionist Californians who expelled him. On his early career, appointment, arrival, convict army, etc., see iv. 285-95; Com. Jones affair, iv. 308-26; rule in '43, iv. 350-67; policy in mission, commercial, and maritime affairs, iv. 368-78; rule in '44, iv. 401-20; revolution against in '44-5; defeat, departure, and later career, iv. 455-517; miscel. mention, iii. 550, 561; iv. 34, 409, 423-33, 448, 521-2, 561, 619, 630, 636, 652. As his career in Cal. is fully recorded in this vol., I need not go further into details here. He was a nat. of Oajaca, a friend of Guerrero, a man of some literary pretensions, and a colonel as early as '33. Elsewhere I say of the gov. that he was 'a strange mixture of good and bad; a most fascinating and popular gentleman; honest, skilful, and efficient as an official in minor matters; utterly weak, unreliable, and even dishonorable in all emergencies;' yet under ordinary circumstances, by reason of his intelligence, experience, and tact in winning friends, he might have been a good ruler for Cal. By his liberality in granting lands as well as by his personal courtesy he made a good impression on most foreigners, who as a rule have given an unfair version of the revolution by which he was overthrown. In the Jones affair at the outset he simply made an ass of himself, and of his acts in the last months nothing can be said in praise; while his breaking the treaty of Sta Teresa, by which he had promised to send away his battalion of cholo ruffians, and his bribing Sutter to arm the foreigners and Indians against the Californians, were in the highest degree dishonorable and unpatriotic. After leaving Cal. he took a somewhat prominent part in the war against the U.S., serving as member of congress in '47 and com. gen. of Yucatan in '50. He seems to have taken a very discreditable part in the Limantour forgeries, though little is known of details. I have found no definite record of his last years or death.   Michael (John), 1844, at S. José. *Sta Clara Co. Hist. Atlas.* Michi (John), 1825, mr of the *Tamaahmaah.* iv. 149; prob. 'Meek,' q. v.

Middleton, 1847, mr of the *Xylon.*   M. (Thomas), 1845, at N. Helv. iv. 578, 587; bought mules of Lassen and Sill, which were driven across the plains eastward in '46; in '76 a resid. of Rohnerville. *Eureka W. C. Signal.* Mier y Teran (José M.), sec. of ayunt. at Mont. (?) '34. iii. 673; sec. of S. Diego ayunt. '35-6. iii. 615-16; síndico '37. iii. 616.   Miguel (José de), 1790, Span. friar, who served chiefly at Sta B. and San Gabriel, dying in 1803. Biog. ii. 355; ment. i. 423, 492, 522, 576-7, 587, 669, 672, 689; ii. 114, 148, 159, 394.   Miles (John), 1832, of the comp. extranjera; still at Mont. '33-4. iii. 221.   M. (Sam.), 1847, Co. B, Morm. Bat. (v. 469); asst alcalde at S. Diego. v. 490; in '81 high councillor and justice of peace in Utah.   Milford (Edmund N.), 1847, Co. F, N. Y. Vol. (v. 499); at Princeton, Mariposa Co., '83.   Millard (Ormon), 1845, disch. from the *Warren*, and shipped on the *Guipuzcoana*, at Mont.

Miller (Augustus), 1847, Co. I, N. Y. Vol. (v. 499); d. before '82.   M. (Chas), 1847, Co. G, ditto.   M. (Daniel), 1832, Engl. sailor from the *Chalcedony*, at Mont. to end of '34.   M. (Edward), 1847, Co. G, N. Y. Vol. (v. 499).   M. (Feltis), 1847, settled on Sac. Riv., at Cache Creek.   M. (Francis), 1847, Co. C, N. Y. Vol. (v. 499).   M. (Henry), 1847, Co. D, ditto.   M. (Hiram O.), 1846, overl. immig. of Bryant's party. v. 528; member of 2d Donner relief. v. 540; settled in Sta Clara Co., where he died in '67.   M. (James), 1844, Irish immig. of the Stevens party, with wife (Mary Murphy), son Wm J., age 12, and 3 daughters. iv. 445-7, 453. He settled in Marin Co., where he still lived in '80 with a large family.   M. (J.), 1845, commander's clerk on the *Savannah*. M. (J. J.), 1845, mid. on the *Savannah*. M. (John), 1847, Co. D, N. Y. Vol. (v. 499). M. (John Morgan), 1848, nat. of Va, who came from Or. to the mines; settled from '50 near Sebastopol, Sonoma Co., where he died in '75 at the age of 61, having been postmaster and justice of the peace. M. (Miles), 1847, Co. E, Morm. Bat. (v. 469). M. (M. R.), 1847, overl. immig., who again crossed the plains in '48, '49, '52, and '73; had an orchard in Pleasant Val., Solano. M. (Valentine), 1847, Co. G, N. Y. Vol. (v. 499). M. (Wm), 1846, deserter from the U. S. *Savannah*.

Millhause (Gustave), 1847, Co. F, N. Y. Vol. (v. 499); at Sta B. '71–82. Milligan (John), see 'Mulligan.' M. (R.), 1841, mid. on the U. S. *St Louis*. Milliken (John), 1847, Co. E, N. Y. Vol. (v. 499); d. Sta Clara Co. about '78. Millington (Chas), 1847, mr of the *Xylon*. v. 581; owner of S. F. lot. Mills (John), 1847, boatswain on the U. S. *Independence*. M. (J. H. A.), 1848, nat. of Mo., at S. José '59–76; livery-stable man. M. (Wm), 1846, Fauntleroy's dragoons (v. 232, 247). Millwright, 1847, doubtful name at N. Helv. Milner (Danell), 1845, signer of the S. José call to foreigners. iv. 599.

Minard (Thos A.), 1847, Co. C, N. Y.Vol. (v. 499). Miner (A. T.), 1848, name in S. F. letter list. Minier, 1846, at Sutter's Fort '46–7 with family; called a volunteer. M., 1845, mid. on the U. S. *Warren*. Mink (Wm), 1846, Co. C, 1st U. S. dragoons, transf. from Co. K. v. 336. Miñon (Juan José), Mex. gen., appointed gov. of Cal. '27; did not come. ii. 515; iii. 8. Minor (Allen B.), 1847, of N. Y., left S. F. for Panamá on the *Charles Drew*. M. (Colville J.), 1847, lieut Co. F, 3d U. S. artill.; d. at Mont. in Aug., age 23; a nat. of Wash., D. C., and graduate of West Point. v. 518, 520. M. (Geo.), 1846, lieut U. S. N. on the *Savannah;* memb. of 1st jury at Mont.; in com. of garrison at S. Diego; in '47 assist q. m. in Stockton's battalion; a witness at Wash. in the Frémont court-martial and Cal. claims. v. 289, 292, 324–6, 328, 385, 420, 456. Minter (J.), 1846, overl. immig. in Bryant's party (v. 526;) Co. F, Cal. Bat. (v. 358).

Miramontes (Candelario), Mex. said to have had a potato-patch in '33 on what was later the plaza at S.F. iii. 709; in '41 or earlier grantee of Pilarcitos, Sta Clara. ii. 616, 664, 672; in '42 at S.F., age 53, wife Guadalupe Briones, child. Miguel b. '19 at S.F., María Dolores '23, Rodolfo '20, José A. '24, José de los Santos '26, Raimundo '29, Guadalupe '31, Cármen '32. M. (Ignacio), soldier of S.F. comp. from '35; corp. '38–44; brought small-pox from Ross '38. iv. 74, 165; age 30 in '44. M. (José Arciano) son of Candelario; soldier of S.F. comp. '44. M. (Juan), soldier of S.F. comp. '19–30. M. (Mariano), soldier of S.F. comp. '37; d. '43. M. (Miguel), sergt in S.F. militia '44, age 26. M. (Raimundo), soldier of S.F. comp. '44, age 20. M. (Ramon), Cal. claim of $15,000 '46–7 (v.462). M. (Rodolfo), son of Candelario; soldier of S.F. comp. '37–44; juez de campo '46. v. 648. M. (Santos), soldier of S.F. militia '44, age 16. M. (Vicente), soldier of S.F. comp. '28–37; in '37 elector. iii. 705; in '39 juez supl. and elected alcalde. *Ib.*; in '42 juez supl. iv. 665; in '42 at S. José, age 32, wife María de Jesus Hernandez, child. Jose María b. '38, Benita '40, and Mariana; in '43 owner of a lot, on which he lived with his fam. '44–8. iv. 669; v. 680; in '44 alférez of militia. iv. 667; in '46 juez supl. v. 648. In '54–5 he lived at the mission, testifying in the Santillan case.

Miranda (Alejo), inval. soldier of S.F. comp. and brevet corporal '19–30; piloted Vancouver's vessels 1792. i. 510; corp. of the guard at S. José mission '97. M. (Antonio), chino settler of Los Ang. 1781. i. 345. M. (Apolinario), soldier of S.F. comp. '19–36; grantee of Ojo de Agua de Figueroa '33, '38. iii. 712, 705; in '42 age 47, wife Juana Briones, child. Presentacion b. '22, Gomez (?) '29, Narcisa '30, Refugio '32, José de Jesus '35, Manuel '37; in '43 in trouble with his wife. vi. 666. See ' Briones' (Juana). M. (Hilario), soldier of S.F. comp. 1797–1824. i. 555–6; in '41 at S. José, age 60. wife Juana Cibrian, child. José Fran. b. '28, José de Jesus '31, Casimiro '33, Alejo (?) '36, Clemente '38, María de Gracia '39. M. (José), soldier of S.F. comp. '34–42. M. (Juan), soldier of S.F. comp. '19–22; sec. at S. José '25. ii. 604–5; in '44, age 52, grantee of Arroyo de S. Antonio, Marin. iv. 673. M. (Juan José), settler on the Colorado 1780–1. i. 359. M. (Manuel), at S. José '41, age 24, wife Cármen Alviso, child. María de los Santos '38, María Rosa '41.   M. (Mariano), soldier of S.F. comp. '37–43. iv. 667; named in '46. v. 162; also had a Cal. claim of $4,400 (v. 462).   M. (Presentacion), daughter of Apolinario; at Mission Dolores '55, and witness in the Santillan case.   M. (Santos), soldier of S.F. comp. '39–43. iv. 667.   M. (Teodoro), at Sonoma '44, age 22.   Mirantes (Ignacio), at S.F. '42, age 31; doubtful name.   Mirayno (Jonathan), 1840, doubtful name in Farnham's list. iv. 17.

Misroon (John S.), 1846, lieut on the U.S. *Portsmouth*, somewhat prominent at the time of the Bear revolt, being sent by Capt. Montgomery to Sonoma and N.Helv. v. 130–1, 154, 156–9, 241, 299.   Owner of a S.F. lot. v. 683. Before his departure in '47 he made arrangements for investing in lands and cattle, and apparently did invest with Larkin, but had a misunderstanding with L. and Sutter, which, perhaps, put an end to the speculation.   I have many of his letters on the matter.   Misteril, 1834, Swiss sailor on the *Natalia*, badly injured at the wreck. iii. 412; worked on a rancho near Mont. '35–6.

Mitchell, 1845, mr of the *Fama*. iv. 565.   M., 1847, mr of the *Providence*. v. 580.   M. (Benj.), 1846, in Napa Val. '69.   M. (Hue), 1842, sailor on the *Admittance;* deserted at S. Diego '44.   M. (Joseph B.), 1845, mr of the *Fannie*, at S.F. Oct.   M. (Wm), 1846, mid. on the U.S. *Congress;* stationed with a garrison at Sta B. Aug.–Sept. v. 267, 287, 630; made a com. U.S.N. '65; d. at Wash. '71.   M. (Wm), 1847, Co. B, N.Y.Vol. (v. 499); d. in Australia before '82.   M. (Wm H.), 1847, Co. E, ditto; in Amador Co. '74.   Mitchener (T.), 1847, from Hon. on the *Francesca*.

Mocho (Dan.), 1831, nickname of an Irishman at Los Ang.   Moerenhaut (Jacob Antonio), 1846, Fr. consul in Cal. '46–8. v. 290, 576, 614; a nat. of Belgium. There is no agreement respecting his initials.   Moffat (Richard), 1847, owner of a S.F. lot. v. 686.   Moffitt (Alfred P.), 1847, Co. F, 3d artill. artificer (v. 518).   M. (James), 1846, nat. of N.Y., sailor on the U.S. *Savannah*, disch. at S.F. '49; in '82 at East Oakland with wife—Margaret Mulgrew, mar. '59—and 9 children, Frank J. (deputy sheriff), Mary, Maggie, Martha, Joseph, Emma, Geo., Harry, and Nellie.   M. (Wm B.), 1847, Co. D, N.Y.Vol. (v. 299).

Mofras (Eugène Duflot de), 1841, French attaché of the Mex. legation, who visited Cal. and Or. in '41–2, commissioned by the govt to examine and report on the country, with its institutions, resources, history, and prospects, the result being published as *Mofras, Exploration, etc.*, a well-known and standard work.   For a full account of his visit and work, including something of Mofras' character, see iv. 248–55; also i. 224; ii. 108, 642; iv. 191, 209–10, 218, 224, 233–4, 297, 329, 343, 564, 618–19, 636, 640, 650, 665.   M. was still in the French diplomatic service, as ministre plenipotentiaire, in '78, and I have not heard of his death down to '85.   Mohr, 1847, Co. F, N.Y.Vol. (v. 499); at S. José '71–4, doubtful name, not in Clark's last list.   Mohron, 1847, mr of the *Com. Shubrick;* perhaps 'Morgan.'   Mojica (Bernardo), at S. José '22. ii. 605.   M. (José Vicente), at Branciforte 1797; alcalde in 1802. i. 569; ii. 156.   M. (Venancio), at S.F. '37–44, age 55.

Molckenbuhr (Henry), 1847, German carpenter at Mont. '47–8; name written in half a dozen ways; perhaps 'Molokenbuker.'   Molina, settler at Mont., taken prisoner by Bouchard '18. ii. 233, 237–41.   M., maj. at S. Rafael '33. iii. 323–4.   M., killed at Jamul, S. Diego '37. iii. 614.   M. (Alejandro), at Los. Ang. '46.   M. (Jesus), at S. Cárlos '40–2, grantee of S. Bernabé. iii. 680; iv. 655.   M. (Joaquin), sirviente at S. F. 1777. i. 297. M. (Vicente), at Mont. '45. iv. 653.   Molini, contract to make adobes for Larkin 1848.   Molteno (Frank), 1848, mr of the *S.S.* v. 580; on the *Julian* from Hon. later in the year.   Molvee (Herman), 1815, sup. of the *Suvarof*. ii. 307.   Molvisto (Nicolai), 1825, pass. on the *Elena*. iii. 146.

Mondojia, 1791, com. of the *Horcasitas*. i. 523.   Mone (Alex.), 1847, overl. immig. from Mo. with wife and father, who settled at Sta Cruz and engaged in the lumber business, with a brief mining experience in '48.   He furnished lumber for Meiggs' wharf S. F. at two hundred dollars per M.   In

'53 settled at Pescadero, where in '78 he gave me the narrative of a *Pioneer of '47.* Monet (John), 1846, Cal. claim $30 (v. 462); owner of S. F. lot '47. Money (Wm), 1843 (?), Scotchman, the date and manner of whose coming are not known; at Los Ang. Feb. '43. iv. 400. He is said to have come as the servant of a scientific man, whose methods and ideas he adopted. His wife was a very handsome Sonoreña. In '46 the couple started with Coronel for Sonora, and were captured by Kearny's force, but perhaps continued their journey, as Mrs M. had a child born on the way, and they returned from the Colorado with the Morm. Bat. Money became an eccentric doctor, artist, and philosopher at S. Gabriel, where his house in '80 was filled with ponderous tomes of his writings, and on the simple condition of buying one thousand dollars' worth of these I was offered his pioneer reminiscences. He died a few years later. His wife, long divorced from M. and married to a Frenchman, was also living at Los Ang. in '80. It was her daughter who killed Chico Forster.

Monneron, 1786, with La Pérouse. i. 435. Monroe, 1845, at Sutter's Fort. Monroy (José de Jesus and Lino), at Los Ang. '46. Montalba (Bernardo), at Los Ang. '46. Montano (Antonio), at Bajada á Huerta Vieja, Mont., 1795. i. 683. M. (José María), at S. Juan Cap. '46, age 40, wife Josefa Gutierrez, child. Apolonio b. '35, Maria '37, Bruno '39. Monteith (Dan.), 1837 (?), at Sta Cruz '81. Montenegro (Eugenio), Mex. corporal of Mont. customhouse guard '34. iii. 378; served under Alvarado's govt as alférez. iii. 508; and in '38–40 was sub-comisario and com. of celadores at Mont. iii. 672; iv. 96–7; owner of S. F. lot '41–5. iv. 669; ministro supl. of the sup. court '42. iv. 296; grantee of Laguna de los Gentiles '44, not serving against Micheltorena. iv. 473, 671; a capt. of aux. cavalry '45–6. v. 41; at S. Luis Ob. '50. Montero (Manuel), soldier of the escolta at S. Miguel 1797. i. 560; at Branciforte '30. ii. 627.

Montgomery, 1844, officer on H. B. M. S. *Modeste.* M. (Allen), 1844, overl. immig. from Mo. in the Stevens party with wife. iv. 445, 453. He was one of the party that at first remained at the mountain camp with Schallenberger. iv. 454. He is mentioned in the *N. Helv. Diary* in '46, and apparently had a rancho on the American Riv. v. 107; but went to Honolulu on the *Julia* in '47, and I find no further record of him. Mrs M.—née Armstrong, sister of Judge A. of Sacramento, and married in '43—was a woman of somewhat remarkable qualities, who in '45–6 lived at S.F. v. 679; married Talbot H. Green, became wealthy, and in '85 as Mrs Wallis resides at Mayfield, taking part sometimes in public meetings of progressive and strong-minded females. M. (Isaac), 1848, liquor dealer from Hon. at S. F.; member of the council '49.

Montgomery (John B.), 1845, capt. U. S. N. in com. of the *Portsmouth* '45–7. His ship was stationed at S. F. during the Bear revolt, and it was he that raised the U. S. flag in July, being commandant of the northern district in July-Dec. iv. 568, 587; v. 102, 127, 129–31, 154, 200, 224, 228–9, 231, 238–41, 294–9, 380, 552, 580, 659, 682. For him Montgomery street was named, and Portsmouth square for his ship. Two sons, John E. and Wm H., were with him on the fleet, and were lost on the *Warren's* launch in Nov. '46. v. 384, 587. The capt. and Wm H. were owners of lots in S. F. v. 682. He later became commodore and admiral, was in command for some years of the Boston navy-yard, and died in '73. M. (John M.), 1847, nat. of Ky and overl. immig., who worked as a carpenter at Mont., went to the mines in '48, and finally engaged in raising cattle, settling in Merced Co. '54, and being a state senator in '75–8. Montijo (Marcos), soldier of the S.F. comp. '39–42. Montreuil (Louis), 1844, of Frémont's party; perhaps did not reach Cal. iv. 437. Montriel (Herman), 1847; Co. G, N. Y. Vol. (v. 499). Monyú (Jaime), 1825, Span. of the *Asia's* crew, who remained in Cal. and married before '28. iii. 51.

Mooar, 1845, mr of a vessel at Mont. '45–6. Moody (Washington), 1847, at Sta Clara '47–8. Moon (Wm C.), 1841, nat. of Tenn. and overl. immig. of the Workman party. iv. 278–9. Named at Los Ang. '42 and Mont. '44. In

'45 he 'mined' for grindstones in the Sac. Val., and in '48-9 for gold, having settled on a rancho in Tehama Co., where he died in '78. He was a famous hunter, and a partner of Ezekiel Merritt.   Mooney (James), 1847, owner of a S. F. lot.

Moore, 1830, mr of the *Globe.* iii. 147.   M., 1837, of the Or. cattle exped. iv. 85.   M., 1795, mr of the *Phœnix.* i. 537, 625, 669.   M., 1848, employed as a shepherd at Sutter's Fort.   M. (Alex.), 1847, son of Eli, overl. immig. with wife, who settled in '53 at Pescadero, where he still lived in '78.   M. (Andrew), 1847, Co. D, N.Y.Vol. (v. 499); in Sta Clara Co. from '67; at Gilroy '82.   M. (Andrew J.), 1847, Co. B, ditto; in Phil. '82.   M. (Benj. D.), 1846, capt. Co. C, 1st U.S. dragoons, killed at the fight of S. Pascual. v. 336, 343-7.   M. (Benj. F.), 1848, nat. of Florida, on the S. Joaquin '48; member of the constit. convention '49; one of the earliest settlers at Sonora.   M. (Calvin W.), 1847, Co. C, Morm. Bat. (v. 469); at Spring City, Utah, '82.   M. (Eli), 1847, overl. immig. with family, who settled at Sta Cruz, buying of Bolcof what is known as Moore's rancho. He died before '78. One of his daughters was Mrs Sam. Besse of Watsonville.   M. (John H.), 1847, Co. E, N.Y.Vol. (v. 499); perhaps at S.F. and S. José '50.   M. (John W.), 1847, Co. D, N.Y.Vol. (v. 499); in the mines '48-51; killed by Ind. near Mariposa in '51.   M. (Otis L.), 1846, sergt Co. C, 1st U.S. dragoons, transf. from Co. K; killed at S. Pascual. v. 346.   M. (Patrick), 1847, Co. F, 3d U.S. artill. (v. 518).   M. (Risdon A.), 1845, one of Frémont's men. iv. 583; v. 453; a blacksmith and nephew of Cyrus Alexander. He served in the Cal. Bat. (v. 358); had a Cal. claim of $524 (v. 462); was at Wash., D. C., Jan. '48; prob. came back with Frémont in his 4th exped.; and in later years lived at Belleville, Ill.   M. (Robert), 1846, Co. C, 1st U.S. dragoons (v. 336).   M. (Thos W.), 1847, son of Eli, and nat. of Tenn.; at Pescadero '53-78.   M. (Wm H.), 1846, Kentuckian immig., who lived in Sonoma Co. to '56. and later in Lake Co. till his death in '67.   M. (Wm), 1816, carpenter on the *Lydia.* ii. 275.   Mora (Regina de la), mentioned in '35. iii. 285.   Morace (Erastus), 1847, Co. I, N.Y.Vol. (v. 499).

Moraga (Domingo), son of Gabriel, sold. distinguido of S.F. comp. from '18. ii. 571; in the Sta B. comp. as corp. before '37.   M. (Fran.), 1st Ind. convert at S.F., named M. for his godfather, the comandante. i. 296.   M. (Fran.), soldier of S. F. comp. '37-9; in '41 at S. José, age 27, wife Josefa Duarte, child. María b. '38, Teodora, '40; in '43 juez de campo. iv. 685; Cal. claim of $3,320 '46-7 (v. 462).   M. (Gabriel), 1776, son of José Joaq. who came as a boy with his parents, enlisting in 1784, and serving as soldier, corporal, sergt, alférez, and lieut of the S.F., Mont., and Sta B. companies till his death in 1823. Biog. ii. 571; ment. i. 470, 549, 559, 569-72, 587, 716-17, 719, 723; ii. 47, 50-7, 91-2, 126, 132, 140, 150, 199, 202, 204, 254, 288, 300-4, 319, 322-30, 334, 336-7, 341, 354, 361, 370, 385, 442, 559, 585, 631. His wife was Ana María Bernal; and later María Joaquina Alvarado at Sta B. in '50; among his children were Domingo, José Guadalupe, and Vicente.   M. (Ignacio María), niece of José Joaq. and wife of José Argüello. i. 470; iii. 11.   M. (Joaquin), prob. a son of Gabriel, soldier of S.F. comp. '19; at S. Mateo '35; grantee of Laguna de Palos Colorados, Contra Costa, '35-41. iii. 712; iv. 671; in '41 a widower, age 48, with the following children: José b. '16, Luisa '18, María '26, María Ant. '29. A part of the Moraga Valley is still owned by D. Joaquin's sons and grandsons, but there has been much trouble about boundaries with squatters.   M. (José), síndico at Sta B. '41. iv. 641; juez at S. Buen. '46. v. 634; justice at Sta B. '52.   M. (José Joaquin), 1776, Mex. alférez who came with Anza, and being made lieut was the 1st comandante of S.F. He was the founder of the presidio, mission, Sta Clara, and the pueblo of S.José. He died in 1785, and his widow, María del Pilar de Leon, in 1808. Gabriel was the only son of whom anything is known. Biog. i. 470; ment. i. 258, 262-4, 266-8, 271, 280-92, 295-7, 305-6, 312, 349-50, 385, 463, 474, 479; ii. 44, 47; iii. 11.   M. (José Guadalupe), son of Gabriel, soldado distinguido at S.F., and cadet at S. Diego '17-20. ii. 341, 571.   M. (Vicente), son of Gabriel; teacher at S. Ant. and Los Ang. '33-5. ii. 571; iii. 630; sec. and

síndico at Los Ang. '33-4. iii. 635, 564-5; admin. at S. Antonio '40. iii. 688;
iv. 61; grantee of Pauba '44. iv. 621; at Los Ang. '46; constable at S. Buen.
'52. His wife was María Ant. Dominguez.
Morah (M.), 1846, Co. F, Cal. Bat. (v. 358). Morales (Bernardo), soldier
on the Colorado, killed by Ind. 1781. i. 359, 362. M. (Francisco), Mex.
teacher at Los Ang. '18-20; 2d sindico of the ayunt. '23, '26-7, '29; ii. 559-61.
M. (Leandro), ment. as having killed Ávila in '31. iii. 208. M. (Pablo), at
S. Bern. '46, age 50. Moran, 1847, mr of the *Com. Shubrick* and *Julian* '47-
8. M. (John H.), 1847, Co. D, N.Y. Vol. (v. 499); d. S. F. '71; a printer
who worked on the *Californian* and was sergt-at-arms of the legislature.
More, 1845, doubtful name at Sta Clara. M. (Andrew B.), 1848, nat. of
Pa who came to Cal. from Mex.; one of the More Bros of Sta B., in '80 a
miner in Idaho, with resid. at Monterey, Cal. M. (John H.), 1847, owner
of a S.F. lot. Morehead (Joseph C.), 1847, lieut Co. D, N.Y. Vol. v. 504;
nat. of Ky; repres. of S. Joaq. in 1st Cal. legislature '49-50; d. before '82.
Morelos (Juan de Dios), surgeon of the Cal. troops at Mont. 1800-3. ii. 140,
147, 150, 153.
Moreno (Antonio), at S. José '41, nat. of L. Cal., age 46, wife Juliana
Tapia, child. Rita b. '18, Cármen '20, Antonia '26, Magdalena '28, Lucia '30,
Manuel '33, Pedro '35, José '37, Pedro 2d '38, —— '39. M. (Cárlos), at S. José
'41 age 29, wife Francisca Garcia; a nat. of U.S.; prob. Chas 'Brown,' q.v.;
grantee of land at S.F. '42. M. (Guadalupe), described in the papers as 115
years old, at Los Ang. '58. M. (Jesus), síndico at S. Diego '36. iii. 615;
juez de paz '41. iv. 619; owner of land at S. Juan Cap. '41. iv. 626; d. at S.
Luis Rey '71. M. (José), mulatto settler of Los Ang. 1781-6. i. 345. M.
(José Matías), Franciscan of Sta Cruz college, Querétaro, killed by Ind. at the
Colorado Riv. pueblos 1781. i. 359, 362. M. (Jose Matías), 1844, nat. of L.
Cal. and son of an Engl. whaler, his real name being Brown. He received
some education from the frontier padres, and lived in Upper Cal. '44-6, being
arrested at Los Ang. '45. iv. 522-3, 631. In '46, ranking as capt. of defensores,
he served as clerk and acting sec. to Gov. Pico for a short time, and escaped
with the gov. to Mex., carrying, as is thought, many doc. of the archives. v. 279.
He returned later to S. Diego, married Prudenciana Lopez, and settled on
the frontier rancho of Guadalupe. In '61-2 he was for a time sub-prefect of
the L. Cal. frontier district; and died at his rancho in '69 at the age of 52,
leaving a widow and 5 children. A search of Moreno's papers, kindly permitted by the widow in '78, resulted in a volume of copies cited as *Moreno,
Doc. Hist. Cal.* M. (Juan), 1836, Swiss who came with Gov. Chico. iv. 118;
at S.F. '40-2. M. (Juan), grantee of Sta Rosa, S. Diego, '46. v. 619; owner
of Los Ang. land '48. M. (Juan), ment. in '80 as living near Los Ang. and
at least 110 years old, having been 12 years old when his father (Jose ?) settled in 1781 at Los Ang.; doubtful. M. (Juan), 1827, Span. friar who served
for short terms at 5 missions, and died at Sta Inés in '45. Biog. iv. 645-6;
ment. ii. 576, 623, 625, 655, 659, 664, 683, 685, 691; iv. 46, 421, 426, 553,
647-8. M. (Juan Bautista), 1844, Sonoran soldier who deserted and came to
Cal., paying his way by gambling and making saddles. In the campaigns of
'46-7 he served as capt. of volunteers, and was wounded at the S. Gabriel
fight. He went to Sonora with Flores, but came back, and in '78 at Sta B.
dictated for me his recollections of a *Vida Militar.* v. 308, 352, 394, 396, 449.
M. (Rafael de Jesus), 1833, Mex. friar of the Zacatecanos, who served at Sta
Clara, and also in '34-8 as president and vice-prefect of the northern missions.
He died at mission S. José in '39. Biog. iii. 726-7; ment. iii. 318-19, 338, 432;
iv. 44, 63-4. M. (Santiago), 1824, nat. of Ecuador and a sailor; went to China
on the *Rover* in '25-6; was collector and síndico of the Mont. ayunt. '27-9.
ii. 612; ment. in connection with the Solis revolt '30. iii. 82; regidor '32-3.
iii. 673; maj. and admin. of S. Luis Ob. '35-9. iii. 354, 587, 682-3; at Mont.
'51. M. (Teodoro), 1829, Mex. who was maj. at Laguna Seca rancho '36,
age 50, wife María Ant. Cantua, child. Tomás b. '31, Juan '33, Francisco '35.
iii. 677.
Morey (Barton, Origin, and Rinaldo), see 'Mowry.' M. (Harley) 1847,

Co. C, Morm. Bat. (v. 469).   M. (Joseph M. W.), 1840, Engl. who got a passport.   M. (Michael), 1847, owner of S.F. lot. v. 685; perhaps 'Murrey.' Morgan, 1837 (?), left an Engl. schr at S.F., and with John Levick built a cabin in which they lived and made a large fortune, till '57, when L. was lost on the *Central America*, and M. drank himself to death in a month or two. *Herald:* iv. 118.   M. (Geo. E.), 1846, mid. U.S.N.; acting lieut Co. B, Stockton's battalion '46–7. v. 386.   M. (Van Rensselaer), 1846, mr on the U.S. *Congress.*

Morillo (Brígido), at S. Juan Cap. '46, age 46; child. María b. '26, Ramona '28, Miguel '30, Paula '32, José Manuel '36.   M. (Hilario), aux. alcalde in Los Ang. dist. '48. v. 626.   M. (Jorge), at Los Ang. '46; cl. for Potrero de Lugo '52. iv. 635.   M. (José Ant.), at Los Ang. '46.   M. (José Justo), at Las Bolsas, Los Ang. dist., '39–52. iii. 633.   M. (Julian, Miguel, and Tomás), at Los Ang. '46.   Morin (A.), 1845, one of Frémont's party. iv. 453, 583; served in Cal. Bat., Co. B, artill. (v. 358); died in the mts in the exped. of '48.   M. (John L.), 1847, Co. D, N.Y. Vol. (v. 499).   Morineau (M. P.), 1833, visitor to Cal. about this year, and author of a *Notice.* iii. 408–9. Morjano, 1833, visiting priest at S.F., prob. chaplain of a Span. vessel. Moro (Faustino), 1842, Mex. director of hospitals, or 'oficial de salud militar,' with the batallon fijo; perhaps did not come till '44. iv. 289, 563. Morphew (J.), 1825–6, mr of the *Eliza.* iii. 146; perhaps 'Murphy.'   Morrell (Benj.), 1825, mr of the *Tartar,* and author of a *Narrative.* ii. 548, 551, 588–90, 592, 610, 614, 616; iii. 25, 28, 149.   M. (Jesse), 1823, nat. of N. H., said to have visited the coast on a trader; later U.S. consul in Australia and a druggist at Sac., where he died in '70, leaving a family.   Morris, 1847, named at S.F.

Morris (Albert F.), 1834, British subject and descendant of a surveyor-gen. of Nova Scotia, for 9 years a sailor. At Los Ang. '36, a bachelor aged 27; one of Graham's riflemen '36–8. In '40 he was exiled with the rest, but came back with a claim for damages. iv. 8–9, 18–22, 24, 27–8, 31, 33, 37, 116. In '42 he went up the Sac. with Capt. Phelps; is mentioned by Mofras; was at Sta Cruz in '43. iv. 356; and in '44 was perhaps grantee of the Arastradero rancho. iv. 655. I find no definite record of his later life, though a newspaper states that he spent the last part of his life with Harvey S. Beal, and died at Ten Mile River (Mendocino Co. ?) before '72, leaving to B. his claim of $30,-000! It was about this time that his *Autobiography of a Crazy Man* fell into my hands. It is a most interesting narrative, and one of the best original authorities on the Graham affair, though marred by bitter prejudice and even falsehood, like all testimony about that matter. The author was in most respects very far from being a 'crazy man,' a term that had been given him by certain enemies, on whom he exhausts his vocabulary of irony and wrath. M. (John S.), 1847, named by Brackett as a lieut. in N.Y. Vol.; not on the roll.   M. (Thos), 1847, Co. B, Morm. Bat. (v. 469); hospital steward at S. Diego; in '82 a gardener near Salt Lake City.

Morrison, 1847, named as a sergt visiting Sutter's Fort.   M. (Bradbury), 1823, sailor on the *Rover.*   M. (Ludlam), 1847, Co. E, N.Y. Vol. (v. 499). M. (Perry), 1848, nat. of Ind., who came from Or. to the mines; in Alameda Co. '49–82; wife Martha Hastings; children Sam. and Geo. P.   M. (Roderick M.), 1847, lieut Co. K, N.Y. Vol. v. 504; killed near Stockton '49.   M. (W.), 1846, Co. F, Cal. Bat. (v. 358), later transferred to Co. B, artill. Wm M. is also said to have settled in Alameda Co. '47.   Morrow (W. J.), 1848, settler in Sonoma Co.   Morse (Henry), 1847, Co. A, N.Y. Vol. (v. 499); d. S. Joaq. '49.   M. (Thompson H.), 1847, owner of S.F. lot.   Morsine (Juan J.), 1848, of N. Mex. caravan. v. 625.   Morton (Freeman), 1847, Co. A, N.Y. Vol. (v. 499); d. at Stockton about '50.   M. (Henry S.), 1847, sergt Co. E, N.Y. Vol. v. 504; d. at Stockton '53.

Mosely (Sam.), 1846, surgeon on the U.S. *Congress;* witness at the Frémont court-martial. v. 420.   Moses (Ambrose T.), 1846, one of the Mormon colony with wife Clarissa and 4 children. v. 546. He left the church or was excommunicated on the voyage. He lived 5 or 6 years at the mission, and then went

to Sta Cruz, where he died, perhaps after '70. His wife died in the faith at
S.F. a little earlier. A son, Norman, still lives, perhaps at Sta Cruz. One
daughter married Eustaquio Valencia and died at S.F.; another became Mrs
Mason, and after her husband's death went to Utah, where she still lived in
'84. Moss (David), 1847, Co. A, Morm. Bat. (v. 469). Mossia (Antonio),
1857, musician N.Y.Vol. (v. 499).
Mota (Antonio Ruiz de la), 1825 (?), Mex. lieut-col in the war of independence, and later a robber chief sent to Cal. as a convict. On the coming of
Gov. Figueroa, an old friend. he was released and became maj. of Jimeno
Casarin's estate. He married and had two sons, Antonio and Maximiano,
acquiring some property as a ranchero and in settling Jimeno's affairs. His
conduct in Cal. was good, and he took but slight part in public affairs, though
mentioned in '46. v. 363. About '53 he went to Cal. by Mrs Jimeno. He rented
property, and in '56 was brought back to Cal. by Mrs Jimeno. He rented
some land near Sta Cruz, was abandoned by his sons, and died in great poverty. M. (Manuel), 1836, Portuguese laborer on Hartnell's rancho, where
he died '38. M. (Rafael), Mex. at rancho S. Felipe, Mont., '36, age 40. iii.
678; still at Mont. '51. Moti, a Sotoyome chief '37. iv. 72. Mott, 1846,
mr of the Vancouver.
Mouet (John), 1847, at Sutter's Fort and the mines '47-8. Moulton (B.
F.), 1848, Soc. Cal. Pion. rolls. M. (Elijah T.), 1846, Co. A, Cal. Bat. (v.
358); said to be living at Los Ang. in late years. M. (Joseph), 1846, French
creole of Frémont's garrison left at Sta B. under Talbot. v. 316. Moultry
(Riley Septimus), 1846, overl. immig. with wife, Mary Lard, married on the
journey, and one of the 1st Donner relief. v. 538. He settled at Sta Clara; I
have no record of what became of him; was possibly still living in Sta Clara
Co. '80-4, as was Mrs M. at Saratoga. A son, Wm Elliott M., born at Sta
Clara Oct. '47, lived at Sta Cruz '84. Mounich (Wm), 1847, Co. B, N.Y.Vol.
(v. 499). Mount (Hiram B.), 1847, Co. B, Morm. Bat. (v. 469); reënl. M.
(Joseph), 1848, said to have come this year; cl. for part of Entre Napa rancho
'52. Mouser (John), 1847, Co. D, N.Y. Vol. (v. 499); drowned in S. Joaq.
Riv. '47. Mover (M), 1846, doubtful name in a Los Ang. list.
Mowatt (Andrew), 1848, passp. from Hon. Mowry (Barton), 1846, one of
the Mormon colony with wife and two sons. v. 546. He, like each of his sons,
was owner of a S.F. lot from '47, and a member of the town council in '48.
v. 649, 679, 686. He left the church and became a spiritualist, dying, I think,
at S.F. many years later. His wife, or widow, with one of the sons, Rinaldo,
went to Utah, where they lived in 84. The other son, Origin, nat. of R.I. and
a mason by trade, was a miner and trader in '48-9, and later a rich farmer in
Alameda Co., where he lived in '85, age 60, with 4 children. Portrait in
Alam. Co. Hist., 616. M. (James), 1847, perhaps of Morm. Bat.; reënl.
M. (John T.), 1847, Co. C, Morm. Bat. (v. 469); at Paris, Id., '82. M.
(Ignacio, Joaquin, José, and Juan), at Los Ang. '46. Moya (Ramon), 1808,
com. of the S. Cárlos. ii. 87. M. (Trinindad), convict tanner in '34; in '41 at
S. José, age 37; in '43 owner of S.F. lot. iv. 669; v. 680. Moz (François), 1833,
Canadian who came perhaps with Walker, iii. 391, or from N. Mex.; naturalized in '40, being than a tanner at Zayante.
Mugártegui (Pablo), 1774, Span. friar who served chiefly at S. Juan Cap.
and retired in '89; at one time vice-president. Biog. i. 459; ment. i. 218,
224, 227, 299, 304, 351, 388, 417, 498-9, 581, 597; ii. 123. Muir (Wm S.),
1847, sergt Co. A, Morm. Bat. v. 477; a farmer in Utah '81. Mulholland,
1847, Co. D, N.Y. Vol. (v. 499). Mulkey (Wesley), 1848, nat. of N.C., who
came overland to Or. in '44, and to the Cal. mines in '48-9; in '62 went to
Idaho, where he still lived, at Lewiston, in '85; married '38 to Mary Black;
no children.
Mulligan (John), 1814-15, Irish sailor who landed, perhaps from the Isaac
Todd, certainly from some vessel before '19, when he was permitted to settle
and marry. ii. 272, 277, 292, 393. At Mont. '23-6. ii. 496, 612; taught the
art of weaving to Ind. at different missions; and later had an interest in
Cooper's rancho on the Salinas, where a sand hill was long known as Mulli-

gan Head. He was a hard drinker, lost his property, and died in '34. His name was properly Milligan, and I have several letters from his father in Ireland. M. (Simpson), 1846, Co. E, Cal. Bat. (v. 358). Mullington (Chas), 1847, owner of S. F. lot. Mulvey (James), 1847, sergt Co. F. N.Y. Vol. v. 504; d. S.F. in '65. Mumm (Christian), 1846, at Los Ang.; Cal. claim $23 (v. 462); at Napa and N. Helv. '47.

Muñoz (Juan Ant.), 1832, Mex. capt. of artill. '32-36, being exiled with Gutierrez in '36, being then 36 years old, wife Manuela Cruz, child. Joaquin b. '27, Jesus '32, Ramona '29. Biog. iii. 467; ment. iii. 239, 445, 455-6, 460, 463-6, 671, 674, 677. M. (Luciano), 1830, capt. appt. to Cal.; prob. did not come. iii. 54. M. (Manuel), ribbon-maker and instructor 1792-5. i. 615. M. (María de la Luz), 1st person buried at S. F. '76; wife of J. M. Valencia. i. 297. M. (Pedro), 1804, Span. friar who served chiefly at S. Fernando, retiring on account of illness in '17. Biog. ii. 357; ment. ii. 52-5, 85-6, 115-16, 149, 159-60, 246, 328, 394, 449. M. (Sebastian), grantee of Orestimba rancho '44. iv. 672.

Munrás (Estévan), 1820, Span. trader at Mont., described in '28 as 8 years a resident; elector de partido and memb. of the dip. in '27; not obliged to quit Cal. on account of his race. ii. 613; iii. 33, 36, 51-2; joined the comp. extranjera in '32, having been prominent in aiding foreigners. iii. 82, 221. In '36 age 46, wife Catalina Manzaneli of Tepic, child. Concepcion b. '23, Antonia '26, Engracia '33, Anastasia '28, José Narciso '35; his position in the Alvarado revolution. iii. 454-5, 469, 524; alcalde in '37 and juez in '40. iii. 675-6; vocal of the junta '43-5. iv. 361, 411, 521, 540, 654. He was the grantee of 3 ranchos, Laguna Seca, S. Francisquito, and S. Vicente, the first two being in his wife's name. iii. 677-8. In '45 Larkin described M. as a man of property and character, disgusted with Mex. politics, and ready for a change of govt. He died about '53. One of his daughters married Dr McKee. M. (Manuel), juez de paz at Mont. '39. iii. 675. M. (Salvador), brother of Estévan who came after '36; síndico at Mont. '44. iv. 653; treasurer in '46. v. 289, 637. Larkin describes him in '45 as an old resident, a man of family and property, disgusted with politics. On the Mont. assessment rolls '50-1; said to have gone to Spain in '58. Munroe (James), 1847, settler at Benicia. M. (John), 1847, Co. D, N.Y.Vol. (v. 499). Munson (Leonard), 1847, Co. A, ditto; at Two Rocks, Sonoma Co., '82.

Murch (Wm B.), 1847, Co. I, N.Y.Vol. (v. 499); d. Mont. '47. Murcilla (Andrés), 1839, mr of the Dan. O'Connell. iv. 103. Murdock (John R.), 1847, Co. B, Morm. Bat. (v. 469). M. (Price), 1847, ditto. Murel (Jean B.), Fr. servant of Estrada at Mont. in 36, age 24. Murey (H.), 1848, from Hon. on the Juliana. Murga (Manuel), 1801, com. of the Activo. ii. 5. Murguía (José Ant. de Jesus), 1773, Span. friar, who served chiefly at Sta Clara, where he died in '84. Biog. i. 476; ment. i .123-4, 194, 196, 297, 299, 304, 306, 351, 385, 388, 410, 631. Murielle (Pierre), Fr. servant of Herrera at Mont. '38, age 19. Murillo (Brígido), maj. at S. Luis Rey '28-30. ii. 553. M. (Eugenio), banished to Texas '35. iii. 674. Muro (Miguel), 1842, Mex. friar of the Zacatecanos, who served at S. José mission, and retired in '45. Biog. iv. 680; ment. iv. 371, 423, 553, 675.

Murphy, 1836, a priest apparently connected with Hartnell's school; ment. by PP. Short and Bachelor at Hon. '39. M. (Bernard), 1844, son of Martin and member of the Stevens overl. immig. party. iv. 445, 453. He settled in Sta Clara Co.; was owner of a S.F. lot '47; was claimant for several ranchos. iii. 712; iv. 674; and was killed in '53 by the explosion of the Jenny Lind in S. F. Bay. M. (Bernard D.), 1844, son of Martin, Jr, who came in the Stevens party at the age of three, being a nat. of Canada. iv. 445, 453. He was educated at Sta Clara, becoming a lawyer and banker; memb. of the assembly '68, and of the senate '77; mayor of S. José '73. He married Annie Mc-Geoghegan in '69, and still lives at San José '85 with 5 children, Mary, Eveline, Martin, Elizabeth, and Gertrude. M. (Daniel), 1844, son of Martin, and nat. of Canada. iv. 445, 453. He served in Co. G, Cal. Bat. (v. 358); had a Cal. claim of $15 for a horse (v. 462); owned a S.F. lot '47; and settled with his father and brothers in Sta Clara Co. He was claimant for Las Llagas rancho, and became the owner of immense tracts of land in Cal., Nev., Ariz., and Mex., being one of the largest stock-raisers in the world. He died in Nev. '82, leaving a widow and two children, Daniel, Jr, age 22, and Diana; another daughter, Mrs Chapman, having died before.   M. (J.), 1825, mr of the *Eliza*. iii. 146.   M. (Jacobo), 1792, alférez in Malaspina's exped. i. 490.   M. (James), 1825, owner of live-stock near S. José; prob. an error in the date.   M. (James), 1837, pass. on the *Europa*. iv. 103.

Murphy (James), 1844, son of Martin, b. in Ireland, accomp. on the overland trip by wife and child. iv. 445, 453. He worked as a lumberman at S. Rafael, and is often named in the *N. Helv. Diary* '45-7; owner of S.F. lots '46-7. He settled in Sta Clara Co. '48; was claimant for Cazadores rancho, Sac. Val., iv. 671, and also with his brothers for Las Llagas. Still living in Sta Clara Co. '85. His wife was Ann Martin, daughter of Patrick M. of the Stevens party, and his children were Mary F., b. '42, Martin B. '45, Wm B. '50, Lizzie A. '53, Julia A. '57, Daniel J. '61.   M. (James), 1844, son of Martin, Jr, who crossed the plains as a boy. iv. 445, 453; ment. at Sutter's Fort '45; perhaps cashier of his brother's bank at S. José '78.   M. (James), 1846, Co. C, 1st U.S. dragoons (v. 336).   M. (John), 1847, Co. B, N.Y. Vol. (v. 499); d. Stockton about '50; also said to be living at S. in '75. *Indep.*   M. (John Landrum), 1846, son of Mrs Lavinia M. of the Donner party; died in the mts. v. 531, 534.

Murphy (John M.), 1844, son of Martin, and memb. of the Stevens party. iv. 445, 453. He was active in raising volunteers in '46 at Sta Clara, and in the Sanchez campaign served as lieut. v. 298, 380; at N. Helv. '47; owner of S.F. lots; and member of the S. José council. v. 664. In '48 associated with Weber in trade at Stockton; also engaged in mining with great success—except in keeping his gold. Murphy's camp took its name from him. In '58 he testified that he had held the offices of treasurer, recorder, and sheriff of Sta Clara Co., and mayor of S. José. Still living at S. José as a trader in '80, and prob. in '85. His wife was Virginia Reed of the Donner party, and they had 6 children.   M. (Lavinia), 1846, widow from Tenn., in the Donner party, with 4 sons and 3 daughters. v. 531, 534-7. She and 2 sons, Lemuel B. and John L., died in the Sierra; 2 sons, Wm G. and Simon P., surviving, as did the daughters Mrs Pike, Mrs Foster, and Mary. The latter married Wm Johnson in '47, and in '48 Chas Covillaud. The city of Marysville was named for her, and she died before '80, leaving 5 children.   M. (Lemuel), 1846, son of Lavinia, who died as above.

Murphy (Martin), 1844, nat. of Ireland who emigrated to Canada in '20, and to Mo. '40. Here he became dissatisfied on account of malaria which killed his wife, and the lack of religious influence for his children, and at the age of 60 resolved to cross the plains to Cal. as a catholic country of fertile soil and salubrious climate. He came in the Stevens party with his children and grandchildren as named in this register, and settled in Sta Clara Co., where the family became prominent and wealthy. He was the owner of a S.F. lot in '47, and in '52 was claimant for a rancho. iv. 672, 684. Several of the sons served under Sutter in the campaign of '45. iv. 486. The old patriarch died in '65 at the age of 80. His daughter Mary was Mrs James Miller; Ellen was Mrs Townsend in '44, and later Mrs C. M. Weber; Johanna was later Mrs Fitzpatrick of Gilroy; and Margaret became Mrs Kell of S. José. M. (Martin, Jr), 1844, son of Martin, accomp. by wife and 4 sons, a daughter being born in camp at Donner Lake. iv. 445, 453. He settled on the Cosumnes, and his visits to New Helv. are often noted in the diary. His rancho is often mentioned by travellers between the bay and Sac. and there it was that Arce's horses were taken and the Bear revolt begun. v. 108. In '50 the family settled in Sta Clara Co., where in '81 the golden wedding was celebrated, and where Martin died in '84 at the age of 78, leaving an immense estate. His sons, Bernard D., Patrick W., James, and Martin, are named in this register. His daughters surviving him were Mrs R. T. Carroll and Mrs Joaquin Arques; another, Mrs Wm P. Taafe, having died. Portrait of M. in *Sta Clara*

Co. Hist.   M. (Martin J.), 1844, son of Martin, Jr, a small boy at arrival; seems to have died before '84.   M. (Patrick W.), 1844, son of Martin, Jr, a boy at arrival, who became a rich farmer in S. Luis Ob., representing that region in the state senate '65-8, '78. Portrait in *S. Luis Ob. Co. Hist.*, 32-3. M. (Simon P.), 1846, son of Lavinia and survivor of the Donner party. v. 531, 535, who returned to Tenn., served in the war of '61-5, and died in '73, leaving a widow and 5 children.   M. (Thomas), 1847, Co. E, N. Y. Vol. (v. 499).

Murphy (Timothy), 1828, Irishman from Lima, who worked for a year or two as clerk for Hartnell & Co. at Mont., subsequently entering the service of Capt. Cooper. iii. 178; ii. 609. From '29 his name appears in various records; joined the comp. extranjera in '32. iii. 221; on Larkin's books '33-5; often engaged in otter-hunting. About '36 he settled north of the bay, and in '37-42 he was admin. of S. Rafael. iii. 718; iv. 117, 676. I have many of his original letters of these years. Don Timoteo was a good penman, but his Spanish was peculiar, and his letters too often contained vulgar expressions and insults to all with whom he did not agree; yet he was on the whole a good-natured and popular man. In '39 he was naturalized; in '40 once put in the calabozo by Vallejo. iv. 171; in '41 ment. by Sir Geo. Simpson, who says he had been a candidate for marriage with one of Vallejo's sisters. iv. 218. As compared with other administrators, M. was a faithful guardian of the neophytes' interest; favored those of Vallejo as he was employed to do; and by no means neglected his own. In '44 he was grantee of the S. Pedro, etc., rancho, later confirmed to him. iv. 676; and he also represented the Ind. in their unsuccessful claim for Tinicasia. Juez de paz in '45. v. 676-7. In the troubles of '46-7 he took no part; owned S. F. lots in '47; took some part in local politics. v. 452, 455, 610; was alcalde, Ind. agent, and land commissioner '47-8. v. 670; and is mentioned by Sherman, Revere, and Mason. He was a liberal giver to several catholic institutions, and died in '53, leaving his property to nephews.   M. (Wm G.), 1846, son of Lavinia and survivor of the Donner party. v. 531, 534. He remained in the Sac. Val. till '49, when he went East to be educated and married, returning in '58. He was a lawyer at Virginia City, Nev., to '66, and since that time at Marysville, Cal., being city attorney, and having a family of 7 children in '80.

Murray, 1848, shoemaker at S. F. Feb. with wife; arriv. at S. F. from Tahiti, March; at the mines from Mont.; had a store at Sutter's Fort, of firm M. & Lappeus—prob. several individuals.   M. (Chas), 1847, purser on the U. S. *Erie.*   M. (Edward), 1847, Co. A, N. Y. Vol. (v. 499); d. Calaveras '55. M. (Ed.), 1847, Co. K, ditto; owner of S. F. lots. He was perhaps the M. who was in trade in Sac. '48, and later lived in the North Beach region of S. F., with a reputation not of the best; still living in '55.   M. (Francis), 1847, Co. H, ditto; owner of a S. F. lot; corp. in S. F. Guards '48; d. before '82. M. (Mary), 1846, one of the Mormon colony. v. 546; left the church; said to live at S. José '84.   M. (Michael), 1846, settler at S. José; in the mines '48; in Sta Clara Co. '60. *Hall; Breen; Carson; Hittell.*   M. (Owen), 1848, Soc. Cal. Pion. rolls; d. Oakland after '81.   M. (Robert), 1847, assist surg. U. S. A., serving with N. Y. Vol. and Co. F, 3d artill. v. 503, 511; at S. F. '71-4; in '82 assist surg.-gen. in N. Y.   M. (R. A.), 1846, Co. B, Cal. Bat. (v. 358). M. (Walter), 1847, Co. A, N. Y. Vol. v. 504-6; serving at Sta B. and in L. Cal. He was a nat. of England, and by trade a printer. Went to the mines '48; established the Sonora *Herald* '52; and in '53 settled at S. Luis Ob., where he practised law and established the *Tribune*, serving also in the legislature. In '73 he was appointed judge of the 1st district, and held that position at the time of his death in '75. His *Narrative of a Cal. Volunteer* is a copy of his original diary, and is one of the best authorities on the history of the regiment.

Muse (Wm), 1847, mid. on the U. S. *Lexington.*   Musgrave (Alfred), 1846, nat. of Tenn. and overl. immig., who served in Co. E, Cal. Bat. v. 358; lived in Napa till '67, when he left Cal.   M. (Charles), 1846, brother of Alfred, who also served in the Cal. Bat. and lived in Napa; in '69 in S. Luis

Ob. Co.; also called Calvin. Musty (John), 1846, Co. C, 1st U. S. dragoons (v. 336). Mutrel (Jean Baptiste), 1827, French pilot on the *Nereid*, wrecked on the L. Cal. coast in a schooner employed by the *Nereid* for seal-hunting. v. 478. He came to Cal. in '27 to drive cattle across the frontier. iii. 176; and in '28–9 became a resident at S. Diego. ii. 545; in '36 at Buenavista rancho, near Mont., age 27; went to Mont. in '40; in '46 at Los Ang.

Myers, 1845, at Sutter's Fort; perhaps 'Meyers.' M., 1845, apothecary at N. Helv. Nov. from below. M., 1848, of firm Adler & M., Sonoma. M. (A. S.), 1847, captain's clerk on the U.S. *Lexington*. M. (Courten), 1847, doubtful name at N. Helv.; called a volunteer; on his way to Salt Lake with a band of horses. M. (Geo. A.), 1846, Co. C, 1st U.S. dragoons (v. 358). M. (Jack), 1847, at Sutter's Fort; perhaps John. M. (John), 1847, Co. G, N.Y. Vol. (v. 499). M. (John J.), 1845, one of Frémont's men, iv. 583, who served as sergt-maj. of the Cal. Bat., v. 360, and was later lieut; Cal. claim of $130 (v. 462). M. (Russell), 1847, Co. A, N.Y. Vol. (v. 499); later trader and deputy sheriff at Sonora; major of vol. in war of '61–5; in N.Y. city '84. M. (Sam.), 1847, Co. B, Morm. Bat. (v. 469); sergt of reenl. comp. v. 495; trial in '48. v. 610–11; in '81 a carpenter in Utah. M. (Wm), 1848, associate of Lassen in Tehama Co., who prob. came earlier; alcalde in '49. M. (Wm H.), 1846, gunner on the U.S. *Dale*. Myler (James), 1847, Co. C, Morm. Bat. (v. 469). Myrick, 1844, mr of the *Sarah* '44–5.

Nachborn (Benj.), 1847, married at S. José to a Sra Mojica. Nactré (Eugenio), neoph. elector of S. Antonia '26–7. ii. 622; iii. 33. Nadal, 1845, from Hon. on the *Fama*. N. (José), 1825, Span. who came on the *Aquiles*, apparently sent away in '30. iii. 51–2. Nagle (Ferdinand), 1847, Co. C, N. Y.Vol. (v. 499). N. (Patrick), 1847, Co. F, 3d U.S. artill. (v. 518). Naglee (Henry Morris), 1847, capt. Co. D, N.Y. Vol. v. 504, 564, 666, 672. A nat. of Pa, graduate of West Point, and lieut 5th U.S. infantry. After being mustered out he became a banker at S.F.; in the war of '61–5 he served as lieut-col of the regular army, and brig.-gen. of volunteers; but returned to Cal. and settled at S. José, where he is well known down to '85 as a man of wealth and manufacturer of brandy. His wife was a daughter of Maj. Ringgold, U.S.A.

Naile (Conrad), 1847, Co. A, Morm. Bat. (v. 469); reenl. N. (Henry), 1836, Amer. trapper from N. Mex., named in a Los Ang. list of the year. iv. 117–18; but soon coming north to join Graham at his distillery. From '38 his name appears in Larkin's accounts and other Mont. records; in '39 with Graham he had a plan to raise a party and cross the mts eastward, which unfortunately failed; and in '40 he was seriously wounded in resisting arrest, and for this reason was not one of the exiles. iv. 14, 17, 18–22. From that time he lived in the Sta Cruz region as a lumberman, being interested with Graham in a saw-mill; in '42 signed an appeal to the U. S. for indemnity; was naturalized in '44; at Branciforte '45, age 36 and single; and in April '46 was killed by James Williams, who had rented his mill, in a quarrel about the contract. v. 641–2. Nalle, 1841, purser on the U.S. *Yorktown*. Nanhozen (Jerome), 1836, named in Larkin's books.

Narciso, Ind. chief in Sac. Val. '40. iv. 137. Narrimore (Mrs Mercy), 1846, of the Mormon colony with her son Edwin. She went back to Hon. on the *D. Quixote*, but returned, and was owner of a S.F. lot in '47. v. 546, 549. Narvaez, 1791, com. of the *Horcasitas*. i. 493. N. (Agustin), alcalde at S. José '21, and regidor '27. ii. 604–5; in '41 age 63, wife Josefa Higuera, child. Antonio b. '31, Lugarda '26, María Guad. '28, Teresa '30, María D. '33. N. (Blas), soldier of the S.F. comp. '39–43; at S. Mateo '35. iv. 667. N. (Joaquin), at S. José '41, age 36, wife María Ant. Sepúlveda, child. Salvador b. '28, Guadalupe '30, Pilar '31, María de los Ang. '33, José de la Luz '34, Francisco '35, Lugardo '37. N. (José Agustin), settler at Branciforte 1797–8. i. 569, 571; grantee of S. Juan B., Mont., '44. iv. 655; perhaps same as Agustin above. N. (José María), 1808, com. of the *Princesa*. ii. 87; in '27 com. of the *S. Carlos*. ii. 456, 458, 470, 474. N. (Miguel), 1822, alférez on the S.

Cárlos. ii. 458.   N. (Miguel), in S. José dist., age 30, wife Raimunda Buelna, child Agustin; at the S. Juan B. rancho '.5.   N. (Pedro), Mex. naval lieut unattached; capt. of the port Mont. '39–44. iii. 672, 676; iv. 97, 307, 339, 357, 408, 431, 653; in '44 grantee of Paso de Robles. iv. 655; in '45 mil. com. at Mont. iv. 652; in '46 served under Castro and was a memb. of the 1st jury. v. 12, 34, 41, 232, 289. I have no later record of him.

Nash, 1846, mr of the *America.* v. 576.   N. (Mrs), 1846, efforts to organize a school for her at N. Helv. in Jan.   N. (John H.), 1845, Amer. lawyer and overl. immig. in the Hastings party. iv. 586–7. Nothing is definitely recorded of him from the time he left N. Helv. for S.F. in Jan. '46 to Oct., when he went to Sonoma with Bryant, but he perhaps took some part in the revolt. In Dec. he was alcalde at Sonoma, being an illiterate, well-meaning old man, who called himself 'chief justice,' and attached great importance to his office. In June '47 he refused to give up the office to Boggs, who was appointed to succeed him, whereupon Lieut Sherman was sent to arrest the recalcitrant alcalde and carry him a prisoner to Mont., where he soon became penitent. v. 608–10, 667–9. With Grigsby and Ide, Nash signed, in May '47, a *Hist. of the Bear Flag Revolt*, having been in Sept. '46 sec. of a meeting of ex-Bears. v. 189, 298. In April '48 he visited the mines as a committee of investigation to report for the benefit of Sonoma residents; and later in the year he returned to Mormon Isl., where he died the same winter. N. (Wm H.), 1846, overl. immig. who settled with his family in Napa Val.; in '49 is said to have built the 1st school-house there; and still lived at St Helena in '69.

Navarrete (Bernardo), 1833, Mex. lieut, attached to Mont. comp.; went to Mex. on the downfall of Gutierrez in '36. iii. 467, 240, 442, 463–6, 671. N. (José Antonio), 1819, Mex. capt. of the S. Blas infantry comp. in Cal. '19 –22, and in '20 com. of the post at Mont. ii. 607–8, 252, 254–5, 265, 379, 422, 451, 461, 463, 609, 675.   N. (Ramon), soldier of the S.F. comp. '21–3; at Mont. '26. ii. 612.   Navarro (José Ant.), mestizo settler of Los Ang. 1786–1800. i. 345, 348–9, 484, 640.   N. (Guillermo), alférez in '39. iii. 583; at Sta B. earlier, wife Dionisia Dominguez, 4 child.; at Los Ang. '46.   N. (Teodoro), soldier of the S.F. comp. '28–34; at Los Ang. '46.   Nay (José), 1832, got a passp. at Los Ang.   Nazario, Ind. cook at S. Diego. ii. 345.

Neail (John), 1847, owner of lot at S.F.   Neal, 1848, miner at Adams' Bar. N. (John), 1845, at Sutter's Fort often in '45–7, several times arriving from the bay and Sonoma with reports of impending hostilities by the Californians. iv. 578, 587; v. 128, 170. As he came from Sonoma June 20th, he may have been one of the original Bears. He was an Irish sailor, a rough character, who lived in Colusa Co. till about '56, when—or earlier, as Bidwell thinks—he killed a man in some dispute about a dog or a mining claim, and escaped from the country.   N. (John C.), 1841, otter-hunter at Sta B. not locally famous for paying his debts.   N. (Joshua A.), 1847, nat. of N. H. who came as a sailor; was a clerk at S.F. '48; went to the mines '49. A resid. of Alameda Co. '50–78, marrying a Bernal and living at Pleasanton.

Neal (Samuel), 1844, nat. of Pa—or of Holstein in one original record—and one of Frémont's men; discharged at his own request early in '44. iv. 437, 439, 453, 229. He was employed by Sutter as a blacksmith; was naturalized in Nov.; and in Dec., in return for services in the Micheltorena campaign, got a land grant on Butte Creek, Butte. iv. 671. In his application he claimed to have been a resid. since '42; and indeed Yates claims to have seen him in '42-3. He still worked much of the time at his trade, aiding Frémont in the autumn of '45. In '46 he guided Gillespie up the Sac. Val. to overtake Frémont, and took part in the following troubles, though there is some confusion between him and John N. in the records. v. 24, 101, 104, 107. After the war he engaged in stock-raising, acquiring some local fame for his fine animals. He never married, and died at his Butte Creek home in '59, leaving his property to brothers whom he had not seen for 20 years.   N. (Wm W.), 1847, on the roll of the Soc. Cal. Pion. as having come in Jan. '49; but he states that he was at S.F. on a whaler in '47; in later years a well-known pilot

of S.F., still living in '85 with a family.   Neale (D.), 1848, passp. from Hon.
Nease (Peter), 1847, with Capt. Hunt of the Morm. Bat. (v. 469), accomp. by
his wife.   N. (Sam.), 1847, Co. F, 3d U.S. artill. (v. 518).
    Ned, 1830, doubtful name, at S. José and Mont. '30-4.   Neddles (John),
1831, steward on the *Catalina*.   Nee (Luis), 1789, apothecary in Malaspina's exped. i. 490.   Neeb (John), 1847, Co. K, N. Y. Vol. (v. 499);
d. Sonoma '74.   Needles (Wm H.), 1847, purser's clerk on the *Columbus*.
Negrete, see 'Castillo Negrete.'   Neiderer, 1847, Co. K, N.Y.Vol. (v. 499);
doubtful name, not in Clark's last list; at S.F. '71-4.   Neif (Joseph Ant.),
1839, German sailor, age 26, captured (?) by Cooper, released by Vallejo, and
employed by Leese at S. F. '40; known as Hen. Richer.   Neill (Wm M.)
1834, mr of the *Llama*. iii. 383; perhaps 'O'Neill.'   Neilson (Thos), 1826,
asst surgeon with Beechey. iii. 121.   Neiman (Hendrick), 1847, Co. D, N.
Y.Vol. (v. 499).   Neligh (Robert B.), 1847, member of the S. José council. v.
664; agent for Com. Stockton in the mines '48; claimant in '52 for rancho in
Mont. dist. v. 637.   Nelson (Chas), 1847, at Hon. from S. F. on the *Francisca*.   Nemesio (Santiago), grantee of Capay '46. v. 675; perhaps an Ind.
named Nemesis.   Neri (Gregorio), soldier in the Hidalgo comp. at Mont. '36,
age 27.   Nero (Joseph), 1847, at Sutter's Fort; prob. 'Verrot,' q.v.   Ness
(Elijah), 1837, Fr. lumberman in the Sta Cruz region '37-43; said to have aided
in the arrest of foreigners '40. iv. 118, 22.
    Neve (Felipe de), 1777, Span. major of cavalry who was gov. of the Cali-
fornias, residing at Loreto from March 4, '75, and—having been promoted to
colonel—at Mont. from Feb. 3, '77, to Sept. 10, '82. He became later brigadier, inspector-general, and comandante-general of Provincias Internas, dying
in '84. He was one of California's ablest rulers. Biog. i. 237-8, 363, 446-8,
487; his rule in Cal., including his reglamento, or system of govt, his founding
of the pueblos, and his controversies with the missionaries, i. 306-83 passim;
ment. i. 296, 389, 393, 405, 608. Gov. Neve had no family.   Nevill (Joseph
M.), 1848, owner of S.F. lots.
    Newell, 1836, named in Larkin's accounts.   N., 1848, mr of the *Hono-
lulu* and *Humboldt*.   N., 1848, of firm N., Brady, & Gilbert, lumberman
at Mont.   N. (Chester), 1847, chaplain of the U. S. *Independence*. v. 657.
Newitt (Sam.), 1847, Co. D, N.Y.Vol. (v. 499).   Newman (James), 1847,
ditto.   N. (John), 1847, Co. H, ditto.   N. (Wm), 1834, Engl. servant of
Wolters at Mont.   Newmayer (Godfrey), 1846, Co. C, 1st U. S. dragoons.
v. 336.   Newson (J. M.), 1848, overl. immig.; memb. of the legislature from
Stanislaus '68.   Newton, 1846, overl. immig. of Bryant's party with wife;
killed by Ind. on the way.   N. (J. W.), chaplain on the U.S. *Columbus*.   N.
(Thomas), 1848, Swiss sailor on the *Isaac Walton;* real name Sjoberg.
    Nicholas, 1842, com. of the U.S. *Yorktown*. iv. 313, 570.   Nicholaus (A.),
1848, passp. from Hon.   Nichols, 1841, of the Walker party with Emmons
of U.S. ex. ex. from Or. iv. 270.   N. (Joseph), 1846, of the Mormon colony,
with wife Jerusha and child, one child having died at sea. v. 546. He left the
church, and in later years lived in Alameda Co. to '82. Mrs N. died in the
faith.   N. (J. M.), 1845, came on a whaler. iv. 587; saloon-keeper at Napa
'52-71. *Napa Register*.   N. (P.), 1848, passp. from Hon.   Nicholson (J.
W.), 1847, mid. on the U.S. *Lexington*.   Nichton (Patrick), 1847, Co. F, 3d
U.S. artill. (v. 518).   Nickerson (Thomas), 1847, Co. I, N.Y.Vol. (v. 499).
    Nidever (Geo.), 1833, nat. of Tenn., from '20 a hunter in the west, making
trips to the Rocky Mts and N. Mex. till '33, when he came over the Sierra
with Walker's party and remained in Cal. iii. 391, 394, 459. Here he continued his hunter's life, taking otter in all parts of the coast under Capt.
Dana's license to '37, and later with one of his own. Occasionally named in
the records from '36, his home being at Sta B.; making frequent raids on the
grizzly bears and killing at least 200; naturalized in '37, and also serving for
a time with Graham's riflemen. iii. 493; having some conflicts with Ind. iv.
90; and escaping arrest in '40. iv. 24. In '41 he married Sinforosa Sanchez,
having bought some land of Joseph Chapman; in '45 refused to join Micheltorena's foreign company; but in '46, having been arrested by the Californians,

v. 317, he served under Stockton in the final campaigns; had some success in mining '48-9; piloted the U.S. coast survey craft in a survey of the Sta B. islands '50; in '53 rescued the famous old Ind. woman of S. Nicolás Isl.; and about the same time bought an interest in S. Miguel Isl., where he raised stock for 17 years, and though wellnigh ruined by the drought of '63-4, sold out in '70 for $10,000. In '78 residing at Sta B. at the age of 76 with his wife and daughter, a man of excellent repute, he gave me a long and most valuable narrative of his *Life and Adventures.* A bit of paper into which the old man at that time put 3 rifle-balls within the space of a square inch at 60 yards forms an appropriate frontispiece of the volume. H. died in '83. A brother John, who died at Sta B. in '73, is sometimes said to have come with Geo. iii. 391; but I think he came after '48. Another brother, Mark, was killed by the Ind. before reaching Cal.

Niebla (Ramon), a hatter at Los Ang. '39, age 47.   Nief, see 'Neif.' Nieto (Antonio), 1830, Mex. alférez who com. a squad of soldiers guarding a party of convicts. iii. 49, 142; prob. not in Cal. '25, as stated in iii. 15.   N. (Antonio María), son of Manuel, owner of Sta Gertrudis, claimed to have been regranted in '34 to his widow Josefa Cota. iv. 635.   N. (Diego), at Los Ang. '46.   N. (Juan José), son of Manuel, b. 1781; mentioned in '11-20. ii. 418; part owner of Los Nietos rancho, Sta Gertrudis, Alamitos, Coyotes, etc., regranted to him '34. ii. 565; iii. 633, 644.   N. (Manuel), grantee of Los Nietos rancho 1784; ment. 1801-16; Las Bolsas and Sta Gertrudis regranted to his widow, Catarina Ruiz, '34. i. 609, 612, 662; ii. 111, 185, 348, 353, 663; iii. 633-4.   N. (Manuela), grantee of Los Cerritos '34. iii. 633.   Nightengell (G. R.), 1875, overl. immig. perhaps of the Grigsby-Ide party. iv. 578-9, 587; at Carson, Nev., '68.   Nikoforof, 1815, sup. of the *Lady.* ii. 307.   Niles (John), 1847, doubtful name of a settler at Benicia.   Ninian (Wm), 1834, English clerk at Mont., age 30.   Niño (Alejo), first man buried at Mont. 1770. i. 175.   Nisbitt (Thomas), 1847, Co. G, N. Y. vol. (v. 499); in '82 at Scott river, Siskiyou Co.   Nixon, 1823, mr of the *Hebe.* ii. 492.

Nobili (John), 1848, Ital. Jesuit who came to the Or. missions in '42 and to Cal. apparently in '48. He was the founder of Sta Clara college in '51, a very able man and popular teacher, who died in '55.   Noble (John E.), 1847, sergt Co. F, 3d U. S. artill. v. 519.   Noboa (Diego), 1783, Span. friar who served at Sta Clara and left Cal. in '94. Biog. i. 722-3; ment. i. 379, 390, 422, 457, 476, 576.   Nocedal (José), 1775, Franciscan chaplain on a Span. ship, visiting the coast several times in '75-8. i. 240, 287, 292, 296, 300, 328.   Noé (José de Jesus), 1834, Mex. who came in the H. and P. colony; iii. 263; and settled at S. F., obtaining a grant of Camaritos in '40, and of S. Miguel in '45. iii. 711; iv. 673. In '42 age 37, wife Guadalupe Gardano, child. Miguel b. '33, Dolores '36, Esperidion (?) '38, Concepcion '40; juez de paz '42 -3. iv. 165-6; owner of a town lot '43. v. 669, 682; alf. of militia '44. iv. 667; alcalde and juez '46. v. 295, 648. He lived at the mission in '55, and his son Miguel still lives in S. F. '85.   N. (Miguel), 1844, Amer. who received naturalization papers; perhaps Michael Noah (?).   N. (Nicolás), 1812, com. of the *Flora* '12-13. ii. 202-3, 268-70, 353.   Noel (Luis), 1848, laborer at Mont. Noler (Christian), 1847, Co. B, Morm. Bat. (v. 469).   Norden (Stephen), 1844, Amer. age 25 at S. F.

Nordhoff (Charles), 1847, nat. of Prussia, educated in Cincinnati, a printer by trade, who in '47 was a sailor-boy on the U. S. *Columbus,* and for a time commander's clerk on the *Warren.* He left the sea in '53, and has since been a prominent newspaper man and author of a dozen books of acknowledged merit. He revisited Cal. several times in '71 and later years; and among his works are *California for Health, Pleasure, and Residence,* and *Northern California, Oregon, and the Sandwich Islands.* In '85 he has been for some years editorially connected with the *N. Y. Herald.*   Noriega (Francisco), 1842, Mex. capt. of the batallon fijo '42-5; a hard case. iv. 289, 357, 364, 633. His marriage with Francisca Sepúlveda was prevented by the woman's friends, and he married a Soberanes whom he afterwards abandoned.   N. (José), 1834, Span. sup. of the vessel bringing the H. and P. colony. iii. 263. In '35 depositario at S. José. iii. 730; in 35 grantee of Los Médanos, Contra Costa, and later of Quito, and half-owner of Los Pozitos. iii. 712; iv. 672-3; alcalde of S. José '39. iii. 731; in '41 age 49, wife Manuela Fernaudez, child Manuel. In '46 he was with Arce when his horses were taken, and on visiting N. Helv. a little later was thrown into prison with Vallejo and the rest, for which the Span. consul tried later to obtain redress. v. 106, 108, 124, 128, 615. After his release he was member of the S. José council. v. 664; and in '60 he still lived at S. José. N. (María Ramona), wife of Pedro Amador, d. 1801. ii. 585. N. (Matias Antonio de Sta Catarina), 1779, Span. friar who served at S. F. and S. Cárlos, retiring in '89. He was perhaps guardian of S. Fern. college later. Biog. i. 469; ment. i. 329, 351, 388, 392, 460, 404, 411, 433, 442. N., see 'Guerra y Noriega.' Norman (F.), 1848, passp. from Hon. N. (J), 1848, at Hon. from Mont. on the *Laura Ann.*

Norris, 1818, negro of Bouchard's force, captured; became a cook at S. Juan Cap. ii. 230, 248, 393. N. (Anderson), 1843, negro deserter from the *Cyane;* killed by the Californians. iv. 400, 565. N. (David), 1844, corp. Co. C, N. Y.Vol. (v. 449); printer and amateur actor, for many years foreman in the S. F. *Bulletin;* from '77 at Centreville, Alameda Co., where he died in '84 at the age of 61; a nat. of N.Y. N. (Jacob W.), 1847, Co. D, N.Y. Vol. (v. 499); at Newark, N. J., '74-82; sergt of police. N. (J. Parker), 1846, com. Stockton's sec., sent East with despatches Sept.; returned on the *Preble* '47. N. (John S.), 1847, lieut Co. K, N.Y.Vol. v. 504; judge of election '48. v. 652; d. in Central America '56. N. (Leo), 1846, nat. of Ky and overl. immig. with his family; at S. José '47-50; and in S. Ramon Val., Contra Costa, from that date to '82, being claimant for the rancho. iii. 713. His wife, Jane Kizzie, died in '55, and there were 5 surviving children in '82. Three daughters became Mrs Lynch, Mrs Perkins, and Mrs Llewelling. N. (Samuel), 1845 (?), trader at N. Helv. and at S.F., of firm Shelly & N. 1847-8, and seems to have come a few years earlier by sea. iv. 587. He was of German or Danish birth. A miner on the Yuba in '48; in '52 claimant for the rancho del Paso. iv. 672. From about '57 he led a wandering life in many parts of the world, though frequently making his appearance at S.F., an intelligent, mildly eccentric man in easy circumstances. Meanwhile the rancho had passed into the hands of Haggin & Tevis; and in '84 Norris began suit against them for the property, claiming that in '57-83, from the effects of a blow on the head, he was not in his right mind, or capable of comprehending the process by which the ranch had passed from his ownership. N. (Wm H.), 1846, son of Leo, and a resident of Contra Costa to '82; married Margaret Nash in '60.

Northgrave (Wm), 1845, Engl. immig. from Or. in the McMahon-Clyman party. v. 572, 587. Served in the Cal. Bat., Co. B, artill. (v. 358); in '47 burned charcoal for Sutter; in '48 mined with Bidwell on Feather River; living near Chico in '84. Northman (Chas), 1847, Co. G, N.Y.Vol. (v. 499). Northrop (Sam.), 1814, mr of the *Pedler.* ii. 305. Norton, 1841, mr of the *Ninfa.* iv. 567. N., 1836, mr of a whaler. iv. 104. N. (Joshua A.) 1848, Engl. jew who came from S. Amer. and was for some years a prosperous speculator and trader. Business reverses affected his mind, and as ' Emperor ' Norton he became a well-known ' crank ' in S.F., where he died in '80. N. Clement), 1845, mr of the *Gustave.* iv. 566. N. (C. B.), 1848, passp. from Hon. N. (Chas C.), 1847, Co. F, 3d U. S. artill. (v. 518). N. (Edward), 1848, overl. immig. with Allsopp. N. (Martin), 1847, Co. H, N.Y.Vol. (v. 499); d. Napa '68. N. (Myron), 1848, lieut Co. C, N.Y. Vol., appointed to fill a vacancy, and not coming with the regiment, but on the *Huntress* in Oct. '48. He was a lawyer, prominent in organizing civil govt at S.F., being justice of the peace and lieut of the City Guards; an active member of the constit. convention of '49; judge of the superior court '51; member of the Los Ang. council '52; county judge from '53, and in '55 and '65 candidate for the supreme court. He died between '67 and '71. N. (Thos A.), 1836, a Honolulu trader, signer of a memorial at Mont. iv. 118, 141; in '43-4 mr of the *Chas M. Morgan.* iv. 564. Norvell (Chester), 1847, chaplain on the U. S. *Independence.* N., 1848, of N. & Co. at Mont.

Noswill (John), 1846, doubtful name of Fauntleroy's dragoons (v. 232, 347). Nott, 1848, mr of the *Sweden*. v. 580. Novales (Manuel), 1789, lieut in Malaspina's exped. i. 490. Nowell, 1848, at Mont.; perhaps 'Norvell.' Nowler (Christian), 1847, of Morm. Bat. (v. 469); reënl. Nowlin (Jabez), 1847, Co. C, ditto. Noyes (Michael S.), 1847, Co. A, N.Y. Vol. (v. 499); at Eureka, Nev. '82.

Nuez (Joaquin Pascual), 1812, Span. friar who served at S. Fern. and S. Gabriel, where he died in '21. Biog. ii. 567; ment. ii. 334, 336–7, 355, 357, 394, 655.   Nuñez, sergt appointed to Cal. '32. iii. 236.   N. (José Antonio), 1833, Fr. sailor who came on the *Gelvichis (Helvetius?)*, and died before Dec. '34.   N. (Sebastian), grantee in '44 of Orestimba, for which he was claimant in '52.   Nuttall (Thomas), 1836, Engl. botanist who visited Cal. iv. 142. N. (Wm H.), 1846, overl. immig. of Bryant's party. v. 528; Cal. claim $63 (v. 462); owner of S.F. lots '47; clerk for McDougall at Sac. '48.   Nutter (Geo. W.), 1845, nat. of N.Y. who visited Cal. on a whaler from Hon. iv. 587; returned later and lived at Sta Cruz in '69.   N. (Noah), 1848, passp. from Hon.   Nutting (Lucy), 1846, one of the Mormon colony. v. 546; owner of S.F. lot '47; in '84 Mrs Ferguson at Lehi, Utah. Nuttman (James E.), 1847, Co. B, N.Y. Vol. (v. 469); owner of S.F. lot; later chief of fire dept in S.F. and Stockton; at S.F. '71; Newark, N.J., 74; New York '82–3.

Nye (Gorham H.), 1830(?), nat. of Mass., who may have visited the coast in '30 as he testified in '68. iii. 180; Peirce says he came to the Isl. from Plymouth in '31; newspapers give a variety of dates; and the 1st definite record is that he was mr of the *Loriot* in '33–5. iii. 383, 381. As mr of the *Bolivar* trading from Hon. and of the *Fama* and *Leonidas* he visited Cal. each year in '35–47. iv. 101, 104, 563, 578. He came on the *Guipuzcoana* in '47, and perhaps remained, as he is said to have made and lost a fortune at S.F., and to have gone East in '53. According to the *Calistoga Tribune* of July 6, '71, Capt. N. had lived many years at Sta Cruz, also spending two years at the Sandwich Isl., where a rich Chinese sugar-planter offered him a home, on account of the captain's kindness to him as steward in old times. Acc. to the *S. J. Pioneer* of Nov. 16, '78, he lived from '71 with Chas Krug at St Helena, where he died in '78 at the age of 76.   N. (Michael C.), 1841, overl. immig. of the Bartleson party, iv. 266, 270, 275, 279, who was naturalized in '44 and got a grant of the Willy rancho on the Yuba, doubtless for services in the Micheltorena campaign. iv. 674, 486. He is often named in the *N. Helv. Diary* '45–8, having also a Cal. claim (v. 462); is said to have entered Cordua's service in '46; in June '47 married Mrs Harriet Pike of the Donner party. N. was a resid. of Marysville in '58, but later went to Or., where his wife died in '70, and where he still lived in '79.

O'Brien (H.), 1845, in Sutter's employ Dec.; went to Or. Apr. '46. iv. 578, 526.   O'B. (James), 1838, Irish resid. of Mont. dist. iv. 119; exiled to S. Blas in '40, but returned in '41 with a pass, which was renewed in '42, iv. 18, 33, 37, when he was, however, banished to the Sonoma frontier. iv. 653. In '44 he died, and I have a letter from his father Daniel in London, in which, with 'hearty thanks for the information' of his son's death, he inquires as to the chances of collecting Jimmy's claim against the govt.   O'B. (John), 1835, Irish sailor who landed from a whaler at Sta B. at the age of 25. iii. 413. He hunted otter on the islands for several years, and in '40 got permission to marry, being then in the employ of Lewis Burton. He was one of the first at the gold mines, but fell ill, and being brought down the river died at Benicia in Oct. '48.   O'B. (John), 1846, Co. C, 1st U. S. dragoons (v. 336); Q. M. sergt.   O'B. (Thos), 1842, at Mont. under sentence of banishment to Sonoma; prob. James.

O'Cain (Joseph), 1795, 'Englishman b. in Ireland from Boston,' sent to S. Blas from Sta B. i. 537.   O'C. (Joseph), 1803, Amer. mr of the *O'Cain*, hunting otter on the coast under Russian contracts 1803–5. ii. 25–6, 32, 38–9, 63, 70–1.   O'Connell (Anthony F.), 1847, Co. H, N.Y.Vol. (v. 499); d. S. F. '66, age 48, leaving a widow and two children. He had been for many years a drayman; known in the later years as O'Connor.   O'C. (John), 1847, accredited to N.Y.Vol., but not on the roll; tarred and feathered at Mont.; drowned on the way to Or. *S. José Pion.*, '82.   O'Connor (Bartholomew), 1847, Co. F, 3d U. S. artill. (v. 518).   O'C. (Owen), 1846, Fauntleroy's dragoons (v. 232, 247).   O'C. (Wm), 1845, at N. Helv. in '46; iv. 578, 587; said to have been in Sta Clara Co. '45.   O'Donnell (Joseph), 1846, Co. E, Cal. Bat. (v. 358).   O'Donojú (José Simon), 1834, Mex. of the H. & B. colony. iii. 263; at Sta B. '41; in '42-4 purveyor of the troops under Micheltorena; at Los Ang. '47.

O'Farrell (Jasper), 1843, Irish surveyor who came to the U. S. in '41 and to Cal. by sea via S. America and Mazatlan. iv. 400. In '44 he signed the order for Weber's arrest, iv. 483, and in '45 served as Q. M. in Sutter's force, iv. 485-6, being mentioned in '44-6 at various places but apparently making S. Rafael his home, being engaged most of the time in making rancho surveys. He seems not to have taken part in the troubles of '46, but is named as a witness of the Haro murder at S. Rafael. v. 171-2. In '47-8 he advertised as a surveyor in the papers, was appointed official surveyor in the northern district, and made the permanent street survey of S. F. v. 455, 648, 653-6, 680, 685. About '48 he exchanged a Marin Co. rancho which he had taken in payment of professional services for that of Jonive in Sonoma Co., purchasing later the adjoining Estero Americano, for which places and for Capay in Yolo he was claimant in '52. iii. 712; iv. 671; v. 675. He married a daughter of Patrick McChristian, and lived chiefly on his rancho, but took also some part in politics, serving in the state senate and also as state harbor commissioner. For so prominent and well known a man there is a remarkable lack of definite information about him. He died at S. F. in '75 at the age of 58. A street in S. F. bears his name.

O'Grady, 1847, perhaps of N.Y.Vol. under another name.   O'G. (Thos), 1846, Irish settler of Sonoma Co. '47-77, when he lived at Bodega.   O'Hara (D. J.), 1847, in S.F. letter list.   O'Neil, 1837, one of the cattle party from Or. iv. 85.   O'N. (John M.), 1847, sergt Co. E, N.Y.Vol. v. 504.   Nat. of N.Y.; maj. of cavalry in war of '61-5, being stationed 4 years in Utah; in '67-83 custom-house officer at S.F.; d. at Mont. '85.   O'N. (Owen), 1847, Co. K, N.Y.Vol. (v. 499); owner of S.F. lot; in Nev. '82.   O'N. (Wm), 1816, said to have touched on the Cal. coast from China in '16. ii. 282; later an employé of the H.B.Co.; died at Victoria '75, at the age of 74; a nat. of Boston.   O'Reilly, 1837, a witness at S.F. Dec.   O'R. (E.), 1847, farmer in S. Mateo Co. '61-78.   O'Rourke (Francis), 1846, Co. C, 1st U.S. dragoons (v. 336).   O'Sullivan (James), 1847, Co. A, N.Y.Vol. (v. 499); a printer who was editor of the Sonora *Herald;* member of the constit. convention of '78; in S.F. '82.

Oakley (Chas H.), 1845, asst surg. on the U.S. *Portsmouth.*   O. (Howard), 1846, of the Mormon colony. v. 546; of the 3d Donner relief. v. 540-1; owner of S.F. lots; no record after '48, but did not go to Utah.   O. (Robert), 1847, Co. F, N.Y.Vol. (v. 499); d. Sta B. '48.   Ober (David), 1848, passp. from Hon.   Obes (Ramon), 1825, Span. who came on the *Aquiles;* perhaps sent away '28-30. iii. '51-2.   Obleie, 1844, doubtful name of a married foreigner.   Oca (Ignacio Montes de), sentenced to presidio 1805. ii. 191.   Ocampo (Francisco), 1834, Mex. of the H. & P. colony. iii. 263; at S. Juan Cap. '41. iv. 626; at Los Ang. '46-8; still at S. Juan Cap. '78.   Ochiltree, 1847, mid. on the U.S. *Independence.*   Odon, neophyte at S. Luis Ob., grantee of land '42. iv. 331.   O., grantee of Escorpion '45.   Ogden, 1828, leader of a party of H.B.Co. trappers who came to Cal. '28-30. iii. 161-2, 174; iv. 263.   O. (Benj.), 1847, Co. B, N.Y.Vol. (v. 499); d. Brooklyn, N. Y. '66.   Ogier (J. S. K.), 1848, nat. of S.C.; member of the 1st Cal. legislature '49-50.   Ogle (Chas A.), 1847, Co. D, N.Y.Vol. (v. 499).

Olavide (Martin), 1791, alférez with Malaspina's exped. i. 490.   Olbés (Ramon), 1812, Span. friar who served for brief terms at four missions, retiring in '21. Biog. ii. 625; ment. ii. 225, 243-6, 364, 369, 387, 389-90, 394, 655.   Olgin (José), settler at the Colorado riv. pueblos, killed by Ind. i. 359,

362.   Olimpio, Ind. majordomo in Sutter's employ '47.   Oliva (Raimundo),
soldier of Sta B. comp. '32; ranchero '45.   O. (Vicente Pascual), 1813, Span.
friar who served at many missions, but chiefly at S. Diego, dying at S. Juan
Cap. in '48. Biog. v. 623; ment. ii. 344, 357, 375, 383-4, 394, 551-2, 655; iii.
96, 619, 622, 641; iv. 422; v. 619.   Olivar (Tomás), soldier of Sta B. comp.
'32.   Olivares (Antonio M.), at Los Ang. '46.   O. (Bonifacio), at Mont. '36,
age 23, wife María del Refugio; banished in '43 to Los Ang., where he took
part in a revolt of '46. iv. 492, 654; v. 308.   O. (Francisco), settler at Los
Ang. '15. ii. 350.   O. (Francisco), 1846, Co. B, Cal. Bat. (v. 358).   O. (Miguel and Tomás), at Los Ang. '46.   Olivas, named as having been killed at S.
Buen. '38. iii. 551.   O. (Cosme), settler at Los Ang. '16. ii. 350.   O. (Domingo), messenger of Gen. Flores '47. v. 387.   O. (Francisco and José), at S.
Bern. '46.   O. (Esculano), comisario de policía at S. Diego '36. iii. 616.   O.
(Ignacio), soldier of the S. F. comp. '28-37; his child murdered '28. iii. 191.
O. (Juan), settler at Los Ang. 1800. ii. 349.   O. (Juan), at Sta B. before '37,
wife Clara Pico, 4 children.   O. (Luis), soldier at Sta B. '32.   O. (Matías),
juez de campo and com. policía at S. Diego '35-6. iii. 615-16.   O. (Nicolás),
at Los Ang. '39.   O. (Raimundo), at S. Fern., age 28, '39; grantee of S.
Miguel '41.
     Oliver, 1835, trapper at Suisun, perhaps of Young's party. iii. 394.   O.
(Jacob), 1843, at S.F., ment. in *Peterson's Diary*.   O. (John), 1834, Engl.,
named in Mont. list of '34-5.   O. (Wm), 1842 (?), doubtful name of a lumberman. iv. 341.   Olivera (Antonio), at Sta B. '32-45. iii. 583, 651; alférez
in '39; grantee of Casmalia, Sta B., '40. iii. 655; wife Concepcion Romero,
5 children before '37.   O. (Desiderio), at Los Ang. '19-48. ii. 355; age 53
in '39.   O. (Diego), b. at Sta B. about 1789, and a soldier down to about
'22; ment. in explor. ii. 57, 326; alcalde at Sta B. '37-8. iii. 654, 569-70;
tithe collector '39. iii. 654; juez in '40. iii. 606; grantee of Guadalupe
rancho '40. iii. 677. He is said to have clung to his old Span. ways, dress,
and ideas to the last, becoming rich in lands and poor again, and dying in
'67. Taylor's *Discov. and Found.* contains some of his reminiscences.   O.
(Ignacio), corp. and sergt of the Sta B. comp. from 1781; d. 1794; i. 463,
465-6, 532, 562; wife María Ant. Félix, who died 1868; child. Lúcas, Anna
M., Diego, and María Estéfana, wife of José V. Ortega.   O. (Josefa), murdered with the Reed family at S. Miguel. v. 620.   O. (Juan de Dios), at Los
Ang. '46.   O. (Juan María), corp. of Sta B. comp. '32; wife Serafina Leiva;
at Los Ang. '46.   O. (Lúcas), at Sta B. '37; wife Manuela Cota; 3 children;
grantee of Jesus María rancho. iii. 655; still a Sta B. ranchero in '45.   O.
(Manuel D.), 1829, Portuguese at Los Ang. '36, age 36. iii. 179; grantee of
land at S. Gabriel '43. iv. 637; majordomo in '45. iv. 637; in charge of the
Mission '47. v. 628-9.   O. (Martin), at Sauzal rancho, Mont., '36, age 56;
wife Josefa Noriega; child. Juan María b. '17, Pedro '19, Nolasco '24,
Lázaro '26, Agustina '21, Melchora '28, Catarina '30. iii. 679; grantee of
Moro Cayucos '42.   O. (Martin), at Los Ang. '39, age 25.   O. (Rosalío), at
Sonoma '44, age 45.   O. (Tomás), at Sta B. before '37; wife María Ant.
Cota, 2 children; grantee of Tepusquet '37. iii. 656; still at Sta B. '45-7.
Olivier (Pierre), 1834, Frenchman of the H. & P. colony. iii. 412. In '42 he
kept a drinking and billiard saloon at Mont.; settled near S. Juan; married
a daughter of Canuto Boronda; and his sons lived near S. Luis Ob. in '78.
Olivor (José), 1847, in S.F. letter list.   Olk (Wm), 1840, Amer. trader, age
24, with passp. from U.S.   Olmstead (Hiram), 1847, Co. C, Mormon Bat.
(v. 469); at Ogden, Utah, '82.   Olole (Chas), 1846, doubtful name in a Los
Ang. list.   Olpstay (Chas), 1847, Co. E, N.Y. Vol. (v. 499).
     Olvera (Agustin), 1834, Mex. who came as a boy with his uncle, Ignacio
Coronel, in the H. & P. colony. iii. 263. In '36 living with C. at Corralitos;
went south in '39, and in '41 was commissioner to distribute lands at S.
Juan Cap., where he was juez in '42-3. iv. 625-7. In '45 he was sec. and
supl. member of the junta, being also the grantee of Mision Vieja and Cuya-
maca ranchos. iv. 495, 522, 540, 621. In '46 he was sec. and member of the
assembly both under Gov. Pico and Flores, being grantee of la Ciénega. v.

38, 264, 321, 627; and in '47 one of the commissioners who signed the treaty
of Cahuenga. v. 404–5.   After the U.S. occupation he became a lawyer, being judge of 1st instance '49, county judge '50–3, supervisor '56–7, presidential elector, and receiver in the land-office, being also claimant for Los
Alamos. Don Agustin was a man of good abilities and reputation, who died
at Los Ang. shortly after '74. His wife was Concepcion Argüello; one of his
daughters married Charles Forbes, and another Juan Toro. His son Cárlos,
living at Chualar in '78, permitted me to copy from his father's papers a valuable collection of *Olvera, Doc. Hist. Cal.*   O. (Diego, Guadalupe, and José), on
S. Luis Ob. assessment rolls '50.   O. (Diego), sirviente at S.F. 1777. i. 297.
O. (Julian), 1829, Mex. convict released in '36.   O. (Santiago), soldier at
S.F. '37–42.   O. (Secundino), soldier at Sta B. before '37.
    Oman (Geo. W.), 1847, lieut Co. A, Morm. Bat. v. 477; in com. of garri-
son at S. Luis Rey. v. 489.   Ombis (Julian), 1845, doubtful name of a
Frenchman in the Branciforte padron; wife Concepcion Espinosa.   Oñate
(Juan), 1604, conqueror of N. Mex., who descending the Colorado to its mouth
must have looked upon Cal. territory. i. 68, 108.   Onge (Joseph S.), 1846,
Cal. Bat. (v. 358).   Ontiveros (José), settler at Los Ang. 1790. i. 461.   O.
(Juan P.), at Los Ang. '37–46, grantee of S. Juan y Cajon de Sta Ana. iii.
678.   O. (Patricio), encargado de justicia at Los Nietos '25.   Opham (Jean),
1825, mr of the *Triton* '25–6. iii. 149.
    Orámas (Cristóbal), 1786, Span. friar who served at Sta B., Purísima, and
S. Gabriel, retiring in 1793. Biog. i. 664; ment. 390, 423, 425, 459, 576, 675.
Orbell (James), 1837, Engl. sailor, age 24, who landed at S. Diego and engaged in trade. iv. 118. There was an order for his arrest in '40, not apparently executed. iv. 15; left in charge of Capt. Fitch's business during the
latter's absence, and his accounts seemed to show a deficit of $6,000 in '42. In
'44–5 he was mr of the *Guipuzcoana*. iv. 566; being naturalized, and in Nov.
'47 ill at Sauzalito.   Ord (Edward O. C.), 1847, nat. of Md, and graduate of
West Point in '38. He came to Cal. as 1st lieut Co. F, 3d U.S. artill. v. 518,
520, 636. After the war he took part in several Ind. campaigns on the Pacific
coast, going East by sea in '50. In the war of '61–5 he was brig.-gen. of volunteers and later in the regular army, with brevet of maj.-gen. For several
years from '68 he commanded the department of the Pacific, and later that
of the Texan frontier, dying at Habana in '83.   O. (James L.), 1847, brother
of E. O. C., who came as surgeon with Co. F, 3d U.S. artill., under contract
and not belonging to the army. v. 518. He remained in Cal. as physician and
farmer, settling at Sta B. and marrying the widow of Manuel Jimeno Casarin,
originally Angustias de la Guerra. He was also claimant for land in Tuolumne.
iv. 674; and later spent some years in Mex., holding about '82 the position of
consul-general. In '74 he resided at Sta B., and in '78 was appointed attending surgeon to the U.S. troops at Ft Point, S.F., still residing in this city '84.
He had one daughter, Rebecca, who in '85 lives with her mother at Salinas.
Mrs O. in her *Ocurrencias de California*, a MS. dictated by her in '78, has furnished one of the most accurate and fascinating narratives in my collection.
The Ords had two brothers, Pacificus and R. B., who came to Cal. after '48
and were somewhat prominent; also a sister.
    Ordaz (Blas), 1820, Span. friar, b. in Castilla la Nueva 1792, who came to
Mex. in 1819 and to Cal. the next year, ii. 375, 394, 328, serving at S.F. '20–1,
and accompanying Argüello on his famous exped. to the north, of which he
wrote a *Diario*. ii. 475–6, 595, 655. In '21–2 he was stationed at S. Miguel. ii.
620; in '23–33 at Sta Inés and Purísima. ii. 490, 529, 581–2; iii. 96, 661; in
'33–8 at S. Buenaventura, being sometimes in trouble and once asking for release from his vows as a friar. iii. 257–8, 658; in '38–47 at S. Fernando. iii.
646; iv. 422, 638; v. 405; and in '47–50 at S. Gabriel, officiating for a short
time also at S. Juan Cap. vi. 623, 628–9. After '48 he was the only survivor
of the Fernandinos, v. 565, and died at S. Gabriel in '50. Padre Blas was
a lively and good-natured man, but his fondness for women involved him
occasionally in scandal and reprimand from his superiors.   Orduno (Ramon),
at Los Ang. '39–48.   Oreña (Gaspar), Span. trader in Cal. '43 or earlier. iv.

364–5; sup. of the *Guipuzcoana* '46; a wealthy resident of Sta B. '50–85. His wife is the widow of Cesário Lataillade and daughter of José de la Guerra y Noriega.   Oribes (Tomás), settler at Los Ang. 1798. ii. 379.   Orozco, ment. in '37. iii. 54.   O. (José María), supl. juez at S. Diego '43. iv. 620; also receptor in the custom-house; grantee of Quejito rancho '45. iv. 621; taking part in the war at S. Diego '46. v. 329.   Orrantes (Bernabé) at Los. Ang. '46.   Orriz (Bernardo), Mex. soldier of the Hidalgo piquete '36.   Orta (José Gabriel), Mex. convict released in '34.

Ortega (Antonio), 1834, one of the H. and P. colony who was maj. at Solano '35–6, and grantee of S. Antonio rancho in '40. iii. 354, 711, 719–20. He died at S.F. about '68.   O. (Antonio), convict settler of 1798. i. 606.   O. (Antonio), soldier of Sta B. comp. before '37.   O. (Antonio María), son of José María, member of the dip.'27–8. iii. 36–7, 41, 63; grantee of Refugio '34. iii. 655; iii. 566–7; capt. at Sta B. '39. iv. 641; proposed for sub-prefect at Sta B. '41. iv. 641, 602; juez in '46. v. 631. He was still at Refugio, for which he was one of the claimants, in '52.   O. (Basilio), settled at Branciforte 1803. ii. 156.   O. (Emilio Miguel), grantee of Punta de la Laguna, S. Luis Ob., '44; also cl. in '52.   O. (Estévan), at Sta B. '37, wife Deogracias Ruiz, one child; collector of taxes Sta B. '46 and juez de policía '48. v. 631; still at Sta B. '50.   O. (Eugenio), admin. at Purísima '40. iii. 666.   O. (Eusebio), at S. Juan Cap. '35.   O. (Faustino), at S. Juan '43.   O. (Felipe? María), sergt of Sta B. comp. 1795, and author of a *Diario* of explor. for mission sites. i. 553; ii. 28. There is some confusion between him and José María.

Ortega (Franciso), musician of the S. F. comp. '39–42.   O. (Francisco), juez de paz at S. Buen. '48. v. 634.   O. (Francisco María), son of Capt. José F.; soldado distinguido 1794; elector at Sta B. '22, and memb. of the dip. '22–4. ii. 454, 462, 486, 510–11, 572.   O. (Guadalupe), wife of Joseph Chapman. ii. 479.   O. (Ignacio), son of Capt. José F., who prob. came with his father in '69–73; soldado distinguido of the S. Diego comp. 1792; wife Gertrudis Arce.   In 1812 he discovered a silver mine near Salinas. ii, 144, 176; and from about '10 to '30 was owner of the S. Isidro rancho in the S. José region. ii. 378, 383, 594, 603–4, 654; though possibly this was not the same man.   There was also an Ign. O. at Sta B. '50.   O. (Isabel), prob. daughter of Ignacio, grantee of La Polka rancho, Sta Clara, '33. iii. 712.   O. (José), at Sta B. before '37 with wife Dolores Quintero and 5 children; in '40 grantee of the Pismo rancho, S. Luis Ob. iii. 678; juez at S. Luis '44, '46. iv. 658–9; v. 638–9; visiting N. Helv. in '46. María Ant. O., cl. of Atascadero '52, was perhaps his daughter.   O. (José Ant.), had a house at S.F. '38–41. v. 684; perhaps Antonio, as above.   O. (José Dolores), son of José María; in '11–20 maj. at Sta B. ii. 364; his daughter Soledad (or probably his sister) marrying Luis Argüello in '19. iii. 11; at Sta B. about '32, wife Dolores Leiva and 4 children; grantee of Cañada del Corral in '41, iv. 642, and still there in '45.

Ortega (José Francisco), 1769, Mex. sergt, nat. of Guanajuato, who came with Portolá and Serra, was lieut from '73, com. of S. Diego, founder and com. of Sta B., com. of Mont., retired as brevet capt. in '95, died near Sta B. '98. He was an officer whose record was an excellent one, the author of several important records of the earlier Cal. events, and founder of one of the leading Cal. families, many of the members of which are named in this register. Biog. i. 670–3; ment. i. 122, 133–6, 140–1, 148, 153, 155, 159–60, 167, 178, 216, 225, 230–1, 236, 249–50, 252–3, 265, 303–4, 312, 315–16, 335, 372–3, 377, 441, 451, 462–3, 468, 484, 501–2, 663, 671, 678, 690; ii. 113.   O. (José Joaquin), son of José María, member of the dip. '30–4. iii. 50, 246, 249–50, 275; diputado and otter-hunter '31–3. iii. 187, 189, 200, 216–18, 246, 374, 394; maj. and admin. of S. Diego '35–40. iii. 353, 499–501, 578, 590, 620, 625; in '42–3 encargado de justicia of the ranchos, elector, juez, and grantee of Pamo. iv. 361, 620–1; in '43–5 maj. at S. Luis Rey, grantee of Sta Isabel, and suplente in the assembly. iv. 540, 621, 623–4; in '46 juez de paz. v. 618–19; cl. for Pamo in '52, and still living in '63. There is some confusion between José, Joaquin, and José J., and more than one man may be referred to.

Ortega (José María), son of Capt. José F., b. 1759, who came to S. Diego a soldier in '69-73; soon made corp. of the Sta B. comp., and com. of the escolta at Purísima. i. 425; marrying María Fran. Lopez in '79. From '91 (appointed in '88) he was sergt of the Sta B. comp. i. 614, 665. About 1797 he was partially relieved from military service in order to aid his father in lifting a load of debt; perhaps retired altogether. He obtained the Refugio rancho, where, as ranchero and trader, he is often mentioned down to about '20. i. 639, 641, 663, 671; ii. 28, 112, 124, 185, 236, 249, 274, 354, 663-4. His children, as named in the *Sta B. Co. Hist.*, were Martin, José Vicente, Antonio María, José Dolores, José de Jesus, Joaquin, Pilar wife of Sant. Argüello, Soledad wife of Luis Argüello, María de Jesus wife of José Ramirez, Concepcion wife of José Ant. de la Guerra, and Catarina wife of José Carrillo. O. (José María), soldier of the S.F. comp. '19-22; a man of same name supervisor at Sta B. '54. O. (José R.), at S. Bern. '46. O. (Josefa), wife of José M. Amador '28. ii. 585. O. (José Vicente), son of Capt. José F.; wife Estefana Olivara; child. Luis (2), Manuel, Pedro b. '15, living '80, Rafaela wife of Daniel Hill.

Ortega (Juan), son of Capt. José F., who came in '69-75; ment. in '75 at S. Diego. i. 255; sergt of the Sta B. comp. '11-18, and comisionado at Los Ang. '18. ii. 326, 350, 361; wife Rafaela Arrellanes; child. Emigdio (married Concepcion Dominguez), María wife of Guadalupe Hernandez, Buenaventura wife of Joaq. Cota, María Ant. wife of Pedro Dejeme, and María de Jesus wife of Fern. Ticó. O. (Juan María), at S. Juan Cap. '46, age 16. O. (Magdalena), Cal. claim $20 '46-7. v. 462. O. (Manuel), at Sta B. about '32; wife Andrea Cota; 1 child; maj. at S. Simeon '39. iii. 685. O. (María Ant.), cl. for Atascadero. iv. 655. O. (María Clara), daughter of Ignacio, and wife of John Gilroy. ii. 444. O. (María Simona), widow at S.F. 1796. i. 603. O. (Mariano), ment. in newspapers as 108 years old in '73, at Agua Mansa, S. Bern. O. (Martin), alcalde at Sta B. '29. ii. 572. O. (Miguel), owner of the Vírgenes rancho, Sta B., 1790-1802. iii. 111-12, 172; at S.F. 1807. ii. 192. O. (Pedro), at Sta B. about '32; wife Lugarda Ortega; 1 child; arrested at Refugio '41. iv. 672; at S. Luis Ob. '58. O. (Quintin), son of Ignacio, b. at S. Diego 1792; ment. in '18. ii. 234; grantee of S. Isidro '33. iii. 670, 713; in '36 juez de campo. iii. 675; wife Vicenta Butron; child. Pilar b. '20, Magdalena '24, Miguel '26, Quintin '32; at S. Juan '37. iii. 512; juez de paz '46. v. 640. Ortiz (Hilario), at Corralitos, age 24, in '36. O. (Nasario), at Los Ang. '46. Orville (James), on Larkin's books '38.

Osborn (Charles), 1847, Co. G, N. Y. Vol. (v. 499). O. (Jeptha), 1846, in Sta Clara Val. with 6 children; at S. José '48. O. (W. B.), 1844, sailor on the *Benj. Morgan.* iv. 453. O. (Wm B.), 1847, Co. G, N. Y. Vol. (v. 499); miner in Placer Co. '49; physician at Los Angeles '49 to '67, the date of his death. He was a famous gardener, and held the offices of postmaster and justice of the peace. Osbourne (James A.), 1846, Co. C, 1st U. S. dragoons (v. 336). Osburn, 1848, of McLean & O. furniture dealers at S.F. v. 678. Oseguera, in trouble 1799. i. 639. Osgood (Henry M.), 1847, Co. I, N.Y. Vol. (v. 499); at S. Luis Obispo '71-82, the date of his death.

Osio (Antonio María), nat. of L. Cal. and said to be of the family that was somewhat famous in very early times in connection with the gulf pearl fisheries. But for the record of offices held by him there is a remarkable lack of information about the man. He first appears as a candidate for treasurer in '27, and as in charge of the Mont. customs '28-30 as sub-comisario, and memb. of the dip. in '30-1. ii. 607; iii. 49-50, 63, 67, 73, 86, 136. In '31 he was contador in charge of the revenue at S.F., taking some slight part in the troubles with Victoria. iii. 187, 189, 376, 700. In '32-3, besides being still vocal of the dip., he was receptor of customs at Los Ang. and S. Pedro. iii. 216-17, 245-6, 377, 635, 641; still in charge of the revenues for some years later. iv. 82. In '35-7 he was a member of the Los Ang. ayunt., sometime síndico. Ment. in connection with the Apalátegui revolt and the vigilance committee, and taking an active part with the sureños against Alvarado. iii. 283, 285, 417-18, 481, 485, 487, 489, 496-8, 501-2, 506, 508-9, 516, 636. Notwithstanding his opposition to

Alvarado, the latter put him again in charge of the revenues at Mont. '38–42; and he was also in '39 vocal and sec. of the dip., partido elector, substitute member of congress, and grantee of Los Angeles Isl. in S.F. bay. iii. 584–5, 590, 672, 711; iv. 91, 96–7, 99, 210, 212, 339, 341. In '40–5 he was justice of the superior court. iii. 605; a partisan of Alvarado against Vallejo '42. iv. 282; grantee of Punta de los Reyes '43. iv. 672; and of S. José mission lands '46. v. 665; again substitute congressman '43. iv. 361; in '44 capt. of defensores, an opponent of Micheltorena, juez at S. Rafael, and of quinterna for gov. iv. 407, 409, 423, 460, 462–3, 530, 652, 676–7. In '46–7 he made a trip to Hono-lulu with wife and 5 children, taking no part in the troubles of those years. Soon after the change of flag he went to L. Cal., and in '58 seems to have been elected gefe político, though forced by ill health to resign. In '68 he lived at S. José del Cabo, and I have not found the date of his death, or any definite information about his family. Don Antonio María was a man of fair ability and education, and of excellent reputation for honesty. As a politi-cian he was somewhat too cautious and timid, disposed to seek safe ground on both sides of a controversy, and in an emergency to have an urgent call to some far-away spot. In his later years he wrote a *Historia de California*, a copy of which I obtained through the kindness of John T. Doyle, the original MS. being after '80 in possession of the writer's daughter in S.F. It is a work of considerable merit, valuable as a supplement to those of Vallejo, Alvarado, and Bandini, as presenting certain events from a different point of view; but like all writings of this class, it is of very uneven quality as a record of facts. None of them, nor all combined, would be a safe guide in the absence of the original records; but with these records they all have a decided value. O. (Antonio), celador of the Mont. custom-house '42–3. iv. 339; suspended for gambling.   O. (José de Jesus), 1847, in trade at S. Diego.   O. (Salva-dor), grantee of Todos Santos, Cosumnes, and Aguas Frias ranchos '41–4. ív. 463, 670.

Osman (Thomas), 1828, Engl. blacksmith, age 21, who deserted from a Fr. whaler at Todos Santos, L. Cal., and came up to S.Diego; ordered to depart '29.   Osmer (Chas H.), 1826, clerk with Beechey '26–7. iii. 121.   Osorno (Pedro), 1798, convict settler. i. 606.   Ossa (Vicente), sec. and regidor of the Los Ang. ayunt. '32–5. iii. 283, 635; in '38 síndico, favoring Alvarado's govt, age 30. iii. 565, 636; in '42–3 grantee of Providencia rancho. iv. 634–5; in '46 at Los Ang., and in '56 justice at Encino.   Ostein, 1817, deserter from Roquefeuil's vessel at S.F. ii. 288.   Ostrander (James), 1847, Co. H, N.Y. Vol. (v. 499); at Kinderhook, N.Y., '74.   Ostwald (August), 1847, Co. B, ditto; at Sac. '82.   Osuna (Juan María), born in Cal. before 1800; a soldier and corporal of the S.Diego comp., and later a settler. In '30 elector, taking part in the revolution of '31. iii. 50, 201, 544; in '35 alcalde. iii. 615; in '36–45 grantee of S. Dieguito. iii. 612, 557; iv. 621; in '39 juez de paz. iii. 584, 616; in '40–3, maj. and admin. of S.Diego mission. iii. 620; iv. 371, 619, 621, 624; in '46 juez de paz. v. 618. He died about '47 at the age of 60, his widow, Juliana Lopez, being cl. for S.Dieguito. His daughter Felipa, widow of J. M. Marron, gave me her *Recuerdos* in '78, as elsewhere noted; and also a collec-tion of her father's *Papeles Originales*.   O. (José Hilario), at Los Ang. '46. O. (Leandro), perhaps son of Juan M.; took part in the fight at S. Pascual '46. v. 329, 352.   O. (Miguel), settler at S. José, 1791; property destroyed by Ind. '95; alcalde in 1801. i. 683, 716; ii. 134.   O. (Ramon), com. de policía at S.Diego '36; collector of tithes '39; grantee of Valle de las Viejas '46. iii. 616–17; v. 619.   O. (Santiago), killed by Ind. at Pauma '46. v. 617.

Otondo (Felipe), sirviente at S. F. 1777. i. 297.   Ousley (Henry) 1846 (?), settler in Napa Val., where he still lived in '68–9; perhaps 'Owsley.'   Owen, 1848, of O. & Wright, liquor dealers at S.F.   O. (Isaac), 1848(?), Methodist preacher; d. S.F. '66.   Owens (Alex.), 1847, Co. E, N.Y.Vol. (v. 499).   O. (Edward), 1845, immig. from Or. in the McMahon-Clyman party with 4 others of the name, perhaps brothers. iv. 572–3; v. 526.   O. (Henry), 1845, ditto; went back to Or. '46.   O. (James), 1845, ditto; went to Or. '46.   O. (John), 1845, ditto; went to Or.   O. (James), 1847, Co. F, N.Y.Vol. (v. 499);

owner of S.F. lot; at S.F.'74.   O. (James), 1847, Co. D, Morm. Bat. (v. 469).
O. (Richard), 1845, nat. of Ohio, and member of Frémont's party. iv. 583; v.
6, 24, 80. From him Owens river and lake derive their name. He served as
capt. of Co. A, Cal. Bat., being in com. at S. Gabriel and somewhat prominently connected with Frémont's controversies. v. 361, 441, 445–6, returning
East with F., and being present as a witness at the court-martial in Washington. v. 453.   O. (Robert), 1847, Co. B, Morm. Bat. (v. 469).   O. (Thos),
1845, from Or. in McMahon party; prob. returned to Or. '46. iv. 572, 526.
Owney, 1847, negro witness at a S.F. trial.   Oxborough (C.), 1848, passp.
from Honolulu.   Oyagüe (J. M.), 1827, doubtful name of mr of the *Huascar*.
iii. 147.

Pace (James), 1847, lieut Co. E, Morm. Bat. v. 477; made an exped. against
the Ind. v. 489; capt. of a hundred on the return to Utah. v. 493.   P. (Wm
B. and Wilson C.), 1847, servants to officers of Morm. Bat.

Pacheco (Antonio), militiaman S.F. '37; in '41 at S. José, age 32, wife María
P. Soto, child. José Prudencio b. '26, José '33, Ventura '35.   P. (Bartolo),
Mex. soldier of S.F. comp. 1790, age 25, wife Soto, 2 children; Ind. exped.
of 1801. ii. 136; inval. of the comp. '19–40; grantee of S. Ramon, Contra
Costa, '33. iii. 713; at S. Mateo '35. · P. (Dolores), alcalde and juez de paz
at S. José '38–41, acting sub-prefect '41, and depositario '43. ii. 729–31; iv.
684, 685–6; grantee of Sta Rita in '39. iii. 713; in '43, age 45, nat. of Cal.,
wife Juana Pacheco (Alviso?), child Salvador b. '36. Again alcalde, juez,
and member of council in '46, and often mentioned in local annals. iv. 685;
v. 8–9, 57, 105, 129, 246, 662, 664. I have much of Pacheco's official and private corresp. He died about '58, and his widow in '75 at the age of 80.   P.
(Francisco), at S. José '41, age 33, nat. of Cal.; wife Paula Sepúlveda, child
Antonio b. '39.

Pacheco (Francisco Perez), 1819, Mex. carriage-maker who came with the
artillery detachment under Ramirez. In '24, for bravery in putting down the
Ind. revolt, he was promoted to brevet alférez. ii. 532, 536; being a memb. of
the dip. in '27. iii. 36; in '29 com. of the custom-house guard and for a time
of the post at Mont. under Solis. iii. 46–7, 50, 74, 136; depositario in '31.
iii. 672; signer of the Zamorano plan as brevet lieut '32. iii. 223, 672; treasurer and grantee of a rancho '33. iii. 673, 679; com. of the guard '33–4. iii.
376, 378; regidor in '35. iii. 673; grantee of Ausaymas and S. Felipe in '36–40.
iii. 711, 678; being at this time 45 years old, wife Feliciana Gonzalez, child.
Jacinta b. '14 in Mex., Isidoro '20 in Cal., Juan '23, Encarnacion '27, and
Isidora '30. In '37 he was arrested at S. Juan. iii. 513; his rancho was sacked
by Ind. '38; in '44 he was capt. of defensores and com. at S. Juan. iv. 407,
652, 654, 662; in '46 tithe collector. v. 637. He was claimant for S. Felipe. v.
678; and also for S. Justo and S. Luis Gonzaga, becoming one of the wealthiest rancheros of Mont. county, besides being always a man of good character
and much influence. His daughter, apparently the only one of his children
surviving him, was the wife of Mariano Malarin.   P. (Guillermo), soldier of
the S.F. comp. '44, age 40.

Pacheco (Ignacio), Mex. soldier of the S. F. comp. 1790, age 30, wife
Cantua, 1 child; before 1800 a settler at S. José, i. 716, where he was alcalde
in 1824. ii. 605.   P. (Ignacio), son of the preceding, b. at S. José 1808;
soldier of the S.F. comp. from '27, and sergt '37. iii. 323, 702; grantee in '40
of S. José rancho. iii. 713; and juez de paz at S. Rafael '45–6. iv. 667; v. 669.
He died on his rancho in '64. Portrait in *Marin Co. Hist.* His wife was María
Loreto Duarte, and his children Salvador b. '43, Gumesindo '52, Catalina '57,
Agustin F. '59, Juan F. '61, and Benjamin '63.   P. (Ignacio), soldier of the
S.F. comp. '28–9.   P. (Jordan), 1829, Portuguese laborer from S. Blas, at
Los Ang. '36, age 50. iii. 179.   P. (José Reyes), soldier at the Colorado pue-
blos 1780–1, not killed. i. 359.   P. (Juan Ign.), ment. in '48. v. 663.   P.
(Juan Sanchez), grantee of Arroyo de las Nueces, Contra Costa, '34. iii. 711.
P. (Lorenzo), in Ind. exped. '29. iii. 111; soldier of S.F. comp. '28–30; in '41
at S. José, age 37, wife Rafaela Soto, child. Nicolás b. '37, Inés '41; juez de

policía '43. iv. 685.   P. (Miguel), corporal of S.F. comp. 1790, age 36, wife Joséfa María Sanchez; inval. and settler at S. José 1797–1829. i. 716.   P. (Pablo), soldier of S.F. comp. '19–26, corp. '27–31, sergt '32–35. iii. 701; alf. of Sta. B. comp. '36. iii. 650.   P. (Rafael), convict settler 1791. i. 606.   P. (Rafael), soldier of the S.F. comp. '37–40; at Sonoma '44.   P. (Rafaela Soto de), grantee of S. Ramon, Contra Costa, '37. iii. 712.

Pacheco (Romualdo), 1825, Mex. sub-lieut of engineers, nat. of Guanajuato, who came with Gov. Echeandía as aide-de-camp, serving in that capacity for 2 years, and also as sec. of the com. gen. in '26–7 at S. Diego, making several exped. to the Colorado and elsewhere, serving as substitute member of the dip., and being often named in connection with military trials. ii. 508–9, 547, 549; iii. 13–14, 36, 61, 63, 102. In '27–8 he was ayudante de plaza and acting com. at Mont., persuading the revolting troops to return to their duty, and making a survey north of the bay to Ross. iii. 40, 66, 115. At the end of '28 he was transferred to Sta B., where he acted as comandante, being promoted to lieut in '29, and being imprisoned on one occasion by the revolting troops. ii. 571–2; iii. 78–84, 99. In '30 he was also com. at Mont. for a short time, ii. 608, and was recommended for promotion to be capt. of the S.F. comp. In '31 he was granted the use of a part of Simí rancho. iii. 656; but marching with a small part of his comp. to support Gov. Victoria, was killed in the fight near Los Angeles in Dec. of the same year. iii. 205–9, 214, 374, 650. Pacheco was a brave and skilful officer, intelligent, courteous, popular, and of unblemished character; a man against whom nothing was ever said, except that some Cal. officers complained of his too rapid promotion as a newcomer. In '29 he married Ramona, daughter of Joaquin Carrillo of S. Diego, being put under arrest for failure to comply with some formalities of military law. The widow married Capt. John Wilson of S. Luis Obispo, and still lives in '85. There were 2 sons b. in '30, '31, both of whom in '38 were sent to Honolulu to be educated, iv. 103, and remained there several years. Of one of them, Mariano, I have no later record than that he was a clerk for Wm H. Davis at S.F. in '43–4. The other son, Romualdo, born about a month before his father's death, after his return from the Sandw. Isl. spent some years on the *Sterling* and other vessels as supercargo's clerk, but in '48 settled on his mother's land in S. Luis Ob. From '53 he was almost constantly in office, holding the positions of assemblyman, state senator, county judge, county treasurer, brigadier-gen. of militia, lieut-governor, and acting governor; being also elected to congress but not admitted. In '78–82 he was a stock-broker in S.F.; and has since lived in Mexico and Texas to '85. His wife was Mary McIntire, married in '63, and there was one surviving child in '82. In respect of official positions, Gov. Pacheco has been more prominent since '48 than any other native Californian; and his record as a citizen, in respect of character, attainments, and social standing, has been a good one.

Pacheco (Salvador), son of Ignacio, b. S. F. '34, who still lived in Marin co. '80; wife Vicenta Saiz; 4 children.   P. (Salvio), soldier of Mont. comp. from about 1810, and corporal of the S. F. comp. '20–4, and perhaps to '29, being corp. of the escolta at S. José in '24. ii. 599; sec. of the S. José ayunt. '27, '29, '32, '34, and alcalde in '28. ii. 605, 730; suplente of the dip. '28–9, '35, '43. iii. '42–3, 111, 291, 293; iv. 361; alcalde '32. iii. 729; in '37–44 grantee of Monte del Diablo rancho. iii. 712; iv. 672; capt. of militia '37. iii. 732; surveyor of pueblo lands '38; iii. 730; grantee of Pozitos and partido elector in '39. iii. 712, 731; juez de paz '43. iv. 685–6, 362; suplente of the superior court '45. iv. 532; síndico '46. v. 662; accused of revolutionary intrigues '48. v. 663. In '41 he is named on the S. José padron as 48 years old, nat. of Cal., wife Juana Flores, child. Fernando b. '18, Padro Ign. '23, Salvador '24, Manuela '27, Concepcion '29. Don Salvio spent his life from '44 on the Mt Diablo rancho, on which the town of Pacheco bears his name, and died in '76 at the age of 83.   P. (Silveria), owner of a house at S. José '46. v. 378.   P. (Tomás), soldier of the S. F. comp. '26–32; in '34 elected regidor at S. José. iii. 730; in '37 alférez of militia. iii. 732; in '39 regidor. iii. 731; in '41 juez de paz. iv. 684; sec. of the juzgado '43. iv. 685; grantee of Potrero de los Cerritos '44. iv. 672.

Pacífico, Ind., executed at Purísima '24.   Packard (Albert), 1845, nat. of R. I., trader and lawyer, who came from Mazatlan. iv. 587; trading at Mont. and S. F. '46–8; still a resident of Sta B. in '76, having been city attorney and held other local offices.   P. (Henry), 1847, sergt Co. A, Morm. Bat. v. 495; in '81 at Springfield, Utah.   P. (P. W.), 1848, passp. from Honolulu.   P. (Thos), 1846, doubtful name at Sta B.   Packwood (Elisha), 1848, nat. of Va, who came overl. to Or. in '45 and by sea to Cal.; a miner '48–9 and trader at Mormon Isl. and Coloma, going East '49 and returning in '50; a stock-raiser till the floods of '61–2, then went to Or., where he died in '76. A son, Parrington P., was in the mines with his father, marrying Matilda Wardle while in Cal.   P. (Sam. T.), 1847, a cousin of Elisha, in Sta Clara Co. '48 and prob. the P. named at N. Helv. '47.   Pacomio (José), leader of neophytes in the revolt of '24. ii. 527, 532; in '36 a carpenter at Mont., age 40, wife María Guevia (?); also com. de policía. iii. 675.

Paddock (Joseph), 1830, mr of the *Whaleman.* iii. 149.   Padilla (Juan), occupant of Chupadero rancho, Mont., 1795. i. 683.   P. (Juan de Dios), trader at Los Ang. '39, age 40; also called captain. iii. 637.   P. (Juan Ne-pomuceno), Mex. barber; at S. José '43. iv. 356; in '44–5 kept a saloon at S. F., was lieut of defensores, alcalde, and grantee of Roblar de la Miseria and Tamales ranchos. iv. 666–7, 673–4. In '46 he was in com. of a party of Californians north of the bay at the time of the Bear revolt. v. 160–4, 680; in '55 a resid. of Los Ang., age 31.   P. (Julian), defender of Apalétegui at Los Ang. '35. iii. 285; accused of passing counterfeit coin. iii. 674; at Los Ang. '46.   P. (Macedonio), 1842, Mex. lieut in the batallon fijo '42–5, re-maining in Cal. after Micheltorena's departure. iv. 289, 513; v. 41.   P. (Mariano), nat. of Cal., b. about '10; at S. José '50–5.   P. (Vicente), soldier of S. F. comp. '27–9; at S. José '45–71.

Padrés (José María), 1830, nat. of Puebla; in '25 lieut of engineers and sec. of the com. gen. at Loreto; acting com. and sub-gefe político after Eche-andía's departure for Cal. In '30, having been promoted to lieut-col, he came to Cal. as ayudante inspector of the troops. ii. 607, 674; iii. 46, 52, 57, 190. In '31 he acted also as inspector of customs; as fiscal in the Rubio case; was the instigator of Echeandía's secularization decree; and was arbitrarily sent to Mex. by Gov. Victoria. iii. 184–5, 192–3, 197, 304–5, 376; iv. 160. In Mex. he devised the H. and P. colonization scheme, and returned to Cal. in '34 with the appointment of director of the colony in addition to his former position as inspector, which latter he soon resigned. In '35 with his associate Híjar he was sent to Mex. by Figueroa to be tried on a charge of revolutionary plots. iii. 259–69, 272–91, 383, 613, 652, 670. Nothing is known of his later career, though a man of the same name figures at Ures, Sonora, as a petty official in '44–8. Padrés was a man of remarkable energy, intelligence, and magnetism, a most radical republican in the Mexican sense of the term; and one whose influence was long felt in Cal., through his teachings to the young men who later controlled the country. So well did they learn their lesson, indeed, that in colony times they turned against their teacher when he seemed to have forgotten their claims to office.   Padushkin (Yakov), 1817, Russ. lieut who visited Cal. on the *Chirikof.* ii. 216, 283, 312–14, 373, 383.   Paele (Pika), 1847, owner of S.F. lot. v. 685.   Paez (Juan), 1542, probable author of Ca-brillo's *Relacion,* and perhaps one of the exped. i. 69.

Page (Hugh N.), 1844, com. of the U.S. *Levant* on the coast '44–6. iv. 567; v. 204, 224, 231.   P. (Rich. L.), 1847, lieut on the U.S. *Independence.*   P. (Thomas), 1847, sheriff in Sonoma dist. '47–8; cl. of the Cotate rancho '52. iv. 671.   Paine (Henry), 1820, named by Michael White as his cousin who aided in building a schr at Sta B. iii. 140.   Painter (Theodore), 1846, Co. E, Cal. Bat., enlisting at Sauzalito Oct. (v. 358).   Palacio (Francisco), 1848 (?), Mex. gefe político of L. Cal. who favored the Amer. during the war, and after the treaty came to Mont., where he died in '73.   Palacios (Geron. M.), 1602, capt. and cosmog. in Vizcaino's exped. i. 98.   P. (Lino), owner of land at Los Ang. '48.   Palani (Keani), 1847, owner of a S.F. lot. v. 678. Pallas (Cayetano), visiting padre at S. Diego 1791–1800. i. 655; perhaps a

274 PIONEER REGISTER AND INDEX.

Dominican from L. Cal. Palma, Yuma chief, 1774-82. i. 221-2, 260-1, 355-7, 361, 370. Palmer (Amasa), 1846, Co. C, 1st U.S. dragoons (v. 336). P. (Joel), 1848, a prominent citizen and official of Or., who came with the Or. miners and spent some months on the Yuba; author of a *Journal* of the trip overland to Or. P. (John), 1846, Co. C, 1st U.S. dragoons (v. 336). P. (Sam. R.), 1847, owner of a Benicia lot. v. 672. P. (Zemira), 1847, servant to officer of the Morm. Bat. (v. 469). Palo (Luis), companion of Brooks in the mines '48; son of a Mex. official at Mont. (?). Palomares (Francisco), son of Cristóbal; b. at Sta B. 1808; from '33 a resid. of S. José, being juez de campo in that year. iii. 729; and juez de policía in '46. v. 662. In the padron of '41 he is named with his wife Margarita Pacheco, and child. Benedita b. '30, María de Jesus '31, Rosario '32, Cristóbal '36, and Felipe '39. In '77 at S. José he gave me a long *Memoria* of his adventures, chiefly as an Ind. fighter—all of them strictly true as is to be hoped. iv. 75-6; v. 313, 566. P. (Francisco G.), at S.F. '38-9; grantee of Corral de Tierra. iii. 711. P. (Ignacio), juez de campo at Los Ang. '34, and regidor '35. iii. 635; in '37-40 grantee of Azuza and S. José ranchos. iii. 633; regidor and a prisoner in '38. iii. 555, 566, 636. He was juez de campo '40, juez de paz '41, elector '43, capt. of defensores '44, and suplente of the assembly '45. iii. 637; iv. 361, 540, 632. In '46 he took part in a movement against Flores, being also elected alcalde. v. 332-3, 626. He was a prominent ranchero in these and in later years, dying at Pomona in '82, at the age of about 70. P. (Jorge), com. of a volunteer cavalry comp. at Los Ang. '46. v. 51. P. (José), soldier and sergt of the Sta B. comp to 1806, from '10 a settler at Los Ang. ii. 117, 349; ment. in '17-19. ii. 354, 425; in '22-4 elector and member of the 1st diputacion. ii. 454, 462, 513, 559; iii. 7; síndico '26, and fiscal in the Fitch trial '30. ii. 560; iii. 142-4. P. (José), possibly same as preceding, or his son; sec. at Los Ang. '28-30. ii. 550-1; in '37 alférez, aiding Bandini in the capture of Los Ang. iii. 519. P. (José Fran.), see P. (Francisco). P. (J. M.), capt. of Los Ang. defensores '44. iv. 407. P. (Luis), soldier at Sta B. before '37. P. (Manuel), at S. José '44.

Palou (Francisco), 1773, Span. friar who was the founder of S.F. mission in 1776, and the successor of Junípero Serra as president in '84. He retired in '85 and became guardian of S. Fernando college. He is best known as the author of the *Vida de Junípero Serra* and *Noticias de las Californias*, standard works on the early mission history. He died about 1790 in Mex. See Biog. i. 473-6; notice of his works. i. 417-20; ment. i. 122-5, 154, 165, 171, 179, 184, 193-6, 198-206, 231-6, 246-7, 254, 280, 287-93, 297, 320, 382, 385-8, 398-407, 410-11, 416-17, 455, 458, 474, 476, 657; ii. 113, 571. Panano (Geo.), 1847, owner of a S.F. lot. v. 678. Panaud (Clement), 1846, Frenchman at S. Juan B. in '47, with a claim for damages by Frémont presented through the French consul. v. 615. He bought a mill in Salinas Valley from' Wm Anderson, and sold it in '48 to Capt. Cooper. In '53 he was claimant for lands in Sta Clara and Mont. counties. iv. 673; v. 637. Panella (José), 1797, Span. friar who served at S. Diego, retiring in 1803. Biog. ii. 107; ment. i. 379, 382, 564, 577, 654-5; ii. 159. Panto, Ind. chief at S. Pascual, S. Diego Co., who rendered much aid to the Cal. authorities in keeping the Ind. quiet; also aiding Stockton in '46-7 with horses, etc., never paid for by the U.S. govt. His claim and that of his people to their land at S. Pascual seems, however, to have been respected by the govt and landsharks down to about the period of his death in '73. P. (José Pedro), 1810, Span. friar whose missionary service was at S. Diego, where he died in '12, being poisoned by his neophyte cook in return for cruelty. ii. 344-5, 107, 159-60, 394. Pantoja (Francisco), regidor of Los Ang. '37. iii. 509, 636; at Sta Gertrudis rancho '39, age 43. P. (Juan), 1782, an officer on the *Princesa*, whose map of S. Diego is copied in i. 455-6, 378. P. (Matias), at S. Gabriel '46.

Pardo, 1831, said to have come from N. Mex. in the Wolfskill party. iii. 387. P. (Roberto), Mex. or Ind. sergt of the Mazatlan comp., at Mont. as early as '20; in '24 posted at Purísima. ii. 533; in '33-4 engaged in otter-hunting (?). iii. 394. From '38 or earlier he was alférez of the Sta B. comp., being acting lieut and comandante '42-5. iii. 566, 589, 630, 651; iv. 282, 641. His wife was Candelaria Cañizares. Parish (De Witt C.), 1847, in S.F. letter list. Park (James), 1847, Co. B, Morm. Bat. (v. 469); reënl.; at Cedar Val., Utah, '81.

Park (Thomas B.), 1826, nat. of Mass., and sup. of the *Harbinger* '26-8. iii. 147, 176. From '35 he was a resident of Cal., coming prob. on the *Alert*, acting as sup., or agent, of the *California* and other vessels from '36, and succeeding Alfred Robinson in charge of the Boston firm's business. iv. 101, 117; iii. 623, 657; often named in commercial records from '39. He was naturalized in '44, aiding the Californians against Micheltorena, and acting as sup. of the *Sterling* in '44-6. iv. 568. He was a man of some education and much business ability, though thought to lack the 'push' displayed by some of his rivals, being addicted to drink and neglecting his business in the later years. He died at Sta B. about '50, leaving a wife in Mass. Parker, 1840, a clergyman on the *Alciope* for Honolulu. iv. 100; prob. B. W. Parker, a Sandw. Isl. missionary who came with a letter of introd. to Larkin. P. (Edward), 1847, Co. E, N.Y.Vol. (v. 499). P. (John), 1840, Engl. deserter from the *Sulphur*, who became a lumberman at S. Antonio; at Bodega '41. P. (Lewis), 1847, Co. E, N. Y. Vol. (v. 499); d. before '82. P. (Robert), 1834, at Mont.

Parker (Robert A.), 1847, nat. of Boston, and sup. of the *Mt Vernon*, introd. by Mellus to Larkin as a 'tough customer'; owner of a S.F. lot and member of the council. v. 648. In '48 he had an adobe store on Dupont St., and from July was keeper of the City Hotel. v. 680-1; being in '49-51 keeper of the famous Parker House. In '54 he lived at Crescent City, but later went to L. Cal., dying at S. Quintin in '65 at the age of 45. His widow died in S.F. '83, age 61, leaving 5 children. P. (Wm C.), 1847, asst surg. of N.Y.Vol. v. 503, 511, 513; owner of S.F. lots. v. 654; surgeon of the S.F. guards '49; also engaged in trade, and named by Colton as owner of New York of the Pacific '49. He lived in S.F. to '76, and in Oakland till '82 or later.

Parks (David), 1848, overl. immig. bound for Or., but turned from his way by reports of gold in Cal.; mined on the Yuba, gave his name to Parks Bar, and went to N. Orleans in '49 with $80,000 in gold-dust. His son David remained in Cal. and became a citizen of Marysville, as did John, who built the 1st hotel at M. P. (Wm), 1846, deserter from U. S. service, for whom Capt. Morrison offered $50 reward. P. (Wm A.), 1848, in S.F. list of letters. Parmo (Luigi), 1834, Ital. sailor at Mont., age 29. Parodi (Nicolás), 1841, Ital. sailor from Salvador on the *Jóven Carolina* as part owner of the cargo.

Parr (Charles), 1846, Engl. overl. immig. with his parents, who settled at Sta Clara in '47, and in '81 still lived as a stock farmer in Almaden township, with wife T. García, and 10 children. P. (Chas H.), 1846, brother of Chas, nat. of Iowa, overl. immig., who died in Sta Clara Co. '77, leaving a widow, Mary A. Kenny, and 2 children. P. (Jonathan), 1846, father of the preceding, who settled in Sta Clara Co., where he died in '67 at Los Gatos, leaving 6 children. P. (Wm J.), 1846, son of Jonathan; nat. of Ohio; farmer near S. José '47-76. Párraga (Francisco), 1803, com. of the *Concepcion*. ii. 19. Parreña (Santiago), 1810, agent for Bonaparte for N. Mex. and Cal.; prob. not in Cal. ii. 88.

Parrilla (Leon), 1793, lieut of the Monterey comp. '93-5, retired for incompetency. Biog. i. 634, 678. Parrish (Joseph), 1845, mid. on the U.S. *Portsmouth*, acting lieut in Co. F, Stockton's battalion, '46-7. v. 385. Parron (Fernando), 1769, Span. friar, third of the missionaries to reach Cal., and founder of S. Diego mission, where he served till his retirement in '71 on account of illness. i. 120, 128, 136-8, 164, 167, 176, 178. Parrott (Enoch G.), 1846, lieut on the U.S. *Congress* '46-8, who served in the war of '61-5 as commander; as commodore was in com. at Mare Isl. '71; rear-admiral '73; and died '79 in N.Y. A nat. of N. H., b. '15. P. (John), 1845, nat. of Va, for many years engaged in trade on the Mex. coast, and U.S. consul at Mazatlan in '45–6, rendering valuable aid to the naval officers in matters relating to the occupation of Cal. iv. 302; v. 13. His first visit to Cal. was in connection with his grand smuggling scheme which ended somewhat disastrously with the wreck of the *Star of the West.* iv. 560, 568, 587. I have many letters written by, to, and about him at that time. After the gold discovery he came with his family to S.F., where he was a shipping merchant to '59, and later a banker and capitalist down to his death in '84 at the age of 73. He was famous for his uniformly successful investments and for never taking any risks, his caution and conservatism being in marked contrast with the prevalent spirit of the times. He left a widow and several children and grandchildren. Parsons (Alonzo P.), 1847, Co. B, N.Y.Vol. (v. 499).   P. (J. H.), 1847, perhaps ditto; not on roll.   Parvin (John B.), 1847, Co. A, ditto; in Nev. '74; at Monticello, Minn., '82; in N.Y. '84.

Pascal (John H.), 1848, mate of the *Rhone;* went to the mines, and later settled on a farm near Ione City, where he died in '72.   Pascual (Juan), 1602, piloto in Vizcaino's exped. i. 98.   P. (Mateo José), 1818, negro of Bouchard's exped.; remained in Cal. ii. 237, 241, 393.   Pask (Francis G.), 1847, artificer in Co. F, 3d U. S. artill. (v. 518).   Pasos (Manuel de Dios), 1822–4, Portuguese nat. of Brazil, who in '29 lived in the Mont. dist, aged 23, single, and a resid. since '24; in '36 at Sta B., a catholic hunter of 'medium' character; in '45 at Los Ang., naturalized, and 23 years a resident. ii. 478.   Pastor (Ignacio), grantee of Milpitas '38. iii. 677.

Paterna (Antonio), 1771, Span. friar who served at S.Gabriel, S.Luis Ob., and Sta B., where he died in '93. Biog. i. 672; ment. i. 173, 176, 178, 181, 189, 193–6, 223, 299, 388, 411, 423, 469, 576.   Patricio, a leader of the neophyte revolt '24. ii. 527.   Patron (Felipe), soldier of S. F. comp. '39–42.   Patry (Peter), 1845, at S.José according to testimony in later litigation.

Patterson, 1846, of P. & Foster who had a Cal. claim of $50 (v. 462); also a P. ment. at Mont. '48; and one in Ione Valley.   P. (Mrs Christina), 1846, overl. immig. whose husband died on the journey; at N. Helv. and in S. Joaq. Val. '47; married Ed. Robinson, and was still living in '78.   P. (F. E.), 1846, at S.Diego.   P. (G.), 1848, passp. from Hon.   P. (Geo.), 1840, Irish sailor who left the *Columbia* at S.F., worked in the redwoods, and in '44 entered Sutter's employ. iv. 120; apparently the man named in *Yuba Co. Hist.* as having occupied a rancho on the Yuba in '45–8; mining in '48–9; later a resid. of S.F., where in '72 he related for me his *Adventures.*   P. (Mrs Isabella), 1844, overl. immig. of the Stevens party with several children, being the daughter of Hitchcock of the same party. iv. 445. In '45 she is named in the Branciforte padron as a widow, age 35; child. Isaac b. '31, Tedra (?) '32, Margaret '33, and Helen '38. A daughter, Mary, was married in Aug. '45 by Larkin to James Williams. iv. 587.   P. (John Alex.), 1847, Co. D, N.Y.Vol. (v. 499); in the mines '48, and later kept a saloon at S.F. acc. to *Swan;* in '49 treasurer of the Regulators, elected to the constit. convention, and to the legislature. *Annals of S.F.;* in '50 at S.José. Swan says he died about this time.   P. (John W.), 1823, nat. of Mass.; resid. of S.F. '67; died at S.F. '79 at the age of 73; arr. '23 acc. to Soc. Cal. Pion. rolls and the *Alta* of '67; perhaps a sailor who touched the coast at the date named and came back later.   P. (Nath. G.), 1846, nat. of Tenn., and overl. immig.; served in Cal. Bat. '46–7 (v. 358); miner in '48; in '50 kept a stable at Stockton; finally settled at Livermore, where he lived in '82 with wife Kate Simpson and 2 children Chas T. and Susan (Mrs Davis). *Alam. Co. Hist.*, 959. P. (Wm), 1846, saloon-keeper with Thos Smith at S.F. '46–8. v. 685.

Pattie (James Ohio), 1828, a young Kentuckian trapper from N. Mex., who spent over a year in Cal., part of the time in jail at S. Diego, and had his *Personal Narrative* of adventures published a few years later. See iii. 162–72; ii. 543, 548, 551, 556, 567, 611, 616, 651; iii. 74, 82–3, 134, 139, 171; iv. 263. I have an autog. letter written by P. in Mex. '30, on his way from Cal.; and he is said to have revisited S. Diego after '50.   P. (Sylvester), 1828, father of James O., who died in prison at S. Diego. iii. 162–5, 178.   Pattison (T.), 1841, mid. on the U.S. *St Louis.* Patton (A. Gwinn), 1841, overl. immig. of the Bartleson party, who went back to Mo. in '42. iv. 270, 275, 342. P. (David), 1846, Fauntleroy's dragoons (v. 232, 247).

Paty (Henry), 1837, nat. of Mass. and merchant at Hon. from '33, of the firm Henry Paty & Co. I have his letters from '34, and he visited Boston in '34–5. In '37 he came to Cal. to sell the *Clarion,* which became the *California.* iii. 531; iv. 101, 106, 117–18. In '38–40 he came again on the *Don Quixote,* owned by his firm, commanding also the *Morse* and perhaps the *Ninfa* in '39–40. iv. 103, 105. In '41 on the way from Valparaiso to Hon. he became demented on account of the ravages of small-pox on board, and cut his own throat with a razor. The firm, after his death, consisted of his brothers John and Wm, and Eli Southworth. P. (John), 1837, brother of Henry, who came on the Haw. schr *Iolani.* iv. 104, 117–18. In '38–48 he made one or more trips each year between Cal. and Hon. as master of the *Don Quixote,* and his name often appears in commercial records, many of his original letters being in my possession. iii. 570; iv. 25, 103, 314, 375, 512, 559, 565; v. 268, 577, 579, 681, 683. Capt. P. owned land at S.F., and his firm of P. & Mc-Kinley kept a store there in '43–5; he rendered occasional aid to the govt, especially in carrying away Micheltorena and his cholos; he was often engaged in smuggling operations, but was known to everybody and liked by all. His wife Mary and daughter came to Cal. occasionally from '42. From '46 he was senior captain, or a kind of commodore, in the Hawaiian navy. After '48 Capt. P. continued his voyages, celebrating in '65 or '66 the 100th trip between Cal. and the Islands; and he died at his Hawaiian home in '68 at the age of 61. His widow visited S. Diego about '80, one of her daughters being the wife of Lieut Benson, U.S.A., and another the wife of a lieut in the navy, living at Vallejo. Capt. Paty was famous for his skill and good luck as a navigator; and few in this list have left so enviable a reputation for business integrity and kindness of heart.

Paul (John A.), 1848 (?), German broker who committed suicide at Oakland in '83. Paulding (Charles), 1833, at Sta B. P. (Joseph), 1832, nat. of Md, trapper and cabinet-maker, who came from N. Mex. in the winter of '32–3, iii. 388, 408, and distinguished himself by making the 1st two billiard-tables in Cal. He was still at Los Ang. in '35, complaining of unjust imprisonment by the alcalde. He went to N. Mex., but returned during the flush times of '48–52, and after a residence of some years in Sonora returned finally to Los Ang., where he died in '60 at the age of 50; perhaps his name should be written 'Pawlding.' Paulet (Lord Geo.), 1843, com. of H. B. M. S. *Carysfort.* iv. 564. Paulina (H.), 1848, passp. from Hon.

Payeras (Mariano), 1796, Span. friar who served chiefly at Purísima, being also president or prefect of the missionaries from 1815 to his death in '22. One of the ablest and most prominent of the Fernandinos. Biog. ii. 489–90; ment. i. 500, 577, 686; ii. 106–7, 123-4, 152, 159, 235–6, 255, 258, 265, 297, 316, 328, 330–2, 335, 338, 351, 366, 394, 397–412, 414, 416, 418, 431–8, 442, 451–2, 458–9, 461, 463–5, 479–80, 496, 562, 571, 580, 587, 591, 597, 631, 643, 655, 657; iii. 11. Paymer (Phil.), 1845, at Sutter's Fort. Payne (R. K.), 1845, immig. from Or. in the McMahon-Clyman party. In the same party was a widow Payne—daughter of Owen Sumner, with 3 children—and the two were married at Sutter's Fort in Feb. '46, prob. returning to Or. or to the East a little later in the year. iv. 572; v. 526. Payson (Sam.), 1878, Co. B, N.Y.Vol. (v. 499).

Peace (James), 1838 (?), nat. of the Orkney Isl., of Scotch and Danish parentage, who in '75–84—and finally in the *S. F. Bulletin* of July 18, '85—claims to have deserted from the H. B. Co.'s ship *Nereid* at S.F. in '18. This vessel came to the N.W. coast in '36, and to Cal. for the 1st time in '38, which I have little doubt was the date of P.'s arrival. The 1st definite record of him is when he was exiled to S Blas in '40 and came back in '41. iv. 18, 33, 119. That he is not heard of in '38-9 is natural enough, and indeed, Brown and Weeks do mention him vaguely about those years; but that he could have lived here in '18–39 without a trace in the records is very unlikely, especially if, as he says,

he married a Valencia in '35, to say nothing of the fact that if he had had a
native wife he would not have been exiled. He worked as a lumberman and
mechanic, and is named in the S.F. padron of '44 as a Scotchman, age 45. For
about 30 years, from '47-8, he lived on a farm at Halfmoon Bay; but since
'78 has navigated S.F. bay in a sloop, earning a living by catching fish and
clams for the S. Mateo Co. market down to '85.   Peacock (John), 1846,
Fauntleroy's dragoons (v. 232, 247).   Peale (T. R.), 1841, naturalist in the
U. S. ex. ex. iv. 241-3.
        Pearce (Geo.), 1846, Co. C, 1st U. S. dragoons. v. 341; nat. of Ky, b. '22.
After his discharge he became a trader at Stockton and Sonoma in '49, also
lobbyist in the 1st legislature; miner and trader in the northern counties '50-
1; deputy sheriff at Sonoma '53-5; and from '55 a lawyer at Petaluma, being
state senator in '63-7. He married Coulter Brown, and was still living in '80
with 3 children—prob. also in '85. Portrait in Sonoma Co. Hist., 48; also biog.
sketch, including his recollections of S. Pascual in Id. 580-5.   P. (Wm),
1844, mate on the Sterling, in care of the consul; d. at Mont. '45.   Peard
(Geo.), 1826, lieut on H. B. M. S. Blossom. iii. 121.   Pearl (Joseph), 1846,
Co. C, 1st U. S. dragoons (v. 336).   Pearsall (Sam. W.), 1847, Co. B, N.Y.
Vol. (v. 499); at Moquelumne Hill '82.   Pearse (John), 1824, carpenter on
the Rover.   Pearson (David C.), 1848, at Benicia.   P. (Ephraim), 1847, Co.
B, Morm. Bat. (v. 469).   P. (Geo.), 1847, Co. F, 3d U. S. artill. (v. 518).
P. (John B.), 1846, Co. C, 1st U.S. dragoons (v. 336).   P. (J.W.), 1848, passp.
from Hon.   P. (Robert H.), 1848 (?), nat. of Me, who brought the Oregon to
Cal., and commanded many steamers down to '64; d. at S.F. '68, age 46.   P.
(W.), 1848, passp. from Hon.   P. (W. S.), 1848, at Benicia.   Pease (Sam.),
1826, sailor on the Rover.   Peasley (Nesmith A.), 1847, Co. A, N.Y. Vol.
(v. 499); d. S. F. '51,
        Peck (Chas L.), 1847, Co. B, N. Y. Vol. (v. 499); d. at Mont. '54.   P.
(Chauncey L.), 1847, corp. Co. B, ditto.   P. (Ed. M.), 1847, Co. D, Morm.
Bat. (v. 469); in Utah '82.   P. (Isaac), 1847, Co. C., ditto; reënl.   P. (Sher-
man), 1833, trader at Hon. who visited Cal. in '33-5 as sup. of the Volunteer
and other vessels, representing J. C. Jones. I have much of his corresp. with
Cal. traders '34-8, and he may have visited Cal. on other occasions.   P.
(Thorit), 1847, Co. C, Morm. Bat. (v. 469); reënl. as corporal.   Peckham (R.
F.), 1846, nat. of R. I., deserting from the whaler Cabinet at S.F. He worked
as lumberman, soldier, farmer, clerk, miner, carpenter, and trader, changing
his occupation and residence half a dozen times a year—but finding time to
marry and study law—until '51, from which time to '70 he practised law at
Sta Cruz and S. José, serving also as district attorney and county judge. In
later years he established a woollen mill at S. José, where he still lived in '81
with wife Ann Smith, and 9 children. Portrait in Sta Clara Co. Hist., 80.
        Pedraza, deserter from a galleon 1791. i. 484.   Pedro y Gil (Rafael),
1774, Span. guarda-almacen at S. Diego '74-81. Biog. i. 451; ment. i. 227,
253.   Pedrorena (Miguel), 1837, Span. sup. of the S. Amer. brigs Delmira
and Juan José '37-40, being also agent for McCall & Co. of Lima. iv. 103-4;
iii. 727; also on the coast '42-3; owner of S.F. lots '45-6. iv. 669; v. 684; had
a claim against the govt for $3,169; declined an appointment to present charges
against Micheltorena. iv. 522. From '45 his home was at S. Diego, where he
married María Ant. Estudillo, being the grantee of S. Jacinto Nuevo in '46,
and his wife of El Cajon in '45. v. 619; iv. 620-1. He strongly favored the
cause of the U. S. in '46-7, acting as juez de paz, as Stockton's aide, with rank
of capt. in the Cal. Bat., and in '47-8 as collector of customs. v. 286, 329,
360, 385, 572, 575, 618-19. In '49 he represented S. Diego in the constit. convention, being one of the most popular and influential members of the Spanish
race. He died in '50, leaving a son, Miguel, and two daughters, Elena and
Isabel, who inherited his large estate, and are still living, I think, in '85.
Don Miguel was of a good Span. family, one of his brothers holding a high
official position at Madrid; and he was himself an intelligent, scholarly man,
of excellent character, who by his courteous affability made friends of all who
knew him.   Peed (John), 1846, sailmaker U. S. N., and acting capt. Co. G,

Stockton's naval battalion '46-7; prob. 'Recd.' Peguero (Alonso Estévan), 1602, capt. in Vizcaino's exped. i. 98. P. (Mariano), sent to Mex. for complicity in the Solis revolt '29-30. iii. 68-71, 85.

Peirce (Henry Augustus), 1828, nat. of Mass., b. 1808, who went to Honolulu in '25, and thence on the same vessel, the *Griffon*, com. by his brother, to the N.W. coast as clerk, touching at S.F. on the return in the autumn of '28. iii. 178. From that time for 14 years he was a trader at Honolulu, being a member of the firm P. & Brewer. Some of his original letters and much of the firm's corresp. are in my possession. Meanwhile he made many voyages as master to China, Kamchatka, and S. America. In '37 he went on the *Peru* from N.Y. to Honolulu, and returned via Lima and overland to Buenos Aires. In '38 he married Susan R. Thompson, whose brother Joseph P. is named in this register. In '39 he went to the Islands as part owner of the *Morse*, and in '41-2 came again to Cal. as mr and owner of the *Maryland*, going from Cal. to Mazatlan and thence overland to Vera Cruz. I have his original *Journals* of voyages in '39-42, including the visit to Cal. iv. 209, 224-5, 235, 250, 300, 348-9, 567, 640, 665. Details of Capt. P.'s subsequent adventures are too complicated for presentation here, but hardly one of the pioneers registered in this list has had so varied an experience. In '42-9 he was a Boston merchant trading with Pacific ports; and in '49 revisited Cal. on the *Montreal*, making extensive and unfortunate purchases of land at Sauzalito and the Islands, and in '50-61 resuming his business at Boston, which was nearly ruined by the war of '61-5. Most of his remaining wealth was lost in a Miss. cotton plantation in '66-7; and in '69 Peirce was made U.S. minister at the Hawaiian Isl., making the trip by rail to S.F. He held this position till '77, and after a brief term as Hawaiian minister of foreign affairs he came in '78 to S.F., where he has since resided down to '85, being in a sense the oldest living pioneer. Besides the journal mentioned, I have several MS. contributions from Mr P. named in my list of authorities. Portrait in *Contemp. Biog.*, ii. 180. His wife resides in Mass. since '70; he has a son and daughter; and is a great-grandfather. (Capt. Peirce died a few days after the above was written, in July '85.) P. (Hardy), 1838, brother of Henry A., who, being mate on a Hon. vessel, died suddenly at Sta B., age 23. iv. 119, 224. P. (Marcus T.), 1828, brother of Henry A., and mr of the *Griffon*. iii. 147. P. (Wm), 1842, mate of the *Sterling* '42-4; died at Mont. '45. iv. 453.

Pelham (Matthew), 1834, a Dane at Mont. iii. 412. Pell (E. Ward), 1846, one of the Mormon colony, with wife and 2 daughters. v. 546; an elder and counsellor, but excommunicated on the voyage. He lived with Robert Ridley in '46. v. 678; and in '47 he was sheriff and inspector of hides and tallow, owning a S.F. lot. v. 648. He still lived to testify in land cases in '65. His daughter Hettie C. married John H. Brown in '46, soon leaving him and becoming apparently Mrs Green. The other daughter is mentioned as the wife of Ed Cohea. Pellan (Antonio), neophyte alcade at S. Diego 1799. i. 655.

Peña (Antonio), 1825, Span. artilleryman, age 50 in '28; prob. sent to Mex. in '30. iii. 51, 85. P. (Antonio), soldier of S.F. comp. '35, sergt '36, alf. '37. iii. 702. P. (Cosme), 1834, Mex. lawyer who came with the H. and P. colony with an appointment as asesor; prominent in Alvarado's revolt of '36; subsequently govt sec., and appointed prefect of the southern district in '39, but not approved in Mex. He left Cal. soon after '39. Biog. iii. 594; ment. iii. 267, 285, 415, 440, 452, 461, 469, 475, 487, 523-5, 585-9, 594, 639-40, 670, 675; iv. 72. He left 2 daughters in Cal., Cármen b. '24, and Cesaría '28. P. (Demetrio), 1840, son of Juan Felipe, with whom he came from N. Mex.; a settler in Solano Co. '41-79; wife Inés Berreyesa, and 6 surviving children in '79. P. (Eustaquio), soldier at Sta B. about '32. P. (Francisco), soldier of the 1st exped. 1769-74; ment. '75-6; killed at the Colorado pueblos '81. i. 250, 303-4, 363. P. (Gerardo), soldier of the 1st exped. '69-74. P. (José), artilleryman and teacher at S.F. '22, elector '30, teacher at Sta Clara '37-41, owner of a S.F. lot '39, grantee of Rincon de S. Francisquito '41, retired soldier as teniente de premio from '44. Possibly more than one of the name. ii. 584, 591; iii. 50, 705, 728; iv. 408, 672, 682. In '41 he is named as a Mex. teacher, age

64, in the S. José padron. His wife was Gertrudis Lorenzana, age 56; she died in '65 at the reputed age of 107 (really 80). P. (José Ant.), soldier of the 1st exped. '69-70; of the S. Juan Cap. guard '76. i. 303. P. (José German), grantee of Tzabaco rancho, Sonoma, '43; his heirs were claimants. iv. 674.

Peña (Juan Felipe), 1840, N. Mex. immigrant with wife and 6 children, who with Vaca settled in Solano Co. '41, and was the grantee of the Putah rancho in '43. iv. 672. He died in '63 at Laguna Val., age 73. P. (Luis), soldier of the 1st exped. '59-74; at Simí rancho 1802. ii. 111. P. (Manuel), soldier of the S.F. comp. '28-34; ment. in '29. iii. 111; in '41 at S. José, age 36, wife Guadalupe Mesa, child. Dolores b. '28, Inés '31, Cármen '32, Encarnacion '33, Hilaria '34, Rosario '38, Paulino '40. P. (Narciso Ant.), juez at Sta Clara '43. iv. 683, 685. P. (Ricardo), land-owner at S. Juan Cap. '41. iv. 626. P. (Romualdo), musician of S.F. comp. '39. P. (Tomás), 1772, Spanish friar who founded and served long at Sta Clara, retiring in '94, holding later the office of guardian at S. Fernando college, and dying in 1806. Biog. i. 722-3; ment. i. 189, 195-6, 227, 289, 291-2, 295, 297, 304-5, 351, 388, 401-3, 474, 476, 484, 496, 511, 576, 578, 581, 631, 720; ii. 166. Peña, see also ' Piña.' Penaud, see ' Panaud.'

Pendleton, 1844, mr of the *Benj. Morgan.* P. (Geo. A.), 1847, lieut Co. D, N.Y.Vol. v. 504. In Tuolumne Co. '49-54; d. in '71 at S. Diego, where he had been county clerk for 14 years. Penhallow (Dav. P.) 1837, mr of the *Alert* '37-9. iv. 68, 101; may have visited Cal. earlier as mate or sup., since on the roll of the Soc. Cal. Pion. '22 is the date of his arrival. In '47 he writes from Honolulu. Pennie (A.), 1848, passp. from Hon. Penny (Moses H.), 1847, Co. A, N.Y.Vol. (v. 499); went to S.C. '50. Penrose (Geo. F.), 1847, lieut Co. A, N.Y.Vol. v. 503, 511; also quartermaster; d. Mont. after '50. Peoples (Geo.), 1847, sailor on the *Ohio;* later a circus-rider; d. in Texas '67. P. (John H.), 1848, chief of a party for relief of snowed-in immig. from Or.; drowned later. Peotrowski (R. K.), 1844, doubtful date; perhaps '54; d. in France '83. Newspapers. Pepper (Thos), 1833, said to have been at S.José. *Hall; Sta Clara Co. Hist. Atlas;* doubtful. iii. 409. Pera (Alexis), 1844, of Frémont's party; did not reach Cal. iv. 437.

Peralta (Antonio María), son of Luis; in '35 at S. Mateo; in '37 alf. of militia at S.F., also elector. iii. 701, 705; in '41 named in the S.José padron (living at S. Antonio rancho), age 39, wife María Ant. García, child. Antonia María b. '32, Guadalupe '33, Fernando '34, Rita '37, Crisanto '38, Inés '40; in '46 juez of the contra costa. v. 662. In '52 he was the claimant with his 3 brothers for S. Antonio. P. (Domingo), son of Luis; in '27 síndico at S.José. ii. 605; in '33 grantee of Cañada del Corte de Madera, Sta Clara. iii. 711; for which, as for S.Ramon and his share of S. Antonio, he was claimant. iii. 713. In '41 named in S.José padron, age 47, wife —— García, child. Angela b. '25, Juan '24, María Ant. '29, Francisca, '36, Ramon '38, Loreto (?) '39. His residence was at Temescal on the S. Antonio rancho. P. (Felipe), at Los Ang. '46. P. (Francisco), soldier of the S. F. comp. '38-9. P. (Gabriel), Mex. corporal of the S.F. comp., at Sta Clara and S.José; an inválido settler at S. José from '90. i. 297, 306, 312, 478. His wife was Francisca J. Valenzuela, and his daughter Gertrudis (i. 312) married Nicolás Berreyesa in '79. P. (Ignacio), son of Luis b. 1791; corp. of S.F. comp. '19-29; elector at S.F. '27, '35, '43. ii. 592; iii. 577, 704; iv. 361; juez of contra costa '39, '41. iii. 705; iv. 684; in '43 supl. of the junta. iv. 361. Named in the S. José padron '41, age 51; wife Rafaela Sanchez, child. Francisco b. '22. Miguel '25, Joaquin '27, Luis M. '31, José de Jesus '33, Juan '35, Gabriel '39, Rafael '40, Lodrivina (?) '29, María Ant. '37. He was claimant for a part of S. Antonio in '53. P. (José), at S.José '17. ii. 425; at S.Mateo '35; of S.F. militia '37; murdered '38. iii. 705. P. (Juan), named in '46. v. 162. P. (Juan José), at S.José 1783. i. 350; inválido at Branciforte '99; comisionado 1811. ii. 390. P. (Juan P.), at Los Ang. '39, age 31.

Peralta (Luis), nat. of Sonora, who probably came as a boy with Anza's exped. of 1776, enlisting in 1782, being a corp. of the S.F. comp. from '91 or earlier, and in com. of the S. José mission guard in 1798-1800. i. 494-5, 556,

PERALTA—PEREZ. 281

598, 716. From 1801 he was a sergt, taking part in several exped. against the Ind., and from 1807 comisionado in charge of S. José pueblo. He showed good qualities as a soldier, and was several times recommended for promotion to alf., but failed to secure it. ii. 35, 126, 132, 134, 138, 370, 378, 584, 604. His wife was María Loreto Alviso, and the birth of a son Ignacio is recorded in 1791. In 1820 he obtained a grant of the S. Antonio rancho, including the sites of the later Oakland and Alameda, which was occupied by his sons perhaps before '25, the rancho buildings—the first erected in Alameda county except at mission S. José—being at S. Antonio, later known as Brooklyn and East Oakland. ii. 375, 594, 664, 712. Peralta retained his position as comisionado till 1822, and his place on the comp. rolls as active sergt to '26, and as inválido to '41; meanwhile continuing to live at S. José and serving as elector, treasurer, and perhaps juez in '30-3. ii. 606; iii. 50, 729. In '41 he appears on the padron as 87 years old, his daughters Josefa and Guadalupe—aged 46 and 23 —living with him. Other daughters were Teodora—grantee of Buacocha, Marin '46, v. 670—and Trinidad. In '42 he divided his S. Antonio rancho between his sons Antonio M., Ignacio, Vicente, and Domingo, and died in '51 at the age of 97. The great value of the lands granted to Peralta, the claim that his daughters were entitled to a share of the property, the alleged insanity of Don Luis at the time of making his will, and various rascalities practised by the land-sharks in later years on some of the heirs, gave rise to complicated litigation which can hardly be regarded as at an end in '85. P. (Miguel), militiaman at S.F. '37. P. (Nicolás N.), at Sta Ana rancho, Los Ang. '39, age 38. The Santiago de Sta Ana rancho had been granted to a Peralta with Yorba in 1809. ii. 112, 172. P. (Pedro), soldier of the S. F. comp. 1785, married a daughter of Lieut Grijalva. ii. 104; corp. of the escolta at Sta Cruz 1797-1800; inválido corp. on the comp. rolls 1819-32. P. (Sebastian), soldier of the S.F. comp. '19-22; in '33 regidor at S. José, making an exped. against the Ind. iii. 359, 390, 394, 729; in '40 grantee of Rinconada de los Gatos and maj. at Sta Clara. iii. 712, 728; in '41 a widower, age 48; in '46 quarrel with Frémont. v. 8, 9. P. (Vicente), son of Luis, whose home was at Temescal on the subdivision of his father's rancho; sergt of militia at S.F. '37; in '41 age 29, wife Encarnacion Galindo, child Guadalupe. In '46 he was one of the Bears' prisoners at Sutter's Fort. v. 124, 128, 298. Percival (John), 1845 (?), com. of the U.S. *Constitution.* iv. 564. Perdu (Joseph L.), 1846, one of the Chino prisoners wounded. v. 313-14; at Mont. '47; Cal. claim $1,305 (v. 462). Pereira (Joaquin), 1826, Portuguese age 20, on the *Jóven Angustias* stranded at Sta B. iii. 176; a vaquero in '36 and '40, when he figured as the revealer of a political plot. iii. 606.

Perez (Cornelio), son of José María, b. at Stá Cruz '11; juez de campo '42. iv. 663, and perhaps in 33; in '45 on the Branciforte padron, wife Rosario Pinto, child. José Ramon b. '37, Celedonia '39, María '41, Juan de Dios '42, Benigna '43. In '77, still at Sta Cruz, he dictated for me a brief *Memoria* chiefly relating to Ind. troubles in early times. P. (Cruz), Mex. convict released in '33. P. (Domingo), at the rancho nacional, Salinas, '36, age 27, wife Fermina Espinosa; claimant for Los Gatos '52. P. (Eulalia), nat. of Loreto, long a resid. of S. Gabriel, and famous for her reputed great age— 140 years—at the time of her death in '78. The evidence respecting her age is too complicated for presentment in detail here; but 30 years at least of the reputed 140 rest on the incorrect assumption that she came with the 1st exped. in 1769. She really came with her husband, Antonio Guillen, a soldier of the S. Diego comp., about 1800, Guillen's name first appearing in 1803. If, as she states, she was married at 15, and her oldest child, Petra, was 11 years old on arrival at S. Diego, she was less than 30 years old in 1800. In the Loreto archives, which exist only in fragments, I have found no record of her birth; but her brother Mariano, son of Diego and Rosalía—whom she names as her parents—was baptized in 1768 and buried in 1777. The S. Diego mission records show the birth of two daughters and the burial of a son in 1810-12. There is some circumstantial confirmation of my supposition that her age was less than 30 in 1800, and therefore less than 108 at her death, and there

282 PIONEER REGISTER AND INDEX.

are numerous inconsistencies in the evidence adduced in support of her great age; 104 is a more accurate figure than 140 for her age in '78. Doña Eulalia was well known as a nurse and midwife at S. Gabriel; had a second husband, Juan Mariné, for a few years from '32; and in the later years was an object of great interest to visitors on account of her age. Mentioned ii. 13, 356, 543; iii. 143, 209. I met her in '74, and in '77 she dictated a narrative of some 30 pages, *Una Vieja y Sus Recuerdos*, full of interesting items. Two of the old woman's daughters lived with her at S. Gabriel in '77, one of them Rosario, b. '14, the wife of Michael White, a pioneer of '29. Her son, Isidoro Guillen, died at Purísima about '64, and her daughter Petra at Los Ang. about '44.

Perez (Francisco), juez de policía at S. José '44. iv. 685. P. (José), regidor at Los Ang. '31–2; iii. 196, 218; suplente of the dip. '33. iii. 246; alcalde '34. iii. 635, 637. One of the vigilantes, and taking part in the sectional troubles '36–7. iii. 432, 495; 2d alcalde '38. iii. 636; grantee of S. Pascual '40. iii. 634; mentioned in '45. iv. 664. P. (Jacinto), at S. Bern. '46, age 24. P. (José Bern. de Jesus), 1833, Mex. friar of the Zacatecanos, who served at Sta Clara and as sec. to Prefect García Diego, disappearing from the Cal. records after '35; but in '42 guardian of the college at Zacatecas. iii. 319, 350; iv. 332. P. (José C.), should be Juan C. iii. 645. P. (José María), Mex. settler 1798. i. 606; in '24 at Branciforte. ii. 627; in '28, wife Margarita Rodriguez, child. Cornelio, Juan, Anita, Rafaela, Ramona, Simon, and Rufino. v. 627. P. (José María), in revolt at Sta B. '29. iii. 78. P. (José María), 1842, cornet in the batallon fijo '42–5. iv. 289. P. (Juan), 1769, com. of the S. Antonio in the 1st exped. to Cal. '69–71; in '74–5 com. of the Santiago. i. 116, 121, 126–7, 129–30, 136, 167–9, 172, 178, 208, 219, 224, 241, 244. P. (Juan), son of José M., b. '13; a soldier of the S.F. comp. '31–4; at Branciforte '45. wife María Ant. Armas, child. José Ant. b. '36, Louisa '37, Ascension '41, Felicidad '44. In '77, still at Sta Cruz, he dictated for me his *Recuerdos*. P. (Juan Crispin), part owner of the Sta Gertrudis rancho, Los Ang., '21–30, and aux. alcalde there '31–6. ii. 565, 635; in '35 grantee of Paso de Bartolo. iii. 633; in '41–5 maj. S. Gabriel. iv. 636–7; in '46 at Los Ang.; age 40 in '39. P. (Manuel Ant.), at S. Gabriel '39, age 42. P. (Marcos), at Los Ang. '46. P. (Pedro), settler at S.F. 1777. i. 297; at Los Ang. 1805. ii. 240; another Pedro, prob. son of the 1st, was at Los Ang. '39, age 42; also in '45. Perez del Campo (José), 1825, Mex. alférez. iii. 15. P. Fernandez (José), 1792, alférez of the S.F. comp. 1792–7, being also habilitado and acting com. '94–6. i. 680, 471, 629, 642–3, 705.

Perkey (J. D.), 1845, Amer. saddler from Or. in the McMahon party. iv. 572, 587. He entered Sutter's service and is often named in the *N. Helv. Diary* '45–8; summoned as a juryman for the trial of B. K. Thompson Feb. '48. Called also Purky, Parky, and Perkins. Perkins (Chas), 1847, Co. E, N.Y.Vol. (v. 499). P. (John G.), 1848, passp. from Hon. P. (Rufus) 1828, sup. of the *Franklin*. iii. 133, 147, 167. Per Lee (Theron R.), 1847, lieut Co. K, N.Y.Vol. v. 504; in '48 a lawyer at S.F., and president of the guards; in '49 justice of the peace and editor of the *Placer Times;* in N.Y. '79–80; Baltimore '83. Perrin (Chas), 1847, Co. D, Morm. Bat. (v. 469). P. (James), 1847, Co. I, N.Y.Vol. (v. 499). Perrot (Baptiste), 1846, teamster with Kearny from N. Mex. v. 337.

Perry, 1844, mr of the *Eagle.* iv. 565. P., 1845, at N. Helv. '45–6; also Mrs P. v. 511. P. (Alex.), 1847, surgeon N.Y.Vol. v. 503, 511, 513; owner of S.F. lots '48; in N.Y. city '74–82. P. (Cornelius), 1845, doubtful name in the Micheltorena campaign. iv. 495. P. (Elijah), 1840, one of the Graham exiles, not known to have returned. iv. 18. P. (John), 1838, Amer. from Realejo, Nic., where he had a family; came on the *Fearnaught* and lived a year or two with Spear at S.F. iii. 709; iv. 119. Acc. to Wm H. Davis, Perry became a Mex. citizen and got a grant of the lot where Spear built his store for the purpose of deeding it to S., going away with the intention of returning with his family, but dying at Realejo in '40; still there was a John P. at Mont. in '44 awaiting a passage to Hon. P. (L.W.), 1848, kept a paint shop at S.F. v. 684. P. (Moses W.), 1847, Co. A, N.Y.Vol. (v. 499); at Los Ang.

'71-6; at Tucson, Ariz. '82.   P. (O. H.), 1841, lieut in U.S. ex. ex. iv. 241.
P. (Peter), 1844, Hawaiian in Larkin's service at Mont.   P. (Wm), 1848,
passp. from Hon.   Persons (Ebenezer), 1847, Co. A, Morm. Bat. (v. 469); in
Sutter's service at the time of the gold discovery; often called Elijah F.   P.
(Harmon D.), 1847, Co. B, ditto.   Pesinger (J. H.), 1847, on the *Henry* at
S.F. from Or.
    Pet, 1837, in the Willamette cattle exped. iv. 85.   Petch (Robert), 1846,
one of the Mormon colony with wife and 2 children. v. 546; owner of S.F.
lot '47. v. 680. He never went to Utah; wife died before '84.   Peters (John),
1847, litigant at S. Diego.   P. (Noah), 1845, at Mont. and N. Helv.; in '46-7
served in Co. G, Cal. Bat. v. 578, 587 (358).   Peterson (Fred.), 1847, Co. C, N.
Y. Vol. (v. 499).   P. (Peter), 1843, mr of the *Admittance* '43-5. iv. 562. He
was a Dane who had perhaps visited the coast earlier as mate with Capt. Arther. Capt. P. is still living at Boston in '85 at the age of 80; and his original
Diary of '43-5 has been shown me by Wm H. Thomes, his son-in-law, who
was a sailor-boy on the *Admittance*.   P. (Peter), 1847, perhaps of Co. C, N.
Y. Vol. (v. 499); at S.F. '74; not in Clark's final list.   P. (Wm H.), 1846,
said to have come with Kearny from N. Mex.; owner of S.F. lot '47. v. 337,
676.   Fetison (Geo.), 1846, at S. Leandro. *Estudillo Doc.;* perhaps 'Patter-
s:in.'   Petitt (Huber), 1846, Cal. claim of $35 (v. 462); bought land of Va-
llejo '47. v. 455.   Petit-Thouars (Abel du), 1837, com. of the French corvette
Vénus, and author of a *Voyage* containing much important matter on Cal. iv.
147-50; also i. 432; iii. 535, 680, 699; iv. 106.   Petrof, 1808, mr of the
Kadiak. ii. 80.   Petrowski (R. K.), 1844, doubtful name and date. iv. 453;
a Pole who was a miner and farmer in Cal., dying in France '83.   Pettegrew
(David), 1847, Co. E, Morm. Bat., who served also as a preacher and spiritual director; at Salt Lake City '55. v. 475, 477, 488, 490, 494.   P. (James
P.), 1847, Co. B, ditto.   Petter (Thos), 1833, at S. José; see also 'Pepper.'
Pettet (Wm), 1847, painter and owner of many lots in S.F. '47-8; also sec. of
the council and somewhat active in town politics. v. 539, 648, 650, 678, 680,
684.   Peyri (Antonio), 1796, Span. friar who served at S. Luis Ob. and at
S. Luis Rey, of which he was the founder, from '98 until his departure in '32;
in Spain '36. Biog. iii. 621-2; ment. i. 564, 577, 587, 657, 689; ii. 108-9, 159,
346-7, 394, 453, 518, 553, 655; iii. 87, 91, 96, 102, 183, 210, 233, 317, 364; iv.
151.
    Pfeiffer (Max W.), 1847, Co. G. N.Y.Vol. (v. 499).   Pfiester (Adolph),
1847, Co. K and G, ditto; settled at S. José, where he was mayor in '75, and
still lived in '82; a German b. '21.   Pfister (Ed. H. von), 1847, mr of the
Com. Shubrick from Hon. in April, and in Aug. bringing up the *Providence*
from the Islands a stock of goods with which he opened a store at Benicia in
Sept. or Oct. v. 672-3. In '48 he went to the mines and kept a store in comp.
with Brannan, and later Vaughan; but returned to Benicia in '49 to keep a
hotel, and still lived there in '80 and later.   P. (John R. von), 1847, brother
of Ed. H., who prob. came with him from Hon.; agent for the *Cal. Star* in
March '48, and murdered by Peter Raymond at Sutter's mill in Oct.
    Phalen (Wm), 1847, Co. F, 3d U.S. artill. (v. 518).   Phelps (Alva), 1847,
of the Morm. Bat. v. 481; died on the way to Cal.   P. (Bethuel), 1848, at
Mont., Benicia, and S. F. '48-55, having business relations with Larkin;
claimant for Pt Reyes rancho. iii. 712.   P. (Geo. H.), 1846, tanner at
Sonoma; with Smith at Bodega '47-9.   P. (Wm D.), 1840, nat of Mass.,
and mr of the *Alert* '40-2, making an exploration of the Sac. River in boats,
and engaging in the Com. Jones war by spiking the guns of the S. Diego fort.
iv. 36, 95, 101, 135-6, 139, 156, 320, 562, 618-19, 665. In '46 he came back as
mr of the *Moscow,* remaining on the coast till '49 as mr and sup. of different
vessels, being com. for a time of the prize schr *Malek Adhel,* affording aid in
divers ways to the Bears and later to the U. S. officers. v. 15, 177-8, 190,
280-2, 467, 579. For one item of his services to Frémont he had a Cal. claim
of $10,000, which was paid after a slight reduction of $9,950. Capt. P. had
exceptional facilities for gaining a knowledge of current events in '46-8, and
his published *Fore and Aft,* besides being a most interesting and oft-quoted

narrative of personal experiences, contains much useful information about Cal.; yet it must be noted that the captain, with all his honesty and zeal, was not on all points an accurate witness. I have many of his original letters of '41-2 and '46-8, with some of later date from Lexington, Mass., where he still lived in '72.   Philip (John V. N.), 1846, act. lieut on the *Cyane;* lieut Co. D, Stockton's Naval Bat. '46-7. v. 386.   Philips (A. B.), 1848, owner of S. F. lot.   P. (David), 1834, Engl. cooper at S. Diego '36 from Sonora with a Mex. wife, age 44. iii. 412.   P. (James), 1847, Co. G, N.Y.Vol. (v. 499).   P. (Joel), 1844, Amer. naturalized in Nov.; 'Joel Felipe' possibly only the baptismal name.   P. (John), 1846, one of the Mormon colony. v. 546; owner of S. F. lots '46-7. v. 678; living in Utah '84.   P. (John B.), 1847, Co. D, N.Y.Vol. (v. 499); at S. F. '71-82.   P. (Joseph), 1846, gunner on the U. S. *Dale.*   P. (Wm D.), 1847, owner of S. F. lot; prob. ' Phelps.'

Piatt (Oliver K.), 1846, Co. C, 1st U. S. dragoons (v. 336).   Pichette (Louis), 1830 (?), Canadian trapper well known in Or. and B.C., who, acc. to notices of his death in '76, made a trip to Cal. from Or. in '20, which is doubtless an error, though he may have come 8 or ten years later.

Pickens, 1841, mr of the *Convoy.* iii. 382.   Pickering (Chas), 1841, naturalist of U. S. ex. ex. iv. 241-3; owner of a S. F. lot '48, perhaps another man.   Pickernell (John), 1837, named in Larkin's accounts.   Pickett, 1815, mr of the *Forrester.* ii. 274.   P. (Chas E.), 1846, Amer. lawyer who had lived several years in Or. and came to Cal. by land in June. In '47 he practised law at S. F., also living at Sonoma and visiting Honolulu; and in '48 kept a store at Sutter's Fort, being tried, and acquitted by a jury on the 2d trial, for killing R. Alderman in a quarrel about an enclosure at the fort. From the first he was an eccentric character, of marked ability but unbalanced mind, always ready to make sacrifices for a friend or abuse an enemy, never tiring of airing his opinions and whims and quarrels in the newspapers; best known as Philosopher Pickett, and the author of pamphlets on all sorts of subjects. He died in Cal. about '80. iv. 395; v. 125, 526, 645, 649, 654, 981. Pickman, 1841, doubtful name of the Workman party of immig. iv. 278. Pickup (Geo.) 1847, Co. C, Morm. Bat. (v. 469).

Pico (Andrés), son of José María, b. at S. Diego in '10. His 1st appearance in the public records is in '36-8, when he was in charge of the Jamul rancho, elector, and receptor of customs. iii. 446, 485, 609, 611, 613; iv. 98.   At the same period he took an active part on behalf of the south in the sectional political strife against the Monterey govt, being half a dozen times a prisoner in that play at warfare and diplomacy. iii. 488, 498, 518-9, 546, 559, 555, 566, 578, 580, 624. In '39-42, ranking as alférez of the S. Diego comp., he served as elector, was for a time in charge of S. Luis Rey, and obtained lands at Sta Margarita, S. Juan Cap., and Temécula. iii. 591, 609, 612, 614, 621, 624, 626-7, 639. He was sent to Mex. in '44 by Gov. Micheltorena to obtain funds. iv. 401-2, 563; and after his return devoted himself, as lieut of the comp. and capt. of defensores, to the organization of the militia at Los Ang. iv. 407, 471, 475-6, 491-2, 619. In '45 he was obliged to join the revolutionists and was in mil. com. for a time at Mont. and at Los Ang. iv. 492-3, 515, 523, 651-2; being subsequently commissioner to make inventories of mission property, and becoming lessee of S. Fernando and purchaser of S. José. iv. 550. 553, 561, 630, 637-8, 643, 665-6, 683. In '46 Don Andrés ranked as capt. of the regular comp.; was left in chief command on the flight of Castro; surrendered and was paroled with other officers; but broke his parole to serve as 3d in rank under Flores; was in com. of the Californians at the victory of S. Pascual—the most notable achievement of his life; took part in the fights of Jan. '47, and being left by Flores in chief command, concluded with Frémont the treaty of Cahuenga closing the war in Cal. v. 49, 143, 264, 266-7, 309, 330-55, 387, 930-1, 403-5, 422, 448. In '48-9 Capt. P. had a company of miners at work on the Mokelumne, was a resid. of S. José in '49-50, but subsequently of Los Ang., being the claimant for several ranchos, iii. 633, 711; v. 675; elected to the assembly in '51; presidential elector in '52; land receiver: brigadier-gen. of militia '58; state senator in '60-1. Much of his time in later years was devoted to land litigation, especially in connection with his S. Fernando estate; and he died in '76. Andrés Pico was a brave, reckless, coarse-grained, jovial, kind-hearted, popular man; abler in several respects than his brother Don Pio, but not overburdened with principle. He was never married. I have a valuable col. of original *Papeles de Mision* from his private achives.

Pico (Antonio María), son of José Dolores, b. at Mont. in 1808. In '33 maj. at S. José; alcalde in '35. iii. 729-30; lieut. of militia '37-8, involved in a conspiracy. iii. 513-14, 573, 732; in '39 suplente of the junta and grantee of Valle de S. José rancho. iii. 590, 713, 731; 2d juez, com. of an Ind. exped., and grantee of Pescadero in '43. iv. 362, 673, 685; in '44-5 juez and alcalde, capt. of defensores taking part in the revolt against Micheltorena, and a suplente of the assembly. iv. 407, 469, 486, 540, 685-6. He was purchaser of the S. Rafael mission estate in '46. v. 561, 670; and was in some trouble through favoring the cause of the U.S.; 2d alcalde in '47, and prefect '49-50, having been a member of the constit. convention. In '61 he was a republican elector, and was appointed by Pres. Lincoln register of the U. S. land-office at Los Ang., resigning in '62. His death occurred in '69. He seems to have been a man of limited abilities and excellent character. His wife was Pilar Bernal, who survived him with 3 sons and 3 daughters, Petra Mrs Gelesch, Marcolina Mrs Campbell, and Vicenta Mrs Castro; or at least, these were the signers of the funeral invitations in '69. Three volumes of *Documentos para la Historia de California* from the private archives of Don Antonio María were added by his family to my collection. P. (Fernando), ranchero at Sta B. '45. P. (Francisco), concerned in the revolt of '45. iv. 487; grantee of Calaveras in '46. v. 665; Cal. claim of $2,950 (v. 462). P. (Francisco Javier), brother of José María; soldier of Sta B. comp. 1786-1806, retiring as inválido; one of the grantees of Simí 1795-1821. i. 663; ii. 566. P. (José), mestizo soldier at Sta B. 1785, age 21. P. (José Ant. Bernardino), son of José María, b. at S. Diego 1794. About '15 he enlisted in the S. Diego comp.; is ment. as clerk in '17. ii. 425. sergt of the comp. from '28. ii. 543; iii. 165; charged with conspiracy '34. iii. 257-8; promoted to alférez '34, and comisionado to secularize S. Juan Cap. in '34-6. iii. 608, 626-7. In '36-8 he was transferred to the Mont. comp.; promoted to lieut in '38; and in '39 transferred to the S. F. comp. at Sonoma. iii. 549, 584, 608, 671, 667-8. He left the mil. service in '43, being the grantee of Agua Caliente, S. Diego, in '40, of S. Luis Rey '46, and also one of the purchasers of· S. José Mission. v. 561, 611, 620-1. Nothing is heard of him in the troubles of '45-8, but he continued to live in the south, dying at S. Diego in '71. He is described as a lively old man, full of jokes, nicknamed Picito on account of his diminutive size; and ridiculed to some extent by Wilkes in his narr. of '41. I know nothing of his family, except that he got permission in '28 to marry Soledad Ibarra.

Pico (José Dolores), Mex. soldier who came to Cal. about 1790, marrying Gertrudis Amézquita in '91, and serving in the Sta B. comp. to '95 or later. Before 1804 he was transferred to the Mont. comp., marrying Isabel Cota, and serving in the Sta Cruz escolta. From '11 he was sergt of the comp., and is ment. in connection with several Ind. exped., being dangerously wounded in '15, obtaining in '19 a grant of the Bolsa de S. Cayetano rancho, and being in charge of the rancho nacional, Salinas, from '21. ii. 56, 335-6, 338-9, 379, 416, 609, 615-16; iii. 43. He died in '27, leaving a good record as a soldier and Indian-fighter, who lacked the education or birth which might have given him promotion. He was the founder of the northern branch of the Pico family, Antonio María and José de Jesus being the most prominent of his sons. There were 13 children. A daughter, María Ant., was claimant for S. Cayetano. iv. 655. The widow died at Castroville in '69 at the age of 86, leaving over a hundred descendants. P. (José de Jesus), son of Dolores, b. at Mont. in 1807. In '27-31 he served as a soldier of the Mont. comp., taking part in the Solis revolts of '28-29. iii. 66-7, 74; but subsequently getting a substitute and living on his father's rancho. In '36-8 he was somewhat prominent in Alvarado's revolution. iii. 457, 461, 491, 501-2, 524, 567, 572, 638; iv. 96; admin. of S. Antonio '38-41; grantee of Piedra Blanca, S. Luis Ob. '40; admin. of S. Miguel '41-3. iii. 678, 688; iv. 252, 660. He took part in the movement of '44-5 against Micheltorena. iv. 458-9, 487, 658, 682. In '46, ranking as capt. of defensores, and being juez de paz at S. Luis Ob., he was paroled with other officers, but broke his parole and supported Flores in the Natividad campaign. He was accordingly arrested by Frémont in Dec. and condemned to death, but pardoned at the intercession of his wife and children. He became a most devoted friend of Frémont, aiding him in bringing about the treaty of Cahuenga, and accompanying him on his famous ride of '47. v. 282, 321, 362-3, 374-5, 403, 443, 638-9. In '48-9 Don Jesus made some successful tours in the mines, and later lived on his S. Luis Ob. rancho with his family, being county assessor and assemblyman in '52-3. In '78 he dictated his recollections for my use, cited as *A contecimientos*, and containing many items of valuable testimony. ii. 230, 232, 339, 384, 417, 427, 446, 624. I have not heard of his death down to '85.

Pico (José María), brother of Dolores, son of Santiago Pico of Sinaloa, and founder of the family in southern Cal.; a soldier of the S. Diego comp. from 1782, corp. of the guard at S. Luis Rey from 1798, and sergt 1805-18, being retired—perhaps with brevet rank of alférez—in '18, and dying at S. Gabriel, where he had long been in com. of the escolta in '19. His wife, married in 1789, was María Eustaquia Lopez, nat. of Sonora. His 3 sons, Andrés, José Ant., and Pio, are named in this register; and there were 7 daughters, of whom Concepcion married Domingo Carrillo, Estefana and Jacinta married José Ant. Carrillo, Isidora was the wife of John Forster, Tomasa of an Alvarado, and a sixth was Feliciana.   P. (Manuel), one of the grantees of Simí '42, prob. son of Javier, Miguel, or Patricio; encargado at Sta Isabel '43. iv. 620, 640.   P. (Miguel), brother of José Maria, soldier of the Sta B. comp.; grantee of Simí rancho 1795, 1821. i. 663; ii. 566; in '32 an inválido, wife Casilda Sinoba, child. María Ignacia, Petra, Apolonia, Juan de Mata, and Mariano. The widow died in '60 at the age of 74, leaving 15 children, 116 grandchildren, and 97 great-grandchildren—116 males, 112 females.   P. (Patricio); brother of José María, one of the grantees of Simí 1795, 1821, '42. i. 663; ii. 354, 663; iv. 643.

Pico (Pio), son of José María, b. at S. Gabriel 1801, moving to S. Diego after the death of his father in '19, where he kept a small shop. For mention of his early life, see ii. 168, 344, 425, 546, 559, 604. In the public records he first appears as clerk at a trial in '26. ii. 549; was a vocal of the dip. from '28. iii. 41-2; being ment. also in connection with the Fitch elopement in '29. iii. 141; and getting the same year some kind of a title to the Jamul rancho. *Dept. Rec.*, vii. 61, 94; confirmed in '31. iii. 611. In '31 he was a leader of the southern opposition to Gov. Victoria. iii. 189, 197, 201, 203-4, 206; and in '32, according to the plan, should have been gov. ad int. as senior vocal and president of the dip., but was unable to secure the place, though he is often erroneously named as gov. in that year. iii. 216-20, 224, 226, 231, 245. He was again member of the dip. '34-5, being a candidate for alcalde and chosen elector '36. iii. 246, 249-50, 275, 300, 483-4, 615; in '34-40 administrator of S. Luis Rey, having also a profitable contract to slaughter cattle on shares at S. Gabriel. iii. 349, 353, 623-4, 628; iv. 54, 61; and in '37-9 an active partisan of the south against Alvarado's govt, being more than once a prisoner, though like most others never in a fight, and playing a not very creditable part in the sectional strife. iii. 495, 499-502, 504, 506, 508-9, 516, 518, 520, 546, 548-50, 555, 558, 564-6, 578, 580, 602, 614. He was again member of the junta in '39-41, protesting against Monterey's claims as capital; also one of the terna for gov., tithe collector at Los Ang., and provisionally grantee of Temécula. iii. 584, 590, 604, 606, 612, 623, 637; iv. 193. In '41 he was the grantee of Sta Margarita and Las Flores. iv. 621, 628; in '42 supposed to be plotting in favor of England. iv. 282; in '44-5 again member of the junta, and capt. of defensores, appointed comandante de escuadron. iv. 361, 403, 407, 410-11, **425, 475. On the downfall of Micheltorena in '45**, having taken some part in the campaign, Don Pio, as president of the junta, became temporary gov. from Feb. 22d. iv. 404, 492-3, 495-9, 503-7, 509, 521, 530. His office was confirmed in Mex., and Apr. 18, '46, he took the oath as constitutional gov. For his rule of '45-6, general acts and controversy with Gen.Castro, see iv. 511-45; v. 30-53; on mission affairs, iv. 546-62; v. 558-64; Frémont affair and Bear revolt, v.5, 138-44; on foreign intervention and McNamara project, v.59-62, 69, 217-19; miscellaneous mention, v. 567, 570, 590, 603, 624. On the approach of the U.S. forces Pico left Cal. for Mexico. v. 261-78; but in '48 returned. v. 588-90; and has since resided at Sta Margarita—sold to John Foster in '64—and at Los Angeles down to '85, having been claimant for other ranchos, iii. 611, 633, and being still a man of some wealth. He married María Ignacia Alvarado in '34, but I find no record of children. Pio Pico is a man who has been abused far beyond his deserts; a man of ordinary intelligence and limited education; of generous, jovial disposition; reckless and indolent; with a weakness for cards and women; disposed to be fair and honorable in his transactions, but without sufficient strength of principle to keep always clear of doubtful complications or avoid being made the tool of knaves; patriotic without the ability to accomplish much for his country. In his controversy of '45-6 with Castro his conduct was foolish in the extreme; in other respects down to 1848 his record is better rather than worse than might be expected of a commonplace man in so prominent a position. Not much fault can be found with his mission policy; he did not, as has been charged, run away in '46 with large sums of money obtained by illegal sales of mission estates; he had a perfect right to favor his friends by land grants in the last days of his power, and to prefer that Cal. should fall into English rather than American possession. That he seems to have antedated some land grants after his return in '48 is the most discreditable feature of his record; yet my study of land litigation leads me to hesitate in condemning or exonerating any official or citizen, native or pioneer, on charges originating in that most unfathomable pool of corruption. In '78 Don Pio dictated for me a *Historia de California*, which in interest and accuracy compares favorably with other pioneer statements; and at the same time gave me two volumes of original *Doc. Hist. Cal.*, including several important papers.

Pico (Rafael), at Simí rancho '29-31. ii. 566; iii. 635. P. (Ramon), son of Antonio María, b. in '27; in '63-6 capt. of Co. A, 1st battalion of native Cal. cavalry, stationed for a time in Arizona. He added to my collection 3 vols of *Doc. Hist. Cal.*, containing many original papers belonging to his father, and others relating to the captain's own military career. Major José Ramon is still a resident of S. F. in '85. P. (Salomon), son of José Dolores, of whom nothing appears before '48 except that a rancho in Tuolumne was later claimed on a grant of '44 to him. iv. 674. After '49 he became a noted highwayman and murderer in the region of S. Luis Ob. and Sta B. About '57 he went to L. Cal., where in '60 he was put to death by order of the sub-gefe político Esparza. P. (Santiago), a settler at Los Ang. 1790. i. 461; at Simí rancho 1802. ii. 111. He seems to have been a soldier of the S. F. and S. Diego comp. in '76-80. It is just possible that he was the father of José Maria and Dolores, though I find no definite record that that Santiago ever came to Cal. P. (Vicente), at Sta B. before '37, wife Estefana García, 4 children.

Pieras (Miguel), 1771, Span. friar, founder of S. Antonio, where he served till his departure from Cal. in 1794. Biog. i. 688-9; ment. i. 173, 176, 188-9, 196, 255, 279, 298, 388, 469, 576. Pierce (Charles), 1847, Co. B, N. Y. Vol. (v. 499); d. before '82. P., 1795, Engl. Nootka commissioner at Mont. i. 527. P. (Harrison M.), 1843 (?), settler in Napa, who landed in Or. from a whaler in '42 acc. to Menefee and Lancey. Bidwell thinks he was in Cal. '41-2. In '68 he testified that he worked for Dr Bale in '45-8; the first definite record is his signature to the S. José call to foreigners in March '45. In '47 named as an Amer. bachelor at N. Helv.; in '48 built the first structure in Napa City, used as a saloon, and still standing in '81. He died in '70. iv. 400, 509; v. 128, 670. P. (Stephen H.), 1846, of the Mormon colony, who prob. did not come to Cal. v. 547. P. (Wm), 1846, Co. C, 1st U. S. dra-

goons (v. 336).   Piercy (Sam. G.), 1847, Irishman of Co. F, 3d U. S. artill.
(v. 518); one of the few who did not desert for the mines; name James G. on
the roll. He worked as copying clerk during the constitutional convention of
'49; and after his discharge in '51 went to N. Y., but returned and lived from
'53 at Oakland, where he died in '77, leaving a widow and married daughter.
Pierola (Arnoldo) at Mont. in '25. iii. 26.   Pierre (Jean), 1806, boatswain of
the *Peacock.* ii. 38.
    Pike (Wm M.), 1846, of the Donner party from Tenn. He was accidentally
killed before reaching the mts, leaving a widow and 2 children. The widow,
Harriet F. Murphy, survived, marrying Michael Nye in '47 and dying in Or.
'70. One of the daughters, Naomi L., also a survivor at the age of 3, married
Dr Mitchell of Marysville in '65, and in '80 was Mrs Schenck at The Dalles,
Or. The other daughter, Catherine, an infant, died at the Sierra camp. v. 531,
533-4.   Pilikin (John), 1844, disabled Amer. sailor of the *Monmouth*, in care
of the consul at Mont.
    Piña (Blas), with Arce's party, 46. v. 106.   P. (Joaquin), Mex. corporal
of artill. at S.F. from '29, when he wrote a *Diario* of an important exped.
against the Ind., the original of which is in my possession; in '44 acting com.
at S.F., also owner of town lands. iii. 75, 111, 113, 212, 702; iv. 463, 660, 672.
P. (Lázaro), Mex. artill. corporal at Mont. '29, at S. Rafael '32. iii. 76, 716;
in '36 at Mont., age 39, wife Plácida Villela, child. José de Jesus b. in Mont.
'26, German '29, Ant. A. at S.F. '31, Feliciano at Mont. '32, Francisco '33,
Luis G. '35. In '37 he was corporal in the S.F. cav. comp., and from '38 sergt
and acting alférez, sometimes in com. at Sonoma, and the grantee of Agua
Caliente in '40, besides being owner of a S.F. lot in '45. iii. 193, 583, 702, 711,
722; iv. 12, 121, 172-4, 669, 684. He is named by Revere in '46. v. 297; but
soon went to Mex., where he is said to have been killed at the battle of Cerro
Gordo.   P. (Máximo), teacher at Los Ang. '17-18. ii. 353.   P. (Pedro),
Mex. soldier in the Hidalgo piquete at Mont. '36, age 28.   Pinard (J. B.),
1848, Canadian farmer at S. José '58-76.   Pineda (Joaquin), Mex. soldier at
Mont., age 26.   P. (Lorenzo), grantee of Los Uvas, Sta Clara, '42. v. 674.
Pinkerton (James), 1846, Co. C, 1st U. S. dragoons (v. 336).   Pinkney (Robert F.), 1846, lieut on the U. S. *Savannah*, in com. of S. José garrison during
the Sanchez campaign of '46-7; also of the U. S. ex. ex. in '41, but not in
Cal. iv. 241; v. 378, 661.   Pino (Miguel), 1770, 2d off. on the Spanish transports '70-3. i. 168, 208.
    Pinto (Antonio), soldier of the S.F. comp. '19-22.   P. (Francisco), son of
Serafin, at S. José '41, age 34, wife Prudenciana Servian (?), child María Ignacia; in '46-7 kept under arrest at Mont. by Maddox for 6 months to prevent his raising a force to join Flores in the south.   P. (Joaquin), resident
of Branciforte '30. ii. 627.   P. (Juan María), soldier of the S. F. comp.
1797-1800. i. 499, 560; of the S.F. comp. '19-27; in '28 at Branciforte with
his wife Apolonia Mesa and 4 child., Claudio, Clara, Cármen, and Rosario,
also at B. '30-6, ii. 627; iii. 697.   P. (Juana F.) married to M. A. Cordew
1776, the first marriage at S.F. i. 296.   P. (Manuel), at S. José '41, age 56,
wife María Amézquita, child. Paulina b. '23, María de la Cruz '25, Estévan
'28, Miguel '33, Felipe '36.   P. (Pablo), corporal of the S.F. comp. i. 297.
P. (Rafael), son of Serafin, b. at Branciforte '18, educated at Mont., and in
'36 joining Alvarado's revolt was made alférez and soon lieut of volunteers,
in which capacity he served in the south '37-9, his regular appointment as
alférez of the Mont. comp. coming from Mex. in '39. ii. 585; iii. 191, 491, 550,
555, 578, 587, 671; iv. 652. In '40 he was one of the officers who went to
Tepic with the foreign exiles, returning in '41. iv. 13, 23, 23, 28, 30. After
serving as an aide to Micheltorena for a year or more he resigned; in '43-4
was a custom-house guard at Mont.; and in '45-6 was receptor of customs at
S.F., refusing to join the movement against Micheltorena, and going south
with Castro after the occupation of S.F. by the U.S. iv. 292, 377, 4 1, 463,
557, 670; v. 68, 135, 239, 659. After the fall of Los Ang. in Aug. P nto returned north, was paroled, and took no further part in the war, becoming a
ranchero in later years; had a 'Cal. claim' of $2,464 (v. 462). His wife was

María, daughter of Juan Amesti, with whom and 4 children he lived in '78 on his rancho near Corralitos, Sta Cruz Co., a man of good reputation. His *Apuntaciones* is a valuable MS. narrative dictated for my use at that time; and he also gave me the original S.F. custom-house records in his possession since '46, a most important col. of *Doc. Hist. Cal.* P. (Serafin), resident of Branciforte '18, and earlier to '30 and later; alcalde in '22, '27. ii. 627. His wife was Ignacia, daughter of Pedro Amador, and his children Francisco, Rafael, Ascension, Antonia, Dolores, María, Ignacia, and Cármen the wife of J. B. Bonifacio.   Pio, one of the grantees of Ulistac, Sta Clara, '45. iv. 674.
Pioche (F. L. A.), 1848, Frenchman who came to S.F. from Chile, engaging in trade and becoming a millionaire, prominently connected with many great enterprises of city, state, and coast. The town of Pioche, Nev., bears his name. Becoming involved in financial troubles, he finally committed suicide in '72.   Pioneer (Jacob A.), 1847, Co. D, N. Y. Vol. (v. 499).   Pioquinto (José Ant.), at Los Ang. '46.   Piper (Asabel D.), 1847, came on the *Loo Choo* from N.Y., but not of N.Y.Vol.; owner of S.F. lot; aided O'Farrel in his survey of the town. In '52 he furnished for the *Alta* his recollections of the city in '47; went in '71 to S. Amer., where he was killed by Ind. in '73. Pistrowski, see 'Petrowski.'
Pitnak (Cárlos), 1828, mr of the *Gen. Sucre.* iii. 147; doubtful name. Pitts (Henry F.), 1844 (?), said by Hall and others to have arrived at Sta Clara in '41. I have a letter purporting to be written by him in April '40, at a quicksilver mine in Cal., doubtless an error. Swan says that Wm P., presumably the same, landed from an Amer. whaler in '44, and from that date he appears on Larkin's books. iv. 453. In '46 he was employed to carry despatches from Mont. to S. José and S.F. v. 238, 245; his receipt for $140 on July 7th appearing in the *Consulate Archives.* ii. 16. In '47-8 he worked at the quicksilver mines; also in the gold-fields '48; in '74 still prospecting for quicksilver in Mont. Co., and still living in '84.   Pixton (Robert), 1847, Co. E, Morm. Bat. (v. 469); in Sutter's employ '47-8; returned to Utah.
Place (Wm), 1833, Amer. sailor left sick at Sta B. by a whaler. iii. 409; still there in '36, age 34; and in '45 permitted to marry a neophyte.   Placencia (Luis), com. de policía at Mont. iii. 675.   Placiat (Antoine), 1827, mr of the *Comète.* iii. 146.   Plaza (Ignacio), 1842, Mex. lieut of the batallon fijo. iv. 289.   Plemmonds (David and John), 1848, came with Col Davis. *Sta Clara Co. Hist.*, 660.   Pliego (José), settler at S. José before 1800. i. 716. P. (Rodrigo), 1825, Mex. alférez of the Mont., Sta B., and S. Diego comp. '25-31; a bad fellow who left Cal. in '32 with Gov. Victoria. Biog. iii. 210-11; ment. ii. 572, 608; iii. 15, 50, 62, 78-9, 84, 186, 191-2, 195, 205, 608, 650, 671. Plino (Louis), 1836, French servant of Abrego at Mont., age 38.   Plummer (Henry), 1835, Engl. cooper who landed from a whaler and became an otter-hunter in the Sta B. region. iii. 413; named in a list of '36 as 38 years old and single; joined Nidever in many hunting trips down to '70.   P. (Wm), 1847, Co. E, N.Y.Vol. (v. 499).   Plucois (Pedro), doubtful name in a Sta B. list of '41.   Plunkett (James), 1847, Co. E, N.Y.Vol. (v. 499).
Poalclcoin (John), 1841, doubtful name of a deserter from the *Juan José,* who worked as a carpenter for Stearns at Los Ang.   Poenicar (José), 1806, doubtful name, mr of the *Reisos.* ii. 39.   Poett (J. Henry), 1848, physician at S.F.; possibly earlier.   Poinsett, 1845, perhaps one of Frémont's party. iv. 583.   Polanco (José), grantee of Conejo, Sta B., soon after 1800; at Los Ang. 1804, '19; a P. owned S. José de Buenos Aires '40; and an Inés (?) P. was sent a prisoner to Mex. in '30. ii. 112, 172, 185, 349, 354, 566, 664; iii. 85, 634. Polley (James H.), 1846, boatswain on the *Dale* '46-7; went East '48 on the *Congress;* returned on the *Vincennes,* deserting for the mines '50; again in the navy '61-66, when he died. *Lancey.*   Pollock (James), 1847, Co. F, 3d U.S. artill. (v. 518); a Scotch weaver supposed by Kooser to have died before '64.   P. (James), 1846, settler in '50 with his family on the Cosumnes, where he died '76 and wife in '80. *Sac. Co. Hist.;* possibly same as preceding.   P. (Lewis), 1840, one of the Graham exiles not known to have returned. iv. 18.   Pollorena, ment. at Los Ang. '47. v. 396.   P. (Juan), at Los Ang.

'19. ii. 355; also in '46. P. (María Ant.), at Los Ang. '48. P. (Pedro), corp. of the S. Diego comp. 1797, and in com. of S. Gabriel escolta. i. 658, 664; settled at Los Ang. 1805. ii. 310. P. (Rosalía), at Los Ang. '48.

Pombert (Louis), 1826, Canadian trapper of Jed. Smith's party, who left the party in '27, lived 18 months on Higuera's rancho, and in Apr. '29 at S. José, age 28. iii. 159-60, 176, 180. In '32 he joined the comp. extranjera at Mont. iii. 221; in '34 had a wife—Filomena, daughter of Dolores Pico—and a son Juan, born in '30, a daughter Isabel being born in '35. He was a sergt in Graham's comp. supporting Alvarado '36. iii. 458, 675. His name, written generally Pombare, appears in Larkin's books to '45 and in other records to '47. His sons are said to have lived at Castroville in '77. Pomeroy (S. D.), 1848(?), nat. of Ohio, in Sonoma Co. '55-77. Pomponio, ex-neophyte and famous outlaw captured near S. Rafael and put to death in '24. ii. 537, 597, 614. Poncabaré (Agustin), 1833, mr of the *Mariquita* '33, '35. iii. 383. Ponce de Leon (Manuel), Mex. clerk at Sta B. in '38-9 and earlier. iii. 656-7; wife Francisca Solórzano, 3 children; in '40 sec. of sub-prefect. iii. 655. Ponton (José M.), Mex. lieut sentenced to 5 years in Cal. as a convict in '36; no record of his coming.   Pool (Peter), 1846, of the Mormon colony, with his mother Mary and sister Elizabeth. v. 546; living in Utah '84.   Pooley, ment. at N. Helv. '47.

Pope (Wm), 1828, Amer. trapper from N. Mex. in Pattie's party, imprisoned for a time at S. Diego. iii. 163, 166-7, 178. He got a pass for Sonora from the gov. in Nov., and subsequently became a naturalized citizen, having a family at Taos. Before '40, perhaps in '36, he came back to Los Ang. with 8 members of his family and a company of 12 men. He was known in Cal. as Julian P., that being prob. the baptismal name received in N. Mex. In '41 he obtained a grant of the Tocoallomi rancho, named for him Pope Valley, Napa Co., and settled there in '42. I have the original passport of March 2, '42, under which he came north, the expenses of the journey being paid by the govt. A little later, prob. in '43, he accidentally killed himself by severing an artery with his axe. iv. 280. His widow married Elias Barnett; his son Joseph was claimant for the rancho. iv. 671; one daughter was Mrs Burton of Pope Valley; and there were 4 or five other children.

Porter (H. F.), 1841, mid. on the U.S. *St Louis*. P. (Sanford), 1847, Co. E, Morm. Bat. (v. 469). Porterfield (Harvey), 1845, nat. of Tenn., and overl. immig. of the Grigsby-Ide party. iv. 579, 587. He worked as a carpenter at Sonoma; prob. joined the Bears in '46. v. 110; went south in Co. B, Cal. Bat., taking part in the fight at S. Pascual, and in Stockton's final campaign; and after his discharge returned to Napa Valley. He went to the mines in '48; was wrecked on Vancouver Isl. in an attempt to reach Trinity River in '49; in '50-1 a stock-raiser in Yolo; in '52 went East by Panamá, returning '53 overland with a wife, Martha Alexander; and from '56 lived in Napa Co. to '81. His wife died in '66, leaving 3 children, and his 2d wife was Mattie Galbraith.

Portilla (Pablo), 1819, Mex. capt. of the Mazatlan cavalry comp. '19-38, being stationed for the most part at S. Diego, and taking part in Ind. exped. and military trials. ii. 253-4, 340-2, 422, 451, 480, 534-6, 540, 543, 547, 549, 551, 675; iii. 62. In '31 he rendered somewhat unwilling and ineffective service against Gov. Victoria, and from that year was nominally comandante of the post at S. Diego. iii. 201, 203-4, 206, 608. As comisionado he secularized San Luis Rey in '33-5. iii. 326, 331-2, 346, 353, 613, 623-4; and in '36-8, after rendering some slight support to Chico and Gutierrez, he joined in the southern intrigues against Alvarado's govt, and finally figured as com.-gen. under Cárlos Carrillo, leaving Cal. after the final defeat of the latter in '38. iii. 440, 446, 459, 463, 515, 520-2, 528, 532-3, 548-9, 565, 568-9, 614, 648; iv. 67-8. Capt. P. was a good-natured, easy-going officer of little force or influence, but of good intentions. He went to Sonora, where he was capt. of the post at Guaymas in '46. In '49 Dr Stillman—*Overl. Monthly*, xv. 247—met him at S. Ignacio, L. Cal., in com. of a party of 30 Sonorans bound for the Cal. gold mines, 75 years old, but 'hale and full of enterprise.' P. (Silvestre), brother of Pablo, ment. in '36 in connection with a proposed Ind. exped., and as grantee of S. José del Valle rancho. iii. 612; iv. 68.   Portolá (Gaspar de), 1769, capt. of dragoons in the Span. army, and gov. of the Californias 1768–70; com.-in-chief of the 1st exped. to Alta Cal., and 1st ruler of that province to July 9, 1770, rather as military commandant than as gov. His *Diario* of the exped. to S.F. and return to S. Diego in '69 is included in my list of authorities. Nine years after he left Cal. he was gov. of Puebla. i. 87, 89, 115–25, 134–6, 140–64 et seq., 172, 225, 231, 376, 486.

Posados (Pedro), prospector at S. Luis Rey '22. ii. 666.   Post (Fred. L.), 1847, Co. A, N.Y.Vol. (v. 499); in '82 at S.F., a clerk in the P.O. for 20 years.   P. (Gabriel B.), 1847, at Hon. from Mont. on the *María Helena;* member of the S.F. firm S. H. Williams & Co. '48; later G. B. Post & Co.; in '49 memb. of the town council and of the state senate. I think Post street, S.F., may have been named for him.

Potiñon, ment. at Los Ang. '36. iii. 419.   Pott (Geo.), 1847, owner of S. F. lot. v. 685.   Potter, 1845, doubtful member of the Grigsby-Ide party. iv. 579; perhaps John.   P. (Andrew), 1848, passp. from Hon.   P. (John), 1844 (?), immig. with a family accredited in newspaper sketches to this year; perhaps of '45. iv. 453. He settled in the Chico region, is noted at Sutter's Fort from June '46; and in '48 gained a fortune in the mines by the aid of Indians. Burnett's party from Or. passed his place and deemed his head somewhat turned by his good fortune. He died there about '51, and is said to have left large sums buried on his farm. His sons—one of them James, said to have been born '46 in Cal.—and daughters were living in Mendocino Co. '74.   Potter (Stephen), 1832, mr of the *Wm Thompson.* iii. 384. Potts (James M.), 1847, mid. on the U.S. *Lexington.*   Poulson (Oliver P.), 1846, Co. B, artill. Cal. Bat. (v. 358); prob. an overl. immig.

Powell (David), 1847, owner of a S.F. lot.   P. (Gilbert), 1846, Co. C, 1st U.S. dragoons (v. 336).   P. (John W.), 1846, Co. E, F, Cal. Bat. (v. 358); ment. in '48 at Sta Cruz. v. 642; at S. José '50.   P. (Wm J.), 1846, surgeon on the U.S. Warren; owner of S.F. lots. v. 682. I think Powell St., S.F., was named for him.   Powells (Wm E.), 1847, Co. A, N.Y.Vol. (v. 499); d. at Mont. '48.   Power (Edward), 1847, Co. F, ditto; d. S.F. about '50. P. (James), 1844, doubtful member of the Frémont party. iv. 437.   P. (John A.), 1847, brother of Ed., sergt Co. F, N.Y.Vol. (v. 499); after his discharge he became a gambler; and later a robber and murderer known as 'Jack Powers.' His associates were chiefly Mexicans, and their depredations were for the most part in S. Luis Ob. and Sta B. counties '51–6. When the vigilantes put an end to their career of crime P. escaped to Sonora, where he was killed in '60.   Poyorena, see ' Pollorena.'

Prado, ment. as a lieut '39. iii. 653; perhaps Prado Mesa.   P. (Tomás), regidor at Branciforte 1802; killed at S.F. 1807. ii. 156, 192.   Prat (Pedro), 1769, surgeon of the 1st exped., who died in Cal. '72–3. i. 128, 130, 136, 140, 168, 210.   Pratt (Addison), 1848, clergyman who married a couple at S.F. P. (Jacob H.), 1847, Co. F, 3d U.S. artill. (v. 518).   Praule (Raphael), 1844, one of Frémont's men 1st and 2d visits; served in Cal. Bat. '46–7. iv. 437, 453, 583; sometimes called ' Prone;' died in the mts of N. Mex. on Frémont's next exped. of '48.   Prause (Wm), 1826, mr of the *Inca.* iii. 147.   Pray (John), 1846, interpreter in Marston's force '46–7. v. 380.   Prendergast (John), 1848, passp. from Hon.   Prentice (Chas), 1847, Co. C, N.Y.Vol. (v. 499).   P. (Samuel), 1830, nat. of R.I. who came on the *Danube* from Lima. iii. 180. A mason by trade, but by preference a hunter; arrested for smuggling '33. iii. 393; one of the vigilantes of Los Ang. '36, being then 37 years old and single; still named as a hunter in '41, and said by Warner to have died on Sta Catalina Isl. about '65.   Monenean (?) Prentis signed a doc. at Los Ang. '46.   Prentiss, 1843, mate of the *Admittance,* discharged by Capt. Peterson; a nat. of Mass.   Prescott, 1846, mr of the *Columbus.*   Presse (Alex.), 1847, surg. of N.Y.Vol. (?); at N.Y. city '84. *S. F. Bulletin.* .   Prestamero (Juan), 1773, Span. friar who served as supernumerary at S. Luis Ob., and retired on account of illness in '74. i. 194, 196, 227.   Preuss (Chas), 1844, artist and draughtsman in Frémont's 2d, 3d, and 4th exped. iv. 437, 583; v. 453.

Price (John), 1833, nat. of Ky, who came with Walker's trappers from Salt Lake, remaining in Cal. as a carpenter; named in Larkin's books '34–5; killed in '37 by a fall from his horse at San José mission. iii. 388, 301, 409. P. (John M.), 1836 (?), Engl. in Mont. dist. '36–8; iv. 118; exiled with Graham in '40, but returned in '41, and in '48 was alcalde at S. Luis Ob. iv. 18, 33, 37; v. 639. Acc. to his own statement in *S. Luis Ob. Co. Hist.*, 63–9, he deserted from the *Kent* at Colima and came to Cal. in '30, going to S. Luis about '36, marrying Andrea Colona in '44, by whom he had 13 children, and serving after '48 as county judge and supervisor. Living in '83 at Pismo rancho.　　P. (Rodman), 1846, nat. of N.Y. and purser on the U.S. *Cyane.* He took part in the ceremonies of raising the U.S. flag at Mont. in July, and for a brief period was a kind of 2d alcalde at that town. v. 231, 287–9, 637; and in Aug. was sent south with despatches for Stockton, taking, however, no part in subsequent military operations. From Mazatlan he was sent with despatches by Mex. and Vera Cruz to Washington. In '49 he came back to S.F. as navy agent; was a member of the town council and of the constit. convention, a candidate for congress, and the owner of city property, including lots obtained in '47, which made him rich. He went East in '50, was elected to congress from N.J., and subsequently became gov. of that state, where he still lives in '85. As a member of pioneer associations, he has taken much interest in annals of the conquest; but in his testimony, as reported in various publications, the governor shows that in all the years that have passed his imagination has at least kept pace with his memory.　　Priest (Albert), 1848, German from Or., of the firm Priest, Lee, & Co. at Sac. '49–50. After '51 he lived chiefly in N.Y. He was an Or. immig. of '43, who shipped lumber to S.F. in '45.　　Prieto, 1822, contador on the S. Cárlos. ii. 458.　　P. (Antonio), at Los Ang. '46.　　Prince (Geo.), 1832, mr of the *Tranquilina.* iii. 384.　　P. (Geo.), 1847, Co. F, 3d U.S. artill. (v. 518).　　Prinon (Sam.), 1828, Amer. bricklayer from N. Mex., at Los Ang. '40, age 43; perhaps 'Prentice.'　　Prior, erroneous ment. '27. iii. 160.　　Prone, see 'Praule.'　　Prouse (Wm), 1826, mr of the *Inca.* iii. 147.　　P. (Wm), 1847, Co. B, Morm. Bat. (v. 469).

Prudhomme (Leon I.), 1835 (?), Fr. cooper said to have come to Los Ang., v. 413, this year in a record of '46. He married a Tapia, and in '52 was claimant for the Habra and Topanga ranchos. iii. 633–4. He died in '71, leaving a family.　　Prudon (Victor), 1834, Frenchman who had lived 7 years in Mex. and came to Cal. as a teacher in the colony at the age of 25. iii. 263, 412. Remaining at S. Gabriel and Los Ang., in '36 he was president of the vigilantes. iii. 418, 432; iv. 116; and in '37–8 was Gov. Alvarado's sec., being also capt. of militia. iii. 506, 523, 529. In '39–40 he lived at S.F., keeping some kind of a shop, or drinking and gambling place. v. 684; and in '41, being grantee of Bodega, he was made sec. of Com. Gen. Vallejo. iv. 204, 670. In this capacity he was sent, in '42, to Mex. in Vallejo's behalf, returning with the rank of capt. and brevet lieut-col in the regular army. iv. 281–5, 319, 563. From '43 he lived at Sonoma, being in '44–5 the grantee of Sac. Isl., and Laguna rancho, Yolo, being also mentioned in connection with various minor affairs. iv. 358, 396, 408, 445, 561, 671, 673, 678. With Vallejo, he favored the cause of the U.S. in '46, and with him was made a prisoner by the Bears. v. 41, 45, 61, 112–21, 298–9, 667; having a 'Cal. claim' of $7,390 (v. 462). He kept a store at Sonoma in '47–8 in partnership with Haan; and in '48–9 made some money in the mines. I have no later record of him than '53, when he was a witness in the Limantour case. His wife, who was separated from him about '48, was Teodocia Bojorques. Victor Prudon—Prudhomme was the original form—was a man of good education, a master of the Spanish and English languages, and an adept in the use of the graceful, flowery language that delights all of Span. race, many of Alvarado's and Vallejo's state papers being for the most part the secretary's work. He was socially an agreeable companion, of attractive personal appearance and fine manners;

impulsive and often imprudent, but never involved, so far as I know, in any-thing very bad or good so far as character and conduct were concerned. Prueth (Chas R.), 1831, clerk or sup. on the *Louisa*.

Pryor (Gabriel), 1840, one of the exiled foreigners, arrested in the south. iv. 14, 18. P. (Nathaniel Miguel), 1828, Kentuckian silversmith and clock-maker who had lived 4 years in N. Mex. and came to Cal. in Pattie's party. iii. 163, 168, 178; ii. 554. After his release from prison he worked at S. Luis Rey, found favor in the eyes of P. Peyri, and in '29 got a carta from Gov. Echeandía, being then 24 years old. From '30 he lived in the vicinity of Los Ang., sometimes mending clocks, but oftener engaged in otter-hunting, not always with due respect to the revenue laws. iii. 393. In '36 he obtained from the ayunt. a certificate of long residence and good character, and a few years later married a Sepúlveda who died in '40. He served against Michel-torena in '45. iv. 495; commanded a comp. of citizen artill. in June '46. v. 50; was arrested for aid to Amer. during the Flores revolt, and in '47 served as regidor. v. 626. He died in '50. A son Paul, born in '37-9, married a daughter of Juan Ávila, and died by accidental poisoning in '78. iv. 119.

Puaani (Kale), 1847, Hawaiian owner of S. F. lot. v. 685. Puga (Joa-quin), sirviente at Sta Clara 1776. i. 306. Puget, 1793, officer of Vancou-ver's exped.; in Cal. '93-4, exploring Bodega. Puget Sound in the north bears his name. i. 513, 518, 533. Puig, 1769, sergt of Cal. volunteers in the 1st exped. i. 136, 160. Pujol (Francisco), 1795, Span. friar who served at S. Cárlos and died at S. Ant. 1801, being poisoned by the Ind. i. 576, 686; ii. 146, 149-50, 159. Pulaski (Albert), 1846, at N. Helv. occasionally '46-8. Pulis (John C.), 1847, sergt Co. F, N.Y.Vol. v. 504; owner of S.F. lots; d. at S.F. '50. Pulpule, Ind. at Sutter's '40. iv. 138. Pulsifer (David), 1847, Co. C, Morm. Bat. (v. 469); in '82 at Concho, Ariz. Purcell (Henry), 1846, Co. C, 1st U. S. dragoons (v. 336). P. (Matthias), 1847, Co. H, N.Y.Vol. (v. 499); d. at S. F. '50. Purdy (Sam. L.), 1847, Co. D, N.Y.Vol. (v. 499); d. in L. Cal. '48. Puter (James), 1828, Amer. trapper, age 20, of Pattie's party. iii. 163, 168; nothing known of him later. Putnam, 1847, mr of the *Susan Drew*. v. 511.

Pyle (Edward), 1846, overl. immig. from Mo., who settled with his family at S.José, where he died in '75. His daughters married B. H. Gordon and J. W. Laird. His son, Edward, Jr, married Mary A. Graves of the Donner party in '47; is ment. in '48 as at N. Helv. raising recruits for service at Maza-tlan (?); also as a member of the Stockton Mining Co. The same year he was murdered near S. José by Valencia, who was hanged for the crime in '49. His widow married J. T. Clark in '51, and in '80 was living at White River, Tulare Co. Another son, John F., was in S. Joaq. Co. '48; Sta Clara Co. '50-76; and in Kern Co. '79. Still another, Thomas, served in Co. B, Cal. Bat. (v. 358); settled with wife and 2 children in Nov. '46 on the Moquelumne; in '47 is ment. as visiting Sutter's Fort; and in '48 moved to Coyote Cr., Sta Clara Co., where he was murdered in '55.

Qudron (Jenckey), 1846, doubtful name, Co. F, Cal. Bat. (v. 358). Queen (Henry W.), 1846, lieut of marines on the U.S. *Savannah;* lieut Fauntleroy's dragoons (v. 232, 247); in com. at S. Juan B., Sept. Q. (James), 1847, sergt Co. F, N.Y.Vol. v. 504; in charge of Brannan's store at Mormon Isl. 48; d. at Napa '79. Quepness (Odilon), at Soledad '26. ii. 623. Quigley, 1847, a Mormon in Kearny's return party. v. 453. Quigley (Robert), 1846, bugler Co. C, 1st U.S. dragoons (v. 336). Quijada (Felipe), soldier at Sta B. '32. Q. (Francisco), grantee of Bolsa de Chemisal, S. Luis Ob., '37. iii. 677. Quijano (Manuel), 1807, surgeon of the troops at Mont. 1807-24. ii. 88, 140, 379, 571, 607.

Quijas (José Lorenzo de la Concepcion), 1833, Mex. friar of the Zacate-canos who served at the 4 northernmost missions, and retired in '44, being vice-prefect in '43-4, perhaps in '57 a parish priest in the state of Guerrero, dying at Querétaro a little later. Padre Q. was a black sheep in the Francis-can flock, yet a good man when sober. Biog. iv. 680-1; ment. iii. 319, 354,

294   PIONEER REGISTER AND INDEX.

713, 716, 719; iv. 48, 86, 171, 195, 224, 371-3, 427, 676-7.   Qnilaguegui (Teodosio), Ind. grantee of Nicasio '35. iii. 712.   Quimby, 1848, mr of the *Wave*.
v. 581.   Quimper (Man.), 1790, alférez of the Span. navy at Mont. from
Nootka. i. 444, 506; see also *Hist. N. W. Coast.*   Quin (Peter), 1848, Irishman shot at Sta B. in Dec. for the murder of the Reed family at S. Miguel.
v. 632, 640.   Quinn (Franklin), 1846, in the Los Ang. region; at Mont. '47-8;
possibly 'Gwinn' of '41.   Quiñones (Manuel), Mex. tanner at Branciforte
'45, age 45, wife Josefa Condesa (?), child. Benito b. Sta Cruz '27, Juan Diego
'29, Mariano '33, Capistrano '34. He had been a convict of '28-34.
Quintana, com. of N. Mexicans in Castro's force '46. v. 363.   Q. (Andrés),
1805, Span. friar who served at Sta Cruz until Oct. 12, '12, when he was murdered by his neophytes. Biog. ii. 387-9; ment. ii. 155, 159-60, 199, 324, 339,
394.   Q. (Antonio), at Los Ang. '46.   Q. (Diego), ditto.   Q. (Francisco
Estévan), grantee of La Vena '42. iv. 656; still at S. Luis Ob. '60.   Q. (Gerónimo), grantee of S. Juan Cap. del Camote, S. Luis Ob., '46. v. 637.   Q.
(Pedro), from N. Mex. '43, a settler of S. Luis Ob. down to '83.   Quintero
(Juan), arrested at S. Juan B. '37. iii. 513.   Q. (Luis), negro settler of Los
Ang. 1781, sent away in '82. i. 345-6.   Q. (Tomás), at Sta. B. '37, wife Vi-
centa Valenzuela.   Quintin, Ind. chief of a Marin Co. tribe for whom Pt
Quintin was named; ment. in '24. ii. 538, 598.   Quirado (Basilio), Los Ang.
land-owner '48.   Quirós (Fernando), 1775, Span. lieut on the *S. Antonio* and
S. Carlos '75-6; made a survey of S.F. bay in boats '76; on the coast again
in '79. i. 241, 287, 289-92, 329.   Quivey (Peter), 1846, overl. immig. from
Mo.; summoned as a witness in N. Helv. Nov. '46; served in Co. B, Cal. Bat.
(v. 358); named at N. Helv. '47; wrote from Los Ang. in March '47 a letter
published in the *Western Expositor* and Liverpool *Millennial Star*. Settled in
Sta Clara Co. with family.

R. ('Il Signor'), 1827, sup. of the *Héros.* iii. 129-30.   Raabes (Claudio), at S. Gabriel '46.   Rabbens, or 'Raben,' 1847, mr of the *Mathilde.* v. 579. Rabbettoile (Pierre), 1847, Co. F, 3d U.S. artill.; 'Rabbittaile' on the roll; living in '64.   Radford, 1847, lieut on the U. S. *Warren,* who went east overland with Kearny. v. 452.   Radon (G.), 1846, mr of the *Narwal.* v. 579.
Rae (Wm Glen), 1841, nat. of Scotland, and agent of the H. B. Co., in charge of the Cal. establishment of the co. at S. F. '41-5.   He was an able man of business, and a jolly, popular bon-vivant.   In '45 he was driven by a complication of causes, arising from business, political, and domestic troubles aggravated by dissipation, to commit suicide at the age of 31. iv. 216-19, 593-4, 665-8; v. 679.   Rae's wife was Eloise, daughter of Dr John McLoughlin, and they had a son and 2 daughters.   The widow became Mrs Harvey, and died at Portland, Or., in '84 at the age of 68.   In a MS. *Life of Dr Mc-Loughlin,* she had furnished me a valuable sketch of her experience in S.F. Her property was left to her son, Joseph McL. Harvey, but the will, acc. to the newspapers, is contested by the daughters of Rae, Mrs Wygant and Mrs Myrick.   Raeckman (Israel), 1846, Cal. Bat. (v. 358).   Rafter (Wm), 1847, Co. F, 3d U. S. artill. (v. 518); still in the service '64. v. 521.   Raggio (Luigi), 1847, Ital. from Mex.; justice of the peace S. Luis Ob. '51; S. Benito Co. '67-81 with family.   Ragsdale, 1837, mr of the *True Blue.* iv. 106.
Rainey (Dav. P.), 1847, Co. B, Morm. Bat. (v. 469).   Rainsford (John), 1829, Irish sailor from the Islands, known as 'Kanaka Jack,' and as Joaquin Solis from his personal resemblance to the convict. iii. 179.   He worked as a lumberman; joined the comp. extranjera in '32. iii. 221; appears on Larkin's books from '34; got a Mont. lot in '35; age 30 in '36; sold out in '37; at S.F. in '39-41, acting as interpreter and mr of a launch on the bay. iv. 130. In '42 he lived at Sonoma, getting naturalization papers, and perhaps visiting the Geysers; grantee of a Napa rancho by the Sonoma alcalde in '45. *Land Com.,* no. 804; died in '46.
Ramirez (Agapito), at Los Ang. '45-6, iv. 522, 541.   R. (Angel), **1834,** Mex. ex-friar and ex-revolutionist, in charge of the Mont. custom-house '34-6; a leading supporter of Alvarado at first and later a conspirator against him; an intriguing, vicious fellow, who died in '40. His wife, or mistress, in '36 was Francisca Gutierrez, who came with him overland from Tepic. Biog. iii. 587-8; ment. iii. 357-8, 261, 297, 370-3, 377, 452, 455, 469, 477, 487, 513, 523-5, 569, 573, 670-2, 677, 683, 688; iv. 96, 163.   R. (Angeles), at Los Ang. '46. R. (Aquilino), killed at S. Buen. '38. iii. 554.   R. (Antonio), at Los Ang. '39, age 25.   R. (Francisco), Chileno at S.F. '43-6; age 40 in '45; collector in '46. v. 648.   R. (Ignacio), first man buried at Mont. 1770. i. 175.
Ramirez (José), 1820, Mex. sub-lieut of artill. '20-26, when he returned to Mex. ii. 263, 371, 381, 422, 470, 510, 537, 674; iii. 25. He was an old man of 60, and soon died, leaving a widow, María de Jesus Ortega, of Sta B., who returned to Cal., and in '75 was still living at Sta Clara.   R. (José), resid. of Branciforte '28-30. ii. 627; wife Margarita Lorenzana, child. Riviano (Bibiano?), Vicente, Victor, Andrés, José Arcadio, Luis, Estefana, Bárbara. R. (José Ant.), carpenter-instructor 1792-5; at Los Ang. '21. i. 615; ii. 351. R. (José Guad.), soldier at S. Juan B. before 1800. i. 558.   R. (José María),

1825, Mex. alférez, who came with Gov. Echeandía, and was soon attached to the S. Diego comp. iii. 13–14, 16, 24, 78. He married Dolores Palomares, and in '30 was tried and acquitted for bigamy. Took part in the revolt of '31, and was the slayer of Vicente Gomez. iii. 204, 673; in '33–4 comisionado to secularize S. Diego mission. iii. 326, 620, 630; in '35–6 admin. of S. Antonio (possibly another man). iii. 354, 687–8; in '36 at Mont.; also comisionado of Sta Inés. iii. 426, 463, 663–4; iv. 46. He was involved in the sectional quarrels of '37–8, being more than once arrested in the south. iii. 504, 555, 566; in '40 was grantee of land at Los Ang. iii. 634; iv. 635; and in '44 is ment. as lieut, being also instructor and adjutant of the Los Ang. comp. of defensores. iv. 407–8. An Alf. Ramirez was wounded at the S. Gabriel in Jan. '47. v. 396. R. (José María), soldier at Mont. '36, age 33, nat. of Oajaca. R. (Juan), at Los Ang. in '36, one of the vigilantes. iii. 432; age 32 in '39; juez de campo '36, '40, '48. iii. 636–7; v. 626; justice of the peace in '50. R. (Manuel), 1801, Mex. convict. ii. 170. R. (María Potenciana), wife of Macario Castro 1777. ii. 141. R. (Miguel), síndico at Branciforte '36. iii. 697; in '45, age 50, nat. of Tepic, wife Margarita Lorenzana, son Canuto b. '26 at B.; prob. same as José above. R. (Ramon), at S. Gabriel '46.   Ramon (José), Ind. grantee of Purísima, Sta Clara.   Ramos (José), Mex. convict settler 1798. i. 606.

Ramsay, mr of the *Good Hope.* ii. 284.   Ramsdale (Geo.), 1846, corp. Co. K, C, 1st U.S. dragoons. Killed at S. Pascual. v. 346.   Ramsey (Chas), 1848, settler in Solano Co., still in Green Valley '78.   R. (Dav.), 1847, corp. Co. H, N.Y.Vol. (v. 499); kept a store at S.F. '48. v. 683.   R. (John W.), 1847, Co. E, N.Y.Vol. (v. 499).   Rand, or Ran (Caleb), 1847, settler in Sta Clara Val. with wife from '46–7; went to Or. '72; d. '79.   R. (Geo.), 1847, perhaps of N.Y.Vol. (v. 499), under another name.   R. (Joshua), 1847, Co. C, N.Y.Vol. (v. 499); d. before '82.   Randall (Andrew), 1847, gunner on the U.S. *Portsmouth;* in '50 called a doctor and scientist; in '53 apparently the claimant for several ranchos. iii. 677, 712; iv. 655, 670, 672.   R. (Chandler G.), 1847, said to have been orderly sergt in N.Y.Vol., but not on the rolls; a carpenter at S. José from '49 to his death in '58, age 36.   R. (Charles G.), 1847, Co. B, N.Y.Vol. (v. 499); d. S. José after '50; doubtless same as preceding.   R. (Eli), 1847, at Stockton. *Tinkham.*   R. (John), 1826, mid. on the *Blossom* '26–7.   Randolph (Isaac N.), 1846, Co. C, 1st U.S. dragoons (v. 336); kept a hotel at Sonoma '48; in Amador Co. from '53 to '63, when he committed suicide.   R. (J. B.), 1847, lieut on the U.S. *Columbus.*   Raney (McKee), 1848, nat. of Va, settler of S. Joaq., apparently living in '84; also called 'Reany.'   Rangel (Juan José), 1829, Mex. convict set at liberty '34.   Ranguel (Manuel), at Los Ang. '46.   Ransch (Joseph A.), 1847, at S.F. asking for land; perhaps 'Rausch.'

Ratiguende (Wm), 1828, doubtful name; mr of the *Fénix.* iii. 147.   Rausch (Nicholas J.), 1847, Co. K, N.Y.Vol. (v. 499); owner of S.F. lot; later a prominent German citizen of S.F. where he died in '63.   Rawson (Dan. B.), 1847, Co. D, Morm. Bat. (v. 469).   Ray (Charles), 1823, mr of the *Plowboy.* ii. 492.   R. (David), 1848, immig. from Or. with wife and 5 children; died on the Yuba the same year. *Burnett.*   R. (John G.), 1846, memb. of the Sonoma council '47. v. 668; Cal. claim of $250 (v. 462); in '60 kept a hotel on the Geyser road. The John Ray who came to Rose Bar with his family in '48, *Yuba Co. Hist.,* 83, may be he or David.   Rayaty (Julian), at Los Ang. '39, age 26.   Raymond (Almon P.), 1847, Co. D, Morm. Bat. (v. 469).   R. (Fred.), 1847, nat. of Mass., who died at S.F. May 27th.   R. (Peter), 1846, Co. E, Cal. Bat. (v. 358); murderer of J. R. von Pfister in the mines Oct. '48, but escaped from jail. I think he may possibly be the Peter Remer executed at Sta B. in Dec. for the Reed murder. v. 632.   Raymore (Thos), 1832, memb. of the comp. extranjera at Mont. iii. 221.   Raynor (Wm), 1846, Co. C, 1st U.S. dragoons (v. 336).

Read (Christina), 1846, of the Mormon colony. v. 546; owner of a S.F. lot. v. 679.   R. (Edward), 1844, Amer. from Mazatlan, who went mad on the voyage, and seems to have died at S. Pedro. iv. 453.   R. (Hannah T.), 1846, of the Morm. colony with a child. v. 546; perhaps Mrs Jimison later. R. (John), 1826 (?), Irish sailor said to have come from Acapulco this year. iii. 176. I find no original record of his presence before '33 except that in '34 several witnesses testified to having known him for 6 years, or since '28. Prevented by Ind. from cultivating the Cotate rancho, and serving for a time as majordomo of S. Rafael, acc. to current sketches he came to Sauzalito in '32. Weeks claims to have visited him in the Sauzalito cabin in '31. His boat running occasionally to Yerba Buena, may be regarded as the 1st ferry. From '33 his name appears on Larkin's books and in various records. iii. 365; iv. 117. He was naturalized in Sept. '34, and in Oct. was grantee of the Corte de Madera del Presidio rancho. iii. 711. In '35 he was godfather at the baptism of Geo. Yount, and in '36 married Hilaria, daughter of José Ant. Sanchez, being appointed admin. of S. Rafael, and perhaps serving as alcalde the next year, when he was visited by Edwards. iii. 718; iv. 86. Henry A. Peirce describes a visit to his place in '41, and he died in '43, leaving 4 children. The widow was still living in '72 with a daughter by a 2d husband. The son, John J., b. in '37, inherited his father's estate and was still living in '80, with wife Carlota Suarez and 2 children. Another son was Richard, b. about '39. One daughter, Inés, Mrs Deffenbach, lived in '80 in the adobe house built by her father; the other, Hilaria, married J. Boyle of S.F. R. (Rachel), 1848, married at S. F. to F. Weaver. R. (Wm B.), 1847, Co. F, 3d U. S. artill. (v. 518).

Reading (Pierson B.), 1843, nat. of N.J. and overl. immig. in the Chiles-Walker party. iv. 393-4, 400. He entered Sutter's service as clerk and chief of trappers, making wide explorations in '44-5, commanding at the fort during Sutter's absence in the Micheltorena campaign, and getting in '44 a grant of the S. Buenaventura rancho. iv. 483, 486, 673. In '46 he was active from the first in promoting the settlers' revolt, and served '46-7 in the Cal. Bat. as paymaster, with rank of major, owning a lot at S.F., and having a 'Cal. claim.' v. 127-8, 170, 179, 360, 404-5, 447, 674, 685. After his discharge he settled on his Shasta Co. rancho, but in '48-9 engaged extensively in mining operations on Trinity River, where Reading Bar bore his name, and in '49 had a store at Sac. in company with Hensley and Snyder, besides taking part in political affairs. In '50 he went east to settle his accounts as paymaster, and to pay a large debt at Vicksburg resulting from a business failure of '37, and returning was candidate for governor in '51, barely missing election. Subsequently he devoted himself to agriculture in northern Cal.; married Fanny Washington in '56, and died in '68 at the age of 52, leaving a widow and 5 children. Maj. Reading was a man of well-balanced mind, honorable, energetic, and courteous; one whose Californian record seems never to have furnished material for adverse criticism.

Real (Antonio Suarez del), 1833, Mex. friar of the Zacatecas college, who served at Sta Cruz '33-44, and retired to his college in the latter year, or perhaps in '45. iii. 319, 693-5; iv. 371, 657, 662, 675. Padre Real was a dissolute man addicted to more than one vice, and even accused of theft, but credited with having been kind and indulgent to his neophytes. Sir Geo. Simpson, Laplace the French voyager, and Josiah Belden have something to say of the friar's character. R. (José María del Refugio Sagrado Suarez del), 1833, brother of Antonio, Mex. friar of the Zacatecanos, missionary at S. Cárlos to '43, and priest at Sta Clara, with charge of S. José and S. Cárlos from '44. iii. 319, 679-80; iv. 5, 427, 549, 638, 651, 657, 682. In '46-7 he was in some difficulty about sales of mission lands and encroachments of immigrants. v. 564, 663, 665-7; and in later years his troubles with the authorities continued to some extent, until in '51 the guardian called on P. Gonzalez to suspend Real if he could not be induced to leave Cal. voluntarily. He went in '52; in '53 writes from S. José del Cabo, L. Cal.; and in '55 he had severed his connection with the college and was serving as parish priest at Mazatlan. Padre José María somewhat resembled his brother in character, though an abler man, with more skill in concealing his irregularities. It was most unfortunate for the general reputation of the Cal. padres—a most excellent body of men, as is fully shown in these volumes—that the Real brothers, Quijas, Mercado, and a few other black sheep of the fold were the friars whose conduct was best known to the foreign immig., and on whom many pioneers have founded their estimate of the missionaries.   Reamer (Wm C.) of the Mormon col. of '46; did not come to Cal.   Reausseau (Charles), 1847, Co. D, N.Y.Vol. (v. 499); d. in S.F. '68.

Recio (Antonio M. Jimenez del), parish priest at Los Ang. '47. v. 625; prob. came in '45 or earlier.   Rector (Geo. W.), 1847, nat. of Ky; resid. of S. Luis Ob. Co. '68-83.   Reddick, 1845, one of Frémont's men perhaps. iv. 583; went east with Sublette in '46, or perhaps to Or. v. 526.   Redmond (John B.), 1848 (?), Irish settler of Marin Co. '64-80.   Reed (B. F.), 1846, Cal. claim of $300 (v. 462).   R. (Edward), 1831, mr of the *Harriet.*   R. (Geo.), 1828, mr of the *Rascow.* iii. 148.

Reed (James Frazier), 1846, nat. of Ireland and a prominent member of the Donner party from Ill., accomp. by his wife, 4 children, and his wife's mother, Mrs Sarah Keyes. The latter died in May at the age of 90. In Oct., before reaching the mts, Reed, in a quarrel, killed John Snyder and was banished from the company. With one companion he crossed the Sierra, and after an unsuccessful attempt to recross with relief, served as lieut in the Sanchez campaign, and in Feb. '47 went back to the lake in the 2d relief. All the family saved their lives and settled at S. José, where R. became wealthy and held local offices, dying in '74, and his wife, Margaret W., in '61. James F. Jr was living at S. José in '80, as was Thomas K., also Virginia E., wife of John M. Murphy, with 6 children, and Martha J., widow of Frank Lewis, with 7 children. Portraits of father, mother, and the daughters in McGlashan's work. v. 508, 530, 532, 534, 664, 666, 668, 676.

Reed (John), see 'Read.'   R. (John), 1837 (?), nat. of N.C., who came from N. Mex.; often accredited to the Workman party, but his name is not in Rowland's list, and Given is positive he was not of the party. iv. 118, 278. Accredited to '37 by the *Los Ang. Co. Hist.*, but perhaps did not come till after '41. Served against Micheltorena in '45. iv. 495; signed the declaration against Castro in June '46, and in Stockton's campaign of 46-7 served as sergt in the Cal. Bat. A visit to Sutter's fort is recorded in '47. He was a son-in-law of John Rowland, and became owner of La Puente rancho, where he died in '74, leaving a widow, but no children.   R. (John), 1846, of the Mormon colony. v. 546; perhaps should be 'Read,' or the others 'Reed.'   R. (John), 1846, lieut in Marston's force Sta Clara campaign. v. 350.   R. (John), 1846, sailmaker on the *Congress*, acting capt. in Stockton's Bat. '46-7. v. 385. R. (Joseph), 1847, accredited to N.Y. Vol., but not on roll; in St Helena '75. R. (Martin), 1830, asked permission to cut timber at S.F.; may be an error for 'John Read.'   R. (P. H.), 1847, on the *Vandalia* at S.F. and Mont.   R. (Rachel), 1846, of the Mormon colony. v. 546; perhaps 'Read.'   R. (Richard), 1845, deserted from the *Hopewell* at S. Diego.   R. (Thos B.), 1845, doubtful name of an overl. immig. iv. 578.   R. (Wm), 1826, claimed to have been with Jed. Smith. iii. 153.   R. (Wm), 1837, Engl. sailor and lumberman in Mont. district '37-8; being also named as pilot and mate of the schr *California* '37-9. iii. 532; iv. 101. He married a native and settled near S. Miguel before '46, in which year, with Petronilo Rios, he got a grant of the mission rancho. v. 561, 637.   Returning to his home from a successful trip to the mines he was murdered in Dec. '48, with wife, children, and servants—11 persons in all—by 4 robbers, some of them discharged N.Y. Volunteers. One of the assassins was killed in the pursuit, and the others, calling themselves Lynch, Remer, and Quinn, were executed at Sta B. Dec. 28th. v. 592, 639-40.   R. (Wm), 1842, trader at S.F. from N. Orleans, aged 32, with wife and 3 children, John, Maria, and Eliza, the last born or S.F. Padron in *Dwinelle.*

Reer (James), 1846, Cal. Bat. (v. 358).   Reese (Dav.), 1847, Co. F, 3d U.S. artill. (v. 518).   R. (Geo.), 1847, ditto.   R. (James), 1846, Co. E, Cal. Bat. (v. 358).   Reeves (S. C.), 1848, Columbia River pilot who came to Cal. on the news of gold, in a long-boat rigged for the trip; returned to Or. as mr of the *Jóven Guipuzcoana*, but came back to navigate S.F. bay on the

Flora, and was drowned in '49. *Hist. Or.*, i. 589, 808.   Reffe (Winchester), 1847, nat. of Ky and overl. immig.; a farmer near Stockton '49–56; settler in Lake Co. '65–80; wife Lucy Maxwell.   Regalado (Pedro) inválido corp. of S. F. comp. '39–40.   R. (Victor), 1848, nat. of Texas who came from Sonora to the mines; later at Los Ang.   Reichart (John), 1847, Co. F, 3d U.S. artill. (v. 518); supposed to be living in '67.

Reid (Hugo Perfecto), 1834, nat. of Scotland, who had been 6 years in Mex., coming to S. Diego in Aug. '34 with a pass from Gefe Pol. Monterde at La Paz. iii. 412. He settled at Los Ang., aged 23, and in '35 was accused of complicity in the Apalátegui revolt. iii. 285; iv. 117. He is ment. in various records from this time, and seems to have been engaged in trade with Leese and Keith. Becoming naturalized in '39, he settled on the Sta Anita rancho, granted to him in '41–5. iv. 635. I have several of his letters to Hartnell, who aided him in getting the land against the efforts of J. A. Carrillo in behalf of the Lopez family. In '39 he had a wife, Victoria, and 3 children, the wife having a grant of the Cuati rancho in '38. iii. 633. He is named as mr of the *Esmeralda* in '42–3. iv. 565; in '43, '46, encargado de justicia at S. Gabriel, iv. 637, of which establishment he was purchaser with Workman in '46. v. 561, 627–9. In '47 he sold Sta Anita to Dalton. v. 628; was owner of a S. F. lot. v. 685; is named as sec. of a meeting at S.F. on land matters; visited the mines in '48, being also Pio Pico's agent to explain the motives of his return. v. 588; and in '49 was a member of the constit. convention. He gave much attention to Ind. manners and customs, on which subject he wrote a valuable series of papers, published in the Los Ang. *Star*. i. 180. His death was in '52. Felipe and José Dolores seem to have been his sons, iv. 119, the former being at S. Juan B. in '49.   R. (Joseph), 1847, Co. H, N.Y.Vol. (v. 499); at Napa '71–82.   R. (Patrick), 1847, corp. Co. F, 3d U.S. artill. v. 519; supposed to be living '64.   R. (Wm), 1835, Amer. physician at Los Ang., accused of complicity in the revolt. iii. 242–5, 285. The ayunt. passed complimentary resol. on his medical services; prob. confounded with 'Keith,' q.v.   Reinhart (John), 1846, Co. F, Cal. Bat. (v. 358).   Reintrie (Henry), 1842, sec. of Com. Jones. iv. 310, 321; a nat. of Cuba of French parentage, who was sec. on the *Independence* in '47; in '68 vice-consul-general at Habana.   Reisch (Jacob), 1847, Co. G, N.Y.Vol. (v. 499).

Remer (Peter), 1848, one of the murderers of the Reed family at S. Miguel, executed at Sta B. in Dec. v. 632, 640. I think he was Raymond of the N.V.Vol., '47, who killed Pfister in Oct. '48.   Remington (Darius C.), 1847, Co. K, N.Y.Vol. (v. 499); in Wash. Ter. '74.   Remon (José Ant.), 1819, at Los Ang. ii. 354.   Renard (Wm), 1840, mr of the *Francis Henrietta;* letters of introd.; perhaps did not come.   Rendall (John), 1826, mid. with Beechey. iii. 121.   Rendon (Guadalupe and Julian), at Los Ang. '46.   R. (Ignacio), settler at Los Ang. '10–19. ii. 349, 354.   Renom, 1817, boatswain on Roquefeuil's vessel, d. at S.F. ii. 288.   Renshaw (Wm B.), 1846; lieut U.S.N., acting capt. in Stockton's bat. '46–7; came from Mazatlan with despatches on the *Malek Adhel* Oct. '46. v. 290, 357–8, 386, 391–5.   Repeto (James), 1846, Co. C, 1st U.S. dragoons (v. 336).   Repoll (Sam. F.), 1846, killed at S. Pascual. v. 346; prob. the following.   Repose (Sam. T.), 1846, Co. C, 1st U.S. dragoons (v. 336).

Requena (Manuel), 1834, nat. of Yucatan, a trader who came by sea from Guaymas, sold his vessel, and remained in Cal. In '35 he was fiscal at the Apalátegui trial. iii. 285; alcalde of Los Ang. '36. iii. 418–19, 431, 481, 636; took a prominent part '36–8 in the southern opposition to Alvarado, and after the affair at Las Flores retired for a time across the frontier. iii. 491, 504, 518, 548–9, 555, 558, 561, 565. In '39–41 he was a member of the junta. iii. 590, 604; iv. 193; in '44 alcalde. iv. 411, 633; and in '45 ministro of the sup. tribunal and suplente congressman. iv. 532, 539–40; v. 50. In the troubles of '46–7 he seems to have taken but slight part; but in '50–67 he was often member of the city council. He died in '76, at the age of about 72, having always been a citizen of excellent standing and much local influence. His wife was Gertrudis Guirado, who died in '74. His daughter married Dav. W.

Alexander, from whom I obtained copies of a small collection of *Requena, Doc. Hist. Cal.*   Retar (Henry), 1840, sailor on the *California.*   Revell (Andrew or Joseph), 1848, S.F. letter list.

Revere (Joseph Warren), 1846, nat. of Mass., and lieut on the *Cyane.* He was the officer sent to raise the U.S. flag at Sonoma in July, and remained in com. of the northern district for several months, making a tour to Clear Lake—the 1st ever described in print—and visiting Sutter's fort to repel the threatened Walla Walla invasion. v. 59–60, 128–9, 238, 242–3, 254, 296–7, 301, 433, 667. In '47 com. of the prize *Admittance.* v. 576; later claimant for a Marin Co. rancho. iv. 673. His *Tour of Duty,* published in '49, contained an interesting narrative of his adventures and observations in Cal. He resigned in '50 to become a ranchero in Mex., soon entering the govt service, but in '61 reëntering that of the U.S. as colonel of a N.J. regiment. He rose to the rank of brig.-gen., but was dismissed from the army by court-martial in '63 for alleged misconduct at Chancellorsville. He resided at Morristown, N.J.; published another book, *Keel and Saddle,* in '72; took much interest in pioneer Cal. matters. v. 148–9; and died in '80.   Revilla (Cristóbal), 1775, mate on transports '75–6. i. 241, 287.

Rey (Chas), 1823, mr of the *Plowboy.* ii. 492.   R. (Cristóbal), in trouble 1797. i. 639.   R. (Joseph), 1842, French lumberman in the contra costa. Reyes (Antonio), at Los Ang. i. '19–39; ii. 355; and Ant. María '46–8, perhaps the same.   R. (Dionisio), in Los Ang. revolt '46. v. 308.   R. (Fecundo), at Los Ang. '46.   R. (Francisco), settler at Los Ang. 1787; alcalde '93–5; owner of ranchos; d. before 1816. i. 461, 553,561–2, 612, 661–3; ii. 172, 185, 349. R. (Ignacio), juez de campo at Los Ang. '45. iv. 634.   R. (Inocencia), ment. at Los Ang. '46. v. 318.   R. (Isidro), aux. alcalde at Los Ang. '38. iii. 636; age 26 in '39; cl. for Boca de Sta Mónica '52. iii. 633.   R. (Jacinto), settler at Los Ang. 1804. ii. 349.   R. (José), saddler-instructor 1792–5. i. 615.   R. (José), convict settler of 1798. i. 606.   R. (José), corp. of S.F. comp. '20–8; perhaps same at Los Ang. '46–8; Sta. B. '50.   R. (Manuel), at Los Ang. '46. R. (Martin), settler at Los Ang. 1790. i. 461.   R. (Saturnino and Seferino), at Los Ang. '46–8.

Reynolds, 1810, mr of the *Sultan* '10–14. ii. 282.   R. (Ed. D.), 1847, purser on the U. S. *Southampton.*   R. (Sam.), 1843, visited Cal. from Hon. R. (Stephen), 1833 (?), Mass. trader at Honolulu, often named in Cal. corresp. of '30–44, many of his original letters being in my collection. I think he visited Cal., but find no positive record. He died insane in Mass. about '53, having lost his property in a sugar plantation at the Islands.   R. (Wm), 1847, Co. C, Morm. Bat. (v. 469).   R. (Wm), 1845, named at S. F.; also as alcalde of S. Rafael, and later claimant for part of Nicasio rancho. iv. 587, 593, 672, 677. There may be some confusion between him and the following. R. (Wm John), 1839, Engl. sailor and carpenter on the *Index,* who left the ship and settled at S.F. in '43. iv. 119. In '44, being 25 years old, he became a Mex. citizen, owner of a lot, iv. 669, and corporal in the defensores. He worked as a carpenter with Davis and Rose, spending much of the time, '45–6, in Napa Valley, where he seems to have worked on a mill, and where he built a small vessel, the *Londresa.* His visits at N. Helv. are recorded in the *Diary* of '45–7; and he is said to have been married in '46 (?) by Alcalde Boggs. There is no reliable record of the part he took in the revolt of '46, though some vague and inaccurate reminiscences are recorded in the Napa *Register* of '72.   He was familiarly known as Chino Reynolds, was rarely detected in telling the truth about early events, and died in '76 at Sonoma. R. (Wm P.), 1845, son of Stephen, b. in Manila, mate on the *Fama.* iv. 565; worked for Davis & Grimes; served in Fauntleroy's dragoons (v. 232, 247); owner of S.F. lot. v. 684; in '49–52 was in charge of Lugo's rancho, Los Ang., and later a trader; still at Los Ang. '58.   Rezánof (Nikolai Petrovich), 1806, Russ. chamberlain, who visited S.F. to establish commercial relations bet Alaska and Cal. ii. 38, 67–80, 182, 219.

Rhea (John), 1831, Amer. trapper from N. Mex. in the Wolfskill party, who settled at Los Ang., where he kept a saloon, with a billiard-table, from

'34 to '36, but is thought to have gone east about '37. iii. 387, 405. Rhett, 1845, perhaps one of Frémont's party. iv. 583. Rheusaw (Hiram), 1845, overl. immig. of the Swasey-Todd party. v. 576, 587. He is ment. at Sutter's fort early in '46; and went south with Frémont in Aug., remaining there with Gillespie, and ranking as lieut in the Cal. Bat. during the final campaign. v. 360, 386, 435; Cal. claim of $15 (v. 462). I have no record of him after his discharge from the service in April '47. Rhinehart (Joseph), 1846, German memb. of the Donner party, who perished in the snow. He had no family. v. 531, 533.

Rhoads (Daniel), 1846, son of Thomas, nat. of Ill., and overl. immig. with wife and his father's family. He worked for Sinclair on the Grimes' rancho, and was a member of the 1st Donner relief, v. 538, of which he has furnished for my use a valuable narrative in MS. Working in the mines '48-9, after a visit east he settled in '51 on a rancho near Gilroy, moving in '57 to the Kings River country, and living in '83 at the age of 62 near Lemoore, Kern Co. He had at that date a son and three daughters. Portrait in *Kern Co. Hist.*, 168. R. (Henry C.), 1846, son of Thomas, in Fresno Co. '72. R. (H.), 1847, visited Cal. on the *Gen. Kearny*. R. (John B.), 1846, oldest son of Thomas; member and perhaps capt. of the 1st Donner relief, and also memb. of the 4th; on the jury in the Keseberg trial. v. 538, 541. He settled in the Sac. Valley, was a memb of the legislature '63, and died in '66. R. (Thomas), 1846, nat. of Ky, a Mormon, and overl. immig. with wife and 12 sons and daughters. He settled on the Cosumnes, and the visits of different members of the family are often recorded at Sutter's fort in '47. In that year Mrs R. died on Sutter's launch while being carried to S.F. for medical aid, and was buried at Benicia. R. subsequently went to Utah, where he died in '69 at the age of 77. The sons, Daniel, Henry, John, Thomas, and Wm B., are named in this register. Of the daughters, Elizabeth married Sebastian Keyser in '46, and in '72, as Mrs Pierce, lived at Kingston, Fresno Co.; Sarah married Wm Daylor in '47, in '51 became the wife of Wm R. Grimshaw, and in '72 lived at the Daylor rancho with 7 children. Grimshaw's narrative has been my chief source of information about the Rhoads family. A 3d daughter married Jared Sheldon in '47, and in '72 lived at Daylor rancho with 2 children. The youngest daughter went to Utah and married John Clawson. The wife of T. Elder is also named as a daughter of R. R. (Thomas Jr), 1846, son of Thomas; prob. the T. Rhoads who served in the Cal. Bat. (v. 358); drowned while crossing the plains in '52. R. (Wm B.), 1846, son of Thomas; in Fresno Co. '72. Rhodes (Jonas B.), 1848, at S. F. from Valparaíso. R. (Stephen C.), 1846, sailor on the U.S. *Dale;* came back to Cal. in '49, and died at S.F. '50 at the age of 40.

Rice (Daniel), 1832, Amer. carpenter from S. Blas. iii. 408; at Los Ang. '40, age 30; married a Romero about '35. R. (Geo. Joseph), 1826, nat. of Mass., who came from Hon. on the *Rover*. iii. 176; ii. 558; and settled at Los Ang. In '28 he made a trip to Hon. on the *Héros* for his health, returning by L. Cal. and S. Diego, obtaining naturalization and a license to marry in '29. His wife was a Lopez, and he was for a time associated in business with John Temple, the partnership being dissolved in '32. I have several of his letters of '31-4. In the later years he kept a billiard-saloon, which he sold to Fran. Figueroa about '35; and he is said to have left Cal. for the east about the same time. R. (John), 1830, Amer. shoemaker from N. Mex. iii. 180; at Los Ang. '36, age 25. R. (Joseph M.), 1846 (?), Soc. Cal. Pion. R. (Thos), 1825, mate on the *Rover*. R. (Wm H.), 1846, died in Alameda Co. '67; said to have been a sailor in the navy '46. R. (Wm), 1826, mr of the *Warren* '26, '29 (?). iii. 149.

Rich (Wm), 1841, botanist in U.S. ex. ex. iv. 241, 243. R. (Wm), 1847, maj. U.S.A., and paymaster '47-8; came on the *Preble*. v. 517, 646. Richards (Henry), 1842, sentenced at Los Ang. to 10 years of presidio in Jalisco for murder; nothing known of the case. iv. 296, 342, 633. R. (James), 1847, Co. E, N.Y. Vol. (v. 499). R. (Q.), 1847, Co. E, Morm. Bat. (v. 469). R. (Nathaniel), 1833, mr of the *N. America*. iii. 383. R. (Pierre), 1844, Frenchman in Mont. district; fined for buying smuggled goods; had a claim for damages done by Frémont. iv. 453, 566; v. 615.   R. (Peter F.), 1847, Co. B, Morm. Bat. (v. 469); reënl.   R. (Wm), 1829, British subject who got a carta. Richardson (A.), 1846, mr of the *Brooklyn*, which brought the Mormon colony. v. 545, 576; d. in N.Y. '84 at the age of 86, and his wife the same day aged 77.   R. (Artemas W.), 1847, Co. C, N.Y. Vol. (v. 499); county surveyor in Tuolumne; d. at Sonora '54.   R. (Benj.), 1848 (?), a capitalist of S.F. and N.Y. whose arrival is doubtfully accredited to this year in newspaper sketches of '84.   R. (Charles), 1847, sergt Co. B, N.Y. Vol. v. 504; d. at sea '55.   R. (Henry), 1844, clerk on the *Sterling;* d. in Cal. iv. 453.   R. (Henry P.), 1847, trader on the coast '47-8; owner of S.F. lot and of property at Benicia.   R. (Paul), 1840 (?), a noted trapper and mountaineer, who several times crossed the continent to Or., and may have entered Cal. before '48, as he did in '49. iv. 120.

Richardson (Wm Antonio), 1822, Engl. mate on the whaler *Orion* who 'left' his vessel at S.F., was permitted by Gov. Sola to remain on condition of teaching his arts of navigation and carpentry, and in '23 was baptized at the mission by P. Esténega, receiving at that time the name of Antonio, and being 27 years old. ii. 478, 495-6, 591. I have his autograph letter of '23 in Spanish, and many of later date. In '24 he was in trouble about debts. ii. 526; and this was by no means the last occurrence of such difficulties; but in '25 he married María Antonia, daughter of Comandante Ignacio Martinez. ii. 592; iii. 29; and in '27-9 he applied for naturalization—obtained in '30— calling himself a piloto, with some ideas of ship-building, speaking Spanish, and having a capital of about $3,000, besides some live-stock, and producing a certificate from P. Altimira of great usefulness to the mission by carpenter-work, and teaching calking to the Ind. He had a boat that traders could hire, served as pilot on the bay, as in the case of Duhaut-Cilly. ii. 590; was more than suspected of smuggling with the support of his father-in-law, and in '29 was employed to vaccinate Ind. at different missions, iii. 168, whence his later title of doctor. At the end of '29 he moved with his family to S. Gabriel, where he made his home till '35, though making trading trips up and down the coast in different vessels. ii. 558; iii. 143, 285, 382. In '35, returning north, after aiding in founding Sonoma, he erected the 1st structure in S.F., a kind of tent, or shanty, replaced in '36 with a large adobe building; became the owner of town lots; declined the office of alcalde in '37; and from the 1st day of '37 served as capt. of the port by Vallejo's appointment. iii. 295, 512, 700, 705, 709; iv. 97-8, 116, 153, 601-2; v. 682. His private business was the collection of country produce by a launch running on the bay. In '36 he became owner of the Sauzalito rancho, granted to Galindo in '35; and in '41 he went there to live, though still holding his office of capt. of the port of S.F. till Nov. '44, with no little trouble arising from his interested leniency to whalers who insisted on going to Sauzalito 'for wood and water.' iv. 245, 314, 376, 430, 665-6, 669-70, 683. In '46 he afforded some slight aid to the Californians against the Bears. v. 176; but under Stockton's appointment served again as capt. of the port and collector in '46-7. v. 572, 659, 433, 539. Had a Cal. claim of $6,683 (v. 462); was claimant for Sauzalito, where he spent the rest of his life, and his wife for Pinole. iii. 713; iv. 672; was a witness in the Limantour and other land cases; and died in '56, leaving a widow, still living in '80, a son, and 2 daughters. Capt. R. was a skilful sailor and an energetic man of business; and though somewhat too often involved in business difficulties, and severely criticised—as who was not?—in land litigations, is still given a good name by men of all classes who knew him in the early days. A biog. sketch is given in the *Marin Co. Hist.*, 386, the very inaccurate nature of which would not be noticed here but for the statement that it is founded on an original diary. R. (Wm B.), 1832, Amer. tailor said to have come on the *Espia*, though I find no other record of such a vessel. iii. 408. Named in Larkin's books from '33; and in '40 at Mont., age 30, and married. In '46 he served in Co. B, Cal. Bat. (v. 358), and was still living in Mont. Co. '50. Called also Rocherson and Rickerson. Sometimes a Wm R. appears

in the records, at Sonoma and elsewhere, who cannot be identified with Wm A. or Wm B., so that there may have been a third of the name   Richer, see 'Nief.'
Richie (Benj.), 1847, Co. C. Morm. Bat. (v. 469). Richmond (Wm), 1847, Co. D, ditto.   Richter (Carl), 1832 (?), writes to Hartwell, in Russian, from Sitka, and seems to have spent some time in Cal., being a friend of the padre prefecto.   Rickman (Robert), 1841, overl. immig. of the Bartleson party; visited Mont. in Jan. '42 with letters from Sutter, but went east the same year. iv. 267, 270, 275, 342.   Rico (Francisco), nat. of Mont. b. about '20; in '42-4 clerk and celador of the Mont. custom-house, being also grantee in '42-3 of S. Lorenzo and Ranchería del Rio Estanislao ranchos. iv. 339, 377, 431, 655, 672. In the revolution against Micheltorena '44-5, Rico took a prominent part from beginning to end. iv. 460, 462, 487, 501, 505, 588. In his Notes of '45 Larkin describes him as an honorable, straightforward man of good standing but little property. In '46-7 as capt. of defensores he was an active supporter of the Flores movement, being 2d in com. in the Natividad campaign, chief of a sub-revolt against Flores, and finally commissioner sent to treat with Frémont. v. 45, 307, 316-18, 321, 333, 362, 365, 368, 372, 404. As late as Feb. '48 he was required to give bonds to commit no hostilities against the U. S. v. 585-6. In later years he was a ranchero in Mont. Co., being apparently supervisor in '56. In '77 he gave me his Memorias, a narrative confined exclusively to the events of '44-7 which fell under his personal observation, the general accuracy of his statements being well attested by original documentary records. In '85 I have not heard of his death. R. (Martin Gonzalez), appointed in Mex. district judge for Cal. in '29, but never came. R. (Vicente), sergt at Sta B. '29-30. iii. 78, 114.   Ricord (John), 1847, N. Y. lawyer who had been attorney-gen. of the king of the Sandwich Isl. An unfavorable letter from Com. Biddle to Gov. Mason respecting his record at Hon. and in the U.S. preceded him in Cal., and he was unable with all his arts to secure a high govt position. He opened a law office at Mont., and in '48 was a speculator in quicksilver mines.
Riddell (D. A.), 1834, mr of the Wm Lye. iii. 384.   R. (Timothy W.), 1834, mr of the Martha. iii. 383.   Ridington (Thomas), 1833, Amer. sailor, who landed from the Ayacucho and settled at S. Diego as a shoemaker, age 33. iii. 409. In '35 he applied for naturalization, and in '38 got provisional papers from Cárlos Carrillo as gov. His arrest was ordered in '40, iv. 15, but he was not exiled; and in '44 and '47 he served as justice of the peace. iv. 618-20. I find no record of him after '48. His wife was Juana Machado, widow of Dámaso Alipás, who still lived at S. Diego in '78, with 4 married daughters, giving me a narrative of Tiempos Pasados.   Ridley (Robert), 1840, Engl. sailor and clerk, who appears on Larkin's books from Jan., being in com. of Sutter's launch, and for a time in charge of Ross '41, acting also as clerk for Spear and Rae at S.F. iv. 117, 120, 129, 138, 186, 233, 668-9, 678-9. In '44 he was naturalized, owner of a lot, corporal of the militia, and married to Juana Briones of North Beach, all at the age of 25. He was a pronounced cockney, a fine-looking fellow, prone to gossip and big stories, capable of drinking prodigious quantities of brandy, and popular with all classes. In '45 he got a grant of Sonoma rancho. iv. 671; and this year or the next built a house in town—the Leidesdorff cottage, at the corner of Montgomery and California streets. He was capt. of the port in '46, and for a time 2d alcalde; but having a fight with Leidesdorff—whose letters are full of denunciation of this 'greatest blaggard in town'—he was removed from the office. v. 648-9. In July, as a Mexican official, he was arrested by the Bears and cast into prison at Sutter's fort, but released in time to get some votes for alcalde in Sept. v. 126, 129, 136, 178, 239, 295, 644-5, 659. In '47 keeping a saloon at S.F.; he went on a voyage of search for the Warren's launch. v. 384, 680; later appears at Mont. for a time; but in '48 was appointed alcalde at S.F. mission, where he spent the rest of his life, dying in '51. His heirs were unsuccessful claimants for the Visitacion rancho. v. 671. His name was prob. Robert T., though the 2d initial is written also J. and F., and he is also called Richard and Joseph.

Riely, 1847, of Lee & R. at Mont. Rielson (Geo.), 1846, at Bernal's rancho near S. Leandro. Riffe (Wm), 1846, Cal. Bat. (v. 328); prob. same as 'Reffe.' Rigby (Geo. F.), 1847, Co. F, N.Y. Vol. (v. 499); at S. José '50. Riley (James), 1846, with Kearny from N. Mex. as asst in the engineer dept. v. 337. R. (James), 1847, Co. D, N.Y. Vol. (v. 499); owner of S.F. lot '48. Ringgold (J.), 1841, lieut U.S.N., com. of the *Porpoise* in U.S. ex. ex. iv. 232, 235, 568. Rins (Louis), 1840, refused grant of Sta Catalina Isl. as a foreigner; doubtful name. Rioboo (Juan Antonio García), 1783, Span. friar who served as supernumerary at S.F. and S. Diego, retiring in '86. Biog. i. 455-7; ment. i. 379, 388, 404, 422, 459.

Rios (A.), land-owner at S. Juan Cap. '43. iv. 621. R. (Cayetano), soldier of S. F., drowned '17-18. v. 202, 382. R. (Gregorio), at Los Ang. '46. C. (Joaquin), sub-majordomo at S. Juan B. '35; land-owner at S. Juan Cap. '41. iii. 692; iv. 626. R. (Petronilo), Mex. sergt of artill. at S.F. '27-40. v. 592; iii. 71, 584, 672, 702; prob. came in '24-5. In '36 named in Mont. padron as 30 years old, wife Catarina Ávila, child. José Camilo b. '34, María Lina '35, José Simon '36. In '42 grantee of S. Bearnabé rancho, Mont. iv. 655; in '46 grantee with Reed of the S. Miguel estate. v. 375, 561, 637, 639-40; and in '52 claimant for Paso de Robles. iv. 655. He still lived in S. Luis Ob. Co. '60; and in '77 his widow, living at Sta Clara, gave me her *Recuerdos* of the Reed murders at S. Miguel in '48. R. (Santiago), juez de paz at San Juan Cap. '42-3, where he was also grantee of land. iv. 627. R. (Severiano), settler at S. Juan Cap. '41. iv. 626. R. (Silverio), at S. Diego '31. iii. 201; in '39 at Sta Ana rancho, Los Ang.; in '46 at S. Juan Cap., age 45, wife Francisca, child. Salvador b. '39, José Dolores '41, José Santos '45. R. (Silverio), at S. Juan Cap. '46, age 32, wife Primitiva (?), child Margarita b. '39, Manuel '42.

Riper (Abraham van), 1847, sergt Co. E, N.Y. Vol. v. 504. Ripley (Francis L.), 1833 (?), nat. of Ga, who in newspaper sketches is said to have visited Mont. this year as mate on a whaler. iii. 409. In '48, being wrecked on the L. Cal. coast he came up to Mont. on the *Ohio*, and, except a short time in the mines, spent the rest of his life in Mont. Co., being city recorder and county surveyor for several terms. He died at Sta Rita '79. Ripoll (Antonio), 1812, Span. friar who served at Purísima and Sta B., and fled from Cal. in '28; a very enthusiastic missionary. Biog. 578; ment. ii. 235, 264, 354, 364, 366, 394, 416, 423, 530-2, 534-5, 655; iii. 92-4. Rippstein (Jacob), 1846, overl. immig. with Hoppe and Buckelew; Co. F, Cal. Bat. (v. 358); owner of S.F. lot '47; in Yuba Co. '85, a farmer. Riser (John J.), 1847, Co. C, Morm. Bat. (v. 469); reënl.; settled in Cal. on discharge, visiting Utah '48-50, and '51-82 in Alameda Co. with wife and 6 children, Catharine, Geo. C., Chas W., May B., Franklin A., and Helen R.

Ritchie (Archibald A.), 1848, a sea-captain who bought land in Solano Co.; later successful cl. for several ranchos. iv. 671, 674; of the S.F. firm R., Osgood, & Co.; d. in '56, leaving a family. R. (M. D.), 1846, nat. of Pa, known as 'colonel' for services in the Blackfoot war, overl. immig. with family. v. 528-9. Working a while for Sutter and being one of the first Donner relief. v. 538-9; he settled at Napa in '47, working on the ranchos of Boggs and Bale, and renting a mill of Vallejo in '48. He died at Napa in '74, having lost his wife in '73, leaving 6 married daughters—Mrs Stark and Poulson of Lake, Mrs Pond, Cooper, and Hecox of Napa, and Mrs Howard of Solano—with 32 grandchildren. Riter (Henry), 1847, Co. B, N.Y. Vol. (v. 499). R. (Levi), 1848, Mormon who went to Salt Lake '49. *Glover.* Rithey (Wm M.), 1846, Co. F, Cal. Bat. (v. 358); at Sutter's fort '47. Ritschard (John), 1848, resid. of Sac. '48-52; d. in Switzerland '77. Rittenhouse (J. B.), 1844, purser on the U.S. *Levant.* Ritter (Henry), 1839, deserter from the schr. *California* at S.F. R. (John), 1847, Co. A, Morm. Bat. (v. 469); reënl.

Rivas (Juan), at Los Ang. '46-8. Rivell (Andrew), 1848, in S.F. letter list. Rivera (Antonio) Mex. sold. in the Hidalgo piquete at Mont. '36, age 27. R. (Francisco), Alvarado's comisionado a Mex. '42. iv. 283; grantee of

S. Luis Gonzaga, Mariposa, '43. iv. 673.   R. (Joaquin), mason-instructor 1792–5. i. 615.   R. (Pascual) corp. at the Col. Riv. pueblos, killed by Ind. i. 359, 362.   R. (Salvador), mason-instructor, 1792. i. 615, 684.   Rivera y Moncada (Fernando Javier), 1769, capt. in com. of the Loreto garrison from 1756 or earlier, and in '69 in com. of the 1st exped. by land to Cal., accompanying Portolá also on the 1st exped. from S. Diego to Mont. and S.F. i. 115–25, 132–6, 140–1, 150–5; returned to L. Cal. '70–1. i. 165, 167, 171–2, 175, 178, 182. In '74, by appointment of Aug. 17, '73, he came back to Cal. to succeed Fages as mil. com. of the province from May 25th. i. 216–18, 220, 225–6, 231, 238, 486, 608. His rule lasted until the arrival of Gov. Neve Feb. 3, '77, and then he went to Loreto to act as lieut-gov. of L. Cal. For events of his rule, including his troubles with Anza and Serra in '76, see i. 230, 232–5, 244–5, 248–9, 255–7, 264–73, 276, 279–80, 286–8, 292, 294–5, 298–309, 683. In '78–9 he was commissioned to raise colonists for Cal., and at the Colorado River on his way was killed by the Indians July 17, '81. i. 319, 339–44, 361–3, 487; ii. 44. On his character and family, see i. 363–4.   Riviere (P.), 1847, doubtful name in N. Helv. Diary '47–8.

Roach (Chas T.), 1848, in S.F. letter list.   R. (John), 1830, Amer. from N. Mex. iii. 180; in the comp. extranjera at Mont. '32. iii. 221; also named in a list of '36.   R. (Thomas), 1846, gunner in Stockton's Bat., campaign of '46–7, according to a newspaper sketch.   R. (Thomas J.), 1847, lieut Co. C, N.Y.Vol. v. 504, 511; deputy collector of the port of S.F., where he engaged in trade after a tour in the mines. In '50 he settled at Trinity bay, and in '52, being county judge elect of Klamath, was drowned in trying to cross a mountain stream, at the age of 28. His brother, Philip A. Roach, is a well-known citizen and official of S.F.   R. (Wm), 1847, sergt Co. D, N.Y.Vol. (v. 504); county sheriff of Mont. for several terms; in Sept. '66 his body was found in a well near Watsonville.   Roan (Francis), 1847, Co. F, 3d U.S. artill. (v. 518).   Roane (Archibald), 1847, Co. F, N.Y.Vol. (v. 499); d. at Georgetown, D.C., '79.   R. (John), 1847, musician of N.Y.Vol.

Robb (James B.), 1847, Co. D, N.Y.Vol. (v. 499).   Robbins, 1842, mentioned as a lieut. with Com. Jones. iv. 308.   R. (Isaac R.), 1846, one of the Mormon colony with wife and 2 children. v. 546; a councillor of the church in Utah '84.   R. (John), 1833, at Mont.   R. (John R.), 1846, one of the Mormon colony, v. 546, with wife and 2 children, 2 children also having died on the voyage; agent to settle affairs of Brannan & Co. 47; owner of a S.F. lot. v. 678; in Utah '84.   R. (Thomas M.), 1823, nat. of Mass. and mate on the Rover '23–5. ii. 495; mate of the Waverly '26–8. iii. 147, 149, 154. About '30 he settled at Sta B., where he opened a store, commanded the Sta Bárbara schooner, and in '34 married Encarnacion, daughter of Cárlos Carrillo. ii. 573; iii. 140, 384; iv. 117. He is named in the padron of '36 as an Amer. trader, age 35, a catholic with wife and child. In '37–9 Capt. R. commanded the govt schr California in the service of Alvarado and Vallejo, winning an honorary commission as capt. in the Mex. navy. iii. 531; iv. 101–2, 552, 569, 580; v. 317. His name does not appear except in private commercial records in 40–4, though I have a copy of his MS. Diary of weather and movements of vessels at Sta B. for the 1st quarter of '43. In '46 he was grantee of La Calera rancho and Sta Catalina Isl. iv. 642; v. 628; being also in some slight trouble with the Flores govt. v. 330, 304; Cal. claim of $143 (v. 462). He was claimant for La Calera in '52, and died in '57, his widow living until '76. Capt. Robbins is remembered as a hospitable, good-natured old salt, whose store was a general rendezvous for seafaring men and traders, who were always welcome at his table.

Roberts (Mrs), 1847, first person buried at Benicia, drawn to the grave by an ox-team. Tustin; perhaps 'Rhoads,' q.v.   R. (Geo.), 1836, nat. of Ga, at Sonoma and Ross; baptized at S. Rafael '38 as Jorge María. iv. 118.   R. (J.), 1846, Cal. Bat. (v. 358); perhaps same as preceding.   R. (James), 1840, at S. Diego.   R. (L.), 1847, Co. E, Morm. Bat. (v. 469); in '82 a farmer at Kaysville, Utah.   R. (Robert), 1847, owner of a S. F. lot. v. 679.   R. (Sam.), 1847, Co. E, N.Y.Vol. (v. 499); chief of the Hounds at S.F. '50, sentenced to 10 years in the penitentiary. *Pop. Trib.*, i. 90, 99-100. R. (Wm), 1847, Or. missionary at S. F. v. 657. R. (Wm), 1848, Amer. sailor at the mines. Robertson, 1848, kept a gambling and grog shop at Sta B. R. (John), 1848, Engl. from Chile on the *Confederacion;* kept a bakery and saloon at Mont., going soon to the mines. Settled in Salinas Val., and died there in '70 at the age of 55. R. (Robert), 1840, at S. Diego '40-8. iv. 15, 120. Robeson (Thomas), 1846, Co. C, 1st U.S. dragoons (v. 326).

Robidoux (Antoine), 1846, nat. of St Louis, Mo., who had lived 15 years in Mexican provinces and married a Mex. wife. He came with Kearny as guide from N. Mex., and was severely wounded at S. Pascual. v. 337, 346-7. Going east in '47 he came back after '49 to remain until '54. From about '56 he lived at St Joseph, Mo.—founded by his brother—where he died in '60 at the age of 66. The name is variously written, but I follow his autograph. R. (Louis), 1844, brother of Antoine, who came from N. Mex. in '44, having possibly visited the country before. iv. 265, 453. He purchased the Jurupa rancho, where he settled with his family, a man of considerable wealth. In the troubles of '46-7, being juez de paz at S. Bernardino, v. 625-6, he favored the Americans, was one of the chino prisoners (v. 311), and served in the Cal. Bat. He was cl. for Jurupa and S. Jacinto. iv. 621, 633; was a prosperous ranchero down to about '62; and died in '68 at the age of 77. Robinson, 1838, mate of the *Llama*. iv. 91.   Robinson, 1841, storekeeper at S. Diego. iv. 619; perhaps 'Robeson.'   R., 1847, of the firm R. & Townsend at Mont. '47-8.

Robinson (Alfred), 1829, nat. of Mass., who at the age of 23 came on the *Brookline* as clerk, and remained in Cal. as agent of Bryant & Sturgis of Boston. He was baptized as José María Alfredo before '33, travelling up and down the coast from S. Diego to S.F. to bargain for the purchase of hides and the sale of goods, often mentioned in commercial records, and many of his original letters—generally signed 'Alfredo' or 'Robinson'—being in my collection. iii. 137, 146, 179, 258, 374; iv. 116; v. 590-1, 619-20. Early in '36—obtaining in his haste a dispensation of two bans with a hint from Padre Duran to contribute $20 to the church—he married Ana María, daughter of Capt. José de la Guerra y Noriega; and in '37 with his wife sailed for Boston via Honolulu. iv. 101. He came back on the *Alert* in '40 to resume his former agency, remaining till '42, when he again went east via Mazatlan, carrying despatches from Com. Jones to the govt, and also gold to the Phil. mint from the Los Ang. placers. iv. 297, 320, 403, 562, 640. While prevented by a certain personal reserve and dignity from achieving the 'hail fellow well met' popularity of some of his contemporaries, Robinson always inspired respect by his straightforward dealings; and his alliance with the leading family of southern Cal. naturally did much to give him a good standing among Californians. In '46 he published anonymously his *Life in California*, a standard work, followed by most writers on the annals of '30-42, and worthy of much praise, though showing here and there the personal and political prejudices of the author and his father-in-law. For notice of the book, with citations on various topics and a sketch of the author, see iv. 343-5; ii. 176, 563, 620-5; iv. 2-3, 6, 20, 35-6, 332-5; v. 98. In '49 he came back to Cal. as agent of the Pacific Mail Steamship Co., in later years becoming agent for the sale and management of several large estates in the south; and in '85 still lives at S.F. —the oldest surviving pioneer so far as my records show. In '80 he furnished a brief *Statement*, which has been found useful in connection with his book and his original correspondence. His wife, after living in the east I think from '37 to '50 or later, died at Sta B. in '55. There were 8 children, 2 of them b. before '40, James (who died at West Point at the age of 17), Alfredo, Miguel, James 2d, Elena, María, Antonia, and Paulina. One of the sons lives at S.F. '85, his wife being a daughter of Horace Hawes.

Robinson (Christopher F.) 1847, at Mont. from Hon. '47-8. R. (Edward R.), 1830 (?), Amer. sailor, said to have touched at Mont. iii. 180; then 'coasted off and on' for 10 years, and settled in the Sac. Val. Mentioned 45-8 in the *N. Helv. Diary;* in '47 married Mrs Christina Patterson and lived on Dry Creek,

S. Joaq. Co.; but went to the mines in '48; testified in a land case '60; near Gilroy '72; and in S. Joaq. Co. '78. R. (Geo.), 1839, mate on the *California* schr, who seems to have died before '42. iii. 532; iv. 101, 119. R. (Geo.), 1842, officer of marines on the *United States. Maxwell.* R. (Geo.), 1846, Co. C, 1st U.S. dragoons (v. 336). R. (Geo.), 1847, sergt Co. G, N.Y. Vol. v. 504. R. (James), 1841, nat. of the Bermudas, sailor disch. from the *Julia Ann;* still at Mont. 42. R. (J. F.), 1848, passp. from Hon. R. (L.), 1846, Co. F, Cal. Bat. (v. 358). R. (Robert), 1835, Scotch sailor, in trade at S. Diego to '50. iii. 423. R. (T.), 1847, gunner on the *Columbus.* R. (Wm), 1847, Co. D, Morm. Bat. (v. 469). R. (Wm), 1847, Co. D, N.Y. Vol. (v. 499). R. (Wm), 1848 (?), sup. of a N.Y. vessel wrecked in S. Amer., said to have arrived this year; at Benicia '49; later county judge of Shasta, and finally a filibuster in Peru. R. (Wm D.), 1847, Co. D, N.Y. Vol.; (v. 499); owner of S.F. lot; watchman at Mont. '48; still at Mont. '72-82. R. (Wm M.), 1847, nat. of Va; member of S. Joaq. Pion. Soc.

Robles (Avelino), soldier S.F. comp. '27-30; killed at Branciforte '39. iii. **588.** R. (Antonio), nat. of Zacatecas; at Branciforte '28, wife Rosalía Merlopes, child. José Raimundo, Teodoro, Secundino, Guadalupe, Nicolás, Fulgencio, and Estefana. In the padron of '45 he appears as José Antonio, age 70, wife Gertrudis Merlopes age 50. He had settled at B. in 1797. i. 569; regidor 1805; comisionado '17; secretary '27; and alcalde '33. ii. 156, 390, 605, 627. iii. 696-7. He died in '42 and his widow in '49. R. (Fulgencio), son of Antonio, a rough character, killed in '42. iv. 663. R. (Juan José), 1769, soldier of the 1st exped.; from '76 sergt of the S. Diego comp.; killed on the Colorado '81 by Ind. i. 342-3, 362, 452. R. (Manuel), soldier at S. Diego '71-2. R. (Miguel), alcalde at S. Luis 1781. R. (Nicolás), son of Antonio, in trouble at Branciforte '39. iii. 588; named in '43. R. (Rafael), soldier of the S.F. comp. '19-30. R. (Ramon), at Mont. '36, age 27; nat. of Branciforte; wife Perfecta Castro, child Felipe b. '33. R. (Secundino), son of Antonio, b. '13; maj. of Sta Clara mission from '41. He claims to have been one of the discoverers of the N. Almaden quicksilver mine about '28; and respecting affairs of the mine, and on the Sanchez campaign of '46-7; in '77 at his rancho of Sta Rita, Sta Clara Co., he gave me a *Relacion.* He was also one of the claimants of Rincon de S. Francisquito. iv. 672. His wife was Antonia García, and they had 29 children. Still living in '81. R. (Teodoro), brother of Secundino, and with him cl. for S. Francisquito. iv. 672. Robredo (José), 1791, lieut in Malaspina's exped. i. 498.

Roca (José), 1796, Mex. sergt of artill., son-in-law of lieut Sal.; mentioned to 1802, and after an absence came back in 1805. i. 540-1, 648, 679; ii. 30-1, 144, 147. R. (Ramon), appointed capt. of the S. Diego comp. '17, but never came to Cal. Rocha (Antonio José), 1815, Portuguese who came on the *Columbia.* ii. 273, 393; naturalized '31; in '36 living at Sta B. with his wife, Josefa Alvarado, and 5 children, age 45; perhaps the grantee of La Brea '28. ii. 350, 565, 633. An Antonio R. was assessor at Los Ang. '69-70. R. (Cornelio), 1798, Mex. convict settler. i. 606. R. (Juan Estévan), corp. at S. Diego, 1775. i. 250-1. R. (Juan José), 1825, Mex. brevet alférez who came with Echeandía under sentence of banishment for 2 years. iii. 13-14. He was put in com. of the Mont. detachment of the S. Blas comp., and is often named in the records of later years, being comisionado for the secularization of S. Juan Cap. in '33-4, in charge of S. Gabriel '36-7, and acting com. of the southern force in the sectional war of '37. ii. 549; iii. 13-14, 36, 61-2, 69, 73, 99, 204, 326, 346, 481-2, 488, 491, 495, 504, 520, 626, 644-5, 648. He died at S. Diego, at a date not recorded. His wife was Elena Dominguez; and a son Manuel died at S. Diego in '54. R. (Ramon), soldier at Sta B. before '37. Roche (Eugene de la), 1845, came from Hon. to S.F. this year or the next acc. to his testimony and that of others in the Santillan case. Rochin (Francisco), soldier of the S.F. comp. '27-37; at S. José '41, age 30, wife María Archuleta, child Francisco b. '40; still at S. José '47. R. (Ignacio), soldier at Sta B. executed for murder 1795. i. 638, 669. His wife was Ana María Bojorques. R. (Leandro), regidor at S. José '35. iii. 730; in '41

named in the padron as 32 years old, wife María Fran. Romero, child. José
Ant. b. '30, Petra '27, Concepcion '28, Efigenia '29. R. (Lúcas), soldier of
Mont. comp. '36, age 15. R. (Miguel), killed by his wife '33. R. (Vicente),
drummer in the Hidalgo piquete at Mont. '36, age 11.   Rochon (Z.), 1846,
came to Sta Clara Co., where he still lived in '82.
    Rock (Geo.), 1836, first appears at Sonoma as a witness against a horse-
thief. iv. 118; seems to have had a rancho near Sonoma, and in '37 was nominal grantee of S. Julian, Sta B., iii. 655-6, being in '37 grantee of Guenoc,
Lake Co. iv. 671. According to the *Lake Co. Hist.*, he lived at Guenoc from
about '48, as agent for Jacob P. Leese.   R. (James), 1841, Amer. deserter
from the U.S. ex. ex. iv. 279; though there is a record that seems to show
the banishment of a woman for *trato ilícito* with Santiago Rock in '40. He
settled at S. José, where in '45 he signed the call to foreigners. iv. 599. In
'46 he served as lieut of Co. G, Cal. Bat., but was cashiered by court-martial
in Jan. '47. v. 361, 366, 434; and was killed by Ind. in S. Joaq. Val., according to the *S.F. Star* of July 24, '47.   Rockwell (Orrin P.), 1848, guide to
the Mormons on the journey east. *Tyler.* 'Rocky Mountain Jack,' 1826,
claims to have been one of Jed. Smith's party. iii. 153.
    Roderick (John), 1841, Engl. mate of the schr *California* '41-2; mr of the
Bolívar '44-5. iv. 279, 563.   Rodford (Wm), 1845, lieut on the U.S. *Warren.* iv. 587.   Rodgers, 1838, mr of the *Flibbertygibbet.* iv. 103.   R.(1843), at
Mont., mr of a vessel. *Peterson.*   R. (Geo.), 1845 (?), lumberman before '46.
iv. 587. *Brown.*   R. (James), 1842, nat. of Md, deserter from the U.S.
Cyane, and captured by Salv. Vallejo March '43.   Rodman (Geo.), 1845,
coxswain of the *Warren's* launch, lost in S.F. bay '46. iv. 587; v. 384.   R.
(Robert C.), 1847, sailmaker on the U.S. *Columbus.*   Rodrian (Chas), 1847,
Co. K, N.Y.Vol. (v. 499); owner of S.F. lot.
    Rodriguez, at S.F. '44, age 20.   R., corp. at Sta Cruz '24. ii. 519, 522.
R., sailor sirviente at Sta Cruz 1795. i. 496.   R. (Alejandro), alcalde of Branciforte '35. iii. 696-7; in '36 at the Trinidad rancho, Mont., age 44, wife
Concepcion Martinez, child. Manuel b. '18, José '23, María del Sacramento
'26, and Juan Buenaventura '32; at Branciforte '45, age 50 (?), with the same
family less Manuel; died in '48.   R. (Antonio), 1829, Mex. convict, liberated '33.   R. (Antonio), drummer in the Hidalgo piquete '36, at Mont., age
13.   R. (Antonio), soldier at Sta B. '32; wife Mariana Arellanes; com-
mended for valor '24. ii. 552; juez or alcalde at Sta B. '39-40, '44. iii. 654-5;
iv. 642; arrested in '45, served under Flores '46, suspected of hostile intentions '48. iv. 542; v. 330, 586; justice of the peace '51-2.   R. (Antonio),
mentioned as 103 years old at Los Ang. '73.   R. (Antonio), alcalde of Branciforte '37, and grantee of S. Vicente rancho '39. iii. 678, 695, 697; also of
Bolsa del Pájaro '36. On the Branciforte padron of '45 he is named as 46
years old, nat. of Cal., wife Dolores Galindo, child. Guadalupe b. '22, Magin
'31, Venancio '34, Miguel '37, José María '43, Balvaneda '35, Adelaida '38,
and María Ant. '41.   R. (Antonio), regidor at S. José '37. iii. 729-30.   R.
(Antonio Catarino), 1809, Span. friar, who served chiefly at S. Luis Ob. and
Purísima, dying in '24. Biog. ii. 580; ment. ii. 155, 159-60, 236, 292, 369, 384,
387, 394, 529, 532-3, 581, 618, 655.
    Rodriguez (Dámaso Antonio), corp. of Mont. comp., transf. to Sta B. comp.
in '18; sergt '21-30, ii. 572, being a leader of insurgents in '29, iii. 78, and
alférez from '31.   From '33 he was alférez of the S.F. comp., sometimes com.
of the post, iii. 396, 573, 701-2, being an inválido at Sonoma on full pay from
'37.   In '44 he was instructor of the Sonoma defensores, grantee of Lac
rancho, and perhaps 2d alcalde of S. Rafael. iv. 407-8, 671, 677.   In '46
named as supl. juez, and as in the Olompali fight with the Bears, which took
place on his land. v. 168, 688; had a Cal. claim of $2,675 (v. 462). He died soon
after '46.   R. (Fecundo), at Mont. '36, nat. of Cal., age 22, wife Guadalupe
Robles, child. Rafaela b. '33, Concepcion '36.   R. (Felipe), at Sta B. before
'37, wife Rafaela Soto; soldier of S.F. comp. '44; prob. 2 men.   R. (Francisco), Sta Cruz poet of '18. ii. 245; in '28 at Branciforte, wife Rafaela Castro,
child. Jesus, Escolástica, Benita, and Antonia; alcalde in '30. ii. 627; grantee

of Arroyo del Rodeo '34. iii. 677; still living in '55. R. (Fran.), at Los
Ang. '43-6; justice at Alamitos '56. R. (Giacundo), at Sta Cruz '43. R.
(Ignacio), grantee of Conejo rancho 1802 et seq. ii. 112, 172, 516, 664.
Rodriguez (Jacinto), nat. of Cal., first mentioned in public records as lieut
of militia and employed by Alvarado in '36. iii. 491. From '39 he was alférez
of the Mont. comp. aiding in the arrest of the foreigners in '40. iii. 671; iv.
23, 282, 652. Celador of the Mont. and S. F. custom-house '43-46, being
grantee of the Jacinto rancho, Colusa, in '44. iv. 377, 431, 463, 557, 570, 671.
Named in the Branciforte padron of '45 as 31 years old, wife Guadalupe —,
child. Rafaela b. '32, Concepcion '35, Guadalupe '36, and Josefa '39. Alcalde
at Mont. in '49 and member of the constit. convention, the reasons for such
a choice by the Montereyans not being very apparent. He still lived in Mont.
Co. '74 and later, a man of some property. I obtained from him a brief Narracion of his recollections of early events. His oldest son, Porfirio, died at
Mont. '77. R. (José), sirviente at S.F. 1777. i. 297. R. (José), soldier at
Sta B. 1832, wife Bernarda Rosas. R. (José), prisoner at Mont. '47; alias
'Letra.' R. (José), síndico at S. F. '38. iii. 705; at S. F. '42, age 35, wife
Romana Miramontes, child. María b. '38, María '40, José and Francisco '37;
perhaps the same who had a Cal. claim of $46 (v. 462), and was at S. José
'50. R. (José), at Branciforte '45, age 21. R. (José), soldier, carpenter,
and teacher at Mont. 1796-1800. i. 643. R. (José Antonio), soldier at S.
Antonio '93 and earlier; corp. of the escolta at S. Miguel '97. i. 560; invál.
at Branciforte from '99, being comisionado of the villa for some years to 1810.
His wife was María Vicenta de Leon, and 6 of his sons were soldiers of the
Mont. comp. after 1800. i. 571; ii. 156, 171, 390. He died in '37. R. (José
Ant.); at Trinidad rancho, Mont., '36, age 26, wife María Elena Castro; juez
at S. Juan B. '44. iv. 661; perhaps was drowned in attempting to save goods
from the Star of the West in '45. R. (José Brígido), son of José Ant., b. at
S. Antonio 1793; soldier of the Mont. comp. 1811-30; a tailor by trade.
From '34 he was a ranchero in Sta Cruz Co., and in '77, at the age of 84, residing near Soquel, he gave me his Recuerdos Históricos. He died in '80, leaving
only one surviving member of his family, an elder sister.
    Rodriguez (José María), at Sta B. before '37 with wife Cármen Dominguez
and 5 children; at Los Ang. '46. R. (Juan), resid. of S. Diego '30. ii. 546.
R. (Luis), at Sta B. before '37 with wife María Arrellanes and 3 children.
R. (Manuel), Mex. soldier of the Mont. comp. at Soledad 1791-1800. i. 499;
in 1819 comisionado of Branciforte. ii. 390; being an invál. corporal; síndico
in '39 and alcalde '44. iii. 697; iv, 408, 664; in '45 on the padron as 68 years
old, nat. of Sinaloa, with a daughter Josefa b. '11.; memb. of town council
'48. v. 642; though this may have been the following. R. (Manuel), at
Branciforte '45, age 28, wife María Gonzalez, child. José b. '42, Santa '44.
R. (Manuel), 1795, Mex. cadet and alférez of the S.F. comp. though serving
in the S. Diego comp., of which he became lieut and comandante. In 1806 he
was made capt. of the S.F. comp. and sent to Mex. as habilitado general, dying in '10. Biog. ii. 98-9; i. 646-7; ment. ii. 11-15, 39, 106, 109, 125, 188-9,
370, 421. R. (María Engracia), at Sta Cruz '47. v. 641. R. (Matias),
soldier at S. Juan B. before 1800. i. 558. R. (Nemesio), soldier of S.F. comp.
'41-2. R. (Norberto), soldier at Sta B. before '37.
    Rodriguez (Pablo), Ind. settler at Los. Ang. 1781-6. i. 346, 348. R.
(Pedro), at Trinidad rancho, Mont., '36, age 25, wife Gertrudis Espinosa,
child. Juan de Parma b. '32, José '35. R. (Ramon), grantee of Agua Puerca
'43 and Cañada de S. Miguel '46. iv. 655; v. 632; killed '48 in attempting to
arrest the murderers of Reed in Sta. B. Co. v. 632, 648. R. (Ramon), in
Branciforte '28, wife Teresa Soto, child José de la Cruz. ii. 627; in '45, age
40, wife María Ignacia Alviso. R. (Sebastian), sergt of the Mont. comp.
'28-30, and comisionado of Sta Cruz '31. ii. 609; iii. 307; in 36 at the Trinidad rancho, Mont., nat. of Cal., age 50, wife María Perfecta Pacheco, child.
José b. '12, Jacinto '13, Francisco '17, Teresa '22, Desiderio '23, Bernabé '26,
María Ant. '28, Cármen '30, Ramona '32. iii. 679. Grantee of Bolsa del
Pájaro in '37, iii. 677, for which he was cl.—as also for Rincon de la Ballena,

310   PIONEER REGISTER AND INDEX.

Marin, iii. 678—and about which there was much litigation between his heirs and those of his brother Alexander. He or another of the name is named as a retired soldier with the rank of alférez in '44-5. iv. 408. He died in '54 or '55. R. (Tomaso A.), grantee of Llajome rancho, Napa. iv. 671. Roe (Chas), 1832, one of the comp. extranjera at Mont. iii. 221. Roeder (Louis), 1847, Co. C, N.Y. Vol. (v. 499). Roether (Chas), 1845, German immig. prob. of Grigsby-Ide party. iv. 579, 587. His name often appears in the *N. Helv. Diary* '45-7; settled at 'Charley's rancho' in Butte Co., moving in '58 to Feather River in Yuba, where he died in '68, leaving a widow and 3 children. Rogenade (Jacob), 1848, nat. of Poland, who came with the U.S. dragoons (v. 522); murdered at Los Ang. '54.

Rogers, 1847, teamster in Sutter's employ. R. (James), 1834; Engl. mr of the *Iolani* '35; on Larkin's books '34-43; arrested in '40 but not exiled. iii. 382, 412; iv. 17, 23. R. (John P.), 1848, from Or. to the mines; brother-in-law of Gov. Burnett. R. (Lewis), 1847, owner of a S.F. lot. v. 684. R. (M.), 1848, passp. from Hon. R. (Sam. H.), 1847, Co. B, Morm. Bat. (v. 469); in Ariz. '81. R. (Seth), 1827, mr of the *Andes* '27-9. R. (Wm.), 1847, Co. F, 3d U.S. artill. (v. 518). R. (Wm H.), 1847, Co. A, N.Y. Vol. (v. 499); at Brooklyn, N.Y., '74-84. R. (Wm J.), 1843, mr of the *John Jay*. iv. 566. Roget (Dr), 1848, intending to settle at Benicia.

Rohlman (John), 1843, Ger. settler in Sta Clara '76; carta '44, then in Sac. Val.; perhaps the name should be 'Rohlan.' iv. 400. Rojas, at Los Ang. '37. iii. 504. R. (Feliciano), at Corralitos rancho, Mont., '36, age 16, nat. of Mex.; in '41 at S. Juan Cap. iv. 626. R. (Justiniano), Ind. said to have been baptized at Sta Cruz in 1791 at the supposed age of 40; d. Sta Cruz 1875, a famous centenarian. Rojo (José María), at Sta B. before '37 with wife Altagracia García, juez de paz in '39. iii. 657-5; grantee of Cuyama in '43. iv. 642.

Roland (Fred. C.), 1828, Engl. sailor, age 23, who landed at S. Pedro, went to Los Ang., and sailed from S. Diego '29 on the *María Ester;* yet apparently at Los Ang. '30. ii. 558. R. (John), 1841, overl. immig. of the Bartleson party, who seems to have returned east in '42. iv. 270, 275. R. (John), 1846, grantee of Los Huecos, Sta Clara, and of land on the S. Joaq., for which ranchos he was cl. in '52. v. 665. At N. Helv. '48. I do not know if this was the same man as the preceding, Rohlman or Rohlan, John Rowland of the south, or distinct from all. Roldan (Mariano), aux. alcalde in Los Ang. dist '36. iii. 636; grantee of La Habra '39, iii. 633, when he was 39 years old; juez de campo '40. iii. 637; at S. Gabriel '46-7. v. 626, 628. He seems to have been a Mex. who came about '36 and went back after '47. Rolfe (Tallman H.), 1847, '48 (?), nat. of Me, who came from Or. '47 or '48, salesman for Brannan & Co. at Sutter's fort '48, and later alcalde in Yuba Co., but was a printer by trade, perhaps working on the *S. F. Star*, and later connected with many papers in Cal. and Nev., being long the editor of the *Austin Reveille* and *Nevada City Gazette*. He died at S. Bern. in '72. Some sketches represent him as having come in '46 and served in the Cal. Bat. Rollin, 1786, surgeon of La Pérouse's exped. i. 435. Rollins (Henry), 1846, according to Glover one of the Mormon colony (v. 546), with son Isaac and a daughter; prob. 'Robbins,' q. v. R. (John), 1843, at Mont.; perhaps 'Robbins.' R. (John), 1847, Co. D, Morm. Bat. (v. 469); in Springville, Utah, '82. R. (John), 1847, Co. E, ditto.

Romaldo, neoph. grantee of land, S. Luis Ob. '42. Roman, tailor of 1798. i. 598. R., neoph. accused of murder '27-8. iii. 193. R. (Richard), 1848, doubtful date; at Vallejo '51; state treasurer '49. Romana (Miguel), 1841, sup. of the *Jóven Carolina.* iv. 566. Romero, a discov. of silver near Mont. '25. ii. 667. R., soldier ment. '34, '37. iii. 257, 638. R. (Abelino), at S. José '41, age 52, nat. of Cal., wife Juana Rubio, child. Matilde b. '24, Pedro Ant. '29, Victoria '31, José Ant. '34, Francisco '37, Rosario '39. R. (Antonio), two sirvientes of the name at Sta Clara 1777. i. 306; one grantee of S. José land 1783. i. 350; regidor '85. i. 478; alcalde '90. i. 478; in '95-7 owner of a rancho near Mont. i. 683, 716. R. (Antonio), perhaps son of the preceding, regidor at Mont. '33–4; grantee of rancho '40. iii. 673, 679. R. (Antonio), soldier at Sta B. before '37; settler at Los Ang. 1807. ii. 350. R. (Balbino), gunner at the Mont. revolution of '36. ii. 461. R. (Domingo), 2d alcalde at Los Ang. '35; in trouble '40. iii. 635, 639. R. (Felipe), blacksmith at S. Diego 1775. i. 250; wife in '78 Rosario Marquez, several children born before '83. R. (Domingo), soldier at Sta B. before '37; at Los Ang. '39, age 47. R. (Florencio), at S. José '41, age 36, wife Encarnacion Miranda, child. José b. '35, Patricio '37, José Ant. '39. R. (Gabriel), soldier at the Colorado pueblos, killed by Ind. 1781. i. 359, 362. R. (Guadalupe), at Los Ang. '46; named in '58 as a centenarian. R. (Ignacio), soldier of the S.F. comp. '28–31. R. (Inocencio), soldier of the S.F. comp. '23–33; in '37 alf. of militia at S. José. iii. 732; in '44 grantee of a Contra Costa rancho. iv. 671. R. (Javier), tanner at S. José '41, age '38, nat. of L. Cal. R. (Joaquin), at Los Ang. '46.

Romero (José), 1823, Mex. capt. who made an exploring exped. from Sonora to Cal. '23–5. ii. 507–9, 542, 568; iii. 14. R. (José), soldier of the S.F. comp. '19–22, '30; in '41 at S. José, nat. of Cal., age 42, wife María García, child. Teodosia b. '30, Estefana '31, García '33, José '32, Lovribano (?) '35, and Poliarno (?) '38. R. (José), at S. Isidro rancho, Mont., '36, age 48, nat. of Cal., wife Paula Cantua, child. José b. '29, Aguilino '32, María '31, Francisco '34, and Juan '35. R. (José), Mex. at Branciforte '45, age 48, child. José b. '37, Dolores '40. R. (José), at Los Ang. '46. R. (José Antonio), settler at the Colorado pueblos, killed by Ind. 1781. i. 359, 362. R. (José Antonio), soldier and settler at S. José 1777. i. 212. R. (José Ant.), teacher at S. José '23. ii. 603; at Mont. '26. ii. 612; maj. and alcalde S. Cárlos '35. iii. 354, 674, 680; being also grantee of Cañada de Laureles. iii. 677. R. (José Ant.), at Sta B. '37, wife Dorotea Alanis, 5 children. R. (José María), soldier of artill. militia 1801–10. ii. 190. He was a son of Juan María, b. about 1788. In '77, living at Los Nietos, he gave me some vague Memorias of the olden times. ii. 237–8.

Romero (José Mariano), 1834, Mex. teacher who came with the H. &. P. colony (iii. 259), and established what he called a normal school at Mont., writing also a Catecismo de Ortología, printed at Mont. in '36. He opposed the Cal. revolutionists, and left the country with Gutierrez in '36. iii. 463. R. (Juan María), corp. of the Sta B. comp. 1788; his wife was Lugarda Salgado. R. (Juan María), 1816, Irish interpreter in the Lydia case at Mont. ii. 276. R. (Manuel), at Los Ang. '39–48. R. (María), miner of Carmelo Vol. '25. ii. 667. R. (Mariano), soldier of the S.F. comp. '22–33. R. (Martin), 1818, Paraguayan of Bouchard's insurgents. ii. 237. R. (Miguel Ant.), soldier at the Colorado pueblos 1780–1. i. 359. R. (Pedro), settler at S. José 1791. i. 716; wife Guadalupe García, child María Guad., in '93. R. (Pedro), settler at Los Ang. 1790. i. 461. R. (Pedro), at Los Ang. '45–6. iv. 541; v. 308, 628. R. (Pierre), 1831, Fr. laborer at Los Ang., age 53, from N. Mex. iii. 387, 405. R. (Rafael), Span. locksmith at Mont. '20–8. iii. 51. R. (Teodoro), grantee of Potrero de Felipe Lugo '45. iv. 635. R. (Tomás), soldier at Sta B. '32, wife Felipa Lugo; sergt '35. iii. 650; alférez '39. iii. 583. R. (Vicente), soldier on the southern frontier from '25; in later years at S. Diego. His Notes of the Past were dictated to Benj. Hayes.

Romeu (José Antonio), 1791, Span. lieut-col and gov. of Cal. from April 16, '91, to his death on April 9, '92. He was an officer from whom much was expected, especially in financial reforms; but though presumably a competent man, and certainly a conservative and amiable one, he was prevented by ill health from attending to any but routine duties during his brief term. Rule and biog. i. 481–500; ment. i. 370, 389, 393, 441, 471, 474, 479, 501–2, 530. Romeu's body was buried at S. Cárlos, and has been multiplied in current newspaper sketches into the remains of dozens of governors. Romie (Ernest), 1841, doubtful name of a German at Mont. Toomes; at S.F. '84. Swan. R. (John F.), 1843, tailor at Mont. '43–8; also visiting Sutter's fort; had a son at school '46. iv. 400. Roody (John L.), 1846, farrier Co. C, 1st U.S. dragoons (v. 336). Rook, 1848, from Hon. on the Sagadahoc. Roper (John),

1832, one of the comp. extranjera at Mont iii. 221. Ropiam, 1816, Hawaiian sailor on the *Albatross*. ii. 275.   Roquefeuil (Camille), 1817, mr of the *Bordelais* '17-18, and author of a narrative of the *Voyage*. ii. 287-91, 222, 251, 331, 373, 419.

Rosa, ment. at Mont. 1798. i. 691.   R. (Cárlos), at S. Diego 1803. ii. 13. R. (José de la), 1834, Mex. printer who came with the H. & P. colony. iii. 263, 289; going to Sonoma and becoming a kind of protegé of Gen. Vallejo; had some skill as a musician, and also worked at mending clothes and tinware. In '45 he was alcalde at Sonoma, being also the grantee of Ulpinos rancho, for which he was the unsuccessful claimant in '54. iv. 674, 678-9. In '46 he was the messenger sent to Capt. Montgomery with news of the Bear revolt, also having a quarrel with Berreyesa. v. 129-30, 668. In 1875 Don Pepe was still living at or near Martinez.   Rosales (Bernardo), settler of 1779-83. i. 350, 605.   R. (Cornelio), soldier at S. José mission 1797-1800. i. 556.   R. (José Ant.), at S. José '30.   R. (Juan), at S. Francisquito rancho, Mont., '36, nat. of Mazatlan, age 48, wife Isidora García, child. José b. '33, María '36; in later years juez de paz. iii. 678, 680; iv. 653; v. 637.   Rosales Pacheco (José María), 1843, Mex. priest who served as curate at S. Buen. till '48, and in '49 at S. Antonio; also as chaplain of Flores' army '46-7. He was sent away by his superior in '49-50 for some ecclesiastical offence. iv. 371, 422, 644-5; v. 400, 632, 635.   Rosalío (Eugenio), owner of Mont. rancho 1795. i. 683.   Rosamel (J. de), 1840, com. of the Fr. corvette *Danaïde*. iv. 35-6, 103.   Rosas (Alejandro), Ind. settler at Los Ang. 1781-6. i. 345, 348. R. (Basilio), ditto. i. 345-6, 348-9, 460.   R. (Feliciano), at Los Ang. '46. R. (José), convict settler of 1798. i. 606.   R. (José), maj. at Soledad '36. iii. 691.   R. (José Ant.), nat. of Los Ang. and soldier, shot and his body burned at Sta B. 1801 for a *crímen nefando*. i. 639-40; ii. 119.   R. (Juan), settler at S. José 1791-1800. i. 716.   R. (Manuel), fifer of S.F. comp. '39-42.   R. (Ramon), at Los Ang. '46.   R. (Sinforoso), at Los Ang. '46.

Rose (John), 1818, Scotchman of Bouchard's insurgents captured at Mont., age 27; in '21 at Purísima, his spiritual welfare being the object of much anxiety to the authorities. ii. 232, 241, 248, 292, 393, 412, 444.   Rose (John), 1841, Scotch carpenter and sailor registered at S. Blas since '39, who touched at Cal. ports in '41-2, and landed permanently at Mont. from the *Clarissa* in Nov. '43, settling at S.F. and going into partnership with Davis and Reynolds as carpenters and builders. iv. 279. In '44, being 36 years of age, he obtained a town lot, was naturalized, and served as corporal in the defensores. iv. 669, 593. In '46-7 he was town treasurer. v. 295, 648; served as lieut in the Sanchez campaign. v. 381; was a member of the council. v. 648. In '46 his firm built a schooner in Napa Creek, and in '47-8 a mill for Salv. Vallejo, going to the mines in '48. Rose gave his name to Rose bar on the Yuba, and was the first settler of Nevada Co., where he had a trading post from '49. Still living at Smartsville in '80 and prob. in '85.   R. (John M.), 1847, Co. G, N.Y.Vol. (v. 499).   R. (Thomas), 1847, employed by Larkin to carry despatches.   R. (Wm), 1843, Engl. naturalized; prob. an error.   Rosecrans (Geo. W.), 1847, lieut Co. C, Morm. Bat. v. 477.   Rosencrantz (Andrew), 1847, Co. F, 3d U. S. artill. (v. 518). *Lancey;* not on the roll.   Rosenberg (N.), 1833, mr of the *Polifemia* '33-5. iii. 383.   Rosentiel (Anton), 1847, musician N. Y. Vol. (v. 499); d. S.F. '55.   Rosete (Marcos), soldier of the Hidalgo piquete. Rosistof, 1838, mr of the *Sitka*. iv. 106.

Ross, 1846, came to Sta Clara Val. *Hall;* went to the mines '48.   R. (Chas L.), 1847, nat. of N.J. who came on the *Whiton* with a cargo of goods for sale, member of the firm Gelston & Co., a prominent merchant and landowner of S.F. '47-9, also taking part in public affairs, and serving as school trustee. v. 650-1, 656-7, 678-9, 681, 683. He lived in S.F. for some years after '50; kept a hotel in Calistoga '66; returned to S.F.; and shortly before '85 went to the Sandwich Isl. In '80 he furnished me a statement of *Experiences of '47*.   R. (Geo. W.), 1842 (?), in S.F. almshouse '81, said to have come in '42. iv. 341. *Chronicle*.   R. (Henry), 1831, sailor on the *Catalina;* at S. Diego again '34 with Hugo Reid.   R. (John), see 'Rose.'   R. (J.)..

1876, Co. F. Cal. Bat.; later Co. B, artill. (v. 358).   R. (Sam. H. P.), 1848, nat. of La, who came on the *Major Tompkins,* and went to the mines, age 18. Afterward trader, county surveyor, assoc. judge, and superintendent of schools in Merced Co.; d. at Hopeton '73.   R. (Wm), 1828, mr of the *Times.* iii. 149.   Rossen (Joseph), 1848, an Or. pioneer of '43 who came to Cal. '48; at Weaverville '73.   Rossignon, 1848, Fr. trader in the mines with Amaador and Suñol, who ran away to Peru with the profits of all three. Prob. ' Roussillon,' q. v.

Rotchef (Alex.), 1836, Russian manager at Ross '36–41. iv. 117–18, 129, 153, 164, 171–6, 179–86; iv. 233.   Roteta (Antonio V.), 1825, naval officer on the *Asia.* iii. 25–6.   Roth (John), 1848, German sailor in the navy, disch. in '48; in the mines '48–51; trader at Mont. '52–73; d. at Castroville '79, leaving a wife.   Roudon (Guadalupe), at S. Bern. '46, age 35.   Rouelle (Jean B.), 1841 (?), Canadian trapper from N. Mex. iv. 278–9. Nothing is known of his coming, but he is named as the discoverer of gold in '42 in the S. Fernando region. iv. 631.   A few years later he moved with his family to the Sac. Val., and was there during the mining excitement, being named in the *N. Helv. Diary.* Finally settled on Feather River.   Rouissillon, 1802, Polish count who sailed with Cleveland and Shaler. ii. 11, 22.   Roulam (Henry), 1846, of the Mormon colony. See 'Rowland.'   Rouleau (François), 1836, Fr. laborer at Los Verjeles rancho, Mont., age 30.   Roulette (Wm R.), 1845, overl. immig. of the Grigsby-Ide party; lived in Capay Valley '45–6; prob. went to Or. '46. iv. 579–80; v. 526.   Round (Joseph), 1845, mr of the *Pacific.*   Rousseau, 1846, with Gillespie when he met Gen. Kearny.   Roussillon (Charles), 1843 (?), Fr. trader who 1st appears at Los Ang. this year, but is said to have come in '37, or even in '33. iv. 400. From '44 he was in the Mont. district, chiefly at Sta Cruz, where he had a mill and dealt in lumber, building a schooner in '46, v. 641, and in '47–8 being a partner of Sainsevain. The 1st jury trial in Cal. was that of Graham vs R. in '46. v. 289. I have some of his business corresp., but no record after '48. Perhaps he went to S. Amer. See 'Rossignon;' age 31 in '45.

Rowan, 1842, doubtful name of a trapper at Los Ang.; came again to Cal. '50. v. 341.   R. (H.), 1847, lieut on the U. S. *Cyane.*   R. (James), 1799, mr of the *Eliza.* i. 545, 706; and of the *Hazard* 1802–4. ii. 11, 17–18, 24–5, 108, 119, 122, 130.   R. (James), 1847, Co. G, N.Y.Vol. (v. 499); in '48 teamster for Brannan & Co. at Sac.   R. (Stephen C.), 1846, lieut U. S. N., and acting maj. of Stockton's Bat.; wounded at the Mesa Jan. '47. v. 385, 395; in later years vice-admiral.   Rowe, 1848, at Sonoma, called one of the N.Y.Vol.   R. 1848, went to Hon. on the *Currency Lass.*   R. (James), 1816, sailor on the *Lydia.* ii. 275.   Rowland (Henry), 1846, of the Mormon colony with his son Isaac and perhaps a daughter. v. 546. They were generally called 'Rollins' by the Mormons. Henry R. died in the faith before '80.   R. (John), 1841, nat. of Pa and leader of the Workman-R. immig. party from N. Mex., where he had lived 18 years, amassing considerable wealth and marrying a native wife. iv. 276–9, 637. He was suspected of complicity in certain revolutionary or filibustering schemes in connection with the Texans, and this was a leading motive of his emigration; indeed, warnings were sent to Cal., but they did not prevent his getting in '42 a grant of La Puente rancho in company with Workman. iv. 331, 635. Then he went to N. Mex. and brought his family, spending the rest of his life on his rancho. iv. 343. In '45 he joined the other southern foreigners in their opposition to Micheltorena. iv. 495, 508; and was one of the Chino prisoners in '46, v. 314, having a Cal. claim of about $1,500 (v. 462); but as a rule took no part in public affairs, being noted for his retiring disposition and fondness for home life. He died in '73 at the age of about 80. His son Wm R. was sheriff in '73, and he or another son married a daughter of Bernardo Yorba.   Roy (C.), 1822, mr of the whaler *Alert.* ii. 474.   R. (Chas), 1823, mr of the *Plowboy.* ii. 492; perhaps Ray.   R. (Pierre), 1782, Fr. sirviente at S. Buen. i. 377.   Royabe (Claudio), at Los Ang. '46.   Royal (B.), 1845, at Sutter's fort '45–6; perhaps one of Sublette's men.

Rub (Geo.), 1847, Co. C, N.Y. Vol. (v. 499).   Rubí (Mariano), 1790, Span. friar whose missionary service was at S. Antonio and Soledad. He retired in '93, and was prob. expelled from the college for immorality. Biog. i. 499; ment. i. 388, 492, 576, 597.   Rubio (Casimiro), at Los Ang. '43–5. iv. 541, 633; fatally wounded at S. Pascual '46. v. 347.   R. (Francisco), soldier of the S.F. comp. '24–31; executed in '31 for crime committed in '28. His was one of the causas célebres of Cal. ii. 592, 594; iii. 191–3, 699.   R. (Francisco), at Los Ang. '46; killed at the S. Gabriel fight Jan. '47. v. 396.   R. (José M. de J. Gonzalez), see 'Gonzalez.' iii. 318, 724.   R. (José), at Los Ang. '46–8. R. (Manuel), at Los Ang. '46.   R. (Mateo), nat. of Flanders, soldier of the S. Diego comp. in 1779 and earlier, and a settler at Los Ang. 1794–1819. i. 454; ii. 349, 354. His wife was Ursula Dominguez, and the birth of 4 children is noted before 1790, one of them being Francisco Ramon.   R. (Nabor), Mex. at Mont. '36, age 40.   R. (Rafael), soldier of the S.F. comp. '24–6.   R. (Santiago), at Los Ang. '19. ii. 355.   R. (Tomás), at San Juan Cap. '46, age 30, child Candelaria; at Los Ang. '48.

Ruckel (Joseph L.), 1847, a prominent trader at S.F., S. José, and Mont. '47–8, of the firms Sherman & R. and R. & Cooke. v. 663. About '55 he went to Or., where he became a steamboatman and pres. of the O. S. N. Co., still there in '74–5.   Rucker (Dan. H.), 1848, capt. of dragoons in Graham's battalion. v. 522.   R. (R. A.), 1848, at S.F. and Mont.   Rudacof, 1846, Russ. naval lieut on the *Baikal* at S.F.   Rudd (John), 1848, came from Callao on the *Lady Adams* and took com. of the U.S. *Dale.* v. 577.   Rudenstein (John), 1846, asst surgeon on the U.S. *Dale,* d. '69.   Rudierkof, 1846, Russ. lieut; prob. same as 'Rudacof.' v. 576.

Rufus (Ernest), 1844, nat. of Germany, about the manner of whose coming, perhaps earlier, nothing appears. iv. 453. He was naturalized in March '44, appointed in July a lieut in Sutter's army, fighting for Micheltorena, and in Dec. got a grant of the Cazadores rancho in Sac. Val. iv. 479, 485, 671, 680. In '45, in partnership with Wm Benitz, he leased the Ross property from Sutter; and in '46 was grantee of the Rancho de German, north of Ross. iv. 679; v. 669. He sold the rancho, or parts of it, to Glein and Hägler in '47, but seems still to have resided in Sonoma Co. as late as '79.   Ruggles (John), 1847, Co. K, N.Y. Vol. (v. 499); at Sac. in '82.

Ruiz, mentioned in 1798. i. 670.   R. (Agaton), wounded at the Olompali fight. v. 166–8.   R. (Anselmo), at Los Ang. '39–46, age 25 in '34.   R. (Cárlos), at Sta B. before '37, wife María Ant. Verdugo, 4 children.   R. (Catarina), widow of M. Nieto, grantee of Las Bolsas '34.   R. (Efigenio), settler at Los Ang. 1790. i. 461.   R. (Eustaquio), killed at Pauma '46. v. 617.   R. (Francisco), com. de policía at S. Diego '36, regidor '37. iii. 616. R. (Francisco), at Los Ang. '39–48.   R. (Francisco María), nat. of L. Cal. and sergt of the Sta B. comp. from 1795, alférez 1801, lieut 1805, and from 1806 comandante at S. Diego, being promoted to capt. in '20 and retired from active service in '27. He received a grant of the Peñasquitos rancho, and died in '39 at the age of about 85. He never married. Biog. ii. 5, 39–41; ment. i. 636, 665; ii. 50, 85, 99–101, 109, 117, 191, 240, 245, 340–1, 345, 451, 457, 546–8, 551–2, 571, 663; iii. 7–8, 612.   R. (Fructuoso), settler at Los. Ang. 1799; regidor 1802. ii. 110, 349.   R. (Gerónimo), zanjero at Carpentería '48. v. 631.   R. (Guadalupe), at S. Gabriel '46.   R. (Hilario), soldier at Sta B. before '37.   R. (Joaquin), grantee of Bolsa Chica, Los Ang., '41, being also claimant '52; at Los Ang. 13, '39, '46; age 47 in '39. ii. 350; iii. 639.   R. (José), inválido settler at Los Ang. '15. ii. 349.   R. (José), soldier at Sta B. '32, wife Isabel Uribe.   R. (José), at Sta B. '32, wife Maria Ign. Lugo, child. Deogracia, Gerónimo, Baltazar, Hilarion, and Gabriel; in '45 a ranchero. R. (José Manuel), brother of Francisco M., lieut in L. Cal., appointed to Cal. in '24 but did not come; he became gov. of L. Cal. ii. 515, 540.   R. (José Pedro), grantee of Calleguas rancho Sta B. '47, his heirs Gabriel et al. cl. iii. 655.   R. (José María), settler at S. José 1791–1800. i. 716.   R. (Juan), settler at Los Ang. '12. ii. 350; at Sta B. '50.   R. (Juan María), mentioned in 1801. ii. 171.   R. (Leon), 1842, Mex. sub-lieut of the batallon fijo '42–5.

iv. 289. R. (Manuel D.), mason-instructor 1792-5. i. 615. R. (Manuel García), made alférez 1789, but did not come to Cal. i. 340. R. (Mariano), at Los Ang. '39, age 25. R. (Martin), settler at Sta B. '32, wife Catalina Lizalde; at Los Ang. '46. R. (Nicolás), at Sta B. '37, wife Encarnacion Pico, and 5 children. R. (Santiago), mason-instructor 1792-5. i. 615, 684-5. R. (Toribio), ditto. i. 615. Ruiz de la Mota, see 'Mota.'
Rule (John H.), 1847, Scotch teacher at Mont., from Callao on the *Guipuzcoana*. Ruinville (Geo. W.), 1839, at Mont., as per Larkin's books. Rumschöttel (Richard), 1847, Co. C, N.Y.Vol. (v. 499); hospital steward at Sac.; at Vallejo '71-4; drowned at Stockton '74. Runyan (Levi), 1847, Co. D, Morm. Bat. (v. 469). Rupe (Henry), 1847, Co. F, 3d U.S. artill. (v. 518); supposed to be living in '64. Ruschenberger (W. S. W.), 1836, surgeon on the U.S. *Peacock*, and author of a *Narrative* of the voyage. iv. 140-2; iii. 680. Rush (Madison), 1847, acting lieut on the U.S. *Columbus*.
Russ (Adolph Gustav), 1847, son of J. C. C., born in Germany '26; of Co. C, N.Y.Vol. (v. 499); owner of a S.F. lot; in the mines '48. He settled in S.F., where he still lived in '82, having been a member of the legislature in '67. His *Biography* and *Remembrances* in my col. of MSS. are brief sketches of the family and of S.F. affairs in early times. He married Frances Simon in '51, and had 5 children surviving in '79. R. (August), 1847, brother of A. G., b. N.Y., drummer of Co. F, N.Y.Vol.; still living in S.F. '82. R. (Chas Christian Ed.), 1847, brother of A. G., b. in Germany '28; fifer of N.Y.Vol.; owner of a S.F. lot. v. 676. After his disch. at Sta B. he went to the mines in '48, making many later mining tours down to that of Frazer River in '58. The intervals were filled in with business enterprises at S.F. He married in '52, and was the father of 7 children. Still a rich and prominent citizen of S.F. in '82; life and portrait in *Contemp. Biog*. R. (Henry B.), 1847, brother of A. G., who came, as a boy, with the family; in later years supervisor of S.F., where he still lives in '85. R. (Jacob), 1846, overl. immig. of Young's party. v. 529. R. (J. C. Christian), 1847, German of Co. C, N.Y.Vol. (v. 499). He had made a fortune as a jeweller in N.Y., and lost it by burglarly one night when he closed his shop and went to see a procession in honor of Gen. Jackson. He enlisted with 3 sons, and was accomp. by his wife and other children. Opening a jeweller's shop at S.F., he obtained, as did his sons, building lots, v. 676, and rapidly regained his fortune during the flush times. He became the owner of much real estate, besides the original lot on which he built the hotel still owned by the family and called the Russ House. His house on this lot was in '47-8 the southern limit of settlement, being separated from the town by a sand hill. He also built a residence on Harrison St in the far-off wilderness, and the Russ Garden near by was from '57 a popular place of suburban resort. He died in '57, and his widow, Christina, in '80. The sons are named in this *Register;* a daughter, Mrs Mebius, died in Dresden '85.
Russell, 1846, mr of the *Sarah Parker*. v. 580. R. (Chas), 1846, of the Mormon colony, but prob. did not come to Cal. v. 547. R. (Eugene), 1845, one of Frémont's men, and of the Sta B. garrison '46. iv. 583; v. 316; later in Co. A, Cal. Bat. (v. 358). He applied for land in the S. José district '46. R. (Geo. W.), 1847, sailor on the *Independence;* applied to Larkin for a clerkship. R. (Henry or Wm), 1847, carpenter and builder at Benicia, a partner of Bryant and of Briggs. v. 672. R. (John), 1845, sailor on the *Benj. Morgan*. R. (J.), 1848, passp. from Hon. R. (Robert E.), 1846, of Cal. Bat. (v. 358); Cal. claim $46 (v. 462); witness at Wash. '48; at S. José '50. Perhaps same as Eugene. R. (Thomas), 1835, Amer. sailor picked up by the *Pilgrim* at Sta B. and landed at S. Diego in '35. iii. 412. He became a permanent resident of S. D., and is named by Dana in his *Two Years*. In '36, with one Weldon, he made an exped. in search of buried treasure at the Colorado River missions, the affair causing more excitement than increase of wealth. iii. 613. The same year he was in trouble through sending a challenge to Lumsden for a duel. iii. 618. In '40 he worked as a carpenter, being married to a native, 37 years old, and a naturalized citizen. Next heard of in '47, when he was in trouble for refusing obedience to the alcalde, or perhaps for an attempt to

commit murder. v. 618; and in '48 ment. by Buffum in the mines at Weber Creek. A man of the same name was cl. for land in Sta Cruz Co. '52.   R. (Wm), 1845, Amer. at Mont.; perhaps the owner of a S.F. lot '47; or one named in Napa Val. '47–8; or as present at Dr Semple's marriage at Benicia '47. v. 672; or some of these may be the following.   R. (Wm), 1847, Co. G, N.Y. Vol. (v. 499).

Russell (Wm H), 1846, nat. of Ky who had been somewhat prominent in local politics, memb. of the legislature, U.S. marshal, etc.; also serving in the Florida war. He came to Cal. overland with Bryant and Jacobs. v. 528; made a flowery oration at the S.F. reception of Com. Stockton in Oct. v. 295–6; served as ordnance officer with rank of major in the Cal. Bat. v. 160, 399; and was one of the commissioners to make the treaty of Cahuenga, v. 404–5, being somewhat active in the Frémont-Kearny controversy, and sec. of state at Los Ang. during Frémont's rule as gov. v. 422–4, 432–3. In March '47 he was sent east with despatches, his chief mission being to secure F.'s appointment as gov. v. 445, 454; and he was one of F.'s principal witnesses at the court-martial. v. 420, 423, 456. He came back to Cal. in '49, and practised law at S. José, Sac., and S.F. to '54 or later; about '61–2 was U.S. consul at Trinidad de Cuba, but resigned and returned to Ky, where he died. A daughter married a grandson of Henry Clay. A second wife was married about '62. Russell was a boastful man of many words, and a hard drinker, but honorable, intelligent, and popular, with much ability.   R. (Wm W.), 1847, lieut of marines on the U.S. *Independence*.   Russum (Thos), 1846, Engl. mr of the *Euphemia* and *Mary Ann* '46–7. v. 578–9; heard of in England in later years. Ruth (John), 1847, Co. G, N.Y. Vol. (v. 499).   Rutledge (John), 1847, acting lieut on the U.S. *Erie*.   Rutter (Henry), 1841, employed on Leese's launch at S.F.   R. (John), 1829, mr of the *Planet*. iii. 148.

Ryan (Edward), 1847, Co. B, N.Y. Vol. (v. 499); d. S.F. '66.   R. (Geo. F.), 1843, Irishman who got a pass in Dec.   R. (Geo. P.), 1847, went to Hon. on the *Gen. Kearny*.   R. (P. H. W.), 1847, Co. A, N.Y. Vol. (v. 499).   R. (Q.), 1847, blacksmith at Mont.   R. (Wm), 1845, sailmaker on the U.S. *Savannah*.   R. (Wm Redmond), 1847, Co. D, N.Y. Vol. (v. 499). He returned east by Panamá, and wrote his *Personal Adventures in Upper and Lower Cal.*, 1848–9, published in London '50. Died at N. Orleans '52.   Ryder (Geo. W.), 1847, arr. Oct., according to Soc. Cal. Pion. roll; died S.F. '68, age 49.

Saavedra (Ramon A.), 1790, Span. com. of transport and exploring vessels on the coast 1790-7. i. 506, 523–4, 542, 706, 728; ii. 184. See also *Hist. N. W. Coast*, through index.   Sabici (Matias), 1834, Ital. sailor who came from Mex. with the H. & P. colony, and settled at Mont. after working for a while at the Palo Colorado as a sawyer. iii. 412. He is mentioned at Los Ang. in '47, and seems to have married a daughter of Wm Wolfskill.   Sabas, (José), at Los Ang. '48.   Saenz (Ignacio), Mex. convict of 1791. i. 606.   S. (Juan), soldier of the S.F. comp. '19–30.   S. (Luis), ditto '42.   S. (Macario), of S.F. militia '37.   S. (Manuel), soldier of S.F. comp. '32–3; militia '37; at Sonoma '44, age 30.   S. (Pablo Pedro), of S.F. militia '37, exiled in '39. iii. 580; perhaps Pablo and Pedro.   S., see also 'Sais,' 'Saez.'   S. de Lucio, see 'Lucio.' Saez (José, Justo, and Miguel), settlers at S. José 1797. i. 717.   S. (Nasario), settler at S. José 786. i. 477; wife Micaela Sotelo, child. in '93, Miguel, Juan, Benedicta, and Felipa.   Sagarra (Eduardo), Peruvian shot for stealing at Mont. '31. iii. 191, 669, 673, 679.   S. (Mateo), 1818, of Bouchard's insurgents, captured at Mont. ii. 232.   Sahr (Albert), 1847, owner of S.F. lot.

Sainsevain (Pierre), 1839, French carpenter, age 20, who arrived at Sta B. on the *Ayacucho*. iv. 117, 119. His passport was dated Bordeaux, Nov. '38. He was a nephew of Louis Vignes, whom he joined for a time in the manufacture of wine at Los Angeles. In '43 he was grantee of the Cañada del Rincon rancho, iv. 655, and from '44 owned a saw-mill at Sta Cruz, being from '46 in partnership with Roussillon, building a schooner in '46, v. 641, and also from '46 having a flour-mill at S. José, which gave rise to some local troubles. iv. 685; v. 660. He went to the mines in '48, Sainsevain Bar being

named for him; and in '49 was a member of the constit. convention. In later
years he became one of the most prominent vineyardists and wine-makers in
the state. His wife, married in '45, was a daughter of Antonio Suñol. St
Clair (Trouett), 1843 (?), trapper who prob. came from N. Mex. about this
year. iv. 400; ment. by Schallenberger and in the N. Helv. Diary '44–5; still
living in Sta Cruz Co. as late as '79. St Germain (Baptiste), 1831, Fr. from
N. Mex.; prob. with Wolfskill. iii. 387. St John (Augustus A.), 1847, Co.
B, N.Y.Vol. (v. 499). St J. (Henry), 1843 (?), Engl. sailor, and later sugar-
planter in the Sandw. Isl., said to have come to Cal. this year. iv. 400. He
was later a miner and cattle-dealer, who attempted suicide at S.F. '83. St
J. (J.), 1848, passport from Hon. St J. (Stephen M.), 1847, Co. E, Morm.
Bat. (v. 469). St Quintin (Joseph), 1847, Co. C, N.Y.Vol. (v. 499). Sais
(Domingo), soldier of the S.F. comp. '26–33; of S.F. militia '37; grantee of
Cañada de Herrera, Marin, '39. iii. 711. He had been elector and regidor of
S.F. '37–9. iii. 705; and his age was '39 in '44. His name is written also
'Saenz' and 'Saez,' which are perhaps more correct forms; at least, it is im-
possible to distinguish between them in Cal. S. (Miguel), settled at Los
Ang. 1806. ii. 350. Saizar de Vitoria, see 'Vitoria.' Sajat (Lewis T.),
1847, owner of S.F. lots.

Sal (Hermenegildo), 1776, Span. soldier who came with Anza; guarda-
almacen at S.F. '78–82; alférez '82; lieut '95. He served at Mont. 1782–1800
(except '91–4 at S.F.); much of the time as habilitado and comandante. In
1800, being retired as capt., he died at Mont. Though a quick-tempered man,
he was a faithful officer, strict disciplinarian, and excellent accountant. Biog.
and fam. i. 678–80; ment. i. 297, 335, 396–7, 441, 463, 467–8, 490, 493–6, 501,
509–11, 514, 516–18, 526, 537, 547, 551–2, 569, 572–3, 588–94, 634, 680, 692–
707, 718; ii. 143, 191; iii. 11. Salamanca (Secundino), 1791, Span. lieut in
Malaspina's exped. i. 490. Salazar, 1796, com. of the Concepcion and
Activo '96–7. i. 540, 544. S. (Alonso Isidro), 1791, Span. friar, who was a
founder of Sta Cruz, where he served until his retirement in '95, writing in
Mex. an important report on the Condicion Actual de Cal. Biog. i. 497–9; ment.
i. 494, 566, 576, 579–80, 603–4, 618, 626, 661. S. (Antonio), at Los Ang.
'46; juez de campo '48. v. 626. S. (Canuto), fifer of the S.F. comp. '39–42;
in '54–5 at S.F., age 28; witness in the Santillan case. S. (Dionisio), at
Branciforte '45, age 28, wife Perfecta Castro, child. Encarnacion b. '40, and
Juan '41. S. (Fulgencio), soldier of the S.F. comp. '38–42. S. (Ignacio
and Jesus), at S. Bern. '46. S. (Isidro), teamster at Mont. '47. S. (Jorge),
soldier at Mont. '36, age 25. S. (José), convict settler 1798. i. 606. S.
(José), soldier of S.F. comp. '38–43. iv. 667; Cal. claim (v. 462). S. (José
Antonio), N. Mexican trader and settler from '39. iv. 81, 278, 387; in '46
supl. juez at S. Feliciano rancho. v. 625; in '47 alcalde at Los Ang. v. 626;
still there in '48. S. (José María), regidor at Branciforte '34. iii. 696, 588;
in '45 on the padron as a nat. of Cal., age 60, wife Hermenegilda Rios,
child. Isidro b. '15, Jorge '19, Juan '25, María Refugio '30, Refugio '33. S.
(Juan), com. of the guard at S. Fern. '23. ii. 570; in '27–30 acting habilitado
at Sta B. and S. Diego. ii. 543, 572; iii. 114. In '31–4 he was promoted from
sergt to alférez, and was once a prisoner during the sectional wars in '37. He
was acting com. of S. Diego, and is ment. as late as '46. iii. 482, 503–4, 541,
608–10; iv. 617; v. 566. S. (Miguel), soldier at S. José mission 1797. i. 556.
S. (Ramon), at Los Ang. '46.

Sales (Alex.), 1833, Amer. hunter from N. Mex., at Los Ang. '36, age 29.
Prob. Cyrus 'Alexander,' q.v.; also ment. in the campaign of '45. iv. 495. S.
(Francisco), grantee of land at S. Gabriel '45. iv. 637. Salgado (Augustin),
at Los Ang. '46. S. (Francisco), ditto; in S. Luis Ob. 50–8. S. (Tomás),
juez aux. Mont. list '44. iv. 653. Salines, 1842, Frenchman in Sutter's employ. iv. 341; prob. the Salinas named in N. Helv. Diary '45–8. Sallalla
(Faustino), soldier at the Colorado Riv. pueblos 1780–1, killed by Ind. i. 359,
362. Salleman, 1847, doubtful name of a Frenchman at S. José. Sallee,
1846, of West's overl. party, killed on the Humboldt. v. 528. Salmon
(Alejo), colegial at Sta Inés '44. iv. 426. S. (James), 1846, Delaware Ind.

in the fight at Natividad. v. 367; at Sutter's fort '47.   Salvador, Cal. Ind.
sent by Sutter to relief of the Donner party '46. He refused to eat human
flesh, but was himself shot and eaten. v. 531-2, 534, 537.   Saly, 1845, at
Sta B.   Samlyn (Henry), 1847, Co. F. Cal. Bat. (v. 358).   Samop (Jaime),
Ind. alcalde at S. Diego 1799. i. 655.   Sam Tetoy, Ind. chief, later called
'Solano,' q.v. ii. 329.   Sampson (Z.), 1848, passp. from Hon.
Sanchez (Antonio), soldier at Sta B. before '37.   S. (Estévan), soldier at
Sta B. '32, wife Romana Lopez.   S. (Francisco), son of José Ant.; soldier of
the S.F. comp. '24-5; in '27-8 elector and sec. at S.F. and S. José. ii. 592,
605; in '35 sec. iii. 704; in '37 sec., capt. of the militia, elector, and grantee
of town lots. iii. 506, 511, 701, 705; v. 683; in '38-9 acting-com. at S.F. and
grantee of S. Pedro rancho, S. Mateo co. iii. 563, 701, 713. He served as juez
de paz in '43. iv. 665; in '42 is named on the padron as a nat. of S. José,
age 35, wife Teodora Higuera, child. Luisa b. '34, Luis '36, Dolores '38, and
Pedro; in '44 capt. of defensores. iv. 407, 468, 667; in '45 capt. of the post,
and grantee of town lot. iv. 666, 669; v. 678. In '46 was acting com. at S.F.,
though absent at the capture by the U.S. v. 4, 17, 61, 239-41, 659; and in
'46-7, provoked by the depredations of the Americans, he headed a kind of
revolt, with a view to obtain guaranties, taking captive Alcalde Bartlett and
his guard, who were making a plundering tour. v. 379-83. Don Francisco
still lived at S.F. mission in '55. He is remembered as a hospitable man,
though somewhat hostile to Amer., and always regarded by them with suspicion.
Sanchez (Francisco de Jesus), 1842 (?), Mex. friar of the Zacatecanos, who
was apparently left behind in L. Cal. when the others came in '33. iii. 319.
He was minister at S. Buenaventura '42-3 and '52-3; at Sta Inés '44-50, being vice-rector of the seminary. iv. 425-6, 644-5; v. 635. He is named occasionally at S. Gabriel and Sta B. to '58, but I have found no later record of
him.   S. (Francisco Miguel), 1774, Span. friar who served at S. Gabriel, and
temporarily at other missions, till his death in 1803. Biog. ii. 113-14; ment.
i. 299, 388, 451, 459, 495-6, 511, 576, 664, 719.   S. (Gil), regidor at Mont.
'36, tithe col. at Branciforte '39, grantee of Arroyo de la Laguna '40, killed
Robles '42, agente de pol. '45. iii. 675, 676, 697; iv. 653, 663.   S. (Hilario),
grantee of Tamalpais '45. iv. 674.   S. (Isidro), son of José Ant., of S. F.
militia '37, age 23 in '42, wife Teodora Alviso, child. Dolores b. '37, Isabel
'40, and Narcisa '41; involved in the assault on Capt. Libby '45.   S. (Jacobo),
in revolt at Los Ang. '45. iv. 538-9.   S. (Joaquin), sirviente at Sta Clara
1776. i. 306.   S. (Joaquin), 1801, sergt sent from Mex. to superintend cultivation of hemp. i. 620-1; ii. 178, 181.   S. (Joaquin), soldier of the S. F.
comp. '23.   S. (José), 1791, piloto in Malaspina's exped. i. 490.
Sanchez (José Antonio), nat. of Sinaloa, soldier of the S.F. comp. from
1791, corp. from 1805, sergt from 1806, brevet alférez from '20, and alférez
from '27, or, as some records indicate, from '32. He was for some years corp.
of the Sta Cruz escolta. i. 496, 526, 535; was later engaged in over 20 Ind.
campaigns and exploring exped., especially in '17-26, being famous for his
skill and courage as an Ind. fighter. ii. 91-2, 126, 232, 322, 329, 335, 339, 371,
445, 497-9, 538, 584; iii. 111-12, 123. In '27-35 he was the grantee of Buri-
buri rancho, S.F. ii. 591-5, 664; iii. 711; in '29-33 com. at S.F., though involved in the revolt of '29. iii. 75, 96, 223-4, 333, 365, 701; but in '32-4 apparently attached nominally to the Mont. comp. iii. 671. In '36 he was retired
from active service, living on his rancho or at the mission; is named on the
padron of '42 as 67 years of age; and died in '43, being denied the comforts of
religion on his death-bed, and for a time Christian burial, through some
quarrel with the friars, to whom he was always hostile. iv. 373. He was a
good man, of known honesty and valor, but very ignorant and unfit for promotion. His sons were José de la Cruz, Francisco, Manuel, and Isidro. His
daughters married Fran. de Haro, two Valencias, and John Read.   S. (José
Ant.), settler at S. José 1791-1800. i. 716.
Sanchez (José Bernardo), 1804, Span. friar who served chiefly at S. Diego
and S. Gabriel till his death in '33. A very prominent missionary and presi-

dent of the Fernandinos in '27-30. Biog. iii. 641-2; ment. ii. 47, 99, 106-7, 110, 159, 344, 366, 394, 442, 487, 560, 564, 567, 569, 580, 655, 657; iii. 87, 91-2, 94, 96, 102, 108, 142-4, 155, 309-10, 315-16, 337-8, 347, 351. S. (José de la Cruz), son of José Ant., elector at S.F. '35, regidor '36-7. iii. 704-5; grantee of S. Mateo rancho '36-41, and admin. of S. F. mission '36-40. iii. 713, 715; named in the padron of '42 as 40 years old, wife María Josefa Merido (?), child. Soledad b. '23, Concepcion '30, José María '34, Ricardo '37, and Francisco. He was supl. juez de paz '43, sergt of defensores '44, 2d alcalde '45, and 2d juez de paz in '46. iv. 665, 666-7; v. 648. He continued to live at the mission till his death in '78.   S. (José Joaquin), at Los Ang. '25. ii. 559. S. (José María), 1824, Mex. who in '35 was grantee of Llano de Tequesquite rancho. iii. 677; age 30 in '36; juez at S. Juan B. '37. iii. 692; his rancho sacked by Ind. '38. iii. 693; iv. 75; Cal. claim '46-7 (v. 462); alcalde at S. Juan B. '47-8. v. 640. He was cl. for Las Ánimas, Sta Clara, '52
    Sanchez (Juan), sirviente at S.F. 1777. i. 297.   S. (Juan), grantee of Sta Clara rancho, Sta B., '37. iii. 656; wife Inés Guevara and 4 children before '37; still in Sta B. Co. '54.   S. (Juana María L.), 2d baptism at S.F. 1776. i. 291.   S. (Macario), at S. José 1800.   S. (Manuel), prob. son of José Ant., elector at S.F. '35 and petitioner for Cañada de Guadalupe rancho. iii. 704, 711; alf. of militia '37. iii. 701; in '42 age 30, wife Francisca Solis, child. Manuel b. '31, Rosario '37, Dolores '38, Juan Francisco '41.   S. (María Josefa), Cal. claim for $9,030 (v. 462).   S. (Miguel), 1829, Mex. convict liberated in '33. S. (Rafael), Ind. executed at Mont. '45. iv. 654.   S. (Rafael), 1842, Mex. sub-lieut of the batallon fijo '42-5, acting also as Micheltorena's sec. He remained in Cal. as custom-house officer in '45; is mentioned in the annals of '46, serving on the 1st jury and getting a grant of S. Lorenzo rancho. iv. 289, 513, 557; v. 35, 41, 45, 61, 289, 637.   S. (Ramon), 1826, Mex. sup. of the Sta Apolonia, and mr of the Magdalena, 27-8. iii. 147-8.   S. (Ramona or Romana), grantee of Butano, Sta Cruz, '44. ii. 591.   S. (Teodoro), juez de campo at Laguna Seca '35. iii. 674.
    Sanchez (Tomás), at Los Coyotes rancho, Los Ang., '39, age 37; collector of taxes at Los Ang. '43. iv. 633. After '49 he was somewhat prominent as sheriff; still living in '77.   S. (Tomito), at S. Pascual '46. v. 352; perhaps same as Tomás.   S. (Urbano), owner of the Sta Apolonia '26. iii. 148, 682; prob. not in Cal.   S. (Vicente), settler at Los Ang. '14-19. ii. 349, 354; arrested and sent to Sta B. in irons '22. ii. 559; elector and prob. alcalde '26-7. ii. 560; iii. 33; member of the dip. '28. iii. 41-2. In '29-32 he as diputado, alcalde, and citizen was involved in a complicated series of troubles, being deposed and imprisoned, and in turn imprisoning others. The details cannot be presented, even if anybody ever understood them. He was a vicious, gambling, quarrelsome fellow, though of some intelligence and wealth; and political quarrels between Echeandía and Victoria had something to do with his troubles, about which suits were pending as was '44. ii. 561; iii. 187-8, 195-6, 200, 205, 212, 230, 630, 634. In '36-9 he had something to do with the vigilance com., and with the sectional quarrel on both sides. iii. 417, 432, 491, 504, 565, 636. In '42-4 his name appears, being the grantee of Ciénega or Paso de la Tijera, and also comis. de zanjas. iv. 295, 629, 633-4; and in '45 he was again alcalde, not free from popular complaints. iv. 497, 523, 633. I have no later record of him.   Sancho (Juan Bautista), 1804, Span. friar who served at S. Antonio till his death in '30. Biog. ii. 621; ment. ii. 152, 385, 388, 655.
    Sandeau, 1846, a mountaineer with Kearny from N. Mex. Lancey.   Sandels (G. M. W.), 1842, Swedish scientist who came from Mex. on the schr California, and went to Hon. on the Diamond in '43. He wrote an account of his observations under the name of 'King's Orphan.' iv. 345-6, 363, 565, 640, 650, 665.   Sanders (Allen), 1845, Amer. blacksmith from Or. in the McMahon party, working for Sutter Jul.-Dec. In the spring of '46 he visited Napa and Sonoma, married Miss Bonney, and in March went with the Bonneys to Or., where he is said to have been living in '80. iv. 572; v. 526.   S. (Horace), 1845, overl. immig. of the Grigsby-Ide party. iv. 579, 587. He was perhaps a

Bear Flag man. v. 110; and served as sergt Co. E, Cal. Bat. v. 361; having a
Cal. claim of $20 (v. 462). Thos Knight states that in '70-1, S. was living near
Carson, Nev.   S. (Richard T.), 1847, Co. E, Morm. Bat. (v. 469).   Sander-
son (Geo. B.), 1847, asst surg. U.S.A., surg. of the Morm. Bat., and an object
of the most intense dislike on the part of the Mormons. He went east with
Gen. Kearny. v. 446, 452, 477, 480-2.   Sandoval (Josefa), 1791, wife of Gov.
Romeu. i. 488, 490.   S. (Luciano), 1842, cornet of the batallon fijo '42-5. iv.
289.   S. (Pánfilo), 1828, Mex. convict liberated '34.
    San Estévan (Antonio), 1831, chief of a N. Mex. caravan. iii. 396.   Sands
(J. R.), 1847, mr of the Benj. Tucker.   Sanford, 1843, at Sutter's fort '45,
and perhaps an overl. immig. of the Chiles party. iv. 393, 578.   S. (Sam.),
1847, Co. D, N.Y.Vol. (v. 499).   Sanger (John), 1844, mr of the Newton; d.
at S. Diego. iv. 567; perhaps 'Sawyer.'   Sangrador (Miguel), tanner-in-
structor 1792-5. i. 615, 725.
    Santa Ana, soldier at Sta B. '24. ii. 532.   Santa Cruz (José Antonio),
com. de policía at Mont. '33, '36, juez de campo '35. iii. 673-5; age 43 in '36,
nat. of Mex., wife Gertrudis Villavicencio, child Juan José.   Santa María,
1815, teacher who came with Gov. Sola. ii. 426.   Sta M., Ind. sirv. at S.
Luis Ob., shot by Frémont. v. 374.   Sta M. (José María), clerk of the court
at Mont. '42; owner of S.F. lot '46. v. 684.   Sta M. (Vicente), 1776, Span.
friar who served chiefly at S. Buen., where he died in 1806. Biog. ii. 121-2;
ment. i. 240-1, 246, 287, 300, 302, 376, 382, 385, 388, 399, 466, 522, 553, 576,
674; ii. 159-60, 490.   Santiago (Juan José Norberto), 1786, Span. friar, who
served at S. Juan Cap. and retired in 1810. Biog. ii. 110; ment. i. 388, 423,
458-9, 474, 563, 576, 657; ii. 114, 159-60, 197.   Santillan (José Prudencio),
1841, Mex. novice of Ind. parentage who came with the bishop and soon became a priest. iv. 195. He was parish priest at S.F. mission in '46-50, though
much of the time absent; and went to Mex. in '50. His chief and only fame
rests on his claim of '50 to the misssion lands under a grant of Gov. Pico in
'46, a grant which after a long and famous litigation, though approved by the
land com. and district court, was finally declared invalid by the U.S. sup.
court, being doubtless fraudulently antedated. v. 558, 659-60. Santillan became asst curate at Mazatlan before '56, and my last record of him is that in
'59 he was arrested for refusal to celebrate the return of peace at the order of
Gov. Pesqueira; yet in '78 the holders of the land claims professed to be able
to produce him as a witness.   Santos, sirv. at Soledad 1791-1800. i. 499.
S., neoph. grantee of Rincon del Alisal, Sta Clara, '44. iv. 672.   S. (Guadalupe), at Mont. '36, age 26.
    Sargent (Constantine), 1846, purser's clerk on the U.S. Congress, committed
suicide at Mont. Dec.   S. (Henry S.), 1848, nat. of Conn. recently from Or.;
d. at S.F. Oct.   S. (James K.), 1847, Co. F, N.Y.Vol. (v. 499).   Sarmiento
(José M.), 1842, Mex. lieut of the batallon fijo; died on the voy. to Cal. iv.
289.   Sarría (Vicente Francisco), 1809, Span. friar whose missionary service
was at S. Cárlos and Soledad until his death in '35. He was prefect in '13-19,
'23-30, and president '23-5; one of the ablest, best, and most prominent of
the Fernandinos. Biog. iii. 688-9; ment. i. list of auth.; iii. 88, 148, 159-60,
217-18, 240, 327-30, 364, 383, 386, 394, 396-409, 451-3, 461, 491, 501-5, 512-
13, 517-18, 521, 525-6, 535, 622-3, 655, 657, 659, 662; iii. 7, 16-19, 87, 89-91,
128, 191, 336, 338, 350-1.   Satte (Juan José), 1827, Moorish servant from S.
Blas an Engl. ship; at S. José '29, age 42.
    Sauerweid (Alex. A.), 1848, Russian, in S. Joaq. Co. '78.   Saunders
(John), 1838, Amer. or Irish sailor at Mont. and Sta Cruz '38, '43; at S.F. '44,
age 30. iv. 119. He went to sea again in '47-8, but returned in '52-3, soon
shipping again.   S. (Theodore R.), 1847, Co. A, N.Y. Vol. (v. 499); in N.Y.
city '82.   S. (Wm L.), 1833, trapper named in Mont. lists of '34. In '34 he
writes Capt. Jos. Walker a severe letter denying any indebtedness and claiming to hold a receipt from Bonneville. He may therefore have come in '33
with Walker (iii. 389), or in '32 with Dye, who mentions a Saunders in his
party.
    Savage (Chas), 1845, at Sutter's fort. iv. 578; went to Or. '46. v. 526; and

was at Jacksonville '81. S. (Eliza), 1846, of the Mormon colony. v. 546; in Utah '84. S. (James D.), 1846, overl. immig. who served in Co. F, Cal. Bat. v. 374 (358); named in the *N. Helv. Diary*, 47–8. He had been a trapper and mountaineer, having great influence among the Ind., by whose aid he is said to have acquired much wealth in the gold mines. In '48–9 he had trading posts on the Mariposa and Fresno; and in later times rendered great service to govt and to settlers as interpreter, commissioner, and major in com. of a volunteer battalion. He was probably the discoverer of the Yosemite Valley. In '52 he was killed at the Kings River reservation in a quarrel with Maj. Harvey, the county judge. An ignorant man of much natural shrewdness, he made many warm friends and bitter foes. It is related of him that he made it a point to marry a chief's daughter in every tribe; exchanged hardware and whiskey by weight, ounce for ounce, with the Ind., for gold-dust; and bet his weight in gold on the turn of a card in a S.F. gambling-house. S. (Levi), 1847, Co. D, Morm. Bat. (v. 469); at Lorqueville, Utah, '82.

Sawis (Nathaniel), 1816, doubtful name of a deserter from the *Albatross*. ii. 275. Sawyer (John), 1844, mr of the *Newton;* d. at S. Diego '45. iv. 453, 567. S. (Joseph), 1828, Scotchman at S. Diego '28–9. Saxton (Chas), 1847, Co. G, N.Y. Vol. (v. 499). Schaffer (J. R.), 1848, nat. of Va; at Hon. from S.F. on the *Tepic;* dist attorney of S. Joaq. Co.; d. in '75, perhaps in Idaho. Schallenberger (Moses), 1844, nat. of Ohio, and overl. immig. as a boy in the Stevens party. His remarkable adventures at Donner Lake, where he was left by the party and passed the winter alone, are noted in iv. 445–7, 453–4, as related in his MS., *Overland in '44*. He appears in various records of '46–8 as clerk and trader at Sutter's fort, S. José, Mont., and Sta Cruz; but finally settled at S. José, where he acquired considerable property, and was still living in '85. I have been unable to obtain information about his career in late years or his family. His sister was the wife of Dr Townsend of the Stevens party, and his daughter Maggie in '84–5 was a teacher, who from her father's notes wrote the MS. narrative of the overland trip. Schenck (James F.), 1846, lieut on the U.S. *Congress*, serving in Stockton's Bat. '46–7; nat. of Ohio; rear-admiral '79. v. 268, 281. S. (Woodhull S.), 1845, lieut on the U.S. *Portsmouth*. Schiller (Ed.), 1847, Co. A, N.Y. Vol. (v. 499); d. Texas '81. Schimer (Earnest), 1847, Co. G, ditto. Schlottour (Karl), 1847, Co. F, ditto; baker at S.F. '48. v. 683; at Rough-and-Ready '82. Schmidt (Geo. W.), 1848, German who died at S. Diego '73; an early steamboat man. S. (Jacob), 1847, cooper at N. Helv. S. (Karl), 1821, Russian manager at Ross, succeeding Kuskof '21–6. ii. 464–5, 506–7, 642, 648. iii. 146. Schmölder (B.), 1846 (?), author of the *Neuer Wegweiser*, who styles himself in June '47 as Capt. 'from Cal.' He sought to organize a German colony. Schneider (Johann), 1846, Co. B, Cal. Bat. (v. 358). Schoa (Juan), at Los Ang. '46. Schoolcraft (Henry A.), 1847, sergt Co. H, N.Y. Vol. v. 504; Sutter's agent, recorder, and alcalde at Sac. '48–9. He went east, and while returning with an appointment as collector of Sac. died at sea near Acapulco '53. Schoonmaker (Jacob J.), 1847, Co. A, N.Y. Vol. (v. 499); at Vineland, N.J., '82. S. (Milton C.), 1847, ditto; d. at Stockton '50. Schreador (Geo.), 1847, Co. D, ditto; d. Napa Co. '82. Schreiber (Chas), 1846, Cal. Bat. v. 358; one of the Sta B. garrison. Schroeder (Martin), 1847, Engl. mr of a vessel, married at Mazatlan, who brought his family in '49 via Hon.; d. at S. José '81, leaving 5 children. Schroth (Chas), 1848, on roll of the Soc. Cal. Pion.; living in S.F. '81.

Schubart (Peter), 1842, Dane naturalized in Feb.; also called 'Serbia.' iv. 341. Schultz (Ernest), 1847, owner of S.F. lot. Schultze (Fred.), 1847, Co. F, N.Y. Vol. (v. 499). Schulz, 1848, cooper at Sutter's fort. Schumacher (John), 1847, Co. G, N.Y. Vol. (v. 499); at Los Ang. '82. Schwartz (John L.), 1841, Dutch immig. of the Bartleson party. 270, 275, 279. In '44–5 he obtained a grant of Nueva Flandria on the Sac. Riv., iv. 672, where he established a fishing station and built a boat. He and his place are described by Bryant in '46 and Buffum in '48; also mentioned in *N. Helv. Diary*, '45–7. He died in '51 or '52, and his brother George was unsuccessful cl. for the rancho in '53. Schweitzer (Philip), 1847, Co. F, 3d U.S. artill. (v. 518).

322   PIONEER REGISTER AND INDEX.

Scollan (John), 1847, Co. A, N.Y. Vol. (v. 499); at Sta B. '82.   Scott
(Andrew), 1847, Co. D, N.Y. Vol. (v. 499).   S. (Antonio J.), 1846, grantee of
S. Luis Rey and Pala.   S. (Chas G.), 1847, sergt Co. B, N.Y. Vol. (v. 499);
treasurer of S.F.; d. in Nicaragua '56.   S. (Felix), 1845, nat. of Va and prob.
overl. immig. iv. 578-9. One of his daughters died at Sutter's fort Jan. '46.
In March he went to Or., v. 526, where he became a prominent settler, visiting Cal. again about '51-3, and being killed by Ind. in '58. See *Hist. Or.*, i.
750.   S. (Gabriel), 1846, had a 'Cal. claim' (v. 462).   S. (G. J.), 1848, had
a cabin on the Capay rancho, Yolo Co.
     Scott (James), 1826, nat. of Scotland, who first visited Cal. as sup. of the
Olive Branch and *Waverly*, being mr of the *Huascar* in '27-8. iii. 176, 154, 147.
From '30 he seems to have considered Sta B. his home, though constantly on
the move, as shown by his business corresp. in my collection. ii. 573; iii. 409;
iv. 117; sup. and mr of various vessels; also otter-hunter. iv. 144, 209, 566;
v. 578. From '39, or earlier, to '47 a partner of Capt. John Wilson; ment. in
mission accounts '40. iii. 657, 660; in '45 purchaser of S. Luis Ob. and grantee
of Cañada de Chorro rancho. iv. 553, 558, 655, 658-9. Not friendly to Amer.
in '46-7, but not much heard of in those years.   He died at Sta B. in '51.
S. (James), 1833, Engl. sailor on the *Catalina*. iii. 409; in Mont. dist. '34-5;
in trouble on the schr *California* '39.   S. (James), 1846, of the Mormon
colony, excommunicated at S.F. v. 546; owner of S.F. lots '47.   S. (James
R.), 1847, Co. E, Morm. Bat. (v. 469).
     Scott (John), 1831, sup. of the *Ayacucho* '31-5. iii. 381; perhaps James.
S. (John), 1845, possibly of Frémont's party, but prob. the following. iv. 583,
587, 453.   S. (John), 1845, overl. immig. of the Grigsby-Ide party. iv. 579,
587. Acc. to the *Yolo Co. Hist.* he lived as a hunter in Capay Val. to June
'46; he was prob. one of the Bears. v. 110; and served as a lieut in the Cal.
Bat. v. 435. Swan remembers a Jack Scott in the mines from Sta Cruz '48.
S. (Leonard M.), 1847, Co. E, Morm. Bat. (v. 469).   S. (Sam.), 1847, nat. of
Ky and overl. immig.; a trader at Sta Clara, successful miner who built the
first house at Placerville, and finally a settler near Snelling, where he died in
'81, leaving one son, Moses.   S. (Wm), 1846, marine on the *Portsmouth*,
wounded at the San Gabriel in '47. v. 395.   S. (Wm), 1847, Co. C, N.Y.
Vol. (v. 499); owner of S.F. lot; county treasurer of S.F.; killed in Nicaragua.
     Scott (Wm W.), 1845, brother of John and overl. immig. of the Grigsby-
Ide party. iv. 579, 587. He came from St Louis mainly for his health, and
took part in the Bear revolt, being also, it is said, the man who in July '46
carried the U.S. flag from Sonoma to Sac. v. 110, 148, 244. In '46-8 he kept
a store at Sonoma, being, I suppose, of the firm S. & Boggs often named, and
sometimes visiting Sac. with goods for sale. In '47 he married Mary Ann
Smith; in Jan. '48 he killed a man named McRice; and I have his autograph
letter of Feb., in which he attributes his bad conduct to the use of liquor, and
solemnly 'swears off' forever. Later in the year he appears as a carpenter in
Sutter's employ, and is said to have been at the Coloma mill when gold was
found. A man of the same name settled in Scott Valley, Lake Co., in '48, and
was still living in '54. The preceding items may refer to more than one man.
Scriver (Chas) see 'Schreiber.' v. 316.   Scullen (John), 1847, Irishman of Sta
B., said to have been killed by Ind. in Ariz. '66; prob. 'Scollan,' q.v.
     Seagrim (Thos), 1839, sailor on the schr *California*.   Seaman (Stephen),
1846, acting sailmaker on the U.S. *Dale*.   Searles (Geo.), 1847, Co. D, N.Y.
Vol. (v. 499).   Searls (Susan A.), 1846, of the Mormon colony, prob. not coming to Cal. v. 547.   Sears (Franklin), 1845, nat. of Mo. who crossed the
plains to Or. in '44, and came to Cal. in the McMahon party, 572-4, 587, gaining an unenviable reputation as an Indian-killer. He is named in the *N. Helv.*
Diary '45-6, and in March '46 was nearly killed by a fall from his horse at
Sutter's fort. Recovering, he joined Frémont and went south, serving at S.
Pascual under Gillespie and in Stockton's campaign. An account of S. Pascual by Boggs in the *Napa Registr*, May 11, '72, seems to be founded on his
statements. In '48-9 he took out large quantities of gold near Bidwell's Bar;
and in '51 settled at Sonoma, where he was living in '80 at the age of 63. His

wife was Margaret Swift, and there were 2 children surviving in '80, one of them, Rachel, being the widow of J. R. Snyder. S. (John), 1845, brother of Franklin, and overl. immig. of the Grigsby-Ide party, iv. 579, 587, with his wife. He was a blacksmith and settled at Sonoma, where he was prob. a Bear Flag man—indeed, Mrs S. is credited with having furnished flannel for the famous flag. v. 110, 147-8. He was capt. of Co. D, Cal. Bat. v. 359, 361; had a Cal. claim (v. 462); and was in the Feather River mines '48. He seems either to have left Cal. or died soon after this date.

Sebastian, Ind. who died at Nicasia '80, said to be about 100 years old. S., 1773, Ind. who was the 1st Christian to make the trip by land from Cal. to Sonora. i. 221. S. (Narcisco), 1844, Canadian at Sta Rosa, having left Ridley's service. Secondi, or Sagondyne (James), 1845, Delaware Ind. of Frémont's party. iv. 583; still in F.'s employ '53. Seely, 1845, in N.Y. '84, claiming to have been one of Frémont's party; also declared by a newspaper corresp. to be the original of Bret Harte's 'Yuba Bill.' Segundo (Angel), sirviente at S.F. 1777. i. 297. Segura (José María), 1842, Mex. capt. of the batallon fijo, who remained in Cal. after Micheltorena's departure, acted as com. at Los Ang. for a time in '46, and seems to have departed with Flores in '47. iv. 289, 364, 492, 513; v. 408. Seibert, 1847, in Sutter's employ '47-8. Seider (Geo. F.), 1847, Co. A, N.Y.Vol. (v. 499). 'Seis Cuartillas' (Theodore), 1834, French carpenter at Mont. Sel, see 'Sells.' Selden (Ed. A.), 1846, mid. on the U.S. Columbus, act. lieut in com. of the prize Julia '46-7. v. 358, 378. Selfridge (Thos O.), 1847, capt U.S.N., com. of the Columbus and later of the Dale. Sellers (Jackson), 1847, sergt Co. K, N.Y.Vol. v. 504. Sells (Joseph), 1846, at Sutter's fort '47-8; also called Selly and Sel; member of the Donner relief parties. v. 538, 541.

Semple (Robert), 1845, nat. of Ky and overl. immig. of the Hastings party. iv. 586-7; a printer and dentist by trade. In '45-6 he was engaged in farming with Johnson and Keyser, first becoming prominent in the Bear revolt. v. 79, 106-7, 110, 114-19, 298, 644. Though a pronounced filibuster and conspirator, he doubtless exerted his influence with much success to restrain the lawless vagabonds of his party from the commission of outrages. In July he went to Mont., served for a time in Fauhtleroy's dragoons (v. 232, 247), and then with Walter Colton published at Mont. the 1st Cal. newspaper, the Monterey Californian. v. 291-3, 658. Early in '47 the paper was transferred to S.F., and Semple, obtaining from Vallejo a large tract of land on Carquines Strait, devoted his energies, in company with Larkin, to the building of a great city at Benicia, as fully recorded in v. 670-4, at the same time taking an interest in various political matters, delivering a 4th of July oration at S.F., and owning a S.F. lot, which he patriotically gave away to show his faith in Benicia as the metropolis. v. 433, 455, 646, 676. His great speculation of city-building was not very successful, but he made a large amount of money in '48-50 by running a ferry-boat across the strait. In '49 he was a member and president of the constit. convention; but does not appear later in public life. He moved to Colusa Co., where he died in '54 at the age of 48, his death being the result of a fall from his horse. Dr S. was a good-natured, popular, and honorable man, of much intelligence and natural ingenuity, of some education, a good speaker—indeed, there were few things he could not do fairly well, though noted for obstinate faith in his way of doing things as always the best. His height was about 6 ft. 8 in., giving rise to no end of amusing stories, true and false, respecting such achievements as wading the strait of Carquines. In '47, being a widower, he married Frances, daughter of Stephen Cooper, by whom he had a daughter, Mary Benicia. His widow is living in '85 as Mrs Van Winkle. A son, John W., came to Cal. in '49, dying in '50; and also a brother, C. D., who was claimant for the Colus rancho. v. 671. Señan (José Francisco de Paula), 1787, Span. friar who served at S. Cárlos and S. Buenaventura until his death in 1823. A model missionary, who was president in 1812-15, and '20-3, being also prefect in '23. Biog. ii. 490-1; ment. i. 388, 469, 572, 576-7, 598, 604-5, 674, 685; ii. 121-2; 159, 209, 240, 258, 270, 317, 326-7, 333, 351, 394, 396, 398, 405, 410-11, 451-3, 479, 487, 493, 497, 499-502, 569, 571,

578, 580, 655, 657.   Senar (Francisco), 1828, doubtfu 'name of an Irish sailor at Mont. '28–9.   Septem (Henry), 1816, sailor of the *Albatross*. ii. 275.

Sepúlveda (Diego), one of the grantees of S. Bernardino rancho '42; somewhat prominent in the Flores revolt at Los Ang. '46–7. v. 312, 320, 407–8. S. (Dolores), son of Juan José, b. S. Diego 1793, settler at Los Ang. 1812, still living there '46–8, having been accidentally wounded in '39. ii. 349, 565, 595.   S. (Dolores), killed by Ind. at Purísima '24. ii. 529.   S. (Dolores), soldier of the S.F. comp. '37.   S. (Encarnacion), grantee of Ojo de Agua '40. iv. 633.   S. (Enrique), prisoner at S. Buen. '38; grantee of S. Pascual '40. iii. 554–5, 634.   S. (Fernando), son of Francisco, at Los Ang. '39–'46; ment. in '40–3. iii. 632–3, 639.   S. (Francisco), settler at Los Ang. '15. ii. 349; in '25 regidor and acting alcalde ii. 559; iii. 11; in '31 in the operations against Victoria, by whom he was imprisoned. iii. 196, 208; in '36–7 comisionado of S. Juan Cap. iii. 626–7; 49 years old in '39, when he was grantee of S. Vicente and Sta Mónica. iii. 634; ment. in '40–3; iii. 639; iv. 629. In '52 he was cl. for the rancho.   S. (Ignacio), killed at the S. Gabriel '47. v. 396.

Sepúlveda (Ignacio), son of José, b. before '48, educated in the east as a lawyer. In later years he became a very prominent lawyer of Los Angeles, and one of the foremost of all the native Californians in respect of both ability and character. He was a member of the legislature in '64; served in Mex. under Maximilian; was county judge in '70–3, district judge from '74, and superior judge from '80, resigning his position in '83 to accept a responsible position as representative of Wells, Fargo, & Co. in Mex., where he has since resided to '85. His *Historical Memoranda*, i. 644, is a valuable contribution to my collection of original MS.; and he has otherwise aided me in my work. His wife, who died before '77, was an American, and there was a daughter.   S. (Isabel), at S. Rafael '42. iv. 237.   S. (José), regidor at Los Ang. '33–4. iii. 635; in '36–8, active among the vigilantes, alcalde, grantee of S. Joaquin rancho, and somewhat prominent on both sides in the sectional quarrels between north and south. iii. 432, 485, 495–9, 509–10, 518–19, 565, 633, 636. His age was 37 acc. to the padron of '39, when he was regidor and took part in a tumulto. iii. 589, 636; iv. 633; sub-prefect in '45. iv. 632–3. He was cl. for S. Joaquin in '52, and died in Sonora '75. His wife was a sister of Juan Ávila.   S. (José), two of the name at Los Ang. '39, a shoemaker and farmer.   S. (José), juez de campo at S. José '43. iv. 685; still there in '55. S. (José del Cármen), at Los Ang. '46–8.   S. (José L.), juez de paz at Los Ang. '42. iv. 632; 2d alcalde '46, '48. v. 625–6; grantee of Palos Colorados '46. v. 627; nominated for prefect '45; memb. of the council '50. I am not sure that he was not the same man as José above.   S. (José Manrico and José Miguel), at Los Ang. '46.   S. (Juan), soldier of the S.F. comp. '20–7; at S. José '41, age 41, wife Francisca Pacheco, child. Demesio b. '29, Silveria '31, Lucía '33, María Ant. '35, Sebastian '38, Bartolomé '39.   S. (Juan), juez de campo at Palos Verdes '40. iii. 637; 2d alcalde at Los Ang. '45, taking some part in politics. iv. 497, 539, 633; age 27 in '39; alcalde in '49; supervisor '54; county assessor '57–8.   S. (Juan María), at Los Ang. '46; justice of the peace '56.   S. (Manuel), at Los Ang. '46–8.   S. (Patricio), soldier at Sta B. before '37.   S. (Rafael), settler at Los Ang. 1789. i. 461.   S. (Vicente), grantee of La Sierra, Los Ang., '46. v. 628.

Serbia (Pedro), 1842, Danish resid. of S.F., age 26; same as 'Schubert,' q.v., and probably intended for 'Sherrebeck,' q.v.   Serer (Domingo) corporal at Mont. '36, age 26.   Serna (Manuel), reputed centenarian of S. Diego '79. S. (Patricio), Mex. soldier of the Hidalgo comp. at Mont. '36, age 33.   Serra (Junípero), 1769, Span. friar, 1st president of the missionaries, and founder of many missions, who died at S. Cárlos Aug. 28, 1784. Biog. i. 409–16; ment. i. 116–23, 129, 134–5, 137–8, 164–8, 170, 175–7, 181, 183–4, 187–94, 199–221, 224, 227, 229–31, 238–9, 244, 246, 248–9, 255, 257, 268, 270–1, 280, 287, 297–304, 309, 320–8, 330–1, 333, 351, 373, 376, 378, 382, 386, 388–400, 414–15, 422, 455, 457, 459, 469, 473–4, 476, 486, 671, 687.   Serrano (Florencio), 1834, Mex. of the Hijar & Padrés colony. iii. 263, 268; who served in '35 as clerk of the admin. at S. Antonio, and as teacher. iii. 687; and from '36 as clerk of

different offices at Mont. taking part in the revolt against Alvarado in '37, and
being sec. of the ayunt. in '38. iii. 524–5, 675. In '44 he was 2d alcalde. iv.
653, 656, 404, 411; and in '45–6 síndico and sec. of the prefecture, serving on
the 1st jury in '46. iv. 652–3; v. 289, 636. In '48–9 he succeeded Colton as
alcalde of Mont. v. 637–8; being before and later engaged in trade. His wife
was Rita, sister of Joaquin de la Torre, and there were several sons who supported Don Florencio in his old age, poverty, and blindness. He died in '77
at the age of 63. He was of Span. parentage, of fair education and good repute. Shortly before his death he dictated for me his *Apuntes*, a full statement
of his life and recollections of Cal. affairs, which throws light on many topics.
S. (Francisco), alcalde at Los Ang. 1799. i. 661.   S. (Ignacio), at Los Ang.
'46.   S. (José), juez de campo, Los Ang. '35. iii. 635; grantee of Cañada de
los Alisos '42–6, iv. 634, being also cl. in '52.   S. (José Antonio), son of Leandro, at S. Juan Cap. '41. iv. 626; grantee of Pauma '44. iv. 621; in the
fight at S. Pascual '46. v. 352; still living at S. Diego '75, age 61. His wife
was a daughter of Rosario Aguilar.   S. (José S.), at Los Ang. '46.   S. (Leandro), son of a soldier of the 1st exped., b. at S. Diego; for many years
majordomo of Pala for the mission S. Luis Reg.; in '28 maj. at S. Juan Cap.,
and grantee of Temescal, ii. 547, 663; iii. 612, where he spent the rest of his
life, dying in '52. His wife was Presentacion Yorba and later Josefa Montalba.
S. (Manuel), killed by Ind. at Pauma '46. v. 617.   S. (Rafaela), at S. Diego
'21, '41. ii. 546; iv. 619.   S. (Tomás), juez de campo at Los Ang. '48. v. 626.
Servin (Ignacio), 1842, Mex. sub-lieut in the batallon fijo '42–5. iv. 289, 513;
still in Cal. '46. v. 41.

Sessions (Wm B.), 1847, Co. A, Morm. Bat. (v. 469).   Sessor (Peter),
1847, Co. F, N.Y. Vol. (v. 499); in S.F. '82.   Settle (Josiah), 1840 (?), nat.
of Ohio said to have crossed the plains to Cal. this year; prob. an error,
though he may have come from N. Mex. iv. 120. Went to Or. '52, to Wash.
Ter. '60, and died at Seattle '76. Sevy (Thomas), see 'Levy.'   Sexton
(Daniel), 1841, nat. of La and overl. immig. of the Workman party. iv. 278–9.
He worked as a carpenter in the Los Ang. region, and finally settled at S.
Bern.; claims to have raised the U.S. flag at his camp '40. iv. 342; served in
the campaign against Micheltorena '45. iv. 495; carried a message from Stockton to Frémont '47. v. 402; married an Ind. woman; cl. for land in Los Ang.
'52; still living in '84.   S. (Geo. S.), 1847, Co. A, Morm. Bat. (v. 469);
Co. reënl.   S. (Lorin), 1847, Co. I, N.Y. Vol. (v. 499).   Seyman (James),
1848, at Sutter's fort.   Seymour (Chas H.), 1848, on roll of Soc. Cal. Pion.;
d. S.F. after '81; an employé in the mint.   S. (Sir Geo. F.), 1846, admiral
in com. of the British Pac. squadron at Mont. on the *Collingwood*, July. v.
199–214, 232, 577.

Shadden (Thos J.), 1843, Amer. immig. of the Hastings party from Or.
accomp. by his family. iv. 390, 400. In '44 he obtained a land grant in Yolo
Co. iv. 674; is named in '45–6 as visiting Sutter's fort from S. José, Sta Cruz,
and other points; and had a 'Cal. claim' of $837 (v. 462). A son is said to
have been born in '47. Shadden settled on the Cosumnes, where he lived in a
cabin of tules in '49, having been before that date a miner and trader in mules.
He went to Or. about '51.   Shaler (Wm), 1803, mr of the *Lelia Byrd* 1803–4,
and author of a *Journal* pub. in 1808, which was prob. the 1st extended account of Cal. published in the U.S. ii. 10–14, 21–4, 102–3, 109, 119, 122, 143–4,
183.   Shannon (John). v. 621; see 'Charbonneau.'   S. (Wm E.), 1847,
capt. Co. I, N.Y. Vol., in com. at S. Diego '47–8, being also collector. v. 504,
514, 617, 619. In '49 a trader, of firm S. & Cady, at Coloma, also alcalde,
member of the constit. convention, and district judge. From Dec. '49 a lawyer at Sac., where he died in '50 of cholera.   Sharkey (Frank L.), 1847, Co.
I, N.Y. Vol. (v. 499); at Norwich, Conn., '82.   Sharnon (John), 1847, alcalde
at S. Diego; prob. 'Charbonneau,' q. v.   Sharp (Matthew W. or A.), 1847,
Co. I, ditto; at S. Diego '48; died near Coloma '50.   Shattuck, 1842, lieut
U.S.N. with Com. Jones at Mont. iv. 308.

Shaw, 1846, overl. immig. who died on the Calaveras in '49.   S. (Charles),
1846, Co. C, 1st U.S. dragoons (v. 336).   S. (James), 1848, guide to return-

ing Mormons. S. (James B.), 1846, nat. of Australia; resid. of Sonoma Co. '51–77. *Son. Co. Hist.* S. (Thomas), 1824 (?), nat. of Mass. I have his autograph letter, apparently written at S. Pedro Oct. 28, 1824, but there may be an error. ii. 526. In '26–8 he was clerk and sup. on the *Courier* and *Waverly.* iii. 154; in 30–1 on the *Pocahontas*, making a contract to carry away Gov. Victoria. iii. 148, 210, 383; in '33–5 sup. and sometimes mr of the *Volunteer, Harriet Blanchard*, and *Lagoda.* iii. 382, 384, 410. He was in Boston '36, not expecting to revisit Cal.; but in '39–40 he came back as sup. of the *Monsoon*, his name often appearing in commercial corresp. and mission accounts. iii. iv. 105; iii. 623, 727. He is said to have died in Boston about '66.

Shea (Wm), 1840, one of the exiled foreigners not known to have returned. iv. 18. Shearman, 1844, mr of the *Menkar.* iv. 567. Shehey, 1847, died at Sutter's fort Oct. Sheldon (Geo.), 1848, passp. from Hon. S. (Henry B.), 1848, editor and part owner of the S.F. *Californian.* v. 658; sec. of the guards; owner of a lot at S. José. Went to the Sandw. Isl. about '65. S. (Jared), 1840, nat. of Vt, who came from N. Mex. or Sonora with a pass dated March 9, '40. iv. 117, 120. Possibly he had visited Cal. before, as his arrival is often credited to '34 or '32. He was naturalized in '43, then describing himself as a carpenter who had arrived in '40, being in '44 grantee of the Omochumne rancho on the Cosumnes. iv. 672; where he was a partner of Wm Daylor, and where he spent the rest of his life but for his service in the Micheltorena campaign, iv. 486, 501, and a brief experience in the mines. In '51 he was killed in a difficulty with miners about a dam. His wife, married in '47, was a daughter of Thomas Rhoads, and survived him with 3 children, Wm b. '48, Sarah '49, and Catherine '51 (drowned in '52). Shelikof (Paul), 1825, Russian manager of Ross '25–9, succeeding Schmidt. ii. 648, 650–1; iii. 213. Shelly (Pearson B.), 1847, mr of the *Gen. Kearny.* v. 518; and trader at S.F. '47–8, of firm S. & Norris. v. 680; also owner of S.F. lot. Shelton, 1842, at S.F.; prob. 'Sheldon,' q.v. S. (Sebert C.), 1847, Q.M. sergt Morm. Bat., but reduced to ranks Co. D. v. 477. Shepherd (Edmund), 1846, mid. U.S.N., acting lieut in Stockton's Bat. '46–7. v. 385. S. (Lafayette), 1847, Co. A, Morm. Bat. (v. 469). Sherman (Heran V. S.), 1847, Co. H, N.Y. Vol. (v. 499); d. before '82. S. (J.), 1837, named in Larkin's accounts.

Sherman (Richard M.), 1846, nat. of R.I., who passed his boyhood on a farm, and then went to sea for 5 or 6 years, coming to Cal. from Honolulu as clerk on the *Euphemia*, leaving the vessel at S.F., where he worked as bookkeeper for Paty & Davis, and in '47–8 made a trip to the Isl. as sup. of the *Euphemia.* He became the owner of a town lot, on which he built a store in which the firm of S. & Ruckel did business in '48–50. v. 681, 686. In '51 he went east, but returned on a business visit in '55–6. He resided in Mass. and at Providence, R.I., till '84, when he returned to S.F. to take charge of his real estate interests, including the 'Sherman building,' on the lot purchased by him in '47, in which he has an office in '85, at the age of 72. In an interview, and also in a letter from R.I., he gave me some information about early S.F. and his own life. His 1st wife, married in '54, was Sally S. Mauran, who died in '65; the 2d, of '69–70, was Emma F. Mitchell; and the 3d, '78–85, Kate Field. Five children survived in '85, Harry M., Elizabeth M., Adeline M., Ethel, and Richard M. Jr.

Sherman (Wm Tecumseh), 1847, nat. of Ohio, graduate of West Point, who came to Cal. as lieut Co. F, 3d U.S. artill., and in '47–50 served most of the time as adj.-gen. under the military governors. v. 444, 450, 492, 518, 520, 609, 636, 646; also of the firm Warner, Sherman, & Bestor at Coloma '48–9. He went east with despatches in '50; but, having resigned his army commission, came back in '53 to conduct as partner the banking business of Lucas, Turner, & Co. until '57. His Californian experience of '47–57 is fully narrated in the early chapters of his *Memoirs*, a most interesting and accurate record, except in a few comparatively unimportant details. Sherman was later superintendent of a La military academy and president of a St Louis street railroad until in '61 he reëntered the military service as colonel. His subsequent career in the war of '61–5 and since is a prominent part of U.S. history, which I make no attempt to summarize. He reached a higher position than any other pioneer named in this register; and in '85 is still living as retired general of the army. His wife, married in '50, is the daughter of Hon. Thomas Ewing. The general has often revisited Cal., taking a deep interest in pioneer matters. Sherreback (Peter), 1840, nat. of Denmark, who came by sea and settled at S.F. as a trader. iv. 117, 120. He was baptized and naturalized in '41-2; síndico '43. iv. 666; agente de policía '44. iv. 666; being married the same year or the next to Mary, sister of John Sullivan. In '45 he was owner of S. F. lands, and aided Sutter in support of Micheltorena. iv. 486, 669, 673; v. 681-2. He was collector in '46-7. v. 295, 648; and memb. of the council '47. v. 678. He still lived at S.F. in '55 and later, but I find no mention of his death. His widow was still living in '60. The original name was probably 'Scherrebach,' but it is written in a great variety of ways. Sherwood (Jeremiah), 1847, lieut Co. G, N.Y.Vol. v. 504, 517. In '48-9 clerk for Brannan & Co. at Sac.; later member of N.Y. legislature; d. N.Y. City '83. Scheuer (Pierre), 1834, Fr. mason at Mont., age 27, married to María J. García. Perhaps same as 'Cheorette,' q.v.

Shields (H.L.), 1847, lieut Co. F, 3d U.S. artill. on muster-roll; but did not come to Cal. (v. 518). S. (Sam.), 1831, Amer. from N. Mex. in the Wolfskill party. iii. 387, 405; d. at Los Ang. a few years later. S. (W.F.), 1847, capt. in com. of U.S. Preble. Shipley (Otto), 1847, Co. F, 3d U.S. artill. (v. 518). Shipp (Wm), 1847, ditto. Shirland (E.D.), 1847, Co. G, N.Y.Vol. (v. 499); nat. of N.Y. and settler in Placer Co. from '50; capt. in war of '61-5; county clerk and recorder of Sac.; at Auburn '82. Shirley (Paul), 1846, on the roll of the Soc. Cal. Pion.; d. in Ohio '76. Shislylind (Gustaff), 1847, musician Co. G, N.Y.Vol. (v. 499).

Shockley, 1846, mr of the Roman. Shoemaker (Sam.), 1846, one of the Donner party from Ohio; died in the Sierra. v. 531, 533. Shoetzof, 1803, in charge of a party of Aleut. hunters. ii. 25, 63, perhaps Shvetzof. Shoive, 1847-8, mr of the Anita. v. 576. Shooks (Wm), 1841, doubtful name at S. Diego. Toomes. Shooter (Chas), 1847, Co. D, N.Y.Vol. (v. 499). Short (J.O.B.), 1846, nat. of Ky, and overl. immig. with his mother—later Mrs Merriner—who settled at S. Rafael, where he still lived in '80 with wife, Mary Miller, and 5 children. S. (Jacob), 1846, brother of J.O.B., and his partner in '80. S. (Patrick), 1832, Irish priest who came in exile from Honolulu with P. Bachelot; in '34-6 an associate of Hartnell in his school near Mont.; left Cal. in '37, and went to Valparaíso, where he still lived in '70. iii. 317-18, 364, 384, 408, 670, 677-8; iv. 102. Shotwell (Geo.), 1841, overl. immig. of the Bartleson party, accidentally killed on the journey. iv. 269. Shreve, 1848, mr of a vessel at S.F. Shrives, 1848, mr of the Anita. Shrives (Dan B.), 1847, Co. F, N.Y.Vol. (v. 499). Shroter (Chas), 1847, Co. G, ditto; at S.F. '82. Shubrick (Wm Bransford), 1846, commodore U.S.N., in com. of Pacific squadron '46-7, on the Independence. v. 428-9, 437, 636. Shulters (John), 1847, Co. H, N.Y.Vol. (v. 499). Shultz (Ernst), 1847, owner of S. F. lot. Shumway (Aurora), 1847, Co. C, N. Y. Vol. (v. 469); reënl. Shurts (Watson), 1847, Co. F, N.Y.Vol. (v. 499).

Sibrian see 'Cibrian.' Sibs (Sam.), 1836, doubtful name of a witness at Sonoma. Sicard (Pierre Théodore), 1833, Fr. sailor and carpenter who on applying for naturalization in '40 claimed a resid. of 7 years. iii. 409. He was in the Mont. dist '34 and at the S. Pablo rancho '40. In '42-4 he worked for Sutter at Hock Farm; and in '44 got a grant of the Nemshas rancho on Bear River adjoining Johnson's, iv. 672, where he settled in '45. His visits from Bear River to Sutter's fort in '45-8 are often recorded in the N.Helv. Diary; in 48-9 a miner and trader on the Yuba, where a flat and bar took his name. Though deemed rich in those days, he became poor; was living with Claude Chana in '71, and died before '79. Sickels (J. F.), 1847, surgeon on the U.S. Independence. Siddons (Wm M.), 1848, on the roll of the Soc. Cal. Pion. Sierra (Benito de la), 1775, Span. friar who visited Cal. as chaplain on the Santiago and S. Antonio, and died at S. Blas '77. He had served in L. Cal. '69-73. i. 240-1, 287, 310. Sigler (Wm), 1845, at Sutter's fort Nov.; prob.

an overl. immig. In the spring of '46 he carried despatches up the valley to Frémont. He was murdered at Moon's rancho Tehama Co. in '49 or '50. iv. 578, 583; v. 24.

Sill (Daniel), 1832, nat. of Conn., trapper and carpenter who came from N. Mex. in the winter of '32-3, settling at Sta B., where he hunted otter under Capt. Dana's license, and was partner in a bakery in '34. iii. 388, 408. In '35 he came to Mont. and got a carta; and from '39 or earlier lived at S.F., building a mill for Spear in '39-40. v. 681; named by Farnham as one of the foreigners arrested in '40. iv. 17. From '44 he spent most of his time in the Sac. Valley, working as a blacksmith for Sutter part of the time. In '46 he bought a rancho of Lassen where he had a cabin. v. 301; and in '49 was joined by his son Daniel and daughter Harriet—later Mrs Mahew. He died in '62, at the age of 66. Sillen (D. S.), 1846, Cal. Bat. (v. 358). Siltzer (Henry), 1847, Co. G, N.Y.Vol. (v. 499). Silva, family at S. Dieguito rancho '31. iii. 612. S. (Antonio), 1840 (?), Portuguese deserter from a whaler, employed for several years at Petaluma by Gen. Vallejo. iv. 120. S. (Mariano), 1840, Mex. capt. of artill. at Mont. '40-6; went to Mazatlan '47 or '48. iv. 31, 198, 293, 307-8, 311, 357, 652; v. 41, 230, 232-3. S. (Mariano), at Los Ang. '39; in '46 at S. Juan Cap., age 37, wife Francisca Perez. S. (Mariano), nat. of Chile, patron of the custom-house boat at Mont. '45. Silvas (Antonio M.), at Los Ang. '39, age 37. S. (Cárlos), owner of land at S. Juan Cap., 41. iv. 626. S. (Clara), at S. Juan Cap. '46, age 40, child. Gerónimo b. '29, Guadalupe '32, Lugarda '37, and Fernando '38. S. (Diego), at S. Bern. '46, age 24. S. (José), settler at Los Ang. 1789. i. 461. S. (Juan), at Mont. '36. iii. 617. S. (Mariano), at Los Ang. '46, age 35. S. (Ramon), owner of land at S. Juan Cap. '41. iv. 626. S. (Teodoro), at Los Ang. '10-16; ii. 110, 350. Silverio, neophyte who killed his wife at Mont. 1798. i. 691.

Sime, 1848, in the legislature '55; John L. in S.F. guard '49. Simental (José C.), 1800, sentenced to 6 years in Cal. as a settler. i. 606. Simeon, Ind., grantee of lot at S. Gabriel '46. v. 627. Simmonds (Stephen), 1835 (?), nat. of N.Y., landing at Sta B. from the whaler Liverpool Packet, and becoming an otter-hunter with Nidever for several years. Named in '39-40 at Sta B. and Mont. Making voyages in different vessels; he was in '44 sick in care of the consulate, and is said to have died at Branch's rancho about '45. iii. 413. Simmons, 1848, lieut on the U.S. Ohio. S. (Alex. R.), 1846, mid. on the U.S. Columbia. '46-7. S. (Bezer), 1843, nat of Vt, mr of the Magnolia '43-6. iv. 400, 567; v. 579. Later of the S.F. firm S., Hutchinson, & Co.; member of the council '49; d. in '50 at the age of 40. His assignees were cl. for the Novato rancho. iii. 712. His wife was a sister of Frederick Billings, and died in '49. S. (Charles), 1847 (?), miner and later trader at Reno, Nev., where he died '79; accredited by the newspapers to N.Y. Vol. Left a daughter at Livermore, Cal. S. (Wm), 1846, clerk in the navy, acting lieut in Stockton's Bat. '46-7. v. 386. S. (Wm A.), 1847, Co. B, Morm. Bat. (v. 469). Simon (Lem.), 1828, Amer. sailor of the Gen. Lucre left at S. Diego drunk. S. (Luis), 1828, Engl. arrested for having no pass; prob. same as preceding. Simons (Maurice), 1846, passed mid. on the U.S. Congress. Simpson, 1827, mr of the Cadboro. iii. 146. S., 1845, doubtful name of an overl. immig. iv. 578. S., 1846, ditto; may have gone to Or. v. 529. S. (Geo.), 1841, at S.F. on the Cowlitz. S. (Sir Geo.) 1841, chief of the H. B. Co., visiting Cal. on his trip round the world, and author of a Narrative which contains much valuable information on the country. ii. 77-8; iv. 191, 209, 218-21, 235-6, 250-3, 259-61, 333, 343, 564, 639-40, 650-1, 665, 678. S. (Henry I.), 1848, author of Three Weeks in the Gold Mines, in the form of a letter written at Mont. in Sept. He claims to be of the N.Y.Vol., but perhaps writes under an assumed name; or still more likely the letter is a fraud concocted in N.Y. S. (Wm), 1844, Engl. who got a passport. S. (Wm), 1828, witness against Capt. Bradshaw. iii. 133. Sims (Jack), 1846, aided in building the Sta Cruz schr. S. J. Patriot. S. (Joseph), 1847, Co. D, N.Y. Vol. (v. 499); Engl. settler in Sac. Co. '79-80, with wife Mary L. Moor, and 3 children.

Sinard ('Major'), 1847, visitor at Sutter's fort. Sinclair (Archibald), 1847, Co. D, N.Y.Vol. (v. 499). S. (John), 1839, Scotchman for some years in employ of the H.B. Co. in Or., later editor of a paper at Honolulu, who in Dec. '39 was at Mont. asking for a carta, and in '40 at Sutter's fort. iv. 117, 119, 139. In '41 he was sent back to the Isl. by Sutter to make arrangement for consignments of goods, going on the *Llama* and returning on the *Julia Ann*. His negotiations for Sutter were not very successful, but he made a bargain with Grimes, by virtue of which on his return in Dec. '41 he obtained naturalization, and in '42 took possession of the El Paso rancho, north of N. Helv., as the representative of Grimes, to whom it was granted in '44. iv. 229, 237, 566. He was visited in '42–3 by Sandels and Yates, who describe him as a very intelligent man fond of grog; also by Frémont in '44, iv. 438, when he was an officer in the N. Helv. militia. iv. 479, 680. He was Sutter's aide in the Micheltorena campaign. iv. 485–6; is often named from '45 in the *N. Helv. Diary;* and in '46–9 he was alcalde of the Sac. district, v. 675, having a Cal. claim of $450 (v. 462), taking part in relief measures for the Donner party, v. 538, 541, and finally dying in '49 on his passage by steamer to the States. S. (Wm), 1845, clerk for Rae at S.F. iv. 593. S. (Wm B.), 1828, Amer. carpenter, age 25, who left his vessel at Sta B., escaping with 3 others in a boat to Sta Catalina Isl. Singleton (A. W.), 1848, passp. from Hon. Sinova (José F.), settler at Los Ang. 1785–6; 2d alcalde in '89. i. 346, 348, 461. Sinton (Rich. H.), 1848, a well-known citizen of S. F. down to '85, whose arrival is accredited, erroneously I suppose, in various publications to '47 or '48.

Sipole (Wm), 1847, Co. F, 3d U.S. artill. (v. 518); d. before '64. Sipp, 1846, Amer. ship-carpenter from Or. in the McMahon party, who prob. went back to Or. in '46. iv. 572; v. 526. Siptler (J.), 1846, in Cal. Bat. (v. 358). Siralde (Mariano). at Sonoma '44, age 27; perhaps 'Lizalde.' Sirey (James), 1847, Co. D, N.Y.Vol. (v. 499); settled at Stockton '48; at S.F. '71–4; Stockton '75; d. before '82. Sirrine (Geo. W.), 1846, of the Mormon colony. v. 546; of Stout, S., & Meder, lumber dealers at Sta Cruz '47; memb. of the town council '48. v. 642. In Ariz., still in the faith, '85. S. (John J.), 1846, ditto, with wife and child. v. 546; in '47 candidate for the council and owner of a S. F. lot. v. 650, 680; an elder and school trustee '48. v. 656; presid. of the council '48; in Ariz. '85. Sisk (Thos J.), 1848(?), survivor of the Texan-Mier massacre; died at Grass Valley '69. Sisson (Reuben), 1847, Co. K, N.Y.Vol. (v. 499); d. S. Rafael '49. Sitjar (Antonio, or Buenaventura), 1771, Span. friar who served at S. Antonio—being also founder of S. Miguel—until his death in 1808. Biog. ii. 151–2; ment. i. 173, 176, 196, 298, 388, 411, 469, 498, 552, 560, 576, 587, 688–9; ii. 147, 159–60. Swarthout (Nathan), 1847, Co. D, Morm. Bat. v. 469.

Skeckett (Job), 1845, Delaware Ind. in Frémont's party '45–7 (iv. 581). Skee (Alex.), 1827, mr of the *Huascar* '27–8. iii. 147. Skein (Joseph), 1847, Co. E, Morm. Bat. (v. 469). Skene (Wm), 1846, one of the chino prisoners, wounded. v. 313–14. Skillington (H.), 1848, at Hon. from Mont. Skinner (Eugene F.), 1845, overl. immig. from N.Y. in the Grigsby-Ide party, with a family. Working for Sutter and visiting S.F. and S. José, he went in '46 to Or., where he founded and named Eugene City, dying there in '64, and leaving a widow and 3 children. iv. 579–80; v. 526. S. (A. A.), 1848, Or. pioneer of '45, judge of the Or. sup. court, brother of Eugene, said to have made a trip to the gold mines; d. at Sta Cruz '77. S. (Horace A.), 1846, of Mormon colony, with wife and child. v. 546; in '47–8 he kept the City Hotel at S.F. v. 680; in Utah '84. S. (John), 1847, Co. A, N.Y.Vol. (v. 499); at S. José '50; at Campo Seco '71–4.

Slocum (Wm A.), 1837, U.S. commissioner on the *Loriot,* and author of a *Report.* iv. 146–7, 165. Slade (Philip O.), 1832, nat. of N. H. who came by sea. iii. 408; in Mont. dist. '33–5; naturalized '39, being a sawyer at S. Rafael; last appears at S.F. '40. S. (Thompson), 1846, Co. F, Cal. Bat. (v. 358. S. (Wm D.), 1847, Co. H, N.Y. Vol. (v. 497). A printer who was city marshal at Yreka; d. before '82, prob. in '63. Slague (John), 1836. Fr. sailor

on the *Ayacucho*, age 19.   Slater (Richard), 1847, Co. E, Morm. Bat. (v.
469); mail-carrier for Brannan '48.   Slausum, 1834, Eng. sailor, age 46, at
Mont.   Sleight (Peter), 1847, Co. K, N.Y. Vol. (v. 499).   Slepe (Jerome),
1834, Eng. hatter in a Mont. list, age 27.   Sloat (John D.), 1846, nat. of
N.Y. in com. of the Pacific squadron, raising the U.S. flag in Cal. July. v.
37, 195–215, 224–54, 411–12, 580.   Com. Sloat was a timid, irresolute man;
but after he decided to take possession of the Cal. ports his policy was entirely
praiseworthy as compared with that of Stockton, his successor.   Biog. note v.
254.   S. (Lewis W.), 1846, son of John D., and his sec. on the *Savannah*. v.
225.   He came back to Cal. about '54 and was a notary public at S.F. for
several years.   Slobodchikof, 1806, chief hunter on the coast from Alaska.
ii. 40; in '13–14 clerk of Kuskof at Ross, visiting S.F. ii. 204, 302, 304, 373.
Slocum, 1844, mate of the *Newton*.   Slover (Isaac), 1828, Kentuckian trapper
of Pattie's party who went back to Sonora with a pass in Nov. iii. 163, 166–7,
178.   He came back with a N. Mex. colony about '41–3, settling at S. Bernardino, where he was killed by a bear in '54, at the age of about 80.   Slover Mt
still bears his name.   Slusser (Levi S. B.), 1847, nat. of Pa; in Sonoma
Co. '48–77.   Sly (James C.), 1847, Co. B, Morm. Bat. (v. 469); a miller in
Sutter's employ, also in the mines '48, exploring a new route and Salt Lake
Val.   S. (John), 1846, Co. F, Cal. Bat. (v. 358).

Smith, naturally many of the name cannot be identified.   S., 1831, sailor
drowned at Sta B. iii. 405.   S., 1831, about to leave Hon. for Cal.   S.,
1844, officer on the *Modeste*.   S., 1845, Engl. who got a pass for Sonora.
S., 1846, from Hon. on the *Euphemia*.   S., 1847, had a project of establishing a colony on the Moquelumne, transferring his claim to McKinstry in '48.
S. Joaq. Co. Hist.   S., 1847, mid. on the U.S. *Independence*.   S., 1847,
owner of a saw-mill near S.F.   S., 1848, at Sutter's fort from Sta Clara;
lately from Or.   S., 1848, mr of the *Haalilo*.

Smith (A. B.), 1837(?), committed suicide at S. Diego '67, said to have been
a resid. for 30 (20?) years; ment. at S.D. '46. iv. 118; v. 329.   S. (Albert),
1847, sergt Co. B, Morm. Bat. v. 477; also Q.M. sergt at Manti, Utah, '81.
S. (Alex.), 1846, ment. by Michael White as in the Los Ang. region, known as
'Stuttering Alec.'   S. (Andrew J.), 1847, capt. in the 1st U.S. dragoons,
who came with the Morm. Bat., of which he was acting com. for a time in the
east. v. 477, 479–83. He was the officer who mustered out the Morm. Bat. and
part of the N.Y.Vol., subsequently taking com. of the dragoons. v. 490, 515,
631. He went east with Sherman in '50; and in the war of '61–5 became a
general.   S. (Azariah), 1847, Co. B, Morm. Bat. (v. 469); author of a song
for the bat.; at the Coloma mill '38 when gold was discovered.   S. (Chas),
1824, named in an archive record as an otter-hunter. ii. 527; perhaps Karl
'Schmidt.'   S. (Chas), 1828, Engl. deserter from a Fr. whaler at Todos
Santos; at S. Diego '28–9.   S. (Chas), 1846, powder-boy on the *Dale*.   S.
(Chas), 1846, Co. G, Cal. Bat. (v. 358).   S. (Chas), 1847, Co. I, N.Y.Vol. (v.
499).   S. (Chas), 1847, with Brannan on trip to Salt Lake. v. 553; perhaps
C.C.   S. (Chas F.), 1847, Co. I, N.Y.Vol. (v. 499); d. before '82.   S. (Chas
R.), 1825 (?), said to have been at Sta B. in charge of Dana's store. *S. Luis Ob.
Co. Hist.*; in '29 writes from Hon., and had visited Cal. before; in '31 came
on the *Louisa* as sup.; in '32 joined the comp. extranjera. iii. 221; ment. in
Larkin's accts '36.   S. (C.C.), 1847, trader at Sutter's fort '47–8, a partner
of Brannan; made a trip to Hon. on the *Tepic* '48.   S. (C. S.), 1848, passp.
from Hon.

Smith (D.), 1847, Co. B, artill. Cal. Bat. (v. 358).   S. (D.), 1848, at Hon.
from Mont.   S. (David), 1847, Co. E, Morm. Bat. (v. 469); d. in April at
S. Luis Rey. v. 481.   S. (D. W.), 1846, Co. G, Cal. Bat. (v. 358).   S. (Edward), 1848, overl. immig. from Mo., with wife, son, and 5 daughters; postmaster at S. Juan B.; died about '57. One of his daughters married John
Breen in '52.   S. (Elijah M.), 1847, Co. I, N.Y.Vol. (v. 499); at Aurora,
Mono Co., '82   S. (Elisha), 1847, Co. E, Morm. Bat. (v. 469).   S. (Ezekiah),
1847, at Sutter's fort; prob. Azariah.   S. (F.), 1846, Cal. Bat. (v. 358).
S. (Frances R.), 1846, married to W. W. Scott at Sonoma, June.   S. (Frazer),

1814, mr of the *Isaac Todd.* ii. 271-2.   S. (Fred.), 1848, German farmer at
S. José '50-76.   S. (Fred C.), 1845 (?), said by his son, Budd S.—U.S. consul at S. Blas—to have come as mr of the bark *Helvetia*, but I have no other
record of such a vessel this year. iv. 587.
    Smith (G. M.), 1845, at Sutter's fort, apparently an overl. immig.; also
the same or another at Sonoma '45-6; perhaps the father of Frances *R.* iv.
579-80, 526.   S. (Geo.), 1825, mr of the *Spy* '25-7. iii. 149.   S. (Geo.), 1846,
Co. C, 1st U.S. dragoons (v. 336).   S. (Geo.), 1846, Co. F, Cal. Bat. (v. 358);
had a fight with Lieut Rock, and was sentenced by court-martial to 22 months
of hard labor. v. 434.   S. (Gerard D.), 1847, Co. C, N.Y. Vol. (v. 499).   S.
(H.), 1848, passp. from Hon.   S. (Henry), 1846, at Sutter's fort; interested
at Benicia. '47-8. v. 672; perhaps Henry C.   S. (Henry), 1846 (?), keeper of a
sailor's boarding-house at S.F., owner of lot, constable, and jail-keeper '47.
v. 648, 685; perhaps same as the following.   S. (Henry), 1847, Co. I, N.Y.
Vol. (v. 499); drowned in Feather River '49.   S. (Henry C.), 1845, nat. of
Ohio, and overl. immig. with the Hastings party. iv. 586-7. He served, perhaps, in the Cal. Bat. (v. 358); had a 'Cal. claim' for $25 (v. 462); was a memb.
of the legislature from Sta Clara Co. '52; cl. for land. iv. 673; supervisor of
Washington, Alameda Co., '55; in Nev. '61-4; in Alameda Co. from '65 to
his death at Livermore in '75, at the age of 51. His wife was Mary van Gordon, married in '46, and his surviving children were Julia A. (Mrs Hargrave),
Emma L., Franklin P., and Charles.   S. (Henry J.), 1847, Co. F, N.Y. Vol.
(v. 499).   S. (Hiram), 1846, Co. F, Cal. Bat. (v. 358).   S. (I.), 1845, at
Sutter's fort Apr. '46.   S. (Isaac P.), 1846, Co. F, Cal. Bat. (v. 358); at Sutter's fort '47.   S. (Israel), 1848, present at the discov. of gold acc. to the
county histories.   S. (I. T.), 1846 (?), nat. of Ia and overl. immig.; a settler
in Sonoma Co. from '51 to his death in '79, leaving a wife and two children;
called also I. P.
    Smith (J.), 1846, Cal. Bat., Co. B, artill. (v. 358).   S. (J. J.), 1846, Co.
F, Cal. Bat. (v. 358).   S. (Jack), 1846, at Sutter's fort from up and down
the valley '46-8.   S. (Jacob), 1816, pilot of the *Lydia.* ii. 275.   S. (James),
1827, capt. of a vessel at S.F.   S. (James), 1841, nat. of Engl., naturalized
in '44, when he had been 3 years in Cal., being then a farmer in the Sac. Val.
iv. 279. Often named in the *N. Helv. Diary* from '45. In Jan. '46 he married
the widow Marshall, and died in '48. Bidwell thinks the widow married
Gregson, and was living in Sonoma Co. '64, having a son named Marshall;
but there may be some confusion here; see 'Gregson.'   S. (James), 1844, mr
of the *Hibernia* '44-5, iv. 566, 587, who in later years established a line of
packets between S.F. and Honolulu, being well known as Capt. 'Jim' Smith.
He died at New London, Conn., in '68, at the age of '65, leaving no family,
as I am informed by Capt. H. H. Watson.   S. (James), 1846, of the Donner
party from Ill., dying in the mountains. v. 530, 533.   S. (James), 1848,
passp. from Hon.   S. (James J.), 1847, Co. F, N.Y. Vol. (v. 499); drowned
in Amer. Riv. '49.   S. (James M.), 1847, Co. K, ditto.
    Smith (Jedediah), 1826, Amer. trapper chief who came from Salt Lake via
Colorado Riv. and Mojave to S. Gabriel. In '27 he went to Salt Lake from
the S. Joaquin Val. and returned, being the 1st to cross the Sierra. From
Cal. he went to Or., and in '31 was killed by the Ind. in N. Mex. See record
of his visit. iii. 152-60; ment. ii. 551, 569, 600; iv. 263.   S. (John), 1834,
Engl. carpenter, age 28, in Spear's service at Mont. iii. 412; also a 'tailor'
Smith the same year. Named in Larkin's accounts '36-40; arrested in '40 but
escaped exile. iv. 17. There may be some confusion between this man and
the following.   S. (John), 1837, nat. of Nova Scotia, who came by sea; asked
for naturalization in '42, being a carpenter in the Sac. Val. and 5 years a resident. iv. 118. Sutter says S. obtained land from him near Marysville; naturalized in '44, and got a grant of land in Yolo Co. iv. 674; living on his
rancho '45-8, ment. in the *N. Helv. Diary*, a partner and neighbor of Michael
Nye.   S. (John), 1845, Amer. sailor on the *Morea* in trouble at S.F.   S.
(John), 1846, Fauntleroy's dragoons (v. 232, 247).   S. (John), 1846, Co. C,
1st U.S. dragoons (v. 336); sentenced by court-martial to imprisonment at

Los Ang. '47.   S. (John), 1847, Co. E, Morm. Bat. (v. 469); in Utah '82. S. (John), 1847, Co. F, 3d U.S. artill. (v. 518); living '64.   S. (John), 1848, passp. from Hon.   S. (John F.), 1838, Fr. carpenter from the Sandw. Isl. at Sta B. iii. 409; where he built the 1st wooden house, and died in '66. *Huse.* S. (John G.), 1847, perhaps of N.Y.Vol. (v. 499), under another name.   S. (John H.), 1848, passp. from Hon.   S. (John M.), 1847, Co. E, N.Y.Vol. (v. 499).   S. (Joseph), 1845, doubtful name of an overl. immig. iv. 578.

Smith (L. H.), 1846, mr of the *Benj. Rush.* v. 576.   S. (Lewis), 1847, Co. B, N.Y.Vol. (v. 499).   S. (Lot), 1847, Co. E, Morm. Bat. (v. 469); re-enl.; in Ariz. '82.   S. (Napoleon B.), 1845, nat. of Ohio, and overl. immig. in the Hastings party with his brother Henry C. iv. 586-7. He worked a while for Sutter, and then became a lumberman in the S. Antonio redwoods, but perhaps took some part in the revolt and war of '46-7. In '48-9 he went to the mines, and kept a store at Mission S. José, being sub-prefect for a time in '49. Later he became a trader at Martinez, being county assessor, and memb. of the legislature in '52. In '57-85 he lived on a rancho in Contra Costa Co. His wife was Margelina, daughter of Elam Brown, and he has 8 children: Frank (b. Jan. '48, the 1st in Contra Costa), Lawrence M., Sarah C., Louis N., Ellen J., Elam, Timothy S., and Warren C. I have a full *Biog. Sketch* of 'Bony' Smith written in '75.   S. (Oliver), 1848, doubtful name at Benicia.   S. (Orrin), 1846, of the Mormon colony, with wife and 6 children, excommunicated on the voy., and perhaps left for a time at Hon. His daughter Amelia was in Utah '84. v. 546, 549.   S. (O. K.), 1848, nat. of N.Y., and overl. immig.; memb. of the legisl. '61, being a farmer at Visalia, age '39.   S. (Persifer F.), 1848. Gov. Smith did not arrive till '49, nevertheless by a slip of his pen he writes at S.F. in March '48, inquiring for Benicia lots. v. 673.

Smith (R.), 1833, mr of the *Fakeja.* iii. 382.   S. (Robert), 1846, of the Mormon colony, with wife and 2 children; teacher of tactics on the *Brooklyn;* owner of S.F. lot '47; died in the faith about '49. v. 546, 550, 679.   S. (Robert), 1847, at Sonoma and N. Helv.; known as 'Growling' Smith, and arrested for outrages on Ind. v. 569, 610. He may have been the 'Badger' Smith of the Bears in '46. v. 167.   S. (Sam.) 1837, named in Larkin's accounts. S. (Sam.), 1845 (?), at Sonoma and N. Helv. '45-8; iv. 587; seems to have had a rancho in the Sac. Val. '47, also working for Larkin. Sam. S. of Baltimore is named in the *El Dorado Co. Hist.* as having come in '43 and kept the 1st store at Kelsey. At S.F. as a witness '47 and owner of a town lot. Acc. to the *Marin Co. Hist.,* a Sam. S. lived in the Pt Reyes region in '46.   S. (Simeon P.), 1847, in S.F. letter-list.

Smith (Stephen), 1841, nat. of Md., who had spent some time in Peru, and who visited Cal., prob. on the *Corsair,* in '41. iv. 279. I have his letter of July written at Callao after his return from Cal. On this 1st visit he made arrangements with Gov. Alvarado to introduce a steam-mill; and in '43 he came back from Baltimore with the engine—the 1st in Cal.—and mill machinery on the *George Henry.* iv. 395-6, 565-6. As soon as he could be naturalized he got a grant in '44 of Bodega, where he had set up his mill, and where he lived for the most part from that time. iv. 186, 392, 670, 679. In '45, visiting S. Blas, Smith was arrested on a charge of being engaged in filibustering schemes for the U.S., but soon released, as there was no proof. iv. 601. As he later told Lieut Sherman that he came to Cal. on the assurance of Webster that the U.S. would surely have the country, it is possible that in the earlier years he talked indiscreetly. In '45-6 he owned lots in S.F., and built a house at the cor. of Dupont and Washington streets. iv. 669, 673; v. 682. In '46 he raised the U.S. flag at Bodega, and in '46-8 served as civil magistrate. v. 242, 670. In the flush times his mill was a very valuable property, and he was cl. for not only Bodega, but the Blucher rancho. iv. 670. He died at S.F. in '55 at the age of 69. His wife was a Peruvian, a sister of Manuel Torres; who married Tyler Curtis in '56; and he left three children, Manuela, Stephen, and James B., all of whom seem to have been living in '75. The daughter, born at Bodega '46, married John M. English, and lived in Oakland '81.

Smith (Theodore), 1847, Co. F, N.Y.Vol. (v. 499). S. (Thomas), 1841, at S. José. iv. 279; naturalized '44, when he claimed to have been a resid. since '42; owner of S.F. lot 45, where he kept a saloon '46–50, a stout and stuttering Englishman. iv. 669; v. 682, 685. S. (Thomas), 1845, overl. immig. of the Swasey-Todd, or possibly the McMahon, party. iv. 576–7, 573; apparently at Sutter's fort '46–7. S. (Thos), 1846, sailor in Stockton's Bat., fatally wounded at the S. Gabriel, Jan. '47. v. 395. S. (Thos), on the roll of the Society of California Pioneers as having arr. in Sept. S. (Thos J.), 1845, ditto, arrived S.F. Dec. iv. 587; perhaps the cl. of S.F. Mission lots in '52; at Gold Hill, Nev., '81. S. (Thos L.), 1829 (?), Kentuckian trapper and mountaineer, known as 'Peg-leg' Smith from his wooden leg. The chronology of his wild career is confusing; but he may have stolen horses in Cal. in '29 and several times later, as he was fond of boasting in late years. iii. 172, 179. In '41 'El Cojo Smit' was reported to be in com. of a party of vagabonds from N. Mex. iv. 208, 278, 342. After '49 he lived in Cal., and died at S.F. in '66.

Smith (W.), 1846, Cal. Bat., Co. B, artill. (v. 358), enlisting at Mont. Oct. S. (Willard), 1847, musician Co. D, Morm. Bat. (v. 469); in '82 at Littleton, Utah, stake president and probate judge. Smith (Wm), 1800, mate of the Hazard, perhaps visiting the coast several times before 1808. ii. 17, 24–5, 95–6. In 1810–11, as mate of the Albatross, he was engaged in fur-hunting on the coast, especially in taking seals at the Farallones. ii. 93. In '16 he came back from China in com. of the Albatross, and was arrested for smuggling at Sta B., though his vessel escaped capture. ii. 275–7, 362, 248, 633. He was a nat. of Va, whose voyages and adventures in all parts of the world would fill a volume. In '36 or earlier he found his way to Cal. again. iv. 103, 141; and now, too old to command, he still made his home on board Boston vessels on the coast or at the Islands, being transferred from one to another according to his whims, and occasionally spending a few months on shore. He died at Sonoma on May 5, '46, at the age of 78. S. (Wm), 1824, mr of the Young Tartar. ii. 519. S. (Wm), 1827, Amer. carpenter in the Mont. dist. '29, age 22. iii. 176. Ment. as a sawyer working for Cooper in '31; 'Bill the Sawyer' at S. José '33, married to a Sais; in Mont. lists of '34; also near Pt Reyes; at Sonoma and S.F. '37–9; one of the arrested foreigners '40. iv. 17; Engl. carpenter, age 42, at S. José '41; wife María Josefa Sais, child. Daniel b. '33, José '36, Patricio '37, José S. '39, María '38; one of Sutter's men in the Micheltorena campaign '45. iv. 495; at S. José, S.F., and in the Sac. Val. '46; owner of a lot at S.F. and settler at Benicia '47—all these may be one or half a dozen Bill Smiths for all that I know.

Smith (Wm H.), 1847, lieut Co. I, N.Y.Vol. v. 504; owner of S.F. lot. Still at S.F. '52; in Tuolumne Co. '74. S. (Wm M.), 1845, nat. of Ga, who came with Capt. Paty from S. Blas. iv. 587. A droll fellow, who had been a circus-rider, known as 'Jim Crow' Smith; in '46–8 member of the S.F. firm of Ward & S., owning lots and building a house, besides serving as capt. of volunteers in Marston's Sta Clara campaign. v. 381, 539, 679, 681, 684. In '48 he married the widow of Capt. Hinckley, and in '49 moved to Martinez. After a while he went to the bad altogether, being a violent and dangerous man when intoxicated, and about '54 he killed himself. S. (Wm Taylor), 1846, lieut on the U.S. Dale. Smyth (Wm), 1826, mate of the Blossom. iii. 121; artist from whose drawings Forbes' California was illustrated. iv. 151.

Snitter (Lewis), 1847, Co. E, N.Y.Vol. (v. 499). Snook (Joseph Francisco), 1830, Engl. mr of the Ayacucho, who had been on the Mex. coast in Virmond's employ since '24. iii. 146, 180. He was naturalized in '33, and in '33–9 mr of the Catalina. iii. 381; iv. 102, 117. In '38 he purchased of Berry a rancho at Pt Reyes or Tomales, confirmed next year by the diputacion. Before this time he had married María Antonia, daughter of J.B. Alvarado of S. Diego, and he talked of quitting the sea and forming a partnership with Fitch; but in '40–2 he commanded the Jóven Guipuzcoana. iv. 12, 104, 305, 566; and the Juanita in '46. In '42 he was grantee of the S. Bernardo rancho,

S. Diego, iv. 621, where he lived with his family, dying suddenly in April '47 or '48. His widow married Henry Clayton.   Snow (A.), 1847, at Benicia. *B. Tribune.*   S. (B. F.), 1848, passp. from Hon.   S. (R. D.), 1848, ditto.   S. (Ze'nora S.), 1846, of the Mormon colony. v. 546; in Utah '84. Snyder (Elijah), 1847, Co. E, N.Y.Vol. (v. 499); at Trenton, N.J., '75. S. (Jacob R.), 1845, nat. of Pa, and overl. immig. of the Swasey-Todd party. iv. 576, 587.   Mentioned at Sta Cruz and various other points in '45–6, employed as a surveyor. v. 654, 641.   He served as quartermaster in Fauntleroy's dragoons. v. 293–4; and later in the Cal. Bat., ranking as major. v. 360.   In '47 he was appointed surveyor for the middle department of Cal., and also commissioned to investigate charges against Alcalde Nash of Sonoma. v. 610, 465.   In '48–9 with Reading and Hensley he had a trading post at Sacramento, and was a member of the constit. convention; from '50 memb. of a S.F. firm; in '52–3 state senator; in '53–60 treasurer of the U.S. mint at S.F.   About '62 he retired for the most part from public life to a rancho at Sonoma, where he died in '78 at the age of 65.   He was a man of fine personal appearance, of good abilities, of excellent character, and of well-deserved popularity.   Portrait in *Colton's Three Years; Sonoma Co. Hist.*   His 1st wife, of '50, was Susan H. Brayton; the 2d, of '74, was Rachel J. Sears; and he had no children.   S. (John), 1846, of the Donner party from Ill., killed by Reed on the Humboldt before reaching Cal. v. 530, 532.   S. (John), 1847, Co. E, Morm. Bat. (v. 469).

Soberanes, occupant of Sauzal rancho '23. ii. 616, 664.   S. (Agustin), sirviente at Sta Clara 1776. i. 306; still at S. José 1794.   S. (Ezequiel), son of Mariano, volunteer officer under Castro at the taking of Los Ang. '45. iv. 492.   S. (Feliciano), at Mont. '26, and regidor '29–30. ii. 612; grantee of Alisal '34. iii. 676; named in the padron of '36 as a nat. of Cal., age 47, wife María Ant. Rodriguez, child. Josefa b. '13, Pánfilo '15, Gabriela '18, Francisco '19, José Ant. '21, José María '23, Cármen '25, Mariano '28, Feliciano '29, José Andrés '31, Francisca '32, and José Mateo '33.   Alcalde in '38–9. iii. 675, 697; grantee of S. Lorenzo in '41. iv. 655; and in '41–5 the admin. of Soledad mission, of which estate he became the owner. iv. 194, 559, 660–1; v. 558, 637, 641; being in '45 juez 2° at Mont., iv. 653, 656, where he still lived in '51.   S. (Francisco), grantee of Sanjon de Sta Rita, Merced, '41. iv. 673. S. (Guadalupe), alférez of auxiliary cavalry '45–6. v. 41; in Mont. Co. '50. S. (José Ant.), mentioned at Sutter's fort '47.   S. (José María), a soldier of the 1st exped. of 1769–74; at Soledad 1791 et seq.; in 1795 an inválido in possession of the Buenavista rancho, Mont. i. 683, 441, 499.   Prob. ancestor of most of the Soberanes here registered.   S. (José M.), son of Feliciano, ment. in '46. v. 41.   S. (Josefa), daughter of Feliciano, grantee of Los Coches '41. iv. 655.   S. (Juan), sub-lieut of militia '46. v. '41; went with Flores to Mex. '47. v. 407.   S. (Mariano), soldier of the S.F. comp. '19–21; in '23 alcalde of Mont., síndico '27, alcalde '29–30. ii. 611–12; iii. 49, 76, 82, 194; in '35 admin. of S. Antonio. iii. 354, 687–8; in '36 living at Alisal, age 40, a widower—his wife had been a daughter of Ignacio Vallejo—7 child. Mariano b. '19, Juan '21, Ezequiel '23, Tomás '25, Guadalupe '28, Victor '29, Ignacio '31.   In '42 he was grantee of Los Ojitos rancho. iv. 655; in '45 juez at S. Miguel. iv. 660.   In '46 he was arrested with his sons, and his property at Los Ojitos destroyed by Frémont, v. 374, 464, for which Don Mariano had a Cal. claim of $19,930, of which $423 was paid (v. 462).   He was cl. for Los Ojitos in '52, and the rancho is still owned by his sons in '85.   S. (Mariano), son of the preceding; grantee of S. Bernardo rancho '41—though this may have been the father. iv. 655.   He was somewhat active in the final campaign of Natividad against the Amer. v. 290, 367; and was still in Mont. Co. '78. His son, Clodomiro, was for a short time employed in my Library, and a small collection of *Doc. Hist. Cal.* bears his name.   S. (Pánfilo), son of Feliciano, juez de paz at Mont. '43; custom-house guard at Mont. and S.F. '44–5. iv. 557, 653, 656.   S. (Tomás), clerk in the Mont. custom-house '44. iv. 431; went to Mex. with Flores '47. v. 407.   Sobradelas (Pablo), 1825, Span. marine from the *Aquiles;* ordered to depart in '28–30. iii. 51–2.   Sohns (John), 1847, Co. D, N.Y.Vol. (v. 499).

Sola (Faustino), 1786, Span. friar who served for brief terms at S. Luis Ob. and S.F., retiring in 1790, and dying at the college of S. Fernando in Mex. 1820. He was a brother of Gov. Sola. i. 388, 423, 469-70, 474; ii. 471. S. (Pablo Vicente), Span. lieut-col, who ruled Cal. as gov. from Aug. 15, '15, to Nov. 22, '22, being promoted to colonel in '19, and leaving Cal. as dip. to the Mex. congress in '22. Except that he was a member of the junta de Cal. in Mex. in '25, iii. 3-5, nothing is definitely known of his later life. For his life and character, see ii. 470-3; on his rule in Cal. ii. 208-470, passim; miscel. mention. i. 662; ii. 78, 188, 479, 485, 514, 562, 565-6, 569, 571, 580, 587, 604, 607, 616, 642, 674, 676; iii. 3, 5, 11, 33, 109.   Solano (Francisco), Ind. chief of the Suisunes, who from '35 was an ally of Vallejo at Sonoma, doing more than any other to keep the Ind. of the northern frontier in order. iii. 295, 360, 598; 71-3, 444, 674. He was the grantee of Suisun rancho in '42. His original name was Numa or Tetoy, and the name Solano, given him at baptism from that of the mission, passed from him to the county. I have no record showing the date of his death. His widow, Isidora, was still living at Sonoma in '74, at an advanced age, and furnished a *Relacion* that is not without interest. Solar (José María), at Branciforte '30. ii. 627.   Solares (Pedro), soldier at the Colorado Riv. pueblos 1780-1. i. 359.   Solas (Matias), sirviente at Soledad 1791-1800. i. 499.

Soler (Juan), 1774, guarda-almacen at Mont. i. 224. There was some complaint of his unfitness for the place in '78-9; and he died at Mont. in '81.   S. (Nicolás), 1781, Span. capt. who held the position of ayudante-inspector of the Cal. troops in '81-8; a prominent officer and inveterate fault-finder, generally in trouble because things were going to the dogs. He became comandante at Tucson, and died in '90. Biog. i. 397-8; ment. i. 334, 370, 383, 385, 392-6, 411, 443, 451, 462-3, 467, 471-2, 479, 484, 676; ii. 571.   S. (Pablo), 1792, surgeon of the Cal. troops at Mont. to 1800. i. 439, 501, 679-80.   Soleto (Juan), doubtful, '46. v. 162.   Solis (Joaquin), 1825, Mex. convict who in '29 headed a revolt of Californian soldiers, and in '30 was sent as a prisoner to Mex. For full account of the revolt, see iii. 68-85; mention of Solis. ii. 576, 591, 604, 615, 664; iii. 16, 149.   Solórzano (Francisco), settler at Los Ang. '16. ii. 350.   S. (José Antonio), sergt of the Mont. comp. '32-3. iii. 671, 673. S. (Ramon), soldier of the S.F. comp. '39-42; at Sonoma '44, age 19.

Somera (José Antonio Fernandez, or Angel), 1771, Span. friar at S. Gabriel, forced by illness to retire in '72. i. 137, 176, 187-9, 192-3.   Somers (Fred.), 1847, Co. B, N.Y.Vol. (v. 499).   Somoza (Antonio María), 1842, Mex. lieut in the batallon fijo '42-5, adjutant, instructor, and com. at Los Ang. '44-5; still in Cal. '46. iv. 289, 354, 407, 538; v. 41.   Soncho (Francisco), juez de paz at S.F. '42. iv. 665, 667.   Soret (Angelina), 1847, owner of a S.F. lot.   Soria (Francisco), alcalde of Mont. (?), '29. ii. 612; in '28 resid. of Branciforte, wife Rita Pinto, child. José, Cecilia, Cármen, and Gregorio; juez de paz at B. '32, regidor '38, juez de campo '43, 2d alcalde '45. iii. 588, 696-7; iv. 663-4; in '45 at B., age '50, wife Guadalupe Juarez, child. José Ant. b. '27, Miguel '33, Cineda (?) '36, José '44, Cecilia '28, Benita '35, Prudencia '37.   S. (José), at Branciforte '45, wife María de Jesus Robles, child. Refugio '43, Teresa '44.   S. (Juan José), alcalde of Mont. '28. ii. 612; and prob. '29.   Sosa (Mariano), visiting Dominican friar at S. Gabriel '31-2. iii. 641.

Sotelo (Francisco), settler at Los Ang. 1803. ii. 350.   S. (Gabriel), ditto '15. ii. 350.   S. (Gabriel), S.F. militiaman '37.   S. (José), at S. Bernardino '46, age 45.   S. (José María), at Branciforte '45, age 50, wife Encarnacion. S. (Juan), soldier in S.F. comp. '42, militia S.F. '37.   S. (Mariano), soldier of S.F. comp. '34-9.   S. (Pedro D.), at Los Ang. '46.   S. (Ramon), settler at Los Ang. 1805; killed at Purísima '24. ii. 350, 412, 529, 566. In '17 P. Payeras writes of him as 'el famoso criminal de California.' Miguel Sotelo, perhaps his descendant, was a famous outlaw killed by the sheriff at Los Ang. in '78.   S. (Venancio), at Los Ang. '48.   S. (Vicente), at S. Bern. '46, age 22.

Soto, sailor sirviente at Sta Cruz. i. 496.   S. (Andrés), at Mont. '38; supl. juez of ranchos '46. v. 637.   S. (Antonio), settler at S. José before 1800, regidor 1809–10, alcalde '18, dying suddenly in that year. i. 716; ii. 134, 378. S. (Antonio), soldier of S.F. comp. '19–29; in '41 at S. José, age 42, wife María G. Briones, child. Ramon b. '22, Raimunda '27, Angel '28, Nieves '30, Concepcion '32, Francisco '39, Felipa '40. S. (Antonio 2d), soldier of the S.F. comp. '19–27. S. (Bernardino), had a Cal. claim '46–7 of $873 (v. 462). S. (Casilda), grantee of La Merced, Los Ang., '44. iv. 635. S. (Casimiro), at Mont. '36, age 28, wife Eleuteria Castro, child María Trinidad b. '34. S. (Domingo), at S. José '41, age 22; and living with him Jesus, age 18, Fernando 12, and José Ant. 14. S. (Eufemio), juez de campo Mont. '37. iii. 675. S. (Eugenio), body found hanging at Sta Cruz '38. iii. 697. S. (Eugenio), at Branciforte '45, age 40, wife ——, child. Ramona b. '35, Juana '37, Rosalía '40, and Josefa '44. S. (Felipe), at S.F. '37; owner of a town lot '45. iv. 669; v. 685. S. (Felipe), at S.F. '37–44. S. (Fernando), owner of a Russian River rancho '46. *Raven.* S. (Flores), at Los Ang. '46.

Soto (Francisco), 1st child b. at S.F. 1776, son of Ignacio. He became a soldier in the S.F. comp., was a corp. in 1810, and was promoted to sergt for bravery in an Ind. campaign of that year; also made an exped. in '13, and another in '20. ii. 91, 204, 324, 339. He was possibly the Fran. S. at S. Matías rancho, Mont., '36, age 57, child Lorenzo b. '21. S. (Francisco), corp. in S.F. comp. '19; sergt '20–9; ment. in '27–8. ii. 584, 592; iii. 66–7, 111, 156. I am unable to distinguish the different men bearing this name. S. (Francisco), grantee of Bolsa Nueva rancho '29. ii. 615, 664. S. (Francisco), corp. died of wounds received in an Ind. exped. '29. iii. 111–13. S. (Francisco), at Mont. '36, age 28, wife María de Los Angeles, child. Ascension b. '32, Trinidad '34, Gertrudis '36. S. (Francisco), at S. José '41, age 34, wife Bárbara Castro, child. Ana María b. '34, Francisco '36, Vicente '38, Encarnacion '39; in '42–4 grantee of S. Lorenzo, Alameda Co., for which his widow was cl. in '52. iv. 673. S. (Francisco), at S. José '41, age 24. S. (Francisco), grantee of S. Vicente, Mont., '35–42. iii. 678. S. (Francisco), prob. some one of the preceding; sergt of the Mont. comp. '35–6. iii. 671; a supporter of Alvarado and comisario de policía. iii. 461, 675; ment. as lieut in '39. iii. 588; admin. of Sta Cruz '39–40. iii. 695; went to Mex. with Covarrubias in '40. iv. 13, 15, 24; but is ment. again in '42. iv. 308.

Soto (Gervasio), soldier of the S.F. comp. '19–31; resid. of Branciforte '36. iii. 697; at S.F. age 54 in '44; at S. José '45. iv. 686. S. (Guillermo), soldier of the S. Buen. escolta 1786, when his wife, Nicolasa Ramirez, died; settled at Los Ang. 1789. ii. 349; alcalde in '98 and 1809. i. 661; ii. 110. S. (Ignacio), soldier of S.F. comp. from 1776; in 1793 at S. José, wife Bárbara Espinosa, child. Antonio b. '76, Francisco María '77, Dámaso '78, Isidoro '80, Josefa (who married José Sanchez) '83, Joaquin '84, José Francisco, Rafaela, Bernarda, Tomás, Juan, Rafael, and Dolores. i. 291, 477. S. (Ignacio), soldier of the S.F. comp. '24–30. S. (Ignacio), corp. at Mont. '36, age 22. S. (Ignacio), soldier at Mont. '36, age 26. S. (Ignacio), at S. José '41, age 33, wife Teresa Martinez. S. (Isidoro), soldier retired with rank of lieut '44. iv. 408; in '36 at Mont., age '55, wife Marcela Linares; married sons Lázaro and Joaquin.

Soto (Jesus), sergt who went to Mex. with Castro '40; aux. de policía '46 at Mont. iv. 13, 30; v. 637. S. (Joaquin), son of Isidoro, at Mont. '36, age 33, wife Dolores Cantua, child. Joaquin b. '24, Luisa '26, Bárbara '27, Josefa '32, Laran (?) '34; possibly the grantee of Piojo in '42. iv. 655; juez de paz at S. Juan B. '46. v. 640; and still in Mont. Co. '51. S. (Joaquin), son of Ignacio; married at S. José 1803 to María de la Luz Berreyesa. ii. 138. S. (Joaquin), resid. of Branciforte '30. ii. 627. S. (Joaquin), juez de campo at Los Carneros, Mont., '35; iii. 674. S. (Joaquin), at S. Matías rancho '36, age 51, wife Juana Butron, child. Bárbara b. '24, Antonia '25, Deogracias '28, María '30, Adelaida '31, María '33, Salvador '34. iii. 678. S. (Joaquin), at S. Bernardino '46, age 35. S. (Joaquin), grantee of Cañada de la Carpintería '45. iv. 655.

Soto (José) soldier of the S.F. comp. '21–9. S. (José María), settler at Los Ang. '15. ii. 349. S. (Josefa), grantee of Capay rancho '35–44. iii. 711;

iv. 671. S. (Juan) soldier of the S.F. comp. '19–24; in '41 at S. José, age 55, wife Petra Pacheco, child. José b. '19, Francisco '25, José Ignacio '30, Guadalupe '33, Silverio '34, and Juana '35. S. (Lázaro), son of Isidro, at Mont. '36, age 34, wife Solecita Cantera, child. Isidro b. '28, General (?) '31, Ramon '34, and Joaquin '35; grantee of Cañada de la Segunda '39. iii. 677; at Mont. '46. S. (Lorenzo), at the Natividad fight '46. v. 368; in the south '47. v. 389–90; cl. for Los Vallecitos '52. iii. 612. S. (Luis), at S.F. '42, age 23. S. (Manuel), soldier of the S.F. comp. '23–31. S. (Manuel), at Branciforte '28. S. (María Ant. Mesa de), widow at S. José '41, age 39, child. Juan Cap. b. '23, Jesus '25, Dolores '27, Juan Cris. '29, Francisco '31, José Ignacio '33, Patricio '35, José Cruz '37, and Celia '39. S. (Mcliton), in the Solis revolt of '29, sent to Mex. iii. 73, 77–8, 82–5. S. (Milano), Mex. soldier at Mont. '36, age 33. S. (Pedro), soldier at S.F. '42. S. (Rejis), settler at Los Ang. 1789. i. 461. S. (Raimundo), worked for Larkin '48 on his rancho. S. (Ramon), at S.F. '44, age 20. S. (Teodora), grantee of Cañada del Hambre and Las Boleus, Contra Costa, in '42. iv. 671. S. (Tiburcio), at Mont. '36, age 30, wife Concepcion Zuñiga, child. José de Jesus b. '29, Raimundo '30, Vicenta '33, Juliana '34, and Miguel '35. Sonervoit (Alex.), 1847, Co. E, N.Y. Vol. (v. 499); at Los Ang. '77. Sout (W.), 1846, Cal. Bat., Co. B, artill. (v. 358). Southward (Chas C.), 1847, clerk for Parker at S.F.; owner of town lots; in '48 trader at Napa in partnership with Swasey. v. 670; at Vallejo after '50; Trinidad '54; Vallejo '77. Southwick (John), 1846, carpenter on the U.S. Congress; capt. and chief engineer in Stockton's Bat. '46–7. v. 385. Southworth (Eli), 1838, nat. of Mass., visited Cal. from Hon. on the D. Quixote, and possibly earlier, '33–5, on the Loriot. iv. 103, 119, 141. In '43–5 he lived at S.F. as a partner in Paty's business, being named in the padron of '44 as 25 years old. After '48 he engaged in the lumber business; and from '53 he lived with William H. Davis at S. Leandro until his death in '57. Souza (Wm), 1847, Portuguese fruit-dealer at Sta Clara '63–76.

Spalding (Josiah), 1840, mr of the Lausanne, in trouble with the authorities. iv. 104, 121, 171–4. A Mass. man who died about '70; his daughter at Mont. in '84. S. (J. C.), 1848, passp. from Hon. Sparks (Isaac J.), 1832, nat. of Me, and long a resid. of St Louis, Mo., who came from N. Mex. with Young's party of trappers. iii. 388, 408. He engaged in otter-hunting on the coast, and in '34 seems to have made a trip to N. Mex., or at least got a pass. iii. 395; in '35 aiding in the removal of Ind. from S. Nicolás isl. iii. 361, 652. From '35 he lived at Sta B., keeping a store from '36 in a house bought of Foxen, but devoting himself mainly to otter-hunting, for which he received several licenses. iv. 81, 117; asked for naturalization in '37, estimating his property at $2,000; grantee of a rancho in '39, he having become a catholic before '36. He was not arrested in '40. iv. 24; but in '41 was in some trouble because of a young woman who bore him two children, iv. 280, being threatened with a fine of $19 (!) if he did not put an end to the scandal, and the woman being finally exiled to Los Ang. In '43 he was grantee of Huasna rancho, S. Luis Ob., for which he was later cl. as also for Pismo. iv. 655; iii. 678. He served rather unwillingly under Frémont for a time in '46–7, had a Cal. claim of some $900 (v. 462), and in '47 was sent to Gov. Mason to explain the state of affairs at Sta B. v. 584. He gave up hunting, except as a pastime, after '48; made an unsuccessful trip to the mines; and later led the life of a prosperous ranchero in S. Luis Ob. Co. till his death in '67 at the age of 63. He was regarded as an honest and active man. His portrait was published in the Hesperian of '59, with a sketch of his early life. A family is mentioned in the later years, but I find no record to show whom he married. S. (Mary), 1846, of the Mormon colony with children. v. 546; daughter of Mrs Hamilton; not named in the Honolulu list; and possibly wife of Q. S. S. (Quartus S.), 1846, of the Mormon colony, with wife and child. v. 546. Called also Q. L. and Q. C.; nat. of Conn., teacher and preacher, who seems to have left the church; said to have been a lawyer at S.F. in later years, but not in the directories. S. (Stephen), 1846, sailor on the Dale. Sparrowhawk, 1846 (?), mr of the Jóven Guipuzcoana, who settled at Stockton, and died '61 acc. to newspapers. Spatz (Conrad), 1847, Co. B, N.Y.Vol. (v. 499); killed in L. Cal, '47.

Spear (Nathan), 1823, nat. of Boston, druggist's clerk with his brother
Paul in B., who made a trip to the Sandw. Isl. in '19, and another on the
Rover in '23, touching at Mont. In '29 he came again to the Islands, in '30
married Jane Holmes, and in '32 came to Cal. in time to join the comp. extranjera at Mont., iii. 221, 408, where he opened a store, obtaining a carta,
and owning a schooner, the *Nicolás*, which ran to Sta Cruz. iv. 83, 141. His
name occurs often in commercial records of each year, and I have many of his
letters. In '36 he formed a partnership with Leese and Hinckley to open a
store at S.F., whither he moved in '38, leaving his Mont. store in charge of
Wm Warren. At this time the partnership was broken up by a quarrel over
$13,000 of profits, but Spear continued the business in the store at the cor. of
Montgomery and Clay streets; transferred the *Nicolás* to S.F. bay for the
collection of produce, adding the *Isabel* to the fleet—Wm H. Davis, his
nephew and clerk, being generally in com. of one of the schooners; and built
a mule-power grist-mill; being arrested as a matter of form in '40. iii. 705,
709; iv. 17, 82, 116, 130, 245, 250, 668; v. 681. In '45 he was injured by Californians in an assault on Capt. Libby. iv. 569, 665-6; and is named as a witness at the Rae inquest. iv. 593. In '46-7 he is named as owner of lots,
candidate for alcalde, and taking some slight part in politics. v. 295, 455,
680-1; but on account of ill-health moved to Napa Val. with his family in
'46, denouncing a quicksilver mine on the Bale rancho. He returned to S.F.
at the end of '48, and died there Oct. '49 at the age of 47. He was an enterprising man of business, honorable in his dealings, gentlemanly in his manners, and scholarly in his tastes though of limited education. He never became
a Mex. citizen, and therefore obtained no land grant. His wife, a half-breed
Hawaiian, died in Napa '48; and there was one son, William N., b. at Napa
'46, who in '78 gave me a valuable collection of his father's *Papers*. He died before '84.   Spect (Jonas), 1848, nat. of Pa, who came overland to Or. in '47,
and to S.F. on the *Henry*, possibly at the end of '47. In '48 he was a very
successful miner, being the discoverer of gold on the Yuba. He kept a store
at Sacramento; was elected to the 1st state senate; was a founder of Frémont,
where he lived till '56; a resid. of Vernon till about '68, when he moved to
Colusa, dying there in '83 at the age of 66. Portrait in *Colusa Co. Hist.*, 42;
Yolo Co. Hist., 26; see also *Hist. Or.*, this series, p. 629.   Spedding (Matthew), 1848, Engl. farmer in Sta Clara '76.   Speiden (Wm), 1846, purser on
the U.S. *Congress;* commissary in Stockton's Bat.; witness at the Frémont
court-martial. v. 385, 420.

Spence (David), 1824, nat. of Scotland, who had lived a few years at Lima,
and came to Cal. on the *Pizarro* to superintend the meat-packing establishment of Begg & Co. at Mont. ii. 519, 526. In '27 he started in business for
himself, iii. 128, and was prosperous from the beginning, being cautious, close,
and energetic. His name often appears in the records of each year, and I have
many of his business letters. In '28 he was baptized at Sta Cruz as David
Estévan; in '29 married Adelaida, daughter of Mariano Estrada, taking an
active part in the protection of Mont. during the Solis revolt. iii. 71, 74, 82, 49;
ii. 609; and was naturalized in '30. In '34-9 he was grantee of Encinal y Buena
Esperanza rancho, of which he was cl. and permanent owner. iii. 677; in '35
alcalde. iii. 673. In '36 he was a member of the diputacion, and in this and
the following years was secretly a supporter of Alvarado's govt, choosing not
to act openly as a member of the 'congress,' yet exerting quietly much influence in municipal and legislative matters. iii. 426, 454-5, 460, 469, 501, 524;
iv. 86, 116, 148. He was elector and juez de paz in '39-40, furnishing information to Laplace, giving Sutter a letter of introduction, and doubtless favoring the exile of Graham and his vagabonds. iii. 675-6; iv. 8-9, 128, 136, 154-
5; ment. '41-2. iv. 212, 309-10; in '43-5 member of the junta departamental.
iv. 361, 411, 425, 521, 540; in '45 in com. of the foreign guard to protect
Mont. during the Micheltorena troubles, being also appointed prefect by Gov.
Pico, but apparently declining the office. iv. 515, 522, 653. In '46, though
popularly believed to have intrigued for an English protectorate, he was regarded by Larkin as friendly to the U.S., was member of the council after the

change of flag, and of the legislative council in '47. v. 28, 61, 68, 234, 289, 433, 637. He subsequently served as prefect in '49–50, and as county supervisor in '58–60. About '48 he gave up his mercantile enterprises, and devoted himself chiefly to the care of his estate and the raising of live-stock. In '73 he furnished me some brief *Historical Notes*, and died in '75 at the age of 77. Don David had an excellent reputation among the pioneers of Cal., few exerting so wide and good an influence. While not exactly popular by reason of his conservatism and closeness in money matters, obstinate as any of his race, and making enemies as well as friends, he yet merited and received the respect of all classes. His wife survived him but a month, and his only son David, born in '30 and educated at Honolulu, iv. 103, died in '68, leaving 3 sons and a daughter, who inherited their grandfather's large estate.

Spence (Geo.), 1846, Co. E, Cal. Bat., enlisting at Sonoma in Oct. (v. 358). S. (Robert), 1846, ditto; in the mines '48. Spencer, 1839 (?), on board the Boston trader *Sophia*, acc. to the S. Diego *World* of Feb. 15, '73, when S. revisited S.D. S., 1809–10 (?), hunter reported to have been in Cal. ii. 89, S. (Oscar H.), 1846, Irishman on roll of Soc. Cal. Pion.; d. at Vallejo '76, age 52. S. (Wm W.), 1847, Co. D, Morm. Bat. (v. 469). Spidle (John), 1847, Co. S, ditto; badly hurt at Los Angeles. Spiel (Henry), 1845, overl. immig. of the Swasey-Todd party. iv. 576, 587 (though John H. Brown says that he went to Or. and came to Cal. in '46). He served in Co. B, artill. of the Cal. Bat. (v. 358), and settled at Sta Cruz, where, acc. to Brown, he was accidentally killed about '53. Spitler (John), 1846, Co. E, Cal. Bat., enlisting at Sonoma in Oct. (v. 358). Spitten (John D.), 1846, Co. C, 1st U.S. dragoons (v. 336). Spitzer (August), 1846, German immig. of the Donner party, who died in the mts. v. 531, 534. Spooner, 1848, from Hon. on the *Sagudahoc;* perhaps Sam. B. at S. José '50.

Sprague (Richard D.), 1847, Co. C, Morm. Bat., musician (v. 469); reënl.; at Brigham City, Utah, '82. S. (Thomas), 1848, doubtful date in a newspaper sketch. Spriggs (Thos), 1847, died in Sonoma Co.'51. Spring, 1848, mr of the *Huntress.* v. 578. Springer (James Peter), 1841, nat. of Ky, and overl. immig. of the Bartleson party. iv. 270, 255, 279. He returned east in '42. iv. 342; is said to have made the overl. trip several times, being engaged in promoting immigration; and finally came to Cal. with his family in '52, settling at Saratoga, Santa Clara Co., and being a member of the legislature of '59. He died in '61, leaving a widow and daughter. An account of the trip of '41, by him, is given in *Taylor's Discov. and Founders.* S. (Lewis), 1847, painter at Mont. '47–50. Sproston, 1847, mid. on the U.S. *Independence.* Squires, 1848, saddler at Sutter's fort.

Stack (Garrett), 1847, Co. E, N.Y. Vol. (v. 499). Stadmuller (Joseph), 1847, Co. F, 1st U.S. artill. (v. 518). Stagg (Wm), 1816, sailor on the *Albatross.* ii. 275. Stall (Alfred B.), 1847, Co. I, N.Y. Vol. (v. 499); d. before '82. Standage (Henry), 1847, Co. E, Morm. Bat. (v. 469); in Ariz. '82. Stanley, 1845, in Sutter's employ '45–6. iv. 578. S. (Fabius), 1846, lieut on the U.S. *Dale;* nat. of N.C.; later rear-admiral; at Washington, D.C., '79. S. (John M.), 1846, nat. of N.Y. and artist with Kearny from N. Mex. v. 337; owner of S.F. lot '47. v. 676; went by sea to Or. and thence to the islands; in '51–2 connected with the survey of the Northern Pac. R. R.; d. at Detroit '72. S. (J. R.), 1846, at Sta Cruz '81. *S. J. Pion.* An R. Stanley of '44 is also mentioned in '78. *Id.* S. (Joseph), 1842, sailor on the *United States;* at Reno, Nev., '83. S. (Simeon), 1846, of the Mormon colony; did not come to Cal. v. 547. Stanly, 1846, overl. immig. v. 528, who joined the Cal. Bat. (v. 358), and died on the march south in Dec. Stanton (Chas Tyler), 1846, nat. of N.Y. and overl. immig. of the Donner party from Chicago. He crossed the Sierra to Sutter's fort and went back to aid the party, though he had no relatives among the number. Again he volunteered to cross the mts for succor, but died in the attempt. v. 531–2, 534, 537. Portrait in *McGlashan's Hist.* I have a long letter from his brother, Philip V. N. Stanton, to Geo. McKinstry in '48, containing much information about the young man's life, character, and family.

Stargenigge (John), 1847, shingle-maker at Mission S. José.   Stark (Benj. F.), 1847, from Hon. on the *Currency Lass*, returning on the *Toulon*. S. (Daniel), 1846, of the Mormon colony, with wife and two children. v. 547; owner of a S. F. lot '47. v. 682; builder of a school-house. v. 656; commissioner to settle the affairs of Brannan & Co.; member of the S. F. council in '49; living in Utah '84.   S. (Henry), 1847, Co. B, N.Y. Vol. (v. 499).   S. (John S.), 1846, nat. of Ky and overl. immig. with M. D. Ritchie, whose daughter, Mary J., was his wife. v. 529. He took part in measures for the relief of the Donner party. v. 540-1; settled in Knights Valley; county judge of Napa '50-1; memb. of the legislature '51, '55-6; lived near Calistoga '51-68; in Lake Co. from '68 to his death at Guenoc in '74, leaving a widow and 8 children.   Starke (Fred.), 1845, German sailor who deserted from a whaler at Sauzalito. iv. 587; a ranchero in different parts of Sonoma Co.; miner in '48-9; in '80 on a farm near Petaluma with his wife Mina Hastler.   Starkey, 1848, Engl. merchant of the S.F. firm of S., Janion, & Co. v. 678, 680; d. at S.F. about '50.   Stayton (James), 1847, Co. B, N.Y. Vol. (v. 499), d. on the Calaveras '52.

Stearns (Abel), 1829, nat. of Mass. who had lived 3 years in Mex., where he was naturalized in '28, and arrived at Monterey in July '29. iii. 179. He came with the intention of obtaining a large tract of land, to be selected in the Sac. or S. Joaq. valleys, which, apparently in payment of some claim, the Mex. govt. had offered him. His associate in this scheme was Geo. W. Ayres, q.v. Being meanwhile for a year or two in the employ of Capt. Cooper, Stearns seems to have selected his land, or at least to have reached a point where the action of the diputacion was required, and in urging a meeting of that body he excited the enmity of Gov. Victoria, by whom he was banished to the frontier to return as one of the leading inciters of the revolution of '31. iii. 49, 179, 193-4, 200-2, 630. Nothing more is heard of the land project; and in '33 S. settled at Los Ang. as a trader. I have much of his business correspondence from year to year. In '34 he obtained a town lot, and also a building at S. Pedro, which he enlarged and used as a warehouse. His dealings were chiefly in hides and liquors; and from '35 he was often in trouble by reason of smuggling operations; and also in '35 severely wounded in a quarrel about a barrel of wine sold to Wm Day. iii. 375, 417, 631-2, 641; iv. 95, 116, 208. Don Abel was, perhaps, not more addicted to contraband trade than Larkin, Fitch, Spence, and others, but he was less cautious and less fortunate in keeping on the right side of the authorities. In '36 he was síndico. iii. 636; and for some reason that is not very clear, but perhaps for his agency in the matter of the vigilantes, was ordered to leave Cal. by Gov. Chico, becoming in this and the next few years a strong supporter, in a quiet way, of Alvarado, even as against Cárlos Carrillo. iii. 197, 424, 428-9, 501, 565. In '39 his name is mentioned in connection with the flag tumult. iii. 589; in '42 entertained Com. Jones. iv. 321; sent gold from the S. Francisquito placers to the Philadelphia mint. iv. 297; and purchased the Alamitos rancho and its live-stock for $6,000 as a foundation for his future landed wealth. He was somewhat active in the movement against Gov. Micheltorena in '45, being also a suplente of the assembly. iv. 495, 497, 508, 540. In '46 he was subprefect and also worked earnestly—both as a foe of Mex. and friend of the U.S.—to further the plans of Larkin, by whom he was formally appointed a sub-confidential agent of the U.S. His efforts and those of his chief were defeated at the last by Stockton's perversity, if, indeed, there was any remaining hope of success after the rascally acts of Frémont and his associates. v. 50, 63, 66, 71, 231, 264, 271-2, 625. In the warlike events of '46-7 he remained neutral as a Mex. official, though he had some small Cal. claims (v. 402), and is mentioned in the annals of '47-8, being síndico in the latter year. v. 329, 435. 448, 610, 626. In '49 he was a member of the constit. convention, and later served as assemblyman, supervisor, justice of the peace, and member of town council. He was cl. for the Laguna and Alamitos ranchos. iii. 633; iv. 621; and the owner of many more, becoming the largest owner of land and cattle in southern Cal. His wealth was somewhat affected by the drought of '63-4 and by other reverses, yet he left an immense estate at his death, which occurred at S.F. in '71, when he was 72 years of age. Don Abel was a shrewd man of business; somewhat tricky in the petty transactions of early years, but apparently honorable in the larger operations of later times; a man of quick temper and strong prejudices, but hospitable, not penurious, a good friend, and kind husband. He hated Mexico and the Mexicans, but liked the Californians to such a degree as to cause at times some hostility on the part of Americans. In person he was very ugly, being known sometimes as Cara de Caballo, and having an impediment in speech from the cut inflicted by Day in '35. His wife was Arcadia, daughter of Juan Bandini, as beautiful as her husband was ugly, raising the personal appearance of the family to a high average, who survived him without children, inherited the bulk of his estate, married Robt S. Baker, and still lives in southern Cal. in '85.   S. (Fred.), 1847, killed at the S. Gabriel. v. 395; perhaps 'Strauss.'

Stebbins (Ira), 1845, overl. immig. of the Hastings party. iv. 586-7; working for Sutter in '45-6, later at Sonoma, and prob. one of the Bears, since he is recorded as having arrived at N. Helv. from Sonoma on June 17th. v. 110, 128; owner of S.F. lot '47. v. 685; said to have been killed in the south by Murieta's men. His name is written Ira H. and Isaac T.; possibly two men. Steel (Austin), 1845, mr of the *Dromio* (?).   S. (James), 1841, an employé of the H. B. Co.   S. (Joseph), 1826, Boston trader, and mr of the *Harbinger* '26-8, of the *Planet* '29-30, *Chalcedony* in '32-3, *Sarah and Caroline* and *Kent* '36-8, and *Roger Williams* in '40.   His name constantly appears in commercial records of all these years, and he was evidently a humorous and popular trader. iii. 93, 146-8, 176, 381, 384, 461, 563; iv. 104-6, 117.   Steele (Geo. E.), 1847, Co. A, Morm. Bat. (v. 469); reënl.   S. (H. A.), 1841, lieut on the *St Louis.*   S. (Isaiah C.), 1847, Co. A, Morm. Bat. (v. 469); reënl.   S. (Seymour G.), 1847, capt. Co. A, N.Y. Vol. v. 503-4; in Humboldt Co. '74; at S. Diego '82.   Steers (Andrew J.), 1847, Co. B, Morm. Bat. (v. 469); reënl.

Steingraudt (Louis), 1846, Co. C, 1st U.S. dragoons (v. 336).   Stenner (Wm), 1831, nat. of Mass. and mate of the *Ayacucho.* iii. 405; for 2 years in charge of the hide-houses at S. Diego; in '33 obtained a passport; perhaps the same who was mr of the *Primavera* in '47, v. 580, having a Cal. claim of $450 (v. 462).   Stenson (J. Fenwick), 1846, passed mid. U.S.N., and acting capt. in Stockton's Bat. '46-7. v. 385.   Stephens, 1848, miner at Coloma. S. (Alex.), 1847, Co. D, Morm. Bat. (v. 469); in Sutter's employ '47-8, and at the Coloma mill when gold was found.   S. (Alfred), 1837, on Larkin's books. S. (Charles), 1848, at Sutter's fort.   S. (John), 1798, Boston sailor at S. Diego. i. 545, 654.   S. (Peter), 1847, Co. F, N.Y.Vol. (v. 499); d. at S.F. '49. S. (Thos H.), 1848, owner of S.F. lots.   S. (Wm), 1836, Engl., age 35, in a Los Ang. list.   Stepp, 1845, one of Frémont's men, separated for a while from the party, but accompanied Gillespie up the valley to rejoin it. His full name was prob. 'Steppenfeldt,' or possibly there may have been another of that name. iv. 583; v. 24, 453.

Sterling, 1840 (?), at Sta Rosa in '77, known as 'Major' S., said to have visited S.F. in very early times on a coasting vessel. iv. 120.   S. (Chas B.), 1847, nat. of La, clerk for naval agent Larkin at Mont. '47-8, and later employed by him in the Sac. Val., where he wrote long letters on his adventures in the mines. He prob. came as purser on a man-of-war; was the 3d settler in Colusa Co.; married Lucinda Stewart '49 in Yolo Co.; and died after '50 at a date not recorded.   Sterrett (Isaac), 1842, lieut in com. of the U.S. *Relief.* iv. 314, 568.   Stetson (Ed. L.), 1841, clerk on the *Don Quixote* '41-2, named in Larkin's accounts and by Davis. iv. 341; mr of the *Warren* at Honolulu and Mazatlan '45-6; in '47-8 clerk for Larkin at Mont. and Benicia, and later for Brannan at Sac.; at S.F. '51.   Stetyel (Geo.), 1848, in S.F. letter-list.

Stevens, 1840, mr of the *Leonidas.* iv. 104.   S., 1845, mr of the *Wm C. Nye.* iv. 570.   S., 1846, mr of the *United States.* v. 580.   S., 1847, mid. on the U.S. *Independence.*   S. (Mrs), 1845, at Mont., went east on the *Admittance.*   S. (Alex.), 1847, Mormon at the Coloma mill when gold was found. S. (Asa), 1847, owner of S.F. lot. v. 679.   S. (Charles), 1847 (?), at S.F. '54.

Annals. S. (Elisha), 1844, nat. of Ga and capt. of the overl. immig. party to which I have given his name. iv. 445–8, 453, 679. I find no record of him in the following years; but in '72–83 he was living on Kern River, with an excellent memory of early times as he wrote, which however he proposed to utilize one of these days to make a book which should bring him money and fame. Alleged portrait and biog. in *S. F. Post*, Dec. 26, '83. I have in '85 received neither a copy of his book nor news of his death.   S. (Geo.), 1847, at Benicia. v. 673.   S. (Geo. A.), 1847, mid. on the U.S. *Dale*.   S. (Isaac), 1842, at Sta Cruz '42–3.   S. (James), 1840, mr of the *Roger Williams* and *Cervantes*. iv. 12, 104; also on the coast in '45 and perhaps in '48.   S. (James), 1845, doubtful name of an overl. immig. iv. 578; also Richard.   S. (John), 1837, at Mont.   S. (John), 1840, on the *Lausanne* acc. to a letter pub. in the county histories. iv. 121; yet not named as a passenger at Hon. and not known to have remained in Cal., unless he may be the following.   S. (John), 1846, Co. A, Cal. Bat. (v. 358), one of the Sta B. garrison. v. 316.   S. (John H.), 1847, Co. G, N.Y.Vol. (v. 499); at Stockton '71–4.   S. (Joshua T.), 1845, mr of the *United States*.   S. (Lyman), 1847, Co. B, Morm. Bat. (v. 469); in '81 at Orderville, Utah.   S. (Thos H.), 1848, owner of S.F. lots.   S. (Wm), 1846, sailor on the U.S. *Dale*.   S. (Wm), 1847, at Sutter's fort.   Stevenson, (B. W.), 1847, mid. on the *Independence*.

Stevenson (Jonathan D.), 1847, nat. of N.Y., democratic politician, and militia officer, who came to Cal. as colonel in com. of the regiment of N.Y. volunteers. For a record of the regimental history, see v. 499–518; and for additional mention of Col Stevenson's career in '47–8, v. 415, 439, 449–50, 489–90, 497, 565, 584, 588–9, 625, 631–2. From May '47 to the end of the war and mustering-out of the volunteers in '48 he was military commandant of the southern district, with headquarters at Los Ang. The colonel never had an opportunity of showing his prowess as a warrior, but he was a man of much energy, of strong will, and good executive ability, a strict disciplinarian, who performed the duties of his position in a very creditable manner. After '48 he settled at S.F. as a real estate agent, and was particularly interested for some years in developing the latent greatness of New York of the Pacific, being the claimant for the rancho of Los Médanos, Contra Costa. iii. 712. From '72 he held the position of U.S. shipping commissioner at S.F., where he still lives in '85 at the venerable age of 85 years. Portrait in *Annals of S. F.*, and *Clarke's Hist.* The public has often been led to expect the publication of his recollections of a long and active life, a work that could not fail to be of deep interest. In '47 Col S. was a widower, having 3 daughters in N.Y.; in '51 he married again and has several daughters born in Cal.   S. (Matthew R.), 1847, son of the colonel and capt. of Co. G, N.Y.Vol. v. 504; died at Sackett Harbor, N.Y., '63.   S. (Wm), 1847, Co. F, 3d U.S. artill. (v. 518); supposed to be living in '64.

Steward (James), 1826, on the *Rover*.   S. (S.), 1848, at Mont.   Stewart (Alfred V.), 1846, at S.F. '46–7.   S. (Chas), 1848, passp. from Hon.   S. (Frank S.), 1847 (?), at a reunion of surviving N.Y. Vol. '84.   S. (J. B.), 1847; mid. on the U.S. *Columbus*.   S. (James), 1847, Co. D, Morm. Bat. (v. 469).   S. (John C.), 1835, sailor on the *Pilgrim* who settled at S. Diego in '38; married Rosa Machado, and still lived at S. D. in '77.   S. (Robert B.), 1847, Co. D, Morm. Bat. (v. 469).   S. (Thomas), 1824, Scotch carpenter on the *Royal George*, arrested at Sta B.; at Mont '29; at S. D. '36. ii. 526.   S. (Thos K.), 1848, on Amer. River; at Sac. '61.   S. (Wm M.), 1848, sec. of Com. Jones, making a trip with Colton to the mines; owner of S.F. lots, memb. of the council, justice of the peace, and candidate for gov. in '49; still at S.F. '54.

Stickney (John), 1836, mr of the *Keat* and perhaps of the *Sarah and Caroline* '36–7. iv. 104, 106.   Stiggere (Ignacio), doubtful name of a Californian at Sonoma. v. 162.   Still (Geo.), 1846, of the Morm. colony, with wife and 3 children. v. 547. Sarah Still, who in '48 was married to J. D. Marston, may have been his daughter. He did not go to Utah.   Stillman (Dexter), 1847, Co. B, Morm. Bat. (v. 469).   Stillwell (Joseph), 1846, overl. immig., who served in Co. E, Cal. Bat., enlisting at S. José in Nov. v. 528 (358); he was a son-in-law of S. C. Young, still at S. Jose in '50.   Stilts (Jesse), 1846, arrived. *Hittell.*   S. (John), 1846, prob. overl. immig., enlisting at Sonoma in Oct. in Co. E. Cal. Bat. (v. 358); settler in Solano Co. '48, and still there in '78.   S. (Marion), 1846, prob. son of John; nat. of Mo.; in Solano Co. '78. Stirling, see 'Sterling.'   Stivers (Simeon), 1846, nat. of N.J. and memb. of the Mormon colony. v. 547. He was a carpenter at S.F., moving in '48 to Mission S. José, where he still lived in '82 with wife, Anna M. Jones, and child. Letitia M. b. '59, Simeon E. '61, Charlotte J. '64, Sam. '66, Champion D. '69, Anna M. '72, Mark '74, and Edward '78.   Stock, 1841, mr of the *Leonidas.* iv. 566.

Stockton (Robert Field), 1846, nat. of N.J. of an old and prominent family, who left Princeton college in 1811 to become a midshipman in the U.S.N.; served with credit in the war of 1812 and later; and in '46 as captain came to Cal. on the *Congress*, succeeding Com. Sloat in command of the Pacific squadron, and holding the position of military gov. of Cal. till Jan. '47. He returned east overland in '47, resigned his commission in '49, was U.S. senator from N.J. in '51-2, was mentioned as a democratic candidate for the presidency several times, and notably in '56, and died '66 at the age of about 70 years. His career in connection with Cal. affairs is fully recorded in v. 232, 251-87, 289-90, 295-6, 302-29, 356, 385-435, 449, 453, 456, 460, 463, 539, 549, 577, 644; iv. 673. It is too complicated and too much the history of the country in '46-7 to be presented en résumé here.   Com. Stockton was brave, resolute, energetic, and in many respects an agreeable gentleman, but an insatiable thirst for popularity and fame was his most marked characteristic, and may be supposed to have determined his policy in Cal.—a policy which, however we may admire some of his acts and qualities, merits nothing but condemnation.   His adoption, in opposition to the views of Sloat and Larkin, of the filibustero plans of Frémont and his associates may charitably be regarded as a mere error of judgment; yet it is hard to resist the conviction that the true state of affairs was known to him, and that his warlike proclamation to a peaceful people, his blustering tirade against imaginary evils, his willingness to identify a criminal revolt of vagabond settlers with the legitimate military occupation, his practical refusal to accept the voluntary submission of the Cal. authorities, his whole policy of conquest which was to produce such unhappy results—that all this was chiefly due to his personal vanity and ambition rather than to his honest opinion respecting the interests of his nation. To the same motive may be ascribed his later policy—not without plausibility and dignity in certain aspects—in the controversies with Gen. Kearny. Stockton was beyond comparison an abler and more honorable man than Frémont, yet his reputation as 'conqueror' of Cal.—notwithstanding his energetic and praiseworthy surmounting of obstacles that but for his folly would not have existed—is as unmerited, though not so fraudulent, as that of the 'pathfinder.'   S. (Wm B.), 1847, Co. F, N.Y. Vol. (v. 499); d. before '82.   Stoddard (Rufus), 1847, Co. B, Morm. Bat. (v. 469); worked as a brick-maker and builder at S. Diego. Stokely (John), 1846, Co. C, 1st U.S. dragoons (v. 336); killed by the explosion at Los Ang. Dec. '47. v. 625.

Stokes (Edward), 1840, Engl. sailor who came from Hon. on the *Fly*, having possibly visited Cal. before. iv. 104, 120. He married Refugio, daughter of José Joaquin Ortega, and in '43-4 was grantee of the Pamo and Sta Isabel ranchos. iv. 621. In '46 he rendered aid to Kearny by carrying despatches to Stockton at S. Diego. v. 339. The date of his death after '50 does not appear, but his widow married Agustin Olvera, and was still living in '70. S. (James), 1834 (?), Engl. sailor who in Cal. became a doctor; first appearing on the records of '35, when he served as consulting physician in the case of Gov. Figueroa, but prob. left some vessel a year or two earlier. iii. 412, 296. He is occasionally named as doctor, druggist, and trader at Mont. in '35-43. iv. 117, 342; married María Josefa Soto in '44; appears at Mont., S. F., N. Helv., and S. José in records of '45, being in com. of a detachment of the

Mont. guard, iv. 515, but appears to have considered S. José his home from this year. In '46 Dr S. is vaguely accredited in tradition with having intrigued for an Engl. protectorate, but was the 1st to raise the U.S. flag at S. José, where by Sloat's appointment he served for a time as alcalde after the change of flag, owning also a lot in S.F., and having a Cal. claim. v. 34, 68, 245–6, 294, 662. He became the owner of the Verjeles and Natividad ranchos, Mont. Co., for which he was later claimant. iii. 679; iv. 656; and in '48 made a trading tour to the mines. I find no record of him or his family after '52. Stolze (Adolphus), 1847, Co. F, N.Y.Vol. (v. 499).

Stone, 1833, at Mont. acc. to Larkin's accounts.   S., 1847, settler in Lake Co. with the Kelseys, killed by the Ind. in '49. Nothing more seems to be known about the man. Possibly he was the following.   S. (Chas), 1847, of the 2d Donner relief party. v. 539–40.   S. (Elisha), 1841, of the original Bartleson party; did not come to Cal. iv. 269.   S. (Heber), 1847, Co. B. N.Y. Vol. (v. 499).   S. (Henry), 1847, owner of S.F. lot.   S. (Joseph M.), 1848, passp. from Hon.   S. (Mahlon), 1846, at Los Ang.   S. (Wm W.), 1808 (?), a resid. of Cal. from '48, and at Angels from '57 to his death in '62; said to have visited the coast in 1808 (prob. an error) and at other dates before '48.   Stoneman (Geo.), 1847, nat. of N.Y., graduate of West Point, and lieut of Co. C, 1st U.S. dragoons, coming to Cal with the Mormon Bat. as quartermaster, but soon rejoining the dragoons. v. 477, 483, 485, 489, 521, 617. Down to '55 or a little later he was engaged in garrison, exploring, or Ind. service on this coast.   At the beginning of the war of '61–5 he was a major in the regular army, reaching the rank of brevet major-general of volunteers, and gaining an enviable reputation as a cavalry officer. After the war he returned to Cal. and settled near Los Angeles, holding later the position of railroad commissioner, and being as I write in '85 governor of California. In these official capacities he will require some notice in a later volume; and in the case of so prominent a pioneer, it is to me a matter of regret that I have no data for a more complete sketch of his earlier Cal. experience. Stope (Gerard), 1836, Engl. at Mont.   Stoppard (Moses), 1847, Co. K, N.Y. Vol. (v. 499).   Storer (Geo.), 1847, nat. of N.Y., from Hon. on the *Francesca;* settled in Sonoma; in Mendocino township '77; there is perhaps confusion between this man and Geo. 'Story.'

Storm (Peter), 1833 (?), Norwegian sailor, whose coming is credited in current sketches to this date with doubtful accuracy. iii. 409. Farnham names him as one of the foreigners arrested in '40. iv. 17. The 1st definite record is that he lived at S.F. in '44, age 40. He settled in Napa Co. in '44–5, and probably took part in the Bear revolt of '46. v. 110, 147–9. He spent the rest of his life mainly in Napa, and died at Calistoga in '77.   Story (Edward), 1848, Amer. lawyer with Brooks in the mines; said to have been alcalde at Mont. earlier (?).   S. (Geo.), 1847, Co. C, N.Y.Vol. (v. 499); near Healdsburg in '80.   Stothers (John E.), 1847, Co. F, ditto; d. at Oakland after '70.   Stout, 1848, mr of the *Bristol.*   S. (Wm), 1846, of the Mormon colony, with wife and child. v. 547. He was one of the founders of New Hope in the San Joaquin Val. v. 550; but left the Mormons, and in '47 was in the lumber business with Sirrine and Meder at Sta Cruz. In '48 had a store at the mines, perhaps of the firm of Brannan & Co.   S. (Wm C.), 1836 (?), agent of P. M. S. S. Co. from '48; died in N.Y. '70 at the age of 69; said to have visited Mont. in '36. iv. 118.   Stow (Aaron), 1847, Co. K, N.Y.Vol. (v. 499); at Davenport, Ia, '82.

Stradspeth, 1845, one of Frémont's men. iv. 583. *Kern.*   Strange (John), 1847, Co. C, N.Y.Vol. (v. 499).   Strauss (Fred.), 1846, sailor on the *Portsmouth,* killed at the S. Gabriel Jan. '47. v. 395; perhaps 'Stearns.'   Streeter (David), 1846, Co. C, 1st U.S. dragoons (v. 336); severely wounded at S. Pascual. v. 346, 355; later a barber at Sta B., where he died in '63.   S. (Wm A.), 1843, nat. of N.Y. and cousin of David; dentist and mechanic, who came from Peru with Stephen Smith as engineer to superintend the construction and running of the Bodega mill. iv. 396, 400. He soon left Smith and went south as dentist or physician till '48. iv. 651, 501. Went to the mines, was in partnership with Weber at Stockton, and leased the S. Buen. mission. Lived at S. Luis Ob. '51–5, and after '55 at Sta B., holding some local offices in both counties. In '78 he gave me his *Recollections of Early Events.* Prob. still living in '85 at the age of '74. Stribling (C. K.), 1836, com. of the U.S. *Cyane* '42 –3, and '45, and of the *Peacock* in '36. iv. 105, 308, 311, 321, 564–5. String-fellow (Jesse A), 1846, nat. of Pa and memb. of the Mormon colony. v. 547. He worked as a carpenter at S.F. (where he owned a lot), Napa, and S. José, going to the mines in '48–9. Later a farmer at S. José, where he died in '78, leaving a widow and 3 grown children. Stroms (John A.), 1846, Co. C, 1st U. S. dragoons (v. 336). Strong (Demas), 1848, Amer. trader at Big Bar and Sutter's mill; alderman and mayor of Sac.; returned to N.Y. '50; in N.Y. senate '64. S. (James H.), 1847, lieut on the U.S. *Columbus.* S. (John M.), 1847, Co. F, 3d U.S. artill. (v. 518). S. (Wm), 1847, Co. E, Morm. Bat. (v. 469).

Stuart (Chauncey), 1848, in S.F. letter-list. S. (María Ant.) 1813, mistress of Capt. Ayers. ii. 269. S. (W. K.), 1848, nat. of Md and overl. immig.; in Nevada co. '51 to his death in '73; widow living in '82. Study (David), 1847, Co. B, Morm. Bat. (v. 469). Stump (David), 1848, miner from Or. at Grass Valley and Placerville '48–9. Stupplebeen (Jacob), 1848, passp. from Hon. Sturgis (Thos), 1831, mr of the *Crusader* '31–2. iii. 382. Sturt (F.), 1848, passp. from Hon. Stuurtzenegger (John), 1846, Co. G, Cal. Bat. (v. 358); owner of S.F. lots '47–8; d. at Oakland about '60–5.

Suarez (Simon), 1797, sub-lieut of the compañía franca at Mont. i. 540–1, 544. S. (Vicente), juez de campo at S. José '44. iv. 685. Sublette (Wm), 1845, came overland with a party of 15 men whose names are not known; at S.F. Jan. '46; went east with Clyman and Hastings. iv. 577–8; v. 526. Succara, chief of the Sotoyomes '37. iv. 72. Suckert (Leon), 1847, Co. D, N.Y. Vol. (v. 499); d. S. F. '71. Sugert, Ind. chief at Sta Cruz 1791. i. 494. Suhr (Albert), 1847, owner of S.F. lot.

Sullivan (Cornelius), 1847, Co. I, N.Y.Vol. (v. 499); locksmith at Mont. '47–8; Sta Clara '71–4; at Lompoc '82. S. (C. G.), 1839, doubtful date in a newspaper sketch. iv. 119; d. in '64, at or near Gold Hill. S. (James), see 'O'Sullivan.' S. (John), 1844, nat. of Ireland, and overl. immig. of the Stevens party with his sister Mary and two brothers. iv. 446, 453. He had come to Canada at the age of 6, and had worked as a stevedore there and as a logger in Me, going to Mo. in '42. After serving under Sutter in the Micheltorena campaign (iv. 476), he settled at S.F., v. 682, where he was teamster, trader, lot-owner, and later capitalist, being founder and president of the Hibernia Bank. He had also kept a store in '48 on Sullivan Cr., Tuolumne. He was a man of upright character, charitable, and well known for his gifts to the church. He died in '82 at the age of 58. His 1st wife was Catherine Farrely in '50, who died in '54; and the 2d was Ada E. Kenna of '60, by whom he had 10 children. There were 2 sons by the 1st marriage, one of whom, Robert, died in '82. The other, Frank J., b. in '52, was educated at St Ignatius College of S.F., in England, and at Columbia law school, N.Y. In '78–85 he practised law at S.F., having been State senator in '82 and a candidate for congress in '84. His wife is Alice, daughter of James Phelan. He has furnished for my use a narrative of his father's life. John Sullivan's sister married Peter Sherreback. S. (John), 1847, Co. G, N.Y.Vol. (v.499); d. S. Luis Rey '48. S. (Michael), 1844, brother of John, and immig. of the Stevens party. iv. 446, 453; owner of S. F. lot '47. S. (Richard), 1847, owner of S.F. lot. S. (Robert), 1844, brother of John, who came as a boy in the Stevens party. iv. 446, 453.

Sumedor (Wm), 1840, permitted to remain in Cal. Summers (W. F.), 1848, at S. Diego. Sumner (N.), 1847, Amer. at N. Helv. S. (Owen), 1845, immig. from Or. in the McM.-Clyman party with his family, including Mrs Payne. He went east with Clyman in '46. iv. 572–3; v. 526. S. (Owen Jr), 1843, son of Owen, who came from Or. with the Hastings party, perhaps with a family. His sister Lizzie married Geo. Davis at Sutter's fort. He prob. went east in '46 with his father. iv. 390–2, 400. S. (Wm), 1826, mr of the

Zamora, and in '32 of the *Waverly*. iii. 149,317, 364, 384, 652.   Suñer (Francisco), 1808, Span. friar who served at 5 different missions, and died at S. Buenaventura in '31. Biog. iii. 658–9; ment. ii. 90, 110, 147, 159–60, 265, 346, 348, 364, 394, 490, 576, 578, 655; iii. 96, 310, 351.

Suñol (Antonio María), 1817, nat. of Spain, who had been a sailor in the French naval service, coming to Cal. on the *Bordelais*, and deserting on her return from the north in '18. ii. 289. He settled at S. José, where he apparently kept a shop and sold liquor in '23. ii. 605; married about '24–5; was postmaster '26, '29. ii. 605; and in '28–30 was the object of some investigation on account of his Span. birth, but was not sent away. iii. 51–2. From about '39 he was owner of the rancho of S. José del Valle, and from about '37 of Los Coches, Alameda Co., selling live-stock to Sutter on credit and having no little trouble to collect the debt. iv. 134, 237; being síndico in '39–40, iii. 731, and sub-prefect '41–4. iv. 274, 684–6. He is mentioned by Mofras in '41 as 'very devoted' to France, and blunderingly by Wilkes; and in the padron of '41 is named as a Span. trader, age 41, wife María Dolores Bernal, child. José b. '26, Paula (later Mrs Sainsevain) '28, Narciso '36 ('35?), and Francisca '38. In '43 he was suplente of the junta. iv. 361; is ment. in the annals of '45–6. iv. 485–6; v. 4, 45; being the purchaser of S. Rafael mission, and a memb. of the S. José council. v. 561, 664, 670. He engaged in mining in '48; was the claimant for his two ranchos in '52. iv. 671, 713; and died in '65, leaving an excellent reputation. His son, José, was probably the man killed in '55 by a squatter on his rancho. He had been juez de policía in '49. Another son, Narciso, was educated in France, and still lives in Suñol Valley, '85, with wife, Rosario Palomares, and 6 child., Margarita, Virginia, Francesca, Eulalia, Josephine, and Juanita. Portrait in *Alam. Co. Hist.*, 176. Other children of Don Antonio María surviving in '83 were Encarnacion (Mrs Etchebarne), Antoneta (Mrs Murphy), and José Dolores.   Suria (Tomás), 1791, artist in Malaspina's exped. i. 490.   Suriano (Juan Fran.), 1602, alférez in Vizcaino's exped. i. 98.   Surok (Francisco), 1845, doubtful name of an applicant for land.   Sutphen (Wm), 1847, Co. A, N.Y.Vol. (v. 499).

Sutter (John Augustus), 1839, German-Swiss trader impelled by bankruptcy in '34 to become an adventurer in America, where, after an unsuccessful career in N. Mex. '35–7, he came to Cal. by way of Or., the Sandwich Isl., and Alaska, and established a trading and trapping post at New Helvetia, obtaining a land grant of 11 leagues, and in '41 the Russian improvements at Ross. Biog. matter relating to Sutter is given elsewhere in these volumes so fully and compactly as to require only reference here. For his early life and arrival in Cal. '39–40, see iv. 122–39, with ment. in iii. 670, 700; iv. 74, 93, 102, 117, 119. Progress of his estab. '41–2. iv. 226–40; also 211, 213, 219–20, 275, 283, 672–3, 679–80. Purchase of the Russian property in '41, with the Muldrow swindle, and efforts of the Russians '42–50 to collect the debt. iv. 177–89. Mention in '43 iv. 356, 366, 387–9, 396. Career in '44. iv. 439, 448–9, 453. Sutter's famous campaign of '44–5 undertaken against the Californians purely as a land speculation. iv. 407, 472, 474, 477–517. Affairs of '45, particularly his efforts to sell his estab. to the Mex. govt. iv. 607–16. Policy and acts of '46 in connection with the Bear revolt, etc. v. 3, 22, 29, 65, 80, 102, 104, 122–5, 359, 538. Mention in '47, when S. had a 'Cal. claim,' served as sub-Ind. agent, and owned a S.F. lot. v. 452, 467, 568, 610, 678. For his experience of '48 and the following years, especially in connection with the gold discovery, see vol. vi. of this series. In '48–9 Sutter was regarded as being very rich, having at least what in the hands of an abler man would have been the basis of an immense fortune; but his wealth, won by good luck without business capacity, could not thus be kept under the new conditions of the flush times, and soon he was reduced to comparative poverty, the successive steps of his downfall being too complicated for presentment here. Doubtless in some instances he was the victim of rascality on the part of sharper adventurers than himself. His original land grant of '41 was confirmed after it had passed for the most part out of his possession; but the Micheltorena grant of '45 was very justly rejected by the supreme court. The end of his public career, in a sense, was in '49, when he was a member of the constitutional convention, and received some 2,000 votes for governor. From '50, being joined by his family from Switzerland, he lived at Hock Farm. From '64, by act of the Cal. legislature, he received a pension of $250 per month till '78, when the bill was defeated. Meanwhile, about '65, he went east, and lived from '71 at Litiz, Pa, making constant but vain efforts to obtain from congress compensation for alleged wrongs of the past; though it does not appear that in his old age and infirmity he ever suffered actual privations. In '76, at his home, he dictated to me his *Personal Recollections*, identical in outline with the story so often told by him, but fuller in most phases than any that has been printed, and most interesting. He died at Washington, D.C., in '80 at the age of 77, leaving a widow who still lives, I think, in '85, two sons, and a daughter. The family seem to have come to Cal. from '44–50 at different dates, though I find but slight information on the subject. Of the sons, Alphonse died some years before '80. One of them seems to have come as early as '44, when the capt. writes to complain of his not being regarded as a naturalized citizen. John A. Jr, to whom his father turned over all his property temporarily in '49, and who was a partner of Hensley, Reading, & Co., was for some years before and prob. after '80 U.S. consul at Acapulco. Emil Victor, identical, I suppose, with E. J., who was Kern's lieut at the fort in '46, v. 298, was for many years to '80 a well-known notary at S.F., and committed suicide in Belgium in '83. The daughter, Anna Eliza, was married in '52 to Geo. Engler, and in '80, as Mrs Dr Link, was living at Acapulco. The biog. matter referred to above contains much of comment on Sutter's character. None of the pioneers named in this register has received so much praise from so many sources; few have deserved so little. Yet it has been by no means a pleasing task, in view of the famous captain's kindly nature and his misfortunes of later years—especially for one who, like myself, has heard from his own lips the story of his wrongs—to reveal the man's true character, as I have deemed it a duty to do. He was but an adventurer from the first, entitled to no admiration or sympathy. His career in N. Mex. was, at the best, discreditable. He came to Cal. in the false character of an ex-capt. of the French army. He was great only in his wonderful personal magnetism and power of making friends for a time of all who could be useful to him; good only in the possession of kindly impulses. His energy was a phase of his visionary and reckless enthusiasm; his executive ability did not extend beyond the skilful control of Indians and the management of an isolated trading post. Of principle, of honor, of respect for the rights of others, we find but slight trace in him. There was no side of any controversy that he would not readily adopt at the call of interest; nationality, religion, friendship, obligation, consistency, counted for little or nothing. There were no classes of his associates, hardly an individual, with whom he did not quarrel, or whom in his anger he did not roundly abuse. For all the favors received at the hands of Californians, he did not hesitate to turn against them, or even to arm foreigners and Indians against them, when a personal advantage seemed within his reach. That his frequent plots and threats of vengeance and revolution and French intervention were for the most more amusing than dangerous does not much increase our respect for the angry plotter. His only capital was money borrowed on the way to Cal., or property obtained on credit from Californians and Russians after his arrival, all on pretences more or less false. He never hesitated to assume any obligation for the future without regard to his ability to meet it; he rarely if ever paid a debt when due; and a general, vague, and kindly purpose to fulfil all his promises in the brilliant future but imperfectly excuses his short-comings. His apparent success in '39–45 was in a sense wonderful, but it rested almost entirely on a fortunate combination of circumstances, and notably on Gov. Alvarado's unwise act—partly inspired by the idea of introducing in the north an element of opposition to Vallejo, with whom he had a temporary quarrel—in permitting a foreigner to found an isolated rendezvous for hostile and uncontrollable elements of a vagabond population in the far interior. Though Sutter's establishment did something to promote the influx of Amer. settlers, it was in no sense beneficial to the interests of the U.S., merely fomenting filibusterism with all its unhappy results. The discovery of gold, often mentioned in this connection, was purely accidental; but I cannot see that its postponement for a time would have done any harm; and I can imagine that its earlier occurrence—likely enough to result from Sutter's settlement—might have been decidedly detrimental to the U.S. in some respects. That the establishment, chiefly by reason of its situation at the foot of the mountains, was of benefit to the immigrants is true; also that Sutter treated them kindly, though not more so than a dozen others; but that he did so at a personal sacrifice, as has been so often claimed, is not true; for Sutter's letters of that time are full of self-gratulations on hisl ucky chance to exchange food and cattle for wagons and implements, to hire mechanics, and to have his land increased in value by the influx of settlers. Neither is it true that Sutter in '45-6 was friendly to the U.S. or to the immigrants as Americans. He did not, as has been claimed by himself and friends, refuse an offer of $100,000 for his property that the immig. might not be deprived of a refuge; on the contrary, he did his best to sell, and failed chiefly because the Mex. govt saw a cheaper way to get the property by buying the Russian mortgage. And as elsewhere stated, I have the captain's original letter, in which he warned Gen. Castro against Gillespie as a secret agent of the U.S., urged the govt to buy his fort, and advised the stationing of a garrison there against the immigrants! Perhaps had this been known pioneers in later times would have been less profuse in their praise of the noble-hearted old patriot. Suwerkrop (E.A.), 1848, at Hon. from S.F. on the *Julian*.

Swab (Emmanuel), 1847, Co. G, N.Y.Vol. (v. 499). Swain, 1848, from Hon. on the *Sagadahoc*. S., 1829, mr of the *Susana*. iii. 149. S. (Chas A.), 1829(?), nat. of Mass., said to have visited the coast in the whaler *American*, iii. 179, and again on the same vessel in '38, though I find no record of such a vessel in either year. He returned in '49 to stay as a farmer, miner, and contractor, dying at S.F. '84 at the age of 71, leaving a widow and son. S. (F. B.), 1848, passp. from Hon. S. (Isaac), 1823(?), on the roll of the Soc. Cal. Pion. S. (Josiah H.), 1847, at Mont. '47-8; perhaps came in '46 on a whaler, and one of Maddox's volunteers, said to be living at S.F. '84. *Swan.* Swaine, 1794, one of Vancouver's men. i. 526.

Swan (John A.), 1843, nat. of England of Scotch parentage, who came as a sailor on the *Soledad* from Mazatlan after 11 years of adventure as a sailor in many parts of the world. iv. 400, 568, 651. He made two trips with Capt. Cooper on the schr *California* in '43-4, then quitting the sea. He kept a little shop and sailors' boarding-house at Mont., his name appearing from '44 on Larkin's books and in other records; made a trip to the gold-mines in '48; went to Fraser River in '59-63; again visited British Columbia in '64-6; and has since resided at Mont. He has written many articles on the olden time for the newspapers, which, with others in MS., have place in my collection, some of them being named in my list of authorities; and he has furnished me besides from time to time many useful items for this register. Swan's writings are not only interesting, but remarkably accurate, his memory being rarely at fault, and the tendency to testify on matters beyond his personal knowledge—too prevalent among pioneer writers—being in his case reduced to a minimum. His work in this direction merits high praise. In the later years down to '85 this kind-hearted old sailor, 73 years old, burdened with poverty and deafness, lives in an old historic adobe at the former capital, delighting in the old ruins that keep alive his dreamy recollections of the past; and occasionally, with 'pioneer of '43' plainly inscribed as credentials on his hatband, he makes a trip to S. José and S.F. to look after the constantly lessening band of his old-time acquaintances. S. (Lyman), 1848, passp. from Hon. S. (Thos M.), 1848(?), in Napa Valley acc. to testimony in later litigation. Swanich (James), 1845, Delaware Ind. of Frémont's party '45-7. iv. 583, 587; said by Martin to have been killed on the Or. frontier '46. Swanson (Joseph), 1848, in S.F. letter list; cl. in '53 for land in Contra Costa. Swartout (Hamilton), 1847, Co. A, Morm. Bat. (v. 469). Swartz (John S.), 1847, Co. E, N.Y.Vol. (v. 499). Swasden, 1847, doubtful name in a Mont. list.

Swasey (Wm F.), 1845, nat. of Maine and overl. immig. from St Louis in the
party that I have called by his name, which was really a division of the Grigsby-
Ide party. iv. 576, 587. For two months he was employed by Sutter as book-keeper, and at the beginning of '46 went by way of S.F. and S. José to Mont., where he
worked for a short time as clerk for Wm H. Davis, and from June to Sept. was
consular clerk for Larkin at $60 per month. v. 16, 60. In Oct. he joined the Cal.
Bat., serving through the southern campaign as asst commissary (v. 358); and
having a 'Cal. claim' of $40 (v. 462). In '47 he came to S.F., where he was
owner of a town lot, clerk of election, and sec. of the council. v. 648, 650.
From '48 he was engaged in trade in partnership with Leighton & Co. at S.F.
and with Southard at Napa. v. 670, 678, 681; also visiting the mines, and in
'49 being a member of the S.F. district legislature and taking some part in
politics. In '51-61 Swasey was a notary public at S.F., being also a witness
in some of the famous land cases; in '61-6 capt. of volunteers and asst quartermaster at Benicia. He has continued to reside at S.F., though I find that
he was appointed in '75 U.S. marshal of Wyoming, and has been a somewhat
prominent member of the Pioneer Society, being the author of many grace-
fully written eulogies of dead pioneers. In '85, at the age of 60 years or more,
though about 45 in appearance, he has received a new appointment as notary
public. Of his family I know nothing except that his mother died recently in
Cal. at a very advanced age. His *View of S. F. in '47* is ment. in v. 676, et
seq. Capt. Swasey has furnished me his recollections of *California in '45-6;*
to him I am indebted for the invaluable *New Helvetia Diary,* of which, as
Sutter's clerk, he was one of the authors; and in several other matters he has
afforded me some assistance.

Sweet (Chas C.), 1847, Co. D, N.Y.Vol. (v. 499). S. (Paul), 1840(?), nat.
of R. I., said to have landed at Mont. this year. iv. 120. In '43-5 a tanner
near Sta Cruz, iv. 356, being named in the Branciforte padron of '45 as Engl.,
age 30, and single; perhaps served in Cal. Bat. '46-7 (v. 358), having a Cal.
claim of $35 (v. 462); and still at Sta Cruz '49-80. Sweeting, 1848, doubt-
ful name of a hotel-keeper at S.F. *Brooks.* Swift (Granville P.), 1844, nat.
of Ky, and immig. from Or. in the Kelsey party, having crossed the plains in
'43. iv. 444-5, 453. He served in Sutter's campaign of '45. iv. 486, 501; was
a leading filibuster of the Bears in '46. v. 95, 104, 107, 110, 147, 153, 168, 172;
and in '46-7 was capt. of Co. C, Cal. Bat. v. 184, 282, 289, 361; having a Cal.
claim of about $2,000 (v. 462). He was a fine-looking man, over 6 ft in height,
a crack shot, and of undoubted bravery, a bitter hater of the Mexicans. He
settled on Stony Cr., Colusa, in '47; made a large fortune in mining on Feather
Riv., with the aid of Ind., in '48-9; later a stock-raiser in Colusa and Tehama;
from '54 ranchero in Sonoma; and from about '68 engaged in fruit-culture
and quicksilver-mining in Solano, where he was accidentally killed in '75, at
the age of about 54. He had a habit of burying his money on his rancho;
several such deposits being accidentally found after he had forgotten them,
and in one instance $24,000 having been stolen by an employee. S., 1807,
mr of the *Derby* and *Hazard;* perhaps on the coast earlier. ii. 17, 78, 84. S.
(Richard), 1846, Co. B, Cal. Bat., enlisting at Mont. in Oct. (v. 358).

Swinburn (Wm), 1839, Engl. mate of the schr *California,* who became a
lumberman in the Mont. district, getting a pass in '41. iv. 119. In '44 in S.
F. dist, age 35. Swinson (Dav.). 1848, at Mont. Swords (Allen J.), 1847,
Co. A, N.Y.Vol. (v. 499); d. at La Paz '48. S. (Thomas), 1846, major U.S.A.,
who came from N. Mex. with Kearny as quartermaster, and returned east
with him in '47, after having made a trip to Honolulu for supplies; witness
in the Frémont court-martial. v. 336, 343-7, 356, 440, 452, 456. In the war
of '61-5 he was chief quartermaster of the western dept, and in '79 lived in
N.Y. as a retired brigadier. Sylvester (Anthony), 1845, one of the men lost
'46 on the *Warren's* launch. iv. 587; v. 384. Syrec, 1848, named as having
kept a store on the Moquelumne.

Tabeau (Baptiste), 1844, one of Frémont's men, killed by Ind. iv. 437,
440. Taber (J. D.), 1846, apparently an overl. immig.; of T. & Hoyt, hotel-

350 PIONEER REGISTER AND INDEX.

keepers at Mont. '47-8; had a family in Contra Costa '60. T., 1847, mr of the *Copia*. v. 577. Tabor (Wm), 1846, in Sta Clara Val. with family. *Hall.* Taforó (José Ignacio), 1819, nat. of S. Amer., soldier of the S. Blas comp. at Mont.; disch. '24; regidor at Mont. '27. ii. 612. Taggart (Geo. W.), 1847, musician Co. B, Morm. Bat. v. 469. T. (Robert), 1848, nephew of Dr Isbel, who killed B. K. Thompson on the way east overland. T. (Sam.), 1842, executed at Los Ang. for murder. iv. 296, 342, 633; called also 'Tagget' and 'Taggett.' Tait (James A.), 1847, Co. A, N.Y.Vol. (v. 499); at Sta Cruz '71-83. T. (Wm G.), 1847, Co. A, ditto. Tajochi (Tomás), Ind. chief of S. Diego '33. iii. 327, 359.

Talamantes (Felipe), settler at Los Ang. 1794; grantee of Sta B. land 1819; at La Ballona '39-40, age 57. ii. 349, 354; iii. 633, 637. T. (Tomás), prob. brother of Felipe, at La Ballona '39, age 47. He took an active part in the fight against Gov. Victoria in '31. iii. 196, 207; was juez de campo '44. iv. 633; and still at Los Ang. '46. Talbot, 1847, of L. & Upham at Mont. '47-8. T. (J. M.), 1846, witness to enlistment in Cal. Bat. T. (Theodore), 1844, nat. of Ky who came with Frémont, and again in '45. iv. 437, 581, 583. He was a young man of good education, who was in a sense com. of that division of the company entering Cal. by the southern route; and in Cal. acted as Frémont's confidential agent. v. 3, 6, 22, 644. He was left in com. of the Sta B. garrison, and later served as lieut and adjutant in the Cal. Bat. v. 287, 304, 316-17, 358, 360, 630. Being sent east with despatches in Feb. '47, he was a witness in the Frémont court-martial. v. 430, 456. Died at Wash., D. C., '62. Talmadge (Abijah D.), 1847, Co. A, N.Y.Vol. (v. 469); killed in '48 by Moquelumne Ind. Tamam (Ig.), 1846, doubtful name, Cal. Bat. (v. 358). Tamanin (Prokop), 1822, mr of the *Volga.* ii. 474. Tamaree (Peter), 1834, at Mont. Tambor (Juan), nickname; killed at Los Ang. 45. iv. 492. Tanferan (Toribio), at S.F. mission from '40; witness in the Santillan case '55. Tanner (Albert), 1847, Co. E, Morm. Bat. (v. 469). T. (John L.), 1848, married at Sonoma to Mary, daughter of J. D. Taber of Mont. Tansill (Robert), 1846, lieut of marines on the *Dale;* in Marston's Sta Clara campaign; com. of the S.F. garrison '47. v. 380, 659.

Tapia (Antonio), juez aux. at S. Cárlos '42. iv. 653. T. (Bartolo), ranchero at Los Ang. 1791-1813. ii. 270, 350-3. T. (Cárlos), at Los Ang. '46. T. (Felipe), soldier at S. José and settler 1786-90. i. 350, 477-8. T. (Fernando), at Los Ang. '48. T. (Francisco), cadet of Sta B. comp. '25-6. ii. 572. T. (Gregorio), grantee of Aguajito rancho '35. iii. 676; at Pilarcitos '36, age 22, wife Martina Vasquez, child María de los Angeles; perhaps at Sta Cruz '54. i. 524. T. (José Ant.), at Los Ang. '46; arrested in '45. iv. 541. T. (José Bartolomé), majordomo of S. Luis Ob. 1789, wife María Lobo; grantee of Topanga Malibu rancho 1804. ii. 112; iii. 634. T. (Mariano), 1792, potter-instructor from Mex. '92-6. i. 615, 715. T. (Ramon), at S. Bern. '46, age 25. T. (Tiburcio), son of José Bartolomé, b. at S. Luis Ob. 1789; later soldier and corporal of the Sta B. comp., being com. of the Purísima guard in '24 at the revolt. ii. 529; member of the diputacion '27, '33. iii. 36-7, 41, 63, 246; alcalde of Los Ang. '30-1, '36; ii. 561; iii. 634, 636; síndico '33, and encargado de Ind. '35. iii. 635; favored Alvarado '38. iii. 565; aux. alcalde '38. iii. 636. In '39 he was alcalde, acting prefect, and grantee of Cucamonga rancho. iii. 586, 589, 633, 636, 640. In '42 he was a supl. ministro of the sup. court; and in '44 2d alcalde. iv. 296, 633. Don Tiburcio was a man of good sense, good character, and some wealth, still at Los Ang. '48 at the age of about 60. A current tradition of later times represented the old man as having buried his treasure on Frémont's approach in '46, and as having died without revealing its exact location. T. (Urcino), settler at Los Ang. 1809. ii. 350. Tapin, 1846, lieut on the U.S. *Savannah.* Tapinto (Mariano), 1792, tailor-instructor '92-5. i. 615.

Tapis (Estévan), 1790, Span. friar who toiled as missionary longest at Sta B. and S. Juan B., and was president of the missions in 1803-12. Biog. ii. 623-4; ment. i. 388, 492, 522, 573-4, 576, 588-90, 594, 640, 669, 672, 689; ii. 7, 9-10, 26, 28, 33-4, 42, 55, 85, 88-90, 108-9, 112-13, 120-1, 140, 148, 159, 161, 165,

168, 175, 182, 326, 346, 366, 369, 378, 383, 386-7, 394, 396, 461, 518, 655. Taplin (Charles), 1844, of Frémont's party; also in '45, returning east in '46 with Sublette. iv. 437, 583. He again joined F. in '48. Tarakánof (Boris), 1806, Russ. chief of Aleut. otter-hunters; captured at Sta B. in '15. ii. 40, 80, 210, 274, 307-13, 353. Tasion (Manuel S.), grantee of a S. Gabriel lot '47. iv. 637. Taufer (Andrew), 1847, German memb. of the Soc. Cal. Pion.; d. at S. F. '79, age 71.

Taylor, 1848, in the mines from Mont. and S. José. T., 1848, at S. F. from the states. T. (Alex. S.), 1848, nat. of S. C., where his father—who had been a lieut on the privateer *Saucy Jack* in the war of 1812—died in '21. The son came to Cal. from China in Sept. '48, but beyond the facts that he was for some years clerk of the U.S. district court at Mont., and later settled at Sta B., marrying Josefa Ortega, and dying in '76, nothing of biog. proper appears in any record that I have seen. He was known as Dr Taylor, but I do not know whether he ever practised medicine. It is not, however, as a pioneer, but as an investigator and writer on the ethnography, bibliography, and history of Cal. that he deserves particular notice; and in these respects he was a remarkable man. Without having any special aptitude by nature or education for such work, he developed a fondness for it almost amounting to a mania. His zeal in face of the most discouraging obstacles is worthy of all praise, though it must be confessed that the result was wellnigh valueless. He was not content with being a collector or even translator and narrator, but had a most unfortunate passion for working the results of his observations and study into what he regarded as a scientific form, the result being too often an absurd jumble of bad Spanish, worse Latin, and unintelligible affectations. While at Monterey he obtained from the priest a valuable collection of old mission documents (later given to the archbishop, and cited by me as *Arch. del Obispado*) which he made the basis of numerous newspaper articles, in which, by reason of faulty translations, typographical blunders, unfounded additions, and the difficulty of locating the dividing line between record and comment, the value of the original was much impaired. His writings from about '53 for the *S. F. Herald, Bulletin, Cal. Farmer, Hutchings' Magazine, Hesperian, Sac. Union*, and other papers were very voluminous. The most extensive of his works and most valuable, being least injured by his peculiar methods, though containing very little original matter, is the *Indianology of Cal.*, published in the *Cal. Farmer* of '60-3, of which most of the linguistic portions are reprinted in *Lucy-Fossarieu, Langues Indiennes de la Cal.*, Paris '81; and which gave Dr T., very properly, an honorary membership in several learned societies of the east. Another of his most ambititious attempts, but least valuable by reason of his utter lack of facilties for bibliographic work, was the *Bibliografía Californica*, pub. in the *Sac. Union*, and noticed in i. 35 of this work. His *Historical Summary of Lower California*, pub. in Ross Browne's *Resources*, ed. of '69, and his *Precis India Californicus*, included by Wm H. Knight in *Bancroft's Hand-book* of '64, are very creditable works, being the only ones that had the advantages of careful editing and proof-reading. His *First Voyage to the Coast of Cal.*, of '53, was a translation of Navarrete's version of Cabrillo's voyage, with comments of little value. i. 69, 72, 77. In his later years Dr Taylor collected all his writings, with numerous MS. additions here and there, into a series of 7 scrap-books, under the titles *Bibliografía California, Indianology of the Californias, Animated Nature of Cal., Odds and Ends of Cal. Life*, and *Discoverers and Founders of Cal., Felix, and Cal. Petra* (the 1st 3 being in '85 in the library of the Soc. Cal. Pion. in S.F.), and issued a descriptive circular, 'The Storehouse of Cal., History and Life,' through which he tried in vain to find in America and Europe a publisher for his collected writings, without a suspicion of the truth that the work and time and ability and resources of data that would enable an editor to put the crude mass in such shape as to do justice to the author's reputation would produce an original work of much greater value. I visited him in '74 at his rancho at La Partera, near Sta B., and found him, though grievously oppressed by illness and poverty, as enthusiastic as ever in all that pertained to early Cal. annals. He pointed sadly but with pride to a wooden box that contained his life work—the 7 volumes mentioned above; and when I sought his advice respecting my own researches, he pointed again to the box as containing all that could ever be gleaned about early Cal.; and he was, I am sure, entirely honest in his belief. 'Test, if you like,' he said, 'the accuracy of my work by examining the documents I gave the archbishop, but I know from long years of earnest research that nowhere else, especially from mission and Spanish sources, will you find a scrap of new information.' Yet only 3 miles away from the rancho where he had lived for many years, at Sta B. mission, I took 6,000 pages of copies of most important missionary correspondence that he had never seen! All honor, nevertheless, to such men as Hayes and Taylor and Lancey, who have toiled under more or less unfavorable auspices to save from destruction the data for our history.

Taylor (Christopher), 1848, came from Or. in Sept. on the *Henry*, engaging in trade at Sutter's fort, as member of the firm of Priest, Lee, & Co.; finally settled at Dayton, Or., where he was in '78. T. (Geo. W.), 1847, nat. of Va, who enlisted in Co. F, 3d artill., at Mont. (v. 518); in the mines '49, and later at Mont.; d. at Napa '84. *Lancey*. T. (Hiram), 1841, Amer. musician in the Workman party from N. Mex. iv. 278-9. I have his original passport dated Sta Fé Aug. 24th. At Los Ang. and on the Cosumnes '42; went to Or. with Leese in '43, but came back in '48. He made money in the mines, and settled at Cloverdale, where he died at a date not given. T. (John), 1846, Co. C, 1st U.S. dragoons (v. 336). T. (John), 1847, Co. E, N.Y. Vol. (v. 499); d. in N.Y. '79. T. (Joseph), 1847, Co. A, Morm. Bat. (v. 469).

Taylor (Nelson), 1847, nat. of Conn., and capt. of Co. E, N.Y. Vol. v. 504, 511. He was a dentist, and after a brief experience in the mines settled at Stockton as a trader, also running a ferry on the Stanislaus; memb. of 1st legislature; trustee of insane asylum from '50; sheriff from '54. In '56 he went to N.Y. and became a lawyer; brig.-gen. in war of '61-5; in '65 memb. of congress; in '71-85 resid. of South Norwalk, Conn. T. (Walter), 1847, sergt Co. G, N.Y. Vol. v. 504. T. (Wm), 1818, Amer. lieut of Bouchard's insurgents. ii. 227, 237. T. (Wm), 1828, Scotch tailor at Mont. '28-32, joining the comp. extranjera; a married man, age 34 in '29. iii. 178, 221. T. (Wm), 1834, mr of the *Magruder*. iii. 412, 383. T. (Wm), 1834, Engl. sailor who landed from the *Margarita* at S. Diego, where he still lived in '40, an unmarried carpenter, age 43. Perhaps the same who voted at S. D. in '48; name written Tela, Telen, and Thell. T. (W. E.), 1847, daughter born to his wife at Sonoma; at S. José '50. T. (W. H.), 1848, passp. from Hon.

Teal (Hiram), 1841, nat. of New England, who brought a stock of goods from Mazatlan, and kept a store at S.F. '41-3, with Titcomb as partner or clerk. iv. 279; v. 683. He went to Hon. in '43 on the *Diamond*, en route for Mex. Tebaca (Gabriel), settler at the Colorado pueblos 1780-1, killed by Ind. i. 359, 362. Teforia (José), 1831, named by Dye as one of Young's party. iii. 388. Tego (Manuel), resid. of Branciforte '30. ii. 627. Tejeda (Juan de A.), 1602, alférez of Vizcaino's exped. i. 98. Tellez (Rafael), 1842, Mex. lieut-col and brevet-col in com. of Micheltorena's batallon fijo; somewhat prominent in Cal. affairs till sent to Mex. for aid in '44. iv. 289, 357, 367, 409, 439, 461, 471-2. In '46 he seems to have started for Cal. with troops, but in Sinaloa engaged in a revolution, v. 32-3, and became acting com. at Mazatlan, where he was when the Amer. took the town in Feb. '48. He seems to have died before the end of that year, and Californians, who did not like him, delight in the tradition that after a drunken debauch he drowned himself in a barrel of mescal!

Temple (Francis Pliny F.), 1841, nat. of Mass., who came on the *Tasso* at the age of 20, engaging in trade at Los Ang. with his brother John. iv. 279. Later he established a stock rancho at S. Emigdio, near Ft Tejon; was a member of the banking firm of Hellman, T., & Co. from '68, and from '72 of T. & Workman. He died in '80 at his rancho of La Merced. iv. 635; v. 320; leaving a widow—the daughter of Wm Workman—and several children. He took but slight part in politics, but was always prominent in business affairs. All his property was lost by the failure of the banking firm in '75. In '77 he gave me a brief narrative of his *Recollections*, and rendered me assistance in

obtaining testimony from others.   T. (John), 1827, nat. of Mass., and brother
of the preceding, who came from Hon. on the *Waverly*, and in the earliest
years signed his name 'Jonathan.' iii. 149, 176-7. He was at once baptized
at S. Diego, and after a few trading trips on the coast obtained naturalization
and married Rafaela, daughter of Francisco Cota, in '30, engaging in trade at
Los Ang., in partnership with Geo. Rice, till '32, and later alone, or with his
brother from '41. ii. 558. I have some of his business corresp., but he does
not figure in public affairs, except that the vigilantes of '36 met at his house.
ii. 418, 539; iv. 117. In the sectional quarrels he took no part, but was glad
in '39 to hear of Alvarado's final success; is named in the following years as
creditor of southern missions; and in '45 was the purchaser of Purísima. iii.
595, 623; iv. 92, 553, 629, 648; v. 558. In the annals of '46-7 he is named in
connection with financial matters, having Cal. claims to the amount of about
$16,000. v. 49-50, 435, 467. From about '48, becoming owner of the Cerritos
rancho, iii. 633, he gave his attention to stock-raising on a large scale; later
he was the builder of the Temple block and other fine structures at Los Angeles; and in Maximilian's time obtained an immensely profitable lease of the
Mexican mint. He died at S.F. in '66, at the age of 68. He had been an able
and successful man of business, socially genial and well liked. His widow survived him, living in Paris with her daughter, Mrs Ajuria, the only child of
whom I find any mention, born in '31.
   Tenchman (Christian), 1846, Co. C, 1st U.S. dragoons (v. 336).   Ten Eck
(Anthony), 1848, U.S. commissioner from Hon. on the *Humboldt*.   Tenid
(Th.), 1846, doubtful name in a Los Ang. list.   Tennent (Archibald), 1848,
passp. from Hon.   T. (Sam. J.), 1848, Engl. surgeon on a whaler, who left
his vessel at the Islands and came to Cal. on hearing of the gold discovery.
He married Rafaela Martinez and settled at Pinole rancho, Contra Costa,
where he still lived in '82 with 5 children, his wife having died in '68. Portrait in *Contra Costa Co. Hist.*, 46.   Tenorio (Ignacio), nat. of S. Amer., who
had been oidor of the audiencia of Quito, and a very rich man, but who, tra-
ditionally, had devoted his fortune to charitable and educational purposes,
and came to Cal. about '15 to live with the friars. Not much is known of him
except that he was buried at S. Juan Cap. in '31 by P. Zalvidea, who in the
record spoke in high terms of his piety.
   Teran (José M.), regidor at Branciforte '34. iii. 696; memb. of the S. Diego
ayunt. '37, and in trouble. iii. 508; perhaps two men.   Termain (James Gilbert), 1843, recommended by the Engl. consul for a carta.   Terrill (Joel J.),
1847, sergt Co. C, Morm. Bat. v. 477; at Ogden, Utah, in '82.   Teschemacher
(Fred. Henry), 1842, clerk and supercargo of Boston trading craft '42-8. iv.
341; v. 579; owner of S.F. lots '46-7; resid. of S.F. after '49; cl. of the Lupyomi rancho, Napa, '52. iv. 671; mayor of S.F.; still living in '85, when he
visited S.F. Portrait and brief biog. notice in *North Pac. Review*. i. 223, 252.
I have a few of his early letters; but for so prominent a pioneer there is a re-
markable lack of information about him.   Tessau, 1837, officer of Petit-
Thouars' exped., making a survey of S.F. bay. iv. 149.
   Thaffer (Andrew), 1847, Co. E, N.Y.Vol. (v. 499); d. S.F. '79.   Thamen
(Henry), 1847, owner of S.F. lot.   Theall (Hiram W.), 1847, lieut Co. D,
N.Y.Vol. v. 504; an early settler of Sonora; d. at White Pine, Nev., before
'82; prob. in '69.   Theyer (Geo.), 1848, from Or., a settler in S. Joaquin.
Thing (Capt.), 1838, left S. Diego for Boston on the *Kent*. iv. 104.
   Thomas, 1845, doubtful immig. of the Grigsby-Ide party. iv. 579.   T.,
1846, at Sta Cruz, June; perhaps same as following.   T., 1847, mr of the
Laura Ann '47-8. v. 579; perhaps L. H.   T., 1847, at Sutter's fort.   T.
(Ambrose), 1836, at S. José Dec.; also Antonio at Los Ang. '35; both prob.
'Tomlinson,' q.v.   T. (Christian), 1847, owner of S.F. lot. v. 685.   T.
(Elijah), 1847, Co. C, Morm. Bat. (v. 469); at Leeds, Utah, '82.   T. (Ig-
nacio), 1818, Engl. sailor who left the *Bordelais*, ii. 393, and in '29 lived at
S. José, age 41, and blind.   T. (John W.), 1847, Co. A, N.Y.Vol. (v. 499);
at S. José '82.   T. (L. H.), 1848, sold piano to Larkin; conducted prayer
at the S.F. school-house. v. 657.   T. (Thomas), 1840, one of the S. Blas

exiles who did not return. iv. 18.   Thomen (Henry), 1846, overl. immig.
who worked for Sutter, and owned S.F. lot '47; at Sac. '60, age 45; perhaps
at S.F. '79.

Thomes (Robert Hasty), 1841, nat. of Me, and overl. immig. of the Bartleson party. iv. 270, 275, 279. With Albert G. Toomes he worked as carpenter and builder at S.F. in '41-2, and later at Mont., where the firm name of
Thomes & Toomes appears often in Larkin's books and other records. In '44
he was naturalized, and obtained a grant of Los Saucos, Tehama. iv. 673;
and may have put some cattle on the place in '45, but did not settle there
till '47, being mentioned at Mont. in '45-7, especially as a member of the 1st
jury. v. 289. He took no part in the war or in politics, but spent his life—
with a brief interval of mining on Feather River—on his Tehama rancho, becoming a wealthy and highly respected and influential citizen. He died in
'78, at the age of 61, leaving no family. A sister resides in Oakland '85 as the
wife of Isaac Given, a pioneer of '41. Portrait in *Tehama Co. Hist.*, 108.   T.
(Wm H.) 1843, nat. of Me, and distant relative of R. H., who came from
Boston as a sailor-boy, age 16, on the *Admittance*, which he left in '45, and
returned east in '46 on the schr *California* to Mazatlan, and thence via England to Boston. Again he came to Cal. in '49 on the *Edward Everett*, returning via Manilla, etc., on the *Alex. Humboldt.* In Boston he was a journalist
on the daily papers, and from '62 a publisher on his own account, making a
comfortable fortune, which was lost in the great fire of '72. In later years of
the firm of Thomes & Talbot, publishers of *Ballou's Monthly;* also author of
many romances of adventure for boys. *On Sea and Land*, one of his latest
works, is a narrative of adventures in Cal. on the *Admittance* in '42-5, full of
interest and bad Spanish, remarkably accurate in its foundation of names and
dates; let us hope that the superstructure of the sailor-boy's personal experiences is equally reliable. A later story of Cal. life, covering the period of the
conquest and now appearing in the *Monthly* is likely to be as fascinating if
somewhat less historic. An excellent account of the trip and company of '49
was also written by Thomes for the magazine, reprinted in the *S.F. Alta* of
Oct. 22, 29, '82. In '85 he revisited Cal. to revive old recollections, at which
time he furnished me many useful items about early men and things, also
permitting me to consult the original *Diary* of Capt. Peterson, his old master on the *Admittance*, and later his father-in-law.

Thompson, 1841, blacksmith at Los Ang. and Sta B.   T. (A.), 1839, passenger from Hon. on the *Clementine.* iv. 102, 127.   T. (Alpheus B.), 1825,
nat. of Me, and sup. on the *Washington* '25-30, having possibly visited the
coast earlier. iii. 29, 139, 149; sup. of the *Convoy* '31; in '33-5 sup. of the
Loriot, being arrested for smuggling in '33, and in '35 carrying prisoners to
Mex. iii. 288, 365, 383, 393. He considered Sta B. his home, and dated his
residence from '34, that being the year in which he married Francisca, daughter of Cárlos Carrillo, by whom he had 3 children before June '36. I have
much of his corresp. from year to year. In '36-7 he was sup. of the *Bolivar*,
on which he went to Hon. and back in '37; from '38 had a hide-house in the
Clark's Point region of S.F.; is named as mr of the *Union* in '40; and also as
creditor of several missions. iii. 657, 660; iv. 101, 106, 117; v. 684-5. He
went to Hon. on the *Julia Ann* '41; was naturalized in '43, being still sup. of
the *Bolivar;* was owner of the *Oajaca* in '44-5, sub-prefect at Sta B. '46,
grantee of a rancho in S. Joaquin Co., having a Cal. claim of some $2,000, and
being in all these years engaged to some extent in otter-hunting. iv. 563,
566-7; v. 282, 330, 455, 675. His name frequently occurs in commercial records down to '48; and after that date continued to reside at Sta B., where,
and throughout the country, he had an excellent reputation for honorable
conduct. He died at Los Ang. in '69 at the age of 74. His wife had died in
'41, but there were 2 daughters and 4 sons who survived. One of the sons,
Francis, is a somewhat prominent citizen of Sta B., and in '78 rendered me
assistance in my search of the mission archives.

Thompson (Bluford K.), 1846, overl. immig. and capt. Co. G, Cal. Bat.,
taking part in the fight at Natividad. v. 361, 364-72. He was a coarse, pro-

fane, reckless fellow, a gambler by profession, with some pretensions to gentlemanly manners when sober; known sometimes as 'Red-headed' or 'Hell Roaring' Thompson. After the war he settled at Stockton, being candidate for Ind. agent in '47. v. 662; where he soon killed James McKee. He was tried for murder at Sutter's fort in Feb. '48, being acquitted; but was obliged to quit the country, and on the way east was killed in a new quarrel with R. Taggart on the Sweetwater.   T. (Ch.), 1847, at Sutter's fort.   T. (Edward), 1844, Amer. sailor on the schr *California*, in trouble at Mont.   T. (Edwin), 1848, at S.F. as he testified in '65.   T. (Frank A.), 1832, mr of the *Roxana* '32-3. iii. 384; mr of the *Pilgrim* and *Alert* '35-6. iii. 381, 383; iv. 100.   T. (Geo. A.), 1839, naturalist who came from Hon. on the *Clementine* with letters from John C. Jones to the gov. and Gen. Vallejo. He was in search of specimens; called also Gordon H. T.   T. (Henry), 1847, Co. D, Morm. Bat. (v. 469).   T. (James), 1828, Irish sailor, age 28, from Acapulco on the *Maria Ester* at S. Diego with a letter from Virmond, intending to settle. ii. 545; iii. 178; got a carta in '29; in his application seems to say he had lived 8 years in Cal., but prob. means in Mex.   T. (James), 1846, sergt-major of Fauntleroy's dragoons (v. 232, 247); perhaps the man at Benicia '47.   T. (James), 1847, Co. A, N.Y.Vol. (v. 499); perhaps the man who on July 4th read the declaration at S.F.; at Brooklyn, N.Y., '82.   T. (James L.), 1847, Co. C, Morm. Bat. (v. 469).

Thompson (John), 1832, joined the comp. extranjera at Mont. iii. 221, 408; perhaps still at Mont. '36.   T. (John), 1843 (?), said to have crossed the plains, to have built a mill on Napa Creek '45, and to have spent 7 years on the coast; revisited Cal. in '76 from Brooklyn, N.Y. iv. 393, 400.   T. (John), 1847, Co. A, Morm. Bat. (v. 469); at Riverdale, Utah, '81; perhaps the owner of a S.F. lot '47. v. 685.   T. (John?), 1847, partner of Finch, and perhaps later of Bennett, in a S.F. saloon '44-8. v. 683; thought to be at S.F. '85.   T. (Joseph P.), 1842, nat. of Mass. who came this year acc. to his own affidavit in '62. iv. 341; perhaps came in '39-40 as sup. on the *Joseph Peabody*. He came again in '44 from Hon. on the *Fama*; at Sta Clara '45; at S.F. '46-7, being owner of a lot and sec. of the council. v. 648, 650; at Napa '47-8, where he kept a store; cl. for Napa lands '52; lost a leg by a street-car accident at S.F. '84. He was a brother-in-law of Henry A. 'Peirce,' q.v.   T. (Josiah), 1836, brother of Joseph P., at Mont. '36; sup. of the *Rasselas* '37-8. iv. 105, 141. T. (Miles), 1847, Co. D, Morm. Bat. (v. 469); reënl.   T. (Peter), 1847, Co. A, N.Y.Vol. (v. 499); d. Los Ang. '79.   T. (Sam.), 1847, lieut Co. C, Morm. Bat. v. 477, 488-9, 496; capt of returning Mormons in '48.   T. (Sam.), see 'Buckle.'   T. (S. S.), 1830, man who ordered a bottle of brandy.   T. (Stephen B.), 1824, doubtful name of Taylor's list.   T. (Wm), see 'Buckle.' T. (Wm), 1840. at Sta B., May.   T. (Wm), 1845, Spear's miller at S.F. '45-6. iv. 587; of 3d Donner relief '47; killed by a bull at Hon. in '50 after 7 years' resid. in Cal. These may be 1, 2, or 3 men.   T. (Wm H.), 1846, mid. on the *Congress;* act. lieut of Stockton's Bat. 41-7. v. 386.   T. (W. T.), 1823 (?), said to have been mr of a trader this year; came to reside in Cal. '49; in '69-70 U.S. gauger at S.F. *Call.*   Thoms (Adalberto), 1846, aux. de policía at Mont. v. 637.

Thorburn (Robert D.), 1847, lieut in com. of the U.S. *Southampton* '47-8. v. 580.   Thorne, 1846, killed at the Natividad fight. v. 371; perhaps an overl. immig., or he may have been the following.   T. (Wm), 1846, of Fauntleroy's dragoons.   Thorner (François), 1847, Co. C, N.Y.Vol. (v. 499); d. at Los Ang. '48.   Thornton (J. Quinn), 1847, a prominent pioneer of Or. who touched at S.F. in Nov. on his way east by sea. Author of *Oregon and Cal. in '48*, a work containing much information on the overl. immig. of '46 and the Donner party. v. 527, 535-6; see also *Hist. Or.*   Thorp (Dav.), 1837, at Mont. Dec.   T. (Lindy), 1845, immig. from Or. in the McMahon party. iv. 572, 587; apparently living in Polk Val. '79. *Yolo Co. Hist.*, 86.   T. (W. S.), 1847, constable at S.F. v. 648; prob. the man who in '48 married Mrs Caroline Warner of the Mormon colony.   Thurning (Henry), 1843, sailor on the *Admittance;* deserted in '44. *Peterson.*   Thursby (Lewis P.), 1847,

Co. A, N.Y.Vol. (v. 499); in Ga '71.   Thurston (Chas H.), 1847, Co. B, N.Y.
Vol. (v. 499); at Marysville '82.   Thusum (Benj. F.), 1845, mr of the *Hannah* '45-6. *Lancey*. Thybury, 1847, shepherd in Sutter's service.
Tibbetts, 1837, in the cattle exped. from Or. iv. 85.   Tibbey (W. H.),
1848, mr of the Hawaiian schr *Mary*. Tibeau, 1841, Fr. Canadian gambler
from N. Mex. in the Workman party. iv. 278; died on the return trip in '42.
Tibian (Fran.), doubtful name of '46. vi. 162.   Tickner (B.), 1847, fleet surgeon on the U.S. *Columbus*.   Ticó (Fernando), son of Joaquin b. at S.F.
1798; settled at Sta B., where in '29 he is ment. as ex-alcalde. iii. 78; grantee
of Ojai rancho '37. iii. 655; juez de paz '41. iv. 641; purchaser of S. Buen.
'45-6. iv. 643, 634. He was constable at S. Buen. '52 and supervisor '54.   T.
(Joaquin), 1796, sergt of Catalan volunteers. i. 540; executor of Alberni's
will 1801. ii. 5. His wife was Juana Carrera, and several children were born
at S.F.   Tierney (John), 1839, Irish carpenter named in Larkin's accounts
'40. iv. 119; naturalized '44, claiming 5 years' residence; at Mont. to '48.
Tieroff (August), 1847, Co. G, N.Y.Vol. (v. 499); owner of S.F. lot '47. v.
685; at S.F. '71-82.   Tighe (John), 1847, Co. H, ditto; dead before '82.·
Tilee (Dan. E.), 1847, Co. D, ditto; d. N.Y. before '80.   Tilghman (Richard L.), 1846, lieut on the U.S. *Congress;* act. capt. of artill. in Stockton's
bat. '46-7. v. 281, 327, 386.   Tillett (James F.), 1847, artificer Co. F, 3d
U.S. artill. v. 518.   Tillotson (John H.), 1845, mid. on the U.S. *Portsmouth.*
Timeans (Charles), 1847, Co. C, N.Y.Vol. (v. 499).   Tindall (Israel C.), 1846,
Co. C, 1st U. S. dragoons (v. 336).   T. (Wm), 1847, Co. F, N. Y.Vol. (v.
499); d. S.F. before '82.   Tinker (John), see 'Finch.'   Tinkerman (Michael),
1847, Co. G, N.Y.Vol. (v. 499).   Tinslar (B.R.), 1841, surgeon on the U.S. *St
Louis.*   Tinson (John), 1847, Co. B, N.Y Vol. (v. 499).   Tipson (Wm H.),
1847, Co. A, ditto; a Canadian printer who dieü at S.F. '79.   Tise (Andrew),
1847, Co. F, 3d U.S. artill. (v. 518).
    Titcomb (Amos A.), 1847, nat. of N.Y. and resid. of S.F. till his death in
'70, having held the office of supervisor. Left a widow and one child.   T.
(Rufus), 1841, nat. of New England, who came from Mazatlan with H. Teal,
whose clerk or partner he was at S.F. '41-3. iv. 279.   Tittel (F. G. Augustus), 1847, Co. G, N.Y.Vol. (v. 499); d. at S.F. '64 (or '68); apparently father
of the 2 following, but there is some confusion about the family; name often
written Tittle.   T. (Fred. Gustavus Ernest), 1847, son of F. G. A., German
fifer of Co. F, 3d U.S. artill. (v. 518), married Miss Winterhalder and settled
at Sta Cruz as a farmer. Later livery-stable keeper, ward politician, supervisor, militia colonel, memb. of the legislature ('61), and cigar-dealer at S.F.
In '70-1 he was engaged in the Alaska fur trade; and died in '77, leaving a
daughter.   T. (F. G. Wm), 1846(?), brother of the preceding, said to have
come this year; a lieut in Mex. under Maximilian; d. at S.F. '70 at the age
of 42, leaving a widow and 2 daughters. The latter are actresses, or danseuses,
in '85 involved in interesting legal complications respecting a lot in S. F.
which was owned by their grandfather, and on which the Maison Dorée,
Kearny St, now stands.
    Toba (Fernando), cadet of the Mont. comp. 1801. ii. 147, 150; in later
years act. com. at Loreto. Tobar, named as a sergt '21. ii. 575.   T. (Albino), settler at S. José 1791-5, sent away for bad conduct. i. 598, 636, 716.
T. (José), 1779, piloto on the *Santiago;* and later com. of the *Favorita* and
other transports and exploring craft on the coast down to 1800. i. 328-9, 378,
430, 444, 540.   T. (Juan José), 1838, Mex. capt. and brevet lieut-col, who
had been somewhat prominent in Sonora as a mil. officer and revolutionist
since '28, and who came to Cal. to support Gov. Carrillo, retiring in disgust
after the campaign of Las Flores. iii. 557-61, 505, 555. Tobias, chief in the
Sonoma region. iv. 72. Tobin (Robt J.), 1848, from Tahiti; at S.F. with
wife; still at S.F. '54. Toca (José M.), ship-boy and teacher at Sta B.
1795-7. i. 643.
    Todd (James J.), 1845, Amer. sailor at Mont.   T. (John), 1848, at Sta
B., May; also in '50. T. (John J.), 1845, Amer. sailor at Mont., perhaps
same as James J. T. (Thos J.), 1844, Amer. sailor at Mont., aided by

the consulate and shipped for Oahu in '45. T. (Wm J.), 1844, Amer. sailor in consular care at Mont. Though the records seem clear, it would seem likely that James J., John J., Thos J., and Wm J. did not represent 4 dif. men. T. (Wm L.), 1845, nat of Ill., nephew of Mrs Abraham Lincoln, and overl. immig. of the Swasey-Todd party. iv. 576, 580, 587. Named in the *N. Helv. Diary* '45–7. Early in '46 he went to Sonoma, where he joined the Bears, gained imperishable fame as the artist who painted the Bear flag, was the messenger sent with the news of revolt to Capt. Montgomery at S.F., and was at one time a captive of the wicked Californians. v. 110, 131, 146–9, 154, 156, 167–8. He lived at Sonoma for several years after '46, not, apparently, serving in the Cal. Bat.; then went to El Dorado Co., where a valley bears his name; and in '78 was living in S. Bernardino, his death not being reported down to '85.

Tole (Thomas), 1836, sailor at Los Ang. from Lima, age 24. Toler (Hopeful), 1847, came to Cal. with despatches, some official appointment, and 2 daughters, on the *Preble.* v. 584–5; worked as a clerk in settling the Leidesdorff estate; went with his family to the mines in '48; in '49 a notary public at S.F. I have no record of what became of him. One of his daughters, Charlotte Catherine, married L. W. Hastings in '48, and died at a date not recorded; the other daughter was still living about '80. T. (Wm P.), 1842, son of Hopeful and mid. U.S.N. with Com. Jones at Mont.; also on the *Savannah* '45–7; returned as lieut on the *St Mary* in '49. He married a Peralta, and still lived at S. Leandro in '85. Tolman (H.), 1848, passp. from Hon. Talmayr (Louis Auguste), 1836, Fr. carpenter from Peru; at Los Ang., age 22. Tometty (Nicholas), 1845, Amer. citizen at Mont. from St Louis Sept. Tomlinson (Ambrose G.), 1832, trapper of Young's party from N. Mex., who remained in Cal. iii. 388, 408. He is also called Thomas L. and Thomason, and known as 'Tom the Trapper.' He had a passp. in '34; was interested from '35 with Job Dye in a distillery near Sta Cruz; signed the letter of thanks to Com. Kennedy at Mont. '36. iv. 141; and apppears on Larkin's books from '37. He was one of Graham's riflemen (iii. 457); was arrested but not exiled in '40, being supposed by some to be the man who, in fear of death, revealed Graham's plot to P. Real at the confessional. iv. 5, 17. In '41 he wrote to Com. Forrest a report on the murder of Anthony Campbell. v. 686. At this time he lived at S. José as a carpenter, age 38, wife María de Jesus Bernal, child Tomás. In '42 Dr Maxwell amputated his leg, and he died before the end of '44. He is called Engl. and Amer., and possibly there were two of the name, but if so I cannot disentangle the records. T. (John J.), 1848, nat. of Md, who came from Or.; trader in Cal. and Ariz., and memb. of a Los Ang. firm; d. S. Bern. '67, age 41. Tompkins (Amos), 1830, at Mont. bound for Guaymas. T. (Christopher Q.), 1847, nat of Va and capt. Co. F, 3d U.S. artill. v. 414–15, 429, 518–20. He went east with Kearny the same year; was a col in the confederate army '61–5; and died in N.Y. '77. T. (Thomas), 1846, of the Mormon colony, with wife and 2 child. v. 547; at Sutter's fort '47–8; did not go to Utah.

Tooms (Geo. W.), 1847, Co. D, N.Y. Vol. (v. 499); treasurer of Stanislaus Co.; at Modesto '82. Toomes (Albert G.), 1841, nat. of Mo. and overl. immig. in the Workman-Rowland party from N. Mex. iv. 278–9. In partnership with R. H. Thomes he worked as carpenter and builder at S.F. for a short time and at Mont. from '43. In '44 he was married to María Isabel Lorenzana, was naturalized, and obtained a grant of the Rio de los Molinos rancho in Tehama Co. iv. 673. He visited the rancho to put cattle on it in '45 and again in '47, but did not settle there till '49, as the firm of T. & T. is ment. at Mont. down to the end of '48. From '49 he lived on the place, becoming a rich and respected citizen, and dying in '73 at the age of 56. His widow, without children, died at Oakland in '78, leaving her large property to a neighbor who had been friendly during her illness. The will was contested by cousins of the Ortega family, with results not known to me.

Toribio, ment. in '18, '33. ii. 383; iii. 323–4. Torre (Estévan de la), son of José Joaquin, who in '36 lived at Mont. age 18; in '44 regidor; in '46 juez de campo. iv. 653; v. 363, 637. He never had much to do with politics; but has always been an industrious, hard-working man, as ranchero and miner. In '76, living on his rancho of Bolsa de las Escarpines—of which Salv. Espinosa, his father-in-law, was grantee and claimant—he gave me a most interesting and valuable dictation of his *Reminiscencias*, which has been frequently cited in these volumes. His narrative is particularly valuable as a picture of manners and customs in Mex. times, but is also a good record of the various public events in which his brothers—more devoted to war and politics than himself—took part. He is a man of excellent repute, and still living in '85 with wife and several children.   T. (Gabriel), brother of Estévan, soldier of the Mont. comp. from '27, taking part in the revolts of '28-30. iii. 67, 69-70; sergt in '34-6, taking part in the movement against Chico. iii. 671, 429; but retired about this time, and in '39 grantee of Zanjones rancho, and agente de policía at Mont. '44. iii. 679; iv. 633, 653. From '45 he was a capt. of defensores, and waʼ active in '45-6 against Micheltorena and the U.S. under Castro and Flores, down to the final treaty of '47. iv. 515, 652, 654-5; v. 41, 362-3; and in '48, during the rumors of intended revolution, was one of the Californians required to give bonds and commit no hostilities. v. 585-6. He was a brave and somewhat reckless man, devoted to the cause of his country. I have no record of the date of his death.   T. (Joaquin), brother of Estévan and Gabriel, b. about '12, educ. at Mont. ii. 429; soon enlisted in the Mont. comp.; corporal in '36; alférez from '39. iii. 583, 671; iv. 13, 652. In '40 he took an active part in arresting the foreigners, and accompanied the exiles to S. Blas, being also grantee of Arroyo Seco rancho. iv. 19-21, 30; iii. 677. In '42-4 he was celador at the Mont. custom-house. iv. 339, 377, 431; and in '45 took a leading part in the revolution against Micheltorena, being made capt. of the Mont. comp., and acting alcalde for a time. iv. 462, 487, 507, 652, 654. In '46 he was in com. of the troops sent by Castro against the Bears, getting the worst of a skirmish at Olompali, but deceiving Frémont by a ruse, he succeeded in crossing the bay and accompanied Castro to the south. v. 41, 134-6, 165-8, 174-7. After the occupation by the U.S. he was paroled, but with the rest broke his parole and fought in the Natividad campaign. v. 289, 331, 362, 366, 370. Don Joaquin was a man of much energy and courage, like his brother Gabriel in many respects, and not friendly to the Amer. invaders. He was cl. for Arroyo Seco in '52, and in '55 was killed by Anastasio García, a murderer whom he was trying to arrest near Sta B.   T. (José Joaquin), 1801, Span. cadet of the Mont. comp. to '22, serving much of the time as governor's sec. ii. 379, 438, 457, 463, 580, 676. In '22 he was grantee of the Bolsa del Potrero, sold to Capt. Cooper in '29. ii. 615, 646; iii. 13; in '23-5 sec. of the junta and diputacion. ii. 486-7, 513, 612; iii. 7, 20; in the lists of Span. of '28-30, but not sent away. iii. 51-2. In '36 he is named in the Mont. padron as 48 years old (prob. 52, as his birth is recorded in 1784 in one doc.), wife María de los Angeles Cota, child. Estévan b. '18, José Ant. '20, Encarnacion (who married Capt. Silva) '22, Rita (who married Florencio Serrano) '26, Pablo '31, José '33, and María de Alta Gracia '34. I find no later record of Don José Joaquin. His widow died at Mont. in '77 at the age of 87, leaving 3 sons, 3 daughters, and 43 grandchildren.   T. (José María), soldier of the Mont. comp. '36, age 19; juez de campo '42. v. 653.   T. (Pablo), in Castro's force '46. v. 363; son of J. J.   T. (Raimundo), son of J. J., at Mont. '26. ii. 612; soldier from '28; corporal of the escolta at S. Miguel '29; involved in the Solis revolt and sent to Mex. '30. iii. 67-85; served in Jalisco and Sonora; and returned to Cal. in '47, to be murdered a little later near Mont.

Torrens (Hilario), 1786, Span. friar who served at S. Diego to '98, when he retired, dying in '99. Biog. i. 651; ment. i. 388, 423, 455-6, 459, 576-7. Torres (Antonio), at Los Ang. '46.   T. (Francisco), 1834, Mex. physician of the H. & P. colony, who was in '35 exiled to Mex. for complicity in the movement at Los Ang. against Gov. Figueroa. iii. 284-90.   T., 1792, mr of the *Sta Gertrudis*. i. 506.   T. (Manuel), 1802, surgeon of the Cal. forces at Mont. 1802-3; and apparently at Mont. again 1805. ii. 31, 140.   T. (Manuel), 1843, nat. of Peru, who came with Stephen Smith, his brother-in-law.

iv. 396; and for some years was employed by Smith at his Bodega mill. In '45 he signed the bonds of Amer. immigrants, iv. 581, and was grantee of the Muniz rancho, Sonoma Co., which was finally confirmed to him. iv. 672, 679. In '48 he married Mariana, daughter of Capt. Wm A. Richardson. He took but slight part in the troubles of '46-7. In '75, residing at S.F., Don Manuel gave me his *Peripecias de la Vida Californiana*, a most interesting MS., devoted to manners and customs and observations on early men rather than to a narrative of events. In '85 he resides at Martinez. Torrey, 1845, doubtful member of Frémont's party. iv. 583. Tosta (Bonifacio), appointed gov. in '23, but did not come to Cal. ii. 484-5. Totten (Matthew), 1846, Co. C, 1st U.S. dragoons (v. 336). Tova (Antonio), 1791, lieut of Malaspina's exped. i. 490.

Towner (Loammi), 1847, Co. B, N.Y.Vol. (v. 499); d. at S. José after '50. Towns (Charles), 1844, one of Frémont's men, who left the party in Cal. iv. 437, 439, 453. Townsend (Alfred A.), 1847, from Valparaíso with letters from Atherton to Larkin; of firm T. & Robinson, bakers and saloon-keepers at Mont. '47-8; went to the mines '48. T. (John), 1844, nat. of Va, a physician and overl. immig. from Mo. in the Stevens party with his wife. iv. 446, 453. He served as Sutter's aid in the Micheltorena campaign. iv. 483, 485, 516; then practised medicine at Mont. for a time in '45. In Clyman's *Diary* he is described as 'much attached to his own opinions, as likewise to the climate and country of Cal. His pleasant wife does not enter into all her husband's chimerical speculations.' In '46-9 Dr T. practised medicine at S.F., visiting Sutter's fort in '46. v. 128; being at Benicia '47, and also prospecting the Marin Co. hills for minerals; the owner of several S. F. lots, on one of which he built a house and office. v. 678; in '48 taking some part in town politics, and serving as school trustee and alcalde, but making a trip to the mines. v. 648-9, 651-2, 656; and in '49 member of the council. Late in '50 he moved to a farm near S. José, where he and his wife (a sister of Moses Schallenberger) died of cholera in Dec. '50 or Jan. '51. Dr T. was a man of excellent character, and of genial, enthusiastic temperament. T. (John M.), 1848, Sta Clara fruit-grower '59-76. T. (J. S.), 1848, passp. from Hon.; perhaps same as preceding. Towson (Thomas), 1846, Co. F, Cal. Bat. (v. 358); enlisting at S. Juan Oct. Toye (H. H. F.), 1847, Co. G. N.Y.Vol. (v. 499); d. in Nicaragua '56.

Trail (G.), 1848, passp. from Hon. Trapin (R. S.), 1845, lieut on the U.S. *Savannah;* performed relig. service at S.F. '46. v. 225. Travers (John) 1847, owner of a S.F. lot. v. 676. T. (Wm B.), 1847, sergt Co. G, N.Y.Vol. v. 504; killed by the Los Ang. explosion. v. 625. Travis (W.), 1848, passp. from Hon. Treadway (P.), 1848, mr of the *Kekanonohi.* v. 579; went back to Hon. on the *Julian.* Treanor (D.), 1848, passp. from Hon. Treat (Thomas), 1847, Co. D, Morm. Bat. (v. 469). Trejo (Entinio), appointed celador at Mont.; perhaps did not come. iv. 557. Tremmels (Wm R.), 1847, lieut Co. C, N.Y.Vol.; died on the voy. to Cal. v. 504, 513.

Tresconi (Alberto), 1844, prob. Italian, named in Larkin's accounts and other records at Mont. from this year. iv. 453; at Sta Cruz '79, owning property in Mont. Co. Trevethan (Wm), 1826, Engl. sailor who came from the Islands on the *Rover*, iii. 176, and worked as boatman at Mont., afterwards becoming lumberman and carpenter, and for a time majordomo of S. Miguel. In '29 his age was 26; and from '33 his name appears in various records as a sawyer in the Mont. dist. In '40 he was arrested, but not exiled. iv. 17, 23; naturalized in '44, and married, perhaps earlier, to María Antonia Perez. In these years he lived in the S. Antonio redwoods, and was for a time sub-alcalde; later he moved to Sta Cruz Co., where he still lived in '70, with 10 children. Trigo (José R.), at Los Ang. '46. Triunfo (José Miguel), grantee of Cahuenga rancho '45. iv. 634. Troutman (James B.), 1857, Co. F, N.Y.Vol. (v. 499). T. (John), 1847, drummer in ditto. Trow (Henry), 1845, Engl. sailor in Sutter's employ '45-6. iv. 578, 587; v. 675; ment. in connection with Benicia affairs '47-8; later in the mines of Trinity or Shasta; and last seen by Bidwell between '56 and '60.

Trubody (John), 1847, nat. of Engl. and overl. immig. from Mo. with family, who, after a short stay at Sutter's fort, settled at S.F., though owning land at Napa. He and his wife were active memb. of the 1st methodist society in Cal.; the latter, Jane Palmer, dying in '77.   T. (Josiah P.), 1847, son of John, b. in Pa, who went from S. F. in '56 to Napa; married Sophronia Ament in '65; at Napa in '80 engaged with his brother in the cultivation of berries.   T. (Wm A.), 1847, son of John, b. in Mo.; educated in the east from '50; married a daughter of T. L. Grigsby '68; at Napa '80.   Truett, 1847, at Sutter's fort; doubtful name.   Truitte (S.), 1846, Co. F, Cal. Bat., enlisting at S. Juan Oct. (v. 358).   Trujillo, half a dozen of the name at Los Ang. '46.   T. (Lorenzo), 1841, chief of a N. Mex. colony settling at S. Bern., where he still lived '46, age 50. iv. 278, 638.   T. (Manuel), Mex. sec. of Cárlos Carrillo as gov. '37–8; perhaps the same who was admin. of S. Luis Ob. '35; left Cal. with Tobar '38. iii. 548-9, 565, 682-3.   Truman (Jacob M.), 1847, Co. C, Morm. Bat. (v. 469); one of the explorers of a new route over the mts '48.   Trusted (Gottfried), 1847, Co. F, 3d U.S. artill. (v. 518).

Tubb (Michael), 1846, Co. C, 1st U.S. dragoons (v. 336); an alcalde at Mormon camp '49; apparently a partner of J. W. Cassin in Tehama Co. in later years.   T. (Wm), 1846, Co. C, ditto; prob. brother of Michael. Tucker (Geo. W.), 1846, nat. of Ohio, son of R. P., memb. of 1st Donner relief. v. 539; miner in '48–9; settler in Napa '47–81; married in '58 to Angelina Kellogg, by whom he has 8 children.   T. (John W.), 1846, brother of G. W., and resid. of Napa '47–81; wife Mrs C. E. Weed '79.   T. (Reasin P.), 1846, overl. immig. with wife and several sons. v. 529; a member of the 1st and 4th Donner relief. v. 538, 541; settled in Napa with his sons, but in '79 living at Soleta, Sta B.; also called Daniel.   T. (S. J.), perhaps another son of R. P., in Napa '47.   T. (Thomas), 1845, in Sutter's employ.   T. (Wm), 1847, Co. I, N.Y.Vol. (v. 499); at Sonora '71; not in Clark's last list. Tuel (James), 1846, Fauntleroy's dragoons (v. 232, 247).

Turcote (François), 1830, Canadian trapper of Young's party; prob. returned to N. Mex. iii. 174.   Turincio (Manuel), 1841, mr of the Columbine. iv. 564.   Turkson (Paul), 1845, trader at S.F.   Turnbull (Thomas), 1841, Engl. sailor on the Braganza, who left the vessel and was at Sta Cruz '42–3. In '48 his relatives in London write for information about him.   Turner, 1848, from Hon. on the Sagadahoc.   T. (Chas C.), 1845, com. of the U.S. Erie '45-7. iv. 565.   T. (David), 1847, Co. D, N.Y. Vol. (v. 499).   T. (Henry S.), 1846, capt. 1st dragoons, who came with Kearny from N. Mex., fought at S. Pascual; com. of 2d bat. of Stockton's force '46–7; went east with Kearny '47; and was a witness at the Frémont court-martial. v. 336, 347, 385, 391–5, 437, 441, 444, 452, 456. He was again at S.F. '52–4, being a member of the banking firm of Lucas, T., & Co.   T. (James M.), capt. of Co. B, N.Y.Vol. v. 503, 511; did not come to Cal. v. 540.   T. (John S.), 1826, one of Jed. Smith's trappers in Cal. '26–7. iii. 153, 159-60, 176; came back with McLeod's party '28. iii. 161; and again before '35, when he went from Cal. to Or., revisiting Cal. with the Cattle party of '37. iv. 85. Bryant met him near Clear Lake in '46; he was one of the 2d Donner relief '47. v. 540; and died the same year in Yolo Co.   T. (Loammi), 1847, Co. B. N.Y. Vol. (v. 499).   T. (Sam.), 1845, one of the men lost on the Warren's launch '46. iv. 587; v. 384.   Turney, 1848, from Or., kept a restaurant at Sutter's fort.

Tustin (Fernandc), 1845, son of Wm I., who came overl. as a child. iv. 579, 587; a blacksmith in S.F. '83.   T. (Wm Isaac), 1845, nat. of Va, and overl. immig. of the Grigsby-Ide party with wife and son. v. 579, 587. He worked for Sutter and remained in the upper Sac. Val. '45–6; iv. 580; and in '47 settled at Benicia, where he built the first adobe house. v. 672. Later he moved to S.F., where he engaged in the manufacture of windmills, and where he still lives in '85 at the age of 65. In '80 he wrote for my use his Reeollections, a MS. which has furnished me not a few items of interest.   Tuttle (Elanson), 1847, Co. C, Morm. Bat. (v. 469).   T. (Luther T.), 1847, sergt Co. D, ditto. v. 477; at Manti, Utah, '81.

Twist (Hilary), 1846, Co. C, 1st U.S. dragoons (v. 336). T. (W.W.), 1847 (?), sheriff of Los Ang. '52–3; killed in Sonora, Mex.; accredited to the N.Y.Vol. by Bell. *Rcmin.*, 58, 288. Twitchell (Anciel), 1847, Co. D, Morm. Bat. (v. 469). Tylee (Dan. E.), 1847, doubtful name Co. D, N.Y.Vol. (v. 499); not in Clark's last list. Tyler (Daniel), 1847, sergt Co. C, Morm. Bat.; also elder in the church, capt. of 50 on the return, and author of an excellent *history of the Morm. Bat.* v. 477, 488, 491, 493; in Utah '85. T. (Henry B.), 1847, capt. of marines on the U.S. *Columbus.* T. (J.), 1846, Co. B, artill. Cal. Bat., enlisting at Sac. Oct. (v. 358).

Uber, 1843, German in charge of Sutter's distillery. *Yates;* iv. 229. Uhrbrook (Henry), 1847, Co. G, N. Y. Vol. (v. 499); in Nicaragua with Walker; d. Sta Clara '75. Ulibarri (Francisco Roman Fernandez), 1809, Span. friar who served chiefly at S. Juan B. and Sta Inés, dying at S. Gabriel, '21. Biog. ii. 569; ment. ii. 154, 159–60, 237, 357, 366, 369, 386, 394, 655. Ulloa (Gonzalo), 1819, com. of the *S. Cárlos.* ii. 253; com. S. Blas '21–2. ii. 441, 456–7. U. (Francisco), 1539, in his navigation of the gulf possibly looked upon Cal. territory. i. 64, 68; *Hist. North Mex. St.*, i. 78 et seq. Unamano (Francisco), 1842, mr of the *Constante.* iv. 564. Underwood (G.L.), 1847, Co. I, N.Y.Vol. (v. 499); at Petaluma '74; d. Portland, Or., '81. Unzueta (José), sergt of artill. at Mont. 1803–4. Upham (Wm), 1847, of U. & Talbot at Mont. '47–8. Upson (Trueman), 1847, Co. G, N.Y.Vol. (v. 499). Uren (Thomas), 1848, d. at Dutch Flat '73. *Placer Co. Hist.*, 411. Ur-guides (Antonio, Dolores, Guillermo, Juan, and Tomás), at Los Ang. '46–8. U. (Encarnacion), settler at Los Ang. '12; alcalde in '24. ii. 349, 354–5, 359. Uría (Francisco Javier de la Concepcion), 1797, Span. friar, whose longest service was at Sta Inés. He died at Sta B. in '34. Biog. iii. 659; ment. i. 562, 577; ii. 29, 115, 155, 159–60, 236, 368, 394, 526, 528–9, 579, 581, 620, 622, 655; iii. 92, 96, 118, 350–1, 657. U. (José Antonio), 1799, Span. friar, who served chiefly at S. José mission, retiring in 1808. Biog. ii. 115; ment. i. 556, 557; ii. 46, 68, 130, 137–8, 155, 159–60. Uribe (Francisco, José M., and Pedro), at Los Ang. '46. U. (Ricardo), soldier of Sta B. comp. before '37; at Los Ang. '45, being a leader in a revolt. iv. 523, 541, 632. Uribes (José Miguel), settler at Branciforte 1797. i. 569. U. (Tomás), regidor at Los Ang. '19. ii. 351, 354. Uriquides (María Magdalena), 1794, wife of Gov. Borica. i. 728. Urrea (José), interpreter at the Col. River pueblos 1780–2. i. 359, 362, 367. Urresti (José Antonio), 1804, Span. friar, who served for brief terms at several missions, and died at S. Fern. in '12. Biog. ii. 357; ment. ii. 109, 114–16, 121–2, 159, 355, 394. Urselino (José), carpenter at S. Diego, killed by Ind. 1775. i. 250, 253. Ursua (Julian), grantee of Panocha rancho '44. iv. 672; chosen alcalde at S. Juan B. '47. v. 640. Usson (Ramon), 1772, Span. friar who was intended for the mission of S. Buenaventura, but after being stationed as supernumerary at S. Diego and S. Antonio, he went away sick as chaplain on the exploring transports in '74, retiring also from that service after one voyage. i. 192–3, 196, 227, 240–1, 455.

Vaca (Manuel), 1841, nat. of N. Mex., prob. of the prominent N. Mex. family of that name—descended from Capt. Vaca, one of the conquerors of 1600, and often absurdly connected with Cabeza de Vaca—who came with his family in the Workman party, settling in Solano Co., where with Peña he obtained a grant of the Putah rancho, where he spent the rest of his life, dying, I think, before '60. iv. 278, 516, 672; v. 119. Don Manuel was a hospitable man of good repute, whose name is borne by the valley and by the town of Vacaville. Of the family there is not much definite information. Juan was killed by Ind. on the Moquelumne in '45. Marcos is named in N. Helv. records from '45; had a Cal. claim of $4,967 (v. 462); and was perhaps grantee of a rancho. iv. 671; being 2d alcalde at Sonoma '45. iv. 678. Nepomuceno is named in a Sonoma list of '44; age 26; perhaps the same as Juan. Teófilo was 19 in '44, and died at the rancho in '77, leaving a family. These

I suppose were all sons of Manuel. In '30 José Ant. Vaca had visited Cal. from N. Mex. iii. 173.   Vail (James M.), 1847, Co. I, N.Y.Vol. (v. 499); killed by Ind. in El Dorado Co. '48.   Vaillant (Jean), 1830, trapper of Young's party from N. Mex. iii. 174.

Valdés (Antonio), settler at Los Ang. '15. ii. 350.   V. (Antonio María), at Los Ang. '36; age 25 in '39 (another Antonio '47); zanjero in '44. iv. 633. V. (Basilio), regidor at Los Ang. '36-7; síndico '40-1, '45. iii. 481, 509, 631-2, 634, 636, 638; still at Los Ang. '48.   V. (Cayetano), 1791, lieut of Malaspina's exped. i. 490; com. of the *Mexicana* 1792. i. 506-7; killed at Trafalgar. V. (Crescencio), soldier of Sta B. comp. before '37; at Los Ang. '39, age 40. V. (Dorotea), an old woman, aged 81, living at Mont. '74, who gave me her *Reminiscences* of very early times. ii. 232. She was a daughter of Juan B. Valdés, one of the early settlers of S. Diego, where she was born in 1793. V. (Eugenio), settler at Los Ang. 1800. ii. 349.   V. (Felix), 1843, Mex. officer of the batallon fijo, who seems to have come later than the main body; is named in several transactions of '43-5, and was the grantee of Temécula rancho in '44. iv. 406, 470, 509, 621, 639.   V. (Francisco), at S. Bern. '46, age 25.   V. (Gervasio), sub-deacon at the Sta Inés seminary '44. iv. 426. V. (Jesus), Sonoran killed at Sta B. '40. iii. 655.   V. (José), soldier of Sta B. comp. '32; at Los Ang. '46-8.   V. (José María), at Los Ang. and S. Bern. '39-46.   V. (José Ramon), b. at Los Ang. 1803; a soldier of '21-32; later ranchero and trader Sta B.; in '38 síndico. iii. 654; in '42-3 juez de paz. iv. 642; in '45 maj. at S. Buen., iv. 645, where in '78 he gave me his *Memorias*. ii. 240; wife Daría Ortega, 3 child. in '37.   V. (Juan B.), an old settler who left some hist. mem. i. 175.   V. (Julian), at Los Ang. '39-48.   V. (Luciano), teacher at Los Ang. '30. ii. 564.   V. (María Rita), grantee of S. Antonio rancho '31.   V. (Melecio), settler at Los Ang. 1789. i. 461.   V. (Miguel), at Los Ang. '48.   V. (Rafael), soldier of Sta B. comp. '32; wife Rafaela Pico; 5 child. in '37.   V. (Rodrigo), shoemaker at Mont. '41.   V. (Salvador), fifer of the S.F. comp. '39-42.   V. (Simplicio), arrested in '45 for conspiracy. iv. 522.   V. (Urita), in revolt at Los Ang. '46. v. 308.

Valencia (Antonio), soldier of S.F. comp. '19-28; hanged in '49 for murder of Pyle near S. José in '47; perhaps 2 men.   V. (Antonio), soldier of Sta B. comp. before '37; arrested in '37, and executed for murder at Los Ang. '42. iii. 638; iv. 632.   V. (Antonio), at Los Ang. '46.   V. (Ascencio), shot for murder at Los Ang. '41. iv.630.   V. (Bruno), soldier of the S.F. comp. '19-27; in '41 at S. José, age 39, wife Bernarda Duarte, child. Francisco b. '31, María Concepcion '30, Meliton '35, José Ramon '38; owner of S.F. lot '43. iv. 669; v. 684; juez de campo '43. iv. 685. He apparently lived at S. Mateo. V. (Candelario), soldier of the S.F. comp. '23-33; in '34 grantee of Acalanes rancho, Contra Costa. iii. 711; S.F. elector '35. iii. 704; owner of lot at S.F. mission '40. iii. 706; juez de campo '42, iv. 665, being named on the S.F. padron as 38 years old, wife Paula Sanchez, child. Eustaquio b. '28, José Ramon '29, María '32, Lucía '43, Tomás '37, Josefa '41. Sergt of defensores '44. iv. 667; juez de campo '46. v. 648; witness in the Santillan case '54. His wife was a cl. for Buri-buri rancho.   V. (Dolores), wife of Lieut Grijalva 1776. ii. 104.   V. (Eustaquio), son of Candelario, resid. at S.F. mission from '37, witness in the Santillan case '55. Grantee and cl. of a mission lot '45-52. iv. 673.   V. (Francisco), regidor at S. José 1802. ji. 134; still at S. José '41, age 68, nat. of Sonora, widower. He was perhaps the father of the S.F. Valencias. The family name is borne by a leading street in S.F.   V. (Gregorio), at S. Bern. '46.   V. (Guadalupe), at S. José '41, age 26, wife Ramona Martinez, child Miguel b. '40.   V. (Ignacio), settler at Los Ang. 1808. ii. 349; at S. Bern. '46, age 25, prob. a son.   V. (José de Jesus), soldier of the S.F. comp. '27-37; in '42 at S.F., age 35, wife Julia Sanchez, child. Catarina b. '35, Riso '37, and Francisco; corp. of defensores '44.   V. (J. M.), his wife the 1st person buried at S.F. '76. i. 296.   V. (José Ramon), b. at S.F. '28, grantee and cl. of mission lots. iv. 673; in Marin Co. '65-76.   V. (Julio), at S. José '41, age 35, wife Concepcion Alviso, child. Cirilo b. '28, Guadalupe '33, Magdalena '45, Manuel '39; in '44 of the S. José guard. iv. 685.   V. (Manuel), settler at S. José 1788, died. i. 477.   V. (Manuel), grantee of Cañada de Pinole, Contra Costa. iv. 672.   V. (Manuel), at Los Ang. '37 in jail; known as 'El Chino.'   V. (Miguel), 2d alcalde at Sta B. '29; soldier before '37, wife Prisca Olivera; alcalde '31-2, iii. 653, 212; maj. at Sta Inés '39. iii. 664.   V. (Ramon), grantee of land at S. Gabriel. iv. 637.   V. (Ritillo), arrested '38. iii. 638; a leader in Los Ang. tumult '45. iv. 523.   V. (Vicente), síndico at Sta B. '27, '39. ii. 572; iii. 52, 654; wife Margarita Valenzuela, 4 child. before '37. Valentin, at Soledad '26. ii. 623.   Valentino, at N. Helv. '47-8.   Valenzuela (Antonio), at Sta B. before '37, wife María Ant. Félix; grantee of land at S. Juan Cap. '41. iv. 626; land at S. Gabriel '43. iv. 637; at S. Gabriel '46. V. (Desiderio and Dolores), at Los Ang. '46-8.   V. (Estanislao), soldier of the S.F. comp. '27-31; at Los Ang. '46.   V. (Felipe and Francisco), at Los Ang. '46.   V. (Gaspar), zanjero at Los Ang. '44. iv. 633; resid. '39-48.   V. (Ignacio), inválido at Sta B, '32, wife Felipa Fernandez, child Juana.   V. (Ignacio), named in '46. v. 162.   V. (Joaquin), at Los Ang. '39, age 29; at S. Gab. '46-7 as juez de campo. v. 628; at Sta B. '50.   V. (José), at Los Ang. '46.   V. (José María), at Los Ang. '15. ii. 350; soldier at Sta B. '32; alcalde at Sta B. '35. iii. 654; maj. at Sta B. mission '38. iii. 656-7; admin. at Purísima '38-41. iii. 666; iv. 648; still at Sta B. '51. His wife was Josefa Cota, with 4 children before '37.   V. (José Sabas), at Los Ang. '46.   V. (Luis), soldier at Sta B. '32, wife Josefa Rocha; at Los Ang. '46-8.   V. (Manuel), soldier of Sta B. 1799; settled at Los Ang. 1800. ii. 349.   V. (Manuel), corp. at Mont. '36, age 22.   V. (Máximo), juez de campo at Los Ang. '38. iii. 636; still there '48.   V. (Pedro), settler at Los Ang. 1798. ii. 350; at Los Ang. '46; d. S. Juan Cap. '68.   V. (Próspero), owner of land at S. Gab. '43. iv. 637.   V. (Ramon), at Los Ang. '46-8.   V. (Salvador), ranchero at Sta B. '45.   V. (Secundino), at Los Ang. '39-46.   V. (Segundo), settler at Los Ang. 1800-19. ii. 349, 354

Valle (Antonio del), 1819, Mex. lieut of the S. Blas infantry comp., stationed at S.F. for a few years. ii. 253, 265, 371; in '22 accompanied the canónigo to Ross, ii. 464, and from that year was in com. of the inf. comp. at Mont. ii. 534, 536, 583, 609, 675, 549; iii. 26. In '23-4 he was in trouble, was tried by a military court for breaches of discipline, and once ordered to S. Blas, but was finally permitted to remain. His troubles seem to have sprung from the hostility of Gov. Argüello, against whom he made many complaints; and he was not released from arrest till '26. Robinson describes him in '31 as 'a little dried-up piece of vanity.' In '32 he supported Zamorano, going to Los Ang. with Ibarra. iii. 227; ment. in '34. iii. 271; in '34-5 he was comisionado for the secularization of S. Fern., where he served also as majordomo to '37. iii. 346, 353, 646-7. He opposed Alvarado in '36, was arrested in '37, and supported Cárlos Carrillo in '38. iii. 488, 504, 545. In '39 he was grantee of S. Francisco rancho, iii. 633, where he died in '41, the same year that gold was discovered on his place.   V. (Antonio), soldier of the Hidalgo batallon at Mont. '36, age 14; juez de paz at Sonoma '46. v. 668.   V. (Ignacio), 1825, son of the lieut and nat. of Jalisco, who came to Cal. with Echeandía, and in '28 became a cadet in the Sta B. comp., going to S. Diego with the gov. and serving as ayudante de plaza. iii. 572, 549. In '31-2 he joined the pronunciados against Victoria and Zamorano, though his father served on the other side, being made alférez in '31, and attached to the Mont. comp. from '32. iii. 201, 204, 227, 671. He was comisionado to secularize S. Gabriel '33, Sta Cruz '34, and S.F. '35. iii. 289, 326, 346, 354, 644, 694-5, 714-15. Don Ignacio supported Gutierrez against Alvarado in '36, going south after G.'s downfall, supporting Carrillo, and being sent to Sonoma as a prisoner in '38. iii. 463, 545, 449, 555, 566, 578. In '39 he is named as alf., habilitado, and supl. vocal of the junta; but was mustered out of the mil. service the same year, iii. 583, 590, 592, 641, 651, though still ment. ac habil. in '40-1. On the death of his father in '41 he settled on the S. Francisco rancho, where in '42 he was appointed juez of the new mining district. iv. 297, 315, 630-1; in '43 elector, suplente of the junta, and grantee of Tejon. iv. 361, 635; in 45-6 still memb. and sec. of the junta, memb. elect of the consejo, and treasurer of the civil govt by Pico's appointment. iv. 519, 521, 547, 558, 631; v. 35. He was alcalde at Los Ang. in '50, recorder in '50-1, member of the council and of the legisl. '52. His record throughout his career is that of a faithful officer and excellent citizen. In '77, living at his rancho of Camulos, he dictated for me his recollections of *Lo Pasado de California*, and gave me a col. of *Doc. Hist. Cal.*, which contains some important papers. He died in '80 at the age of 72. Of his family I know only that a son, R. F., is in '85 prominent in Cal. politics, having been member of the assembly and state senator. V. (Luis), 1834, com. of the *Morelos*. iii. 269, 383. V. (Rafael), teacher at S. José '21. ii. 379.

Vallejo (Ignacio Vicente Ferrer), 1774, nat. of Jalisco, Mex., son of Gerónimo V. and Antonia Gomez, b. in 1748, of pure Span. blood, and of a family which included many persons of education, especially several priests, friars, and nuns of some prominence, as is proved by a certificate of limpieza de sangre founded on testimony taken in Jalisco 1806 at the petition of Juan José V., a priest and brother of Ignacio. The latter, however, had no inclination for education or the church; nothing definite is known of his early life; but in '73, at the age of 25, he enlisted at Compostela under Rivera for Cal. service, and arrived at S. Diego in Sept. '74 with Lieut Ortega. He was a somewhat unmanageable soldier, often in trouble; but was praised for bravery in connection with the Ind. rising at S. D. in '75. i. 255; and in '76 was given leave of absence from mil. service to become an employé at S. Luis Ob. i. 299, 428; being formally discharged, I suppose, at the expiration of his enlistment term. From '81 he was employed at S. Cárlos, having, it seems, much skill and energy in directing agric. and irrigation works, though by no means a model of regular conduct, as is shown by occasional charges and reprimands. In '85 he was appointed comisionado of S. José; reënlisted in '87 for 10 years in the Mont. comp.; was promoted to corporal '89; and in '95 was removed from his position at S.José on complaint of the citizens; being corp. of the escolta at Soledad in '93-5; returning to S. José as superintendent of flax culture '95-6, and holding again the post of comisionado, or perhaps corp. of the guard, in '97-9. i. 439, 478-9, 499, 543, 552, 587, 620, 710-11, 716-19, 725. In 1799 he was made comisionado at Branciforte, holding that place for several years, or more than once, the records not being quite clear. i. 571; ii. 156; in 1805 was promoted to sergt, and in 1807—having obtained the certificate of gentle blood in 1806, as mentioned above—was declared sargento distinguido. ii. 140-1, 182; iii. 451. I have his hojas de servicio of dif. dates, showing him to have been engaged in several Ind. campaigns, and to have been recommended for promotion, which—prob. on account of his intractability and early irregularities—he did not get. In '18 he is ment. in connection with the Bouchard affair, subsequently being employed on certain public works at Mont. ii. 230-1, 339, 379, 381, 609. In '24 he was sent to S. Luis Ob. on service connected with the Ind. revolt of that year; asking the same year for retirement, which was apparently not granted, though he got a grant of the Bolsa de S. Cayetano rancho, on which his cattle had been for some years. ii. 536-7, 615-16, 619, 664; iii. 43, 678; ment. in '30. iii. 83. He died at Mont. in '31 at the age of 83. Don Ignacio is described in his enlistment papers as 5 ft 5½ in. in height, with brown hair, gray eyes, short nose, full beard, and fair complexion. He was a rough, coarse-grained, uneducated man; proud of his Spanish blood and family; haughty in manner, insubordinate and unmanageable as a soldier, and often in trouble with his superiors; careless in his morals; but endowed with considerable force and executive ability, and honorable and straightforward, I think, in his dealings with other men. His wife was María Antonia, daughter of Francisco Lugo, married in 1790, who died in '53. There were 13 children, 5 sons—4 of whom survived their father, and are named in this register—and 8 daughters—3 of whom, including Magdalena b. 1833, Isidora, and the wife of Mariano Soberanes, died before 31. The survivors were Prudenciana, who married José Amesti, and died after '77. Encarnacion, who married Capt. J. B. R. Cooper, and still lives in '85; Rosalía, Mrs J. P. Leese, living in '85;

Josefa, wife of Alvarado (ii. 141), Estrada, and Madariaga successively; and María de Jesus, still living in '53.

Vallejo (José de Jesus), son of Ignacio, b. at S. José in 1798; 1st named in records of the Bouchard affair of 1818, when he perhaps commanded a battery at Mont. ii. 229–32, 234. From about '24 he seems to have lived at the Bolsa de S. Cayetano, belonging to his father and after '31 to himself, till '36, being suplente of the diputacion in '33, regidor at Mont. in '35, and capt. of militia artill. under Alvarado in '36–8. ii. 615; iii. 82, 246, 430, 457, 474, 511, 525, 567, 673, 678, 732. From '36 he was comisionado and admin. of S. José mission. iii. 725; iv. 47, 194; in '39 suplente of the junta. iii. 590; in '40 engaged in an Ind. campaign. iv. 76, 138; and in '40–2 grantee of the Arroyo de la Alameda, for which in later years he was the successful claimant. iii. 711; iv. 670. He was mil. com. at S. José '41–2, and is ment. in '44. iv. 201, 465, 684, 686; delegate to the consejo general '46. v. 45; Cal. claim of $2,825 '46–7 (v. 462). He spent the rest of his life at Mission S. José, where he was postmaster in '52, and in '75 dictated for my use his *Reminiscencias Históricas*. He died in '82 at the age of '84. His wife was Soledad Sanchez, and two daughters, Teresa and Guadalupe, survived him. V. (Juan Antonio), son of Ignacio, owner of S.F. lot '40. iii. 706; v. 681; suplente juez at Mont. '43. iv. 653; aux. de policía '46. v. 637. He was later a ranchero in the Pájaro Valley, having but little to do with public affairs at any time. Died at Mont. '57. Larkin describes him as the most popular of the brothers.

Vallejo (Mariano Guadalupe), son of Ignacio, b. at Mont. in 1808, and educated at the same town. ii. 429; see a sketch of his life to '36 in iii. 471–3. He entered the mil. service in '23 (or from Jan. 1, '24) as cadet of the Mont. comp., and in '27 was promoted to alférez of the S.F. comp., though remaining at Mont. till '30 as habilitado and sometimes acting com., being in '27 a suplente of the dip., and in '29 a prisoner of the Solis revolters, besides making a somewhat famous exped. against the Ind. ii. 583–4, 608; iii. 36, 65, 69, 73, 89, 112–14. From '30 he served at S.F., being com. from '31; but as memb. of the dip. during the revolution against Victoria, of which he was an active promoter, and the Zamorano-Echeandía régime of '32, he was absent in the south much of the time. iii. 50, 99, 187, 189, 192–3, 200, 212, 216–19, 365, 399,701. In '33, though denied a place in the dip. on account of his mil. rank, V. was sent to the northern frontier to select a presidio site and to inspect the Russian establishment, on which he made a report; and was also occupied by troubles with his soldiers and with the missionaries. iii. 245–8, 254–5, 321–4, 393, 631, 699, 716; iv. 161–2. In '34 he was promoted to lieut, sent as comisionado to secularize Solano mission, and was grantee of the Petaluma rancho, besides being intrusted with the preliminary steps toward establishing a civil govt at S.F., and being elected a substitute member of congress. iii. 256–8, 279, 292, 712, 719–20. In '35 he was the founder of Sonoma, being made com. mil. and director of colonization on the northern frontier, engaging also in Ind. campaigns. iii. 286–7, 294, 354, 360, 363, 721–3; and from this time was indefatigable in his efforts to promote the settlement and development of the north, efforts that were none the less praiseworthy because they tended to advance his own personal interests. From '35 he was the most independent and in some respects the most powerful man in Cal. The year '36 brought new advancement, for though Lieut V. took no active part in the revolution, yet after the first success had been achieved, such was the weight of his name, that under Alvarado's new govt he was made comandante general of Cal., taking the office on Nov. 29th, and was advanced to the rank of colonel by the Cal. authorities; and in the sectional strife of '37–9, though not personally taking part in mil. operations, he had more influence than any other man in sustaining Alvarado, being advanced by the Mex. govt in '38 to the rank of capt. of the comp. and colonel of defensores, his position as comandante militar being recognized by Mex. from '39. iii. 423, 429–30, 440–3, 456–7, 471–4, 488–9, 511–14, 523–5, 531–4, 541–4, 546–7, 561–2, 567, 570,–4, 579–83, 590–2, 594, 670, 718; iv. 47, 67, 70–4, 86–7, 145. The new admin.

being fully established, Gen. V. gave his attention not only to the development of his frontera del norte, but to an attempted reorganization of the presidial companies in anticipation of foreign invasion, and to the commercial interests of Cal.; but insuperable obstacles were encountered, the general's views being in some respects extravagant, the powers at Mont. not being in sympathy with his reforms, and a quarrel with Alvarado being the result. Meanwhile no man's name is more prominent in the annals of '39-42, space permitting special reference here only to his relations with Sutter and with the Russians. iii. 595-604; iv. 11-12, 61, 92, 121, 128-9, 133-4, 165, 171-8, 196, 198-206, 208, 213-14, 218-20, 237-9, 249-52, 273-5. After several years of controversy with the gov., and large sacrifices of private means in fruitless efforts to serve his country, the general induced the Mex. govt to unite the mil. and civil commands in one officer from abroad, and turned over his command to Micheltorena in '42. There is no foundation for the current charge that he sought the governorship and overreached himself. Under the new admin. he was promoted to lieut-colonel and made com. mil. of the linea del norte, his jurisdiction extending south to Sta Inés. iv. 281-93, 312-17, 338. In '43 he was granted the Soscol rancho for supplies furnished the govt, his grant of Petaluma being extended; and was engaged in '43-4 not only in his routine duties and efforts for progress, but in minor controversies with Micheltorena, Mercado, and Sutter. iv. 351-3, 356-7, 373, 386-8, 396, 402, 407-8, 423, 444-5, 672, 674. From this time the general clearly foresaw the fate of his country, and became more and more satisfied with the prospects, though still conscientiously performing his duties as a Mex. officer. In the movement against Micheltorena in '44-5 he decided to remain neutral, unwilling and believing it unnecessary to act against a ruler appointed through his influence, and still less disposed to engage in a campaign, the expense of which he would have to bear, in support of a treacherous governor; but he discharged his soldiers to take sides as they chose, and warmly protested against Sutter's villany in arming foreigners and Ind. against his country, the only phase of the affair likely to give a serious aspect to the expulsion of the cholos. Meanwhile he was a faithful friend to the immigrants. iv. 459-60, 462-5, 481-2, 486, 516, 519, 530, 561, 603, 608. In the spring of '46 he was an open friend of the U.S. as against the schemes for an English protectorate, though his famous speech on that subject must be regarded as purely imaginary. v. 17, 28, 36, 41, 43, 46, 59-63, 66, 105-6; and in June-Aug., perhaps because of his devotion to the cause of the U.S. in its more legitimate form, he was cast into prison at Sutter's fort by the Bears, being rather tardily released by the U.S. authorities, and even awarded some slight honors, and a considerable amount of his 'Cal. claim' being later allowed as partial recompense for his losses. v. 111-21, 123-6, 157, 297-300, 467-8. Commissions of brevet colonel and colonel were issued to him in Mex. in July and Sept. Still mindful of the interests of his section, he gave the site on which Benicia was founded, the town being named for his wife. v. 670-1; and in '47 he received the appointments of legislative councillor and Ind. agent. v. 433, 539, 568, 610, 667-8. In '49 Vallejo was a member of the constit. convention, in '50 a member of the 1st state senate; from that time he was engaged in brilliant and financially disastrous schemes to make Benicia the permanent capital of Cal., of which more will be found in vol. vi. of this work; and in '52 et seq. the claimant for several ranchos, with varying success. In later years Gen. V. has continued to reside at Sonoma to '85, often called upon to take part in public affairs, though reduced financially to what, in comparison with the wealth that once seemed secure in his grasp, must seem like poverty. That he has been from 1830 one of the leading figures in Cal. annals is clearly shown in the records to which I have referred above; and in connection with the narrative thus referred to will be found much of comment on his acts and character. Here it must suffice to say that without by any means having approved his course in every case, I have found none among the Californians whose public record in respect of honorable conduct, patriotic zeal, executive ability, and freedom from petty prejudices of race, religion, or sectional politics is more evenly favorable than his. As a private citizen he was always generous and kind-hearted, maintaining his self-respect as a gentleman and commanding the respect of others, never a gambler or addicted to strong drink, though by no means strict in his relations with women. In the earlier times he was not in all respects a popular man by reason of his haughty, aristocratic, overbearing ways that resulted from pride of race, of wealth, and of military rank. Experience, however, and long before the time of his comparative adversity, effected a gradual disappearance of his least pleasing characteristics, though the general still retained a pompous air and grandiloquence of speech that unfavorably impress those who know him but slightly. He is in a sense the last survivor of old-time Californians of his class; and none will begrudge him the honor that is popularly accorded, even if praise sometimes degenerates into flattery. He is a man of some literary culture, and has always taken a deep interest in his country's history. Many of his writings are named in my list of authorities. His services to me in this connection have been often and most gladly acknowledged. His collection of *Doc. Hist. Cal.* is a contribution of original data that has never been equalled in this or any other state. His MS. *Historia de Cal.*, while of course not to be compared with the original documents, is not only the most extensive but the most fascinating of its class; and while, like the works of Bandini, Osio, Alvarado, Pico, and the rest, it is a strange mixture of fact and fancy, yet to a student who has the key to its cipher, it is a most useful aid; and moreover it should be stated that its defects are not all fairly attributable to the author. In '32 Vallejo married Francisca, daughter of Joaquin Carrillo of S. Diego, who still lives in '85. They had 13 children. None of the sons has ever been prominent in public life; one of them, Platon, is a well-known physician of Vallejo—a town that, like a street in S. F., bears his father's name; and two others still reside in Cal. Two of the daughters married the Frisbie brothers and two others the Haraszthys all well-known men, and four or five I think still live in Cal.

Vallejo (Salvador), son of Ignacio, b. in '14. His early years were passed as a ranchero, but in '36 his brother established him at Sonoma, where he ranked as capt. of militia, was often in com. of the post, engaged in many Ind. campaigns, went south to serve Alvarado in the Las Flores campaign of '38, served as juez de paz in '39, when he also had an appointment as admin. of Solano mission; was capt. of defensores from '44. iii. 511–12, 522, 547, 552, 529, 561, 591, 720–3, 71–2, 163, 197, 252, 355, 362–3, 407, 444, 465, 678. He was grantee of the Napa rancho in '38, of Salvador's rancho in '39, and of Lupyomi in '44. iii. 705, 712; iv. 671. In '46 he was a prisoner of the Bears. v. 112–21, 298–9; is named in connection with the Walla Walla affair. v. 302; and had a Cal. claim, $11,000 of which was paid. v. 467. He is said to have made a large amount of money in '48-9 by the aid of Ind. miners; but his lands passed gradually out of his possession, though he was a successful cl. for Llajome. iv. 671. In '63 he was commissioned major of the native Cal. cavalry, going to Ariz., but engaging in no active service. He died at Sonoma, where he had long lived with the general, in '76. Don Salvador was a rough, hard-drinking, unprincipled fellow; recklessly brave, and often inhumanly cruel in his Ind. warfare; very popular among his countrymen, though easily provoked to quarrel; generous and hospitable to the early immigrants, though hostile to Americans and to all foreigners as a rule. He dictated some *Notas Históricas* for my use, but his good qualities as a historian did not include truthfulness. His wife was María de la Luz Carrillo, but I have no further information about his family.   Vallely (John), 1847, Co. G, N.Y.Vol. (v. 499).   Vallivode (Stephen), 1839-40, doubtful name, mr of the *Elena*. iv. 103. Vallobodski (Stephen), 1837, mr of the *Sitka*. iv. 106; doubtful name, prob. same as preceding.   Valois (Antoine), 1846, Frenchman at Los Ang.   Valverde (Agustin), tailor at Los Ang. '39, age 27.   V. (José M.), Mex. tailor at Los Ang. '36, age 29, wife Francisca, child José.

Vanallen (John), at Sta Cruz.   Vanaken (Paul), 1846, Co. C, 1st U.S. dragoons (v. 336).   Vanauken (Philander), 1847, Co. D, N.Y.Vol. (v. 499). Vanbussum (J.V.), 1847, Co. B, ditto; d. before '82.   Vance (Robert), 1847,

Co. F, 3d U.S. artill. (v. 518); living in '64.   Vancoeur (Francis), 1846, from
N. Mex. with Kearny. *Lancey.*   Vancouver (Geo.), 1792, English navigator
who accompanied Capt. Cook in his famous voyages; and in 1792-4 three
times visited Cal. in com. of an exploring exped. to the N.W. coast and round
the world. His *Voyage* contains much of interest on Cal., and is a standard
work on the regions farther north. Capt. V. died in 1798. For his visits to
Cal. and his book, see i. 510-29; ment. i. 503, 506, 533, 538, 602, 619, 623, 645–
6, 649, 653, 658-9, 667-9, 674-5, 681-2, 685-6, 696, 698, 702-5, 714, 724; ii. 23,
121-2, 206; see also *Hist N.W. Coast*, i., this series.   Vanderbeck (J), 1847,
owner of a S.F. lot.   Vandussey, 1847, at Sutter's fort.   Vanegas (Cosme),
inválido at Sta B. '32, wife Bernardina Álvarez, child Estefana; ranchero at
Sta B. '45.   V. (José), Ind. settler at Los Ang. 1781; alcalde '88, '96. i. 345,
348, 461, 661.   V. (Pablo), at Sta B. before '37, wife Rita Rodriguez, and 4
children.   Vanhorn (Barnett), 1847, Co. F, 3d U.S. artill. (v. 518); d. before
'64.   Vankensen (Jeremiah), 1847, Co. I, N.Y.Vol. (v. 499); d. Aroca, N.Y.,
'55.   Vanness (Henry), 1848, nat. of N.J., who came from the Society Isl.,
became a pilot on S.F. Bay, and was lost in '67 on the pilot-boat *Caleb Curtis*,
age 47, leaving a widow and 3 children.   Vanpelt (Jacob), 1847, Co. E, N.
Y.Vol. (v. 499); owner of S.F. lot; d. at S.F. '49.   Vanriper (Abraham),
1847, sergt Co. E, N.Y.Vol. (v. 499); d. on the Mokelumne '48-9.   Van-
vechten (Geo.), 1847, Co. H, ditto; at New Brunswick, N.J., '74-82.   Van-
zandt (R. H.), 1847, mid. on the U.S. *Columbus.*
    Varela, 1818, mr of the *S. Ruperto*. ii. 291-2.   V. (Casimiro), one of the
1st settlers at S.F. 1777. i. 297.   V. (Hilario), ringleader with his brother in
a Los Ang. revolt. '44-5; also in '46. iv. 476, 538, 540-1; v. 308.   V. (Manuel), killed by Pomponio before '24. ii. 537.   V. (Sérbulo), brother of Hilario, a turbulent character at Los Ang. '38-9, age 26; engaged in revolts of '45-
6; and taking part in the last campaigns against the U.S. iii. 564, 589; iv.
540-1; v. 307-14, 325.   Varelas (Casimiro), settler at Los Ang. 1790; d. before 1816.   V. (Cayetano), settler at Los Ang. 1809-19; still there in '46. ii.
349, 354.   V. (Ignacio), settler at Los Ang. '15. ii. 349.   Vargas (Francisco), Los Ang. trader '39, age 37; alférez of Mont. comp. '43, and appointed
instructor of the S. Juan comp. of defensores '44. iv. 652, 407.   V. (Josefa
Rodriguez de), wife of Capt. Soler. i. 398.   V. (José Manuel), 1828, Mex.
convict, liberated in '34.   V. (Julian), 1831, perhaps of Young's party from
N. Mex. iii. 388.   V. (Manuel), 1781, soldier of the Mont. comp.; cabo distinguido in 1787; sergt of the comp. from about '87 to '94, being generally
employed by Gov. Fages as a clerk. On retiring from the service he taught
school at S. José, S. Diego, and Sta B. down to 1800 or later. i. 468, 484,
642-4, 680, 688. His wife, married at S.F. 1783, was María Gertrudis Linares,
and in '95 there was a daughter named Micaela.   V. (Mariano), friar named
for Cal. 1801; did not come. ii. 159.   Vargas Machuca, 1834, named by
Janssens as a Mex. alférez who came with the colony.   Varney, 1841, mr of
the *Thos Perkins.* iv. 569.   V. (Sam.), 1846, mr of the *Angola.* v. 576; and
trader at S.F. '46-8.
    Vasquez, at Mont. '28. ii. 615.   V., at S.F. '44, age 48.   V., mr of the
Flecha '48.   V. (Antonio), soldier of the Mont. comp. '36, age 20; perhaps
the man killed at Los Ang. '45. iv. 492.   V. (Atanasio), settler at S. José
1786. i. 477.   V. (Felipe), of the Mont. policía '33. iii. 673; grantee of
Chamizal '35. iii. 677; in '36 at Pilarcitos, age 54, wife María Nicanor Lugo,
child. José Ant. b. '20, Pedro '22, Dionisio '24, Sinforosa '26, and Manuel '32.
V. (Hermenegildo), soldier at Mont. 1809; regidor at S. José '27. ii. 605;
grantee of land '35.   V. (José), soldier of S.F. comp. '19-24; at Mont. '48;
S. Luis Ob. '51.   V. (José Ign.), settler at S. José 1777. i. 312.   V. (José
María), 1829, Mex. convict set a liberty '33; at S. José '41, age 31, wife An-
drea García, child Susana b. '36.   V. (Julio), at Mont. '36, nat. of Cal., age
40, wife of Brigida German, child. Ambrosia b. '16, Apolonia '18, Ramon '23,
Gregorio '26, Domingo '28, María Guad. '30, Altagracia '32, Perseverancia '33,
Juan '34, Marcos '35.   V. (Pedro), applic. for land '45. iv. 656; cl. for Son-
lajule '52. iv. 674; Cal. claim $3,375 '46-7 (v. 462).   Vasquez (Tiburcio),

Mex. settler at S.F. 1777, and at S. José '83. i. 297, 350 (another named as a convict of '98. i. 606); named in the S. José padron of '93, wife María Bohorques, child. Felipe, María, Hermenegildo, Rosalía, Faustino, and Félix; alcalde 1802, 1807. ii. 134, 192; síndico '24. ii. 605. He seems to have died in '27. The famous bandit of later years was prob. his grandson. V. (Tiburcio), prob. son of the preceding; soldier of the S.F. comp. '19–25; in '39 regidor at S.F., and grantee of Corral de Tierra rancho. iii. 705, 711; in '40–6 admin. and maj. of S.F. mission. iii. 715; iv. 675; v. 660; named in the padron of '42, b. at S. José, age 49, wife Alvira Hernandez, child. Juan José b. '25, Bárbara '27, Josefa '29, Siriaca '31, José María '32, Purificacion '33, Luciano '34, Francisco '36, Francisca '38, and Pablo '40. He was still at S.F., a witness in the Santillan case, '55. V. (Timoteo), at Branciforte 1803. ii. 156. Vassilief, 1820, com. of Russ. vessels. ii. 319.

Vealy (John), 1829, Amer. cooper, age 34, who landed at S. Pedro ill from a Hon. vessel. Vedder (Peter G.), 1847, Co. H, N.Y.Vol. (v. 499); d. in Nicaragua '56. Vega (José), sergt killed by Ind. at the Colorado Riv. pueblos. i. 359–62. V. (Matías), soldier at S. Juan Cap. 1776; killed at Colorado Riv. pueblos 1781. i. 303, 359–62. V. (Victoriano), 1834, came from Mex. in the H. & P. colony at the age of 24; in '77 at S. Gabriel gaining a living by making cigarettes. He gave me a MS. dictation of 62 p. on *Vida Californiana*. His real name was Esparza. V. (José M.), 1769, Span. arriero killed by Ind. at S. Diego. i. 138. V. (Emigdio), juez de campo at Los Ang. '38; juez de paz at S. Juan '44–5; grantee of Boca de la Playa '46. iii. 636; iv. 627. In '46 living at S. Juan Cap. He was 35 years old, wife Rafaela Ávila, child. María de Jesus b. '38, Jesus '43, Ramon '45. V. (Emilio), aided in taking Los Ang. '37. iii. 519. V. Enrique), juez de campo at Los Ang. '40. ii. 637. V. (Francisco), settler at S. José 1791–5. i. 716–17; man of same name, son of Ricardo, at Los Ang. '46–77. V. (Juan Crisóstomo), regidor at Los Ang. '39, age 25. iii. 636; member of the council '65–70. V. (Lázaro and Manuel), at Los Ang. '46. V. (Pablo), son of Salvador, b. at S. Diego in 1802; soldier of the S. D. comp. from '21, but soon sent to Mont. for an attempt to desert. In '28–9 he was a leader in the revolt, and was sent to Mex. in '30, but returned in '33. iii. 66–7, 69, 74, 85; again ment. in '37. iii. 519; and in a revolt of '46, being taken prisoner at S. Pascual. v. 308, 347. His wife was a daughter of Juan M. Félix and Isabel Cota. In '77, living near Spadra with his brother Ricardo, with a large family and in great poverty, he dictated 90 pages of the *Recuerdos de un Viejo* for my use. V. (Ramon), at Los Ang. '46. V. (Ricardo), son of Salvador; in '33 juez de campo Los Ang. iii. 635; grantee of S. José, or Azuza, '37–40. iii. 633; age 28 in '39. He became a rich man, but was reduced to poverty, and in '77 lived near Spadra with a large family. V. (Salvador), 1792, Mex. carpenter-instructor at S. Diego '92–5; at Mont. '96. i. 615, 684. His wife was María Josefa Lopez. Vela (Martin), at Branciforte '28–30. ii. 627; wife María de la Luz Fuentes. Velarde (Baltasar), at S. Bern. '46, age 34. V. (Desiderio), Los Ang. hatter, age 38, in '39. V. (Jacobo), settler at S. José 1791–1800. i. 716; alcalde in '98. Velasquez (José), 1781, alférez of the S. Diego comp., engaged in explorations to the Colorado Riv. and in other directions; d. at S. Gabriel 1785. i. 340, 367, 451, 454–5; ii. 44. V. (José), 1798, convict settler at Branciforte 1798–1803. i. 606; ii. 156. V. (José), corporal of the S. Diego comp. 1803. ii. 14, 103. Velez (Miguel), sirviente at S.F. 1777. i. 297. V. (Rafael), appointed sec. of the com. gen. '29; did not come. iii. 54. Velsor (Stephen), 1847, Co. A, N.Y.Vol. (v. 499); d. before '82. Vendurm, 1846, doubtful name in a Los Ang. list.

Verdia (José), died in '16, leaving his property to the mission fund. ii. 407; iv. 338. Verdugo (Crisóstomo), at Los Ang. 46. V. (Francisco), at Los Ang. '39, age 38. V. (José Antonio), at S. Bern. '46, age 20. V. (José María), retired corp. of the S. Diego comp. and S. Gabriel escolta, who was grantee of the S. Rafael rancho in 1784, '98, and is often named down to 1816 in connection with farming operations. i. 553, 609, 612, 661, 664; ii. 111, 185, 350, 353, 663; iii. 634. V. (Juan Diego), at S. Diego 1776; wife María Ign.

de la Concepcion Carrillo, who in '50 was cl. for the Félix rancho, granted in
'43. iv. 634; daughter Rosalía, married to Sergt Góngora.   V. (Julio), son
of José María; aux. alcalde at S. Rafael rancho '31, '33, '36, and juez de
campo '40. iii. 635-7; cl. for the rancho '52.   V. (Manuel), juez de campo
at S. Diego '41. iv. 619; soldier, retired with rank of lieut '44. iv. 408.   V.
(Mariano), 1769, soldier of the 1st exped., serving in the S. Diego comp.;
sergt at Mont. '81-7; settler at Los Ang. 1787-1819 or later, being alcalde in
1790-3, 1802; grantee of Portezuelo rancho 1795. i. 252-3, 461, 468, 661-2;
ii. 110, 350, 353-4, 663.   V. (Miguel), at Sta Ana rancho Los Ang. '39, age
26; at S. Juan Cap. '41. iv. 626.   V. (Pedro and Teodoro), at Los Ang. '46.
Verduzco (Francisco), 1834, Mex. ex-capt., who was connected with the H.
& P. colony; but being implicated in the alleged revolt of '35 was sent to
Mex. as a prisoner. iii. 281, 286, 288.   Vergara (Quirino), 1842, cornet in
the batallon fijo '42-5. iv. 289.
    Vermeule (Thomas L.), 1847, lieut Co. E, N.Y. Vol. v. 504, 511; nat. of
N.J.; memb. of the constit. convention '49; lawyer, politician, and writer for
the newspapers. He died at S. José before '67.   Vermilion (John), 1840, one
of the exiles not known to have returned. iv. 18.   Vernon (Richard), 1848,
overl. immig. with Allsopp.   Verrot (Joseph), 1844, Canadian of Frémont's
party, remaining in Cal. iv. 437, 439, 453; named in the N. Helv. Diary, '46
-8; an early settler of Yuba Co.; connected with the Donner relief. v. 537;
married Mary Luther in '48, and a son, Charles, was born in '50. Usually
called 'Vero' or 'Varro.'   Vevis (Joseph), 1847, chief musician of N.Y. Vol.
v. 503; d. before '82.   Vhor (Christopher), 1836, Arabian, age 49, at Mont.
    Viader (José), 1796, Span. friar who served for 37 years at Sta Clara, leav-
ing Cal. in '33. Biog. iii. 726-7; ment. i. 577, 719-20, 723; ii. 56-7, 135, 137,
153, 159, 168, 218, 387, 394, 577, 585, 600, 623, 655; iii. 20, 88-9, 96, 318,
338, 365, 727.   Viana (Francisco), 1791, lieut in Malaspina's exped. i. 490.
Vice (James), 1846, sailor on the Dale.   Vicente, corp. at Sta B. '38. iii.
656.   Vich (Chris.), 1845, Amer. at Branciforte, age 20; doubtful name.
Vichilman, 1823, mr of the Buldakof. ii. 492.   Victoria (Manuel), 1830,
Mex. lieut-colonel, who came in '30 as gov. and com. gen. of Cal.—appointment March 8th, arrival Dec.—and held that office from Jan. 31, '31, to Dec.
9th, when he yielded to a successful revolutionary movement, and sailed for
Mex. Jan. 17, '32. He was an honest and energetic officer, who as general
forgot that he was also governor; ignored the diputacion and all civil authorities and precedents; and by his well-meant short cuts to justice by military
methods soon provoked a revolution that overwhelmed him. All that is known
of the man is contained in the narrative of his rule and downfall. iii. 181-
212. See also ment. in ii. 549, 551, 594; iii. 26, 54, 216-17, 233, 306-8, 364,
367-8, 374-6, 647, 652, 669-70; iv. 160.   Vidal (Francisco), 1602, corp. in
Vizcaino's exped. i. 98.   V. (John A.), 1847, Co. F, N.Y. Vol. (v. 499); settled at Sta B., where in '53 he was killed in a fight over the possession of a
rancho. See Sta B. Co. Hist., 82.   V. (Mariano), 1776, purveyor of Anza's
exped. to Cal. i. 258, 266.
    Vigil (Francisco Estévan), 1841, in com. of a trading caravan from N.
Mex. '41-2, and again in '48. iv. 207, 343; v. 625.   Vignes (Jean), 1834,
nephew of Louis, age 22, who came from Hon. on the D. Quixote to join his
relatives at Los Ang.   V. (Jean Louis), 1831, Fr. cooper and distiller, who
came from Hon. on the Louisa at the age of 48. iii. 405. His Fr. passp. was
dated Bordeaux '26. He at once applied for naturalization; in '32 joined the
comp. extranjera at Mont. iii. 221; but soon settled at Los Ang., where
he was in a sense the pioneer vineyardist and wine-maker, being joined by
his nephew in '34. His name is occasionally mentioned in '36 et seq., he being
one of the vigilantes in '36, an applicant for Sta Catalina Isl. in '40, and rid-
ing in the campaign against Micheltorena '45. iii. 417, 634; iv. 117, 495,
629; v. 49, 283, 365; had a Cal. claim of about $1,000 '46-7 (v. 462). He was
founder of the wine-making firm of Sainsevain & Co.; was the cl. for Temécula—of which he had been in reality the grantee in '45, and of Pauba; and
died at Los Ang. '62 at the age of 79 (or 82). He had no family in Cal., was

an excellent and popular citizen, and was familiarly known as Don Luis del Aliso, from an immense sycamore, or cottonwood, on his land at Los Ang. V. (Pierre E.), Fr. at Branciforte '45, age 50; at S. José '47. Vila (Vicente), 1769, com. of the *S. Cárlos* in the 1st exped. '69–70. i. 116, 128–9, 136, 165–8. Villa (Antonio M.), prob. son of Joaquin; cl. for Tequepis rancho, Sta B. iv. 643. V. (Buenaventura), soldier of the Mont. comp. '36, age 26. V. (Demetrio), at Los·Ang. 39-48. V. (Diego), colegial at Sta Inés '44. iv. 426. V. (Eleuterio), inválido soldier '44–5. iv. 408. V. (Francisco), at Los Ang. 19. ii. 354; in charge of S. José del Valle '36. iii. 612; zanjero at S. Gabriel '47. v. 628; juez de campo at S. Luis Ob. '49; still at S. Luis '51. V. (Joaquin), soldier at Sta B. before '37; maj. at Sta. Inés '39. iii. 664; grantee of Tequepis '45. iv. 643. V. (José), settler at Los Ang. 1790. i. 461. V. (Luis), at Los Ang. '46. V. (María del Rosario), executed by vigilantes at Los Ang. '36. iii. 417–19. V. (Manuel), soldier of S.F. comp. '32–3. V. (Mariano), at Los Ang. '39, age 22; also in '46. V. (Mariano), 1842, Mex. lieut of the batallon fijo '42–5; remained in Cal. '46. iv. 289, 513; v. 41. V. (Miguel), settler for Los Ang., who deserted before reaching Cal. i. 345. V. (Rafael), cabo invál. 1793 at S. José, wife Ildefonsa, child. Pascual, Eleuterio, Rafael Gertrudis, María Ign., and Juana. The full name was prob. 'Villavicencio,' q.v. V. (Rafael), son of preceding, at S. Luis Ob. '42–60. V. (Vicente), at Los Ang. '19; regidor in '27. ii 354, 560.

Villagrana (José Félix), Mex. at S. José '41, age 52, wife Bernardina Martinez, child. Guadalupe b. '26, Juana '31, Lucia '36, Dolores '38; d. in '47. V. (Manuel), regidor at Branciforte '32. iii. 696. V. (Miguel), Mex. resid. of Branciforte from '28, alcalde '36, grantee of Aguagito '37, juez de campo '38. ii. 637; iii. 676, 697. In the padron of '45 named as 66 years old, wife Francisca Juarez, child. Carpio b. '25, Eugenio '27, Dorotea '29, Ignacia '31, Leandro '31, José Ign. '34, Andrés '33, Ponciana '40. V. (Miguel), at Branciforte '45, age 23, wife Concepcion, child. Julian b. '40, José '44. Villalba (Nicolas), settler of the Colorado Riv. pueblos, killed by Ind. 1781. i. 359–62. Villalobos (José), at Los Ang. '48. Villapando (Juan de J), mule-thief '33. iii. 396. Villarasa (Francis S.), 1848, said to have preached at Stockton. Villaroel (Francisco), 1777, com. of the *S. Antonio.* i. 310. Villaverde (Alonso), lieut for Cal. 1779; did not come. i. 340. V. (José), 1782, chaplain on the *Favorita.* i. 378. Villavicencio (Félix), Span. settler of Los Ang. 1781–6. i. 345, 348. V. (José María), resid. of Mont. '36, age 36, wife Rafaela Rodriguez, child. José Ant. b. '34, José Ramon '35; being at the time juez de campo. iii. 675. As capt. in Alvarado's force, and at times com. at Sta B., he was prominent in the operations of '36–8. iii. 460, 481, 505, 524–5, 546, 550, 552–3, 561, 565, 651, 672; also admin. of S. Antonio and S. Fernando '37–8, '40–3. iii. 647–8, 688; iv. 61, 638; acting prefect at Mont. '40. iii. 675; grantee of Corral de Piedra, S. Luis Ob., '41, '46. iv. 655; in '44 juez de paz at S. Luis Ob., and capt of defensores. iv. 407, 462, 658–9; also serving against the U.S. at S. Diego '46. v. 267. Still at S. Luis '51–2, and later a prosperous ranchero. Often called by himself and others 'Villa.' V. (Rafael), weaver at S. José 1791-1811. i. 716, 718; ii. 378. V. (Rafael), grantee of S. Gerónimo, S. Luis Ob., in 42. iv. 655; and cl. in '52. Villela (Felipe), soldier at Sta B. before '37; at Los Ang. '39, age '35. V. (Juan M. M.), settler at S. José 1777; did not remain. i. 312. V. (Marcos), soldier at Soledad 1791 et seq.; invál. at Branciforte '99. i. 499, 511.

Viñals (José), 1798, Span. friar who served at S. Cárlos, retiring in 1804. Biog. ii. 146–7; ment. i. 577, 686; ii. 159–60, 166. Vincent, 1848, mr of the *Zach Taylor,* built at Sta Cruz. *Fresno Co. Hist.,* 51. V. (Calvin), 1846, came to Sta Clara. *Hall.* V. (E. C.), 1848, passp. from Hon. V. (Geo. W.), 1826, nat. of Mass. and mate of the *Courier.* He came back as mr of the *Monsoon* '39–40; and in '44–6 com. the *Sterling;* owner of a S.F. lot and of a Cal. claim '46–7. In '48 he was mr of the *Sabine,* and remained at S.F., where he was killed in the fire of '51. iii. 146, 176; iv. 105, 568; v. 296, 580. A son, Geo. W., lives, I think, in S.F. '85. V. (Joshua S.), 1847, sergt Co. I,

N.Y.Vol. v. 504; at Linn Creek, Mo., '82.   Vincenthaler (L. C.), 1846, in
Cal. during the war of '46-7; prob. went east with Frémont or Stockton. v.
454; one of Frémont's men '48.   Vines (Bartlett), 1843, overl. immig.
of the Walker-Chiles party with his wife, who was a daughter of Geo. Yount.
iv. 393, 400, 448. He settled in Napa Val., and still lived there in '81. A
daughter was born in '45.   Vinson (Wm), 1847, Co. E, N.Y. Vol. (v. 499).
Vioget (Jean Jacques), 1837, Swiss sailor and surveyor who came as mr of
the *Delmira* '37-9. iv. 103, 117-18. He settled at S.F., where he made the 1st
town survey, owned a lot, and built a house in '39-40. iii. 706, 710; v. 679.
In '40 he was naturalized, and from that time appears in various records as a
trader, keeping also a billiard-saloon, and being employed by Sutter in '41 to
make a survey of his N. Helvetia grant, having of course much trouble to
collect his pay. iv. 179, 229-30, 237, 668. In '44-5, renting his saloon or hir-
ing a man to keep it, he was mr of the *Clarita;* was employed to carry
Micheltorena to Mex., and was grantee of the Blucher rancho, Sonoma
Co. iv. 480, 564, 670. In '46-7 he made a trip to Hon. and back on the
Don Quixote; and in '47-8 was mr of the *Euphemia,* running to the
Islands, being judge of election, and advertising his hotel—The Portsmouth
House—for sale. v. 578, 650, 680. He lived at S. José '49, and in '54
at S.F., age 55. I find no later record of him. His wife was apparently a
Benavides. Vioget was a jolly, musical sort of fellow, speaking several lan-
guages, a sailor and surveyor and hotel-keeper of some skill.   Virgen
(Leonardo), soldier at Sta B. '24. ii. 532.   Virgin (Thomas), 1827, Amer. at
S. Diego.
     Virmond (Henry), 1828, German merchant of Acapulco and the city of
Mex., who did a large business with Cal., where he was well known to nearly
everybody before he visited the country in '28-30. He was a skilful intriguer,
had extraordinary facilities for obtaining the ear of Mex. officials, and was
always the man first sought to solicit any favor, commercial, military, civil, or
ecclesiastical, for his many Cal. friends. He owned the *Leonor*, *Maria Ester,*
Catalina, Clarita, and many other vessels well known in the Cal. trade. He was
the tallest man ever seen here till the coming of Dr Semple; was a business man
of great enterprise; had many accomplishments and a Mex. wife; and had,
also, his leg broken by the kick of a mule while in Cal. ii. 594; iii. 58, 141-3,
147, 149, 233, 313, 398, 572; iv. 249, 285.   Vischer (Edward), 1842, Ger.
clerk in Virmond's employ at Acapulco, who came to Cal. on the schr *California.* iv. 341, 349. After '49 he became a resident, being an artist, and his
Pictorial of Cal. was a series of photographs from pencil sketches, with descriptive matter, published under the title of *Missions of Upper Cal.* His drawings, however, were all made after '65. He died at S.F. after '70.
     Victoria (Marcos Antonio Saizar de), 1805, nat. of the province of Álava,
Spain, b. in 1760; became a Franciscan in '76; came to Mex. in 1804. His
missionary service was at Sta B. 1805-6, S. Buen. 1805-17 and '20-24, S. Fernando '18-20, Purísima '24-35, and Sta Inés '35-6. His death occurred on July
25, '36, at Sta Inés. Padre Vitoria was a most virtuous and exemplary man,
always in feeble health, not accredited by his superiors with great ability, but
beloved by his neophytes. *Autobig. Autog. de los Padres,* MS.; *Arch. Sta B.*
iii. 48-50, 128; *Sta Inés Lib. Mis.,* 19-21. See mention in ii. 109, 121-2, 357,
490, 530, 578-9; iii. 96, 661-2, 664; iv. 63.   Vivaldo (Feliciano), 1842, sub-
lieut of the batallon fijo '42-5. iv. 289.   Vivero, 1800, com. of the *Princesa.*
i. 546.   Vizcaino (Juan), 1769, Span. friar who served for a brief term at S.
Diego; was wounded by the Ind. in Aug.; and retired on account of illness
in '70. i. 127, 136, 138, 164-5.   V. (Sebastian), 1602, Span. navigator in com.
of an exped. that explored the Cal. coast 1602-3. See complete record of his
visit, and mention of a later one of 1613, in i. 97-105, 111, 151-2, 158, 169;
ii. 1.   Vizcarra (José), soldier at Sta Cruz 1795. i. 496.
     Vonks (Stephen), 1837, doubtful name of mr of the *Baical.* iv. 101.   Vor-
hees (John), 1847, Co. E, N.Y.Vol. (v. 499).   Vorhies (Wm Van), 1848(?),
postal agent for the govt; memb. of the 1st senate, and sec. of state under
Gov. Burnett and his successors; prominent in later years as politician, law-

year, and editor, residing many years in Oakland. He died at Eureka in '84.
Vrandenburg (Adna), 1847, Co. A, Morm. Bat. (v. 469).   Vyer (John), 1846,
Co. C, 1st U.S. dragoons (v. 336).

Waccodzy, or Wacoocky (Basil), 1835, doubtful name of mr of the *Sitka*
'35–6. iii. 384; iv. 106.   Waddell (Archibald), 1847, Co. E, N.Y. Vol. (v.
499).   Wade, 1847, at Sutter's fort '47–8, prob. one of the Mormons.   W.
(Edward W.), 1847, Co. C, Morm. Bat. (v. 469); at Ogden, Utah, '82.   W.
(Isaac), 1847, Co. F, 3d U.S. artill. (v. 518); d. before '64.   W. (Moses),
1847, Co. C, Morm. Bat. (v. 469).   W. (Wm), 1844, deserter from the U.S.
Warren.   Wadleigh (Joseph), 1848, maker of pans at Sutter's fort '48–9;
went east with a fortune '49. *Grimshaw.*   Wadsworth (James C. L.), 1847,
came from N.Y. on the *Whiton;* became sutler's clerk of N.Y. Vol. v. 503;
alcalde at Stockton '49; a resident of S.F. in later years to '85, being a well-
known mining man. He gave me his testimony on matters connected with the
Vigilance Committee.   W. (Samuel), 1847, nat. of N.Y. and settler at Sta
Clara; d. at Pleasanton '82 at the age of 62.   Waggoner (P. W.), 1846, Cal.
Bat., Co. B, artill. (v. 358); enlisting at Sta Cruz Oct.   Wagner (Thomas),
1848, nat. of Va, who died at Snelling '77.   Waine, 1846, lieut on the *Levant.*
Wainwright (John), 1826, lieut on H. B. M. S. *Blossom* '26–7. iii. 121.   W.
(J. M.), 1847, acting mr of the U.S. *Columbus;* perhaps J. W.   Wakefield
(Benj.), 1847, act. boatswain on the *Preble.*

Walcott (Ephraim), 1844, Amer. deserter from a vessel who worked at S.
F. for Fink, going into business for himself as a blacksmith in '47. iv. 453,
683; also at Sutter's fort '46–7.   Wald (Wm), 1846, arrested at Los Ang.
iv. 14.   Waldo (Geo.), 1846, officer of the Cal. Bat. (v. 361).   W. (Giles),
1848, passp. from Hon.   Waldron, 1846, at Sutter's fort from S.F. June.
W. (J. W. and R. R.), 1841, brothers and officers on the U.S. *Vincennes.*
Walker, 1843, mate of the *Admittance* discharged at S. Diego; in '45 mr of
the *John and Elizabeth;* perhaps two men.   W. (Edwin), 1847, Co. D, Morm.
Bat. (v. 469); reënl.   W. (Henry D.), 1846, Co. C, 1st U.S. dragoons (v.
336).

Walker (James T.), 1848, nat. of Tenn. and nephew of Capt. Joe W., who
came overland, starting in '47, but being obliged to winter on the way, through
having, with the true family instinct, sought a new route. v. 556–7. Working
as teamster, cattle-trader, and miner in '48–9, he went east by sea and came
back across the plains in '50. The next year he went to Mo. via N. Mex., and
in '52 made his 3d overl. trip to Cal. In '53 he settled in Contra Costa, where
he still lived in '82, at the age of 57, with wife and 3 children. Portrait in
Contra Costa Co. Hist., 88.   W. (Joel P.), 1841, nat. of Va, brother of Joseph, Ind. fighter from '14 in the Seminole and other wars, later in the Sta Fé
trade, overl. immig. to Or. '40, who came to Cal. with his family from Or.,
accompanying a detachment of the U.S. Ex. Ex. After working for Sutter, and
later for Yount, he returned to Or. with a drove of cattle, remaining there for
5 years, though he appears as owner of a S.F. lot in '45. iv. 233, 278–9, 347,
377, 390. He came back to Cal. in '48, lived at Napa till '53, being a member
of the constit. convention in '49, and 1st assessor of Napa Co. In '53 he moved
to Sonoma Co., where he still lived in '78 at the age of 81. His wife, Mary
Young of Mo., was the 1st white woman to arrive in Cal. by land or to settle
north of the bay. They had a daughter Louisa born in Or. '41; and the other
children who came to Cal. in '41 were John, Joseph, Newton, and Isabella.
The 1st was living at Sebastopol in '77. A MS. *Narrative* furnished by Joel
P. to Robt A. Thompson is in my collection.

Walker (Joseph Reddeford), 1833, nat. of Tenn. who went to Mo. in '19,
where he served as sheriff, and became one of the most skilful and famous of
the guides, mountaineers, Ind.-fighters, and trappers of the far west. His 1st
visit to Cal. was as com. of a party of Bonneville's trappers, spending the
winter of '33–4 at Mont. Walker's lake, river, and pass were named for his
discoveries on this trip. iii. 389–92, 409, 669; iv. 264, 434. In '41, unless
there is an error in archive records, he came to Los Ang., prob. from N. Mex.,

to buy horses. iv. 278. In '43 he guided a division of Chiles' immig. party by a southern route to Cal., going back in '44. iv. 393-5, 679. His next visit was in '45-6 as guide to Frémont's party, a portion of which he brought through his original Walker pass. iv. 582-5; v. 3, 6. In July '46 he was met by Bryant at Ft Bridger on his return from Cal. Capt. W. continued his wanderings, with intervals of ranchero life and stock-trading experience in Cal., for 20 years, making extensive explorations in Arizona as well as in other sections; and then in '66-7 he settled in Contra Costa Co., living with his nephew James T., and dying in '76 at the age of 78. Capt. Joe Walker was one of the bravest and most skilful of the mountain men; none was better acquainted than he with the geography or the native tribes of the great basin; and he was withal less boastful and pretentious than most of his class. In his old age he was moved by the absurd praise accorded to a 'pathfinder' who had merely followed the tracks of himself and his trapper associates, to say many bitter and doubtless unjust things against Frémont, but his prejudice on this point was natural and merits but slight censure. W. (R.), 1848, passp. from Hon. W. (W. M.), 1841, lieut in U.S. Ex. Ex. iv. 241. W. (Wm), 1846, sailor on the Dale. W. (Wm), 1847, Co. B, Morm. Bat. (v. 469). Walkinshaw (Robert), 1847, nat. of Scotland and long resid. of Mex., who came as sup. of the William, and took charge of the N. Almaden quicksilver mine; cl. for Sta Clara lands '52. iv. 673; left Cal. in '58 and died in Scotland '59. A man of the same name and apparently of the same family resided at S.F. in '85.

Wall (Richard), 1847, Co. B, N.Y.Vol. (v. 499); d. in S. Joaq. Co. after '50. W. (Wm), 1847, owner of a S. F. lot. Wallace (Geo.), 1845, Amer, at Mont.; in prison '47. iv. 587. Wallen (Edward), 1846, Co. A, Cal. Bat. (v. 358). Wallis (Wm), 1846, Co. F, ditto, enlisting at S. Juan Oct. Walpole (Fred.), 1846, lieut on the Collingwood, and author of Four Years in the Pacific. v. 213-14. Walsh (James), 1847, Co. A, N.Y.Vol. (v. 499). W. (John), 1818 (?), resident of Benicia '78-84, said to have visited S.F. in '18; prob. an error. W. (Robert A.), 1838 (?), priest at Hon. '39, who had apparently visited Cal. with his associate, Murphy.

Walter, see 'Wolter.' W. (Geo.), 1846, one of the Chino prisoners. v. 314; Co. A, Cal. Bat. (v. 358). W. (John), 1847, perhaps of N.Y.Vol.; not on roll. W. (Philip J.), 1832, Engl. carpenter and naturalized citizen at Mont. '32-6. iii. 408; perhaps 'Watson.' Waltham (Henry), 1848, passp. from Hon. Walther (Geo.), 1847, Co. K, N.Y.Vol. (v. 499); at Los Ang. '71-4. Walton (Ambrose), 1841, overl. immig. of the Bartleson party, who prob. returned east in '42. iv. 270, 275, 342. W. (Major), 1841, ditto; or, acc. to some sketches, was drowned in the Sac. Riv.; also named as one of the Chiles party of '43. iv. 393. Walz (Geo.), 1847, Co. D, N.Y.Vol. (v. 499).

Wambough (M. M.), 1846, apparently from Or. in June. v. 526; enlisting at S. Juan Oct. in Co. F, Cal. Bat., of which he became lieut. v. 361. In '47 he became the owner of land in Sta Clara Co.; and in July, while on his way to Stockton's camp, was robbed and perhaps wounded near Altgeier's place in the Sac. Val.; though in later years, when he attempted to get relief from the gov't, some doubt was thrown on the robbery. I do not know if he was the senator to whom Wm B. Ide directed his famous letter on the Bear revolt. Wanec (Wm), 1845, doubtful name of an Irish resid. of Branciforte, age 45, single. Warbas (Thos A.), 1840 (?), on roll of Soc. Cal. Pion. iv. 120; in '42, acc. to list in the Herald of '51; at S. F. '54. Warbeck (Henry K.), 1847, Co. I, N.Y.Vol. (v. 499); d. at S.F. after '50. Warburton (Henry H.), 1847, Engl. physician who came as surgeon on the Corea (?), and settled at Sta Clara, where he still lived in '81, with wife, Catherine Pennell, and 5 child., Caroline, Ellen, John, Charles, and Henry.

Ward, 1848, of the ship Confederacion at S.F. W. (Andrew J.), 1847, Co. I, N.Y.Vol. (v. 499); a physician at Sutter's fort '47-8; at Madison, Wis., '82. W. (C. L.), 1848, at S.F. in August. W. (Edward C.), 1847, officer on the U.S. Preble. W. (Frank), 1846, came from N. Y. on the Brooklyn,

though not a Mormon, and opened a store at S.F. as a member of the firm W.
& Smith, which became prominent for several years; owner of town lots, inspector of election, marshal at the public reception of Com. Stockton, acting
alcalde, etc. v. 295-6, 455, 539, 546-7, 648, 679, 681, 685. In '48 he testified
on the Cal. claims at Wash., D.C., but came back to Cal. with his wife, Henrietta Zimmerman, who died at S.F. in '49. A little later, in business reverses,
he shot himself, but not fatally; went east about '53; came back soon after
'70, married the widow of Dr Bale, and some years later started east by sea,
drowning himself on the way. He was not a very dissipated man, but stylish
and extravagant. W. (Geo. R.), 1839, owner of a S.F. lot (?). W. (Henry),
1847, gunner on the *Preble.* W. (James C.), 1847, brother of Frank, who
came in March with letters to Larkin; owner of lots at S.F., and member of
the firm W. & Wells; inspector of election; lieut of S. F. guard, somewhat
prominent in politics '47-8. v. 650-2. It was perhaps he instead of his brother
who shot himself. He lived in Mass. '55-78, then returning to S.F., where he
was a notary, and published his *Diary* of earlier times in the *Argonaut.* He
had a shock of paralysis, and was taken back to Mass., where he died in '83,
leaving a widow. W. (John), 1832 (?), nat. of Va, said to have been at Los
Ang. '32-3. iii. 408; again in Cal. '43-6, returning in '49, and dying at Los
Ang. '59. *Los Ang. Co. Hist.,* 35. The only original record that I find is a
pass. for Sonora in '45. W. (John B.), 1840, nat. of Ireland, who came as a
boy on the U.S. *St Louis,* visiting Mont. and S. F. He came back in '49 on
the steamer *California;* married Arcadia Concepcion Estudillo; was one of
the founders of S. Leandro; and still lives at S.F. in '85. W. (O. R.), 1847,
at Mont. from Hon. on the *D. Quixote.* Wardell (Geo. S.), 1847, left S.F.
on the *Chas Drew.* Warden (Wm), 1829, mr of the *Dhaulle,* or *Dolly.* iii.
146. Wardlow (Joseph), 1846, overl. immig. with family. v. 328; owner of
Sonoma Co. lands in '47.
    Ware, 1847, blacksmith at S. Buen. W. (T. H.), 1845, purser of the
Warren '45-8. W. (Wm), 1832 (?), Irishman, who prob. came this year
from N. Mex., but possibly with Walker in '33. iii. 388, 391, 408. He worked
as distiller, tanner, and lumberman in the Sta Cruz region, his name often
appearing on Larkin's books and other records from '34. In '40 he was arrested.
iv. 17; but got a license to remain; and in '44 was naturalized. Wm H. Ware
testified in Alameda Co. '68 that he had been in Cal. since '32; and acc. to
the newspapers, Uncle Billy lived at his Zayante farm till his death in Feb.
'68. Warfield, 1841, one of Lieut Emmons' guides from Or., with wife and
child; perhaps remained. Waring (Richard), 1837, perhaps at Mont.
Warley (Alex. F.), 1847, mid. on the U.S. *Independence.* Warner (Caroline), 1846, of the Mormon colony, with 3 children. v. 547; she married at
S.F. a man named Thorp, and died some years before '84. W. (Cornelius),
1834, Amer. in a Mont. list. W. (John), 1840, Engl. exile, who returned
from S. Blas in '41. iv. 18, 33, 120.
    Warner (Jonathan Trumbull, known in Cal. as Juan José, or John J.),
1831, nat. of Conn., who went to St Louis and N. Mex. in '30, was a clerk
for Jed. Smith at the time of the latter's death, and came to Cal. in Jackson's
party of trappers. iii. 387, 405; iv. 264. He continued his occupation as a
trapper in the Cal. valleys during '31-3, iii. 357, 393, and settled, '34, at Los
Ang., where he is occasionally named in records of the following years, taking part with the vigilantes in '36, obtaining from the ayunt. a certificate of
long residence the same year, and in '38 having an arm broken in resisting a
search of his house during the political wars. iii. 566. In '39 he went east via
Acapulco, and thence overland to V. Cruz; and during his stay he delivered
at Rochester, N.Y., an interesting lecture on the far west, with special reference to a Pacific railroad, returning to Cal. in '41 on the *Julia Ann.* iv. 37,
223, 280, 566. In '43 he got a license to hunt goats and seals on the Sta B.
islands. iv. 642; and in '44, being naturalized, he was grantee of the Agua
Caliente rancho, S. Diego district, where he lived with his family from '45 to
'57, the place being known as Warner's rancho, and another, Camajal y el
Palomar. being perhaps granted in '46. iii. 611, 620; v. 619. Here Gen.

Kearny's force camped in '46 just before the fight of S. Pascual. v. 339; also the Mormon battalion in '47. v. 486; and here W. had much trouble with the Ind., notably at the time of the Pauma massacre. To a certain extent Warner was a confidential agent of Larkin for the U.S. in '46. v. 63. In his *Notes* of '45, Larkin described W. as a man of good information, addicted to politics, with some influence likely to increase. Since '57 he has resided at Los Ang., holding at times the positions of federal assessor and notary public, but much reduced financially. He has written much for the papers on topics of early history, respecting some phases of which, involving the trappers' explorations, he is recognized as one of the best authorities. He was selected to write the earliest annals for the centennial *Los Ang. Hist.*; and he has furnished for my use a brief *Biog. Sketch*, and a more extended book of *Reminiscences*, which I have often had occasion to cite. He still lives at Los Ang. in '85, age 78. About '37 he married Anita, daughter of Wm A. Gale, who died in '59, leaving a son.   W. (Richard), 1836, one of the Los Ang. vigilantes.   W. (Wm H.), 1846, capt. U.S. top. engineers, who came from N. Mex. with Kearny, and was wounded at S. Pascual. v. 336, 343–7. In '47 he came to Mont. and S.F., where he obtained a lot; and then engaged in trade with Sherman and Bestor at Coloma in '48, having previously made a survey of Sacramento City. He was killed in '49 by the Pit River Ind.

Warre (John), 1843, Sutter writes that he is not at N.Helv., but prob. at Sonoma.   Warren (James), 1847, Co. G, N.Y.Vol. (v. 499).   Warren (Wm), 1828 (?), negro known as 'Uncle Billy,' who died at S. José '75; said in newspaper sketches to have come in '28. iii. 178.   W. (Wm R.), 1836, nat. of Mass. who had lived at Hon. some 10 years or more, being known as 'Major.' iv. 118. He signed the memorial to Com. Kennedy at Mont. in Oct., unless Wm M. may have been another man. iv. 141; his name appears on Larkin's books in '37–42; and he was for some years in charge of Spear's store at Mont. In '40–1 he made a trip to Hon. and back. iv. 100, 567; and his daughter Mary, a quarter-breed Hawaiian, coming to Cal. about that time, married W. D. M. 'Howard,' q.v. Warren went back to Hon. and apparently died before '48.   Warrington, 1846 (?), connected with the legislature of '55. W. (John), 1847, Co. D, N.Y.Vol. (v. 499); at S. José '50; d. in Mendocino before '82.   W. (John H.), 1848, porter in U.S. naval store at Mont. '48–9.

Wasden (Stephen J.), 1844, Amer. who got a pass.   Washburn (Benjamin), 1844 (?), nat. of N.Y. who had lived in Ill. and Iowa, signed the call to foreigners at S. José in March '45, and prob. came overland in '43 or '44. iv. 453, 599. In April occurred the death of his wife, Elizabeth Woodred, at S. José; and in Nov. W. was ill at Perry's farm near N. Helv. In April '46 he was at S. José; and in July is named as one of the prisoners carried south by Castro. v. 136. I have no later record, but W. is thought by Given to have died at S. José.   W. (J.), 1845, at Sutter's fort; also at S. José. *Hall;* perhaps an error. iv. 578, 587.   W. (Lysander E.), 1847, Co. C, N.Y.Vol. (v. 499); at N. Helv. and Sonoma '47, taking part in a dramatic performance at Sonoma; capt. of Cal. volunteers in the war of '61–5; at S.F. '71–82.   Washington (Geo.), 1844, sailor on the *Monmouth.*

Watawha, or Wetowah, 1845, Delaware Ind. of Frémont's party; died in the service. iv. 583.   Waterfall (Christian), 1847, Co. F, 3d U.S. artill. (v. 518).   Waterman, 1841, mr of the *Braganza.* iv. 563; perhaps same as the following.   W. (Robert H.), 1848, nat. of N.Y., and for many years a sea-captain; founder of Fairfield, Solano Co., where he still lived in '79. His wife was Cordelia Sterling.   Waters (C.), 1848, from Hon.; clerk for Ross, Benton, & Co. at S.F.   W. (James), 1844, nat. of N.Y. and Rocky Mt trapper, who settled in S. Bern. Co., where he lived in '76.   Watkins (Adolphus), 1846, came from Hon. on the *Elizabeth;* owner of a S.F. lot '47.   W. (B. F.), 1847, from N.Y.; a fruit-grower at Sta Clara '76.   W. (Francis D.), 1847, owner of a S. F. lot; d. at Mission S. José '48, age 33.   W. (James T.), 1832 (?), com. of steamers from about '55, said to have touched at S. Diego in '32; died in China '67; a nat. of Md age 59. Also called James W., and accredited to '44. iv. 453.   W. (Richard), 1846, one of the party captured with

Alcalde Bartlett by Sanchez; in '82 a judge in Mono Co. Watmough (James H.), 1846, purser on the U.S. *Portsmouth*, who was com. of the Sta Clara garrison in Aug. and made a successful campaign against the Ind. on the Stanislaus. v. 102, 239-40, 294, 378, 567, 661. He was owner of a S.F. lot. v. 685; and in '47 bought land in Sonoma Co. from Vallejo, being in '53 an un-successful cl. for part of the Petaluma rancho. In later years he was a pay-master in the U.S.N., and in '77 chief of the dept of provisions and clothing. W. (Pendleton G.), 1846, mid. on the *Portsmouth*, who served in the S. José garrison under Lieut Pinckney.

Watson (Andrew), 1834, Engl. sailor named in several Mont. records, age 34; at S. José '36; on Larkin's books '39-41, and said by Farnham to have been arrested in '40. iii. 412; iv. 17. W. (Edward), 1828, Engl. carpenter who joined the comp. extranjera at Mont. in '32, and in '33 was baptized as José Eduardo María. iii. 178, 221. His name appears in various records from '34, and in '36 he is named in the Mont. padron as 31 years old, with a wife María Guadalupe Castillo, age 16; in '37 bought land of John Rainsford; in '40 was arrested but not exiled. iv. 17, 23; in '41 naturalized, being a trader and memb. of the ayunt. After the discov. of gold he went to the mines, and died at Dry Creek, near the Cosumnes in '48. W. (Francis), son of James, b. at Mont. about '30; educated at Hon. from '40. iii. 180; iv. 103. In the mines '48; married a daughter of Santiago Estrada; and in '75 still lived in Mont. Co. with 8 children. I have a brief *Narrative* from him. W. (Henry), 1846, Co. G, Cal. Bat. (v. 358), enlisting at S. José Nov. W. (Henry B.), 1846, lieut of marines on the U.S. *Portsmouth*, in com. of S.F. garrison; also with Stockton in the southern campaign of '46-7. v. 239-40, 295, 392, 436, 659.

Watson (James or David), 1824(?), Engl. sailor who left a whaler at Sta B. or S.F. about this time and settled as a trader at Mont. His original name seems to have been David, but was prob. called Santiago at baptism; also called Felipe Santiago, and in one record James Peter. ii. 495, 526. The 1st original record is in '30; in '32 he joined the comp. extranjera. iii. 221-2; and in '34 he had a wife, Mariana Escamilla, and 2 children—a number increased to 4 in '36, when he was a naturalized citizen, age 33. A lot was granted him in '35, and in '36 he bought a house of Luis Beltran, afterwards sold to Fuller and bought back. He was often a memb. of the ayunt. from '36, being a respected citizen and merchant frequently named in the records down to '48. iii. 675; iv. 117, 136, 218, 403, 653. Sir Geo. Simpson describes him as a Lon-doner from Redriff, whose father had been 'in the public line,' keeping the 'Noah's Hark between Globe Stairs and the 'Orse Ferry;' and Larkin, in his *Notes* of '45, as an uneducated, unambitious, honest man, who did not meddle in politics. He acquired a fortune, and is named by Willey and others in '49 as a very generous man. About '50 he bought the S. Benito rancho, for which he was successful claimant. iv. 655; but he was ruined by the drought of '63, and died the same year. His children were Francis b. abt '30; Catalina in '33; Tomás in '35 (later sheriff of Mont. where he still lived in '75); and Santiago Jr, born in '36. W. (J. B.), 1848, passp. from Hon. W. (J. M.), 1847, lieut U.S.N., who brought despatches to Gen. Kearny; later in com. of the *Erie;* d. at Vallejo '73, age 66. W. (Wm), 1836, Engl. lumberman in Mont. dist, age 30. W. (Wm), 1847, at Benicia. v. 673; at Napa '48. Watt (James), 1836, juez de campo at Mont. iii. 675; 'Santiago Guat,' prob. 'Wat-son,' q.v.; and Felipe Guati, an Engl. catholic mariner, at Mont. in '29, age 25, was also prob. the same 'Watson.' Watts (John), 1847, Co. B, Morm. Bat. (v. 469); reënl.; a man of the same name at S. José '50. W. (Wm), 1827, doubtful name of sup. of the *Karimoko*. iii. 147. W. (Wm), 1841, doubtful name at Mont. *Toomes.* Watty, 1845, at Larkin's soap-factory. Wayne (W.A.), 1845, lieut on the U.S. *Savannah.*

Weaitz (John), 1846, Co. B, Cal. Bat. (v. 358), enlisting at Mont. Oct. Weaver, 1831, a trapper, said by Nidever to have been in Young's party; called Powell W. by Dye. iii. 388; perhaps Pauline W., a noted mountain man of Ariz. later. He was also possibly the man who served as guide to the

Morm. Bat. v. 483; and a Paulino W. is named at S. Bern. in '46, age 40.
W. (Daniel), 1846, Co. C, 1st U.S. dragoons (v. 336).   W. (Franklin), 1847,
Co. A, Morm. Bat. (v. 469); in Utah '81; married Miss R. Reed at S.F. '48.
W. (M.), 1846, doubtful name in a Los Ang. list.   W. (Miles), 1847, Co. A,
Morm. Bat. (v. 469).   W. (Vance), 1846, Co. E, Cal. Bat. (v. 358), enlist-
ing at Sonoma in Oct.; Cal. claim (v. 462).   W. (Wm E.), 1848, part owner
of the S.F. *Californian;* perhaps same as the following.   W. (Wm J.), 1847,
Co. C, N.Y.Vol. (v. 499); a printer.   Webb (Chas Y.), 1847, Co. A, Morm.
Bat. (v. 469); at Parowan, Utah, '81.   W. (Wm), 1832, memb. of the comp.
extranjera. iii. 221; still at Mont. '33-4.
    Weber (Charles M.), 1841, nat. of Germany, who came to N. Orleans in
'36, and in '41 was an overl. immig. of the Bartleson party from St Louis.
He worked through the winter for Sutter, who had signed his bond on arrival. iv. 270, 275, 279; and in '42 settled at S. José as trader, miller, baker,
and a little later salt-producer and shoemaker, also acquiring land and live-
stock, all in partnership with Wm Gulnac. In '43 they obtained, in G.'s
name, as W. was not naturalized till '44, a grant of the Campo de los Franceses rancho, G.'s share of which was bought by W. in '45. Weber was an
active business man, and well liked at this time by the Californians, to whom
he afforded valuable support in their movement of '44 against Micheltorena's cholos, raising a comp. of foreign volunteers, being imprisoned at Sutter's fort on account of his efforts for his country without regard to the Swiss
adventurer's personal schemes, being made capt. of militia in '45, and taking
a prominent part in issuing the call for an assembly of foreign residents. iv.
462, 468-9, 483, 599, 604-5. His position in all these matters was consistent
and praiseworthy, though his influence at this time and his prominence in
events of the next year have been grossly exaggerated in the newspapers and
county histories of late years. In '46 Weber was in sympathy with Larkin's
plans rather than with those of the filibusters; but on hearing of the Bear
rising he seems to have taken some steps for the protection of the settlers
south of the bay, and on the discovery of his plans was arrested by Castro,
who carried him south as a prisoner, but released him on leaving Cal. for
Mex. I am inclined to think, however, that Castro did this at the request
of W., who, having made enemies on both sides of the pending troubles,
deemed it wise to absent himself for a time. v. 16, 136-7, 245, 277. He returned in Oct. in time to engage actively, to the great displeasure of many
Californians, in the work of collecting horses and supplies for the Cal. Bat.,
in which he declined to serve on account of hostility to Frémont; but was
made capt. of volunteers and took part in the final campaign against Sanchez,
being ordered to discharge his men and thanked for past services in Feb. '47.
v. 294-5, 377-8, 380, 382, 661. In '47 he settled on his French Camp rancho,
and founded a settlement which he afterwards had laid out as a town and
named Stockton. v. 674-5. In '48-9 he added to his wealth by successful
gold-mining, with the aid of Ind., at Weber Creek and elsewhere; and his
lands were vastly increased in value during the flush times. He was claimant
for Campo de los Franceses and Cañada de S. Felipe. iii. 677, 711; iv. 671.
He spent the rest of his life at Stockton, where he died in '81 at the age of 67,
leaving a widow, the daughter of Martin Murphy, and 3 children. Weber
was an intelligent, energetic, and honorable man of business; generous in his
many gifts to his town and to his friends; but in his later life eccentric to the
verge of insanity, morbidly sensitive, avoiding his fellow-men.   There is
nothing apparent in his record, that of a successful man, who was neither the
author nor victim of any great wrongs, to account for his peculiarities. *Tinkham's Hist. of Stockton* contains a portrait, and is the best source of information outside of original records.   An early MS. copy of *Halleck's Land Laws,*
to which were appended some of Weber's correspondence of considerable interest, was for a short time in my possession.   W. (John), 1847, of N.Y.
Vol.(?); at S.F. '74.   Webster (Charles A.), 1847, Co. G, N.Y. Vol. (v. 499);
d. at Los Ang. '47.   W. (Ed. C.), 1848, at Mont.   W. (John H.) 1847, Co.
F, N.Y. Vol. (v. 499); notary at Stockton, where he died in '81, leaving a
family.

Weed (John W.), 1841, Amer. passenger on the *Julia Ann*, who came from N.Y. for his health, and went back in '42. iv. 566. Weeks (Elbert), 1847, Co. B, N.Y. Vol. (v. 499); d. before '82. Weeks (James W.), 1831, Engl. sailor who deserted from the whaler *Fanny*, at S.F. in Oct., while the crew were occupied in cutting wood at Pt Quintin. iii. 405. Spending some time at Read's, and then working for the Castros at S. Pablo, he lived for some months on the beach at S.F. trying with others to repair an old boat, tried a ranchero's life with Narvaez in Sta Clara Valley, cooked for a while in the Pulgas redwoods, joined Ewing Young's trappers, and returned via Ross to the redwoods. In '40 he was arrested but not exiled, having married a native wife. iv. 9, 17, 23; in '41-5 lived at Sta Cruz, iv. 280, 356, 663, being named in the padron of '45, age 32, wife Ramona Pinto, child. María Ana b. '41, Blas Antonio '43, Teodoro '44. He signed the S. José call to foreigners. iv. 599; in '46 was coroner in the Naile case. v. 641; was clerk for Alcalde Stokes and in charge of the archives, and later member of the council. v. 664; and in '47-8 alcalde of S. José. v. 662; went to the mines in '48; was sec. of the prefecture in '49; and continued to live in Sta Clara Co., being cl. for a part of S. Antonio rancho. In '77 he wrote for me his *Reminiscences*, a detailed narrative of his career in early times; and having fulfilled this part of his destiny, he died in '81, leaving 4 sons. He was an intelligent man with but slight education, of good character, though at times addicted to intemperance. Wehler (Edward), 1847, musician of N.Y. Vol. (v. 499).

Weidney (Anthony), 1847, Co. K, N. Y. Vol. (v. 499). Weifenback (Philip), 1847, Co. E, ditto. Weimar (James), see 'Wimmer.' Weir (James), 1847, Co. F, 3d U.S. artill. (v. 518). W. (Thomas), 1847, Co. A, Morm. Bat. (v. 469); employed by Sutter as a tanner. Weirick (Wm H.), 1847, lieut Co. F, G, N.Y. Vol. v. 504. Weirgen (Christian), 1847, Co. A, ditto. Weiss (Wm), 1847, Co. B, ditto; at S.F. '83. Weit (John), 1847, Co. F, 3d U.S. artill. v. 518.

Welburn (Benj.), see 'Washburn,' signer of the S. José call to foreigners of '45, the name being incorrectly given in several county histories. Welch, see 'Welsh.' Welder (Anthony), 1847, Co. C, N.Y. Vol. (v. 499). Weldon (Peter), 1835, Amer. carpenter, age 24, who came on the *Framen* (?); an anabaptist who joined Russell in his exped. from S. Diego to the Colorado in '36. iii. 613. Weller (C. M.), 1846, Cal. claim $297 (v. 462); prob. an error for 'Weber.' W. (Edward H.), 1847, Co. A, N.Y. Vol. (v. 499); at S.F. '71-4. Wells, 1847, married by Sutter and remarried at Sta Clara. *Alexander;* prob. 'West.' W., 1848, on the *Sagadahoc* from Hon.; perhaps Robert. W. (Benj. F.), 1846, mid. on the U.S. *Congress;* acting lieut in Stockton's Bat. '46-7. v. 386. W. (David), 1848, came from Or. and settled in S. Joaq. Co. W. (Robert), 1847, from N.Y. by sea; owner of S.F. lot; of firm W. & Co., merchants at S.F.; still here in '54. W. (Thos J.), 1847, Co. G, N.Y. Vol. (v. 499); in N.Y. '71-82. W. (Wm M.), 1847, Co. G, ditto. Welsh, 1847, doubtful name or date of a justice at S. Buen. W. (Charles), 1848, Amer. sea capt. said to have been educated in Spain and to have served in the Span. mail service; d. at S.F. '83. He married a sister of Philip A. Roach. W. (John H.), 1847, Co. E, N.Y. Vol. (v. 499); in N.Y. '71-84. W. (Wm), 1821, Scotch sailor on the *Lady Blackwood* discharged at Bodega. ii. 478. He was at Los Ang. '29-30. ii. 558; is often named in northern records from '30. ii. 616; lived at S. José from '32, and in '44 was grantee of Las Juntas, Contra Costa. iv. 671. He seems to have been a brother-in-law of James A. Forbes, and to have been living in the S. José district '47; but died before '52, when the rancho was claimed by the admin. of his estate. He left a wife and 8 children.

Wescott (Joseph F. R.), 1836, nat. of Conn., baptized at S. Rafael in Oct. iv. 118. In '42 Francis Wescott is named as gunsmith of the S.F. comp.; and in '48 Conway & W. were proprietors of the Colonnade House at S.F., W. leaving his debtors in the lurch; perhaps not he of '36. v. 683. Wesley, 1847, visitor at Sutter's fort. West (Benj.), 1847, Co. E, Morm. Bat., reënl. (v. 469). W. (Henry S.), 1843, mr of the *Rafak.* iv. 568. W. (T.), 1846,

Fauntleroy's dragoons (v. 232, 247), enlisting at Mont. July.   W. (Thomas), 1846, overl. immig. with Bryant, sometime capt. of the party, accompanied by his wife and 4 sons. v. 528. He settled at S. José, and acc. to Hittell became wealthy and went east before '60. His sons Francis T. and Thomas M. kept a livery-stable at S. José in '47. Another, Wm T., served in Co. B, artill. Cal. Bat. (v. 358); and the 4th was Geo. R. The grave of Ann W. was passed on the overl. route by Bigler in '47.   W. (Thos J.), 1847, Co. G, N. Y. Vol. (v. 499); d. before '82.   W. (Wm C.), 1846, Co. C, 1st U.S. dragoons (v. 336); killed at S. Pascual. v. 346.

West (Wm Mark), 1832, Engl. carpenter, lumberman, and farmer, who had lived 7 years in Mex. territory before coming to Cal. iii. 408. In '34 he obtained naturalization, having been baptized at Sta Cruz, and owning property to the value of $1,500. From '33 he appears on Larkin's books, generally as a lumberman working with Trevethan in the redwoods. In the Mont. padron of '36 he is named as 40 years old, wife Guadalupe Vasquez, child María Luisa b. '33. In '40, being arrested but not exiled, he was grantee of the S. Miguel rancho, Sonoma, and of Llano de Sta Rosa in '44. iii. 713; iv. 17, 23, 673. I have no record of him after '48, but he died before '52, when his widow appears as cl. for the rancho, on which a stream still bears the name of Mark West Creek.   Westfall (Jacob), 1846, Co. C, 1st U.S. dragoons (v. 336).   Westgate (Francis J.), 1839, blacksmith and carpenter at Sonoma and S.F. '39–42, working for Spear & Hinckley and Salv. Vallejo. iv. 119; perhaps the man named as having lived at Pt Reyes in '46.   W. (Obadiah), 1833, gunsmith at S.F.; perhaps same as preceding.   Westlake (Richard), 1840, one of the exiles to S. Blas who did not return. iv. 18.   Weston, 1846, mr of the *Wm Neilson*. v. 581.   Wetmarsh, see 'Whitmarsh.'   Wetmore (C. E.), 1848, S.F. merchant of firm W. & Gilman. v. 680; member of the council '49; settled at Benicia with his wife. Wetowah, see 'Watawha.' Wettermark (Chas P.), 1847, Co. A, N.Y.Vol. (v. 499).   Weyland (John), 1848, at S.F., advertising tents for sale.

Whalen (John), 1847, musician of N.Y.Vol. (v. 499); d. at Los Ang. '53. Whally (Scotch), 1840(?), a man known only by this name, who lived for several years in the redwoods near Mont., engaged in making shingles. iv. 120. About '45 he was killed by the Tulare Ind.   Wheeler (Alfred), 1847 (?), nat. of N.Y., and memb. of 1st Cal. legislature. *Anaheim Gazette*, Oct. 16. '75. W. (Geo.), 1848, on roll of Soc. Cal. Pion.   W. (Henry), 1847, Co. C, Morm. Bat. (v. 469); reënl.   W. (John), 1847, Co. K, N. Y. Vol. (v. 499).   W. (John L.), 1847, Co. B, Morm. Bat. (v. 469); reënl.   W. (Merrill W.), 1847, Co. A, ditto.   W. (Wm), 1845, boy on the *Warren*, living at S. José '77, when he gave me a narrative on the *Loss of the Warren's Launch* in '46. iv. 587; v. 384.   W. (Wm H. H.), 1847, Co. D, N.Y.Vol. (v. 499); d. in L. Cal. '48. Wheelock (Lyman), 1847, Co. K, ditto.

Whisman (Andrew), 1847, nat. of Mo., who came overl. with his father, John W. (?), and in '47–8 kept an inn bet. S. José and S.F.; later a farmer in Sta Clara and Alameda counties. He died at Harrisburg '79. His 1st wife was Serelda Lynn, by whom he had 11 children; the 2d Catherine Smith '72.   W. (John), 1848, cousin of J. W. at Sta Clara.   W. (John W.), 1847, nat. of Va and overl. immig. with wife and son, settling in Sta Clara.   Whistler (Geo. R.), 1846(?), said to have come as a soldier; later in the mines; murdered in Ariz. '74; known as Geo. Reese.   Whitaker, 1845, doubtful name of an overl. immig. iv. 578.   W. (Amison), 1847, Co. F, N.Y.Vol. (v. 499); at Sac. '82.   W. (John Geo.), 1845, mid. on the U.S. *Savannah, Columbus,* and *Warren* '45–8.   Whitcomb (Wm N.), 1847 (?), said to have come with Capt. Brackett's comp. in '46; committed suicide at Napa in '71. *N. Register.*

White, 1845, named as having come with McDowell and also with Frémont. iv. 578, 583.   W., 1847, at Stockton '47–8.   W. (Arthur F.), 1845, at Mont. from R.I.; bought goods from the wreck of the *Star of the West.* W. (Charles), 1846, overl. immig. who settled with his wife at S. José, where he was councilman in '46 and alcalde in '48–9, becoming the owner of a large estate and cl. for Arroyo de S.Antonio. He was killed in the *Jenny Lind* explosion in '53; his widow married Gen. C. Allen, and was the cl. for several ranchos. iii. 678, 711-12; iv. 655; v. 529, 662, 664. His son, Chas E., was a lawyer at S. José '81. W. (Chris. S.), 1847, Co. B, N.Y.Vol. (v. 499). W. (Henry), 1847, Co. F, 3d U.S. artill. (v. 518); d. before '82. W. (J.), 1846, Co. F, Cal. Bat. (v. 358), enlisting at S. Juan in Oct. W. (J.), 1848, passp. from Hon. W. (John), 1846, Co. C, 1st U.S. dragoons (v. 336). W. (John C.), 1847, Co. C, Morm. Bat. (v. 469). W. (Joseph), 1847, Co. A, ditto. W. (Joseph), 1848 (?), trapper in the mines with Brooks who claimed to have come with Capt. Weber '41 (?).

White (Michael), 1829, Engl. or Irish sailor who came from Hon. on the *Dolly* or *Dhaulle.* iii. 179; having touched on the L. Cal. coast in '17, and sailed, sometimes as mate and mr, on Mex. and Hawaiian vessels from that date according to his own statement. He settled at Sta B., where he built a schooner in '30. ii. 573; iii. 140. Except from his own testimony nothing is known of him till '36, when his name appears in a Los Ang. list as an Irishman aged 30; though he may have been the White accused of smuggling at S.F. in '33. iii. 393. He says he made a trip to Mazatlan in the schr *Guadalupe,* which he had built for S.Gabriel mission, returning in '32, marrying María del Rosario Guillen, daughter of the famous old woman Eulalia Perez, opening a little store at Los Nietos, and keeping aloof from politics. In '38 he signed a petition against Carrillo. iii. 565; and in '39 went to N. Mex., but returned with the Workman party in '41. iv. 278. In '43 he was grantee of Muscupiabe rancho and a S. Gabriel lot. iv. 635, 637; served in the foreign comp. against Micheltorena '45. iv. 495, 595; and was one of the Chino prisoners in '46. v. 314. In later years he continued to live at S. Gabriel; was the successful cl. for his lands, which, however, in one way or another he finally lost; and occasionally indulged in a sea voyage. In '77, at the age of 75, somewhat feeble in health and very poor, having a large family of children and grandchildren, Miguel Blanco gave me his interesting reminiscences of *Cal. All the Way Back to '28.* His memory was good, and he seemed to be a truthful man. He died in or before '85. W. (Milton), 1840, one of the exiles to S. Blas, arrested in the south; did not return. iv. 14, 18. W. (Moses), 1847, Co. E, N. Y. Vol. (v. 499). W. (Philander), 1847, Co. K, ditto. W. (Sam. S.), 1847, Co. A, Morm. Bat. (v. 469); in Sutter's employ '47-8; at Pleasant Grove, Utah, '81. W. (Thomas), 1840, deserter from the *St Louis,* who became a lumberman, married, and in '48 lived on the Salinas. He died about '50. iv. 120. W. (Wm), 1836, named in Larkin's books. W. (Wm), 1847, shoemaker in Sutter's employ. W. (W.), 1846, Co. F, Cal. Bat. (v. 358), enlisting at S. Juan Nov.; perhaps same as one or both of the preceding. Whitehouse (Benj.), 1847, Co. B, N.Y.Vol. (v. 499); perhaps the 'Dad' W. at Stockton '48-9; d. at S.F. after '50. W. (Geo. W.), 1846, Co. C, 1st U.S. dragoons (v. 336); at Los Ang. '79. W. (Joseph), 1840, one of the exiles to S. Blas who did not return. iv. 18. Whitehurst, 1846, sergt, killed at S. Pascual (?). *Frémont Court-martial,* 169. See 'Whitness.' Whiteman (Wm), 1846, overl. immig. who settled at S. José with his family; drowned in the S. Joaq. River '48. His widow lived at S. José '77, in the house built by W. in '46. A daughter was the wife of Waldo Lowe. A son, John T., who came as a child in '46, was a farmer in Sta Clara Co., and died at S. Luis Ob. in '77, leaving a widow. Whiting (Wm J.), 1830, trader on the coast '30-1. Whitlock (Geo. W.), 1847, clerk for Wm H. Davis '47-9. v. 651; sergt of S.F. guard '48; at Sac. about '74-5. W. (Jacob H.), 1847, Co. A, N.Y.Vol. (v. 499); d. at S.F. '49. W. (Mervin R.), 1847, ditto; drowned in S. Joaq. River '49. Whitmarsh (James), 1833, Amer. sailor who came from Mazatlan on the *Sta Bárbara.* iii. 409. In '37 a lumberman near S. Rafael; passp. in '40. Called 'Wetmarsh' and 'Webmarch,' but I have his autograph. Whitness (Wm), 1846, sergt Co. K, 1st U.S. dragoons, killed at S. Pascual. v. 346; perhaps his name was 'Whitress;' also called 'Whitehurst.' Whitney (Francis T.), 1847, Co. B, Morm. Bat. (v. 469). W. (Wm), 1848, nat. of Engl., who came from Or. to the mines, and went back; died at Butterville, Or., '78. Whittaker (Robert), 1845, boatswain on the

U.S. *Portsmouth;* owner of a S.F. lot '46. v. 685. Whittemore, 1810, mr of the *Avon* and *Charon* '10–14; trader and fur-hunter. ii. 96, 267, 282, 328. Whittle, 1846, named as a physician at the Mont. hospital. W. (W.), 1815 (?), said to be mentioned in a doc. of '35, in the Los Ang. arch., as a resid. for 20 years, doubtless an error. My copy makes the name 'Wittle,' and the time 25 years, perhaps another error. Whittmer (L. C.), 1847, at Sutter's fort from Sonoma, Sept. Whitton (1845), one of Frémont's men, who perhaps did not come to Cal. iv. 583. W. (Ezekiel or Jerry), 1834, Amer. named on Larkin's books at Mont. '34–6. iii. 412. Whitworth (Wm), 1847, Co. E, Morm. Bat. (v. 469).

Widger (Benj.), 1847, Co. I, N.Y.Vol. (v. 499). Wierzbicki (Felix P.), 1847, Co. H, ditto; a Polish physician and author; owner of lots and participant in a political meeting at S.F. '47. v. 455. In '48 he sends Gen. Vallejo a copy of his work entitled *The Ideal Man.* He was also the author of *California as It is and as It may be, or A Guide to the Gold Region,* S.F., 1849, 8vo, 60 pp., published in 2 editions by Washington Bartlett (mayor of S.F. as I write, in '85), and the 1st book ever printed in this city. Dr W. died at S. F. in '60. Wiggins (Wm), 1840, nat. of N.Y., who crossed the plains from Mo. to Or. in '39 and come to Cal. on the *Lausanne,* landing at Bodega and proceeding to Sutter's fort, and thence to Marsh's rancho. iv. 120–1, 136, 173. In '42–4 he was with Graham at Sta Cruz; served in Gantt's comp. to support Micheltorena in '45. iv. 486; is named in the Branciforte padron of '45 as 29 years old and single; went east overland in '46; returned at the head of an immig. party in '47, but taking a cut-off was obliged, after great dangers, to go to Or. v. 556; and came down to Cal. on the *Henry* in '48. He was perhaps the man who is named at Benicia in '48. v. 673; is said to have owned at one time part of the Capitancillos rancho, Sta Clara Co.; lived at S. Juan B. '53–68, and later at Mont., where in '77 he gave me his *Reminiscences.* He died at S. José in '80, at the age of 63. He was called 'doctor,' had no family, and was a man of somewhat eccentric ways. Wight (David), 1847, carpenter and lumberman at Mont. '47–8. W. (Randolph H.), 1848, nat. of N.Y., who came from Or. on the *Sterling,* working in the mines, and going east in '49. He came back in '52 to settle in Contra Costa, where he lived in '82 with wife and two daughters. Wigman (Lewis), 1845, blacksmith and trader at Mont., S.F., and Sutter's fort '45–8, serving also in Fauntleroy's dragoons '48. iv. 578, 587; (v. 232, 247).

Wilber (James H.), 1847, Methodist preacher, touching at S.F. on his way to Or. on the *Whiton,* who organized a Sunday-school at S. F. v. 657. W. (Jacob), 1846, Co. C, 1st U.S. dragoons (v. 336). Wilbur, 1846, mr of the *Magnet.* v. 579. W., 1848, in charge of Sutter's launch. W. (Jeremiah P.), 1846 (?), nat. of Conn.; owner of S. F. lots '48; married in '48 to Amanda Hoit; died at S.F. '64. Wilcox (Edward), 1847, Co. B, Morm. Bat. (v. 469); nat. of Pa who went to the mines, and in '52–81 was a farmer in Mont. Co. W. (Frank), 1846, Co. F, Cal. Bat. (v. 358), enlisting at S. Juan Oct. W. (Henry), 1847, Co. B, Morm. Bat. (v. 469). W. (James Smith), 1816, Amer. mr of the *Caminante,* or *Traveller,* '16–17, who was suspected of revolutionary designs, and wished to marry Concepcion Argüello. ii. 78, 216–17, 285–7, 291, 310, 362, 365, 382, 399. W. (Matthew), 1847, Co. C, Morm. Bat. (v. 469). Wilder (Peter), 1848, voter at S. Diego, and perhaps the P. Wilde of '44 at S.D., hired by Capt. Peterson of the *Admittance* to look for deserters. Wiley (James), 1848, lieut of marines at Mont.; passp. from Hon. Wilkes (Charles), 1841, lieut U.S.N. and com. of the U.S. ex. ex., and author of the *Narrative* of that exped., a work that, as far as Cal. is concerned, cannot be very highly praised. iv. 241–8; also iv. 2, 6, 20, 191, 208–9, 214, 227, 434, 569, 665. W. (E. P.), 1847, owner of S.F. lot. W. (James), 1846, came to S. José. *Hall;* also J.P.W., named at S. José '47. W. (John), 1847, Co. K, N.Y.Vol. (v. 499).

Wilkin (David), 1847, sergt Co. C, Morm. Bat. v. 477; at Pioche, Nev., '82. Wilkins (C. P.), 1848, in Q. M. dept Los Ang.; prob. same as preceding. W. (Edward), 1847, at Sutter's fort. Wilkinson, 1848, went from

Mont. to the mines with Colton; said to be a son of a U.S. minister to Russia.
W. (James), 1831, named by Dye and Nidever as one of Young's trappers;
perhaps did not come to Cal. iii. 388.   W. (John), 1845, act. mr of the U.S.
Portsmouth.   Willard, 1843, nat. of Mass. and mate under Capt. Cooper,
who had been naturalized and got a land grant in the Sac. Val. Doubtful
mention by Thomes. W. (Fannie), 1846 (?), nat. of Mass. Married later to
Alfred Baldwin of Sta Cruz.   W. (Henry or Isaac), 1847, Co, A, N.Y.Vol.
(v. 499); miner in '48–9; farmer and trader in Marin Co. to '56; and later a
farmer in Mendocino, living at Sanel in '80 with wife and 10 children.
Willey (Jeremiah), 1847, Co. A, Morm. Bat. (v. 469).   Willhart (Louis),
1847, Co. C, N.Y.Vol. (v. 499).
    William, 1845, Chinook Ind. of Frémont's party; in Sta B. garrison. v.
316.   Williams, 1846, with Kearny from N. Mex. (v. 337); perhaps Geo. N.
W., 1846, Amer. at S. Luis Ob. v. 639.   W., 1848, arrested at S. José. v.
663.   W. (Aaron W.), 1828, mr of the *Clio.* iii. 146, 165.   W. (Albert),
1840, one of the exiles to S.Blas, who did not return. iv. 14, 18.   W. (Alonzo),
1846, applicant for land at S. José. *Sta Clara Co. Hist.*, 331.   W. (Alex.),
1836, Engl. sailor who landed at Sta B. from a whaler.   W. (B.), 1837, said
to have been one of the party driving cattle to Or. iv. 85.   W. (Baylis),
1846, one of the Donner party from Ill., who died in the Sierra. His half-
sister, Eliza, survived, and in '49 was living at S. José, married, but I do not
know what became of her. v. 530, 533–4.   W. (Benj.), 1847, owner of a S.
F. lot, perhaps at Sutter's fort '48, and on the first jury at S. José '48.   W.
(Charles), 1839, at Mont.; one of the exiles of '40 who did not return. v. 18.
W. (Edward), 1847, lieut of Co. E, N.Y.Vol. v. 504; in '82 a resid. of Oakland.   W. (Elonzo), 1846, came from N. Helv. to S. Juan B. in Jan.; served
in Fauntleroy dragoons (v. 232, 247); prob. same as Alonzo above.   W.
(Geo.), 1829 (?), Engl. sawyer named in Mont. lists of '34, who in '41 claimed a
resid. of 12 years; at S.F. '42, age 39. iii. 179; possibly same as the following.   W. (Geo.), 1832, nat. of Demerara, naturalized in '41, claiming a resid.
of 9 years. iii. 408.   W. (Geo.), 1845, overl. immig., perhaps of the Grigsby-
Ide party. iv. 579; settled at Sta Cruz and served in the Cal. Bat. '46. (v.
358).   W. (Geo. N.), 1846, Co. C, 1st. U.S. dragoons (v. 336).   W. (Henry
E.), 1846, Fauntleroy's dragoons (v. 232, 247).
    Williams (Isaac), 1832, nat. of N.Y. and one of Young's trappers from
N. Mex., where he had lived several years. iii. 388, 408. He settled at Los
Ang. as a trader, though occupied for some years as a hunter; built a house
in '34; aided in '35 in removing the Ind. from S. Nicolás Isl. iii. 361, 652; is
named in lists of '36 as 25, 38, and 50 years of age, obtaining that year a
certificate of residence from the ayunt. and joining the vigilance com. (iii.
430). He was generally known in Cal. as Julian W., often signing in that
way. In '39 he was naturalized, and about this time married María de Jesus,
daughter of Antonio M. Lugo, becoming the owner of the Chino rancho
granted to Lugo in '41, and being himself the grantee of an addition to the
rancho in '43. iv. 634, 117. His house in town was sold to the city govt. In
'46 he proposed to build a fort at the Cajon. v. 37; on the fight at Chino,
when W. was taken prisoner, see v. 312–14. He had a Cal. claim for property
destroyed for $133,000, which was not allowed (v. 462). In '47 he advertised
in the *Californian* for a large no. of men to build an adobe fence round his
rancho; and Col. Coutts says that the men all ran away to the mines in '48
just before the work was completed. He died in '56 at the age of '57, leaving
as heiresses of his large estate two daughters, María Merced, wife of John
Rains, and Francisca, wife of Robert Carlisle. His wife had died in '42, leaving the 2 daughters and apparently a son. Col. Williams was one of the typi-
cal rancheros of southern Cal., enterprising, hospitable, and generally of good
repute.   W. (Isaac), 1843, overl. imming. of the Chiles-Walker party, iv.
393–4, 400, who settled at Sta Cruz and later moved to Los Ang., where he
died about '70.   W. (James), 1843, brother of Isaac and memb. of the same
party. iv. 393–4, 400. He also settled at Sta Cruz as a lumberman and blacksmith, being naturalized in '45, and married by Larkin in Aug. to Mary Pat-

terson. In '46 he killed Henry Naile. v. 641; and is often named in records of '47-8, being a miner in the latter year. In '52 he was cl. for ranchos in Sta Cruz and the Sac. Val. iii. 677; iv. 670; and he died at Sta Cruz in '58 at the age of 45. W. (James V.), 1847, Co. E, Morm. Bat. (v. 469); reënl.; in Utah '82. W. (J. H.), 1848, passp. from Hon. W. (John), 1826, sailor on the *Rover*. W. (John), 1846, doubtful name of an overl. immig. v. 529.

Williams (John S.), 1843, brother of Isaac and James, and overl. immig. of the Chiles party. iv. 393-4, 400. He was a tanner by trade, and I find no original record of his presence till '45, when he is named in the Branciforte padron as 26 years old (Isabel and Esculla Williams living with him—prob. the Cal. rendering of Isaac and Squire!), and is mentioned at Sutter's fort. In Feb. '46 he asked for naturalization, continuing to work for Sutter, but travelling much up and down the valley, visiting Mont. and Sta Cruz, and perhaps serving with the Bears. v. 167. In '47, besides buying lots and building at Benicia, v. 672, he took charge of Larkin's rancho in Colusa, and was married in June to María Louisa, daughter of Joseph Gordon, at Wm Gordon's place on Cache Creek, by Alcalde Ide. I have many of his original letters. He went to the mines in '48; moved to Butte Co. in '49; and died in May of that year. His widow married Lindsay Carson in '50, was one of the cl. for the Arroyo Chico rancho '52, and still lived in Sonoma Co. '80. A son, John S., Jr, was born in Cal. '48, and was also one of the claimants. He went east, and in '70-80 lived in Texas. W. (N. L.), 1848, passp. from Hon. W. (Richard), 1846, sergt Co. C, 1st U.S. dragoons (v. 336), 341. W. (Robert), 1844, doubtful name of a man who came with his family. *Ariz. Hist.*, 268. W. (Squire), 1843, brother of John S. and James. v. 393-4, 400; Co. F, Cal. Bat. (v. 358); died at the Yuba mines '48; yet named as a cl. for Arroyo de la Laguna in '52. iii. 677. W. (S. H.), 1848, of S. H. W. & Co. at S.F. v. 678. W. (Thomas), 1847, sergt Co. D, Morm. Bat. v. 477, 481; perhaps did not come to Cal. W. (Wm), 1838, Engl. sailor who landed at S. Diego. iv. 119; in charge of Capt. Fitch's house '40; sub-Ind. agent at S. Luis Rey '48. v. 621-2; claimant for Valle de las Viejas '52. v. 619. W. (Wm H.), 1847, Co. A, N.Y.Vol. (v. 499); at Nyack, N.Y., '74-84.

Williamson (Benj.), 1846, Co. B, Cal. Bat. (v. 358), enlisting at Mont. Nov. W. (Daniel or David), 1846, Co. F, ditto, enlisting at S. Juan Oct.; at S. José '48; d. in '49. *Swan*. W. (James), 1826, on the *Rover*. W. (J. C.), 1838 (?), nat. of Mass., said to have come via N. Mex. in '38, iv. 119, and, returning, to have started in '41 with his family, killed by Ind. on the way. Then he turned Ind.-fighter; was with Frémont in '46 (?); was a sharpshooter in the war of '61-5; a scout under Custer later; then a hunter in Cal. known as Grizzly Dan; at Oroville '80. *Sac. Union*, July 3, '80. How much truth there may be in all this I do not know. W. (Thomas), 1833, at Mont. '33-4. W. (Thomas D.), 1847, Co. K, N.Y.Vol. (v. 499); at Sta Rosa '71-4; d. before '80. Willie (Henry), 1847, Co. H, ditto.

Willis (Ira), 1847, Co. B, Morm. Bat. (v. 469); later in Sutter's service, and at the Coloma mill when gold was found. W. (Otis W.), 1847, Co. F, N.Y.Vol. (v. 499); at S. Andrés '74. W. (Wm), 1827 (?), Englishman, owning cattle and applying for land at S. José in '28. ii. 595, 605; iii. 178. In '30 Wm With got permission to keep cattle at Mt Diablo. ii. 602. As Wilk and Villa he is named in '34, age 31, with wife and 3 children. In '41 Guillermo Wil is named in the S. José padron as an Amer., age 46, wife María Ant. Galindo, child. Guillermo b. '33, Concepcion '28, and Anastasio '30. There is also a Julian Wil named as a militiaman of S.F. in '37. There is a strange lack of definite information about this Wm Willis. W. (W. S. S.), 1847, known as Sidney W.; Co. B, Morm. Bat. (v. 469); in Sutter's employ '47-8, and at the Coloma mill when gold was discovered. Wilmot (James), 1845, perhaps overl. immig. of the Grigsby-Ide party. iv. 579; named at Sutter's fort '46. W. (Lewis), 1846, Cal. Bat. (v. 358); also Lewis A. W., sailor on the *Elizabeth* '48. Wilmoth (Geo.), 1845, boatswain on the U.S. *Savannah*. Wilson, 1845, in Sutter's employ; went east with Clyman in '46. v. 526. W., 1847, at S.F. from Hon., with wife and 2 children, on the *Julia*. W., 1847, owner of land at Benicia. W., 1848, at S.F. from Tahiti. W., 1848, of Hood & W., carpenters at S.F. v. 684. W. (A.), 1824, sailor on the *Rover*. W. (Alfred G.), 1847, Co. A, Morm. Bat. (v. 469); at Moab, Utah, '81. W. (Amariah), 1847, owner of S.F. lots. W. (Alvin), 1840, nat. of Conn., who landed from Capt. Hinckley's vessel and became a lumberman in the Sta Cruz district. He was arrested with the other foreigners, but not exiled; and in '42 signed an appeal to the U.S. govt. He was killed by Ind. near Gilroy in July '44. W. (B.), 1848, at Hon. from S.F., on the *Julian*.

Wilson (Benj. Davis), 1841, known in Cal. as Benito, nat. of Tenn., and immig. of the Workman party from N. Mex., where he had resided for 8 years as trapper and trader. iv. 277-9. In '43 he purchased the Jurupa rancho, iv. 635, and from this frontier station in the following years engaged in several campaigns against hostile Indians. In '45 he was prominent among the southern foreigners who served against Micheltorena. iv. 495, 504, 506-7. In '46 he acted as juez for the district ranchos; commanded a comp. of citizen riflemen intended to resist Castro; was in com. of the foreigners at the Chino fight; and after the U.S. occupation served as lieut in the Cal. Bat. v. 50-1, 265, 312-14, 360, 625. He was the 1st county clerk and 1st mayor of Los Ang.; Ind. agent in '52, taking pride in having been the 1st to urge the settling of the Ind. on reservations at the old missions; cl. for S. José de Buenos Aires rancho. iv. 635; and was state senator for two terms. Don Benito was a prosperous ranchero and fruit-raiser, an influential and respected citizen. In '77 he dictated for my use his *Observations* on early Cal. events, a MS. of considerable value, though on some points I have found Wilson's testimony less accurate than I had deemed it at first. I notice that a copy, left with the family at their request, has been consulted by some of the county history and newspaper men. W. died at his rancho of Lake Vineyard in '78, at the age of 67, leaving a widow—a 2d wife, the 1st having been Ramona, daughter of Bernardo Yorba, married in '44—and 3 daughters. W. (Charles), 1848, carpenter at S.F. W. (Dorsey), 1847, owner of S.F. lot. W. (Henry), 1847, purser on the U.S. *Preble*. W. (Henry J.), 1847, sergt Co. D, N.Y. Vol. v. 504. W. (James), 1824, Engl. trader at Mont.; age 25 in '29; also at Mont. '30-3. ii. 609. W. (James), 1844 (?), Engl. soldier, veteran of Waterloo, said to have come to Sta Clara and to have died in '70. v. 453. W. (James), 1847, Co. A, N.Y.Vol. (v. 499).

Wilson (John), 1826, Scotch shipmaster and trader on the roll of the Soc. Cal. Pion. as having arrived in April '26, and who in '37 claimed a residence of 12 years; the 1st original record being '28, when he was master of the *Thos Nowlan*. iii. 149. In '31-7 he was mr of the *Index* '38-9, '41-3; of the *Fly* '40; of the *Juanita* in '44-5. iii. 381; iv. 101, 104, 566. Before '36 he married Ramona Carrillo de Pacheco, and from that time considered Sta B. his home; naturalized in '37, and from '39 to '47 a partner of James Scott; about '41 engaged in otter-hunting. In '45 Capt. W. took some part in the troubles with Micheltorena. iv. 498; and with Scott was the purchaser of the S. Luis Ob. estate, and grantee of the ranchos Cañada del Chorro and Cañada de los Osos, where he spent the rest of his life. iv. 553, 655, 658-9; v. 375, 558, 566. He died in '60 at the age of 65, leaving a widow, still living in '85, a son John who settled in England, and a daughter. There were few of the old pioneers better known or more respected than Capt. John Wilson. W. (John), 1826, Amer. trapper, apparently of Jed. Smith's party. iii. 155, 190, 176. Ment. in '27-30; on Larkin's books '38-9; in '41 permitted to marry María F. Mendoza of S. Cárlos. W. (John), 1837, grantee of Guilicos rancho, Sonoma, for which he was cl. in 53. iii. 712; iv. 118; ment. at Sonoma '43. W. (John), 1841, deserter from the U.S. Ex. Ex. at N. Helv. July. W. (John), 1844, owner of a lighter on S.F. bay; perhaps John of '37, or the captain. W. (John), 1847, wounded at the S. Gabriel fight. v. 395; prob. Joseph. W. (John), 1847, Co. D, N.Y. Vol. (v. 499); perhaps at Stockton '48-9. W. (J. B.), 1847, carpenter at Mont. '47-8; perhaps the initials were E. B. or O. B. W. (John E.), 1846, on roll of Soc. Cal.

Pion.; nat. of Sweden; d. at S.F. '77, age 63.   W. (John Henry), 1826, negro who landed from a whaler, and was still at Los Ang. '29 and '37. iii. 196. W. (John K.), 1845, mid. on the U.S. *Savannah* '45–7; lieut, and later capt., of the artill. comp. of the Cal. Bat. v. 361, 434, 446; in '48 a witness at Wash. on the Cal. claims.   W. (J. T.), 1847, owner of a S.F. lot.

Wilson (Joseph), 1845, asst-surg. on the U.S. *Savannah* '45–7.   W. (Joseph), 1846, seaman wounded at the S. Gabriel fight '47.   W. (Joseph), 1847, purser on the U.S. *Lexington*.   W. (Julian), 1828, partner of Exter in a trapping project. iii. 172–3, 178; named in the Branciforte padron of '28, wife Josefa Arbito (?), child María. ii. 627.   W. (Lorenzo), 1830 (?), brother of Julian, said by Vallejo to have had personal encounters with Pliego and José Castro.   W. (Mariano), 1846, had a Cal. claim (v. 462).   W. (Oliver C.), 1846, Co. C, 1st U.S. dragoons (v. 336).   W. (Robert), 1847, Co. G, N.Y. Vol. (v. 499); at Vallejo '82.   W. (Thomas), 1832, at Purísima, a farmer.   W. (Thomas A.), 1848, overl. immig., son of Wm D., settler in S. Joaquin Co., where he still lived with a family in '84.   W. (Wm), 1822, Amer. carpenter at Mont. '29, aged 27, married; also at Mont. '34. ii. 478. There way be some confusion between him and Wm 'Willis,' q. v.   W. (Wm), 1847, at S.F. from Tahiti.   W. (Wm C.), 1845 (?), nat. of Tenn. said to have come from Sonora this year; a well-known horseman who died at S. José '82, leaving a widow and son. iv. 587.   W. (Wm D.), 1848, nat. of Ky and overl. immig. who settled on the Cosumnes, where he built a wire bridge. He was rich at one time, but lost his fortune by floods and other misfortunes. He died near Gilroy in '75 at the age of 65, leaving a widow and son.   Wilt (John), 1847, sergt Co. B, N.Y. Vol. v. 504; d. before '82.

Wimmer (Peter L.) 1846, nat. of Ohio and overl. immig. with his wife, Elizabeth J. Bays. He may have served in the Cal. Bat. (v. 358); and in '47 was owner of a S.F. lot. v. 685. He worked for Sutter as a millwright in '47–8, and was one of the men employed at the Coloma mill when gold was discovered, being perhaps with Marshall on the eventful morning when 'they' picked up the 1st nugget. At any rate, Mrs W., ranking as cook and laundress of the camp, tested that nugget by boiling it in her soap-kettle, and still claimed to have it in her possession in '85. After the discovery the family kept a boarding-house, having also a choice assortment of pigs. A child was born in Aug. '48; in '49 W. went to Calaveras; in '55 he had 10 children. In '78–85 be resided in Southern Cal.   W. (John M.), 1847 (?), perhaps a brother of Peter, teamster at N. Helv. and Coloma '47–8.   G.W. and family are also ment. in the *N. Nelv. Diary;* prob. error.

Winckley (J. F.), 1848, passp. from Hon.   Winders (John), 1847, nat. of Va; d. at Stockton '72, age 67.   Windmeyer (Richard), 1847, Co. F, N.Y. Vol. (v. 499).   Wing, 1847, mr of the *Obed Mitchell*. v. 579; on the *Sagadahoc* '48.   Winkley, 1847, at S.F. from Or. on the *Henry;* at Benicia. Winkworth (Wm), 1836, mr of the *Europa* '36–7. iv. 103.   Winn (Dennis), 1847, Co. A, Morm. Bat. (v. 469); laborer at Mont. '48; at Richmond, Utah, '81.   Winner (Geo. K.), 1846, one of the Mormon colony, with wife and 6 children. v. 547; owner of S.F. lot '47. v. 679.   Winnie (James), 1847, sergt Co. H, N.Y. Vol. v. 504; sergt of S. José guard '48; d. before '82. W. (Wm), 1847, Co. E, N.Y. Vol. (v. 499); carpenter and miner in Calaveras Co. '48–56; at Portland, Or., to '74, and at Oakland, Cal., to '85.   Winship, 1848, trader in the mines and at S.F.   W. (Charles), 1850, mr of the *Betsey*. i. 546, 656.   W. (Jonathan), 1806, mr of the *O'Cain;* a famous trader and smuggler on the coast 1806–12. ii. 25, 39–40, 78–9, 82, 84–5, 92–4, 267, 633. W. (Nathan), 1806, brother of Jonathan, mate of the *O'Cain;* mr of the *Albatross* 1807–12. ii. 39, 82, 84, 92–5, 148, 199, 267, 296.   Winslow, 1848, from Hon. on the *Sagadahoc*.   Winter (Jacob), 1847, Co. B, Morm. Bat. (v. 469); reënl.   W. (John D.), 1848, hotel-keeper at Coloma, of firm W. & Cromwell, owning an interest in Sutter's mill; later a resid. of S. Joaquin.   W. (Wm H.), 1843(?), nat. of Ind. and overl. immig. of the Walker-Chiles party. iv. 393–4, 400; or possibly came to Or. '43 and to Cal. '44. He is said to have gone east in '45 and returned in '49, but is named in N. Helv. in '47.   He made other trips east, but in '53 settled in Cal. with his family, living in Colusa and Lake to '55, in Napa to '71, and in Shasta until his death in '79 at the age of 60, leaving 5 sons, one of them a lawyer at Napa. W., 1843, mr of the whaler *Ana Maria. Peterson.*

Wise (Henry A.), 1847, lieut on the U.S. *Independence,* and author of *Los Gringos,* pub. in N.Y. '49, in which his experience is described. v. 100. I have also some MS. *Notes on Cal.* by him, but cannot say how or when they were obtained. W. (Marion), 1845, apparently one of Frémont's men. iv. 583; at N. Helv. '46, and perhaps one of the Bears. v. 110, 128, 453; a witness at Wash. in Feb. '48. He perished in Frémont's exped. of '48–9. Wismon (John), 1846, in Hittell's list. Wisner (Geo.), 1845, carpenter on the U.S. *Portsmouth* '45–7; owner of a S.F. lot. v. 683. Wissell (Fred.), 1847, Co. H, N.Y. Vol. (v. 499). Wiswell (James), 1846, a doctor who became rich and went east. *Hittell.* Withrell (Adolphus), 1846, sailor on the *Dale.* Wittam (Isaac), 1847, Co. I, N.Y. Vol. (v. 499). Wittmer (Jacob), 1847, Swiss in Sutter's employ '47–8, often named in the *N. Helv. Diary.* On Feb. 14, '48, he arrived at the fort with glowing reports from the gold mines. Witmarsh (Benj. H.), 1845, Amer. at Mont. Wittengstein (David), 1847, Co. F, 3d U.S. artill. (v. 518).

Wodwarck, 1815, mr of the *Lady.* ii. 307. Wohler (Herman), 1848, German who married a daughter of Capt. Cooper, and was a member of the legislature of '55. He lived on Mark West Creek, and later at Sonoma, where he had a vineyard. An accomplished musician, famous as an entertainer. He died in '77. Vohlgemouth (Henry J.), 1847, Co. E, N.Y. Vol. (v. 499); at S.F. '82. Wolcott, 1845(?), d. at Hon. '50; said to have lived 5 years in Cal.; prob. 'Walcott.' Wolfe (James), 1826, mate of the *Blossom* '26–7. iii. 121. W. (John), 1847, Co. D, N.Y. Vol. (v. 499); trader at Mont., Stockton, and in the mines; in N.Y. '71–82. Wolfinger, 1846, German of the Donner party, who died before reaching the Sierra. His wife survived and was married in '47 at Sutter's fort to Geo. Zinns. v. 531–2, 534.

Wolfskill (John R.), 1838, nat. of Ky, who came from N. Mex., after some years residence in Mex. iv. 117, 119. After working for several years for his brother Wm in the south, he came north in '42 and settled on a rancho on Putah Creek—granted to Francisco Guerrero and owned by Wm Wolfskill. Here he has lived down to '85, his name rarely appearing in any early records that I have seen, possibly serving with the Bears and Cal. Bat., but not tempted away from his rancho and cattle by the gold excitement of '48–9. In the later years he has been one of the best known fruit-growers of Yolo and Solano, a man of wealth, and a citizen of the most excellent reputation, now 81 years of age. Portrait in *Yolo Co. Hist.,* 26. By his first wife, whose name I have not found, he had a son, Edward, who in later years was his business manager. In '58 he married Susan, daughter of Stephen Cooper, by whom he had 3 daughters living in '80. I have a brief *Biog. Sketch* of 'Uncle John,' taken by G. W. Boggs in '83. W. (Sarchel), 1838(?), nat. of Mo., brother of John R., who may have come from N. Mex. '38–41; in Solano Co. '80. W. (Wm), 1831, brother of John R., nat. of Ky, and for several years a trapper and trader in N. Mex., coming to Cal. in com. of a trapping party by a new route. iii. 386, 405, 630; iv. 263–4. He had been naturalized in N. Mex. '30; and in Cal. for several years was engaged in hunting otter on the coast, building a schooner for that purpose. iii. 363, 393. In '36 he settled at Los Ang. as a carpenter, getting a lot, being named as one of the vigilantes, giving much attention to the raising of vines, and from '38 devoting himself wholly to the vineyards which were to make him rich and famous. iv. 117. He married in '41; in '42 became the owner of the Putah Creek rancho occupied from that time by his brother. iv. 673; in '44 was regidor at Los Ang. iv. 633; and is hardly mentioned in the political troubles of '45–7 or in public matters of later years. He died in '66 at the age of 68, leaving an enviable reputation as an honest, enterprising, generous, unassuming, intelligent man. He and Louis Vignes may be regarded as the pioneers of California's greatest industry, the production of wine and fruit. His wife Magdalena, daughter of

José Ign. Lugo, died in '62; a daughter Juana, Mrs Henry D. Barrows, died in '63, and another daughter in '55. The surviving children and heirs of his large estate were Joseph W. born in '44, Luis, Madelina (wife of Matias Sabici), and Francisca, apparently Mrs Cardwell. Wm had 3 brothers, perhaps including Sarchel, who came after '48.   Wolter (Charles), 1833, German mr of a Mex. vessel, who in Dec. obtained a certificate of Mex. citizenship, having been for 2 years a citizen of Peru. iii. 409. It is not unlikely that he visited Cal. before '33. He was mr of the *Leonor* '36-8, of the *Clara* or *Clarita* '40-3, of the *Julia* '44-5, and of *El Placer* '48. iii. 383; iv. 102, 104, 403, 563-4; v. 577. Capt. Wolter married an Estrada, settled at Mont., and was cl. for the Toro rancho. iii. 679. He died in '56 at the age of 65.

Wood, 1841, with Douglas. iv. 212; named at Sutter's fort.   W. 1846, at Sutter's fort from Or. in June. v. 526.   W., 1846, mr of the *Pandora*. v. 579.   W., 1847, juryman and constable at Sutter's fort. v. 542.   W., 1848, in the mines; discov. of Wood Creek; perhaps the man who came from Or. with Capt. Martin, and was killed by Ind.   W., 1848, builder at Benicia. v. 673.   W. (Geo.), 1831, mr of the *Louisa*. iii. 383.   W. (Geo. T.), 1844, deserter from the U.S. *Warren* at S.F., who lived among the Ind. of Marin Co. near Tomales, where Wood Point bears his name. iv. 453. The ex-sailor became an expert horseman, widely known as Tom Vaquero. He died at S. Rafael in '79.   W. (Henry), 1833, Amer. named in Larkin's books '33-7, known as the 'deacon.' iii. 409; in the Or. cattle party of '37. iv. 85; served in Cal. Bat. '46 (v. 358), and had a Cal. claim of $30 (v. 462); owner of S.F. lot '47; a carpenter at S.F. '51-4; perhaps several different men.   W. (John), 1847, Co. I, N.Y.Vol. (v. 499); at Hanford, Tulare Co., '82.   W. (Joseph), 1845, overl. immig. of the Grigsby-Ide party, who probably returned east in '46. iv. 579; but may have been one of the Woods named at Sutter's fort at the beginning of this paragraph.   W. (O. R.), 1848, at Hon. from Mont.; seems to have married a daughter of W. H. Merrill at S.F.   W. (Paul D.), 1846, Co. C, 1st U. S. dragoons (v. 336).   W. (Wm), 1840, sup. of the *Columbia* '40-1. iv. 102-3, 564.   W. (Wm), 1846, Co. E, Cal. Bat., enlisting at Sutter's fort Oct. (v. 358).   W. (Wm), 1847, Co. C, Morm. Bat. (v. 469). W. (Wm A.), 1847, Co. F, 3d U.S. artill. (v. 518).   W. (Wm Maxwell), 1844, fleet-surgeon of the Pacific squadron U.S.N. '44-6, who, on his way overland across Mex. in '46, sent to Com. Sloat at Mazatlan news of the outbreak of war. He published a narrative of his adventures under the title of *Wandering Sketches*. iv. 452-3, 460, 479, 661.

Woodard (John), 1832, witness at Mont.   Wooden (John), 1843, doubtful name of the Chiles-Walker immig. party. iv. 393-4.   Woodruff (Wilford), 1848, Mormon, and one of the discov. of gold at Mormon Isl.; perhaps 'Wilford.'   Woods (Henry), 1838, in Sta Clara; perhaps 'Wood.'   W. (Isaiah C.), 1848, nat. of Me, who came as sup. of a trader, and from '49 was prominent as manager of Adams & Co.'s express and banking business. He went east after the failure of that comp. in '55; among other enterprises established an overland mail from Texas to S. Diego; served as commissary of transportation in the war of '61-5; and returned to Cal. about '68. He died in '80, leaving a widow and 3 children.   W. (John), 1848, at Sta Cruz '81.   Woodside (Preston K.), 1847, Co. D, N.Y.Vol. (v. 499); clerk of the naval agency at Mont. '48; later clerk of supreme court. In '81 at Tucson, Ariz.   Woodward (E.), 1840, steward of the schr *California*.   W. (Francis), 1847, Co. C, Morm. Bat. (v. 469).   Woodworth, 1847, a Mormon in Sutter's employ '47-8, teaming between the fort and mill.   W. (John), 1834, Engl. at Mont. '34-5.

Woodworth (Selim E.), 1847, nat. of N.Y., and lieut U.S.N., who came overland to Or. in '46, and to Cal. in the winter of '46-7, taking some part in an exped. for the relief of the Donner party. v. 539; owning S.F. lots, joining the *Warren*, and in '48 acting as mr of the transport *Anita*. v. 576. In '49 he resigned his commission, engaged in trade in comp. with P. A. Roach, and was a member of the 1st state senate. Later he became a business man at S. F., being prominent in the vigilance com. of '51. In the war of '61-5 he rejoined the navy, reaching the rank of commodore, resigning about '67, and residing for the most part at S. F., where he died in '71, at the age of 55, leaving a widow and 5 children. Portrait in *Annals of S.F.* Woolard (Henry), 1847, Co. K, N.Y.Vol. (v. 499); 58 lashes and a month in jail at S. José '48 for attempted murder.   Wooldridge, 1846, com. of the *Spy.* v. 580. Wooley (Wm), 1847, Co. A, N. Y. Vol. (v. 499); at Campo Seco '71-82. Wooster (Charles W.), 1847, nat. of N. Y., who came as sup. of the *Confederacion*, having been admiral in the Chilean navy.   He presided at the 1st thanksgiving dinner at S.F. '47, being owner of lots here and at Benicia. v. 646, 672, 678. Partner of Ward and Fourgeaud in the Yuba mines; dying at Hock farm Aug. '48.

Worden (John L.), 1847, lieut on the *Southampton*.   W. (Stephen), 1844, doubtful name of an Amer. at S.F., age 25.   Work (John), 1833, a trapper applying for supplies. iii. 392.   Workman (Andrew J.), 1847, Co. B, Morm. Bat. (v. 469); at Virgin City, Utah, '82.   W., 1809, doubtful record of a hunter. ii. 89.   W. (Oliver G.), 1847, Co. B, Morm. Bat. (v. 469); reënl.; at Salt Lake City '82.   W. (Wm), 1841, nat. of England, who came from N. Mex. in com. of an immig. party with his family. iv. 276-9, 637. He had long been a trader at Taos, and at the time of his coming to Cal. was somewhat compromised in the eyes of the Mex. govt by his supposed connection with Texan political or revolutionary schemes. He obtained, with John Roland, the Puente rancho, confirmed in '45. iv. 331, 635; was a leader of the foreigners against Micheltorena in '45. iv. 495, 505; took some part in '46-7 in the direction of preventing warfare. v. 50-1, 332-3, 387, 396; and was the purchaser of S. Gabriel mission. v. 561, 627-9. In '52 he was cl. for the Cajon de los Negros and La Puente ranchos. From about '68 he was a banker in company with Temple at Los Ang., and in '76, on the failure of the bank, he committed suicide, at the age of 76. I know nothing of his family, except that a brother David died at La Puente in '55.   Wort (Geo.), 1847, Co. G, N.Y.Vol. (v. 499); d. at S.F. '47.   Worth (Caroline), 1848, nat. of Ind., resid. of Sonoma Co. '74-7.

Wrangell (Baron F. von), 1833, gov. of the Russian colonies in Alaska, at Ross in '33, and at Mont '35 on his way to Mex. iv. 160-9. See also *Hist. Alaska.*   Wright, 1845, doubtful member of the Grigsby-Ide party. iv. 579. W., 1847, had a hospital on Cooper St., Mont.   W., 1848, from Hon. on the *Sagadahoc.*   W., 1848, at Sta Cruz, buying C. C. Smith's interest in a store, which was perhaps in the mines.   W., 1848, partner of Dav. Ray in the Yuba mines.   W., 1848, of W. & Owen, liquor dealers at S.F.   W. (Chas), 1847, Co. B, Morm. Bat. (v. 469).   W. (David), 1847, carpenter at Mont.; cl. in '52 for Roblar de la Miseria rancho. iv. 673.   W. (Harry), 1846, Co. G, Cal. Bat., enlisting at S. José Nov. (v. 358).   W. (J.), 1840, passenger on the *Lausanne* perhaps, who went to Hon. iv. 104, 121.   W. (Jonathan), 1846, at Mont. '74, said by McPherson to have come this year.   W. (J. H.), 1848, passp. from Hon.   W. (Phineas R.), 1847, sergt Co. A, Morm. Bat. v. 477.   W. (Stephen A.), 1847, prob. overl. immig., perhaps of '46; at Mont. '47-8, of W. & Dickenson, lumber dealers; owner of S.F. lot '49. v. 685; and member of S.F. council '49; later a banker who failed and went to Ariz. before '60.   W. (Tiery), 1844 (?), perhaps one of Frémont's men. iv. 337. Wümsen (John), 1823, appears as a witness at Sta B.; prob. a sailor. ii. 495.   Wunderlich (F. H.), 1848 (?), biog. in *Eureka Humboldt Times,* June 25, '79.   Wybourn (Robert), 1847, Co. I, N. Y.Vol. (v. 499); in Calaveras '71-4.   Wylie (John), 1847, Co. E, ditto.   Wylis (Richard), 1845, doubtful name of an overl. immig. iv. 578.   Wyman (Gardner), 1847, at Mont. '47-8. W. (Geo. F.), 1844 (?), sent by Sutter to raise recruits for the Micheltorena campaign in Dec. iv. 453, 486, 501; often named in the *N. Helv. Diary* '45-8; His wife, ment. in '47, was America, daughter of David Kelsey, still living in '85. In '78-84 W. was living at Spanishtown, S. Mateo Co., and in newspaper sketches and county histories is said to have left a whaler in '36.   W. (T. W.), 1847, capt. on the U.S. *Columbus.* v. 577.

Yame (Blas), 1806, sailor on the *Peacock.* ii. 38.   Yanonalit, Ind. chief at Sta B. 1782. i. 377.   Yard (Edward M.), 1846, lieut on the U.S. *Dale;*

at Trenton, N.J., '78.   Yarnall (Mordecai), 1847, prof. of mathematics on the *Columʰus*.   Yates (John), 1842, Engl. sailor who came from Mazatlan and was employed by Sutter as mr of his launch. iv. 229, 341. In '43 he was in some trouble at Sonoma, Sutter furnishing bail; in Nov. '44 his launch was wrecked at Ross; he is named in the *N. Helv. Diary* '45-7, and seems to have been the owner of land in the Chico region '46-7, having also a Cal. claim of $50 (v. 462). In '51 he went to the Sandwich Isl., where he was living in '72, in which year he sent me his *Sketch of a Journey to the Sacramento Valley in '42*, including a narrative of earlier adventures. It is a most interesting and useful MS., though there are indications that the valley trip may have been antedated by a year or two.   Y. (John D.), 1847, Co. H, N.Y.Vol. (v. 499); in '82 at Albany, N.Y.; a printer.   Ybarra, etc., see 'Ibarra,' etc.

Yeamans (Edward), 1847, Co. E, N. Y. Vol. (v. 499).   Yellow Serpent, Or. Ind. at Sutter's fort '44-6. v. 300-2.   Yems, 1817, sailor at Sta B., doubtful name. ii. 286.   Yergeens (Fred.), 1847, Co. F, 3d U. S. artill. (v. 518); living in '64.   Yetch (August), 1847, perhaps of N. Y. Vol. under another name.   Yim (James), 1828, Amer. pilot at Mont. '28-9, age 23; name doubtful; prob. 'Jim.'   Yndarte (J. D.), 1845, mr of the *Farici*. iv. 565.   Ynitia (Camilo), grantee of Olompali '43.   Yonkins (Wm), 1847, Co. F, 3d U. S. artill. (v. 528); in the S. José hospital '64, suffering from an incurable cancer.

Yorba (Antonio), 1769, one of Fages' original Catalan volunteers; in 1777 corp. of the S. F. comp.; in 1782 corp. of the Mont. comp.; and in 1789 of the S. Diego comp. In 1797 he was retired as inválido sergt; and in 1809-10 grantee of the Santiago de Sta Ana rancho, Los Ang., which he or a son of the same name occupied down to '30, and the family later. i. 647, 663; ii. 104, 112, 172, 353, 565, 664; iii. 634. His wife, from 1782, was María Josefa, daughter of Alférez Grijalva; and the children named in early years were Isabel María, Cecilia, Raimunda (who married J. B. Alvarado), Francisca, and José Domingo who died in 1796.   Y. (Bernardo), son of Antonio, age 35 in '39, aux. alcalde or juez de campo at St Ana '33, '36, '40, '44. iii. 635-7; iv. 633; grantee of Cañada de Sta Ana '34 and of Sierra '46. iii. 633; v. 628. His daughter Ramona married B. D. Wilson.   Y. (Isabel), grantee of Guadalasca '46, and cl. in '52. iii. 655.   Y. (José Ant.), son of Antonio, age 27 in '39; aux. alcalde and juez de campo at Sta Ana Abajo '36, '40. iii. 636-7; in '41 at S. Juan Cap. iv. 626, 628; in '47 regidor at Los Ang. v. 626. Y. (José Domingo), son of José Ant., b. at S. Diego 1795; cl. of S. Vicente Cañada '52. v. 629.   Y. (Ramon), cl. for Las Bolsas '52. iii. 633.   Y. (Teodosio), son of José Ant., age 22 in '39, aux. alcalde at Sta Ana '36 and '47. iii. 636; a prisoner in '38. iii. 554-5; grantee of Arroyo Seco '40. iii. 711; at S. Juan Cap. '41. iv. 626; grantee of Lomas de Santiago '46. v. 627.   Y. (Tomás Ant.), son of José Ant., age 55 in '39, supl. of the diputacion '30, '32. iii. 50, 216-18; aux. alcalde at Sta Ana '31-2, '35. iii. 635; ment. in '39, '40, '43. iii. 589, 629, 637.

Yorgens (Joseph), 1828, Amer. trapper of Pattie's party. iii. 163, 168; age 24 in '29. Either Y. and Ferguson were the same, or one of them could not have belonged to this party.   York, 1834, Engl. sailor, age 23, in a Mont. list.   Y. (John), 1845, nat. of Tenn. and overl. immig. of the Grigsby-Ide party, with his wife Lucinda Hudson and 2 sons, Wm E. and David, the latter being apparently born on the trip. iv. 579, 587. He settled at the head of Napa Valley; was at Sonoma during the Bear revolt; went to the mines in '48-9; and in '49-82 lived on his farm in Napa. There were 9 surviving children in '82, including those named above. Portrait in *Napa Co. Hist.*, 62. Y. (Wm), 1846, Co. F, Cal. Bat. v. 358; at S. José '48-50.

Young, 1833, at S. Diego '33-4, in Ebbetts' service, called capt.   Y., 1647, mr of the *Com. Stockton*, at S.F. and Bodega. v. 577.   Y. (Alpheus), 1847, Co. D, N.Y.Vol. (v. 499); at S.F. '82.   Y. (Charles B.), 1847, lieut Co. A, ditto. v. 503.   Y. (Chas D.), 1847, musician, ditto.   Y. (Ewing), 1830, capt. of trappers, who came to Cal. from N. Mex., and again in '31-2, going to Or. in '34, returning in '37, to purchase cattle, and dying in Or. '41. ii. 600; iii. 174-5, 180, 357, 387-8, 393-4, 410, 630; iv. 85-7, 263-4; see also

Hist. Or., i. **90** et seq. Y. (Francis), 1837, lumberman in the Mont. dist. '37-44. iv. 118. He failed in business '44; and nothing more is known of him unless he was with Ford at Olompali '46. v. 166. Y. (John), 1844, on roll of Soc. Cal. Pion.; nat. of Scotland, and nephew of Capt. John Wilson; perhaps did not come from Valparaíso till '45. He was a trader and mr of vessels on the coast; and later superintendent of the N. Almaden mine. Died at S.F. '64. Y. (Jonathan), 1847, mid. on the *Columbus*. Y. (J. E.), 1848, miner at Mormon Isl., etc.; later a farmer in Placer Co. to '68. Y. (Lewis or Levi), 1833, mr of the *Enriqueta*. iii. 382. Y. (Nathan), 1847, of Morm. Bat. (v. 469); reënl. at Los Ang. Y. (Rom⁰), Mex. citizen at N. Helv. Y. (Sam. C.), 1846, nat. of Tenn., and overl. immig. with his family. v. 528-30. He settled as a farmer at Sta Clara, where he died in '78, leaving 3 sons— Leander C., who died in '82, M. D., at S. José '81, and R. J., ditto.

Yount (George C.), 1831, nat. of N.C. who came as a trapper in Wolfskill's party from N. Mex. iii. 386, 405, 166, 363. For several years he hunted otter chiefly on S.F. bay and its tributaries, also making shingles at odd jobs. His name appears on Larkin's books in '33. In '35 he was baptized at S. Rafael as Jorge Concepcion, and worked for Vallejo at Sonoma. In '36 he obtained a grant of the Caymus rancho in Napa Valley, where he built a cabin, or block-house, and for years was the only representative of the gente de razon in the valley. iii. 711; iv. 117. He still spent much of his time in hunting, and had many encounters with the Ind., though by his long experience with the natives, his fearless character, and by his tact in forming alliances with the strongest rancherías, he managed to keep all under good control. In '43 he was grantee of the La Jota rancho, an extension of Caymus, iv. 671, where he soon built a saw-mill, having also a flour-mill on his place; and the same year he was joined by two daughters who came overland with Chiles, the latter having in his visit of '41 brought news from the family and been commissioned to bring them. iv. 393. In several of the old trapper's experiences, as related by him and embellished by others, a trace of faith in dreams and omens is shown; but the oft-repeated story that a dream of his led to the relief of the Donner party has no foundation in fact. In later years the old pioneer found the squatters and land-lawyers somewhat more formidable foes than had been the Ind. and grizzlies of earlier times; but he saved a portion of his land, and died at his Napa home—called Yountville in his honor—in '65 at the age of 71. Portraits in *Hesperian*, ii.; *Napa Co. Hist.*, 54; *Menefee's Sketch-book*, 160. Y. (Lot G.), 1844, ranchero named in Larkin's papers; prob. error for Geo. C. Youin (Juan), 1846, owner of S.F. lot. v. 684.

Zabriskie (Jerome), 1847, Co. B, Morm. Bat. (v. 469); reënl.; in Utah '82. Zaldíbar (Pedro), 1818, deserter from Bouchard's insurgents. ii. 241. Zalvidea (José María), 1805, Span. friar whose missionary service was chiefly at S. Gabriel and S. Juan Cap. He died at S. Luis Rey in '46. Biog. v. 620-1; ment. ii. 48-50, 109, 114-15, 159-60, 352, 355-6, 394, 555, 567-8, 655; iii. 91, 96, 102, 317, 358, 625, 627; iv. 371, 422, 622-4. Zamora (Ignacio), soldier at the Colorado pueblos 1780-1; killed by Ind. i. 359, 362. Z. (Juan), capt. appointed for Cal.; did not come. iii. 54. Z. (Manuel), Mex. soldier of the Hidalgo piquete at Mont. '30, age 26. Z. (Nicanor), supl. com. de policía at Mont. '36. iii. 675. Zamorano (Agustin Vicente), 1825, Mex. alférez who came with Echeandía; nat. of Florida, of Spanish parentage; capt. of the Mont. comp. from '31, and of the S. Diego comp. from '35. He left Cal. in '38, but returned in '42 as lieut-col, and died in that year at S. Diego. He is named in the Mont. padron of '36 as 36 years old, wife Luisa Argüello, child. Dolores b. '27 (married J. M. Flores), Luis '29, Gonzalo '32, Guadalupe '33 (married Henry Dalton), Josefa '34, and Agustin '36. An Eulalia is also named by Hayes as having married Vicente Estudillo. Of the sons I have no record. Biog. of the capt. iii. 559-61; ment. ii. 543-4, 549, 608, 669, 676; iii. 13-14, 33, 44, 47, 50, 61-2, 81, 84, 91, 99, 102, 205, 214, 220-32, 239, 243, 347, 364, 441, 445, 463, 515-20, 533, 549, 556, 568-9, 608, 614, 669-71; iv. 68, 290, 408, 619; v. 365. Zampay, chief of the Yolo Ind. '36. iv. 72.

Zarembo (Dionisio), 1827, mr of the *Okhotsk* '27-9. iii. 148; and of the *Urup* '31-2. iii. 213, 384; again in Cal.' 45 as Russian agent. iv. 187-8. Zavaleta (Aniceto María), Mex. artilleryman at S. Diego '21 and earlier, a somewhat unmanageable fellow, though a good soldier. He became sergt, and about '28 was retired as teniente de premio; serious charges against him in '31; had much trouble in collecting his pay in later years; sec. of the ayunt. at S. D. '41. iv. 619; ment. in '45. iv. 508. Zavalishin (W.), 1824, Russ. agent who visited Cal.; author of a work on the Russ. colony, *Delo o Koloniy Ross.* ii. 641, 647. Zeballos (Areaco), 1791, Span. lieut in Malaspina's exped. i. 490. Zeilin (Jacob), 1846, lieut of marines on the *Congress;* acting capt. in Stockton's Bat. '46-7. v. 281, 385, 391-5; perhaps 'Zielin.' Zenon, Ind. leader of a plot at S. José '42. iv. 338. Zerman (John Napoleon), 1846 (?), Fr. lieut at Waterloo; veteran of many campaigns: in Mex. war; in Cal. '49 et seq. and in '74; possibly in '46. Zertaje, 1821, mr or sup. of the *S.F. Javier.* ii. 440, 202. Zetch (August), 1847, gen. accredited to N.Y. Vol. (v. 499); settled at Petaluma; d. at S. F. '79; prob. the following. Zetschsky (Charles), 1847, Co. C, N.Y. Vol. (v. 499); at Petaluma '83. *Clark.*

Zimmerman (Bernard), 1847, Co. F, 3d U.S. artill., (v. 518). Z. (W.), 1847, ditto; in Cal. '64. Zindel (Louis), 1844, one of Frémont's party; prob. did not come to Cal. iv. 437. Zinky (D.), 1846, doubtful name of the Cal. Bat. (v. 358). Zinns (Geo.), 1846, nat. of Lorraine, and overl. immig.; Cal. Bat. (v. 358); married Mrs Wolfinger at Sutter's fort '47, and is said to have built the first brick house at Sac. He was later a brewer and fruit-grower, but being ruined by fire and again by slickens, he lived on a chicken ranch from '72, and died at Oakland in '85 at the age of '86. Zittle (Michael), 1847, Co. I, N.Y. Vol. (v. 499). Zorrilla (Francisco), 1842, named as in charge of the Los Ang. gold mines. iv. 630. Zúñiga (José), 1781, lieut of the S. Diego comp., acting as habilitado and com. to 1793. Later capt. at Tucson, Sonora; lieut-col 1810. He was one of the most efficient of the old presidio officers. Biog. i. 645-6; ment. i. 335, 340, 343, 372, 396, 398, 400, 441, 454, 461-3, 467, 484, 502, 522, 653; ii. 78. Z. (Guillermo), land-owner at Los Ang. '39, age 48. Z. (Nicolás), soldier of the Mont. comp. '36, age '21. Z. (Pio Quinto), soldier of the S. Juan Cap. escolta 1776-9. i. 303. Z. (Ramon), soldier at Mont. '36, age 25. Z. (Valentin), at Los Ang. '39, age 42. Z. (Ventura), boy at Los Ang. 1802; soldier in '10. ii. 91. Zurrillaga 1824, mr of the *Constancia.* ii. 519. Zurita (José), murderer at S. Juan B. '44. iv. 662.

END OF PIONEER REGISTER.